D0781021

Karl Popper – The Formative Years, 1902–1945

Karl Popper (1902–1994) is one of this century's most influential philosophers, but his life in fin-de-siècle and interwar Vienna, and his exile in New Zealand during World War II, have so far remained shrouded in mystery. This intellectual biography recovers the legacy of the young Popper, the progressive, cosmopolitan, Viennese socialist who combated fascism, revolutionized the philosophy of science, and envisioned the Open Society. Malachi Hacohen delves into his archives (as well as the archives of his colleagues) and draws a compelling portrait of the philosopher, the assimilated Jewish intelligentsia, and the vanished culture of Red Vienna, which was decimated by Nazism. Seeking to rescue Popper from his postwar conservative and anticommunist reputation, Hacohen restores his works to their original Central European contexts and, at the same time, shows that they have urgent messages for contemporary politics and philosophy. Long before poststructuralism, Popper and his colleagues answered "poststructuralist" queries, demonstrating that nonfoundationist philosophy – philosophy that has no firm absolutes – is compatible with the Enlightenment's legacy and the pursuit of human emancipation. They formed cosmopolitan visions that, once a dream, may now provide guidelines for moving beyond the nation-state. Hacohen's is an adventurous biography that recovers the historical origins and meanings of ideas and renders them relevant to the present.

Malachi Haim Hacohen is associate professor of history at Duke University. He has also taught at Columbia University and Reed College. His articles have appeared in the *Journal of Modern History*, the *Journal of the History of Ideas*, *History and Theory*, *Philosophy of the Social Sciences*, and similar publications. He is a coordinator of the Triangle Intellectual History Program (Duke, NCSU at Raleigh, UNC at Chapel Hill) and serves on the Program Board of the Vienna International Summer University.

For my mother and father:
"Mine and yours is theirs."
(*Babylonian Talmud*, Ketuvot 63a, Nedarim 50a)

KARL POPPER – THE FORMATIVE YEARS, 1902–1945

Politics and Philosophy in Interwar Vienna

MALACHI HAIM HACOHEN

Duke University

PUBLISHED BY THE PRESS SYNDICATE OF THE UNIVERSITY OF CAMBRIDGE
The Pitt Building, Trumpington Street, Cambridge, United Kingdom

CAMBRIDGE UNIVERSITY PRESS
The Edinburgh Building, Cambridge CB2 2RU, UK
40 West 20th Street, New York, NY 10011-4211, USA
10 Stamford Road, Oakleigh, Melbourne 3166, Australia
Ruiz de Alarcón 13, 28014 Madrid, Spain
Dock House, The Waterfront, Cape Town 8001, South Africa

http://www.cambridge.org

© Malachi Haim Hacohen 2000

This book is in copyright. Subject to statutory exception
and to the provisions of relevant collective licensing agreements,
no reproduction of any part may take place without
the written permission of Cambridge University Press.

First published 2000
First paperback edition 2002

Printed in the United States of America

Typeface Bembo 11/12 pt.   System QuarkXPress™ [BTS]

A catalog record for this book is available from the British Library

Library of Congress Cataloging in Publication data is available

ISBN 0 521 47053 6 hardback
ISBN 0 521 89055 1 paperback

Contents

Acknowledgments

This book has been long in the making, and I have incurred many debts while writing it. I take pleasure in acknowledging them, but fear that I may not recall them all and will be able to pay back only a few. As an Israeli youth, I received an intensive education in Jewish studies. My teachers taught me to love learning for its own sake and, through Talmudic study, to read a text closely. I have since explored fields they did not expect I would, and this book advances precisely the ideas they sought to combat. Nonetheless, my work owes more to them, I suspect, than to my academic education. In odd ways, I still feel close to them. Nowhere in the academy have I found a genuine love of learning comparable to theirs.

My teachers at Bar-Ilan University, Ramat-Gan, Israel, provided me with a comprehensive, classical European, historical education that has served me well ever since. At Columbia University, where I completed my entire graduate education, the faculty – both the U.S. and European historians – were supportive of my work. They allowed a young student, who thought he knew better, to stumble and learn, and to do things his own way. I would like to thank Fritz Stern for supervising the dissertation with his usual elegance; Bob Paxton for providing sound advice, and for diligently reading my work and correcting my mistakes; and István Deák for always being generous with me. I learned most, however, through arguing with Larry Dickey about method in intellectual history. I struggled to develop my own mode, integrating the history of ideas with social and discursive contexts. In writing an intellectual biography of a liberal philosopher in the late 1980s and 1990s, when biography and liberalism alike – to say nothing of Karl Popper – were out of fashion in the U.S. academy, I also had to come to terms with poststructuralism. Larry Dickey's concern with conceptual moves that thinkers make in response to historical problems has remained a constant motif in my own work.

My Ph.D. dissertation, "The Making of the Open Society," served as a draft for this book. Nancy Moody in New York and Antonia Larsen in Portland typed early versions of the dissertation, with talent and patience. I completed the dissertation while teaching as a visiting assistant professor at Reed College, Portland, Oregon, a wonderful, intellectually intense, liberal arts college. My time there was the most exciting period thus far in my academic career, mostly owing to interdisciplinary teaching in the humanities program. I learned a great deal by listening to exquisite lectures by colleagues on topics as varied as the *Oresteia*, late-antique architecture, and *The Divine Comedy*. Both my practice of literary analysis and my ability to argue with Popper's classical scholarship – for whatever they are worth – I owe to my Reed experience.

I interviewed Karl Popper (1902–94) in January 1984 for four hours at his home in Penn, west of London. He was hospitable and charming, serious and interesting, but he did not remember Vienna well. The interview was invaluable, all the same, but I needed to see the archives. The 1990s have seen the opening not only of Popper's papers but also those of other Viennese intellectuals. It is a measure of the Central European catastrophe that none of the original archives are in Austria: The papers are dispersed in universities all over Western Europe and North America. Altogether, I have consulted about twenty collections. This would have been impossible without the generous help, well beyond the call of duty, of many archivists: Carol Leadenham and the staff at the Hoover Institute Archives, Stanford; Dr. Brigitte Uhlemann at the *Philosophisches Archiv*, Constance, Germany; Gerald Heverly at the Archives of Scientific Philosophy, Pittsburgh; Dr. Hubert Knoblauch at the *Sozialwissenschaftliches Archiv*, Constance; Ana Gomez at the Karl Polanyi Institute, Concordia University, Montreal; Danielle Green at the Harvard University Archives; Mary Osielski at Special Collections, State University of New York at Albany; Yakov at the Central Archives for the History of the Jewish People, Hebrew University of Jerusalem; Herbert Koch at the Meldearchiv, Wiener Stadt- und Landesarchiv, Vienna; and Frau H. Weiss at the *Israelitische Kultusgemeinde*, Vienna. Philippe Rosenberg, Steve Rowe, Matthew Specter, and Daniel Villanueva, at the time graduate students at Duke, helped with my research. (Other debts I have tried to acknowledge in my notes.) I am deeply thankful to all.

While writing the book, I have enjoyed the friendship and support of many of Popper's former students. Ian Jarvie (York University, Toronto) and Jeremy Shearmur (Australian National University, Canberra) offered extremely valuable criticism, first of my dissertation, then of the book manuscript. Joseph Agassi (Tel Aviv University and York University) commented on my essays and parts of the manuscript, reported on his conversations with Popper, and offered unparalleled psychological insight into Popper's personality. The late Colin Simkin (University of Sydney), Popper's closest colleague during his sojourn in New Zealand, provided indispensable first-hand knowledge of Popper's life there and the formation of his political philosophy. Peter Munz (Victoria University, Wellington), Popper's favorite student at Canterbury University College, added an invaluable perspective on his life and teaching there. The late John Watkins (University of London) offered criticism on both my essays and the entire manuscript, correcting with special care my treatment of probability. Troels Eggers

Hansen (University of Copenhagen) contributed his incomparable expertise in Popper's early manuscripts, offering important criticism of two "final versions" of Chapters 5 and 6. Karl Milford (University of Vienna) commented on several chapters and shared impressions of Popper's ambivalent relationship to Vienna. Stefano Gattei (University of Milan) commented on the first six chapters and corrected several mistakes. (I have acknowledged other help in my notes.) I am deeply grateful to all and so regret that Colin Simkin and John Watkins will not be here to see the book's publication.

Popper was a genius polymath, and it would be pretentious for most historians to claim expertise enabling them to provide an adequate account of his entire oeuvre, let alone pass judgment on it. I have no specialized training in mathematics or the natural sciences, and so the more technical details of Popper's work in probability theory and physics remain beyond my grasp. Fortunately, these do not represent the most significant part of his work to 1945, and, where they are relevant, I have had the good fortune of having the late John Watkins and Joseph Agassi check my account. (Any remaining errors are, of course, my own.) The literature on Popper is abundant, and discussion of his contributions to mathematical logic and scientific theory is available elsewhere. This is, however, the first comprehensive historical work on his early life and work, and I have sought to illuminate the contribution of the Viennese milieu to his philosophy. Born and buried in Vienna, Popper was the foremost philosopher to carry the legacy of Viennese progressivism to the postwar trans-Atlantic world. I have emphasized the intimate relationship between his philosophy of science and political philosophy. Both represent radical reformulation of the liberal ideal of free and critical scientific and political communities pursuing (uncertain, but real) knowledge and reform. Both answer current quandaries about the possibility of knowledge and a cosmopolitan world order.

The Duke history department and its chair, Alex Roland, have provided a supportive and congenial setting for the writing of this book. I would especially like to thank my colleagues Warren Lerner, Seymour Mauskopf, Martin Miller, Kristen Neuschel, and Joseph Shatzmiller for making me feel at home, and Claudia Koonz, Bill Reddy, Kären Wigen, and Ron Witt for supporting my work. I have greatly enjoyed and learned much from my conversations with Catherine Peyroux. My graduate students have been a delight, a constant source for intellectual interaction and stimulation. Jan French, Matthew Specter, Patrick Wilkinson, and other students have commented on significant parts of my work. In the context of discussions at Duke, I have expanded my interest in Popper and interwar Viennese culture to the assimilated-Jewish intelligentsia, Central European cosmopolitanism, and the workings of national and cosmopolitan identities in a multicultural setting. My recent essays (see the Bibliography) have drawn attention to the sociocultural conditions that made a transnational "Central European culture" possible – and also to its limits. I have argued that Central European cosmopolitanism should be understood against the background of ethnonationalism and the dilemmas of national integration of the assimilated Jewish intelligentsia. This view informs my understanding of the making of Popper's Open Society, but the essays foreground it better, I suspect, than this intellectual biography.

While I have written against the grain of much of contemporary modern European intellectual history, I was lucky to have some of its leading practitioners treat my work kindly. Allan Megill (University of Virginia), especially, read both my dissertation and the book and has provided most helpful and detailed comments and much needed support, for which I am grateful. Since the spring of 1995, the monthly meetings of the Triangle Intellectual History Seminar at the National Humanities Center have provided an exceptional scholarly forum for discussing current work in intellectual history. I would especially like to thank Tony La Vopa and K. Steven Vincent (both of North Carolina State University at Raleigh) for having closely read my work, for providing invaluable comments and advice, and for constant moral support. The seminar is a source of hope that the practice of intellectual history may yet be reinvigorated in the U.S. academy.

Readers may wonder whether a second volume, an intellectual biography of the mature Popper, is forthcoming, and the answer is definitely no. The mature Popper is better known, and there are a good number of people, more qualified than I, to evaluate his postwar achievements. The formative context for Popper's work was the interwar socialist struggle against fascism in Central Europe, but his philosophy became popular in the postwar trans-Atlantic world, preoccupied with the cold war. I have attempted to rescue Popper from his postwar conservative reputation and recover the legacy of the young socialist who pursued radical reform and revolutionized the philosophy of science. I may still try to explain in detail the postwar reception of Popper among the philosophers of science, but, for the rest, I am leaving Popper and returning to the project that first gave rise to my interest in his philosophy: the Congress for Cultural Freedom, postwar trans-Atlantic liberalism, and the generation of liberal intellectuals who began their career as leftist antifascists, turned cold war liberals, and then, in the aftermath of 1968, became neoconservatives. Only recently have I realized that the appeals to me of postwar liberalism and the interwar assimilated-Jewish intelligentsia were actually one. Acculturated Jewish intellectuals and Central European Jewish émigrés played a prominent role in the Congress for Cultural Freedom, the international organization of postwar liberals. What made the liberal anticommunist crusade an international phenomenon was not only NATO and the CIA funding but also the cosmopolitanism of congress activists – many of them Jewish émigrés and ex-Communists – who envisioned a humanity that would fulfill, at the end of the day, the Marxist promise on which communism reneged.

One's debts to family and personal friends are always the greatest, but also the most difficult to speak of. Yerra Sugarman accompanied this project in its early stages and has remained a model of artistic sensitivity and good writing. My good friends Wim-Haim, Moishe, Blondie, Gikattila, and Shmulik Kipod-Igel have stood by me in difficult times, their support unwavering. Julie Mell, my spouse, has lived with the book through good and bad times. She has read and commented on numerous versions of most chapters and has been a constant source of intellectual and moral support, unfailing scholarly judgment and good advice, and, most importantly, wonderful companionship. Of my debt to my parents, Moshe and Zehava Hacohen, I can only say that which the Jewish midrash attributes to Rabbi Akiva. Upon his return home from a twenty-four-year sojourn of Torah study, Rabbi Akiva tells the students he brings with him about Rachel, his wife: "Mine and yours is hers."

Malachi Haim Hacohen
Duke University, Durham, N. C.
December 1999

Introduction

Why write an intellectual biography of Karl Popper (1902–1994)? To his many admirers, the answer may be obvious. He has been one of the most widely known philosophers of the twentieth century and may one day be recognized as its greatest. His philosophy, critical rationalism, resolved long-standing problems in the philosophy of science, and his cosmopolitanism inspires our age to look beyond the nation-state. He contributed to virtually every field of philosophy. Terms that he coined, or redefined, have become salient in contemporary discourse: Open Society, social engineering, essentialism, falsifiability, psychologism, World 3. He has been translated into more than forty languages, and additional translations continue to appear every month. Open Society projects and Popper centers have been proliferating around the world. He has become one of the most influential twentieth-century philosophers.

Born and raised in Vienna, Popper emigrated to New Zealand in 1937, settling in England in 1946. *The Open Society and Its Enemies* (1945), his major work in political philosophy, transformed him, almost overnight, from an unknown Viennese philosopher into a trans-Atlantic intellectual.[1] He wrote the book during World War II in his New Zealand exile, intending it as a defense of democracy against fascism, but it quickly became, with his full support, a charter of cold war liberalism. He regarded his political philosophy as the application of the philosophy of science that he had developed in interwar Vienna. His *The Logic of Scientific Discovery* (1935; 1959) is arguably the most important work in twentieth-century philosophy of science.[2] He drew a vision of science as an adventurous revolutionary project, an unending quest for growing, but never certain knowledge. Nobel laureates in physics and biology, seldom appreciative of philosophers of science, admired him: "incomparably the greatest philosopher of science ever," said biologist Peter Medawar of Popper.

For a time in the 1970s, leaders of all three major West German parties, notably former chancellor Helmut Schmidt, declared themselves Popper followers.[3] *Samizdat* editions of his works circulated in Eastern Europe

---

[1] Two vols. (London: Routledge, 1945). The work has remained in print for more than half a century, reissued in six editions and numerous reprints.

[2] Karl Popper, *Logik der Forschung: Zur Erkenntnistheorie der modernen Naturwissenschaft* (Vienna: Julius Springer, 1935); *The Logic of Scientific Discovery*, trans. Karl Popper (London: Hutchinson, 1959).

[3] Helmut Spinner, *Popper und die Politik* (Berlin: Dietz, 1978).

before the fall of communism. He has been less of a household name in the United States than in Europe, and his influence among English and North American philosophers has always lagged behind his following among the educated public, but recent surveys of scholarly literature on totalitarianism and on social science methodology found him mentioned more often than any philosopher, including Hannah Arendt, Ludwig Wittgenstein, and Thomas Kuhn.[4] Having always been at odds with the prevailing philosophical fashions – whether analytic philosophy, existentialism, or neomarxism – his popularity at any one period may not have matched that of the contemporary gurus, but the public interest in his work has remained high for half a century and is on the rise. No debate on the philosophy of science today takes place without a mention of his ideas.

I have endeavored to trace the formation of Popper's philosophy and to resolve many of the riddles that have preoccupied Popper's students about the young philosopher and his early works. I hope that the Popperians find interest in my account of the fin-de-siècle and interwar Viennese milieus and marvel, as I do, at how Popper struggled with problems, failing as often as succeeding, always with unparalleled ingenuity. My book is not directed, however, primarily to the Popperians. Nor do I simply wish to redress the current political imbalance in the reception of Popper's work. To be sure, I take exception with the uses to which the political right, in Austria no less, has put Popper. Recovering the historical Popper, whether the committed young socialist or the old, more conservative, Popper who remained supportive of the welfare state, is the best antidote to the political misappropriation of his work. But I have little to say to the right. My major audience is the academic left that has been, in my view, on the wrong track since it took the poststructuralist turn in the late 1970s. I hope to convince them that Popper saw more clearly than they have through the philosophical and political problems preoccupying them and that he provides a more promising direction in the search for answers. In short, I hope that Popper can help the academic left set a new progressive liberal agenda that will seek to recoup the social losses of the last two decades.

In *Philosophy and the Mirror of Nature*, a book that heralded the poststructuralist turn in the United States, Richard Rorty celebrated non-

---

[4] Peter Hedström, Richard Swedberg, and Lars Udéhn ("Popper's Situational Analysis and Contemporary Sociology," *Philosophy of the Social Sciences* 28 [1998]: 342–3) surveyed the five leading sociology journals in the United States, Britain, France, Germany, and Italy (1960–96). Popper was mentioned more frequently than Thomas Kuhn, Carl Hempel, or Ludwig Wittgenstein. He trailed Kuhn badly in the United States but led greatly in Germany and slightly in Britain, and was about equal in France and almost so in Italy. Christian Fleck, "Sieg der *Offenen Gesellschaft?*" in *Heinrich Gomperz, Karl Popper und die Österreichische Philosophie*, ed. Martin Seiler and Friedrich Stadler (Amsterdam: Rodopi, 1994), pp. 201–22 includes some statistics on references to *The Open Society* and Hannah Arendt's *The Origins of Totalitarianism* (New York: HBJ, 1951).

foundationist philosophy, philosophy that no longer sought a firm foundation in unshakable truths but, rather, recognized its practices as pragmatic
communal conventions.[5] Nonfoundationism reflected the crisis of representation, the recognition that language not only described the world but
also created it. Subjects did not conceive of objects; rather, subjectivity and
objectivity were themselves historically contingent discursive chimeras, a
product of modern philosophy since Descartes. The postmodern rid itself
of them. Rorty used Dewey, Heidegger, and Wittgenstein to illustrate nonfoundationist options. Had he used Popper, he might have saved the contemporary academy some detours. Contemporary debates are a *déjà vu* to
anyone familiar with the fin-de-siècle and interwar scenes, especially in
Vienna. Popper and his interwar interlocutors recognized "poststructuralist" dilemmas – they simply opted for different solutions. I am eager to recommend their solutions as against poststructuralist ones.

"Where we believed that we were standing on firm and safe ground,"
said Popper, "all things are, in truth, insecure and in a state of flux."[6]
"Objectivity" meant intersubjectivity: Rationality was a product of critical
debate, criticism the acid test of political and scientific rationality. Acknowledging linguistic self-referentiality – statements and reality could not be
compared – Popper permitted experience to inform theory (language)
through falsification. One statement about experience could contradict
another:

> [K]nowledge of the world is . . . to some extent . . . our invention. [S]o far
> idealism [or, he might have added, poststructuralism] is right. *But* it is not
> only an invention. . . . [O]ur theories are inventions for certain purposes
> and whether or not they fit the purposes *does not* depend on us. There are
> thus two elements in knowledge. Our experience (realism) tests and selects
> theories. This is not a criticism of Kant but just [an] illustration.[7]

Falsification in an experiment was conventional – it depended on a public
consensus that an event actually occurred and that it contradicted a proposed theory – but it was not arbitrary: A decision to accept a refutation
was informed, albeit not determined, by logic and methodology. We can
and do learn from experience, especially from errors. This idea distinguishes
Popper from the poststructuralists. He suggests a promising direction in the
search for knowledge: a modified conventionalism that sheds absolutism,
but safeguards rationalism.

Establishing free public debate as the *conditio sine qua non* of the Open

[5] Princeton: Princeton University Press, 1979.

[6] Karl Popper, "The Logic of the Social Sciences," in Theodor W. Adorno et al., *The Positivist Dispute in German Sociology*, trans. Glyn Adey and David Frisby (London: Heinemann, 1976), p. 87.

[7] Canterbury College lectures, 1941, Hoover Institute Archives, Karl Popper Papers, box 366, file 24. Henceforth: Popper Archives (box no., file no.). The catalog is now available electronically through The Karl Popper Web: www.eeng.dcu.ie/~tkpw/.

Society, Popper innovated on a familiar liberal motif, shared by thinkers as different as Immanuel Kant, Germaine de Staël, François Guizot, John Stuart Mill, and Jürgen Habermas. Including him with Habermas in the same genealogy may seem surprising. Their exchanges were hostile and exemplified what critical dialogue should *not* be like.[8] To the young Habermas, Popper was a positivist; to Popper, Habermas was a "Hegelian," a representative of German obscurantism. Both misunderstood each other. Both were Kantian liberals, using variations of the ideal speech situation to provide a nonfoundationist criterion of rationality and envision a deliberative democracy.[9] Habermas, engaged in Germany's political battles, has been more keenly aware than Popper of the socioeconomic and political preconditions for restoring the public sphere in postwar Europe. The burden of German politics, however, prevented Habermas until recently from espousing a vision similar to Popper's Open Society. In the Federal Republic, conservatives appropriated the liberal discourses of social technology and *Rechtsstaat* to fight the cold war and obstruct democratization and socialization. Just as one needed to be (and Popper was) a radical socialist in interwar Central Europe in order to promote the Open Society, so also was Habermas in postwar West Germany. By the early 1990s, however, Habermas brought together the *Rechtsstaat* and the *Sozialstaat*, constitutionalism and social reform, making the previously implicit explicit: Like Popper, he was a progressive cosmopolitan liberal, a bridge builder between liberalism and socialism.[10]

Not as well versed in natural science as Popper, and accepting of Max Weber's and Max Horkheimer's dark vision of "rationalization," Habermas was content to let the "positivist" view of natural science stand. He consigned natural science to "instrumental reason," radically separated instrumental and communicative rationality, and castigated Popper as a positivist who extended instrumental rationality to the social life world, the field of communicative action. Habermas achieved a pluralism of life spheres, or "a functionally differentiated society," but only at the cost of homogenizing each life sphere and giving up on emancipatory technology.[11] Popper

---

[8] Jürgen Habermas, "A Positivistically Bisected Rationalism," and Karl Popper, "Reason or Revolution?" both in Theodor Adorno et al., *The Positivist Dispute*; Popper, "Against Big Words," in his *In Search of a Better World* (London: Routledge, 1992).

[9] Jürgen Habermas, *Communication and the Evolution of Society*, trans. Thomas McCarthy (Boston: Beacon Press, 1974); Karl Popper, *The Open Society*, chaps. 23–4. Jeremy Shearmur draws further parallels in his admirable *The Political Thought of Karl Popper* (London: Routledge, 1996), esp. pp. 165–6.

[10] Ernst Forsthoff, ed., *Rechtsstaatlichkeit und Sozialstaatlichkeit: Aufsätze und Essays* (Darmstadt: Wissenschaftliche Buchgesellschaft, 1968); Arnold Gehlen, "Antropologische Ansicht der Technik," in *Technik im technischen Zeitalter*, ed. Hans Freyer et al. (Düsseldorf: Schilling, 1965); Jürgen Habermas, *Faktizität und Geltung: Beiträge zur Diskurstheorie des Rechts und des demokratischen Rechtsstaats* (Frankfurt: Suhrkamp, 1992). Matthew Specter's dissertation in progress evoked these reflections.

[11] Jürgen Habermas, *Technik und Wissenschaft als "Ideologie"* (Frankfurt: Suhrkamp, 1968); *The Theory of Communicative Action*, 2 vols. (Boston: Beacon Press, 1984–7).

refused to split the life of reason or action, or give up on the "scientific worldview" that he had inherited from the Viennese late enlightenment (*Spätaufklärung*):

> Science is nothing but enlightened and responsible common sense – common sense broadened by imaginative critical thinking. But it is more. It represents our wish to know, our hope of emancipating ourselves from ignorance and narrow-mindedness, from fear and superstition. . . . The nuclear bomb [has], I think, shown us the shallowness of the worship of science as an "instrument," of our "command over nature": . . . [T]his command, this control, is apt to be self-defeating, and apt to enslave us rather than to make us free – if it does not do away with us altogether.[12]

Only restoration of the "tradition of rationality" could save us from science as a means of control. This meant reclaiming science and philosophy for the public from the experts and the professionals. Long before cultural studies began deconstructing science, Popper countered philosophers' and scientists' claims of expertise. There was no philosophical or scientific method, he said. Every person was a problem solver; hence, every person was a philosopher-scientist. Demystifying science, he never gave up on the growth of knowledge and its emancipatory potential. Habermas regarded Marxism and psychoanalysis as emancipatory sciences, removing obstacles to liberation by calling attention to them. Popper's science performed a similar function – but did more: It guided social engineering in reconstructing society. The rules obtaining in the ideal scientific and political communities were similar – those making free criticism possible. To be sure, there were differences. In science, hypotheses, not humans, died, and so permanent revolution was welcomed. Politics should not likewise experiment with human lives. Social engineering must be piecemeal. Still, science and politics worked hand in hand to enable humans to take charge of their destiny, and thereby complete the Enlightenment project.

The Popper emerging from the previous paragraphs may not be the one most people have known over the past half century. The obscurity of his early life in Vienna, the cold war, his growing conservatism in the postwar years, and his disinterest in engaging most contemporary philosophers are largely to blame. Born and buried in Vienna, he was the foremost philosopher to carry the legacy of Viennese progressivism to the postwar trans-Atlantic world. His cosmopolitanism originated as a solution to the dilemmas of ethnic identity faced by the assimilated Jewish-Viennese intelligentsia. His Open Society expressed their hopes of integration into a community that discounted religion, ethnicity, and nationality.[13] During World

---

[12] Karl Popper, *Realism and the Aim of Science* (London: Hutchinson, 1982), p. 260.

[13] Malachi Hacohen, "Dilemmas of Cosmopolitanism: Karl Popper, Jewish Identity, and 'Central European Culture,'" *Journal of Modern History* 71 (1999): 105–49.

War II in his New Zealand exile, he drew a vision of a cosmopolitan empire that reflected the Viennese progressives' lost hopes for the Habsburg monarchy. The empire had its counterpart in a cosmopolitan scientific community laboring for human progress. Fascism destroyed cosmopolitan science and democratic politics in Central Europe. The progressive Viennese imagination preserved them as universal ideals in exile.

During the interwar years, Popper was involved in socialist reform and in Viennese circles developing scientific philosophy. He began as an unorthodox socialist and a critic of logical positivism, the philosophy of the Vienna Circle. The circle's efforts to transform philosophy into science, the defeat of Austrian socialism, and the collapse of Central European democracies were the major experiences informing his philosophy. Reception of his work in the postwar trans-Atlantic world occurred in radically different contexts. Red Vienna vanished from memory; the postwar Austrian socialists preferred to forget their Marxist predecessors. Communism, not fascism, became the overwhelming political issue. The circle's emigration to the West, and the triumph of analytic philosophy in the Anglo-American academy, transformed positivism from a Central European movement into a trans-Atlantic one. The "fugue of exile's disruptions" severed the thread connecting Popper to Austria.[14]

Popper launched his critique of the Vienna Circle from a marginal Kantian perspective foreign to logical positivism. He developed his philosophy in dialogue with the circle, but he adamantly refused to take their linguistic turn. His critique of positivism constituted a Kantian rejoinder. Against their platform for linguistic reform, he counterposed a revolutionary epistemology that rehabilitated philosophy, and even metaphysics, and made the search for ever-uncertain yet "true" knowledge a compelling task. The circle regarded his work as contributing to their scientific philosophy and made publication of his book, *Logik der Forschung*, possible. The book appeared in the circle's famed *Schriften zur Wissenschaflichen Weltauffassung* (Writings on the Scientific Conception of the World) series. Most discussions of Popper's philosophy of science in the immediate postwar period relied on the secondary reports of Vienna Circle émigrés. Popper protested to no end that he was their critic, not their friend, but his protests were in vain. What he called the "Positivist Legend" emerged.

Likewise, the reception of his political philosophy had little to do with its original intent. It was Red Vienna, not Soviet communism, that provided the grounds for his critique of Marx. When writing *The Open Society*, he knew next to nothing about the Soviet Union. He felt ambivalent about the Austrian socialist party whose policies he deemed suicidal. Fascism, he thought, reflected a primeval urge to return to the closed "tribal" society, and Marxist mistakes prevented the working class from resisting effectively

[14] Breyten Breytenbach, "The Long March from Hearth to Heart," *Social Research* 58 (1991): 81.

the fascist assault on democracy. Historians have corroborated much of his critique: Socialist trust in the Marxist grand narrative was a major reason that the Austrian socialists did not take up arms early to defend parliamentary democracy. Popper proposed a "United Front" of socialists and liberals to combat the prospective resurgence of fascism in postwar Central Europe. Within two years of the publication of *The Open Society*, he discovered that he had actually written the platform for the postwar Social Democratic Consensus in the West, a consensus that legislated for the welfare state and mobilized to contain communism.

During the cold war, Popper made a few naive pronouncements on deterrence and the free world that may reflect badly on his political philosophy.[15] Conceding that he had never anticipated the Soviet expansion in Europe, he gave, nonetheless, his blessings to appropriating *The Open Society* for containment. As the postwar economic miracle diminished poverty in Western democracies, his reform enthusiasm waned. Increasingly secluded in his house in Buckinghamshire, west of London, he devoted himself to the philosophy of science, paying little attention to social theory, all the more so because he thought little of its current proponents. His growing conservatism and retreat from politics obscured *The Open Society's* radical potential. The work was subject to trenchant critiques from the left and, worse, false liberal affirmations that the "West" approximated Popper's utopia. Precisely because the "West" was not, and is not, an open society, Popper's liberal utopia is relevant today. He refused to give up on cosmopolitanism in the bipolar world, when *Machtpolitik* (power politics) seemed the order of the day. Almost alone among postwar liberals, he retained a belief in an international legal order, and challenged national self-determination. His vision has regained relevance today.

The cold war is over, and analytic philosophy has long been in decline. The cold warrior and critic of logical positivism is dead. But he never was the only Popper. The intellectual and political circumstances that brought Popper his great renown may turn out, upon examination, to have distorted his legacy. My biography restores Popper to fin-de-siècle Vienna and interwar Central Europe, the vanished world of the assimilated Jewish intelligentsia. By historicizing Popper, I hope to recover the legacy of progressive and socialist Vienna for the post–cold war world. That which history tore apart historiography cannot mend. There may never be a revival of the flourishing cultures of cosmopolitan Habsburg centers. Central European cosmopolitanism represented the dreams of ethnopolitics' losers. They went into exile, or up Auschwitz's chimneys in flames. Historians can only work

---

[15] Popper, "The History of Our Time: An Optimist's View," in his *Conjectures and Refutations* (New York: Basic Books, 1963), pp. 364–76; "What Does the West Believe In?" (1959), in *In Search of a Better World*, pp. 204–22; "Zum Thema Freiheit," *Die Philosophie und die Wissenschaften*, ed. Ernst Oldemeyer (Meisenheim am Glan: Anton Hain, 1967), pp. 1–12.

toward realizing their dreams in different contexts. This is what I have attempted to do.

Having begun my work on Popper in the mid-1980s, I faced major difficulties in reconstructing his intellectual biography. I first considered him a member of the postwar liberal cohort, but quickly discovered that the two foundational texts, *The Open Society* and *The Poverty of Historicism*, made no sense when read in the cold war context.[16] One had to go back to interwar Vienna to find their roots. This was more easily undertaken than done. A young generation of Austrian scholars, usually on the left and on the margins of Austrian universities, was only then beginning to turn out the wonderful works that, in the past two decades, have recovered interwar Viennese culture. Popper's archives were not available yet, and his *Autobiography*, anachronistic on some issues, scarce in historical detail on others, proved less helpful than I had hoped.[17] I interviewed Popper once, for four hours, and he was kind and hospitable, but he did not remember very well the interwar years and seemed reluctant to talk about them. I read his 1928 dissertation and his articles, published from 1925 to 1931, in two organs of the Austrian school reform movement. They made it clear that the *Autobiography* could not have accurately described his intellectual progress, but in as much as they touched on unfamiliar problems and contexts, they left me as much in the dark as before. There was no choice but to follow leads in Popper's works and *Autobiography*, delve into interwar Viennese culture and politics, and reconstruct the institutional and discursive contexts relevant to his work from scratch.

I soon recognized that I was writing as much a book on interwar Viennese culture as on Popper. Biography opened a window to intellectual milieus that repeatedly surprised me with their richness, sophistication, and creativity. Interwar Vienna, capital of a tiny republic, could not compete with Habsburg Vienna for social and political splendor, but it was its intellectual match. As in fin-de-siècle years, intellectual innovation took place mostly in circles on the academy's margins, not at the university itself. Their economic base was, however, thinner; the socialist municipality substituted only partially for lost private funds. With limited resources, in a

---

[16] Karl Popper, "The Poverty of Historicism, I, II, III," *Economica* 11–12 (1944–5): 86–103, 119–37, 69–89; *The Poverty of Historicism* (London: Routledge, 1957).

[17] *Unended Quest: An Intellectual Autobiography* (La Salle, Ill.: Open Court, 1976). Henceforth: *Autobiography*. This is a slightly revised version of the original, published in the first Popper volume of the Library of Living Philosophers: *The Philosophy of Karl Popper*, ed. Paul Arthur Schilpp, 2 vols. (La Salle, Ill.: Open Court, 1974), 1:3–181.

tense political atmosphere suffused with anti-Semitism, these circles created much of what the postwar trans-Atlantic world would recognize as its own art history, economics, jurisprudence, mathematics, music, philosophy, political theory, sociology – and the list is by no means complete. Popper worked on the margins of these circles. Always a stranger in his homeland, he saw more presciently than most Austrian intellectuals what was in store for Central Europe and left early in 1937, joining the intellectual migration that enriched the Anglo-American academy and turned Vienna into an intellectual province.[18]

The various pieces of the biographical puzzle gradually fell into place. The picture that formed was surprising. It sharply diverged from both the autobiographical self-portrait and the familiar antileftist polemicist and disgruntled positivist. Whence, I wondered, the divergence? The disjunction between interwar Central Europe and the postwar trans-Atlantic world surely formed part of the explanation, but it seemed insufficient. The reception of other émigrés' works did not seem to raise as many problems. Further coincidences, I discovered, complicated the Popper reception. The sequence of publication of his English works upset the chronology of their formation and accentuated the chasm between the contexts of formation and reception. Until 1957, "The Poverty of Historicism," his treatise on planning and social science methodology, was buried in wartime issues of the journal *Economica*. Until *Logik der Forschung* appeared in English in 1959, his philosophy of science was known primarily through hearsay. His three-volume *Postscript to The Logic of Scientific Discovery*, written in the 1950s, remained unpublished until the early 1980s.[19] Until his archives opened in November 1990, his early manuscripts were inaccessible even to researchers. Much of the evidence for his intellectual trajectory was unavailable for a long time and, when it became available, seemed to speak to concerns widely different from the original ones.

Popper regarded his 1920s work on psychology and pedagogy as immature, made few references to it until his *Autobiography* (1974), and was reluctant to have others read it.[20] In 1929, he moved from cognitive psychology

---

[18] Friedrich Stadler, ed., *Vertriebene Vernunft*, 2 vols. (Vienna: Jugend und Volk, 1987–8); *Vertreibung der Vernunft: The Cultural Exodus from Austria*, ed. Friedrich Stadler and Peter Weibl, 2d ed. (New York: Springer, 1995) includes comprehensive biographical indexes on the Austrian migration. The older collection, Bernard Bailyn and Donald Fleming, eds., *The Intellectual Migration* (Cambridge: Harvard University Press, 1969) also includes essays on Austrian intellectuals.

[19] The *Postscript* came out as *Realism and the Aim of Science; The Open Universe; Quantum Theory and the Schism in Physics* (London: Hutchinson, 1981–2).

[20] Popper had the only copy of the incomplete 1927 thesis " 'Gewohnheit' und 'Gesetzerlebnis' in der Erziehung" (Popper archives [12, 11]). The 1928 dissertation was available through the University of Vienna: "Zur Methodenfrage der Denkpsychologie" (Ph.D. diss., 1928). The Austrian National Library (ÖNB) seems to be the only one to have the complete *Die Quelle*, where Popper published three of his four articles on psychology and pedagogy. (The Dollfuss government banned this school reform organ in 1934.)

to the logic of science. His geometry thesis, signaling the move, became accessible only when his archives opened.[21] His first book, *Die beiden Grundprobleme der Erkenntnistheorie* (The two fundamental problems of epistemology), written between 1930 and 1932, remained unpublished until 1979.[22] It is still not available in English. Reading *Grundprobleme*, one sees Popper's novel vision of science emerging from his critique of Kant and his epigones, Jakob Fries and Leonard Nelson. *Logik der Forschung* radically compressed this critique, and then to make things worse, took a quarter of a century to appear in English. During the time that elapsed, Popper's philosophy came to form part of logical positivist discourse. The positivists knew and cared nothing about Fries and Nelson, and Popper himself forgot about them.[23] His published work seemed to obscure, rather than illuminate, the intellectual transformations that he had undergone as a young intellectual.

Popper helped the confusion by first omitting historical signposts from his work, then reconstructing his intellectual autobiography in a manner that concealed most turns and dead ends. While writing "The Poverty of Historicism" in New Zealand, he was already reshaping Central European discourses so as to make them relevant also to Western Europe, rarely mentioning Viennese intellectuals and seldom referring to Central European methodological controversies (*Methodenstreit*). He had conceived of "Poverty" before leaving Europe; he wrote a draft in New Zealand before the war, and rewrote most of the work for publication in 1944–5, after he had already completed *The Open Society*. Most people read "Poverty" only when it was published as a book, dedicated to the victims of Nazism and communism. As it came out the year after the Soviet repression of the Hungarian and Polish uprisings, and as Popper had the reputation of Marx's foremost critic, it became another contribution to the cold war. Many of Popper's arguments made little sense in this context – but no other existed. A book formed at three intervals, in between cultures, with moving targets of criticism and few historical markers represented a nightmare for the historian seeking to identify its "original" aims.

Popper has not found his biographer until now and has rarely been the subject of historical study. In the boundless literature on his ideas, there is not one historical monograph. His breadth of interests would not deter historians – we often write about fields in which we have less than ade-

---

[21] "Axiome, Definitionen und Postulate der Geometrie," 2 vols., Popper Archives (4, 6).

[22] Ed. Troels Eggers Hansen (Tübingen: Mohr, 1979). Popper completed only the first volume of *Die beiden Grundprobleme* on induction. The second, on demarcation, was never completed. Hansen collected in *Grundprobleme* all extant material, dating from late 1932 and early 1933. In July 1933, Popper began work on *Logik der Forschung*. See my discussion in Chapters 5–6.

[23] He mentioned them in *Autobiography*, pp. 74–5, 85, and in "Julius Kraft: 1898–1960," *Ratio* 4 (1962): 2–10, but it is not clear that he was fully cognizant of the role they played in his intellectual development. Compare: *Die beiden Grundprobleme*, Section 11; *Logik der Forschung*, Sections 25, 29.

quate competence. It is rather that, with Popper, one does not quite know where to begin. Virtually everyone who knows him recognizes that one must go back to interwar Vienna, but outside Austria, the interwar Viennese milieu is not well known. Not surprisingly, the few attempts at historical study of Popper have been made by Austrian scholars and Popper students who read German. They have produced work that I have found most helpful for my own.

Young Austrian scholars took advantage of the Second Republic's effort, beginning in the 1980s, to reclaim the interwar cultural heritage and proclaim Popper, an eternal exile who escaped the country for his life, an "Austrian philosopher." With remarkable energy, they have painstakingly reconstructed the life of fin-de-siècle and interwar Central European networks, thereby throwing light on the context for Popper's work. They have put us – and their compatriots who still feel uneasy about their projects – in debt. They recognize Austrian socialism as the crucial context for Popper's political philosophy. Using evidence yielded by the opening of the archives of the Vienna Circle and its affiliates, they have emphasized Popper's ambivalent relationship to the circle.[24] The Popper archives have recently been made available to the Austrians. I look forward to their forthcoming works.

A few Popper students endeavored to explore his early intellectual development. William W. Bartley, III, philosopher and biographer of Wittgenstein, undertook in the 1980s to write Popper's biography. He interviewed many of his early Viennese acquaintances, and had the still unorganized archives at his disposal. If the one chapter from his prospective biography, circulating among Popper scholars, is evidence enough, he collected a great amount of useful material and would have written an interesting biography.[25] Unfortunately, he died in 1990, and to the best of my knowledge, the material has not been released to other scholars. Philosopher John Wettersten wrote, with William Berkson, a book on Popper's early psychology, then followed up with another, *The Roots of Critical Rationalism*, using all

---

[24] Friedrich Stadler, *Studien zum Wiener Kreis* (Frankfurt: Suhrkamp, 1997), chap. 10; Friedrich Wallner, "Popper und die österreichische Philosophie," in *Karl Popper – Philosophie und Wissenschaft: Beiträge zum Popper-Kolloquium*, ed. Friedrich Wallner (Vienna: Braumüller, 1985); Johann Dvorák, "Karl Popper und die Wissenschaft von der Geschichte in der Epoche des Faschismus," in *Versuche und Widerlegungen offene Probleme im Werk Karl Poppers*, ed. Karl Müller, Friedrich Stadler, and Friedrich Wallner (Vienna: Geyer, 1986); see also the essays by Müller in the last volume.

[25] William W. Bartley, III, "Rehearsing a Revolution: Music and Politics" (extract from "Karl Popper: A Life"), a paper delivered at the Pacific Regional Meeting of the Mont Pèlerin Society, Christchurch, New Zealand, November 27–30, 1989. I have found this paper most informative on Popper's involvement with communism and the Schoenberg circle. See also: "Theory of Language and Philosophy of Science as Instruments of Educational Reform: Wittgenstein and Popper as Austrian School Teachers," in *Methodological and Historical Essays in the Natural and Social Sciences, Boston Studies in the Philosophy of Science* 14 (1972): 307–37; *Wittgenstein* (Philadelphia: Lippincott, 1973).

of Popper's early published works.[26] Wettersten reconstituted many of the psychological theories available to the young Popper, and offered an insightful treatment of *Die beiden Grundprobleme*. The archives tend to corroborate his conclusions about *Grundprobleme*'s composition, but my view of Popper's early intellectual development, presented in Chapters 3 and 4, diverges from his.

Having completed my dissertation early in 1993, I had the opportunity to consult the opened archives.[27] They were, in many respects, a dream come true, including every manuscript that I could not access before, and more. Although Popper did not release most personal material, such as correspondence with family members, to the archives, and although he seemed to have done – perhaps with his wife Hennie (Josefine Henninger, 1906–85) – minor editing of some material (for example, correcting wrong dates), the archives convey a vivid picture of the person, with all his eccentricities, anxieties, and moods. I have gotten to know him much better than I had before. The archives corroborated some of my conjectures, but falsified a few, especially with regard to *The Poverty of Historicism*, and corrected and refined others. Archives of other Viennese intellectuals have been opened in recent years, and they include illuminating correspondence not only *with* Popper but also *about* Popper, rendering a fuller picture of his place in Viennese and Central European debates. I have accordingly rewritten my dissertation into a new book. This is the first biography of Popper to have taken his archives into account, and the first monograph on his work by an intellectual historian.[28]

Popper aptly called his *Autobiography* an *intellectual* autobiography. It is the history of his ideas, his progress from one philosophical problem to another. Precious little of the person and the context found its way into the work. For all of its clarity, simplicity, and elegance of style, the *Autobiography* frustrates the historian's effort to identify the debates and the people Popper engaged in his work. It can sometimes be misleading. Popper imposed the *telos* of his mature philosophy on his intellectual development. His progress from youth politics to psychology in the 1920s to the logic of science in the 1930s to the Open Society during World War II seems linear. The "rationality of scientific revolution" dominates the narrative. Only the theories that withstood the test of time and criticism – above all,

[26] William Berkson and John Wettersten, *Learning from Error: Karl Popper's Psychology of Learning* (La Salle, Ill.: Open Court, 1984); John Wettersten, *The Roots of Critical Rationalism* (Amsterdam: Rodopi, 1992).

[27] Malachi Hacohen, "The Making of the Open Society: Karl Popper, Philosophy and Politics in Interwar Vienna" (Ph.D diss., Columbia University, 1993).

[28] Rumor has it that Professor Brian Boyd of Auckland University, New Zealand (biographer of Vladimir Nabokov), has been entrusted by the executors with the writing of Popper's official biography. One hopes that the remaining material that Popper willed to his archives would soon be made available to the scholarly community.

Popper's own criticism – made it into the *Autobiography*. He projects a coherence of philosophy and life that seems almost unworldly. It conceals the plurality of directions in which his thought developed, the intellectual impasses, the options foreclosed, and the decisive turning points. His auto-biography dehistoricized his life and philosophy.

Readers may trace in my complaints against Popper's *Autobiography* the poststructuralists' grievances against biography as such. Biography, they believe, presumes the author's stable identity. As the subject, or the self, is discursively constructed, even alterably performed, deconstruction of iden-tity seems a more promising strategy than biographical assemblage, or uni-fication. Biography also seems to imply a linear narrative of life rather than plurality of directions, coherence of experience rather than multiplicity of contexts, teleology rather than contingency. In my view, however, histori-ography, biography included, moves between stability and change, unity and dispersal, determinance and indeterminance, either radical position ren-dering it impossible, or superfluous. The poststructuralists have appropri-ately put the fear of premature coherence in the heart of every methodologically aware historian, but they have also rendered problematic, even illegitimate, modes of scholarship, intellectual biography among them, that I am eager to recommend. This is not the place for a methodological manifesto, and readers will have to judge for themselves whether my account of Popper does justice to the complexity of his life and work. I may be able, however, to arbitrate some of the poststructuralist complaints by explaining why my own biography is not open to the objections I raise against Popper's.

We commonly tell stories of our lives with particular purposes in mind. Already in the early 1930s, Popper was using his biography to argue a pri-ority claim on nonfoundationism against the Vienna Circle. He had, however, little time or inclination in interwar years to take a longer view of his life. A young philosopher in search of recognition, convinced that he had a revolutionary message, he was absorbed in his projects. Only after the war, when he became a leading trans-Atlantic philosopher, did he begin systematic reflection on the history of his ideas. By the early 1950s, he had solved many of his philosophy's thorny problems. He was fighting the prevalent "positivist" reading of his work, determined to show that, intel-lectually, he owed nothing to the circle. He was also beginning to have private priority disputes with his students, philosophers Joseph Agassi and Paul Feyerabend. His recollection of his early intellectual life was no longer vivid. The past was traumatic, not only on account of fascism and exile but also because his progress was a story of repeated emotional crises, radical shifts between elation and depression. He endeavored to present his own development as a model for the growth of knowledge. As a result, he pro-duced an anachronistic account of his intellectual development, reading his later philosophy back into the interwar years. While writing my dissertation, I suspected either amnesia or a willful distortion, but neither seems necessary to explain his account (and neither is likely). Autobiographical anachronism is common, and Popper's memory failure may not even be as surprising as I still occasionally find it.

Popper's main story line for the interwar years runs as follows: After a brief youthful engagement with communism in 1919, he rejected it. Responding to the corroboration of Albert Einstein's relativity theory in a major experiment the same year, he demarcated science from pseudo-science through testability: Marxism and psychoanalysis were not testable, hence pseudosciences; Newtonian and Einsteinian physics were testable, hence scientific (although they may be "wrong"). His explorations in psychology in the early 1920s led him to reject the prevailing empiricist and behaviorist doctrines and overthrow induction, the view that science progressed by generalizing particular observations into laws. Rather, science progressed through conjectures and refutations, offering theories (laws) that went beyond experience, then subjecting them to criticism and tests. In 1929, he realized that his solution to the two problems, demarcation and induction, actually converged into a revolutionary view of science. Scientists and philosophers used induction to demarcate science because they had no better criterion of demarcation. He did – testability. He also recognized that arguments he sought to make in psychology were best made in the logic of science. His philosophy of science emerged from his psychology. In the later 1930s, he began applying his philosophy of science to politics. From 1919 on, he had been elaborating fundamentally the same philosophy.[29]

This is not the way things happened, however. Popper formulated neither the induction nor the demarcation problem before 1930, and his intellectual breakthrough in the logic of science required him to renounce his previous research program for psychology as "psychologism." He also gained more than he was willing to acknowledge from his encounter with the Vienna Circle. All the same, the 1950s set the road marks for Popper's *Autobiography*. He settled on a narrative that clarified, to him and others, the significance of his experiences as a young Viennese intellectual. That the narrative did little justice to his intellectual confusion during the 1920s did not matter.

Not all was lost – yet. Having learned in May 1963 from Paul Arthur Schilpp, editor of the noted Library of Living Philosophers, that Schilpp was planning a volume on his philosophy, Popper enthusiastically responded that "I have actually started writing my autobiography."[30] (Each Schilpp

---

[29] "Science: Conjectures and Refutations," in his *Conjectures and Refutations*, pp. 33–59. This began as a 1953 lecture to a Cambridge seminar, first published in 1957 under the title: "Philosophy of Science: A Personal Report." Fifteen years later, Popper reconstructed his intellectual development along similar lines in *Autobiography*.

[30] Schilpp to Popper, 7 May 1963; Popper to Schilpp, 12 June 1963, Popper Archives (334, 2).

volume begins with an autobiography, followed by contributors' critical essays, to which the philosopher has replied.) But Popper had difficulties writing. In the following years, he produced a number of outlines (which the archives contain) and wrote occasional fragments that he hoped would eventually find their place in the *Autobiography*.[31] His outlines included references to Viennese intellectuals, political events, and books about which we hear nothing later in the drafts, and even less in the published version. Had he carried out his original plans, we would have had a different auto-biography from the one we possess. But he did not. He sensed that the *Autobiography* was his great chance to shape his image and legacy, had great expectations for public recognition, yet was reticent about speaking of himself and revealing the life behind his philosophy. "I find it greatly embar-rassing to write my intellectual autobiography. So far, arguments were the very life of what I have written." "[I]t is more interesting to go on trying to solve problems than to look back on one's failures. . . . [T]here is too much material, and too little confidence that it will interest anybody." "[I]t takes such an effort to write one's intellectual autobiography."[32]

There are signs that his undertaking to write an autobiography gave occasion to introspection that he found unpleasant. He was aware of the literary artistry of shaping the self and astute about people's psychological motives; at the same time, he had high moral expectations of himself. He now needed to present himself and his mission, and may have reflected on his "true self" and motives. With images of childhood, youth, and family "pressing before [his] mind, for the first time in many, many years," he revis-ited almost forgotten issues – "know thyself," authenticity, and the existen-tialist philosopher Søren Kierkegaard (1813–55). He recoiled, a bit startled. The search for pure motives, he said, was self-defeating and narcissistic. "The idea must lead to hysteria; and it must lead to lying and to the adoption of a pose – precisely those things it wants to avoid; and to self-centeredness." Kierkegaard "was almost pathologically vain. . . . He wrote: 'Not only my work will be studied and studied, but especially my life, the intriguing secrecy of its whole machinery.' " Kant "speaks of the good will; but he does not admonish you to analyse. In fact, as Schiller has shown, any self-analysis leads to nonsense."[33]

Popper endeavored to explain Kierkegaard's obsession with authenticity by his relationship to his father.[34] He never completed the argument (which

---

[31] Popper Archives (134, 4, 6).

[32] Fragments of the *Autobiography* (134, 4). The first quotation is from a ten-page holograph, the begin-ning of an early draft of the autobiography, the second and third from an incomplete one-page type-script, possibly intended to introduce the autobiography.

[33] "A Digression: Know Thyself and the Purity of Heart" (134, 4, 8). Popper's opposition to preoccu-pation with pure motives was evident already in his Canterbury College lectures on Kant's ethics (366, 24).

[34] Kierkegaard repeatedly reconfigured the biblical story of Abraham's near-sacrifice of Isaac. (Søren

was also to include a discussion of Simone Weil [1909–43], the French socialist Jewish-Catholic philosopher). He probably caught himself in the middle, realizing that his psychoanalysis was not leading to an easy dismissal of authenticity, but, rather, was delegitimizing Kierkegaard on account of his motives. This, indeed, would be self-defeating. He would be claiming superiority for his own autobiography, written as a history of ideas, over Kierkegaard's journals, a self-involved search for authenticity, based on precisely the kind of analysis and moral judgment he rejected. He dropped the digression altogether, and proceeded to shape the only self that he thought was not narcissistic or self-aggrandizing, that of a philosopher engaging (for whatever reason) problems of interest to humanity.

Kierkegaard was not the only thinker Popper castigated for obsessive unmasking of motives. His rejection of Sigmund Freud and Karl Mannheim reflected similar objections. His brief critique of psychoanalysis never accounted for his intense hostility toward it. He actually conceded the importance and correctness of much of Freud's interpretation of dreams.[35] He was less persuaded of the sociology of knowledge's importance: It said correct, but trivial, things about ideas' historical conditioning.[36] But here, too, what irked him most was delegitimizing opponents (like diagnosing patients) without giving them a chance of challenging the analysis. This undermined rationality, by eliminating criticism in science's name. His critiques of psychoanalysis and the sociology of knowledge were excellent, but he closed himself to contributions they could make to critical rationalism, above all, the understanding of the conditions likely to promote a free and secure public sphere. Like critical rationalism, they, too, had an emancipatory impetus. His *Autobiography* showed that exorcising introspection did not prevent self-aggrandizement; indeed, a measure of self-reflection might have restrained it and produced a narrative closer to life.

Why did he, Popper, deserve recognition, he wondered? Only because he had worked so hard on problems of interest to humanity and managed to solve some, he thought. Was he a genius? He was not sure (though I am). He hoped for public recognition as one, but dismissed the question as irrelevant. In 1964, he was rethinking his early involvement with composer Arnold Schoenberg and his circle. He posed them as a countermodel for the pursuit of fame. Modernism in music demonstrated "the triviality of the expressionist idea." To expressionists, "if I am somebody worthwhile (a genius) then my work will be worthwhile." On the contrary, said Popper,

---

Kierkegaard, *Fear and Trembling, Kierkegaard's Writings*, trans. Howard and Edna Wong, vol. 6 [Princeton: Princeton University Press, 1983].) Popper suggested that, having found out that his father cursed God, Kierkegaard faced the dilemma of whether to sacrifice himself to atone for his father's sin.

[35] "Science: Conjectures and Refutations," pp. 33–9; *Realism and the Aim of Science*, pp. 163–74.

[36] *The Open Society*, chap. 23.

"if I can produce something worthwhile, then, perhaps, I may even grow, in so doing, into somebody worthwhile; but clearly only if I put [in] the work first."[37] Did he put in the work! He told the story of the engraver who used to wake up in the middle of the night to add one line to the engraving and added, "I did the same." He worked 360 days a year, morning to night. Genius was controversial; his hard work was not. Its results the public must judge. He would not bother them with personal life, but focus his *Autobiography* on philosophy, demonstrating exemplary dedication to it.

"How often have I heard the doctor himself say those very words as he was packing his little black bag to go on a voyage: 'what to leave out and what to put in? That's the problem.'"[38] Memories of sixty years over-whelmed Popper. It was not that he remembered too much. Indeed, he would complain at various points that he did not recall his childhood and family well enough.[39] Rather, he had difficulty making sense of it all as intellectual history. "Intellectual history . . . is a fascinating subject precisely because we have to guess, to reconstruct, to discover the surprising logical interplay of problems and their proposed solutions." Life, especially early life, was not easily susceptible to such organization. He did not find the process pleasant. "In one's autobiography . . . the only thing that one finds surprising are one's blind spots, one's stupidities."[40] How could he, earlier, not have seen things that later became so clear?

Returning to the Vienna of his youth, a vanished world, Popper also rec-ollected personal losses. "Ghosts walk Vienna's streets," he told philosopher John Watkins, his student.[41] He now had to converse with the ghosts. He was always frightfully busy, and so faced with an unpleasant and seemingly unmanageable task, he procrastinated writing his *Autobiography*, ignoring Schilpp's pleas. He experimented a good deal with the *Autobiography*'s first section, seeking to recount an episode in his life that would capture his philosophy. At one point, he considered his now famous October 1946 con-frontation with Wittgenstein in Cambridge's Moral Sciences Club, a strug-gle between giants that he felt he had won.[42] He wisely decided that it would look like self-glorification and gave up on it, as he did on a story,

---

[37] Fragment of autobiography dated 8 December 1964 (134, 4).

[38] Motto of *Autobiography*, quoted from Hugh Luftig, *Doctor Dolittle's Zoo*. (Dr. Dolittle stories were one of Popper's favorite pastime readings.)

[39] Draft of *Autobiography* (134, 4); *Offene Gesellschaft – offenes Universum: Franz Kreuzer im Gespräch mit Karl R. Popper* (Vienna: Deuticke, 1982), p. 23.

[40] Both quotations are from a fragment (134, 4).

[41] My conversation with Watkins, London, 8 March 1996.

[42] *Autobiography*, pp. 122–4; Peter Munz, *Our Knowledge of the Growth of Knowledge* (London: Routledge and Kegan Paul, 1985), pp. 1–2. See the correspondence in the February and March 1998 issues of the *Times Literary Supplement* and Watkins, "The Truth Will Out," *The Philosophers' Magazine* (Spring 1999).

told tongue in cheek, of a childhood injury to his head that prevented him from a future understanding of Hegelianism, existentialism, language philosophy, and other twentieth-century intellectual fashions. This was as far as he got by April, or even October, 1967. He settled on the opening episode, but had not yet begun the narrative.[43]

He began seeing his way through the dark, however. In January 1967, he happily reported the discovery that a youthful dispute he had had with his father was actually over essentialism: He rejected the notion that words, or definitions, had an essential meaning and were something other than conventional instruments, malleable with context.[44] He began writing about essentialism, rather apologetically, as a digression, emphasizing that the terms he was using had not been available to him as a youth. Both the apologies and the caveats gradually disappeared. With growing confidence, he discovered a series of early philosophical problems (one, the problem of infinity, at the age of eight), and extended the digressions, as well as discussions of his current theories, until they constituted the bulk of the text. He reported to Schilpp that he was writing a "philosophical autobiography." If the extant drafts are evidence enough, he spent more time on the early sections, to World War I, than on the rest. He did most of the writing during the spring and summer of 1969.[45] Pressed for time, writing with lightning speed, he latched onto a narrative of philosophical problems. "Earlier generations," he said gleefully, "used texts as their point of departure. . . . Nowadays, one starts with a problem situation, a problématique."[46]

Once Popper had turned his life into a story of intellectual progress, he was in familiar territory. He had ready-made models for the history of philosophy and science. He may not have thought over their methodology yet, but he had long favored problem-oriented historical narratives. Already in his 1929 geometry thesis, he modeled his history of geometry on Max Born's *Einstein's Relativity Theory*.[47] Born had begun with classical mechanics, moved to Newtonian mechanics, optics, and electrodynamics, and ended with Einstein's relativity. He had outlined each theory, and explained how discoveries in related fields problematized it, thereby creating conditions for the next scientific advance. Popper adopted his explanatory model, used it whenever he discussed scientific progress, and now applied it to his

---

[43] Popper to Schilpp, 8 April 1967; outline, October 1967, indicating that Popper had not yet begun even the preliminary drafts.

[44] Note to John Watkins, 19 January 1967 (134, 4).

[45] Drafts and timetable (134, 4, 6, 8–9, 11, 12); Schilpp to Popper, 31 December 1968, and 6 June, 4 August, and 20 September 1969; Popper to Schilpp, 12 June, 23 July 1969.

[46] Fragment (134, 4), quoting Franz Tietze's editor's introduction to Hermann Ferdinand Fränkel, *Wege und Formen frühgriechischen Denkens* (Munich: Beck, 1955).

[47] Trans. Henry L. Brose (London: Methuen, 1924); Max Born, *Die Relativitätstheorie Einstein und ihre physikalischen Grundlagen*, 3d ed. (Berlin: Springer, 1922).

autobiography. He thought the result a major success. Where he had no biographical narrative before, he now had one that wonderfully shaped his life into an unended quest for growing knowledge, endowing it with supreme philosophical significance. Greatly heartened, he elaborated further, in several essays, on the relationship between intellectual history and the "logic of the situation," his method for constructing social science models. In the 1980s, he urged Bartley to adopt a problem-focused narrative for his planned Popper biography.

Born's explanatory model was powerful. It represented a traditional history of ideas, explaining ideas' development by focusing on tensions in theories and thinkers' efforts to resolve them. It is a crucial intellectual history method, and I have argued elsewhere that, having been neglected in recent years, it must be recovered.[48] But it has limits. The problem situations that thinkers face are not solely theoretical, but reflect a variety of contexts – political, social, cultural. The art of intellectual history is the coordinating of internal (theoretical) and external (contextual) explanation. Leonard Krieger, the previous generation's brilliant intellectual historian, let the theoretical explanation run its course until a theory reached a crisis, its logic breaking down, then permitted other contexts to explain its transformation. This, however, constrains historical explanation, or "historicization." The theoretical problem situation is rarely closed to history. Theories, texts, and authors respond to "history" at all times, historical changes translating into theoretical tensions and new problems.

It is tempting to describe my intellectual biography of Popper as historicizing the antihistoricist thinker par excellence, but it would be misleading. Popper's critique of historicism has little to do with historicization. He distinguished between "historicism" (*Historizismus*) and "historism" (*Historismus*). The first entailed "inexorable historical laws," the latter the "historical dependence of our opinion."[49] The first was a dangerous theory, the major subject of his political critique; the latter was nebulous. He thought that *Historismus* contained an "undeniable but rather trivial kernel of truth" and usually reflected conservative resistance to scientific endeavors to rationalize the world.[50] His stance against *Historismus* depended, however, on the historicization in question. He opposed the social determination of ideas, but not the use of social context in explaining the formation of ideas. He himself produced wonderful historical scholarship on Plato, classical Athens, and the philosophy of science. His conclusions were controversial, but his manner of relating text, biography, and contexts was

---

[48] "Leonard Krieger: Historicization and Political Engagement in Intellectual History," *History and Theory* 35 (1996): 80–130.

[49] *The Poverty of Historicism*, p. 3: "an approach to the social sciences which assumes that *historical prediction* is their principal aim, and . . . that this aim is attainable by discovering . . . the 'laws' . . . that underlie the evolution of history." *The Open Society and Its Enemies*, vol. 2, p. 196.

[50] *The Open Society*, vol. 2, pp. 242–3.

exemplary, showing sensitivity to literary clues, psychology, institutions, and intellectual development.

Indeed, Popper himself developed a mode of historicization – "situational logic."[51] He suggested that we account for theoretical advances (or theoretical "moves" thinkers made) by constructing the problem situation they faced, then explaining the solution they came up with as a response to the problem. This disposes of determinism. Agents "move." Problem situations explain the relative constraints under which they operate. The extent of freedom varies from one situation to another. Admittedly, Popper was inclined toward an "internalist" philosophical explanation: The intellectual problem situation was the one he considered most valuable. He was suspicious of sociological and psychological explanations and usually used them to delegitimize opponents or to explain philosophical failures, that is, to clarify the reasons that thinkers did not see things right, or failed to make the correct "moves." There was something undignified about historicization. One psychologized and sociologized failure, not success.[52] This was an unnecessarily defensive move. Popper argued, at the same time, that ideas' origins have nothing whatsoever to do with their validity. Intersubjective criticism was the criterion for acceptance, not freedom from prejudice (of whatever sort), which, in any case, was impossible. If his criterion for "objectivity" is accepted, historicization poses no threat to universal validity. Popper could have cast a wider contextual net.

I have attempted to do so in this intellectual biography of Popper. I see myself as extending his method, not challenging it. I do not think, however, that excluding historical origins from discussions of validity is useful, or that questions of genesis are theoretically trivial. There is no need to privilege the context of an idea's genesis to recognize that it is often appropriate to test and criticize the idea. The situational logic explaining an idea's formation is often easier to grasp than its other contexts of application. This facilitates criticism. That a particular context gave rise to Popper's cosmopolitanism does not impinge on cosmopolitanism's universality, that is, on its claim to be a valid solution for the rest of humanity, but it may alert us to some of its problems. Cosmopolitanism tended to be the ideology of those who lived in between cultures and saw no ethnic future for themselves. Neither the majority of German-Austrians nor the Czechs nor the Zionists went for it. Reception was not the only problem. Emerging from a life-and-death struggle against ethnonationalism, Popper's cosmopoli-

---

[51] *The Poverty of Historicism*, secs. 31–2; "Models, Instruments, and Truth" [1963] and "A Pluralist Approach to the Philosophy of History" [1969], in *The Myth of the Framework* (London: Routledge, 1994); "On the Theory of the Objective Mind," *Objective Knowledge* (Oxford: Clarendon Press, 1972).

[52] *Locus classicus*: "I admire Socrates in spite of the fact that in some respects he may justly be interpreted as a forerunner of language philosophy. I look upon this aspect of Socrates as something to be explained, and even to be excused by historical considerations": "Replies to My Critics," in *The Philosophy of Karl Popper*, 2:1181 n. 5.

tanism ignored the legitimate claims of community. Aware of how the original context both enabled and disabled the cosmopolitan idea, we may want to negotiate universalism and particularism a little differently.[53]

This is not to suggest that Popper would have approved of my biography. In all likelihood, he would have objected to much of it. He did what he could to control his image and shape his reputation, and he showed less than exemplary openness to criticism and to efforts to reconstruct his intellectual history that did not tally with his *Autobiography*. To explain his intellectual formation, I call on contexts that he considered irrelevant – above all, the assimilated Jewish intelligentsia – and on others that he overlooked, or diminished, in his autobiography. I rehistoricize the life that he dehistoricized. My aim is not only to provide a fuller and more accurate account and recover a rich culture that vanished but also to rescue the young Popper for the present, to see how the adventurous socialist who revolutionized the philosophy of science and formed a compelling vision of the Open Society can help us rethink our problems today. I believe that my biography and mode of historicization are not open to the charge of premature closure of authorial identity and formative experience. I have constructed Popper's identity from historical materials, not presupposed it, and assembled multiple contexts in order to create the problems that he addressed, not reduced his philosophy to a unitary context. I have endeavored to show that an intellectual biography is possible after poststructuralism. Rumors of the death of the subject and the eclipse of experience have been greatly exaggerated.

I take Popper to the end of his New Zealand exile in 1945 – and no further. The postwar mature Popper is well known. A number of his students have provided accounts of the postwar philosopher and have done so with a philosophical expertise and personal knowledge that I do not pretend to have.[54] More biographies will undoubtedly come out soon. I also think that the young Popper, much like the young Hegel and Marx, is the more interesting and creative. It is not that the old Popper was resting on his laurels, or "reliving the drama of [his] own youth."[55] He advanced new ideas, like evolutionary epistemology and World 3 (neither objective

---

[53] Malachi Hacohen, "Dilemmas of Cosmopolitanism."

[54] Joseph Agassi, *A Philosopher's Apprentice* (Amsterdam: Rodopi, 1993) draws a splendid critical portrait of the postwar philosopher and projects well the excitement that Popper generated among young philosophers in the 1950s. David Miller, "Sir Karl Raimund Popper," *Biographical Memoirs of Fellows of the Royal Society* 43 (1997): 367–409 provides a brief overview of Popper's career and philosophy, as does John Watkins, "Karl Raimund Popper 1902–1994," *Proceedings of the British Academy* 94 (1997): 645–84. (Watkins was working on a fuller memoir at the time of his death in July 1999.) Readers interested in ongoing developments in Popper's philosophy and in the wide spectrum of Popperian influences can consult *Philosophy of the Social Sciences*, established in 1971, edited by Popper's student, philosopher and social scientist Ian Jarvie.

[55] Karl Mannheim, "The Problem of Generations," in his *Essays on the Sociology of Knowledge* (New York: Oxford University Press, 1952), p. 301.

nor subjective, but intersubjective – discourse, theories, books), into the 1970s, and beyond. But, whereas the young Popper was open to new influences, willing to adapt and change, the old Popper focused on developing an already established philosophy, the sources of innovation almost all internal. He made wonderful contributions. Indeed, his later philosophy of science is more thoroughly nonfoundationist and antideterminist, less insistent on the boundaries between science and history, more attuned, I think, with contemporary views. But it is the politics and intellectual engagement of the young Popper that is most relevant today, and it alone can explain the formation of the philosophy that flourished, often in appropriations I do not appreciate, in postwar years.

Popper engaged the past in a manner that I propose as a model for contemporary intellectuals. He rejected, on the one hand, the authority of the past and of tradition. His critique of Plato dethroned him in a manner that recent critics of Western metaphysics could only aspire to emulate. But he refused to join in a wholesale dismissal of the past and of tradition, because such dismissal inevitably involved arrogant pretension to knowledge. In the intellectual avant-gardes of his day, he found what I still find in our own: not skepticism, but certitude that "now we know." We do not know, and therefore have no more right to treat our predecessors as if we did, than they have to claim our allegiance. We can engage them critically, and learn. Popper upheld Kant against Wittgenstein and the Vienna Circle not because he thought that Kant had the right answers but because he thought that Kant was on the right track to discover better answers, whereas the attack on Western metaphysics manifested old philosophical absolutism and would lead to a dead end. Throughout his life, he rejected all temptation to "ride the next wave." I identify with his stance. Academic avant-gardes have "treated [Popper] as a 'dead dog.' I therefore openly avow myself the pupil of that mighty thinker"[56] so that we can critically engage him to rethink a better future.

---

[56] Karl Marx, speaking of his debt to Hegel, "Nachwort" [1873] to *Das Kapital*, 2d ed. (*Capital*, trans. Samuel Moore and Edward Eveling, 2 vols. [London: Sonnenschein, Lowrey, 1887].)

Chapter 1

Progressive Philosophy and the Politics of Jewish Assimilation in Late Imperial Vienna

"It is difficult – nay impossible – to recreate the atmosphere in which I grew up," wrote Popper in a draft of his *Autobiography*.[1] He was unhappy with most historical portrayals of fin-de-siècle Vienna, and took special exception to *Wittgenstein's Vienna*.[2] Not Ludwig Wittgenstein's prominence alone irritated him. The focus on Viennese modernism, he felt, produced a distorted picture of fin-de-siècle culture. The Vienna he knew – progressive, optimistic, reform oriented – virtually disappeared from accounts of modernism. Social reform, not cultural crisis, prevailed in his Vienna 1900. A generation of scholars, primarily Austrian, has meanwhile recovered his milieu, the Viennese late enlightenment.[3] He is *Spätaufklärung's* most renowned twentieth-century representative.

Karl Raimund Popper was born on 28 July 1902 in Vienna. He was a first-generation Viennese. His father, Simon Carl Siegmund (1856–1932), came from Bohemia, and his maternal grandparents from Silesia and Hungary. (His mother, Jenny Schiff [1864–1938], was born in Vienna.) All adopted German culture and made a rapid social climb. Having earned a law degree, Simon Popper became the legal partner of Vienna's last liberal mayor, Raimund Grübl (1847–98). Their relations must have been close: Karl Popper received his middle name, Raimund, from the mayor. After Grübl had died, Simon Popper took over the firm, and the family moved into a huge apartment with adjoining offices, across from the Stephan Cathedral in the Innere Stadt. The Popper household embodied the ideals

---

[1] Karl Popper, "Autobiography: Draft," Hoover Institute Archives, Popper Papers (134, 4). (Henceforth: Popper Archives.)

[2] Allan Janik and Stephen Toulmin, *Wittgenstein's Vienna* (New York: Touchstone, 1972). In my view, the book was a major contribution.

[3] Friedrich Stadler introduced the term "late enlightenment" (*Spätaufklärung*) in "Spätaufklärung und Sozialdemokratie in Wien, 1918–1938," in *Aufbruch und Untergang: österreichische Kultur zwischen 1918 und 1938*, ed. Franz Kadrnoska (Vienna: Europaverlag, 1981), pp. 441–73. See also: Ingrid Belke, *Die sozialreformerischen Ideen von Josef Popper-Lynkeus (1838–1921) in Zusammenhang mit allgemeinen Reformbestrebungen des Wiener Bürgertums um die Jahrhundertwende* (Tübingen: Mohr, 1978). In a letter to the editor of *Austria Today*, Popper recommended Belke's work as a counterbalance to *Wittgenstein's Vienna* (Popper Archives [270, 30]).

of *Besitz* (property), *Recht* (law), and *Kultur* (culture) that were held in the highest esteem by Viennese liberals.[4]

In 1900 Simon and Jenny Popper renounced their membership in the Jewish community and converted to Lutheranism. (Their two daughters, Dora [Emilie Dorothea, 1893–1932] and Annie [Anna Lydia, 1898–1975], perfunctorily became Protestants, too.)[5] Vienna was overwhelmingly Catholic, but Simon Popper shared the vehement anticlericalism of Viennese progressives. He preferred the *Aufklärung's* religion. Neither acculturation nor religious conversion broke, however, the barriers of ethnicity. The assimilated Jewish intelligentsia constructed bridges to progressive secular Austrians opposed to anti-Semitism, but there were relatively few of these. Together they formed the utopian visions of a secular commonwealth that became the hallmark of fin-de-siècle Viennese progressivism. In such a state, free of religious superstition and ethnic prejudice, the assimilated Jewish intelligentsia hoped finally to find their home: No one there would probe their ethnic origin or challenge their claims to be German. But reality defied utopia. Secular progressive Germans were marginal to their own ethnic group. German-Austrians did not accept Jews into their social networks. The Poppers spent much of their life in the company of other Jews.

Throughout his youth, Popper was surrounded by progressive intellectuals. They rebelled against the social conservatism of mainstream liberalism and sought an opening to the workers. They opted for a bourgeois-proletarian alliance, under the auspices of an enlightened bureaucracy, that would promote social legislation, economic modernization, and scientific education. In 1891 they founded the Viennese Fabian Society and, in 1896, the *Sozialpolitische Partei*. The party advocated universal male suffrage and welfare reforms. It ran against the twin obstacles of Catholicism and anti-Semitism, and remained very small, its constituency limited to Viennese districts populated with Jews.[6] The progressives, finding the political path obstructed, increasingly channeled their efforts to a large network of associations for educational reform, social welfare, economic planning, and women's rights.[7] Militantly secular, politically radical, trusting in social reform, popular education, and technological progress – this was the young Popper's social and intellectual milieu.

[4] On *Besitz* and *Kultur.* Carl Schorske, *Fin-de-siècle Vienna: Politics and Culture* (New York: Knopf, 1980).

[5] *Israelitische Kultusgemeinde (IKG)*, Matrikelamt, Vienna; *Verlassenschaftsakt* of Simon Popper, Meldearchiv, Wiener stadt- und Landesarchiv. Troels Eggers Hansen of the University of Copenhagen kindly provided me with Anna Popper's date of death.

[6] Eva Holleis, *Die Sozialpolitische Partei: Sozialliberale Bestrebungen in Wien um 1900* (Munich: Oldenbourg, 1978).

[7] Ingrid Belke, *Josef Popper-Lynkeus*, esp. pp. 5–56; Albert Fuchs, *Geistige Strömungen in Österreich, 1867–1918* (Vienna: Löcker, 1949), pp. 133–62; John Boyer, "Freud, Marriage, and Late Viennese Liberalism," *Journal of Modern History* 50 (1978): 72–102.

Popper would spend much of his life refashioning progressive philosophy and politics. Deeply committed to historical progress, he nonetheless discarded progressive utopianism and constructed a new liberal framework for reform and social planning. Carrying progressive opposition to ethnonationalism one step further, he rejected *Deutschtum* (Germanness), dissociated the Enlightenment from Germany, and advocated radical cosmopolitanism. His relentless hostility toward any nationalism (Zionism was his favorite example), his rejection of any and all religion (Judaism more than Christianity), his belief in an international legal order (rare among a generation witnessing the League of Nations failure), his passionate defense of the Enlightenment and the Open Society: all were a metamorphosis of progressive Vienna. He remained an assimilated progressive Jew to the end of his life. Through migration and exile, his own as well as others, progressive Viennese philosophy – a product of marginal milieus – made cosmopolitan dreams part of mainstream Western culture.

VIENNESE JEWRY IN THE AGE OF FRANZ JOSEPH

Central European Jewish émigrés, nostalgic about the Habsburg Empire, described life under Franz Joseph (1830–1916) as a golden age. It was a short golden age. Prior to 1848, Austria had never enjoyed a good reputation among Jews. After the expropriation, mass execution, and expulsion of Vienna's Jews in 1420–1 (still commemorated by a plaque in Vienna's Judenplatz, across from the Lessing sculpture), Austria had been known as the "land of blood."[8] In 1671, Vienna again expelled its three thousand Jews. Joseph II's 1782 Edict of Toleration, which stipulated a measure of German education for Jews, was greeted in Galicia, where two-thirds of Habsburg Jewry lived, as an "evil decree" (גזירה ; *Gzeyre*). In the first half of the nineteenth century, emancipation in Prussia and other German states progressed further than in Austria. Until 1848, only two hundred Jewish families with special privilege were permitted to reside in the capital, although a few thousand Jews lived there unofficially. The authorities recognized no official Viennese Jewish organization.

The revolution of 1848 emancipated the Jews, granted them equal citizenship, and lifted residential and occupational restrictions throughout the empire. When imperial authority was restored, emancipation was abolished, but not all of its achievements were reversed. Previous restrictions were no longer enforced, and this made a massive migration of Jews to the capital possible. In 1867, the *Grundgesetz* (constitutional law) granted Jews civil

---

[8] See Maharil's responsa (c. 1365–1427): Jacob ben Moses Moellin, *Sheelot u-Teshuvot Maharil* (Jerusalem: Mifal Torah Hakhame Ashkenaz, 1979); Samuel Krauss, *Die Wiener Geserah vom Jahre 1421* (Vienna: Braumüller, 1920).

equality. By the 1880s, their "special relationship" with Austria was well established. All Jews – poor Galician traditionalists and refined Viennese assimilationists, orthodox rabbis and liberal scholars, Zionists and socialists – declared unswerving loyalty to the dynasty and the supranational empire.

The Popper and Schiff families reflected general migration patterns for Habsburg Jews. The name Popper was common among Czech, and also Hungarian, Jews. From the seventeenth century on, we know of rabbis in Prague, community leaders, and, in the eighteenth century, even nobles, carrying the name Poppers (פאפרש).[9] Karl Popper's paternal grandfather, Israel Popper (1821–1900), apparently came from Kolin which, in the mid-nineteenth century had the second largest, and largely impoverished, Czech Jewish community.[10] The famous Viennese reformer Josef Popper-Lynkeus (1838–1921) also came from Kolin, and may have been related to Israel Popper.[11] Passersby on the Vienna street often confused Popper's uncle, Siegfried (d. 1927), for Lynkeus, their looks were so similar.[12] Sometime after 1848, Israel Popper must have left economically depressed Kolin in search of a better life. Moravian Jews often emigrated directly to Vienna, but German-Czech towns were the first beneficiaries of the post-1848 Bohemian Jewish migration, which turned, within a generation, a predominantly rural and poor population into an urban and prosperous one.[13] Israel Popper apparently found himself in Raudnitz (Roudnice nad Labem) in northern Bohemia, which was, in the mid-1850s, right on the linguistic boundary between the Czech- and German-speaking areas. Raudnitz, too, had a large Jewish community. Economic prospects in this trade and transportation center – where German was probably still the

---

[9] Most likely, the name signals a Frankfurt origin. Jewish last names often reflect the practice of identifying a person as: *x*, son (or daughter) of *y*, from city *z*. City names were often shortened to acronyms (*FF* for Frankfurt [פפ, or *pp* in Hebrew]) that later became family names. The *er* ending is common (like Ascher out of Altschul), and the *o* was added to facilitate phonetic pronunciation. The *s* was commonly dropped toward the end of the eighteenth century. Where Popper was common, Frankfurter was not, corroborating evidence. Samuel Krauss, *Joachim Edler von Popper: Ein Zeit- und Lebensbild aus der Geschichte der Juden in Böhmen* (Vienna: Selbstverlag des Verfassers, 1926), p. 6 n. 9. The Poppers were often Kohanim (כהנים), i.e., presumed descendants of the priestly caste (e. g., Frankfurt Rabbi Jacob ben Benjamin Hakohen Poppers, born in Prague, died 1740).

[10] *Autobiography*, p. 10.

[11] Josef Popper-Lynkeus, *Mein Leben und Wirken* (Dresden: Carl Reissner, 1924), pp. 1–4.

[12] Draft of *Autobiography*, Popper Archives (134, 4).

[13] On Czech Jewry see Hillel Kieval, *The Making of Czech Jewry* (New York: Oxford University Press, 1988); the older Ruth Kestenberg-Gladstein, "The Jews between Czechs and Germans in the Historic Lands, 1848–1918," in *The Jews of Czechoslovakia*, 3 vols. (Philadelphia: Jewish Publication Society, 1966), 1:21–71; and Jan Heřman, "The Evolution of Jewish Population in Bohemia and Moravia, 1754–1953," in U. O. Schmelz, P. Glikson, and S. Della Pergolia, eds., *Papers in Jewish Demography, 1973* (Jerusalem: Hebrew University of Jerusalem, 1977), pp. 255–65. I wish to thank my assistant, Matthew Specter, for research on Czech-Jewish demographic patterns.

language of commerce – may have looked, at the time, brighter than they proved later.[14]

In 1856, Anna Löwner (c. 1828–1910), Israel Popper's wife, gave birth to Simon Popper, Karl's father, in Raudnitz.[15] Simon was apparently brought up separately from his two brothers, Leopold and Siegfried.[16] The family seems to have moved around. Siegfried Popper was born in Karlburg, near Pressburg (Bratislava). Eventually, the entire family – parents, three brothers, and two sisters, Camilla and Hedwig – made their way to Vienna.[17] Simon Popper arrived there no later than the mid-1870s, probably earlier. Israel Popper never reached the level of affluence enabling him to pay the substantial Jewish community poll tax. Jewish community tax rolls and voter lists have no record of him. His son Simon seems to have been the first member of the family to climb to the upper middle class.

Karl Popper's maternal family, the Schiffs, belonged to a different social world, the Viennese high bourgeoisie. Max Schiff (1829–1903) came from Breslau and apparently made a small fortune in the textile commerce. He first appeared on the Jewish community voter list in 1862, remained there at all times, and, in 1900, was included in the list of the highest-paying members. He probably performed some services for influential members of the court: From 1898 on, he carried the title "imperial councilor" (*Kaiserlicher Ratsherr*).[18] He married Karoline Schlesinger (1839–1908) from Budapest, daughter to another leading Viennese Jewish family. They had six children: Helene (1861–1943), Otto (1863–1916), Jenny (1864–1938), Walter (1866–1950), Dora (d. 1926), and Arthur (1871–1939). The third, Jenny, was Karl Popper's mother. By the end of the century, the Schiffs apparently had a thriving umbrella factory, apartments in Vienna's first, then ninth, district, and a villa in Pressbaum, on the city's western outskirts, where their

[14] I owe this information to Professor Karl Bahm, University of Southern Mississippi (E-mail communication 6 November 1995).

[15] *Verlassenschaftsakt* of Simon Popper, Meldearchiv, Wiener stadt- und Landesarchiv; *IKG*, Matrikelamt.

[16] David Miller, "Sir Karl Raimund Popper," *Biographical Memoirs of Fellows of the Royal Society* 43 (1997): 370.

[17] Some, perhaps all, of Israel Popper's siblings emigrated to Vienna, as well. To reconstitute the family, I used the computerized burial records of the Central Cemetery (Zentralfriedhof) at the *IKG*, Matrikelamt, in conjunction with obituaries in the *Neue Freie Presse*. (The Viennese residential register begins only in 1910.) I wish to thank Frau H. Weiss, the *IKG Matrikelführerin*, for her kind cooperation, and Steven Beller for suggesting, when I nearly gave up, that I check the *NFP* obituaries. For Viennese Jewish cemeteries, see Patricia Steine, *Hunderttausende Steine* (Vienna: Falter, 1993).

[18] *IKG* archives, Central Archives for the History of the Jewish People, Hebrew University of Jerusalem (A/W 33–38, 40–50, 3078–85, 3152). Popper suggested (draft of *Autobiography* [134, 4]) that the Viennese Schiffs were related to the famous American branch, rooted in Frankfurt. Some Schiffs maintained a family genealogy going back to fourteenth-century Frankfurt, including numerous Judaic scholars (e. g., Meir ben Jacob Hakohen Schif [Maharam Schif], a Talmudic commentator [Frankfurt, 1608–Prague, 1644]) and prosperous community leaders.

grandchildren spent vacations and weekends with friends. They were supporters of the arts, founders of the *Gesellschaft der Musikfreunde* that built
the Musikvereinsaal. Lina Schiff headed charity organizations; Max was
honorary chair of a loan association. Their children distinguished themselves in music, the academy, and the professions, although none came into
wealth comparable to that of the parents. Walter Schiff was professor of economics and statistics at the University of Vienna; Arthur Schiff (who
married Margarethe Breuer, daughter of Freud's collaborator) was a medical
doctor and a *Dozent* (lecturer) in internal medicine; the three daughters, as
well as Arthur and many grandchildren, played the piano or the violin, or
composed, some professionally.[19]

Simon Popper married "up," his meteoric social rise mirroring the
remarkable success of some Jewish immigrants. Owing to the German-
Jewish school system in Bohemia and Moravia, introduced during the
Josephist reforms of the 1780s, Czech Jews were more secular and
"Western" than Jews in Galicia and Hungary, and frequently bilingual in
Czech and German. In Vienna, they sent their children to German educational institutions, moved into white-collar clerical positions, and transformed Vienna's professional elite.[20] All three Popper brothers earned law
degrees from the university, and became *Hof-und Gerichtsadvokaten*, barris-
ters and solicitors transacting, among other things, official city business. By
1887, Simon Popper was sufficiently well-off to pay the Jewish community's (*Israelitische Kultusgemeinde*) minimum tax of 10 florins. (Siegfried
Popper began paying in 1892, Leopold Popper in 1905.) Only the solid
middle class could afford the tax. Sometime in the next decade, Simon
Popper increased his contribution to 20 florins, something only a minority of well-to-do taxpayers did.[21] (Dropping from the rolls for inability to
meet the minimum tax was as frequent as an increased contribution.)
According to the social conventions among the upwardly mobile professionals, it was now time to have a family.

On April 3, 1892, Simon Popper married Jenny Schiff in the magnificent main synagogue in Vienna (on Seitenstettengasse).[22] They may have
lived first on Castellezgasse, next to the Augarten, in the second district,

[19] *Verlassenschaftsakt* of Max Schiff, Meldearchiv, Wiener Stadt- und Landesarchiv; Popper, *Autobiography*, pp. 53, 82; draft, Popper Archives (134, 4); photos, Popper Archives (86039-10, A and BB).

[20] For Viennese Jews' immigration and educational and professional patterns: Marsha Rozenblit, *The
Jews of Vienna: Identity and Assimilation, 1867–1914* (Albany: State University of New York Press, 1983);
Steven Beller, *Vienna and the Jews: A Cultural History, 1867–1938* (New York: Cambridge University
Press, 1989).

[21] Tax records for Simon, Siegfried, and Leopold Popper, *IKG* Archives, Central Archives for the History
of the Jewish People (A/W 805, 23). Tax records for two Leopold Poppers seem to match the profile
of Karl Popper's uncle, and so the data for him is uncertain.

[22] *IKG* Vienna, Matrikelamt.

then moved to Hörlgasse in Alsergrund, in the ninth district; finally, in 1898, they moved, together with their two daughters, to the Innere Stadt, the first district, where the most affluent lived.[23] They rented from the city that had owned the impressive, eclectic-style, four-story building on the corner of Freisingergasse and Bauernmarkt since 1891. Grübl, the last liberal mayor, had lived there, and Simon Popper shared his offices. Now that the mayor was deceased, Simon Popper inherited liberal Vienna's grandiose but precarious legacy, and took over both the residence and the legal offices. The apartment looked down a narrow street to the western doors of the Stephan Cathedral. It occupied an entire floor, had well over twenty rooms richly decorated in the high bourgeois fashion, and included also a secretary's and servants' residential quarters, as well as offices of charitable organizations that Simon Popper ran.

Simon Popper joined *Besitz* with *Kultur.* He worked long hours at his legal practice but remained intellectually engaged. He spent his limited leisure time writing political satire, studying history, and translating Latin poetry. He had a large library – twelve to fourteen thousand volumes, apparently – spilling over from the reading room to the entire apartment. The library included a large history collection, classical works, contemporary philosophy and literature, and recent Viennese publications on politics, social reform, and psychoanalysis. In the dining room stood a Bösendorfer concert grand with volumes of classical music. The young Popper found himself surrounded with culture at its best.[24]

The Jewish rise to economic, social, and cultural prominence in Vienna was mercurial. The capital served as a magnet first to German-acculturated Czech and Hungarian Jews, then, from 1890 on, to poor traditional Galician Jews. The 1857 census listed just over 6,000 Jews in Vienna. This increased to more than 72,000 by 1880, ten percent of the population, and to more than 175,000 in 1910.[25] Anti-Semites exaggerated the number and power of Jews in finance and commerce – for every Jewish merchant in fin-de-siècle Vienna there were four Catholic ones – but Jews did control major banks and high finance, and were disproportionately represented among the upper bourgeoisie. They dominated the liberal professions. In the 1880s, they constituted over half of the medical doctors in Vienna, and about three-fifths of the lawyers. Jews owned the major Viennese papers,

---

[23] William W. Bartley, III, "Rehearsing a Revolution: Music and Politics" (extract from "Karl Popper: A Life"), a paper delivered at the Pacific Regional Meeting of the Mont Pèlerin Society, Christchurch, New Zealand, November 27–30, 1989, pp. 7–8. (I have not managed to corroborate the first address [Castellezgasse]. The Poppers' residential pattern reflected a rapid social climb.

[24] Popper, *Autobiography*, pp. 8–11; draft, Popper Archives (134, 4, 9).

[25] Ivar Oxaal and Walter Weitzmann, "The Jews of Pre-1914 Vienna," *Leo Baeck Institute Yearbook* 30 (1985): 395–432; Marsha Rozenblit, *The Jews of Vienna*, chap. 2; Robert Wistrich, *The Jews of Vienna in the Age of Franz Joseph* (New York: Oxford University Press, 1990), chap. 2.

notably the *Neue Freie Presse*, the organ of liberal public opinion. Jewish journalists were a lightning rod for the anti-Semites.[26]

Socioeconomic prominence translated into cultural hegemony – transient and fragile, to be sure. Intellectuals of Jewish origin were predominant in literature, philosophy, political and social theory, economics, legal theory, and the theater, and had a significant, albeit minority, representation in music, art, and architecture.[27] Around 1880, Jews constituted almost a third of both university and gymnasia students. Nearly half of the faculty in medicine, a quarter in law, and between 15 percent (1890) and 34 percent (1920) in philosophy were of Jewish origin. The Jewish bourgeoisie competed with the aristocracy in cultural salons and patronage of the arts. Coffeehouse culture was "Jewish." Vienna without Jews, quipped Hugo Bettauer in a 1922 utopian satire, would be a deadly boring city. He would not live to see the joke turning into a nightmare.[28]

The Jewish rise to cultural prominence, says Steven Beller, was due to a particular educational pattern.[29] Viennese gymnasia were traditionally preparatory grounds for a civil service or a teaching career. Only a minority of the non-Jewish middle classes sent their sons to gymnasium, which was a prerequisite for university admission and a professional career, but virtually all middle-class Jews did so. Jewish girls, like Dora Popper, comprised almost half of Viennese lycées' students, over two-thirds in progressive ones.[30] Jewish boys shared the classroom with sons of Austrian officials. Once they were out of school, most officials' sons chose an administrative or a teaching career, whereas the Jews opted for the professions. As a result, the Viennese intelligentsia were predominantly of Jewish origin.

Acculturation to German culture created a crisis of identity. Jews responded variously, some endeavoring to assimilate, others reaffirming traditional identity, yet others inventing secular Jewish nationalism. The spectrum of responses within the Popper and Schiff families seems to have been

---

[26] Steven Beller, *Vienna and the Jews, 1867–1938*, pt. 1; Marsha Rozenblit, *The Jews of Vienna*, chap. 3.

[27] Steven Beller, *Vienna and the Jews*, pp. 1–32.

[28] *Die Stadt ohne Juden* (Vienna: Gloriette, 1922). See also Stefan Zweig, *The World of Yesterday* (New York: Viking, 1943), chaps. 1–4. Bettauer, who campaigned for sexual diversity, was murdered by a fascist in 1925.

[29] Steven Beller, *Vienna and the Jews*, pp. 33–70. Beller's explanation of Jewish educational patterns in his path-breaking book is controversial. He puts a premium on Jews' longtime passion for education, especially Talmudic study, that was now redirected to German culture. There is something to it, but German-acculturated Jews, who had shown limited passion for education under the oppressive social conditions in Bohemia and Moravia (and not Galician traditionalists), first filled Viennese gymnasia. The modernizing economy and state presented unique professional opportunities that required academic education. The Jewish minority of mobile immigrants was well poised to exploit them.

[30] Eugenie Schwarzwald opened her famous Lyzeum in 1901 to prepare Jewish (and progressive German) middle-class girls for the day when the academy's gates might open to them. The fight for women's education was central to fin-de-siècle feminism and progressivism.

narrower, ranging from German acculturation and limited engagement with the Jewish community to outright rejection of Judaism. Max Schiff did not play a role commensurate with his social status in the Jewish community, and normally he did not even bother to vote, but highly charged elections to the *Kultusgemeinde*, such as those in 1887, could still draw him out to cast his ballot. Israel Popper gave his sons and daughters distinctly non-Jewish names (Leopold; Hedwig), but the Popper and Schiff grandparents all died Jewish. Simon Popper seems to have waited until his father had died before his family converted to Lutheranism in 1900. The conversion probably reflected not only his conviction but also his vulnerability: A prominent lawyer, he lived in a luxurious city apartment, his office transacting city business under a popular anti-Semitic mayor, Karl Lueger. Vienna had the highest conversion rate of any European urban center, and Lutheranism was the religion of choice for upper-class Jewish converts.[31] Two, probably three, of the Schiff children (Otto, Jenny, and, probably, Walter) converted to Lutheranism. Still, assimilated Jews remained a small minority. The rest of the Popper family seem to have all remained Jewish, as did the two other Schiff sisters and the youngest Schiff brother. Both Siegfried Popper and Arthur Schiff continued to be sufficiently engaged in Jewish affairs to cast a vote in the 1920 *Kultusgemeinde* elections. Religious differences seem to have created no major fissures in family relations. All Schiffs and Poppers seemed to partake in family vacations, socials, and the like.[32]

Certain sociological trends militated against Jewish assimilation. For one, most Austrian-Germans were not willing to accept the Jews. Assimilated and nonassimilated upper-class Jews belonged to the same social networks.[33] Intermarriages seemed to have actually been less common in

---

[31] Lutherans were a tiny minority in Vienna, but a quarter of the Jews entering intermarriage chose Lutheranism. (Marsha Rozenbilt, *The Jews of Vienna*, chap. 6.)

The tax record for Simon Popper (*IKG* Archives, Jerusalem [A/W 805, 23]) gives 1900 as his conversion date (*ausgetreten*). That year saw a record number (627) of Jews convert. The Poppers acted in the nick of time. By law, parents' conversion included their children, but only up to the age of seven. A few more months, and the seven-year-old Dora would not have been included.

[32] *Neue Freie Presse* obituaries for the Popper and Schiff grandparents, and burial records for the Schiff grandparents and for Siegfried Popper's family, indicate that they all died Jewish (*IKG*, Matrikelamt, Vienna). Max Schiff's *Verlassenschaftsakt* (Meldearchiv, Vienna) indicates that Otto and Jenny Schiff converted, and Helene, Dora, and Arthur remained Jewish. Both Simon Popper and Otto Schiff last appear on the *IKG* voter list in 1898 (*IKG* Archives, Jerusalem [A/W 49, 2; 50, 2]). Walter Schiff never shows up. Arthur Schiff appears on all lists after 1902 (51, 1). Siegfried Popper's and Leopold Popper's tax records indicate that they remained *IKG* members to their death. The 1920 *Stimmeliste* (list of votes actually cast, not available for all elections) recorded Siegfried Popper's and Arthur Schiff's ballots (*IKG* Archives, Jerusalem [A/W 57, 7]). Photo negatives at the Popper Archives (86039-10, BB) show Schiff family gatherings. A draft of Popper's *Autobiography* indicates that, at his father's encouragement, he frequently engaged his paternal uncles.

[33] The Poppers spent summer vacations in the Alps with members of the Freud family. (Popper,

Vienna than in other European cities.[34] Ethnicity determined residential patterns more than class: Middle- and lower-class Jews often lived in the same neighborhoods. Newly arrived Czech Jews and non-Jewish Czechs – the capital's other major ethnic minority – lived near each other in Vienna's second district, Leopoldstadt, but in separate neighborhoods.[35] A similar situation existed at work: The white-collar Jewish middle class tended to concentrate in Jewish firms (which usually did do business on Saturday). Thus, even Jews who maintained but loose connection to the religious community continued to live, work, and socialize together.

The educational patterns of Viennese Jews, too, worked against assimilation. Since Jews concentrated in three districts (the first, second, and ninth), Jewish students often constituted a majority in their schools. From 1908 to 1913, Karl Popper went to the *Freie Schule*, a private school established in 1905 by progressives and socialists to provide an education free from clerical influence. Jewish children were probably a plurality. Almost half of the students in the three gymnasia he attended between 1913 and 1918 were Jewish.[36] Scattered information about his companions from kindergarten to gymnasium to university suggests that he had non-Jewish friends – some, like Konrad Lorenz, lifelong – but a majority were of Jewish origin. There was nothing Jewish about the Popper children's education; it was progressive German education in the *Freie Schule* and in the Schwarzwald *Lyzeum*, and classical German, with a scientific bent, in the *Realgymnasium*. But "a certain separation of Gentiles and Jews into groups," recalled Arthur Schnitzler, "could be felt always and everywhere, also therefore in school."[37] Contrary to their aspirations, neither assimilated nor acculturated Viennese Jews became Austrian-Germans. Much like their predecessors in nineteenth-century Germany, they constituted a German-

---

Autobiography, p. 13.) Friedrich von Hayek mentioned years later that no one in his family circle would associate with the Freuds. Separate social circles existed for Jews and non-Jews, with established intermarried families moving in between. F. A. Hayek, *Hayek on Hayek*, ed. Stephen Kresge and Leif Wenar (Chicago: University of Chicago Press, 1988), pp. 57–62. I owe this information to Jeremy Shearmur.

[34] They required that one member of the couple convert to the other's religion, or declare himself/herself *konfessionslos* (without religious affiliation; atheist). This did occur, and some cases of Jewish marriage into the lower aristocracy and the non-Jewish bourgeoisie became famous, but the number was smaller than in Berlin. Rozenblit, *The Jews of Vienna*, chap. 6. Ivar Oxaal and Walter Weitzmann, "The Jews of Pre-1914 Vienna," disagree.

[35] For Jewish residential patterns and social life: Marsha Rozenblit, *The Jews of Vienna*, chap. 4. For the Czechs in Vienna: Monika Glettler, *Die Wiener Tschechen um 1900* (Munich: Oldenbourg, 1972).

[36] William Bartley, "Rehearsing a Revolution," reports that Popper went to the small *Realgymnasium* in the third district (1912–14), where almost half of the students were Jewish, moved on (1914–15) to the *Franz Joseph Gymnasium* in the first district, where Jewish students had always constituted over forty percent, and, after two years in another (unidentified) gymnasium (1915–17), returned to the *Realgymnasium*. I have not been able to corroborate the school trajectory, but the statistics can be found in Beller and Rozenblit.

[37] Arthur Schnitzler, *My Youth in Vienna* (New York: Holt, Rinehart and Winston, 1970), p. 63.

Popper devoted his political philosophy to reconstructing liberalism, and provided a radical cosmopolitan solution to the predicament of his youth: the Open Society.

Austrian liberalism suffered a major blow in the aftermath of the 1848 revolution. The restored imperial authority abrogated all constitutional arrangements, establishing, in the 1850s, a neoabsolutist government. Even at its nadir, however, liberalism continued to gather strength at the local level through club activities, while Alexander Bach's Josephist-styled ministry modernized the Austrian administration and economy. Neoabsolutism enjoyed little popular support, and the 1859 defeat in the Italian war threw the monarchy into a political and financial crisis. It resulted first in the federalist 1860 October Diploma, then in the centralist 1861 February Patent, introducing a liberal Germanocentric parliament (*Reichsrat*). Thus began two decades of liberal hegemony in Austrian politics.

Defeat in the war against Prussia in 1866 led to the *Ausgleich* (compromise) with Hungary and to the December 1867 constitution, which recognized the legal equality of all citizens. The *Ausgleich* made Austria into a dual monarchy, giving the government in Budapest control of domestic affairs in much of the eastern half of the empire. The jurisdiction of liberal ministries in Vienna was limited from then on to the territories lying nowadays in Austria proper (plus southern Tyrol), as well as Slovenia, Dalmatia, Trieste, Czechia (Bohemia, Moravia, and Austrian Silesia), Galicia (stretching east past Lemberg [Lvov]), and Bukovina. In return for the liberals' agreement to the *Ausgleich*, the 1867 constitution expanded parliamentary prerogatives, making ministers individually responsible to parliament. (Cabinets, however, remained responsible to the emperor alone.) There were three imperial ministries − war, foreign affairs, and finance − and the emperor retained command of the army, the imperial bureaucracy (*Verwaltung*), and foreign policy, with the *Reichsrat* exercising budgetary control over them. The Dual Monarchy represented a compromise between the *Obrigkeitsstaat* (authoritarian state) and the *Rechtsstaat* (constitutional regime).

Liberals led almost all Austrian cabinets between 1867 and 1879. They promoted economic modernization, undid the 1855 Concordat, expanded secular public education, rebuilt Vienna as a modern city, and shaped its cultural life. They effected a rapprochement with the *Verwaltung*. They were proud of having gained a measure of autonomy for local communities (*Gemeinde*) and the *Länder*, but intent on securing a centralized progressive administration against federalism. In 1870–1, while briefly out of power, they failed the conservative cabinet's effort to reach an agreement with the Czechs that could have turned the empire from dualist into trilateralist, and resolved the conflict over the administrative language in the Bohemian crown lands. They spoke of cosmopolitan *Deutschtum*: Full citizenship was open to all who exhibited the solid character of German *Bürger*.

Deutschtum was culturally and socially acquired – Jews who attained property and education were, in principle, welcome. German culture must spread to backward nationalities in Central and Eastern Europe. Czech nationalist claims were retrogressive. History was on their side; in Central Europe as elsewhere, the progress of enlightenment, constitutional government, and economic modernization reflected humankind's betterment.

The liberals fancied themselves the state's party, above the fray of particular interests: provincial, aristocratic, clerical. The loose coalition of liberal clubs in parliament called themselves the *Verfassungspartei*, the Constitution Party. Truly, their electoral base was narrow, largely the propertied German-speaking bourgeoisie (*Besitzbürgertum*), urban and rural, affluent professionals, and civil servants. Prior to 1873, provincial diets had chosen the *Reichsrat*. Elections became direct in 1873, but a curia system, narrow suffrage (about six percent of the adult male population), and administrative manipulation guaranteed liberal majorities throughout the 1870s. As demands for the extension of suffrage were rising, the liberals found themselves the major force resisting them. In 1879, the emperor dismissed the liberal cabinet over liberal objections to the occupation of Bosnia and Herzegovina, an occupation that would further complicate, the liberals argued, the Germans' status as a *Staatsnation* by adding Slavs to the empire.[42] Out of power, the liberals lost their majority in elections the same year. The new premier, the emperor's friend, Count Edward Taaffe, put together a strange coalition of marginal groups, known as the "Iron Ring": conservative aristocrats and clericals together with the Poles and Czechs, everyone but the liberals (and the Ruthenians). The intransigent liberals were confident that such a motley coalition would not survive for long and disrupt historical progress. Instead, Taaffe stayed in power for fourteen tumultuous years. *Fortwursteln*, "muddling through," he said, when asked for the strategy that kept him in power for so long.[43]

Taaffe had a lot to "muddle through." During his ministry, radical nationalist German and Czech parties emerged, threatening the empire's integrity. The emperor's lieutenants observed in the early 1880s that further extension of the suffrage was likely to produce majorities more amenable than the liberals. In 1882 Taaffe extended the suffrage further down into the middle class, still within a complicated curia system. Another extension came in 1896. In 1907, after a major socialist campaign, Austria introduced universal male suffrage. Each successive election led to liberal losses. The liberals desperately sought a new vision to unify the middle classes under their leadership. They found it in German nationalism. Throughout Europe,

---

[42] The two provinces remained under Austrian occupation until 1908 when the decision to annex them almost precipitated a general European war.

[43] On Taaffe's ministry: William A. Jenks, *Austria under the Iron Ring, 1879–1893* (Charlottesville: University of Virginia, 1965).

liberal elites facing democratization deployed social reform or nationalism, or both, to fashion new communities. In Austria, where ethnonationalist tensions prevailed, the combination was deadly. As a rule, the more socially progressive a liberal party was, the more nationalist. Resurgent populist German and Czech nationalism collided, and the Jews were caught in between. In 1880 the liberals established the *Deutscher Schulverein* (German School Association) to advance German language and culture in ethnically contested areas. They relinquished pretensions to being the state's party and became advocates of particular ethnic interests. They now aimed to secure, they said, the *National Besitzstand* (national property ownership). Within two decades, an ever-diminishing and fragmented liberal camp normalized anti-Semitism and undermined its own previous universalist ideals.[44]

The liberals faced the ineluctable dilemmas of Austrian-German national identity. In a multinational empire, German nationalism could only mean the dismemberment of the Austrian state that liberals aspired to lead. In 1885 the United Left (*Vereinigte Linke*) split over including "Austrian" in its title. The populist nationalists left, establishing their own *Deutscher Club* (German Club). Who belonged in their German nation? The progressive nationalist 1882 Linz program still included both Jews and anti-Semites among its promoters: historian Heinrich Friedjung, future socialist leader Victor Adler, future Pan-German leader Georg von Schönerer. Soon, local branches of the *Deutscher Schulverein* opted to exclude Jews from membership. The liberal leadership dissolved them. In response, Schönerer left in 1886, Otto Steinwender and the populist nationalists the year after. To them, Jews were not German: *Deutschtum* was ethnic (or racial), not cultural. Schönerer's style – demagogic, impulsive, crowd oriented, contemptuous of legality, harping on ethnic resentment, appealing to the imagination rather than to the intellect, to emotion rather than to interest – was a harbinger of nationalist mass politics.[45] He called for a break with Rome, dissolution of the empire, and unification with Germany. German nationalism collided openly with the state, and the liberals were increasingly forced to choose. They finally toppled Taaffe and entered a coalition government, but a proposed Slovenian school in a southern Styrian town, Cilli, aroused a storm of German nationalist protests, bringing down the government in 1895 after a mere year and a half. Nationalism made Austria parliamentarily ungovernable.

---

[44] Pieter Judson, *Exclusive Revolutionaries* (Ann Arbor: University of Michigan Press, 1996); Lothar Höbelt, *Kornblume und Kaiseradler: Die deutschfreiheitlichen Parteien Altösterreichs 1882–1918* (Vienna: Verlag für Geschichte und Politik, 1993).

[45] Carl Schorske speaks of "politics in a new key": *Fin-de-siècle Vienna*, chap. 3. He argues that it appeared in Austria earlier than elsewhere in Europe. On Schönerer and his party see: Andrew Whiteside, *The Socialism of the Fools* (Berkeley: University of California, 1975); Peter Pulzer, *The Rise of Political Anti-Semitism in Germany and Austria*, rev. ed. (Cambridge: Harvard University Press, 1988), chap. 17.

Liberal nationalists managed to hang on to the German middle classes in the Bohemian crown lands, but a competing populist movement undermined them in their fortress, the capital. Karl Lueger, who had begun his career as a social liberal, founded the anti-Semitic Christian-Social Party in 1888. Against liberal elitism, laissez-faire, and secularism, he presented a vision of a popular, protective, Catholic community. He captured first the support of the Viennese lower middle class – artisans, shopkeepers, and tradesmen – long seeking relief from modernization and Jewish competition, resentful of the liberals who had refused them a voice in politics. He rapidly extended his electoral base to the rest of the liberal constituency and, by 1895, controlled the third and second curia (teachers and civil servants), and split the first, the wealthiest, with the liberals. He was elected five times as mayor with increasing majorities, but the emperor regarded him as a rabble-rouser and refused to confirm him in office. Freud toasted the emperor – never before a liberal idol – on his refusal in 1895. He celebrated prematurely, for in 1897, the emperor relented, and Vienna welcomed an anti-Semitic mayor.[46]

No community felt the consequences of the liberal failure as profoundly as the Jews. The liberals were the only party committed to retaining Jewish emancipation. (The socialists were, until the 1890s, a negligible political force, in conflict with the Jewish bourgeoisie.) Anticlericalism, laissez-faire, and the attack on aristocratic privilege served nicely an expanding Jewish bourgeoisie that looked forward to the day when religion and ethnicity would play no role in determining social status and political power. To be sure, the liberals always did their best not to appear the Jews' party: They elided the Jews' active role in their clubs and reluctantly rewarded them with leadership. Jewish liberal leader Ignaz Kuranda (1812–84) noted how conscious his colleagues were of ethnic boundaries. All the same, liberalism's decline closed gates that had only recently opened. Kuranda's son, Camillo, elected to the *Reichsrat* in 1907 as a representative of the German Progress Party (*Deutsche Fortschrittspartei*), faced exclusion from the parliamentary German National Union (*Deutschnationaler Verband*). By 1899, the *Deutscher Schulverein* was permitting branches to determine membership criteria (and exclude Jews). The liberals declined to divide their constituents by taking a firm stand against anti-Semitism. Pushed to choose, many crossed over to the radical nationalists. This was liberalism's end, and it put Jewish emancipation at grave risk.[47]

---

[46] John Boyer, *Political Radicalism in Late Imperial Vienna* (Chicago: University of Chicago, 1981), provides a detailed and nuanced account of Lueger's progress and the waning of the liberal electorate. In contrast to Schorske and Pulzer, he views the Christian-Socials as a traditional middle-class party.

[47] Against Schorske's picture of liberalism in retreat, defeated by nationalism and Christian socialism, recent works have emphasized the continuity between the old liberalism and the new movements. Boyer, Höbelt, and Judson maintain, albeit from very different perspectives, that Lueger and the

Liberal Jews increasingly recognized that they shared a common interest with the government, the emperor, and the *Verwaltung* in preserving the multinational empire's integrity, even against the German nationalists. "Thou shall always be praying for the welfare of the monarchy," commanded ancient Jewish authorities, "for without the fear of the authorities, people would devour each other alive."[48] This fit perfectly 1890s Habsburg politics. Radical German nationalism triggered a Czech reaction. In 1889, the Young Czechs won a majority in the Bohemian diet (already boycotted by the Germans). Alarmed, Taaffe negotiated, in 1890, an armistice in the linguistic war in Bohemia between the German liberals and the Old Czechs. The Young Czechs torpedoed it. Realizing the difficulty of securing parliamentary support for a compromise, premier Casimir Badeni issued in 1897 his famous language decrees, establishing both Czech and German as administrative languages in Bohemia and Moravia, requiring all officials in ethnically diverse areas to be bilingual by 1901. Most Czech officials knew German, but few Germans knew Czech, and they had no inclination to learn it. Badeni hoped to compensate the Germans with a division of the Bohemian crown lands into German and Czech spheres, seen as a protection against Czech advances, but Germans throughout Austria, taking their cue from a militant *Reichsrat* delegation, rose in uproar, creating civil disorder and forcing the decrees' repeal. Germans and Czechs alternately used obstructionist tactics in parliament, turning the assembly into chaos. The government began ruling through imperial emergency decrees, and negotiated deals with *Reichsrat* factions behind closed doors. Austrian parliamentarism reached a dead end. Imperial authority seemed the only alternative. Only enlightened absolutism could secure the achievements of liberal constitutionalism.

Viennese progressives had had it with "liberalism." They represented a small liberal minority that remained largely immune to anti-Semitic populism. They continued their close cooperation with the Jewish intelligentsia

nationalists carried out the liberal project of uniting the middle classes, but with a modified ideology. They serve as an important corrective, but the novelty of populist anti-Semitism should not be underestimated. Of the three, Judson is the most critical of the movement he discusses. He traces the transformation of liberalism into nationalism with great sensitivity, but believes that liberal meritocracy opened the door to ethnic exclusion by promoting hierarchy. This is problematic: It is difficult to see how meritocracy, having an open door as its rationale (all were invited; few were chosen because few, an increasing number, proved worthy through their good works), could be translated into ethnic exclusion, premised on closed doors. Liberal and racial hierarchies radically diverged. (Not all exclusions are interchangeable, and the absence of hierarchy is no guarantee against exclusion.) The middle classes could be unified on liberal and illiberal principles. "Liberals" who endorsed ethnic exclusion were no longer liberal.

[48] Mishnah *Avot*, III:2. This tractate recites sayings and dicta of Jewish sages. Jewish communities have recited for ages – in Hebrew, Yiddish, or German – a weekly prayer (on Saturday morning, just before the torah scrolls are returned to the ark) for the monarch's and the kingdom's welfare. They did so even under the oppressive tsars.

and were moving toward the socialists. They occupied the space on the political map that democratic, reform-oriented, social liberalism filled in Britain and the United States, an exceedingly narrow space in Austria. Many were members of the Vienna Fabian Society, modeled after the English one. They advocated state management of cartels, social insurance, a maximum workday, and universal suffrage, but rejected revolution, the dictatorship of the proletariat, and total socialization. From the 1880s on, they founded a series of small parties as an alternative to conservative liberalism: *Deutsche Volkspartei* in 1882, *Wiener Demokratische Partei* in the late 1880s, *Sozialpolitische Partei* in 1896. The latter managed to elect in 1896 three representatives to the Lower Austrian *Landtag* and, in 1901, two to the *Reichsrat*. They found themselves collaborating with the socialists rather than the liberals. Progressive-socialist collaboration increased, during the 1900s, in educational organizations in Vienna. *Die Bereitschaft* (Preparation), established in 1913 and dedicated to popular education (*Volksbildung*), had, with socialist support, more than ten thousand members. Inheriting the liberal belief in emancipation through knowledge – *Wissen macht frei* – socialists and progressives hoped for social transformation through education and technology. Social engineering (*Sozialtechnik*) would give rise to socialism – nonviolently.[49]

John Boyer notes the progressives' Josephist predilection, seemingly in conflict with their call for democratization. It reflected the peculiar circumstances of fin-de-siècle politics.[50] In 1900, the emperor appointed an unrepresentative *Beamtenministerium* (cabinet of civil servants), a group of enlightened officials headed by Ernest von Koerber. With little support from the conservative court and none from the unruly parliament, they tried innovative schemes for economic development, especially in transportation (railroads and canals), hoping that they would ameliorate national tensions. Koerber demonstrated respect for legality and freedom of the press, and recommended moving toward universal suffrage. In supporting economic modernization, civil rights, cosmopolitan culture, and a dialogue with the socialists, the Koerber ministry (1900–4) was Josephism redivivus with a liberal spirit, not dissimilar to Viennese progressivism.[51] Koerber's plans failed, but they were kept alive in progressive dreams for a cosmopolitan empire and in utopian plans for a new society. Both would inform Popper's political philosophy.

Karl Popper remembered his father as "a radical liberal of the school of

[49] Ingrid Belke, *Josef Popper-Lynkeus*; Albert Fuchs, *Geistige Strömungen in Österreich*; Eva Holleis, *Die Sozialpolitische Partei*; Friedrich Stadler, "Spätaufklärung und Sozialdemokratie in Wien, 1918–1938."
[50] "Freud, Marriage, and Late Viennese Liberalism."
[51] Alexander Gerschenkron, *An Economic Spurt That Failed* (Princeton: Princeton University Press, 1977) contains four charming essays on Koerber's ministry; Carl Schorske, *Fin-de-siècle Vienna*, pp. 236–43 discusses the program of Koerber's minister of culture, Wilhelm Ritter von Hartel, to countervail nationalist discourses with state support for modernist movements, like the Secession, reflecting cosmopolitan influences.

John Stuart Mill," but there was little that was radical about Simon Popper, other than his anticlericalism.[52] He remained attached to the high-bourgeois liberalism of his partner Grübl, a leader of the *Fortschrittspartei*. He seemed to shy away from political engagement, perhaps out of the conviction, expressed by his son many years later, that Jews should keep away from politics so as not to provoke anti-Semitism.[53] He left no political statement, but his satire *Anno Neunzehnhundertdrei in Freilichtmalerei* (The Year 1903 in Plein-Air Painting) ridiculed the aristocracy, the church, the anti-Semites, and other enemies of liberalism.[54] It expressed no progressive reform urge. Indeed, he caricatured the socialists and, at one point, the *Sozialpolitiker*. Karl Popper said that the censor had prohibited the work, which was published under a pseudonym, on account of its disrespectful portrayal of the German emperor, but Simon Popper's mockery of imperial pomp, aristocratic mores, clerical hypocrisy, and anti-Semitic hysteria reflected old-fashioned liberalism, not democratic or socialist sentiments. Bourgeois resentment toward the aristocracy and church was long lasting, and the liberals continued their *Gründerzeit* fights into the new century, rarely recognizing that they had a stake in the old social order. Freud's political dream, in which Count Franz Thun's imperious conduct recalled Freud's democratic nationalist youth, was symptomatic.[55] The premier and Freud were both engaged in a fight for their life against the nationalists. Simon Popper did not seem to recognize it any more than Freud did.

Ironically, the book celebrated Simon Popper's entry into the Order of Franz Joseph. The emperor knighted him for his charity work, which was carried out – again ironically – under the auspices of the illegal freemasons. Simon Popper did not deride Franz Joseph as he did Wilhelm II, but he assured his brethren at the Masonic lodge that the surprising event had not changed his bourgeois convictions, and his honor was theirs.

Sometime after 1904, Simon Popper apparently became master (*Meister vom Stuhl*) of the Masonic lodge *Humanitas*.[56] Established in 1871,

---

[52] *Autobiography*, p. 9. In draft (Popper Archives [134, 4]), Popper wrote "a somewhat radical liberal."

[53] *Autobiography*, pp. 105–7.

[54] Siegmund Pflug (Simon Popper), *Anno Neunzehnhundertdrei in Freilichtmalerei* (Leipzig: Eisenstein, 1904).

[55] Sigmund Freud, *The Interpretation of Dreams*, trans. James Strachey (New York: Avon Books, 1965), pp. 241–52.

[56] My repeated inquiries with the *Grossloge von Österreich* concerning Simon Popper have remained unanswered. Karl Popper indicated (draft of *Autobiography*) that his father was master "for many years." In *Offene Gesellschaft – offenes Universum: Franz Kreuzer im Gespräch mit Karl R. Popper* (Vienna: Deuticke, 1982), p. 23, as well as in a questionnaire for the Research Foundation for Jewish Immigration, *Zentrum für Antisemitismusforschung*, Technische Universität, Berlin, Popper mentioned specifically *Humanitas*. As Hugo Warmholz was master of *Humanitas*, 1900–4, and Adolf Kapralik, 1915–28, it is likely that Simon Popper was master sometime in between. (Vienna's mayor Eduard Uhl was master, 1885–93.) Alfred Nimmerrichter's forthcoming *Loge Humanitas – Chronik des Überlebens, Quatuor-Coronati-Berichte* 17 (1997) may provide further information.

Humanitas was the oldest and largest lodge, and had a few hundred members. Masonic lodges provided the bourgeoisie with an alternative to the established social hierarchy. Their leadership came from the bourgeoisie's upper echelons, and their members from the solid middle classes: affluent merchants and bankers, well-to-do professionals, and professors. Jews were heavily represented, giving Austrian lodges a very different profile from their German counterparts.[57] The church prevented the Freemasons' legalization in Austria, and the battle constant between the two reached its peak in the late 1890s when the church organized mass anti-Masonic protests.[58] This partially explains Simon Popper's anticlericalism, as well as the salience of cultural issues in Austrian politics that drove a wedge between the progressives and the government, undermining the coalition of forces seeking to maintain the empire's integrity.

As the Freemasons were legal in Hungary, Humanitas officially had its headquarters across the border, first in Neudörfl (near Wiener Neustadt), then, after 1880, in Pressburg (Bratislava). The "brothers" would take the train to Wiener Neustadt or Pressburg once a month on Sunday morning to conduct their rituals. In Vienna, the Freemasons organized as charitable and educational societies, promoting social welfare and secular popular education. They were especially proud of the orphanage (*Kinderasyl Humanitas*) they opened in 1875 in Kahlenbergerdorf near Vienna for about sixty children. Simon Popper ran the association's affairs from his office, as he did with other non-Masonic, charitable organizations. Around the turn of the century, socialism and social reform became major subjects of debate among Freemasons. Members participated in progressive organizations, from the Ethical Society to the *Verein Freie Schule* to the pacifist *Friedensgesellschaft* to *Die Bereitschaft*. Their views on social reform ranged from liberal to progressive. Simon Popper's charity organizations reflected his: a homeless shelter (*Asylverein für Obdachlose*), a loan association (*Wiener Selbsthilfverein*; Vienna Self-help Association), and the Association for the Prevention of Poverty and Begging (*Verein gegen Verarmung und Bettelei*).[59] The

[57] Rainer Hubert, "Freimaurerei in Österreich 1871 bis 1938," in *Zirkel und Winkelmass* (Vienna: Eigenverlag der Museen der Stadt Wien, 1984), pp. 31–46. On German lodges: Jacob Katz, *Jews and Freemasons in Europe, 1723–1939* (Cambridge: Harvard University Press, 1970), esp. pp. 163–70. In contrast to some eighteenth-century lodges elsewhere in Europe (Margaret Jacob, *Living the Enlightenment* [New York: Oxford University Press, 1991]), women do not seem to have been regular members, but some lodges had close connections to the Viennese feminists and were at the forefront of the struggle for women's rights.

[58] Gustav Kuéss and Bernhard Scheichelbauer, *200 Jahre Freimaurerei in Österreich* (Vienna: Kerry, 1959); John Boyer, *Culture and Political Crisis in Vienna: Christian Socialism in Power, 1897–1918* (Chicago: Chicago University Press, 1995), chap. 4. Freemasons' active role in the *Freie Schule*, opened in 1905 in Vienna, and the ensuing fight over religious instruction in the school galvanized the struggle in the 1900s.

[59] William Bartley, "Rehearsing a Revolution," p. 28, indicates the last two as Simon Popper's charity organizations. For the others: *Autobiography*, p. 9, and Berlin questionnaire.

underlying vision was liberal self-help, not progressive institutional reform. Toward the end of his book, Simon Popper presented himself as a self-made man who had climbed to the *Bürgertum* through his own efforts. Self-reliance and *Bürgertum* were his guiding ideals.

There were others around the family who could inspire Karl Popper with a more progressive vision. His uncle, Walter Schiff, an expert on agrarian questions, was an admirer of the socialist thinker Anton Menger, and a member of the *Sozialpolitische Partei*. Arthur Arndt, a socialist family friend and his personal guide in his youth, took him to meetings of the Monists, an association founded by Ernst Mach's disciples in 1913, dedicated to the "scientific" reform of philosophy, education, and law.[60] Virtually all Viennese reformers belonged.[61] Many Monists advocated radical economic restructuring, even socialization, while at the same time rejecting Marxism. Unlike the Berlin Monists, who were German nationalists, the Vienna leadership – Rudolf Goldscheid (president) and Wilhelm Börner – was pacifist. Two figures towered above the progressive reform effort: Friedrich Jodl (1849–1914) and Josef Popper Lynkeus. Jodl, a professor of philosophy, had come to Vienna from Prague in 1896. He was a staunch proponent of secular "scientific" education and supportive of feminist causes. In 1894, he cofounded with sociologist Wilhelm Jerusalem the Vienna Ethical Society, advocating, like its American counterpart, an altruistic, humanistic, scientific ethic, combating religious education, social Darwinism, and racism. Most progressives were members.[62] Even more famous was Josef Popper, known under his pseudonym Lynkeus, whose plan for resolving the "social question" epitomized fin-de-siècle progressive utopianism.[63]

Lynkeus believed that the abject poverty around him resulted from the faulty organization of production and distribution: The current state of technology should allow an adequate standard of living to the entire population. He proposed a general draft of young citizens – men and women alike – to a nutrition army (*Nährarmee*) for five to eleven years. Upon completing their service, the "soldiers" would be guaranteed a basic standard of living (*Existenzminimum*) for the rest of their lives. A ministry of living standards (*Ministerium für Lebenshaltung*), independent of government or party, would administer the *Nährarmee*. Natural resources necessary for providing the *Existenzminimum*, including land, would be nationalized, but a vital

---

[60] *Autobiography*, pp. 12–13.

[61] Friedrich Stadler, *Vom Positivismus zur "Wissenschaftliche Weltauffassung"* (Vienna: Löcker, 1982).

[62] Friedrich Jodl, *Geschichte der Ethik als philosophischer Wissenschaft*, 4th ed., 2 vols. (Darmstadt: Wissenschaftliche Buchgesellschaft, 1965); Margarete Forster Jodl, *Friedrich Jodl* (Stuttgart: Cotta, 1920); Albert Fuchs, *Geistige Strömungen*, pp. 147–55, 213–15; Friedrich Stadler, "Spätaufklärung," pp. 445–51; Harriet Anderson, *Utopian Feminism: Women Movements in Fin-de-siècle Vienna* (New Haven: Yale University Press, 1992), esp. pp. 19–20.

[63] *Die Allgemeine Nährpflicht als Lösung der sozialen Frage* [1912] (The duty of providing nutrition to all as a solution to the social question), 2d ed. (Vienna: Rikola, 1923).

capitalist sector (and a traditional civil service) would remain to absorb the released "soldiers." Karl Ballod, a Protestant missionary–turned–political scientist at the University of Berlin, reworked Lynkeus's program, introducing total socialization of production and consumption.[64] Anton Menger, professor of jurisprudence in Vienna, proposed another blueprint for a socialist commonwealth, a *volkstümlicher Arbeitsstaat* (popular workers' state).[65]

Lynkeus and other progressives expressed great optimism about social technology. They were living through the second industrial revolution in the chemical and electric industries, witnessing the great increase in production as industrialized areas of the monarchy grew in wealth and population. (As an engineer and inventor, interested in aviation technology, Lynkeus was intimately familiar with industrial machinery.) Technological advances were changing Vienna's face.[66] Electric trams replaced horse-drawn buses in 1897, and a steam-powered metropolitan railway network was growing. The municipal water supply system expanded; gasworks came in 1899. The telephone was introduced in 1881. With electrification, technology moved from the work sphere to private life. Science's triumphs were human, leading to tangible improvements in the quality of life. Technology was applied science, science was knowledge, and its acquisition and spread meant emancipation. Established religion and nonscientific traditions were obstacles, to be fought and removed. Secular popular education was the way. Church and state obstructed it, but expanding print media and adult education in "popular universities" (*Volkshochschulen*) – the first, *Volksheim*, founded in 1901 in the working-class district of Ottakring – provided channels for enlightenment.[67] Owing to the intelligentsia's dedication, education at the popular universities was often better informed by recent scientific advances than at the University of Vienna. The day when society would undertake to reform itself along scientific lines, when the scientific worldview would triumph in ethics, economics, and politics, was not far off.

---

[64] Karl Ballod, *Die Zukunftsstaat–Produktion und Konsum im Sozialstaat* [1898], 2d ed. (Stuttgart: Dietz, 1919); Ingrid Belke, *Josef Popper-Lynkeus*, pp. 155–63, 182–204. Economist and journalist Theodor Hertzka published in the late 1880s and early 1890s a popular series on *Freiland* (Freeland) a future state in East Africa that would be ruled by syndicates of production: *Freiland. Ein soziales Zukunftsbild*, 4th ed. (Dresden: Pierson, 1890).

[65] Anton Menger, *The Right to the Whole Produce of Labor* [1886], trans. M. E. Tanner (New York: Augustus Kelley, 1962); *Neue Staatslehre* (Jena: Fischer, 1904).

[66] *Wiener Beiträge zur Moderne*, ed. Roman Horak, Wolfgang Maderthaner, and Michaela Maier (Vienna: WUV, 1999). See the introductions by the project group.

[67] Ulrike Felt, "Lire de la science à Vienne, 1900–1938," in Bernadette Bensaude-Vincent and Anne Rasmussen, eds., *La science populaire dans la presse et l'édition, XIXe et XXe sieclès* (Paris: CNRS éditions, 1997), pp. 237–55; Klaus Taschwer, "Wissenschaft für alle. 'Volksuniversitäten' als Vermittlungsorte zwischen Wissenschaft und Öffentlichkeit im Wien um 1900" (Ph.D. diss., University of Vienna, 1999).

There was no conflict between commitment to individual rights and technological control, thought the progressives, no insurmountable difficulty in translating scientific into ethical principles, or technological into social engineering, no tension between scientific progress and aesthetic pleasure.[68] Science studies would nowadays interrogate the political paradigm (and social interests) giving rise to such scientific claims, and readers of Foucault could easily trace technologies of power and disciplinary practices associated with modernity in progressive discourse. They would not be the first to challenge the progressives' scientific *Weltanschaaung*. Karl Popper did. His philosophy represented a lifelong engagement with the progressive worldview. He shared the progressives' ideals, and aimed to solve their problems. Science, he insisted, was not knowledge, at least not in the sense progressives meant, but a search for knowledge; not *episteme*, but problems and conjectures. All the same, it represented humanity's greatest achievements and hopes. There was no scientific ethic – this would end freedom – but a scientifically inspired ethic, such as the "negative utilitarianism" (the principle of minimizing suffering) guiding Popper's political reform, was desirable. The progressives' grand narrative was false. History was not a story of progress, and the triumph of reason was anything but inevitable, but critical rationalists should nonetheless keep fighting for both.[69]

Popper had a soft spot for Lynkeus. They were both individualists, committed to civil rights, a utilitarian state, and social welfare (*Existenzminimum*).[70] He recommended to Marxists Lynkeus's and Menger's social engineering. When conservative libertarians, like Hayek, argued the dangers

[68] Indeed, they were one, said Lynkeus: *Die technischen Fortschritte nach ihrer aesthetischen und kulturellen Bedeutung* (Leipzig: Carl Reissner, 1888). He proposed also to reform the penal code (eliminating the retribution principle) and to abolish compulsory military service.

[69] Siegfried Mattl explores socialist cultural politics with a view to its disciplinary strategies in "Politik gegen den Tod: Der Stellenwert von Kunst und Kultur in der frühen sozialdemokratischen Bewegung. Eine Skizze," in *Die Bewegung*, ed. Erich Fröschl, Maria Mesner, and Helge Zoitl (Vienna: Passagen, 1990), pp. 53–75. Popper did not pay attention to the discipline forming the "bourgeois individual" (although he protested against teaching science as authority), but this did not constrain his individualism or liberty. The aim of progressive science and education was to form an "individual" that we *may* find today gendered or class specific, defying the progressives' claims for universal humanity. Their vision had, however, emancipatory potential for women, the proletariat, and the sexually different. Popper recognized, I think, its historical specificity, not least because it was advanced by a minority and defeated, in Central Europe, by the fascists. He insisted that the practices of science and education alike were open to debate and revision. The problem with his inattentiveness to socialization (or the formation of the "bourgeois individual") is not that it legitimized coercive discipline, but that it omitted a debate on the practices most conducive to shaping individuals who would be eager to abide by the rules of democratic public debate (or the public sphere).

[70] Karl Popper introduced his book (coauthored with John Eccles) *The Self and Its Brain* (New York: Springer, 1977), p. 3, with a quotation from Lynkeus: "[E]very time a man dies, a whole universe is destroyed." Lynkeus also suggested, however, that if a demographic explosion threatened his planned society with famine, infanticide might be inevitable.

of social technology, Popper outlined a vision of piecemeal social engineering compatible with liberty. He was unwilling to trust the free market to ameliorate the poverty that he had witnessed in his youth and during the depression, but his proposed reforms did not involve socialism or a major social transformation. Lynkeus's naïveté about the compatibility of a Spartan nutrition army and personal autonomy reinforced Popper's ambiguity about socialism and liberalism. He no longer took for granted the harmony of social control and individual rights that Lynkeus had assumed, but he longed for it, all the same.

VIENNESE COSMOPOLITANISM:
GERMAN, AUSTRIAN, AND JEWISH

Ethnonationalism was the progressives' greatest enemy, but they underestimated its danger and responded ambivalently to it. Their ranks included pacifists, but also German nationalists. They fought anti-Semitism, which offended their humanity and excluded their Jewish members from the nation, but they could see no harm in expanding the German cultural sphere (*Kulturbereich*) in Central Europe and regarded Slavic nationalism as reactionary. The *Sozialpolitiker* declined to endorse federalism, or Badeni's language decrees. Instead, they suggested that democratic reforms would facilitate agreement among the nationalities. (The opposite proved true.) Analyzing the Czech-German conflict, they found it rooted in divergent socioeconomic development among the empire's provinces, hence a transitional problem. Ethnopolitics was a passing frenzy. An enlightened administration, encouraging economic development in German areas, could resolve the conflict.[71] They refused to implicate German nationalism with anti-Semitism. They believed that anti-Semitism was rooted in religious prejudice – amply demonstrated by the Christian-Social Party – and secular education was its proper antidote. Clericalism, not nationalism, was their major enemy. They contested anti-Semitic rhetoric with German *Aufklärung*, rather than with multinationalism.

All the same, their imagined communities were universalist, rather than German nationalist. They divested their utopias of any national attribute. Neither Hertzka's *Freiland* nor Menger's *Arbeitsstaat* nor Lynkeus's *Nährarmee* was tailored to the Habsburg monarchy. This reflected the progressives' inability to negotiate imperial problems, but also their universalism. They did not design cosmopolitan federations as openly as Kant did, or as polemically as Popper would, but they denationalized the state. The

[71] Michael Hainisch, *Die Zukunft der Deutsch-Österreicher* (Vienna: Deuticke, 1892); Otto Wittelshöfer, *Politische und wirtschaftliche Gesichtspunkte in der österreichischen Nationalitätenfrage, Preußische Jahrbücher*, 76, no. 3 (1894).

Talmudic saying, "the foundation of the earth is one," perfectly expresses their conviction.[72] The requirements of a good social order were not a matter of cultural difference. Even to most nationalists among them, nationalism remained secondary to popular education. Undoubtedly, they confounded *Aufklärung* and *Deutschtum*, but, for many, it seems, *Deutschtum* was an instrument for realizing *Aufklärung*, rather than the opposite. They were less nationalists in a cosmopolitan guise than cosmopolitans in a German guise.[73]

The Popper family circle represented the cosmopolitan-pacifist pole on the progressive spectrum. Relatives and friends were identified with the Austrian peace movement.[74] Freemasons and pacifists gave the clearest expression of Austrian cosmopolitanism. To Viennese Freemasons, humankind was advancing toward cosmopolitanism. Nationality and religion did not matter, only universal humanity. As a multinational empire, Austria represented a higher developmental stage than national states. Cosmopolitans were the Austrian patriots par excellence. They contributed to political harmony and internal peace. "If Austria had had no Freemasons," argued Carlos von Gagern, "the government should have called them from abroad, facilitated the formation of lodges with all the means at its disposal, and supported their expansion with all its powers – in the empire's obvious interest!"[75] Unlike the socialists whose party structure forced confrontation with the nationality problem, the Freemasons drew no plan for imperial reform. They were content to "think of themselves as guardians of liberal values and as the intellectual elite of a huge state whose composition gave it the appearance of the international order of humankind in miniature."[76]

Such pronounced cosmopolitanism was rare in Central Europe.[77] Habsburg court circles and bureaucratic and military elites propagated varieties of the Austrian imperial idea (*Staatsgedanke*), or dynastic patriotism, emphasizing the blessings of imperial rule in a multinational empire. The Josephist bureaucracy provided a measure of administrative uniformity throughout

---

[72] *Babylonian Talmud, Kiddushin*, p. 27b, *Baba Kama*, p. 12b: "Sadana d'ara chad hu (סדנא דארעא חד הוא)."

[73] Steven Beller, "Patriotism and the National Identity of Habsburg Jewry, 1860–1914," *Leo Baeck Institute Year Book* 41 (1996): 215–38.

[74] *Autobiography*, pp. 11, 13–14.

[75] *Zirkel*, no. 11 (1878), quoted in Rainer Hubert and Ferdinand Zörrer, "Die österreichischen Grenzlogen," *Quatuor Coronati Jahrbuch* (1983): 153; Gustav Kuéss and Bernhard Scheichelbauer, *200 Jahre Freimaurerei in Österreich*, pp. 137–73; Richard Laurence, "Bertha von Suttner and the Peace Movement in Austria to World War I," *Austrian History Yearbook* 23 (1992): 181–201.

[76] Paul Silverman, "Law and Economics in Interwar Vienna: Kelsen, Mises and the Regeneration of Austrian Liberalism" (Ph.D. diss., University of Chicago, 1984), p. 26.

[77] For socialist and Catholic cosmopolitanism and their limits, see my "Dilemmas of Cosmopolitanism: Karl Popper, Jewish Identity, and 'Central European Culture,' " *Journal of Modern History* 71 (1999): 105–49. The essay includes further bibliographic references.

Austria's diverse regions, and the military integrated nationally diverse troops into a loyal imperial force. Both the administrative and officer corps were multinational. They enjoyed a reputation of relative impartiality and occasionally made admirable efforts to settle fairly provincial conflicts. But neither they nor the court developed a cosmopolitan ideology. Their frame of mind was usually traditional, looking backward to prenationalism, rather than beyond it.[78] Their commitment to supranational ideals remained superficial: They could not quite agree on a unified strategy for confronting varieties of ethnopolitics, usually preferring accommodation and divide-and-rule measures to an all-out attack. Plans for reorganizing the empire along multinational principles, giving the Slavic nationalities a voice equal to that of the Germans and Hungarians, faced German protests and Hungarian vetoes. German and Hungarian hegemonies, combined with rising ethnonationalism, rendered any genuine cosmopolitanism a dream.

Jews were the only ethnic group to adopt enthusiastically the official *Staatsgedanke*. "Jews are the standard-bearers of the Austrian idea of unity," stated liberal Rabbi Jellinek.[79] "If one could construct a specifically Austrian nationality," echoed his modern orthodox colleague, Joseph Bloch (1850–1923), "Jews would form its foundation."[80] They were not just "the most loyal supporters of the monarchy, [but] the only ones who were unconditionally Austrian."[81] Indeed, they were the only minority whose "golden age of security" depended wholly on the multinational empire's survival.[82] Well into the final days of World War I, when the empire already lay in ruins, Viennese Jewish papers insisted that, federally reorganized, the multinational empire was viable.[83] Later, in their exile, Jewish émigrés portrayed Central Europe under the Habsburgs as a vanished cosmopolitan dream.[84]

Liberal Jews were slower than others to join the cult of the emperor. German imperial hegemony and the ambiguity of Austrian nationality per-

---

[78] István Deák, *Beyond Nationalism: The Social and Political History of the Habsburg Officer Corps, 1848–1918* (New York: Oxford University Press, 1990). Deák argues that the multinational officer corps did not succumb to ethnonational tensions precisely because they depended on dynastic "feudal" traditions. Refusing to enter the modern age, they were beyond nationalism's reach.

[79] Adolf Jellinek, "Jüdisch-österreichisch," *Die Neuzeit* (15 June 1883): 225: "Die Juden . . . sind die Träger des österreichischen Einheitsgedankens."

[80] Joseph Bloch, *Der nationale Zwist und die Juden in Österreich* (Vienna: Gottlieb, 1886), p. 41: "Wenn eine specifisch österreichische Nationalität construirt werden könnte, so würden die Juden ihren Grundstock bilden."

[81] Idem, "Nichts gelernt und nichts vergessen," *Oesterreichische Wochenschrift* (22 June 1917): 390: "In der Tat sind die Juden nicht etwa die treusten Anhänger der Monarchie, sie sind die einzigen bedingungslosen Oesterreicher in diesem Staatsverband."

[82] On the "golden age of security": Stefan Zweig, *The World of Yesterday*. Hannah Arendt presents the Jews as the state-people par excellence in *The Origins of Totalitarianism* (New York: HBJ, 1951).

[83] David Rechter, "Neither East nor West: Viennese Jewish Politics in World War One" (Ph.D. diss., Hebrew University of Jerusalem, 1994).

[84] Malachi Hacohen, "Dilemmas of Cosmopolitanism."

mitted initially both German and Jewish liberals to declare themselves, at one and the same time, good Austrians (imperial patriots) and German nationalists. Often making, within a generation, a radical transition from *Shtetljuden* to German-speaking intelligentsia, liberal Jews could not understand the discrepancy between their dreams and those of other nationalities. Why would Czechs not be equally content with integration into the German cultural sphere? Once the Germans faced showdowns with Taaffe and Badeni, lost their hegemony, and got outflanked by the populists, the German liberals opted for German over Austrian nationalism. Very few Jews did. The Austrian *Staatsgedanke* offered a patriotism the underlying rationale of which was not ethnonational but multinational, making Jewish participation unproblematic. It gave Jews an opportunity missing elsewhere for negotiating Jewish and national identity, and this became crucial once rifts opened between them and the Germans. They were not going to give it up.

Was Jewish imperial patriotism cosmopolitanism by default? Hardly. The one-sided love affair that the masses of orthodox Galician *Kaisertreuen* (imperial patriots) had with Franz Joseph reflected their recognition of Austro-Hungary as a "kingdom of grace," contrasted with the pogroms and "evil edicts" across the Russian border.[85] Franz Joseph was beloved because he permitted the "Chosen People" a respite in the Diaspora, not because he represented a supranational idea. "[I]n the person of his Holy Majesty Franz Joseph [is the] guarantee of our protection," declared the orthodox Viennese paper, *Jüdisches Weltblatt*.[86] The traditionalists' more articulate representatives, such as Rabbi Bloch, *Reichsrat* representative from Kolomea in eastern Galicia, made special efforts to reconcile orthodox Judaism with multinationalism, but neither he nor orthodoxy's more conservative leaders developed imperial cosmopolitan designs.[87]

In contrast, liberal Jews professed cosmopolitanism, but their cosmopolitanism conflicted with their German nationalism, and anti-Semitism brought their Jewish-German synthesis, a mark of genuine cross-cultural interaction, into crisis. As long as *Deutschtum* was defined culturally, liberal Jews could regard themselves as its messengers to the *Ostjuden*

---

[85] Joseph Roth, *Radetzkymarsch* (Berlin: Kiepenheuer, 1932); Asher Barash, *Kitve Asher Barash* (Collected Works), 3 vols. (Tel-Aviv: Massada, 1952); Shmuel Yosef Agnon, *Tmol Shilshom* (Heretofore) (Tel-Aviv: Schocken, 1968), introductory chapter. The last two were Zionists but remembered life in Galicia under Franz Joseph with great fondness. (Moshe Hacohen encouraged me to pursue leads in Barash; Yaakov Ariel of the University of North Carolina, Chapel Hill, in Agnon.) Barash described the emotional ties that Jews felt to the imperial family whose tragedies – from the crown prince's suicide (1889) to the empress's murder (1898) to the emperor's nephew and heir's assassination (1914) – they followed with concern and sympathy. In Barash's "Rikma" (רִקְמָה ; Embroidery) the poor hunchbacked Jewish tailoress, living in a Galician town, identifies her own fate with the empress and dies shortly after she does (vol. 1, pp. 228–51).

[86] "Unser Programm!" *Jüdisches Weltblatt* (1 June 1882), quoted in Wistrich, *The Jews of Vienna*, p. 272.

[87] Joseph Bloch, *Israel and the Nations* (Berlin: Harz, 1927).

and Slavs. Once it became racially defined, they faced exclusion from the German nation. Jews active in the nationalist German student association in the 1870s – Freud, Adler, Friedjung – were the first to discover that nationalism began at home, in their fraternity, with exclusion of the Jews. A decade later, Friedjung realized that Schönerer and Steinwender would reject even hypernationalist assimilated Jews, like himself.[88] Jellinek insisted that those advancing racial, as opposed to cultural, *Deutschtum* would destroy the German cause: True *Deutschtum* was Enlightenment cosmopolitanism.[89] To no avail. Bloch drew the conclusion. The politics of *Deutschtum* was a disaster. Nationalist tensions weakened the multinational empire, and Jews would be the main losers of any explosion. To the liberals' chagrin, he and the orthodox community endorsed Taaffe and his conciliatory policies toward the Czechs.[90] By the mid-1890s, however, even liberal Jews had second thoughts. A February 1897 meeting of the *Oesterreichisch-Israelitische Union* called for a "return to the program of reconciliation of peoples (*Völker*) and nationalities (*Stämme*), of all denominations, estates and classes in our fatherland, in the name of free thought and progress, of justice and equal rights of all citizens."[91]

Liberals affirmed cosmopolitanism most strongly, not against German nationalism but Zionism. Zionists claimed that Jews were a people (*Volksstamm*) and a nation (*Nationalität*) like any other. In 1882, only months after pogroms in Russia had triggered the *Hibbat Zion* (חיבת ציון; Love of Zion) movement among Russian Jewish youth, Jewish students established a national organization *Kadimah* (קדימה; Forward) at the University of Vienna. Illustrious Zionist thinkers Perez Smolenskin, Nathan Birenbaum, and Leon Pinsker participated in its activities.[92] Combining the legacy of the *Haskalah* (השכלה; Jewish enlightenment) with ancient memories of lost statehood and a commitment to rebuild a Jewish community in Palestine, they promoted a secular Jewish national identity, calling assimilation a sham. Some, like Birenbaum, shifted later to Diaspora nationalism, seeking to guarantee Jewish cultural autonomy in Europe. They were a vocal and embattled minority. Both orthodox and liberal Jews fought them, the former provoked by their secularism, the latter by their nationalism. Liberals feared that the nationalists would vindicate the anti-Semites' platform

---

[88] William McGrath, *Dionysian Art and Populist Politic in Austria* (New Haven: Yale University Press, 1974); Carl Schorske, "Generational Tension and Cultural Change: Reflections on the Case of Vienna," *Daedalus* (fall 1978): 111–22.

[89] On similar grounds, Victor Klemperer insisted half a century later in his diaries that he, a cosmopolitan "German-European," was the true German, not the Nazis. *Ich will Zeugnis ablegen bis zum letzten*, 2 vols. (Berlin: Aufbau, 1995).

[90] Joseph Bloch, *Der nationale Zwist und die Juden in Österreich*.

[91] Gustav Kohn, addressing a meeting concerning the coming parliamentary elections, 20 February 1897: *Mittheilungen der Oesterreichisch-Israelitischen Union* 9, no. 92 (March 1897): 3. See also: Werner Cahnman, "Adolf Fischhof and his Jewish Followers," *Leo Baeck Institute Year Book*, 4 (1959).

[92] Robert Wistrich, *The Jews of Vienna*, chaps. 11–12.

and place Jewish integration in jeopardy. Jellinek denounced the new cult of power and nationalism that distorted Jewish cosmopolitanism and sought a return to the tribe, but he could not be German in an age of ethnona-tionalism and had nowhere to turn politically.[93] Cosmopolitanism repre-sented the aspirations of the prospective losers of ethnopolitics.

Kadimah proved a prelude to the main show, the "King of the Jews."[94] No one touched the Jewish liberals' exposed nerves as pointedly as Theodor Herzl (1860–1904). The *Neue Freie Presse* editor had begun his career as an avowed liberal assimilationist, but then turned against his class and, with *Der Judenstaat* (The Jewish State), became almost overnight Zionism's world leader.[95] He adopted the despised *Ostjuden* and, organizing the first World Zionist Congress in Basel in 1897, set them on a utopian renewal of Jewish statehood in Palestine. His dramatic style and utopian vision, observes Schorske, resembled anti-Semitic mass politics. Like the anti-Semites, he exposed the liberal dream of Jewish emancipation as hopeless. To Simon Popper, a committed assimilationist and a staunch anti-Zionist, he must have seemed Judas incarnated. Karl Popper recalled how, at the age of ten, he had argued with a son of a Zionist friend in defense of his father's posi-tion: "Are there no Arabs in Palestine?" – he asked.[96] He would rarely mention Zionism in his future work, pouring his wrath on the Zionists only in private, but his political philosophy would attack all the tenets of Herzl's program.[97]

The young Karl Popper's milieu was thoroughly anti-Zionist. Socialists and progressives alike denied that Jews were a nationality. In his *National-itätenfrage*, Bauer rejected the claims of Galician Jewish socialists for Jewish autonomy. What future could a nation without territory, common history, and culture have, he asked? Jews should, and would, assimilate in the major-ity nationality wherever they lived. This conflicted with Bauer's major thesis concerning other nationalities, that is, that the autonomy of the *Kulturna-tion* did not depend on territory. In denying Jews the rights of other nation-alities, he sought to avoid not only an organizational problem for the Polish section but also challenges to his own identity as a German (of Jewish

---

[93] Likewise, his successor as Vienna's chief rabbi, Moritz Güdemann, responded to Theodor Herzl's *Der Judenstaat* (Leipzig: Breitenstein, 1896) by reaffirming the cosmopolitan Jewish mission, rejecting Zionism and nationalism as backward: *Nationaljudentum* (Leipzig: Breitenstein, 1897). See also his *Jüdische Apologetik* (Glogau: Flemming, 1906), esp. chaps. 3, 7.

[94] Karl Kraus, in *Eine Krone für Zion* (Vienna: Frisch, 1898), denounced Herzl.

[95] *A Jewish State*, trans. Sylvie d'Avigdor (London: Nutt, 1896); David Vital, *The Origins of Zionism* (New York: Oxford University Press, 1975); Amos Elon, *Herzl* (New York: Holt, Rinehart and Winston, 1975); the older Alex Bein, *Theodore Herzl* (Philadelphia: Jewish Publication Society of America, 1941); Schorske, *Fin-de-siècle Vienna*, chap. 3.

[96] Draft of *Autobiography* (135, 1): "As a schoolboy I had a good friend in Vienna whose father was a Zionist: and I remember that when I was 10 we had an argument about these matters . . . in which I asked him: Are there no Arabs in Palestine?"; my interview with Popper, 26 January 1984.

[97] See my discussion in Chapter 7.

origin).[98] Similarly, when a 1905 electoral reform in Bukovina, the center of Jewish Diaspora nationalism, established a Jewish curia, progressive Viennese Jews led the charge against the "electoral ghetto" (*Wahl-Ghetto*).[99] They felt that their German identity was at stake. Striving for recognition as German-Austrians, they sought to strip religion and ethnicity of significance – their own first and foremost. Their non-Jewish colleagues were happy to oblige. The progressive intelligentsia represented a group that, to emancipate itself from its own ethnicity, needed to dissolve all ethnicity and recover universal humanity – Marx's universal class.[100]

The progressives' denial of ethnonationalism flew in the face of historical reality. Progressive culture remained marginal. It conflicted with the religious beliefs, nationalist values, and ethnic identity of most Germans. There was nothing *essentially* Jewish about it. Progressive Germans recognized it as their own. Almost every progressive circle had both Jewish and non-Jewish members, but there were few progressive German-Austrians, and the marginality of progressive culture cannot be overemphasized. It made few inroads into the court, the civil service, and aristocratic circles. Class and education limited it to the intelligentsia. Even in the academy, where Jews were heavily represented, progressivism represented a minority. Virulent German nationalism dominated much of the student body, and conservative Catholic and nationalist traditions prevailed in the humanities and social sciences. Through their organizational network, the liberal professions, and Vienna's salons and coffeehouses, the progressives contributed to the legendary cultural intensity of fin-de-siècle Vienna, but they remained a narrow segment of the German intelligentsia allied with a subgroup of an ethnic minority who posed for a short time as a social and cultural elite: Vienna's "non-Jewish Jews."

Notwithstanding the best efforts of intelligent government officials, ethnonationalism resisted imperial management. Occasional provincial compromises during the 1900s still reflected the search for equal rights of nationalities (*Gleichberechtigung der Nationalitäten*). Electoral reforms and national curiae were negotiated for Moravia (1905–6), Bukovina (1909–10), and Galicia (1914), but ethnonational struggles turned even the golem of national autonomy against its maker.[101] How was the national identity (and curia membership) of bilingual representatives to be decided? A sensitive 1879 decision of the administrative high court

[98] Otto Bauer, *Die Nationalitätenfrage und die Sozialdemokratie* [1907] (Vienna: Volksbuchhandlung, 1924), pp. 366–81; Robert Wistrich, *Socialism and the Jews: The Dilemmas of Assimilation in Germany and Austria-Hungary* (London: Associated University Presses, 1982), chap. 8.

[99] Gerald Stourzh, "Galten die Juden als Nationalität Altösterreichs?" in Anna Drabek, Mordechai Eliav, and Gerald Stourzh, *Prag-Czernowitz-Jerusalem* (Eisenstadt: Roetzer, 1984), pp. 73–117.

[100] Karl Marx, "Zur Kritik der Hegelschen Rechtsphilosophie. Einleitung," *Werke* (Berlin: Dietz, 1961), 1:390.

[101] Gerald Stourzh, *Die Gleichberechtigung der Nationalitäten in der Verfassung und Verwaltung Österreichs 1848–1918* (Vienna: Österreichische Akademie, 1985).

(*Verwaltungsgerichtshof*) in Vienna privileged "subjective" factors: "[B]elong-ing (*Zugehörigkeit*) to a certain nationality [is] essentially a matter of consciousness and feeling."[102] But hypernationalist efforts to exclude dissenting representatives from one's own curia, or place Trojan horses in the enemy's camp, led the courts to rely increasingly on "tangible evidence" in determining nationality. This all ended, during the interwar period, with Austrian courts excluding German-speaking Galician Jews from citizenship on racial grounds.[103] Ethnonationalism turned multiculturalism on its head by reifying national identity as race. Is it any surprise that Karl Popper wished to cut through the knot of national identity by declaring it false?

Popper regarded the dissolution of the Habsburg Empire as an unmitigated disaster and held nationalism, especially German nationalism, responsible. His response to the predicament of the Jewish liberal and progressive syntheses of German nationalism and cosmopolitanism was to reject both German and Jewish nationalism in favor of uncompromising cosmopolitanism. This was an extremely rare response. It required an individual to give up both Jewish and German identity. Such radicalism left Popper a permanent exile, a citizen only in an imaginary Republic of Science.[104] He freed progressivism from ambivalence about nationalism, making good on cosmopolitanism, but still inherited progressive dilemmas. He was just as impatient as they had been with multinational diversity. As an antinationalist, he defended diversity in the strongest terms, but it existed almost by default, a result of humanity's failure to realize cosmopolitanism fully. Discounting all national, ethnic, and religious identity as culturally primitive and politically reactionary, Popper posited a universalist vision of the scientific community and the Open Society where none of them counted.

PROGRESSIVISM AND AUSTRIAN PHILOSOPHY

"There is a distinct Austrian philosophy," says Rudolf Haller, "that leads from Bolzano to the Vienna Circle," a philosophy "opposed to the philo-

---

[102] Ibid., p. 205.

[103] Gerald Stourzh, "Ethnic Attribution in Late Imperial Austria: Good Intentions, Evil Consequences," *Austrian Studies* 5 (1994): 67–83.

[104] Michael Polanyi, a cosmopolitan fugitive from Central Europe and, like Popper, an assimilated Jew, popularized the term in postwar years: "The Republic of Science" [1962], in his *Knowing and Being* (Chicago: University of Chicago, 1969), pp. 49–72. French scholars have recently attributed the dissolution of the "self" in Viennese modernism to crises of identity exacerbated by the ambiguity of Austrian nationality. Of course, the crisis of Austrian identity could, and did, also lead to reassertion of coherent, even monolithic, selves, nationalist or universalist. See: Jacques Le Rider, *Modernité viennoise et crises de l'identité* (Paris: Presses universitaires de France, 1990); Manuel Durand-Barthez, *Être Autrichien: La problématique de la faute chez les écrivains autrichiens du début du siècle* (Bern: Peter Lang, 1997).

sophical currents of the rest of the German-speaking world."[105] "Austrian philosophy" rejected Kantian metaphysics; insisted on empiricism, inductive methods, and the methodological unity of the sciences; emphasized the close relationship between science and philosophy; and focused on logical, and then linguistic, analysis. Its foremost representatives around the turn of the century were philosopher and psychologist Franz Brentano (1838–1917) and philosopher and physicist Ernst Mach (1838–1916). The latter was influential among the Viennese progressives who joined a crusade against metaphysics to their campaign against the church. Social and educational reform, they believed, depended on a scientific philosophy that would substitute empiricism for German idealism. Mach's positivism set forth many of the problems that Popper and the Vienna Circle would later address. Adequate answers to these problems became a precondition for recognition as an Austrian philosopher.[106]

Paradoxically, it was government repression of Kantianism during the French Revolution, the severe limits imposed on teaching philosophy in Austrian universities during the *Vormärz* period (pre-1848), and the sanctioning of an official anti-idealist educational philosophy in the aftermath of the great educational reform of 1853 that created the background for the emergence of scientific philosophy. Catholic, scholastic, Leibnizian traditions that regarded the universe as a rational order and language as reflecting a universal logic survived in Austria long after Kant's Copernican revolution had decimated them in Germany. Prague philosopher and priest Bernard Bolzano (1781–1848), who articulated them, had a lasting influence.[107] Bolzano's influence was joined, in the 1850s, by that of the anti-Kantian, empiricist, Prussian philosopher Johann Friedrich Herbart (1776–1841), whom Austrian educational reformers adopted as their guiding light. The education ministry promoted a young philosopher, Robert Zimmermann (1824–98), who had done work on Leibniz and Herbart, and who, in 1861, became a professor in Vienna. His "Philosophical Propaedeutics" (1853), a textbook for teachers, synthesized Herbart and

---

[105] Rudolf Haller, "Einleitung" and "Gibt es eine Österreichische Philosophie?" in his *Fragen zu Wittgenstein und Aufsätze zur Österreichischen Philosophie* (Amsterdam: Rodopi, 1986), pp. 11–43; "Wittgenstein and Austrian Philosophy," in his *Questions on Wittgenstein* (Lincoln: University of Nebraska Press, 1988), pp. 1–26. The quotations are from "Einleitung," p. 22, and "Wittgenstein," p. 2, respectively.

[106] John T. Blackmore, *Ernst Mach: His Life, Work, and Influence* (Berkeley: University of California, 1972); Friedrich Stadler, *Vom Positivismus zur "Wissenschaftliche Weltauffassung."*

[107] His *Wissenschaftslehre* (Scientific Theory) contained what many consider as the first modern theory of logic. Propositions (to Bolzano, merely one species of *intelligibilia*) existed outside of space and time, whether known or not. Popper regarded this as an early version of "World 3," the theory of objective knowledge he developed in the 1960s. *Bernard Bolzanos Wissenschaftslehre* [1837], 2nd. ed., 4 vols. (Leipzig: Felix Meiner, 1929–31); Eduard Winter, *Bernard Bolzano – Ein Lebensbild* (Stuttgart: Frommann, 1969).

Bolzano.[108] Until the 1890s, he was the most powerful academic philosopher in the empire. This ensured that Austrian philosophy would develop along paths different from that in Germany.

Austria remained a philosophical backwater until Brentano established his school. In *Psychology from an Empirical Standpoint* (1873), he used intentionality to distinguish between mental and physical states, opening the door both to empirical inductive approaches (Meinong) and to phenomenology (Husserl).[109] Through his students in the Graz School, he exercised great influence on Austrian philosophy in the next generation, and was a key figure in introducing English empiricism to Austria. He became familiar with Mill's *Logic* through classicist Theodor Gomperz's translation, went on to visit England, and referred to English philosophers in his book.[110] He was not an uncritical recipient of empiricism, but he commended the English for their opposition to metaphysics, shared their interest in induction and probability, and encouraged his students to study them. Alexius Meinong wrote his *Habilitation* on Hume, and expressed distaste for Kant and Hegel. At the turn of the century, Cambridge philosophers, led by G. E. Moore and Bertrand Russell, in revolting against their predecessors' Hegelianism, discovered Brentano and, especially, Meinong, and had them translated into English. In turn, Moore's and Russell's logic influenced the Vienna Circle, both directly and indirectly, through Wittgenstein's *Tractatus Logico-Philosophicus*.[111] An Anglo-Austrian analytic axis emerged, empirical in its method, realist (anti-idealist) in epistemology, respectful of natural science and pretheoretical common sense, and concerned with logical analysis.[112]

---

[108] Eduard Winter, ed., *Robert Zimmermanns Philosophische Propädeutik und die Vorlagen aus der Wissenschaftslehre Bernard Bolzanos* (Vienna: Österreichische Akademie, 1975). See also Robert Zimmermann, "Philosophie und Philosophen in Österreich," *Österreichisch-Ungarische Revue* 6 (1889): 177–98. On Herbart and Austrian school reform, see my discussion in Chapter 3.

[109] Franz Brentano, *Psychologie vom empirischen Standpunkt*, 2 vols. (Leipzig: Felix Meiner, 1924–5); *Psychology from an Empirical Standpoint*, trans. Antos Rancurello, D. B. Terrell, and Linda McAlister (London: Routledge, 1995). Rudolf Haller, "Zur Historiographie der Österreichischen Philosophie," in *From Bolzano to Wittgenstein: The Tradition of Austrian Philosophy*, ed. J. C. Nyíri (Vienna: Hölder-Pichler-Tempsky, 1986), pp. 41–53. See also the other articles on Brentano in this collection. For the divergence of the Brentanian heritage: Franziska Mayer-Hillebrand, "Franz Brentano: Der Werdegang seines philosophischen Denkens" emphasizes the phenomenological inheritance, and Karl Wolf, "Der Grazer Schule: Gegenstandstheorie und Wertlehre" emphasizes the empiricism of Meinong and the Graz School, both in *Wissenschaft und Weltbild* 21 (July–September 1968): 12–30, 31–56, respectively.

[110] Gomperz, Mill's admirer and friend, later supervised the translation of Mill's complete *œuvre*. Adelaide Weinberg, *Theodor Gomperz and John Stuart Mill* (Geneva: Librairie Droz, 1963).

[111] Trans. C. K. Ogden (London: Routledge, 1990).

[112] Peter Simons, "The Anglo-Austrian Analytic Axis," in *From Bolzano to Wittgenstein*, pp. 98–107. Wittgenstein studied with Russell in Cambridge. Brian McGuinness, *Wittgenstein: A Life* (Berkeley: University of California, 1988), chaps. 4–5. I discuss the *Tractatus* and the Vienna Circle in detail in Chapter 5.

The Anglo-Austrian connection made Hume the favorite thinker of many Austrians. For both the Austrian empiricists and their few Kantian opponents, such as Alois Riehl (1844–1924) and Robert Reininger (1869–1955), the confrontation between Kant and Hume became epistemology's central question. Reininger devoted a number of studies to it. It became Popper's epistemological point of departure. Beginning in 1930, he radically reconfigured the Hume–Kant problem. Against the majority of progressive philosophers, he declared his allegiance to Kant, arguing for an empirically oriented but nonfoundationist Kantianism.[113]

Mach was even closer home than Hume, and Popper regarded his radical positivism, known also as "neutral monism," "sensationalism," or "phenomenalism," as pernicious. To Mach, experience was nothing but a stream of sensations (*Fluß der Empfindungen*). Science described sense data. "Reality" or "substance" were unknown. In science, the world appeared as a constellation of elements (*Weltelemente*), a structure of functional relationships of phenomena. Scientific theories described them in the simplest and most economical terms, simplifying experience, and making prediction easier. Theories described, rather than judged, sense data. They were conventional, not true or false, but more or less useful. Causality, lawfulness, so-called natural laws, were scientists' creation, hypotheses facilitating the organization of experience and the making of predictions. Knowledge's sole criterion was reduction to experience. (Mach inveighed against the "metaphysical" theory of atoms.) Immediate experience alone sanctioned a transition from common sense to scientific knowledge. Any attempt to go beyond experience would result in errors. Philosophy outside of science was futile.[114]

Mach rejected the Cartesian dualism of subject and object. Subjectivity (the "I" or the ego) was a philosophical construction, a figment of imagination. He attacked idealist philosophy. Kant's question, how knowledge of reality was possible, presupposed an inquiring subject and pursued fantasy. Kant's synthetic a priori suppositions, that is, the attempt to derive the notions making our knowledge of reality possible from the fact that such knowledge was already available, was a target for Mach's derision. Neutral monism – neither subject nor object, but a neutral stream of sensations – abolished also the distinction between mind and body, the psychical and

---

[113] David Hume, *A Treatise of Human Nature* (Oxford: Oxford University Press, 1960); Immanuel Kant, *Critique of Pure Reason*, trans. Norman Kemp Smith (New York: Macmillan, 1929); Robert Reininger, "Das Causalproblem bei Hume und Kant," *Kant Studien* 6 (1901): 427–58. Popper respected Reininger's *Metaphysik der Wirklichkeit* (Vienna: Braumüller, 1931). See Popper, *Logik der Forschung*, pp. 53–4. For Reininger, see also: *Philosophie der Wirklichkeitsnähe: Festschrift zum 80. Geburtstag Robert Reiningers* (Vienna: Sexl, 1949). Wolfgang Röd, "Alois Riehl und der Herbartianismus in Österreich," in *From Bolzano to Wittgenstein*, pp. 132–40 emphasizes the empiricist dimensions in Riehl's Kantianism.

[114] Ernst Mach, *Die Analyse der Empfindungen und das Verhaltniss des Physischen zum Psychischen*, 2. ed. (Jena: Fischer, 1900); Allan Janik and Stephen Toulmin, *Wittgenstein's Vienna*, pp. 133–45.

the physical. Science's methodological unity required that all phenomena be described in physiological terms.

The task of science can only be

1. to determine the laws of the association (*Verbindung*) of representations (*Vorstellungen*) (psychology);
2. to discover the laws of the association of sensations (physics);
3. to clarify the laws of the association between sensations and representations (psychophysics).[115]

Popper would reject this view as early as his 1928 dissertation on the methodology of cognitive psychology. Later, he would develop an interactionist view of body and mind, supporting objective knowledge. His solution to the synthetic a priori would give rise, in the early 1930s, to his novel vision of science: Kantian presuppositions were unnecessary because science was conjectural. Popper was a dualist and a realist, and considered Mach's monism and phenomenalism a reversion to idealism, a mark of the decay in twentieth-century philosophy. He opposed Mach every step of the way.[116]

Mach was a popular teacher, and his students, among them Heinrich Gomperz and Wilhelm Jerusalem, spread his philosophy, as did the Monists. His influence extended to many fields: psychology, social theory, literature, and, with Fritz Mauthner (1849–1923), the critique of language. Robert Musil thought of his philosophical novel as an attempt to come to terms with sensationalism. Austrian socialist Friedrich Adler (1879–1960) sought to synthesize Marxism and positivism. Lenin's *Materialism and Empirio-Criticism* (1904), written in Switzerland, did the same, and later became the Russian communists' fundamental philosophical work.[117] (Popper thought that it was excellent.) Max Adler and Otto Bauer rejected Mach, but they sought to address his concerns. Mach was active in progressive organizations and developed a lifelong friendship with Joseph Popper-Lynkeus. He sympathized with the Viennese Fabians, took active part in *Volksheim*, the popular university, and fought Christian-Social influences in the Viennese public schools. He left part of his inheritance to *Volksheim* and the *Arbeiter-Zeitung*, the socialist paper. He virtually became the official philosopher of Viennese progressivism.

---

[115] Ernst Mach, *Die Geschichte und die Wurzel des Satzes von der Erhaltung der Arbeit* (Prague: Calve, 1872), p. 57. For Mach's developing views on psychophysical parallelism, see briefly in Blackmore, *Ernst Mach*, pp. 63–5.

[116] Karl Popper, "Zur Methodenfrage der Denkpsychologie" (Ph.D. diss., University of Vienna, 1928); Karl Popper and John Eccles, *The Self and Its Brain; Autobiography*, chaps. 7, 18–20, 31–2, 34–5, 38–9.

[117] Robert Musil, *Der Mann ohne Eigenschaften, Roman* (Hamburg: Rowohlt, 1952); David Luft, *Robert Musil and the Crisis of European Culture* (Berkeley: University of California, 1980). Musil wrote his dissertation (1908) on Mach, but later became a critic of positivism. For Lenin: Vladimir Ilich Lenin, *Materialism and Empirio-Criticism*, 4th ed. (Moscow: Progress Publishers, 1964). For Mach's other influences: Friedrich Stadler, *Vom Positivismus*, pp. 41–125.

Hegel, the German romantics, and Kant fared badly in Austria. First, the authorities declared Hegel a revolutionary, then the progressives dismissed him as obscurantist and reactionary. "A few decades ago," said Brentano of Hegel's philosophy in 1895, "it was generally held to be the highest achievement of the power of human research; it is now generally damned as the most extreme degeneration of human thought. That is a good sign."[118] (Popper concurred.) There was also no interest in Fichte or Schelling, or in speculative idealist philosophy, in Austria. Things were somewhat different with Kant. Karl Reinhold had introduced his philosophy during the 1780s, and it made a promising beginning, but reaction to the French Revolution stemmed the rising philosophy. Kant was (wrongly) accused of being a revolutionary instigator, and (correctly) regarded as a heretic deifying humanity. In 1803, his works were prohibited, and textbooks disclosing his influence censored. In *Vormärz* Austria, Kantianism survived only as an undercurrent.[119] When Herbart's influence, enshrined through Leo Thun's educational reforms, began waning in the 1880s, Brentano and Mach were already leading the campaign against idealist metaphysics, a grand finale of which was played by the Vienna Circle during the interwar period. At no time did Kantian philosophy gain a firm foothold in the Austrian academy.[120]

"Austria saved itself the interlude with Kant," said Otto Neurath, a Vienna Circle leader, in 1936.[121] Saved itself the interlude? Generation after generation, Austrian philosophers argued against Kant, sought to assure themselves that they were not Kantians, and competed in explaining why. The spectacle of a culture constantly endeavoring to exorcise a dead philosopher provides the best testimony to his influence. It was in confrontation with Kant that Austrian intellectuals formulated their philosophies. They may have reached anti-Kantian conclusions, but they made Kant the most widely read philosopher in Austria. Friedrich Stadler's survey

---

[118] A 1895 lecture quoted in Peter Simons, "The Anglo-Austrian Analytic Axis," p. 101.

[119] Werner Sauer, *Österreichische Philosophie zwischen Aufklärung und Restauration. Beiträge zur Geschichte des Frühkantianismus in der Donaumonarchie* (Amsterdam: Rodopi, 1982); Ernst Topitsch, "Kant in Österreich," in *Philosophie der Wirklichkeitsnähe*, pp. 236–53. Even Bolzano, who developed a Leibnizian response to the Kantianism that he had absorbed in his youth, was accused of Kantianism and dismissed from his Prague position in 1819.

[120] To be sure, Vienna appointed its first Kantian philosopher, Reininger, in 1913. In interwar years, Hans Kelsen's legal theory endeavored to synthesize legal positivism and Kantian ethics, and philosopher Max Adler combined Kantian ethics and Marxist sociology. Still, Haller's view holds. Max Adler, *Kant und der Marxismus* (Berlin: Laub, 1925); Hans Kelsen, *General Theory of Law and State* (Cambridge: Harvard University Press, 1945), esp. the Appendix, "Natural Law Doctrine and Legal Positivism." See also: William Johnston, "Neo-Idealists from Austria 1870–1938," *Modern Austrian Literature* 4 (1971): 7–17 and, on the panorama of characters discussed in this section, his *The Austrian Mind: An Intellectual and Social History, 1848–1938* (Berkeley: University of California, 1972).

[121] Otto Neurath, *Le développement du Cercle de Vienne et l'avenir de l'empirisme logique* (Paris: Hermann & Cie, 1936), sec. 2.

of philosophy curricula in prewar and interwar years shows Kant to have been the most popular subject in Vienna by far.[122] Among the first philosophical works that Karl Popper read were *Critique of Pure Reason* and *Prolegomena to Any Future Metaphysics*. The crusade against metaphysics ensured that there would be few Kantians in Austria, but the engagement with Kant made Popper's philosophy possible.

Not all Austrian philosophy had a progressive outlook. Pessimism about the limits of science prevailed among the critics of language. Of the major critics of language, Karl Kraus (1874–1938) and Wittgenstein had the greatest influence, but Mauthner was the one who initiated the critique and pushed it to its limits – severing the ties between language and reality. He never lived in Vienna, but had roots in Austrian philosophy, played a role in shaping Wittgenstein's project, and maintained correspondence with Mach. His work reverberated among Viennese intellectuals, such as Otto Weininger.[123] An assimilated Bohemian Jew, an atheist, and a German nationalist, Mauthner attended university in Prague, came under Mach's influence, but also found Nietzsche's critique of *Historismus* and Schopenhauer's critique of Kant appealing. He moved to Berlin at the age of twenty-seven, worked as a journalist, freelance writer, and literary critic, educated himself in philosophy and linguistics, and, for twenty-five years, developed his critique of language. His point of departure was radical skepticism and nominalism (concepts were but names for individual or aggregate phenomena), extending Hume's and Mach's epistemological critique to language. He ended up undermining the scientific worldview.

If thought and speech were one, said Mauthner, language was not an instrument of thought but "nothing other than its use (*Gebrauch*). Language is the use of language."[124] No knowledge was possible apart from language,

[122] Friedrich Stadler, "Aspekte des gesellschaftlichen Hintergrunds und Standorts des Wiener Kreises am Beispiel der Universität Wien," in *Wittgenstein, The Vienna Circle and Critical Rationalism*, ed. H. Berghel et al. (Vienna: Hölder-Pichler-Tempsky, 1979), pp. 41–59.

[123] Gershon Weiler, *Mauthner's Critique of Language* (Cambridge: Cambridge University Press, 1970) wonderfully elucidates the Wittgenstein-Mauthner relationship. See also: Allan Janik and Stephen Toulmin, *Wittgenstein's Vienna*. Elisabeth Leinfellner, "Fritz Mauthner im historischen Kontext der empiristischen, analytischen und sprachkritischen Philosophie," in *Fritz Mauthner*, ed. Elisabeth Leinfellner and Hubert Schleichert (Vienna: Böhlau, 1995), pp. 145–63, argues Mauthner's Austrian "identity" as does Rudolf Haller, "Philosophy and the Critique of Language: Wittgenstein and Mauthner," in his *Questions on Wittgenstein*, pp. 57–72. Rudolf Haller and Friedrich Stadler, eds., *Ernst Mach* (Vienna: Hölder-Pichler-Tempsky, 1988), pp. 229–43 published the Mach-Mauthner correspondence. Weininger dismissed Mauthner in *Geschlecht und Charakter* (Vienna: Braumüller, 1903), p. 176. Popper emphasized Mauthner's influence on Wittgenstein in *Autobiography*, p. 11, and in his copy of the *Tractatus*: Sotheby's sale catalogue, *The Library of Karl Popper* (London: Sotheby's, 1995), pp. 92–3.

[124] *Beiträge zu einer Kritik der Sprache* [1901], 3rd ed. (Leipzig: Felix Meiner, 1923), 1:24.

yet language was inadequate to the task. Sensations were contingent, the meaning people gave them stable: The same words were used to describe invariably different sensations. This made it impossible for language to describe the world with any precision, and rendered all language metaphorical. Everyday language was a pragmatic communal arrangement, "a pseudostandard, like a rule of a game [*Spielregel*] . . . that aims neither to change nor grasp the real world."[125] There was no correspondence between statements (language) and states of affairs (facts). Philosophy could not know the world; it could only criticize the limits of language. Since the critique itself did not escape language's metaphorical traps, but only called attention to them, it "would surely be the redeeming act, if [it] could be carried out with the quietly despairing suicide of thought or language."[126] Mauthner's critique began as an emancipatory project, endeavoring to free thought from verbal superstition (religion and metaphysics), but ended, like Wittgenstein, with mysticism and a call for silence.

Spätaufklärung could not proceed on such grounds. Both the Vienna Circle and Popper had to find answers. The circle sought to reconstruct scientific language. Popper thought this a mistake, but had to offer some way of closing the gap between reality and language. Experience (or scientific experiment), he argued, could show language (or theory) to have been wrong. No guarantee it would do so, but one could learn from error.

The critique of language discloses the proximity of late enlightenment and Viennese modernism. It raises questions about portrayals of Viennese culture that originated in the 1960s and 1970s, above all in Schorske's work. To Schorske, liberalism's retreat and "politics in a new key" gave rise to modernism in literature and the arts. Modernism reflected the dissolution of bourgeois orderliness and progress. *Bildung* foundered; the ideal of a well-formed character, of psychological balance and ethical responsibility, vanished. In stepped visions of a chaotic universe, social decadence, instinctual life, psychological torment, and morbidity. Self-expression became the guiding principle. Intellectuals withdrew from politics to their studies and studios, surreptitiously disclosing their political anxieties in science, art, and literature.

Few people in Popper's milieu fit Schorske's picture. The progressives revealed a greater continuity with the old liberalism. Philosophers, econo-

---

[125] Ibid., p. 25: "Die Sprache ist nur ein Scheinwert wie eine Spielregel . . . die aber die Wirklichkeitswelt weder ändern noch begreifen will." This became the late Wittgenstein's underlying assumption in *Philosophical Investigations*. In the *Tractatus* (4.0031), he still rejected Mauthner's assumption that the critique of language targeted everyday language, and aimed to construct an ideal scientific language.

[126] Fritz Mauthner, *Die Sprache* (Frankfurt: Rütten and Loening, 1907), p. 120: "Das wäre freilich die erlösende Tat, wenn Kritik geübt werden könnte mit dem ruhig verzweifelnden Freitode des Denkens oder Sprechens."

mists, and social scientists exuded confidence and hope in humankind's future and dedicated themselves to social reform. Their effusive optimism in the face of intractable imperial problems was distinctive. Enlightenment and liberalism were very much alive for them. Their responses to modernism varied. No doubt many were shocked by some of its aspects, but the very people who rejected modernism in art formulated philosophical problems that we associate with postmodernity. Philosophers who envisioned a chaotic universe and challenged scientific certitude – Mach, for example – often led efforts for social reform and popular education. In Schorske's beautiful essay on Klimt, Jodl plays the bewildered liberal who delved into the *Modernismusstreit* (modernism controversy) to reaffirm old enlightenment against modernism.[127] Yet he was a politically engaged philosopher, whose vice was not cultural despair but dogmatism, political naïveté, and German nationalism. For some, Schopenhauer and Nietzsche heralded liberalism's collapse, but they caused no Dionysian explosion among philosophers. They were widely read, and calmly absorbed.[128] Late enlightenment and Viennese modernism were intertwined.

Popper faced the dilemmas of late enlightenment with serenity. He espoused aspects of Austrian philosophy but spent his life combating others. He shared the progressives' contempt for Hegel and the German romantics, and condemned antinominalist philosophies as "essentialist" – a term much used nowadays, which he coined.[129] But, an unorthodox Kantian, he rejected the crusade against metaphysics and sought to relegitimize aspects of traditional philosophy. Whether in confrontation with his past or in an agreement with it, Popper, in his work, addressed questions and problems that had first been put on the agenda in fin-de-siècle Vienna.

CHILDHOOD: HOME AND SCHOOL IN FIN-DE-SIÈCLE VIENNA

Photographs of Karl Popper as a child in his parents' apartment, the Schiffs' villa, and vacation places in the Alps show him a content, intelligent-looking, neatly dressed child, often under his sisters' wings, in surroundings projecting affluence and civility. Photos can be misleading. Few of his earliest recollections, as he recounted them in his *Autobiography*, seemed particularly pleasant or cheerful, whether they touched on family,

---

[127] *Fin-de-siècle Vienna*, pp. 231–45.

[128] For Nietzsche's revolutionary reception: William McGrath, *Dionysian Art and Populist Politics in Austria*. Jodl and Jerusalem "domesticated" Schopenhauer. The Kantian philosopher Robert Reininger attempted to reconcile Kant's and Nietzsche's diametrically opposed positions on ethics: *Philosophie der Wirklichkeitsnähe: Festschrift zum 80. Geburtstag Robert Reiningers*, esp. pp. 192–7. Both Schopenhauer and Nietzsche became essential components of the academic curriculum.

[129] "The Poverty of Historicism, I," *Economica* 11 (1944): sec. 10.

kindergarten, or city streets. He told of encounters with poverty and suffering, and expressed nothing of the warmth of family relations. Was it just that he was private? Unlikely. His story is quiet and distant in tone, but it is moving, all the same, revealing a sensitive soul.

Karl Popper remembered his father as tolerant and good-humored, but recalled also his stringent working habits – he often worked until midnight – and his exacting moral and intellectual standards.[130] The father's photographs represent a formidable figure: tall, robust, stern, and – as the son was quick to note – not very Jewish looking (unlike his mother and most of the Schiffs).[131] His huge library – vast, dark, mysterious – reaching to the ceiling, requiring even adults to use a moving ladder, seemed to embody his authority and personality. Even before he could use it, Karl spent time there, pondering its mysteries. Having had to sell most of it when his father died, he sought to reconstitute, nay, supersede it when he finally became affluent in the 1980s. The father seemed to devote little time to his children. He never discussed with Karl his scholarly interests and only rarely his social views. The precocious child's questions were first redirected to "Uncle Poldi" and, a little later, to his friend Arthur Arndt. Karl seemed to cherish the memory of the few philosophical and political discussions he had had with his father. He greatly respected him, but seemed to have derived little intellectual support or emotional comfort from him.

He seemed to have had closer emotional ties to his mother. If the father represented the scholarly and political world, the mother represented music and literature. She wrote some poetry, and Popper mentioned her beautiful piano playing, which had deeply influenced him.[132] She read to him and to his sisters a great deal. At the age of five, she read them *The Wonderful Adventures of Nils*, a book that he kept rereading at least once a year for many years.[133] "No other book had such a decisive influence . . . on my character. . . . I fell in love with Selma Lagerlöf and her books."[134] One wonders if, hearing his mother's voice narrating Nils's flight with the geese, it was Lagerlöf alone that he was in love with, but there is no way to probe further; he barely mentioned his mother in the *Autobiography*. She did spend much time with him (and his sisters) during summer vacations in the Alps, her husband rarely around. Karl Popper recalled her leading him the first day into the kindergarten, then, noticing his distress, taking him back. After his father's death, he sought to protect her. His expressions

[130] Popper, *Autobiography*, pp. 9–15, 17, 83, and drafts.

[131] Photos in Popper Archives, 86039-10, A–V (BB, negatives); draft of *Autobiography*, emigration chapter (135, 1).

[132] *Autobiography*, p. 53; *Offene Gesellschaft*, p. 23.

[133] Selma Lagerlöf, *Wunderbare Reise des kleinen Nils Holgersson mit den Wildgänsen*, 3 vols. (Munich: Langen, 1907–9).

[134] Popper, *In Search of a Better World* (London: Routledge, 1992), p. 99. He read, and loved, Lagerlöf's other works as well (except for *Gösta Berling*).

of concern for her from his New Zealand exile in 1937–8 were as emotional as he ever got in his correspondence about matters not related to his work.

His two sisters, Dora and Annie, vanished completely from the *Autobiography*. In a draft, Popper described them as strong willed, unbending, of "great vitality," and he claimed to have been suppressed by them. This is difficult to imagine; he always hated discipline (other than the iron one he imposed on himself) and took orders from no one. If his future behavioral patterns were any indication of his youth, he had been used to getting his way, and threw temper tantrums when he had not. To such a fiercely independent spirit, older sisters – Dora was almost nine years older, Annie four – would certainly seem suppressive, if they were half as headstrong as he was.

Both sisters wrote: Dora poetry, Annie stories. Popper remembered that they all took part in frequent drama productions at home. Dora attended *Lyzeum*, wild Annie did not. Dora would end her life with a suicide, shortly after her father's death in 1932. Anna would marry three times (twice in Vienna), and be rumored to have also had lovers.[135] She would escape to France without passport or money after her mother's death in 1938, then go on to Switzerland, still without money. In postwar years, living in Ascona, Switzerland, she would write popular romances and mysteries, primarily for illustrated magazines, one of which would become a best-seller and a film: *Liane: Das Mädchen aus dem Urwald* (Liane: The Girl from the Jungle).[136] Her love stories, which take rich protagonists all over the globe, often to colonial settings, contain all the gender and race stereotypes one would expect, but especially noticeable are the powerful female figures. They exercised power through sex appeal, as did the young, blond, illiterate Liane, discovered among the apes in an African jungle, or they outperformed men in their own sphere, as did the older French laureate writer, Olympia, member of the academy, a heavy smoker and drinker. Both seemed Annie's imaginary role models; both seemed to reflect her dreams. Popper, in contrast, would disavow smoking, drinking, and, I believe, sex. The precise family relations and atmosphere that produced such diverse

---

[135] She married first Josef Häussler, an editor, then, apparently, one Helveg (adopting the name Anna Grüner-Helveg) (Meldearchiv, Wiener Stadt- und Landesarchiv). Hollywood director Leon Askin (b. 1907) told historian Friedrich Stadler that they had an affair in the 1930s, and he frequented the Poppers' home. (However, he seems to have been in Vienna only from 1936 to 1938.) The relationship ended, apparently, when he left for France immediately after the *Anschluss*, whereas Annie stayed with her mother for another three months. According to Bartley, "Rehearsing a Revolution," Annie married Fred Lothringer, most likely in postwar years.

[136] Anne Day-Helveg, *Liane: Das Mädchen aus dem Urwald* (Bayreuth: Heros, 1958). The romance was reissued in many editions, most under Anne Day, in illustrated magazines, revised. The 1956 German film featured Marion Michael (It is available from Deutschland Video U.S.A.). Some of her other romances: *Liane: Zwischen zwei Welten* (Bayreuth: Heros, 1958); *Getrennt und doch vereint, Jüwellen-Roman 879* (1961). For mystery: Anne Day, *Fünf gläserne Särge* (Munich: Lentz, 1974).

responses remain a mystery, but they are unlikely to have been utterly conventional.

Popper remembered himself a puritanical and somewhat priggish child. The sight of a drunken man run over by a carriage, he said, weaned him forever from alcohol. He envied his cousin, Erich Schiff (1901–92), to whom he felt inferior in age, looks, and tidiness, "gifts which I always regarded as important and unattainable."[137] In later years, he would use these "deficiencies" to demonstrate that fanatic egalitarianism was wrongheaded: There was nothing he, or anyone, could do to change his or her looks, he said. Apparently, he also felt that he did not measure up to parental (or social) demands for neatness and orderliness.

He also remembered himself as a "softy." He feared the drunken and violent people on Vienna's streets (as much, he said, as he feared anesthesia).[138] The sight of hopeless men, women, and children on the city streets, suffering hunger and cold, touched him deeply and left indelible impressions on his memory. Eliminating poverty would be the major goal of his future proposed reforms, and he would see the disappearance of poverty from much of the Western Hemisphere as one of humanity's greatest achievements. The libertarians' lesser concern for poverty, and their willingness to trust the market to relieve it, he would regard as mistaken, if not callous. In his childhood, however, he could only ask his parents for a few coppers to give the poor. His sympathy, perhaps identification, with the victims was not limited to the poor. One of his earliest memories, from the first day of kindergarten, was falling in love with a beautiful, blind, helpless girl whom he had seen for only an hour or two. He felt deeply sorry for her. It is not true, he said using himself as an example, "that children are cruel by nature."[139] Avoiding cruelty would become his guiding moral principle, indeed, one of the few examples of a moral law he would later offer.[140]

In an interview at the age of ninety, Popper again emphasized the need for politics "not to be cruel."[141] This did not prevent him from suggesting, in the same interview, the use of military power to control dangers to the West. Nor did it prevent him from treating students with cruelty, albeit never intentionally. (He would be deeply offended if anyone suggested he was cruel.) Children may or may not be cruel, but oedipal fears and recognition of dependence on the agents of socialization normally contribute to the domestication, even inversion, of aggression. Children who perceive themselves as particularly vulnerable, or feel especially inadequate, may internalize the aggression all the more strongly, becoming "saints," identi-

[137] *Autobiography*, p. 8.   [138] Draft of *Autobiography* (134, 4).   [139] *Autobiography*, pp. 8–9.

[140] Addendum to the fourth edition of *The Open Society* (London: Routledge, 1962), 2:386.

[141] Interview, *Der Spiegel* (June 1992), trans. in הארץ (*Ha-aretz*) (27 September 1992). Zehava Hacohen provided me with this reference.

fying with the blind and the poor and trying to care for them. Popper's recollections may testify to such intense internalization of aggression and parental norms. That this gentle and kind person could also, in the future, be merciless in intellectual combat, taking no hostages, may not be surprising.

Popper fled discipline and reality in his imagination, and books served this flight. He was, he said, a "typical day dreamer," joining Nils Holgersson and polar explorer Nansen on their adventures. A streak of the child always remained in him: Doctor Dolittle, who opened the animal kingdom to humans by speaking their language and traveling with them around the globe, was his favorite reading in his adult years. Mostly, however, self-discipline channeled imagination into theory. Even the emancipatory message of books he read was not unambiguous, but, rather, conflated freedom and disciplinary threat. Lagerlöf's Swedish geography textbook, which quickly became a children's classic, expressed an austere view of life and harsh moral and educational demands. Before Nils's adventures with the wild geese began, he had failed to study the Sunday sermon, treated cruelly a magical manikin, and became himself a midget. He returned to his natural size only after improving during the trip and bringing his friend, the goose, back home for slaughter. The goose was fortunately saved, but the moral, the danger of disobedience, could hardly be lost on the reader. The story Popper recalled so fondly, his recollection of childhood puritanism, and his concern about his own figure complement one another.

In a draft of his *Autobiography*, Popper said that he had wished to emigrate since childhood. It is doubtful that Austrian politics alone was the reason. Asked years later to recall early family life, he said that he had difficulties recollecting. It is likely that he forgot a period he did not wish to remember. Dora's suicide and Anna's lifestyle, of which he certainly disapproved, may partially explain why they vanished from his *Autobiography*. This still leaves the virtually absent mother and rather ephemeral father unexplained. Some major aspect of family life, or his personal life, may have gone wrong, but it is unlikely that we will ever know. His severe moralism in sexual matters was interestingly accompanied by aversion to judging other people's character, or, at least, to voicing publicly his disapprobation of them.

Popper went to the *Freie Schule* for five years, from 1908 to 1913. It was a private elementary school providing an alternative educational environment, free from clerical influence. It represented an outgrowth of a decade of fighting between progressives and socialists, on the one hand, and the Christian-Social city administration on the other. In 1896, Otto Glöckel (1874–1935), future leader of socialist school reform, established, with like-minded instructors, the *Zentralverein der Wiener Lehrerschaft* (Central Association of Viennese Teachers) and its organ *Freie Lehrerstimme* (Voice of the

Nonconfessional Teacher). They aimed to improve schools and teachers' pay. A year later, Lueger fired Glöckel and four of his colleagues. Together with Karl Seitz, Vienna's mayor in interwar years, Glöckel now led the socialist *Jungen*, establishing a platform for school reform. It called for eight years of compulsory schooling; free tuition and books; kindergartens and day-care centers; a maximum of thirty students to a class; and scientific education. When Christian-Social–inspired school laws took effect in Lower Austria in 1905, a coalition of Freemasons (especially the lodge *Pionier*), liberal *Freisinnigen*, progressives, and socialists established the *Verein Freie Schule*. It grew to 26,000 members in Austria (including Bohemia) and, in 1906, opened a school in Vienna.[142]

The *Freie Schule* used advanced pedagogy rather than old-fashioned drilling, encouraging children's natural curiosity and permitting their freedom of movement in the classroom. It had smaller classes, sixteen to twenty students. Most students came from affluent progressive families. Popper, who hated discipline but loved learning, recalled fondly his teacher Emma Goldberger, who first taught him reading and writing. She was the only teacher whom he ever remembered sympathetically (with the possible exception of one Freud, a mathematics teacher in high school). Likewise, the *Freie Schule* was the only teaching environment in which he ever felt comfortable as a student. In interwar years, he would join the socialist school-reform effort, designed to extend the *Freie Schule*'s educational methods throughout Viennese schools.

The *Freie Schule* became entangled immediately in a series of legal battles with the church and school board over religious instruction. The 1869 school bill separated school and church, but it required schools to provide religious instruction, commonly handled by priests. School director Josef Enslein, a *konfessionslos* socialist, refused to permit priests. The court ordered him to do so in 1909, or else the authorities would close the school. He relented, and the church appointed Father Josef Wolny, an anti-Semite and antisocialist, as religious instructor. The *Israelitische Kultusgemeinde* appointed its own instructor, and so did, one assumes, the tiny Lutheran community as well, for the likes of Karl Popper. Enslein refused to pay either of them. Wolny took him to court, and the case dragged on until 1914 when the court ruled for Enslein: He had no obligation to pay for religious instruction, only make it possible. The *Freie Schule* became a cause célèbre. Similar battles over confessional issues gave rise, during the decade preceding World War I, to an anticlerical alliance of progressives and socialists. Religious identity became the contested terrain of antagonistic cultural politics that continued into the First Republic.[143]

---

[142] Ernst Glaser, *Im Umfeld des Austromarxismus* (Vienna: Europaverlag, 1981), pp. 301–6; John Boyer, *Culture and Political Crisis in Vienna*, pp. 174–86.

[143] John Boyer, *Culture and Political Crisis in Vienna*, chap. 4.

Karl Popper thus received some religious instruction, however superficial. He discovered that he had little patience for it. At home, they most likely celebrated (as he would in future years) Christmas and Easter, put up a Christmas tree, and exchanged greetings and presents. It is unlikely that he ever attended church services regularly, other than through school. (Wolny took the Catholic students to confession.) If his father could have avoided baptism as part of his family's conversion to Protestantism, he probably would have, but it is unlikely. Popper recalled hearing in school for the first time the biblical story of the golden calf that the Hebrews worshiped in the desert in Moses' absence. Moses purged the idolaters upon his return. Initially, Popper said, he had thought the purge justified, but, subsequently, he realized that this was precisely the root of intolerance and genocide. Moses' Torah, he said in later years, "was the source of religious intolerance and tribal nationalism, and nationalism is a terrible danger, especially the connection between religion and nationalism."[144]

Those around Popper delivered an unequivocally antireligious message, but not a consistent antinationalist or prosocialist one. The *Verein Freie Schule* had as its secretary the socialist historian Ludo Moritz Hartmann, an assimilated Jew who was, like Glöckel, a German nationalist who could be caught cooperating with the *Deutscher Schulverein*. There were others: *Los von Rom* (Break with Rome) united both nationalist and cosmopolitan progressives, although no open anti-Semite would take part in the *Freie Schule*. In contrast, Wladimir (and Olga) Misař and Wilhelm Börner, whom Popper met at the Monists, were leading pacifists (and feminists).[145] So also were Arndt, relatives, and family friends. Popper met the thirty-year-old Arndt when he was ten. Arndt seemed to have been single and became, apparently with the approval of Popper's parents, his companion and lifelong friend. He was of German descent, but had grown up in Moscow and studied engineering in Riga. He was a student leader during the 1905 revolution, turned against the Bolsheviks, but remained a socialist, and turned Popper into one.[146] In 1912, he began taking Popper to the Monists, especially on their Sunday excursions into the Vienna woods. He explained Marxism and Darwinism to Popper. Popper also read, around 1914, the semisocialist utopian novel *Looking Backward*, by American progressive

---

[144] My interview with Karl Popper, 26 January 1984; he told the story also in "Toleration and Intellectual Responsibility" [1981], *In Search of a Better World*, pp. 188–90, where he declared the Bible the source for twentieth-century genocide.

[145] Draft and outline of *Autobiography* (134, 9, 4).

[146] *Autobiography*, pp. 12, 33; photo Arndt sent to Popper, 11 May 1914, suggesting they meet (86039-10, BB, roll 7, no. 9). Arndt tried to dissuade Popper from joining the communists during the Austrian revolution, tried later to help publish Popper's first book, and, having spent World War II in Vienna, renewed their correspondence in postwar years. Popper to Anon., 18 July 1932 (17, 6); Otto Lange (Springer Press) and Victor Kraft to Popper, 1946 (352, 1) and (316, 24), respectively.

Edward Bellamy.[147] His father had little interest in the Monists and no sympathy for socialism, but he was content to let the boy find his own way – for the time.

Socialism and nationalism would remain Popper's preoccupation throughout life, but he would relegate clericalism to the margins. Just as he had reservations about the progressives' attack on metaphysics, he disliked their antireligious crusade, though for different reasons. He had a major interest in metaphysics – he wished to reform it, rather than eliminate it – but had no faith, or interest, in traditional religion. His objections to anticlericalism were pragmatic: The progressives' crusade for the secularization of culture alienated the Catholic middle classes and drove them to the fascists' and anti-Semites' arms. In *The Open Society*, and in a series of lectures with ministers in New Zealand, he made feeble attempts to construct bridges between critical rationalism and Christianity. Accepting the liberal Protestant view, he regarded early Christianity as a universalist emancipation from Jewish tribalism, and sought to assure religious believers that philosophy left space for belief. He offered them a modus vivendi, but emphasized that politics must remain free of confession, in the interest of all believers and the antifascist coalition. In his old age, when he underscored the need to control demographic growth in developing nations, he somehow believed that the Catholic Church could be persuaded to cooperate.

Not a religious believer himself, his dissent from the progressives extended, however, to the question of religious belief itself. Just as his philosophy criticized their scientific hubris, so it criticized also their proud atheism:

> So far as religion is testable, it seems to be false. This is not an accusation because religion is not science. . . . Because something is not science, however, does not mean that it is meaningless.
>
> I don't know whether God exists or not. We may know how little we know, but this must not be turned or twisted into a positive knowledge of the existence of an unfathomable secret. . . . I do not think that it is admissible to make a theology out of a lack of knowledge. . . . Some forms of atheism are arrogant and ignorant and should be rejected, but agnosticism – to admit that we don't know and to search – is all right.[148]

Theologians "who go on treating religion as if it were science" shared responsibility for wars and cruelty, as did philosophers. Monotheism was

---

[147] *Looking Backward, 2000–1887* (New York: Regent, 1887); *Ein Rückblick aus dem Jahre 2000 aus 1887* (Leipzig: Philipp Reclam, 1890).

[148] Edward Zerin, "Karl Popper on God. The Lost Interview" [1969], *Skeptic* 6, no. 2 (1998): 47–8. (I have reversed the original order of the first and second paragraphs. In the interview, the first paragraph is an answer to a later question.) Dr. Roger Mell drew my attention to this interview.

"philosophically and emotionally superior to polytheism," but the latter had the considerable advantage of being more tolerant. "I do think that all men, including myself, are religious. We all believe in something more important . . . than ourselves . . . a Third World, something which is beyond us and with which we do interact . . . and through which we can transcend ourselves."[149]

Popper's statement would have horrified Mach and many progressives. They exemplified Nietzsche's "brave atheists," scientists and philosophers refusing to acknowledge that their belief in "truth" transposed divinity from the Christian God to science. Popper did not challenge the progressive enterprise; he sought to defend it. This could not be done within the confines of dogmatic atheism; it required critical rationalism. Lest this serve current efforts to open Popper's philosophy to traditional religion, it must be emphasized that he thought contemporary history told against God:

> If [one could] keep up his courage under the worst conditions, that would be an argument for God. I don't think that any human being can stand up against the tortures in concentration camps which break the spirit. . . . I can't account for [radical evil]. It is evil which turns me against God and makes me doubtful whether a God or anything like it exists, and which makes me even more certain that one shouldn't talk about God.[150]

At the turn of the century, the evil of which Popper speaks was still being prepared – all around him. The forces challenging *Spätaufklärung* and Jewish emancipation were gathering strength. The progressives and the Jews depended increasingly on imperial authority, and hoped that, should it fail, the socialists would prevail and vindicate the Enlightenment and emancipation. National and social strife mounted throughout the empire, the growth of Slavic nationalism in the Balkans reinforcing internal strain. The Serb government fostered anti-Habsburg feelings among the southern Slavs, encouraging their national aspirations. After the Austrian annexation of Bosnia and Herzegovina in 1908, an act that had nearly plunged Europe into a general war, tensions increased. When in June 1914 a Serb nationalist shot the Austrian crown prince in Sarajevo, European controls could no longer prevent a war. Unable to solve its problems at home, the Habsburg Empire went into a war that it did not survive.

Popper's philosophy would confront the disaster's consequences. The intellectual resources that he would mobilize for solutions predated the crisis: They originated in fin-de-siècle Vienna. His responses to clericalism, nationalism, and socialism were often remarkable for their originality and sound judgment, but their motivating ethos remains Viennese *Spätaufklärung*. Science, he said years later, was "nothing but enlightened and respon-

---

[149] Loc. cit.   [150] Loc. cit.

sible common sense – common sense broadened by imaginative critical thinking. . . . It represents our wish to know, our hope of emancipating ourselves from ignorance and narrow-mindedness, from fear and superstition."[151] For all of his criticism, no one has done more than he to vindicate the progressives' "scientific worldview."

[151] Karl Popper, *Realism and the Aim of Science* (London: Hutchinson, 1982), p. 260.

Chapter 2

The Great War, the Austrian Revolution, and Communism

"The First World War destroyed not only the commonwealth of learning; it very nearly destroyed science and the tradition of rationalism. For it made science technical, instrumental. It . . . estranged from science what ought to be its true users – the amateur, the lover of wisdom, the ordinary, responsible citizen who has a wish to know."[1] Popper thus bemoaned the loss of the popular scientific culture that he had experienced in progressive Vienna. He would spend his life trying to restore "the tradition of rationalism," shattered by war and Central European ethnonationalism. He ended up envisioning science and politics in the image of the lost culture: free cosmopolitan communities, engaged in critical debates. In exile, he recovered progressive Vienna as the Open Society and the Republic of Science. This was, however, a desperate move, signaling the community's historical collapse. As a youth, he still attempted to shape a new community in political action. The Austrian revolution represented the period of his most intense political engagement. Only when politics failed did he withdraw into philosophy and science.

Popper came of age during World War I and the ensuing revolution. At a time when most (middle-class) teens stage their rebellion against the parental and social order, that order collapsed, right before his eyes. Few things are more disenchanting, or disorienting, than a war that begins in a patriotic mood, reinforcing traditional authority, and ends with patriotism and authority exposed as corrupt and impotent. Few things encourage more youthful experimentation and dreaming. Nothing liberates more from tradition. When Popper began to develop a distinct intellectual and political identity, he had an unusual freedom to think things anew. The cost in human life and misery, present and future, however, was abysmal. Popper's philosophy reflected both – pain in face of destruction and freedom to invent, with a view to a better world.

YOUTH IN WAR

Popper remembered vividly the war breaking out. On June 28, 1914, he was on a Sunday hike in the Vienna woods with the Monists. When they

---

[1] Popper, *Realism and the Aim of Science* (London: Hutchinson, 1982), p. 260.

returned to the city, they heard that the Archduke Franz Ferdinand and his wife had been shot. A long month of waiting followed. Popper spent the first half of July in Vienna, the second half with his mother and sisters in Altaussee in the Salzkammergut, halfway between Vienna and Salzburg, their summer vacation place in the Alps. On his birthday, the 28th, he got a letter from his father, explaining that he could not join them "denn es ist leider Krieg," since, unfortunately, it is war.[2] Learning of the ultimatum given to Serbia, and having a few political connections, Simon Popper knew that Austria would declare war, no matter what the Serb response was.

Simon Popper was depressed, his mood contrasting with the wave of patriotism that the war initially aroused, a wave that swept over even the family's pacifist friends. Popper was surprised by their reaction; only yesterday they had spoken ill of the alliance with Germany and Austria's expansion in the Balkans: "Today I understand these things a little better. It was . . . the problem of divided loyalties," especially among Jews.[3] The Monist leadership remained surprisingly immune to the hysteria, but even they could protest the chauvinism of their Berlin colleagues only in private letters. Arndt did not celebrate, either, but he did foresee some good coming out of the war: the possible downfall of Russian autocracy. The Franz Joseph Gymnasium in the first district, which Popper attended, was full of war propaganda. Popper joined in by writing a poem, "Auf, auf zum Frieden-fest," "Forward to Celebrating the Peace," which he remembered by heart in old age and considered "the lowest point of my political development" (he was twelve).[4] In it he commended Austria for resisting aggression, thanked the "German brothers" for their support, and expressed the hope that the war would soon end and the victorious Austrian army restore peace in Europe.

For the first two years of the war, life continued largely undisturbed for the Poppers, just as it did for other affluent Viennese families.[5] Summer vacations in the Alps continued. The level of comfort to which Popper had been accustomed until his midteens led to a taste for the good things in life that would remain even when he was later impoverished and could not afford them. He would not settle for less than a Bösendorfer piano, for example. But the life of luxury was about to end. Signs of war were already around Popper in 1914. The war was going badly for the empire, the

---

[2] *Autobiography*, p. 13.   [3] *Autobiography*, p. 14.

[4] Draft of *Autobiography*, Popper Archives (134, 4); William W. Bartley, III, "Rehearsing a Revolution: Music and Politics," p. 19.

[5] Stefan Zweig captured the stark difference between life on the front and back home in *The World of Yesterday* (New York: Viking, 1943), pp. 249–51. Karl Kraus dwelled on it in *Die letzten Tage der Menschheit* [1922] (Zurich: Pegasus, 1945). He reflected critically on the public's changing moods from jubilation at the war's beginning to despair at the end, and on the working of imperial propaganda.

Russian army running over eastern Galicia before the Germans could rush to the rescue. An influx of refugees, well over two hundred thousand, arrived in Vienna. A majority were Jews, mostly poor. They were initially well received, and both the authorities and Jewish organizations made efforts to provide them with food and shelter. They were expected to return home soon. When this did not happen, and frustration over the long war and food shortages increased, Viennese anti-Semitism resurged, and the refugees were regarded as parasites. Western Viennese Jews feared that their influx would intensify – as it actually did – anti-Semitic feelings, and treated them haughtily. Popper was appalled. He shared the liberal view that the *Ostjuden* needed to be "civilized," but charged that Viennese Jews did not do nearly enough for them.[6]

The war hit even closer to home: Three of his cousins (among them Georg Schiff), only a few years older, served in the army, and one of his uncles (probably Arthur Schiff) was a medical officer. Toward the end of the war, his sister Dora served as a nurse on the southern front. The officer corps were decimated during the first few months of the war. His close relatives were mercifully saved, but not all their friends. In the summer of 1916, they had their vacation in Bad Ischl with Rosa Graf, Freud's sister. Her son, who had just completed his training, came in his officer's uniform before going to the front. Shortly thereafter, the news arrived of his death. His mother's grief struck Popper forcefully: This was war. By that time, he had already become critical of Austrian war policies. Belatedly persuaded by prewar socialist propaganda, he approached his father, in 1915 or 1916, with a reasoned argument why Austria and Germany were culpable in the war and should lose it. His father was reluctant to discuss the subject and skeptical of his moral absolutism, but he shared his sentiments. Arthur Arndt, too, agreed. Popper became convinced of the malevolence of imperial designs. For the rest of his life, he blamed the Austrian aristocrats for starting the war.[7]

Popper dared not express his dissent in public; students who expressed antiwar sentiments in school were severely reprimanded, even expelled. He had had enough trouble in the gymnasium as it was. Having completed five years at the Freie Schule, he would normally take an exam to determine whether he could go on to a gymnasium. This was probably no problem, but, interestingly, he chose the Realgymnasium in the third district over a conventional humanistic gymnasium.[8] Both programs had a

---

[6] David Rechter, "Neither East nor West: Viennese Jewish Politics in World War One" (Ph.D. diss., Hebrew University of Jerusalem, 1994), chap. 2; Arieh Tartakower, "Jewish Migratory Movements in Austria in Recent Generations," in *The Jews of Austria: Essays on their Life, History and Destruction* (London: Vallentine, 1967), pp. 289–92.

[7] E-mail communication from Colin Simkin, 9 June 1997.

[8] William Bartley, "Rehearsing a Revolution," p. 20. Again, I was not able to corroborate much of Bartley's information concerning Popper's school shifts.

fairly traditional curriculum, but the Realgymnasium put less of an emphasis on classical languages and more on mathematics and natural science. This may have reflected Popper's own preference. He was relatively happy in at the Realgymnasium, he told Bartley, but it was distant from his home at the city center, and so after a year, in 1914, he moved to the Franz Joseph Gymnasium in the first district. This proved disastrous, because he encountered there an anti-Semitic Latin teacher who harassed him. Psychologically depressed, he fell ill with rheumatic fever in the winter of 1915. When he was well, he apparently transferred to a new (unidentified) gymnasium for two years. He found the classes in all three schools unstimulating and pursued extracurricular interests. The archives contain, at this time, no transcripts, but it seems that he was not an unproblematic student. Bouts of depression, accompanied by illness, real or imaginary, would accompany him for the rest of his life. His mental and physical health reflected also the general atmosphere. War propaganda, continuing unabated in school until 1917, was a sobering experience. He found himself critical of official opinion, having to make up his own mind. He fell back on the values that he had never questioned, those of *Spätaufklärung*. Even before the war had its full impact on his social world, his intellectual universe had been shaken.

The war went from bad to worse; the empire's losses were staggering.[9] In the Balkans, it took well over a year, until the fall of 1915, to subdue tiny Serbia. In the east, two successful Russian offensives in 1914 and 1916 brought the Russian army deep into Galicia. Only Russian exhaustion and German counterattacks saved the empire and temporarily relieved the military pressure. From early on, rumors circulated about the Slavs' dubious allegiance. Czech and Croatian exiles abroad were urging the allies to recognize their national rights, and national committees were established at home by the Czechs, Slovaks, Poles, and South Slavs to advance their claims, first for autonomy, then for independence. The multinational army held together surprisingly well, but when the Russians formed a contingent of Czech prisoners of war to fight on their side, tensions in the military and the empire mounted. Growing agitation led the government, in 1917, to crack down heavily on nationalist organizations. Some of their leaders were put on trial, a few executed.

The Popper family was well aware of these repressive policies. Attorney Dr. Karl Schmidt, an older brother of one of Popper's classmates (Oscar) and a friend of Simon Popper, worked for the military, preparing charges against "traitors" for tribunals. In long after-dinner conversations, he told

---

[9] István Deák, "The Habsburg army in the first and last days of World War I: A Comparative Analysis," and Gunther Rothenberg, "The Habsburg army in the First World War: 1914–1918," both in B. K. Király and N. F. Dreisinger, eds., *East Central European Society in World War I* (New York: Columbia University Press, 1985), pp. 301–12, 289–300, respectively.

the Poppers, in a quiet voice, about the violation of constitutional procedures and human rights in the crown lands. To his distress, he was preparing to try in absentia Thomas Masaryk (1850–1937), future founder and
president of Czechoslovakia, the only nationalist politician Karl Popper ever
admired.[10] Popper now faced the problem of nationalism in its acuity.
Neither then nor later did he favor dismembering the empire that embodied, for him, an almost idyllic multiculturalism: Its "dissolution proved a disaster for Europe and the world." "But I did abhor the way in which these
individuals and movements were suppressed."[11]

At the outset of the war, the Austrian socialists declared a "civil peace,"
but a growing leftist opposition in the party rejected the pro-war stance.
On October 21, 1916, Friedrich Adler, son of the party's venerable leader,
Victor Adler, murdered the imperial minister-president Count Karl von
Stürgkh. The act first shocked everyone in Vienna, but Adler became the
Viennese workers' hero. When he stood for trial in May 1917, only half a
year later, public demonstrations revealed popular support for him, and
he escaped execution (and was later released). He left an indelible impression on Popper, who admired his courage and forthright defense. In
an unpublished excerpt of Popper's *Autobiography*, Adler exemplified
democratic theory.[12] Popper permitted violence if it meant disposing of a
tyranny blocking democratic change, with an eye to restoring constitutional procedures. He saw Adler as a model citizen, peace loving and
law-abiding, but ready to take up arms to defend life and liberty. Years later,
he recognized that Stürgkh represented the party in court seeking a way
out of the war. But even his growing appreciation for the empire, his
opposition to violence from below, the controversial character of the
deed among friends – Hayek thought it murder, pure and simple – and his
recognition that Adler's despair over his love affair with Sofie Lazarsfeld
may have been a partial motive did not change his mind. The murder
crystallized opposition to the terrible war – it remained for him a noble
deed.

The death of the old emperor in November 1916 deprived the monarchy of its great symbol of unity. Simon Popper and his family stood at
attention in their apartment as the emperor's funeral procession passed by
their window, recognizing that an epoch was coming to an end.[13] The army
held the empire together for two more years, but escalating nationalist

[10] Karl Popper, "Prague Lecture" (1994), www.lf3.cuni.cz/aff/p2_e.html (access through the Karl Popper Web: www.eeng.dcu.ie/~tkpw/); "Epistemology and Industrialization," in *The Myth of the Framework* (London: Routledge, 1994), pp. 185–7.

[11] Idem, "Epistemology and Industrialization," p. 186; William Bartley, "Rehearsing a Revolution," p. 22, respectively. See also: Popper, "On Culture Clash," in his *In Search of a Better World* (London: Routledge, 1992), esp. p. 124.

[12] Popper Archives (134, 4, 5).

[13] William Bartley, "Rehearsing a Revolution," p. 9.

demands were leading, as if by inexorable force, toward dissolution.[14] The Bolshevik revolution sent an electrifying shock throughout the empire, and communist peace propaganda found a willing ear among the tired, starved, and cold population. The winter of 1917–18 was harsh, and conditions in Vienna were worse than almost anywhere else. Food and fuel shortages were severe because the Hungarians and Czechs refused to supply the capital. Social tensions were mounting. On December 7, students and the socialist left organized a day on "academic youth and the peace." When the government decided in January 1918 to cut the already inadequate ration of grain by half, spontaneous strikes broke out and spread like fire throughout lower Austria, especially in Vienna and surrounding industrial centers. They were led by young intellectuals, mostly in their late teens, the "left radicals," who encouraged the workers to set up Soviet-style councils. The workers demanded an immediate armistice on all fronts. The socialist party, which controlled the central council of Vienna's workers, was caught by surprise. Even the party's antiwar left, led by Otto Bauer, was apprehensive about the unruly nature of the events. In return for some political and economic concessions, the party assisted the government in quelling the strikes, and the left-radical leaders were arrested.[15]

The empire was, however, lost. Between January and October 1918, the various nationalities moved rapidly toward independence from Vienna, encouraged by President Wilson's fourteen points, and by the allies' recognition, in the spring of 1918, of the Czech and Southern Slav National Committees as cobelligerents. The young Emperor Karl understood the urgent need for federal reform, but he was helpless in the face of the different nationalities' conflicting claims. Any recognition of the Slavs would have led to a breakup with Hungary, and the different Slav committees presented conflicting territorial demands. Meanwhile, the desertion of minorities on the front became endemic, and complete units disintegrated. In February, naval units at Cattaro mutinied. Austria lost the battle on the Italian front, where it had earlier had its only major success. When the defeat of the Central Powers became clear, revolutions broke out in Prague, Zagreb, Cracow, and Budapest, and the Czechs and Slovaks, the Southern Slavs, the Poles, and the Hungarians declared national independence. In Vienna, the Socialists (as well as the Christian-Socials and German nationalists) set up a provisional government on October 21. The imperial government signed the armistice on November 3, and the Emperor Karl

---

[14] The Empire's breakup is recounted in detail in Z. A. B. Zeman, *The Break-Up of the Habsburg Empire, 1914–1918* (New York: Oxford University Press, 1961). István Deák, *Beyond Nationalism: The Social and Political History of the Habsburg Officer Corps, 1848–1918* (New York: Oxford University Press, 1990) explains how the army managed to hold the empire together until the war's end.

[15] Hans Hautmann, *Die verlorene Räterepublik: Am Beispiel der Kommunistischen Partei Deutschösterreichs* (Vienna: Europa, 1971), pp. 19–61.

renounced participation in state affairs on November 11. Six hundred years of Habsburg rule were at an end.

REVOLUTION: POPPER AS A COMMUNIST

The late war years witnessed the increasing politicization of students. Youth groups provided a major channel for radical political action during the war. Popper appears to have been a member of one, the *Jung-Wandervogel* (Youth Scout) group led by Karl Frank (1893–1969). They were socialist pacifist youth who withdrew from the scout movement after it had adopted, in 1913, an Aryan clause excluding Jews. Their leader in prewar years had been Siegfried Bernfeld (1892–1953), who combined Gustav Wyneken's ideas on the purity of youth with psychoanalysis and socialism to produce a plat-form for a *Jugendkulturbewegung* (Youth Cultural Movement) that would reform education and rebuild community. When, after the outbreak of the war, Bernfeld became a Zionist, Frank and Max Ermers took over. During the war years, the group went through political radicalization and became thoroughly Marxist. They included future communist and socialist leaders, friends of Popper. Popper himself was younger than the leaders and seemed to have joined late; he remembered most members in the context of the revolution.[16]

In the fall of 1917, Popper changed schools once again, returning to the Realgymnasium in the third district. He felt that his education was useless. School represented the disintegrating social order and failed to address the crisis outside its walls. Socialist students argued among themselves whether to continue their education or leave school and staff the barricades. Students were among the leaders of the great strike of January 1918. After their arrest, the police disbanded their organizations. The revolution made open political debates in school possible. Popper challenged, apparently, a teacher of German who vowed eternal hatred to the Allies. A few days later, the teacher caught him leading a student debate, and commented that the class had found its *Führer*. It was unacceptable for a "Jew" to lead, and Popper never wished to; "neither willing to lead nor be led," socialist student leader and future sociologist Paul Lazarsfeld (1901–75) would soon complain about him.[17] Rather than confront the situation, Popper staged a rebellion against his parents and left school. He enrolled immediately as a nonma-

---

[16] Questionnaire, Research Foundation for Jewish Immigration, *Zentrum für Antisemitismusforschung*, Technische Universität, Berlin, indicates Popper was a member. He seemed to remember the Eisler siblings, who had been members before the war, in the context of the revolution. On Bernfeld, Frank, and the *Jugendkulturbewegung*: Friedrich Scheu, *Ein Band der Freundschaft: Schwarzwald-Kreis und die Entstehung der Vereinigung Sozialistischer Mittelschüler* (Vienna: Böhlau, 1985), pp. 13–27, 55–66.

[17] Bartley, "Rehearsing a Revolution," pp. 26–7, 31, recounts the episode in detail, and Popper, more obliquely, in draft of *Autobiography* (134, 9).

triculated student at the University of Vienna, intending to study on his own for the *Matura,* or *Reifeprüfung,* the final gymnasium examinations that served as an entry ticket to the university. The exams were difficult, and his father doubted that he would make it. Popper broke the career pattern for an upper-middle-class boy, but, then, the world of the Jewish bourgeoisie was falling apart. Popper just got the message earlier.

On November 12, the provisional government declared the Republic of German Austria, making it clear that it would later seek to unify with Germany. Sneaking into the parliament building through the backdoor, and climbing a few floors to the top of the front stairs, Karl Popper found himself among the ministers declaring the republic, then ducked the flying bullets, fired by communist soldiers, that put a quick end to the ceremony.[18] He was going around Vienna dressed in an old military uniform, eager to partake in the revolution. He joined the *Freie Vereinigung sozialistischer Mittelschüler* (Free Association of Socialist High-School Students), founded on December 14, 1918, under Ludwig Wagner's and Lazarsfeld's leadership. They included both communists and socialists and cooperated with the *Freie Vereinigung sozialistischer Studenten,* reestablished by Frank on October 30–1, 1918. The university students turned communist within a few weeks, providing the nucleus for the Austrian Communist Party. Popper found himself in the hotbed of Central European communism.[19]

Members of student organizations comprised the Who's Who of interwar Austrian and German socialism. Wagner, distinguished among the predominantly bourgeois Jewish students for his proletarian Aryan origins, would lead the left-wing opposition in the Socialist Party in the early 1930s. Frank, also a non-Jew, would move to Germany after the failure of the Austrian revolution and become first a leading communist, then a member of the communist opposition. He would later leave the party but, after 1933, would lead first *Neu Beginnen,* then the Spark group, pursuing a united communist-socialist front to fight fascism in Germany and Austria. Popper, who came to despise most youth leaders, considered him a good friend, a decent person, and a fine communist. Both Frank and Wagner were protégés of Eugenia Schwarzwald (1872–1940), a leading Viennese benefactor, organizer of charity and youth projects, whose *lycée* provided most of the women members of the socialist *Mittelschüler.*

Most famous were, however, the three Eisler siblings: Elfriede (1895–1961), Gerhart (1897–1968), and Hanns (1898–1962). Children of an erudite philosopher and sociologist who had never found a job, they grew up in poverty. The twenty-three-year-old Elfriede was the dynamic leader of the young, mostly Jewish, intellectuals who founded the communist party. In interwar years, she would become known as Ruth Fischer, leader

---

[18] William Bartley, "Rehearsing a Revolution," pp. 17–18.
[19] Friedrich Scheu, *Ein Band der Freundschaft,* pp. 68–77.

of the militantly sectarian left-opposition in the German Communist Party. An enfant terrible of the Communist International, she would eventually be expelled. Gerhart, a Comintern agent, would jump bail in 1946 in the United States and return to Germany to assume leading party posts, eventually becoming minister of communication and information. Ruth would testify before the House Committee on Un-American Activities against her brother Hanns in 1948, at the time a successful Hollywood musician. He would be deported, end up in East Germany, and become one of its leading cultural lights, composer of the national anthem.[20]

The Eislers would disappear from Popper's life by the mid-1920s by moving, one after another, to Germany. In contrast, his path would cross with Lazarsfeld's throughout the 1920s and, occasionally, in postwar years. Lazarsfeld was an energetic and charismatic organizer of socialist youth, involved in "socialist education" and in research projects on socialist youth and the unemployed. Popper knew him already from childhood. Lazarsfeld grew up in a progressive Jewish family, his mother active in feminist and psychoanalytic circles. When his father left for the war, first Friedrich Adler, then Rudolf Hilferding became his mentors. Aware of the peculiarities of his own progressive culture, he said, half-jokingly, that humankind's redemption would come from *Homo Judaicus Viennensis*, yet shrewdly consented to Wagner as the *Mittelschüler's* president. Popper disapproved of Lazarsfeld's leadership both during the revolution and, later, in school reform. He saw him as a power monger who would sacrifice those around him, including women companions, when it suited him. He came to think much the same of the Eislers.

Still, the revolutionary students provided a new circle of friends. Some would remain lifelong friends: Joseph Burstein, whom Popper would save from a Nazi camp and bring to New Zealand; Hilde Elkan (later Braunthal); Max Elstein (1901–22), a Zionist, member of Bernfeld's group, who would shortly explain relativity to him; Fritz Hellin (1901–81), in charge of student propaganda, his best friend at the time; socialist educator Ernst Papanek (1900–75); Ilsa Pollak (later Barea, 1902–75), in charge of student finance, who would later write on fin-de-siècle Vienna and help with *The Open Society;* future physicist Alexander Weissberg(-Cybelski); future biologist Bertold Wiesner (b. 1901). The socialist students would form his central social network to the mid-1920s.[21]

---

[20] Elfriede was married, at the time of the revolution, to communist intellectual Paul Friedländer. Interview with Popper, 26 January 1984; Hautmann, *Die verlorene Räterepublik*, pp. 23–68; Franz Borkenau, *World Communism: A History of the Communist International* (Ann Arbor: University of Michigan, 1962), chaps. 14–15; Ruth Fischer, *Stalin and German Communism* (Cambridge, Mass.: Harvard University Press, 1948).

[21] Friedrich Scheu, *Ein Band der Freundschaft*; William Bartley, "Rehearsing a Revolution"; Friedrich Stadler kindly reported to me Popper's view of Lazarsfeld as expressed in an unpublished portion of his interview with him.

The *Mittelschüler* were moving left toward the communists in early 1919. The tiny Austrian Communist Party (KPDÖ) was established on November 3, 1918. It demanded, as the Bolsheviks had previously done, an immediate transfer of power from the provisional government to the councils of workers and soldiers. Soldiers returning from the Russian front provided the party with a military force, the *Rote Garde*. Initially, the communists had only a small following among workers and soldiers. Once the war was over and the socialists were in power, it made no sense for the workers to abandon their established party for a dubious newcomer. The superbly organized socialists dominated the councils. Unlike the German socialists, the Austrians had their own military force, the *Volkswehr*, that absorbed, after November 1918, most returning soldiers. In the February 1919 elections, they came out as the largest party with 34 percent of the vote. They won handsomely in Vienna; the rural provinces supported the Christian-Social Party. The communists failed to win a single delegate. Only a sweeping Central European revolution, or bad socialist mistakes, could open up an opportunity for a communist putsch.

In March 1919, a coalition government was set up, the socialists exercising the dominant influence in it. The conservatives understood that the socialists alone could control the unemployed, the soldiers, the radical crowds, and the councils, voicing increasingly revolutionary demands. The socialists were more radical than their German counterparts, but their leaders, especially Otto Bauer, argued that the large, conservative, peasant class in Austria did not permit a socialist revolution. A socialist dictatorship would also likely trigger the Allies' intervention. He preferred to use the revolutionary situation and the socialists' extraparliamentary support to extract concessions from the conservatives and push through parliament a radical program of social legislation.[22]

Vienna's streets were unruly throughout the spring of 1919. Despite the armistice, the Allies did not lift the food blockade, and the Hungarians and Czechs did not, or could not, renew food shipments. The city reached near-famine conditions. Economic production dropped to a fraction of its prewar levels, and unemployment peaked. Returning soldiers, disabled veterans, and the unemployed crowded the streets and the councils, demonstrated in front of parliament, and voiced radical demands. In March, a Soviet republic was established by Béla Kun and the communists in Hungary, and in April in Bavaria. The prospect of a radical Central European communist-socialist bloc seemed imminent, and Kun sent urgent appeals for military assistance to the Austrian socialists. Bauer refused. The communists were making, however, inroads among workers and soldiers, encouraging

---

[22] Norbert Leser, *Zwischen Reformismus und Bolschewismus: Der Austromarxismus als Theorie und Praxis*, 2nd ed. (Vienna: Böhlaus, 1985), pp. 135–73; Otto Bauer, *Der Weg zum Sozialismus* (Vienna: Wiener Volksbuchhandlung, 1919).

demonstrations, strikes, and confrontations with the Vienna police and the *Volkswehr*. On April 17, 1919, a demonstration of four thousand unemployed workers, soldiers, and disabled veterans in front of parliament led to a clash with the police, and demonstrators set fire to parts of the building. The *Volkwehr* soon restored order, and only a few people – mostly policemen – were killed. Persistent rumors had it that the demonstration was part of a communist putsch. While events seemed to have caught most of the party by surprise, a faction supported by the Hungarians planned to use such occasions for initiating a takeover. They hoped that, in the event, the socialist left would remain neutral. They were disappointed when Friedrich Adler used his enormous popularity to dissuade the workers from revolting.[23]

The *Mittelschüler* followed closely the developing European scene, especially events in Bavaria. The twenty-four issues of *Sozialistische Jugend*, published between January and June 1919, testified to the constant communication between revolutionaries in Vienna and Munich. Elstein, Hellin, and Lazarsfeld were frequent contributors. In March, the *Mittelschüler* appointed section leaders for the different schools. Karl Popper represented the Realgymnasium in the third district. He now sought engagement with the communists. Arndt warned him that "the Bolsheviks were prepared for every crime," but in April 1919 or thereabouts, Frank used Soviet peace propaganda to convince him of the justice of the communist cause, and with a few friends, including Wagner, Popper "converted" to communism.[24]

It is not clear whether Popper actually became a communist party member, but he was working as an office boy at communist headquarters, precisely when the party was staging its coup attempts. At headquarters, he got to know the Eislers well and, apparently, "loved them like cousins."[25] There he also met an old acquaintance from prewar Pressbaum days, musician Max Deutsch (1892–1982). The constant communication passing between Vienna, Budapest, and Moscow caught his attention, as did the activities of Dr. Ernö Bettelheim (1889–1959), the Hungarian emissary who took over the communist organization in April. Popper's family, hearing about his activities, was alarmed. His uncle, Walter Schiff, was undersecretary of finance and president of the statistics bureau in Bauer's government. Uncle Walter thought he could use his socialist and academic credentials to force communism out of the headstrong youth; "as a scientist, I can assure you that communism is false," he told Popper.[26] Popper was in no mood

---

[23] Hans Hautmann, *Die verlorene Räterepublik*, pp. 75–152.

[24] Friedrich Scheu, *Ein Band der Freundschaft*, pp. 71–6; *Autobiography*, pp. 32–3 and draft (134, 11); my interview.

[25] William Bartley, "Rehearsing a Revolution," p. 61.

[26] "Popper und der Wiener Kreis – Aus einem Gespräch mit Sir Karl Popper (1991)," in Friedrich Stadler, *Studien zum Wiener Kreis* (Frankfurt: Suhrkamp, 1997), p. 541.

to accept anything on authority, least of all from his family. His father's partner, Raimund Grübl, had built the new *Rathaus* (town hall) opposite the Hofburg Palace to rival it in splendor while people were rotting in poverty on the streets. What right did liberals have to speak? Frank persuaded him that Bauer's socialism, too, was futile. Only revolution would end poverty and war.

Béla Kun, disappointed with the Austrian socialists and thinking the communists incompetent, sent Bettelheim to organize a coup. Bettelheim realized that he had no time to capture the councils: The Bavarian revolution was brutally put down in May and the Hungarian revolution was in serious trouble because of Romanian military intervention. He planned to use several units of released soldiers, the most volatile element in interwar Central Europe, to stage a putsch. The armistice commission, learning of the communist plan, postponed the soldiers' release, and the Vienna police, tipped off about the coup, arrested the communist leaders on its eve. The next day, June 15, 1919, thousands of unarmed, unemployed workers marched to begin the takeover. Popper was with them. They soon learned of their leaders' arrest, and hundreds of them attacked the police station in the Hörlgasse to release them. The police opened fire, killing twelve workers and injuring eighty. The coup failed, and support for the communists dissolved over the summer. With the ouster of the Hungarian Soviet Republic in July, the revolutionary wave in Central Europe receded.[27]

Popper grew unhappy with the communists in the late spring, and the attack on the jail brought about his break with the party: This was, he said, "one of the most important incidents in my life."[28] Like most of the people involved in the demonstration, he did not realize that it was part of a coup.[29] Having been spared the Great War's bloodiest scenes, and not yet seventeen, he was horrified by the loss of life and, as a communist, felt guilty for inciting the unarmed workers. He learned to distrust the communists; "they would reverse their theses on the situation in Austria overnight, when the Russians so demanded," he would recall later, and "they took it for granted that they were the political leaders of the working class and of the future."[30] How could intellectuals so easily claim to represent the proletariat? Not their presumptuousness, however, frightened him most, but their callousness in demanding intensification of the class struggle. The logic that justified violence for the sake of an elusive final aim, socialism, was deadly.

[27] Hautmann, *Die verlorene Räterepublik*, pp. 183–91; Franz Borkenau, *World Communism*, pp. 128–9.

[28] *Autobiography*, p. 33.

[29] This is obvious in the draft of *Autobiography* (134, 11), p. 33 (of typescript).

[30] My interview and *Autobiography*, pp. 34–5, respectively. See also draft (134, 11). Was Popper projecting his impressions of the Austrian communists during the 1920s onto the 1919 scene? There was Russian influence in the party, but not major. Hungarian influence was much greater. Popper knew little about the party's internal workings.

Once communist premises were accepted, one was drawn into a process whereby moral and intellectual autonomy were sacrificed to fulfill an imagined historical destiny. "With every moral or intellectual sacrifice, one gets more deeply involved," he said. "One becomes ready to back one's moral or intellectual investment in the cause with further investments."[31] The Eislers told him that, like good soldiers, they all had to obey orders if socialism were to come. Rereading Marx, he found the arguments on socialism's inevitability unpersuasive. He began listening again to Arndt, who harped on the Bolshevik terror. He now doubted that the classless society could justify terror: "It was a terrible thing to arrogate to oneself a kind of knowledge which made it a duty to risk the lives of other people for an uncritically accepted dogma, for a dream which might turn out not to be realizable."[32]

This critique of communism may reflect his considered opinion in later years, rather than his immediate response. (One can see him progressively formulating his views on the significance of the Hörlgasse event in drafts of the *Autobiography*.) Still, it is almost certain that after the shock of seeing people fall dead or wounded right next to him, he recoiled when asked to accept communism on faith. He was independent and rebellious, not one to accept party discipline and dogma. If his future friendships tell anything, it is that he was inclined toward suspicion of friends, and was a harsh judge of their human failings. Lazarsfeld was right: He was not made to be either a political leader, or a disciple.

Beset by doubts about communism, an ideology that he had only yesterday defended to parents, relatives, and friends, Popper turned to the Danish existentialist philosopher and theologian Søren Kierkegaard. Kierkegaard was not popular in Germany or Austria, but Simon Popper's library included his works, and Karl reported that his father had actually read them. He himself read, apparently, *Stages on the Way of Life, Journals*, and *Fear and Trembling*. Much of it was beyond him, but *Stages*, wherein Kierkegaard recounted the transition (partially biographical) from aesthetic to ethical to religious life, left a profound impression on him. To many readers, Kierkegaard's long, introspective, self-involved discourse on religion, occasioned by the turmoil of a terminated love affair, was less than compelling, but it touched Popper at the right moment, when he was questioning his friends' and his own motives in espousing communism. The irrationality of faith was Kierkegaard's motif. In *Fear and Trembling*, he explored, almost obsessively, the religious and ethical significance of Abraham's obedience to the Lord's command to sacrifice his beloved son

---

[31] *Autobiography*, p. 34, and interview. Compare Popper, "Science: Conjectures and Refutations," in his *Conjectures and Refutations* (New York: Basic Books, 1963), chap. 1. The communist believer's fateful psychology was Arthur Koestler's theme in *Darkness at Noon* (New York: Bantam Books, 1941).

[32] *Autobiography*, p. 34.

– the theological suspension of the ethical. This struck a chord in Popper. Marxism seemed to demand a similar suspension of the ethical, a leap of faith. For a few months, he apparently adopted the existentialist credo: There was no way to knowledge but through a leap of faith. Bartley claims that this credo was still apparent in *The Open Society*, where Popper declared the commitment to rationalism "irrational."[33]

There seemed to be a psychoanalytic dimension to Popper's fascination with Kierkegaard. Wishing to explain Kierkegaard's obsession with "purity of the heart," he used, in a draft of *Autobiography*, Kierkegaard's relationship with his father to illuminate his discourse on Abraham and Isaac:

> Søren, who was only ten years old when his father was sixty-six, was a constant worry to his old father, Michael Pederson. But they loved each other, and often they had long discussions, and "they talked to each other like two men of superior understanding rather than like father and son." [W]hen the son was still a little child, the father had told him . . . the story of his own despair. . . . [O]nce, in his extreme misery, he raised his fist against heaven and cursed the Lord. . . . [T]he father told his sons . . . to become servants of God . . . in order to remove the curse . . . to make up for the sin of the father.[34]

The similarity of Popper's and "Kierkegaard's" relationships with an old father, to whom they were "a constant worry," is striking, especially when considered in the context of Popper's rebellion in 1918–19 – his withdrawal from school and espousal of communism. Whether Popper had already been sensitive to Kierkegaard's biography in 1919, as he was when writing his *Autobiography*, cannot be known. Whether the affinities he discovered with "Kierkegaard" were "real," or imaginary, reflecting his wishes for a close egalitarian relationship with his father; whether his father, too, had a secret that he divulged to the son (or the son only wished there were one, or neither), there is no way to know. But, it is interesting to note that Popper, not Kierkegaard, drew the connections between Kierkegaard's biography and the biblical story. Popper, not Kierkegaard, described what Michael Kierkegaard did as "sacrificing his son." Popper, not Kierkegaard, dwelled on "the son's problem whether to sacrifice himself to atone for the sin of the father – to be Isaac to his father Abraham."[35] Kierkegaard never configured, to my knowledge, the Abraham–Isaac relationship in this manner. It seems that Popper's recognition of the irrationality of political commit-

[33] Draft of *Autobiography*, sec. 8, pp. 10–15 (134, 11); William Bartley, "Rehearsing a Revolution," pp. 63–70; Søren Kierkegaard, *Fear and Trembling* and *Stages on Life's Way*, *Kierkegaard's Writings*, trans. Howard and Edna Wong (Princeton, N. J.: Princeton University Press, 1983, 1988), vols. 6, 11, respectively; *Journals and Papers*, 5 vols. (Bloomington: Indiana University Press, 1970.)

[34] Draft of *Autobiography*, "A Digression: Know Thyself and the Purity of Heart" (134, 4).

[35] Draft of *Autobiography*, sec. 8, pp. 11–12.

ment (to communism) joined a claim that such commitment somehow constituted a self-sacrifice, designed to make up for his father's sin. A psychoanalytically trained historian may be able to probe further. I can only point out what seems as a conflation of intellectual and psychological issues in the aftermath of the communist episode.

Popper was unsure about Marxism, but his rejection of it was a prolonged process, stretching over years, not months, as the *Autobiography* might suggest. He continued to spend his time with communist youth. In the summer of 1919, he was a member of a vacation colony in Bad Ischl, organized by Schwarzwald. Frau Doctor Schwarzwald (doctorate from Zurich, 1902 – Vienna did not admit women at the time) was married to a well-paid civil servant, Hermann, at the finance ministry, and anything but a socialist, but she extended beneficence to the cultural and political avant-garde. Oskar Kokoschka, Adolf Loos, and Arnold Schoenberg taught in her school. Karl Frank lived in her home. Of the two coeducational colonies she sponsored in 1919, the first, of about thirty members, was thoroughly communist. (The nonpolitical Erich Schiff stuck out among the members; Popper did not.) To Friedrich Scheu, the seventeen- and eighteen-year-olds seemed a bunch of lunatics. They were angry at the socialists for collaborating with the Christian-Socials and planning a new communist putsch. The "wild" Lazarsfeld led, Wagner presenting himself lightly as leader of the *Mittelschüler's* Aryan section. (Ernst Papanek led the second colony.) Wagner gave a seminar on political economy. Hilde and Vera Elkan, Max Elstein, Fritz Hellin, Olga and Vera Misař (daughters of the feminist-pacifist couple), pianist Rudi Serkin (1903–91), Alex Weissberg, and Berti Wiesner, in short, Popper's associates among the *Mittelschüler*, all participated.

Back in Vienna, the socialist reform wave reached its high point in the summer of 1919, then began to recede. Parliament passed extensive social-welfare legislation: unemployment compensation, social insurance, an eight-hour working day, regulation of labor conditions, collective bargaining, worker councils in factories. Once a semblance of order was restored, however, conservative social forces revived, and populist antisocialist currents spread in rural areas. A broad new coalition was formed in October, but the socialists now lost their hegemony. In June 1920, they left the government. The elections of October 1920 made the Christian-Socials the largest party in Austria. If the federal course of reform seemed blocked after 1920, however, a new one opened. In the May 1919 municipal elections, the socialists won an absolute majority in Vienna (and other industrial centers). The constitution gave Vienna a provincial status, and so the socialists were now free to focus their reform effort on the capital, inhabited by well over a third of the truncated Austria's population. They would build Vienna in the next decade into a model socialist community. Red Vienna would become a mecca for visitors coming to see humanity's socialist future in the making. Popper would participate in the socialist project. Red Vienna would be his Vienna.

THE SOCIALIZATION DEBATE

War and revolution were the midwives of socialization. During World War I, most warring states instituted some form of centralized corporate economy to meet the needs of total mobilization. The state allocated resources to the most efficient factories, usually the largest ones, set production quotas in accordance with war needs, and arbitrated the demands of labor and business to assure domestic peace. Some intellectuals called these corporatist arrangements war socialism (*Kriegsozialismus*).[36] To progressives and socialists, however, socialization meant moving toward public management, and possibly ownership, of the means of production, with a view to guaranteeing more equal distribution of resources and eventually dissolving the class structure. In Germany and Austria, defeat in the war discredited prewar social arrangements to such an extent that even such antisocialists as German industrialist Alfred Hugenberg or Christian-Social leader Seipel felt compelled to appear, for a while, as endorsing "socialization."

Socialization (*Sozialisierung*) was a new concept in the Marxist lexicon. Prior to World War I, Marxists had given little thought to the transition from capitalism to socialism. During the revolutionary years, the Soviets presented one model: mobilization of the workers and peasants around a "peace and land" program, forceful expropriation, the dictatorship of the proletariat. In Central Europe, only the Hungarian and Bavarian communists attempted to implement the Soviet model, and both were crushed, the Bavarians in three weeks, the Hungarians in four months. The German and Austrian socialists opted instead for a transition to socialism within the framework of bourgeois democracy. The Austrians hoped to use the revolutionary situation, and the pressure of the councils, to induce the conservative elites to accept extensive social reforms and a measure of socialization. In March 1919, a parliamentary "socialization committee" was set up to consider proposals for nationalizing the coal, steel, and iron industries and for regulating the banks. Socialization committees worked also in Germany and semiautonomous Bavaria and Saxony. But the socialization of devastated economies proved problematic. The socialists were not alto-

---

[36] For the wartime debate on the socioeconomic effects of mobilization, see the *Archiv für Sozialwissenschaft und Sozialpolitik*, beginning with Edgar Jaffé's article, "Die Militarisierung unseres Wirtschaftsleben" 40 (1915): 511–47. For some of the major figures involved: Dieter Krüger, *Nationalökonomen im wilhelmischen Deutschland* (Göttingen: Vandenhoeck & Ruprecht, 1983). For an unsympathetic overview of Walter Rathenau and *Kriegsozialismus:* Walter Struve, *Elites Against Democracy* (Princeton, N.J.: Princeton University Press, 1973).

gether clear on what they wanted, or could hope, to achieve, the Catholics (and other conservatives) put obstacles in the way, and the opposition of the peasantry and middle class mounted. So socialization came to little. The Austrian and German committees recommended, in February and May 1919, respectively, moderate plans for nationalizing heavy industries and recognizing a limited role for the councils in the factories, but they remained largely unapplied. In Austria, the Christian–Socials rolled back any achievement in the early 1920s.[37]

In contrast to socialization's meager accomplishments, the literature on the subject exploded in 1918–20. Socialists (Bauer, Renner, Emil Lederer, and, unorthodoxly, Joseph Schumpeter), progressives (Otto Neurath, Rudolf Goldscheid), and liberal advocates of economic planning (Rathenau) competed in offering socialization schemes. Even when it became clear that socialization would amount to nothing in Germany, and to little more in Austria, the arguments continued. The Calculation (*Zurechnung*) Debate on the viability of a monetary socialist economy was their offshoot, and, in its course, issues relating to social-science methodology became central. Methodology and politics became intertwined. The debates continued throughout the interwar period, and provided a first major forum for discussing problems of social planning and welfare economics that would preoccupy industrial societies for the rest of the century. Communists, socialists, progressives, and libertarians (Ludwig von Mises, Friedrich Hayek), all participated. They drew on traditional discourses – Marxism, German *Historismus*, and subjectivist Austrian economics – but refashioned them radically. World War II put an end to these debates, and with the disintegration of Central Europe, they were soon forgotten. Postwar intellectuals had no knowledge of them. Only in the 1970s, with the revival of interest in some of the protagonists, especially in the Austrian economists and Neurath, did historians begin to reconstruct these debates.

When Popper, in his old age, wished to give an example of the futility of utopian social schemes, socialization came readily to his mind.[38] As a youth, he followed with interest the revolutionary debates. Their terminology – social engineering, technological social science, scientific prediction – would reverberate in *The Poverty of Historicism* (1944–5). The

---

[37] For detailed accounts of socialization in Austria that include some comparisons with Germany, see Erwin Weissel, *Die Ohnmacht des Sieges: Arbeiterschaft und Sozialisierung nach dem Ersten Weltkrieg in Österreich* (Vienna: Europaverlag, 1976) and Rudolf Gerlich, *Die gescheiterte Alternative: Sozialisierung in Österreich nach dem Ersten Weltkrieg* (Vienna: Braumüller, 1980). I used also William Smaldone, *Rudolf Hilferding: The Tragedy of a German Social Democrat* (DeKalb, Ill.: Northern Illinois University Press, 1998).

[38] "Gespräch mit Karl Popper," in *Theorie und Politik aus kritisch-rationaler Sicht*, ed. Georg Lührs et al. (Berlin: Dietz, 1978), p. 23: "[T]he naive belief in a general formula, for example, 'socialization' or 'nationalization' . . . must be fought; the idea, that socializing is good and not socializing bad."

work explored the connection between social-science methodology and the politics of planning, and deployed the socialization debate's concepts to shape a novel vision of planning. Written in exile, with a view to postwar Europe, it never invoked, however, the debate openly. Otto Neurath (1882–1945), a progressive-socialist reformer and, later, a Vienna Circle leader, provided Popper with a negative model of planning. Neurath felt, during the revolution, that humankind stood at the gates of heaven. The mission of science was to take charge of the situation and, through social engineering, transform society into utopia. Utopias, he said, had acquired since Marx an undeserved reputation as useless dreams. Actually, they were anticipatory: Technological progress made them possible. In *The Poverty of Historicism*, Popper turned Neurath upside down. He criticized "holistic" schemes for transforming society and offered his alternative: piecemeal social engineering. Holistic planning was dangerously utopian. Science ought to shape society, but not the way Neurath and the Marxists thought. Popper never extended to Neurath, or to the socialists, the sympathy he showed Lynkeus and the old progressives.[39]

Neurath had been fascinated by the administrative war economy (*Kriegswirtschaft*) even before the Great War. He thought that it could provide a model for peacetime central planning. In an administrative economy, there would be no use for money, only for calculation in kind (*in natura*): "To socialize therefore means to further the natural economy. . . . [M]oney cannot be directed. . . . [Our] economic plans . . . force [us] . . . to do away with monetary calculation and engage in natural calculation. Production and consumption draw closer, and objects and men appear more graphically. . . . Everything becomes transparent and controllable."[40]

Science and technology would end market capriciousness. In 1916–17, he recommended introducing a "converse Taylor system," based on the American model of technological efficiency, but adopted to a socialist society. He denied that omnipotent administration would shape life uniformly; rather, when capitalist competition ceased enforcing its ruthless rationality, greater pluralism would become possible. Efficiency and humane economy were compatible, the only obstacles to administrative economy political.

During the winter of 1919, Neurath moved among the centers of socialization in Germany, preaching the virtues of socialization to worker councils, civil servants, and politicians. In late March 1919, he became head of the Bavarian socialization commission. To Lynkeus in Vienna, he sent a

---

[39] Karl Popper, "The Poverty of Historicism, I, II, III," *Economica*, 11–12 (1944–5): 86–103, 119–37, 69–89; *The Poverty of Historicism* (London: Routledge, 1957). Otto Neurath, *Durch die Kriegswirtschaft zur Naturalwirtschaft* (Munich: Callwey, 1919); *Vollsozialisierung* (Jena: Diederichs, 1920).

[40] Neurath, *Durch die Kriegswirtschaft*, pp. 216, 213, respectively.

famous telegram: "Your idea is being realized; we are carrying out full socialization."[41] He sought to bridge the gap between workers and industrialists, socialists and statists, by emphasizing that the central administrative board could represent varieties of social bodies. State agencies and worker councils could together manage the factories, and even older social forms, like guilds and communal cooperatives, would find their place. "Economic tolerance" was important. Intensification of the class struggle or Bolshevik imposition of socialism would alienate supporters of the planned society. He remained in charge of socialization through April 1919, as governments in Munich rose and fell. When the Soviet republic was declared on April 7, he stayed on and remained at his post even when, a week later, the communists purged the government. A right-wing military coup put a bloody end to the Soviet experiment on April 27. Neurath was arrested and put on trial. He argued that, as a civil servant, he was immune from prosecution. Ernst Niekisch and Max Weber testified on his behalf. Weber's highminded testimony did as much damage as good, but Neurath was acquitted and deported to Austria. Back in Vienna, he became involved once more in the public debate on socialization.[42]

Popper left us a brief memoir of his encounters with Neurath in 1920 in Vienna. He impressed him as

> a most unusual personality . . . a man who believed passionately in his social, political and philosophical theories, but who believed even more in himself . . . a man who was immensely attractive, but cared nothing about it; who would not look behind him or, when rushing ahead care very much about whom his big stride might knock down.[43]

For a few months Popper saw him at Akazienhof, a pleasant not-for-profit eatery (*Gemeinschaftsküche*) that Schwarzwald opened near the university for students and professors, a meeting place for the radical intelligentsia, including Hungarian émigrés. The two met again eight years later, during Neurath's lecture to the *Verein Ernst Mach*, and, apparently, once or twice when Popper had his class visit the Neurath's Economic Museum. Later, when Popper formed his critique of the Vienna Circle, they collided: "Neurath and I had disagreed deeply on many important matters, historical, political, and philosophical; in fact on almost all matters."[44] He would

[41] Popper, "Memories of Otto Neurath," in *Empiricism and Sociology*, ed. Marie Neurath and Robert S. Cohen (Boston: Reidel, 1972), p. 51.

[42] Otto Neurath, "Experiences of Socialization in Bavaria," in *Empiricism and Sociology*, pp. 18–28; Ernst Niekisch and Karl Popper, "Memories of Otto Neurath," ibid., pp. 28–9, 51–6; Elizabeth Nemeth, *Otto Neurath und der Wiener Kreis: Revolutionäre Wissenschaftlichkeit als politischer Anspruch* (Frankfurt: Campus, 1981), pp. 3–20; Lola Fleck, "A Life Between Science and Politics," in Nancy Cartwright et al., *Otto Neurath: Philosophy between Science and Politics* (Cambridge: Cambridge University Press, 1996), esp. pp. 22–56.

[43] Popper, "Memories of Otto Neurath," p. 52.

[44] Ibid., p. 56.

shape both his philosophy of science and political philosophy in confrontation with Neurath and the Marxists.

SCIENCE AND REVOLUTIONARY INTELLECTUALS, 1919–1920

"They who did not know the Grinzing barracks, did not know well Vienna of the post–World War I period," said Friedrich Scheu in his recollections.[45] The Grinzing barracks were a huge military hospital, built during the war. After the war, they became residences for impoverished students, intellectuals, and German and Hungarian exiles. Each barrack acquired a distinct identity: Nationalist German students took residence in one; socialist youth, the *Kinderfreunde*, in another; communist refugees and students in a third, Barrack 43. A medical doctor, Ernst Kulka, bought Barrack 43 and rented the forty rooms at no cost to friends and people they recommended. Popper lived there. In the winter of 1919–20, he left home to live with an eccentric group of political outcasts and wayward students.[46] They converted the barrack into primitive student living, cooked breakfast together, and shared cleaning duties. The barracks' leading figure was Emil Karl Männer, the Bavarian republic's finance minister. Frank got him in, and he lived there for eight to ten years. Paul and Elfriede (Eisler) Friedländer, Hanns Eisler, Fritz Hellin, and Hungarian communists lived there, too. Georg Lukács came to visit his fiancée, Max Ermers and Karl Frank led the social circle. Schwarzwald soon got involved, assisting with organization (and possibly money). Paul Ostersetzer, the son of an artistic family who would become a lifelong friend of Popper, was also a leading figure. At the time, he was a carpenter, making toys for a Montessori orphanage directed by Kulka's wife. Popper would soon follow his example and become a cabinetmaker.[47]

In the summer of 1920, Popper was one of the leaders of the Kaltenbach colony. Like its predecessor in Bad Ischl, it was an educational experiment, the youth running their own coeducational camp with minimal adult supervision. Only the leadership changed, the eighteen-year-olds now including Popper's friends: Hellin, Serkin, and Wiesner. The thirty-five to forty members included the Misař sisters and Hilde Elkan, and psychologist Alfred Adler's son, Kurt. Ernst Papanek supervised, but when floods required an emergency evacuation, Popper and his friends, all wearing military uniforms, were in charge.[48]

[45] *Ein Band der Freundschaft*, p. 83.

[46] *Autobiography*, p. 39; draft of *Autobiography* (134, 11). I am not certain about the date of Popper's move.

[47] *Ein Band der Freundschaft*, pp. 83–4.   [48] Ibid., pp. 93–5.

Aware of the gap separating intellectuals and workers, and critical of the former's pretensions to lead the latter, Popper decided to experience worker life firsthand. He had already worked in a factory during the war. Now he sought another manual job. For a short time, probably in 1920, he worked in road construction, found the job exhausting, and had to quit. He tried a variety of social work. First, in 1919, he worked in Schwarzwald's *Haus in der Sonne* (House in the Sun), a large villa in Küb, near Semmering, converted into a convalescence home for "children of all classes" who were suffering the effects of postwar hunger and cold. There Director Helly Baumgarten applied Bernfeld's antiauthoritarian educational philosophy.[49] Next, Popper may have worked, or was somehow involved, in Bernfeld's orphanage *Kinderheim Baumgarten*.[50] During the war, Bernfeld had led Zionist youth, combining the ideas of youth, national revival, and educational reform. By the summer of 1919, however, he withdrew from the Zionist leadership and dedicated himself to opening an orphanage for Jewish youth where a psychoanalytically inspired educational reform would be tried, and the youth would be given significant control over their lives, with a view to building a democratic community, the older helping the younger. In October 1919, the orphanage opened in a former military hospital, with Bernfeld as director. It had three hundred children of Jewish refugees, ranging in age from three to sixteen. Popper was no Zionist, but it is obvious why he would take interest in Bernfeld's educational reform. The orphanage encountered difficulties. In December, Bernfeld fell sick, and his involvement diminished. The people financing the project disagreed with the orphanage's direction and pulled the rug from under it in April 1920.[51] This would not be the last time Popper witnessed the failure of educational reform, but at least for the next five years, he would remain committed to it.

Social work and educational reform forced Popper to confront Sigmund Freud (1856–1939) and Alfred Adler (1870–1937), psychoanalysis and individual psychology. Socialists deployed psychology to shape their reforms, and arguments between Adler's and Freud's disciples were frequent. Bernfeld and his associates used Freudian approaches at Kinderheim Baum-

---

[49] Ibid., pp. 78–9; draft of *Autobiography* (134, 11), sec. 9, p. 2. Popper may have had a romantic interest in Helly Baumgarten. Also, he first met in Küb Peter Hilferding (b. 1908), son of socialist economist and Weimar finance minister Rudolf Hilferding (1877–1941). They had, for a few months, a very close relationship, then continued to see each other periodically during the interwar period. (My interview with Peter Milford [Hilferding], 30 January 1999.)

[50] Popper mentioned *Kinderheim Baumgarten* in outlines of *Autobiography*, and also Bernfeld and his associates, Otto Fenichel (1897–1946) and Willi Hoffer (1897–1967), psychoanalysts, medical doctors, the latter also a pedagogue. In a letter to Achim Aschbach, 1 December 1982 (293, 22), Popper indicated that he was friendly with Bernfeld.

[51] Bernfeld, *Kinderheim Baumgarten: Bericht über einen ernsthaften Versuch mit neuer Erziehung* (Berlin: Jüdischer Verlag, 1921); Philip Utley, "Siegfried Bernfeld's Jewish Order of Youth, 1914–1922," *Leo Baeck Institute Year Book* 24 (1979): 349–68.

garten, but Adler, not Freud, became the official philosopher of socialist educational reform. Socialist reformers Otto Kanitz, Karl Furtmüller, Papanek, even Julius Tandler, admired him. Adler focused on inferiority feelings as the source of psychological malaise and found them rooted in the prevailing social hierarchy. He later argued that restriction of individuals' life space in bourgeois society resulted in "the breakdown of personality." Privileging social and cultural factors in the formation of subjectivity, Adler vindicated socialist dreams of shaping a "new individual." He was a faculty at the *Kinderfreundeschule* at Schönbrunn, training teachers. His medical-pedagogical counseling clinic (*Beratungsstelle*) for teachers and parents at *Volksheim* was considered so successful that twenty-eight such clinics opened in schools around Vienna. His psychology dominated the socialist kindergartens and, later, the *Horte*, after-school centers for youth. Only when Bernfeld and others challenged the Horte in the late 1920s did Freud make a comeback in socialist reform pedagogy.[52]

In the spring of 1919 Popper heard Adler lecture. At the lecture's end, Adler asked for volunteers to work in his clinic. Popper volunteered and formed a fairly close relationship with him. He got to know his family and seemed to have hung around his house. He heard Adler sing and thought his voice much superior to his psychology, and the person – kind, warm, and socially responsible – much superior to the theories. Adler gave him two of his books to read. Popper did not find them persuasive, and interrogated him. Adler was responsive, but at some point, Popper may have exceeded boundaries, challenging Adler's method of adducing evidence to support his theories. Adler's daughter reported, years later, that Popper had suddenly disappeared one day from their lives.[53] The pattern was not atypical. When disappointed in people whom he approached first as authorities, then found to have fallen short of his unreasonable expectations of cogency and integrity, Popper often made sudden clean breaks.

---

[52] Otto Kanitz, "Alfred Adler und die sozialistische Erziehung," *Sozialistische Erziehung* 10 (1930); Johannes Reichmayr, "Sozialistische Erziehung und Psychoanalyse in der Ersten Republik," in Erik Adam, ed., *Die österreichische Reformpädagogik 1918–1938* (Vienna: Böhlaus, 1981), pp. 149–61; Kurt Adler, "Ursprünge und Ausstrahlungen der Individualpsychologie," in *Das geistige Leben Wiens in der Zwischenkriegszeit*, ed. Norbert Leser (Vienna: ÖBV, 1981), p. 161–73. For Adler's views: Alfred Adler, *Studie über Minderwertigkeit von Organen* (Berlin: Urban & Schwarzenberg, 1907); *Über den nervösen Charakter: Grundzüge einer vergleichenden Individual-Psychologie und Psychotherapie*, 4th ed. (Munich: Bergmann, 1928); *What Life Should Mean to You* (Boston: Little, Brown, 1931.) Popper read the first two in 1919–20.

[53] Kurt Salamun of the University of Graz spoke to Adler's daughter, and Joseph Agassi communicated the information to me, E-mail, 6 June 1998. Draft of *Autobiography* (134, 11), sec. 10, eventually deleted; Popper, "Science: Conjectures and Refutations," p. 35. Popper recounted having reported to Adler a case that did not seem to conform to his theory; Adler then interpreted the evidence with great ease, and without examining the child, so that it conformed. "How can you be so sure?" Popper asked. "My thousandfold experience," Adler apparently responded. "Now thousand and one," Popper may have retorted.

Freud was familiar to Popper; family connections to his circle were multiple and close. Paul Federn (1871–1950), Freud's collaborator, was a close friend of the Popper family, and Josef Breuer (1842–1925), who split with Freud early on, was the father of Karl Popper's youngest aunt.[54] Simon Popper had Freud's early works in their original edition, but Popper reported that Breuer's critical attitude toward Freud had prevailed in the family. (He may have meant that neither he nor his father were well disposed toward psychoanalysis, or simply that although they vacationed with Freud's relatives, they did not care for him personally.) At one point or another, probably around 1919–20, he read, or looked at, or may have just heard discussed, *The Interpretation of Dreams, Introductory Lectures on Psychoanalysis, The Psychopathology of Everyday Life*, and *Totem and Taboo*. He remained skeptical. It was not that psychoanalysis shocked him, it seems, but, rather, that he thought it incredible. He did not doubt that the unconscious existed, or that dreams had latent content that was revelatory of the unconscious. He thought Freud's interpretation of dreams "fundamentally correct." Nor did he question that oedipal conflicts and Adlerian inferiority feelings existed and were significant. He had inferiority feelings himself, he said – his lack of good looks and small figure – and, just as Adler suggested, he tried to compensate, or overcompensate, for them. But not everyone did. The universality that Freud and Adler claimed for their interpretations, and their pretension to explain everything, drove him frenetic. Neither seemed amenable to correction by "experience."[55]

Bernfeld wrote, Popper recounted years later, that psychoanalysis can predict that people will either suppress or sublimate, but not which they will do. He found this unacceptable. Both Freud and Adler were able to explain a person who pushes a child into the water, intending to drown it, and another who jumps into the water to save it, by repression and sublimation of the same drives, or the overcoming of inferiority feelings. Under what conditions were Freud and Adler willing to concede that their theories failed? "It seemed to me only too obvious from many symptoms that

---

[54] Draft of *Autobiography* (134, 4); Popper to Achim Aschbach, 1 December 1982 (293, 22). Connections went further. Physicist Franz Urbach (1902–68), who, while working at the Radium Institute, helped Popper with quantum theory, was engaged to Popper's cousin (and, apparently, also first love), physicist Käthe Schiff (b. 1909), who helped even more with *Logik der Forschung*, but he eventually married Federn's daughter Anni (the first woman court clerk in Austria, later a physicist at the Radium Institute) in the early 1930s. (Wolfgang Reiter, "The Year 1938 and Its Consequences for the Sciences in Austria," in *Vertreibung der Vernunft*, ed. Friedrich Stadler and Peter Weibel, 2nd. ed. [New York: Springer, 1995], p. 198.) Ernst Federn was mentioned in the Popper-Gombrich correspondence during World War II.

[55] Outline and draft of *Autobiography* (134, 4, 11); "Science: Conjectures and Refutations," pp. 33–9; *Realism and the Aim of Science*, pp. 163–74. Inasmuch as I had to rely primarily on Popper's recollections of his early views on psychology, with no contemporary documents to corroborate, or correct, his recollections, my judgments on the aspects of his account likely to reflect "authentic" 1919 responses are particularly tentative.

Adler was an Adlerian case; and although I did not know Freud, there could be little doubt for any reader of his *Interpretation of Dreams* that Freud was a Freudian case," wrote Popper in a draft of *Autobiography*.[56] Freud and Adler were not wrong: there were both Freudian and Adlerian cases, but neither proceeded scientifically about generalization; neither could claim that their theories were, like science, "based on experience."

A few years later he discussed the subject with Edgar Zilsel (1891–1944), a socialist educator, student of mathematics, philosophy, and sociology, later associated with the Vienna Circle and known for his Marxist account of the social origins of "genius." Zilsel was skeptical of psychoanalysis and individual psychology and proposed that they, and philosophy, be excluded from socialist curricula as unscientific. Popper met him first as a *Matura* examiner, later probably as a friend of a cousin who had a crush on Zilsel. Zilsel suggested to Popper that there were multiple psychological types and that Freud's and Adler's classifications were not helpful. Popper's report of their conversation is all too brief, but he thought Zilsel's critique excellent, and it decided the issue for him. Never again would he be interested in Freud or Adler. In his incomplete 1927 thesis, he dismissed them as unscientific. Other than in his autobiographical accounts, he returned to Freud only once, in the mid-1950s, in a brief critique, demarcating science from psychoanalysis.[57]

As a youth, in 1919–20, he faced a crisis. He questioned the socialist reformers' prophets, Marx, Adler, and Freud, but believed in reform itself. What was he to do? No wonder he grasped at existentialism for a while, accepting a leap of faith to reform politics. Salvation came shortly from natural science, theoretical physics in particular. In the gymnasium, Newtonian cosmology and mechanics reigned supreme, but in May 1919, A. S. Eddington's eclipse observations appeared to corroborate Albert Einstein's theory of gravitation and precipitated a revolution in physics. According to Einstein, light must be drawn by heavy bodies, such as the sun, just as other material bodies were. He predicted that the light of a distant "fixed" star,

---

[56] Section 10 (134, 11; 137, 1).

[57] Ibid.; Popper, *Realism and the Aim of Science*, pp. 163–74; "Gespräch mit Sir Karl Popper (1991)," p. 528; Edgar Zilsel, "Der einführende Philosophieunterricht an den neuen Oberschulen," *Volkserziehung, Pädagogischer Teil 2* (1921): 324–41. Popper mentioned Zilsel repeatedly in his outlines, but never elaborated. The conservative Vienna philosophy faculty failed Zilsel on his *Habilitation* in 1923. He taught at the *Pädagogisches Institut*, where Popper studied between 1925 and 1927, and also in one of the *Volkshochschulen* (people's universities), socialist adult-education institutions. (Walter Schiff, Popper's uncle, also played a role in the latter.) His work *Das Anwendungsproblem* (Leipzig: Barth, 1916) helped Popper formulate his geometry thesis in 1929 and the induction problem the year after. (See discussion in Chapter 5.) He invited Popper to his seminar in 1934, and tried to smooth his relations with the Vienna Circle. (Outlines of *Autobiography* [134, 4, 6]; *Autobiography*, pp. 82–4.) I wish to thank Paul Zilsel for an informative phone conversation on 20 June 1994. See his touching memorial essay: "Über Edgar Zilsel," in *Vertriebene Vernunft II*, ed. Friedrich Stadler (Vienna: Jugend und Volk, 1988), pp. 929–32.

seemingly "close" to the sun, would reach the earth so that its location would seem slightly shifted from the one observed at night. Normally, the sun's brightness rendered stars invisible by day, but Eddington's eclipse expedition in the Pacific corroborated Einstein.[58] The excitement among Popper's friends was immense.

Einstein came to Vienna to lecture. Popper went to hear him but did not understand a thing. He heard that a proponent of relativity theory, Hans Thirring, had recently been appointed professor at the university, and went to his lectures, but they, too, were too difficult. He helped himself to Einstein's popular exposition, *Relativity: The Special and the General Theory*, Erwin Freundlich's *The Foundations of Einstein's Theory of Gravitation*, and Max Born's *Einstein's Relativity Theory*.[59] He also found an intellectual guide in the gentle, dreamy, Sephardic Jew from Jerusalem, Max Elstein. Only one year his senior, Elstein was, apparently, exceptionally gifted, and patiently explained relativity to him. He finally grasped it. For the rest of his life, no scientific question would deter him. He would inspire his students with confidence that all human endeavors were within their reach, if only they put their mind and effort to it. He would also endeavor to write his books with the same clarity and simplicity that he found in Einstein and his popularizers.

Einstein opened *Relativity* with a basic exposition of geometrical physics, questioning the classical Euclidean geometry that Popper had been taught in the gymnasium. "By reason of your past experience," Einstein said, "you would certainly regard everyone with disdain who should pronounce [a] proposition of this science to be untrue. But perhaps this feeling of proud certainty would leave you immediately if someone were to ask you: 'What, then, do you mean by the assertion that these propositions are true?'"[60] Theoretical physics worked with competing geometries, the choice among which was difficult. The problem captured Popper's interest. A decade later, it became the focus of his 1929 thesis. His solution, to entrust testing with arbitrating the choice of geometry, was the centerpiece of his epistemological revolution. A vision of adventurous and revolutionary science emerged. As Neurath perceptively observed in 1935, Popper turned Eddington's experiment into a scientific model.[61]

---

[58] For a brief account of Eddington's experiment with a view to Popper's later emphasis on testability, see David Oldroyd, *The Arch of Knowledge* (New York: Methuen, 1987).

[59] Draft of *Autobiography*, sec. 10 (134, 11); Albert Einstein, *Über die spezielle und die allgemeine Relativitätstheorie: (Gemeinverständlich)*, 9th ed. (Braunschweig: Friedrich Vieweg, 1920); *Relativity: The Special and the General Theory*, trans. Robert Lawson (London: Methuen, 1920); Erwin Freundlich, *Die Grundlagen der Einsteinschen Gravitationstheorie* (Berlin: Springer, 1916); *The Foundations of Einstein's Theory of Gravitation*, trans. Henry Brose, 2d ed. (London: Methuen, 1924); Max Born, *Die Relativitätstheorie Einstein und ihre physikalischen Grundlagen*, 3d ed. (Berlin: Springer, 1922).

[60] Einstein, *Relativity*, p. 1.

[61] "Pseudorationalismus der 'Falsifikation'," *Erkenntnis* 5 (1935): 353–65.

Science progressed by leaps, an *experimentum crucis* deciding between two competing theories.

Einstein's undercutting of "proud certainty" appealed to Popper, just as the adventure and risk of theoretical physics did. He thought some of his communist friends smug. The hypercritical youth – "I was critical even of Elstein" – was tired of infallible philosophies. Marxism, psychoanalysis, and individual psychology seemed to discover confirmations wherever they looked and explained away contradictory evidence. Such hubris seemed out of place in a world where centuries-old empires had just collapsed and Newtonian cosmology had been overthrown. Certainty should be exceedingly difficult to come by, Popper reasoned. He looked for a philosophy promising progress, but remaining modest and vulnerable, open to correction and change. Einstein and theoretical physics embodied it. After all, Einstein had just subjected his theory to a severe test and emphasized its precursory character. Relativity theory, Einstein said, was an approximation, a better one, to be sure, than Newton's, but not conclusive, not a final word.[62]

In 1919–20, there was still much that Popper found confusing about science and philosophy. Contrary to his autobiographical accounts, he had not yet settled on testability, or falsifiability, as the demarcation between science and pseudoscience, or science and metaphysics. Indeed, he had not even formulated the question yet. There is no reason to doubt, however, that in the aftermath of the political and scientific revolutions, he began to regard openness to criticism and refutation as marking the "scientific attitude." What was it, he wondered, that made Newtonian mechanics "science," even though it proved "wrong," and Marxism, psychoanalysis, and individual psychology "nonscientific"? By 1920, or shortly thereafter, he reached some understanding of his discomfort with Marxism and psychology. He did not quite put it this way at the time, but he sensed that theories immunized to refutation were pseudoscientific.

In his *Autobiography*, Popper described the immediate post–World War I period as one of the most crucial in his life. He was right. The revolutionary upheaval settled nothing, but it set him on his political and philosophical trajectories. The political and scientific revolutions taking place around him promised new cosmology and polity. In natural science alone, however, not in politics, he found a stance toward life and knowledge that

---

[62] *Autobiography*, pp. 33–44 and draft; "Science: Conjectures and Refutations," pp. 33–9; "On Reason and the Open Society," *Encounter* 38 (1972): 13–18. In "Induktion und Deduktion in der Logik," *Berliner Tageblatt* (25 December 1919), Einstein stated that a theory's truth can never be proved, as future experience may contradict it. A theory can only be shown incorrect, through a logical failure, or contradiction by a fact. Intuition alone can decide between two competing theories agreeing with the facts. Popper wrote Einstein's archivist, John Stachel (15 March 1984 [292, 12]) that he had never before seen the article. After 1919, it took him at least another decade, I believe, to reach the first two of Einstein's conclusions and find a way to reject the third.

he could adopt. His stance represented a combination of commitment and distance, belief and suspense. It was not one revolutionary politics or "Normal Science" easily tolerated, but they both stood to benefit from it. Popper's fierce independence would have likely gotten him into trouble with his elders, at home and in school, no matter what history did, but World War I and the Austrian revolution rechanneled his rebellion. The old order had disappeared. It was no longer a target of criticism. Instead, Popper developed a lifelong suspicion of the political avant-garde, of intellectuals' claims to leadership: "I resisted the idea that we, young people, should be . . . the future leaders of the working class."[63]

Experiencing the mass hunger and cold of the immediate postwar years, Popper saw his sheltered life as an upper-middle-class boy come to an end. He would remain politically engaged for another five years, but retain an outsider's perspective. In this sense (and, perhaps, only in this), his critique of Marxism in *The Open Society* and *The Poverty of Historicism* began with his political experience in 1919. Science and politics were joined in his life from the start. The revolutionary experience made it clear that, when in doubt, he would privilege the former over the latter. But he would always retain the hope that, somehow, he might harness science to politics without putting either at risk.

[63] *Offene Gesellschaft – offenes Universum: Franz Kreuzer im Gespräch mit Karl R. Popper* (Vienna: Deuticke, 1982), p. 8.

Chapter 3

The Early 1920s: School Reform, Socialism, and Cosmopolitanism

"The breakdown of the Austrian Empire and the aftermath of the First World War," said Popper, "the famine, the hunger riots in Vienna and the runaway inflation destroyed the world in which I had grown up."[1] Although the revolution was over by early 1920, there was no return to prewar days. A "cold civil war" between the Christian-Socials and the socialists began, occasionally flaring up into hot outbursts. Postwar inflation wiped out the Popper family's savings. It is not clear whether Simon Popper, now well over sixty, remained active as a lawyer or kept his offices open after the war. If he did, he had less commerce, perhaps because he no longer transacted city business.[2] Although catastrophic inflation had been unthinkable in prewar days, it is surprising that the Poppers had not diversified their investments. Other upper-class families had. It is difficult to know how badly off inflation left them, but there are hints. When Karl Popper married in 1930, he moved in with Hennie and her mother, who were living in a small house in Hietzing. Apparently, the Poppers could provide no help. Two years later, upon his father's death, he had to sell his magnificent library for next to nothing to provide for his mother. Throughout the interwar years, the Poppers managed to retain their huge apartment in the inner city, rented from the municipality, probably because socialist rent control saved them from eviction. (No wonder the liberal father became a socialist.) These economic dislocations left an indelible impression on Popper. Even when he later abandoned socialism for liberalism, he did not trust the "free market." Post–World War II welfare liberalism had its roots in interwar economic catastrophes.

At the end of the revolution, Popper faced the question of a career. He broke with the traditional pattern of a young man's progress in his social class – from high school to university to profession – when he left the gymnasium in the fall of 1918, but, then, the war greatly diminished both his social class and his career prospects. He refused to consider the professions. Law bored him to death. In his father's legal library, he found of interest only Savigny and the Napoleonic Code.[3] He would not think of a banking

---

[1] *Autobiography*, p. 32.
[2] Peter Milford told me (interview, 30 January 1999) that Simon Popper kept his office open, but apparently no longer had a secretary.
[3] Draft of *Autobiography*, Popper Archives (134, 9), p. 30.

career, like that of his cousin, Erich Schiff. In his early years at the university he considered medicine, but decided against it. He drew some income from guiding American students around the university and city. Like most socialist reformers, he did not drink or smoke. He lived rent-free in the barracks, eating from virtually no earnings. Modest as his needs were, however, his income was hardly sufficient to sustain even a meager existence. What was he to do with his life?

POPPER S APPRENTICESHIP: MUSIC, MATHEMATICS, AND CARPENTRY, 1920–1924

For two years, between 1920 and 1922, he thought seriously of becoming a musician. His mother was a pianist of considerable talent and her family had a rich musical tradition. The Schiff grandparents were among the founders of the *Gesellschaft der Musikfreunde* (Society of Music Lovers). Renowned composer and conductor Bruno Walter (Schlesinger) belonged to his maternal grandmother's family. (Popper sang once under his direction, probably during his studies in the *Konservatorium*, and disliked him.) His aunt Helene Schnabl was a professional pianist. Her three children – Sophie, Otto, and Ludwig Sebastian Amadeus – were all musicians.[4] His other maternal aunt Dora played the piano, too. His uncle Arthur Schiff, a medical doctor and *Dozent* at the university, played the violin in "an excellent Viennese quartet." Cousin Gertrud (b. 1901, daughter of Walter Schiff) was a professional musician.[5] Cousin Georg Schiff asked for musical scores to read in the trenches during World War I.[6] Popper himself had taken a few violin lessons, but no piano instruction. Somehow he learned to play both piano and organ, and some old Viennese friends recalled with pleasure, in the 1980s, his organ performances. Music came naturally to him, but he had a tough act to follow.[7]

In later years Popper was conservative in his musical tastes, considering Schubert the last great composer.[8] But, in his youth, he appreciated Mahler,

---

[4] Popper remembered his aunt Helli as an extraordinary personality. In 1943, at the age of 82, she was deported to Theresienstadt. Her daughter survived the Holocaust and lived in postwar Vienna as Sophie Tempel.

[5] She married Gottlieb Kadleck (b. 1866), the second husband of her aunt Dora (née Schiff). Both emigrated to England with her daughter Rosa after the *Anschluss*. Gertrud returned to Vienna with her daughter after the war.

[6] The Nazis arrested Georg Schiff immediately after the *Anschluss* and took him to Berlin for investigation. He disappeared.

[7] Draft of *Autobiography* (134, 12); *Verlassenschaftsakt* of Max Schiff, Meldearchiv, Wiener Stadt- und Landesarchiv. William Bartley recorded the Viennese friends' recollections of Popper's performances, and economist Colin Simkin, Popper's closest friend in New Zealand, told me of Bartley's report in May 1998.

[8] He adored Bach, loved Beethoven, but despised Wagner and (Richard) Strauss. When circumstances

and decided to learn about contemporary music. In the fall of 1919, he joined Arnold Schoenberg's Society for Private Musical Performances (*Verein für musikalische Privataufführungen*). The society was popular among his friends. Fritz Deutsch, a childhood friend from the Schiff's villa in Pressbaum, was there, and his older brother Max served on the executive board. His friend from revolutionary days, Hanns Eisler, was Schoenberg's beloved student. Schoenberg found Eisler a job during the terrible winter of 1919–20 and gave him free lessons until 1923. Eisler ended their friendship in 1925, joining the German Communist Party and moving to Berlin. Popper continued to see him occasionally until then. Popper's close friend Rudi Serkin became one of the society's pianists. They met in the summer of 1919 in the Ischl colony. Serkin, who would become a world-renowned pianist, was playing at the time in the Schwarzwald *Lyzeum*, and Popper admired his talent. He both shared the initial hope and eventual disappointment with Schoenberg.[9]

The Society for Private Musical Performances was established on November 23, 1918. Schoenberg (1874–1951) was president. Alban Berg (1885–1935), Anton von Webern (1883–1945), Edward Steuermann (1892–1964) and, later, Erwin Stein (1885–1958) – all Schoenberg's students – were the major rehearsal directors. The society performed modern works "from Mahler and Strauss to the newest": Bartók, Debussy, Ravel, Reger, Scriabin, and, of course, Berg, Webern, and Schoenberg. The first performance was on December 29, 1918. By February 1919, the society had 320 members. Many of the rehearsals took place in the *Festsaal* (ceremonial hall) of the Schwarzwald Lyzeum. (Schoenberg, like Loos and Kokoschka, taught in the school.) He was developing, at the time, his twelve-tone method. Popper got to know closely his *Kammernsymphonie* and *Pierrot Lunaire*, performed in January and April 1921. He went also to performances of Berg and Webern. He helped Erwin Stein with rehearsals, and considered himself his student. But he remained an outsider, maintaining distance from the inner circle.[10] After about two years, he became disenchanted: "I found that I had succeeded in getting to know something – about a kind of music which now I liked even less than I had to begin with."[11] He took exception to the circle's *esprit de partie* and internal squabbling. "The society," he said, "was like a Communist cell, full of conspiracy."[12] He had no need to resign his membership. Financial problems, due mostly to inflation, forced Schoenberg to suspend the society in December 1921.[13]

forced him to attend a Strauss performance, he plugged his ears. John Watkins, "Karl Popper: A Memoir," *The American Scholar* 66 (1997): 207.

[9] William W. Bartley, III, "Rehearsing a Revolution: Music and Politics," pp. 10–17.

[10] Member Lona Truding remembered him as an outsider: Ibid., p. 17.

[11] *Autobiography*, p. 54.

[12] William W. Bartley, "Rehearsing a Revolution," p. 14.

[13] Joan Allen Smith, *Schoenberg and His Circle: A Viennese Portrait* (New York: Macmillan, 1986), pp. 81–102 and Appendix 3 (a calendar of performances).

Schoenberg designed the private performances to protect the musician from the public and the market. In his view, publicity and competition made it impossible for musical talent to thrive. Artistic genius was not easily communicable. Modern music was complex, and the public was incapable of understanding it. Yet, this very public determined musicians' fates through applause or censure. Organizers, publishers, and trade middlemen further limited musicians' control over their work and deprived them of just rewards. Private performances would establish a new, direct relationship with the audience, preserving musicians' autonomy. "The public . . . will no longer be the haughty judge, deciding between hunger and the laurels," he said. "The correct relationship [will be] restored: 'there is a performance: those who want to listen are permitted.' "[14] Press critics would be proscribed from attending performances, and members from discussing them publicly. Performances would become endless rehearsals. Relieved of public pressure, musicians would be free to perfect their output and, according to Alban Berg, make "the work, and therewith its composer, intelligible" to the audience.[15] Private rehearsals of modern music would gradually substitute for public performances of chamber symphonies.

Until the triumph of national socialism, Schoenberg was a German nationalist and cultural chauvinist.[16] But the 1918 revolution brought anticipation of growing state involvement in cultural life. In this context, his anticompetition rhetoric sounded almost socialist: "Concert life must gradually cease to be commercial business. . . . Competition, the need to win, brings pettiness into the business of art. . . . The true artist . . . receives so little in his lifetime that he is in no position to apply all his working energy to creation."[17] He followed Loos in calling for a state musical theater, a national music-school system, and regulation of trade in art. His major concern was promoting the "true musician." A state theater, to which everyone got only one admission per year, would establish a direct relationship with the public, independent of traders. Most importantly,

> it will be possible to find a way of paying artists appropriately, while still holding adequate rehearsals. . . . Musicians' social position must be improved. . . . An artist in his own field needs a higher degree of infallibility than do

[14] Arnold Schönberg, "Musik," in *Stil und Gedanke: Aufsätze zur Musik* (Frankfurt: Fischer, 1976), p. 186. This was his contribution to Adolf Loos, *Richtlinien für ein Kunstamt* (Guidelines for a ministry of art) (Vienna: Lanyi, 1919), pp. 10–11.

[15] Alban Berg, Statement of Aims for the "Society for Private Music Performances in Vienna," in Joan Allen Smith, *Schoenberg and His Circle*, Appendix 1, p. 246.

[16] "The most important task is . . . to secure the German nation's superiority in the realm of music." Arnold Schönberg, "Musik," p. 185.

[17] Ibid., p. 186. English translation: Leonard Stein, ed., *Style and Idea: Selected Writings of Arnold Schoenberg* (London: Faber, 1975), pp. 370–1. The "preliminary remark" to the 1924 reprint, *Von Neuer Musik* (Cologne: Marcan, 1924), p. 33 hr. ff., disavowed the socialist original as a fantasy.

most top civil servants. . . . He should be numbered among the truly elect on the social ladder.[18]

Schoenberg was acutely aware of his place in history. He made two radical breaks with tradition: the "emancipation of dissonance" before the war and the twelve-tone method after. He then sought reintegration into German music, but critics made it difficult. Ernst Krenek (1900–91) and young composers attacked him as an old-fashioned romantic. German critics denounced him as a revolutionary "rootless Jew."[19] In response, he emphasized the evolutionary growth of his music, distanced himself from Wagner, and tied himself to Bach, Mozart, and Brahms.[20] He argued that his music served Germany in "the battle of nations." "In music the national personality emerged in a particularly striking way."[21] The "power of genius" grasped the essence of the people's spirit and expressed it in art. Schoenberg combined aesthetic modernism, German nationalism, and the avant-garde.[22]

Popper found this combination deadly. His future critique would link "historicism" and aesthetic modernism. A historicist imperative underlay aesthetic modernism: Act always so that your actions reflect the coming new age.[23] This meant complicity in history's travesties. Rather than fight history, Schoenberg colluded with it. Popper regarded him as a successor to Wagner and the German romantics – and despised them all:

> There was nothing quite like the Wagnerians: . . . a pressure group, a party, a church with rituals. . . . I saw some of these things at close quarters in Schönberg's Society for Private Performances. . . . [Schönberg's] problem . . . became . . . "How can we supersede Wagner?" . . . Still later: "How can we remain ahead of everybody else?" . . . I feel that the will to be ahead of one's time has nothing to do with . . . music.[24]

Schoenberg had a more nuanced view of tradition than Popper recalled, but just as Popper suggested, he defined his identity, and those of other musicians, against Wagner. His "historicism" was elitist and chauvinistic. His effort to foreclose criticism did not protect fledgling music; it promoted

---

[18] Ibid., pp. 186–7 (German); ibid., pp. 371–2 (English).

[19] Joseph Auner, "Schoenberg's Handel Concerto and the Ruins of Tradition," *Journal of the American Musicological Society* 49 (1996): 264–313.

[20] Arnold Schoenberg, "New Music" [1923], in *Style and Idea*, pp. 137–9; "Nationalmusik" [1931], "Neue und veraltete Musik" [1933], "Brahms, der Fortschrittliche" [1933; 1947] in *Stil und Gedanke*, pp. 250–4, 466–77, 35–71, respectively.

[21] Idem, "Folk-Music and Art-Music," in *Style and Idea*, p. 168.

[22] Schoenberg was born a Jew, converted to Catholicism, then, after the National Socialist triumph, converted back to Judaism, and became a Zionist for a while. Alexander Ringer, *Arnold Schoenberg: The Composer as Jew* (Oxford: Clarendon, 1990).

[23] Popper, *The Poverty of Historicism* (London: Routledge, 1957), p. 54.

[24] *Autobiography*, p. 71.

infallibility and self-aggrandizement. Popper's experience with Schoenberg recapitulated the one with the Marxists. He distrusted artists' claims to superior talent, just as he doubted revolutionaries' claim for special knowledge. All achievement reflected hard work and incessant improvement: "I felt that these people were swindlers. You can get hysterically involved in what you are doing, but true understanding was impossible."[25] To Popper, both the political and cultural avant-garde became forever suspect.

Popper left the Schoenberg circle late in 1921, but he still contemplated a career in music. For about a year, he became a student of church music in the Vienna *Konservatorium* (Academy of Music). He had been composing, intermittently, for years. He was admitted on the basis of a fugue "honoring Bach through its second subject, 'a quotation from Bach's *Passion Music according to St. Matthew.*' "[26] A noted composer recently described it as "a composition of romantic impulse vested in baroque form. It would have been a most credible piece of work to have submitted at the end of his studies at the *Konservatorium*, let alone at the beginning."[27] Popper seemed to think differently: "As with so many other things . . . I felt in the end that I was not really good enough."[28] He gave up on a musical career: "I have done a little composing throughout my life . . . but never deceived myself about the merits of my compositions."[29]

Throughout the early 1920s Popper was also studying at the university. He began as a nonmatriculated student (*ausserordentlicher Hörer*). In an essay written just weeks before his death, he recalled how in January or February 1919, furnished with "an identity card and a registration book (in which the professors confirmed that I had attended lectures) . . . I first set foot, hesitantly and almost trembling, on the sacred ground of the Mathematical Institute of the University of Vienna." The first semester was difficult. "I knew not a soul and I was afraid . . . of asking . . . an *ordentlicher Hörer* . . . for information or assistance."[30] He would feel more comfortable once he became a matriculated student, but this took three years. In 1921, on his first attempt at the *Matura* he failed in both Latin and logic. In Latin, he had difficulties translating a Horace ode from memory.[31] In logic, the examiner, Edgar Zilsel, found his understanding of Aristotle inadequate. Popper was in no position to win the argument. "I found Zilsel always anxious to put me in my place," he recalled.[32] He passed the *Matura* on his

---

[25] William W. Bartley, "Rehearsing a Revolution," p. 17.

[26] Popper, quoted in David Miller, "Sir Karl Raimund Popper," *Biographical Memoirs of Fellows of the Royal Society* 43 (1997): 371.

[27] Julien Musafia, quoted in *loc. cit.* The fugue in F-sharp Minor for organ, arranged by Musafia as a piano work for four hands, was first performed by Gillian Weir in 1992.

[28] *Autobiography*, p. 54. [29] Loc. cit.

[30] Popper, "In Memory of Hans Hahn," in *Hans Hahn: Collected Works* (Vienna: Springer, 1995), 1: 11.

[31] David Miller, "Sir Karl Raimund Popper": 370.

[32] Outline of *Autobiography* (134, 4).

second try in 1922. At the university, he sampled courses in different fields, "nibbling like a mouse everywhere." He found most courses disappointing. Reading the professors' books proved more rewarding than listening to their lectures. There was no contact at all between professors and students until the dissertation. He had two uncles teaching at the university: Walter Schiff taught economics and statistics, and Arthur Schiff medicine. His cousin, Erich Schiff, participated in Ludwig von Mises's seminar. None of this appealed to him. Academic life seemed trivial, almost a bore.

Popper stopped going to most lectures and began studying with a group of socialist friends he had known since the revolution. They composed their own reading list, discussed books, debated politics, climbed the Alps, and went to concerts. Circles of young intellectuals who found the university stifling were common in Vienna both before and after the war, but socialist students moved the center of activities from the coffeehouse to the scoutlike group. (Popper, especially, despised the coffeehouse milieu. He spoke of it contemptuously as a waste of time.) Years later, when writing his *Autobiography*, Popper would trace many of his views on psychology and science to his extracurricular activities during this period. The problems he formulated and the terms he used in the *Autobiography* could not have been available to him in the early 1920s, but his narrative reflected the rich intellectual life among gymnasium-educated socialist youth.

In contrast with his attitude toward most academic studies, Popper found mathematics exciting. He spent long hours in the library of the Vienna Mathematical Institute. The institute included world-renowned mathematicians: Wilhelm Wirtinger, Philipp Furtwängler, Hans Hahn, Eduard Helly, and, for a while, Kurt Reidemeister. Popper took courses with all of them. He first attended, in the winter of 1919, Wirtinger's lectures on infinitesimal calculus, but found him difficult to follow. Furtwängler's lectures in algebra and number theory were, in contrast, amazingly clear. He studied probability theory with Helly, heard Rudmeister on the Pythagorean Theorem, but learned the most from Hans Hahn (1879–1934). He took his courses on calculus and the theory of natural numbers sometime in 1922. His lectures were "a work of art: dramatic in logical structure; not a word too much; of perfect clarity; [introduced] by an exciting historical sketch; delivered in beautiful and civilized language."[33] Hahn went through the history of infinitesimal calculus focusing on the great innovators' problem situation, emphasizing that mathematical problems reflected larger concern with the universe's logical structure. "Many years later," noted Popper, "I wrote that history should be an account of problem situations. . . . I recognize that [this was] perhaps a result of the great impression he made upon me."[34]

[33] *Autobiography*, p. 40.   [34] "In Memory of Hans Hahn," p. 13.

Hahn ended the course with Alfred Whitehead's and Bertrand Russell's *Principia Mathematica* and David Hilbert's axiomatic theory, that is, with mathematical logic. He was enthusiastic about "logicism," the view that mathematics was logically founded, its problems translatable into logical ones. Popper read the *Principia* and found it difficult, but Russell's revolutionary attempt to translate mathematical into logical rules provoked his reflections on the rational foundation of science. He heard first in 1920 about Brouwer and intuitionist mathematics. Brouwer seemed to him to challenge mathematical rationality: "I was stunned, found it irritating and depressing, but could do nothing with it."[35] On Hahn's authority, he trusted the *Principia*, "and looked at Weyl and Brouwer with suspicion." The subject remained for a while beyond his reach. He needed some guidance but could get none at the university. The mathematics professors were demigods whose lectures, with the exception of Reidemeister's, could not be interrupted. Nonetheless, his mathematical studies introduced him, however vaguely, to philosophical problems that remained of permanent concern.

"Why did I study mathematics?" wondered Popper in later years. It is "a huge and difficult subject, and, had I ever thought of becoming a professional mathematician, I might soon have been discouraged."[36] "I was not particularly good – none of my colleagues were quite outstanding."[37] But Max Elstein showed him the interdependence of mathematics and theoretical physics, and physics continued to capture his imagination. He attended lectures by Ernst Lecher, Felix Ehrenhaft, and Hans Thirring, found them uninspiring, but remained interested all the same. All his life he admired creative mathematicians and physicists. Joining Karl Menger's *Mathematisches Kolloquium* late in 1934 was the high point of his intellectual life in Vienna. When asked, years later, to record achievements of which he was proud, he listed his election to the Royal Society and a lecture he had given at Princeton in 1950, when, after six hours, he remained alone with Bohr and Einstein – the audience had long dispersed – debating indeterminism.[38] He was as lenient with scientists as he was harsh with philosophers.[39] With the exception of Russell, no contemporary philosopher earned his admiration. In contrast, he was in awe of physicists and biolo-

---

[35] Popper, "Some Memories of Gödel and Some Problems" (Speech at the Gödel Symposium), July 1983, Hoover Archives (249, 15), p. 4.

[36] Ibid., p. 40.

[37] Draft of *Autobiography*, sec. 9 (134, 11), p. 4. Sitting in a university lecture hall, probably in fall 1921, an older friend drew his attention to a student of his age, already in his fourth year, a "coming light": Karl Menger (1902–85). Menger was Hahn's student, and had recently made a contribution to curve theory.

[38] Questionnaire, Research Foundation for Jewish Immigration, *Zentrum für Antisemitismusforschung*, Technische Universität, Berlin; John Watkins, "Karl Raimund Popper 1902–1994," *Proceedings of the British Academy* 94 (1997): 666.

[39] Joseph Agassi, "Celebrating *The Open Society*," *Philosophy of the Social Sciences* 27 (1997): 505. Agassi is quoting Jagdish Hattiangadi.

gists, thrilled when they welcomed him as a colleague. Respect did not mean, of course, acceptance of their authority. He argued with leading mathematicians and scientists as an equal, venturing into every field he had regarded as closed in the early 1920s: mathematics, physics, biology.

"Looking back I always felt how stupid I had been only a few years ago. This never left me," he wrote.[40] Nothing he did during the early 1920s seemed successful: music, mathematics, physics. He was capable of great insight into his own psychology. He recognized that his contempt for the professional *cursus honorum* and the pursuit of money and pleasure reflected, in part, his feeling that he was not up to par. He remained attached to a puritan socialist ethic for life, and judged harshly academic careerism: He or she is "not a true seeker," he would say of a colleague or a student. But he knew that a crusade against ambition would be hypocritical, a power ploy. "Both my ambition and my anti-ambition died early," he said.[41] Truly, not all his ambitions died. His aspirations in mathematics and physics – fields in which he declared himself inadequate – merely lay dormant. Once he had acquired confidence in the philosophy of science – the one field where his genius was incontrovertible – these ambitions resurged, with wonderful results.

At the end of 1922, Popper was still drifting. His friend at the barracks, Paul Oster, was a carpenter for an orphanage. Recalling his own commitment to manual labor, Popper decided to become a cabinetmaker. For the next two years he worked as an apprentice to a cabinetmaker, Adalbert Pösch. His family's distress is easy to imagine. Freemasons always paid tribute to labor, but this was certainly not what Simon Popper had envisioned for his son. Pösch was proud to have a university student as an apprentice, but Popper quickly acquired the nickname "the philosopher." His class background created tensions with other workers. He discovered the obvious: He was interested in philosophy more than in cabinetmaking. He concluded his apprenticeship in October 1924, receiving a diploma. The only furniture he would ever make would be for his house in New Zealand.

Popper decided to become a teacher. Given his interest in educational reform, this was understandable. A teaching position, especially in a gymnasium, provided a relatively secure, though not comfortable, living. While still an apprentice, he took a second *Matura* at a teacher's training college, probably the *Kinderfreundeschule* in Schloss Schönbrunn. It qualified him to teach in primary schools, but he found no teaching position. Declining enrollments in the early 1920s reduced available positions in Viennese schools, and openings were reserved for war veterans. This placed severe limits on socialist school reform. The old guard of teachers remained entrenched – the socialists would not supplant them – and eager young

[40] Outline of *Autobiography* (134, 4).   [41] Loc. cit.

reformers did not get in. Positions first opened in 1929. Popper received his teaching position the year after. Meanwhile, upon completing his apprenticeship, he became, for a year, a *Horterzieher*, an educator (and social worker) in a socialist center running after-school programs for working-class youth.

The first years after World War I were for Popper a period of loss of direction and constant experimentation. The immediate postwar era, he recalled, was grim. Like most Viennese, he lived in poverty, had little to eat and wear, and had no prospects for a career. Like most of his socialist friends, he was full of resentment toward the government and the academy. But he also remembered the period as an exhilarating time of companionship, intellectual pursuit, and exciting exchanges with friends. He found intellectual freedom in the harsh circumstances and was dreaming of a better world. He may have been drifting, but he drifted in a way unique to Viennese intellectuals, learning and experimenting with the various fields of Viennese culture.[42]

POPPER AND VIENNESE SCHOOL REFORM

The Association of Socialist Students remained active until Austrian fascism triumphed in February 1934. With few exceptions, Popper's friends returned to the socialist party in the early 1920s, but continued their contact with the communists. As the revolution failed, they committed themselves to reform. In 1923, Lazarsfeld and Wagner reorganized the socialist students with the support of Alfred Magaziner, a socialist functionary of the *Arbeiterjugend*. Magaziner allowed them wide autonomy, and they now enjoyed superior party organization. Their activities combined the ideals of the prewar youth movement with socialist educational work and school reform. Popper was in complete sympathy with their ideals. His fierce independence and bad gymnasium experience made him receptive both to Bernfeld's ideas on antiauthoritarian education and to Glöckel's school reforms. He, too, dreamt of founding a school where a community of students and teachers would explore the intellectual world. He no longer played an active role among the students, but he did social work with the *Kinderfreunde*, the socialist educational association for working-class youth. From day-care centers in the early 1920s, to social work with proletarian youth in 1924–5, to the Pedagogical Institute in 1925–7, his social network consisted of school reformers. Moreover, between 1925 and 1931, he contributed three essays on educational philosophy to the journals of the school-reform movement.

The movement's undisputed leader was Otto Glöckel, the president of

---

[42] *Autobiography*, pp. 38–40; outline (134, 4).

the Vienna School Council in interwar years.[43] As a socialist member of parliament, he had published a pamphlet in 1917, detailing the proposals for postwar school reforms.[44] Their principles were democratic and anticlerical, not distinctly socialist. They did emphasize social mobility and endeavored to annul the bourgeoisie's educational advantage by making *Bildung* available to all, but they reflected progressive educational theories and opted for a merit system. This was in line with the socialists' nonrevolutionary course in interwar years. Indeed, school reform was essential to socialism. If a socialist society were ever to emerge from bourgeois democracy, education would have to play a transformative role.

The prewar Austrian school system had an excellent reputation throughout Europe, but it was due primarily to gymnasiums and universities. Elementary schools in rural areas and working-class districts were often neglected. Teachers were poorly trained and paid. The 1869 school bill limited compulsory education to five years. After completing the *Volksschule* (elementary school), the ten- or eleven-year-old sat for a single examination that determined his future. Successful performance directed him to the seven-year gymnasium; failure, to a vocational school. The latter foreclosed, forever, academic education or a high profession. It trained lower-level civil servants, clerks, and tradespeople. Workers' children rarely completed a secondary school. There was no required education for women, and they were excluded from the gymnasium and university. The system curtailed social mobility and reinforced class and gender hierarchies.

Class mobility and anticlericalism were the core of school reform from the start. Progressives and socialists believed that real educational opportunity was key to working-class progress. They tried to extend the period of uniform education, and postpone career tracking to an older age, giving lower-class children a better chance at a professional career. Glöckel's first action as an undersecretary of education in April 1919, however, was to release children from attending religious exercises in school and teachers from supervising them. This proved not the final act in the *Freie Schule* drama, but the first act in interwar culture wars. In October 1920, when the socialist-Catholic coalition fell apart, Glöckel left office as the person most hated by the Christian Socials. The Catholic-led government shelved his reform proposals. Reform efforts now shifted from the nation to Red Vienna, where the socialists enjoyed an absolute majority and provincial autonomy. School reform became the centerpiece of socialist cultural politics.[45]

[43] Otto Glöckel, *Selbstbiographie; sein Lebenswerk: die Wiener Schulreform* (Zurich: Genossenschaftsdruckerei, 1939).

[44] Idem, *Das Tor der Zukunft* (Vienna: Verein Freie Schule, 1917).

[45] Ernst Glaser, *Im Umfeld des Austromarxismus* (Vienna: Europaverlag, 1981), pp. 301–41; Erik Adam, "Austromarxismus und Schulreform," in Erik Adam, Primus-Heinz Kucher, Eva Reitmann, and Josef Weidenholzer, *Die Schul- und Bildungspolitik der österreichischen Sozialdemokratie in der Ersten Republik* (Vienna: ÖBV, 1983), pp. 271–314.

Glöckel managed to apply fully his reforms in only twelve secondary schools, including about a tenth of Viennese students. He abolished the old-fashioned military and "girl schools," converting them into model *Einheitsschulen* (uniform schools). They offered uniform instruction to all students, boys and girls, for eight years. A four-year *Allgemeinemittelschule* (general middle school) followed the four-year *Volksschule*. The curriculum included core subjects, such as German and mathematics, with sufficient instruction in foreign languages and specialized fields to prepare for the gymnasium. Tracking occurred at age fourteen, and workers were offered opportunities for postgraduate education. Glöckel strove also to unify the secondary schools' curricula. He hoped to extend reforms gradually to other Viennese schools, and beyond.[46]

The hopes for school reform died, however, in 1927. A Christian Social education bill, which represented Social Democracy's retreat in the aftermath of the July 15th events, dismantled Glöckel's reforms. Tracking was to occur at age ten. A new, universally open secondary school, the *Hauptschule*, was founded alongside the various gymnasiums and vocational schools. It precluded higher education. All the socialists could salvage was a provision for later examinations for the best *Hauptschule* students, so that they could transfer to a gymnasium. Viennese teachers obstructed Glöckel's other changes. Only one-fifth of the teachers were socialist. The rest were equally divided between the Christian Socials and Pan-Germans. No one had done more than Glöckel to improve teacher and teaching conditions, but he could not overcome the teachers' hostility to socialist cultural politics. Glöckel was the first Viennese official to be dismissed and arrested after the socialist uprising in February 1934. The clerical-fascist government threw him into a concentration camp. By the time he was released later that year, he was a broken person, and died the year after. The government took pains to undo whatever remained of his reforms.[47]

Viennese school reform may have had limited practical achievements, but it generated extensive literature on educational philosophy. Philosophically, the reformers found themselves in a peculiar situation. The educational philosophy that underlay Austrian pedagogy before the war had been shaped by disciples of the progressive German philosopher Johann Friedrich Herbart (1776–1841). Herbart developed an empiricist, associationist, and sensationalist psychology of learning. Education was to construct the child's intellectual universe by implanting proper representations on the mind and transforming basic experience into knowledge. By using social intercourse to generate sympathy, education built the moral will and

---

[46] Richard Olechowski, "Schulpolitik," in *Österreich 1918–1938*, ed. Erika Weinzierl and Kurt Skalnik (Graz: Styria, 1983), pp. 589–607. Glöckel introduced other improvements in Viennese schools. He provided first-rate medical care, built libraries, distributed free educational material, removed barriers to women's education, and established parent associations in each district.

[47] Erik Adam, "Austromarxismus und Schulreform"; Helmut Gruber, *Red Vienna: Experiment in Working-Class Culture, 1919–1934* (New York: Oxford University Press, 1991), pp. 73–80.

formed character.[48] As Kant's successor in Königsberg (1809–33), Herbart had promoted reforms in Prussian schools. But complaints against his reforms found an ear among conservative Prussian officials, and eventually drove him back to Göttingen.[49] Ironically, within a decade of his death, he was lauded as an almost official state philosopher in conservative Catholic Austria. His disciple Franz Exner (1802–53) headed the commission in the Austrian ministry of education in 1848–9 that worked out a plan for reorganizing Austrian gymnasiums and *Realschulen*. Count Leo Thun implemented these reforms during the 1850s. They made Austrian schools the envy of many European countries. Herbart's philosophy remained dominant in Austrian universities for four decades.[50] School reformers thus confronted a progressive philosophy that had been put to conservative pedagogical uses and enjoyed an excellent reputation.

Until World War I, most Austrian schools aimed to form submissive subjects who accepted the hierarchical social order and were loyal to the army and the church. Classes were never interactive. The teacher remained an unchallenged authority figure, possessing knowledge that needed to be imprinted on the child's mind. Instructor guides explained that character formation entailed patient and persistent taming of the student's desire, accompanied by firm refusal to negotiate with him. Intellectual curiosity was discouraged as precociousness. Such pedagogy created alienation among talented students. The gymnasium's trademarks became strict discipline, tedious memorization, and infinite boredom. Fin-de-siècle reform pedagogy decried both passive instruction and pedagogical authoritarianism. Reformers drew parallels between hierarchy in society and in the classroom. School needed to become an education for democracy, emphasizing both individuality and social integration. Such a philosophy required, however, recognition of the child as an autonomous subject, or at least an emerging one. Herbart provided no such vision. Neither did Mach. His psychology and epistemology displaced Herbart's among progressives, but rendered the autonomous subject problematic. Austrian reformers remained without a progressive educational philosophy.[51]

---

[48] Johann Friedrich Herbart, *Outlines of Educational Doctrine* (New York: Macmillan, 1909).

[49] Henry and Emmie Felkin, "Biography of Herbart," in Johann Friedrich Herbart, *The Science of Education* (Boston: Heath, 1908), pp. 1–23.

[50] Edward Castle, "Unterrichtsreform," and Carl Siegel, "Philosophie," in *Geschichte der deutschen Literatur in Österreich-Ungarn im Zeitalter Franz Joseph I*, ed. Edward Castle, 2 vols. (Vienna: Earl Fromme, 1936), 1: 12–16, 28–32.

[51] William W. Bartley, III, "Theory of Language and Philosophy of Science as Instruments of Educational Reform: Wittgenstein and Popper as Austrian School Teachers," in *Methodological and Historical Essays in the Natural and Social Sciences*, ed. Robert S. Cohen and Marx W. Wartofsky, Boston Studies in the Philosophy of Science, vol. 14 (Boston: Reidel, 1974).

In the mid-1920s, Otto Neurath, organizer of the *Verein Ernst Mach* and member of the Vienna Circle, promoted educational reform based on sensationalist and associationist principles. He developed a universal language of isotypes (simplified pictures) for use in visual education. The idea did

In searching for an educational philosophy, the reformers "did not try to develop a special new theory of their own, nor did they base their practical work on any single theory," said school reformer Ernst Papanek.[52] They were eclectic. They borrowed a great deal from contemporary German reformers, especially Georg Kerschensteiner (1854–1932). During the interwar period, Dewey became popular. Since a "naturally developing," spontaneous, intellectually curious student was the reformers' ideal, there were obligatory references to Pestalozzi and, more significantly, to his student Friedrich Froebel (1782–1852). For child psychology they looked in different directions: Alfred Adler, William Stern (1870–1931), and Karl Bühler (1879–1964). Journals, such as *Schulreform, Der Schulkampf,* and *Die Quelle,* regularly discussed theoretical and practical issues of school reform.

By the early 1920s certain ideas became common among reformers. First, there was the *Einheitsschule* (comprehensive school), domesticated from German reformers.[53] Industrial nations and modern armies, reckoned Kerschensteiner, required a cohesive citizenry, but class conflict tore them apart. Uniform education would reunify the German nation. The Austrians gave his ideas a progressive socialist twist. The Einheitsschule would end the bourgeoisie's *Bildung* privilege, advancing the workers. *Gesamtunterricht* (comprehensive instruction) was the Einheitsschule's guiding principle. It had a plurality of meanings. It could refer to the core instruction of reading, writing and arithmetic, implying that it was done innovatively, integrating the various skills. In higher grades it suggested an interdisciplinary program, preparing students both for gymnasiums and vocational schools. It intimated two other reform ideas: *Bodenständigkeit,* or teaching rooted in the native environment, and *Selbsttätigkeit* (self-activity). Both owed much to Froebel. Instruction should be attuned to the student's spontaneous growth. By using children's natural curiosity, interactive teaching could impart learning. Students needed to work out the material themselves and experiment. Reform pedagogy aspired to take the student as its point of departure: *Pädagogik vom Kinde aus.*

Glöckel described socialist school reform as the culmination of historical progress, leading from the imperial Drilling School to the bourgeois Learning School, and on to the socialist Laboring School (*Arbeitsschule*).[54] Austrian reformer Eduard Bürger transformed Kerschensteiner's idea of vocational training in an industrially oriented *Arbeitsschule* into a compre-

---

not appeal to school reformers. Otto Neurath, "From Vienna Method to Isotope," in his *Empiricism and Sociology,* ed. Marie Neurath and Robert S. Cohen (Boston: Reidel, 1972).

[52] Ernst Papanek, *The Austrian School Reform* (New York: Fell, 1962).

[53] Georg Kerschensteiner, *Staatsbürgerliche Erziehung der deutschen Jugend,* 5th ed. (Erfurt: Villaret, 1911); idem, *Das einheitliche deutsche Schulsystem,* 2d. ed. (Leipzig: Teubner, 1922).

[54] Otto Glöckel, *Drillschule, Lernschule, Arbeitsschule* (Vienna: Organisation Wien der Sozialdemokratischen Partei, 1928).

hensive *Arbeitspädagogik* (work pedagogy).[55] The term's popularity was due to the multifarious meanings of Arbeit. It implied, first, that students processed the material, rather than memorized it: the idea of self-activity. But it also meant, literally, instruction in manual crafts that would increase labor's respectability. (Glöckel introduced such instruction in the *Volksschule* to the Christian-Socials' chagrin and endless derision.) Glöckel's reform team, Viktor Fadrus, Hans Fischl, and Karl Furtmüller, added another essential idea, borrowed from Wyneken, the German scouts, and the Viennese youth movement: the "school community" (*Schulgemeinde*).[56] It contrasted the traditional authoritarian school with the reform school where a non-hierarchical community of teacher and students pursued knowledge and contemplated social improvement. The idea gave expression to the hope that the reform school would presage the socialist society.

Socialist educational efforts were not limited to school reform. Socialist educators recognized that a network of communal institutions was essential to transforming working-class culture. Otto Felix Kanitz redirected the *Kinderfreunde* from welfare activities to pedagogical work among working-class youth. The association was responsible for both the kindergartens and the centers for after-school programs (*Horte*) that the socialists opened around Vienna. They aimed both to facilitate life for working parents and to draw youth away from street culture to an educational environment. The association's center was a training institute for socialist educators, the *Kinder-freundeschule*. Kanitz defined its mission as "socialist education." Austro-Marxist theoretician Max Adler best articulated the concept in his *Neue Menschen*. Socialist education would prepare the proletariat to lead a future socialist society. The proletariat would appropriate the bourgeoisie's *Bildung* traditions, and form a new humanity.[57]

Popper became a *Horte* educator late in 1924. Among his colleagues, he acquired a new circle of friends, the "young proletarians," as he called them. Their leader was Fritz Kolb (1902–83). Son of a postal worker, he grew up in poverty and obtained education only with great effort. He first attended a Catholic seminar, then the Kinderfreundeschule, then the university. He organized a growing group of radical socialist educators in the *Arbeitsge-meinschaft sozialistischer Erzieher* (Working Community of Socialist Educators). They challenged the party's educational policies. When Popper spoke of his admiration for Viennese workers "who substituted mountaineering

[55] Georg Kerschensteiner, *Der Begriff der Arbeitsschule*, 2nd ed. (Leipzig: Teubner, 1913); Eduard Bürger, *Arbeitspädagogik: Geschichte, Kritik, Wegweisung*, 2d. ed. (Leipzig: Engelmann, 1923).

[56] Hans Fischl, "Zweck und Form der Schulgemeinde," in *Mittelschülerbewegung und Schulgemeinde* (Vienna: Vereinigung sozialistischer Mittelschüler, 1919), vol. 2; Karl Furtmüller, *Auf dem Weg zur Schulgemeinde* (Vienna: Jugend und Volk, 1926).

[57] Max Adler, *Neue Menschen* (Berlin: Laub, 1924). Adler was not a member of the *Kinderfreunde*. Helmut Uitz, *Die österreichischen Kinderfreunde und Roten Falken 1908–1938: Beiträge zur sozialistischen Erziehung* (Vienna: Geyer, 1975).

for alcohol, classical music for swing, serious reading for thrillers," he most likely had Fritz Kolb before his eyes.[58] His experience with Hort children taught him that "socialist culture" encountered resistance among workers, but Fritz Kolb remained a living proof of its potential success. He had great respect for Kolb's character and leadership abilities (not to mention his good looks and superior mountaineering, which he compared favorably with his own).[59]

Kolb and Popper shared the Hort's frustrations. Popper found the children extremely difficult. He was a young intellectual, confronting street culture and youth who did not trust him. His difficulties were by no means unique. When Lazarsfeld first led his educators into a working-class district to meet their pupils, the kids welcomed them with a shower of stones that sent them into retreat.[60] "These kids," Popper recalled later, "were constantly in danger of becoming enemies of humanity." He called them *verwahrloste Jugend*, "wayward youth." Barriers of class culture (and prejudice) separated educators and educated. Recent critics of progressive reform rejoice that street culture successfully resisted socialist efforts to shape *Neue Menschen*, but Kolb and Popper saw the failure as a tragedy. Popper did his best, he said, "to bring the kids back to civilization." He soon recognized that his efforts were no match for the task.[61]

Throughout the year, he found the Viennese civil service unresponsive to frontline social workers. Progressive educational theory disappointed him, too. It had little relevance to the social reality he was facing. To function as a teacher, he had to employ tactics that had nothing to do with "educational community" or "self-activity." He challenged the students' leader to a boxing match. The youth proved more amenable afterward. He learned to read constantly the children's faces to anticipate trouble, never to turn his back to them, and always to speak slowly and articulately to reinforce his authority.[62] This was helpful training for future teaching. Students would marvel at his extraordinary ability to read doubt or confusion on their faces, and respond. At the time, however, it was a hellish experience that made him skeptical of the "cant of school reform."

The Hort's problems unsettled Kolb and his colleagues, too. In a path-breaking article in the *Kinderfreunde*'s organ, Kolb demanded a change of course. Most children avoided the Hort, he said, because they regarded the

---

[58] *Autobiography*, p. 36.   [59] Fritz Kolb, *Es kam ganz anders* (Vienna: ÖBV, 1981), pp. 7–24.

[60] Hans Zeisel, "The Vienna Years," in *Qualitative and Quantitative Social Research*, ed. by Robert Merton, James Coleman, and Peter Rossi (New York: Free Press, 1979), p. 13.

[61] My interview with Popper, 26 January 1984; Popper, *Autobiography*, pp. 8, 41, 72; outline, (134, 4). On street culture and the *Hort*, see: J. Robert Wegs, *Growing Up Working Class: Continuity and Change Among Viennese Youth, 1890–1938* (London: Pennsylvania State University Press, 1989), chaps. 3, 4, 6, esp. pp. 79–80.

[62] My interview with Popper, 26 January 1984.

institution as an imposition. The party was failing to reach the great majority of proletarian youth. To attract them, the authoritarian Hort had to be converted into a voluntary *Arbeitskinderheim* (working home for children) where youth were permitted to develop freely.[63] Several months later, Lazarsfeld's and Wagner's popular "green booklet" raised further concerns about socialist education. Under the Kinderfreunde's sponsorship, they organized a summer vacation colony in Lind. The colony was supposed to provide a model of an educational community that had overcome class and age differences and resolved problems of authority. They ended up with 110 elementary-school proletarian students and 60 middle-class *Mittelschüler*. Their report spoke of mistrust among youth of different classes, deference shown by working-class kids to the better-dressed bourgeois, and the absence of any revolutionary consciousness. They detailed major problems of management and discipline. Socialists had their work cut out before an educational community could emerge.[64]

Socialist functionaries were listening. Perturbed by the Horte's low appeal, Anton Tesarek, the Kinderfreunde's second-in-line, launched in 1925 the *Rote Falken* (Red Hawks), a socialist scout movement. Kolb and the *Arbeitsgemeinschaft* remained unhappy. They protested that the "new course" was turning the Kinderfreunde into another bourgeois youth movement. Socialist education was becoming bourgeois instead of preparing for revolution.[65] They wanted a socialist community that would be both revolutionary and nonauthoritarian; pluralist, yet capable of collective action. Popper did not share their revolutionary sentiments. He saw socialist education as a progressive project, bringing liberals and socialists together under a platform of democratic reform, not revolution. But he shared Kolb's antipathy to the "institutionalized leaders at the center." He would join any protest against authority and hypocrisy.

Popper's first published article, "On the Teacher's Position toward School and Student," echoed the school-reform debates. It appeared in 1925 in *Schulreform*.[66] In a draft of his *Autobiography*, Popper called it "immature."[67]

---

[63] Fritz Kolb, "Klares Wollen!" *Sozialistische Erziehung*, 4 (January 1924): 2–5. Anton Tsarek, the *Kinderfreunde* official responsible for the *Horte*, responded in: "Die praktische Arbeit in der Erziehungsbewegung IV," ibid.: 194–8.

[64] Paul Lazarsfeld and Ludwig Wagner, *Gemeinschaftserziehung durch Erziehungsgemeinschaften* (Vienna, 1924). This became a guide for future socialist youth activities. Friedrich Scheu, *Ein Band der Freundschaft* (Vienna: Böhlau, 1985), pp. 115–21, 130–8.

[65] Fritz Kolb, "Erziehung zur Revolution," *Sozialistische Erziehung* 6 (September 1926): 208–10. Party ideologists and Siegfried Bernfeld agreed. Bernfeld, "Sozialistische Erziehungskritik," ibid. 6 (May 1926): 106–8; Johannes Reichmayr, "Sozialistische Erziehung und Psychoanalyse in der Ersten Republik," in *Die Österreichische Reformpädagogik 1918–1938*, ed. Erik Adam (Vienna: Böhlau, 1981), pp. 149–61.

[66] Karl Popper, "Über die Stellung des Lehrers zu Schule und Schüler. Gesellschaftliche oder individualistische Erziehung?" *Schulreform* 4 (1925): 204–8.

[67] Idem, draft of *Autobiography* (134, 12), sec. 15.

It was actually a lovely short piece that provides hints about his theoretical queries and political dispositions in the mid-1920s. The article addressed a paramount issue for school reformers. Against the enforced uniformity of traditional education, reformers wished to cultivate individuality. At the same time, they regarded education as an instrument of social integration, preparing individuals for life under socialism. Were these goals compatible? Could an educational community realize both?

The controversy over individual versus collective orientation in education, said Popper, always ended up with a metaphysical question: Is society prior to the individual, or vice versa? The debate was founded on a misunderstanding. Education always dealt with individuals; the question was only whether they should be viewed in their individuality or as social types.[68] Popper distinguished between the school as a social institution and as an educational community. Social institutions had to view the individual as a type. As school was an institution designed for socialization, individuals had to be made aware that society viewed them as social types and adjust their behavior accordingly. Overestimation of one's own needs, excessive individualism, or crime made it impossible for school to accommodate individuality. As an institution, school dealt with students as social types.

Popper sought, however, to free the relationship between teacher and student from institutional pressures. He wished to maintain it as an individual relationship. There were occasions when even teachers had to treat pupils as types: seating arrangements, grading, and the like. Popper sought to minimize these occasions. School programs were best constructed, he said, when they imparted "social experience" indirectly, by facilitating free interaction of student and teacher. The less school requirements intruded on personal relationships, the better off the educational community would be. It was essential that teachers not appear to be representatives of school authority. When authority was exercised, it had to be clear that it was not personal: Teachers were as much subject to it as students. A social relationship ignoring the student's individuality was authoritarian. A personal relationship respectful of individuality was free, and encouraged trust and good feeling. Reformulating Kant's postulate to treat all individuals as ends rather than as means, he implored teachers to view students as individuals rather than as social types. This would create a true educational community, and the classroom would become a microcosm of socialist society.

No doubt Popper's convictions reflected his bad experience with gymnasium teachers. His growing skepticism about the "institutionalized leaders

---

[68] His investigation, said Popper, would be purely formal; his results should be valid for education in any society. He preferred the concept of *Individualität*, he added, to value-laden concepts, such as William Stern's "personality," or Georg Kerschensteiner's "character." But, of course, *Individualität* had romantic investments that Popper underplayed.

at the center" reinforced his suspicion of school authority. But there was more than impatience with socialist bureaucracy here. There was liberal aversion to social authority intervening in "personal" relationships, and liberal disregard of possible abuses of power in individual relationships. There was a pronounced liberal proclivity to set the legal framework, so that it deferred social questions to individual relationships, and trust that adequate socialization could thus be achieved. Furthermore, there was anxiety that collective goals might enforce uniformity and endanger individuality. Uniformity, emphasized Popper, would be no achievement. It marked a bad, not a good, school. He did not engage (and could not answer) Kolb's and Lazarsfeld's problem: How did one create an educational community in the context of class difference? But he seemed to suggest that, to the extent that their question involved the use of class types as a criterion for educational success, it was badly put. Still, he remained convinced that school reform could contribute to building a socialist community, and that such a community was compatible with individuality.

Popper wrote the article prior to his worst experience as a social worker, and one of the most difficult in his life. One of the children under his supervision fell from a ladder and fractured his skull. Popper remembered previously asking for the ladder to be removed, but the city sued him for negligence. Ernst Papanek testified on his behalf. His father defended him, the only opportunity Karl ever had to hear his father speak in court. The judge acquitted him, placing responsibility for the accident on the city.[69] But all this was too much for him. He ended his involvement with socialist educational reform.

His correspondence of later years disclosed ambivalence about school reform and the Kinderfreunde. "In the hands of highly gifted teachers," he said, "school reform was a *great* success."[70] He dismissed Glöckel, however, as "a party-politician," and reform pedagogy as "cant." He was not merely repeating the social workers' litanies. The 1925 tragedy made him think social reform anew. "I learned the futility of any party program," he said.[71] "I found how much wrong there was with government and party bureaucracy."[72] School reform was a great idea. It had idealist protagonists. Nonetheless, bureaucracy failed it. His socialism did not survive the trauma unscathed. To Rudolf Carnap he complained in 1947 that the atmosphere among the Kinderfreunde was "totalitarian."[73] This unfair – and untrue – accusation testified to the lasting impact of the 1925 tragedy.

[69] *Autobiography*, pp. 10, 197 n. 2.
[70] Popper to Alexander Gerschenkron, 24 August 1974, Hoover Archives (298, 31).
[71] My interview with Popper, 26 January 1984.   [72] Draft of *Autobiography*, segment (134, 6).
[73] Popper to Carnap, 6 January 1947, Carnap Collection, Archives of Scientific Philosophy, University of Pittsburgh.

POLITICS AND PHILOSOPHY AT THE MARGINS OF
GERMAN CULTURE: POLANYI, KRAFT, NELSON,
AND THE *FRIES'SCHEN SCHULE*

Even before entering the Pedagogical Institute in 1925, Popper had expanded his intellectual network beyond socialist youth. No later than 1924, he became a friend of economist and social theorist Karl Polanyi (1886–1964). The same year, he met philosopher Julius Kraft (1898–1960). Polanyi introduced him to social science methodology, and Kraft to the unorthodox Kantian philosophy of Jakob Fries (1775–1843) and Leonard Nelson (1882–1927). Both Polanyi and Kraft represented marginal traditions in Central European culture, but they contributed significantly to Popper's intellectual development.

Polanyi is recognized today as a social thinker of great originality who made major contributions to history, economics, and anthropology. He had an unusual career. A scion of an assimilated Hungarian Jewish family, he was active among the pre–World War I Budapest radical intelligentsia, serving as president of the Galileo Circle and secretary of Oskar Jászi's Radical Party. He was critical of Bolshevism and kept his distance from the Hungarian revolution, leaving for Vienna in June 1919. The ensuing white terror made a return to Budapest unthinkable, and he spent most of the interwar years in Vienna. His exile coincided with a spiritual crisis that transformed him into a religious socialist. He joined the association of religious socialists (*Bund der religiösen Sozialisten*) in the Austrian Socialist Party, led by the "little" Otto Bauer. He greatly admired Red Vienna and critically engaged Marxism, searching for a humanistic socialism compatible with individuality and freedom. In 1933 he left for England, where he spent World War II teaching for the Workers' Educational Association. His celebrated *The Great Transformation* (1944) reflected both his Viennese and English experiences.[74] Providing an overview of two centuries of industrial society, Polanyi emphasized the revolutionary and destructive character of laissez-faire, presented Red Vienna as a noble effort to recreate community, and explained fascism as a response to the failure of laissez-faire. During the first postwar decade, he taught in the United States, but lived in Canada. (His wife, Ilona Duczynska [1896–1978], was proscribed from the United States on account of her previous affiliation with the Hungarian and Austrian communist parties.) He refused to endorse Western mobilization against communism and, especially after 1956, sought reconciliation with communist Hungary. Much of his work in economics and anthropology was published posthumously.[75]

---

[74] Karl Polanyi, *The Great Transformation* (New York: Farrar and Rinehart, 1944).

[75] For example, *Primitive, Archaic, and Modern Economies: Essays of Karl Polanyi* (Garden City, N.Y.: Anchor, 1968). For Polanyi's biography: Kari Polanyi-Levitt, ed., *The Life and Work of Karl Polanyi* (Montreal: Black Rose, 1990).

In Vienna, Polanyi was a foreign affairs editor for the *Österreichische Volks-swirt* (Austrian Economist). He also taught at the *Volkshochschule*, a social-ist adult-education institute. Popper's uncle, Walter Schiff, professor of economics and statistics, invited him to offer seminars there. He gradually distanced himself from the politics of the Hungarian exile community, devoted himself to scholarship, and developed an intellectual circle that met frequently in his apartment on Vorgartenstrasse. His wife, Ilona Duczyn-ska, remained a socialist activist, but she never complied with party disci-pline. She was expelled, consecutively, from the Hungarian Communist (1922), Austrian Socialist (1929), and Austrian Communist (c. 1938) Parties. Polanyi was involved in the socialization debate. Socialism and the method-ology of economics and social science were frequent subjects of discussion at his home gatherings. Participants included, among others, the Hungar-ian émigré Aurel Kolnai, and younger Austrian students Peter Drucker, Felix Schafer, Hans Zeisel – and Karl Popper.[76]

Polanyi's socialism and social science were sui generis. He sided with the Austrian economists against the German historical school and accepted Bohm-Bawerk's critique of Marx. Marx neglected, he thought, consumer demand. Austrian marginalism and "subjectivism" provided a superior theory of value, based on consumer preferences. But his political conclu-sions conflicted with those of the Austrians. He challenged the assumption held by virtually all protagonists in the socialization debate that a socialist economy required a central planning board to fix prices. Efforts to imitate the market through an administrative economy, he thought, would not allow for adequate input of consumer and producer preferences. He argued for "functional socialism" (*funktioneller Sozialismus*) in the tradition of British guild socialism. Different branches of industry would remain autonomous, do their own accounting, and collect consumer (and pro-ducer) information. Final prices would be negotiated among the units, allowing consideration of maximum productivity and social purpose to overcome the drive for profit. Capitalism's major crime was not wage labor but unequal distribution. Socialism should respond by organizing the con-sumers and negotiating prices. Society would gain control over the economy through coordination, not centralized administration. Individu-ality and liberty would be safe with socialism.[77]

---

[76] Kari Polanyi-Levitt, ed., *The Life and Work of Karl Polanyi*, esp. essays by Dalós, Congdon, Mendell, Polanyi-Levitt, and Rosner. Felix Schafer described the Polanyi Circle in "Karl Polanyi's Life in Vienna: Memoirs by Felix Shaffer," typescript (1960s), Karl Polanyi Institute, Concordia University, Montreal (9, 4). I wish to thank Kari Polanyi-Levitt and Marguerite Mendell (institute director) for informative phone conversations on 24 November 1993, and Ana Gomez (administrative assistant) for providing a copy of Schafer's manuscript.

[77] Karl Polanyi, "Sozialistische Rechnungslegung" and "Die funktionelle Theorie der Gesellschaft und das Problem der sozialistische Rechnungslegung," *Archiv für Sozialwissenschaft und Sozialpolitik* 49 (1922), 377–418, and 52 (1924), 218–28, respectively; idem, "Neue Erwangungen zu unserer Theorie

It is likely that Popper met Polanyi early in 1924, when the latter gave lectures on guild socialism at the socialist students' headquarters. As attendance at the lectures declined, Polanyi moved the "seminar" to his apartment. In his *Autobiography*, Popper said little about their relationship, but he knew the Polanyi family well and kept in touch with circle members years later.[78] Polanyi thought highly of Popper, introduced him to philosopher Heinrich Gomperz, and tried to help him publish his first book, *Die beiden Grundprobleme der Erkenntnistheorie* in 1932.[79] In 1924–5 Popper discussed Marxism and social-science methodology with him. Polanyi clarified some of the differences between the social and natural sciences. He also explained that Marxism was useful for analyzing the unintended consequences of social action, because it demonstrated how capitalist relations of production unintentionally led to dehumanization.[80] Popper showed only modest interest in socialization, but already in 1924, he was telling Peter Hilferding that Eduard Bernstein's revisionism and Menger's marginalism provided an alternative to Austro-Marxism.[81] He reaffirmed this conviction to friends in the late 1920s: Marginalism could substitute for Marx's theory of value as a foundation for socialism.[82] Also, it is not coincidental that Bohm-Bawerk was the single Austrian economist Popper read.[83] In *The Open Society*, he expressed enthusiasm about the Swedish socialists' reliance on consumer cooperatives, as opposed to centralized production.[84] Polanyi confirmed the possibility of a socialism informed by "bourgeois" theoretical economics. Critical of Marx, yet a committed socialist, Popper thought it was the way to go. Polanyi was his single major exposure to social-science methodology prior to *The Poverty of Historicism*.

There seemed to have been little communication between Popper and Polanyi once the latter had left Vienna. Popper felt that Polanyi did not help him sufficiently to publish *Grundprobleme*: He "failed me badly. . . . He

---

von Praxis" [1925], in *Austromarxistische Positionen*, ed. Gerald Mozetic (Vienna: Böhlau, 1983), pp. 439–49.

[78] Hennie Popper to William Bartley, 31 January 1985, Hoover Archives (273, 5). He was, recalls Kari Polanyi-Levitt, "a household name."

[79] *Autobiography*, p. 74. Popper to Michael Polanyi, 17 September and 18 October 1932, Hoover Archives (339, 1); Popper to Egon Friedell, June 1932–January 1933, Hoover Archives (297, 2).

[80] Popper, *The Open Society*, chap. 3 n. 30, chap. 15 n. 11; *Autobiography*, p. 20.

[81] My interview with Peter Milford (Hilferding), 30 January 1999.

[82] Fritz Kolb, "Karl Popper und der Sozialismus," in *Theorie und Politik aus kritisch-rationaler Sicht*, ed. by Georg Lühr et al. (Berlin: Dietz, 1978), pp. 33–4.

[83] Communication from Colin Simkin, 18 March 1997. Karl Milford (son of Peter) reports (conversation with author, 27 January 1999) that Popper also read a pamphlet by Eugen von Philippovich (1858–1917), the Austrian economist who straddled the boundary between the German historical school and marginalism. The (unidentified) pamphlet seems to have been his first encounter with Austrian economics.

[84] Popper, *The Open Society*, chap. 18 n. 10. Simkin drew Popper's attention to the Swedish experiment. He found him receptive. Polanyi had prepared the ground well.

[was] extremely nice but no help whatever in such a matter like the book."[85] Polanyi was helpful, however, with Popper's New Zealand appointment. His collaborator, religious philosopher John Macmurry, was chair of Popper's appointment committee, and once Popper was appointed, Polanyi tried to facilitate his move by providing contacts with previous New Zealanders.[86] After the *Anschluss*, Popper mobilized, at Polanyi's urging, faculty and immigration officials in New Zealand to secure an emigration permit for Felix Schafer, a Polanyi circle member who had been arrested by the Nazis and sent to a concentration camp. He was successful, and Schafer and his family spent the war in New Zealand. Returning to England from the United States in 1943, Karl and Ilona Polanyi inquired after Popper. In postwar London, again at Polanyi's urging, Popper tried to assist Schafer in finding a job. Their politics grew wide apart, but the old ties, although relaxed, still bound.[87]

Popper's friendship with Kraft was always close. Kraft was apparently a distant German relative of Popper. He came to Vienna in 1924 after completing a dissertation, under Nelson in Göttingen, on the method of legal theory in Kant and Fries. In Vienna, he studied with Nelson's bête noire, legal positivist Hans Kelsen. Kelsen became a lifelong friend, but Kraft failed to gain *Habilitation*.[88] After almost two years, he left for Frankfurt to become the assistant of sociologist Franz Oppenheimer. He and Popper developed a close friendship and conducted intensive discussions of philosophy and politics. Popper was gratified that the older Kraft, who had both a doctorate and a number of publications, showed interest in his ideas, but, typically, he responded to Kraft's instruction in "critical philosophy" by sharply criticizing him.[89] When Kraft left Vienna, the two continued their correspondence. In 1932, Kraft tried to help Popper publish *Grundprobleme*.[90] He thought highly of the young philosopher, predicting

---

[85] Popper to Gombrich, 4 December 1943, Hoover Archives (300, 2). See also: Popper to Fritz Hellin, 16 May 1943, Hoover Archives (28, 6). Popper probably expected Polanyi to intervene decisively with his brother to secure publication. At the time, Michael Polanyi was already a well-known chemist at the Kaiser Wilhelm-Institut in Berlin.

[86] Gombrich to Popper, 29 October 1943 (300, 2); Popper to Condliffe, 19 May 1943, Hoover Archives (28, 4).

[87] Felix Schafer, "Memoirs." Peter Drucker, another Polanyi circle member, tried to help publish *The Open Society*: Braunthal to Popper, 11 November 1943, Hoover Archives (28, 2). Popper wrote a reference for a UN position for Felix Schafer, 10 November 1946, Karl Polanyi subject file, Hoover Archives (391, 25; see also Popper to Carnap, 1 March 1947, Hoover Archives [282, 24]). He wrote another letter to the Nuffield Foundation for Aurel Kolnai. "I have known him for nearly thirty years," he said: 27 November 1954, Aurel Kolnai's subject file, Hoover Archives (387, 25).

[88] Julius Kraft to Karl Popper, 10 November 1949, Hoover Archives (316, 23).

[89] Popper to Kraft, 21 August 1925, Julius Kraft Papers, State University of New York at Albany. He also complained that his hard work prevented him from responding in a timely fashion to Kraft's letters.

[90] Popper–Kraft correspondence, September 1932–July 1933 (1932 letters without date), Hoover Archives (316, 24, under Victor Kraft).

a bright future for him.[91] This may explain his willingness to accept Popper's criticism and near-insults − such as being invited to obtain his own copy of *Logik der Forschung* for a review.[92] They lost contact during World War II, when Popper was in New Zealand and Kraft in the United States, but renewed correspondence after the war. Their cooperation led to the founding of *Ratio*, a philosophical journal in the Kant-Fries-Nelson tradition.[93]

Popper remembered his early discussions with Kraft as focusing on two subjects: the critique of Marxism and Social Democratic policies, and Kant's epistemology, especially Fries's psychological critique of it. They reached a prompt agreement on politics: Both regarded themselves as social reformers and unorthodox socialists, and both were critical of Marxism. Nonetheless, they supported the Social Democrats, the sole democratic force capable of resisting fascism. On Kant's epistemology and Fries's psychological procedure, they disagreed. Kraft accepted Fries's critique of Kant and his alternative foundation for knowledge. Popper dismissed Fries's proposal as psychologistic and, by the early 1930s, disposed altogether of foundationism. But theirs was a family quarrel: noisy, passionate, yet evincing closeness. They regarded themselves as Kantians, rejected logical positivism, and were hostile to German historical thought.[94]

In Leonard Nelson, Kraft and Popper found a model of critical philosophy and progressive politics. Nelson was an untypical German mandarin.[95] Of Jewish origin, he was a militant left-liberal and cosmopolite who preached a universal Kantian ethics and called for the establishment of an international legal system. He ridiculed the German mission in Central Europe, opposed German imperialism, and advocated pacifism. In the midst of World War I, he published a critique of positivist jurisprudence that challenged the moral and legal claims of all combatants, Germany included.[96] At the end of the war, he founded the *Internationaler Jugendbund* (*IJB*), a youth league promoting educational and political reform. Initially, the league included mainly his students, but it gradually extended its reach from Göttingen to most German universities. It established its own school, the *Walkmühle Schule*, near Kassel. Nelson introduced there a modified Montessori method that he renamed the "Socratic Method." It emphasized the dialogical nature of education. Nelson hoped that the school would serve

---

[91] Kraft to Popper, 27 July 1945, Hoover Archives (316, 23), recalling his earlier prediction in Vienna of Popper's future success.

[92] Popper to Kraft, 11 January 1935, Hoover Archives (316, 24). Popper reported that he had no copies of *Logik der Forschung* left and suggested that Kraft obtain one "at my cost."

[93] Karl Popper, "Julius Kraft, 1898−1960," *Ratio* 4 (1962): 2−15.

[94] Popper, "Julius Kraft," 5−8; *Autobiography*, pp. 74−5.

[95] The term "German mandarins" belongs to Fritz Ringer: *The Decline of the German Mandarins: The German Academic Community, 1890−1933* (Cambridge, Mass.: Harvard University Press, 1969).

[96] Leonard Nelson, *Die Rechtswissenschaft ohne Recht* (Jurisprudence without justice) (Leipzig: Veit, 1917).

as a model for socialist educational reform, cultivate enlightened citizens, and create leaders for the Weimar Republic. He doubted that parliamentary democracy was capable of producing responsible leaders, or of resisting fascism. He considered popular control absurd and majority rule incompatible with liberty and justice. Against democracy, he posed the Platonic "rule of the wise."[97] He rejected Marxism, believing that the postulate of social justice was incompatible with "economic determinism." The league first joined the independent socialists (*USPD*), then the mainstream socialists (*SPD*), but was expelled from the party in 1925. It continued to exist after Nelson's death in 1927. Members used the network to stage opposition to the Nazis. Some were arrested on the eve of World War II.[98]

Nelson's cosmopolitanism informed Popper's own, but it was his epistemology that proved essential to Popper's intellectual development. As a student, Nelson discovered the nearly forgotten Kantian philosopher Jakob Friedrich Fries. Fries considered himself Kant's true successor. He formed a critique of Kant's transcendental proofs in epistemology, ethics, and religion. Kant held that certain propositions had an a priori validity because no conception of reality or morality was possible without them. Fries thought that these synthetic a priori propositions left too much of the world closed to the human mind and, at the same time, ran the risk of subjectivism. He developed a methodological procedure for grounding knowledge in a universal human psychology, thereby eliminating much of Kant's agnosticism and "subjectivism."[99] In his dissertation, Nelson defended Fries against contemporary Neo-Kantians.[100] In 1904, he reestablished the *Annals of the Friesian School*, a journal where he and like-minded colleagues published their work.[101] His voluminous work in epistemology, ethics, and jurisprudence carried the imprint of Fries's

[97] Idem, *Politics and Education* (London: Allen & Unwin, 1928); "The Socratic Method," in his *Socratic Method and Critical Philosophy*, trans. Thomas K. Brown III (New Haven, Conn.: Yale University Press, 1949), pp. 1–40. A sympathetic critique: Ludwig Grünebaum, "Führerschaft, Demokratie, Ethik: Eine Kritik von Leonard Nelsons *Demokratie und Führerschaft*," *Zeitschrift für die gesamte Staatswissenschaft* 107 (1951): 36–89.

[98] Brand Blanshard, "Foreword," and Julius Kraft, "Introduction" to Leonard Nelson, *Socratic Method*; Werner Link, *Die Geschichte des Internationalen Jugend-Bundes (IJB) und des Internationalen Sozialistischen Kampf-Bundes (ISK)* (Meisenheim am Glan: Hain, 1964); Walter Struve, "Leonard Nelson: The Rule of the Just," in his *Elites Against Democracy: Leadership Ideals in Bourgeois Political Thought in Germany, 1890–1933* (Princeton, N.J.: Princeton University Press, 1973), pp. 186–215.

[99] Jakob Friedrich Fries, *Neue oder anthropologische Kritik der Vernunft* [1828–31], *Sämtliche Schriften*, 26 vols. (Aalen: Scientia, 1969), vols. 4–6.

[100] Leonard Nelson, "Jakob Friedrich Fries und seine jüngsten Kritiker" [1904], *Gesammelte Schriften*, 9 vols. (Hamburg: Felix Meiner, 1970), 1: 79–150.

[101] Ernst Apelt, Fries's student, began the first *Abhandlungen der Fries'schen Schule*. It lasted only two years. The publication of Nelson's new series was interrupted in 1937. Kraft conceived of *Ratio*, begun in 1957, as a renewal.

"Kantianism with a greater confidence of reason."[102] Popper rejected precisely this "confidence." He shared Fries's and Nelson's critique of Kant but declined their solution, and offered his own: ever uncertain knowledge. His arguments with Kraft over Fries and Nelson set the context for his epistemological revolution.[103]

Nelson also shaped Popper's view of the history of philosophy. He did not need to teach Popper admiration for Kant and contempt for Hegel, but he vindicated his predilections. Already Fries had recounted the history of "scientific philosophy" from the Greeks to his own time as a story of progress and regress. Classical Greek and Hellenistic philosophies made promising beginnings, he said, but could not explain how one arrived at synthetic judgments (that is, judgments not analytically derived from others). Medieval church doctrines, informed by Jewish magic and Neo-Platonic mysticism, stymied free thinking and arrested scientific philosophy. Bacon and Galileo built philosophy anew and Kant established it on firm foundations. Post-Kantian philosophy represented a regress. Fichte, Schelling, Schlegel, and Hegel betrayed Kant. Nelson updated Fries, adding varieties of contemporary Neo-Kantians to the enemy's list. Socrates and Kant were idols; Hume, a respected, but mistaken opponent. Nelson identified progressive philosophy with Kant and Fries, and dogmatic regress with Hegel and the romantics. A new philosophical tradition was formed under the banner of "critical philosophy."[104]

Kraft and Popper inherited the tradition. They applied Nelson's criticism to later-day opponents as well: positivism, Marxism and Neo-Kantianism.[105] Kraft wrote *Von Husserl zu Heidegger* (1932), a relentless attack on phenomenology, existentialism, and Hegelianism. He held them responsible for the current intellectual crisis and associated them with authoritarian politics.[106] He extended his critique to social-science methodologies in *Die Unmöglichkeit der Geisteswissenschaft* (1934: The

---

[102] Nelson spoke of the "Grundsatz des Selbstvertrauens der Vernunft" (principle of the self-confidence of reason): "Die Kritische Methode und das Verhältnis der Psychologie zur Philosophie" [1904], *Gesammelte Schriften*, 1: 33. Also: Leonard Nelson, *Über das sogennante Erkenntnisproblem* (Göttingen: Vandenhoeck und Ruprecht, 1908).

[103] Popper, *Die beiden Grundprobleme der Erkenntnistheorie* [1930–3] (Tübingen: Mohr, 1979), chap. 5; "Julius Kraft."

[104] Jakob Friedrich Fries, *Die Geschichte der Philosophie, dargestellt nach den Fortschritten ihrer wissenschaftlichen Entwickelung* [1837–40], *Sämtliche Schriften*, vols. 18–19; Leonard Nelson, *Über das sogennante Erkenntnisproblem*; idem, *Socratic Method*; idem, *Progress and Regress in Philosophy: From Hume and Kant to Hegel and Fries*, ed. Julius Kraft, trans. Humphrey Palmer, 2 vols. (Oxford: Basil Blackwell, 1970).

[105] Popper mentioned Nelson as "the first" to have pointed out, in his critique of Spengler, the danger of "historicism." Popper, *The Open Society*, chap. 4 n. 45. Leonard Nelson, *Spuk. Einweihung in das Geheimnis der Wahrsagerkunst Oswald Spenglers* [1921] (Spook. Initiation into the secret of the prophetic art of Oswald Spengler), *Gesammelte Schriften*, 3: 349–552.

[106] Julius Kraft, *Von Husserl zu Heidegger*, 2d ed. (Frankfurt: Öffentliches Leben, 1957).

impossibility of the *Geisteswissenschaft*).[107] Today, these books read almost as sequels to *The Open Society*. After World War II, Kraft and Popper sought to use *Ratio* to revive enlightenment discourse in Germany and complete Nelson's project.[108] They established a genealogy of progressive Kantianism, from Kant to Fries to Nelson to themselves.

Ratio conveyed the impression of a unified Kantian camp fighting for cosmopolitanism and liberal politics. The enemy was likewise homogenized: Hegelian dogmatism, German nationalism, and Prussian authoritarianism were interchangeable. But genealogies rarely maintain such a consistent meaning through shifting historical contexts. Popper was aware of the differences separating him, an Austrian progressive, from Nelson, a German mandarin. For both, socialism was a means to a liberal end. But for Nelson, liberalism and *Bildung* were one; for Popper, liberalism and radical democracy. They differed radically on Plato and political leadership. Popper commended Nelson for his cosmopolitanism, but dissented from his elitism.[109] *Ratio* restored the Friesian School, he said, but with a decidedly democratic orientation.[110] Popper was unaware, however, how badly Fries's politics fit with progressive Kantianism. For all his emphasis on rights, justice, and state limits, Fries was an anti-Semitic German nationalist.[111] He became part of the liberal, cosmopolitan, antinationalist camp only because Nelson, Kraft, and Popper focused on his enemies' politics, rather than his own.

During the early restoration years, Fries was a leading nationalist intellectual, seconding the clamors of the *Burschenschaften* (student fraternities) for German unification. Future liberals would regard the students as martyrs for national liberation, but they were also xenophobic romantics who excelled at burning books and attacking Jews. In 1816, Fries added to his nationalist pamphlets a treatise "On the Danger [Posed] to the Welfare and Character of the German People by the Jews."[112] In 1817, he gave a rousing speech at the student festival in Wartburg. The Saxon government, under Austrian and Prussian pressure, deposed him from his Jena chair. Hegel

---

[107] Idem, *Die Unmöglichkeit der Geisteswissenschaft*, 2d ed. (Frankfurt: Öffentliches Leben, 1957).

[108] Editorial statement in *Ratio* 1 (1957–8); Popper, "Julius Kraft," 2–10.

[109] Popper, *The Open Society*, chap. 7 n. 3, 25 (2). Popper's criticism of Nelson was mild. He insisted that Nelson's elitism be viewed within the liberal context of his philosophy.

[110] Popper to Martin Hollis (*Ratio*'s new editor), 22 October 1979, Hoover Archives (341, 6).

[111] Recently, Kant's critics have implicated his universalism with nationalism and anti-Semitism. In my "Dilemmas of Cosmopolitanism: Karl Popper, Jewish Identity, and 'Central European Culture,'" *Journal of Modern History* 71 (1999): 105–49, I argue for the emancipationist potential of Kant's universalism, and lay the blame for anti-Semitism primarily with nationalist appropriations, like that of Fries.

[112] Jakob Fries, "Über die Gefährdung des Wohlstandes und Charakteres der Deutschen durch die Juden," *Heidelberger Jahrbücher* 16–17 (1816). For his political program: *Von deutschem Bund und deutscher Staatsverfassung* (Heidelberg: Mohr und Winter, 1816). Popper probably did not know these writings, and Nelson and Kraft may have chosen to ignore them.

attacked Fries and justified Prussian repression of the nationalists in his preface to *The Philosophy of Right* (1821). He contended that Fries's politics resulted from his Kantian subjectivism, agnosticism, and romanticism. Hegel thus tied Kantian epistemology and politics together and bound his own philosophy to the Prussian government.[113]

Later nineteenth-century interpreters turned Hegel into both a German nationalist and a Prussian reactionary. Karl Rosenkranz (1805–79) defended him as a moderate philosopher. But, in his influential *Hegel und seine Zeit* (1857, Hegel and his times), Rudolf Haym (1821–1901) condemned him as the restoration philosopher par excellence.[114] A disappointed liberal nationalist of 1848, Haym criticized Hegel as an "accomodationist" acquiescing in Prussian repression. After 1870, Constantin Rössler (1820–96) described Hegel as a prophet of Bismarckian *Machtpolitik*. More liberal mandarins of the next generation criticized Hegel on similar grounds. As Prussia gradually came to symbolize aggressive German nationalism, Hegel was transformed from a reactionary antinationalist to a reactionary nationalist. Erich Kaufmann, Eduard Spranger, and other conservative mandarins completed Hegel's transformation into an authoritarian state philosopher during the early years of this century.[115]

For Nelson, Kraft, and Popper, Hegel's reactionary politics were conventional wisdom. They assumed that all Kantian enemies of Hegel and Prussia were friends of liberty and cosmopolitanism. Those who shared their Kantian epistemology also shared their progressive politics. Early German nationalism appeared to them progressive: It opposed reactionary Austria and Prussia. Notwithstanding Fries's lapses, they projected his epistemology onto liberal politics. Kraft searched for additional anti-Hegelian links, drafting Haym into his camp.[116] Popper, in contrast, had little interest in claiming liberal nationalists for his position. Whereas Haym criticized Hegel for defending antinationalist Prussia, Popper condemned him as a representative of "tribal nationalism."[117] All the same, Nelson's history of philosophy informed *The Open Society*. Philosophical and political progress went hand in hand. The history of correct epistemology and methodology and their opponents was also the history of the Open Society and its enemies.

Nelson's influence on Popper was formidable. Popper probably bor-

---

[113] G. W. F. Hegel, "Preface" to *Elements of the Philosophy of Right*, ed. Allen W. Wood, trans. H. B. Nisbet (Cambridge: Cambridge University Press, 1991), pp. 9–23. On the confrontation between Hegel and Fries: Shlomo Avineri, *Hegel's Theory of the Modern State* (New York: Cambridge University Press, 1972), pp. 115–31. See also the essays on Hegel and Prussia by Carrit, Hook, Knox, and Kaufmann, in *Hegel's Political Philosophy*, ed. Walter Kaufmann (New York: Atherton, 1970).

[114] Rudolf Haym, *Hegel und seine Zeit*, ed. Hans Rosenberg, 2d ed. (Leipzig: Heims, 1927).

[115] Henning Ottmann, *Individuum und Gemeinschaft bei Hegel* (Berlin: Gruyter, 1977), vol. 1.

[116] Julius Kraft, introduction to Haym selections, *Ratio* 2 (1960), 42–3.

[117] Popper, *The Open Society*, chap. 12.

rowed from him the "Socratic Method." Both Nelson and Popper identified the method with critical dialogue and awareness of the limits of cognition. Nelson emphasized similarities between Socrates' and Fries's search for the foundation of knowledge. Popper emphasized the Socratic claim for "not knowing."[118] Unlike Nelson, Popper dissociated Plato completely from the "Socratic Method." Socrates was a critical democratic philosopher; Plato a totalitarian enemy of the Open Society. Nelson's Platonic ideal of leadership elicited Popper's prompt dissent. The rest of his politics, however, he found admirable. Already in 1927 he was using Nelson to buttress his cosmopolitanism.[119] He would refer to Fries and Nelson in all his early works. Their philosophy was a departure point to which he continuously returned to check his own developing views, first on the psychology of learning, then on the logic of science.

Popper's incomplete 1927 paper on the psychology of lawfulness deployed Nelsonian terminology.[120] He applied Nelson's distinction between critical and dogmatic thinking to child psychology, arguing that dogmatism prevailed in children's mental life. Nelson distinguished between habit (*Gewohnheit*) and psychological association in his critique of Hume, and between cognition and judgment in his critique of Kant.[121] Popper suggested that neither habit nor judgment played a role in children's thinking. But he was at a loss as to what else to do with these terms and formed no epistemological argument of his own. Nelson's influence was still apparent in Popper's 1928 dissertation on cognitive psychology.[122] Nelson used the "regressive method," the method of Kant's *Critique* modified by Fries's psychological interpretation, to outline the interaction of epistemology and psychology in the acquisition of knowledge.[123] Mentioning Fries as a predecessor, Popper explored questions relating to the interaction in his dissertation.

Nelson's lifelong effort to vindicate Fries's solution to the foundation of knowledge proved essential to Popper once he turned, in 1929, from the psychology to the logic of the sciences. His 1929 teacher-qualifying thesis reflected Nelson's interest in non-Euclidean geometry and his intention of

---

[118] Nelson, "The Socratic Method"; Popper, *The Open Society*, vol. 1, chap. 7; idem, "Replies to My Critics," *The Philosophy of Karl Popper*, ed. Paul Arthur Schilpp, 2 vols. (La Salle, Ill.: Open Court, 1974), pp. 961–3; idem, "Einleitung 1978: das wissenschaftliche Wissen als ein sokratisches Nichtwissen," in his *Die beiden Grundprobleme*, pp. xv–xxi.

[119] Popper, "Zur Philosophie des Heimatgedankens," *Die Quelle* 77 (1927): 906. He used Nelson to support an internationalist standpoint in the education of youth.

[120] Karl Popper, " 'Gewohnheit' und 'Gesetzerlebnis' in der Erziehung: Eine pädagogisch- strukturpsychologische Monographie," submitted as *Hausarbeit* to the Pädagogisches Institut, Vienna, 1927, Hoover Archives (12, 11).

[121] Nelson, "Die Kritische Methode," pp. 20–3, 55–7.

[122] Karl Popper, "Zur Methodenfrage der Denkpsychologie" (Ph.D. diss.: University of Vienna, summer 1928).

[123] Nelson, "Die Kritische Methode," pp. 11–64.

using it as a test case for epistemology. Many of his terms (and references) were Nelsonian. The 1929 epistemological setting pointed toward the philosophical problematic of the early 1930s.[124] In *Die beiden Grundprobleme* (1930–3), Popper devoted the longest chapter to Fries's Kant critique.[125] It constituted the core of his epistemological revolution. The radically short-ened discussion of the empirical basis of science in *Logik der Forschung* still evinced Nelson's and Fries's role in the long-winded passage to the new philosophy.[126] "Critical philosophy" set the problem situation that enabled Popper to make his radical theoretical move, reformulate the question of the validity of knowledge, and achieve his great breakthrough in the phi-losophy of science.

HEIMAT, SOCIALISM, AND COSMOPOLITANISM

Nelson's influence on the young Popper was evident in Popper's second published article: "On the Philosophy of the *Heimat* Idea."[127] The essay emerged from a 1927 seminar on the *Heimat* (homeland) idea at the Ped-agogical Institute. City councillor Eduard Bürger, *Die Quelle's* editor, directed the seminar. Its goal was to examine the educational significance of Heimat. Reform pedagogy emphasized that learning should be rooted in the children's home environment, their Heimat, and come naturally. But Heimat was a politically loaded term, intimating also local and national patriotism. This could not have been lost on seminar organizers. They sought rapprochement between socialism and Heimat. School reform always aimed at forming a modern nation. In its German version, it was hypernationalistic. Glöckel and other members of the *Verein Freie Schule* were also not beyond cooperating with the nationalist and anti-Semitic *Deutsche Schulverein*. Popper would have none of it. He used the essay to criticize the educational limits and political dangers of Heimat, defining a cosmopolitan socialist vision for progressive education.

Heimat, a convergence of country and home, originated with the German romantics. It denoted patriotism and civic culture to nineteenth-century liberals. But in interwar years, it became the Austrian fascists' leit-motiv. They used it to express local patriotism, attachment to provincial customs, family and religion, hatred of urban industrial society, parliamen-tary politics, and Viennese culture.[128] The provincial armed units that con-

---

[124] Karl Popper, "Axiome, Definitionen und Postulate der Geometrie," 2 vols., Hoover Archives (4, 6).

[125] Idem, *Grundprobleme*, chap. V. This is discussed in detail in Chapter 5.

[126] Idem, *Logik der Forschung* (Vienna: Springer, 1935), p. 51 hr. f.

[127] Karl Popper, "Zur Philosophie des Heimatgedankens," *Die Quelle* 77 (1927): 899–908.

[128] For a more positive evaluation of *Heimat*, emphasizing its role in bridging local community and national identity, see Celia Applegate's study of the Palatinate: *A Nation of Provincials: The German Idea of Heimat* (Berkeley: University of California Press, 1990), chap. 1.

stituted the hard core of Austrian fascism assumed the name *Heimwehr* (Home Guard).[129] In the November 1930 elections, the Austrian fascists, first organized as a political movement, ran under the *Heimatblock* banner. The socialists were hoping to reappropriate the concept, but Popper offered them no help. Noting the amorphous character of Heimat, he moved to define the concept, purging it of mystical nationalist meanings. He founded Heimat on individuals' psychological relationship to their environment and spoke of school as an educational Heimat. But he remained suspicious even of this "native" environment. It connoted a rejection of the new and different as "foreign." *Bodenständigkeit* was acceptable as a point of departure, but education should open Heimat to new experiences and ideas. Pedagogy that closed the student's Heimat to external influences, like Plato's, was countereducational. Heimat existed, but it needed to be overcome.

The argument was as much about political culture as about education. Popper recognized that individuals' psychological relationship to their environment established a "naturally given primitive *Kulturverband* [cultural community]" that supported larger cultural units. But he did not investigate the transformation of multiple local communities into a nation. Instead, he defined the nation as a *Rechtsverband* (legal association). Legal systems, not cultural heritage, set national boundaries. Popper insisted that a universal ethic must shape national legal codes, so that citizenship is compatible with internationalism. Education should cultivate respect for law, a sense of justice, and a critical awareness of social iniquities. But it should not foster patriotism, or *Heimatliebe*. Love is an aesthetic feeling, not a virtue, and so there is no duty to love. Patriotic actions violating internationalism are unethical. Threatened by the fascist Heimat, Popper contained its political force and emotional appeal first by restricting it to individuals and their environment, then by transforming national collectives into legal associations to protect universal rights.

Popper's cosmopolitanism was already full-blown in this uneven early essay. So also were his difficulties in negotiating national identity. He recognized cultural-historical communities, but divorced nationality and citizenship from them: The latter were legal concepts. National differences appeared insignificant. All nations must conform to the legal code of a yet-to-come world federation. "From good Germans to good cosmopolites [*Weltbürger*]," he quoted Eduard Bürger.[130] For socialists, the dictum justified a German national focus. For Popper, good Germans virtually ceased being German, becoming cosmopolites. He heaped abuse on German epis-

---

[129] On the *Heimwehr* and Austrian fascism, see: C. Earl Edmondson, *The Heimwehr and Austrian Politics, 1918–1936* (Athens, Ga.: University of Georgia, 1978).

[130] Popper, "Zur Philosophie des Heimatgedankens": 906.

temology and *Naturphilosophie* that reflected, in his view, something of a German national character. Their superstition, making truth relative to national circumstances, could bring philosophy down. But, Popper seemed to suggest, education could change "national character" by transforming affective relationships and aesthetic feelings into legal relationships and ethical actions. Love of Heimat might develop into an appreciation of nature's beauty, anxieties about "bad" outsiders into ethical judgments, native (*bodenständige*) art and music into high culture. His suggestions reflected not so much cultural elitism, or authoritarian universalism, as an assimilated Jew's mortal fear of German ethnonationalism. Excluded from Heimat on ethnic grounds, Popper responded by subjecting ethnic and national identities to a universal humanity.

Democratic socialism was an essential complement to cosmopolitanism. Democracy was founded on respect for law and justice. "The meaning of democracy is that individuals' sense of justice guides legal life," he wrote.[131] Justice alone was the source of duty to obey the law. The struggle for social justice took precedence over obedience to the law. Citizens had a duty to fight for workers' rights and socialism because injustice eroded the proletariat's trust in the legal order and could lead to its dissolution. Poor living conditions, Popper seemed to suggest, could prevent workers from exercising their citizenship. Egalitarian citizenship required a socioeconomic base. Working-class integration into the nation demanded socialism. "To me," Popper recalled years later, "socialism was an ethical postulate – nothing more or less than the idea of justice."[132] Already in the mid-1920s, he had grounded socialism in Kantian principles of law and justice, and not in Marxism.

These were daring moves for a young student to make. Viennese progressive cosmopolitanism lost much of its force in interwar years. The empire was gone, and Versailles (or St. Germain) discredited the Austrian peace movement. Eccentric aristocrats and Freemasons, such as Coudehove-Kalergi, could still dream of Pan-Europe. Conservative proponents of the Austrian idea from Hugo von Hofmannstahl to Joseph Roth expressed anti-German sentiments and opposition to nationalism, but they were not progressive universalists. As for the socialists, German nationalism always tempered their internationalism. Prior to 1914, many believed in the German cultural mission in Central Europe. During the interwar period, they supported unification with Germany. Popper stood almost alone.

His Kantian socialism was less anomalous, but it had unique features. Austro-Marxists, notably Max Adler, assimilated Kant to socialism. But they worked in a Marxist framework. Popper lectured to a Marxist audience,

---

[131] Loc. cit.   [132] Popper, "On Reason and the Open Society," *Encounter* 38 (1972): 13.

but made no mention of Marx. His socialism expressed the ethos of Viennese progressivism (and the future welfare state), but gave it a radical twist by placing social justice above obedience to the law and demanding socialism. The editor of *Die Quelle* may have gotten more than he bargained for when he requested Popper to open the Heimat seminar. He provided a platform for a progressive who had made a clean break with German nationalism, refused to compromise cosmopolitanism, and had little use for Marx.[133]

To be sure, Popper's cosmopolitanism and socialism involved limited conceptual innovation. His central ideas belonged to Kant: the state as a legal and political entity (not a cultural-historical one); the parallel between civil, national and cosmopolitan rights; the universality of the moral imperative and its expression in law; citizenship as equality of rights and duties; and the division between aesthetics and ethics (ruling out derivation of moral imperatives from aesthetic judgment).[134] But political realism and government pressure had constrained Kant's cosmopolitanism. His republican government and international federation were a future prospect, a conjecture about historical progress that would lead humankind to enlightenment and cosmopolitanism. In reality he faced an absolutist monarchy, first an enlightened one (under Frederick II), then a reactionary one. He provided many escape clauses for an absolutist monarch. The security of the state was a supreme imperative. Under no circumstances was resistance to the monarch permitted. Rebellion was "the greatest crime." A country in the midst of Europe (that is, Prussia), subject to pressures from powerful neighbors, was exempt from a republican constitution.[135] The moral imperative was universal, but its political fulfillment was problematic and required caution.

Young Popper would have none of it. With typical single-mindedness – reflecting philosophical consistency, moral uprightness, intellectual inflexibility, psychological obstinacy, and more than a touch of political naïveté – he collapsed Kant's future and present, conjecture and reality. He extended Kant's political rights into the social and economic spheres, making obedience to the law conditional upon their recognition, and authorizing resistance. He freed Kant's cosmopolitanism from its historical and political limits, and realized the socialist potential of his republicanism, daringly pro-

---

[133] Responding to Popper's criticism of native art and music (Popper included the *Reigentanze*, popular in socialist colonies), Bürger, in an editorial note, drew the reader's attention to conflicting views in other essays. Popper, "Heimatgedankens": 905.

[134] Immanuel Kant, "Über den Gemeinspruch: Das mag in der Theorie richtig sein, taugt aber nicht für die Praxis" [1793] and "Zum ewigen Frieden" [1795], in vol. 8 of *Gesammelte Schriften (Akademieausgabe)*, 29 vols. (Berlin: Reimer, 1912); *Critique of Judgement* (Oxford: Clarendon Press, 1952), bk. 2: "Critique of Aesthetic Judgement."

[135] Idem, "Theorie [und] Praxis," esp. pp. 297–300; "Zum ewigen Frieden," esp. pp. 372–3; "Der Streit der Fakultäten" [1798], in *Gesammelte Schriften*, 7: 79–94, esp. p. 86 n.

claiming the universal validity of cosmopolitanism and socialism, here and now.

Drifting on the margins of the Schoenberg circle, the university, and the *Kinderfreunde* until the mid-1920s, Popper seemed always the odd man out. He did not commit himself, but maintained a critical distance from all movements, remaining out of power and influence. Neither modern music nor school reform left a positive impression on his philosophy. Schoenberg's musicology became a negative model of historicism; school reform, an example of bureaucratic spoilage of good pedagogy. All the intellectuals who played a formative role in his philosophy, Kraft, Nelson, and Polanyi, took pride in going against the current. So did he: "I never followed intellectual fashions, but always combated them."[136] With *The Open Society*, however, his philosophy enjoyed a success of which they could only dream. Through him, marginal Central European traditions became formative of postwar Atlantic liberalism, moving into the Western mainstream.

Popper was active in social reform until the mid-1920s in a manner he would never again repeat. His retreat from reform in the aftermath of the 1925 tragedy was no temporary withdrawal of a frustrated youth. It lasted for life. From 1925 on, he had no active political engagement, and participated in no social reform. He focused on his intellectual interests and professional career. His years of rebellion, of antibourgeois lifestyle and unconventional career pattern, had ended. From now on, he led a conventional life, completing his university studies, getting a teaching job, then marrying. Significantly, the court drama that ended his rebellion brought back the father figure. Popper himself linked his rebellion against the father with the collapse of the bourgeois world in the Austrian revolution: "The revolution incited me to stage my own private revolution."[137] Having successfully defended his son in court, Simon Popper regained some authority, as did the bourgeois world. Popper now loathed revolutionary intellectuals, despised the cultural avant-garde, disrespected socialist politicians, and feared bureaucracy. Retreating from politics to intellectual life, however, he was not giving up on changing the world. He was merely shifting fronts. His intellectual battles would always bear the character of a political crusade.

---

[136] Questionnaire, Research Foundation for Jewish Immigration.　　[137] *Autobiography*, p. 32.

Chapter 4

The Pedagogic Institute and the Psychology of Knowledge, 1925–1928

The analogies between Popper's philosophy of science and his psychology are obvious. In both, theory, or expectation, precedes experience; trial and error weeds out false theories; thus, knowledge grows. Popper's psychology is often considered a mere extension of his philosophy. His *Autobiography* supports such a view. He spoke of his early recognition of the "principle of transference" from philosophy to psychology: Whatever is true in logic must also be true in psychology.[1] In a draft, he cautioned that "for a considerable time, these things were not as clear to me as they are stated here; and [throughout the 1920s] I continued to work on the psychology of the formation of theories and expectations."[2] However, he did not recall precisely his intellectual development, and read back to the 1920s problems and solutions of later years. For the late Popper, logic, psychology, and evolutionary biology formed congruous parts of a unified philosophy, or at least so he thought. He projected this unity back to the 1920s. Even a cursory reading of his early work in psychology would show that no such unified philosophy existed.

Contrary to Popper's recollections, his logic and psychology collided during the 1920s, making his intellectual progress impossible. In his 1928 dissertation on cognitive psychology, he rejected "transference" as "logicism," and sought to maintain the autonomy of *both* psychology and epistemology. Yet, his psychology could not explain thinking without encroaching on the autonomy of epistemology. He reached an impasse. In 1929, he shifted his inquiry from psychology to the logic of science. There, he achieved a major breakthrough – by radically separating logic from psychology. For almost two decades, he left psychology aside. Only in postwar years did he bring logic and psychology back together. His *Autobiography* overlooked the detour.

Popper provided two fairly consistent accounts of his intellectual development during the 1920s. In the first, he traced his psychological refuta-

---

[1] *Autobiography*, p. 60. Further discussion: *Objective Knowledge* (Oxford: Clarendon Press, 1972), pp. 23–7, 67–8, esp. n. 30; "Replies to My Critics," *The Philosophy of Karl Popper*, ed. Paul Arthur Schilpp, 2 vols. (La Salle, Ill.: Open Court, 1974), 2:1020–4. William Berkson and John Wettersten, *Learning from Error: Karl Popper's Psychology of Learning* (La Salle, Ill.: Open Court, 1984), pp. 79–83 point out nicely the methodological problems with transference.

[2] Draft of *Autobiography*, Hoover Archives (134, 12).

tion of induction.[3] The conventional empiricist view was that scientists proceeded from particular statements, which were based on observation or experiment, to general hypotheses and theories. In *A Treatise of Human Nature*, Hume had already undermined the logical foundation of induction by demonstrating that there was no valid progression from particular experiences to general laws. Having to provide an alternative foundation for induction, Hume turned to psychology. Although repetitious observations and experiments could not lead logically to scientific generalizations, they did so in reality through habit. One got used to the sun rising in the morning and expected it the next day. Knowledge, said Popper, became a matter of belief. Popper was dissatisfied with Hume. Psychological induction, he contended, was as dubious as the logical original:

> The kind of repetition envisaged by Hume can never be perfect; the cases he has in mind cannot be cases of perfect sameness; they can only be cases of similarity. Thus, *they are repetitions only from a certain point of view.* . . . But this means that, for logical reasons, there must always be a point of view – such as a system of expectations, anticipations, assumptions, or interests – *before* there can be any repetition.[4]

He dated his critique of Hume to the 1920s. He first became interested in induction, he said, in 1923. He meditated over the problem during his apprenticeship in 1923–4, and formulated a solution. He presented his views in an unfinished thesis titled "On Habit and Belief in Laws," submitted to the Pedagogic Institute in 1927:[5]

> I was led by purely logical considerations [recalled Popper in the 1950s] to replace the psychological theory of induction by the following view. Without waiting, passively, for repetitions to impress or impose regulations upon us, we actively try to impose regularities upon the world. We try to discover similarities in it, and to interpret it in terms of laws invented by us. These may have to be discarded later, should observations show us that they are wrong.[6]

This is *not* the way things really happened. The 1927 and 1928 theses were not concerned with the psychology of induction, or questions related to epistemology and the logic of science. Popper unproblematically accepted induction (and verification) as the standard scientific method up

---

[3] "Science: Conjectures and Refutations" [1957], in *Conjectures and Refutations* (New York: Basic Books, 1963), pp. 42–52. See also: *Autobiography*, pp. 44–60, 75–8.

[4] *Conjectures and Refutations*, pp. 44–5.

[5] " 'Gewohnheit' und 'Gesetzerlebnis' in der Erziehung. Eine pädagogisch-strukturpsychologische Monographie," Popper Archives (12, 11). Popper translated the title as "On Habit and Belief in Laws," in *Conjectures and Refutations*, p. 50, and in *Autobiography*, p. 205. However, "Habit and the Experience of Lawfulness [or Laws] in Education" would seem more appropriate.

[6] *Conjectures and Refutations*, p. 46.

to 1929. He was more partial to inductive (or associationist) psychology than his mentor Bühler or the Würzburg psychologists. He formulated neither the problem of induction nor the solution until 1929. His *Autobiography* read his later views on the logic of science into his psychology of the 1920s. More significantly, it missed the intellectual stalemate of the late 1920s, and the great breakthrough of 1929–30. The first is this chapter's subject, the latter the subject of the next.

THE PEDAGOGIC INSTITUTE

One of school reform's main goals was to improve teachers' training and education. Glöckel was eager to train a new generation of teachers. He knew that this was key to transforming Viennese schools. Until 1925, however, there were no prospects of new teaching jobs, and hence no teachers to train. Demand for teachers was projected first for 1927–8. Glöckel thought they should all receive academic training, preferably in a psychology department. Teachers ought to be familiar, he argued, with recent research in child development. But the conservative university faculty would not hear of training teachers. Scholarship and professional training did not mix, they said. In July 1925, the city council merged Vienna's pedagogic and psychological institutes, and established a two-year teacher-training program, combining academic and practical training.[7] Students took a minimum of ten semestral hours at the university, the rest at the institute: lectures, recitations, practical work. The program emphasized psychology and reform pedagogy. Upon completing their course work, students submitted a protothesis, the *Hausarbeit*, and took a qualifying exam in a seminary or a secondary school. The program survived only five years. It was suspended in 1930 when it became clear that no more teaching posts would be available. It matriculated 299 teachers (155 women, 144 men). Some would distinguish themselves later in fields far removed from school instruction.[8]

Popper and his friends received the news of the program with dismay. Most of them had already qualified as teachers and looked at their present jobs as social workers as a stopgap measure. Now they had to study for another two years, without compensation, to requalify. They felt that the program of studies was overambitious and had doubts about its efficacy. To top it all, they learned that only eighty students were to be admitted, and no one was sure that they would be among them. Popper knew Viktor Fadrus, the institute's director and editor of *Schulreform*. He asked for an

[7] Viktor Fadrus, "Die Neugestaltung der Lehrerbildung in Deutschland und Österreich," *Schulreform* 5 (1926): 1–42.

[8] Gerhard Benetka, *Psychologie in Wien: Sozial- und Theoriegeschichte des Wiener Psychologischen Instituts 1922–1938* (Vienna: WUV-Universitätsverlag, 1995), pp. 30–9.

interview. Fadrus assured him that the social workers' applications would be favorably reviewed.[9] They were, and Popper's friends were all admitted. School reformers were not about to let go of the avant-garde of socialist education.

At the institute, Popper expanded his social and intellectual circle. His class included Robert Lammer, who would help him write his first book; Otto Haas, to whom he would entrust his papers, upon leaving Vienna; Ludwig Krenek; and Fritz Kolb. He established long-term friendships with all. Most significantly, he met his future wife, Josefine Anna Henninger (1906–85) there. She and Karl were members of a student group that studied, hiked, and mountaineered together. Karl became their intellectual leader. He was intellectually way ahead of most of them: Only 17% of his class had a gymnasium education. (A seminary or secondary school diploma was the program's admission basis.) Popper gave the group informal seminars, reviewing class material and helping them prepare for exams. He did well. Karl Bühler, the institute's foremost academic authority, complimented him on his teaching. Upon reading the group's final exams, he related to Popper, in their first personal conversation, that these were the best-prepared students he had ever encountered.[10]

At the institute, Popper finally found an academic milieu conducive to a systematic development of his theoretical interests. However, the courses were, again, disappointing. He and his friends grew tired of the teachers' pedagogical preaching and questioned their credentials. Aside from the informal seminars that he led, and loved, he had good intellectual rapport with Bühler, who was professor of philosophy and psychology at the university and the institute. He learned much from Bühler and greatly admired him.

Bühler (1879–1964) was a prominent European psychologist of the interwar period. Born in humble circumstances in Meckesheim near Heidelberg, he first obtained a medical degree in 1903, then, two years later, joined psychologist Oswald Külpe in Würzburg. The Würzburg school was known for its *Denkpsychologie* (cognitive psychology), the investigation of high-level thought processes.[11] Külpe was leading a revolt against Wilhelm Wundt and associationist psychology, and Bühler became the point person when his published *Habilitationschrift* evolved into a sharp exchange with Wundt.[12] He defended introspection as an experimental method; rejected

---

[9] Draft of *Autobiography*, sec. 15 (134, 12), pp. 1–4. The entering class was larger than planned: 115 students.

[10] *Autobiography*, pp. 73–4.

[11] The term "cognitive psychology" was not available at the time. But there is sufficient proximity between the "psychology of thought" *(Denkpsychologie)* and cognitive psychology to permit my use of the less cumbersome term.

[12] Karl Bühler, "Tatsachen und Probleme zu einer Psychologie der Denkvorgänge," *Archiv für die gesamte Psychologie* 9 (1907): 297–365; 12 (1908): 1–23, 24–92, 93–123. The final section includes Bühler's response to Wundt's critique.

reduction of thought to sensations, images, and feelings; and increasingly emphasized the mind's creative role. When Külpe died unexpectedly in December 1915, Bühler was called back from the western front to Munich to teach his courses, then, in 1918, appointed to a chair in Dresden. *Die geistige Entwicklung des Kindes* (1918; *The Mental Development of the Child*) established him as a leading child psychologist.[13] He used a biologically informed developmental approach to trace concept formation in children. An abridged version became the standard textbook in child psychology for the next fifteen years.[14] It earned Bühler the invitation to Vienna.

The University of Vienna had no psychology department. Glöckel was eager for the university to appoint a philosophy professor with expertise in experimental psychology, and Bühler proved an acceptable candidate to both the faculty and the education ministry. He needed a laboratory, and the university did not have one. His wife, Charlotte Bühler (née Malachowski, 1893–1974), was also a child psychologist. School reformers realized that acquiring two noted child psychologists for their training program would establish its academic credentials and turn Vienna into a center for psychological research. Negotiating for the city, Glöckel guaranteed Bühler a laboratory in the Vienna School Council's building, and allocated resources for a new psychological institute. He further proposed to employ the couple to teach psychology in a reorganized pedagogic institute, supplementing Karl Bühler's university salary. The Bühlers arrived in the fall of 1922. In January 1923, the new Psychological Institute opened. It represented a unique collaboration of university and city, and served a double function: academic research and pedagogical training. It became one of the leading psychological institutes in Central Europe.[15]

Karl Bühler proved a popular lecturer, drawing crowds in psychology, logic and, later, linguistics. Students from all over Europe came to study with him. His Wednesday night psychology colloquium at the institute, which frequently moved, later in the evening, to the Regina Hotel for dinner, became legendary. The institute's elite – Charlotte Bühler, assistants, doctoral students, visiting scholars – attended and set research agendas. Popper participated for at least four years but, typically, did not enter the inner circle.[16] A warm, spontaneous person, Bühler cultivated colleagues and students alike. He worked well with his philosophy colleagues, Reininger and Schlick, cosponsoring many dissertations (Popper's

[13] Karl Bühler, *Die geistige Entwicklung des Kindes* [1918], 3rd ed. (Jena: Fischer, 1922).

[14] Idem, *Abriß der geistigen Entwicklung des Kindes* (Leipzig: Quelle and Meyer, 1919). English: *The Mental Development of the Child* (New York: Harcourt, Brace & Company, 1930).

[15] Mitchell Ash, "Psychology and Politics in Interwar Vienna: The Vienna Psychological Institute, 1922–1942," in *Psychology in Twentieth-Century Thought and Society*, ed. Mitchell Ash and William Woodward (New York: Cambridge University Press, 1987), pp. 143–64; Gerhard Benetka, *Psychologie in Wien*, pp. 16–29.

[16] Popper to Achim Eschbach, 5 July and 5 August 1981, Popper Archives (293, 22).

included). About half of the 185 dissertations he supervised were published. At the institute, he oversaw experimental work in cognitive psychology, through assistants Helmut Boksch and, beginning in 1927, Egon Brunswik. His interests shifted, in interwar years, from cognitive and child psychology to psychological methodology and linguistic theory. *Die Krise der Psychologie* (1927; The crisis in psychology), which provided the focus for Popper's 1928 dissertation, was an important methodological work, integrating conflicting approaches to psychology.[17] Throughout the 1920s, he was also developing a biologically oriented linguistics, culminating in 1934 in *Sprachtheorie*.[18] Popper took notice of his linguistic theory in his dissertation, and it became important for his work in later years.[19] With antagonists Freud and Adler, Bühler made Vienna a psychological mecca it had never been before, or after.[20]

Charlotte Bühler taught courses in child psychology and social psychology and took charge of most research on children and youth at the institute. She pioneered the use of youth diaries for research on adolescents. For children, she used minute observation and free play. She also made innovative use of statistics. Her major project, beginning in 1926, took place in the city's adoption center. The city was applying policies for preventing child abuse in working-class families. The authorities gathered neglected youth for psychological evaluation at the center. Bühler's staff observed them, and administered intelligence and development tests. The result was a series of books on child development from the first year to adolescence. They drew full pictures of children's social, intellectual, and mental life during different periods in their development.[21]

Women played unusually prominent roles at the institute. Hildegard Hetzer and, after 1931, Lotte Danziger were Charlotte Bühler's assistants. Else Köhler offered courses in child psychology. Else Frenkel, Marie Jahoda, and Käthe Wolf did research. Not everyone was happy with the institute's direction. Assistants often complained that Charlotte Bühler took advantage of their services to further her own career. School reformers protested that her research proved largely irrelevant to classroom instruction.[22] At the university, she suffered from triple jeopardy: She was a woman (of Jewish

---

[17] Karl Bühler, *Die Krise der Psychologie* (Jena: Fischer, 1927).

[18] Idem, *Sprachtheorie* (Jena: Fischer, 1934).

[19] Popper, "Language and the Body–Mind Problem" [1953], *Conjectures and Refutations*, pp. 293–8.

[20] James Bugental, ed., "Symposium on Karl Bühler's Contributions to Psychology," *The Journal of General Psychology* 75 (1966): 181–219; Gerhard Benetka, *Psychologie in Wien*, pp. 9–67.

[21] Charlotte Bühler, *Das Seelenleben des Jugendlichen*, 4th ed. (Jena: Fischer, 1927); idem, *Kindheit und Jugend* (Leipzig: Hirzel, 1928); Charlotte Bühler, Hildegard Hetzer, and Beatrix Tudor-Hart, *Soziologische und psychologische Studien über das erste Lebensjahr* (Jena: Fischer, 1927). Some historians find the city's policies on working-class child abuse prejudicial, and the psychologists' collusion in them disturbing: Gerhard Benetka, *Psychologie in Wien*, pp. 132–45.

[22] Mitchell Ash, "Psychology and Politics," pp. 150–3.

origin) who had received her appointment through her husband; a psychologist in a university that had no psychology department; and associated with socialist reform in a conservative atmosphere. Only in 1929 did the faculty recognize her as an associate (*ausserordentlicher*) professor. At the institute, even her critics recognized that she was opening gates for women and sponsoring innovative projects.

The Bühlers were the predominant intellectual influence at the institute, but there were others. Virtually every progressive intellectual in Vienna gave a guest lecture at some point. Alfred Adler taught regularly and had a formative influence on many students. His views on the constraints that bourgeois society imposed on the proletarian psyche informed research in social psychology. Paul Lazarsfeld's study of youth's occupational choices reflected the Bühlers' and Adler's influence. Lazarsfeld argued that Charlotte Bühler's concept of adolescent culture was insensitive to class. Working-class youth had a shortened adolescence because of early entry into the workforce. In early adolescence, they were open to various careers, but circumstances directed them to labor. This diminished their life possibilities in ways similar to traumatized bourgeois youth. By transforming economic structure, socialism could open up new possibilities. Charlotte Bühler tempered Lazarsfeld's socialist rhetoric, but she conceded that class differences were essential to psychology. She herself had no warm feelings for Adler or socialism, but her researchers were young radicals, and she was open enough to learn.[23]

One had to study previously ignored proletarian youth. But how? Proletarian youth rarely wrote diaries. Lazarsfeld and colleagues developed questionnaires. In 1931 they participated in an experimental study of responses to a radio broadcast, and in doing so discovered mass polling. Now they wanted to do statistical research on proletarian youth and workers. (Lazarsfeld had been semiofficially teaching statistics at the institute for a couple of years.) Economists whom they mobilized for the project directed them, however, to commercial market research, which gathered statistics on consumer preferences for clients. The group founded the Research Center for Psycho-Economics (*Wirtschaftspsychologische Forschungsstelle*). The young socialists hoped that it would generate sufficient money for social research. It did not, but they nonetheless proceeded to organize a study of the unemployed community of Marienthal, an industrially based village south of Vienna. They were eager to learn the social and cultural effect of prolonged unemployment, widely experienced during the Great Depression. They found that unemployment increased apathy instead of revolutionary sentiments. *Marienthal* became a milestone in quantitative social research. After their emigration west, Lazarsfeld and his col-

---

[23] Paul Lazarsfeld, ed., *Jugend und Beruf* (Jena: Fischer, 1931), pp. 1–87, 157–74. See also: Hildegard Hetzer, *Kindheit und Armut* (Leipzig: Hirzel, 1929).

leagues helped make market research the hallmark of capitalism, and quantitative social science the pride of the academy.[24]

The institute's growing international reputation could not shield it from Central European politics. The sight of a thriving socialist institute, supported by Rockefeller fellowships, run by a well-paid academic couple, contrasted with the background of growing economic misery and political tensions. After 1933, German periodicals and publishers, the channels for the institute's publications, were closed to Jewish writers. In Austria, the government crackdown, following the February 1934 socialist uprising, transformed the institute. Director Fadrus was deposed, funds were cut, and the institute was moved to the university. Trying to save their school, the Bühlers played a tough, and unedifying, balancing act.[25] The institute got a respite, but faced mounting financial problems. In 1937, the Bühlers reluctantly gave up, accepting jobs in New York for fall 1938. Events caught up with them: Ten days after the Anschluss, Karl Bühler was arrested, suspended from his job, and held in custody for more than six weeks. To the Nazis, he represented the worst combination: socialism, philo-Semitism, and Austrian patriotism. Charlotte Bühler avowed that they were both "completely unpolitical." They "just wanted to see people respected as people."[26] In interwar Europe, this was a profoundly political stance.[27] Bühler was told that he had to divorce his wife to rehabilitate. Instead, he left Vienna with a backpack, having lost his library, papers, and property. In the United States, neither he nor his wife ever received recognition. He died virtually forgotten in exile in 1963. Charlotte Bühler died eleven years later in Germany.[28]

---

[24] Marie Jahoda and Hans Zeisel, *Die Arbeitslosen von Marienthal* (Leipzig: Hirzel, 1933). The standard account of the *Wirtschaftspsychologische Forschungsstelle* was: Paul Lazarsfeld, "An Episode in the History of Social Research," in *The Intellectual Migration*, ed. Bernard Bailyn and Donald Fleming (Cambridge, Mass.: Harvard University Press, 1969), pp. 270–337. However, historians have recently revised it: Christian Fleck, *Rund um "Marienthal"* (Vienna: Gesellschaftskritik, 1990); Gerhard Benetka, *Psychologie in Wien*, pp. 197–227. Much *Forschungsstelle* material is available in the Lazarsfeld papers, Columbia University (Series 1, boxes 33–5, 38–9).

[25] They assured the institute's new director that socialists were no longer on the staff and that Adler's psychology had no part in the curriculum. Karl Bühler published in periodicals supporting the government. To him, it was a choice between clerical-fascist Austria and the Nazis. Gerhard Benetka, *Psychologie in Wien*, pp. 261–2.

[26] Charlotte Bühler, "Selbstdarstellung," in *Psychologie in Selbstdarstellungen*, ed. Ludwig Pongratz, Werner Traxel, and Ernst Wehner (Bern: Huber, 1972), p. 24.

[27] It was also a touch disingenuous. In 1927 Karl Bühler signed a major petition of Viennese intellectuals supporting socialist cultural policies. Running their institute from the headquarters of the Vienna School Council, both Bühlers were implicated in socialist reform. Their student circle was overwhelmingly socialist (and Jewish). Bühler resigned his membership in the German Psychological Society in 1933, shortly after it had been "Aryanized." He was a firm Schuschnigg supporter.

[28] Gustav Lebzeltern, "Karl Bühler – Lebens und Werke," in Karl Bühler, *Die Uhren der Lebewesen* (Vienna: Böhlau, 1969), pp. 9–70; Achim Eschbach, "Karl Bühler: Sematologist," editor's introduc-

Karl Bühler was the first professor Popper managed to engage. Their styles of thinking differed from the start, but Bühler's spontaneous generosity drew Popper. He felt that he could learn much from the erudite and cultivated master. Bühler's politics made him comfortable, too: "About half of his circle consisted of people of Jewish origin. He was very liberal, anti-anti-Semitic, antifascist."[29] He sat in on all his lectures in psychology and logic and managed to find his way to his colloquium as early as in the first semester. (He also took Charlotte Bühler's courses in youth and social psychology.) In dialogue with Bühler's work, he systematically explored the psychology of learning. During his 1928 Ph.D. examination, Bühler encouraged him to express his ideas and charmingly accepted his criticism. Years later, he wrote Popper a strong recommendation for his job applications abroad, describing his thesis as theoretically "sagacious" and innovative.[30] Popper reciprocated his high esteem: "Bühler was an original thinker, a man of wide reading and culture, a splendid teacher, and a man who acted bravely under fascism. Few men are better, and few are more genuine."[31]

Working with Bühler on cognitive psychology, Popper found himself in the only field in progressive Viennese culture where Kant was taken seriously. As I pointed out in Chapter 1, Viennese progressives grounded their reforms in varieties of empiricist philosophies, and regarded Kantian idealism as reactionary. The Würzburg school's psychologists were, in contrast, decidedly Kantian, and insisted on autonomous thought and a creative mind. Neither empiricism nor Kantianism were progressive or reactionary in themselves. Just as Herbart's radical empiricism could turn out conservative, Kantianism could prove progressive. Bühler introduced to socialist Vienna a competing reform discourse. Popper, who worked his way through Kant and Nelson, felt comfortable with Bühler. He had not yet formulated his philosophical objections to inductivism or associationism, but his own inquiries and those of the Würzburg school converged.

The Würzburg school put an end to the hegemony of Wundt's associationist psychology in Germany. Oswald Külpe and his disciples, Narziss Ach, Karl Bühler, and Otto Selz, opposed the reduction of psychology to physiology. They rejected Wundt's (and Mach's) view that the task of psychology was to establish functional relations among sensations. Külpe demonstrated that not all sensations registered on the mind. A prior selection must have taken place. Association could not alone explain thought.[32] Mental processes were not pictures. Thought could be imageless. Külpe

tion to Karl Bühler, *Theory of Language*, trans. Donald Fraser Goodwin (Amsterdam: John Benjamins, 1990), pp. xiii–xliii.

[29] Popper, fragment of "Bemerkungen über Sprachtheorie und ihre Geschichte" (4, 8).

[30] Karl Bühler, letter of reference for Popper, 1936 (406, 1).

[31] Popper, a single page fragment (3, 37).

[32] Oswald Külpe, *Outlines of Psychology*, trans. E. B. Titchener (New York: Macmillan, 1895), pp. 169–225; *Vorlesungen über Psychologie*, 2nd. ed. (Leipzig: Hirzel, 1922), pp. 187–215.

could not quite show how, but Bühler and Selz did. Their radicalism increased with the years, as the *Gestalt* psychologists (Wertheimer, Köhler, Koffka) joined in rejecting association. The two groups concurred that disparate sensations made no sense. Mental structures, "wholes," or *Gestalten*, constituted thinking's basic elements, organizing data provided by the senses. Selz showed further that the *Gestalten* were task oriented. The mind was a problem solver. For the passive mind learning through association, the Würzburg school substituted an active mind forming knowledge.[33]

Karl Bühler contributed to the Würzburg school a developmental perspective, informed by comparative evolutionary biology. He strove to resolve questions of concept formation by turning to the child's intellectual development. In *The Mental Development of the Child*, he distinguished among three levels of mental development: instinct, training, and intellect. A newly born baby was a bundle of instincts. Like many animals, it gradually acquired sensory and motor skills through training, but a problem-solving intellect distinguished humans and the higher primates. By age three, a child had surpassed all others in development. Intellect was not reducible to training. Association theories could not account for it. Würzburg-style cognitive psychology (*Denkpsychologie*) was needed to explain it.

Language, recognized Bühler, was the key to intellectual development. The sensationalist "picture theory of language" was inadequate: "As soon as objects have received their names, the formation of concepts begins, and these take the place of concrete images. Conceptual knowledge, which is formulated in language, dominates the memory of the child."[34] His study of children's drawings showed that they were products of organized knowledge, a schematic memory, not merely pictorial replication. Reproducing (retelling) fairy tales also involved creative imagination, not mere recollection. The advent of writing put an end to most drawings and fairy tales. Both ontogenetically and philogenetically, writing was an advance over the earlier representational stage. It was an invention, a move from schematic representation (drawing) to symbol to organized symbolic system. Writing "first spoilt drawing, then swallowed it up completely."[35] The growth of knowledge was a result of constant confrontation with new tasks, conceptual reorganization, and creation of new theoretical complexes. Human motivation had as much to do with the simple pleasure of creativity as with the satisfaction of basic needs.

Popper read the major works of Gestalt and Würzburg psychologists. Both his 1927 *Hausarbeit* and his 1928 dissertation referred to them. The first focused on the psychology of learning. He submitted it unfinished to

---

[33] William Berkson and John Wettersten, *Learning from Error*, pp. 13–20, 103–11; John Wettersten, *The Roots of Critical Rationalism* (Amsterdam: Rodopi, 1992), pp. 102–36.

[34] Karl Bühler, *The Mental Development of the Child*, p. 114.

[35] Ibid., p. 120.

the institute. The second focused on cognitive psychology. It was a brief methodological introduction to a study he never completed. The Bühlers' work on child and youth psychology, as well as Else Köhler's book on child development, provided the material for his theoretical reflections on the psychology of learning.[36] *Die Krise der Psychologie* was at the center of his meditations on cognitive psychology. His theses showed, however, no discipleship. He brought Bühler's work to bear on questions that were genuinely his. Unlike Nelson and Gomperz – Gomperz will be discussed shortly – Bühler did not quite set the problems that made Popper's intellectual breakthrough possible. But Bühler did provide rich meditations, on the relationship between logic, psychology, and biology, which Popper could use to try and answer theoretical queries emerging from his study of Nelson and Gomperz. Bühler also provided essential intellectual and emotional support to a brilliant student who had not yet found his way. No more could be asked of a teacher.[37]

" 'HABIT' AND THE 'EXPERIENCE OF LAWFULNESS' IN EDUCATION" (1927)

Popper submitted " 'Gewohnheit' und 'Gesetzerlebnis' " to the Pedagogic Institute in summer 1927. This was the final quasi thesis required of all students completing the two-year program. The founders expected it to bridge academic and pedagogical training, by drawing lessons from scholarly literature for classroom instruction. Josefine Henninger's essay, for example, focused on gymnastics in the first two grades of elementary school.[38] Popper did not abide by this restrictive vision. He conceived of his project as a Kantian critique of the limits of scientific pedagogy. He wished to refocus cognitive psychology on the conflict between dogmatic and critical thinking, so that it better informed reform pedagogy. He apologized profusely for the theoretical character of the thesis. He emphasized that his previous work as a social worker provided the material for his theory and that the practical implications of the thesis were significant. These were rhetorical efforts to fit an innovative theoretical project into the straitjacket of a practical-training thesis. The thesis was maddeningly ambitious. Popper always thought big. From pedagogy to psychology, natural science, social science, and political philosophy, he conceived of his projects as Kantian

---

[36] Elsa Köhler, *Die Personlichkeit des dreijahrigen Kindes (Annchen)* (Leipzig: Hirzel, 1926).

[37] William W. Bartley, III, elaborated on the Bühler–Popper connection in: "Theory of Language and Philosophy of Science as Instruments of Educational Reform: Wittgenstein and Popper as Austrian School Teachers," *Methodological and Historical Essays in the Natural and Social Sciences*, ed. Robert S. Cohen and Marx W. Wartofsky (Boston: Reidel, 1974), esp. pp. 313–15, 320–4.

[38] Josefine Henninger, "Turnen und Gesamtunterricht in der ersten und zweiten Grundschulklasse" (Hausarbeit: Pädagogisches Institut der Stadt Wien, summer 1927), Hoover Archives (443, 14).

critiques that would transform the sciences. That, at the age of twenty-five, he was unable to come anywhere close to completing the thesis is understandable.[39]

Popper thought that his experience as a social worker disclosed the inefficacy of reform pedagogy. The reformers hoped to shape free, self-determining agents, endowed with a firm will and a discerning judgment. Their *Arbeitspädagogik* promoted self-activity and spontaneous learning, but they underestimated the resistance that children's natural conservatism offered to self-activity. Psychologists and pedagogues had failed to distinguish, as Nelson did, between dogmatic and critical thinking. Children were captives of dogmatic thinking. Bühler's child psychology and Bürger's reform pedagogy treated children's mental processes as if they involved a critical intellect, capable of forming judgments.[40] They were wrong. Both philogenetically and ontogenetically, dogmatic thinking preceded critical thinking. Children identified "is" with "ought," searched for order, rejected the unfamiliar, and tended to accept authority. Critical thinking and judgment developed at a fairly late stage of human evolution and life. They entailed a challenge to the perceived order of things: Are things really this way? Must they be? Children, and many adults, never broke with dogmatism to challenge order. School reform faced major obstacles.[41]

Could reform overcome dogmatic thinking? Popper was not optimistic. Children's passivity was not, as commonly assumed, mere attachment to "habits" that education might change. Rather, passivity was grounded in children's search for an orderly universe. The search for lawfulness dominated their mental life. They resisted change and refused to recognize difference because they wished to safeguard lawfulness. Reform pedagogy must recognize that this led to distortion and prejudice. Cognitive psychology must refocus on analyzing experiences of lawfulness, and reform pedagogy must draw implications for instruction. Otherwise, the hopes put on self-activity would be crushed against the walls of dogmatic thinking.[42]

Popper spent forty-four pages, over a third of the thesis, on methodological and theoretical introductions, descriptions of the pedagogical and psychological problem situations, and a definition of his task. The thesis was to have three parts: empirical description – a "phenomenology of the experience of lawfulness" – followed by theory, then by practical "applications." But the project got out of control. Popper completed only the first part, and barely that; the last subsection (pp. 124–7), on the reification of law-

[39] Popper, " 'Gewohnheit' und 'Gesetzerlebnis,' " pp. 3–17, 33, 42–3.
[40] Karl Bühler, *Die geistige Entwicklung des Kindes*; Eduard Bürger, *Arbeitspädagogik*, 2nd. ed. (Leipzig: Engelmann, 1923).
[41] Popper, " 'Gewohnheit' und 'Gesetzerlebnis,' " pp. 15–17, 33–42, 109–18.
[42] Ibid., pp. 3–17, 37, 64–71, 109–17.

fulness and irrational attachments, the *Festhalten*, was cursory. Later in 1927–8, he may have written the theoretical part, intending it to be his dissertation, but he seemed to have run again into difficulties and set the manuscript aside. In *Die beiden Grundprobleme*, he referred to an unpublished work, "Theorie des Intellekts," that could provide empirical support for a deductivist psychology of knowledge, the view that the mind continuously tested human expectations (or "theories") against reality, revising them when frustrated. This may have been the theoretical part of the 1927 thesis.[43] As his interests shifted from psychology to the logic of science, the manuscript – in whatever state of completion – was abandoned and eventually lost.

The 1927 thesis shows that Popper had yet to travel a long distance before he made his breakthrough in the logic of science. He advanced methodological positions that he would repudiate in a few years. He undertook to provide a phenomenology – "not in Husserl's sense" – of dogmatic thinking: a comprehensive description of the psychology of lawfulness among children.[44] Such description, he said, must remain pure, unadulterated by theory. Induction was the scientific method. Psychological theory merely established causal connections among phenomena. Causality was transcendentally deduced and a priori true: The world was inconceivable without it. However, causal explanations in psychology were subject to verification, just as in the natural sciences. Psychological observations required confirmation through introspection. Since the totality of the subject, the "I," was not available in introspection, "personality" was no subject of psychology. Freud's psychoanalysis and Adler's individual psychology violated scientific strictures. They presumed to explain the "I," and imposed theory on empirical data. Trying to emulate physics, they provided a single explanation for psychological phenomena. But psychology was not physics. Its explanations were plural. It did not search for overarching laws, but for typical experiences. It maintained a place between the natural sciences and the *Geisteswissenschaften*. Popper's "method" was a melange of inductivism, a priorism, and psychologism, much influenced by Nelson and Bühler.[45]

Popper faced a problem that would eventually drive him from psychology to the logic of science. Psychology could not explain the growth of knowledge. He regarded the search for lawfulness as typical of dogmatic

---

[43] This is the view of Troels Eggers Hansen, editor of *Die beiden Grundprobleme der Erkenntnistheorie* (Tübingen: Mohr, 1979), pp. 28–9 n. 23. See also Popper, *Autobiography*, p. 78. In " 'Gewohnheit' und 'Gesetzerlebnis' " Popper indicated (p. 87 n.) that the theoretical part would discuss, among others, the problem of psychological association.

[44] " 'Gewohnheit' und 'Gesetzerlebnis,' " pp. 3, 18, 39–43.

[45] Ibid., pp. 18–32, 80 n. Popper also suggested (pp. 31–2) that the notion of the "unconscious" was "mystical," and tantamount to a "death sentence" to scientific methodology. But Freud and Adler failed the test of induction, not falsification. Popper had not yet conceived of falsification.

thinking and discerned three stages in it: anxiety about unfamiliar phenomena; creation of a framework (*Setzung*) to incorporate the new data and re-create lawfulness; attachment (*Festhalten*) to the framework, making it immune to change. Among adults he discerned a fourth stage, identified with critical thinking: revision of the framework in response to conflicting experiences. Yet adults, too, were often captives of dogmatism. In later years, he considered the interchange between dogmatic and critical thinking as a trial-and-error process, essential to the growth of knowledge. In 1927, however, dogmatic thinking represented to Popper an obstacle to learning, not a necessary stage. It remained confined to psychology, never crossing the boundary into logic, the realm of critical thinking. How did one move from dogmatic to critical thinking? Somehow, psychological development brought the child to a point where logic overcame psychology. How could it do so? No transference between psychology and logic, dogmatic and critical thinking, was possible. So long as Popper searched for the production of knowledge in psychology, he could not explain growth.[46]

Popper viewed the child's mind as passive. He made wide use of association psychology to explain lawfulness. The child's "interest" in lawfulness did not mean, he insisted, that constructing a framework was the same as learning. The framework had been latent in the child's mind. New experiences motivated the child to restore lawfulness, but produced no knowledge, no intellectual growth. Contrary to Bühler's theory, the framework did not abstract from reality, but distorted it. It rendered the specific general and the individual typical, thereby creating similarity and familiarity where alterity and difference were appropriate. The child merely associated familiar dimensions of reality with new "foreign" ones, transposing difference into similarity. This was a strangely restrictive view of children's capacities. Bühler and the Würzburg school allowed for much greater freedom and creativity in children's mental life. Popper had also read Selz by this time, but there was no hint in the 1927 thesis of the active, problem-solving Selzian mind that would dominate his later views.[47] The child's passivity, conservatism, and dogmatism contrasted with critical thinking. Intellectual development proved difficult to explain.[48]

Why did Popper deny critical thinking to children? What convinced him of their conservatism and dogmatism? Undoubtedly, his experiences as a social worker played a role. Socialist reform encountered resistance. Proletarian youth mistrusted bourgeois reformers attempting to transform street culture.[49] Popper recounted children's mistrust of "outsiders" and

[46] Ibid., pp. 9–11, 15–17, 33–42, 92–6, 109–27.

[47] Otto Selz, *Über die Gesetze des geordneten Denkverlaufs*, vol. 1 (Stuttgart: Spemann, 1913); Karl Popper, "Die Gedächtnispflege unter dem Gesichtpunkt der Selbsttätigkeit," *Die Quelle* 81 (1931): 607–19.

[48] Popper, " 'Gewohnheit' und 'Gesetzerlebnis,' " pp. 92–117.

[49] Helmut Gruber, *Red Vienna* (New York: Oxford University Press, 1991), chaps. 4–5; J. Robert Wegs, *Growing Up Working Class* (London: Pennsylvania State University Press, 1989), chaps. 3, 4, 6.

attributed it to their psychology.[50] Outsiders were suspect because they were different, and difference threatened lawfulness. Children's refusal to modify their behavior and abide by educational requirements revealed their attachment to order. Natural conservatism explained the refusal of street culture to retreat in the face of *Bildung*. A revolutionary transformation of working-class culture had proved arduous because children were dogmatic.

Children's conservatism was rooted in their anxiety about the unfamiliar (*Angst vor den Fremden*). Anxiety was a typical response to the confrontation with the unknown. It explained children's rejection of novelty (*Ablehnung des Neuen*) and their rush to restore orderliness by establishing a framework. Popper devoted his phenomenology to this motif (pp. 46–92). He borrowed Kierkegaard's distinction between fear (of the known) and anxiety (about the unknown) and proceeded to trace anxiety in the classics of literature (Dostoyevsky, Shakespeare, Strindberg, Lagerlöf), philosophy (James and Jaspers), and psychology (Adler, Bühler). He argued that it played a rarely acknowledged role in a range of psychological, physiological, and political phenomena, among them curiosity, fear of death and pain, heart constriction, helplessness, homesickness, mistrust of strangers. Kierkegaard's response to anxiety – a leap of faith – revealed its danger. Like ancient oracles, religious belief sought to secure protection against destiny from a divinity that was identified with the cosmic order. Superstition did not give in easily. On the contrary, challenges led to conservative reification of the present order. Children objected to any change of rules in their games; adults rejected the Austrian revolution and the republic and hung on to bureaucratic pedantry and church rituals. Anxiety about change produced dogmatic thinking and reactionary politics.[51]

Joy at novelty and change, the welcoming of risks, and a trust in the future were prerequisites for revolution and reform. They were characteristic of critical thinking and a precious rarity among children. Children expressed joy when they managed to reestablish order: "Aha! So must it be." Popper rejected any positive portrayal of the search for order. Adler's idea that children's mental life reflected a quest for protection (*Sicherung*) against painful experience was "speculative." Such "protection" often veiled cowardice and mistrust. It signified reluctance to take risks and rejection of anything foreign to the children's *Heimat*.[52] But Heimat needed opening to the unfamiliar, not protection. Comfort in closure, satisfaction in lawfulness, or rest in order were impermissible. Homesickness (*Heimweh*), mistrust, and attachment to habit reflected fear of the unknown; one fought and conquered them.[53] "We must go on into the unknown, courageously," Popper would say in *The Open Society*.[54] The sentiments and ideas that

---

[50] Popper, " 'Gewohnheit' und 'Gesetzerlebnis,' " pp. 53, 65–6.

[51] Ibid., pp. 46–61, 71–9, 125–7.   [52] Ibid., pp. 62–9, 79–84.   [53] Ibid., pp. 53–61.

[54] *The Open Society*, vol. 1, p. 177.

would motivate his political philosophy had already informed the 1927 thesis.

Indeed, the psychology of dogmatism required only historicization and sociologization to yield the central thesis of *The Open Society*. Dogmatism reflected anxiety about change and difference. Conflation of *is* and *ought* was central to it and led to efforts to sanction the status quo. Political conservatism and philosophical dogmatism, exemplified by Aristotle and Hegel, demonstrated its reach beyond childhood.[55] Repeated efforts to control destiny through religious superstition and oracles testified to anxiety about the unknown. Popper needed only to translate these anxieties from the individual to society and history to reach "the burden of civilization," his explanation for totalitarian philosophy and politics. To be sure, his politics in 1927 was more radical than in *The Open Society*. His socialist sympathies were never in doubt. His reservations about school reform, party functionaries, and civil servants had not yet developed into ambivalence about socialism. Historicism and Marxism were not yet oracular philosophies. All the same, his refusal of Heimat and his demand that it be transformed into an open society were already there.

The motif of anxiety about the "alien" may testify to the origin of Popper's vision of the Open Society. Popper was sensitive enough to recognize that the resistance of working-class youth to reformers was rooted in suspicion of outsiders, but his psychological explanation ignored class and culture and focused on anxiety about the "foreign." An assimilated Jew, he had anxieties about acceptance that sensitized him to the youths' rejection of outsiders. He tied together his own plight and the difficulties of school reform. Anxieties about difference and change produced dogmatism, authoritarianism, and an enclosed Heimat. There was no room for compromise with them; they needed to be fought and overcome. The prospects for scientific pedagogy, school reform, socialism, and Jewish assimilation all depended on the triumph of critical thinking and the Open Society.[56]

The analyst of anxiety was himself an anxious person. His attraction to Kierkegaard may have been brief, limited to a short period after his disillusion with communism, but he conducted a lifelong battle against Kierkegaard's existential dilemmas. He never considered religious commitment a viable option and commended Jaspers for rendering Kierkegaard's concept of anxiety useful for psychology.[57] But Kierkegaard's description

[55] Popper, " 'Gewohnheit' und 'Gesetzerlebnis,' " pp. 109–17.

[56] Malachi Hacohen, "Dilemmas of Cosmopolitanism: Karl Popper, Jewish Identity, and 'Central European Culture,' " *Journal of Modern History* 71 (1999): 105–49.

[57] Popper, " 'Gewohnheit' und 'Gesetzerlebnis,' " p. 47. The works in question were Søren Kierkegaard, *The Concept of Anxiety* and *Fear and Trembling, Kierkegaard's Writings*, trans. Howard and Edna Wong, vols. 8 and 6, respectively (Princeton, N.J.: Princeton University Press, 1980, 1983); Karl Jaspers, *Psychologie der Weltanschauungen*, 3d ed. (Berlin: Springer, 1925).

of the human condition and his search for authenticity clearly struck a chord in him. In *The Open Society*, he described the commitment to rationalism in much the same way as Kierkegaard did his leap of faith.[58] Years later, writing his *Autobiography*, he returned to Kierkegaard and his quest for authenticity. He presented Kierkegaard's quest as self-involved and contrasted it with his own philosophical commitment to the "real" world.[59] Eventually, he chose not to frame the *Autobiography* in this manner. He cared deeply about these issues, but felt uncomfortable speaking about them.

His internal strife nevertheless expressed itself surreptitiously in his work. The struggle between fear and hope, suspicion and trust, order and change, which he discerned in children and in society, was also his own. His life represented a singular fusion of hope and anxiety, openness to change and attachment to habit, critical awareness of one's self and mistrust of friends who refused him blind protection. The 1927 thesis condemned those who distrusted everything and counted on the worst possible future. Throughout the interwar period, however, he himself expected the worst for Central Europe.[60] He was proved right, and his emigration saved his life. Leaving Vienna behind, he relocated to New Zealand, a provincial society on the other side of the globe, adjusting quickly to the English-speaking world, learning the language with remarkable speed. In postwar England, however, he was notoriously attached to routine, to a rhythm of ceaseless work in his secluded rural house. His correspondence, especially when a new publication hung in the balance, or confrontations with colleagues or students emerged, expressed extraordinary anxiety and mistrust of friends.[61] He embodied the tensions he traced in his subjects.

Popper negotiated these tensions brilliantly in his work. His philosophy arbitrated the claims of order and change, certitude and criticism, universality and difference. The resolution was unique. In 1927, at twenty-five, having broken all rules of the bourgeois *cursus honorum*, he was more impatient with lawfulness than ever after. At this moment, he found virtue only in change and difference, taking pleasure at deconstructing intellectual frameworks and destabilizing political order. Even here, however, he was engaged in demarcation, delineating the boundaries of scientific pedagogy, demarcating the limits of a possible rational order. Permanent negotiation

---

[58] Vol. 2, chap. 24.   [59] Draft of *Autobiography*, Hoover Archives (134, 4).

[60] *Autobiography*, pp. 104–5; Frederick Dorian (Fritz Deutsch) to Popper, 10 April 1942, Popper Archives (28, 6, under Hellin). See also my "Karl Popper in Exile: The Viennese Progressive Imagination and the Making of *The Open Society*," *Philosophy of the Social Sciences* 26 (December 1996): esp. 455–7.

[61] Three examples: correspondence with Julius Kraft, 1932–5, concerning *Die beiden Grundprobleme* and *Logik der Forschung* (316, 24, under Victor Kraft); with Alfred Braunthal, 1943–4, concerning *The Open Society* (28, 2–3); with Paul Arthur Schilpp, 1971, concerning *The Philosophy of Karl Popper*, students, and critics (334, 3).

of freedom, difference, and change with rationality, universality, and order, constant experimentation with theories and traditions: This was his philosophy's great appeal. He provided a liberal response to both dogmatism and "poststructuralism" by finding a place for both in a process of perpetual revision and rethinking.

IN HEINRICH GOMPERZ'S ORBIT: LIBERALISM AND SCIENCE, OLD AND NEW

Popper's 1927 thesis demonstrated an interest in the relationship between logic and psychology. Bühler and Nelson both wrote on the subject, but Popper followed the lead of a third thinker, Heinrich Gomperz (1873–1942). Gomperz was a professor of philosophy at the university. He had an enormous breadth of interests and published extensively on epistemology and classical philosophy. Polanyi introduced Popper to him in 1926, and he became a mentor of sorts to the aspiring student. A circle of intellectuals met on Saturdays at his Viennese villa, but Popper did not participate in these meetings.[62] Rather, for the next two years, he met Gomperz privately to discuss psychology. He usually gave Gomperz a manuscript to read, receiving it back with comments. They got along quite well, it seems. Gomperz was never scathing and ironical with him, Popper said, as he had been with other students. All in all, they may have met only eight to ten times.[63] But Popper also took Gomperz's course on Plato in the spring of 1926 and read all his works.[64] They provided Popper with an incomparable guide to epistemology, psychology, and the methodology of science.

Gomperz made no effort to mold Popper intellectually. He saw equally the faults of all philosophies and never succeeded in forming his own, and so he imposed nothing on the young student. But he clarified complex issues to Popper, drew his attention to different approaches, and provided useful references. Popper's 1928 dissertation, "Zur Methodenfrage der Denkpsychologie" (On the Methodological Problem of Cognitive Psychology), testified to his influence.[65] Following Gomperz, Popper searched for a secondary science (*sekundäre Wissenschaft*) that would delineate the boundaries between disciplines. He shared Gomperz's interest in the biological bases of learning. This would become a lifelong concern for him.

---

[62] Friedrich Stadler, "Heinrich Gomperz und Karl Popper im Kontext des Logischen Empirismus," in *Heinrich Gomperz, Karl Popper und die Österreichische Philosophie*, ed. Martin Seiler and Friedrich Stadler (Amsterdam: Rodopi, 1994), esp. pp. 5–6.

[63] *Autobiography*, pp. 20–1, 74–5, 81–5; draft of *Autobiography*, p. 72 (corrected typescript, 134, 12).

[64] Transcripts, Hoover Archives (335, 19).

[65] Karl Popper, "Zur Methodenfrage der Denkpsychologie" (Ph.D. diss.: University of Vienna, 1928).

Heinrich Gomperz was a scion of a patrician Viennese Jewish family. His father, Theodor Gomperz, was a famous classicist whose *Griechische Denker* (*Greek Thinkers*) popularized classical philosophy throughout the German- and English-speaking worlds.[66] Theodor Gomperz regarded Greek philosophy as presaging the Enlightenment and modern utilitarianism and was responsible for translating Mill's works into German. The son followed the father's classical pursuits. At eighteen, he organized with his gymnasium friends a Socratic circle (*Sokratiker-Kreis*) to discuss politics, economics, and science. Identifying their progressive Viennese milieu with the Periclean age, members took the names of Greek sophists. Later in life, Heinrich distanced himself from both classical Greece and his father's scholarship: "While my father had been supremely interested in all these early thinkers insofar as they had had glimpses of 'the truth,' my chief aim has been to realize to what extent their ways of looking at nature and life had been different from ours."[67] Contrary to his father's views, he said, Greek ideals of freedom and knowledge, especially the notion of "inner freedom," differed radically from modern ones. Popper appreciated Heinrich Gomperz's classical scholarship, but in *The Open Society*, he preferred the older Gomperz's approach. Identifying the Athenians' war with Sparta with the Open Society's war with fascism, Popper reaffirmed the abiding relevance of classical Greece to the modern world.

Viennese Jewish patricians had educated their children in German culture with fervor. Theodor Gomperz had been brought up this way and, in turn, tried to transmit the legacy to his children.[68] His daughter recalled the austere intellectual atmosphere of their childhood. Their house was cut off from the "real things in life. . . . Until my fourteenth year [my father] appeared to me as a ghost, residing in a big library."[69] Heinrich's own education in philosophy began with English positivism (Mill and Spencer) and Herbart's metaphysics. Then came the encounter with Mach, a "Buddha of science," "the incarnation of the scientific spirit."[70] Gomperz accepted the monistic world view. He conceived of the monumental project of *Weltanschauungslehre* (The Theory of Worldview) as constructing a new worldview in light of Mach's monism. The project signaled both an end and a beginning in the history of philosophy. One of the last major efforts at nineteenth-century system building, it also denoted the end of the "phi-

[66] Theodor Gomperz, *Griechische Denker*, 3 vols. (Leipzig: Veit, 1896–1906).

[67] Heinrich Gomperz, "Autobiographical Remarks," in his *Philosophical Studies*, ed. Daniel S. Robinson (Boston: Christopher Publishing House, 1953), p. 20.

[68] Theodor Gomperz, *Essays und Errinerungen* (Stuttgart: Deutsche Verlags-Anstalt, 1905), pp. 1–9.

[69] Bettina Holzapfel-Gomperz, *Reisnerstraße 13. Meine Jugend im Wien der Jahrhundertwende* (Vienna: Österreichische Verlagsanstalt & Schroll, 1980), p. 14.

[70] Heinrich Gomperz, "Autobiographical Remarks," p. 18.

losophy of consciousness." It explored new paths: the analysis of language and meaning.[71]

Weltanschauungslehre, said Gomperz, would "establish a relationship free of contradictions [*Widersprüchslos*] of all those ideas, [emerging] from different scientific disciplines as well as practical life, [and] used in the reproduction of facts."[72] It was not a practical science, establishing facts, but a theoretical one, setting the preconditions for the different sciences, and seeking their integration into a unified *Weltanschauung*. He planned four volumes, methodology, noology (science of cognition), ontology, and cosmology, but completed only the methodology volume and the first half of noology. He lost interest in the project – it did not evoke sufficient response, he said – and abandoned it. The project itself resisted closure. Mach's dissolution of the "Subject" mitigated against traditional system building, bound with the totalizing "I." Gomperz was also disinclined to impose closure. His changing interests and developing theories made completion difficult. The cloud of *Weltanschauungslehre* hung over his head for the rest of his life. It marked his loss of confidence in the ability of philosophy to overcome contemporary problems. He became an image of his own melancholic philosophy.

Weltanschauungslehre remained, however, a magnificent account of the state of philosophy at the turn of the century. The methodology volume defined the tasks, basic concepts, and method of *Weltanschauung* theory. Gomperz ran four metaconcepts through analytical and historical examinations: substance, identity, relation, and form. Analytically, he discussed them from the perspectives of epistemology, concept construction (*Begriffsumbildung*), and meaning, emphasizing the relationship between the last two. Historically, he established a four-stage view of philosophy: animistic-theological, metaphysical, ideological (empirical), and critical. In this, he followed Comte's and Hegel's example, but used different criteria for periodization: transitions in emotive dispositions toward self and reality. In both first stages, mental representations reflected attachment to objects. A chasm separated these stages from both the empirical and critical periods when representations reflected subjective feelings and were bound with consciousness and self. Now philosophy was approaching a new caesura. Subjectivity was running its course, and unified consciousness was dissolving into discontinuous feelings. All concepts had to be grounded in feelings. Gomperz's philosophy, *Pathempirismus* (emotive empiricism), represented the transition to a fifth period, a new *Weltanschauung*.

---

[71] Idem, *Weltanschauungslehre. Ein Versuch die Hauptprobleme der allgemeinen theoretischen Philosophie geschictlich zu entwickeln und sachlich zu bearbeiten*, vol. 1, *Methodologie*, and vol. 2, pt. 1, *Noologie – Einleitung und Semasiologie* (Jena: Diederichs, 1905–8).

[72] Ibid., vol. 1, p. 17.

Pathempiricism was a response to the crisis of "immanence." Mach's monism stipulated that there was no difference between reality and mental states, no going beyond sensations to "consciousness," "experience," or "objects." The knowing subject, the *I*, became problematic. Somehow the stream of sensations merged into consciousness of "the world as an organized event." But how? Gomperz held on to empiricism: Concepts were rooted in experience. At the same time, he accepted Kant's critique of Hume: Concepts were no mere representation of experience. The subject's spontaneous activities (*Ich-Tätigkeiten*) modified experience. Yet Kant's powerful cognition no longer seemed a possibility. Gomperz suggested that feelings – not living emotives, but cognitive feelings – gave experience forms and produced representations: "According to the path-empirical concept of form, all form is feeling, so that, in consciousness, the total contents of experience are represented through ideas, as against all their forms [that] are represented through feelings."[73] Analytic psychology explained the working of cognitive feelings, and evolutionary biology explained their genesis:

> Every theoretical urge serves initially to preserve and protect life. But it tends to acquire independent biological significance as a functional stimulus to the main purpose of developed organs or faculties. . . . Theoretical urges appear above all as a double challenge to the organism, human or animal, to know the environment and to understand the interdependence [of organism and environment].[74]

The organism's progress determined the limits of consciousness. Pathempiricism moved from epistemology to psychology and biology.

The "naturalization" of knowledge problematized the autonomy of science, epistemology, and logic. The second volume of *Weltanschauungslehre*, noology, devoted an extended discussion to the relationship of psychology and logic.[75] Gomperz separated radically between thought (*Gedachte*) and thinking (*Denken*), objective and subjective ideas (*Gedanken*), logical relationships among statements and cognitive psychological processes (experiences of consciousness). He rejected as metaphysical the realistic view that statements existed independent of experiences creating them, the *Gedachte* independently of the *Denken*.[76] But if he accepted monism epistemologi-

---

[73] Ibid., vol. 1, p. 274.   [74] Ibid., vol. 1, p. 9.

[75] Ibid., vol. 2, pp. 2–53. Noology dealt fundamentally with epistemology, but Gomperz insisted (vol. 1, pp. 21–2) that pathempiricism no longer pursued consciousness, but cognitive processes. The new term denoted the science of mental phenomena.

[76] Ibid., vol. 2, p. 140: "Realism's distinctive mark is conceiving of the logical contents of statements as an existing reality, standing on their own, independently of their formative experiences." Popper would later adopt precisely this realism with his notion of World 3 (*Objective Knowledge*, chaps. 2–4). In his *Autobiography* (pp. 20–1), he reported that Gomperz had told him that his belief in an orderly

cally, he rejected it methodologically. Logic and psychology represented divergent modes of investigation:

> The relations of order that logic and psychology establish among ideas differ from each other. In logic we speak, for example, of higher and lower concepts, of statements which, in regard to their validity, are necessary through each other. One does not find comparable [relations] in psychology. It would be meaningless to say that the facts of consciousness are higher or lower, or that one [fact] must be valid, if the other is. On the other hand, psychology treats of the temporal development of particular thoughts and of causal laws, according to which one [thought] gives rise to the other. This manner of observation finds no application in logic, since concepts, statements and proofs do not develop temporally and therefore cannot act as causes and influences on one another.[77]

Gomperz argued at length against all efforts to confound logical and psychological explanations. He especially contested psychologism, that is, the reduction of logical categories to psychological ones, and inveighed against psychological explanations of scientific procedures. When analyzing observations, he said, psychology and physics could construct parallel sequences of psychological and physical events, but it was impossible to explain one causal sequence through the other: "Scientific explanation of the interdependence of objective ideas is a logical and not psychological task."[78]

Having separated logic and psychology radically, Gomperz needed to reunite them in his *Weltanschauung*. This was especially the case since he insisted, in accordance with "neutral monism," that they treated of the same subject matter. He trusted noology to reconcile contradictions between the two, but the negotiations remained at a preliminary stage. Gomperz proceeded instead to distinguish between what he called semasiology (*Semasiologie;* semantics), which was to investigate the formation and meaning of statements, and alethology, which was to ascribe truth and falsity to them. He completed the part on semasiology alone. Taking a linguistic turn, he argued that thought was accessible only through language. He formulated a series of problems concerning the formation and meaning of statements, which traditional epistemologies could not solve. Realism, nominalism and rationalism represented historically the metaphysical, ideological (empirical), and critical ages. Pathempiricism represented their "dialectical" synthesis, and solved the problems of semasiology. Demonstrating the role of cognitive feelings in constituting statements, Gomperz showed how logic and psychology interacted, but his arbitration between logic and psychol-

---

external world was "realist." It is not clear, however, how precisely he recalled his epistemological positions of the mid-1920s.

[77] Ibid., vol. 2, pp. 9–10. [78] Ibid., vol. 2, p. 11.

ogy was limited to theoretical resolution of epistemological problems. Otherwise, semasiology merely prevented collisions between incompatible methods. The system remained decidedly pluralistic. A monistic worldview did not emerge.

Weltanschauungslehre represented a bundle of tensions, theoretically resolved, but historically ready to explode. Could theoretical philosophy survive without a knowing Subject? Was a grand Hegelian synthesis possible once consciousness dissolved into sensations? Whence the belief in a progressive unified history? It was no surprise, perhaps, that *Weltanschauungslehre* remained unfinished. Gomperz was not one to swim against the current. His linguistic turn, reinforced by his contacts with the Vienna Circle, culminated, during the interwar period, in a shift to analytic philosophy. Philosophy could not confront great questions; it may perhaps explain them away as terminological pseudoproblems. He did not accept logical positivism wholesale and dissented especially from the crusade against metaphysics, but he left theoretical philosophy to young believers, like Popper, who took *Weltanschauungslehre* seriously.

Gomperz recognized a remarkable philosophical achievement when he saw one. Having read *Die beiden Grundprobleme* late in 1932, he accepted the major tenets of Popper's revolutionary science, but drew a different philosophy of life from it.[79] Popper confidently confronted the challenge of conjectural fallibilistic science. He rejoiced at the endless striving for scientific truth that never reached certainty. Moreover, he believed his science provided a model for social reform. "You do have to act," he said many years later.[80] "For acting you have to believe in certain things, even if sometimes they are not true. . . . Afterwards, perhaps, you can revise your beliefs, although you may not really have enough time." There was no cause for despair. In contrast, Gomperz emphasized the unbridgeable gap between science and life. Science provided no cognitive certainties. It was forever open to revision. Life demanded immediate action, based on partial knowledge. Action's consequences were often irreversible. Physicians faced the situation daily, and so did politicians. Politics demanded belief and loyalty, not skepticism and questioning. The "tragedy of the scientific spirit [is] its conflict with the 'exigencies of action,'" he concluded.[81]

The march of fascism echoed in Gomperz's philosophy. His pessimism and "decisionism" betrayed resignation in the face of an impending doom. He was unable to offer resistance to the decline of Austrian liberal culture. As was the case with other twentieth-century thinkers, pessimism surrep-

---

[79] Gomperz to Oskar Siebeck (Mohr publishing house), 21 December 1932; Gomperz to Popper, 27 December 1932, Popper Archives (300, 9).

[80] Edward Zerin, "Karl Popper on God" [1969], *Skeptic* 6:2 (1998): 48.

[81] Gomperz, "Autobiographical Remarks," p. 19; "Die Wissenschaft und die Tat" [1934], in *Werturteilsstreit*, ed. Hans Albert and Ernst Topitsch (Darmstadt: Wissenschaftliche Buchgesellschaft, 1971), pp. 383–414; *The Limits of Cognition and the Exigencies of Action* (Berkeley: University of California, 1938). Both works made explicit references to Popper's scientific model.

titiously offered an excuse for wrong political choices. Gomperz represented the old guard of Jewish Pan-German nationalists. Prior to World War I, he was committed to limiting the Slavs' influence in the Habsburg Empire. His World War I essays on the philosophy of war were exemplary for their detachment, but they made war acceptable for the like-minded: those who considered themselves both cosmopolites and patriots.[82] The assumptions underlying his essays – inadequate global resources could not sustain the world's population; ergo, war and power politics were inevitable – made a mockery of cosmopolitanism. In 1920 he attacked Wilsonian cosmopolitanism and postwar treaties.[83] He supported unification with Germany all the way to the Anschluss and World War II.[84] In 1934, he refused to join the Christian-Social "Fatherland Front" because of its opposition to unification. Fired from his position as a professor, he found himself teaching in California, developing his political philosophy.[85] He could be kind to socialists, like Polanyi, but was skeptical of democracy, sympathetic to the free market, and supportive of an inegalitarian distribution of wealth. All the malaise of the old Austrian liberalism metamorphosed in Gomperz. Pessimism and "decisionism" shifted responsibility for the catastrophe from his own hypernationalism to the irrationality of politics. They were the luxury of a declining genius who was wrong all the way.

Popper stipulated that we must be optimistic in spite of it all.[86] Progressive liberalism could find salvation only in a new generation, ready "to start all over again."[87] Gomperz's opposition to psychologism and his exploration of evolutionary epistemology struck chords in Popper, but entangled in Gomperz's myriad of problems, his 1928 dissertation reached a dead end. Shortly after, he cut through the knot of Gomperz's problems with a renewed belief in the logic of science. He redefined the grounds of philosophy to make them invincible to the challenges that had defeated Gomperz. Later he would complete Gomperz's project, by constructing a unified realistic worldview on the basis of his new epistemology. The "conquest of nihilism" had to begin, however, with a credo that the tired, beleaguered, and skeptical Gomperz was unwilling to accept. Rationality could be saved, provided it was declared first a matter of logic alone, then of critical discourse in general. Psychology – "cognitive feelings" not excepted – had to be excluded as immaterial. Intellectual virtuosity alone was insufficient for this rescue operation. Youthful confidence, rational belief,[88] and a measure of blindness were necessary. Popper had them all.

---

[82] *Philosophie des Krieges in Umrissen* (Gotha: Perthes, 1915).

[83] *Die Idee der überstaatlichen Rechtsordnung* (Vienna: Strache, 1920).

[84] "Autobiographical Remarks," pp. 15–16, 23–4.

[85] See the essays collected in *Philosophical Studies*.

[86] Popper, *The Myth of the Framework* (London: Routledge, 1994), p. xiii.

[87] Popper, *Logik der Forschung*, p. iii.

[88] This refers to Kant's *Vernunftglaube*: "Was heißt: Sich im Denken orienti(e)ren?" [1786], *Gesammelte Schriften (Akademieausgabe)* (Berlin: Reimer, 1912), 8:131–47.

"ON THE METHODOLOGICAL PROBLEM OF
COGNITIVE PSYCHOLOGY" (1928):
POPPER'S INTELLECTUAL STALEMATE

Popper submitted his dissertation to the University of Vienna in summer 1928. In his *Autobiography*, he described the thesis as a haphazard affair. He dropped large portions of the manuscript, based on years of research in psychology, and submitted instead a methodological introduction, written at the last minute.[89] The thesis's ninety-odd pages reflected this erratic composition. Popper often discussed ideas and approaches cursorily. He digressed a great deal, neglecting to tie the digressions tightly to the thesis's major methodological concerns. The frequent shifts in the thesis's foci were difficult to follow. The second part especially (pp. 46–78) was not fully thought out. Popper's effort to establish Bühler's methodology as a prerequisite for cognitive psychology did little to advance his larger project: understanding the relationship among logic, psychology, and biology. He probed questions of tremendous significance but faced overwhelming difficulties. Gomperz's *Weltanschaaungslehre* crumbled under the effort to relate the explanatory frameworks of the different sciences. What hope could a twenty-six-year-old have to answer such questions? No wonder the dissertation became a turning point. Shortly after, Popper confined his interest to the logic of science, then to natural science methodology. There, the problem of the growth of knowledge became manageable.

The purpose of the thesis, stated Popper, was to outline some of the methodological preconditions for scientific practice in cognitive psychology. In *Die Krise der Psychologie* (The Crisis in Psychology) Bühler established his methodology as a prerequisite for a theory of language.[90] Popper intended to show that the same methodology was equally necessary for cognitive psychology. Külpe had already pursued, said Popper, a "transcendental method" for psychology, but he, Popper, was developing Gomperz's idea of a secondary science that would establish methodological ground rules for all sciences. Such a metascience would neither produce knowledge nor prescribe any one method. Rather, it would clarify the relationship among the different sciences, compare their methods, criticize their practices, and suggest new orientations. Schlick assigned similar functions to epistemology vis-à-vis natural science. He, Popper, wished to extend them to psychology through Gomperz's semasiology. He was aware of the problematic nature of his "Kantian" procedure – Fries had criticized it – but he was not claiming a synthetic a priori validity for his methodology. On the contrary, he would subject its ramifications for research to exami-

---

[89] *Autobiography*, p. 78.   [90] Karl Bühler, *Die Krise der Psychologie* (Jena: Fischer, 1927), esp. p. 29.

nation. Bühler's method would answer Külpe's, Gomperz's, and Schlick's quest for a secondary science.[91]

As Bühler's interests shifted, during the 1920s, from child psychology to linguistic theory, he was adjusting his methodology. In *Die Krise der Psychologie* he focused on the social significance of language. He formed the concept of *Steuerung*, the steering of the community through discourse, the social control and modification of behavior that the community exercised through language. He argued that *Steuerung* required a different conception of linguistic functions from those currently prevailing among psychologists. One could not limit language, as Wundt did, to individual "expression." It was a system of communication, involving an exchange of signs. In contrast to animals, human communication also contained representations of reality, entailing a descriptive function of language (*Darstellungsfunktion*). This function accounted for culture, the context of meaning for human behavior. Bühler suggested that no contemporary methodology could alone develop linguistic theory. A synthesis was necessary. He adjusted his own methodology, he said, to take account of behaviorism and other approaches. He now offered his synthesis as a solution to the current crisis in psychology.[92]

The current methodological crisis resulted from the collapse of the associationist paradigm, especially Mach's positivist, sensationalist psychology. There was now a proliferation of methodologies that often addressed aspects of psychology effectively, but extended themselves improperly to the entire field. Linguistic theory demonstrated that no one method was capable of addressing the different levels of human psychology. Understanding subjective experiences (*Erlebnisse*) was as essential as interpreting behavior (*Benehmen*), or analyzing thought structures (*objektive geistige Gebilde*). They were all interrelated. The unity of psychology demanded methodological pluralism, but also coordination. Behaviorism dealt effectively with aspects of behavior, but was unable to address questions about its meaning. It was of no help with inner experience and intellectual processes. *Geisteswissenschaftliche* psychology from Dilthey to Spranger interpreted thought structures well, but ignored the role of instincts in behavior. Only a methodological synthesis integrating the three levels of

---

[91] Popper, "Zur Methodenfrage der Denkpsychologie," pp. ii–v.

[92] Bühler, *Die Krise der Psychologie*, esp. pp. 29–62. In his articles from 1918 on, as well as in his groundbreaking *Sprachtheorie* (Jena: Fischer, 1934), pp. 24–33, Bühler spoke explicitly of three linguistic functions (which he reformulated occasionally): expression (*Ausdruck*), appeal (*Appell*), and description. The first consisted of uncontrolled signs, released in response to instinctual stimulation. The second was communicative, directed at others, aiming to elicit response. The third was representational and descriptive, an intellectual operation requiring a degree of abstraction, describing states of affairs, or symbolically representing objects. Popper deployed this classification in his work (e.g, "Denkpsychologie," pp. 46–7; *Conjectures and Refutations*, pp. 134–5, 293–5) and recognized its importance in *Autobiography* (p. 74).

psychology – experience, behavior, and intellectual structure – could over-come the methodological confusion in psychology.[93]

Popper toed Bühler's line, accepting his program and defending it against his enemies, but he aimed higher. He used his program as a site for rethink-ing scientific theory. He sought to demonstrate that the methodological problems raised by Bühler would not reach resolution until a secondary science had arbitrated the relationship between the sciences. His critique of Schlick combined the two tasks. Bühler criticized *Gestalt* psychology for physicalism, the translation of psychological structures into physiological ones. Popper defended Bühler's methodological pluralism against Schlick's (and the Gestaltists') "physicalism" and showed that Schlick's reduction of psychology to physics was no alternative to semasiology. Psychophysics was impossible, and physicalism was not a secondary science. Bühler's method-ology, in contrast, opened psychology to biological perspectives, making a promising beginning to a metascience linking logic, psychology, and biology.[94]

Popper presented Schlick's *Allgemeine Erkenntnislehre (General Theory of Knowledge)* as a countermodel to Bühler's *Die Krise der Psychologie*.[95] Both Bühler and Schlick were Popper's Ph.D. examiners, but in contrast to the tribute Popper paid to Bühler, he singled out Schlick for criticism. Schlick had come to Vienna from Bonn in 1922 to occupy Mach's chair in the philosophy of the inductive sciences. His *Allgemeine Erkenntnislehre* reflected his views prior to Wittgenstein's influence and the Vienna Circle. Popper read the book first about 1922, then again with the publication of the second edition (1925). It facilitated his understanding of major epistemo-logical problems from Hume and Kant to Mach and Husserl. He greatly admired its clarity and, in later years, called it "a milestone," "one of the greatest epistemological works since Kant."[96] Yet, he gave few signs of his admiration in the dissertation. Schlick represented the enemy.

Schlick devoted a long chapter in *Allgemeine Erkenntnislehre* to criticism of simplistic physicalist views, such as Mach's neutral monism and phe-nomenalism, but he demanded that psychology model its methods on the natural sciences and, more specifically, on physics. He rejected separate physical and mental realms, body and mind. There were no special laws governing the mind. The physical universe extended to "the mental," and

[93] Bühler, *Die Krise der Psychologie*, esp. pp. 1–62. Bühler devoted the rest of the work to critiques of different psychological approaches. Psychoanalysis was the one approach he refused to integrate into scientific psychology. He used his expertise as a child psychologist to launch an attack on the psy-choanalytic developmental model, and especially on the pleasure principle (p. 162 hr. ff.).

[94] Popper, "Denkpsychologie," pp. ii–v, 1–5, 46–8, 62–70.

[95] Moritz Schlick, *Allgemeine Erkenntnislehre*, 2d ed. (Berlin: Springer, 1925).

[96] Popper to Albert Blumberg, 2 November 1974, Hoover Archives (277, 27); Popper, draft of *Autobi-ography*, Hoover Archives (136, 1), p. 40a; idem, "Erinnerungen an Schlick" [1984], Hoover Archives (252, 1).

physical laws applied to the mind. He allowed for two conceptual systems, psychological and physiological, but required that psychological concepts be expressed in quantitative physical terms. Psychologists must dispose of introspection and other "prescientific" methods: "The reduction of psychology to brain physiology is the demand made by our parallelism."[97]

Popper objected strongly to both physicalism and psychophysical parallelism. He conceded that the choice between Bühler's pluralism, which recognized the interaction of body and mind, and Schlick's physicalism could not be logically decided. Interactionism and parallelism were both logically possible. Still, a methodological separation between physics and psychology was essential. Transference of methods from physics to psychology was impractical. The Gestaltists succeeded in translating psychological laws into physical terms, but only after obtaining these laws in psychological research. One could not begin with a physiological hypothesis and search for psychological laws. Schlick's physicalism, insisted Popper, offered no working hypothesis for psychology. There were no practical applications for quantitative methods and physiological explanations in psychology, or the *Geisteswissenschaften*. The positivist ideal of methodological unity of the sciences was, at least for the time being, logically problematic and methodologically impractical. It was founded on belief in the empiricist worldview and an imposition of the natural science model on other sciences. An attempt to limit psychology to physiological explanations would spell out the end of the discipline. Psychology must remain autonomous.[98]

The critique of physicalism took more than half of the dissertation. In the rest, Popper showed that, like linguistic theory, cognitive psychology operated on three levels: experience, behavior, and intellectual structure. Bühler thought that he demonstrated their necessity through a "Kantian" critique. Popper emulated his procedure, showing that each level was indispensable and required different methods. His discussion revealed his theoretical queries and methodological dilemmas during this period. He would reformulate, and resolve, these dilemmas in natural science methodology a few years later. As outlined in the dissertation, they were unlikely to reach a satisfactory resolution. He was reaching an impasse in psychology.

The necessity of behavior for cognitive psychology was clearly the most difficult to demonstrate, but Popper argued that functional (*Zweckmässig*) behavior was purposeful behavior, and cognitive psychology could help explain functional failures or blunders. Mach and Gomperz had already noticed, said Popper, that, occasionally, different situations trigger similar emotional reactions. A response appropriate to one situation repeated itself

---

[97] Schlick, *Allgemeine Erkenntnislehre*, chaps. 25–6, 31–4. Quotation is on p. 288.

[98] "Denkpsychologie," pp. 6–45. The section on parallelism (pp. 39–45) is possibly the most cogent and insightful part of the thesis.

in another, inappropriate one. The animal and child psychologist Volkelt explained the mistake as rooted in a biological inability to make distinctions. Both situations meant the same for the animal. The behaviorist Morgan clarified the association mechanism operating in such cases. Particular concepts were associated with particular emotions. When the animal mistakenly established an identity of situations, its emotional response led to dysfunctional behavior. If cognitive psychology was to explain such mistakes, argued Popper, it needed to consider both situation and behavior and interpret their meaning for the animal.[99]

It was obvious that intellectual structures were a subject matter of cognitive psychology.[100] Popper focused, therefore, on the appropriate methodology for their study. He wondered how the various elements of language and thought, chaotic perceptions and words, were organized into meaningful statements and conceptual structures.[101] He rejected the "nominalist view" that mere association of facts could give rise to meaningful statements. Bühler's discovery of imageless thought, he said, demonstrated the possibility of active thinking, but he refused the opposite view, too. Sympathetic though he was to Selz's task-oriented mind, he declined to assign it an active role in organizing perceptions into meaningful structures. He maintained, against Selz, the partial validity of association. The mind's operation, he insisted, did not abide by logical procedures. These refusals left him in a bind. He described "objective intellectual structures" as logical in character, in a manner not dissimilar to his later views of science and World 3. At the same time, he maintained that the mind, and psychological processes, did not conform to logic. Yet, he wanted psychology to explain the formation of intellectual structures. How could it? He opened a gap between logic and psychology that seemed impossible to bridge.[102]

Popper was anxious, above all, about "logicism." He resisted all efforts to impose logical structures on psychological experiences. Concepts and judgments, he insisted, did not shape experience: "The axiom that subjective experiences [that are involved] in the formation of representation have a fairly similar, or parallel structure to the objective structure of the 'repre-

---

[99] Ibid., pp. 48–55.

[100] Popper did spend time, however, showing that interpretation of meaning was essential to cognitive psychology (pp. 59–62). In contrast, he thought that the role of inner experience was obvious and required no further discussion (p. 70). He probably relied on Bühler's earlier rejoinders to Wundt on introspection.

[101] Popper seemed to be discussing a number of related issues concerning the formation of statements at one and the same time. The first was universal names; the second universal statements (universal laws); the third a statement's syntax, or semantics. The problems of formation and meaning are different in each case. Popper seemed to distinguish clearly among them at some points, and disregard the differences at others.

[102] Ibid., pp. 62–70, 77.

sentation' [itself, which is] set forth by the logician, has little to recommend itself."[103]

There was no logic of transference in either direction. He regarded logicism as a greater danger than psychologism, but rejected psychologism all the same. He expressed reservations about Selz's use of psychological experiences to explain scientific breakthroughs. Yet, logical-psychological and biological-psychological parallels fascinated him.[104] He was searching for a method to explore them that would, at one and the same time, translate from one discipline to another and guard the integrity of each. Semasiology was his answer:

> I maintain that the investigation of thought from the perspective of the intellectual structures (that is, representation) cannot be concluded without first resolving the problem of the boundaries among psychology, logic and epistemology.[105]
>
> . . . A psychology of thought cannot be complete without a preliminary semasiological investigation of "representation."[106]

Semasiology was a counsel of despair. It reflected his inability to deploy psychology to investigate intellectual structures. Logic and psychology seemed self-contained realms, closed to each other. In his two theses he tried to establish a dialogue between them to explain the production of knowledge. He failed. Now he hoped that semasiology would somehow open them to dialogue. This was hope against hope.

His impasse became evident when he pursued parallels between prescientific and scientific thinking. He regarded science as a prototype of objective intellectual structures. Scientific procedures were logical and autonomous. Their determination was epistemology's task. In contrast, prescientific thinking reflected psychological experience. In a manner prescient of his future work, he distinguished between scientific representation (or theory) and research. The first abided by logic, the second by psychology. He insisted that epistemological and psychological issues be kept strictly separate. Still, Selz's concept of "trying-out behavior" (*probierenden Verhalten*), a self-correcting psychological mechanism for exploring the world, appealed to him. "Science tests its theories, too," he said, "in a manner corresponding to the Selzian scheme."[107] But he hastened to add that, "of course," the logic of science controlled neither research nor Selz's trial-and-error behavior. Wishing to preserve the logical integrity of science, he neutralized any psychology of discovery. Cognitive psychology could not possibly explain science.

---

[103] Ibid., p. 65.   [104] Ibid., pp. 66–70, 76–9.

[105] Ibid., p. 63: "Ich behaupte, daß eine Untersuchung des Denkens innerhalb der 1. Position (Darstellungsposition) des 'G' Aspektes nicht zu Ende geführt werden kann, ohne diese Grenzprobleme der Psychologie, Logik und Erkenntnistheorie zu bearbeiten."

[106] Ibid., p. 64.   [107] Ibid., p. 69.

All Popper could do was defer the investigation of scientific and prescientific parallels until the demarcation of epistemology from psychology was complete: "Our proposal to compare scientific and prescientific induction procedures trespasses on the domain of epistemology. It is probably not completely feasible without first working a sharp demarcation between epistemological and psychological [issues] in each semasiological domain."[108]

Such demarcation was unlikely, however, to advance his investigation. His real problem was not fuzzy disciplinary boundaries, but the incompatible explanatory frameworks of psychology and epistemology. One framework had to give in before a solution emerged. In 1928, it was clear that Popper was not willing to give up on scientific autonomy. The question was how long he would persist in attempting to reach a solution in psychology. Semasiology and demarcation merely bought him time. They did not provide solutions.

His fascination with biological explanations of thought processes complicated his tasks further. He suggested, as he had done the year before, that progress from dogmatic speculation to critical science occurred in the life of both the individual and the species.[109] Could a genetic theory of the intellect explain thought processes in a manner psychology could not?[110] Selz's biologically guided mind, advancing from one task to another through trial and error, provided a partial explanation. The mind reworked knowledge into new schemes to resolve problems, but how did the mind create new material that had not previously been there?[111] *Logik der Forschung* provided an epistemological explanation, but the psychological and biological production of new knowledge remained problematic until the late 1940s. Popper would not commit to biology because he rejected transference from biology to psychology to logic. In 1928, biology did not resolve but only accentuated his problem. A biologically generated science was no more compatible with logic and epistemology than a psychologically produced one. Semasiology was to negotiate between explanations that might be (but had not yet been) produced in each discipline.

Popper must have realized shortly after the dissertation that semasiology was not a cure-all. He never tried his hand at it. He chose the only practical way out, by shifting his inquiry to the logic of natural science, and later to epistemology and methodology. Once he had separated radically between psychology and epistemology, declaring the former irrelevant to the latter, a stalemate in psychology no longer inhibited progress in the logic of science. In *Logik der Forschung*, he created a model of natural science,

---

[108] Ibid., p. 70.
[109] Ibid., p. 68. He now recognized also that dogmatic and critical thinking struggled continuously in intellectual life, but he could not yet find a place for dogmatic speculation in science.
[110] Ibid., pp. 69–70, 76–9.   [111] Idem, *Die beiden Grundprobleme*, pp. 26–30.

then extended it to social science in *The Poverty of Historicism*, and finally drew implications for political philosophy in *The Open Society*. Reversing his 1928 position, he pronounced the methodological unity of the sciences, and rejected any *Geisteswissenschaft*.[112] In postwar years, he again confronted the psychology of knowledge head-on. Conjecture and refutation in science had parallels in expectation, disappointment, and correction in psychology.[113] With growing confidence, he formulated, in 1970, the principle of transference, affirming "logicism": "what holds in logic must hold in genetics or in psychology."[114] This permitted the development of an evolutionary epistemology. All life, from the ameba to Einstein, from childhood to death, was problem solving. Biology, psychology, epistemology, and logic came together. Popper completed the ambitious program of semasiology he had suggested in 1928.

Critical rationalism was not, however, the semasiology envisioned in 1928. Semasiology was pluralistic. It arbitrated among sciences, the diverse methodologies of which reflected different perspectives and produced disparate explanations. It was necessary precisely because transference did not work among logic, psychology, physics, and biology. Popper's 1929 credo – that epistemology and logic must be radically separated from psychology – was essential to epistemology, but future leaps of faith would be more problematic. Popper knew no more psychology in 1970, when he declared his belief in transference, than he did in 1928, when he rejected logicism. His newly found faith privileged epistemology, imposing its terms on psychology and biology. It created a monolithic science. It also stifled discussion of the psychological and sociological preconditions for scientific and political practice. By narrowing down the field of inquiry and foreclosing intellectual options, Popper made philosophical breakthrough possible. But he left permanently unanswered the interesting, if intractable, questions about the interaction of logic and psychology in scientific practice. His great breakthrough was achieved at the cost of diminishing horizons.

PSYCHOLOGY AFTER THE BREAKTHROUGH:
"MEMORIZATION FROM THE PERSPECTIVE OF
SELF-ACTIVITY" (1931)

Popper provided two explanations for his shift of fields in the late 1920s. He recognized the priority of logic over psychology, and concluded that the psychology of discovery must have a logical base. He also rejected psychologism and efforts to ground epistemology in psychology.[115] Com-

---

[112] Idem, *The Poverty of Historicism*, chaps. 29–30.

[113] Idem, *Conjectures and Refutations*, chap. 1, esp. pp. 42–52; *Objective Knowledge*, Appendix, pp. 341–8.

[114] Idem, *Objective Knowledge*, p. 68 n. 30.   [115] *Autobiography*, pp. 59–60, 75–8.

mentators suggest that the two explanations were inconsistent: The first attributed the shift to his recognition of transference, the second to its abuse in psychologism.[116] Actually, it was not until forty years later that Popper stated strongly the case for transference. In contrast, a deeper rejection of psychologism accompanied his shift to epistemology. He desisted from any endeavor to trace the psychological genesis of theories. He was pursuing a new course in the logic of science.

As a secondary motivation for shifting fields, Popper mentioned his realization that Otto Selz (1881–1943) "had already anticipated" most of his psychological views. "Anticipated" may not be the best term to describe his debt to Selz. Selz shaped his psychology during his great epistemological breakthrough from 1928 to 1932 and beyond.[117] It is true, however, that Selz's psychology left an impression on him only because it seemed a tight fit with his emerging epistemology. His 1931 article on the psychology of school reform, "Memorization from the Perspective of Self-Activity," was couched in Selzian concepts.[118] Likewise, his brief sketch of deductivist psychology in *Die beiden Grundprobleme* deployed Selzian ideas.[119] After lying dormant for two decades, these ideas reemerged in Popper's postwar psychology and, later, in his evolutionary epistemology.

Among Würzburg psychologists, Selz assigned the mind the most active role. He, too, was a Külpe student. In 1923, he became a professor at Mannheim's commercial academy (*Handelshochschule*). Dismissed in April 1933 on account of his Jewish origin, and arrested after *Kristallnacht*, he reluctantly left Germany for Holland. In 1943, he refused pleas to escape deportation and perished in Auschwitz. He had few students and remained little known, but he was an innovative cognitive psychologist. He created the concepts of "productive thinking" (*produktives Denken*), "trying-out behavior," and "problem-solving method" (*Lösungsmethode*) to explain intellectual growth. He was the only psychologist Popper found relevant to his inquiries on scientific discovery and progress.[120]

A relentless enemy of associationist psychology, Selz began his career by demonstrating, based on a detailed analysis of experimental protocols, that mental processes were task oriented.[121] Structural ("schematic") anticipation of an outcome led to selection and arrangement of data to complete a new thought structure. Mental processes constituted problem-solving mechanisms, using trial and error. When a routine mental operation failed to fulfill a new task, the thought structure was revised. This process was

[116] Berkson and Wettersten, *Learning From Error*, pp. 79–83.

[117] This agrees with John Wettersten, *The Roots of Critical Rationalism*, p. 142.

[118] "Die Gedächtnispflege unter dem Gesichtpunkt der Selbsttätigkeit," *Die Quelle* 81 (1931): 607–19.

[119] Pp. 19–32.

[120] For Selz's biography and selections from his work, see: *Otto Selz: His Contribution to Psychology*, ed. Nico Frijda and Adriaan De Groot (The Hague: Mouton, 1982).

[121] Otto Selz, *Über die Gesetze des geordneten Denkverlaufs* (Stuttgart: Spemann, 1913).

endless. Responding to successive problems, the mind constantly created new structures, new knowledge. "Scientific methods are especially accomplished cases of sensible solving methods," he wrote.[122] Scientific routine was not a matter of "habit," but of continuous successful actualization. Discovery of new solving methods occurred when, confronting new tasks, old means attained only partial results. The growth of knowledge was biologically grounded: "An organism's new modes of reaction, . . . new psychic functional modes, arise . . . always on the foundation of previously formed task-oriented, life-sustaining operations."[123] Biology, psychology, and epistemology conformed to a unified logic.

The combined effect of Popper's reception of Selz's psychology and his recent breakthrough in the logic of science was evident in his 1931 essay on memorization. It was his single contribution to the psychology of school reform. Responding to a June 1931 conference of Viennese school teachers on memorization and self-activity, he brought a new psychology of learning to bear on reform pedagogy. He expressed himself with glee. In his dissertation, he had left unanswered the question of how chaotic perceptions were organized into meaningful structures. Now he knew: The mind imposed order in chaos, revising constantly the structures to accommodate new data.

The article focused on the role of memorization in the *Arbeitschule*. Most school reformers believed that traditional schools emphasized tedious memorization. "Self-activity" was their alternative to memorization. Pedagogy should no longer be guided, they claimed, by the *Stoffprinzip* (memorization of material), but by the *Kraftprinzip*, the development of the student's faculties. Popper suggested that reformers ought to rethink their position. Memorization was neither a product of continuous imprinting on a passive mind nor a matter for obsolete school training. This view reflected the mistaken belief in association. It assumed that meaningless sensations and impressions, imprinted on the mind, somehow increased gradually in complexity to form thoughts. But psychological association was nothing but a myth. Kant, Külpe, Bühler, and Selz had already refuted it. Memorization was a complex intellectual operation. It required a discriminating mind that simplified a mass of material and selected among an infinite number of facts. The mind reorganized them into meaningful thought structures, making them manageable for memory. Memorization was a matter of "learning how to learn," a prime task for the *Kraftprinzip* and a worthy goal for the Arbeitschule.[124]

If memorization entailed building a thought structure, then difficulties in memorizing were not a result of insufficient training, intellectual laziness, or shortsightedness. Rather, as Selz and Bühler implied, they reflected

---

[122] Idem, *Die Gesetze der produktiven und reproduktiven Geistestätigkeit* (Bonn: Cohen, 1924), p. 11.
[123] Ibid., p. 30. [124] Popper, "Gedächtnispflege": 607–17.

an inability to complete a gestalt, or, once it was complete, to identify the precise location of elements in the thought structure. The clearer and simpler the thought structure, the better the prospects for memorization. Popper devoted the article's final section to suggestions for classroom instruction that would enhance the ability to memorize. He emphasized that the Arbeitschule, which sought the students' active participation in learning, was superior to traditional schools in developing memorization capabilities.[125]

Popper's exposition of the psychology of learning in 1931 already bore the marks of his developing philosophy of science. His concerns may seem those of a school reformer, but both exposition and solution were informed by his new ideas on scientific procedures. The article was a compendium of his intellectual progress in the previous six years: a school reformer first, a student of cognitive psychology later, and finally a philosopher. Still, in *Die beiden Grundprobleme*, he felt compelled to return, if only for a moment, to the psychology of knowledge. He was apprehensive, he said, lest the hegemony of inductive, or associationist, psychology would rule out prima facie his deductivist epistemology, the view that scientists confirmed or falsified theories through their logical consequences, that is, through test statements deduced from them. He was not interested in refuting inductive psychology, he said. Indeed, he was not interested in psychology at all. He merely proposed that a deductivist psychology (*deduktivistische Erkenntnispsychologie*) was possible in principle, and deductivist epistemology could not be ruled out on psychological grounds. He drew major features of the psychology he would advance, with fewer qualms, many years later.

Inductivist epistemologists, suggested Popper, showed a proclivity for inductivist psychology, and believed that association governed thought processes. In contrast, biologically oriented psychologists – Bühler, Jennings, Selz, even Mach, in certain works – believed that thought processes were testing mechanisms. Organisms responded to biological anticipation, but often failed. Having misjudged different situations as identical, and responded habitually, they either perished or revised their anticipation and response. Intellect performed similarly. Revised psychological anticipation was knowledge. "Habit," or repetition, was no guarantee of knowledge, but of failure. This was a Kantian psychology. "Anticipation" corresponded to the synthetic a priori judgment, psychologically interpreted, but, contrary to Kant's assumption, anticipation often proved a posteriori false. Trial and error governed both psychology and epistemology. "Deductivism" provided a rational selection mechanism, a "method of trial and error" for the psychology of knowledge.[126]

---

[125] Ibid., 615–19.

[126] Popper attributed "trial and error" to Shaw (*Die beiden Grundprobleme*, p. 26; George Bernard Shaw, *Zurück zu Methusalem: ein Metabiologischer Pentateuch* [Berlin: Fischer, 1922], p. 218.) He had read Shaw in the mid-1920s.

Popper admitted that his proposal could still not solve the problem of the growth of knowledge. He was unable to explain how anticipation was initially formed, and, hence, the psychological genesis of new hypotheses. To say that new anticipations were biologically based, like mutations, he said, was no answer.[127] (This would be precisely the response he would give in later years.) Moreover, he insisted that revisions could not be the single source of new anticipation. An inexplicable, irrational moment was involved in all anticipation. There was no automatic growth of knowledge. The logic of transference had limits. It permitted the constructing of inductivist and deductivist epistemologies as parallel psychologies of knowledge, but biology, psychology, and epistemology remained autonomous.

Whether his psychological model worked in reality, said Popper, he did not know. His own previous work, a "Theory of the Intellect," could provide some evidence for it, but inductivist psychology remained a possibility, although not one that he liked. It was possible, he said, to combine an inductivist psychology with a deductivist epistemology. He had already rejected induction on logical grounds, but he was not quite sure about the implications for psychology. Deductivist psychology could not explain scientific progress, and logical transference still did not work fully.

Just over a year later, in the fall of 1932, when Popper wrote the final chapter of *Grundprobleme*, he went further. Explaining why the search for laws in science did not imply metaphysical belief in the lawfulness of the universe, he suggested that the search for laws was biologically grounded. "Biologically, we are told: you want to know – search for laws. But that there are laws must [and cannot conclusively] be shown."[128] He gave to Kant's question of how it was that our subjective epistemological apparatus conformed to objective relationships in the universe a genetic-biological answer: Organisms adapted to their environment. Preconditions for adaptation were inborn. The search for lawfulness was part of biological adaptation. Selection took place among intellectual adaptations. *Pace* Kant, our subjective ordering of the world was neither epistemological nor a priori valid. It was part of practical adaptation that could prove a failure. Popper deployed biology to diffuse an epistemological problem.

Still, he moved cautiously. He brought biology, psychology, and epistemology together for a moment, only to separate them all the more effectively. Kant confused, he said, epistemological and psychobiological questions. The biological a priori could prove epistemologically wrong. Evolution appeared too irrational and erratic a process to explain the growth of knowledge. Inborn expectations were a mere tentative hypothesis. He now possessed virtually all the conceptual tools that would make his postwar psychology of knowledge, but he declined to use them. The

---

[127] Popper, *Die beiden Grundprobleme*, p. 27.   [128] Ibid., p. 105. See also pp. 87–90, 99–106.

struggle against psychologism made him suspicious of transference. Were his suspicions unfounded? The old Popper never adequately addressed the young Popper's reservations about transference.

FROM PSYCHOLOGY TO PHILOSOPHY:
AUTOBIOGRAPHY AND INTELLECTUAL HISTORY

In his *Autobiography*, Popper remembered formulating and solving – tentatively and "in clumsy terminology"[129] – both the problems of demarcation and induction before 1928. However, he did not recognize, he said, the connection between the two, or the revolutionary implications of his solutions. He failed to realize that in order to guard the privileged status of scientific knowledge, philosophers used induction to demarcate scientific from nonscientific theories. But induction was false. His idea of falsifiability provided a superior criterion of demarcation. Science did not grow through cumulative observations, but through conjectures and refutations. Only after he had completed his dissertation did he "put two and two together." Things fell into place, and the new conception of science emerged.[130]

My reconstruction of Popper's intellectual development corroborates crucial aspects of his narrative, but revises others. The postdissertation period was, indeed, a period of crucial transition, giving rise to his revolutionary science, but he understated the transition. By 1929, he had not yet formulated the problems of demarcation and induction. His recollection that he made no significant progress on demarcation during the 1920s seems correct. This was not, however, because he had solved the problem in 1919 by settling on falsifiability as a demarcation criterion. Falsifiability did not become his demarcation criterion until 1932. He accepted induction and verifiability unproblematically throughout the 1920s. He was simply not concerned with methodological distinctions between scientific and nonscientific theories. There is little doubt that, after 1919–20, he had all along a vague sense that, for a theory to be scientific, it had to be open to questioning, but he had no inkling that anything was wrong with induction. His autobiographical account of progress on induction during the 1920s must be radically revised.

The various tenets of Popper's later psychological refutation of induction (and association) already existed in the Popperian intellectual universe in the mid-1920s. By 1927–8, he had read Selz. Even more significantly, around 1925, he read Nelson's critique of Hume, and by 1929, Zilsel's critique. Both Nelson and Zilsel refuted Hume with similar arguments to the

---

[129] *Autobiography*, p. 52.   [130] Ibid., pp. 79–81; *Conjectures and Refutations*, pp. 42–52.

one Popper would advance against induction in the 1950s. Hume hypothesized that habit, or repetition of phenomena, led through association to judgments about causality and laws. But habit and repetition, said Nelson, could never explain association itself. The expectation of future repetitions based on past events, the very "connection of ideas," had first to be explained. Hume could not do it. His psychological foundation for knowledge was ephemeral.[131] Zilsel distinguished, as Popper would in 1953, between Hume's subjective theory of induction, that is, induction as habit, and objective theory. As natural phenomena were never uniform, any generalization involved a preexisting conception of similarity. Such conception was rooted in biological expectation of regularity, but epistemologically, remained unfounded. No objective theory of induction existed.[132] Somehow, these critiques did not fully register with Popper. Even in 1930–2, when he had already rejected association, he did not use their arguments to refute "inductive" psychology, or undermine scientific induction.[133] Only in the 1950s did he use the critiques, by then developed as his own, to refute inductivism.

Contrary to the autobiographical account, antiassociationist, or anti-inductivist, psychology did not lead to anti-inductivist epistemology, certainly not before 1928. Just the opposite: After Popper had formulated induction as an epistemological problem in the early 1930s, he began exploring the relationship between deductivist epistemology and antiassociationist psychology. First, in 1930–2, he attempted, rather tentatively, to reconstruct psychology in light of his new epistemology. He left the project incomplete, and psychology took a back seat to epistemology for fifteen years. Then, in the late 1940s, he began using his psychology, incomplete though it was, to support his epistemological positions.[134] It was then that he also began reconstructing his intellectual autobiography. When he looked back to the 1920s, he could not make sense of the vicious cycle of arguments he was unable to break. Now that he had completed his scientific epistemology and methodology, the solution seemed so much at hand. He found in the psychological theories of the 1920s all the building blocks

---

[131] Leonard Nelson, "Die Unmöglichkeit der Erkenntnistheorie," *Gesammelte Schriften*, 9 vols. (Hamburg: Felix Meiner, 1973), 2:478–9; idem, *Über das sogennante Erkenntnisproblem* (Göttingen: Vandenhoeck und Ruprecht, 1908), pp. 742–56. Popper read these works as early as 1925 (Popper, *Autobiography*, p. 75) and quoted the latter in his 1927 thesis. Notwithstanding Nelson's antiassociationist stance, he accepted induction unproblematically: "Die Kritische Methode," *Gesammelte Schriften*, vol. 1, pp. 11–15.

[132] Edgar Zilsel, *Das Anwendungsproblem* (Leipzig: Barth, 1916), pp. 78–80, 93–4. But Zilsel considered induction, however problematic, indispensable for science. Popper used his work in his 1929 thesis, and found it helpful in formulating his critique of induction around 1930.

[133] He came closest in *Die beiden Grundprobleme*, p. 104. The psychological argument against induction is almost there, but neither Hume nor association are the target.

[134] Popper's first use of psychology to support his epistemology was: "The Bucket and the Searchlight: Two Theories of Knowledge" [1948], *Objective Knowledge*, pp. 341–61.

for his logical solution. He used them to construct a picture comprehensible to him in 1950.

Many years later, Popper would add confidently that "what is true in logic, must, by and large, be true in psychology."[135] We should take Popper's methodological dictum as a clue to his intellectual development: Having found solutions in epistemology to previously intractable problems in psychology, he "translated" (transferred) the epistemological solution to psychology. At the beginning he did so hesitantly, fully aware of the psychological problems that remained unresolved. By 1948, he confidently rejected inductivist psychology, stating that his new psychology and epistemology explained the growth of knowledge. For the first time, he used psychology to refute induction. He then naturally read back his concerns with the logic of science into the psychology of the 1920s, antedating his solutions. The disjunction between psychology and logic disappeared. Antiassociationist psychology paved the way to *Logik der Forschung* in a teleological biographical narrative.

[135] Popper, "Replies to My Critics," *The Philosophy of Karl Popper*, p. 1024.

Chapter 5

The Philosophical Breakthrough, 1929–1932

When did Popper become Popper – the philosopher articulating the familiar ideas of critical rationalism? Two decades ago, intellectual biographies raised such questions with relish. Historians assumed that authors achieved a fairly stable identity at a certain point in their lives, and tried to determine that point. Dating the "mature" Marx, for example, was a perennial issue, and a politically loaded one. Conflicting politics were invested in shaping Marx's identity. If Marx of the 1844 Paris Manuscripts was a "real" Marx, then the New Left's critique of the Old Left would be vindicated. But the question "who is Marx?" depended on "when does Marx become Marx?" Scholars traced concepts, ideas, and doctrines "essential" to Marxism in the young Marx's writings.

Such inquiries have disappeared from recent intellectual history. In an exaggerated response to "essentialism," critics have destabilized authorial identity and dissolved doctrine into discourse. Tracing the formation (or contours) of authorial identity may now seem futile. Yet, some authors are easier to track than others. A reader of Popper's 1928 dissertation would not identify the writer as Popper. A reader of *Die beiden Grundprobleme der Erkenntnistheorie* (1930–33; The two fundamental problems of epistemology) could make no mistake.[1] Some of Popper's major ideas, awkwardly expressed and incompletely developed, are there. Popper's transition from an "unfamiliar" psychologist of knowledge to a "familiar" philosopher of science took place between 1929 and 1932. The transition – Popper becoming Popper – is this chapter's subject.

French Marxist critic Louis Althusser used the notion of "epistemological break" (*coupure epistemologique*) to describe the young Marx's transition from philosophy to economics (or, as Althusser would have it, from ideology to science).[2] Something similar happened to Popper. Rearranging previous concepts, themes, and questions to form a new problem situation (or, to use Althusser again, a new *problématique*), he made a breakthrough in the logic of science. Pre-1928 sources, especially Nelson and Gomperz, initially

---

[1] Karl Popper, *Die beiden Grundprobleme der Erkenntnistheorie*, ed. Troels Eggers Hansen (Tübingen: Mohr, 1979). The book contains Popper's manuscripts from 1930 to 1933. Hansen's careful editing and scholarship have put all Popper scholars in debt. (I will be referring to the complete manuscript of the first volume of *Grundprobleme* as *Grundprobleme* I, and to the fragments of the second volume as *Grundprobleme* II).

[2] Louis Althusser, "Sur le jeune Marx," in *Pour Marx* (Paris: Maspero, 1965), pp. 45–83; reformulated in

informed his inquiry, but beginning in 1930, he constantly checked his progress against logical positivism and the Vienna Circle. His philosophy took shape as a critique of positivism. Until the summer of 1932, he was only infrequently in touch with the circle. He worked virtually alone, surrounded by old friends from the Pedagogic Institute. But engagement with the works of Carnap, Reichenbach, and Schlick contributed to his philosophy. By late 1932, a new vision of science emerged. The epistemological break ended in a paradigmatic shift.

"AXIOMS, DEFINITIONS, AND POSTULATES OF GEOMETRY" (1929)

Having submitted his doctoral dissertation, Popper was subject, on July 24, 1928, to the awesome *Rigorosum*, a public oral exam. He chose philosophy (including psychology) and the history of music as his two subjects. Karl Bühler and Moritz Schlick were the examiners.[3] Although his dissertation criticized Schlick's views on physicalism, his critique had not become an issue during the exam. Schlick probably had not read the dissertation. He examined Popper on the history of philosophy. Popper thought that he failed to answer adequately the question of whether Leibniz was a realist. Schlick was, indeed, unimpressed with his performance, but Popper was Bühler's student, not his, and Schlick would not pick a fight with a good colleague over a student. Bühler was well disposed toward Popper. Rather than properly examine him, he encouraged him to elaborate his ideas. So Schlick joined in passing Popper *einstimmig mit Auszeichnung*, unanimously with distinction. Popper, who felt badly about both thesis and exam, was surprised. He thought he had failed.[4]

A doctorate with distinction did not change Popper's career. He did not think he was cut out for the academy and still hoped for a school teach-

---

"Sur l'évolution du jeune Marx," *Éléments d'autocritique* (Paris: Hachette, 1974). Althusser argued that the continuity of themes between Marx's early works and *The German Ideology* concealed a structural change in 1845: the emergence of a new *problématique* (theoretical framework). An epistemological break separated Marx's prescientific early writings from post-1845 historical materialism. Althusser borrowed "epistemological obstacle" and "break" from Gaston Bachelard, *Le nouvel esprit scientifique* (Paris: Felix Alcan, 1934) and *La Philosophie du non* (Paris: Presses Universitaires de France, 1940).

[3] Popper had taken at least three lecture courses with Schlick in previous years, more than with any professor other than Bühler. Schlick was not an inspiring lecturer, however, and it is not clear that Popper attended most lectures. "Popper und der Wiener Kreis – Aus einem Gespräch mit Sir Karl Popper (1991)," in Friedrich Stadler, *Studien zum Wiener Kreis* (Frankfurt: Suhrkamp, 1997), p. 534. Popper may have also had a critical exchange with Schlick in the years prior to the exam. He surmised that Schlick had forgotten about it. Popper, "Erinnerungen an Schlick" [1984], Hoover Archives (252, 1).

[4] *Autobiography*, p. 78.

ing position. At twenty-six, he was an educated, talented, intellectually sharp young person, but not accomplished. Nothing he had done throughout the past decade had been successful. Social engagement ended in frustration, if not worse. The intellectual world proved unwieldy. He had written voluminously, but failed to complete either of his theses in an orderly manner. He lacked a specific intellectual direction and felt overwhelmed by philosophical problems. He had few academic contacts and no source of consistent intellectual and emotional support. Bühler was kind, but rarely within reach. The acerbic Gomperz could give criticism, but no encouragement. Above all, Popper had no job and no financial support.

Things began to improve in 1929. That year he wrote an additional thesis on axiomatics in geometry, qualifying him to teach mathematics and physics in secondary school (*Hauptschule*).[5] It was a fairly polished product, limited in scope and aim, not, perhaps, original, but perceptive all the same. In contrast with the more ambitious, but unfinished, theses of 1927–8 that were hastily pulled together – or not quite – and messily typed, the geometry thesis was clearly organized, and neatly typed and bound. Popper surveyed the history of geometry, elucidated axiomatic principles, explained non-Euclidean geometry, and presented conflicting views on the foundation of geometry. While discussing the applicability of geometry to reality, he made important observations on the methodology of science. His breadth of knowledge and theoretical sophistication clearly exceeded the teaching requirements for the *Hauptschule*. Hauptschule students were gymnasium rejects who did not plan on academic study. Popper would have little use for advanced geometry in teaching. But his inquiry first formulated the problem of scientific rationality, enabling his future philosophical progress.

The 1929 thesis reflected Popper's turn from cognitive psychology to the logic and methodology of science. Victor Kraft's work on the basic forms of scientific methods and Edgar Zilsel's work on the "application problem" may have suggested the topic to him.[6] Both works explored the applicability of mathematics to reality, tying together logical, epistemological, and, in Kraft's case, methodological issues. Kraft emphasized the axiomatic and hypothetico-deductive character of mathematics. He explored the application of mathematical models in scientific theory, most significantly, the application of geometrical space in physics. Zilsel discussed the universe's lawfulness, determinism, and induction and raised the problem of scientific rationality. Popper used some of Zilsel's distinctions, but disagreed with his view on the experiential foundation of logic and

---

[5] Popper, "Axiome, Definitionen und Postulate der Geometrie," 2 vols., Popper Archives (4, 6).
[6] Viktor Kraft, *Die Grundformen der Wissenschaftlichen Methoden* (Vienna: Hölder-Pichler-Tempsky, 1925); Edgar Zilsel, *Das Anwendungsproblem* (Leipzig: Barth, 1916). Gomperz recommended the first work. Popper, *Autobiography*, p. 81.

mathematics. Following Kraft, he directed his investigation toward scientific methodology. He became familiar, at about the same time, with the French mathematician and conventionalist philosopher Henri Poincaré. Poincaré classified different geometries, and concluded that preference for one over the other could not be logically or experientially decided.[7] Popper agreed, but felt that application of geometrical space in physics required a clear methodological decision, because relativity theory was at stake. He probed the question. His epistemological and methodological inquiries were not essential to the thesis. But they were of the greatest interest to him – and they were new.

New was also the Vienna Circle's influence. In the preface, Popper declared that his orientation was similar to theirs. He lauded their effort to reform scientific language. His elaborate discussion of basic terms, he said, may seem superfluous. But recent work on logistic (mathematical logic) made clear the field's sorry state of terminological confusion. Clarification of terms was the order of the day. He was moving away from Gomperz into the circle's orbit. His vocabulary still belonged to Gomperz and Nelson. He still conceived of scientific methodology as a secondary science. His metadiscourse on geometry clarified the relationship among logic, geometry, and physics. Likewise, his classification of epistemologies – rationalism, empiricism, and critical thought (*Kritizismus*) – followed Gomperz. But, using Carnap's work on logistic and Kraft's on hypothetico-deductive scientific models, he explored methodological procedures in physics, and was groping to reformulate Nelson's question on the foundation of knowledge. He was finally carving his own philosophical path.

Some long-term philosophical commitments were evident already in 1929. He rejected psychologism in no uncertain terms. "Genetic speculation," he echoed Gomperz, "has become an asylum of choice for the ignorant."[8] The sources of knowledge, historical or psychological, were irrelevant to its validity. For two thousand years, philosophers tried to explain geometrical space by analyzing "space consciousness" (*Raumbewußtsein*). Confusion between subjective conviction and objective grounding of knowledge was the root of evil – and widespread. Popper himself was not clear, however, how knowledge may be grounded. He was looking for contact points between theory (or language) and reality, but found none. He conceded that perceptual experience verified theory, but was aware that verification was difficult, and inclined toward a modified conventionalism. He accepted Poincaré, but pointed out that methodological preference (for

[7] Henri Poincaré, *La Science et l'hypothèse* (Paris: Flammarion, 1903). (German: *Wissenschaft und Hypothese* [Leipzig: Teubner, 1906].) The thesis discussed Poincaré extensively, but without direct reference to his work.

[8] Popper, "Axiome, Definitionen, und Postulate der Geometrie," p. 31.

the simplest theory) could still determine choice of one geometry (or theory of space) over another.[9] Convention ruled, but choice was not arbitrary.

The thesis had three parts. The first introduced two sets of problems, mathematical-logical and scientific-theoretical. The former were axiomatic and could be resolved with no reference to reality. The latter were methodological, involved epistemological issues, and raised the foundation problem. The second part discussed the historical development of both groups of problems. Popper focused on the parallel postulate, outlined the rise of non-Euclidean geometries, and analyzed their space conceptions. The third part developed the problems systematically. Popper explored the grounds of geometrical validity, geometry's applicability to reality, and methodological rules governing geometrical space in physics. Much of the thesis, he said, was mere exposition of secondary literature. Only his final methodological observations were original.

Popper thought that recent advances in axiomatics and mathematical logic had already solved all questions concerning the validity of pure (that is, nonapplied) geometry.[10] Following Pasch and Hilbert, he identified four prerequisites to any axiomatic system. It must be contradiction-free and complete (i.e., contain all presuppositions essential for deriving theorems); its axioms must be indispensable (i.e., necessary for deriving theorems) and independent (i.e., not derived one from another). Euclid's system was contradiction-free, but not complete, and replete with concealed assumptions. Its definitions seemed superfluous. The fifth postulate, known as the parallels postulate, proved, historically, the most problematic, but all efforts to demonstrate its dependence or dispensability failed.[11] Gauss (1777–1855), (Johann) Bolyai (1802–60), and Lobachevskii (1793–1856) gave the parallels postulate up and developed a geometry independent of it. Their "non-Euclidean geometry emerged," emphasized Popper, "as a completely nongraphic (*unanschaulich*) theoretical construction," grounded in no experience, or perception.[12] Epistemology was irrelevant to these developments. They were purely conceptual and logical.

A plurality of geometries emerged in the nineteenth century. Projective

---

[9] Poincaré himself established the methodological preference for simplicity, but Popper understood it differently.

[10] Two years later came Gödel's proof that there exist some well-formulated statements within any presumably consistent, sufficiently developed system (one that has prime numbers in it) that neither follow from the axioms nor conflict with them. One such example is the assertion of the consistency of the system. (Joseph Agassi helped me here.) Kurt Gödel, "Über formal unentscheidbare Sätze der Principia Mathematica und verwandter Systeme I," *Monatshefte für Mathematik und Physik* 38 (1931): 173–98. This did not shake Popper's confidence.

[11] Euclids' fifth postulate: If a straight line falling on two straight lines makes the interior angles on the same side less than two straight angles, the two straight lines, if produced indefinitely, meet on that side on which the angles are less than two right angles.

[12] Popper, "Axiome, Definitionen und Postulate der Geometrie," p. 61.

geometry disposed of metric measurement of geometric configurations (size and distance). It established relationships of position, incidence, and coincidence, unalterable by space transformation, among geometric configurations. It freed itself from the parallel postulate, but plane, line, and point remained essential concepts. Topology disposed of them, too. This "rubber-sheet geometry" investigated properties of spatial configurations that remained unaltered when the configuration was subject to one-to-one transformation in both directions. (Deforming an inflated balloon is an example of a topological transformation.) All geometrical configurations were topologically equivalent. Non-Euclidean geometries did not, however, replace Euclid. In *Foundations of Geometry* (1899), David Hilbert (1862–1943) radically reformulated the Euclidean system, establishing it on a purely formal axiomatic basis.[13] Still, the doubts cast on Euclidean geometry translated quickly into questions about its applicability to physical space. Theoretical physics faced choice among competing geometries, offering alternative space conceptions. All were internally consistent. How could they all be valid?

Geometry represented an especially difficult case of Zilsel's "application problem." How come the statements of logic, arithmetic, and geometry were applicable to reality, yet always unconditionally true? For logic, the answer was that it never involved questions of conformity to reality. The relationships logic established among objects were conceptual, not real: It simply grouped objects into concepts. Only the internal consistency of logic was at issue. The same applied to most branches of mathematics. Russell and Whitehead attempted to show the purely logical character of mathematics in *Principia Mathematica* (1913).[14] They did not achieve complete formalization, but Popper accepted their conclusion, at least for arithmetic and algebra. Pure geometry, too, was no problem. All geometric theorems were analytic, derived from axioms. As long as the axioms were accepted, the theorems were valid a priori. Applied geometry, however, was different. It established real, not conceptual, relationships among objects. Its theorems were, at least in part, synthetic, and valid a posteriori. Their proof required observational verification. It involved scientific procedure and raised epistemological and methodological issues. Scientific theory needed to adjudicate applied geometry's problems.

Geometry's most striking applications were in theoretical physics. Divergent concepts of geometrical-physical space competed in physics. Methodological choice among them absorbed Popper. Einstein's relativity theory deployed Riemann's curved space. Could Einstein's preference for non-Euclidean geometry be justified? Helmholtz, said Popper, expected physi-

---

[13] David Hilbert, *Grundlagen der Geometrie*, 6th ed. (Leipzig: Teubner, 1923).

[14] Alfred North Whitehead and Bertrand Russell, *Principia Mathematica*, 3 vols. (Cambridge: The University Press, 1910–13).

cal experiments to determine geometrical space.[15] Poincaré insisted they could not. Experience did not determine choice of geometry. On the contrary: Geometry formed experience. It was possible to describe geometrical space with various mathematical expressions. These expressions, containing data about form, measure, or position, were interpretive of the reality they described. Physical theories were couched in a preselected geometry's terms, and unanticipated experimental results could always be reinterpreted to suit this geometry. Geometrical-physical space was conventional, and choice among competing geometries logically undecidable.

Popper largely agreed with Poincaré, but added a major caveat that restored authority to experience and experiment. Choice of geometry for physical space was, indeed, free. Physical theories could always be reinterpreted in the light of geometry, but such reinterpretation often required introducing so many ad hoc hypotheses that it became impractical. Relativity theory worked best with non-Euclidean curved space. Attempts to adjust it to Euclidean space, though possible in principle, would require speculation about additional physical forces. They would produce a highly complex, even grotesque, worldview. Scientific theory required the greatest economy in the use of hypotheses, the smallest number of assumptions: The simpler the theory, the better.[16] Popper was not clear, at this point, whether this was a matter of logic or methodology, but even if only a methodological convention, it was a forceful one. Helmholtz was partially right: Experience may induce us to accept a non-Euclidean worldview. This happened with Einstein's relativity theory. Poincaré was partially right, too: Acceptance of a particular geometrical space was conventional. Choice among applied geometries was methodologically decidable.

This was Popper's first statement on natural science methodology. It expressed a clear methodological orientation that would remain consistent throughout his epistemological revolution.[17] He accepted a strong con-

---

[15] Like Mill, German physicist Hermann Helmholtz (1821–94) endeavored to turn geometry into an experimental science. Popper rejected his effort. Hilbert's axiomatics and Russell's mathematical logic demonstrated to his satisfaction that a geometry independent of experience was possible. But if radical empiricism proved irrelevant to pure geometry, it could still contribute to geometrical physics (*Raumphysik*).

[16] Popper gave Mach's "economy of theory" and Poincaré's "simplicity" a twist: Not the simplicity of geometry (or theory) itself counted, but of all its applications. (This concurred with Kraft, *Grundformen*, p. 164.) Ernst Mach, "Die ökonomische Natur der physikalischen Forschung," in his *Populärwissenschaftliche Vorlesungen*, 3d ed. (Leipzig: Barth, 1903); Poincaré, *La Science et l'hypothèse*.

[17] To be sure, Popper was still groping. Applied topology, he said, was valid a posteriori, based on perceptual judgment (*Wahrnehmungsurteil*). This conflicted with every tenet of his later epistemology. He hastened to add that anyway, most statements in applied geometry were not "pure applied geometry," but part of geometrical physics, and subject to normal verification procedures. Einstein's statement remained his motto: "Insofar as the statements of mathematics are strictly valid, they do not refer to reality; insofar as they refer to reality, they are not strictly valid." Albert Einstein, *Geometrie und Erfahrung* (Berlin: Springer, 1921), p. 3.

ventionalist component in methodology, but endeavored to make tests the arbitrators of decisions. He would shortly apply the hypothetico–deductive model to all natural science, as an alternative to inductivism. Unlike geometry, however, science was not axiomatic. How could scientific theories be grounded? Applied geometry set the context for Popper's discussion of scientific rationality and brought together his long-held interests in theoretical physics, mathematics, and epistemology. It provided the launching pad for his epistemological revolution.

SETTLING DOWN? MARRIAGE AND PHILOSOPHICAL REVOLUTION

In 1930 Popper finally obtained a teaching position at the Schwegler Hauptschule in the fifteenth district. A generation earlier, few intellectuals had opted for school teaching as a career, but economic circumstances, and enthusiasm for school reform, made teaching a popular career among Popper's cohort. The stagnating interwar economy offered few opportunities to the intelligentsia. The market was saturated with professionals and academics. A teaching position provided a modest but secure income (the equivalent of 110 British pounds per annum, Popper said late in 1936). A family of two teachers could sustain a middle-class standard of living. Karl's friend of five years, Josefine Henninger (Hennie), obtained a teaching position, too. They could now marry. The ceremony took place on April 11, 1930. A modest reception followed in the piano room of the downtown apartment, which had seen better days. Karl moved into the small house where Hennie and her mother lived, in Hietzing, a single-family residence area – distinctly non-Jewish – in the westernmost part of Vienna. This meant a daily commute of over two hours to and from school in southeast Vienna. For the time, however, he was happy to have a job. After a turbulent decade, he seemed to be settling down.

Teaching middle school was not, to be sure, an accomplishment reminiscent of his father's feat. Karl Popper's generation could not emulate, during interwar years, their parents' achievement. Of Simon Popper's children, Dora became a civil servant and a nurse. Such a professional career had been impossible for women of previous generations, but in terms of social class, it represented no advance. She remained single until 1922, when she moved to Merseburg in Germany, possibly after marrying. Annie became a dance teacher, but seemed to have had neither stable family life nor financial security until she became a popular romance writer in postwar Switzerland. Neither sister seemed to have had children, and, with Karl Popper's death, this branch of the family reached an end. The psychological and cultural makeup of the second generation of bourgeois newcomers was different from that of the first, but their talents were not inferior. Rather, transitory socioeconomic and political circumstances created the Viennese Jewish bourgeoisie. Its meteoric rise had barely been completed when war and imperial dissolution triggered its decline. Cultural warfare (anti-Semitism) precipitated the decline, and the Nazis finalized it.

Karl Popper married down. Hennie was the only daughter of Josefine Gussl (1871–c. 1949) and Josef Henninger (1849–1923), a senior elementary school teacher (*Oberlehrer*) in Speising (on the western outskirts of Vienna).[18] Both parents were Roman Catholic, the father descended from lower Austrian peasant origin. From photographs, Hennie grew up in middle-class comfort (which included stuffed toys and tennis).[19] She completed secondary school, then joined the first class of women training at the Pedagogic Institute. She received a teaching certificate from one of Glöckel's model schools, the *Bundeserziehungsanstalt* in the third district.[20] Her sociocultural background diverged radically from Karl's, but he was fortunate in his choice of a life companion. Their relationship was codependent. It is difficult to imagine another woman sustaining a lifelong relationship with this difficult man.

What could have attracted Karl and Hennie to each other? Reports are that he went a long way to woo her. At first sight, they seemed an unlikely match. He was intellectually intense and contentious, small in figure but, perhaps, not unattractive. She was quiet and withdrawn, tall, pleasant-looking but not striking. The convention that in Central Europe, Jews marry down to cross over, non-Jews cross over to move up may apply, but not completely. His family was no longer well off. Both he and Hennie were training to become socialist teachers. The cliché about Jewish men's physical attraction to prohibited non-Jewish women may partially hold, too. A contemporary commented acerbically that Karl thought Hennie was "the sun, the moon, and the stars."[21] It is unlikely, however, that Karl's attraction was sexual per se. He admired beauty in men, women, and children, but was sexually anxious. He subscribed to the puritan ethos of socialist education and the scout movement. They preached abstinence from alcohol, smoking, and sex to bourgeois and proletarian youth alike. Sexual and intellectual activities were incompatible. Popper commended the Viennese workers for having substituted cultural endeavors and sports for alcohol and smoking (respectability prohibited his mentioning of sex). In New Zealand, he harped on the danger of premature sexual activity to his student Peter Munz. He warned him that playing tennis was insufficient

---

[18] Meldearchiv, Wiener Stadt- und Landesarchiv.

[19] Photos, Popper Archives (86039–10, BB).

[20] Karl Popper, questionnaire, Research Foundation for Jewish Immigration, *Zentrum für Antisemitismusforschung*, Technische Universität, Berlin.

[21] Peter Milford (Hilferding) related this to Colin Simkin many years later. Communication from Simkin to author, 28 May 1997.

to contain sexual urges.[22] Mutual attraction certainly existed between Karl and Hennie, but it was not the usual sort.

Hennie's ambitions were modest. Her 1927 thesis was everything that Karl's was not: a self-contained project, neatly organized, meshed in socialist rhetoric, with little pretension to originality – but complete, all the same. Her later correspondence reveals a refined sensibility, a poetic touch, a melancholic soul. She wrote simply and beautifully, though not effortlessly. She wanted a calm middle-class Viennese life. She had nothing like it with Karl. He was ambitious, egocentric, and restless, and he had the added liability of Jewish origin, which made staying in Vienna impossible. She first resisted his intellectual endeavors, then gave up – always. She opposed his writing his first book, but relented. She taught herself to type, and typed numerous versions of his manuscripts up to *The Open Society*. She resisted his search for a job abroad, but financed it from her own resources. Then, she reconciled herself to a painful exile. She made the fortunes of his philosophy and career her paramount concern. She could not inspire his work, or advise him on theoretical issues, but she was an astute commentator on nontechnical expositions, pointing out where he lacked clarity. She did not play the homemaker, relieving him of daily concerns – she despised house chores, and rarely cooked – but became instead a collaborator in his work. She advised on relations with publishers, colleagues, and students. She expressed strong views on his choice of fields, reinforcing his turn back from political philosophy to the philosophy of science in the immediate postwar years. For many years, she handled virtually all his correspondence with friends. She perused all his writings, counseling when she thought they might adversely affect his stature, or badly reflect on his (or their) personal history. He listened to her. She had, he told Colin Simkin, a mind sharp as a needle. She became an instrument for advancing his philosophy.

Hennie sometimes had a better sense of reality than Karl, but not always. Often enough, her anxieties – which focused increasingly on *his* reputation – merely reinforced his. Like him, she had a foreboding sense that things might turn out for the worse. She led a sad existence. After leaving Vienna, she became a loner. New Zealand was exile, and London proved no better. She hated the metropolitan bustle, and despised social obligations. Like her husband, she sought a secluded life in a rural area. Until the 1960s, she took an interest in his students and friends. Later, she complained that their visits to the house in Penn created commotion. (He, in contrast, seemed to take pleasure in them.) She enjoyed his growing reputation. She liked being called Frau Professor, something a young woman of her class could only dream of, but his success did not bring her (or him) great joy of life or calmness of soul. She was melancholic, even depressive.

---

[22] Communication from Peter Munz to author, 25 February 1997.

Her resentment at having been taken away from Vienna broke out periodically. In her depression during the early 1950s, she blamed Karl for her miserable life.[23]

We may never know why the couple had no children: They were both extremely private. In his archives, Popper did not include material not pertaining to his intellectual production. Infertility, or exiles' anxiety about the future, could explain not having children. Popper suggested as much in a posthumously published interview, when, in response to a question about children, he spoke obliquely about his Jewish origin and the torture of the camps.[24] Still, his response seemed to conceal as much as reveal. He seemed to like children, even adore them. The general picture of life emerging from the couple's correspondence contains no hint of amorous relations and leaves little room for them, but this is no *argumentum in silentium*. In drafts of the *Autobiography*, Popper toyed a little too much with puritanism.[25] One's feeling of superiority for being puritan, he said, had to be contained. His murderous work ethic and his abstinence from smoking and alcohol may account for his perverse pride, but they seem insufficient. Sexual abstinence, or near abstinence, could help explain it. Dedicating *Die beiden Grundprobleme* to Hennie in 1978, he wrote that "she made great sacrifices for this book . . . more than I should have accepted."[26] Hennie was suffering at the time from cancer, and so his uncharacteristically emotional dedication may have simply acknowledged her untiring labor on his behalf. More likely, Popper was hinting at greater sacrifices. They may have extended to conjugal life itself.

Marriage, job, and house meant settling down, but they came in strange proximity to a new adventure. Sometime in 1930, Popper embarked on a book on the logic of science. His interest in natural science methodology, especially physics, was already evident in the geometry thesis. He now endeavored to extend the deductive models of geometry to natural science. He read avidly the Vienna Circle's works as they were coming out. He soon recognized that his deductivism provided a corrective to the circle's views, and he sought to develop it into an alternative scientific model. He formulated the problem of induction and made it the center of his critique of logical positivism. The circle, he argued, failed to resolve the problem. His deductivism offered a solution.

Zilsel's work may have first suggested the induction problem to Popper. Hume's critique of induction, said Zilsel, demonstrated that human expec-

[23] Popper to Hayek, February 1951–September 1952, Hayek Archives (44, 1).
[24] Edward Zerin, "Karl Popper on God. The Lost Interview" [in 1969], *Skeptic* 6:2 (1998): 48. "We got married in the worst time of Hitler. My wife also is not Jewish, and we decided not to have children. I think that it was perhaps a cowardly but in a way a right decision." He proceeded to mention the concentration camps and his loss of friends and relatives.
[25] See especially: outline (134, 4).   [26] P. v.

tation of natural lawfulness, or uniformity, was logically unfounded. Expectation of future regularity was based on induction already completed, on a pattern already established. This pattern, in turn, required its own justification. None existed. Could science verify inductive patterns, once they were formed, using deductive procedures similar to geometry? No, deductive reasoning was precise and its judgment final, whereas scientific theories were approximate and alterable. Inductive procedures could never lead to deductive results. Zilsel settled for a biologically programmed induction in a determinist universe. Organisms anticipated regularities, made mistakes in establishing similarities, but made progress all the same. Still, he had no theory of induction. It is insufficient to believe, he said, that science was getting closer to truth. Inductive theory needed to provide a measure of proximity, but he could not see how. Induction accounted for science's enormous success but faced major difficulties. A viable theory of induction had to be found.[27]

Popper benefited from Zilsel's setting of the induction problem. By linking induction and lawfulness, Zilsel called his attention to the circle's difficulties in dealing with natural laws. He set starkly the contrast between deductive and inductive models, and associated theoretical change with scientific growth, but he remained wedded to the ideals of induction and certainty. Popper was moving quickly toward renouncing both, and making deductive hypotheses the crux of science. He now returned to the foundation debate in the Fries–Nelson tradition, and interjected Nelson's epistemological critique into Zilsel's setting. He thereby radically transformed Zilsel's problem situation.

Nelson had noted that as all intellectual judgments had to be justified, induction was no exception. The notion that observed phenomena were somehow connected and could be formed into laws required justification. Judgments could be deferred to other judgments, but those, in turn, required justification. We risk either infinite regress, or alternatively, dogmatism, that is, accepting judgments on faith or authority. Kant's way out was to substitute the laws of consciousness for the laws of reality. His "transcendental deduction," or "transcendental proof" – the central philosoph-

---

[27] Zilsel, *Das Anwendungsproblem*, pp. 75–100. Popper used Zilsel in his 1929 dissertation and mentioned him in his preparatory outlines for the *Autobiography* (Popper Archives [134, 4, 6]) in connection with the Kant–Hume problem. Joseph Agassi objects here (E-mail communication to author, 22 June 1998) that "everything you ascribe to Zilsel is already in [Bertrand] Russell's slim volume, *The Problems of Philosophy* [London: Butterworth, 1912]." Yes and no: Russell may have informed Viennese discussions of induction, but Zilsel's English was not the best, and he did not use Russell's book (a German translation of which, *Die Probleme der Philosophie*, trans. Paul Hertz [Erlangen: Weltkreis]) appeared only in 1926). Popper did read Russell's book in translation, quoting it in *Die beiden Grundprobleme*, p. 96. Still, *Grundprobleme* seems to me informed by Zilsel more than by Russell. Russell does not confront inductive and deductive procedures in the manner Zilsel and Popper do, nor does he consider biological grounding. Popper mentions neither Russell nor Zilsel as helpful in formulating the problem of induction.

ical procedure of the *Critique of Pure Reason* – showed that both a lawful universe and causality were prerequisites for experience and knowledge. The world was inconceivable without them. They were synthetic propositions: They could not be derived analytically from other propositions. On the contrary, they contained the very knowledge upon which other propositions were based. They were a priori valid: They were not products of experience, not empirical, but constituted the preconditions for experiencing reality. Induction was vindicated as a by-product of lawfulness and causality. Fries and Nelson found Kant problematic. They thought that he confused intellectual judgment and psychological cognition. There was no synthetic a priori in epistemology. Epistemology could not solve the problem of knowledge. The only way out was a turn to psychology. Fries's "immediate knowledge," cognition preceding any judgment, provided the foundation of knowledge.[28]

Popper accepted Nelson's formulation of the foundation problem, but rejected his solution. Fries and Nelson were justly critical of Hume and Kant: Induction led to infinite regress. No synthetic statement was a priori valid. Kant's transcendental deduction led to an antinomy: Who said experience was always possible? The contrary position (the universe is unlawful; experience is impossible) could also be advanced, and no arbitration between the two was possible. Still, said Popper, Kant had made a considerable advance, now threatened by positivism. He recognized lawfulness as a scientific prerequisite: Only repeatable events were verifiable, and they alone assured intersubjectivity. Fries and Nelson were wrong to turn from epistemology to psychology. Immediate knowledge was subjective and provided no foundation for science.[29]

Popper had a better solution. Let the synthetic a priori remain forever hypothetical. Scientific theories (or natural laws) could never be conclusively verified, or declared true. They were regulative ideals, or logical "fictions," constructed for heuristic purposes: the deduction of prognoses and their testing.[30] In Victor Kraft's work, he found elaborate discussions of hypothetico-deductive models, including provisions for forming and testing theories.[31] He became familiar also with the deductivism of French physicist and conventionalist philosopher Pierre Duhem.[32] Science, he decided, proceeded deductively, not inductively. There were no inductive scientific procedures. Scientists deduced prognoses from theories (natural laws) and

[28] Leonard Nelson, "Die Unmöglichkeit der Erkenntnistheorie" [1911], vol. 2 of *Gesammelte Schriften*, 9 vols. (Hamburg: Felix Meiner, 1973).

[29] *Die beiden Grundprobleme* I, secs. 3–5, 9–10.

[30] Popper borrowed the term "heuristic fiction" from neo-Kantian philosopher Hans Vaihinger, *Die Philosophie des Als Ob*, 4th ed. (Leipzig: Meiner, 1920).

[31] Kraft, *Die Grundformen der wissenschaftlichen Methoden*, pp. 86–192.

[32] Pierre Duhem, *La Théorie physique: Son objet et sa structure* (Paris: Chevalier & Rivière, 1906). (German: *Ziel und Struktur der physikalischen Theorien*, trans. Friedrich Adler [Leipzig: Barth, 1908].)

tested them. Prognoses were "specific statements about reality." Their verification confirmed the theory; their falsification contradicted it. Popper drew no antifoundationist conclusions – yet. He merely substituted an empirico-deductivist model of science for inductive ones. He declared parts – but only parts – of science hypothetical (or "fictional"). Falsification of theories had not yet become the prime goal of science. Verification of prognoses assured a foundation for science.[33]

Popper's alternative scientific model proved significant to methodological debates in the Vienna Circle. He posed as the circle's critic from the start. He carefully studied Wittgenstein's *Tractatus*, the circle's "Bible," and rejected it as a dangerous combination of dogmatic rationalism and mysticism.[34] He was disappointed when his teacher, Schlick, the circle's head, renounced his early work under Wittgenstein's influence.[35] He had known Neurath since 1919 and visited him, with his class, at the Vienna Social and Economic Museum. In 1927 or so, he heard Neurath speak about socialism and the circle to a socialist youth group.[36] He had important conversations with Zilsel about Freud and, possibly, the Hume–Kant problem, during the 1920s. He read Carnap's works as they came out, and visited his seminar in the late 1920s. He used Carnap and Hahn in his geometry thesis. His mentor Gomperz was never a member of the inner circle but, nevertheless, informative about it. In short, he had been familiar with the circle long before he initiated intellectual exchange with its members.

Beginning in 1929, Popper met circle members for lengthy discussions. Having read Victor Kraft for his geometry thesis, Popper wrote him (or Gomperz may have introduced them), and they met several times in Vienna's Volksgarten.[37] Kraft (1880–1975) was one of the circle's elders, but not a leader. Like Popper, he was influenced by neo-Kantian currents, and his attitude toward traditional philosophy was more positive than the circle's. His book was a survey of deductive and inductive procedures in science. He presented them as mutually exclusive. Inductive procedures did not lead to theory, which was deductive. He was aware of induction's logical problems but, unlike Zilsel and Popper, took them in stride. Generalizations based on inductive inference were incomplete, but valuable, nonethe-

---

[33] *Grundprobleme* I, esp. secs. 3–6, 34, 37–8, 47.   [34] *Grundprobleme* I, secs. 43–6.

[35] He expressed his disappointment to Schlick: "Erinnerungen an Schlick" [1984], (252, 1). His recollection of their early confrontation may also reflect his later concerns, but Heinrich Neider ("Persönliche Erinnerungen an den Wiener Kreis," *Conceptus* 11 (1977): 22) reported a similar encounter. Having praised *Allgemeine Erkenntnislehre* to Schlick, the latter related to him that under Wittgenstein's influence, he renounced the book. Neider and Popper alike were taken aback.

[36] "Memories of Otto Neurath," in Otto Neurath, *Empiricism and Sociology*, ed. Marie Neurath and Robert S. Cohen (Boston: Reidel, 1973), pp. 52–5.

[37] *Autobiography*, pp. 81–2; "Replies to My Critics," *The Philosophy of Karl Popper*, ed. Paul Arthur Schilpp, 2 vols. (La Salle, Ill.: Open Court, 1974), 2: 974–5.

less. He was open to Popper's criticism, and became his closest friend among the circle. They remained friends until Kraft's death.[38]

Popper's meeting with young Herbert Feigl (1902–88) later that year proved crucial. Feigl, a Schlick student, had just published a book on theory and experience in physics. He reviewed models for forming and testing theories, and discussed the problem of verification. Theories, he concluded, were approximations the probability of which increased with repeated confirmation. Induction was the standard scientific procedure: "Although theories are not obtained through induction, their validity is assessed inductively."[39] He tied together the problems of induction, theory formation, testing, verification, and natural law, thereby providing the focus for Popper's critique of the circle.

Popper's uncle, Walter Schiff, arranged the first Feigl–Popper meeting by inviting Feigl and his fiancée, Maria Kaspar. Popper took no time in criticizing Carnap's *The Logical Structure of the World* for disallowing synthetic statements.[40] The two set out on a nightlong walk around Vienna, ending in Feigl's apartment. Other all-night sessions followed. Popper drove home every intellectual victory. Feigl was impressed, but exasperated. He suggested that Popper publish his ideas in a book. Popper had previously ruled out a career as a professional philosopher. Gomperz had discouraged him from trying to publish, recalling that Kraft's book was printed only with grant support. His father and wife, too, dissuaded him from undertaking a book. They simply did not see the point. An academic career was as remote a possibility as anything. Hennie was happy with their new life as teachers. She wished to continue their skiing and mountain climbing. But Popper was possessed. He now recognized how significant his innovation on a moribund Kantian discourse was to ascendant logical positivism. Sometime in 1930, he began writing.[41]

Feigl set the pattern for Popper's relationship with the Vienna Circle.

[38] Popper–Kraft postwar correspondence, Popper Archives (316, 24); "Popper und der Wiener Kreis – Gespräch," in Friedrich Stadler, op. cit., pp. 531–2.

[39] Herbert Feigl, *Theorie und Erfahrung in der Physik* (Karlsruhe: Braun, 1929), p. 116: "Die Theorien sind somit, wenn sie auch in der Forschung nicht durch Induktion gefunden werden, ihrer Gültigkeit nach dennoch als Induktionen zu bewerten."

[40] Carnap defined concepts extensionally: "Red" was the class of "red experiences." His purely nominalistic language, opined Popper, left no room for "genuine" universals, i.e., concepts going beyond a given list of experiences. No hypothesis could be formulated this way, since every hypothesis must include universals, or concepts with indeterminate extension, refering to instances not yet enumerated. Carnap's sentences were all analytically true or contradictory, their truth easily checked by comparing their words (concepts) with the enumerated lists. "Popper und der Wiener Kreis – Gespräch," pp. 526–7.

[41] *Autobiography*, pp. 82–3; Herbert Feigl to Moritz Schlick, 14 September 1933, *Schlick Nachlaß*, *Philosophisches Archiv*, University of Constance. (Original at the *Wiener-Kreis Archiv*, Haarlem, Netherlands.)

His philosophical development in the early 1930s would owe much to his critical dialogue with them. Recognizing his contribution, they provided him with outstanding opportunities. But the disjunction between their positivism and his Kantianism remained a source of constant tension. His anxiety that their reception would diminish his originality, and his perturbing insistence that he had learned nothing from them, made things worse. Neither he nor they appreciated that theories formulated in one tradition of discourse could make their major mark in another. The cunning of discourse, however, had beneficial effects. It contributed to both logical positivism and critical rationalism. Popper could have easily been forgotten as a marginal commentator in a neglected Kantian tradition. He became, due to his encounter with the circle, the most renowned philosopher of science in this century.

THE VIENNA CIRCLE

The legendary intensity of Viennese intellectual life in fin-de-siècle and interwar years owed much to intellectual circles that flourished on the margins of the academy. The university was too traditional and small to absorb urban life's intellectual creativity. Semiformal groups provided a network for intellectuals without institutional affiliation, and a refuge for academics who found the university stifling. The Vienna Circle was one such group. It consisted of philosophers and scientists committed to a radical reform of philosophy. They sought to apply recent advances in logic, mathematics, and scientific theory to philosophy. Among the more famous were Rudolf Carnap (1891–1970), Otto Neurath (1883–1945), and Moritz Schlick (1882–1936). Their philosophy became known as "logical positivism."[42] They were by no means the most influential or well-known group in Vienna, but they established links to like-minded groups in Central Europe's urban centers: Berlin, Prague, Warsaw, Budapest, Lvov, Bratislava. They had disciples throughout Europe and North America. Many of their members emigrated west in the 1930s, and had tremendous influence on postwar Anglo-American analytic philosophy.[43]

---

[42] Albert Blumberg and Herbert Feigl, "Logical Positivism: A New Movement in European Philosophy," *Journal of Philosophy* 28 (1931), 281–96. Other members preferred "logical empiricism," "scientific," "consistent," or "radical empiricism."

[43] Friedrich Stadler, *Studien zum Wiener Kreis* (Frankfurt: Suhrkamp, 1997), includes biographies, bibliographies, and documentation on proceedings and conferences. Secondary literature is bountiful: Herbert Feigl, "The 'Wiener Kreis' in America," in *The Intellectual Migration: Europe and America, 1930–1960,* ed. Donald Fleming and Bernard Bailyn (Cambridge, Mass.: Harvard University Press, 1969); Rudolf Haller and Friedrich Stadler, eds., *Wien–Berlin–Prag: Der Aufstieg der wissenschaftlichen Philosophie* (Vienna: Hölder-Pichler-Tempsky, 1993); Victor Kraft, *The Vienna Circle* (New York: Philosophical Library, 1953). English selections: Alfred Ayer, ed., *Logical Positivism* (New York: Free Press, 1959).

Already in prewar years, four of the circle's elders, physicist Philipp Frank (1884–1966), mathematician Hans Hahn (1879–1934), mathematician Richard von Mises (1883–1953), and Otto Neurath (1882–1945) had met regularly in Vienna's cafés to discuss philosophy and scientific method. Their hero was Mach. French conventionalists, Duhem and Poincaré, influenced their thinking, too. The group held together for only two years, 1907–9. Hahn left Vienna for Czernowitz and Bonn in 1909, von Mises for Strasbourg the same year, and Frank for Prague in 1912. The "First Vienna Circle" thus came to an end, but many of their ideas concerning the methodology of science reemerged in interwar years.[44]

Hahn returned to Vienna for a chair in mathematics in 1921. He organized those interested in "scientific philosophy" around the university, and facilitated Schlick's appointment in 1922. Against mounting conservative resistance, the two arranged several additional appointments. Kraft became associate professor in 1924. Carnap arrived from Berlin as a *Privatdozent* in 1926, winning a competition with Hans Reichenbach (1891–1953). Hahn's student, Karl Menger (1902–85), became associate professor of mathematics in 1928. Other circle members had to content themselves with minor administrative positions – Schlick's student, Friedrich Waismann (1896–1959), was a university librarian – or seek employment outside the academy, most often as school teachers. Thus formed a group of scientifically minded philosophers and mathematicians.

Beginning in 1924, the group met weekly for a Thursday evening seminar at the Mathematical Institute on Boltzmann Strasse. As the holder of Mach's chair in philosophy, Schlick presided as *primus inter pares*. Regular participants included Carnap, Feigl, Hahn, Olga Hahn-Neurath (1882–1937), Kraft, Menger, Neurath, and Waismann; social theorist Felix Kaufmann (1895–1949); young mathematicians Gustav Bergmann (1906–87) and Kurt Gödel (1906–78); Schlick's students Béla Juhos (1901–71), Marcel Natkin (1904–63), Heinrich Neider (1907–90), Rose Rand (1903–80), and Josef Schächter (1901–95).[45] Zilsel maintained a critical distance, but kept current. Gomperz made an occasional appearance. Frank came frequently from Prague, von Mises and Reichenbach

---

[44] Rudolf Haller, "Der Erste Wiener Kreis," in his *Fragen zu Wittgenstein und Aufsätze zur Österreichischen Philosophie* (Amsterdam: Rodopi, 1986).

[45] Rose Rand transcribed the meetings. Women were just entering the philosophical and mathematical professions in interwar years, and both were very much man's domain. The circle was open to women. In addition to Hahn-Neurath and Rand, mathematician Olga Taussky (1906–95) and psychologist Else Frenkel (1908–58) occasionally attended meetings. The presence of women was insignificant, however, in comparison with other liberal circles, such as those around Bühler and Ludwig von Mises. (In the latter case, the men responded by establishing an exclusively male *Geist Kreis*.) Philosophy was not, in interwar years, an expanding profession, likely to attract women. However, it is also true that some circle members did not take the women seriously. See, for example, Neider's account of Hahn-Neurath and Rand in: "Erinnerungen an den Wiener Kreis": 22, 34.

from Berlin. Visitors from abroad abounded with the years: philosopher A. J. Ayer and mathematician Frank Ramsey from England, philosophers Ernest Nagel and W. V. O. Quine from the United States, Kurt Grelling and Carl Hempel from Berlin, Polish logician Alfred Tarski, Danish philosopher Jørgen Jørgensen, and Norwegian philosopher Arne Naess. A number of epicycles formed around Schlick's seminar, most notably Karl Menger's Mathematical Colloquium. The core group, however, remained quite exclusive. A personal invitation by Schlick was required to attend. Popper never received one.

Like fin-de-siècle progressives before them, Hahn, Neurath, and other circle members saw a social mission for scientific philosophy: popular education and social transformation. Virtually all circle members participated in progressive organizations. Neurath had bigger plans. He wanted the circle to become the avant-garde of socialist culture. In 1928, he persuaded the militantly secularist Free Thinkers (*Freidenker*), now numbering most circle associates among them, to establish the Ernst Mach Society.[46] Schlick was elected president, apparently without his prior knowledge, and other circle members chief officers. The society's aim was to spread the new "scientific worldview." The next year, when Schlick returned to Vienna from the United States, his colleagues presented him with a slender volume: "The Scientific Worldview – The Vienna Circle." The booklet declared the circle's "independence from traditional philosophy," and outlined its program.[47] Schlick was now, reluctantly, the leader of a philosophical movement.

The same year, the Society for Empirical Philosophy in Berlin and the Ernst Mach Society jointly took over a philosophical journal, *Annalen der Philosophie*. They changed its name to *Erkenntnis*, and turned it into the movement's organ. It began publishing a year later, under the joint editorship of Reichenbach and Carnap. Seven volumes appeared until 1938, when political circumstances forced *Felix Meiner Verlag* in Leipzig to stop.[48] A book series, under the joint editorship of Schlick and Frank, began in 1929 in Vienna: *Schriften zur Wissenschaftlichen Weltauffassung* (Writings on the Scientific Worldview). Ten books, most written by circle members, were published to 1937. Popper's *Logik der Forschung* appeared as Volume 9 in

[46] Friedrich Stadler, *Vom Positivismus zur "Wissenschaftliche Weltauffassung"* (Vienna: Löcker, 1982), p. 2; Rainer Hegselmann, "Otto Neurath – Emiristischer Aufklärer und Sozialreformer," editor's introduction to *Otto Neurath: Wissenschaftliche Weltauffassung, Sozialismus und Logischer Empirismus* (Frankfurt: Suhrkamp, 1979), pp. 7–77.

[47] Rudolf Carnap, Hans Hahn, and Otto Neurath, *Wissenschaftliche Weltauffassung: Der Wiener Kreis* (Vienna: Wolf, 1929). (English: "The Scientific Conception of the World: The Vienna Circle," in Otto Neurath, *Empiricism and Sociology*, pp. 299–318.) On "declaring independence from traditional philosophy": Feigl, "The 'Wiener Kreis' in America," p. 646.

[48] Given the circle's political profile, and *Erkenntnis*'s many Jewish contributors, it was surprising that Meiner persisted until 1938. In 1939–40, the *Journal of Unified Science (Erkenntnis)* appeared in The Hague, under Neurath's editorship. Only one volume had been published before the German invasion in May 1940 terminated the journal.

December 1934. The circle also began organizing Central European conferences: in September 1929 in Prague and in September 1930 in Königsberg. Their international network testified to the vitality of cosmopolitan culture in interwar Central Europe – and its limits.[49]

The Vienna Circle was neither philosophically nor politically homogeneous. Some members, notably Frank, Hahn, Neurath, Neider, and Zilsel, were active, committed socialists. Others, such as Kraft, von Mises, and Schlick, were politically disengaged liberals. Schlick and Neurath represented polarities. Schlick spoke of a "turn in philosophy," but remained a foundationist philosopher, suspicious of Neurath's "radical physicalism" and "unified science." A refined grand bourgeois, he disliked the "loud" Neurath, and felt uncomfortable about the circle's close association with the Ernst Mach Society, whose activities were attended by socialist youth and considered part of the socialists' educational program. To Neurath, the circle was contributing to a new culture. The scientific worldview provided ideals and instruments for socialist reform, and would accomplish in the long run what the 1919 revolution had failed to achieve in the short. Schlick and others resisted, if only halfheartedly, his "politicization" of philosophy.[50] Even Carnap – previously a member of the soldiers' councils and the independent German socialists (USPD) – felt uneasy. Popper thought such politicization reprehensible. It became his model of what a philosopher should not do.[51]

In the polarized political culture of interwar Austria, a group that preached a militantly secular worldview, sought to eliminate metaphysics and theology, and believed in scientific progress could hardly expect to maintain cordial relations with the Christian-Social right. A majority of the Vienna Circle, and almost all of Schlick's students, were of Jewish origin. Liberal and socialist alike, they recognized that their fortunes depended on the socialists' ability to hold the line against fascism. When the socialists failed in March 1933, then again in February 1934, their "community of reason" was in great peril. Schlick could try to assure the government, in 1933–4, that the Ernst Mach Society was an academic, and not political, organization. He could even join the Fatherland Front and express his

---

[49] Malachi Hacohen, "Dilemmas of Cosmopolitanism: Karl Popper, Jewish Identity, and 'Central European Culture,'" *Journal of Modern History* 71 (1999): 105–49.

[50] Otto Neurath, *Empirische Soziologie* (Vienna: Springer, 1931); Elizabeth Nemeth, *Otto Neurath und der Wiener Kreis* (Frankfurt: Campus, 1981); Friedrich Stadler, "Otto Neurath – Moritz Schlick," in *Grazer Philosophische Studien* 16/17 (1982): 451–63.

 Radical politics and radical philosophy did not always overlap. Zilsel was skeptical about the linguistic turn, and Hahn made light of "unified science." Encountering resistance to using *Erkenntnis* to articulate his agenda, Neurath edited (with Carnap, Frank, and Hahn) a separate monograph series: Unified Science (*Einheitswissenschaft*). Seven slim volumes appeared from 1933 to 1938. (All seven are included in *Unified Science*, ed. Brian McGuinness [Boston: Reidel, 1987], with an introduction by Rainer Hegselmann. The series continued later in different formats.)

[51] "Popper und der Wiener Kreis – Gespräch," pp. 531–2, 536–7.

support for the fascist chancellor Dollfuss, whom he regarded as the only alternative to the Nazis.[52] To no avail. The government dissolved both the Free Thinkers and the Ernst Mach Society, harassed Schlick's colleagues, and fired his librarian (Waismann). After Schlick's murder by a deranged student in June 1936, a Christian-Social paper carried an article complaining that Schlick had poisoned Austrian youth with a secular, Jewish, socialist philosophy.[53] Ethnonationalism and clerical fascism were leading a concerted attack on the enlightenment heritage. Socialists and progressive liberals stood unified against it, but they constituted far too small a community of reason to resist the fascist onslaught.[54]

The circle's future was in the West. It attracted growing attention among philosophers, physicists, and mathematicians across Europe and North America. After a preparatory conference in September 1934 in Prague, a major international congress for scientific philosophy met in September 1935 at the Sorbonne. It received some support from French foundations and the government. One hundred seventy philosophers and scientists from twenty countries, among them such dignitaries as Bertrand Russell, attended. The proceedings came out in eight volumes.[55] Four smaller annual congresses followed until 1939: in Copenhagen, Paris, Cambridge (England), and Cambridge (Mass.). The war put an end to the meetings.[56]

The congresses solidified British and American interest in scientific philosophy and facilitated the circle's migration. Even in the best interwar years, academic appointments in Austria were scarce and competitive. For scholars of Jewish origin, or those tainted by socialism and positivism, they were increasingly difficult to obtain. Circle members were drawn to the United States: Schlick was visiting professor at Stanford in 1929, and Berkeley in 1931–2. Feigl left for a position in Iowa in 1931. Carnap left for Prague in 1931, then for Chicago in 1936. After 1933, the circle could no longer operate openly in Germany. Reichenbach and von Mises lost their positions and left, first for Ataturk's university in Istanbul, later for

---

[52] Schlick to Dollfuss, 1 June 1933; to the education ministry, 16 June 1933, 29 February 1936; to the Vienna police chief, 2 March 1934; to the security commissioner for Vienna, 23 February 1934, *Schlick Nachlaß*. Friedrich Stadler, "Aspekte des gesellschaftlichen Hintergrunds und Standorts des Wiener Kreises am Beispiel der Universität Wien," in *Wittgenstein, The Vienna Circle and Critical Rationalism*, ed. H. Berghel et al. (Vienna: Hölder-Pichler-Tempsky, 1979), pp. 41–59.

[53] Prof. Dr. Austriacus (Johann Sauter), "Der Fall des Wiener Professors Schlick – eine Mahnung zur Gewissenserforschung," *Schönere Zukunft*, 12 July 1936; reprinted in Stadler, *Studien zum Wiener Kreis*, pp. 924–9.

[54] The expression "community of reason" is borrowed from Peter Gay, *Weimar Culture* (New York: Harper, 1968). It is more appropriate for Vienna than Weimar. Otto Neurath's exclamation at the 1935 Paris Congress, "long live the new encyclopedists," captured well the circle's spirit, as does Stadler's rubric "late enlightenment."

[55] *Actes du Congrès International de Philosophie Scientifique*, 8 vols. (Paris: Hermann & Cie, 1936).

[56] The Nazi invasion forced the cancellation of the 1940 Oslo congress. An American congress met in September 1941 in Chicago.

the United States. In Austria and other Central European countries, the circle and its affiliates were under attack by semifascist academies and regimes.

If this were not enough, a chain of tragedies beset the circle: Hahn's premature death in 1934, Schlick's murder in 1936. Waismann, who took over from Schlick, left for England (Cambridge) in the fall of 1937. Gomperz left in 1935, and Menger in 1937, both for the United States. The worst was yet to come. The Anschluss in March 1938 sent members of Jewish origin scrambling to emigrate: Bergmann, Kaufmann, and Zilsel to the United States, Natkin to France, Rand to England, Schächter to Palestine.[57] The circle's publications were now banned. Kraft, the single senior member to remain in Vienna, was relieved of his teaching position (on account of his wife's Jewish origin) and relegated to librarian. Restored to his position in 1946, he would report to Popper that scientific philosophy was dead in Vienna.[58] The contrast with the Anglo-American academy, where the émigrés were shaping postwar analytic philosophy, was stark. Few, if any, movements left a greater mark on twentieth-century Atlantic philosophy.

The circle's program responded to the fin-de-siècle and interwar crisis of traditional philosophy. Helmholtz, Mach, and the critics of language had already demolished romantic *Naturphilosophie*, and cast doubt on Kant and empiricism. French conventionalists Duhem, Poincaré, and Rey undermined trust in traditional scientific views, demonstrating that testing could not arbitrate among competing theories. But the major impetus for philosophical reform came from advances in logic, mathematics, and physics. Frege, Hilbert, and Russell demonstrated that logic, arithmetic, and geometry were purely formal, and had nothing to do with experience, or intuition.[59] Their propositions were tautologies, constructed in closed hypothetico-deductive systems. Relativity theory undermined trust in perception and Kant's intuition of space and time. Science was advancing by leaps, yet philosophy could not explain its procedures and remained out of step. World War I accentuated the need for philosophical reform. Traditional belief in reason and progress proved illusory. If reason and progress were to be saved – and the Vienna Circle and Popper were both committed to salvage operations – they had to be reestablished on a scientific basis: their claims cut to size, purged of metaphysical nonsense. Philosophy had to explain scientific knowledge.

To accomplish the task, the circle took a linguistic turn. By joining mathematical logic and empiricism, they aimed to reconstruct a new

---

[57] Kurt Grelling of the Berlin group got caught in wartime France and died in Auschwitz.

[58] Victor Kraft to Karl Popper, 20 July 1946, 12 December 1946, 1 June 1947, and 22 December 1947, Popper Archives (316, 24).

[59] Gottlob Frege, *The Foundation of Arithmetic: A Logico-Mathematical Enquiry into the Concept of Number* (Oxford: Basil Blackwell, 1968). Frege had a decisive influence on Carnap.

"disinfected" language that would make science explicable. Only the statements of logic – analytic and formal – and empirical statements, designating discernible facts, were permissible. Statements about "unobservables" (or scientific theories) had to be logically reconstructed from empirical statements – intersubjective and testable – through induction. In *The Logical Structure of the World*, Carnap built an edifice of a scientific language that demonstrated the logical base for scientific claims to knowledge and their constitution from immediate experience.[60] He started with the definition of basic concepts and relations, progressing into composite, more complex ones. He considered statements not abiding by scientific discourse meaningless. Philosophy was to become a servant of natural science, constructing its language, or clarifying its concepts and procedures. The futile competition of philosophies that had lasted for two millennia would end. Real progress would become possible.

As members of the circle were struggling to formulate an agenda for reform in the mid-1920s, Wittgenstein's *Tractatus Logico-Philosophicus* offered them a program.[61] The *Tractatus* was an inquiry into the relationship between language and reality and a critique of the limits of language. Language, thought the young Wittgenstein, constituted a symbolic representation of reality. Reality consisted of the totality of facts (or states of affairs).[62] Thought and language, when properly functioning, represented them accurately. Language provided a logical picture, a model of reality. The basic units of language were elementary propositions (*Elementarsätze*) that described atomic facts (or states of affairs). They could be compared with reality. They were true when the facts they described existed, false when they did not. The totality of true elementary propositions fully described the world. Through logical procedures (truth operations), compound propositions could be constructed from elementary ones. The totality of propositions was language. Language set the world's limits.

"All philosophy is 'critique of language,'" wrote Wittgenstein (proposition 4.0031). Natural, science already contained all true propositions. Philosophy had nothing to add to them, no subject matter of its own. It was an activity, the task of which was logical clarification of thought. Traditional philosophical problems arose from faulty construction, "failure to understand the logic of our language" (4.003). They were not false, but

---

[60] Rudolf Carnap, *Der logische Aufbau der Welt* (Berlin: Weltkreis, 1928), esp. iii–vi, 1–33. (English: *The Logical Structure of the World and Pseudoproblems in Philosophy* [Berkeley: University of California, 1967].)

[61] Ludwig Wittgenstein, *Tractatus Logico-Philosophicus* [1922], German and English, trans. C. K. Ogden (London: Routledge, 1990). (Originally: "Logisch-Philosophische Abhandlung," *Annalen der Naturphilosophie* 14 [1921]: 185–262.)

[62] It was difficult to fathom what Wittgenstein meant precisely by *Sachverhalten*, or "atomic facts." Pears and McGuinness translate: "state of affairs." *Tractatus* (London: Routledge and Kegan Paul, 1961).

nonsensical, meaningless. "The riddle does not exist: If a question can be put at all, then it can also be answered" (6.5). Questions of ethics and religion lay beyond language and thought, "the sense of the world must lie outside the world" (6.41). "When someone wished to say something metaphysical [it is incumbent upon us] to demonstrate to him that he had given no meaning to certain signs in his propositions," they were meaningless (6.53). "Whereof one cannot speak, thereof one must be silent" (7).

In circle meetings in 1926–7, the *Tractatus* was read aloud sentence by sentence. (Only one, or few copies were available.) Schlick and Waismann found in it a working program for a scientific philosophy.[63] In "The Turn in Philosophy," the programmatic statement opening *Erkenntnis*, Schlick announced that, in principle, science could provide solutions to all existing problems.[64] Old philosophy's problems were pseudoproblems. They could receive no final answers, and diminished philosophy's stature. Philosophy was not a science, or a system of knowledge, but a series of acts. It did not determine statements' truth – science did – but their meaning. Its dignity was its clarity and finality. To outsiders, the *Tractatus* was the bible of logical positivism, and Wittgenstein the circle's patron saint. Participants in the 1929 Prague conference inquired why the philosopher behind the circle, Wittgenstein, was not present.[65]

In reality, the *Tractatus* was controversial within the circle. Neurath was highly critical. Some *Tractatus* propositions (6.423 on) openly endorsed mysticism: "There are, indeed, things that cannot be put into words. They make themselves manifest. They are what is mystical" (6.522).[66] What was the significance of the "unsayable," or the mystical, for Wittgenstein? English philosopher Ramsey suggested that metaphysics was "nonsense, but important nonsense." Was Wittgenstein exposing the inability of rationalism to address life's profound questions, or purging metaphysical nonsense with a view to constructing scientific language? Both the circle and Wittgenstein's early English disciples assumed the latter.[67] Neurath insisted that, even so,

---

[63] Brian McGuinness, ed., *Wittgenstein and the Vienna Circle: Conversations recorded by Friedrich Waismann* (Oxford: Basil Blackwell, 1979).

[64] Moritz Schlick, "Die Wende in der Philosophie," *Erkenntnis* 1 (1930): 4–11.

[65] Heinrich Neider, "Memories of Otto Neurath," in *Empiricism and Sociology*, p. 47.

[66] "Es gibt allerdings Unaussprechechliches. Dies *zeigt* sich, es ist das Mystische." I used the Pears-McGuinness translation here.

[67] Rudolf Carnap, "Intellectual Autobiography," *The Philosophy of Rudolf Carnap*, ed. Paul Arthur Schilpp (La Salle, Ill.: Open Court, 1963), pp. 24–9, conceded the circle's predisposition to discount the "metaphysical" dimensions of the *Tractatus*. Allan Janik and Stephen Toulmin, *Wittgenstein's Vienna* (New York: Touchstone, 1972), chaps. 6–8 argue for the *Tractatus* as "an ethical deed," and against the positivist reception. Norman Malcolm, *Nothing is Hidden* (Oxford: Basil Blackwell, 1986); David Pears, *Wittgenstein* (London: Fontana, 1969); and many others accept the positivist reading. See also: W. W. Bartley, III, *Wittgenstein* (Philadelphia: Lippincott, 1973), esp. chap. 2; Brian McGuinness, *Wittgenstein: A Life* (Berkeley: University of California, 1988); and Ray Monk, *Ludwig Wittgenstein* (New York: Free Press, 1990).

the entire project was metaphysical.[68] Any foundationist attempt to confront language and reality, construct an ideal language, and establish one true picture of the world was reenacting Cartesian First Philosophy. As the circle was reading the *Tractatus* aloud, Neurath repeatedly growled "metaphysics," to Schlick's consternation.[69]

Wittgenstein reinforced the circle's strategy for overthrowing (*überwinden*) metaphysics: logico-linguistic analysis, demonstrating that metaphysical propositions were improperly formed, and hence, meaningless pseudosentences (*Scheinsätze*).[70] Wittgenstein's *Tractatus* and Carnap's *Logical Structure* both showed the logical constitution of propositions and concepts. Properly constructed propositions were reducible to elementary ones, compound concepts to basic ones. Nonformal (factual) propositions and concepts – that is, those not belonging in logic or mathematics – could be checked against reality. When either reduction or verification proved impossible, an error in logical syntax was at fault. Either a concept was improperly defined, or a connection among the concepts violated syntactic rules. The proposition was meaningless.[71]

Around 1930, circle members thus held a twofold criterion of demarcation between science and metaphysics. Metaphysical statements were meaningless because they failed to conform to scientific language's formal rules, but also because they could never be confirmed by reality. Waismann introduced, in 1930, the verifiability criterion, implicit in the views of other members for a long time: "[T]he sense of a proposition is the method of its verification."[72] Verification attracted varied degrees of attention. Carnap and Neurath were mostly preoccupied with constructing a new language, not epistemological questions. In contrast, the Wittgensteinian wing, Schlick and Waismann, and also Feigl, sought to clarify the implications of the linguistic turn for constructing and testing scientific theory. For all that Schlick announced the end of epistemology, he remained concerned with causality, probability, and natural laws. Verification was a live issue.

Neither the problems of induction nor of verification were new to

---

[68] Wittgenstein conceded as much. The *Tractatus* was the metaphysical ladder which one had to climb to see the world aright, then discard (proposition 6.54). Neurath disagreed: "We need no metaphysical ladder of elucidation": "Soziologie im Physikalismus," *Erkenntnis* 2 (1931): 395.

[69] Carnap, "Intellectual Autobiography," pp. 24–9; Neider, "Erinnerungen an den Wiener Kreis," pp. 23–30; Otto Neurath, "Einheitswissenschaft und Psychologie" [1933], *Gesammelte philosophische und methodologische Schriften* (Vienna: Hölder-Pichler-Tempsky, 1981), 2: 588–9. Neurath's criticism of Wittgenstein was even sharper in private correspondence: Carnap Collection, Archives of Scientific Philosophy, University of Pittsburgh.

[70] Rudolf Carnap, "Überwindung der Metaphysik durch logische Analyse der Sprache," *Erkenntnis* 2 (1932): 219–41.

[71] Idem, "Die alte und die neue Logik," *Erkenntnis* 1 (1930): 12–26.

[72] Friedrich Waismann, "Logische Analyse des Wahrscheinlichkeitsbegriffs," *Erkenntnis* 1 (1930): 229. The phrase may have been extracted from a conversation with Wittgenstein (at the time in his positivist phase): *Wittgenstein and the Vienna Circle*, pp. 47–8.

Schlick or his students.[73] Still, Popper was right to state that, prior to his criticism, the entire circle had taken them for granted.[74] They recognized that theories went beyond "the given" and could not be verified, but they tried to work around the problems, rather than dispose of induction and verification. Feigl suggested that theories were approximations, but Waismann's analysis of probability showed that determining approximation required prior verification. Schlick, in consultation with Wittgenstein, concluded that natural laws, or universal theories, were not genuine statements but "directives for forming statements" of lower generality that could be verified.[75] Sometime later, Carnap realized that natural laws were not susceptible to being reduced logico-linguistically to "the given," the reduction demarcating science from metaphysics. Scientific theories passed neither the logico-linguistic nor the verification test. The circle began the attack on metaphysics by seeking to explicate science's claims to knowledge and vindicate them. It ended up nearly shattering the scientific edifice.

"THE TWO FUNDAMENTAL PROBLEMS OF EPISTEMOLOGY": THE CRITIQUE OF INDUCTION (1930–1932)

Popper sought to overcome the gap the circle had opened between science and philosophy. His empirico-deductivism resolved the difficulties the circle was encountering with natural laws. Initially, he limited his task to substituting deductive for inductive procedures, so as to secure improved logical status and methodological role for scientific theories. Only gradually did he develop an alternative scientific vision, but, somehow, he sensed from the start that major issues divided him from the positivists. He despised Wittgenstein. He was not merely jealous but furious that Wittgenstein had managed to divert enlightened thinkers from critical philosophy to language. How could an obscurantist mystic turn Schlick's head?[76] To be sure, Popper was also an aspiring young philosopher, seeking to catch Carnap and Schlick in logical absurdities and be recognized as an original thinker. His studied Kantian pose reflected, at one and the same time, deep philo-

---

[73] Moritz Schlick, *Allgemeine Erkenntnislehre*, pp. 353–67; Feigl, *Erfahrung und Theorie in der Physik*, chap. 3.

[74] Schlick, *Erkenntnislehre*, pp. 148–56; Carnap, *Aufbau*, pp. 252–3; Feigl, *Erfahrung*, chap. 3; Kraft, *Grundformen der Wissenschaftlichen Methoden*, pp. 192–258; Waismann, "Wahrscheinlichkeitsbegriff," 228–48.

[75] Moritz Schlick, "Die Kausalität in der gegenwärtigen Physik," *Die Naturwissenschaften* 19 (1931): 151: "ein Naturgesetz [trägt] nicht den logischen Charakter einer 'Aussage,' sondern [stellt] vielmehr eine 'Anweisung zur Bildung von Aussagen' dar. (Diesen Gedanken und Terminus verdanke ich Ludwig Wittgenstein.)"

[76] He considered "The Turn in Philosophy" a disaster. Draft of *Autobiography* (136, 1), pp. 40 A/B; *Grundprobleme*, pp. 297–9, 314–15.

sophical conviction and thinly veiled self-promotion. He established a convoluted relationship to the circle that haunted him almost to the end of
his life.

"The Two Fundamental Problems of Epistemology" (henceforth, *Grundprobleme*) began as one: the problem of induction. Popper intended to follow
Gomperz's model of a "dialectical critique": a critique exposing internal
contradictions in the positivist views of induction, and leading to his own
solution. He found the project difficult. For one, he was learning to write
a book. *Grundprobleme* was crystal clear, but long-winded. The compact style
that became Popper's trademark from *Logik der Forschung* on was still in the
making. His friend from the Pedagogic Institute, Robert Lammer, assisted
in the writing.[77] Not a professional philosopher or a scientist, he insisted
that Popper elaborate whenever he was unclear. Popper's writing became
clear and simple, but it was slow, repetitive, and inordinately long. In
February 1931, Schlick's "Causality in Contemporary Physics," addressing
the natural law problem, appeared.[78] Popper had to confront a new sophisticated alternative to his empirico-deductivism. His critique of Schlick
extended to conventionalism and to Wittgenstein's meaning criterion. It
also had implications for probability and virtually every aspect of his book.
This must have thrown the project off balance: The critique of Schlick
occupied about half of the manuscript, and references to his essay appeared
in all but a few sections. Popper did not get to explicating his empirico-
deductive model until the end (Section 47), by which time he had discovered the demarcation problem. A second volume became necessary. He
had a lengthy manuscript (about 300 printed pages), mostly a critique of
positivism, that proved difficult to publish.

As Troels Eggers Hansen points out, Popper wrote most of *Grundprobleme* I in just over one year, between February 1931 and June 1932. This
must have involved intensive work, done mostly on weekends and during
the summer. Part of the summer, he and Hennie would spend in the Alps.
This was one way of gaining privacy: They lived with Hennie's mother.
On weekends they went on outings to the surroundings of Vienna, Popper
carrying the typewriter with him. They would stop at a small restaurant
for a meal. He would write, she type. The people at the restaurant called
him "the man with the gramophone."[79]

Early into the project, Popper discovered that the internal "dialectical"
critique of positivist epistemology that he had planned would not do. He

---

[77] Robert Lammer to Karl and Hennie Popper, 20 August 1968 (318, 12); *Autobiography*, pp. 83–4.

[78] Moritz Schlick, *Philosophical Papers* (Boston: Reidel, 1979), 2: 176–209; "Die Kausalität in der gegenwärtigen Physik," *Die Naturwissenschaften* 19 (1931): 145–62. Troels Eggers Hansen drew my attention to the precise publication date, February 13, 1931, and its implications for *Grundprobleme*:
"Popper's Early Work on the Theory of Knowledge," *Ringvorlesung*, 30 October 1998, *Karl Popper
Institut*, Vienna.

[79] Hansen, "Popper's Early Work on the Theory of Knowledge," pp. 3, 16.

accepted, at this point, the circle's view that epistemology had no method of its own. Logical and empirical critiques, "immanent critiques," were the only legitimate ones. The first confronted statements with statements; the second, statements' "factual content" with reality. Logically, however, some of the epistemologies he criticized were proof. He needed to subject them to an external or "transcendental," critique. What external criteria could he use to arbitrate between conflicting epistemologies? Kant had asked the same question, but Popper did not like his answer, the transcendental deduction (consciousness is impossible without X; there is consciousness; hence X). He found another: an empirical method in epistemology. Just as scientific statements must correspond to reality, so must epistemology correspond to scientific practice. Positivism, sanctioning only statements about "the given," did not conform to the scientific practice that made wide use of hypotheses and prognoses. In contrast, his empirico–deductivism was both prescriptive and descriptive. By means of an "immanent transcendental" method, his critique demonstrated deductivism's superiority.[80]

Inductivist models of science, argued Popper, were logically deficient and methodologically unviable because they failed to address the problem of natural laws. Science went beyond particular experiential statements (*besonderen Erfahrungssätze*) to establish universal theories, or natural laws. To inductivists, theories generalized particulars, but there was no logical basis for generalization, unless inductivists presupposed natural lawfulness.[81] Such presupposition (for example, a determinist universe) was metaphysical. Positivists, aware of the problem, devised a series of solutions by redefining natural laws. The first regarded natural laws as mere summaries, not laws. The second submitted that they had no universal, but probable, validity. The third suggested that they were useful pseudopropositions, "directives for forming [genuine scientific] statements." Popper criticized each solution in detail, demonstrating either that redefinition failed to circumvent the induction problem or that it conflicted with scientific practice (testing). Natural laws were genuine statements. Induction was impossible. Deductive testing was the sole solution.

---

[80] He used this awkward vocabulary to mid-1933. Then, having demonstrated to his satisfaction that there was space for philosophy on the side of science, he dropped all talk about transcendental and immanent methods. In *Logik der Forschung*, he spoke simply of methodology. Popper, *Grundprobleme* II.

[81] In 1930–2, Popper assumed that lawfulness was necessary and sufficient to sustain induction. In later years, he concluded that even if lawfulness had been shown, it would have been insufficient to sustain induction. *Grundprobleme*, p. 35 n. *3. (Popper marked with an asterisk the notes that he added to *Grundprobleme* for the 1979 publication.) Hansen (letter to author, 15 March 1999) reads the text differently. As *Grundprobleme* focuses solely on demonstrating that it is impossible to prove that the *necessary* condition – the lawfulness of nature – is fulfilled, and Popper thereby levels a devastating critique against "naïve inductivism," the question of sufficiency is irrelevantly raised (although, philosophically, "it is better, of course, to present a condition which is both necessary and sufficient"). I do think that, in *Grundprobleme*, sufficiency is implied.

Initially, Popper considered empirico-deductivism his greatest contribution. He liberated deductivism from its traditional dogmatic-rationalist presuppositions, and empiricism from its inductivist associations. Scientific theories were hypothetico-deductive but empirically testable. While criticizing Schlick, however, he developed a critique of conventionalism, asserting the possible falsification of a natural law in a crucial experiment. Natural laws were not mere conventions. They could not be verified, but they could be falsified. This was a good enough reason to consider them a genuine part of science. Falsifiability became a marker of scientific statements. To complete his critique of Schlick, Popper engaged Wittgenstein, assailing the view that natural laws were metaphysical and meaningless. He discovered the problem of demarcating science from metaphysics, and recognized that falsifiability was an alternative demarcation criterion to induction. It dawned on him – it was the spring of 1932, or thereabouts, and he was at the end of the book – that scientists and philosophers clung so desperately to induction because it provided their demarcation criterion, their way of vindicating science against metaphysics. Induction and demarcation now came together. The concept of two fundamental problems of epistemology emerged.[82]

The discovery of demarcation shifted the focus of Popper's revolution. Induction now dissolved into demarcation. As falsifiability moved from margins to center, the hypothetical character of science became evident.

---

[82] In his *Autobiography*, p. 79, and *Conjectures and Refutations* (New York: Basic Books, 1963), pp. 33–59, Popper dated the linkage between induction and demarcation to about 1929, "after my dissertation." Having antedated his solutions to both demarcation and induction, he remembered 1929 to 1934 as one revolution, whereas there were a series of them.

Troels Eggers Hansen disagrees, writing that "it is *not* true that 'until the end' Popper was unaware of the problem of demarcation. Throughout the first volume he knew of the problem of demarcation, and – as it appears from many of the places I refer to in my 'Nachwort' – he also from the outset planned to write about this problem" (letter to author, 15 March 1999). Hansen kindly enclosed a list of references to the "demarcation problem" in *Grundprobleme* (Section 6 of his "Nachwort des Herausgebers"), distinguishing between typed references and those inserted in ink after the section had been completed. Of the typed references, I consider eight (Section 3, text to note 3; Section 10, text to notes 6, 7, 12, 13; Section 24, text to note 1; Section 30, text to note 1; Section 31, text to note 5) problematic for my argument. Popper first discovers that "inductivism is nothing else but a (primitive) solution to the demarcation problem" in Section 44 (p. 288), discussing Wittgenstein's meaning criterion. All references to demarcation in Sections 46–8, or in *Grundprobleme* II, or in Sections 1, 2, and 11, which were rewritten after the manuscript had been completed (see my note 83), do not contradict my account. Most of the references in Sections 3, 10, 24, 30, and 31 defer particular issues to a future discussion of the demarcation problem and appear as later insertions (sometime in parentheses). There is no significant discussion of demarcation. I do think that Sections 3 and 10 were among the earliest written, but the great number of references to later sections, especially in Section 10, makes it clear that they were retouched and retyped at a later stage.

Popper had had a vague sense of the demarcation problem since 1919. Is it possible that he formulated it as a philosophical problem, even in a preliminary fashion, in 1929–30 and contemplated tackling it in his project but, as he was writing on induction, found it impossible to address issues relating to demarcation? I find it unlikely, but, of course, it is not impossible.

Empirico-deductivist procedures, the inquiry's previous focus, now supported a new scientific vision. Sometime between the late spring and the fall of 1932, Popper rewrote *Grundprobleme*'s first two sections, the last section (48), and Sections 33 to 35, as well. In these, he took account of demarcation, and tried to create a new framework for a book that had been superseded.[83] Moreover, in response to the circle's debate on protocol sentences, he radicalized his revolution.[84] He recognized that even "basic statements" (*Basissätze*) – a new term he coined – remained hypothetical, and their acceptance was conventional. Returning to the foundation debate in the Nelson–Fries tradition, he extensively rewrote his earlier critique of Kant and Fries (Section 11), formulating a nonfoundationist vision of science. He completed the new Kant–Fries critique, and the manuscript of the first volume as it currently stands, late in November, or December, of 1932.[85] The book now offered a new paradigm: a deductive science that was empirical but not inductive, testable and confirmable but not certain, demarcated from metaphysics by falsifiability but not deeming metaphysics meaningless. Science left space for epistemology, methodology, and "non-scientific" philosophy.

Grundprobleme makes fascinating reading for the historian. Popper grapples with fundamental epistemological and methodological problems, and

---

[83] Themes, terminology, and *Fragestellung* distinguish between the rewritten Sections 1 and 2 and subsequent sections in *Grundprobleme*. Sections 1 and 2 reflect the results of Popper's inquiry – what he had learned while writing the book – not its origin. Their terminology seems to correspond generally to "A Criterion of the Empirical Character of Theoretical Systems" (*The Logic of Scientific Discovery*, pp. 312–14), written in the early summer of 1932. The earlier versions of these and other sections have not been preserved. (Hansen indicates [letter to author, 15 March 1999] that the earlier versions of Sections 1 and 2 reported in his "Nachwort," *Grundprobleme*, p. 443, note 7, are carbon copies of the final version, missing only insertions in ink.)

The copy Popper sent to England in late May, or June, 1932 did not include the final section (48) and Sections 34–5. Susan Stebbing, who read the manuscript a year later, inquired after them. (Popper to Stebbing, 3 February 1934 [352, 15].) In all four manuscripts of *Grundprobleme* I, Popper prefaced Sections 33–5 and 48 with a note stating that they were being rewritten, providing the contents of the prospective revised sections. The version we have seems to correspond well to his plans for revision. (See Hansen's editorial notes in *Grundprobleme*, pp. 230–1, 241, 245, 326–7, 443.) In his letter of 30 November 1932 to the German publisher Buske (281, 8), Popper wrote that he was shortening Sections 33–5 and 48. It is not clear whether he ever got to it, but the length he anticipated corresponds to the current version. Hansen reports (letter to author, 15 March 1999) that these sections have a different type style from that of all other sections of *Grundprobleme* I and II. Popper sent an extract, or an abstract, of Section 33 to Bertold Wiesner in England on 7 January 1933 (362, 8).

[84] He met Carnap and Feigl in the Tyrolian Alps in August 1932, and learned about Neurath's view that even protocols, elementary scientific reports, were subject to change. I discuss this in detail in Chapter 6.

[85] Popper to Julius Kraft, early December 1932 (316, 24). This concurs with John Wettersten, *The Roots of Critical Rationalism* (Amsterdam: Rodopi, 1992), chap. 8. It corrects my earlier account (Malachi Hacohen, "The Making of the Open Society" [Ph.D. diss., Columbia University, 1993], chap. 5), which conflated the intellectual revolutions of 1929 and 1932.

defines his position relative to other schools. He explores, trips, and changes his mind. Gradually, he emancipates himself from Gomperz's terminology. Discussions of Carnap, Duhem, Fries, Kant, Schlick, and Wittgenstein provide signposts for his intellectual development that will disappear from his later work. *Grundprobleme* shows Popper progressively becoming the philosopher familiar from *Logik der Forschung*, but it includes surprising turns that show also that Popper could have ended otherwise. His protracted path in *Grundprobleme* is my next subject.

"Knowing is searching for lawfulness, or, more accurately, positing laws and methodically testing them," said Popper.[86] He attributed this insight to Kant. Kant had recognized science's intersubjective character. Subjective perceptions played no role in it. Repetition (hence lawfulness) was essential to intersubjectivity. Kant was equally insightful in noting that experience was a scientific problem, not, as Hume thought, a program. If experience was problematic, how did it yield laws? How do we know? Kant's quest for knowledge, thought Popper, represented philosophy's high point. His Copernican revolution – turning from the laws of reality to those of consciousness – was valid, up to a point. Lawfulness was a precondition to knowledge; no experiential, nontheoretical knowledge was possible. But the "synthetic turn," establishing the a priori validity of lawfulness and vindicating induction, was an error. The "psychological turn," Kant's tendency to conflate the origins of consciousness with epistemological validity, was an even greater mistake. The first error threatened to drag philosophy back to metaphysical dogmatism, the second to psychologism. One had to concede that a chaotic universe was possible. It was not necessary for science to assume a lawful universe to search for laws. Science operated "as if" the world were lawful. This was sufficient for positing natural laws and testing them. All the same, Kant had made great progress in epistemology.[87]

Positivism threatened Kant's achievement by undermining natural laws. Popper made a short dismissal of "strict" positivism. Strict positivists adamantly refused to go beyond experience. They considered natural laws simply summary reports of experiential statements. They established no universal lawfulness and made no prediction. Schlick had already criticized this position in *General Theory of Knowledge*, and Popper quoted him widely. Laws were crucial to science. Strict positivism established none. Testing of summaries was impossible, they could never be falsified. Logically, strict positivism may be proof, but, epistemologically, it was a disaster.[88]

Positivists seeking to retain natural laws, yet recognizing that they could not be verified, sought a way out in probability. Natural laws were not true or false, but more or less probable. Induction, suggested Reichenbach, can

---

[86] *Grundprobleme*, p. 78.   [87] Ibid., secs. 9–10.   [88] Ibid., secs. 7–8.

provide no certainty, but can produce probability. This, responded Popper (and Waismann), was misunderstanding probability. Probability statements were hypotheses about series of events. They had to be validated just like any other. Their validity was *not* somewhere between true and false. Saying "this statement is valid with a certain degree of probability" required the same validation as "this statement is true." Knowing with a certain probability that natural laws would be valid tomorrow was equally beyond induction as knowing it with certainty. Natural laws had actually a rather low probability. The more they proscribed, the lower their probability, but the greater their value for science: They said more about the world. Laws that proscribed little had a high probability, but a diminished scientific value. Science was not about highly probable natural laws. Popper had not yet drawn the radical conclusion that science was all hypothetical, but he was moving in this direction.[89]

The "most recent and sophisticated" attempt of logical positivism to save inductivism was the "pseudostatements" position, articulated in Schlick's "Causality in Contemporary Physics." Schlick attempted to rethink causality in light of quantum physics. He thought, like Popper, that lawfulness was essential to science, but quantum theory seemed to throw earlier views of an orderly universe overboard. Heisenberg's uncertainty principle suggested that causality was inapplicable at least to some fields in physics. Schlick tried to use scientific practice to reformulate causality. Scientists formulated the simplest connection among observed events – a causal law. They made predictions based on this law. Their fulfillment confirmed the law. Scientists assumed it was likely that future tests would confirm the law, too, but expectation of future regularity, Schlick agreed with Hume, had no logical basis. It was a matter of custom and belief. Absolute verification of a natural law was impossible. Logically, verification applied only to individual cases. Natural laws were "directives" (*Anweisungen*) for scientific activities: deriving and testing predictions. Causality had a similar status. It was not a postulate that lawfulness always obtained, but a directive to search for it. The induction problem was, indeed, logically insoluble, but a redefinition of causality and natural law saved science.

Schlick defended eloquently the scientific model Popper wished to displace. He presented Popper with his toughest, yet most productive, challenge. Popper developed a twofold attack strategy. First, he interpreted Schlick to be saying that "directives" were "pseudostatements," and argued that they were actually normal statements with no special logical status. Second, he argued that Schlick's directives could support two methodologies, conventionalism and positivism, traces of both of which he found in Schlick. Neither methodology conformed to scientific practice. Schlick was out.

[89] Ibid., secs. 12–17.

Schlick opined that directives appeared "in the grammatical guise of ordinary statements."[90] Popper argued that this was inaccurate, confusing, and said nothing about natural laws. Specific statements, which were verifiable, also served for deriving other statements. If natural laws contained information about reality, and verifiable statements could be deduced from them, then they were – the play on Schlick's wording was evident – "genuine statements in the guise of pragmatic directives."[91] There was another possibility. In suggesting that natural laws were "neither true, nor false, but good or bad, useful or useless,"[92] Schlick was moving toward a pragmatic-instrumentalist, or conventionalist, view. Laws were then the equivalent of mathematical functions (*Aussagefunktionen*), not really statements about reality. They were neither informed nor contradicted by experience, but mere conceptual relationships that scientists found convenient in organizing reality. Schlick had to choose. If natural laws were about reality, then he faced the positivist dilemmas of verifying natural laws. If they were functions, then he, Popper, would like to offer an empiricist critique of conventionalism.[93]

Popper regarded conventionalism as a respectable adversary. Logical positivism was a passing fashion: logically cogent, perhaps, but methodologically flawed. Conventionalism, in contrast, represented a scientific vision that Popper found dangerous, but tenable. He stood with the "empiricist" Galileo against the "conventionalist" Cardinal Bellarmino, and his successor Duhem, in insisting that laws were not just instruments for organizing reality but had empirical content, but he admitted one could believe, and live, otherwise. He sought to contain conventionalist relativism through falsification, but conceded a great deal to it. Conventionalism was contestable, but irrefutable.

Poincaré's deliberations on geometry started Popper on his methodological explorations in 1929, and Duhem's views on physical experiments drove his inquiry in 1931–3. Like Poincaré, Duhem emptied physical theory of empirical content: "A true theory [does not] give an explanation of physical appearances in conformity with reality. . . . [It is] a system of mathematical propositions, deduced from a small number of principles that aim to represent as simply, completely, and precisely as possible a group of experimental laws."[94] Laws abstracted common properties of facts, forming them as single propositions. These propositions were further condensed into theories through deductive processes, classifying and establishing hierarchies and relations among them. Scientific growth meant multiplication of facts and laws of which theory took account by ever greater condensation. Growing orderliness gave rise to scientists' belief that somehow "the exact

[90] "Die Kausalität in der gegenwärtigen Physik": 156: "grammatisch in der Verhüllung gewöhnlicher Sätze."
[91] *Grundprobleme*, p. 268.　　[92] Schlick, "Kausalität": 155.
[93] *Grundprobleme*, secs. 18–23, 36.　　[94] Duhem, *La Théorie physique*, pp. 28, 26.

ordering of this system [reflects] natural classification."[95] Physical theory neither explained laws nor revealed reality's essence. This belonged to metaphysics. Still, the logical order that science established mysteriously corresponded to real relations among things.

Experiments, the fulfillment of predictions, further sustained scientists' belief in "natural classification," Duhem continued. Indeed, experiment was sole judge of a theory's viability. Judgment was difficult, however, because testing was complicated. First, physical experiment was no mere observation, but interpretation. Interpretation alone made measurement possible. Second, physical laws were not true or false, but approximate, because symbolic representation never corresponded completely to reality. Laws always remained provisional. Third – and this was Duhem's major innovation – testing of single hypotheses was impossible. An entire theoretical complex was always at stake. Consequently, an *experimentum crucis*, deciding the fate of an hypothesis, was impossible. Scientists never knew which part of the theory to credit for the success, or blame for the failure. They could amend a refuted theory, or opt for another. Logic could not decide in such matters. Good sense did. Experiment was complex, but it was the heart of physics, all the same.

Popper probably had no firsthand knowledge of Duhem and Poincaré. He formed his formidable critique of conventionalism without ever having read their works.[96] As the French conventionalists were widely known in Vienna, he had easily absorbed summaries by Carnap, Kraft, Reichenbach, and Schlick. He tended to collapse Poincaré and Duhem together, confounding Poincaré's a priorism and antiexperimentalism with Duhem's antiessentialism and criticism of *experimentum crucis*. He did not recognize that against Poincaré, Duhem held the hypothetical nature of physical the-

---

[95] Ibid., p. 36.

[96] Popper mentioned Duhem and Poincaré numerous times, but prior to the postwar era, he quoted Poincaré only once *(Grundprobleme*, p. 207) and cited Duhem twice (ibid., p. 23, n. 9; *Logik der Forschung*, sec. 1, p. 225 n. 5). There are no page references to either Duhem or Poincaré.

Troels Eggers Hansen comments (letter to author, 7 April 1999): "I have just discovered that [Popper's] references to Poincaré [in his bibliography to the 1929 dissertation] must have been 'cribbed' from Carnap's *Der Raum* (1922): 75. However Popper's *discussion* of Poincaré is *not* 'cribbed' from Carnap." The single Poincaré quote in *Grundprobleme*, Hansen adds in another letter (17 June 1999), *may* originate in Reichenbach's *Philosophie der Raum-Zeit-Lehre* (Berlin: Gruyter, 1928), p. 49. Popper quoted from this page in Reichenbach (p. 211) shortly after he had quoted Poincaré. All the same, Hansen does not regard this as conclusive evidence that Popper had not read Poincaré (or Duhem).

Joseph Agassi reports that a draft of his 1956 review of Duhem's English translation surprised Popper. (Communication to author, 4 August 1997.) Although Popper addressed Duhem's views on the difficulties of falsification (later known as the "Duhem-Quine-Thesis"; see *Grundprobleme*, p. 390 n. *1), he had not realized until the 1950s how close their views were. Duhem had elaborated on methodological problems that Popper believed to have formulated and solved first. He borrowed Agassi's copy and eagerly read it. His critique of conventionalism in "Three Views Concerning Human Knowledge," *Conjectures and Refutations*, pp. 97–119, sought to distance his views from Duhem's.

ories, their testability and refutability.[97] These inaccuracies had little bearing, however, on Popper's empirico-deductivism. Even a more generous reading of Duhem would leave his response to conventionalism intact.

Conventionalism, stated Popper, was deductive, but nonempirical. Experience could not decide on natural laws, because they were not testable. They were a priori valid analytical judgments, concealed definitions, conventional rules, chosen for their efficiency in organizing reality. Conventionalist and empiricist theories both applied to reality – but in different ways. No real prognoses could be drawn from conventionalist theory. Interpretation framed events and processes, and so they could not contradict a theory. Simplicity of organization was the single criterion for accepting a theory.

To demonstrate the contrast between conventionalism and empiricism, Popper recalled his 1929 argument on geometrical space in physics. He compared two concepts of simplicity, the conventionalist and empiricist. Viennese physicist Hugo Dingler, a Poincaré disciple, criticized relativity theory for its preference for Riemann's four-dimensional, curved space. Choice of geometry was independent of experience, he thought. Greater simplicity meant progress. When experimental measurements differed from prognoses, introducing ad hoc hypotheses to correct them was appropriate. Why opt instead for a more complex geometry (and theory)? In contrast, empiricists insisted that not the simplicity of the theory alone had to be considered, but all of its testable derivations as well. "Economy of thought" meant sparing use of ad hoc hypotheses. When the structure necessary to support a simple geometry grew increasingly complex, it was likely that not experience but the theory required correction. Hence, relativity theory.[98]

Popper acknowledged his debt to the conventionalists' deductive models, and accepted their pragmatic methodological orientation. But he insisted, first, that experience was crucial to methodological decisions (which Duhem readily conceded); second, that clear methodological rules had to be established to define "usefulness" (including an empiricist concept of simplicity); third, that logic did play a role, if a diminished one, in methodological decisions. Falsification in an *experimentum crucis* was possible. Duhem was correct that testing involved not a single natural law but a series of limiting conditions, that is, additional hypotheses. It was not always possible to point out immediately the hypothesis responsible for falsification, but it was possible to test suspected hypotheses, clear those confirmed, and, through gradual elimination, reach the culprit. Denial of such a possibility, said Popper, should not be taken seriously. It would be tantamount to rejecting verification of specific statements. They, too, were lower-level hypotheses, the testing of which included limiting conditions. He would

---

[97] Duhem, *La Théorie physique*, pp. 342–9.   [98] *Grundprobleme*, secs. 24, 29–30.

shortly recognize (in the fall of 1932) that, indeed, verification of specific statements was problematic, and they remained provisional. His central argument, however, would remain intact. Falsification was technically difficult but logically possible. Deductive testing of hypotheses and empirical falsification provided a viable model.

Theoretical physics, the most advanced science, demonstrated the power of falsification. Relativity theory triumphed in a series of crucial experiments. Falsification of prognoses threw into crisis an entire theoretical structure, Newtonian physics. Scientists isolated the hypothesis at fault, substituting Einstein's relativity. Or better, as Popper put it two years later, scientists searching for falsification had an alternative theory (relativity) to guide them, and designed experiments so that they could decide between the two theories. Falsification made choice among theories possible. If natural laws could not be falsified, science would revert to chaos, just like metaphysics. No arbitration would be possible between two contradictory theories. Empirical refutation held science together. Scientists were united in rejecting falsified theories, or ones that had become so cumbersome through ad hoc hypotheses as to be useless. Scientific progress, the growing approximation (*Annäherung*) of natural laws (universal theories), depended on falsification.

Science never verified a natural law, opined Popper, because it never excluded the possibility of future contradictory experience. Verification and falsification were asymmetrical. Verification of natural laws was forever impossible. They remained hypothetical and could only be assigned a provisional truth value. Their falsification, however, was final. They were partially, or one-sidedly, decidable: never true, but sometimes false. This was sufficient to retain them as part of science. Induction was impossible. There were no bridges to verifying natural laws, but there were bridges to falsification. Natural laws could be falsified through their consequences, specific statements, and prognoses that were both verifiable and falsifiable. Falsification characterized both universal and specific scientific theories.[99]

What was the logical status of natural laws? Popper was wavering. In *Logik der Forschung*, he no longer had any doubt. All science was falsifiable and hypothetical. In 1932, he was not sure. He had a sense that scientific knowledge must be true, not hypothetical. Natural laws seemed to have a peculiar, not altogether scientific, character. Any assertion of their truth would evoke an antinomy by implying universal lawfulness. He argued that they were "normal statements," but felt he had to find them a special logical status. He suggested that they were "heuristic fictions," or Kantian "regulative ideals."[100] Formed "as if" lawfulness existed, they were used for

---

[99] Ibid., secs. 31, 34, 37–8, 46.

[100] Ibid., secs. 34, 47. Hans Vaihinger, *Die Philosophie des Als Ob*, thought that scientific hypotheses were verifiable, hence no fiction, but Popper suggested that his notion be extended to natural laws.

deducting prognoses "as if" they were true. They were important, instrumental in allowing deductions, yet not quite scientific. His ambiguous position did not escape the criticism he leveled at Schlick's "directives." Both he and Schlick thought of natural laws as facilitating other, "real" scientific statements. Both could not find a place in science for natural laws.

Popper abandoned the idea of natural laws as "logical fiction" by the end of 1932. Many years later, he attributed his conflation of validity and decidability, that is, his failure to recognize that natural laws could be true and valid, and yet remain hypothetical and falsifiable, to a faulty theory of truth. Until he learned of Tarski's semantic theory of truth early in 1935, he said, he did not understand what validity actually meant.[101] It seems, however, that he had solved his problem even earlier. In the summer of 1932, he accepted falsifiability as a demarcation criterion and recognized that verifying specific statements was problematic. As his consciousness of science's hypothetical character grew, natural laws seemed less and less peculiar. His project had begun as an attempt to solve the problem of natural laws. It turned out that the problem was the norm for science. Science was hypothetical.

For hypothetical science to emerge, falsifiability had to substitute for validity (truth) as demarcator of science. In his sharp polemic against Wittgenstein, Popper extended falsifiability from a decidability criterion (for natural laws) to a demarcation criterion (for science). He engaged Wittgenstein because Schlick's directives and Waismann's verifiability represented epistemological applications of the *Tractatus*, but he was also apprehensive lest his critique be summarily dismissed as metaphysical by those arguing, with Wittgenstein, that epistemological critique was impossible. He needed to show who the real metaphysician was. He established an alternative demarcation criterion between science and metaphysics: falsifiability.

To Schlick, natural laws were not genuine statements because they failed the *Tractatus's* dual test of meaning. They neither described specific facts nor were truth functions of elementary propositions. But the concept of meaning, argued Popper, was blurred, and the test dogmatic-metaphysical. No evidence could be adduced to support the meaning test. It was a priori, without Wittgenstein availing himself even of Kant's transcendental deduction (showing that science was inconceivable without it). Like Hegelian dialectic, Wittgenstein's metaphysical ladder (the one he needed to climb to see the world aright, then discard) was an attempt to immunize oneself to criticism. Any proposal of an alternative demarcation criterion would be rejected as metaphysical. Carnap criticized Wittgenstein for asserting "the omnipotence of modern science" ("if a question can be put, it can also be answered"). Like Neurath, Popper sensed that not scientific omnipotence

---

[101] "Einleitung 1978," *Grundprobleme*, pp. xxii–vi. More on Tarski in Chapter 6.

but scientific limits were Wittgenstein's true aim. Paradoxically, the prophet of positivism was interested more in what science could not do than in what it could. It was not surprising that he ended the *Tractatus* with a mystical call for silence.[102]

Popper "therefore propose[d] to eliminate the concept of meaning from epistemology."[103] Traditional philosophy needed radical reform, but philosophers should reformulate its problems, not dismiss them as meaningless. A viable demarcation between science and metaphysics was available without "meaning": falsifiability. Falsifiability solved not only a particular problem – the status of natural laws – but a general one: demarcation. Induction and demarcation were essentially one problem. He suspected all along that inductive logic underlay Wittgenstein's meaning criterion. This was how verifiability and meaning disastrously combined to put natural laws at risk. Now he understood why the circle held tenaciously to induction (and verification): They needed a demarcation criterion for science.[104] Falsifiability solved both problems. Philosophers could put induction to rest, and substitute falsifiability for verifiability as a demarcation criterion.

"Demarcation is epistemology's basic problem," said Popper in *Grundprobleme*'s final section (48). Surely he would have written the volume on induction differently if he had recognized as much from the start.[105] He now reframed his project according to the results, rewriting *Grundprobleme*'s first two sections and resetting the *Problemstellung*. Induction and demarcation both appeared as epistemology's fundamental problems. Popper knew, however, that publication of the large manuscript on induction would be difficult. He wrote a short "Exposé," three paragraphs long, presenting the book to prospective publishers as a new epistemology that, through a critique of logical positivism, solved philosophy's basic problems.[106] To his friend, biologist Berti Wiesner, in England, he wrote excitedly in May 1932 that his book was "probably one of the richest in ideas and most radical of its kind. It could be an epoch-making book."[107]

Popper sensed increasingly that his main contribution would be less in the critique of positivism and more in his radical vision of a falsifiable science. He summarized, in a two-page report, the results of his epistemo-

---

[102] Ibid., secs. 42–5.   [103] Ibid., p. 300.   [104] Ibid., p. 288.

[105] Troels Eggers Hansen disagrees: "Your description of the development of Popper's ideas is too schematic: [first induction, then demarcation, then the two put together]. When Popper wrote *Grundprobleme*, he was breaking new ground, and it is very unlikely that it happened in such a systematic way. Whether from the outset Popper realized that the problem of demarcation is *the fundamental* problem (that there is only *one* problem – and not two problems), I do not know. But I do think that this possibility cannot be excluded" (letter to author, 15 March 1999).

[106] A later (1933) version of the "Exposé" is available in *Grundprobleme*, p. xxxv. One can reconstruct the 1932 "Exposé" based on this version and Hansen's editorial comments on pp. 443 and 454–5. Popper first sent it to Wiesner, 22 May 1932 (362, 8). (Wiesner was a childhood friend from the socialist colonies.)   [107] Popper to Wiesner, 22 May 1932 (362, 8).

logical revolution. In July 1932, he sent an early version of "A [Formal] Criterion of the Empirical Character of Theoretical Systems" to *Die Naturwissenschaften*, Germany's premier scientific journal.[108] It was declined. *Erkenntnis* published a slightly revised version in 1933.[109] The report in *Erkenntnis* stated briefly the problem of induction and its implications for natural law, and dismissed Schlick's solution as verbal. Schlick, and others, assumed that scientific statements had to be fully decidable. If one substituted partial decidability, or falsifiability, for full decidability, natural laws would become unproblematic. The problem of induction would dissolve, and epistemology's second fundamental problem, demarcation, would find resolution, too. Falsifiability would demarcate testable statements as scientific, nontestable ones as metaphysical. Metaphysics was historically a fountain of scientific theories, and so it was not meaningless. Wittgenstein's meaning criterion annihilated not only metaphysics but also science (natural laws).

The note in *Erkenntnis* was Popper's first publication in the philosophy of science. It constituted an end – and a beginning. It closed the chapter on induction and natural laws, and opened a new chapter – falsificationist methodology. It reflected *Grundprobleme*'s final stage. Partial versus full decidability would no longer be a major issue in *Logik der Forschung*. Falsifiability would absorb decidability. But the report's concise style was already pointing toward *Logik*. Popper included it later in the book's English edition (prefacing it with an inaccurate historical note).[110] He considered it in sufficient conformity with his mature philosophy. By mid-1932, Popper's vision of hypothetical science had emerged. In a letter of 30 June 1932, asking Viennese cultural critic Egon Friedell to recommend *Grundprobleme* for publication, Popper stated that his book was "a child of the crisis in physics. . . . Crisis is the permanent condition of a highly developed rational science."[111] The young Popper had become the familiar Popper of later years.

POPPER AND THE VIENNA CIRCLE: THE POSITIVIST LEGEND

Critical dialogue with logical positivism propelled Popper's epistemological revolution from beginning to end. He wrote *Grundprobleme* in virtual

---

[108] Popper to Arnold Berliner *(Naturwissenschaften)*, 30 July 1932 (276, 11).

[109] Popper, "Ein Kriterium des empirischen Charakters theoretischer Systeme," *Erkenntnis* 3 (1933): 426–7. (English: "A Criterion of the Empirical Character of Theoretical Systems," *The Logic of Scientific Discovery*, pp. 312–14.)

[110] His preface *(Logic*, pp. 311–12) insisted that he had formulated the problem of demarcation in 1919 in confrontation with Marxism, and not in 1931–2 in criticism of Wittgenstein.

[111] Popper to Egon Friedell, 30 June 1932 (297, 22).

isolation, and consulted only mathematicians and physicists while writing *Logik der Forschung*. Unlike Feigl, Hempel, or Waismann, who thrived on collaborative work, he was proud of his independence. His was an individual path.[112] He withdrew into seclusion for lengthy periods, then reappeared to confront the circle with new ideas. Nonetheless, even in seclusion, he was responding to the circle. Circle members were, at intervals, a source of critical feedback that led to crucial developments in his philosophy. He did not accept their challenges but, rather, worked out innovative responses. They were a crucial context for his philosophy.

Popper's differences with the circle were paradigmatic. Historians have tended to accept the circle's contention that Popper exaggerated his disagreements with positivism. Recent historiography has pluralized logical positivism, drawing a picture of competing philosophies in the circle.[113] But Popper does *not* belong in this picture. Historians often find that certain circle members shared his position on one issue or another. They miss, however, the paradigmatic disagreement.[114] Popper adamantly refused to take the linguistic turn. He understood it perfectly, but rather than take the turn, he found a way to cross the junction, forging his way straight ahead. He demarcated science from metaphysics but resisted the attack on philosophy. Even in 1932–3, when he showed he could do one better than the positivists on demarcation, he sought to establish the legitimacy of philosophy. He pursued reform, not an overthrow of metaphysics. He regarded himself a heterodox Kantian, and the positivists as precritical philosophers. His attack on Plato, Aristotle, and Hegel in *The Open Society* marked not a logical positivist seeking to eliminate metaphysics but a Kantian trying to prevent its contamination.

Paradigmatic theoretical differences still did not mean that collaboration between Popper and the circle was impossible, but his personality made collaboration difficult. Even Popper's defenders, Carnap and Kraft, admitted that he was a social problem.[115] He was brilliant, but self-focused, both insecure and arrogant, irascible and self-righteous. He was a terrible listener, and bent on winning arguments at all cost. He had no understand-

---

[112] He did not collaborate easily. In later years, collaboration with brilliant students, willing to dedicate themselves to the master, was an exception. But as few disciples could practice total abnegation for long, collaboration rarely lasted. Joseph Agassi, *A Philosopher's Apprentice* (Amsterdam: Rodopi, 1993) provides a wonderful description of Popper and his students.

[113] Friedrich Stadler, *Studien zum Wiener Kreis*; Thomas Uebel, *Overcoming Logical Positivism from Within* (Amsterdam: Rodopi, 1992).

[114] Stadler's outstanding *Studien*, pp. 512–24 follows Victor Kraft, "Popper and the Vienna Circle," *The Philosophy of Karl Popper*, ed. Schilpp, pp.185–204, in examining Popper's differences with the circle issue by issue. Both are correct in arguing that the circle was essential to Popper's intellectual development, but by placing Popper within the spectrum of opinions on various issues in the circle, they seem to overlook the different problem situations underlying the disagreements.

[115] Carnap reported in his diary, 13 December 1932, Carnap Collection, that Schlick did not want Popper in his circle and that Kraft conceded that he was difficult.

ing of group dynamics and no ability to negotiate them. His resistance of circle pressures to conform may have been admirable, but he also behaved as if he had learned nothing from them and insisted on his priority on every idea.[116] He mentioned approvingly philosophers with whom he shared little, like conservative Kantian Robert Reininger, but poured sarcasm on the circle.[117] He later admitted that both he and they were the last laggards of enlightenment. Yet, he emphasized their differences, not their common ground. He defined his mission as giving positivism a Kantian coup de grâce.

Popper towered above circle philosophers – old and young alike. He had Schlick's erudition, and was acquiring his lucidity. He had Carnap's logical precision, and intellectual agility to add. He had Neurath's imagination, and ingeniously translated it into methodology. He was developing an alternative to positivism, seeking to redirect the philosophy of science from language to problems. His chances of changing the course of logical positivism were small, but not nonexistent.[118] Kraft said that he took Wittgenstein's place as the major external influence on the circle in the early 1930s.[119] Neurath called him, in the 1935 Paris congress, the circle's "official opposition." In later years, Neurath spoke of a Popper phase in the circle's life, 1932–5.[120] Schlick conceded that *Logik der Forschung* was "an exceptionally clever work." Popper, he said, got "almost everything right."[121] This was some admission from the circle's magisterial head, who was just beginning to release himself from his self-imposed Wittgenstein tutelage. Was a second turn of positivism, away from language, impossible?

Perhaps, but a more congenial Popper might have further influenced the movement. It was unfortunate that he was not present in circle meetings. Gomperz accepted his revolution completely, but remained an outsider. Kraft was sympathetic all along, but never outspoken. Carnap proved adept at absorbing his methodology, but was too far into his linguistic project to change course. Neurath was beyond persuasion, but an open competition between their nonfoundationist visions of science could have saved the phi-

---

[116] Schlick reported to Carnap, 1 November 1934, *Schlick Nachlaß*, that he had censored *Logik der Forschung*. Neurath urged Popper to demonstrate unity and fraternity: Neurath–Popper correspondence, 1935–6, esp. 11 December 1935, *Neurath Nachlaß, Philosophisches Archiv*, University of Constance. (Original at the *Wiener-Kreis Archiv*, Haarlem, Netherlands.) Feigl described Popper's arrogance to Schlick, 14 September 1933, *Schlick Nachlaß*. Popper, *Logik der Forschung*, p. 227 (Section 10, note 6, added in proof), asserted that he, not Carnap, first suggested conventional demarcation.

[117] Popper, *Logik der Forschung*, pp. 53–4, 232 (sec. 26 nn. 3, 4, 10).

[118] "It was Feigl's belief that an earlier publication of the *Logik der Forschung* or of some other abridged version of the 'Grundprobleme' would have decisively changed the history of the Vienna Circle." Paul Feyerabend, "Herbert Feigl," in Feyerabend and Grover Maxwell, eds., *Mind, Matter, and Method* (Minneapolis, Minn.: University of Minnesota, 1966), p. 7 n. 3.

[119] Victor Kraft, "Popper and the Vienna Circle," p. 200.

[120] Neurath to Carnap, 18 November 1944, 16 June 1945, Carnap Collection.

[121] Schlick to Carnap, 1 November 1934, *Schlick Nachlaß*.

losophy of science some detours, and produced a viable alternative to the relativism that would triumph two generations later. In philosophical style, Schlick and Feigl were close to Popper. If the master changed direction, all bets would be off. Changing the course of scientific philosophy required a politician as well as a philosopher. It was a problem of human relations as much as of philosophy. Popper was ingenious in dealing with the latter, incompetent with the first.

Nonetheless, collaboration between Popper and the circle did take place. Both he and they reformulated their positions in response to mutual criticism. This was exemplary of the way philosophy and science should work, but Popper did not feel this way. The positivists, especially Carnap, appropriated his ideas and used them to advance their own project: a new scientific language. This was not what Popper had intended, but he had no right to complain. If Carnap wanted to use falsifiability as a meaning, rather than a demarcation criterion, it was Carnap's business. Popper had no exclusive proprietorship on his ideas, and no one had to accept his framework to use them. He himself used positivism to develop his philosophy. Neither he nor the circle grasped what was happening: Two philosophies were in dialogue. The circle denied that there were two. Popper, they claimed, belonged to their movement.[122] They were wrong. Popper believed that the positivists plagiarized his philosophy. He, too, was wrong – with a caveat. Their appropriation was legitimate. With some exceptions, Popper's claims of plagiarism reflected misunderstanding of the way ideas move in the public sphere, not to say a touch of paranoia, but the inadvertent result of the circle's reception of Popper was his absorption into positivism. This distorted his philosophy for the next generation, obscuring its revolutionary implications. The "legend" of a positivist Popper would emerge.

Popper's anger at the "positivist legend" was understandable.[123] The circle's interpretation of his work prevailed against his. He was one; they were many. Outsiders almost always preferred their version. *Logik der Forschung* came out in the circle's series, addressed positivist issues, and evoked a lively debate in the circle's international network. Could Popper be anything but a dissenting positivist? Shortly after publication, Popper wrote Jørgen Jørgensen in Copenhagen, clarifying his objections to positivism. To no avail.[124] In 1937, he went into exile in New Zealand for nine years. Logical positivism was meanwhile making headway in Western academies. Most discussions of Popper during and after the war relied on secondary reports by circle émigrés. The "positivist myth" became a convention.

[122] Ibid.: "ganz und gar unserer Richtung angehört"; Carnap, "Besprechung: *Logik der Forschung*," *Erkenntnis* 5 (1935): 293: "Den Auffassungen des Wiener Kreises steht Popper ganz besonders nahe."

[123] Popper, "Replies to My Critics," *The Philosophy of Karl Popper*, pp. 961–76.

[124] Popper to Jørgen Jørgensen, 31 March 1935 (313, 23). Jørgensen's *The Development of Logical Empiricism* (Chicago: University of Chicago Press, 1951), reflected the circle's view.

Finally, in 1959, *Logik der Forschung* appeared in English. Popper hoped that the myth would now dissolve, but two years later, he got tangled in the positivism dispute in German sociology. Habermas, employing a broad definition of positivism, criticized Popper as a positivist.[125] Popper's critique of positivism, *Die beiden Grundprobleme*, was not published until 1979 – and then only in German. His *Autobiography* increased confusion by providing an anachronistic account of his intellectual development. The debate on his philosophical identity remained inconclusive. Public recognition of his radical message remained limited. His exasperation was evident: "I am resigned to the fact that . . . the label of positivist will stick to me to the end of my days."[126]

In his *Autobiography*, Popper posed as a murderer, confessing to have killed logical positivism. "Logical positivism is dead. . . . Who has done it? . . . I fear that I must admit responsibility."[127] His ambivalence toward the Vienna Circle was immense. He alleged that they had misrepresented his positions and distorted his philosophy. At the same time, he expressed admiration for the circle, thanked them for their help, and acknowledged that they shared with him the enlightenment legacy. He recognized that the circle made his career possible, but thought they had diminished his achievement. He knew he was a superior philosopher, and resented having been at their mercy, subject to their authority, begging to be published. He somehow expected to go after them, relentlessly pointing out their errors, with no attention to personality or movement, and yet be thanked for his criticism. He never forgot, or forgave, not being invited to Schlick's seminar. Carnap promoted his work. Popper showed him later that no good deed goes unpunished. In postwar years, he pursued him mercilessly, winning one battle after another, pretending all along that truth alone, not rivalry, was at stake. From beginning to end, he wished to be known as the philosopher who "killed" logical positivism.

Internal battles in the community of reason are not a pretty sight. They should not obscure the merit of the philosophies involved. Asked in the 1950s for his view on the Popper–Carnap debate, Tarski responded that he thought Popper had the better argument, but that the people on the other side were much nicer.[128] Not all circle members were open, or even nice, but for an embattled movement, the logical positivists proved remarkably receptive to their most formidable critic. Their tolerance paid off handsomely. Popper's criticism enabled them to reformulate their positions, reinforcing the movement. In time, they reached a dead end. Popper sensed early that they were going nowhere, but their demise had little to do with

[125] Theodore W. Adorno et al., *The Positivist Dispute in German Sociology* (London: Heinemann, 1976).
[126] Popper, *Realism and the Aim of Science* (London: Hutchinson, 1982), p. 177.
[127] *Autobiography*, p. 88.
[128] John Watkins, "Karl Popper: A Memoir," *The American Scholar* 66 (1997): 215.

his critique. He did not need the dubious distinction of an intellectual murderer to feel vindicated. His critique of positivism gave rise to a novel philosophy that transformed radically the way we view human knowledge. Knowledge was hypothetical, open to change, yet growing. Practicing the intellectual openness that Popper only preached, the circle gave a contentious young philosopher, a social misfit, a chance to develop and articulate the most compelling philosophy to emerge from the interwar Viennese milieu. Popper was the true inheritor of the Vienna Circle's legacy.

Chapter 6

The Logic of Scientific Discovery *and*
the Philosophical Revolution, 1932–1935

"Today, I would like to make a request on behalf of a previous student of mine who has meanwhile become a thinker in his own right," Heinrich Gomperz wrote to the Mohr publishing house in December 1932. "Dr. Karl Popper completed [a book] on epistemology. . . . All those familiar with its contents consider it of major significance for the progress of science."[1] A few days later, Gomperz added in a letter to Popper: "Dr. Herbert Feigl told me already during the summer that the book contains the single epistemology he would take seriously. Professor Carnap, too, seems ready to take your objections into consideration. . . . It would be desirable for [the] book to be published. . . . Notwithstanding its original-ity and scientific seriousness, the presentation in the parts I have seen is so light, lucid, and understandable that one could certainly expect a wider circle of readers than [is common] for 'philosophical' books."[2]

Gomperz had no success in obtaining a publisher. Mohr promptly rejected Popper's manuscript. The search for a publisher went on for another half year, until Springer accepted the work in June 1933. The book that emerged in the fall of 1934, *Logik der Forschung (The Logic of Scientific Discovery)*, bore little resemblance to the manuscript that Gomperz had seen. The manuscript, consisting of *Die beiden Grundprobleme*'s first volume, represented an epistemological breakthrough. *Logik der Forschung* was a philosophical revolution, and that revolution took place in two stages. First, in fragments of a projected second volume of *Grundprobleme* II, dating to the fall and winter of 1932–3, Popper drew a new vision of science and philosophy. Second, in *Logik*, written between the summer of 1933 and the summer of 1934, he developed an innovative methodology to support his vision, applying it to probability and quantum physics. Popper had gone beyond Gomperz's wildest expectations.

Gomperz's letters reflected a radical change in Popper's life. He had come into his own as an original thinker and was gaining recognition as a philoso-pher. The splendid isolation of *Grundprobleme*'s first volume came to an end. His encounter with Carnap in early August 1932 transformed the circum-stances of his intellectual production. He continued to work alone, but from then on, he engaged a growing number of circle members, and circle con-

---

[1] Heinrich Gomperz to Oskar Siebeck (Mohr), 21 December 1932, Popper Archives (300, 9).
[2] Gomperz to Popper, 27 December 1932 (300, 9).

nections proved essential in getting his work published. He entered the public sphere as a member of the logical positivist avant-garde.

PUBLICATION: PRIVATE AND PUBLIC DRAMA

The circle gave Popper a reception he could hardly expect. The positivists, not their Kantian critics, turned out to be his main audience. He was surprised, gratified, confused, resentful, all at the same time. He did not plan it this way. Having written a critique of positivism, he first tried antipositivist channels as avenues to publication. Karl Polanyi provided a connection to cultural critic Egon Friedell, but Friedell had little time and interest in Popper's work. After months of delay, he offered only kind words.[3] Michael Polanyi, Karl's brother, a well-known chemist at the Kaiser Wilhelm Institut in Berlin, was of no help, either. He suggested, in October 1932, that Popper send the manuscript to Philipp Frank in Prague.[4] In postwar years, he and Popper would write each other as if they were best friends, but neither thought much of the other's philosophy. Popper mobilized other friends. His old mentor, Arthur Arndt, interceded on his behalf with a Berlin acquaintance – apparently with no results.[5] Popper asked economist and labor-law expert Alfred Braunthal, brother of the *Arbeiter-Zeitung*'s editor, Julius Braunthal, to see whether he could do something.[6] He could not. In the fall of 1932, publication prospects looked bleak.[7]

Popper pinned his greatest hopes on his Frankfurt friend Julius Kraft, who shared his malevolent contempt for positivism. Kraft had connections to a Leipzig publisher, Buske. In a series of self-involved, emotional, desperate letters, Popper pleaded with Kraft to lean on Buske. In December, Buske responded that he was ready to publish, but Popper needed to assume part of the production costs. The manuscript was long, the market was limited, and Germany was in the midst of a political crisis and an economic depression. Books of this sort required grants to be published, and Popper had little money to offer. Early in 1933, Wiesner promoted the book with several British academics and, apparently, got access to Wittgenstein. Popper

---

[3] Popper's letters to Friedell, 30 June and 17 September 1932, 19 January 1933 (297, 2).

[4] Popper to Michael Polanyi, 17 September and 18 October 1932 (339, 1).

[5] Popper to Anon., 18 July 1932 (17, 6).

[6] Popper to Hilde Braunthal, 10 January 1933 (279, 9).

[7] In the summer of 1932, Popper also sent two copies of the manuscript abroad, hoping to obtain both a translator and a publisher. One copy went in late May, or June, 1932 to Berti Wiesner in England and, through him, to biologist Joseph Needham; the other, in August or September, with Feigl to the United States. Susan Stebbing read Needham's copy late in 1933 and was duly impressed. Nothing came of her publication effort, but in 1935 she invited Popper to give lectures in London. Popper to Wiesner, 22 May 1932 (362, 8); Popper to Julius Kraft, late September or early October 1932 (316, 24); Popper to Feigl, 25 May 1933 (316, 24); Popper to Stebbing, 3 February 1934 (352, 15).

told him not to try Wittgenstein, and the two gloomily contemplated bringing the book out in a private edition. In the spring of 1933, Popper and Kraft explored publication in Nelson's journal, *Abhandlungen der Fries'schen Schule*. Plans were not quite set when Springer, the circle's publisher, accepted.[8]

In the background of the yearlong pursuit of a publisher, May 1932 to June 1933, a family tragedy played out. On June 22, 1932, Simon Popper died at 76. His life drew a trajectory of the rise and fall of the Viennese Jewish bourgeoisie. Having emerged from a modest provincial background to become the partner of Vienna's last liberal mayor and the chair of Austria's leading Masonic lodge, Simon Popper died leaving his wife with insufficient means. A few months after his death, Karl interjected a rare personal note in his letter to Kraft. He told him he had to sell his father's library, "a true monument to his personality and universal interests, for a ridiculous amount."[9] He did keep selected books, taking them all the way to New Zealand, then back to England after World War II. (They fetched a better price when, after his death, the University of Klagenfurt [Austria] established a Popper Center, and bought his library.)[10] The remnants of Simon Popper's library were the only enduring material testimony to his family's affluence and culture in fin-de-siècle years.

Worse was to come. Karl's sister, Dora, was back in Vienna from Merseburg (Germany). A photograph from September 1932 shows her, still a young and pleasant-looking woman, with a calm and dignified expression. Her bearing bespoke fine *Bildung* – solid character, generosity, intelligence, and remarkable civility.[11] She was at that time suffering from tuberculosis. Her pain was great, and depression ensued. Sometime in the fall of 1932, she took her own life.[12] Karl became responsible for his mother's welfare and any remaining family business, but he was woefully inadequate to the task. "He was never a great adept in making money," wrote Ernst Gombrich to Hayek in 1943, explaining how Popper could approach destitution on an academic salary in New Zealand.[13] There was no one else, however, to take care of the family. Karl's second sister, Annie, was always irresponsible. He had to assume the burden as well as he could.

His correspondence gave no hint of the family tragedy, and his *Autobi-*

[8] Popper's letters to Julius Kraft, September 1932–July 1933 (316, 24, under Victor Kraft; the letters from the fall of 1932 have no date); Popper to Buske, 30 November and 28 December 1932 (281, 8; 316, 24, respectively); Popper to Wiesner, 7 January, mid-January, 14 February 1933 (362, 8).

[9] Popper to Julius Kraft, early December 1932 (316, 24).

[10] Sotheby's sale catalog, *The Library of Karl Popper* (London: Sotheby's, 1995); *Autobiography*, p. 11.

[11] Photo (negative), Popper Archives (86039-10, BB, roll 1, no. 3). Date entered by William Bartley (list, no. 162).

[12] David Miller, "Sir Karl Raimund Popper," *Biographical Memoirs of Fellows of the Royal Society* 43 (1997): 370.

[13] Ernst Gombrich to Friedrich Hayek, 20 October 1943, Hayek Archives, Hoover Institute (44, 1). Popper's financial situation may not have been quite as grim, but it seemed so from his and Hennie's letters.

ography remained silent about it. This should come as no surprise. He did not include personal correspondence in his archives, and the *Autobiography* ignored happier family affairs. But the publication drama of 1932–3, and confrontations with the circle, seemed to absorb and, in turn, reflect private life's emotional turmoil. He acted, at points, as if crazed. Letters complaining about plagiarism, beseeching help with publication, and expressing ambivalence about the circle's reception reflected excessive responses to the circumstances. Psychologists may observe that Karl was pursuing publication of a book his father had always resisted. In Carnap, he confronted an authority figure who, like his father, was tall, handsome, and critical. A transfer of ambivalence was not impossible, but there is little evidence for proceeding further. Under the trying circumstances of exile in New Zealand, Popper was equally impassioned, unreasonable, suspicious when trying to publish *The Open Society*. Precisely which aspects of his private life contributed to the public drama is difficult to determine, but his anxieties always focused on the public theater. Private drama vanished into a public one.

In the summer of 1932, Popper had a crucial encounter with the Vienna Circle. Feigl, who came back from the United States for a visit, read his manuscript. Greatly impressed, he reported to Carnap. Carnap, now associate professor in Prague, was spending his summer vacation in Burgstein in the Tyrolian Alps. Early in August, Feigl, Popper, and their wives joined him for a few days. Popper was in top form, recounting his philosophical breakthrough. He found that the circle had meanwhile moved ahead and was now deep into physicalism and protocol sentences. Isolation had its cost: Some works he had criticized were no longer considered current. But he could not be easily thrown off balance. Incredibly quick in responding to new challenges, he may have improvised on the spot some of his new ideas on testing and falsification. In fragments and miscellaneous pieces from late 1932 (and possibly early 1933), he developed these ideas into a consistent methodology.

Popper lectured Carnap as if neither age nor position separated them. He insisted that his work was free of positivism. Carnap mildly reproached him, saying that the recognition he deserved, but had not yet received, made him exaggerate his independence. Still, Popper left a deep impression on him. Carnap accepted his methodological views, using them to advance his linguistic project. Shortly after, he wrote Neurath, suggesting that he draw Popper into the circle. "He is not easy to have an exchange with," he said. "He talks a lot and fervently, but, then," he teased Neurath, "what is it to you?"[14] Others were less kind. Feigl related to Schlick a year later that the encounter left him with a bad taste in his mouth.[15] Carnap's companion,

[14] Rudolf Carnap to Otto Neurath, 24 October 1932, Carnap Collection.
[15] Herbert Feigl to Moritz Schlick, 14 September 1933, *Schlick Nachlaß, Philosophisches Archiv*, University of Constance. (Original: *Wiener-Kreis Stichting*, Haarlem, Netherlands).

Ina, took an immediate dislike to Popper, complaining to Hempel that his forceful rhetoric got on everyone's nerves.[16] Popper was oblivious to the scene he created. This was his time of glory. Years later, he cherished memories of the time when he had finally broken out of anonymity to slay the positivist giant.[17]

Carnap reported on Popper's manuscript in his December 1932 article in *Erkenntnis*, "On Protocol Sentences."[18] He endorsed Popper's deductivist model of testing, and expressed the hope that his work would be published soon. Intense exchanges behind the scene preceded publication. Carnap's article described Neurath's and Popper's positions as fairly close. He sent a draft to both; both objected that they actually disagreed. Popper claimed priority over nonfoundationism: recognizing basic statements as provisional. Carnap told him that Neurath also claimed priority.[19] Popper was chagrined. His originality and independence were at stake. "I almost appear as a good student of Neurath," he complained.[20] Carnap's promotion of his work was gratifying, but he resented Carnap's use of his ideas to improve on Neurath. He asked Carnap to emphasize his independence, and Carnap agreed. He also sent Carnap "A Criterion of the Empirical Character of Theoretical Systems" for publication in *Erkenntnis*. This, he hoped, would clarify his divergent point of departure. Again, Carnap graciously accepted.

Popper derived little comfort from Carnap's cooperation. If Neurath disputed his priority, Gomperz, he suspected, was plagiarizing his work. He had discussed his ideas with Gomperz the previous spring, and he was surprised to hear him repeat them, without acknowledgment, in a public lecture in the fall.[21] He was about to be robbed, he feared, of his great philosophical achievement. He rushed to write a statement summarizing his philosophical revolution, including his recent advances and responses to the circle, and deposited it with the notary public of Vienna, Dr. Ludwig Willig. His statement provided a synopsis (*zusammenfassender Auszug*) of his projected two-volume work, *Die beiden Grundprobleme*. He thought of depositing a copy also with the *Wiener Akademie*, but apparently gave

---

[16] Ina Carnap to Carl Hempel, 7 September 1932, Carnap Collection, Archives of Scientific Philosophy, University of Pittsburgh.

[17] Popper, "The Demarcation between Science and Metaphysics," in his *Conjectures and Refutations* (New York: Basic Books, 1963), pp. 253–4.

[18] Rudolf Carnap, "Über Protokollsätze," *Erkenntnis* 3 (1932): 223–8.

[19] Carnap to Popper, 18 October and 28 October 1932; Popper to Carnap, 22 October and 1 November 1932; Neurath to Carnap, 26 October 1932, all in Carnap Collection. Neurath objected to "going hand in hand with Popper," but did not question Popper's independence. It is surprising that Carnap reported such a challenge to Popper.

[20] Popper to Julius Kraft, c. 2 November 1932 (316, 24).

[21] Loc. cit. Popper told Kraft that he did not want to disclose the plagiarist's name (a "well-known Vienna philosophy professor"). Joseph Agassi facilitated my identification by relating Popper's account of the episode twenty-five years later.

up.[22] Gomperz's ringing endorsement of his manuscript in December, his invitation to Popper to present his work to his circle, and a reference to Popper in his published lecture resolved the matter.[23] All the same, Popper thought that he had learned his lesson. He would be secretive with future work. Meanwhile, the only solution, he told Kraft, was quick publication of his book.

Easier said than done. He tried to approach Hahn through both Victor Kraft and Carnap. Hahn said he would be happy to read his work but declined to discuss it with him. In any case, he told Carnap, no further publication in the circle's series was possible before Friedrich Waismann's book came out. This could take a long time.[24] Popper daringly tried to approach Springer on his own. Director Otto Lange referred him to Schlick.[25] Everything depended on the head of the circle, but for some reason, he did not take to Popper from the start. Was it memories of Popper as a student? Reports on his difficult personality? Or, most likely, news that he targeted Schlick's and Wittgenstein's view on natural law for criticism? When the two finally met in mid-December, it was a disaster. Popper gave a lecture to the Gomperz circle at which Schlick, Carnap, Kraft, and other circle members were present. Popper was nervous, and this brought out the worst in him. He targeted Wittgenstein for criticism and, during the discussion, confronted Schlick. Wittgenstein, he told Schlick, was a dogmatist. Like the Catholic Church, he prohibited discussion of philosophical problems that he could not solve, declaring them nonexistent. Schlick left angrily in the middle of the discussion. He told Carnap later that Popper had misinterpreted Wittgenstein, and there was nothing new in his paper. He did not want Popper around. He promised Carnap not to reject publication outright, but he was clearly unenthused.[26] Publication prospects looked poor, indeed.

---

[22] Troels Eggers Hansen kindly provided me with this information: letters to author, 20 December 1998 and 30 March 1999. The *Auszug* is available in *Grundprobleme*, pp. 421–39.

[23] Heinrich Gomperz, "Die Wissenschaft und die Tat" [1934], in *Werturteilsstreit*, ed. Hans Albert and Ernst Topitsch (Darmstadt: Wissenschaftliche Buchgesellschaft, 1971).

[24] Carnap to Popper, 10 November 1932, Carnap Collection. Waismann's *Logik, Sprache, Philosophie* was planned as volume one in the circle's series. It was published only posthumously: *The Principles of Linguistic Philosophy* (London: Macmillan, 1965). Waismann had difficulty completing his works. Wittgenstein made things worse by objecting to Waismann's reporting his views and alleging plagiarism.

[25] Popper to Carnap, 17 June 1933, Carnap Collection; Popper to Anon. (Schlick), 16 March 1933 (17, 6). Joseph Agassi told me of Popper's recollection of his encounter with Lange. The letters confirm that they met, but provide no detail.

[26] Popper told Julius Kraft in early December 1932 (316, 24) that he dreaded the coming lecture. He described the meeting in his letter to Wiesner of mid-January 1933 (362, 8). Carnap reported on the meeting and on Schlick's response in his diary, 13 December 1932, Carnap Collection, and mentioned it again to Feigl, 4 July 1933, Feigl Collection, Archives of Scientific Philosophy. As the Gomperz circle met occasionally in Zilsel's apartment, this may have been the meeting that Popper described in *Autobiography*, p. 84. However, in a preparatory chronology for the *Autobiography* (405,

Throughout the fall of 1932, Popper was writing a new Kant–Fries critique.[27] He was casting himself as a Kantian philosopher. Neurath – whose "Protocol Sentences" he had discussed in Burgstein – may have clarified to him things that had been dim in his mind before. Statements can be compared only with statements, language with language. Experience cannot provide an indisputable foundation for science. Popper now understood how nonfoundationism resolved the nagging problem of the synthetic a priori. He did not appreciate, however, Neurath's contribution, and ascribed Neurath's position to Fries, Nelson, and the Kantian philosopher Robert Reininger.[28] They recognized first, he said, the problematic character of comparison between statement and experience. The positivists were rehearsing earlier Kantians. His epistemology owed much to Kant and Fries, not the circle. He was not wrong, but his reconstruction concealed the positivist contribution to his revolution. He was performing Kantianism to convince a positivist audience that he was not staging their own show.

In the fall and the winter of 1932–3, Popper also wrote several methodological expositions and a draft of an introduction to *Grundprobleme*. He sought to facilitate publishers' consideration of *Grundprobleme* by placing his project in the context of contemporary philosophy and outlining the methodological issues that his projected second volume would address. But the writings reflected even more his eagerness to vindicate his philosophy against objections that circle members, from Carnap to Neurath to Reichenbach to Schlick, had recently raised. He implicated Neurath's protocols with psychologism, that is, reliance on subjective experience to

---

1), Popper dated the lecture at Zilsel's place to 1935. He did lecture in Zilsel's apartment early in 1935, and it is possible that he confounded the two. He made two presentations at meetings chaired by Gomperz in the fall of 1932. It is possible that one took place at Zilsel's, the other elsewhere. (Popper to Wiesner, late December 1932.)

27 John Wettersten (*The Roots of Critical Rationalism* [Amsterdam: Rodopi, 1992], chap. 8) noted the peculiarities of Section 11 of *Grundprobleme* (the new Kant critique). It is fifty-six pages long, by far the longest section, about a fifth of the manuscript. It seems to stand on its own, the transition to the succeeding section abrupt. It includes terminology (empirical basis; basic statement; observation statement) absent elsewhere in *Grundprobleme* I (and standard in *Logik*), and its nonfoundationism conflicts with statements in other sections that accept "singular reality statements" as final. Wettersten concluded that this was the last section to be written, and the correspondence between Popper and Julius Kraft corroborates his view. Troels Eggers Hansen examined, however, all of Popper's cross-references to Section 11 in the manuscript. He counted nine typed references, and eleven inserted in ink. He concludes that there must have been an earlier version of Section 11. (Hansen to author, 20 December 1998 and 31 January 1999.) I concur. However, with the exception of the reference in Section 2 (rewritten sometime between the late spring and the fall of 1932), none of the typed references touch on testing, or falsification, or the empirical basis, i. e., the epistemological revolution of the fall of 1932. Could Popper have coined the term "empirical basis" and written on it prior to Burgstein? I doubt very much, but his fury when Neurath denied him priority over nonfoundationism would become less unreasonable.

28 Popper, *Logik der Forschung*, secs. 25–6, 30 n. 4.

justify statements. He countered "protocol" with a new term, "basic statement" (*Basissatz*), referring to a singular statement that could be intersubjectively tested. He also made several defensive moves. Apprehensive lest the positivist effort to diminish philosophy put his own work at risk, he tried to carve a living space for philosophy in between science and metaphysics, by legitimizing epistemology and methodology as fields outside the scientific purview. He also responded to conventionalist objections to his demarcation criterion (falsification) by developing methodological rules for testing. As he was moving from epistemology to methodology, his nonfoundationism became progressively radical. He transformed his epistemological breakthrough into a revolution. By early 1933, the revolution was complete. He needed a methodology to support it. *Logik der Forschung* would supply it.

Troels Eggers Hansen surmises that the miscellaneous pieces and fragments from the fall and the winter of 1932–3 represent a more complete manuscript, now lost, of *Grundprobleme*'s second volume.[29] I doubt that such a manuscript existed, but there is little doubt that Popper thought of his current writings as addressing problems that he was planning to discuss in *Grundprobleme* II.[30] The writings include an introduction outlining the task of philosophy; two brief *Problemstellungen*, setting the problems of induction and demarcation; three methodological outlines, focusing on falsification (the first an appendix to *Grundprobleme* I); and a synopsis (*Auszug*) of the two volumes as Popper projected them in November 1932.[31] Together with *Grundprobleme* I, Popper probably submitted to Schlick, around Christmas of 1932, the methodological appendix "Transition to Methodological Theory" and, possibly, the

---

[29] He collected these writings under the title "Book II: The Demarcation Problem (Experience and Metaphysics)" (*II. Buch: Das Abgrenzungsproblem [Erfahrung und Metaphysik]*). This was the title Popper projected for *Grundprobleme*'s second volume in November 1932: *Grundprobleme*, "Auszug," p. 421.

[30] Between the spring of 1932 and the spring of 1933, Popper intended to write a second volume, but there is significant evidence in his correspondence that he never undertook the task. Until his letter to Susan Stebbing of February 3, 1934, he mentioned nowhere having written any part of *Grundprobleme* II. On the Stebbing letter, see my discussion of Popper's lost manuscripts later in this chapter.

[31] Introduction ("Entwurf einer Einführung"), *Grundprobleme*, pp. 341–6 (Popper used the introduction's first paragraph as the preface to *Logik der Forschung*); two problem settings ("Problemstellung" and "Philosophie"), pp. 347–9, 385–8; three methodological outlines ("Übergang zur Methodentheorie," "Grundriß einer Theorie der empirisch-wissenschaftlichen Methoden," "Das Problem der Methodenlehre"), pp. 353–74, 378–82, 389–95; synopsis (*zusammenfassender Auszug*), pp. 419–39. (The synopsis is published as an appendix to both volumes of *Grundprobleme*, not as a fragment of volume II.) As Hansen indicates in his "Nachwort" (*Grundprobleme*, p. 445), precise dating of some of the fragments is difficult. I think that "Philosophie" and "Das Problem der Methodenlehre" *may* date from later in 1933 when Popper was already working on *Logik der Forschung*. The later date seems even more probable for the final three fragments, collected in *Grundprobleme* II, on "freedom of the will" and "probability" (pp. 396–418). Hansen believes, however, that they all belong in *Grundprobleme* II and points out similarities of terminology and themes with *Grundprobleme* I (letter to author, 14 May 1999).

introduction.[32] If we trust his protestations to Carnap, (Julius) Kraft, and Schlick, he was not working on *Grundprobleme* II in a sustained manner during the winter and the spring of 1933.[33] He could put no more effort into the project, he said, unless publication became possible. Fragmented as his contemporary writings were, however, they represented a major theoretical advance.[34] With few exceptions, they settled all epistemological issues, leaving to *Logik der Forschung* technical and methodological questions.

Popper's capacity for endless work was legendary. He worked 360 days a year, day and night. Observers rarely noticed the spasmodic pattern of his literary production. He alternated between productive periods, characterized by tension and elation, and barren ones, characterized by nonintellectual concerns, anxiety, and depression. During the first, he worked for weeks and months with little sleep. During the latter, he made little headway. To be sure, he was always frightfully busy, whether teaching (1932–3), searching for a job (1935–6), or procuring visas for refugees (1938–9), but impediments to writing were as much psychological as external. In early May 1933, he told Carnap that teaching prevented him not only from making progress on his work, but also from writing the article that Carnap promised to publish in *Erkenntnis*. He was even unable to comment on Carnap's *Logical Syntax*.[35] This must be compared with the incredible amount of work he did on *Logik der Forschung* during the next year. The problem was psychology, not teaching. In the spring of 1933, he thought that his previ-

---

[32] One of the two manuscripts of *Grundprobleme* I remaining in Vienna includes (in Section 30) a reference to "Übergang" as an appendix. Popper described his visit to Schlick's apartment to Wiesner in a letter, mid-January 1933 (362, 8). He sent the introduction to Wiesner, Braunthal, and Friedell (together with selections from Carnap's "Protokollsätze" and Gomperz's letter) on January 7, January 10, and January 19, 1933, respectively (362, 8; 279, 9). He also sent the introduction and the synopsis to Julius Kraft on July 11, 1933.

[33] Popper to Carnap, 7 May 1933, Carnap Collection; Popper to Julius Kraft, 26 May 1933 (316, 24); Popper to Anon. (Schlick), 16 March 1933 (17, 6). Thus, to Carnap, on May 7: "I am under the painful pressure of nonscholarly obligations, above all teaching. I do get to work, but this consists only in thinking through certain questions, sometimes also reading or sketching something, here and there. For continuous work I simply find no time. Having made a few unproductive efforts to work through the night, I had to give it up. I thus accomplished *very* little this past winter, carrying out virtually no part of my plan."

[34] Some of the material on methodology, conventionalism, and the foundation problem would appear in *Logik der Forschung*, if rarely in recognizable form. Popper rewrote everything: *Logik der Forschung* (Vienna: Julius Springer, 1935), Preface and Sections 6, 10, 11, 19, 29, 30, 46.

[35] Popper to Carnap, 7 May 1933, Carnap Collection. They spoke about the article in Burgstein (Popper to Carnap, 22 October 1932). On November 1, Popper said that he would soon send a draft of "On the Discussion of Protocol Sentences." Carnap inquired about it twice: March 3 and April 17, 1933. Popper promised comments on "Semantik" (later: *Logische Syntax der Sprache* [Vienna: Julius Springer, 1934]) in January 1933. He sent brief comments on June 20. (See also *Grundprobleme* II, pp. 371–4, which discusses "Semantik," and the editor's notes there.)

ous work had been in vain. Political catastrophes worsened his publication chances and ominously clouded his future. The Nazis came to power in Germany on January 30. Dollfuss ended parliamentary democracy in Austria on March 4. Director Lange told him late in March that, under the circumstances, publication was unlikely. Until Popper heard of Schlick's favorable recommendation to Springer in early May, he was depressed and doing little writing.

Schlick's recommendation changed Popper's prospects overnight. The problem all along had been to get Schlick to read the manuscript. He had promised Popper a decision in January.[36] Carnap, supporting himself with Gomperz's recommendation, sent him a letter, urging publication.[37] The letter may have dissuaded Schlick from dismissing the book without reading it, but, in mid-March, he had still not read it.[38] When he finally did in April 1933, he recognized that Popper had the sharpest mind around. The level of analysis and presentation, he told Frank, was exceptionally high.[39] Nevertheless, he still disliked Popper. Having held the manuscript for half a year, he complained that Popper seemed in a terrible rush.[40] He kept referring to Popper and his work as "clever" (*klug*), a term often used to describe Jews.[41] Still, he was no anti-Semite – his most beloved students were Jewish – and did not let personal dislike stand in the way of philosophical judgment.

Popper's joy at the publication contract was immense. He did not quite believe it until he signed it on June 30.[42] To Julius Kraft he apologized for consenting to publish his work in a positivist series: Writings on the Scientific Worldview.[43] Truly, he was granted an entry into the most prestigious club of Viennese avant-garde philosophy. The contract stipulated a maximum length of twelve sheets (about 200 pages) and delivery by March 1, 1934. The title was to be determined later. Popper was to heed Schlick's advice on abridgment. Apparently, he agreed with Schlick to provide a summary of *Grundprobleme* I but to cut short his criticism and elaborate his solution. Already in July 1933 he had a different plan: His brief exchanges with Reichenbach convinced him that, to vindicate his epistemology, he had to develop both a new concept of probability and a methodology of falsification. He had not written much during the previous spring, but he seems to have thought some questions through. The *Exposé* he sent Julius

[36] Popper to Carnap, 16 January 1933, Carnap Collection.
[37] Carnap to Schlick, 19 January 1933, *Schlick Nachlaß*.
[38] Popper to Anon. (Schlick), 16 March 1933 (17, 6).
[39] Schlick to Frank, 9 June 1933, *Schlick Nachlaß*.
[40] Schlick to Carnap, 18 June 1933, Carnap Collection.
[41] Schlick to Carnap, 9 June 1933 and 1 November 1934, *Schlick Nachlaß*.
[42] Springer to Popper, 30 June 1933, *Schlick Nachlaß*.
[43] Popper to Julius Kraft, 25 May 1933 and 11 July 1933 (316, 24).

Kraft suggested his new foci: investigating the simplicity, economy, and degree of testability of hypotheses, lawfulness and chance, causality and probability.[44]

In his postcontract elation, Popper felt omnipotent. He would show circle philosophers, who considered themselves arbiters of physics and mathematics, that he could do one better. On July 11 he told Julius Kraft that he would be writing a virtually new book. He did not quite know yet how true this would prove, and what a tall order he was setting for himself. All the same, *Logik der Forschung* built on the epistemological revolution of *"Grundprobleme* II," 1932–3. Reconstructing this revolution and setting the intellectual scene in which Popper found himself in July 1933, as he was beginning *Logik*, is my next task.

NONFOUNDATIONIST PHILOSOPHY: THE EPISTEMOLOGICAL REVOLUTION, 1932–1933

Logical positivism traveled some distance between 1930 and 1932. From 1931 on, the circle's "left wing" – above all Carnap and Neurath – undertook to create a universal scientific language. The project originated in critiques of Carnap's *The Logical Structure of the World*.[45] Following Wittgenstein, Schlick and his students protested that language could not speak about its own logical forms. Representation's forms were not themselves representable. Gödel gave Carnap a way out. He showed, Carnap thought, that arithmetization of syntax was possible: "A theory of the forms of expressions could be formulated with the help of concepts of arithmetic" by "correlating numbers with signs and expressions."[46] This should make it possible for language to talk about its own syntax, for a metalogic to be formulated in scientific language itself. Carnap turned to forming universal logical syntax for scientific languages. As Gödel showed that no linguistic system was complete, more than one language could be constructed based on syntactic rules. Choice was conventional. In principle, this gave rise to "linguistic tolerance."[47] In practice, as Menger complained, the opposite was true.[48] Efforts to exclude metaphysics intensified. Carnap hoped

---

[44] *Grundprobleme*, p. 453; enclosure to Popper's letter to Kraft (316, 24). Hansen drew my attention to the *Exposé* (letter of 30 March 1999).

[45] Rudolf Carnap, *Der logische Aufbau der Welt* (Berlin: Weltkreis, 1928), esp. pp. iii–vi, 1–33. (English: *The Logical Structure of the World and Pseudoproblems in Philosophy* [Berkeley: University of California, 1967].)

[46] Rudolf Carnap, "Intellectual Autobiography," *The Philosophy of Rudolf Carnap*, ed. Paul Arthur Schilpp (La Salle, Ill.: Open Court, 1963), p. 53.

[47] Carnap, *Logische Syntax der Sprache* (Vienna: Springer, 1934), pp. 44–5.

[48] Karl Menger, "Memories of Moritz Schlick," in *Rationality and Science*, ed. Eugene Gadol (New York: Springer, 1982), pp. 83–103.

that scientific logic would replace philosophy. Neurath sought to limit linguistic choice to one universal language of unified science: physicalism. Statements that could not be expressed in physicalism were meaningless from the scientific vantage point, even if they remained meaningful in less restrictive ordinary languages.

Physicalism was Neurath's response to *Logical Construction*. Carnap described his own epistemology as solipsistic. He reconstructed scientific concepts based on "the given," the world as available to the self. Neurath and Neider pointed out that individual psychological concepts did not conform to science's collective and intersubjective character.[49] They were not testable. An avowed materialist, Neurath was convinced that only statements referring exclusively to physical objects (or data) and their location and movement in space and time were intersubjective. He acknowledged that opting for physicalism was not a logical matter, but a practical decision. Science was an instrument of social transformation, and a universal language of unified science best suited the battle against metaphysics, and the fight for human mastery over history and nature. Linguistic reform had to conform to emancipatory scientific practice. Carnap's attempt in *Logical Construction* to construct an ideal scientific language presupposed going outside natural language to create a pure one. This was impossible, a vestige of metaphysics. Instead, clarity of imprecise scientific concepts (*Ballungen*) should be increased through piecemeal physicalist reform.[50]

Carnap accepted intersubjectivity and physicalism, but was reluctant to give up on grounding statements in experience. He devised primitive protocols: reports in phenomenal, autopsychological language, to be translated later into physicalist language. Verification against reality meant confronting physicalist with phenomenalist sentences.[51] Neurath rejected such a comparison between language and reality as metaphysical: "It is impossible to go back behind language."[52] "Statements are always compared with statements, not with some 'reality,' or 'things,' as the Vienna Circle has so far done."[53] Solipsistic ("mental") protocols were nonscientific. Protocols should be physicalist: "observation statements" on observers in relation to their environment. Neurath never expressed himself with clarity, however, and Carnap remained skeptical: No intersubjective protocols were possible. In early 1932, he recognized that even singular (physicalist) statements

[49] Heinrich Neider, "Persönliche Erinnerungen an den Wiener Kreis," *Conceptus* 11 (1977): 29–30.

[50] Otto Neurath, "Physikalismus" [1931], *Gesammelte philosophische und methodologische Schriften*, 2 vols. (Vienna: Hölder-Pichler-Tempsky, 1981), 1: 417–21; "Soziologie im Physikalismus," *Erkenntnis* 2 (1931): 393–431. Thomas Uebel's reconstruction of circle debates in *Overcoming Logical Positivism from within* (Amsterdam: Rodopi, 1992), chaps. 3–6, is helpful.

[51] Rudolf Carnap, "Die physikalische Sprache als Universalsprache der Wissenschaft," *Erkenntnis* 2 (1932): 432–65; "Psychologie in physikalischer Sprache," *Erkenntnis* 3 (1932): 107–42.

[52] "Physikalismus," p. 419: "hinter die Sprache kann man nicht zurück."

[53] Ibid., p. 418.

were hypothetical and could not be reduced to primitive protocols. Their acceptance was conventional.[54] This made Carnap all the more reluctant to give up on experiential protocols as a measure of empirical control.

Neurath remained adamant. All experiences were "processed" the moment they were put into language. There were no primitive protocols, no "first language," "language of experience," or "phenomenalist language." "There is no way to establish final, secure, neat protocol sentences as the sciences' starting point. There is no *tabula rasa*. We are like sailors who have to rebuild their ship on the open sea, without ever being able to take it apart on the dock and reconstruct it from the best components."[55] All that we can do is let physicalism, "the one scientific language, speak about itself" in "an incontestable [*einwandfrei*] syntax," purging its metaphysical elements.[56] Scientists confronted each protocol with existing scientific statements. If they agreed, the protocol became part of science. If they disagreed, the protocol could be rejected as false, or science could be modified. This became known as the "Neurath Principle."[57] Experience did modify scientific statements, but science had no unshakable foundation.

Prior to his encounter with Carnap in August 1932, Popper had not thought through the foundation problem. He took it for granted that singular statements could serve as science's foundation. But he could immediately see Neurath's point. Singular statements could no more be compared with reality than could theories. He also saw where he and Neurath disagreed. Neurath had no way of arbitrating acceptance and rejection of protocols. He, Popper, had a testing method to decide among conflicting statements. Carnap concurred, and adopted his method, but Popper went further. He demanded that Carnap give up "psychologistic" protocols. Carnap refused. Instead, he designated Popper's test statements as protocols. He could now safely give up foundationism because testability provided an empirical check on conventionalism.[58] He conceded that any statement could serve as a protocol, and protocols, too, were subject to change. Neurath disagreed. To him, both Carnap and Popper were abandoning empiricism. By refusing to recognize protocols' special form and finality, they undermined empirical control.[59] Popper, too, remained unhappy. In

---

[54] Carnap, "Die physikalische Sprache als Universalsprache."

[55] Neurath, "Protokollsätze," *Erkenntnis* 3 (1932): 205.

[56] Neurath, "Physikalismus," vol. 1, p. 419.

[57] Rudolf Haller, "The Neurath Principle," in *Rediscovering the Forgotten Vienna Circle*, ed. Thomas Uebel (Boston: Kluwer, 1991), pp. 117–29.

[58] Uebel, *Overcoming Logical Positivism*, chap. 7 concedes that Carnap adopted Popper's view of "protocols," but argues that Popper's contribution to the debate was limited to reinforcing Carnap's antipsychologism. I disagree. Carnap accepted Popper's testing method. Popper, not Neurath, convinced him to relinquish his lingering foundationism (psychologism) and espouse a more radical conventionalism. Carnap himself saw things this way: "Über Protokollsätze," *Erkenntnis* 3 (1932): 223–8.

[59] Neurath to Carnap, 26 October 1932, Carnap Collection.

his view, both Carnap and Neurath fell back on psychologism and foundationism by retaining protocols.[60]

Carnap responded to Neurath in "On Protocol Sentences."[61] Both phenomenalist protocols, formulated outside scientific language, and physicalist ones, formulated inside it, represented legitimate methods of constructing scientific language. The first method allowed greater freedom to "private" languages, but required complicated translation into physicalism. It also retained protocols' absolutism: If protocols contradicted a hypothesis, either the hypothesis or the translation rules would be modified, but the protocols would remain unchanged. Accepting much of Neurath's and Popper's criticism, Carnap was inclined toward one scientific language, and an all-hypothetical science. This required, however, that particular statements be chosen as protocols, or test statements. They could assume a determined form − Neurath's "observation statements." Or, they could remain conventional − Popper's test statements. Popper was in better conformity with scientific practice, Carnap said, because he let current scientific test statements stand. Neurath was the first to turn against absolutism, but Popper did one better. In his system, there were no final sentences. Protocols could be put to the test, too. Popper's nonfoundationism was more radical.

Carnap's article was a coup for Popper, but he needed to clarify his differences with the positivists. His ideas first saw light, he complained to Carnap, incorporated into a foreign system:

> You frame the question as: "protocol sentences inside or outside the system's language?" In this problem situation, Neurath's answer and mine seem closely related. I see the question from a different perspective: demarcation of metaphysics, deductivism, epistemological methodological procedures. From this perspective, Neurath's and Carnap's answers seem closely related, whereas my answer assumes an *entirely* different position.[62]

He was denied recognition for single-handedly overcoming foundationism: "Neurath's antiabsolutism is at best a pious wish. Mine, a thought-out consequence of a deductivist system."[63] (He overlooked the fact that Neurath's antiabsolutism prompted his own nonfoundationism.) He, and he alone, was antiabsolutist.

Popper returned to the Kant–Fries–Nelson tradition to reset and resolve the foundation problem. Humans may be biologically programmed to search for lawfulness, he said, but the biological a priori had no epistemological equivalent. There was no synthetic a priori. Lawfulness could not be conclusively demonstrated, but this did not mean complete skepticism.

---

[60] Popper to Carnap, 22 October 1932, Carnap Collection; *Logik der Forschung*, pp. 53–5.
[61] Carnap, "Über Protokollsätze," pp. 215–28.
[62] Popper to Carnap, 22 October 1932, Carnap Collection.   [63] Loc. cit.

Scientists increasingly purged prejudicial lawfulness by replacing deficient theories with better ones. This meant the growing approximation (*Annährung*) of knowledge to truth. *Annährung* retained a measure of Kant's optimism about universal lawfulness, but made it contingent on the permanent "incompleteness of our knowledge of reality."[64]

This view, said Popper, represented a development of Fries's "anthropological critique of reason."[65] Fries was the first to notice the confusion of psychology and epistemology in Kant. Kant's transcendental proof showed synthetic propositions to be logically necessary, but did not prove them valid:

> He demonstrates [said Fries] the basic metaphysical statements of natural science through the possibility of experience. But this does not constitute ontological justification of a natural law. Rather, [it is] psychological justification of . . . human reason's need to presuppose laws' truth in order to regard appearances as unified in experience. The entire observation is correctly understood as psychic-anthropological.[66]

The transcendental proof had to be psychologically grounded, or it would be caught in a circular argument. Epistemology could clarify knowledge's presuppositions, but not justify them. Any attempt to justify synthetic statements led to an infinite regress. Thinking could not beget its own principle. Epistemology independent of psychology was impossible.[67]

Fries used what Nelson called the "regressive method" to ground epistemology in psychology. He began, as Kant did, by analyzing philosophical presuppositions, regressing into ever more fundamental and abstract principles. Kant had demonstrated that certain principles were indispensable for knowledge. Fries showed that they were cognitions (*Apperception*) "immediately given" by the human psyche. They were initially obscure, but once reflection brought them to consciousness, they required no justification or verification. They had limits: They remained subjective, incapable of settling epistemological issues. They provided experience's forms – lawfulness – not its "contents." Their translation into objective statements could prove erroneous. All the same, they were universal, as every psyche yielded them. Those who distrusted their cognitions did not have a logical, but a

---

[64] *Grundprobleme*, p. 101. This part of Popper's critique of Kant preceded, I believe, Burgstein. A year later, Feigl, recalling Burgstein, commended Popper's "pragmatic biological orientation" to Schlick. (Feigl to Schlick, 14 September 1933, *Schlick Nachlaß*.)

[65] Jakob Friedrich Fries, *Neue oder anthropologische Kritik der Vernunft*, 2nd ed., 3 vols. (Heidelberg: Winter, 1828–31). Popper read some Fries, but his direct references were sparse. He used Nelson and (Julius) Kraft as his major sources.

[66] Ibid., vol. 1, p. xvii.

[67] Ibid., vol. 1, pp. 21–30; Leonard Nelson, "Die kritische Methode und das Verhältnis der Psychologie zur Philosophie," *Gesammelte Schriften*, vol. 1 (Hamburg: Felix Meiner, 1970), pp. 41–2, 57–60; "Die Unmöglichkeit der Erkenntnistheorie," vol. 2, pp. 474–6.

psychological, problem. They would better avail themselves of a psychiatrist, suggested Nelson. To him, Fries dispelled Kant's agnosticism concerning the "thing in itself" (*Ding-an-sich*), renewing the "self-confidence of reason." "Immediate knowledge" (*unmittelbare Erkenntnis*) provided epistemology's foundation.[68]

Popper thought that Fries's and Nelson's demonstration of endless regress in epistemology was impeccable. Indeed, it served as epistemology's point of departure. Contrary to Nelson, however, Popper maintained that epistemology was not impossible. Fries and Nelson were wrong to assume that epistemology's task was grounding knowledge. Their "foundationism," not endless regress, made epistemology impossible. Truly, epistemology was nothing but general scientific methodology. It did not justify statements, but investigated methods and criticized procedures, pointing out contradictions and misapplications. As its subject matter was scientific practice, it required no foundation. It sought to clarify, criticize, and improve practice. This concept of epistemology underlay *Logik der Forschung*.

Fries's epistemological critique was pathbreaking, but his solution a disaster. He accomplished nothing, said Popper, by deferring lawfulness from Kant's consciousness (*Verstandesgesetzlichkeit*) to psychology. Insofar as epistemology and science were concerned, immediate knowledge became accessible only in statements. These required justification, ending in infinite regress. The psychological turn forewent Kant's great advance: establishing intersubjective scrutiny (*Nachprüfbarkeit*) as the criterion of scientific objectivity. Immediate knowledge was intuitionist, dogmatic, irrational. It mattered not that Fries carefully separated subjective psychological cognition and objective epistemological proof. Any appeal to a foundation beyond language was "psychologism."[69] Fries, Carnap, and Neurath committed the same mistake. Protocols were psychological reports in physicalist guise. Experience, or experiential language, could not directly exercise empirical control over science. Science had no absolute empirical basis.

Popper now recast epistemology's basic problem. All epistemologists, he said, confronted "Fries's Trilemma." They could reconcile themselves to dogmatism, that is, accept basic propositions without justification. Or, they could admit infinite regress, whereby no statement would ever reach conclusive validation. Or, they could opt for psychologism, justifying

---

[68] Fries, *Kritik der Vernunft*, vol. 2, secs. 88–95, pp. 16–42; Nelson, "Die kritische Methode," pp. 11–14, 27–37; "Die Unmöglichkeit der Erkenntnistheorie," pp. 467–9; "Von der Kunst, zu philosophieren," vol. 1, pp. 239–45.

[69] John Wettersten questions Popper's rendering of Fries. Fries recognized, he says, that immediate knowledge could not justify statements. Wettersten is correct, but his critique is not decisive. To Popper, if immediate knowledge could not justify, it was epistemologically irrelevant. (Wettersten, *The Roots of Critical Rationalism*, pp. 159–60 n. 26.)

statements by appealing to "experience." With the exception of conventionalists, epistemologists had historically chosen, as had Fries, psychologism. To avoid dogmatism, they called on experience, perceptions, or immediate knowledge to justify statements. Popper dissented. Observation and experiential reports were scientifically admissible only if they could be intersubjectively checked. Scientists had strong convictions about theories, but this was trivial. Convictions were of genetic-historical, not epistemological significance. They could contribute to a theory's discovery, or explain subjective preference for it. They could not justify it. Psychological data did not arbitrate statements. It required justification, just as the rest of science did. To retain objectivity, epistemology had to exclude psychologism.

Popper offered a revolutionary solution. Earlier, he had believed that infinite regress ended with verification or falsification of specific prognoses. He now recognized that even these prognoses, or, as he began calling them, singular (or basic) statements, were theories of a lower degree of universality. Their testing did not always produce incontrovertible results. They could become testable hypotheses of their own. Testing had no natural end point. It could continue, in principle, ad infinitum. A decision to stop and accept a statement was conventional. The accepted statements remained without conclusive verification, or foundation. They could be falsified in the future. Their acceptance was "dogmatic," but this was undangerous dogmatism. When doubts emerged, scientists renewed testing. Subjective convictions contributed to the consensus that ended testing, but this was harmless psychologism. Scientists did not ground statements. They accepted them in accordance with an objective methodological rule, stipulating admission of confirmed test statements into science. Dogmatism, endless regress, and psychologism all played roles in scientific work, but they were rendered innocuous by science's hypothetical, falsifiable character.

Popper's solution to Fries's trilemma radicalized his position in *Grundprobleme* I. Science's foundation became ever shifting. He continued to speak, for a while, of acceptance of basic statements as "verification," and called them "foundation statements" (*Basissätze*). They alone – not nonverifiable universal statements – could be true, but their truth and status were provisional. Testing could resume at any moment, falsifying them. In *Logik der Forschung*, he assiduously avoided the questions of whether acceptance of test statements constituted verification, and whether scientific theories could be true. In 1935, having adopted Tarski's theory of truth, he recognized nonverifiable statements as true. This put to rest any logical distinction between universal and basic statements: All were hypothetical and nonverifiable. Science progressed not by discovering unshakable truths but by eliminating errors. Change was its hallmark. Intersubjectivity was the sole guarantor of progress. Basic statements, a temporary end point to testing, constituted science's relative, transitional, conventional "foundation." This was the end of foundationist philosophy.[70]

"Foundationism" was not Popper's only concern in the fall and winter of 1932–3. In the fragments of *Grundprobleme* II, he assailed positivist efforts to dissolve philosophy into science. He declared philosophy a science of demarcation, concerned with establishing boundaries between science and metaphysics. Science could not establish its own boundaries. Carnap showed that logic consisted of metaconcepts that were not part of science. They belonged to epistemology. Hence, philosophy had a body of knowledge, and was not just an activity, as Schlick surmised. As methodology transcended science, and scientific practice was its object, scientific language could not express methodological rules, as Carnap suggested. Science needed philosophy. Philosophy was a theory of knowledge (*Erkenntnistheorie*), a methodology, a secondary science, both descriptive and prescriptive. It did not accept uncritically scientific practice, but directed it to procedures that had proved successful. Learning from the most advanced science, physics, it helped less advanced ones: biology, psychology, sociology. Philosophy was a critical theory of science.[71]

Popper expressed buoyant optimism about scientific philosophy. It could reformulate and solve traditional problems. Notwithstanding current "philosophical fashion," they were not pseudoproblems. The epigrams to *Grundprobleme* and *Logik der Forschung* contrasted Schlick and Kant.[72] Schlick was quoted to the effect that it was unlikely that philosophy would ever pose a genuine problem. Kant held, on the contrary, that where verbal disputes had been raging, there was surely a genuine problem. Popper sided with Kant against Schlick. Both logical positivism and *Weltanschauung* philosophy (Heidegger, Jaspers, Scheler), he said, dismissed efforts to rethink traditional philosophy. They were intolerant. Traditional philosophy may be "a heap of ruins," but "a philosopher who avows none of the contending schools and does not wish to give up on changing the sorry state of philosophical discussion [can] start anew."[73] This was a self-aggrandizing posture, but also a true statement. Contrary to prevailing fashion, he showed that scientific reconstruction of traditional philosophy was possible. Rather than pronounce a (false) break with it, he reconsidered its problems in light of contemporary science, building bridges to the past.

---

[70] *Grundprobleme* I, pp. 107–36.   [71] *Grundprobleme* II, pp. 344–6, 364–8, 385–6, 390–5.

[72] Ibid., pp. 443, 447–8; *Logik der Forschung*, p. iii.

[73] *Grundprobleme* II, p. 342: "So bleibt dem Philosophen, der sich zu keiner der streitenden Schulen bekennen und auf eine Änderung des traurigen Zustandes der philosophischen Diskussion nicht verzichten will, nichts anderes übrig, als vom Anfang anzufangen." This concludes the first section of "Entwurf einer Einführung: Gibt es eine philosophische Wissenschaft?" ("Outline of an Introduction: Is there a Philosophical Science?"). Revised, the first section became the preface to *Logik der Forschung*, p. iii. The rest (*Grundprobleme* II, pp. 342–6) was cut.

Popper's conception of philosophy remained, however, restrictive. He may have thought that all carefully formulated problems from cosmology to ethics were of interest to philosophers. (He would say so in future years.)[74] But his definition of philosophy, a "science of demarcation," limited it to epistemology and scientific methodology. Positivist discourse overpowered him. His brilliant demonstration that positivists could not do science without philosophy came at the cost of a diminished philosophical sphere. Scientific philosophy became an instrument for excluding metaphysics. The only way out was to let metaphysics back into philosophy by relaxing the boundaries between science and metaphysics. He gradually did so. In *The Open Society*, he engaged in nonscientific historical interpretation that was excellent political philosophy.[75] Moreover, he extended the criterion of scientific objectivity from intersubjective testing to public criticism.[76] A decade later, he showed that criticism of metaphysical theories was possible.[77] Metaphysics reentered philosophy.

In late 1932, however, philosophy's legitimacy depended on his demarcation against metaphysics. Reichenbach told him in November that, a few years earlier, the circle had briefly considered falsifiability as a demarcation criterion and rejected it.[78] They concluded that the conventionalist stratagem of saving a falsified theory by adding an ad hoc hypothesis was always possible. Popper knew as much. When a theory was in crisis, he said, the empiricist, learning from experience, sought theoretical revision; the conventionalist corrected measurements. Still, he had to construct methodological procedures for testing that would make the empiricist's approach viable. This was a tough balancing act. He agreed with conventionalism against positivism that logical or linguistic demarcation was impossible. Acceptance of a basic statement that falsified a theory was a methodological decision, and methodology was conventional. If empiricism was to contain conventionalism, methodological decision had to be empirically and logically guided (and yet, not determined). Ground rules for accepting a basic statement had to be clear. Demarcation depended on methodological conventions that were empirically and logically informed.[79]

Popper devoted the next two years to developing a methodology of falsification. In the fragments of 1932–3, he established ground rules. Universal theories, or systems of statements, were considered confirmed as long

[74] Preface to *The Logic of Scientific Discovery*, pp. 15–23.

[75] *The Open Society*, chapter 25, for his theory of historical interpretation.

[76] Ibid., vol. 1, pp. 109–11; vol. 2, pp. 204–6, 224–6.

[77] "On the Status of Science and Metaphysics" [1958], *Conjectures and Refutations*, pp. 184–200.

[78] Reichenbach to Popper, 24 November 1932, Reichenbach Collection; "Bemerkung" (a rejoinder to Popper's "Kriterium"), *Erkenntnis* 3 (1933): 426–7.

[79] *Grundprobleme* II, pp. 353–74: "Übergang zur Methodentheorie."

as all possible falsification efforts failed. A theory was falsifiable (that is, scientific) when at least one basic statement could be deduced from it.[80] Basic statement was a testable theory of lower generality, a specific prognosis the universality of which was so low that a test could easily determine "yes" or "no." Logically speaking, testing confronted a basic statement with its contradiction, determining which to accept. Acceptance of the contradiction falsified the entire theory. A new basic statement, agreeing with the falsifying statement and not deducible from the falsified theory, had to be used to reconstruct the theory. Only testable statements (or theories from which they could easily be deduced) were acceptable as ad hoc hypotheses. As testing always involved limiting conditions, that is, a statement in relation to other statements, there was, in principle, no end to testing, no verification of theory. Scientists accepted basic statements as true only when no doubt remained. When a basic statement falsified an especially well-tested theory, or testing conditions were not ideal, or results were controversial, testing continued. But Popper implored scientists to accept a surprising falsification of a "safe" theory as great progress. The revolution in contemporary physics exemplified falsification's virtues.[81] He strove to make falsification into a comprehensive methodology for natural science.

The public first became familiar with Popper's epistemological revolution through *Logik der Forschung*. Truly, the revolution was complete by the end of 1932. The Kant–Fries critique reshaped Popper's epistemology, introducing issues and concepts that gained permanent hold on his philosophy: Fries's trilemma; exclusion of psychologism; theory as a system of statements; basic (singular) statement; empirical basis; methodological decision. He negotiated convention, experience, and logic, forming a unique synthesis of conventionalism and empiricism. He showed that convention and experience modified, rather than determined, each other. Experience always remained problematic, but one could learn from it all the same.

Popper retained a vocabulary of foundationism. He spoke of empirical basis and *Basissätze*, but he transformed their meaning:

---

[80] John Watkins, *Science and Scepticism* (Princeton, N.J.: Princeton University Press, 1984), pp. 144–6, points out that, strictly speaking, one cannot deduce a basic statement from a universal one. A universal statement is equivalent to a negative existential statement (e.g., "All ravens are black" is equivalent to "there does not exist a nonblack raven"). A basic statement is a positive existential statement plus a spatio-temporal location (e.g., "There exists a nonblack raven at space region k"). There is no way to deduce it from the universal statement. One can deduce, however, what Watkins calls a singular predictive implication: "If the thing at k is a raven, then it is black." This is testable. A theory is falsifiable as long as one can deduce at least one singular predictive implication from it.

[81] Ibid., pp. 378–82, 389–95, 432–8: "Grundriß einer Theorie der empirisch-wissenschaftlichen Methoden (Theorie der Erfahrung)," "Das Problem der Methodenlehre," "Auszug." I concur with Hansen that "Methodenlehre" is the last of the three. It was incorporated into *Logik*, Sections 4, 10, 11.

The empirical basis of objective science is *nothing absolute*. Science does not rest on a rockbed. Its towering edifice, an amazingly bold structure of theories, rises over a swamp. The foundations are piers going down into the swamp from above. They do not reach a natural base, but go only as deep as is necessary to carry the structure. One does not stop driving them down because one reached firm ground. Rather, one resolves to be satisfied with their firmness, hoping they will carry the structure. (If the structure proves too heavy, and begins tottering, it sometimes does not help to drive the piers further down. It may be necessary to have a new building, which must be constructed on the ruins of the collapsed structure's piers.) . . . *The objectivity of science can be bought only at the cost of relativity.* (He who seeks the absolute must seek it in the subjective.)[82]

Antifoundationism has become today almost an article of faith. Science studies may consider Popper's edifice over a swamp an insufficiently radical metaphor for science, but his edifice was no Cartesian First Philosophy.[83] Foundations (basic statements) were neither stable nor certain. They were not interesting in themselves, but only insofar as they said something about theories. (Popper considered excluding them from science altogether.) Knowledge was theory, always hypothetical. Scientists did not prove theories (*Begründung*), only resolved to accept them (*Beschluß*). There is something to be said for leaving foundations hanging over a swamp, rather than demolishing them. Experience is a problem, and all knowledge is theoretical, but parts of knowledge seem closer to experience, and we try to derive some instruction from this proximity.[84] They may prove more remote from experience than we thought, or completely wrong, but, so long as we main-

---

[82] *Grundprobleme* I, p. 136. Revised, the first half of the quotation (to "they will carry the structure") concluded Section 30 of *Logik der Forschung*, pp. 66–7.

[83] In later years, Popper became uncomfortable with foundationist traces in his philosophy. In *The Logic of Scientific Discovery*, he rendered *Basissätz* as "basic statement," eliminating any hint of foundation. Joseph Agassi, "Sensationalism," *Mind* 75 (1966): 1–24 thinks that this did not solve the problem. So long as Popper regarded accepted basic statements as (tentatively) true, sensationalism (and foundationism) lurked behind.

[84] This proximity grants, however, no epistemological privilege. Repeatable observation reports facilitate a consensus on basic statements because, among others, perceptual judgment often proves convincing, but intersubjective criticism, not perception, is epistemologically relevant. John Watkins thinks otherwise. Finding hints in Popper's late work that perceptual experience may be not only (psychological) motive but also inconclusive (epistemological) reason for accepting a basic statement, he endeavors to demonstrate the quasi-rationality of perceptual judgment and acceptance of observation reports. Otherwise, he argues, Popper has no rationale better than Neurath's for preferring one theory over another. Testing concludes with a testable statement: *Why* do we accept one statement and reject another? (*Science and Scepticism*, pp. 247–69).

In contrast, Agassi believes that "the philosophical problem of the acceptability or otherwise of observation reports can be entirely ignored by non-sensationalists" ("Sensationalism": 20). "We need speak neither of acceptance, nor of justification of acceptance, of observation reports" (19). "[They] ought to be accepted as a task, as something which we should try to explain" (16). "We merely . . . demand that account be taken of the fact that some observation reports were made repeatedly, and that this fact be explained by some testable hypothesis" (19). "This proposal . . . severs

tain their hypothetical character, they pose no risk of traditional foundationism. Popper got it right. His epistemological revolution was a high point in twentieth-century philosophy.

WRITING *LOGIK DER FORSCHUNG*, 1933–1934: THE LIMITS OF FRIENDSHIP AND MEMORY

Logik der Forschung consolidated Popper's epistemological revolution by providing a methodology to guide scientific work. Popper wrote *Logik* in a year of incredibly intensive work. Well over half the book was new. The longest chapters, on probability and quantum physics, addressed issues that Popper had barely broached before. He devoted the greatest effort to them, so much so that one wonders when he found time to revise the old material.[85] He transformed *Grundprobleme*'s long-winded discussions into concise, fast-moving, sharp arguments. Space limitations dictated the new style, but more significantly, Popper found his voice. In *Logik der Forschung*, one hears for the first time a confident and mature philosopher.

Popper was tempting fate by adding material to a book that required radical shortening. He spent most of the summer and fall of 1933 and the winter of 1933–4 on a new interpretation of probability. From his summer "vacation" in Achensee in Tyrol, he sent Carnap requests for offprints of Gödel and Reichenbach. Carnap was alarmed. Playing the *Doktorvater*, he urged Popper to put closure on his work and explore no new avenues. He told him that he had more than enough material. In February 1934, he urgently repeated his advice.[86] In vain. Popper could do no other. Flirting with catastrophe was a life habit. Somehow, he always made it in the end.

---

the last connection between the philosophy of experience and sensationalism. . . . The problem of the empirical basis is thereby disposed of" (20).

Agassi seems to discount the role perceptual judgment and observation reports play in forming the consensus. Watkins seems to move toward psychologism by granting them epistemological privilege. To me, intersubjective acceptance (for whatever reason) of a repeatable observation seems a good enough reason to declare it rational, even if Popper does not provide, as Watkins argues, tight procedures for testing.

[85] Did Popper take a leave from his school job in 1933–4? In contrast with the 1935–6 leave, which he announced to all his friends, he kept silent about this one (if, indeed, he took one). He told Julius Kraft (11 July 1933 [316, 24]) that he must finish the bulk of the book by the summer's end because, on September 10, the school year would begin. But in a letter to Felix Kaufmann from early November 1936 (*Kaufmann Nachlaß, Sozialwissenschaftliches Archiv*, University of Constance), he wrote that "in order to complete my book, which had already been extensively rewritten many times, I had to take a leave from my job, with my pay and promotion suspended. . . . As I did not accomplish my goal in the allotted time, I had to devote the summer vacation to completing my book." Karl Milford told me (conversation, 31 January 1999) that his father (Peter Milford [Hilferding]) thought that Popper had taken out a mortgage on the house owned by his mother-in-law in order to publish *Grundprobleme*. If Popper took a leave without pay, they obviously needed the money.

[86] Popper to Carnap, 26 July 1933, 5 August 1933; Carnap to Popper, 14 August 1933, 10 February 1934, Carnap Collection.

Writing *Logik*, Popper closed himself off to the world, neglecting professional contacts and friends. Once he had completed his probability chapter early in 1934, he showed it to Waismann, Menger, Hahn, and Helly. He still felt insecure about his mathematical abilities and was exceedingly pleased when they approved, but they had no active role in developing his work. He opened up to the circle in Burgstein, maintained fairly close contacts for a couple of months, then withdrew into the private sphere. He ignored his friends, too. Robert Lammer, who had helped him with *Grundprobleme* I, learned about *Logik* and the circle only years later by reading Popper's books. "Why did we grow so far apart?" asked the old Lammer.[87]

Lammer fell victim to Popper's common practice in friendship. Few, if any, of his relationships were personal or social in the common sense of these words. His ideas and work were always at the center. When the relationships proved no longer instrumental, they usually ended. He did not set out to use people. Indeed, the suggestion would have offended him. He was calculative in making gestures to people whose favor he needed, but no long-term planning was involved. It was simply that work was his life's center and left little room for family, friends, or community. He did little, or nothing, to keep friends. Even his closest acquaintances found that they had to abide by his schedule. Popper would not see them, or write, if this seriously interrupted his work. Philosophy took precedence over life.

On occasion Popper could be sensitive to people's suffering and needs. In 1937, he helped Waismann, who was unemployed in Vienna and in dire need, get the fellowship he himself declined at Cambridge. In the immediate postwar period, he was the only person connected with the circle to take interest in the welfare of Victor Kraft and Rose Rand.[88] His sympathetic correspondence, during the early 1970s, with the old and dying Kraft is touching, disclosing rarely revealed dimensions of his personality. But this was not his common approach to friends. He developed few deep friendships. In the early 1970s, he complained that he had almost no one left in England. Art historian Ernst Gombrich, social theorist Friedrich Hayek – both Viennese émigrés – a few friends from his youth, colleagues who stood by him in New Zealand, a student or two who survived his tutelage: these were his friends in old age. They were, for the most part, incredibly loyal. They knew his faults, adjusted themselves to his caprices and egoism, and overcame his suspicion. To none was he as good a friend as they were to

---

[87] Robert Lammer to Karl and Hennie Popper, 20 August 1968, Popper Archives (318, 12). Popper acknowledged Lammer in his *Autobiography*, p. 83.

[88] Popper sent food packages to Kraft, who was suffering from the acute shortages in occupied Vienna. For Rand, who was starving in London, he tried to find a job. Kraft to Popper, 1946–8, Popper Archives (316, 24); Popper to Carnap, 1 March 1947, Popper Archives (282, 24); and Carnap to Popper, 27 May 1947, Carnap Collection.

him. Most he rarely visited, and wrote to infrequently. He thought that developing his philosophy was of monumental significance. It justified the great sacrifices he made, and those he demanded of others. Blindly tying together the fortunes of his philosophy and humanity, he sacrificed everything and everyone on his philosophy's altar.[89]

For philosophy's sake, Popper took incredible risks. By Springer's deadline, March 1, 1934, he was still working on probability. He was able to settle only the book's new title – *Logik der Forschung*.[90] He also had only a rudimentary version of the chapter on quantum physics. He handed in the manuscript on April 9, leaving a copy in Schlick's apartment, but he was not really ready.[91] He was still drawing the implications of his new concept of probability for falsifiability and testability. To his delight, Schlick was recovering from the flu in Italy. He took back the manuscript ten days later, returning it on May 9.[92] This was not the end. Springer held the manuscript for a while. Popper continued to work on quantum physics, consulting his friend Franz Urbach (1902–69), Urbach's friend in Zurich Viktor Weisskopf (b. 1908), and his cousin Käthe Schiff (b. 1909).[93] Sometime in June or early July, Springer returned the manuscript, demanding that it be cut by one-third. Popper had the opportunity to revise the physics chapter, indeed, the entire book, but he was utterly exhausted. He reports that his uncle Walter Schiff did much of the editing.[94] A look at the contents clarifies where the major cuts were made. The technical chapters tolerated no significant abbreviation. Indeed, Popper added new material. The first five chapters, outlining *Grundprobleme*, bore the brunt of the cuts.[95]

Schiff was a fine stylist. His *Die Planwirtschaft* (1932) and *Logik der Forschung* both display an uncommon style for German academic writing: short clauses, simple grammatical structures, rapidly moving arguments.[96]

---

[89] The best portrayal of Popper's attitudes toward life and work is: Joseph Agassi, *A Philosopher's Apprentice* (Amsterdam: Rodopi, 1993).

[90] Popper to Carnap, 17 February and 12 March 1934, Carnap Collection. He agreed with Schlick on the new title.

[91] Popper to Otto Lange (Springer), 9 April 1934, Popper Archives (352, 1).

[92] Popper to Anon. (Schlick), 24 April 1934, Popper Archives (17, 6); Popper to Carnap, mid-August 1934, Carnap Collection.

[93] He received some help but constantly argued with them. Popper to Anon. (Weisskopf), 10 June 1934, Popper Archives (17, 6); Weisskopf to Popper, 26 June 1934 (360, 21); Popper to Käthe Schiff, 16 March 1934 (346, 34); and *Logik der Forschung*, p. 246, note 1 to Appendix VII.

[94] *Autobiography*, p. 85.

[95] *Logik* (1935) has ten chapters. The total length of the first five chapters is 66 pages; the last five, 143 pages; appendixes and notes, 39 pages. Extant drafts of earlier versions of *Logik*'s last five chapters (Popper Archives [17, 9–10]) suggest that Popper barely cut them and added technical sections at the last minute. No draft is available of the first four chapters. Popper later remembered that the manuscript was cut by one-half (*Autobiography*, p. 85), but told Carnap in mid-August 1934 (Carnap Collection) that he shortened it by one-third. Most likely, the first five chapters were cut by about half to produce the one-third cut Springer required.

[96] Walter Schiff, *Die Planwirtschaft und ihre ökonomischen Hauptprobleme* (Berlin: Heymanns, 1932).

The style was partly Popper's, or at least he had made it his own while writing *Logik*, but partly it was not. Schiff broadly used the semicolon to separate clauses in compound sentences. This structure, not typical of Popper's writing before or after, is apparent especially in *Logik*'s first five chapters. It seems less frequent in the technical chapters. The pace is also quicker in the earlier chapters. Still, Schiff probably did *not* rewrite *Logik*. He "ruthlessly cut" and pasted the first five chapters, reducing them by half. Hennie was there to retype. Popper must have gone once more through the manuscript, polishing the final draft. Somehow, the quick cuts did not make the arguments less cogent or lucid. On August 8, Popper brought the final manuscript to Springer. Later in the fall, he added a few notes in proof, and introduced minor changes in the table of contents, but the August manuscript remained otherwise unchanged.

Tracing *Logik der Forschung*'s emergence from *Grundprobleme* remains problematic. Popper reworked *Grundprobleme* into *Logik* quickly. Many sections in *Logik* betray a debt to *Grundprobleme*, but few paragraphs appear verbatim. The fragments of "*Grundprobleme* II" do not easily find their place in *Logik*. Popper must have radically revised them. We do not possess all the material necessary for a reconstruction. The archives contain drafts of the chapters on the empirical basis, testability, simplicity, probability, quantum physics, and corroboration.[97] Some are incomplete. Those on testability and simplicity, and segments of probability, still carry the original section numbering of ur-*Logik* (the April–May 1934 manuscript). They are fairly close to the final version. No draft remains of *Logik*'s first four chapters. Without drafts of the chapters most informed by *Grundprobleme*, the historian can trace the Herculean editing job of 1933–4 only in broad outline.

Intending, until mid-1933, to complete a second volume of *Grundprobleme*, Popper ended up writing a new book. His changing plans gave rise to the postwar search for the lost manuscript of *Grundprobleme* II. When Hansen examined *Grundprobleme* I in the early 1970s, he looked, as every reader would, for the second volume. He found none, because none, I believe, existed. Popper did not remember his project's development very well. Until Hansen inventoried his manuscripts and recovered his correspondence in the mid-1970s, Popper had not been clear as to whether a manuscript of *Grundprobleme* II, separate from *Logik*'s early version, existed.[98] In his mind, ur-*Logik* and *Grundprobleme* II overlapped. "I must

---

[97] Popper Archives (17, 9–10; 18, 1), files under the titles: *Logik der Forschung: Ur-version* and *Urfassung: Logik der Forschung*. The files also include fragments of "*Grundprobleme* II."

[98] Hansen and Robert Lammer conducted a thorough search for any remaining manuscript and retrieved two copies of *Grundprobleme* I as well as a collection of papers, fragments, and correspondence from 1932–5. On Popper's vague recollections of the 1930s, Hansen writes: "Popper could not remember [in 1972] much of the story; he told me that I knew more about his old manuscripts than he did. I doubt that this was actually the case. Later – when he and I received detailed letters

rewrite my book completely," he told Kraft in July 1933, "or, more precisely, write a completely new book."[99] A few months later, just before
he finished the early version of *Logik*, he told English philosopher Susan
Stebbing that *Grundprobleme* II was "almost complete, but some spots
required further work." He compressed the second volume, he said, into a
new book, *Logik der Forschung*.[100] In the tumult of 1934, *Logik* rapidly
changed form under different editors. The relationship between the old and
new project became confused. Twenty years later, when Popper's student,
philosopher Paul Feyerabend, searched for the manuscript of ur-*Logik* in
Vienna, Popper suggested that he might look for it under *Das Abgrenzungsproblem*, the prospective title of *Grundprobleme* II.[101] *Logik* was both a
rewritten *Grundprobleme* and a new book. Is it surprising that Popper, who
had indeed completed, and lost, an expansive ur-*Logik*, eventually concluded that he must have also (almost) completed *Grundprobleme* II?[102]

If my account is correct, Popper lost no *Grundprobleme* II, but may have
lost a (complete) manuscript of *Logik*'s early version. Correspondence suggests that extant *"Grundprobleme* II" fragments are almost all that Popper
wrote in connection with the second volume prior to July 1933. Discussing,

---

from Robert Lammer – he could remember much more about this affair" (letter to author, 20
December 1998).

[99] 11 July 1933 (316, 24). In May 1933, Popper and Kraft were discussing publishing *Grundprobleme* I's
critique of positivism in Nelson's *Abhandlungen*. On July 11, Popper inquired of Kraft whether he
was still interested, and enclosed the old *Exposé* of two prospective volumes of *Grundprobleme*,
amended. The amendment elaborated on the critique of positivism, but included also the new
themes that Popper would shortly undertake in *Logik*. (He gave no indication that he had written
anything on these themes. All the chapters he offered to send Kraft belong in *Grundprobleme* I.)
Undertaking a new book (*Logik*), Popper still seemed to contemplate a complete *Grundprobleme*,
and the themes he envisioned for the second volume are those at the center of *Logik*.

[100] The letter to Stebbing (3 February 1934 [352, 15]) is the single piece of evidence that can be adduced
for an "almost complete" manuscript of *Grundprobleme* II. Stebbing read *Grundprobleme*'s first volume
and inquired as to whether the second was complete. She wished to facilitate a translation. In his
response, Popper wrote in some detail about *Grundprobleme* I, but he said nothing about the
second volume's contents. Hansen regards this, nonetheless, as decisive evidence that a manuscript
of *Grundprobleme* II, separate from ur-*Logik*, existed. I think that Popper, eager to have the complete
Grundprobleme published, exaggerated his completed work while remaining vague about it. (He did
the same later in life, e.g., *Autobiography*, when pressed by editor's deadlines.) As *Logik* entailed
progressive shortening and reworking of *Grundprobleme*, Popper probably had expansive sections on
epistemology, some only in draft, which he had already abbreviated for ur-*Logik*. These could have
constituted parts of an English *Grundprobleme* II. In Popper's mind, he did almost complete a
Grundprobleme II. (Popper Archives [352, 15].)

[101] Popper to Feyerabend, 11 January 1954 (294, 16). In the spring of 1954, Feyerabend, too, assumed
that ur-*Logik* and *Grundprobleme* II were one. He told Popper that the fragments that he had found
and inventoried seemed to belong to *Das Abgrenzungsproblem*, and that through them (and other
fragments he expected to find), he hoped to reconstitute the manuscript of *Logik*'s early version.
(Feyerabend to Popper, 10 June 1954 [294, 13]. I am grateful to Hansen for drawing my attention
to this important letter and for his comments on it.)

[102] *Autobiography*, pp. 85, 212 n. 108.

in May and July 1933, publication plans with Kraft, Popper spoke of the manuscript that Schlick had read (*Grundprobleme* I) as "the book." He did not mention that a second volume existed.[103] From July 1933 on, he wrote *Logik*. Nothing suggests further work on *Grundprobleme* (separate from *Logik*).[104] It is improbable that while writing *Logik*, Popper completed (or "almost completed") another manuscript, prior to ur-*Logik* of April–May 1934. It is not impossible that, late in 1933, he still conceived of *Logik* as fulfilling his plans for *Das Abgrenzungsproblem* (that is, *Grundprobleme* II) and had expansive sections, later shortened, arranged sequentially. This manuscript would not be, however, very different from ur-*Logik*. Popper took to New Zealand one copy of *Grundprobleme* I and, probably, his 1929 geometry thesis and his incomplete 1927 *Hausarbeit*.[105] He did not take *Logik*'s early drafts because he probably considered them fairly close to the book. Would he have left behind an "almost complete" manuscript substantially different from *Logik*? All four copies of *Grundprobleme* I survived. Popper made four copies of other significant manuscripts. I find it difficult to believe that four copies of a nearly completed volume, under whatever title, could have been lost.[106]

---

[103] Popper to Kraft, 25 May, 26 May, 11 July 1933.

[104] Hansen agrees as much. He feels that *Grundprobleme* II must have been written earlier. Is it conceivable that Popper completed *Grundprobleme* II without ever hinting, in his correspondence, that he was engaged in writing it, and while reporting other engagements for the second halves of 1932 and 1933, and complaining, throughout the first half of 1933, that he got no significant work done? I find it improbable. (Nothing is, of course, impossible.)

My conclusions agree with Wettersten, *The Roots of Critical Rationalism*, p. 161, but see Hansen's "Nachwort," *Grundprobleme*, esp. pp. 448–9 for the opposite view. Hansen is currently completing a collection of documents relevant to the search for Popper's lost manuscripts, including Hansen's correspondence with Feyerabend, Lammer, and Popper. He is writing an introduction to the collection and may also write a paper based on this material, presenting a well-informed account, an alternative to the one I propose here.

[105] Feyerabend does not mention either work among the manuscripts he found in Vienna. It cannot be ruled out, however, that he delivered them to Popper without a written comment.

[106] In 1953, when Popper was planning *Logik*'s English translation, he sent Feyerabend to fetch the manuscripts that he had deposited with Otto Haas, a socialist friend, prior to his emigration to New Zealand in 1937. (He thought of translating the early expansive version of *Logik* in order to settle controversies on his views in the 1930s.) He remembered depositing a "wardrobe full of manuscripts" in Haas's apartment (Hansen to author, 20 December 1998). Haas, a member of the resistance, fell victim to the Nazis. Lammer and Feyerabend visited his mother in the summer of 1953. She let them into his apartment, and they fetched some of the manuscripts, including one or two copies of *Grundprobleme* I and two copies of *Logik* (mistakenly identified by Feyerabend as the early version, inasmuch as he had, at the time, no printed copy of *Logik* against which to check the manuscript). (Feyerabend to Popper, c. July 1953 [294, 13].) Urged repeatedly by Popper to find the early version of *Logik*, Feyerabend returned to Frau Haas later that fall, and possibly also the following spring, and took more manuscripts, possibly everything left. (Popper to Feyerabend, 11 January and 6 May 1954. Feyerabend to Popper, 10 September 1953; 25 January, 12 March, and 10 June 1954 [294, 13 – undated correspondence; 294, 15; 294, 16]. Lammer to Hansen, 30 November 1975 [letter in Hansen's possession]. Hansen, "Popper's Early Work on the Theory of Knowledge," *Ringvorlesung*, 30 October 1998, *Karl Popper Institut*, Vienna.)

The situation is different for ur-*Logik*. Such a manuscript undoubtedly existed and was submitted to Springer. Schiff and Popper may have used some of the copies to reconstitute the final version, but it is unlikely, although not impossible, that they used all four, and Popper did not retain

Looking at *Grundprobleme* I, Feyerabend expected, as Hansen would twenty years later, to find a second volume. Lammer told him that "there was no such volume" (Feyerabend to Popper, 12 March 1954), but, then, Lammer's collaboration with Popper had ceased after the summer of 1932 – he was not aware of Popper's contacts with the circle – and so his knowledge was not definitive. (He changed his view later when Popper and Hansen told him the story of the manuscripts.) Feyerabend repeatedly reported to Popper having found fragments of *Grundprobleme* II and ur-*Logik*, but not a complete manuscript of either. In January or February 1954, he sent Popper (possibly with positivist philosopher Arthur Pap, who left Vienna for London [Hansen to author, 14 May 1999]) copies of *Grundprobleme* I and *Logik* (hoping that it was ur-*Logik*), and possibly also a file with the fragments currently collected under "*Grundprobleme* II," including ur-*Logik* material. (Feyerabend to Popper, 24 February and 12 March 1954. It is possible, however, that the file was delivered sometime later.) In June 1954, Feyerabend went through many, or all, of the manuscripts that he still had and provided Popper with a partial inventory of fragments from 1932–3 (*Einführung, Problemstellung, Übergang zur Methodentheorie, Orientierung, Auszug*), ur-*Logik* (chapters 1 [in a separate portfolio], 6, 8, 9, 10 [I have used *LSD*'s, rather than *Logik*'s, chapter numbers here; they are simpler], some chapters incomplete, others in more than one version), and papers related to quantum theory and Popper's dispute with Heisenberg in 1934–5. (Feyerabend to Popper, 10 June 1954.) Feyerabend may or may not have delivered any of this material to Popper in 1954, but he did not deliver all of it. A couple of years later, he left for England (Bristol) and later for Berkeley. He left the undelivered manuscripts in his apartment in Vienna. After his father's death in 1962, the apartment was sold. Some of the manuscripts were sent to Feyerabend; others apparently disappeared. (Hansen to Popper, 29 January 1976 [217, 6].) In 1975, Hansen and Lammer asked Feyerabend to send all the material he had. He sent another copy of *Grundprobleme* I, another copy of *Logik*, parts of the material that he had reported in June 1954, and a collection of letters, 1932–5 (reported in his postcard to Popper, c. July 1953). He had meanwhile lost, it seems, material for which no other copy exists (notably chap. 1 of ur-*Logik*).

Did Feyerabend lose an "almost complete" *Grundprobleme* II or ur-*Logik*? On their visit to Frau Haas, Lammer and Feyerabend found two parcels in pale gray cover, with a label: "Für Robert Lammer." Lammer took one, which contained a *Grundprobleme* I manuscript, with its sections indexed (1_1, 2_1, 3_1 . . . 48_1). The second package was returned to the drawer, those present assuming that it contained a duplicate of the first parcel. Hansen ("Popper's Early Work on the Theory of Knowledge") surmises that it contained *Grundprobleme* II (indexed: 1_2, 2_2, 3_2 . . .). Based on his later correspondence with Feyerabend, Lammer, and Popper, he concludes that the parcel was not delivered to Popper and was lost. I think it likely that the package contained another *Grundprobleme* I. (The indexing, too, makes better sense this way: the section comes first, then the copy number. Popper may have intended to distinguish between the two copies – no indexing of the second was thus necessary. Had a volume number been involved, it would have probably come first, not second.) Feyerabend reported twice in 1953–4 (10 September 1953; 12 March 1954) of having found "a second copy" of *Grundprobleme* I. (The second report concerned the copy that Popper had sent to England in 1932. Feyerabend sent it to Lammer in 1975.) His efforts to trace ur-*Logik* or *Das Abgrenzungsproblem* in the spring of 1954 seem to have been, for once, genuine and fairly thorough. (He had just disappointed Popper by declining to become his assistant and was eager to oblige him.) I find it improbable that he did not pick up and open the second package. (Frau Haas said, many years later, that he took all of the remaining manuscripts.) Still, it is not impossible that he did not. It is also not impossible that the second package contained an ur-*Logik* copy, possibly even under the title *Das Abgrenzungsproblem*. Hansen (letter to author, 14 May 1999) remains

one complete manuscript.[107] At least in 1953–4, he seemed certain that a copy of ur-*Logik* existed and had been deposited with his friend in Vienna. Whether in the emigration rush of January 1937, or later through Feyerabend's negligence, or some unfortunate mishap, an ur-*Logik* manuscript may have been lost. Only parts seem to have survived. To the historian, ur-*Logik*'s missing chapters could have clarified how Popper acquired, within a few months, his mature style and voice. They could have also provided evidence of Schiff's role in editing the manuscript. For the philosopher, they may not be a great loss. They surely contained a more elaborate discussion of epistemology than *Logik*, but Popper was editing *Grundprobleme*, occasionally bringing it up to date. It is improbable that significant new material was lost through shortening. Substantively, we may possess everything Popper produced between 1932 and 1934.

Having completed *Logik*, Popper felt it was a monumental achievement. He hoped that habilitation as a *Dozent* might follow.[108] Chances were remote, but perhaps not nonexistent. Vienna had four philosophy chairs. Two, Gomperz and Bühler, thought highly of Popper. Schlick's high regard for his work might overcome his personal dislike. *Logik* paid tribute to Reininger, the fourth.[109] Reininger supported the *Ständestaat*, but was known as a "philo-Semite." (He had a Jewish assistant – Amalie Rosenblüth – and helped Schlick's students after the Anschluss.) Just a few days before his death in July 1934, Hahn, too, spoke to Popper appreciatively about *Logik*.[110] If Austrian politics had not intruded into the academy, the situation would not have been altogether hopeless. As they did, it was, but Popper did not realize that. In any event, *Logik* had first to be published.

Carnap was prudent in rushing Popper to finish. In July 1934, Neurath

---

convinced that this is the case and offers a rationale the details of which are too elaborate to be repeated here.

Hearing from Lammer in the early 1960s about the second parcel, Popper told him that it must have contained the missing manuscript. (Lammer to Hansen, 30 November 1975.) Some of the material that Feyerabend fetched clearly disappeared, but I think it improbable that it included a complete manuscript of either *Grundprobleme* II or ur-*Logik*.

[107] A caveat: The chapters of ur-*Logik* missing, the first four, were probably those subjected to the heaviest editing, and possibly dismembering. In my 1998 manuscript, I argued that abbreviating *Logik* probably consumed all four copies of these chapters. I have modified my position in light of Feyerabend's letters and Hansen's comments for which I am grateful.

[108] Popper to Julius Kraft, March or April 1934, Popper Archives (316, 24).

[109] *Logik der Forschung*, pp. 53–4; *The Logic of Scientific Discovery*, p. 95. Popper credited Reininger (*Metaphysik der Wirklichkeit* [Vienna: Braumüller, 1931]) with Neurath's idea of protocols. Indeed, Reininger did one better than Neurath (or Carnap) by providing a testing method. Neurath was incensed. He suspected that Popper was solicitous of metaphysicians. (Neurath to Popper, 4 July 1935, *Neurath Nachlaß*.) In his response (10 July 1935), Popper feigned uprightness. He may have been more concerned with covering his tracks, so that he owed nothing to Neurath, than with ingratiating himself to Reininger, but perhaps not.

[110] Popper, "In Memory of Hans Hahn," in *Hans Hahn: Collected Works*, vol. 1 (Vienna: Springer, 1995), p. 19.

resisted Carnap's proposal to invite Popper to the Prague conference. Prague, he said, was an intimate gathering of the circle. Popper did not belong. Besides, Popper would do well to publish something already. Neurath relented, however, extending an invitation.[111] Popper showed up in Prague on August 31, carrying his completed *Logik*. The conference treated him as an unknown. The discrepancy between his expectation for recognition and the audience's response was enormous. This brought out the worst in him. He behaved horribly. Eva Hempel, a kind observer, remembered him as "frightfully arrogant."[112] He was not scheduled to lecture, but participated actively in discussions. On September 2, Reichenbach opened a debate on induction and probability. Neurath and Carnap responded, arguing that no "induction machine" was possible, but it was Popper who delivered the most pointed critique.[113] Reichenbach refused to shake his hand. All the same, Popper was finally becoming part of the circle's Central European network. He met Tarski, Janina Hosiasson, and other Polish logicians, and they read parts of his manuscript.[114] He was emerging from anonymity.

Now that Popper had submitted his manuscript, he complained that Springer was taking its time. In September, he went over the galley proofs, introducing brief comments on Carnap's *Logical Syntax*, which he had read in August. He was concerned lest his book be seen as derivative of Carnap. The earlier it was out, the better. He received the formatted pages in sequence through late October and early November, corrected them speedily, the last two sheets on November 16. In late November, the book was ready. Springer even gave him his complimentary copies, but requested that he await official publication before giving them away. Popper was impatient.[115]

Meanwhile, Popper became entangled in a dramatic confrontation with quantum theorist Werner Heisenberg. Early in the summer of 1934, Popper designed an imaginary experiment, measuring simultaneously an electron's momentum and position. (Contemporary physics could not test single particles, and so quantum theorists commonly used imaginary experiments.)

---

[111] Carnap to Neurath, 13 April, 8 July, 14 July 1934, *Neurath Nachlaß*; Neurath to Carnap, 12 July and 16 July 1934, Carnap Collection; Neurath to Popper, 27 July 1934, *Neurath Nachlaß*.

[112] Eva Hempel to Ina Carnap, 27 January and 7 July 1936, Carnap Collection.

[113] Popper, " 'Induktionslogik' und 'Hypothesenwahrscheinlichkeit,' " *Erkenntnis* 5 (1935): 170–2. Friedrich Stadler, *Studien zum Wiener Kreis* (Frankfurt: Suhrkamp, 1997), pp. 395–402, provides an overview of the conference. Correspondence between Neurath and Popper discusses Popper's participation: Neurath to Popper, 22 November 1934; 3 January, 22 January, 11 February 1935. Popper to Neurath, December 1934, 28 February 1935, *Neurath Nachlaß*.

[114] Popper, *Ausgangspunkte* (Hamburg: Hoffman und Campe, 1979), p. 305 n. 114b. (This was an addition to the *Autobiography*'s German edition.) Idem, *A World of Propensities* (Bristol: Thoemmes, 1990), pp. 3–5.

[115] Popper to (Julius) Kraft, incomplete draft, c. 7 December 1934, verso of letter to Heisenberg, 16 December 1934, Popper Archives (305, 32).

He attempted to show that, contrary to Heisenberg, the interference of one measurement with the other did not make calculation of the electron's path impossible. This sustained his interpretation of quantum theory. He included the experiment in *Logik*. In August, he produced a synopsis and sent it to *Die Naturwissenschaften*.[116] The editorial board recognized the contribution's potential significance, but was unsure that it was scientifically sound. They sent it to Heisenberg for comment. Heisenberg entrusted his protégé, Carl August von Weizsäcker, with answering Popper in the journal. He then wrote Popper himself, suggesting that he withdraw his piece. Popper thought that Heisenberg misunderstood him and treated him as a novice. As the pace of their exchange increased, the tone became less civil.[117] Popper hoped that *Logik's* discussion of quantum and probability would establish his credentials. Ignoring Springer's request, he sent Heisenberg the book on December 6. A few days later, *Logik der Forschung* came out.

LOGIK DER FORSCHUNG: REVOLUTIONARY METHODOLOGY

The titles of both *Logik der Forschung* and its English translation, *The Logic of Scientific Discovery*, can be misleading. They seem to contradict Popper's contention that no logic unique to science exists. Science cannot be demarcated logically, he argued, only methodologically. Methodological rules were conventions, rules of the scientific game. These rules constituted the so-called logic of research. They were not logic proper. Even so, they applied only to testing theories, not their invention. Constructing a theory required metaphysical ideas and artistic insight. Discovery was not a matter of logic. But Popper mounted, at the same time, a compelling defense of the rationality of scientific conventions and their ability to guide scientists through experience in the search for knowledge. There was "logic" to the "logic of research." It was the book's subject. It became its title.

Popper offered his methodological vision as an alternative to two others: the positivist and the conventionalist. He cast the positivists as naive empiricists who propounded a psychologistic view of science. He cast the conventionalists as antiempiricists who threatened genuine knowledge. He posed as a conventionalist in his criticism of positivists, and as an empiricist in his criticism of conventionalists. To the first, he argued that

---

[116] Popper, "Zur Kritik der Ungenauigkeitsrelationen," *Die Naturwissenschaften* 22 (30 November 1934): 807. Section 77 in *Logik* provides a fuller account.

[117] Heisenberg to Popper, 23 November, 10 December, 19 December 1934; Popper to Heisenberg, 26 November, 6 December, 16 December 1934; Carl Friedrich von Weizsäcker to Popper, 6 December 1934, all in Popper Archives (305, 32).

(conventional) methodology alone demarcated science; to the latter that testability and falsifiability set limits to convention. Both positivism and conventionalism were tinged with subjectivism. His own methodological proposals offered the best guarantee of scientific objectivity (that is, intersubjectivity).

Popper reconfigured the opponents he had criticized in *Grundprobleme*. Familiar positivist figures reappeared in *Logik*, but wore different mantles, and performed different roles. Reichenbach moved to center stage. His inductive "probability logic" challenged Popper, motivating his reinterpretation of probability and quantum theory. As Schlick and his students Waismann and Feigl pronounced on both probability and physics, Schlick, too, loomed large in Popper's account. No wonder Reichenbach and Schlick were the circle members most furious with *Logik*. Popper attributed to them a "naturalist" metaphysics. They believed, he said, that science was successful because theories captured "real" lawfulness in the universe. This was metaphysics. His own methodology was free of metaphysical commitments. All he assumed was that scientists searched for lawfulness. Why scientists had proved so successful in finding lawfulness – that is, why the universe yielded to scientific theories – was not a question "scientific philosophy" could answer. He, Popper, did one better than the positivists in excluding metaphysics from science.

Logik der Forschung opened with two chapters outlining Popper's scientific methodology and its fundamental problems: induction, demarcation, falsification, deductive testing, empirical basis, psychologism, and objectivity (intersubjectivity). Popper fine-tuned *Grundprobleme*, saying little that was new, but saying it better. Supporting himself with quotations from Bergson and Einstein, he opined that no rational reconstruction of scientific discovery was possible: "The formation of theories seems to me neither to call for logical analysis nor to be susceptible of it."[118] Every discovery contained a "creative intuition," an "irrationalist element," going beyond method. He emphasized this to exclude psychologism forcefully. Questions of the genesis of knowledge had no bearing on epistemology or methodology. Positivists accepted this in principle, but resorted to psychologism in

---

[118] *Logik der Forschung*, p. 4: "Das Aufstellen der Theorien scheint uns einer logischen Analyse weder fähig noch bedürftig zu sein." (*The Logic of Scientific Discovery*, p. 31. Henceforth: *LSD*.)

Popper's translation of *Logik* (with the help of Julius and Lan Freed) was a masterpiece. It superseded two or three unpublished translations that had failed to satisfy him. The translation was rather free. Occasionally, it reflected recent developments in Popper's ideas that clarified, or even corrected, *Logik*. He was translating his own book, and so it was his prerogative to decide on the presentation best suited to his ideas. But *Logik* is also a historical document, testifying to Popper's views in 1933–4. Where the German seemed to me to suggest a different meaning, my translation diverged from his. (Here, Popper translated *Aufstellen der Theorie* as "conceiving or inventing a theory," because "formation," the literal translation, suggested more than he found acceptable in 1959: Certain stages in theory formation *were* subject to logical control.) I provide the German original wherever I diverge from Popper's translation.

practice, seeking to ground theory in "experience" – subjective perceptions. He, Popper, recognized that "in demanding objectivity for . . . scientific statements, we deprive ourselves of any logical means by which . . . to reduce the truth ("*Wahrheitentscheid*") of scientific statements to our experiences."[119] "Experiences can *motivate a decision*, and hence an acceptance or a rejection of a statement, but a basic statement cannot be *justified* by them – no more than by thumping the table."[120]

Popper used jury trial to demonstrate his point. Courts present juries with a case and a question formulated according to legal rules. Guided by procedures, the jury reaches a verdict, "a true statement of fact." No doubt convictions motivate the decision to accept a particular story as "fact," but convictions do not *justify* the decision. Indeed, the verdict may be wrong. In contrast, judges justify their judgment. They determine punishment by "deducing" the judgment from the laws. Scientific parallels are close. Basic statements can no more be justified by scientists' convictions than a jury's verdict. Questions posed to, and decisions reached by, both juries and scientists represent applications of a system, legal or theoretical, not unadulterated facts, or experience. Only "arbitrary" acceptance of a basic statement makes further application of the system – one that can be justified – possible. Theory informs all action and decision. Decision can not be justified.[121]

Positivism failed to grasp the fundamental difference between decision and justification. Popper used Frank and Hahn as positivist straw persons. (They represented the least nuanced empiricism among the circle.) Their appeal to experience as final arbitrator of scientific questions, Popper opined, was naive: There was no such thing as experience unadulterated by theory. Theory dominated experiments from their initial planning to their final execution in the laboratory. The language used to report experience was full of theories. Even basic statements were interpretive. They used universal concepts, if only because language contained universal names that were not reducible to experience. Transcendence was inherent in every description, every report of observation or sensory perception. Trying to justify decisions by appealing to experience ignored the unbridgeable gap between language and fact, theory and experience. It was an appeal to conviction, pure subjectivism, and psychologism.

Conviction could not justify but could initiate a discovery: "Scientific research is probably impossible without . . . 'metaphysical' faith in some-

---

[119] *Logik*, p. 18; *LSD*, pp. 46–7.

[120] *Logik*, p. 62; *LSD*, p. 105. I used Popper's translation, but it is not completely literal: "Erlebnisse können Entschlüsse, also auch Festsetzungen [conventions] *motivieren*, aber sie können einen Basissatz ebensowenig begründen wie ein Faustschlag auf den Tisch."

[121] The analogy of science and court was, of course, limited. The legal system was not empirical, but prescriptive. Unlike a basic statement, no jury verdict could contradict a law. *Logik*, pp. 51–3, 62–7; *LSD*, pp. 93–5, 106–11; *Grundprobleme*, 128–31.

times hazy theoretical ideas," initial speculation that becomes scientific once formulated as a testable hypothesis.[122] Eradicating speculation and faith from science was impossible. To be sure, science represented more advanced knowledge than metaphysics. Speculative, that is, untestable, theories were none of its business. All empirical sciences developed historically from metaphysics. Scientists may exclude, in a piecemeal fashion, the remaining metaphysical elements in theories, by demarcating them through testability.[123] Still, metaphysics was not meaningless. "Meaningless" meant for positivists "not susceptible to inductive inference," but scientific theories were just as vulnerable as metaphysics.[124] Positivists eradicated science along with metaphysics.

The project of logically demarcating science failed. Science's boundaries were conventional, not "natural."[125] Methodological conventions set them. Which practitioners were designated "scientists" and what activities were defined "scientific" had changed throughout history. When positivists proposed rules, they were offering conventions, not establishing facts. Proposals had to be debated and accepted by the scientific community. Methodology did not replicate but set the rules of science. It was not descriptive but prescriptive. Whether induction was used in practice or not made little difference. It was invalid. "The despised defenders of 'traditional philosophy'" had to teach positivists that science was a problem, not a program.[126]

Popper's emphasis on methodology's prescriptive character represented a change of position from *Grundprobleme*. *Grundprobleme* I's major claim to fame, as Gomperz and Carnap understood it, was the correspondence between its epistemology and scientific practice, but already in *Grundprobleme* II, Popper was arguing for a critical theory of science.[127] In *Logik*, he completed the shift. His demarcation was superior, he said, *not* because it corresponded to scientific practice, but because it clarified and resolved its problems. In *Grundprobleme* I, he largely limited himself to internal criticism. He was now leaving the "critical-dialectical" path behind, he said, to

---

[122] *Logik*, p. 11; *LSD*, p. 38: "wissenschaftliche Forschung . . . ohne einen . . . 'metaphysischen' Glauben an manchmal höchst unklare theoretische Ideen wohl gar nicht möglich ist."

[123] In his *Autobiography*, Popper claimed that he was more interested in demarcating science from pseudoscience than from metaphysics, but at least in the early 1930s, there was little evidence of it. In *Logik*, he claimed to provide the single effective criterion for excluding metaphysics.

[124] *Logik*, p. 9; *LSD*, p. 36.

[125] In *Logical Syntax*, Carnap, too, acknowledged that demarcation was conventional. In response, Popper added in proof that he had held this position for years and that *Syntax* appeared too late to be discussed in *Logik*. Apparently, Carnap's draft, "Semantik," which Popper had read in 1932, did not hold this position. Popper was politely asserting his priority.

[126] *Logik*, sections 4, 9–11.

[127] Gomperz noted in his 1932 recommendation for Popper that where Popper disagreed with the circle, his proposals were closer to scientific practice. Gomperz to Mohr, 21 December 1932 (300, 9). Carnap concurred. Rudolf Carnap, "Über Protokollsätze," *Erkenntnis* 3 (1932): 228.

focus on methodology. Was he doing philosophy? It did not matter. Many philosophical problems, for example, objectivity and causality, were methodological in character. *Logik der Forschung* offered a philosophy the task of which was the shaping of scientific methodology.

Popper divided *Logik*'s second, and much longer, part – "some structural components for a theory of experience" – into eight chapters. The first three, "theories," "falsifiability," and "empirical basis," the fifth, "simplicity," and the last, "corroboration," betrayed a debt to *Grundprobleme*; the other three, on testability, probability, and quantum theory, almost none. All eight chapters investigated the structure and forms of scientific theory, the range of scientific concepts, and the rules governing scientific procedures. Popper erected a scientific edifice that, though constructed of methodological conventions, was logically tight like few others in the history of philosophy.

In the first chapter, Popper suggested that few scientific fields ever approached axiomatization, or displayed as firmly constructed a system of theories as geometry. Nonetheless, an axiomatic system remained a regulative ideal. Theories should be formulated as tightly as possible so that any new assumption would be easily recognizable. Physics could not be axiomatized, but connections among different theories were sufficiently clear for scientists to decide, in case of a falsifying experiment, which part of the system was to blame. Axiomatic systems, such as geometry, included concepts that could not be empirically defined (point, line, and the like), and had to remain undefined. But geometrical concepts could be correlated with, or interpreted by, the concepts of another system, such as physics. This was especially important when a new system of hypotheses (for example, relativity) explained an earlier one (Newtonian physics). It was possible to use some of the old concepts of geometrical physics to define the new ones. Popper thus resolved a problem that had preoccupied him ever since his geometry thesis. Geometry was nontestable and, yet, proved crucial to experimental physics. He now understood how and why.

Scientific theories were strictly universal statements, not limited by space and time. They aimed to capture natural laws. The statement "all planets revolve in orbits" was strictly universal.[128] It meant: "there is no planet not revolving in an orbit." It was falsifiable, but nonverifiable. The discovery of a planet not revolving in an orbit would falsify the statement – it prohibited such an occurrence – but no number of planets circulating in orbits could verify it. Existential "there is" statements, such as "there are planets

---

[128] In contrast, "all planets in system *x* revolve in orbits" was a numerical statement. As the planets, limited by space or time, could be counted, the statement was not truly universal, but singular. Inductive inference could be used to verify numerical statements, but it was Popper's contention (and criticism of Carnap) that individual concepts could not constitute universal ones, or singular statements universal ones.

revolving in orbits," were verifiable, but nonfalsifiable. They prohibited nothing. Observation of planets circulating in orbits could repeatedly verify the statement, but a planet not revolving in an orbit would not falsify it. Logically, strictly universal and existential statements were symmetrical, unilaterally decidable, the former falsifiable, the latter verifiable. Moreover, negation of a strictly universal statement produced an existential statement ("there are planets not revolving in orbits"), and vice versa, negation of an existential statement produced a natural law ("no planet revolves in an orbit"). Only methodological demarcation declared the former scientific, the latter metaphysical.

Theories provided causal explanations. To give a causal explanation of an event was to deduce a statement describing it, subject to initial conditions, from one or more universal statements (natural laws). From universal laws governing the planets' movement, one may deduce that "on day and time x, planet y would be (is) at point z on orbit u." This could serve as a basic test statement. All test statements were singular existential statements. In a crucial test, scientists confronted such a statement with one deduced from a competing theory: "on day and time x, planet y would be at point r (outside orbit u)." (More accurately, scientists confronted the competing statement with its negation – "planet y would *not* be at point r" – a singular nonexistence statement that was compatible with the prevailing theory.) If observation provided, and scientists accepted, that "planet y is at point r," the universal statements regarding the planets' revolution were falsified, and required reconstruction in accordance with the corroborated theory.[129]

Popper moved next to investigate falsifiability. Here, he mostly restated *Grundprobleme* II's arguments against conventionalism. He created a conventionalist straw person in the figure of conservative Viennese physicist Hugo Dingler, who bemoaned the "collapse of science" with the triumph of relativity.[130] (Circle members complained later that this was not a fair representation of conventionalism.) The sarcasm Popper poured on Dingler could not conceal the conventionalist character of his own critique of positivism. He therefore emphasized more than ever that falsification radically broke with conventionalism. Conventionalists ignored the methodological significance of the distinction between universal and basic statements, collapsing theory and test: "Convention or decision does not immediately determine our acceptance of *universal* statements but [of] basic statements." "Choice of any particular theory is . . . decisively influenced by the application of the theory." Utility and practicality determined, indeed, acceptance, but their chief measure was the severity of tests the theory survived.

---

[129] *Logik*, Section 12 for causality, Section 28 for basic statements.

[130] Hugo Dingler, *Der Zusammenbruch der Wissenschaft und der Primat der Philosophie* (Munich: Reinhardt, 1926).

"What ultimately decides the fate of a theory is the result of a test, i.e., an agreement about basic statements."[131]

Moving beyond *Grundprobleme*, Popper used testability to define falsifiability.[132] A theory was falsifiable if it could distinguish clearly between the classes of statements that potentially falsified it and those that did not. (If it could not, it was metaphysical at best, self-contradictory at worst.) If the class of potential falsifiers was larger for one theory than for another, it was more testable. It had greater empirical content because it prohibited more. Science aimed at obtaining easily falsifiable theories that restricted the range of permitted events to a minimum. In lengthy technical sections, some of which Popper added to the book at the last minute, he demonstrated that classes of potential falsifiers of different theories, that is, theories' degree of testability, could be compared. Scientists now had a clear criterion for selecting among competing theories.

Scientists' preference for theoretical simplicity was equivalent to a requirement of the greatest possible degree of testability (and falsifiability). Marcel Natkin (1904–63), who preceded Popper as the circle's *Wunderkind*, discussed simplicity in an unpublished dissertation that circulated widely.[133] Popper argued that he, not Natkin, explained for the first time why simplicity was desirable. Not, as Wittgenstein and the positivists (Feigl, Natkin, Schlick) assumed, for aesthetic or pragmatic reasons (Duhem's and Mach's "economy of thought"), but rather because a theory's universality and precision increased with simplicity. The simpler the theory, the more informative and testable it was. A theory's applications must be taken into consideration in evaluating simplicity. Conventionalists were wrong to erect complex systems to defend purportedly simple theories, the degree of falsifiability of which approached zero.

Popper now succeeded in logically defining the epistemological position that he had been arguing against conventionalists since his 1929 dissertation. His joy at having established simplicity as a purely logical concept, identical with falsifiability, was great. Whether he rendered testability and simplicity methodologically usable was a different question. Actual comparison of competing theories' degree of falsifiability required measurement of the "logical space" occupied by their potential

---

[131] *Logik*, pp. 64–5; *LSD*, p. 109. Until the galley proofs, Section 30 was part of the testability (4), not foundation (3) chapter. The positivists were the major target in 3; the conventionalists in 2, 4, and 5 – all dealing with falsifiability. (Chapter numbers here refer to *Logik*.)

[132] John Watkins points out (E-mail communication to author, 26 June 1998) that testability and falsifiability are not equivalent. Falsifiability is purely logical. "All dinosaurs are yellow" has potential falsifiers, but they are hardly testable. However, in *Logic*, Popper treats the two interchangeably. See especially his introduction to "Degrees of Testability."

[133] Marcel Natkin, "Einfachheit, Kausalität und Induktion" (Ph.D. diss.: University of Vienna, 1928). Popper did not see Natkin's dissertation, only Feigl's and Schlick's reports on it: *Grundprobleme*, pp. 148–9; *Logik*, p. 89; *LSD*, pp. 138–9.

falsifiers. When one theory was clearly more universal than another (that is, prohibited more), this did not represent a problem, but this was rarely the case. In practice, the degree of falsifiabilty proved difficult to measure with any precision.[134] Counting and evaluating all basic statements that could be deduced from a theory was a difficult task. Popper acknowledged as much, but insisted that his prescriptions remained effective as rules.

As scientists searched for highly falsifiable theories, the probability of their theories was low; indeed, universal theories with infinite domain had zero probability. Falsifiability and probability were inversely related. Probability decreased as falsifiability (and testability) increased. This represented a direct challenge to Reichenbach. Reichenbach believed that science required a new logic, compatible with the probabilistic universe of modern physics. Quantum theory shattered causality and demonstrated the inexactitude of measurement, but it successfully used probability. As probability statements were neither verifiable nor falsifiable – no test could refute, or conclusively verify, a probability – Reichenbach concluded that classical logic, which assigned truth and falsity to statements, was approaching an end. Physical theories were probability statements, not true or false, but somewhere in between, more or less probable. Scientists searched for highly probable theories. To determine a theory's probability, they inducted results of repeated tests.[135] Inductive "probability logic" contrasted strikingly with Popper's "falsifiability logic."

Popper regarded inductive probability logic as completely untenable but could not ignore it. *Logik's* final three chapters were an elaborate response to Reichenbach. Popper insisted that corroboration (or confirmation[136]) of hypotheses and probability of events were completely different. A probability statement determined the relative truth frequency of a statement ("the throw is six") within a sequence of statements (describing results of throws). Such probability of events could not be translated into one of hypotheses. Against what sequence of statements could scientists assign probability to a hypothesis? None existed, or worked in practice.[137]

---

[134] For a technical discussion of the problems and an effort to resolve them see: John Watkins, *Science and Scepticism*, Chapter 5.

[135] Popper used primarily: Hans Reichenbach, "Kausalität und Wahrscheinlichkeit," *Erkenntnis* 1 (1930): 158–88; "Wahrscheinlichkeitslogik," *Sitzungsberichte der Preussischen Akademie der Wissenschaften*, Physik.–mathem. Klasse 29 (1932): 476–90; and the more technical "Axiomatik der Wahrscheinlichkeitsrechnung," *Mathematische Zeitschrift* 34 (1932): 568–619.

[136] I have translated *Bewährung* as "corroboration" in accordance with *LSD*. Initially, Popper accepted Carnap's rendering: "confirmation." (Rudolf Carnap, "Testability and Meaning," *Philosophy of Science* 3 [1936]: 427.) In postwar years, Popper shifted to "corroboration" to distinguish his views from Carnap's. Carnap used confirmation as a weak "verification," which Popper insisted corroboration was not.

[137] Popper thought that there were two possibilities, and he rejected both. The first was that scientists would count the testable statements belonging to a theory and determine the relative frequency of

Hypotheses were not sequences of statements. Probability was no measure of corroboration.

Corroboration was an assessment of how well a theory stood up to tests. That it had stood up well did not mean that its probability had been raised. Routine confirmation meant little. Theories rarely, if ever, broke down because familiar experiments produced new results. Rather, new experiments produced refutations. A high degree of corroboration meant that a theory had survived severe tests. Severity depended on the degree of testability and simplicity. The most falsifiable theory was often also the most corroborated, but not always: A falsifiable hypothesis could remain only slightly corroborated. (Falsifiability was a logical concept, but attempted falsifications depended on experimenters.) Comparing theories' degree of corroboration was difficult. Corroboration represented a rough estimate that had no "truth" or probability value. (It was not a new hypothesis.) Whereas a false theory remained forever false, a theory's degree of corroboration changed with experiments. There was no need to be precise in such matters, said Popper, for methodological rules to guide scientific decisions. Intersubjective falsification, in a crucial experiment, was final. It overthrew one theory, corroborated another. Theories opened ways to new knowledge; tests saved scientists from following tracks that led nowhere.

This was all well stated, but Popper still faced a major problem. Probability statements were nonfalsifiable. They did not rule out anything observable, and could not be contradicted by a basic statement. (Only an infinite sequence of events could contradict a probability estimate.) Yet, contemporary physics achieved great success with predictions obtained from hypothetical estimates of probabilities. Reichenbach's probability logic was seductive. A probabilistic universe seemed to vindicate induction at the same time as it disposed of causality and verification. Objective probabil-

those turning true. But, then, scientists needed to limit themselves to statements actually tested (otherwise probability would approach zero), and probability became dangerously subjective. It depended on experimenters' skill and training, not on reproducible effects. The second possibility was that scientists could consider the theory as one of a class of competing theories in a field, and determine frequencies in this class. But, then, irrespective of problems in establishing the class (how would scientists decide which theories belonged?), there was no way of knowing whether any one hypothesis was true or false. (If there were, there would be no need for a frequency at all.) Neither possibility significantly reduced the probability of a hypothesis when a refutation occurred. Neither worked.

Reichenbach was initially unclear what the frequency of hypotheses meant. In his 1935 review of *Logik*, he adopted the above proposals, proposals that Grelling and Popper had made during the debate in Prague the previous fall, and Popper had discussed (and rejected) in *Logik* (Section 80, pp. 188–95). (Hans Reichenbach, "Über Induktion und Wahrscheinlichkeit. Bemerkungen zu Karl Poppers *Logik der Forschung*," *Erkenntnis* 5 [1935]: 267–84, esp. 274.) Popper thought that this was outright plagiarism *(LSD,* p. 260 n. ★5. See also: Popper, "'Induktionslogik' und 'Hypothesen-wahrscheinlichkeit,'" *Erkenntnis* 5 [1935]: 170–2.)

ity theories seemed to presuppose lawfulness as an axiom, validating induction. No scientist could conceive of giving up induction, stated Reichenbach in 1930, expressing the hegemonic view. By allowing a weaker verification, a degree of confirmation, his probability logic retained induction. Popper faced a Herculean task. Not only did he need to make probability statements falsifiable, but he also had to demonstrate that a theory of probability free of any assumption of lawfulness was possible. Else, probability would deal a fatal blow to falsifiability.

Opening the long probability chapter, Popper stated his intention to clarify the relationship between theory and experience in probability. Physicists had been making use of probabilities without being able to explain what they meant by them. He, Popper, would show how mathematical probability statements – neither verifiable nor falsifiable – became methodologically falsifiable. He would modify Richard von Mises's frequency (*Häufigkeit*) interpretation so as to create a new objective concept of probability, and lay the foundations for axiomatization of the calculus of probability.

Probability made random events calculable. How could probability make the unpredictable predictable? This represented the fundamental problem of the theory of chance (*Zufalltheorie*). There were two major answers, which Popper called subjective and objective. He associated the subjective with Keynes and Waismann.[138] They thought that probability did not calculate predictions but stated incomplete knowledge, establishing a "degree of rational belief." The next throw with a die was unpredictable. No testable statement about it could be made. The objective answer, which Popper identified with Richard von Mises, was that probability did not make the unpredictable predictable, only calculated probabilities that were not given from given ones. Scientific and popular use of probability did not correspond. Probability said nothing to the gambler about the next throw. It established the relative frequency of a particular result in a series of throws or, generally, the relative frequency with which an event occurred within a sequence. Any probability statement about a single event was actually a statement about the entire class, in which the event was an element. From an initial collective (sequence) with a certain distribution, the calculus of probability inferred a collective with derived distributions. That was all.[139]

---

[138] This was problematic. Keynes and Waismann thought of probability as a logical relationship between two statements. It denoted, said Waismann, "logical proximity" (*logische Nähe*), rather than derivability and contradiction. Popper remained convinced, however, that their conceptions were "psychologistic" (*LSD*, p. 148 n. ★1). John Maynard Keynes, *A Treatise on Probability* (London: Macmillan, 1921). (Trans.: *Über Wahrscheinlichkeit* [Leipzig: Barth, 1926].) Friedrich Waismann, "Logische Analyse des Wahrscheinlichkeitsbegriffs," *Erkenntnis* 1 (1930): 228–48.

[139] Richard von Mises, "Grundlagen der Wahrscheinlichkeitsrechnung," *Mathematische Zeitschrift* 5 (1919): 52–99; *Wahrscheinlichkeit, Statistik, und Wahrheit* (Vienna: Springer, 1928); *Wahrscheinlichkeit-*

Popper did not think that Mises's explanation was altogether adequate. Frequency hypotheses did make random events predictable. They did not predict single events, but they predicted the relative frequencies of different events in long sequences. All the same, Popper adopted the frequency interpretation, intending to improve on it. Only an objective interpretation allowed probability statements to become empirical (that is, testable). A statement of incomplete knowledge that made no predictions was useless to scientists. He sought, however, to purge the frequency interpretation of axioms that introduced metaphysical lawfulness. Mises defined a random sequence of events (*zufallsartige Ereignisfolge*) by means of two axiomatic conditions: the "limit axiom" (*Grenzwertsaxiom;* Popper later called it "convergence axiom"), and the "randomness axiom" (*Regellosigkeitsaxiom*). The limit axiom stipulated that as the event sequence (for example, repeated throws with a die) became longer, the frequency sequence would tend toward a definite limit. (If 1 to 6 were possible results, actual frequencies of 1 will fluctuate, but tend toward one fixed value: 1/6.) Probability was this limit, the one fixed frequency value. The randomness axiom excluded the possibility of a "gambling system," that is, any systematic method of selection (for example, "after a run of 10 successive tails, predict heads") that would give better results than random selection. The longer the sequence, the closer the limit would be approached. If a sequence of events satisfied both of these conditions, Mises called it a "collective."

Criticism of Mises's axioms, especially their combination, was common: How could a mathematical rule, Mises's limit, apply to a sequence defined as random? Popper thought he could relax the randomness requirement. He regarded the problem as primarily mathematical. The limit axiom, however, he sought to eliminate for epistemological reasons. He wanted to show that the "quasi-convergent behavior" (*konvergenzartiges Verhalten*), or statistical stability, of long sequences – their tendency to approach Mises's limit – was neither an empirical fact, as inductivists believed, nor a necessary axiom of probability. It was simply a feature of sequences' random character, a mathematical tautology. He strove to free probability from metaphysical assumptions about lawfulness. In 1934, he was predisposed toward determinism. He insisted that probability was compatible with a determinist universe. He was suspicious of the stringent randomness axiom. Still, he refused to admit determinist metaphysics into

srechnung und ihre Anwendung in der Statistik und theoretischen Physik (Leipzig: Deuticke, 1931). Reichenbach was also a leading frequency theoretician. Popper de-emphasized his role.

John Watkins alerted me to the debate on whether probabilities can be assigned to single events. In 1934, Popper, following Richard von Mises, answered in the negative. His later interpretation of probability made assigning probability to single events possible. (See: David Miller, *Critical Rationalism* [Chicago: Open Court, 1994], p. 182 ff.) Watkins wisely suggested that I stay away from the debate. I did, and I thank him also for a good number of corrections to my discussion of probability.

probability, or induction would be vindicated. He had to dispose of the limit axiom.

He performed both tasks by first deriving Bernoulli's theorem, the "Law of Great Numbers," from a modified randomness axiom, then demonstrating that the limit axiom was neither sufficient nor necessary for deriving this law. Bernoulli's theorem asserted that the probability of chancing upon a "fair sample" of a random sequence approached 1 the longer the sample was.[140] This quasi-convergent behavior – disorder and randomness in short sequences, order and stability in long ones – was statistically ascertainable. Popper showed that, to derive the law, it was not necessary to exclude all systems of selection ("gambling systems"). It was sufficient if the sequence was insensitive to its predecessors, that is, free from the "aftereffects" (*nachwirkungsfreie*) of an earlier sequence, or, as he put it later, "absolutely free." Relaxing the randomness requirement in this manner made construction of model sequences possible, thereby showing that such sequences, indeed, existed. Although models were constructed according to mathematical rules, such rules no longer violated the randomness requirement.

Next, Popper proceeded to demonstrate that the limit, or convergence, axiom was insufficient to derive Bernoulli. There were sequences that satisfied the convergence requirement without satisfying Bernoulli, because arbitrarily long segments did not constitute "fair samples." These sequences were not "absolutely free." Popper's randomness – "absolute freedom" – was indispensable for Bernoulli, but convergence was not. Indeed, it seemed that Bernoulli could be derived without convergence even for free finite sequences, provided the sequences were sufficiently long. Popper now replaced the limit (convergence) axiom with a "uniqueness" (*Eindeutigkeit*) requirement: For any one property (for example, numerical result of a throw) in a random sequence there was only one middle ("average") frequency, its probability. (In a sequence representing results of throws with a die, each result from 1 to 6 had only one average frequency: its probability.) This was necessary because certain sequences could have more than one middle frequency, and mathematicians worked with a single probability. From the randomness and uniqueness axioms, Bernoulli and the entire calculus of probability could be deduced.[141]

---

[140] I followed here Popper's account in *LSD*, p. 179. As he notes there (n. ★1), *Logik's* exposition (p. 123) was cursory and did not use the notion of a "fair sample."

[141] Popper was aware that introducing the uniqueness requirement was problematic. He could be seen as readmitting the limit axiom by the back door. He suggested that this was not the case, because he introduced uniqueness *after* postulating randomness (i. e., establishing a free sequence) (*Logik*, pp. 129–30; *LSD*, p. 186). All the same, the status and function of uniqueness remained ambiguous. In Section 63 (*Logik*, pp. 126–7; *LSD*, pp. 183–4), he implied that randomness was sufficient for deriving Bernoulli, and in Section 64 *(Logik*, p. 129; *LSD*, p. 185), he proposed to eliminate convergence without replacing it. But later in this section *(Logik*, p. 130; *LSD*, p. 187), he spoke of uniqueness as an axiom required for Bernoulli, and, in n. 7 (*Logik*, p. 240; *LSD*, p. 189), said that he replaced the

Convergence eliminated, long sequences' statistical stability became a logical result of axiomatic independence (randomness). From disorder in short random sequences, order in long ones followed logically. Quasi-convergent behavior was no longer an epistemological issue, but an axiomatic-logical one. It was not an "empirical fact," or a "natural law," that could become an axiom of probability and a foundation for inductive logic. Popper could also explain now how probability made the unpredictable predictable. As statistical stability in large subsections of a random sequence was normal, it was permissible to express it by means of a frequency *hypothesis* (prediction). Subjective interpretations, lacking a frequency concept, could not formulate such predictions. Mises's frequency theory sidestepped the issue by postulating regularity. There was nothing to predict. Popper's interpretation relaxed probability so that it permitted, but not legislated, regularity in randomness. Order was possible, even likely, but never certain, always a matter of hypothetical prediction. Frequency hypotheses made the incalculable calculable.

How could frequency hypotheses be corroborated or falsified? Without methodological intervention, mathematical probability statements were nonfalsifiable and metaphysical. As they prohibited nothing, any arbitrarily chosen basic statement could "confirm" them. In principle, they could "explain" any and all phenomena as an accumulation of accidents. Frequencies could express all regularity – including the law of gravity – as randomness, provided the sequence was extended sufficiently to include an irregular section. Probability's scientific application had to be narrowed down.

Popper proposed a methodological postulate: Never explain reproducible regularities as accidental. Physicists used probability to explain "macroeffects," such as gas pressure, resulting from hypothetical, nonobservable, nonmeasurable "microprocesses" (molecular collisions). Had "microprocesses" been measurable and experiments' results consistent, law and causality would have been appropriate. As repeated controlled experiments produced varying results, probability, relative frequency in randomness, was the best science could do. To render probability statements falsifiable, if an experiment of a "fair sample" consistently yielded a fre-

limit axiom with a uniqueness requirement. In Section 66, the logical form and function of uniqueness proved problematic. Critics could understandably wonder whether it was wise to perform all these acrobatics to exclude convergence. But Popper had no choice. Falsifiability had little chance against inductive logic, if convergence were retained.

Popper knew he had a problem. In *LSD* (pp. 165–6 n. *1; p. 185 n. *1; p. 187 n. *2; p. 188 n. *3; p. 195 n. *4), he suggested that further analysis of randomness (Appendix *VI and n. *2 to Appendix *IV) would have rendered the uniqueness requirement superfluous. He could have constructed finite, shortest *n*-free sequences, and demonstrated that if *n* grew without bounds, the sequences became infinite, and the frequencies turned without further assumption into limits.

quency deviating by more than a methodologically established minimum from a predicted probability, it constituted falsification. The minimum did not need to be set tolerantly. Scientists opted for the best possible conformity, given attainable measurements, between a predicted probability and frequencies of tested fair samples. By definition, deviations, even an atypical segment, were permitted. Systematic deviations, predictable and reproducible, were prohibited. Mathematical and physical probability were not the same. Methodological rules rendered probability statements empirical and falsifiable.[142]

As Popper completed developing his probability concept, he realized that its application to quantum mechanics might resolve theoretical difficulties. Quantum theory constituted a problem for Popper's "objective science." It represented a recent, much admired revolution in physics, one in which probability found remarkably successful application. At the same time, positivist and subjectivist interpretations of the theory – by its founder, Heisenberg, no less – prevailed. An indeterminist picture of the universe, which Popper thought detrimental to modern science, was threatening to become hegemonic. With his new probability concept, Popper thought that he could reinterpret quantum theory in accordance with objective science. Here was an obvious site to demonstrate his methodology's practical significance and show the enemy, the positivists, for what they were: misguided metaphysicians whose antimetaphysical crusade threatened to render science a subjective enterprise.

A positivist agenda, suggested Popper, underlay Heisenberg's interpretation of quantum theory. Heisenberg sought to eliminate all unobservable magnitudes from atomic theory as metaphysical. Every measurement involved an exchange of energy between object and observer. Its effects were usually negligible, but in atomic particles' case, measurement altered electrons to such an extent that their state could not be determined. It was possible, while measuring, to limit interference with either the particles' momentum or position, but only at the cost of severe interference with the other. Both could not be simultaneously measured. Momentum-cum-position relations were indeterminate (*Unbestimmtheitsrelationen*). Predicting an electron's path was impossible. It was a matter of belief. Schlick proposed to eliminate the "path" altogether as nonverifiable. Indeterminancy became a basic quantum principle. To Heisenberg, it accounted for the

---

[142] In later years, Popper integrated falsifiability into probability itself, rather than into its application. As a result of his further investigation into randomness (see n. 141), he substituted finitude for uniqueness as a requirement for probability: the shortest random sequence possible. This made probability statements falsifiable without any further methodological rule. Empirical sequences could be expected only to approximate shortest sequences. Mathematical statistics and the theory of corroboration determined the acceptable degree of approximation. *LSD*, p. 187 n. *2; p. 191, n. *1; p. 199, n. *2.

theory's statistical character. To obtain precise measurement would not be to resolve a technical problem, but to falsify quantum theory.[143]

Popper considered quantum theory "one of the greatest achievements in the history of science," but he disputed Heisenberg's indeterminancy. The indeterminacy formula, he suggested, should be statistically interpreted. It did not refer to subjective limits of knowledge of a single particle's behavior. Rather, it predicted results of particles' selection (measurement) by establishing objective relations between ranges of statistical scatter (*Streuungsrelationen*). Any selection (measurement) of an aggregate of electrons with a certain momentum will produce a range of random scattering of their position. The smaller the selection's imprecision, or the smaller the range it permitted the momentum, the greater the range of position that will result (and vice versa). Thus interpreted, Heisenberg's formula asserted only that selection interfered with scattering and constituted a barrier to obtaining a homogeneous aggregate of particles for experiment. It did not prohibit precise measurement of momentum-cum-position.[144] On the contrary, it required it so that the hypothesis might be tested. Heisenberg's indeterminacy was no part of quantum theory. It was an added assumption, a dogma that threatened to turn the theory metaphysical.

Popper suggested that Heisenberg's program for purging metaphysics from quantum theory be inverted. Rather than exclude unobservable magnitudes, Popper proposed to show that they were testable. A particle's path between measurements could be calculated with precision by ascertaining two consecutive positions, or measuring first position, then momentum, or first momentum, then position. To be sure, these were nonpredictive measurements. They could not predict particles' future path, because the initial conditions for experiment (selection) could not be set. Scatter relations between momentum and position were all that could be predicted. But Heisenberg had to choose. Either the path existed, making the indeterminacy principle subjective (merely human knowledge's limits), or it did not exist, rendering calculations of past "paths" metaphysical. The problem vanished if the indeterminacy formula was statistically interpreted as scatter relations, and falsification substituted for verification as a demarcation criterion. The scatter-relations hypothesis, presupposing a "path," was testable and falsifiable. Quantum mechanics was free of metaphysical elements. Heisenberg's subjectivist, indeterminist, verificationist program failed. Popper vindicated objective probability and falsificationist science.

[143] Werner Heisenberg, *Die physikalischen Prinzipien der Quantentheorie* (Leipzig: Hirzel, 1930). Also: idem, "Über quantentheoretische Umdeutung kinematischer und mechanischer Beziehungen," *Zeitschrift für Physik* 33 (1925): 879–93. For the history of quantum theory: Max Jammer, *The Philosophy of Quantum Mechanics* (New York: John Wiley, 1974).

[144] In any case, probability hypotheses did not prohibit single events. A single electron's measurement (translated into a singular probability statement) could not contradict a probability hypothesis.

This was persuasive enough, but Popper wanted to top off his theoretical achievement with a hard scientific accomplishment. He would design an imaginary *experimentum crucis* that would simultaneously measure momentum and position and rout any doubt about his interpretation. However, his experiment contained an error.[145] A letter from Einstein, with whom he corresponded in summer 1935, convinced him that the experiment was untenable. This was a sad end to a year of bitter struggle with Heisenberg and his entourage. The failure dimmed his interpretive achievement and shook him badly, but at least one historian of quantum theory, Max Jammer, thinks it possible that Popper's failed experiment inspired the famous Einstein–Rosen–Podolsky experiment the following year.[146] This last experiment accomplished what Popper had tried: simultaneous measurement of momentum and position. Whether *Logik* reached Einstein in time to leave a mark on his developing experiment, or not, Popper's and E-P-R's reasoning were close. "In fact," says Jammer, "one may say that Popper's is an over-determined Einstein-Podolsky-Rosen argument."[147]

Popper retreated from physics for a decade. He returned to quantum theory in 1950, and his *Postscript to The Logic of Scientific Discovery*, written in the mid-1950s, addressed issues emerging from *Logik's* quantum chapter.[148] He had to come to terms with the metaphysics underlying quantum theory. Throughout *Logik*, he refused to get involved in speculation about the universe's structure. This was in part scientific pose, in part theoretical necessity. If the universe were lawful, he feared, induction might be possible.[149] If it were random, objectivity might be at risk. For falsifiable science to work, he needed to keep the universe in suspense by relegating any speculation about its structure to metaphysics. He, Popper, might be a realist – upholding the world's objective existence separately from consciousness – and a determinist. As a methodologist, he was metaphysically neutral.

---

[145] Popper assumed that in an experiment where measurement of momentum preceded position, an electron's past path, prior to the first measurement, could be reconstructed. Not so.

[146] Albert Einstein, Boris Podolsky, and Nathan Rosen, "Can Quantum-Mechanical Description of Physical Reality be Considered Complete?" *Physical Review* 47 (1935): 777–80.

[147] Max Jammer, *The Philosophy of Quantum Mechanics*, p. 178 n. 30. John Stachel, Einstein archivist, wrote Popper (15 July 1977) that a draft of E-P-R was complete by 25 March 1935, whereas *Logik* did not reach Einstein until 28 April 1935. Popper Archives (292, 12).

[148] "Indeterminism in Quantum Physics and in Classical Physics, Part I," *British Journal for the Philosophy of Science* 1 (1950): 117–33; "Part II," 1 (1950): 173–95. (This was an extended version of his Princeton lecture, attended by Einstein and Bohr. Hansen drew my attention to it.) Extensively rewritten, the *Postscript* came out in three volumes in 1981–2 (London: Hutchinson): *Realism and the Aim of Science; The Open Universe: An Argument for Indeterminism; Quantum Theory and the Schism in Physics.*

[149] John Watkins comments here: "Hume's problem is the same whether there are exceptionless regularities or only statistical regularities. A methodology ought to be impartial with regard to such metaphysical issues" (*Science and Scepticism*, pp. 124–5).

Still, Popper took pains to demonstrate that quantum theory did not imply indeterminism. Indeterminist metaphysics was an understandable response to the failure of the atom's mechanical model, but it could have crippling effects on research. Science's basic rule was: Never cease searching for laws. To deny causality was to tell scientists to give up. Determinism might hypostatize a methodological rule into a metaphysical principle, but at least faith in regularities was productive: It guided scientific pursuits. Science opted for perfect lawfulness, and limits of knowledge alone prevented it from reaching it. The die's throw was no different from the planets' movement. If scientists knew all the throw's initial conditions, they would produce a law, not a probability. Still, how could scientists opt for perfect lawfulness if the universe was not lawful? Popper pretended that *expectation* of lawfulness did not imply determinism, or realism, but the tension between methodological hope and metaphysical agnosticism was great.

Popper had to close the gap he had opened between methodology and metaphysics, science and the universe. He needed a realist metaphysics compatible with falsificationist science. In 1934, only fear of induction prevented him from confessing realism and determinism. Later, he had second thoughts about determinism. During his New Zealand exile, he developed a political philosophy that combated historical determinism. Nature and history were radically different – there were no historical laws, only trends which did not allow for predictions – but natural laws did not remain unscathed. Popper's antiessentialism was central to his critique of historicism. Theories were constructs; they did *not* grasp an essential reality behind appearances. Why did some theories prove successful, others not? Popper's metaphysical quandary grew.

In the mid-1950s, as Popper was working again on probability and quantum theory, he envisioned a world of propensities. The universe was neither determined nor chaotic, but had inherent physical dispositions. Probability, or frequencies, expressed physical tendencies. A throw had an inherent tendency to produce a particular result. The propensity interpretation of probability and quantum theory now substituted for the frequency interpretation.[150] Propensities could still be measured and tested only statistically. Methodologically, *Logik* held well, but the metaphysics changed. Probabilities and laws were guesses about the universe's inherent tendencies.[151] They sometimes proved good approximations. Induction was impos-

---

[150] Popper, "The Propensity Interpretation of the Calculus of Probability, and the Quantum Theory," in *Observation and Interpretation*, ed. Stephen Körner (London: Butterworths, 1957), pp. 65–70, 88–9; "The Propensity Interpretation of Probability," *British Journal for the Philosophy of Science* 10 (1959): 25–42.

[151] But, as reality had many layers, theories did not grasp an "ultimate reality." Popper, "Three Views Concerning Human Knowledge" [1956], *Conjectures and Refutations*, esp. pp. 114–19. A reviewer called this view: "modified essentialism" (*TLS* 55 [1956]: 527). Popper initially accepted ("The Aim

sible, but not regularity. Scientific success became comprehensible. Propensity reduced the tension between the indeterminist universe of modern physics and a successful science.[152] Popper finally found a metaphysics for falsificationist science. As he was no longer worried about the positivists, he could relax the boundary between science and metaphysics, demonstrating that both were criticizable. The universe became progressively harmonious.[153]

FALSIFICATION VS. PROTOCOLS: CRITICAL RATIONALISM, LOGICAL POSITIVISM, AND THE POSTSTRUCTURALIST CONUNDRUM

As Popper was rushing to complete *Logik der Forschung*, prolonged tensions in the circle broke into the open. Throughout 1933, Schlick had grown increasingly agitated about the circle's left wing. He disliked "radical physicalism" and Neurath's politics. Both, he felt, made defending the circle before a hostile academy and government difficult. Finally, he broke the taboo on making circle disputes public. Recovering from a bad flu in April 1934 in Salerno, Italy, he wrote "On the Foundation of Knowledge." Radical physicalism was his target, and Neurath the major antagonist. His attack did not remain unanswered. Carnap responded in private, Hempel and Neurath in public. The summer and fall issues of *Erkenntnis* carried the sharp exchange. It has become known as the "protocol sentences debate."[154]

of Science" [1957], *Objective Knowledge* [Oxford: Clarendon Press, 1972], p. 195), but later expressed reservations (*The Philosophy of Karl Popper*, pp. 1114–17, 1193 n. 167). For an interesting discussion: Joseph Agassi, "Modified Conventionalism," in his *Science in Flux* (Boston: Reidel, 1975), esp. pp. 366–70.

[152] But propensity did not resolve the tension: "If the picture of the world which modern science draws comes anywhere near to the truth . . . then the conditions obtaining almost everywhere in the universe make the discovery of structural laws of the kind we are seeking . . . almost impossible. For almost all regions of the universe are filled by chaotic radiation, and almost all the rest by matter in a likewise chaotic state. In spite of this, science has been miraculously successful." Karl Popper, *Realism and the Aim of Science* (London: Hutchinson, 1982), p. 146.

[153] Nowhere was the universe more harmonious than in his late statement: *A World of Propensities* (Bristol: Thoemmes, 1990). Propensity also eased tensions of which Popper was little aware. His critique of historicism, separating radically between determined nature and contingent history, created a breach in the human world. Kant overcame such a breach by lending a pattern to history, Popper by relaxing nature. (See: Leonard Krieger, "Kant and the Crisis of Natural Law," *Journal of the History of Ideas* 26 (1965): 191–210, and my elucidation, "Leonard Krieger: Historicization and Political Engagement in Intellectual History," *History and Theory* 35 [1996]: 90–8.)

[154] Moritz Schlick, "Über das Fundament der Erkenntnis," *Erkenntnis* 4 (1934): 79–99. (English: "On the Foundation of Knowledge," *Philosophical Papers*, vol. 2 [Boston: Reidel, 1979], pp. 370–87.) Neurath, "Radikaler Physikalismus und 'wirkliche Welt,'" *Erkenntnis* 4 (1934): 346–62; Hempel, "On the Logical Positivists' Theory of Truth," *Analysis* 2 (1935): 49–59. Carnap-Schlick correspondence, March–June 1934, Carnap Collection.

Popper was initially oblivious to the debate. *Logik* included a sharp critique of Carnap's and Neurath's protocols, but took no account of Schlick's and Neurath's reformulated positions. Popper designed his rhetorical strategies against the positivism he had known in 1932, not 1934. Neurath eventually directed him to the exchange in *Erkenntnis*. Popper did not change his mind. On the contrary, the debate provided him with new ammunition for his attack on positivist psychologism and subjectivism. Neurath's review of *Logik* in 1935 brought out in sharp relief the contrast between protocols and falsification, the positivist-physicalist and critical Kantian programs for philosophical reform. Popper thought little of Neurath but was grateful for his critique all the same.[155] He appreciated the engagement, and delighted in being called a Kantian by a positivist. He was apprehensive lest Carnap's "official" favorable review in *Erkenntnis* once again assimilate his philosophy into positivism. To Carnap and Schlick, his methodology did not seem revolutionary. "He is completely of our persuasion," wrote Schlick to Carnap.[156] Neurath disagreed. He took seriously their metaphysical differences. His critique illuminated *Logik*'s significance for the protocol sentences debate.

During the past decade, the debate has become the major site for investigating logical positivism. Excavating the positivist citadel, historians and philosophers have discovered "poststructuralist" layers: sophisticated debates on language and method that pertain to current critiques of Western science and metaphysics.[157] I myself have participated in this quarry. Historicizing the postmodern predicament is an antidote to current false consciousness of its uniqueness. But caution is well advised. Scholars have used ingenious but strained interpretations to turn the Vienna Circle into poststructuralists of a sort. In Neurath's case especially, they have imposed coherence on an imaginative but unsystematic mind, making him voice each scholar's preferred alternative to traditional scientific philosophy. This is counterproductive. If the past is to inform rather than vindicate the present, its alterity must be preserved. Popper and the Vienna Circle did address "poststructuralist" problems, but their answers were different and, in my view, better than ours. They did not echo poststructuralism, but voiced an alternative to it.

Neurath has become the darling of circle scholarship. He forms an attrac-

---

[155] Popper to Neurath, 28 February 1935, *Neurath Nachlaß*; "Popper und der Wiener Kreis – Gespräch," in Friedrich Stadler, *Studien*, p. 536.

[156] Schlick to Carnap, 1 November 1934, *Schlick Nachlaß*.

[157] Nancy Cartwright, Jordi Cat, Lola Fleck, and Thomas Uebel, *Otto Neurath: Philosophy between Science and Politics* (Cambridge: Cambridge University Press, 1996); Jordi Cat, "The Popper–Neurath Debate and Neurath's Attack on Scientific Method," *Studies in History and Philosophy of Science* 26 (1995): 219–50; Malachi Hacohen, "The Making of the Open Society" (Ph.D. diss.: Columbia University, 1993), chap. 6; Thomas Uebel, *Overcoming Logical Positivism*; Danilo Zolo, *Reflexive Epistemology: The Philosophical Legacy of Otto Neurath* (Boston: Reidel, 1989).

tive figure, catering to current tastes: an imaginative thinker, political radical, and philosophical iconoclast, who berated (Western) metaphysics. In contrast, scholars have accorded Popper a rough treatment. Nancy Cartwright and Thomas Uebel represent him as a foundationist philosopher, an enemy. My view is that, on the contrary, Popper was an original nonfoundationist philosopher. Focusing on the foundation and protocol sentences debates, I hope to show that Popper provided the most viable response to "poststructuralist" dilemmas among the disputants: a modified conventionalist, nonfoundationist philosophy that safeguarded rationalism, but skirted the dangers of absolutism.[158]

Schlick's 1934 essay moved the foundation problem to the center of circle debates. Most circle members recognized that scientific access to reality was problematic, but they held, nonetheless, to verification, without being clear what it entailed methodologically. Popper caught them at their most careless moments when they sounded like old-fashioned empiricists. But they were not all, *pace* Popper, pre-Kantian foundationists. Recognizing the difficulty of confronting theory and experience, Neurath and Carnap tried to confront theory and physicalist protocols. To Popper, they merely translated experience into protocols and remained subjective foundationists. To Schlick, on the contrary, they severed the relationship between theory and experience, science and reality.

Like Neurath and Popper, Schlick recognized the gap between psychological experience and scientific language. Observations confirming predictions generated feelings of certitude – "aha!" experiences – among scientists, but "as soon as the soul *speaks*, alas, it is no longer the *soul*."[159] Neither observation nor certitude were fully translatable into scientific language. An "aha!" put into a statement was no longer an "aha!" Schlick resisted, however, the conclusion that statements could only be compared with statements: Assertions, or affirmations (*Konstantierungen*) of "what is immediately observed" were "unshakable points of contact between language and reality."[160] They verified predictions and theories. They were the only scientific synthetic propositions that were a priori valid. They constituted both science's end point and a new beginning, an occasion for forming new hypotheses.

Affirmations did not quite amount to statements. Translated into scientific language, the assertion "here now blue" became a protocol, but lost its affirmative character: "at time *x*, place *y*, Schlick perceived blue." Like all scientific statements, protocols were hypothetical. To Schlick, Neurath confused affirmation and protocol, and made science's foundation

[158] The term "modified conventionalism" belongs to Joseph Agassi: *Science in Flux*, pp. 365–403.
[159] This is actually Popper, *Logik*, p. 233, section 30 n. 4 (*LSD*, p. 111), quoting Robert Reininger, *Das psycho-physische Problem* (Vienna: Braumüller, 1916), p. 291: "*Spricht* die Seele, so spricht, ach! schon die *Seele* nicht mehr." Schlick made the same point: "Über das Fundament der Erkenntnis": 97–9.
[160] Schlick, "Fundament": 93, 99, respectively.

hypothetical and relative. His suggestion that protocols be accepted or deleted based on their conformity with a system of statements overthrew empiricism. Russell had already criticized formal, or "coherence," theories of truth. They defined truth by consistency of statements, not correspondence to reality, leaving scientists unable to choose among internally coherent but conflicting scientific theories. If reality could not serve as the final judge of truth, modern science would end up with a very "peculiar relativism."[161] Immediate, certain, and final, affirmations provided science with an unequivocal criterion of truth, a foundation of sort.

Neurath responded that "reality" could not sit as a judge in any scientific dispute. In science, reality, too, appeared as a linguistic construct. Competing theories portrayed not "one true world" but several possible worlds. Statements contradicted one another, not "reality." Any talk about "correspondence" to reality was metaphysical. Science did not lay down conditions for "truth," but for the acceptance of statements. Schlick's complaint that "coherence" did not provide an unambiguous truth criterion was thus irrelevant. Indeed, no such criterion was possible. Science never escaped ambiguity. When protocols translated personal experience, or observations, into statements, they did not simply establish facts. They included imprecise concepts (*Ballungen*) and perception terms. Extralogical criteria, such as economy of time, prompted decisions to adopt or reject protocols. But this implied no surrender of empiricism. Scientists strove for agreement between hypotheses and as many protocols as possible, amending hypotheses contradicted by protocols. Physicalism purged nonempirical statements. "Certainty," however, was metaphysical. Affirmations were available to science only as protocols. (The notion that they were untranslatable was mystical. It echoed Wittgenstein's "unsayable.") Translated into protocols, affirmations were first reconciled with each other, then with a plurality of theories. Modern science represented diverse worlds.[162]

Popper and Neurath were epistemologically closer to each other than to other circle members. They represented modified conventionalism, antiabsolutism, and nonfoundationism. Both insisted that language could not be compared with reality and considered Schlick's "immediate observations" scientifically irrelevant. (Carnap wavered.) Both believed that observation reports were theoretically loaded and regarded them as provisional.[163] Extralogical factors played a role in the decision to accept them.

---

[161] "Fundament": 83.
[162] Neurath, "Radikaler Physikalismus": 346–62.
[163] Protocols were not, as Carnap thought, "primitive." Popper showed that universal, lawlike concepts, such as "glass," could not be reduced to singular "experience." Neurath concurred. But, for him, the problem was linguistic imprecision. Everyday language contained conceptual clusters (*Ballungen*), lacking the precision of axiomatized theories. To Popper, growing precision would never overcome the gap between concepts and experience. Neurath seemed to entertain the hope of eventually closing the gap through linguistic reform.

Both sought ways of bridging the gap between experience and language so that experience informed scientific theory. Popper demonstrated his genius as a methodologist by keeping science and reality separate, and yet allowing experience to arbitrate theoretical questions through falsification, that is, through a conventional decision, logically and methodologically informed, to accept a falsifying statement. In contrast, Neurath's linguistic control, protocols that testified to their own empirical formation,[164] was cumbersome and ineffective. Popper was so successful because he recognized that the linguistic turn made it impossible for language to guard empiricism. Instead, he sought a measure of empirical control in methodological conventions.

To Popper, positivism grounded science in perceptions and experiences. Schlick's "Foundation" was a perfect example.[165] Placing a premium on the scientist's feeling of certainty, Schlick recapitulated Fries's "immediate knowledge." Such "knowledge" was irrelevant to science. "We must distinguish between our *subjective experience of conviction . . .* and *objective-logical relations* among systems of scientific statements," wrote Popper.[166] Carnap and Neurath made an unsuccessful attempt to overcome the gap between psychology and logic by translating psychological behavior into physicalist language. Whether phenomenalist or physicalist, their protocols were logical constructions of experience, "perception statements," records of sense data, translations of observations into formal speech. They gained nothing by changing the mode of expression. They remained attached to the psychological basis.[167]

Popper's critics claim that he misunderstood Neurath, assimilating his position on protocols to that of Carnap.[168] Neurath, they say, rejected Carnap's phenomenalism. Protocols did not record "immediate experience," but "stimulation states," "changes in certain areas of perception in the brain" in response to the environment. For example: Malachi's protocol at 7 P.M., 24 January 1998: (Malachi's speech thinking at 6:59 P.M. was: [at 6:58 P.M. there was a UFO in space region *x* perceived by Malachi].) Neurath thought that behaviorist, or physicalist, language escaped the phenomenalist trap. Malachi's protocol reported physical events and states of

---

[164] Jordi Cat, "The Popper–Neurath Debate": 234.

[165] Uebel argues (*Overcoming*, pp. 214–17) that since affirmations stood outside the system of scientific statements, their importance was not logical and epistemic, but psychological and motivational. "To call them 'foundations' is to court serious misunderstanding." I share this misunderstanding. Schlick's argument is not only foundationist, but psychologistic and subjectivist. Uebel's efforts to exonerate the circle from foundationism stand in marked contrast to his easy dismissal of Popper as a foundationist. Critics' impatience is understandable. (Joseph Agassi, "To Salvage Neurath," *Philosophy of the Social Sciences* 28 [1998]: 83–101.)

[166] Popper, *Logik*, p. 16; *LSD*, p. 44.

[167] Idem, *Grundprobleme*, pp. 429–32, 438–9; *Logik*, section 26.

[168] Thomas Uebel, *Overcoming*, pp. 265–67. Jordi Cat, "The Popper–Neurath Debate," suggests the same, in a more nuanced fashion.

affairs, not personal experience. Popper denied precisely that, and Carnap accepted his verdict.[169] Behaviorist trappings notwithstanding, Neurath's protocols related psychological experience. Neurath occasionally spoke of protocols as statements of personal experience (*Erlebnisaussagen*).[170] He insisted that they include both the observer's name and observational terms (*see, perceive*). To Popper, this suggested psychologism. His reading of Neurath was neither generous nor thorough, but was correct all the same. Behaviorism could claim no dispensation from psychologism.

Neurath claimed such a dispensation but did not articulate a coherent defense.[171] His protagonists have developed one for him. Uebel regards physicalism as liberal "naturalism." Neurath stipulated that science may invoke events and states of affairs only if they could be naturalistically described and explained.[172] Physicalist, or behaviorist, protocols enforced the provision. By definition, they were anything but experiential. But were they? The aforementioned protocol indicated that Malachi's perception was that "there is a UFO in space region x," and his "speech thinking" converted it into a protocol. Did this transform the statement into a behavioral description? Or did it, on the contrary, psychologize an intersubjective observation? Popper thought the latter. Neurath showed nothing to justify his high hope for linguistic reform. Why should Popper have made the behaviorist leap?

In contrast to Uebel, Cartwright suggests that protocols were both about individual experience and public matter-of-fact. Information about the conditions of observer and observation served as "entitlement" for making the statement. Neurath required both entitlement and intersubjectivity. (This explains protocols' awkward structure). Popper demanded only intersubjectivity, dropping all reference to observer and observation: "there is a UFO in space region x." "No one would be led into foolish mistakes by Popper's 'shorthand' version," says Cartwright: Every scientific statement requires entitlement.[173] Perhaps. For Popper, intersubjectivity (observability) was necessary and sufficient "entitlement." Without reproducible UFO observation, no entitlement would make Malachi's protocol scientific. Cartwright simply refuses to take seriously his radical antipsychologism (and antifoundationism). She disregards, at the same time, Neurath's difficulties in moving from individual experience to public matter-of-fact. Neurath used "speech thinking" (*Sprechdenken*) to explain how experience

[169] Carnap to Neurath, 13 February 1935, Carnap Collection.

[170] Neurath, "Radikaler Physikalismus": 347–8.

[171] When Carnap and Popper resisted, Neurath could only say that psychologism was not a bad word. Neurath to Popper, 22 January 1935, *Neurath Nachlaß*; Neurath to Carnap, 18 January and 28 January 1935, Carnap Collection.

[172] Thomas Uebel, *Overcoming*, esp. pp. 2–3, 226–8.

[173] Nancy Cartwright et al., *Otto Neurath*, p. 201. (Jordi Cat coauthored the chapter quoted.)

became protocol. The notion embodied psychologism's basic problem: the gap between language and perception. Having separated the two, Neurath could not quite break with the psychological basis, and tried behaviorist reunification. He reintroduced the psychologistic dilemma in speech-thinking protocols.

Popper could therefore rightfully claim to have been the only one to make a true break with psychologism. Knowledge was grounded in particular dispositions, biological, psychological, or whatnot. This was of interest to evolutionary biology and psychology. It had no bearing on logic or epistemology. Testing, a combination of logical procedures, methodological rules (conventions), and rhetorical persuasion, arbitrated scientific questions. It did not stop at protocol, or perception, but at easily testable statements that scientists decided to accept provisionally. Science was free of subjective psychological foundation.

Testing held together Popper's science. Without it, language and reality, theory and experience were hopelessly severed. Neither Carnap nor Neurath provided a testing method. How, asked Popper, were decisions on protocols to be made? The Neurath Principle permitted arbitrary deletion of protocols, or amendment of theories. Any theory could be so salvaged, or even confirmed. Protocols were also difficult to test. Malachi's observation of a UFO was testable, but not his brain stimuli.[174] Test statements concerned observable facts, such as the movement and position of physical bodies, not psychological experience. Observability (*Beobachbarkeit*) was intersubjectivity's sole guarantee.[175] Science's empirical dimension consisted in testing theories through observable basic statements. A theory of lower generality (basic statement), closer to experience, but never quite reality –"the thing" – itself, could knock out a theory of greater generality. Protocols provided no comparable method, neither demarcation nor objectivity (intersubjectivity). Neurath overthrew empiricism.

Neurath responded to Popper in a 1935 review of *Logik* that has become

---

[174] Jordi Cat, "The Popper–Neurath Debate," proposes that not Malachi's brain stimuli, or speech thinking, were subject to test, but his observation. Entitlement was not part of the statement. This would make protocols testable, but entitlement irrelevant.

[175] Popper insisted that "observation" was a psychological event, but "observability" a logical concept. Not observation's psychology was significant, but its intersubjectivity. I find the distinction persuasive, as do most Popperians. But to Victor Kraft ("Popper and the Vienna Circle," *The Philosophy of Karl Popper*, pp. 195–6), the concept remained problematic. Psychological experience convinced people that statements were true. Was the refusal of psychology not question begging? "When do we see experience as conforming to our expectations (our theory), and when do we see it as conflicting?" ask William Berkson and John Wettersten. "In other words, what is the psychological correlate of the contradiction (between a basic statement and a theory) which Popper describes?" (Berkson and Wettersten, *Learning From Error* (La Salle, Ill.: Open Court, 1984, p. 20). These questions had to remain unanswered if Popper was to solve epistemology's problems. An attempt to reformulate the relationship between logic and psychology would have resurrected the problems that ran his dissertation aground.

a classic, "Pseudorationalism of Falsification."[176] Against the backdrop of *Logik*, Neurath made an "encyclopedic turn."[177] Science, he argued, was not a hierarchically structured body of knowledge, a closed, coherent, homogenous system. Rather, there existed multiple sciences, loosely connected, if at all, each with its own practices. To Popper's system of well-defined theories, constructed of clean statements and striving toward simplicity, Neurath counterposed his own model, the encyclopedia. It consisted of porous bodies of statements, linked "sometimes more closely, sometimes more loosely. Systematic deductions are attempted at certain places, but the nexus in its entirety is not transparent."[178] Clarity, simplicity, and coherence were metaphysical ideals because multiplicity, diversity, and indeterminacy characterized science: "'The' system is the great scientific lie."[179]

Physicalist language alone unified science. Falsification could not set methodological rules, because no common rules existed. Testing could not carry the burden Popper put onto it: Experiments played little role in many sciences. Popper's *experimentum crucis* flew in the face of practice. Testing provided no certainty of falsification because Duhem's conventionalist stratagems applied. When a theory served scientists well, an apparent refutation would not convince them to abandon it, only shake their confidence (*Erschütterung*). Popper's view of science as a permanent revolution neither reflected scientific practice nor served it well.

Why, then, did Popper desperately attempt to found scientific logic on falsification? Neurath thought he knew the answer: Popper wanted to maintain at all cost the logical choice among theories. Falsification was a salvage operation for the "old philosophical absolutism," or "pseudorationalism," that appealed to the "real world" to resolve scientific disputes: "The pseudorationalism in Popper's basic view would quickly make us understand why he could feel drawn to traditional philosophy [*Schulphilosophie*] and its absolutism, while his book contains so much of that

---

[176] Otto Neurath, "Pseudorationalismus der Falsifikation," *Erkenntnis* 5 (1935): 353–65. (English: "Pseudorationalism of 'Falsification,'" *Philosophical Papers*, pp. 121–31.)

[177] Neurath's "anti-system" rhetoric in Prague began the encyclopedic turn ("Einheit der Wissenschaft als Aufgabe," *Erkenntnis* 5 [1935]: 16–22), but it became clear only in his review of *Logik*.

[178] "Pseudorationalismus": 354. Popper, too, recognized that scientific theories rarely approached axiomatization, but he insisted that scientists aim for the greatest possible clarity and cogency so as to facilitate the operation of methodological rules guiding negotiation over basic statements. In contrast, Neurath maintained that science remained ambiguous on every level: Concepts had rough edges; clean statements did not exist; systems of statements were loose; fields were separate.

[179] Neurath, "Einheit der Wissenschaft als Aufgabe," 17. Popper's and Neurath's scientific metaphors mirrored their intellectual and political life. Neurath took personal risks lightly, cared little about appearance and conditions of life, was talkative, warm, and open. Spreading over disciplines with little patience for detail, he wrote with ease, but not clarity. Popper had little trust in people or the world, led a structured and secluded life, and incessantly rewrote his manuscripts to diminish the prospect of being misunderstood. He wrote with difficulty but achieved incomparable clarity.

analytical technique advocated precisely by the Vienna Circle," and why he is so much kinder to Kant than to the positivists.[180]

Alone among the circle, Neurath recognized the limits of Popper's partaking of positivist discourse. His rhetoric concealed their broad agreement on conventionalism, but illuminated the chasm between linguistic and critical philosophy. This did not make him a sound judge, let alone an unbiased arbitrator. To him, Popper was positivism's nemesis. He clashed with Popper in the Paris and Copenhagen congresses in 1935 and 1936. Popper then went to New Zealand and was out of touch and without influence. Neurath did not relent. In his correspondence with Carnap, he harped on pseudorationalism's becoming a metaphysical fifth column amidst the circle.[181] He fought the legend of the "positivist Popper" tooth and nail from the start. His premature death in 1945 left the legend uncontested in postwar years.

Neurath's protagonists second his judgment of Popper, but recognize that he lacked method. "Popper is perfectly justified," says Cat, "in noting that 'Neurath gives no method [to] delete a protocol sentence which contradicts a system.'"[182] They offer Neurath two divergent ways out. Uebel constructs a Neurath method. He searches for methodological clues in Neurath's works, skillfully establishing rules that Neurath would have enunciated, if only he had put his mind to method.[183] His suggestions are so reasonable that when he is done, one wonders why Neurath needed obfuscating protocols as empirical control. Uebel moves the debate to the methodological terrain. Popper is there at his best: agile, precise, systematic. Neurath is imprecise, diffuse, unclear.

In contrast to Uebel, Cartwright and Cat argue that Neurath ejected all method, and it is good he did. "Scientific method is logically open-ended," they write.[184] Extralogical considerations determine scientific decisions. "We always start from historical, natural language. Its sentences are *Ballungen*, and that means mixtures of forms of expression (precise and imprecise concepts)."[185] There are "no fixed connections" between theory and basic statements. "Theoretical hypotheses and protocol statements can[not] endure an unambiguous logical confrontation with testing value," insists Cat.[186] Deduction and comparison of basic statements are impossible. But, then, any comparison of theory and protocol is in jeopardy. Confirmation and shaking are impossible as well! There is no more basis for tentative shaking than for definite falsification. Indeed, how can Neurath even decide

---

[180] "Pseudorationalismus": 365.

[181] Carnap–Neurath correspondence, 1935–7, 1942–5, Carnap Collection.

[182] Jordi Cat, "The Popper–Neurath Debate": 227.   [183] Thomas Uebel, *Overcoming*, chap. 11.

[184] Nancy Cartwright, *Otto Neurath*, p. 205; Jordi Cat, "The Popper–Neurath Debate": 245.

[185] Cartwright, *Otto Neurath*, p. 195, quoting Neurath's "Besprechung über Physikalismus," 4 March 1931, Carnap Collection (RC 029-17-03).

[186] Cat, "The Popper–Neurath Debate": 243.

whether he has confirmation or shaking? Imprecision must be measured before any conclusion is possible. Logical imprecision can be no reason for tentativeness. Overthrowing method, Cartwright and Cat overthrow Neurath, too.

To Popper, to the extent that method was logical, it was *not* open-ended. Language was "imprecise" in that both universals and undefined terms occurred in basic statements, but this was no obstacle to logical procedures. Method *was* open-ended, because it was conventional, dependent upon decisions. His position was nuanced. He distinguished between logical falsifiability and methodological falsification. Falsification depended on both logical and extralogical criteria. There was little disagreement between him and Neurath concerning the extralogical character of scientific decisions. He would gladly second Cartwright's and Cat's view that "every application requires judgment, local knowledge and free decision. . . . Every concrete prediction is a matter of construction."[187] Scientists negotiated acceptance and rejection of basic statements, but this did not imply giving up on method. Cartwright insists that science can provide no rule to resolve logically undecidable questions. Popper was more sensible: Methodology provided guidelines for negotiation. It was stupid, he said on occasion, to attempt to make such rules precise.[188] It was equally unwise to think that they were dispensable.

Popper's insistence that choice among theories could be informed by rules irks Cartwright and Cat. Any implication that we are not at sea, they say, is absolutist and metaphysical. Indeterminacy is a positive good, determinacy "pseudorationalism." Neurath's great virtue is to have permitted coexistence of multiple encyclopedias as opposed to Popper's one theoretical system.[189] But Popper, too, thought that we were at sea. He acknowledged that choice among theories was rarely clear, and not always possible, but he insisted that where tests were possible, a decision may also be. To pursue knowledge meant to seek falsification not to avoid it. Neurath challenged falsification but, unlike his protagonists, did not cherish indeterminacy. Logical indeterminacy was scientific reality. He countered it with linguistic rules. "Open-ended method" is Cartwright's and Cat's, not Neurath's, idea. Seek no rule, they say; negotiate. They are determined to reconfigure Neurath as a poststructuralist.

Neurath claimed to be a consistent empiricist. Poststructuralism has made a laughing matter of traditional scientific and historical empiricism. Yet, Neurath's admirers are all scientifically inclined philosophers, seeking

---

[187] Cartwright, *Otto Neurath*, p. 222. Cartwright thinks Popper disagreed. She is wrong.

[188] Popper to Herbert Feigl, 4 November 1969, Feigl Collection, Archives of Scientific Philosophy.

[189] Admittedly, the system metaphor may not best describe science, but Popper focused on competing theories within particular fields, rather than on relationships among disciplines. His system of theories was ever changing, not a stable body of knowledge.

to salvage some empirical practice from the poststructuralist ruins. Having charged Popper with excessive logical determinacy, Cat turns the tables and accuses him of empirical indeterminacy. Falsification, he concurs with Neurath, was a pseudorationalist substitute for protocols. It failed to secure empiricism. "At the level of the empirical basis," he acutely observes, "Popper is no less conventionalist than Neurath."[190] But Neurath's protocols secured science's empirical foundation by establishing strict data-admission criteria: "statements that wear their own observational genealogy (perception terms) and public doxatic coordinates (institutional encoding) on their sleeve." Popper's test statements "fail to make explicit the ultimate agreeable element on which science can possibly stand, namely our experience."[191] All Popper required was "observability" – vague and undefined. "Decisions to determine what is accepted on an empirical basis are largely immaterial."[192] Excluding empirical "entitlement," Popper overthrew empiricism.

A careful reader, Cat recognizes that Popper was no foundationist, but he misunderstands observability. He confounds preconditions for tests with their results, collapsing observability and falsification. Observability made tests possible; it said nothing about results. It provided no grounds for a basic statement's acceptance. It guaranteed intersubjectivity, not empiricism. Should observability be contested, there would be no recourse to experience: Another statement would have to be tested. As Neurath had no testing method, he made conformity with linguistic rules a precondition for admitting a statement. Cat searches for similar rules in Popper, but he had none. Scientists used whatever (intersubjective) language they preferred. Testing determined acceptance. Only if Cat denies that tests *may* persuade us to accept falsification can he claim that Popper overthrew empiricism. Nothing, of course, guaranteed statements' "empirical character." Why should nonfoundationists seek guarantees? Why should they entrust empirical guards to behaviorist language, translate experience into awkward protocols, try to circumvent *decision* on evidence by lending statements empirical character? Cat's Neurath demonstrates Popper's charge: Positivism was in search of an empirical basis.

Neurath condemned falsifiability as "old philosophical absolutism," but offered no demarcation criterion of his own.[193] His protagonists concur with his critique and insist that confronting hypotheses with protocols adequately demarcated science against metaphysics, but they feel ambivalent about demarcation. They share Neurath's antipathy to metaphysics, but not his scientism, his belief in science's exclusive legitimacy. They are

[190] Cat, "The Popper–Neurath Debate": 234.   [191] Ibid., 246.   [192] Loc. cit.
[193] More correctly: Neurath collapsed together falsification and falsifiability and spoke of falsification as a demarcation criterion.

apprehensive lest demarcation exclude too much, and prefer blurred boundaries. Uebel argues that Neurath's naturalism was broader than Quine's, recognizing "all human cognitive endeavors." Cat concedes that Neurath's protocols "may be too strict," but, fortunately, they are "not decisive for theory choice."[194] This is all too generous to Neurath, too harsh on Popper. Popper represented their convictions better than Neurath did. There was nothing absolute about falsifiability. "My demarcation criterion," Popper said, is "a *proposal of a convention*. People can differ on its usefulness."[195] Reasonable people *may* accept it. Science had conventional boundaries, and they were anything but clear. Neurath's linguistic demarcation, in contrast, was draconian. He recognized that linguistic choice was pragmatic, but this did not make his physicalist strictures any less dogmatic. He had no doubt what science was and was not. Neurath was the demarcator par excellence.

Metaphysical disagreement underlay the Neurath–Popper exchange. To Neurath, Popper's commitment to the "one and only world" spelled out metaphysics. Behind Popper's methodological realism, he correctly discerned a metaphysical one, but he overlooked his own metaphysical commitment.[196] He deluded himself that protocols avoided the "real world" problem. They did not. Linguistic reform depended on a monistic metaphysics – be it materialist, naturalist, or physicalist. Neurath correctly suspected that linguistic choice often entailed a metaphysical one. In response, he launched a linguistic purge to secure an official language. Popper demurred: Argue, do not silence; criticize, for you may persuade. (In postwar years, he recognized that this applied to metaphysics, too, not only to science.) Whether his scientific method was metaphysically neutral, or not, his science permitted a dialogue between statements informed by conflicting metaphysics. Neurath and Popper were both wrong to assume that their philosophy was metaphysics-free, but, then, there is good and bad metaphysics. Popper's realism was liberal, Neurath's monism absolutist.

Popper and Neurath subscribed to similar progressive historical narratives. Both considered science the peak of human achievement. Both recognized, at the same time, that science was conventional. They experimented with liberalizing science, relaxing its boundaries and method. Popper went further than Neurath, because his historical narrative was

---

[194] Cat suggests that Neurath's linguistic "warrant for theoretical beliefs" was more liberal than Popper's testability, but Popper required no warrant for "theoretical belief." None existed. Theory construction was not subject to scientific control. Who was more liberal?

[195] *Logik*, p. 10; *LSD*, p. 37.

[196] In *Logik*, Popper claimed metaphysical neutrality. In postwar years, he claimed to have always been a realist. Having demonstrated, by the mid-1950s, that metaphysical theories were criticizable, he validated inquiries into the nature of the universe, previously excluded as a tactical move against positivism.

more contingent, and his politics more liberal. A vicious grand narrative underlay Neurath's linguistic reform. He consigned physicalism's opponents to the dust bin of history, delegitimizing Popper's mode of engaging the past. Popper made some scientific progress, he said, but then fell into serious error, regressing to traditional philosophy. Falsification was a pseudorationalist "residue." The scientific worldview and revolutionary politics both depended on physicalism. He, Neurath, was pronouncing history's judgment. Future science and politics spoke through him. History was moving his way.

Neurath's protagonists ingeniously liberalize him, softening his scientism by loosening his science. They are not "wrong"; rather, they develop tendencies in his philosophy. Still, their interpretations are strained. They override resistance – linguistic dogmatism, monistic metaphysics, historical determinism. Their hostility to Popper makes their partiality to Neurath all the more objectionable. To present Neurath as a tolerant empiricist, pluralist, and pragmatist, and Popper as a regimented metaphysician is unfair and untrue. Of the two, Popper liberalized science more thoroughly. His nonfoundationism was more radical, his method more ecumenical. In postwar years, he declared scientific method simply a systematic application of trial and error, the problem-solving approach to life. Unlike Neurath, he rejected scientism. As a person, Neurath may have been more open and tolerant.[197] As a philosopher, Popper was, by far.

Neurath's protagonists cast Popper off because he resisted the linguistic turn, opposed the crusade against metaphysics, and sustained method. His stance on all three issues is currently unpopular. I find him persuasive, all the same. Recognizing the gap between language and reality, he nonetheless refused the myth of the prison house of language. He validated dialogue across languages, in science and everyday life alike. Criticism of empirical evidence and methodologically informed decision were possible in any language. On metaphysics, his philosophy resists the positivist-poststructuralist alliance, demanding that both positivists and poststructuralists acknowledge their own metaphysics (or, to use non-Popperian parlance, their own historicity). At the same time, he admits metaphysics to the critical dialogue. We can argue about metaphysics, and persuade. Critical rationalism shuts no one and nothing out of the conversation, whether on account of language or non-empirical evidence.

Critical dialogue has, to be sure, a few ground rules. They are more explicit in science than elsewhere. Current animus toward rules, even liberal ones, is so great that for Cat and Cartwright, Popper's method classifies him immediately as the "other." Yet, in indeterminacy's name, Cat is willing to put pluralism itself at risk. "Neurath leaves the door open to the possibil-

---

[197] Neurath could also be dogmatic. Against critics of the circle's left wing, he asserted, loud and clear, a party line.

ity of extra-scientific sources of dogmatism upon scientific practice," he rejoices. "That is one reason why for Neurath it is important that scientists share the same worldview." So much for diversity! Neurath's alternative to liberal rules, it appears, is not Feyerabend's anarchism, but dogma that derives its legitimacy from the community. (Whether Feyerabend's anarchism, or any view rejecting critical dialogue, does not end up in dogmatism is a different question.) Given a choice between Cat's Neurath and absolutist rationalism, I would opt for absolutism. Fortunately, my choice is not so limited. There is Popper. Conflicting perspectives are in vigorous debate, no decision guaranteed, none ruled out.

My critique of Neurath's protagonists does not diminish, but reinforces, their achievement. They have made obscure debates in interwar scientific philosophy speak to the present so movingly that we take sides in them. My own work on Popper endeavors to do the same. Their achievement comes, however, at the cost of "presentism." Had they trusted Popper rather than Neurath to lead them out of the poststructuralist conundrum, they would not have violated the past's alterity.

No member of the Vienna Circle subscribed to Cartwright's and Cat's worldview. All remained committed to progressive historical narratives. All believed that science was humanity's crowning achievement. Most made nonfoundationist gestures but remained empiricists, refusing to sever the relationship between language and experience. None followed the late Wittgenstein's move from scientific language to language game. None viewed language as a culturally bound artifact, a historical product, with changing rules difficult for an outsider to grasp and impossible to translate.[198] None thought local languages deserved protection. Neurath designed educational programs to eliminate any but the universal scientific language. Carnap persisted in efforts to develop a scientific metalanguage even after realizing, in 1935, that rules for concepts' use were not syntactic, that is, logical and formal, but semantic, that is, dependent on meaning. For good or bad, the Vienna Circle represented *Spätaufklärung*, not poststructuralism.

Popper weeded illiberalism out of late enlightenment, but preserved its emancipatory potential. His political philosophy targeted progressive grand narratives for criticism, but retained the hopes for progress and freedom. His cultural politics was pluralist. He readily accepted multilingualism – even in science – and multiculturalism. But a diversity of closed cultures was not the best humankind could do. Culture clash in an open society was. Languages had different rules and presented divergent pictures of reality, but they were not self-contained and self-referential. Dialogue across languages was essential. Popper eschewed any certainty, any finality of

---

[198] Ludwig Wittgenstein, *Philosophical Investigations*, ed. G. E. M. Anscombe and Rush Rhees (London: Macmillan, 1958).

empirical evidence. He, too, traveled on Neurath's boat. But uncertainty did not inhibit the growth of knowledge. If decision was not always possible, criticism was. Openness to criticism helped eliminate error. Conventions set the rules of debate, and traditions set its terms, but they, too, were subject to change. Popper may have been overconfident about methodology's capacity to guide critical debate and produce a consensus. Neurath's objection that scientific practice never followed Popper's prescriptions remained largely unanswered. Neither Popper nor his students inquired after the conditions facilitating criticism and consensus. Such inquiry, however, need not undermine Popper's belief in learning from error. This is the issue dividing him from both positivists and poststructuralists. Popper was as instructive in refusing "poststructuralism" as he was in reshaping late enlightenment.

AMBIGUOUS RECEPTION? *LOGIK DER FORSCHUNG* 1935

Logik der Forschung created a stir in Vienna and beyond, wherever the circle's network reached. For a specialized book on scientific philosophy, it was widely read and reviewed.[199] A day or two after publication, Viennese economist Oskar Morgenstern (1902–77) reported in his diary that he, too, had already read the book, and "recht gut!"[200] Not all reactions were positive. Frank, Neurath, Reichenbach, and Schlick within the circle, and physicists outside it, especially Heisenberg's entourage, were critical, even outraged. But Popper had defenders and admirers. Einstein praised the book, and Carnap regarded it an outstanding achievement. Polish logicians Kotarbinski and Tarski thought it extraordinary, and young philosophers

---

[199] Examples of reviews: Anon., *Revue des sciences philosophiques et théologiques* 24, no. 4 (1935); Gaston Bachelard, *Recherches Philosophiques* 5 (1936): 447; Max Black, *Mind* 45 (1936): 104–6; Ludovico Geymonat, "Logica e filosofia delle scienze," *Rivista di filosofia* 28 (1936): 3–16 (reviewed together with Josef Schächter, *Prolegomena zu einer kritischen Grammatik* and Hans Reichenbach, *Wahrscheinlichkeitslehre*); Kurt Grelling, *Theoria* 1 (1937): 134–43; Carl G. Hempel, *Deutsche Literaturzeitung* 58 (1937): 309–14; Grete Hermann, *Physikalische Zeitschrift* 13 (1935): 481–2; Helen Knight, "Philosophy in Germany," *Philosophy* 11 (January 1936); Ernest Nagel, *Journal of Philosophy* 32 (1935): 107–8; Dina Sztéjnbarg, *Rocznika Przeglądau Filozoficznego* 37 (1935): 269–78; Julius Weinberg, *Philosophical Review* 45 (1936): 511–14; Edgar Zilsel, *Die Naturwissenschaften* 23 (1935): 531 f.

Although *Logik* was widely read, it did not sell very well. Springer printed 860 copies, of which sixty were complimentary (author and journals). Like most books of its kind, it was affordable only to well-paid academics. Priced at 13.5 RM (about 75 pence), it cost a *Hauptschule* teacher, like Popper, a two- to three-day salary. Hempel borrowed Neurath's copy for his review. Springer sold about 200 copies by July 1935, 415 by October 1937, 449 by August 1939. (Director Lange to Popper [352, 1].) Sale of 442 copies covered the publisher's expenses, and so Popper received no proceeds. The Nazis prohibited sale of *Logik* (author of Jewish origin). Springer retained the stock, but an Allies bombardment set it on fire (Lange to Popper, 2 March 1946).

[200] Oskar Morgenstern's diary, 9 December 1934, Morgenstern Papers, Special Collections, Duke University.

Ayer, Hempel, and Nagel were in awe. *Logik* received three reviews in *Erkenntnis*, and the reviewers' intense exchange demonstrated its vitality. Popper began corresponding now with philosophers, physicists, and mathematicians in Central Europe, England, and the United States. He joined Karl Menger's *Mathematisches Kolloquium* where, in company with mathematicians from all over Central Europe, he contributed to probability theory. *Logik* did not bring him the academic job he dreamed about, but it made Central European culture a living reality for him during his final years in Vienna.

Popper took little pleasure in his success. In winter 1934–5, he fell into a depression.[201] He had thought that *Logik* would capture the philosophical world overnight and change its course. An epigram to *Grundprobleme*, borrowed from Kant's *Critique of Pure Reason*, intimated that, like Kant, he had solved every major problem of philosophy.[202] He may have come close, but it still took time for *Logik* to catch on. Initial responses were not all encouraging. Earlier in the fall, Schlick lectured Popper about his willful attacks on positivism, making it clear that he had damaged irreparably his relations with the circle.[203] Carnap did not write him for a while, and when he did, late in January, he, too, suggested that Popper had exaggerated his differences with the circle. Exhausted and disappointed, Popper was in despair. No one was reading his book, he complained.[204] He sought attention and validation, and asked Julius Kraft to write a detailed review of *Logik*.[205] Political circumstances, Gomperz's dismissal, and Schlick's response made it clear that no academic job would be forthcoming. He was back in school teaching, distressed about Central European developments, anxious about his future. All seemed hopeless.

Viennese philosopher and social theorist Felix Kaufmann came to the rescue. He was a *Privatdozent* in the philosophy of law at the university, but made a living as the general manager of the Austrian branch of the Anglo-Iranian Oil Company. His interests included mathematics, legal philosophy, phenomenology, and social science methodology. He was active in many intellectual circles and known for helping colleagues in distress.[206] Greatly

---

[201] Felix Kaufmann to Carnap, 23 January 1935, Carnap Collection.

[202] *Grundprobleme*, pp. xii, 447–8. (Kant, *Critique of Pure Reason*, trans. Norman Kemp Smith [New York: Macmillan, 1929], p. 10.)

[203] Popper related to Agassi the story of his painful meeting with Schlick. Its echoes can be heard in Schlick to Carnap, 1 November 1934, *Schlick Nachlaß*, and Popper to Carnap, 31 March 1935, Carnap Collection. When Popper came to give a paper in Zilsel's apartment in the spring of 1935, he asked Zilsel to facilitate reconciliation with the circle. (After the socialist uprising, the government closed down the Volkshochschule where Zilsel was teaching, and so he moved his class to his apartment and invited Popper to lecture: phone conversation with Paul Zilsel, 20 June 1994.)

[204] Popper to Carnap, 31 March 1935, Carnap Collection.

[205] Popper to Julius Kraft, 11 January 1935 (316, 24). Popper was concerned that if the positivists alone reviewed his book, his critique would be missed.

[206] Harry P. Reeder, *The Work of Felix Kaufmann* (Lanham, Md.: University Press of America, 1991).

impressed with *Logik der Forschung,* he contacted Popper and heard his *historia calamitatum.* He took his situation to heart, began a propaganda campaign, as Popper described it, to promote his work, and explored possible fellowships for him so that he could devote himself to work. He recommended the book warmly to whoever would listen – economist Gottfried Haberler, for example, who later told Hayek to read the book. He encouraged Carnap to write Popper, asked Hempel to review *Logik,* and reported news about the book's growing favorable reception to Popper.[207] In vain. Until the late spring, when Popper learned of the forthcoming reviews in *Erkenntnis,* he was in low spirits.

The failed experiment continued to weigh on him and mar his book. Most physicists thought that he was out of his league in quantum debates. The editor of the circle's series, Philipp Frank, himself a physicist, was embarrassed about the failed experiment and chagrined that Popper had put it into the final version without consulting him.[208] Weisskopf refused to engage Popper, stating that he shared Heisenberg's views.[209] Viennese physicist Arthur Haas, father of a friend, was discouraging and unsympathetic. Only Thirring seemed interested, and invited him to address his seminar.[210] Sometime in January, Popper sent Heisenberg a draft of a response to Weizsäcker, intended for *Die Naturwissenschaften.* Neither Heisenberg nor Weizsäcker wanted to deal with him anymore. They entrusted Heisenberg's assistant, Hans Euler, with the response. Popper regarded Euler's response as insulting, considered terminating the debate, then responded all the same.[211] He continued to work on a published response throughout the spring of 1935, expanding it into an article, "Zur Kritik der Ungenauigkeitsrelationen" (critique of indeterminacy relations).[212] But he sensed that he was losing ground. He always felt that his intrusion into physics was a transgression. Having engaged the greatest

---

[207] Kaufmann wrote Carnap (22 December 1934) that he was impressed with *Logik* and would do anything he could to promote Popper. He urged Carnap to write him (23 January 1935, Carnap Collection). He solicited Hempel's opinion of *Logik* (26 February 1935). When Hempel reported (25 March 1935) the book's favorable reception among German philosophers of science, Kaufmann suggested he review it, and quickly told Popper. He asked Felix Ehrenhaft (1879–1952) to forward Popper's letter to Einstein (28 March 1935). He spoke to Cassirer about *Logik* (12 July 1935). *Kaufmann Nachlaß.*

[208] Philipp Frank to Otto Neurath, mid- to late July 1935, two letters, *Neurath Nachlaß.*

[209] Viktor Weisskopf to Popper, 21 January 1935, Popper Archives (360, 21). Later, he renewed their discussions but was critical (24 October 1935).

[210] Popper to Max Jammer, 26 April 1967, Popper Archives (313, 3).

[211] Draft of response to Weizsäcker, dated 6 December 1934, Popper Archives (305, 32). Euler to Popper, 4 February 1935 (293, 29). Popper drafted, but probably did not send, a furious response on February 14, then another on March 12. Heisenberg sent a final letter on 19 March 1935 (305, 32).

[212] He sent "Zur Kritik der Ungenauigkeitsrelationen" to Carnap, Ehrenhaft, Heisenberg, and Schrödinger, hoping that Ehrenhaft would forward it to Einstein. (Popper to Carnap, 10 June 1935, Carnap Collection; Popper to Richard von Mises, 26 June 1935, Popper Archives [329, 4].)

physicists, and then been found wrong, he was filled with anxiety, his exhilaration now gone.

In the early spring Popper sent *Logik* to Einstein. Popper's friend, pianist Rudolf Serkin, gave the book to his mother-in-law, Frida Busch (wife of violinist Adolf Busch, Einstein's friend), who forwarded it to Einstein with the note that the author is a young man without an academic position who could use any help Einstein might offer. Einstein responded on June 15. He told Popper that his experiment was flawed, but warmly endorsed his philosophy, expressing agreement on all essential points: falsifiability, rejection of induction and probability of hypotheses, objective probability.[213] He concluded by asking what he could do to promote the book. Popper was overwhelmed. Kaufmann advised him to focus his response on his need for a fellowship.[214] Popper declined; it was unconscionable to impose on Einstein. (He would, however, have no hesitation imposing on other people whose time he did not consider as precious.) But he would not accept Einstein's verdict without an argument. In an eight-page letter, he defended a reformulated experiment, clarified his position on probability, and ended with a note saying he would appreciate whatever Einstein could do for him.[215] On August 29, he sent Einstein his critique of indeterminacy relations.[216] Einstein responded on September 11. He disposed of Popper's experiment, explained E-P-R, but confirmed Popper's interpretation of quantum theory.[217] Popper finally relented. The experiment was "a great mistake for which I have been deeply sorry and ashamed ever since."[218]

---

[213] Einstein to Popper, 15 June 1935, Popper Archives (292, 12). There was one further dissent: Einstein thought that frequency hypotheses could be derived from precise laws. A determinist universe was compatible with probability. Popper disagreed. In the 1930s he sought to contain probability; in the 1950s, determinism. In both cases, it was essential to keep the two separate.

[214] Kaufmann to Popper, 12 July 1935, *Kaufmann Nachlaß*.

[215] Popper to Einstein, 18 July 1935, Popper Archives (292, 12).

[216] Popper to Einstein, 29 August 1935 (from Galtür in Tyrol) (292, 12). He told Einstein that he heard about the E-P-R experiment but had not read the report. Having discussed the revised manuscript with Weisskopf and reached no agreement, he was now sending it to him.

The manuscript, just over thirty pages long, is in the Popper Archives (27, 1; 27, 2, the latter retyped and partially edited by Troels Eggers Hansen in 1982–3 [Hansen to Popper, 11 January 1983, 27, 4]). Popper elaborated his statistical interpretation of quantum theory and, while defending the experiment, sought to diminish its significance. There was nothing unique to "indeterminacy," or scatter, relations, he said. They were equivalent to statistical relations obtained in a die's throws, and permitting prognoses. In a long epistemological appendix, he discussed causality in quantum theory, engaging works by Jordan, Neumann, and Schrödinger not discussed in *Logik*. He insisted that his interpretation was metaphysically neutral, and implied neither determinism nor realism. As statistical hypotheses could not be deduced from laws, the charge that he viewed quantum mechanics as causal did not hold.

[217] A facsimile of the four-page letter, and an English translation, are available in *LSD*, pp. 457–64. Einstein also reaffirmed that it was possible to infer statistical conclusions from a deterministic theory.

[218] Popper to Max Jammer, 13 April 1967, Popper Archives (313, 3). He was insecure about his contribution to physics to the end of his life, grateful to Jammer (25 April 1980) for suggesting that he

All the same, the exchange with Einstein was a moral boost, and a badly needed one. Throughout the spring, Carnap kept Popper in suspense. Neurath wrote in January that he was reading *Logik* with great interest. Popper rejoiced. Neurath expressed disagreement, but Popper sought engagement, not agreement.[219] He got no engagement from Carnap, who was taking time to think his way through *Logik*.[220] On physics or probability, Carnap could pass no judgment. He admired, and begrudged, Popper's guts, but the "experts," Frank and Reichenbach, dismissed *Logik* offhand.[221] Neurath wrote that Popper was gifted, but his epistemology unfounded, and his massive critique of positivism unjust.[222] Schlick had already made the latter point. Carnap himself could not but be offended by Popper's relentless attack. Still, he found *Logik* increasingly persuasive.[223]

For the next half year, *Logik* became the center of backstage *Erkenntnis* politics. A furious Reichenbach decided to let Carnap review *Logik* and write his own essay against Popper. He told Neurath in February that *Logik* was a naive, senseless book, marred by mathematical mistakes.[224] Why had Schlick taken the book? Neurath responded that *Logik* made him angry, too: It was not pleasant to hear Kant talking back to him. But *Logik* was a comprehensive work, and Popper had his right of speech. They needed simultaneously to promote and fight gifted youth like Popper.[225] Await Carnap's judgment, he suggested. When Carnap declared for Popper, Neurath was beside himself and changed his tune. In January, Popper was still the circle's "official opposition." In February, he led a metaphysical

---

played a crucial role in quantum debates, and thankful to Weizsäcker (letters in 1971 and 1980 [360, 22]) for remembering their exchange.

[219] Neurath to Popper, 22 January 1935, *Neurath Nachlaß*. Neurath expressed agreement on induction and methodological conventionalism, rejected realism, thought falsification was never decisive, and insisted that Popper confounded physicalism and psychologism. Popper responded only on February 28, enclosing "'Induktionslogik' und 'Hypothesenswahrscheinlichkeit'," long overdue, for *Erkenntnis*. Neurath's letter pleased him enormously, he said, since he had had barely any response to his book.

[220] Carnap was impressed but unsure. To Kaufmann, he wrote (16 January 1935) that *Logik* was "clear and informative," to Schlick and Neurath (23 January 1935) that it was a good book, but full of unnecessary criticism. (All in Carnap Collection.) He tried to be as supportive of Popper as someone with his unforgiving sense of fairness could be. He told him (29 January 1935) that his book was "a notable achievement" and that Nagel was enthusiastic about it. He suggested that he write a summary for *Erkenntnis*. He generally agreed with his views, but thought they would have come out more clearly if he had not emphasized his differences with the circle.

[221] On January 13, Carnap's wife, Ina, wrote Olga Hahn-Neurath that "views on Popper's book are divided. The physicists (Frank, Reichenbach) do not think much of it; the philosophers (Kaufmann, Nagel) think better." *Neurath Nachlaß*.

[222] Neurath to Carnap, 18 January 1935, Carnap Collection.

[223] Carnap to Neurath, 13 February 1935, Carnap Collection.

[224] Reichenbach to Neurath, 4 February and 25 February 1935, *Neurath Nachlaß*.

[225] Neurath to Reichenbach, 11 February and 5 March 1935, *Neurath Nachlaß*.

attack on physicalism, now besieged from all sides: Kaufmann, Popper, Waismann. Are you with me, Carnap? asked Neurath. In March, he warned Carnap not to commend Popper in his review, but rather emphasize their own viewpoint. No wonder Kaufmann liked *Logik*, he said; metaphysicians flock together. Mark my word, Carnap: Popper will not make you happy.[226]

Carnap's "official review" was an act of political balancing. He pronounced *Logik* "one of the most important contemporary works on scientific logic," demonstrating the mutual influences Popper and the circle had exercised on each other.[227] He sent a draft to Neurath. Neurath protested that the review was too favorable.[228] Popper's critique not only broke their scholarly ranks, he said, but let metaphysics loose after they had spilled blood trying to exorcise the demon. He reminded Carnap that he had been right all along about allies and enemies. Popper was another Wittgenstein at the door. Do not let him in. The circle's "correct line" – Frank, Neurath, perhaps also Carnap – did not square with Popper's scientific logic. Contrary to Carnap, said Neurath, Popper had not influenced recent circle developments but had picked up others' ideas, and criticized positions long superseded, pretending he did not know recent literature. Do not reward his aggressiveness. It is nice that you play Popper's advocate. But we need advocacy even more:

> A Viennese who grew up in an atmosphere that is familiar to Frank and me . . . wants to appear as a genius. No way. Having had the misfortune of growing up in such an intensive environment, one is [condemned to be] a pathbreaker. I find it pedagogically important that Popper understand it, above all, because his polemic is so contemptible.[229]

---

[226] "Du wirst aus Popper wenig Freude erleben." Neurath to Carnap, 28 January, 9 February, 16 March 1935, Carnap Collection.

[227] *Erkenntnis* 5 (1935): 290–4. Just as he told Popper (28 May 1935), the review was detailed and positive. Carnap suggested that conventional syntactic rules may transform probability of hypotheses into degree of confirmation, but generally, he defended Popper against Reichenbach. He sent the proofs of Reichenbach's "Über Induktion und Wahrscheinlichkeit. Bemerkungen zu Karl Poppers *Logik der Forschung*," *Erkenntnis* 5 [1935]: 267–84 to Popper and told him not to worry. Reichenbach was notoriously jealous of his territory and misunderstood *Logik*.

Popper responded cheerfully on June 10 that he was not worried. He was pleased that Reichenbach devoted sixteen *Erkenntnis* pages to refute such a bad book. His rendering of *Logik* was so outrageous that anyone reading the book would see it. Reichenbach had also plagiarized his theory. He enclosed a brief response to Reichenbach to help Carnap with his review. (Reichenbach's essay became a minor embarrassment. Hempel dismissed it in a draft review for *Jahrbuch über die Fortschritte der Mathematik* 63 [1937] [Popper Archives, 20, 2]. Neurath wrote Frank [1 August 1935] that Popper's endless slandering [*masslosen schimferei*] provoked Reichenbach, who may not have Popper's logical ability, but at least had a feeling for research. He encouraged Reichenbach "for fraternity's sake." *Neurath Nachlaß.*)

[228] Neurath to Carnap, 3 June 1935, Carnap Collection.

[229] Neurath to Carnap, 25 June 1935, Carnap Collection. Carnap responded that he had spent much

Neurath now determined to write his own review and arrest the metaphysical tide threatening to overwhelm the circle. He chose falsification and *experimentum crucis* as his central themes. He now called them "absolutism" and, against them, clarified his own encyclopedic vision of science. Having received authorization from Reichenbach for an additional review, he wrote Carnap that a third review would surely do Popper an honor. In less than ten days, he produced an angry draft of "Pseudorationalism of Falsification" and sent it to Carnap and Frank for comments. He completed the final, toned-down version in mid-August. Reichenbach encouraged him to "get rid" of the "naive youth," and complained that he now had to respond to Carnap's positive review. He did, and Carnap responded briefly again. No other book, before or after, received such extensive coverage in *Erkenntnis*. While the circle was preparing for the greatest event in their history, the International Congress of Scientific Philosophy in Paris, *Logik der Forschung* was on everyone's mind.[230]

In 1935, another newcomer to the circle began exercising great influence: mathematical logician Alfred Tarski. Tarski spent the spring and summer of 1935 in Vienna, attending Menger's and Schlick's seminars. He and Popper became friends. It was an unusual friendship for Popper: He revered Tarski and dreaded his judgment.[231] Early in 1935, in a meeting in Vienna's Volksgarten, Tarski expounded his theory of truth to Popper, solving the major problem inhibiting his realism.[232] Popper was forever grateful and repeatedly acknowledged Tarski in his work.[233]

To Popper, Tarski had rehabilitated Aristotle's correspondence theory of truth. In *Logik*, he insisted that as language could never be compared with reality, a statement could not "correspond" to facts. What did truth and

time trying to address Neurath's concerns and do justice to the variety of perspectives in the circle. Popper might develop into a metaphysician, but there was much to learn even from metaphysicians.

[230] Neurath to Reichenbach and to Susan Stebbing, 3 July 1935; to Carnap, 8 July and 12 July 1935; and to Frank, 8 August and 12 August 1935, *Neurath Nachlaß*. Reichenbach to Neurath, 8 July 1935, *Neurath Nachlaß*.

[231] Popper to Tarski, 25 February 1964, Popper Archives (270, 35, under Alfred Ayer). Tarski respected *Logik* but remained evasive about Popper's later work. He warmly recommended Popper for the New Zealand job. (Popper Archives [406, 5]. As Tarski was apprehensive about his German, Popper drafted the letter, following Tarski's instructions as to contents. Tarski to Popper, 11 October 1936 [354, 8].) Popper let Tarski down in 1936, going back on a promise to edit his forthcoming *Einführung in die Mathematische Logik und die Methodologie der Mathematik* (Vienna: Springer, 1937). But he tried to promote Tarski's work and career, something he did for few people. He offered to facilitate his emigration to New Zealand. (Popper to Tarski, July 1938 or shortly thereafter [draft, 354, 8].) They lost contact during the war, and their friendship never resumed afterward.

[232] Alfred Tarski, "Der Wahrheitsbegriff in den formalisierten Sprachen," *Studia Philosophica* 1 (1935): 261–405.

[233] *Conjectures and Refutations*, pp. 223–8; *Objective Knowledge*, pp. 308–40; *Autobiography*, pp. 88, 98–9, 141–4. Popper dedicated *Objective Knowledge* to Tarski.

falsity mean then? He reduced them to logical deductibility and contradiction: If statement *A* followed from a conjunction of *B* and *C*, one may say that, if *B* and *C* are true, *A* is true, and *non-A* false. But this was awkward, and one might as well dispose of true and false. There was no "empirical truth," or verification against reality: Basic scientific statements were conventional. Falsification consisted in *acceptance* of a basic statement contradicting a theory. One need not assert that the statement was true. Still, it was strange for falsifiability to be empirical science's touchstone, when Popper disposed of "false." It was even stranger for science to be in "quest for truth," when Popper disposed of "truth."[234] Experience did falsify theories, and falsification implied some relation between language and reality. What could it be like?

Popper understood Tarski to be saying that the correspondence of statement to facts required a "semantical metalanguage." A metalanguage spoke, at one and the same time, about another language and the facts to which the other language referred. It set semantical rules for the relationship between them. A metalanguage had "names" for all of the linguistic expressions of the other language (that is, it could translate them), described the facts to which the other language referred, and used higher-order terms – such as "correspondence" – to set semantical rules. Popper opined that most modern languages could function as a semantical metalanguage.[235] One could speak about correspondence of statement and "fact" in one language. Access to reality remained problematic, as there was no way of knowing for sure what the facts were, and whether a statement actually corresponded to them. Truth (correspondence) was a regulative ideal, always sought, never obtained. But Tarski relegitimized "commonsense" truth, the demand to a witness to tell it "just the way it was." The linguistic turn no longer threatened realist metaphysics and objective science. Popper's relief was immense.

He was making progress on probability, too. Karl Menger invited him to his mathematical colloquium, which met biweekly from 1928 to 1937, on alternate weeks with Schlick's seminar. From 1931 on, the colloquium published its proceedings in a special journal.[236] Members included some of this century's greatest mathematicians and logicians:

[234] *Logik*, p. 209.

[235] Popper's favorite example was the statement "grass is green." Let English be the metalanguage, German the other. The sentence "The statement in German 'Gras ist grün' is true (or corresponds to the facts), if and only if grass is green" may seem trivial, but makes perfect sense. "Gras ist grün" in German is easily translatable into English as "grass is green"; "grass is green" at the end of the sentence refers to the same facts as in German; "statement," "true" (or "correspond to the fact"), and "if and only if" are semantical terms setting the confrontation between (German) language and "reality."

[236] *Ergebnisse eines Mathematischen Kolloquiums*, ed. Karl Menger, 8 vols.; the last one, containing the papers of 1935–6, was published in 1937.

Gödel and Abraham Wald (1903–50) attended regularly, Tarski and John von Neumann (1903–57), when visiting Vienna. Popper's delight at the invitation was still evident in his report forty years later. On February 6, he gave a paper on probability, presenting his ideas on constructing finite random sequences.[237] Wald found it interesting and used it to develop his own solution.[238] He was working on mathematical economics, and statistical problems drew him to probability, where his interests converged with Popper's. Popper thought Wald's solution did not address his problem, but was delighted at the reception Wald accorded his views. He discussed with him the axiomatization of the probability calculus, and the two became friends.[239]

Menger, Morgenstern, Neumann, Wald, and Viennese economist and financier Karl Schlesinger all had interest in mathematical economics. Without fully recognizing it, Popper was witnessing the making of a social science. Morgenstern's essays from the mid-1930s combined subjectivist Austrian economics, emphasizing consumer preferences as determining value, with Walras's general equilibrium theory, explaining mathematically the market's tendency toward equilibrium of supply and demand. Morgenstern showed that general equilibrium analysis was dependent on imperfect foresight and varying expectations among economic agents. Under market conditions, agents operated in a permanent state of limited knowledge and uncertainty. In making decisions, they relied on interpreting others' actions and on conjectures about their future behavior.[240] Menger pointed out that rational economic conduct actually created uncertainty of prediction, since other economic agents, aware of competitors' expectations, might seek to defeat them.[241] Economics was a "game" of expectations that could be understood

---

[237] Karl Popper, "Über nachwirkungsfreie Folgen," *Ergebnisse* 7 (1936): 12. No manuscript available. Wald gave a paper on the concept of the collective the same day.

[238] Wald was a Romanian Jew, who began his studies in Vienna in 1927. From 1930 on, he studied mathematics with Menger. Everyone recognized him as an exceptional talent. In 1933, he began working at the Austrian Institute for Trade-Cycle Research under Morgenstern.

[239] Popper, *Autobiography*, pp. 99–105. Menger ("The Formative Years of Abraham Wald," *Annals of Mathematical Statistics* 23 [1952]: 18–19) testified to Popper's inspiring Wald's paper: "Die Widerspruchsfreiheit des Kollektivbegriffes der Wahrscheinlichkeitsrechnung," *Ergebnisse* 8 (1937): 38–72. See also: Wald to Richard von Mises, 27 April 1936, Mises Papers, Harvard University Archives; Wald to Popper, early in 1938, Popper Archives (359, 8). Popper inquired after Wald in his letters to Kaufmann from New Zealand. The two later lost touch.

[240] Oskar Morgenstern, "The Time Moment in Value Theory" [1933] and "Perfect Foresight and Economic Equilibrium" [1935], in *Selected Writings of Oskar Morgenstern*, ed. Andrew Schotter (New York: New York University Press, 1976), pp. 151–67, 169–83, respectively. See also: E. Roy Weintraub, "On the Existence of a Competitive Equilibrium: 1930–1954," *Journal of Economic Literature* 21 (1983): 1–39, esp. 5–17.

[241] Karl Menger, "The Role of Uncertainty in Economics" [1934], in his *Selected Papers in Logic, Foundations, Didactics, Economics* (Boston: Reidel, 1979), pp. 259–78. (Menger was the son of Carl Menger [1840–1921], founder of Austrian marginalist [subjectivist] economics.) Both the economic agent

only with the aid of game theory and probability. This gave rise later to Morgenstern's and Neumann's theory of games.[242]

The extent of Popper's exposure to economic theory remains unclear. Economic issues were on the colloquium's agenda, but they were not his major concern. Morgenstern presented an early version of "Perfect Foresight and Competitive Equilibrium" early in 1935, but Popper's argument on market predictions in an early version of *The Poverty of Historicism* showed no awareness of it.[243] All the same, he came out of the colloquium with a heightened consciousness of the problematic nature of prediction in social science and an exalted view of economics. Mathematical economics showed what social science could be. When he bemoaned the sorry state of social science in *The Poverty of Historicism*, he excluded economics.[244] "The success of mathematical economics shows," he said, "that one social science at least has gone through its Newtonian revolution."[245] His recommendations for model building in social science drew on economics, displaying methods he could recollect from the mathematical colloquium.[246]

A couple of months after his initiation into Menger's colloquium, Popper became persona grata in Richard von Mises's circle. He met Mises during Easter 1935 at Café Central, where Mises held court on his frequent visits to Vienna. Mises expressed reservations about the falsifiability of probability hypotheses. Following their meeting, he wrote Popper a long letter, detailing his objections. Popper responded two months later with a fourteen-page draft of an article, vindicating his position. "I do not think I have achieved something final," he said, "but I have cleared the only possible way to resolving probability's problems."[247] During the summer, he incorporated his Menger presentation, response to Mises, and quantum article into a paper

and economist were caught in what Morgenstern called the Sherlock Holmes paradox. Holmes, pursuing his opponent Moriarty, caught him at the right train station because he correctly guessed his intentions. But what, asked Morgenstern, if Moriarty, aware that he was being pursued, figured out correctly Holmes's expectations about his conduct and sought to frustrate them? The determination of the proper course of action in a situation of "I think that he thinks that I think . . . etc." admitted no rational solution, no certainty, and this was precisely the situation in which economic agents found themselves.

[242] John von Neumann and Oskar Morgenstern, *Theory of Games and Economic Behavior* [1944], 2nd ed. (Princeton, N.J.: Princeton University Press, 1947). Robert J. Leonard, "From Parlor Games to Social Science: von Neumann, Morgenstern and the Creation of Game Theory, 1928–1944," *Journal of Economic Literature* 33 (1995): 730–61.

[243] See Hayek's proofs for Part 1 of "The Poverty of Historicism" in Popper Archives (47, 4), p. 36. Hayek excised this discussion from Section 5 on "the inexactitude of predictions."

[244] Popper, *The Poverty of Historicism*, pp. 1–2, 56, 59–60, 116 n. 2.

[245] Ibid., p. 60 n. 1.

[246] *Autobiography*, pp. 117–18; *The Poverty of Historicism*, pp. 141–3; *The Open Society*, vol. 2, pp. 89–90.

[247] Popper to Anon. (Richard von Mises), 26 June 1935 (329, 4); "Popper und der Wiener Kreis – Aus einem Gespräch mit Sir Karl Popper (1991)," in Friedrich Stadler, *Studien zum Wiener Kreis* (Frankfurt: Suhrkamp, 1997), pp. 532–3.

he hoped to deliver at the Paris congress: "Die Prüfbarkeit von statistischen Hypothesen" (The testability of statistical hypotheses).[248]

Carnap urged Popper to come to Paris, promising to introduce him to English philosophers. Popper offered to present two papers at the congress.[249] Neurath allowed him only one, but assigned him to a respectable panel with Carnap, Reichenbach, Schlick, and American philosopher Morris Cohen.[250] In haste, Popper produced lengthy, incomplete drafts of "Empirical Method and the Concept of Experience."[251] He lectured on the afternoon of September 19. Neurath presided, introducing him as the "circle's official opposition."[252] He confronted Neurath. The only thing they shared, he said, was the conviction that the other was *not* an empiricist. He distinguished between falsification and falsifiability: The first was methodological, the latter logical. Falsifiability was not open to conventionalist objections about falsification's ambiguity.[253] He suggested that falsifiability be made the criterion of empiricism. Discussion followed. Neider opposed his restrictive criterion. Popper expanded on verification and falsification and on the impossibility of identifying the degree of confirmation with probability.[254] In another discussion, he opposed Neurath's encyclopedic model of science. Physicists endeavored to increase systematization, he said, so as to facilitate deducing and testing prognoses. Neurath undermined their effort.[255] His voice was heard, but few people paid attention. Russell was the weeklong congress's major attraction.[256] Neurath's report in *Erkenntnis*, synthetic in character, further muffled Popper's dissent.

---

[248] Popper, "Die Prüfbarkeit von statistischen Hypothesen," Popper Archives (15, 19), with draft. Popper reargued both his frequency interpretation of probability and the methodological falsifiability of statistical hypotheses, developing further his solution for finite random sequences.

[249] Popper to Neurath, 10 July 1935, *Neurath Nachlaß*. Carnap thought it best for Popper to speak on empirical method; Neurath, who disagreed with Popper's method, preferred that he speak about quantum theory. He complained to Frank that Carnap was pushing for a second paper for Popper, and asked for his opinion. (Neurath to Frank, 13 July 1935, *Neurath Nachlaß*.) Frank was blunt: Popper was a dilettante in physics, and should not speak on quantum theory. He urged Neurath to resist pressure to give Popper a prominent role. (Frank to Otto Neurath, mid- to late July 1935, two letters, *Neurath Nachlaß*.)

[250] Neurath to Popper, 10 August and 24 August 1935, *Neurath Nachlaß*. Announcement in *Erkenntnis* 5 (1935): 302. Schlick did not show up, and there were last-minute schedule changes. Popper still ended up paired with Carnap and Reichenbach.

[251] Popper, "Über die empirische Methode und den Begriff der Erfahrung," Popper Archives (16, 31), with drafts. He showed up in Paris also ready to deliver "Die Prüfbarkeit von statistischen Hypothesen," incomplete.

[252] Popper, *Conjectures and Refutations*, p. 269 n. 44. Neurath also criticized Popper, without mentioning his name, in "Einzelwissenschaften, Einheitswissenschaft, Pseudorationalismus," *Actes du Congress Internationale de Philosophie Scientifique*, 8 vols. (Paris: Hermann & Cie, 1936), 1:57–64.

[253] *Logik* implied the distinction, but Popper first made it explicit in his letter to Neurath, 10 July 1935, *Neurath Nachlaß*.

[254] Neurath's report: *Erkenntnis* 5 (1935): 377–406, esp. 397–8.

[255] Ibid., 390.

[256] My interview with Alfred Ayer, 21 November 1983. At the time, Ayer admired Popper.

Popper's contribution to the congress was not limited, however, to his own interventions. Two of Carnap's three papers were indebted to *Logik*.[257] In "Wahrheit und Bewährung" (Truth and confirmation), he revisited the protocols and foundation debate in light of Popper and Tarski. He suggested that as truth was timeless and contextless, and scientific statements conventional, no truth talk should be permitted in science. But, just as Popper observed, Tarski's metalanguage made correspondence between statements and facts possible without resorting to psychologism. Protocols were reports of observable physical states, first formulated in a lower-level language, then compared with other statements through the scientific metalanguage. Testing meant comparison with both fact (observation) and other statements. It was essential to science; it alone produced confirmation. Confirmation, not truth, was science's aim. Carnap adopted testability as the demarcation criterion for science, but interpreted testability as confirmability rather than falsifiability. Popper's critique of induction put an end to verification and psychologism. But Carnap retained confirmation as a weaker verification, raising the host of problems (natural law) that had started Popper on his way to falsifiability.[258]

Carnap excelled at rigorous rethinking and judicious adaptation of others' bold moves. His rendering of Popper proved more influential than Popper's own. He was already a leading continental philosopher and, in a few years, would influence the American academy. Popper was emerging as a maverick star but, with his emigration to New Zealand, would virtually fall silent for a decade. He avoided any open criticism of Carnap until the 1950s. In his correspondence with Neurath in 1935–6, Neurath repeatedly called on him to show fraternity and cooperate. They were a beleaguered camp, he said, and one gave no comfort and aid to enemies. Criticism should remain inside the community. Popper insisted that one criticized friends, not enemies. "I do not like schools of thought," he said, hinting that positivism, while fighting *Schulphilosophie*, was becoming itself

---

[257] "Von der Erkenntnistheorie zur Wissenschaftslogik" and "Wahrheit und Bewährung," *Actes*, vol. 1, pp. 36–41, and vol. 4, pp. 18–23, respectively. The first responded to Popper's effort to delineate a philosophical sphere between science and metaphysics (without mentioning his name). Carnap insisted that radical antipsychologism entailed transformation of all epistemological questions into logical ones.

[258] "Testability and Meaning," *Philosophy of Science* 3 (October 1936): 419–71; 4 (January 1937): 1–40.
    The circle met to discuss the theory of truth before the second Paris congress in 1937. Neurath was distressed at Popper's and Tarski's influence on Carnap and Hempel. He rejected truth as metaphysical and objected to the semantic turn. The Polish logicians' admiration for Popper corroborated his suspicion that they were all metaphysicians. Kotarbinski defended falsifiability. (Kotarbinski to Neurath, 12 April 1936; Neurath to Kotarbinski, 6 May 1936, *Neurath Nachlaß*.) Neurath spoke later of the Popper and Tarski periods in the circle's history: Neurath to Carnap, 18 November 1944, Carnap Collection.

an orthodoxy.[259] Both he and Neurath conflated personal and communal interest. Neurath was imposing his line on critics; Popper was using criticism to assert independence. He was a dissenter in the community of reason. Neurath disciplined dissenters; Popper ignored community. Reading *Logik*, one might forget that fascism, not positivism, haunted intellectual life in the 1930s. (*The Open Society* set the record straight.) But circle criticism took its toll on Popper. He needed the circle's reputation to get a job abroad. Once in exile, they were his major contact with the world. They silenced his criticism – for a while.

In 1935–6, Neurath repeatedly spoke of the circle as a republic of scholars (*Gelehrtersrepublik*). It mattered not that he was in The Hague, and not in Vienna – he could not return to Austria after February 1934 on pain of arrest – that Reichenbach was in Istanbul and Hempel in Brussels, not in Berlin, and that Carnap was leaving Prague for the United States. The Paris congress showed that their republic was spreading all over the globe, becoming American, British, French, Polish, Scandinavian. They were re-creating the enlightenment's republic of letters. In Paris, Neurath launched the International Encyclopedia of Unified Science, concluding his address with "vive les nouveaux encyclopédistes!"[260] But his optimism was a counsel of despair. Central European culture was living on borrowed time. None of the annual congresses for scientific philosophy could be held in Central Europe. Viennese cosmopolitanism was always utopian, the response of a marginal intelligentsia to the ethnonationalism that condemned it to extinction.[261] Trying to snatch victory from the jaws of defeat, Neurath imagined the circle's diaspora as a cosmopolitan triumph.

Writing Popper in October 1936, Tarski reported that the political situation in Poland was getting worse by the day. He no longer had any prospect of a professorial appointment, and soon, he feared, everything would be *gleichgeschaltet* (coordinated) after the German example. His next letter mentioned the likely dismissal of all junior faculty of "non-Aryan origin."[262] He did not explain why this should be of concern to him – the words "Jew" and "anti-Semitism" rarely surfaced in assimilated Jews'

---

[259] Popper to Neurath, 10 July 1935, *Neurath Nachlaß*. Neurath to Popper, 4 July, 24 August, 11 December 1935, and 4 February 1936, *Neurath Nachlaß*.

[260] Neurath thought that the encyclopedia was a particularly suitable medium for unified science because it reflected its very structure. Neurath, "Une encyclopédie internationale de la science unitaire," *Actes*, vol. 2, pp. 54–9; "L'encyclopédie comme 'modèle,'" *Revue de Synthèse* 12 (1936): 187–201. (Both available also in *Philosophical Papers*.) Popper opposed the encyclopedia: It would turn out to be another series of *Erkenntnis* articles. (Popper, *Conjectures and Refutations*, p. 269 n. 44.)

[261] Malachi Hacohen, "Dilemmas of Cosmopolitanism: Karl Popper, Jewish Identity, and 'Central European Culture,'" *Journal of Modern History* 71 (1999): 105–49.

[262] Tarski to Popper, 11 October and 5 December 1936, Popper Archives (354, 8).

discourse – but Popper understood well. He himself had no chance of an academic appointment in Austria, and he, too, sensed the impending doom. Hoping for a fellowship that would free him from his job, he obtained a leave without pay from his school for the year 1935–6. However, he received no fellowship.[263] He left for the Paris congress thinking of possible international connections, perhaps a position in England or the United States. He was searching for a way out of Central Europe.

A brief report on the second Paris congress from summer 1937 mentioned that "Popper, one of scientific philosophy's greatest hopes, went to New Zealand."[264] This was an appropriate epithet. Popper had solved some of epistemology's most intractable problems, creating a wonderful vision of science as a rational, adventurous, progressive enterprise, a vision reuniting science and the best of traditional philosophy. Paving his path amidst political and intellectual turmoil, he refused authority and order, without succumbing to relativism and mystification. He first carried out a philosophical revolution in *Grundprobleme*, then established a postrevolutionary order in *Logik*, providing methodological guidelines for future revolutions. His ingenious synthesis of objectivity and incertitude, tradition and change, truth and convention, rationality and criticism constituted a novel view of human knowledge. We do not know, he said, we guess, and our guesses are guided by beliefs that often prove wrong. Science is not an *episteme*. It remains tentative forever. Rationality requires no foundation, only critical dialogue.

To science studies critics, Popper's effort to direct revolution through methodology, control arbitrariness, and retain rationality may seem futile. Whereas conventionalists from Poincaré to Carnap sought to isolate science from culture through pragmatic prescriptions (simplicity) and ideal language, science studies have shown that culture permeates science. Relativism seems an inevitable result, and sociology, not methodology, the key to understanding science. But Popper saw through old and new conventionalism alike. Science could *not* be separated from culture, but this had no bearing on scientific objectivity. So long as science retained intersubjective criticism, testability, and falsification, it was alive and well:

> I readily concede that my conventional rules are guided, in the last analysis, by value judgments and predilections. Those who value, like me, logical rigor and freedom from dogmas, who seek practical applicability, who are captivated by the adventure of research, which puts us once and again to the test

---

[263] He asked Carnap (10 June 1935) about possible fellowships. Thirring inquired on his behalf with the Rockefeller Foundation, to no avail. Popper to Kaufmann, 5 January 1936, *Kaufmann Nachlaß*.

[264] "Die Philosophen in Paris," 5 August 1937, unidentified newspaper, Hoover Archives (18, 2).

by [yielding] new, previously unanticipated answers, they will probably be able to agree with the conventional rules I shall propose.[265]

The legacy of the progressive Viennese intelligentsia underlay Popper's science. For those still committed to its values, Popper's vision is as relevant today as it was in its time. In the late 1930s, progressive Central European culture went into exile. Popper recognized that if it were ever to return to Central Europe, it would require a new politics. He would devote the next decade to fashioning this new politics.

[265] *Logik*, p. 10; *LSD*, p. 38. "Wir geben also offen zu, daß wir uns bei unseren Festsetzungen in letzter Linie von unserer Wertschätzung, von unserer Vorliebe leiten lassen. Wer, wie wir, logische Strenge und Dogmenfreiheit schätzt, wer praktische Anwendbarkeit sucht, wer gefesselt wird von dem Abenteuer der Forschung, die uns immer wieder vor neue, vorher ungeahnte Antworten zu erproben, der wird den Festsetzungen, die wir vorschlagen werden, wohl zustimmen können."

Chapter 7

Red Vienna, the "Jewish Question," and Emigration, 1936–1937

Conventional wisdom has it that when the cannons thunder, the muses fall silent. Writing to Carnap on February 17, 1934, just a couple of days after Dollfuss had shelled the Karl-Marx-Hof in Vienna and put down the socialist uprising, Popper included a brief handwritten postscript: "on the events in Vienna, better talk only in person." The muses of philosophy, it appears, continued singing on condition that they avoid politics. Popper recognized that the day when they would fall completely silent was near, and he fled into exile. Far from the cannons' thunder he could dream a new politics.

There was no escaping politics in interwar Vienna. As Popper was writing *Grundprobleme*, the university closed for long periods because of nationalist student riots. The economic depression was bottoming out, the Austrian Nazis emerged as a major force, and the fascist *Heimwehr* sometimes participated in the government, at other times conspiring to overthrow it. Popper was pursuing *Grundprobleme*'s publication as Hitler came to power and Dollfuss put an end to democracy. He was writing *Logik* as Dollfuss crushed the socialists. Just days after *Logik* had gone into print, an abortive Nazi putsch killed Dollfuss. By the time the book came out, the clerical-fascist regime had completed the first round of academic dismissals and was pressuring schoolteachers, like Popper, to adapt their pedagogy to the regime. Another Nazi putsch was widely feared.

None of these events echoed in *Logik*. Scientific logic is not open, prima facie, to political considerations, but the absence of political referents also reflected Popper's withdrawal from the public sphere. He remained a socialist party member until he left Austria in 1937, but grew increasingly critical of socialist policies and was inactive. In postwar years, he was almost apologetic about his previous socialist affiliation. He had no choice but to be a socialist, he said; the social democrats were "the only democratic party."[1] At the same time, he felt that he owed an explanation for disengaging from the struggle against fascism, a struggle that became the central motif of his political philosophy. In his *Autobiography*, he said that he withdrew from politics because Jews' high public profile contributed to anti-

---

[1] Popper, "Vorwort" to Fritz Kolb, *Es kam ganz anders. Betrachtungen eines alt gewordenen Sozialisten* (Vienna: ÖBV, 1981), p. 7: "Ich war mitglied der sozialdemokratische Partei – man konnte nichts anders sein, es war die einzige demokratische Partei."

Semitism.[2] He tied together the "Jewish question," his political withdrawal, his critique of socialism, and his emigration. Socialists and Jews alike made political mistakes which he, Popper, could not correct, but whose consequences he had to bear. Some of his views on Jews, anti–Semitism, and socialist politics may be untenable, at points even skewed, but they are a key to the origins of the Open Society.

Popper thought that his political philosophy represented an application of his scientific one. In New Zealand during World War II, he envisioned the Open Society in the image of the scientific community, and used methodological arguments to dissolve political myths he held responsible for the Central European catastrophe. Notwithstanding his political withdrawal, political and scientific revolution remained intimately tied in his philosophy. After the Anschluss, when public criticism of socialism could no longer hurt the democratic cause, he launched "The Poverty of Historicism." The critique of Austrian socialism provided the impetus for his political project. We owe *The Open Society* to interwar Austrian politics.

RED VIENNA AND INTERWAR AUSTRIAN POLITICS

The first Austrian republic was the republic no one wanted.[3] It was implicated from the start with the Saint Germain treaty's unfavorable terms. "L'Autriche, c'est ce qui reste," Austria is what remains (after the empire is divided), declared French premier Clemenceau at Versailles. Before the war, Vienna was the administrative and financial capital of a multinational empire of more than fifty million people. Afterward, the capital's two million residents constituted over a third of the population. Most of Austria's economic resources lay beyond its borders, and the empire's commercial and financial network was in disarray. Few people believed in Austria's viability.[4] Disbelief was grounded as much in politics as in economics. Both nationalists and socialists resented Saint Germain's interdiction of unification with Germany. The Catholics harbored reservations about parliamentary democracy. The republic confronted overwhelming odds.

Like the Weimar Republic, the first Austrian republic had an admirably

---

[2] Popper, *Autobiography*, pp. 106–7.

[3] *Österreich 1918–1938. Geschichte der Ersten Republik*, ed. Erika Weinzierl and Kurt Skalnik, 2 vols. (Graz: Styria, 1983) includes detailed assessments of the first republic.

[4] Economists today believe that Austria's economic prospects were not nearly as bleak. For a discussion of the *Lebensfähigkeit* (ability to survive) question, see: Hans Kernbauer, Eduard März, and Fritz Weber, "Die wirtschaftliche Entwicklung," in *Österreich 1918–1938*, esp. pp. 343–6; Frederick Hertz, *The Economic Problems of the Danubian States: A Study in Economic Nationalism* [1947] (New York: Howard Fertig, 1970), pp. 53–91.

democratic constitution. A lower house, the *Nationalrat,* elected by universal suffrage and proportional representation, had full legislative power and
control over the executive and the army. An indirectly elected upper house,
the *Bundesrat,* had only a suspensive veto. The Constitutional Court
reviewed federal and provincial legislation and administrative ordinances.
But the republic lacked a democratic political culture. Political life was
dominated by the Social Democrats (*Sozialdemokratische Arbeiterspartei
Deutschösterreichs*) and the Christian-Socials (*Christlichsoziale Partei*), two
"parties of integration," each representing a *Weltanschauung* antagonistic to
the other, each having separate social and cultural institutions, and a paramilitary organization to boot.[5] The Christian-Socials led all governmental
coalitions but never managed to get an absolute majority. With the Social
Democrats permanently in opposition after 1920, political conflicts intensified until no modus vivendi was possible.[6]

Polarized politics made the formation of a ruling coalition progressively
difficult. The Social Democrats drew their electoral support from the capital
and industrial centers, increasing their share to 42 percent of the vote in
1927. The Christian-Socials lost their electoral base in Vienna, and their
support came mostly from rural Austria and provincial towns. After 1920,
they lost seats in every election. The Pan-Germans (*Grossdeutsche Volkspartei*)
had a hold on the non-Jewish professional middle class, the civil servants,
and the students. The Agrarian League (*Landbund*) and, later, the fascist
Heimatblock dug into the Christian-Socials' electoral base. Christian-Social
leader Monsignor Ignaz Seipel, the pivotal figure in Austrian politics during
the 1920s, initially represented an accommodationist stance toward democracy and modernity. But once the threat of social revolution vanished, and
the republic failed to serve the church, he gradually moved toward "true
democracy," a clerical-fascist state, a *Ständestaat,* which would restore
authority, rid Austria of class tension, and remove the threat of revolution
and socialization.[7]

Neither socialist revolution nor socialization had real prospects in the
1920s. Socialist leaders Bauer and Renner believed that bourgeois democ-

---

[5] Sigmund Neumann developed the concept of "parties of integration" to analyze the socialist and
Catholic parties in Weimar: *Modern Political Parties* (Chicago: University of Chicago, 1956). It befits
Austria even better. He distinguished between democratic and totalitarian parties of integration, but
considered even the former harmful. The Christian-Socials were neither as democratic nor as "in-
tegrative" as the socialists: They could not match the socialist institutional network. They lacked an
official paramilitary organization, but, from 1922 on, supported the *Heimwehr.*

[6] Klemens von Klemperer, *Ignaz Seipel: Christian Statesman in a Time of Crisis* (Princeton, N.J.:
Princeton University Press, 1972), pp. 94–156; Norbert Leser, *Zwischen Reformismus und Bolschewismus: Der Austromarxismus als Theorie und Praxis,* 2d ed. (Vienna: Böhlaus, 1985), pp. 181–244.

[7] Viennese sociologist Othmar Spann was the most influential intellectual advocating a corporate state.
Alfred Diamant, *Austrian Catholics and the First Republic: Democracy, Capitalism, and the Social Order,
1918–1934* (Princeton, N.J.: Princeton University Press, 1960), esp. pp. 73–106, 153–255, surveys the
spectrum of Catholic thought.

racy was the best they could achieve for the time. They had deep aversion to violence, and endeavored to pave a "third way" between Soviet communism and German social democracy. They considered the Soviet model inapplicable to developed economies with "bourgeois democratic" institutions. Bauer defended bolshevism as heroic, but pointed out very early (1920) that it established a bureaucratic dictatorship over the proletariat. Bourgeois democracy was not socialist "functional democracy" – Bauer emphasized that to Renner's and Popper's chagrin – and socialist reformism was wrong to permit integration of socialist parties into the bourgeois system. But a socialist revolution against parliamentary democracy would issue in civil war. "The democratic way may seem to take longer than that of violence," he wrote, "but it is undoubtedly one requiring smaller sacrifices in welfare, freedom, and human life."[8]

Excluded from the national government, the socialists focused on building a model community in Vienna. They developed an extensive network of social services: a comprehensive public health system, with advanced medical facilities for children (including Adler's mental health clinics); a comprehensive educational system, including kindergartens, adult education, municipal libraries, and local *Bildungskommissionen*, organizing cultural, sport, and leisure activities; and huge housing projects, financed by heavy income and property taxes, relieving the city's acute housing shortage. Recent critics have sought to diminish their achievement and demonstrate the authoritarian nature of their efforts to bring high culture to the workers. But to contemporaries, Red Vienna was a socialist mecca where visitors came to observe "the abundance of new forms of community life in which the socialist idea expressed itself."[9] It "was something like a new civilization in the making," a pioneering community, permeated with unbound optimism: "mit Uns zieht die neue Zeit," the new age is marching with us.[10]

Red Vienna led, however, a precarious existence. The capital's provincial status enabled the socialists to run its affairs with little concern for the federal government, the church, and the provinces, but drew fire from all three. Deep animosity toward the capital prevailed in the provinces.

---

[8] Otto Bauer, *Kapitalismus und Sozialismus nach dem Weltkrieg* (Vienna: Wiener Volksbuchhandlung, 1931), p. 225. See also his *Zwischen zwei Weltkriegen?* (Bratislava: Eugen Prager, 1936), p. 2 (The Crisis of Democracy). Anson Rabinbach, *The Crisis of Austrian Socialism: From Red Vienna to Civil War, 1927–1934* (Chicago: University of Chicago, 1983), pp. 24–58.

[9] Julius Braunthal, *In Search of the Millennium* (London: Gollancz, 1945), p. 255.

[10] *Mit uns zieht die neue Zeit: Arbeiterkultur in Österreich 1918–1934* (Vienna: Habarta, 1981). Exhibition catalogue. Charles Gulick, *Austria: From Habsburg to Hitler*, 2 vols. (Berkeley: University of California, 1948), chaps. 18–19, provides a comprehensive account of socialist programs and a laudation to Red Vienna. Helmut Gruber, *Red Vienna: Experiment in Working-Class Culture, 1919–1934* (New York: Oxford University Press, 1991) describes socialist popular culture, and emphasizes the social and cultural gap between the bourgeois Jewish leadership and the workers. He also recounts (pp. 69–72) serious infractions of proletarian families' rights by social workers and clinical staff.

WasserkopfWien allegedly lived off them, its secular, socialist, "Jewish" culture threatening toiling, family-oriented, God-fearing, patriotic, provincial Germans. Catholic congregations around Vienna suffered heavy membership losses in 1923 after the socialists had called upon the workers to disaffiliate. To Seipel, the modus vivendi with socialism diminished the church's influence. He searched for an alternative. So long as he believed that an attack on the constitution would trigger an armed socialist uprising, Red Vienna was safe. But he suspected all along that notwithstanding their bellicose rhetoric, the socialists would shrink from a civil war. He was testing them.

Postwar economic stabilization gave Seipel his first opportunity to weaken the socialists. The Geneva Protocols of 1922 provided an international loan to Austria under draconian conditions, mandating deflationary policies. They restored the currency's viability but solved none of Austria's long-term problems. Socialist leaders regarded them as an instrument for restoring lost bourgeois domination. In parliamentary debates, they protested that Seipel had sold the country to the Western capitalists, and ought to be tried for high treason. But when the crucial vote came, they balked, abstained, and allowed the protocols' approval. The contrast between their rhetoric and vote was telling: Geneva undermined their power, but they could offer no alternative and were too responsible to throw Austria into havoc.

Postwar inflation pauperized large segments of the middle classes, wiping out long-term savings, impoverishing pensioners and renters living on fixed incomes. Geneva forced Seipel to reduce the huge bureaucracy, and so laid-off civil servants joined the unemployed. Bauer and the socialists made a fateful mistake in hoping to capitalize on middle-class discontent. To Bauer, pauperization represented growing polarization under capitalism that would eventually force the middle classes into the socialist camp. But the middle classes, anxious about their loss of status, were distrustful of the republic, fearful of socialism, and vehemently anti-Semitic. Inflation profiteers and stock-market speculators of the early 1920s included a good number of Jews. Financial scandals unveiled after the 1925 stock-market crash centered on Jews as well. All Austrian parties, the socialists included, used the Jew's image as an alien conspirator in their propaganda. In the bourgeois imagination, the Jew embodied capitalism, socialism, and the republic, all at the same time. The fascist press described the regime as "a miserable Jew republic." Paradoxically, socialist workers alone remained loyal to "bourgeois democracy."[11]

---

[11] Fritz Weber, "Hauptprobleme der wirtschaftlichen und sozialen Entwicklung Österreichs in der Zwischenkriegzeit," in *Aufbruch und Untergang*, ed. Franz Kadrnoska (Vienna: Europa, 1981); Martin Kitchen, *The Coming of Austrian Fascism* (London: Croom Helm, 1980), chaps. 2–4; Bruce Pauley, *From Prejudice to Persecution: A History of Austrian Antisemitism* (Chapel Hill, N.C.: University of North Carolina, 1992).

The army remained under socialist influence during the early 1920s, and was too weak to impose order until the early 1930s. Seipel needed a "secular arm" against the socialists and found it in the paramilitary *Heimwehr*. In 1922, he began channeling funds to them through major industrialists. The socialists, mindful of the recent march on Rome that brought Mussolini to power, established, in 1923, the Republican Defense League, or *Schutzbund*. It grew into a formidable trained force, secretly armed. Its very presence, the socialists hoped, would deter aggression from the right. But the Catholics charged that the Schutzbund were a revolutionary vanguard, and bloody street collisions between the Schutzbund and the Heimwehr began. In an atmosphere of heightened tension, Seipel headed a unified bourgeois bloc in the 1927 elections: the Christian-Socials, the Pan-Germans, and a small agrarian party. He spared no effort in describing the perils of the dictatorship of the proletariat to the middle classes. Bauer responded with "democratic as long as we can, dictatorial only when we are forced, and insofar as we are forced."[12] As Popper noted, this allowed the enemy to choose the opportune moment for confrontation. They chose well, and put an end to both democracy and Red Vienna.

The crisis of July 1927 tested socialist strategy. On July 12, a Viennese jury acquitted several members of the Heimwehr of the charges of killing a socialist veteran and a child. The *Neue Freie Presse* expressed dismay, and the *Arbeiter-Zeitung* carried inflammatory editorials. The socialist leadership planned no action, but on Friday, July 15, a spontaneous demonstration in front of the court went out of control, and the unprepared police opened fire. The crowd reacted violently, set the Justizpalast ablaze, and prevented the fire engines from approaching the building. The police intensified the shooting, killing eighty-five workers and injuring many more. The socialists restrained the *Schutzbündler* from colliding with the police, and rushed to police headquarters and to the government to negotiate.[13] Seipel made it clear that he was willing to raise the stakes, and privately dared Bauer to make a real revolution for once. The socialists declared a one-day general strike and a two-day transportation strike: Both had only limited success. Seipel used the police to control the situation in Vienna, and Heimwehr units to break the strike in the provinces. The socialists relented and called off the protests, thereby exposing the impotence of a strategy that built up force as a deterrence, then refused to meet violence with violence.

"Bloody Friday" was a turning point of the first republic. The Schutzbund, the unions, and the party could not protect the workers from the government and the Heimwehr. Bauer revised his evaluation of the historical situation – the 1920s were a period of capitalist stabilization, not of class equilibrium, as he had earlier surmised – but not socialist strategy.

---

[12] *Protokoll des sozialdemokratischen Parteitages 1926* (Vienna: Volksbuchhandlung, 1926), p. 272.

[13] Charles Gulick, *Austria*, chap. 20, recounts the events in considerable detail.

As fascism was growing, he remained convinced that the bourgeoisie would act "rationally" and avoid dragging the country into a civil war. If the socialists maintained their strength, the bourgeoisie would "come to us to share the power of the state."[14] The "bourgeoisie" had no intention of doing such a thing. The Christian-Socials became more aggressive, more open about their relationship with the fascists, more insolent in demanding constitutional reform. The Heimwehr groups patched up their differences, enjoyed greater popular support, received increased financial contributions, and coordinated their strategies. They organized marches in predominantly socialist areas, bringing the latent civil war into the open. In December 1929, the socialists agreed to constitutional reform that strengthened the presidency and curtailed the autonomy of Vienna and the constitutional court. They hoped reform would broaden the consensus to defend the constitution. Instead, the fascists and the Christian-Social right, Seipel included, regarded it as "a first payment" toward a corporate state.

Beginning in 1929, the economic depression reinforced right-wing extremism, weakened the trade unions, and made the country more difficult to rule. Between 1929 and 1932, industrial production dropped by 39 percent, and unemployment doubled, reaching 557,000, or 26 percent of the workforce in the winter of 1932–3. Socialist party membership dropped by one-third. The government enacted deflationary policies, cutting unemployment and welfare benefits, and using force to control workers' protest. The collapse of the *Creditanstalt* in June 1931, the failure of the custom union with Germany, and mounting public disorder made Seipel offer the socialists an emergency coalition. Bauer rejected the offer: He suspected, correctly, that Seipel wished to implicate the socialists in unpopular budget cuts, and thought socialists had no business managing the affairs of a collapsing capitalism. He continued to view historical events through the prism of the struggle between capitalism and socialism, and had no appreciation of fascism's appeal to the middle classes. He expected the classical, Marxist revolutionary situation to develop, whereby increasing alienation of ever broader classes from a failing capitalism carries a unified working class to power.[15]

In the early 1930s, the National Socialists rapidly became the predominant force on the right. In local elections in April 1932, they wiped out the Pan-Germans and drew much of the Heimwehr's and the Peasant League's electorate. In Vienna, they won thirteen out of fifteen Christian-Social seats. The white-collar German middle class, the civil servants, the

---

[14] Peter Loewenberg, "Otto Bauer as an Ambivalent Party Leader," in *The Austrian Socialist Experiment: Social Democracy and Austromarxism, 1918–1934*, ed. Anson Rabinbach (Boulder, Colo.: Westview Press, 1985), pp. 71–9; Leser, *Zwischen Reformismus und Bolschewismus*, chap. 14.

[15] Otto Bauer, *Kapitalismus und Sozialismus nach dem Weltkrieg*. For statistics of unemployment and socialist membership, see: Gulick, *Austria*, esp. pp. 685, 698, and Fritz Weber, "Hauptprobleme," in *Aufbruch und Untergang*, pp. 606–17.

German intelligentsia, the non-Jewish professionals, and the petty bourgeoisie all voted Nazi. When Engelbert Dollfuss became prime minister in
May 1932, both the Nazis and the socialists were clamoring for national
elections. The socialists mistakenly believed that elections would increase
their strength, and were willing to risk a substantial increase in Nazi power.
Dollfuss offered them a coalition, probably pro forma rather than bona fide,
but they rejected it. Events in Germany still failed to register with them.
Dollfuss turned to the *Heimatblock*, and appointed their Vienna leader,
Emil Fey, as minister for internal security, thereby unifying Viennese
Heimwehr forces with the police. As Dollfuss looked for support to Austria's
neighbors, Italy and Hungary, their leaders, Mussolini and Gömbös,
urged him to move against the socialists and put an end to parliamentary
democracy.[16]

The coming to power of German National Socialists on January 30,
1933, changed the equation of political forces in Austria overnight. The
threat to Austrian independence seemed imminent. It finally dawned on
the socialists that in seeking to undermine the government, they were doing
the Nazis' work. They were now eager to cooperate with the Christian-
Socials. Dollfuss, however, was already set on fighting both the socialists and
the Nazis. In February 1933, the government announced wage cuts for
railway workers. The unions declared a strike, and on March 1, Dollfuss
moved the army to break it. The socialists summoned an emergency session
of parliament on March 4. When the vote reached a deadlock, the socialist, Christian-Social, and Pan-German presidents of the assembly resigned
successively so that they could vote. There was no one to preside, and so
Dollfuss suspended parliament. On March 7, he declared presidential rule.
On March 15, police surrounded parliament, preventing the socialist and
Pan-German delegates from reopening it. Dollfuss banned mass meetings
and demonstrations, outlawed strikes, imposed press censorship, and, on
March 31, ordered the Schutzbund to disband. He carried out an open
coup against parliamentary democracy.

This was the moment for which the socialists had been preparing for
years: the moment when the Schutzbund and militant unions would take
up arms to defend democracy. Yet when the day of reckoning came, they
did nothing, not even call a general strike. If earlier they had been crimi-
nally casual about national socialism, they were now convinced that a civil
war would mostly benefit the Nazis. They were apprehensive about foreign
intervention by Italy, Hungary, even Germany, and persuaded themselves
that the Nazis, not they, were Dollfuss's main target. So long as the party,
the unions, the Schutzbund, and Red Vienna remained intact, they would

---

[16] C. Earl Edmondson, *The Heimwehr and Austrian Politics, 1918–1936* (Athens, Ga.: University of
Georgia, 1978); Bruce Pauley, *Hitler and the Forgotten Nazis: A History of Austrian National Socialism*
(Chapel Hill, N.C.: University of North Carolina, 1981).

be able to ward off an attack on the workers.[17] But Dollfuss skillfully broke the socialists through a combination of authoritarian political measures and deflationary economic policies. He cut social security, controlled negotiations over wages, prohibited strikes and protests, censored the *Arbeiter-Zeitung*, and eventually moved against the Schutzbund. Impoverished, defeated, and demoralized, Austrian workers no longer trusted the socialist leadership, and the party lost an additional third of its membership in less than one year. The decision not to offer military resistance, or call a general strike, in response to Dollfuss's coup was a disastrous mistake.[18] "Armed resistance would have almost surely brought down the Dollfuss government," Ernst Fischer, leader of the left-socialist opposition, later observed. "What would have then ensued could not be predicted, and cannot be retrospectively construed. . . . Nonetheless, we should have fought."[19]

Dollfuss's wager that the socialists would not fight was successful, but he still had his hands full with the Nazis. In June 1933, he outlawed them and established detention camps. This left his government without a popular base, at the Heimwehr's mercy. Attempting to form a mass movement and contain the Heimwehr, Dollfuss launched, in May 1933, the Fatherland Front (*Vaterländische Front*). In early February 1934, police and Heimwehr units began invading Schutzbund arms depots, confiscating their weapons, and arresting their leaders. On February 12, a Heimwehr unit entered the depot in Linz. The socialist leadership urged restraint, but the militant Upper Austrians gave the sign for the uprising, disconnecting electricity in the capital and declaring a general strike. The uprising was badly planned and managed: The moderate Lower Austrians did not participate, and many workers – notably railway workers – remained unorganized. The transportation strike, which should have immobilized the army, failed. Dollfuss acted quickly, disrupting the *Schutzbündler*'s mobilization. Socialist fighting was uncoordinated; the workers fought more to preserve their honor than to win. Within two days, Dollfuss had put down all resistance. Close to two hundred people were killed. A few socialist leaders, including Bauer, fled to Czechoslovakia; many who stayed behind were arrested. Renner and moderate socialists who took no part in the uprising remained free.[20]

Dollfuss now outlawed the socialists, purged Vienna's ruling councils, confiscated socialist property, arrested militants, and banned the *Arbeiter-*

---

[17] Rabinbach, *The Crisis of Austrian Socialism*, chaps. 4–5.

[18] Already in 1934, Bauer acknowledged that it was "the most fatal of our errors." Otto Bauer, *Der Aufstand der österreichischen Arbeiter* (Prague: Verlag der deutschen sozialdemokratischen Arbeiterpartei in der Tschechoslowakischen Republik, 1934).

[19] Ernst Fischer, *Erinnerungen und Reflexionen* (Reinbek bei Hamburg: Rowohlt, 1969), p. 248. Fischer was leader of the Austrian Communist Party in postwar years.

[20] Kitchen, *The Coming of Austrian Fascism*, chaps. 2–3, 8, 10; Rabinbach, *The Crisis of Austrian Socialism*, chaps. 4–8.

Zeitung. But he left the trade unions alone, and on the eve of the Anschluss, Renner offered the government their support, should it decide to resist. In May 1934, Dollfuss promulgated a corporatist constitution, establishing the legal prerequisites for a fascist regime, but never fully capitalized on them.[21] On July 25, 1934, the Nazis carried out a botched putsch that killed Dollfuss and made Mussolini, fearing German intervention, rush troops to the Brenner. But the international situation was turning increasingly unfavorable to Austrian independence. Dollfuss's successor, Kurt Schuschnigg, tried to drum up support for Austria among the Western powers and the Little Entente (Yugoslavia, Romania, Czechoslovakia), but failed. The story of the final diplomatic moves leading to the Anschluss in March 1938 has been told many times. Ernst Karl Winter, a Catholic dissenter, had warned Dollfuss in 1933 that an independent fascist Austria was an illusion: The alternative was "democracy in Austria or the swastika on the Brenner."[22] Dollfuss overthrew democracy, and the swastika reached the Brenner, and beyond.

THE "JEWISH QUESTION"

The only socialist meeting Popper remembered attending after 1925 was Neurath's lecture on the Vienna Circle to the Ernst Mach Society, probably in 1928.[23] But he remained informed about socialist politics. A group of friends from the Pedagogic Institute, including Fritz Kolb and Otto Haas, all socialist activists, were frequent guests at his house in the early 1930s.[24] He was a fairly close friend of economist and labor historian Alfred Braunthal (b. 1897), director of the German socialist party's school. He knew remotely his brother Julius (1891–1972), editor of the *Arbeiter-Zeitung*, as well. At least once, in 1927, he exchanged views on socialist politics with Friedrich Adler. Adler withdrew from party affairs during the 1920s but returned later, at crucial moments, to unify warring factions. Popper thought their views agreed.[25]

Popper was a socialist dissenter. He grew increasingly anti-Marxist. In 1924, he announced his commitment to Bernstein's revisionism. In 1927,

---

[21] Hans Mommsen, "Theorie und Praxis des österreichischen Ständestaats 1934 bis 1938," in *Das geistige Leben Wiens in der Zwischenkriegzeit*, ed. Norbert Leser (Vienna: ÖBV, 1981), pp. 174–92.

[22] Winter is quoted in Kitchen, *The Coming of Austrian Fascism*, p. 6, but see also his "Die Staatskrise in Österreich," *Wiener Politische Blätter* 1 (16 April 1933).

[23] Popper, "Memories of Otto Neurath," in Otto Neurath, *Empiricism and Sociology* (Boston: Reidel, 1972), pp. 53–4; my interview with Popper, 26 January 1984.

[24] Fritz Kolb, "Karl Popper und der Sozialismus," in *Theorie und Politik aus kritisch-rationaler Sicht*, ed. Georg Lührs et al. (Berlin: Dietz, 1978), pp. 33–4.

[25] My interview with Popper, 26 January 1984. Adler represented the radical left in opposing the war but, in interwar years, often supported conciliatory policies toward the right.

Kant, not Marx, showed the way to socialism. Around 1930, Popper told friends that "there is no bourgeois social science distinct from a socialist one. . . . The dialectic is nothing but metaphysics, and so is also dialectical materialism."[26] But he remained a socialist, all the same. In his circles, socialism was almost taken for granted. Referring a New Zealand colleague to Carnap in 1938, he commended his leftist politics, concluding: "a truly excellent person."[27] In 1946, Carnap told him that Hayek expressed surprise to hear that he had been a socialist in interwar years. Carnap inquired whether he still considered himself one. Popper gave an ambiguous answer the import of which was that he was a progressive liberal, or a welfare-state social democrat, but no longer a socialist in the interwar sense.[28] In interwar years, his socialist commitment was clear.

Popper and his wife were among the crowd in front of the Justizpalast on Bloody Friday, July 15, 1927. They watched incredulously as the police opened fire on "peaceful and unarmed social democratic workers and bystanders. We were lucky to escape."[29] He thought the police's attack unprovoked, but, all the same, blamed the socialist leaders for the "massacre." Their "suicidal" policies gave the government opportunity to use violence. He understood well the event's historical significance. From then on, he was sure of the demise of Austrian democracy. He distrusted the Schutzbund, sensing they would not fight. He supported Theodor Körner's strategy of training the workers for guerrilla warfare rather than establishing, as Julius Deutsch did, a traditional military force, centralized and hierarchical, accumulating weapons in secret depots.[30] Arming the workers at the Karl-Marx-Hof was a folly, he thought. The workers were untrained in the use of weapons, and the action provoked the right.[31] Bauer was leading the workers right into the trap set by the fascists.[32]

"Although I was not active in the party," Popper said years later, "I attempted to influence its course through discussions with friends."[33]

---

[26] Kolb, "Popper und der Sozialismus," pp. 33–4. In their correspondence in 1943, Alfred Braunthal and Popper recalled their interwar discussions of social science and criticism of Marxism. (Popper to Braunthal, 21 May 1943; Braunthal to Popper, 24 August 1943, Popper Archives [28, 2].)

[27] The colleague was philosopher John Findlay from Dunedin. Popper to Carnap, 11 November 1938, Carnap Collection, Archives of Scientific Philosophy, University of Pittsburgh.

[28] Carnap to Popper, 17 November 1946; Popper to Carnap, 6 January 1947, Carnap Collection.

[29] Draft of *Autobiography*, Popper Archives (135, 1).

[30] This emerges from the still unpublished part of Friedrich Stadler's and Hans-Joachim Dahms's 1991 interview with Popper. (My conversation with Friedrich Stadler, 7 December 1998. Published excerpt: "Gespräch mit Sir Karl Popper [1991]," in Friedrich Stadler, *Studien zum Wiener Kreis* [Frankfurt: Suhrkamp, 1997], pp. 525–45.)

[31] Colin Simkin's recollections, E-mail communication, 9 June 1997; John Watkins, "Karl Raimund Popper 1902–1994," *Proceedings of the British Academy* 94 (1997): 650.

[32] Popper, "On Reason and the Open Society," *Encounter* 38 (1972): 13; "Gespräch," in *Theorie und Politik*, ed. Georg Lührs et al., pp. 24–5; Fritz Kolb, "Karl Popper und der Sozialismus," pp. 32–9.

[33] My interview with Popper, 26 January 1984.

Apparently, he asked Peter Hilferding, who had access to party officials, to arrange interviews for him, but had little power, of course, to change their policies.[34] Still, his views were well represented, for the most part, within the party. Renner and right-wing socialists proffered policies that concurred with his views: unambiguous defense of parliamentary democracy; unequivocal renunciation of the dictatorship of the proletariat; discarding of the class struggle; peaceful, gradual reform as the way to socialism; the toning down of political rhetoric; a coalition with the Christian-Socials.[35] Popper's Cassandra-like cries echoed Renner's warnings that Bauer's policies would end in a catastrophe. Popper was not alone: He chose not to join the chorus.

During his years at the university, Popper had experienced growing campus clashes between nationalist and socialist students. The German Student Association (*Deutsche Studentenschaft*) dominated campus politics and grew increasingly violent. They sought to defend the "German character of the university" by excluding "foreign" elements (that is, Jews and Slavs). At a minimum, they demanded a restriction of the number of Jewish students and professors through a *Numerus Clausus* (proportional ethnic admission) and the organization of students into national corporations to counteract Jewish assimilation. They pushed professors to block appointments of liberal and Jewish faculty. In 1930, the university's profascist (and later Nazi) rector, Wenzel Gleichspach, ordered national incorporation. A year later, the constitutional court ruled the order unconstitutional. Riots broke out on campus, and the university closed for months. The German students now entered national politics, joined the Heimwehr, then the Nazis. Dollfuss declared them illegal in 1933, but they were there five years later to carry out swiftly the *Gleichschaltung* of the university following the Anschluss.[36]

Socialist students fought back. In 1923, they established an academic legion of the Schutzbund, and associations of socialist faculty and students. Nonsocialist democratic students, Jews, and Slavs joined. But they remained a minority, fighting for equal rights, ethnically blind admission and appointment policies, and exclusion of racism from the lecture halls. They resisted nationalist efforts to turn the university into a *völkisch* cultural center, a base for political action against the "republic of Jews and socialists." Nationalists prevented the university from recognizing the commemoration days for 1848 and the republic's founding as official holidays.[37] Socialists celebrated

[34] Conversation with Karl Milford, 27 January 1999.

[35] Popper had warm recollections of Viktor Adler (1852–1918), the socialists' reformist leader prior to World War I. His politics did have one major difference with Adler and Renner: They were German nationalists; he was an internationalist.

[36] Erika Weinzierl, "Hochschulleben und Hochschulpolitik zwischen den Kriegen," in *Das geistige Leben Wiens*, pp. 72–86.

[37] The pretext was that they were "political" holidays. In contrast, nationalists turned commemorations

both holidays, honoring bourgeois revolutions. Nowhere else was it as clear as on Austrian campuses that by the 1920s, socialism had become the true inheritor of bourgeois liberalism.

Popper recognized as much but remained uninvolved. His disengagement was especially surprising in light of the social activism of progressive intellectuals. Progressivism's last show in Austrian politics was in February 1919, when the *bürgerliche Demokraten* elected one representative, Michael Hainisch, to the constituent assembly. He became a consensus candidate of socialists and Catholics for president because he had no political base. After the war, the *Deutschliberale* shed any liberal pretension and joined with nationalists to form the anti-Semitic Pan-German People's Party.[38] Progressive intellectuals' only choice was to cooperate with the socialists. In 1919, they established an umbrella organization, the *Freier Bund kultureller Vereine* (Free Union of Cultural Associations), to coordinate their activities. It included the Ethical Society and the Monists, focusing increasingly on socialization and economic planning; the *Bereitschaft*, dedicated to popular education among working-class youth; the Austrian feminist association; and organizations for special causes, such as marriage-law reform. Another umbrella organization, the *Freidenkerbund* (Free Thinkers Association), included 310 organizations with 45,000 members, all advocating separation of church and state, school reform, and legal dispensation from marriage – all controversial issues in the early 1920s. Their organ, *Pionier*, had a circulation of about fifty thousand. Devoid of political power, Viennese progressives remained a well-organized, activist community, imbedded in Red Vienna.[39]

Few progressive intellectuals kept aloof from organizational life. Hans Kelsen, the liberal intellectual par excellence, critical of Marxism, was active in the socialist-oriented Sociological Society. Among circle members, the relatively disengaged Carnap, Kraft, and Schlick still participated in the Ethical Society and the *Allgemeine Nährpflicht*. Frank, Hahn, Neurath, and Zilsel were involved in socialist politics. Popper's circle associates, teachers, and friends at the Pedagogic Institute, relatives – uncle Walter Schiff – were all involved in socialist and progressive organizations embodying the Open Society's ideals. Popper's withdrawal stood out.

Why did Popper take no part in the struggle against fascism? In his *Autobiography*, he answered potential critics that "with much latent popular anti-Semitism about, the best service which a good socialist who happened to

of German national events into riotous festivals, where anti-Semitism and antirepublicanism had free rein. Helge Zoitl, "Akademische Festkultur," *Aufbruch und Untergang*, pp. 167–204.

[38] Adam Wandruszka, "Deutschliberale und deutschnationale Strömungen," in *Das geistige Leben Wiens*, ed. Norbert Leser; idem, "Das 'nationale Lager,'" in *Österreich 1918–1938*, esp. pp. 277–85.

[39] Friedrich Stadler, "Spätaufklärung und Sozialdemokratie in Wien 1918–1938," in *Aufbruch und Untergang*, pp. 441–74; *Vom Positivismus zur "Wissenschaftliche Weltauffassung"* (Vienna: Löcker, 1982), pp. 151–66.

be of Jewish origin could render to his party was not to try to play a role in it."[40] Prudence dictated that he withdraw from public affairs so as not to provoke anti-Semitism. His anti-Semitic alibi was self-serving, but not disingenuous. His withdrawal was not contingent on anti-Semitism but established a life-long pattern that served him, an eternal dissenter and intellectual loner, well. At the same time, it did reflect deep fears of anti-Semitic persecution and was a well-thought-out conclusion of his stance on the Jewish question. It was a questionable political strategy that violated his ideal of universal citizenship, but it is telling of Jewish assimilationist politics and revealing about the origins of his cosmopolitanism.

Anti-Semitism was never far from the surface in fin-de-siècle and interwar Vienna. Jews' fear of anti-Semitism was rooted in daily experience. At the age of twelve, Popper was harassed by an anti-Semitic teacher to such an extent that he had to leave the gymnasium. In 1918, a teacher caught him preaching an antinationalist message to fellow students, and commented acerbically that the class finally had a leader. Non-Jewish students showed their resentment, and Popper left school.[41] Still, similar experiences did not deter other assimilated Jewish intellectuals from entering politics. Fears originating in personal or family experience must have reinforced Popper's feeling of vulnerability. His fears of persecution were not limited to anti-Semites but extended to fellow academics. Eva Hempel, who liked him, observed in 1936–7 his "persecution mania."[42] In postwar years, he was convinced that an academic conspiracy existed to diminish his philosophy.[43] That he was erroneously singled out for prosecution by the city in 1925 did not inspire in him confidence that the world would treat him kindly. As Central European politics sent alarming signals to Austrians of Jewish origin, Popper was receptive. He foresaw things others did not, and was among the first to leave Austria. He predicted the worst possible course of events – and was proved right. His prophecies of doom were accompanied by paralysis: He did nothing to fight anti-Semitism.

Personal psychology reinforced Popper's political instincts, but assimilationist politics directed them. The fears and hopes of the assimilated Jewish

---

[40] *Autobiography*, p. 107.

[41] William W. Bartley, III, "Rehearsing a Revolution: Music and Politics" (extract from "Karl Popper: A Life"), a paper delivered at the Pacific Regional Meeting of the Mont Pèlerin Society, Christchurch, New Zealand, November 27–30, 1989, 26–7.

[42] Eva Hempel to Ina Carnap, 7 July 1936, Carnap Collection; Eva Hempel to Popper, 21 March 1937, Popper Archives (306, 2). She discussed with Popper his *Verfolgungswahnsinn*, first in Copenhagen, then in correspondence. She pointed out astutely how his behavior triggered responses that he interpreted as conspiratorial, and made suggestions for changes.

[43] Popper had grounds for complaint about inattention to his philosophy. Academics are not generous about competing schools, and he had no clue about self-promotion. He was irascible, regarded professional activities as wasted time, and declined many invitations to speak. As a result, he was often "the big man who was *not* invited." (John Watkins, "Karl Raimund Popper 1902–1994": 672.) But his critique of conspiracy theories in *The Open Society* could dispel his own.

intelligentsia informed his political philosophy in ways he did not fathom. He presented his views on the Jewish question as flowing from his cosmopolitanism. He thought that anti-Semitism disclosed the natural hostility of an indigenous community toward strangers. Assimilation was a moral imperative, and Jewish nationality and religion were impediments to cosmopolitanism. He got the relationship between assimilation and cosmopolitanism wrong: Assimilation under threat violated cosmopolitanism. It was precisely assimilation's failure that gave rise to cosmopolitanism. Assimilated Central European Jews rejected Jewish identity but failed to gain acceptance into their nations. Imagined cosmopolitan communities were the only societies that they hoped would accept Jews. Cosmopolitanism was a precondition to assimilation, not vice versa.

Both assimilation and cosmopolitanism reached a dead end in interwar years. The republic formally removed all barriers to Jewish integration, opening positions in government and society to Austrian citizens equally. But anti-Semitism made appointment of Jews in the academy, civil service, and cabinet exceedingly difficult. Resistance to Jewish integration increased. (Municipal socialist institutions were the only notable exception.) With the empire's collapse, cosmopolitanism became more utopian than ever. Zionism was still a wild wager, but seemed increasingly a hopeful alternative. In 1932, the Zionists gained a majority in the *Kultusgemeinde*, and opted to turn it from a religious organization into a *Volksgemeinde*, a national association.[44] As an assimilated Jew, equally critical of Judaism and Zionism, Popper was not involved. In his view, Jewish religious organizations still carried the stigma of an ethnic, or national, community. Better go the extra step, as his father had done, and dissolve the community altogether.

Popper thought that there was little worth saving in Judaism. He regarded the Hebrew Bible as the fountainhead of tribal nationalism. Oppressed and persecuted, he said, Jews in the Babylonian exile created the doctrine of the "Chosen People," presaging modern visions of chosen class and race.[45] Both Roman imperialism and early Christian humanitarianism threatened the Jews' tribal exclusivity. Jewish orthodoxy reacted by reinforcing tribal bonds, shutting Jews off from the world for two millennia. The ghetto was the ultimate closed society, a "petrified form of Jewish tribalism."[46] Its inhabitants lived in misery, ignorance, and superstition. Their separate existence evoked the suspicion and hatred of non-Jews and fueled anti-Semitism. Enlightened Jews should help their unfortunate coreligionists make the transition to the modern world. Integration into non-

---

[44] Harriet Pass Freidenreich, *Jewish Politics in Vienna, 1918–1938* (Bloomington, Ind.: Indiana University Press, 1991).

[45] Popper, "Toleration and Intellectual Responsibility," in his *In Search of a Better World* (London: Routledge, 1992), pp. 188–90; *The Open Society*, vol. 1, pp. 6–8, 179 (n. 3); vol. 2, pp. 21–2.

[46] Popper, *The Open Society*, vol. 2, chap. 11, n. 56.

Jewish society was the only solution to the Jewish problem. "Assimilation worked."

To Popper, Zionism was a colossal mistake, and Israel a tragic error. They retarded solution of the Jewish question and incited a national conflict between Jews and Arabs. "The *status quo* is the only possible policy in that maze of nations which peoples Europe and the Near East."[47] Zionism disrupted the *status quo* in Palestine. Once Israel was established, Popper recognized the need to prevent annihilation of the Jewish community there, and "strongly opposed all those who sympathize with the Arab attempts to expel them."[48] But Israel's treatment of Arabs elicited his harsh condemnation:

> Of all the countries benefiting from European civilization, only South Africa and Israel have racial laws that distinguish between rights of different groups of citizens. The Jews were against Hitler's racism, but theirs goes one step further. They determine Jewishness by mother alone. I opposed Zionism initially because I was against any form of nationalism, but I never expected the Zionists to become racists. It makes me feel ashamed in my origin: I feel responsible for the deeds of Israeli nationalists.[49]

Popper treated Jewish religion, nationality, and ethnicity as if they were interchangeable and reducible to race, but in fact they were not. Rather, they were intricately related both historically and theologically. Divergent Jewish communities viewed the relationship differently. Liberal Jews discovered enlightenment cosmopolitanism in Judaism. Zionist socialists rejected traditional religion, but negotiated between Jewish nationality and socialist internationalism. Even traditional Jews defined themselves more as a religious community bound by belief and practice than in ethnic terms. Besides, Jewish ethnicity was no more incompatible with the Open Society than other ethnicities whose continued existence Popper tolerated. He was prescient in observing the emergence of Jewish racism under the conditions of ethnonational conflict in Israel. "The connection between religion and nationalism is most dangerous," he said, especially when the Hebrew

---

[47] Draft of *Autobiography* (135, 1), section 20.   [48] Loc. cit.

[49] My interview with Popper, 26 January 1984. Popper gave little public expression to his anti-Zionism: a fleeting condemnation of Jewish nationalism in his *Autobiography* (p. 105); a footnote in *The Open Society*, endorsing Toynbee's "attack upon nationalist attempts to revive ancient languages, especially in Palestine" (chap. 24, n. 54); a comparison, in passing, of the Arab refugees with Pol Pot's victims ("Toleration," pp. 188–9); a sentence added to the German version of his *Autobiography*, pointing out (correctly, I think) that Jews in the Habsburg empire had more rights than Arabs in Israel (*Ausgangspunkte* [Hamburg: Hoffmann und Campe, 1979], p. 147). He repeated the latter point in my interview: "[T]hose Jews who criticize me for my tolerance of remaining inequalities under the Habsburgs should show me how many Arab university professors, army officers, and cabinet members the Jewish state has today."

Bible sanctioned genocide.[50] Still, as obnoxious, discriminatory, and oppressive as Israeli laws and policies have been, physical genocide has been (so far) neither their goal nor end result, so they cannot be regarded as "one step further than Hitler's racism."

Many assimilated Viennese Jews shared Popper's anti-Jewish convictions. Liberal Jews' critique of Zionism and Jewish orthodoxy was almost as fierce. Such discourses have prompted scholars to hypothesize about Jewish self-hatred and its origin in the assimilationists' acceptance of enlightenment pseudocosmopolitanism.[51] Admittedly, Popper expressed ambivalence about his Jewish background. He claimed to have cut his ties to Jews, yet felt "ashamed" in his origin and "responsible" for Zionists. Nonetheless, an explanation in terms of the "pathology" of assimilation is inadequate. Popper's rhetoric expressed not hatred of the self, but concern for it. He did not internalize anti-Semitic norms, trying to transform a despised Jewish self into a respectable one. He was anxious lest Jewishness and Zionism provoke ugly and contemptible anti-Semitism. Not cosmopolitanism but anti-Semitism made it impossible for him to negotiate between Jewish identity and cosmopolitan principles. Jews, he knew, would not be accepted as such. They had to disappear as Jews. They could only become cosmopolitan citizens in a Kantian Kingdom of Ends. Central European reality intruded into cosmopolitan dreams.

Popper's analysis of anti-Semitism explains his fervent assimilationism:

> My father had decided that living in an overwhelmingly Christian society imposed the obligation to give as little offense as possible – to become assimilated. This needed some courage, for it meant to arouse the hatred, and the attacks, of organized Judaism. . . . [But] anti-semitism was to be feared, and it was the task of all people of Jewish origin to do their best not to provoke it. It was most understandable that people who were despised for their racial origin should insist that they were proud of it. But the logic of this racial pride was, obviously, mutual contempt, and ultimately racial war. . . .
>
> In Austria, anti-Semitism was very largely the resistance of an autochthonous population against infiltration from outside. . . . Not only did many

[50] My interview and "Toleration," pp. 188–90.

[51] Sander Gilman, *Jewish Self-Hatred* (Baltimore, Md.: Johns Hopkins University Press, 1985) focuses on the detrimental consequences of the enlightenment's unfulfilled promises for assimilated Jews. Paul Rose, *Revolutionary Antisemitism in Germany: From Kant to Wagner* (Princeton, N.J.: Princeton University Press, 1990) shows how enlightenment philosophers posed the Jew as the counteruniversal. The assimilationists were prisoners of hostile discourses. Zionism appears the only answer. Zygmunt Bauman, "Strangers: The Social Construction of Universality and Particularity," *New German Critique* 78 (1989): 7–42 collapses together modernity, liberalism, and Jewish assimilation, and ascribes exclusionary universalism to all three. Daniel Boyarin, *Unheroic Conduct: The Rise of Heterosexuality and the Invention of the Jewish Man* (Berkeley: University of California Press, 1997) opines that Freud and assimilated Jews sought to overcome the queer character of Jewish orthodoxy (the effeminate Jewish scholar) through masculine Protestant Aryan images, product of the *Aufklärung*.

Jews look different from the "autochthonous" population (my father's family did not – they all looked typically Austrian), but some acted in a way which made the rest blush. . . . Some of the rich were typically and odiously nouveaux riches. . . .

The Jews *were* "guests" in Austria. . . . I believe that the Jews were treated as well, or better, than one could expect. There was almost every career open to Jews. . . . When I heard [Jews] complain that they were held back by anti-semitism, I felt that they were both ridiculously conceited and unwise in their assessment of what could be expected of society. The situation changed radically for the worse with the dissolution of the Austrian Empire. . . . The Jews achieved full equality, at least before the law and, understandably but not wisely, invaded politics and journalism. . . . The influx of the Jews into the parties of the left contributed to the downfall of these parties.[52]

In these staggering statements, Popper draws us back from cosmopolitan dreams to ethnopolitical realities: Anti-Semitism was to be feared at all times and places. Jews were not to expect fulfillment of cosmopolitanism's promise, but accommodate themselves to anti-Semitism. They were wrong to take advantage of openings in society and stupid to draw attention to their wealth and success. Popper reversed the roles of persecutor and victim. Jews infiltrated Austria, invaded politics and journalism, attacked assimilationists, provoked anti-Semitism. By assuming leadership positions among the socialists, they contributed to the triumph of fascism. Retaining Jewish identity, they triggered a racial war that brought upon them their own destruction. Popper's discourse descended from cosmopolitanism dangerously close to anti-Semitism.

Mortal fear of anti-Semitism accounts for Popper's willingness to tamper with cosmopolitanism. Jewish marginality first gave rise to cosmopolitan dreams, then made their realization impossible. Liberal and assimilationist Jews imagined a cosmopolitan community accepting them. But anti-Semitism constantly reminded them of cosmopolitanism's hopelessness. Reality conflicted with dream. Anti-Semitism was a given, an immutable fact, a natural, if regrettable, response of a native population to strangers. Jewish identity, in contrast, seemed a variable, subject to change. Popper,

---

[52] Popper, first draft of *Autobiography*, Popper Archives (135, 1). I used the corrected typescript (pp. 140–1), but retained phrases that appeared in the earlier holograph (21 pp.). See also p. 142 of the later version (137, 3).

Popper was aware that his statement was controversial. He rarely spoke of anti-Semitism and had never before done so in print. Aside from this statement, occasional correspondence (see especially Popper to Hayek, 24 October 1969, Popper Archives [305, 15]) and students' recollections are the only sources. He felt compelled to express his views in *Autobiography* because the subject was too important to gloss over, and both postwar critiques of assimilation and Zionist triumphalism needed to be answered. In the published version, *Autobiography*, pp. 105–7, he eliminated some polemical terms but retained all the essentials.

like many progressives, thought the price of integration right. Confusing assimilation with cosmopolitanism and pretending that humanity would remain intact if threats forced Jews to disappear, he gave up a tribal religion to join humanity. The refusal of most Jews to join seemed reactionary and treacherous, putting assimilation at risk by fueling anti-Semitism. Recalcitrant Jews, rather than anti-Semites, became the Jewish problem. The polemics of traditional Jews and Zionists against assimilation reminded Popper constantly of its precariousness. His response was to lash out at his Jewish opponents in rhetoric reminiscent of the anti-Semites whose victim, like all Jews, he was.

The triumph of ethnonationalism throughout Central Europe made the reconciling of German and Jewish identities impossible. The result was an indeterminate identity for assimilated Jews. If assimilation were possible, Popper would become a German Austrian. But neither would anyone but progressives accept him as German anytime after 1880, nor would he, sworn enemy of nationalism, wish to become one. Cosmopolitanism appealed to Popper and liberal Jews precisely because of their life in between cultures and their indeterminate identity. The German *Aufklärung* may have been their cosmopolitanism's source. But few Austrians secure in their German identity promoted cosmopolitanism. Jewish intellectuals appropriated enlightenment traditions because they promised a home for them, an alternative to the ethnonational *Heimat*.

Claiming membership in an imagined cosmopolitan community, Popper rejected Jewish identity. "I do not consider myself 'an assimilated German Jew,'" he told a critic of his *Autobiography*: "[T]his is how 'the *Führer*' would have considered me."[53] Could he be included in the *Jewish Year Book*, inquired an editor in 1969. No, answered Popper, "I am of Jewish descent, but . . . I abhor any form of racialism or nationalism; and I never belonged to the Jewish faith. Thus I do not see on what grounds I could possibly consider myself a Jew."[54] He was right to refuse an ethnic reification of his identity. Living in between Germans and Jews, assimilated Jews did not belong clearly to either group. Their own profession of identity must be respected.

The historian has the right, however, to interrogate Popper's claim to have overcome the conditions of an "assimilated Jew." In an open society, those declining to belong to any nationality might be recognized as *Weltbürger*. Popper did not live in such a society. From childhood to death, his closest friends were assimilated Jews. He grew up in an assimilated Jewish family. Progressive Viennese circles were essential to his intellectual forma-

---

[53] Popper to M. Smith, 7 August 1982, Popper Archives (407, 17).

[54] Popper to Michael Wallach, 6 January 1969, Popper Archives (313, 10). He softened his stance in later years, agreeing to be included in Herlinde Koelbl's *Jüdische Portraits: Photographien und Interviews* (Frankfurt: Fischer, 1989), pp. 189–90.

tion and Central European networks to his intellectual growth. Both were preponderantly Jewish. His cosmopolitanism emerged from Jewish marginality and reflected the assimilated Jews' dilemmas. Anti-Semitism drove him to exile. He retained a special relationship to Jewish nationality, condemning it, yet feeling responsible for it. Using the category of "assimilated Jew" to describe and analyze Popper, I neither follow in "the *Führer's*" steps nor deny cosmopolitanism. Rather, I use the dilemmas of assimilation to explain cosmopolitanism's emergence, demise, and constraints. To do so simply recognizes that Central Europe set limits to cosmopolitanism. I hope with Popper for a world where such limits will no longer exist.

EMIGRATION

"Although I loved Vienna and Austria . . . I had dreamt of emigration since childhood," Popper wrote in a draft of his *Autobiography*.[55] In Central Europe, he could find no intellectual or political home. The intellectual networks in which he was active were culturally marginal, their members, like him, predominantly progressive intelligentsia of Jewish descent. With Hitler's first success in Germany, he expected the Nazi triumph, the Anschluss, the European war. In his old age he may have been oblivious, even naive, about matters politic. But a friend's letter from 1942 corroborates his foreboding of the impending Central European disaster: "[We] often recall your remarkable predictions of the catastrophe in its totality as well as in more detailed features."[56]

Notwithstanding *Logik*'s success, Popper had no prospects for an academic position in Austria. Under Schuschnigg's dictatorship, the appointment of a *Dozent* of Jewish origin, associated with the circle, was unthinkable, *ausgeschloßen* (out of the question) in contemporary parlance. "The unfavorable circumstances of the time," as Felix Kaufmann delicately put it in a recommendation for Popper, prevented *Habilitation*.[57] Popper was exasperated with Hauptschule teaching. School was far from home; transportation and work consumed his time during the school year.[58] Delinquency ran high among his students. The only Jew among the instructors, he had clashes with "loud Nazi colleagues." His wife, teaching in

[55] Draft of *Autobiography*, "Emigration" chapter, p. 18, Popper Archives, Hoover Institute (135, 1). Popper later deleted this statement.

[56] Frederick Dorian (Fritz Deutsch) to Popper, 10 April 1942, Popper Archives (28, 6, under Hellin). The "we" are Dorian and Fritz Hellin, Viennese friends of Popper from his youth.

[57] Kaufmann to the Academic Assistance Council, 28 October 1936, *Felix Kaufmann Nachlaß, Sozialwissenschaftliches Archiv*, Constance.

[58] Eva Hempel to Ina Carnap, 7 July 1936, Carnap Collection.

another school, suffered on account of his Jewish origin as well.[59] Professionally and politically it was time to get out.

The relative civility of British politics and academic life served as a magnet for Popper. Later in his life he gave private expression to his dislike for the German language and culture. Already in the 1930s, he considered most of German philosophy decadent. His disagreements with British philosophers were, in contrast, a family affair, not unsimilar to his quarrels with the circle. The circle had British admirers, and Popper himself had already been in touch with one, Susan Stebbing. He wanted to try his luck in England. Émigré physicist Eugen Weissenberg, in Southhampton, heard of his job search and offered to take him on as his assistant. Weissenberg had previously worked on short wave therapy (medical application of electric waves). Now he turned to mechanical wave theory, and wanted Popper's help with mathematics. Popper felt that his mathematical abilities were not up to par. He declined, recommending a Viennese acquaintance, Hans Motz.[60] But he needed somehow to finance his trip abroad. His wife opposed the trip. Ethnic marginality was no part of her background, and her relationship to Austria was relatively free of ambivalence.[61] She was deeply attached to her mother, did not want to leave Vienna, and was skeptical about his professional prospects. But, as always, she gave in and procured cash for his trip by taking a risky mortgage on her family's house.[62] She herself stayed in Vienna to earn money for both.

In August, they went on a summer vacation in Galtür, Tyrol. They always rented modest accommodations and dearly loved the vacations. Popper planned to meet Julius Kraft there and introduce him to Tarski's work. He spent the vacation studying Tarski.[63] On September 8, he continued to the Paris congress.[64] There, he met young English philosopher Alfred J. Ayer (1910–89). Ayer had visited Schlick's seminar before but had never met Popper. Duly impressed with *Logik*, he disregarded Popper's reputation for

---

[59] Draft of *Autobiography*, sec. 20, Popper Archives (135, 1). Questionnaire, Research Foundation for Jewish Immigration, *Zentrum für Antisemitismusforschung*, Technische Universität, Berlin.

[60] Popper to Weissenberg, 8 September 1935, Popper Archives (360, 19, under Weiselberg). Popper to Kaufmann, 8 September 1935 and 5 January 1936, *Kaufmann Nachlaß*.

[61] Karl Milford comments here: No secular socialist educator who went to the Pädagogisches Institut had a relationship free of ambivalence toward Catholic Austria. (Conversation with author, 27 January 1999.)

[62] Eva Hempel to Ina Carnap, 7 July 1936, Carnap Collection; Popper to Kaufmann, 5 January 1936, *Kaufmann Nachlaß*. Did Hennie, or her mother (who apparently owned the house), take out a second mortgage? The precise nature of the transaction remains unclear, but it got the family into trouble within months.

[63] Popper to Julius Kraft, 11 July 1935 (316, 24); Popper to Tarski, 20 August 1935, from the Alpenrose Inn, Hoover Archives (353, 8).

[64] Popper to Kaufmann, 8 September 1935, from the border station at Bregenz, thanking him for helping with Einstein, asking for advice on Weissenberg, and requesting help for his friend, Fritz Hellin.

being difficult, and initiated a friendship. Throughout Popper's stay in England, he looked after him "as a hen looks after a chick."[65] In Paris, he introduced him to Isaiah Berlin and Gilbert Ryle, the Oxford philosopher of mind, and facilitated Susan Stebbing's invitation to him to give lectures at Bedford College, the University of London.[66] Stebbing (1885–1943) was a remarkable logician and scientific philosopher in an age that still regarded women philosophers as quixotic. Like Ayer and Ryle, she knew German, and had long been a major channel for circle influences in England. In 1934, she had invited Carnap to lecture. She had read both *Grundprobleme* and *Logik*, and now invited Popper. He was officially on an English "lecture tour."[67]

He came to England late in September 1935. He was under Tarski's spell, and in his two lectures at Bedford College, drew the implications of Tarski's semantics and theory of truth for scientific philosophy. This introduced Tarski to the British, a boon for a Polish intellectual with limited Viennese connections and no English publications.[68] But Popper had to take care of himself first. His friend Berti Wiesner introduced him to mathematician and popular leftist writer Hyman Levy, who invited him to give three public lectures on probability at Imperial College.[69] He may also have given a paper at Oxford at Berlin's and Ryle's invitation. Ayer took him to a meeting of the Aristotelian Society. Russell spoke about "The Limits of Empiricism."[70] He suggested that the impossibility of justifying the induc-

[65] Popper, introductory remarks to Ayer's public lecture, "Man as a subject for science," Popper Archives (101, 13). Jeremy Shearmur drew my attention to the remarks.

[66] My interview with A. J. Ayer, 21 November 1983. Stebbing thought highly of Popper: Hayek to Carr-Saunders, 7 August 1943; Hayek to Horton, 14 March 1945, Hayek Archives (44, 1).

[67] Before leaving Paris for London, Popper updated Carnap about his situation and asked whether he could do an *Habilitation* with him in Prague. It is not clear whether he had in mind a Prague appointment or wished to improve his chances outside Central Europe. Probably both. Carnap explored the possibility with his dean and responded that it was difficult, and likely impractical. Carnap to Popper, 5 November 1935, Carnap Collection.

[68] Mathematical logician and biologist Joseph Henry Woodger (1894–1981), whom Popper had met in Paris, was mesmerized by his presentation. He contacted Tarski, spent the next summer's vacation with him in the Tatra mountains, and decided to rewrite his manuscript (*The Axiomatic Method in Biology*, with appendixes by Alfred Tarski and W. F. Floyd [Cambridge: The University Press, 1937]) in light of Tarski's comments. (Carl and Eva Hempel to the Carnaps, 7 July and 2 September 1936.) Both Stebbing and Woodger inquired with Tarski about a possible visit for lecures. (Tarski to Popper, 1 February and 11 October 1936 [354, 8].) Surprisingly, there was insufficient interest in Tarski's work, and no formal invitation was issued. Woodger tried unsuccessfully to get him a position. (Tarski to Popper, 3 January 1937; Woodger to Popper, 30 May 1938 [363, 17].)

[69] Popper to Levy, 22 July 1943, Popper Archives (300, 2) dated this to 1936.

[70] *Proceedings of the Aristotelian Society* 36 (1935–6): 131–50. The date is not clear. *Proceedings* reports the society meeting in "London, April 6, 1936 at 8pm." Popper dated the meeting to 1936 in *Autobiography*, p. 109, but in *Realism and the Aim of Science* (p. 12), written in the mid-1950s, he wrote: "Not long after I came to London, in the autumn of 1935 . . . I was taken to a meeting of the Aristotelian Society." William Bartley, having researched Popper's biography, reported to Popper (25 July 1981 [273, 1]) that the meeting, where Russell spoke and Popper commented, took place in November

tive principle represented the absolute limit of empiricism. This was the problem that had started Popper on his way to *Logik*, and he was encouraged by Ayer to intervene in the discussion:

> I formulated [my objections] as briefly and as pointedly as I could with the halting English at my disposal. . . . I said first that I did not believe in induction at all, even though I believed in learning from experience. . . . [T]he audience . . . took it as a joke, and laughed. In my second attempt I suggested that . . . what we call "scientific knowledge" was hypothetical, and often not true, let alone certainly or probably true. . . . Again . . . they laughed and clapped.[71]

The audience was responding graciously to novel ideas, seemingly paradoxical, expressed in a thick Viennese accent and broken English. Other audiences were less generous. Popper had learned English in the gymnasium but, other than occasional coaching of American students around 1920, had had no opportunity to use the language. He could read English but, as a rule, did not, using translations whenever possible.[72] Now he wanted to make quick progress so that he could find a job and emigrate. He communicated in his mother tongue with English friends who had any German, but insisted, apparently, on lecturing in English, even when encouraged to speak German.[73] His English greatly improved during his nine months abroad. He told Carnap in September 1936 that he spoke English freely.[74] He may have exaggerated. (He was asking Carnap to find him a job in the United States.) Half a year later, from aboard the ship taking him to New Zealand, he revealed his fear that because of his imperfect (*recht mangelhaftes*) English, he would be sent back.[75] He did not shift to English in correspondence until the war, but he liked the language,

---

1935, and Wittgenstein attended. Popper did not remember Wittgenstein attending, and this seems strange. Russell may have given the paper on several occasions.

[71] *Autobiography*, p. 110.

[72] Questionnaire, Research Foundation for Jewish Immigration. The only frequent English reference in his manuscripts from the 1920s is to Hume's *Treatise of Human Nature*, but he never quoted Hume, and I am not certain that he read him. *Logik* included only two English references to Compton's works in experimental physics (the first with a spelling error: French *revue* for the English Review, section 77, note 2).

[73] Eva Hempel to Popper, 21 March 1937, Popper Archives (306, 2).

[74] Popper to Carnap, 5 September 1936, Carnap Collection.

[75] Popper to Carnap, 15 February 1937, Carnap Collection. His ability in English probably fell somewhere in between his two self-evaluations. His cover letters for the New Zealand job from October 1936 were still in awkward English, using German structures. The rest of the application was much more fluent and may have been corrected by someone else. (Popper Archives [366, 3].) His first available English letter, from January 1937, was in nice, if occasionally nonidiomatic, English. (Popper to G. E. Moore, 5 January 1937, Moore Papers, Cambridge University Library, 8P/18/1.) His notes for his first seminar in New Zealand, on the Vienna Circle, were in serviceable English. (Popper Archives [366, 21].)

wanted to learn it, made tremendous efforts, and learned quickly. Those reading his wonderful English prose cannot imagine the struggle that went into its acquisition. He privately described his move to English as traumatic.[76]

Financial, or legal, problems with his house back home interrupted his trip. He was back in Vienna for Christmas. Hennie accompanied him to the border on his trip back to England on January 5. He sent a letter with her to Kaufmann, reporting that his housing situation had improved but that the house problem could yet come to a trial. What happened precisely I do not know, but it seems that they lost their house. From then on they moved, with Hennie's mother, from their house to an apartment in the same district.[77] Hennie's family had been in the little house, surrounded by a garden, for at least a generation. Karl's parents and friends had visited it during their first years of marriage. Leaving it may have been the first good-bye to Vienna.

On his way to England, Popper went through Brussels, spending January 8 and 9 there, meeting with the Braunthals, the Hempels, and other friends. The first evening a discussion group gathered at the house of Paul Oppen-heim, an independent scholar, mathematician, and scientist; the second evening they met at Alfred Braunthal's. Discussion ranged over many issues, but on the second evening, it focused on themes that would later be at the center of "The Poverty of Historicism": causal explanation and historical laws. Popper criticized sociologist Karl Mannheim (1893–1947), proponent of the sociology of knowledge.[78] He was becoming aware of *Logik's* potential implications for social science, and was seeking to increase his job prospects by expanding into new fields. In his 1936 resume, he listed the methodology of sociology as an expertise.[79] But, as he sat among Central European exiles in Brussels, contemplating the deteriorating situation back home, the critique of historical "laws" may have also reflected his meditation on socialist mistakes that had brought them all to where they were.

He stayed in Britain until after the middle of June 1936, living with a friend in a dreadful bed-sitter, in the Paddington area of London. He told the Hempels that space was so limited that he had difficulty opening his suitcase. He could do no work under such conditions. Neurath chased him for months to get his Paris paper for publication in the congress's pro-

[76] John Watkins, "Karl Raimund Popper 1902–1994": 653.

[77] The old address: 46 Anton Langergasse; the new, 8 Neukräftengasse, both in Wien 13. See also: Robert Lammer to Karl Popper, 20 August 1968 (318, 12).

[78] Eva Hempel to Ina Carnap, 27 January 1936, Carnap Collection; Popper to Braunthal, 21 May 1943 and 19 July 1944, Popper Archives (28, 2, 3); chronology (405, 1). See the detailed discussion in Chapter 8.

[79] SPSL (Society for the Protection of Science and Learning) Papers, Bodleian Library, Oxford University.

ceedings, to no avail.[80] He published none of the work that he had completed in 1935. Einstein's letters canceled his publication plan for the quantum article, and he never polished his probability papers. In search of a job and in low spirits, he completed no work until landing in New Zealand.

He was naturally seeking the company of Central European exiles. He saw Hempel when the latter visited London, and spent time with Hempel's friend, mathematician Olaf Helmer, who was completing a dissertation with Stebbing. His closest new friend, however, was a young Austrian émigré, future art historian Ernst Gombrich (b. 1909). They would become lifelong friends. Gombrich was at the time a junior research fellow at the Warburg Institute. Like Popper, he came from an assimilated Jewish family, the father a Freemason. Like Popper, he could find no job in Austria. Their families knew each other well. Gombrich's father had been Simon Popper's apprentice before the war and helped Karl's mother, Jenny, after her husband had died. They had met on at least one social occasion in Vienna, but Popper paid no attention to Gombrich, focusing his attention on the pianist performing at the party instead. Now he was much in need of company. They discussed philosophy and politics, Popper, seven years older, very much the leader. Like Popper's other friends of this period, Gombrich recorded his great anxiety about Austria, his desire to emigrate, and, at the same time, his apprehension about leaving Vienna.[81]

Popper made some essential academic contacts in spring 1936. Ayer introduced him to leading British philosophers R. B. Braithwaite and G. E. Moore, and to A. C. Ewing, head of Cambridge's famed Moral Sciences Club. He received an invitation to lecture. He chose probability, hoping Keynes would be present. Neither Keynes nor Braithwaite made it to the presentation, but Moore did, and Popper may have had the opportunity to expound Tarski to him.[82] He gave, apparently, a second paper in Cambridge, with Moore and American philosopher C. H. Langford in the audience.[83] He left a good impression. Moore wrote Ayer a fortnight later that Popper could use him as a reference. Later that year, he had Ewing issue an offer of academic hospitality for him.[84] Braithwaite was always respectful. In 1943, he tried unsuccessfully to sway the board of Cambridge University Press to publish *The Open Society.*

Popper returned to Oxford, too. He had met Erwin Schrödinger

---

[80] Popper left Neurath's letters, beginning December 11, 1935, and ending June 6, 1936, unanswered. (Popper Archives [331, 28].) The last one, a postcard of June 6, 1936, was forwarded from Austria to his London address: 5 Devonport Street, Hyde Park, London W2.

[81] Interviews with A. J. Ayer, 21 November 1983, Ernst Gombrich, 7 December 1983, and Ernest Nagel, March 1984; Ernst Gombrich, *The Open Society and Its Enemies: Remembering Its Publication Fifty Years Ago* (London: LSE Discussion Paper Series, 1995), pp. 1–2.

[82] Braithwaite to Popper, 12 March 1936, Popper Archives (279, 3).

[83] *Autobiography*, p. 108.   [84] Moore to Ayer, 24 March 1936, Popper Archives (270, 35).

(1887–1961) the previous fall (probably through Thirring), and Schrödinger invited him to Oxford. They had "long conversations and heated quarrels," and took a liking to each other.[85] In Berlin, Schrödinger had led a seminar attended by Einstein, Planck, and other famous physicists. He did not find similar interest in theoretical physics in Oxford and was happy to talk to Popper. Like Bohr, he thought E-P-R unconvincing. But he rejected Bohr's Copenhagen interpretation of quantum theory, and was skeptical about the field. Popper got to know him and his wife well. They renewed their intense exchanges after the war in Alpbach, a Tyrolian village where previous members of the tiny Austrian resistance established a summer school to promote internationalism among European youth.

In the spring of 1936, Popper met the Countess von Zeppelin at least once. Carnap had referred him to her in 1934 in connection with *Grundprobleme*.[86] She was interested in scientific philosophy and had publishing connections, and Popper hoped she could facilitate the translation and publication of *Logik*. (She was now translating Carnap's *Logical Syntax of Language*.) They clearly got along well. In April, in a very friendly letter, she asked to see him again.[87] Unlike many of his generation, Popper did not condescend to women with a keen intellect (especially not, one suspects, to women of aristocratic lineage). In discussions, he cut quickly through national, class, and gender differences to reach substance. But gender did make a difference. His conversations with women were often more relaxed, less competitive. In his postwar seminar at the LSE, the few women occasionally attending were the only participants allowed to complete their statements without being interrupted. This did reflect Popper's prejudice that women were not suited for intellectual combat, but the net effect was that he treated women as he should have treated everyone. Colin Simkin, who knew him well in New Zealand, testified that he could be infinitely charming with women, presenting to them his best social self.

In search of a job, Popper was displaying rather than acquiring knowledge, but one encounter may have proved crucial to "The Poverty of Historicism." He recalled a "meeting at the old windmill at Hunstanton, in some of the most pleasant surroundings," lasting a couple of days, with a group of philosophically inclined leftist scientists, primarily young biologists, some already distinguished: J. D. Bernal, W. F. Floyd, J. B. S. Haldane, Dorothy Hodgkin, Hyman Levy, Joseph Needham, C. H. Waddington, Bertold Wiesner, and J. H. Woodger.[88] Wiesner or Woodger most likely

---

[85] Popper to Max Jammer, 26 April 1967 (313, 3).

[86] Popper to Carnap, 23 April 1934; Carnap to Popper, 24 April 1934, Carnap Collection.

[87] Amethe (Smeaton), Countess von Zeppelin to Popper, 6 April 1936 (365, 15).

[88] Popper to Gombrich, 22 July 1943; Popper to Levy (Gombrich's copy), 22 July 1943 (300, 2); Levy to Popper, 15 September 1943 (319, 31); "Chronology," 1935–6, Popper Archives (405, 1). In the letter to Gombrich, Popper said that Berti Wiesner "encouraged me greatly, during my stay in England, to write a book on the very topic of the present MS. [*The Open Society*]."

invited him. Participants were concerned with the history and social organization of science, and with the social implications of evolutionary theory.
All were persuaded that the traditional view of scientific activity as socially
neutral was wrong. Some were outright Marxists, others deeply engaged
with Marxism. Many held positions Popper later called "historicist."[89] He
did not mention the gathering in his *Autobiography*, and we may never
know what discussions took place, but he apparently participated actively,
and Wiesner encouraged him to develop his ideas further. In "The Poverty
of Historicism," he assailed Waddington for his moral futurism – the
assumption that evolution and progress must be good – and used Bernal
and Haldane to sustain his criticism. If sociology was the discussion's
center in Brussels, biology provided a model for "historicist laws" "at the
windmill."[90]

Historical "laws" and the methodology of sociology were the subject of
a paper Popper delivered that spring, probably from notes, at the London
School of Economics: "The Poverty of Historicism." Austrian émigré economist Friedrich von Hayek (1899–1992) invited him to address the seminar
he ran jointly with the LSE's leading economist, Lionel Robbins
(1898–1984). The seminar "was usually attended by some thirty or forty
members of staff and postgraduate students as well as by visiting Europeans
and Americans."[91] It is not clear how many showed up for the unknown
Viennese philosopher. In addition to Hayek and Robbins, present were also
economists G. L. S. Shackle and Abba Lerner, Ernst Gombrich, and possibly Karl Mannheim, a reader in sociology at the LSE.[92] There were likely
other LSE economists whom Popper could not remember. A discussion
followed. Lerner asked about "Marxist time limited truth," laws confined
to historical periods. In *Poverty*, Popper would reject the possibility. The
theoretical problems that historicization of laws would present aside, Tarski
had just rehabilitated "absolute truth." Popper was not inclined to relativize
truth after it had been rescued from the linguistic turn.

Popper's encounter with Hayek turned out to be one of the most important in his life. Fifty years later, he would recall their first meeting in Hayek's

---

[89] J. D. Bernal, *The Social Function of Science* (London: Routledge, 1939); J. B. S. Haldane, *The Marxist Philosophy and the Sciences* (New York: Random House, 1939); C. H. Waddington, *The Scientific Atti- tude* (London: Penguin, 1941). Hyman Levy had just edited a collection of essays and discussions with noted evolutionary biologist Julian Huxley, *Science and Social Needs* (New York: Harper, 1935).

[90] However, the early version of "Poverty" (1938–40) did not seem to contain a systematic critique of leftist evolutionary thinking. Popper seemed to have developed it only after having read Hayek's cri- tique of "Scientism" and Waddington's *Science and Ethics* in 1943–4. (Popper to Hayek, 17 January 1944, Hayek Archives [44, 1]; Popper to Gombrich, 11 January 1944, Popper Archives [300, 3]. See the discussion of "Poverty's" composition in Chapters 8 and 10.)

[91] B. J. McCormick, *Hayek and the Keynesian Avalanche* (New York: St. Martin's, 1992), p. 45.

[92] Popper told Alfred Braunthal (19 July 1944 [28, 3]) that Mannheim had attended, but did not include him among the attendees mentioned in his *Autobiography*. Abba Lerner to Popper, 1951 (no exact date), Popper Archives (260, 1).

office at the LSE. They had not known each other in Vienna where Hayek had been head of the Institute for Trade Cycle Research. Popper now came to seek his advice on emigration. Hayek was a full professor; Popper was, outside the circle of scientific philosophers, an unknown. Renowned jurist Hans Kelsen, to whom Julius Kraft had introduced Popper in Paris, had given him a letter to Hayek, urging his case. He was anxious not to take up Hayek's time.[93] Respect for authority, however temporary, brought out his best behavior. They took to each other from their first meeting. Hayek remembered him as quiet, modest, pleasant, and exceptionally lucid.[94] He remembered Hayek as kind, attentive, helpful, and very serious. He left a formidable impression on Hayek. After hearing him in his seminar and reading *Logik*, Hayek was ready to vouch for him.

Popper fit well into Hayek's vision of a scholarly community committed to libertarian principles at the LSE. Fabian reformers, who had founded the LSE in 1895, intended it to serve as a progressive alternative to Cambridge, a center for economics and public administration with a collectivist orientation. They sought to overcome the hegemony of Marshall's classical individualist economics. But by the late 1920s, trends had been reversed. Keynesian economics was emerging at Cambridge, presaging the end of laissez-faire, and neoclassical liberal political economy was becoming predominant at the LSE. Robbins came under the influence of the Austrian marginalists, especially Hayek's teacher Ludwig von Mises (1881–1972). In 1931, he drafted Hayek to the LSE. The social science faculty still included prominent labor intellectuals, and even the economists numbered socialists, like Lerner, amongst them. But Robbins shaped the field. Together with Hayek he led the LSE resistance to Keynes.

In 1935–6, Hayek was wary of rising mathematical economics, and attributing it to positivist influences. (Morgenstern was attending Schlick's seminar and preaching the virtues of exact economics.) Hayek voiced his distaste for the circle to Austrian economist Gottfried Haberler. Haberler told him that the positivists were not all bad, offering *Logik der Forschung* as an example. It is not clear whether Hayek read *Logik* prior to meeting Popper, but when he did, he was enthralled. It seemed to him to dissolve the positivist myth of natural science threatening subjectivist economics.[95]

---

[93] Popper to Hayek, 30 April 1984, Popper Archives (305, 17); "Gespräch mit Sir Karl Popper (1991)," in Friedrich Stadler, *Studien zum Wiener Kreis*, p. 543. Hayek recalled Susan Stebbing introducing them: Hayek to Horton, 14 March 1945, Hayek Archives (44, 1).

[94] Hayek to the LSE Director, 7 August 1943; Hayek's evaluation of candidates for the readership in logic and scientific method, 14 March 1945, Hayek Archives, Hoover Institute (44, 1).

[95] For Hayek's recollections: *Markt, Plan, Freiheit. Franz Kreuzer im Gespräch mit Friedrich von Hayek und Ralf Dahrendorf* (Vienna: Deuticke, 1983), esp. p. 18; F. A. Hayek, *Hayek on Hayek*, ed. Stephen Kresge and Leif Wenar (Chicago: University of Chicago Press, 1988), pp. 49–51. (I owe the latter reference to John Watkins.) Hayek remembered having read *Logik* "some years before I made [Popper's] acquaintance" (actually, at most one year). Colin Simkin, *Popper's Views on Natural and Social Science*

A brilliant antipositivist philosopher of science was just what was ordered. To be sure, reading an early version of *The Open Society* in 1943, Hayek would learn that Popper was no libertarian, but he was adept at building alliances, tolerant of differences of opinion so long as they served his vision. Lerner's social market economy was preferable to Marxism. Hayek supported him. Popper's piecemeal social engineering was preferable to socialism. Hayek wanted him around. In 1936, there was no position available at the LSE, but Hayek would keep Popper in mind.

Hayek told Popper about the Academic Assistance Council, the major organization facilitating academic refugees' employment in British and Commonwealth universities. Established at the initiative of William Beveridge, director of LSE, in June 1933, the AAC worked closely with the American Refugee Aid Committee, and became the clearinghouse for jobs all over the world. It was supported by the Rockefeller Foundation.[96] Hayek introduced him to the council's head, Walter Adams, and its secretary, Esther Simpson.[97] Both were kind and helpful, but Popper did not qualify as a refugee: He had a job in Austria. They could provide him information on positions, but no financial assistance.

He found no job. With many Central European intellectuals knocking on Western doors, the times were difficult. He had never held an academic appointment in Austria and had no English publications. His entire reputation was founded on reports of his Austrian colleagues, the few English philosophers who had read *Logik der Forschung*, and, now, his English lectures and contacts. Apparently, some of his lectures did not go well. He often spoke from notes, in a language he had not mastered, to an audience unfamiliar with the material. He paid little attention to time limits or discussion etiquette. Even Stebbing, who thought the world of him, apparently rebuked him for his conduct. He complained to Eva Hempel that his reputation for being difficult had preceded him.[98] Alone, insecure, without money, in a foreign country whose manners no Viennese, he least of all, could understand, he let his worst character traits, a combination of arrogance and contentiousness, occasionally come out. He left England empty-handed. When the Hempels saw him in Copenhagen in June 1936, he was in despair.[99]

(Leiden: Brill, 1993), p. 2, believed that Hayek's "Economics and Knowledge," *Economica* 4 (1937): 33–54, a turning point in his career, reflects *Logik*'s influence.

[96] For the Academic Assistance Council see Claus-Dieter Krohn, *Intellectuals in Exile* (Amherst, Mass.: University of Massachusetts Press, 1993), chapter 3.

[97] *Autobiography*, p. 110; Popper to Walter Adams, 28 July 1969, Popper Archives (266, 20). Popper had already heard about the AAC from Helmer, who was seeking the council's help. (Popper to Carnap, 5 October 1936, Carnap Collection.)

[98] Eva Hempel to Karl Popper, 21 March 1937.

[99] Eva Hempel to Ina Carnap, 7 July 1936, Carnap Collection. Popper never had the aptitude for academic politics. In Copenhagen, he met Warren Weaver, a representative of the Rockefeller

He wanted badly to stay in England. It was foreign, but it was the first society he encountered where anti-Semitism rarely surfaced. Most English academics sympathized with Central European refugees. He would later recall their kindness and decency.[100] England was also his first experience of Western European democracy. Parliamentary institutions enjoyed a public consensus, rarely threatened by ideological divisions. It was a "breath of fresh air."

Still, his judgment of England was not uncritical. English politicians and public opinion, he thought, did not grasp the German threat. Churchill alone did. Rapid rearmament and a realistic foreign policy were necessary to deter German aggression. Instead, calls for rearmament were considered belligerent; Hitler's remilitarization of the Rhine a matter of German sovereignty; and the Hoare-Laval pact with Mussolini, which would have prevented Italy's shift to the German alliance, a cynical betrayal of Ethiopia.[101] Popper's analysis was astute, but he went far in accommodating anti-Nazi fascist regimes. Ernst Gombrich remembers that they both blasted the Austrian socialists for undermining Schuschnigg and doing the Nazis' job. "No one liked Schuschnigg," says Gombrich, "but he was not the problem; Hitler was."[102] Their judgment was shared by many nonfascist Austrians, but their criticism of the socialists repeated an unattractive pattern in Popper's life. Once again, he made the victims of aggression the target of criticism. The aggressors, the Christian-Socials, were beyond reach. He criticized "friends."

He left London for the Copenhagen congress, from June 21 to 26.[103] Officially, the congress's theme was causality in biology and physics, but most speakers ignored the theme and spoke about their own interests.[104] There were about eighty to one hundred participants, more than antici-

Foundation's European division, who was screening continental scholars for American universities. Unfamiliar with the operation, Popper never pursued him. *Autobiography*, p. 218 n. 165.

[100] Popper to Walter Adams, 28 July 1969 (266, 20); Popper, "On Reason and the Open Society," *Encounter* 38 (1972): 13–18.

[101] *Autobiography*, pp. 111–12; Popper, "Public Opinion and Liberal Principles" and "The History of Our Time: An Optimist's View," in his *Conjectures and Refutations* (New York: Basic Books, 1963), esp. pp. 347–8, 353, 371.

[102] Interview with Ernst Gombrich, 7 December 1983.

[103] Popper received a last-minute invitation. To Hempel, who visited London in early June, he complained that Neurath had not invited him. Neurath was surprised. He asked Jørgenson to clear a lecture on quantum mechanics for Popper with Bohr. Jørgenson (and Frank) advised against Popper speaking. Neurath offered him another lecture on June 10. "You fell silent after Paris," he wrote. "You need to cooperate more and keep in touch. Publication [of your Paris paper] would have done you good." Neurath to Popper, 10 June 1936, *Neurath Nachlaß*, University of Constance. (Original in the *Wiener-Kreis Stichting*, Haarlem, Netherlands.) See also: Neurath to Jørgenson, 5 June 1936; Frank to Neurath, June 1936.

[104] Thus, the congress ended having had sections on psychology, sociology, and scientific logic. J. B. S. Haldane gave a lecture on causal analysis in genetics. For the program: *Erkenntnis* 6 (1936): 275–442; briefly, Friedrich Stadler, *Studien zum Wiener Kreis*, pp. 416–18.

pated. Niels Bohr was the central figure, giving a lengthy opening talk that few understood. At the end of the first day, news arrived of Schlick's murder in Vienna. The shock was great, but the congress continued, devoting a session to Schlick's work. Popper spoke about syntax and semantics, using Tarski to argue the impossibility of one universal language, unified science, and protocols. Carnap's syntax must be part of a semantic metalanguage, he said, and so physicalist syntax was outside physicalist language.[105] He was allotted thirty minutes but spoke for seventy. Still, other speakers did the same, and the audience found his talk interesting. "It was the congress's high point," Hempel told Kaufmann.[106] Then came the discussion. An upset Neurath, eager to rescue physicalism, said sharply that Tarski might well be wrong. Popper responded arrogantly and angrily, way out of line, losing the admiration his talk had gained him. To the astounded Hempels he explained later that he had simply lost control. He was in a terrible state.

He departed Copenhagen on a slightly higher note. Victor Weisskopf was working with Bohr at his institute. He introduced Popper to Bohr, who invited him to stay for a couple of days to discuss quantum theory. Popper felt so obliged, and so defeated, that he offered little resistance to Bohr's views. Bohr's overwhelming and generous personality won him over, but he did make an effort to advance his statistical interpretation, and told Carnap later that he had reached an understanding with Bohr. His deference paid handsomely. The next fall, Bohr wrote him a reference.[107] He had now corresponded with Einstein, and engaged Schrödinger and Bohr, but still had no job. After the congress, he desolately returned to Vienna, traveling through Hitler's Germany, possessed more than ever with the wish to leave Central Europe for the Open Society.

Back in Vienna, he decided to try his luck in the United States. In August and September, he wrote Carnap, Feigl, Lazarsfeld, Charles Morris, and Nagel, asking them to organize a lecture tour for him so that he could come and search for a job. He mentioned to Carnap, who had just arrived in Chicago, that he would need an affidavit of support for a visa.[108] Ayer encouraged him, offering to introduce him to Quine. Woodger urged him, at the same time, to apply for two advertised positions, professor and lecturer in philosophy and psychology, at Canterbury University College in Christchurch, New Zealand. The Universities Bureau of the British Empire in London handled English applications. Walter Adams of the AAC

---

[105] Eva Hempel to Ina Carnap, 7 July 1936, Carnap Collection; Carl Hempel, circular letter reporting on the 1938 Cambridge congress, late summer 1938 (306, 2); Popper, "The Demarcation between Science and Metaphysics," in *Conjectures and Refutations*, p. 269 n. 44; Stadler, *Studien*, p. 510.

[106] Hempel to Kaufmann, 2 December 1936, *Kaufmann Nachlaß*.

[107] *Autobiography*, pp. 92–4, 110; Victor Weisskopf to Popper, 8 August and 17 October 1936, Popper Archives (360, 21); Popper to Carnap, 5 September 1936, Carnap Collection; Bohr's testimonial, Hayek Archives (44, 1).

[108] Popper to Carnap, 5 September and 20 September 1936, Carnap Collection.

promised to help but was pessimistic: New Zealanders preferred local or British candidates.[109] Meanwhile, Popper's job situation in Vienna was worsening. Whether at his request or at the authorities' decision, he was moved to a school in Meidling, in the twelfth district. (Hennie taught in the same district.) This was closer to home, but his curriculum now included instruction in composition, handicraft, and singing.[110] He was at his wits' end.

Popper's friends in the United States saw no urgency in his situation, however. Unlike Waismann and Zilsel, who had been fired, he at least had a job. It took no time to find out that he was a chronic complainer, unhappy wherever he was. Carnap knew that he was brilliant, but the problem was, as Ina Carnap said cruelly to Eva Hempel, that no one wanted him around where they were.[111] A newcomer, Carnap was not quite able to work the network yet. The year after, he tried strenuously, but unsuccessfully, to get a position for Hempel. Feigl, Lazarsfeld, and Nagel were junior scholars with little influence. But it was also true that no one had sufficiently warm feelings for Popper to dedicate themselves to helping him. The Carnaps were not going to sign an emigration affidavit, making them responsible for his welfare, should he fail to find a job. Carnap wrote Popper that he understood that "the ground in Vienna is burning under your feet," but any search for a U.S. position must be carefully prepared. Both he and his Chicago colleague Morris recommended that Popper publish in leading American journals. Carnap offered to find a translator. He urged Popper to apply to the Rockefeller Foundation and the IIE (Institute of International Education) through their European branches.[112] To Neurath he wrote at the end of October that he was looking for something suitable for Popper, but could do little for Waismann who had to complete his doctorate and learn English.[113] He was taking care of those closest and dearest to him first. He obtained a one-year Rockefeller fellowship for Hempel, and extended an invitation for Chicago for 1937 both to him and to Helmer (who had received a fellowship from the AAC). Years later, realizing that early emigration had saved his life, Popper almost suspected that circle members wanted him left behind.

---

[109] Walter Adams to Popper, 19 August 1936 (266, 20).

[110] Popper to Kaufmann, early November 1936; Kaufmann to Council, 28 October 1936, *Kaufmann Nachlaß*; Franz Wiehart to Popper, 18 May 1983, Hennie Popper subject file (391, 28). Hennie taught in the Hauptschule on Steinbauergasse.

[111] Ina Carnap to Eva Hempel, 15 November 1936, Carnap Collection.

[112] Carnap to Popper, 3 October 1936, Carnap Collection; Charles Morris to Popper, 10 October 1936, Popper Archives (329, 37).

[113] Carnap to Olga Hahn-Neurath, 31 October 1936, Carnap Collection. Neurath wrote Carnap from New York, 7 October 1936, that Popper, Waismann, and Zilsel were all in a bad way, and that he and Carnap needed to find something for them. Popper had told Neurath of his American search on August 3. Neurath asked repeatedly (July 2, August 20) for his "Copenhagen contribution and comments on the Bohr-Frank debate," but received none.

Felix Kaufmann came to the rescue. In October and November 1936, while in London, he negotiated with the Academic Assistance Council on Popper's behalf for a fellowship at Cambridge. (Popper hoped to get an English degree that would facilitate a permanent position in England.) Adams hinted that if Popper were to lose his teaching position in Austria for anything that could be deemed persecution, the council would extend its help.[114] Popper took an enormous risk: To qualify for assistance as a refugee, he resigned his position in mid-November 1936, and declared his intention to leave Austria.[115] The AAC responded immediately by offering him a one-year fellowship of £150. But it took another month before A. C. Ewing, through G. E. Moore's intervention, issued an invitation to Cambridge for him.[116] He was to give eight lectures in the spring of 1937, but focus on his own work so that publication and contacts might finally yield a permanent job. Kaufmann had meanwhile arranged for £50 to be put toward his initial expenses in London.[117] Thanking Kaufmann, a grateful Popper wrote:

> It is nothing new to me that you take care of me as only rarely a father does of his son. . . . I wish to take this opportunity to thank you once again for the great achievement you attained in your struggle on my behalf. Through it, you stepped into my life in a decisive manner. I shall never forget what you have done for me, and the way you did it.[118]

But Popper did forget Kaufmann. He undermined most father figures almost as soon as he had created them. A few years later, he concluded that Kaufmann had not dealt with him honestly.[119] Asked in 1982 for his "recollections of Felix Kaufmann," he responded curtly, creating the impression of a distant relationship, omitting any word of Kaufmann's tireless efforts on his behalf.[120] His emigration correspondence with Kaufmann has yet to make it into his archives. Other friends who helped with his job search also found that he could be ungrateful. Ayer provided him with contacts to British academics (especially G. E. Moore), and was a source of encouragement. In September 1936, after his *Language, Truth and Logic* had already

---

[114] Walter Adams to Kaufmann, 6 November and 11 November 1936, *Kaufmann Nachlaß*.

[115] Trying to move Carnap to action, Popper told him (18 November 1936) that he had "lost" his position.

[116] Adams to Kaufmann, 16 November and 28 November 1936; Popper to Kaufmann, 21 December 1936, with a transcribed copy of the Cambridge invitation, just received from A. C. Ewing, all in *Kaufmann Nachlaß*. The £150 was probably sufficient for Popper, but not for a couple. In Vienna, he made £100 a year, and his wife £92.

[117] Hayek to Popper, 7 December 1936, Popper Archives (305, 12); Popper to Kaufmann, 12 December 1936, *Kaufmann Nachlaß*. Popper intended to use the money to defray partially the costs of an English translation of *Logik der Forschung*.

[118] Popper to Kaufmann, 1 December 1936, *Kaufmann Nachlaß*.

[119] Popper to Braunthal, 19 July 1944, Popper Archives (28, 3).

[120] Popper to Ingeborg Helling, Kaufmann subject file, Popper Archives (387, 15).

become a success, Ayer expressed his admiration to Popper for "the intensity of your interest in philosophical problems which made me feel very much a dilettante."[121] This was precisely what Popper thought of him, and, in later years, he did not conceal it. Like Ayer, the Hempels recognized that Popper was a genius. "His book is so much better than anything we do around here," Eva Hempel wrote the Carnaps in December 1936. She persistently pushed them to help Popper, and remonstrated with Ina for her unkindness to him.[122] Both Hempels would write him encouraging letters in New Zealand. He rarely responded. In 1944, realizing that Hempel had capitalized on his explanation of causality in *Logik* without proper acknowledgment, he came close to charging him with plagiarism.[123] He often rewarded his best friends with pain.

Popper ended up, however, going to New Zealand, and not to England. While Kaufmann was negotiating with the AAC, he also assisted Popper with his New Zealand application.[124] Popper submitted testimonials by Bohr, Bühler, Carnap, Russell, and Tarski. (Russell had not read *Logik*, but was happy to write a brief note for the talented young émigré.) He used Moore and Woodger as additional referees, submitting all material by the end of October.[125] The chair of the appointment committee in England was leftist Christian philosopher John Macmurray, a friend of Karl Polanyi, who, apparently, pushed hard for Popper.[126] The board of Canterbury College rarely received applications from candidates as well published and supported. Still, they preferred a local anthropologist, Ivan Sutherland, for the professorship, and assigned Popper the lectureship.[127] On Christmas Eve 1936, he received a telegram offering him the position. The AAC grant was contingent on his not receiving another job offer, but he could probably have declined and gone to Cambridge.[128] He had to make up his mind in no time: He was expected in Christchurch at or near the beginning of the

---

[121] A. J. Ayer to Popper, 25 September 1936 (270, 35). A. J. Ayer, *Language, Truth and Logic* (London: Gollancz, 1936). The book popularized logical positivism in England.

[122] Eva Hempel to Ina Carnap, 7 December 1936, Carnap Collection.

[123] Popper, *The Open Society*, vol. 1, chap. 25, n. 7 (3), added in September 1944.

[124] So did also Ayer and Woodger: Woodger to Popper, 24 September 1936, Popper Archives (363, 17); Ayer to Popper, 12 October 1936 (270, 35).

[125] Application and resume: Popper Archives (366, 3). Testimonials: Bühler (406, 1); Carnap (406, 2); Russell (406, 4); Tarski (406, 5). Bühler's letter, in bad English, was complimentary; Carnap's was understated; Tarski's, written by Popper himself under Tarski's instructions, was laudatory.

[126] SPSL Secretary Esther Simpson related to Gombrich a few years later that Macmurray "was chiefly responsible for getting Popper his present job": Gombrich to Popper, 29 October 1943 (300, 2). Popper criticized Macmurray's historicism in *The Open Society*.

[127] Their letter to their office in London indicated that Sutherland and Popper were judged equal, but Sutherland was preferred on account of his psychological expertise and New Zealand citizenship. (Registrar of Canterbury College to the Secretary of the Universities Bureau of the British Empire, 21 December 1936, enclosure to Bartley's letter to Popper of 15 September 1983 [273, 3].)

[128] Walter Adams to Kaufmann, 16 November 1936.

academic year in the first week of March 1937.[129] There was security and better pay (£320 to £400 per annum) in the New Zealand position. The country was "halfway to the moon," but Popper, who had collected information about it, thought that both he and Hennie might take to it.[130] Someone else, such as his friend Friedrich Waismann, might use his Cambridge offer, he reasoned.[131] On January 5, 1937, he wrote Moore to thank him for the Cambridge offer – "I know how much I owe to you and I always shall keep it in mind" – and told him he was going to New Zealand.[132] He needed a clean break from his past, Austrian politics, and German culture.

In less than a month, in a mad rush that brought to a crescendo the drama of emigration and exile, Popper wrapped up his family's three generations in Vienna and left. The couple sold the little property they had, made whatever arrangements they could for their mothers, and bid goodbye to their friends.[133] Popper took as many books as he could – Harrop forewarned him about the bad library situation in New Zealand – and some of his manuscripts.[134] This was all he could save from his father's glorious library, his family's past fortune, and Vienna's flourishing culture. Only his philosophy would give testimony to their legacy. They traveled to London for final financial arrangements and documents, passing for one day through Brussels to see the Hempels and other friends. Five more days of mad rush (*Hetzjagd*) in London, and on February 4, 1937, they boarded the freighter *Rangitata* and sailed.[135]

Partir, say the French, *c'est mourir un peu* (There is a bit of death in depar-

---

[129] A. J. Harrop (representative of the University of New Zealand in London) to Popper, 2 January 1937 (366, 3).

[130] Popper to Kaufmann, two letters (no date), mid- to late October and early November 1936. He learned a lot about New Zealand from books: Questionnaire, Research Foundation for Jewish Immigration. "[B]ooks on New Zealand are very alluring. Karl fell for the country when he saw an illustrated N.Z. paper during his stay in England": Hennie Popper to Ernst and Ilse Gombrich, 28 March 1944 (300, 3).

[131] Popper, *Autobiography*, p.111; letters to Kaufmann, 4 February 1937 from London, and 14 February 1937 from aboard the ship to New Zealand, reporting his efforts in London on Waismann's behalf. This was no simple "transfer" of fellowship. But Kaufmann's and Popper's action on Waismann's behalf in the wake of Popper's decline gave Waismann a foot in the door.

[132] Popper to Moore, 5 January 1937, Moore Papers, Cambridge University Library.

[133] Shortly after the couple had left, Hennie's mother moved from their apartment to another residence in the thirteenth district, and later to Salzburg. I have seen no evidence of a real estate transaction taking place, and the Poppers seem not to have taken any furniture to speak of with them. The terms of the position provided £64 to £80 for transportation. Popper told Carnap (15 February 1937) that this covered about half of their moving expenses.

[134] The rest he deposited with his socialist friend, Dr. Otto Haas, who was arrested and sent to Dachau after the Anschluss and executed in 1944.

[135] Draft of *Autobiography*, Popper Archives (135, 1); Popper to Kaufmann, 4 February and 14 February 1937; Popper to Carnap, 15 February 1937, Carnap Collection. In London, Popper saw Hayek and AAC secretary Simpson, and spoke to Stebbing about Waismann.

ture). Unlike other intellectuals emigrating from Central Europe, Popper seemed to sense that he was leaving Austria forever. He wanted out – away from the political madness, from anti-semitism, from the daily struggle, to a quiet place where he could be a philosopher and where a harsh reality did not intrude every moment into philosophy. Yet he could not but feel ambivalent about leaving Vienna, and departed with a heavy heart. Austria was his homeland. "I loved Austria – there is no more beautiful country," he recalled.[136] Viennese culture, with its Central European links, was very much his culture, providing the sources, the impetus, and the major audiences for his work. He was apprehensive about intellectural isolation in New Zealand, and sorry to lose his friends. Please, keep sending me your works, he begged of them.[137] But the immediacy of a vital intellectual world and a bustling urban culture were never essential to his work. He wrote his major works in virtual isolation. In his dream, New Zealand was likely cast in the image of semirural Penn, to which he would withdraw from London a few years after his return to England in 1946.

Even the separation from family was not, it seems, free of ambivalence. The worst of it was leaving his sick mother whom he would not see again. He also left behind his sister Annie, who survived the war by escaping first to France in 1938, then to Switzerland in 1941. Left behind were also uncles, aunts, and cousins, some rather close to him, sixteen of whom would die at the Nazis' hands, before and during the war.[138] With those who survived the war he would maintain only a distant relationship. As a child, he said, he had dreamed of emigration. Why? At the time he enjoyed a secure and comfortable existence. Was it not the family that he wished to escape? His obstructed academic path and the triumph of fascism were undoubtedly the major reasons for his leaving Austria, but setting him apart from other émigrés, these reasons seemed to reinforce an earlier psychological drive. On the ship to New Zealand his relief about escaping Central Europe was immense.[139] Nothing seemed to die in him on his departure from Austria. Was Popper leaving his homeland, escaping the fatherland, or

---

[136] Draft of *Autobiography*, first version, sec. 20, Popper Archives (135, 1).

[137] Correspondence with Carnap, especially 15 February 1937; with Kaufmann, 1937–8; and with Hempel, 1937–8, Popper Archives (306, 2).

[138] Draft of *Autobiography*, first version, sec. 20, Popper Archives (135, 1). At the request of his secretary, Melitta Mew, Popper jotted down, at the bottom of a handwritten page of a draft manuscript, a list of his lost family members: "my father's two sisters [Camilla Kohn and Hedwig Mass], one with her husband, the other with two of her three daughters. The widow of my uncle Dr. Siegfried Popper and her brother-in-law (Auschwitz). [Dr.] Arthur Schiff and his wife [Margarethe] died (probably suicide), one daughter was deported, the other committed suicide [Hannah and Lili]. My mother's sister [Helene Schnabl] and her elder son (Auschwitz). My cousin Georg [Schiff] and his wife. My cousin Bruno disappeared in a mental hospital." I wish to thank Michelle-Irene Brundy of the University of Lille for the list.

[139] Popper to Carnap, 15 February and 17 April 1937; Popper to Kaufmann, 14 February and 17 April 1937.

neither? Was he really going into exile, or was he reaching for a promised land?

The true exile was Hennie. For her, emigration held no promise and was an unmitigated disaster. Austria was her homeland, Vienna her city. Married to an intellectual of Jewish origin, she recognized, in 1936, that life was becoming problematic. But she had no share in her husband's professional ambitions and would rather have stuck it out in Vienna. All the same, she did what he wanted, reluctantly bade her mother, city, and country good-bye, and accompanied him to New Zealand. Her Viennese teaching career interrupted, she never assumed another job. Wherever they went for the next half century, she was profoundly homesick.[140] Exile's bitterness showed in her personality. She was a loner, restless and unhappy. Never sharing fully in her husband's "Central European culture," she became as much a victim of its demise as he was. But his dreams migrated with him; hers were destroyed.

POPPER'S CRITIQUE OF AUSTRIAN SOCIALISM

"I am deeply concerned about the European developments," Popper told Kaufmann late in 1937. "There is no use in running away from Europe when one has left behind one's relatives and friends."[141] While he was living and writing in exile, his concerns remained focused on Central Europe. The Nazi occupation of Austria in March 1938 shook him badly. In his *Autobiography*, he dated his decision to publish a critique of Marxism to the Anschluss. Now that the anti-Nazi battle had been lost, he reasoned, there was no longer any fear that his critique would weaken the socialists. He proceeded to write "The Poverty of Historicism."[142]

His turn from the philosophy of science, logic, and probability to social science, political theory, and the history of philosophy was anything but natural. His knowledge of social science was limited, as was his interest in history. But at least since 1936, he was convinced that the model of natural science developed in *Logik der Forschung* could help solve major social

---

[140] *Heimweh*, or homesickness, was diagnosed as a killer disease by sixteenth-century doctors treating Swiss mercenaries away from their homes. Joseph Rykwert, "House and Home," *Social Research* 58 (Spring 1991): 53.

[141] Popper to Kaufmann, 27 November 1937, *Kaufmann Nachlaß*.

[142] *Autobiography*, p. 113. I have found no evidence for this line of thinking in Popper's correspondence. But he did complete a preliminary draft of "The Poverty of Historicism" by October 1938, and wrote "What is Dialectic?" over the antipodal summer break of 1938–9.

   In a letter to Hayek (14 March 1944, Hayek Archives [44, 1]), Popper suggested that he had virtually completed his critique of Marx by 1930: The critique of Marx "is mainly an elaboration of a draft begun in 1920 and brought to some kind of finality as early as 1927." In my interview, he dated the critique's completion to 1930. As the critique represented an application of *Logik*, this could hardly have been the case. His archives contain no draft of the critique prior to an early version of *The Open Society* from February 1943. Still, his political orientation had remained constant since the mid-1920s, and he certainly thought over some of the issues, and most likely wrote his thoughts down.

science problems. Moreover, he was persuaded that these problems were responsible for the political drama unfolding before his eyes. The "historicist" mistakes of Marxist parties accounted for their failure to resist fascism. He wanted to explain socialism's failure as a preamble to reconstructing social science and politics.

Decades later, historian Anson Rabinbach would inquire: "Why was Austrian Social Democracy, with its powerful organizational structure, its vast cultural and institutional framework and a private army double the size of the federal army unable to survive the onslaught of the right?"[143] Popper thought that he knew the answer all along: dogmatic Marxism. He, apparently, read no Marxist literature after 1922 and was not familiar with the Austro-Marxists' theoretical works.[144] Everything he said about the Austrian socialists could be, and probably was, derived from his early involvement with socialist reform, his talks with socialist friends, and his reading of the *Arbeiter-Zeitung*. (He commended the *Arbeiter-Zeitung* as an exceptional newspaper. It included theoretical debates.) He was an acute observer. His critique anticipated analyses of postwar historians, socialist and liberal alike.

Popper wrote his critique with enormous passion. He shared Marx's vision for humanity. He challenged socialism's methods, not its aim. He expressed admiration for the Viennese workers, and pain and anger at Red Vienna's destruction. He attributed the socialists' failure to their leaders' Marxist beliefs.[145] Well intentioned though the leaders were, they misled the workers and were responsible for their calamities. Marxism presented itself as the science of society, establishing inexorable historical laws. Truly, it offered a deficient historical interpretation, depriving Marxists of effective reform politics, and jeopardizing socialist victory. Three chapters of *The Open Society* explored the effects of Marxist doctrines on socialist strategy. Each concluded with a demonstration of the doctrines' disastrous consequences for the struggle against fascism.[146]

Marxism predicted that growing misery and antagonism under capitalism would lead to its final economic collapse, carrying the working class to power. This never occurred. When the Austrian and German socialists found themselves in power in 1918, they were at a loss. Marxism gave no guidelines for sharing political power with nonsocialists, no instructions for managing a capitalist economy. The Russian communists were as ill prepared as other Marxists. But they had "an irrational faith in Marxism," made a revolution, and carried it out through a bloody civil war. The German and Austrian socialists, in contrast, shrank from revolution, and fell back on

---

[143] *The Crisis of Austrian Socialism*, pp. 1–2.   [144] My interview with Popper, 26 January 1984.

[145] But note that he is at odds with currently popular critiques of the socialist leaders. He does *not* censure reform from above. "The socialists, convinced that the working class would come to rule, resolved to prepare them by education," Popper told Colin Simkin. Popper thought this was splendid. Communication from Colin Simkin, 28 May 1998.

[146] Karl Popper, *The Open Society*, chaps. 17–20, especially each chapter's final section; idem, "Vorwort" to Fritz Kolb, *Es kam ganz anders*, pp. 7–9.

an unrealistic scheme, socialization. What is there in Austria that we can socialize? Bauer asked economist Walter Schiff, Popper's uncle. Marxism provided no effective program to transform society. All it did was assure believers that, eventually, history would make their dream come true.[147]

To Popper:

> [The Marxist leaders] had learned from Marxism to organize the workers and to inspire them with a truly wonderful faith in their task, the liberation of mankind. But they were unable to prepare for the realization of their promises. . . . "Workers of all countries, unite!" – that exhausted their practical program. When . . . there was an opportunity of assuming the responsibility for a better world, when their hour had struck, they left the workers high and dry. . . . They waited for the promised suicide of capitalism.[148]

"Economic historicism" had even worse effects: It encouraged skepticism about the socialists' ability to reverse historical trends, weakening their resolve to fight fascism. Socialist leaders interpreted fascism as the bourgeoisie's last stand, and welcomed the Great Depression as capitalism's final gasp. They fought the fascists halfheartedly. This demoralized the workers, and they lost their faith in the leadership. Too late, the leaders recognized their mistake. The Viennese workers offered a heroic, but badly organized, resistance to the fascist dictatorship and were crushed. Their leaders failed them, wrote Popper; "they functioned like cicerones, as guides through the hills (and valleys) of history rather than as political leaders of action."[149]

Most destructive was the socialists' ambiguous stance on democracy and violence. Popper traced it to the positions of Marx and Engels on the dictatorship of the proletariat. In an erudite discussion, he concluded that both had remained ambivalent about violence. Although they had a rather poor view of bourgeois democracy with its "formal freedoms," they insisted, at least in some of their writings, that the working class would adhere to democratic rules. But they expected that, faced with an electoral victory of the working class, the bourgeoisie would initiate a counterrevolution, forcing the socialists to establish a dictatorship. Even when they conceded that the proletariat might come to power peacefully – in Great Britain, for example – they still spoke of electoral victory as "the conquest of power," a term connoting violence and illegality.[150]

The Russian communists were open about their contempt for democracy. The Austrian socialists, in contrast, preserved the ambiguity of Marx

[147] Popper, *The Open Society*, vol. 2, chap. 18, esp. sec. 5, pp. 132–4; Fritz Kolb, "Popper und der Sozialismus," pp. 40–9.

[148] Popper, *The Open Society*, vol. 2, pp. 133–4.

[149] Ibid., chap. 18, n. 22: Popper is paraphrasing Karl Kraus's statement.

[150] Ibid., chap. 19, pp. 135–54. Having witnessed the first electoral successes of socialist parties in the

and Engels. They acted democratically and proved incapable of violence. They ought, said Popper, to have joined "the battle of democracy," allied themselves with democratic bourgeois elements, and stated that they would use force only to defend democracy.[151] Instead, they remained forever equivocal. They emphasized democracy's limitations, and made the workers suspicious of it. The 1926 Linz Program virtually paraphrased Engels: "[I]f the bourgeoisie should resist the social revolutionary change . . . then the working class would be compelled to break the resistance of the bourgeoisie by the instrument of dictatorship."[152] This was the worst strategy possible. The threat of violence permitted Seipel and Dollfuss to use the government's resources to prepare a coup, mobilize the frightened bourgeoisie, then choose the opportune moment to strike. They chose wisely, catching the workers in a vulnerable position. The "ambiguity of violence" was a prescription for disaster.

Anticipating bourgeois violence, the socialists helped bring it forth: a self-fulfilling prophecy. Having threatened violence, they not only lost the moral grounds but also played into the fascists' hands. They scared away potential bourgeois voters. The bourgeoisie, convinced that the socialists would force socialization, turned to the fascists. "Every opposition," said Popper cruelly, "has the majority it deserves."[153] The socialists armed the workers, used strikes as a political weapon, and inflamed the atmosphere with revolutionary rhetoric: "The[y] taught the theory of class war to the workers, but the practice of it to the reactionary bourgeoisie."[154] Their policy was "talking big and doing nothing in the face of real and increasing danger to democratic institutions. It is a policy of talking war and acting peace: and it taught the fascists the invaluable method of talking peace and making war."[155]

Popper's critique of Austrian socialism demonstrated brilliantly how Marxism confined the socialists' intellectual universe, entrapping them in a conceptual system that limited their capacity to adapt. He accomplished his goal: demonstrating that Marxism was implicated in the Austrian socialists' major policy mistakes. But he underestimated the constraints under which the socialists worked, ignored Austro-Marxist contributions to the analysis of fascism, and misjudged the German "bourgeoisie." He placed a greater share of responsibility for the catastrophe on Marxism and

1890s, Engels insisted that the "gentlemen of the bourgeoisie," not the workers, would be the first to shoot. Marx never put things quite so clearly. Marxian and Engelsian ambiguities were thus different. I owe this clarification to Robert Paxton.

[151] Both Popper and the socialists developed theories of defensive violence, committing the working class to use force only in case of a coup against a democracy. However, Popper limited the working class to restoring democracy; Bauer spoke about establishing a dictatorship.

[152] *Protokoll des sozialdemokratischen Parteitages 1926* (Vienna: Volksbuchhandlung, 1926), p. 248.

[153] *The Open Society*, vol. 2, p. 150.   [154] Ibid., p. 153.   [155] Ibid., p. 152.

the socialists than was theirs. His critique was acute, but severe, and at points unfair.

Marxist theory did leave the transition from capitalism to socialism in the dark. But any party reaching power on the empire's ruins would have experienced a loss of direction. (All parties did.) The Austrian socialists adapted quickly, and passed, in 1919–20, comprehensive social legislation that protected the workers until the early 1930s, sustaining them under hostile governments. Socialization proved, indeed, unsuccessful, but the problems were daunting. Bauer recognized that the major problem in 1919 was how to spur production, not who owned the factories, and acted accordingly. To argue that the socialist leaders "left the workers high and dry" is simply untrue.[156]

The socialists were, indeed, uncomfortable exercising power in a situation for which Marxist theory provided no guidelines. This partially explains their reluctance to participate in a coalition after 1920. Bauer saw opposition as the natural stance of a socialist party in bourgeois society. He underestimated the threat of leaving the bourgeoisie in control of the state. In *The Austrian Revolution* (1923), he argued that the working class and the bourgeoisie reached an equilibrium of forces (*Gleichgewicht der Klassenkräfte*).[157] The state was no longer a bourgeois instrument. The socialist infrastructure, especially Red Vienna, would protect the working class against aggression, and further growth would carry them back to power. He was delighted at the prospect of a peaceful transition because he had neither taste nor nerve for violence. He was enough of a political realist, however, to recognize that in a crisis situation, the government would use force. The *Schutzbund*, the unions, and the party were his answer. He trusted that the state would not conduct a war against society. He was proved dead wrong. Popper's argument about the adverse consequences of the Marxist theory of the state holds, but even here, Bauer modified Marxist concepts in precisely the direction Popper suggested: recognition of the relative autonomy of politics, and a peaceful transition to socialism.

The debilitating effects of the Marxist theory of history were most evident in socialist policies in the early 1930s. The socialists thought that the current political and economic crises presaged capitalism's collapse. They did not realize that fascism, not socialism, lurked behind. They refused to enter a coalition, and left the government at the *Heimwehr*'s mercy. Later, they viewed Dollfuss's coup and the Nazis' seizure of power as the bourgeois dictatorship they had anticipated in the twilight of capitalism. Popper correctly discerned their defeatism: Democracy could not be saved. His cri-

---

[156] For Bauer on socialization: *Der Weg zum Sozialismus* (Vienna: Wiener Volksbuchhandlung, 1919).

[157] Otto Bauer, *Die österreichische Revolution* (Vienna: Wiener Volksbuchhandlung, 1923). (*The Austrian Revolution* [London: Parsons, 1925].) Bauer further developed Marx's theory of the state, as presented in *The Eighteenth Brumaire of Louis Bonaparte*, trans. Eden & Cedar Paul (New York: International Publishers, 1926).

tique of their ineptitude in fighting the fascists was uncharitable, but it was correct. If he disregarded objective constraints on their actions – in 1933–4, any response to fascist provocations would have triggered, and eventually did trigger, a government attack – it is also true that, in hindsight, they had nothing to lose, and should have fought. They grossly misunderstood fascism and "gazed at [it] rising like hypnotized rabbits."[158] But, then, fascism was the great surprise of the twentieth century.

During the 1930s, Bauer made strides in understanding fascism. He distinguished among various fascist constituents: the paramilitary déclassés, the petty bourgeoisie, the nationalist intelligentsia, and the big capitalists. He described how their interests and ideologies converged and diverged at different stages in the development of fascism. Socialist tendencies predominated in fascism prior to the seizure of power. From the very beginning (1919–20), however, the capitalists used the movement to break the working class. They succeeded in rolling back the revolution in the early postwar years, but at least in Germany and Austria, the workers were strong enough to limit their influence. For a while, a balance of powers existed, and the socialists used parliamentary democracy to defend the working class. Growing economic difficulties in the late 1920s made the industrialists shift their support to the fascists. Catching the workers at their weakest moment, the fascists overthrew democracy. Once in power, the big industrialists (and, in Italy, landowners) moved to control the government, weeding out socialist elements. In the last analysis, fascism served the upper bourgeoisie.[159]

Aspects of Bauer's theory, especially his insistence on capitalist control of fascist juntas, are certainly debatable. Others, for example, his social analysis of early fascism, have by now become commonplace in historiography. Marxism did confine socialist horizons, but it also provided analytical tools. Popper's summary judgment on Austro-Marxism was harsh.

Popper underestimated the socialists' commitment to bourgeois democracy. They repeatedly came to its rescue in times of crisis. In 1919, 1927, and 1933, when the threats of communist revolution, civil war, and Nazism hung over the republic, they offered to enter a coalition to ride over the crisis. Bauer argued consistently against violence, and spoke warmly of parliamentary democracy as embodying civilization's best ideals.[160] His doubts about Austrian democracy derived as much from his assessment of the Austrian right as from his Marxist heritage.

Indeed, Popper's view of the interwar bourgeoisie seems less sound than Bauer's. His assumption that "the influence [of fascist groups] within the

---

[158] Ernst Gombrich to Popper, 11 August 1943, Popper Archives (300, 2).

[159] Otto Bauer, "Der Faschismus," *Der Sozialistische Kampf* 1(1938): 75–83. The basic tenets appeared already in *Zwischen zwei Weltkriegen* (1936).

[160] Even in *Zwischen zwei Weltkriegen*, where he admitted the failure of previous nonviolent strategies, he insisted that some others may have worked.

so-called bourgeoisie will depend largely on the policy adopted by the workers' parties" was downright wrong.[161] The Austrian middle classes were not potentially democratic. The German socialists were moderate, and this made no difference in the middle classes' disposition toward them, or toward the Weimar republic. With the Great Depression, they flocked to the Nazis. Some of Popper's policy proposals represented wishful thinking. The socialists could make no major inroads into the bourgeoisie. (They had some success among the Jewish middle classes in Vienna, but it is doubtful they could extend it further.) Toward the end of the republic, they tried to form democratic alliances with the bourgeoisie and were rebuffed. Not socialist ambiguity on violence produced a bourgeois coup. Failure to respond to violence did.

Contrary to Popper, the "reactionary bourgeoisie" needed no lesson on how to conduct a class war. Dollfuss exemplified, indeed, the duplicitous conduct of "talking peace and making war," but he did not learn his tactics from the socialists. Popper turned victims into aggressors: The socialists were said to have encouraged and instructed the fascists. Still, "talking war and acting peace" was Austrian socialism's Achilles' heel. "Bauer always weighed the alternatives carefully, but never failed to come to the conclusion that no real action on the part of the Social Democrats could effect a decisive change in the situation," writes Rabinbach.[162] The socialist leaders were flowers of the European intelligentsia, humanists and visionaries, lovers of peace and civility, an inimitable model of political leadership. They were not fighters. An insufficient commitment to democracy was *not* their problem; an excessive one was. Had the Nazi bullet that killed Chancellor Dollfuss on July 25, 1934, been fired earlier by a socialist, democracy might have had a fighting chance. "Even a temporary victory of the working class, in a country as small as Austria," said Ernst Fischer, "would have encouraged and empowered anti-fascist forces throughout Europe."[163]

Popper's critique mentioned, at points, the Russian communists and, on other occasions, the German communists and socialists. But the Austrian socialists provided most of his evidence, and his theoretical discussions were most relevant to Austria. In dismissing Marxist attempts to restore autonomy to politics through the theory of class equilibrium, he implicated Bauer in all but name.[164] His discussion of Engels's "ambiguity of violence" addressed the 1926 Linz Program without mentioning it.[165] He was settling disputes with the Austrian socialists. Why did he not mention them by name? He referred to them as the "Social Democrats of Central Europe," "the moderate wing of Marxism," "certain more 'radical' Social Democratic parties," and "the Marxist movement in Central Europe."[166] These labels

[161] Popper, *The Open Society*, vol. 2, p. 152.   [162] *The Crisis of Austrian Socialism*, p. 45.

[163] *Erinnerungen und Reflexionen* (Reinbek bei Hamburg: Rowohlt, 1969), p. 248.

[164] Popper, *The Open Society*, vol. 2, pp. 111–12.   [165] Ibid., pp. 147–9.

[166] Ibid., pp. 133, 111–12 and 147, 153, and 319–20 n. 20, respectively.

meant little more than the interwar Austrian and German socialists.[167] Why did Popper use general rather than specific categories? Why did he not identify the political parties and personalities who were the targets of his criticism?

Popper wished to make his critique of Marxism as universal as possible. The use of general categories made it possible to present a broad critique, while drawing on the Austrian experience. Moreover, the Austrian party was not made of one skin: It included reformists and radicals, representing conflicting Marxist positions. Using general categories, such as "moderate" and "radical," that applied to the German and Russian Marxists as well, Popper was able to address both positions without entering into party politics. But avoiding specificity also reflected his effort to make the critique as inoffensive as possible. He was writing about friends and victims of fascism. He asked Braunthal in 1943 if there was anything unfair in his comments about Central Europe: "I shall cut it out," he promised.[168] He need not have worried. Braunthal, a thorough Marxist in the 1920s, had meanwhile moved just as far from Marxism as Popper had. He understood well who Popper's targets were, and agreed wholeheartedly.[169]

Different considerations moved Popper to show restraint in his criticism of the Soviet communists. He cared little about Russia. His criticism was mingled with occasional praise, and reflected respect for Soviet achievements. When Braunthal asked him to apply his critique to Russia, he responded that he simply did not know enough.[170] The Great Purges and Stalin were not mentioned even once.[171] Russia carried the brunt of the war against Hitler. He would not jeopardize the war effort.

In later years, Popper spoke of the intimate relationship between his Austrian socialist experience and the critique of Marxism. In his *Autobiography*, he directed the reader to *The Open Society* to explain why he felt

---

[167] The first and second references were to the Austrian and German socialists; the third, to the Austrian alone; the fourth, primarily to the Austrian socialists, possibly also to the German. At one point (pp. 153 and 326 n. 39), Popper referred to "the radical wing of Marxism" as including not only the communists but "even some of the leaders of the Viennese workers."

[168] Popper to Braunthal, 20 July and 12 October 1943, Popper Archives (28, 2). See also: Popper to Gombrich, 19 July 1943 (300, 2).

[169] Popper's caution also reflected ambivalence. He was attached to Red Vienna and socialist ideals, but angry about the socialist leaders and pseudoscientific Marxism. He preferred to avoid confrontation. Similarly, in later years, he criticized Hayek for his utilitarian justification of capitalism, without mentioning his name. (Popper, Preface to *Miseria dello storicismo*, trans. Carlo Montaleone, 2d ed. [Milano: Feltrinelli, 1975]. I owe this reference to Jeremy Shearmur. Popper, "Vorwort" to Fritz Kolb, *Es kam ganz anders*, pp. 8–9.)

[170] Braunthal to Popper, 24 August 1943; Popper to Braunthal, 14 December 1943 (28, 2). See, however, his brief book reviews on Russian schools and Soviet educational policies: "Pädagogische Zeitschriftenschau," *Die Quelle* 82 (1932): 712–33. I discuss Popper and Soviet Russia further in Chapter 9.

[171] "The Poverty of Historicism, II" *Economica* 11 (1944): 132 (p. 91 of the book edition; see also Index, p. 165, under "Stalin") included an opaque reference to Stalin. Popper rewrote this part in 1944 after having read Hayek on economic planning.

apprehensive about Austrian socialism and democracy from early on. But his efforts to underplay the "Austrian connection" were successful. During the cold war, his critique of socialism became the standard anti-Marxist critique. Convinced of an imminent communist threat to democracy, postwar liberals regarded the Marxist equivocation on democracy and violence as dangerous. Like Popper, they wanted socialists to give up Marxism and form a wide democratic alliance, this time against communism rather than fascism. Adherence to democratic rules became the ultimate test for any party's political legitimacy. Popper's critique catered to the postwar outlook.

Postwar Austrian socialists remembered the interwar party, especially Otto Bauer, with embarrassment. It ended in a political disaster, and represented a different type of socialism from the postwar one. Interwar socialists were more radical; most of their leaders were of Jewish origin. Karl Renner, the Second Republic's first president – a reformist who took no part in the February 1934 uprising, a nationalist who voted for the Anschluss, an Aryan who promoted Austria as Hitler's first victim – became a hero to postwar socialists. They participated for two decades in a grand coalition with the conservatives, including previous Christian-Social leaders.[172] They were anticommunist. Bauer and the interwar party did not fit the new mold. Their efforts to pave a third way between communism and reformism seemed out of place in a world sharply divided between "democrats" and "totalitarians." Failing to place them on either side of the totalitarian divide, postwar socialists and liberals regarded them, like Popper, as "ambiguous," insufficiently committed to democracy, prone to revolutionary rhetoric. They preferred to forget them. It took both the New Left and a young generation, no longer invested in protecting Austria from its past, to recover Austro-Marxism and Red Vienna.

The Open Society was the work of an unorthodox socialist coming to terms with his ambivalence about socialism. The critique worked well as therapy: Once completed, Popper separated himself from the Austrian socialist past, and embarked on a new political course in the West. The nexus of progressivism and socialism was unique to Vienna. In England, Popper felt comfortable almost with the entire political spectrum. His social

---

[172] The postwar historiographical consensus among conservatives and socialists in Austria held both interwar parties responsible for democracy's collapse. See: Heinrich Benedikt, ed., *Geschichte der Republik Österreich* (Munich: Oldenbourg, 1954); Norbert Leser, *Zwischen Reformismus und Bolschewismus* (1968). This remains the view of most historians in the West: Mary MacDonald, *The Republic of Austria, 1918–1934* (London: Oxford University Press, 1946); Klemens von Klemperer, *Seipel* (1972); Barbara Jelavich, *Modern Austria: Empire and Republic, 1800–1986* (New York: Cambridge University Press, 1987). The New Left challenged this consensus: Hans Hautmann and Rudolf Kropf, *Die österreichische Arbeiterbewegung vom Vormärz bis 1945* (Vienna: Europa, 1974); Tom Bottomore and Patrick Goode, eds., *Austro-Marxism* (Oxford: Clarendon Press, 1978); Anson Rabinbach, *The Crisis of Austrian Socialism* (1983).

circle was no longer socialist. Hayek, an avowed antisocialist, was a close friend. They never agreed completely, but Popper found some of his arguments persuasive. He became increasingly conservative and lost interest in social questions. "Few people now living in one of the Western democracies," he said in his *Autobiography*, "know what poverty meant at the beginning of the twentieth century."[173] The abject poverty of fin-de-siècle Vienna had disappeared (or so, at least, he believed), and he was content. Little was left of the enchanting socialist vision of interwar Vienna.

[173] *Autobiography*, p. 9.

Chapter 8

Social Science in Exile, 1938–1939

The world the Poppers encountered upon landing in New Zealand in March 1937 was radically different from anything they previously had known. In the 1930s New Zealand was still a provincial colonial society, almost "cut away from the world" *(abgeschnitten,* as Popper complained profusely). Foreign economic and intellectual contacts were virtually limited to Britain, a five-week sail away (there were no air connections). Correspondence with Europe and the United States was conducted at three-month intervals.[1] Christchurch was at the time a town of one hundred thousand people, and Canterbury College was the smallest of the four colleges of the University of New Zealand, with an enrollment of about eleven hundred students. The college was underfinanced, short of staff, and without adequate academic facilities, neither a research library, nor laboratories, nor large lecture halls. It had close ties to the town, and the board thought of its mission in terms of basic education and practical training for careers in the trades and professions. Faculty research was considered an extracurricular activity, never funded and often discouraged, a far cry, indeed, from any European institution of higher learning.[2]

Nonetheless, Popper seemed initially to settle down well. He was finally a full-time philosopher, had a job, enjoyed lecturing, and was a member of an academic community. Hennie, in contrast, was miserable from the start. She was alone in a foreign country, without a permanent house or a job. She did not fit in. Local informality of manners and the absence of class distinctions did not appeal to her as they did to her husband. He told Kaufmann that the people were "incredibly nice."[3] "New Zealand was the best-governed country in the world, and the most easily governed."[4]

He exaggerated the ease of governing New Zealand. The dominion went through difficult times during the Great Depression. It had a militant labor tradition that reached a peak in the unemployment riots of 1932. Natural bounty and increasingly mechanized farming had previously allowed for a

---

[1] "Airmail" (through Australia) was expensive and took two to three weeks in each direction. During much of the war, it was not available.

[2] W. J. Gardner, E. T. Beardsley, and T. E. Carter, *A History of the University of Canterbury, 1873–1973* (Christchurch, N.Z.: University of Canterbury, 1973).

[3] Popper to Kaufmann, 27 November 1937, *Kaufmann Nachlaß, Sozialwissenschaftliches Archiv,* University of Constance.

[4] Popper, *Autobiography,* p. 112.

comparatively high standard of living, but the economy was dependent on world prices for its major agricultural exports. As prices for farm products fell in the early 1930s, New Zealand slipped into a crisis. Economic discontent brought the Labor Party to power for a fourteen-year rule. Through welfare reforms, and projects such as public housing, the government reshaped society. Popper was impressed. Life in New Zealand reinforced his conviction that the Open Society was possible.[5] All the same, Central Europe remained a focal concern. New Zealand was not mentioned even once in *The Open Society* and "The Poverty of Historicism."

Popper did not come to New Zealand with a political project in mind. His excursion into political philosophy was a lengthy but unplanned detour that lasted only for the duration of the war. He was "neither by inclination nor by training a student of society or politics."[6] If he thought for a moment in 1943 of becoming a political philosopher, by the war's end he was impatient to move back into his natural habitat, the sciences. His political project was a response to the European catastrophe. He moved from science to politics by way of logical and methodological critiques of political ideologies. By late 1938 he had written a draft of "The Poverty of Historicism" and, over the antipodal summer break of 1938–9, he completed "What is Dialectic?" With the outbreak of the war, he began conceiving of a new political philosophy. It was no coincidence that epistemological and methodological critiques gave rise to a political philosophy. Viennese intellectuals have long believed that "problems of logic and methodology have a close bearing on the life of every individual and on the fate of our entire culture."[7]

LIFE IN EXILE, 1937–1939

Popper was first appointed a lecturer in education and philosophy. The process leading to his appointment reveals much about the college. The education department, which played an important role in a college oriented toward community service, shared its staff, from the 1920s on, with philosophy. In the mid-1930s, plans were made to shift positions from philosophy to psychology, but a few administrators, as well as the local presbytery, whose elders exercised influence on the college, intervened, urging that "it would be a disaster if philosophy were replaced by one or more of the modern systems of psychology. . . . Those based on sex psychology

---

[5] Peter Munz suggests (E-mail communication, 25 February 1997) that Popper was largely oblivious to his surrounding. Colin Simkin believes that New Zealand's welfare reforms served nonetheless as one model for Popper's "piecemeal social engineering."

[6] Popper, "Response Upon Receiving the Award of the Fondation Tocqueville" (5 November 1984), Popper Archives (253, 1).

[7] Ludwig von Mises, *Epistemological Problems of Economics* (Princeton, N.J.: Van Nostrand, 1960), p. xvii.

would be most objectionable since . . . [they] may explain and suit the crank but are not suitable for the sons and daughters of commonsense people."[8] The plans were canceled, and in 1936 a unified department of education and philosophy was established. Two new professors were appointed as chairs of education and philosophy, respectively, and Popper as a lecturer. His senior colleague, I. G. L. Sutherland (1897–1952), taught psychology and had no interest in philosophy. He left Popper in charge of the philosophy curriculum. This meant greater freedom, but also an increased burden.

The New Zealand school year began in early March and ended in late October. There were three ten-week terms, with a week's vacation between them. The department had eighty to one hundred students, many with a major interest in theology. They expressed shock when Popper told them that he doubted scientific ethics existed, apart from psychology and history.[9] Few students, if any, were as well educated as Viennese gymnasium graduates. Many were part-time students with jobs, and most lectures were held in the evening to facilitate their attendance. The board of the University of New Zealand set the curriculum for all four colleges, and there were joint examinations at the end of each year. Popper taught six courses: two lecture courses in logic, and one each in ethics, the history of philosophy, and introduction to philosophy, as well as one seminar, led initially by Sutherland. (Popper complained of its low level: "The idea is to get the students to read," he told Carnap.) Aristotle's syllogisms and Mill's inductive method were the major topics in logic. Popper had to teach them, but enlivened his courses with a good dose of contemporary material, ridiculing Carnap's views on induction and probability and elucidating Tarski's theory of truth. He did also a fair amount of tutorial work, both with students writing papers and those needing special help.

By all accounts, Popper was an exceptional teacher, a wonderful lecturer, drawing enthusiastic responses from varied audiences. He lectured from notes, rarely repeating himself. Students saw him thinking his way through the material, thoroughly familiar to him but new to them. He modeled his lectures on his view of the history of science. Each began with a problem. He constructed a theory to solve it, discussed it, compared the solution to those of other philosophers, and, at the end, invited questions and criticism. The lectures, delivered in a thick Viennese accent, were simple in structure, clear, and direct. He had an unusual capacity to simplify esoteric thought and dramatize philosophical problems, using metaphors, such as "bucket" and "searchlight," to describe theories of the mind. After his first

---

[8] W. J. Gardner et al., *A History of the University of Canterbury*, p. 261.

[9] Popper to Carnap, 17 April 1937, Carnap Collection, Archives of Scientific Philosophy, University of Pittsburgh. Popper would refine his position in *The Open Society*.

(and also second) year, he eagerly awaited exam results. His students were very successful. All passed.[10]

He brought to Canterbury the European tradition of academic research. This was exceptionally difficult. The library's holdings were 15,000 books (about the size of his father's library). They included no more than forty philosophy books written in the twentieth century; the latest was ten years old.[11] The latest physics book was from 1928. There was one philosophical periodical: *Mind*. (Popper ordered *Philosophy of Science*.) There was no catalogue. The administration discouraged research: Time spent on research was filched from teaching. Popper's research became a source of much misunderstanding. After one year, he told Hempel that he would have to conceal his research activities because his colleague Sutherland frowned upon them. During the war, Sutherland made Popper pay for paper Hennie used to type his book. In 1945, Popper and fellow scientists would lead a rebellion that would change the situation for the better in postwar years.

To the college's young scientists, Popper's arrival on campus was a breath of fresh air. They had so far had little contact with the philosophy department. Now they had the avant-garde of scientific philosophy among them, and they were eager to learn. With no inhibition, Popper propagated his philosophy, organizing research seminars for the faculty. In 1938 he gave a lecture, "Philosophy for Scientists," to the New Zealand Royal Society. It was enthusiastically received. Beginning in 1939, he taught a course on "Science in the Making" to the Workers' Educational Association. (This replicated the Viennese tradition of *Volksbildung*, and he badly needed the extra income.) His close friends in Canterbury were physical chemist Hugh Parton (the only professor; the others were, like him, lecturers); geologist Robert Allen (also a neighbor); physicist Frederick White; economists Harold Larsen (to late 1938) and Colin Simkin; lawyer Alan Reed; George Roth, an Austrian pharmacist whom Popper got appointed as a radiation technician at the Cancer Research Institute, and who taught physics for the post; and Otto Frankael, a German émigré botanist who worked at the Wheat Research Institute, a downtrodden, two-story wooden building on the second floor of which Popper had his office. Philosopher John Findlay from Dunedin made the trip to Christchurch many times to converse with

[10] Popper to Carnap, 7 March 1938, Carnap Collection; typed notes, taken at Popper's lectures on the history of philosophy in 1941, Canterbury College file, Popper Archives (366, 24; see also: 366, 20); testimonials by rector James Hight (1943) and philosopher J. N. Findlay (1944), Hayek Archives, Hoover Institute (44, 1); Gardner et al., *A History of the University of Canterbury*, esp. p. 263; Peter Munz, "Transformation in Philosophy Through the Teaching Methods of Wittgenstein and Popper," in *The Search for Absolute Values and the Creation of the New World*, Proceedings of the Tenth International Conference on the Unity of the Sciences, vol. 2 (New York: International Cultural Foundation, 1982).

[11] They included Russell and Whitehead, but not even all of *Principia Mathematica*.

him. Popper also corresponded with Auckland mathematician Henry Forder, who showed interest in modern logic. In short, he was generally well liked around the college, had a small congenial community around him, and made quite a name for himself, first around town, later throughout the academic community in New Zealand.[12]

Not everyone was happy with Popper. He initially deferred to Sutherland, who welcomed him to the department. To Carnap and Kaufmann he reported, shortly after his arrival, that Sutherland was a very fine person who treated him as an equal, and that they were getting along wonderfully.[13] The idyll did not last. Rank and pay-scale differences between professors and lecturers at Canterbury were pronounced.[14] Trained as a moral psychologist at the University of Glasgow, Sutherland had become, by the mid-1930s, a cultural anthropologist, an early champion of Maori ethnic revival.[15] Contemporaries remembered him as an especially kind person, but he was not Popper's intellectual equal. Popper thought it outrageous that Sutherland was above him, better paid, and he could not conceal his feelings for long. Sutherland, jealous and insecure, felt threatened. Mutual distrust developed. Within a year, the department split into two programs, but departmental conflicts kept increasing nonetheless. Popper made it no secret that he had no interest in New Zealand affairs and read only foreign news in the paper. (There was exceedingly little of this, he complained, only one page of political news, mostly about New Zealand and England, virtually nothing about Central Europe.) Sutherland took offense at what he probably regarded as snobbism toward the provincials. He vowed, apparently, to push Popper out of New Zealand and made his life miserable.[16]

Karl and Hennie both complained bitterly, from the start, that they were in financial straits. Eva Hempel wondered how it was that other lecturers

---

[12]　For details on Popper's colleagues, and other aspects of Popper's life in New Zealand, I am indebted to Colin Simkin.

[13]　Popper to Carnap, 17 April 1937; Popper to Kaufmann, 17 April 1937, *Kaufmann Nachlaß, Sozialwissenschaftliches Archiv*, University of Constance.

[14]　Professors earned up to 1,000 NZ pounds, double the amount of lecturers. Popper reminisced about rank and status differences in a preparatory chronology for the *Autobiography* (405, 1).

[15]　I. L. G. Sutherland, *The Maori Situation* (Wellington, N.Z.: Tombs, 1935), published through the New Zealand Native Affairs Commission; I. L. G. Sutherland, ed., *The Maori People Today: A General Survey* (London: Oxford University Press, 1940), issued under the auspices of the New Zealand Institute of International Affairs & the New Zealand Council for Educational Research. Sutherland became a hero to the Ngati Porou people. (J. C. Beaglehole et al., "I. L. G. Sutherland, 1897–1952," *Journal of Polynesian Society* 61 [1952]: 120–9). Roger Sandall argues in "Karl Popper," *Salisbury Review* 15 (1996): 12–17 that the Popper–Sutherland tension was due, in part, to ideological disagreement about ethnic communal life. (Popper sought to open "closed societies" and viewed fascism as a revival of "tribalism.")

　　David Miller kindly sent me the Sutherland obituaries, and Peter Munz drew my attention to Sandall's article. Together with John Watkins, they provided helpful hints to the Sutherland question.

[16]　Popper Archives (366, 5); communication from Peter Munz, 3 February 1997.

managed on the same salary. The Poppers had arrived with little or no initial capital, had an unusually high rent for their temporary residence (175 NZ pounds per annum), and had to purchase furniture and other start-up items that were expensive (twice their price in England, Popper complained).[17] The advertisement for the N.Z. job indicated a salary of 400 pounds annually, to be increased by two annual increments to 500. It did not specify whether the denomination was NZ or British pounds (500 NZ pounds equaled £400). In August 1937, Popper told the council, the college's lay governing body, that he had assumed the latter and tried to make inquiries before his departure. The council was still well disposed toward him and fixed his salary at £400 (500 NZ pounds), the top of the lecturer scale, as of the date of his appointment. This remained his salary for the duration of his stay in New Zealand. He prodded the council for the two increment increases in 1939 without success. They were not going to deviate from the lecturer pay scale. They were also malevolent. In 1941, the university introduced a new rank, senior lecturer, with a pay scale of 500 to 650 NZ pounds. Popper was promoted immediately but placed at the bottom of the scale, never receiving an increase. He had enemies on the council, including a powerful registrar who sided with Sutherland. Popper's complaints, said Sutherland, were "typical of behavior that no Britisher or New Zealander would ever adopt." There was more than a grain of truth in it, but the council was wrong all the same.[18]

Popper made some bad financial decisions that aggravated his situation. Acutely aware of Hennie's vulnerability in case he died, he purchased an expensive life insurance policy.[19] He bought a car in 1937 (other lecturers had to be content with bicycles) and gave it up in 1942 when wartime fuel control made it virtually unusable beyond Christchurch. They changed their residence several times. On arrival, they stayed for a month in a hotel, then rented a bad but expensive apartment for a couple of months. In the winter of 1937, they moved to a rented house, repaired it, but had to vacate the premises in 1941. They then bought a house in Cashmere Hills, on the southern outskirts of Christchurch, overlooking the Canterbury plains to the beautiful Southern Alps. It was a nicer house, and in a better neighborhood, than most lecturers could afford. Karl bought it to make Hennie happier: The backyard allowed a wider scope for gardening – the one activity she enjoyed – and the Alps reminded her of Austria. But this house, too, needed repair, and the mortgage weighed heavily on their finances.

Their house was sparsely furnished. (Karl put his carpentry skills to use

[17] However, Peter Munz reports (3 February 1997) that he and his mother arrived in 1939 with £150, put a down payment on a house, and managed just fine.

[18] Canterbury College file, Popper Archives (366, 2, 4, 5, 11); Eva Hempel to Popper, 31 January 1938, Popper Archives (306, 2); Popper to Ernst Gombrich, 28 March 1945, Popper Archives (300, 4).

[19] She did some German teaching privately, but had no job, and apparently did not look for one.

and made some furniture.) They had neither a radio nor a gramophone, to say nothing of a piano.[20] (He bought an old harmonium and composed on it.) Books and journals were beyond their reach. Carnap and Hempel sent Karl their works, offprints, old copies of *Erkenntnis*, and a few additional books. Paul Oppenheim subscribed for him, in 1942, to the *Journal of Symbolic Logic*. Their life was not easy, but they were not quite poverty stricken, as their correspondence would lead one to believe.[21] Popper would regularly indulge his sweet tooth with ice cream and, on special occasions, a chocolate cake generously layered with cream. He frequently took his students out for milkshakes – the one food which his sensitive stomach would tolerate, he told them – and paid for everyone. He was impractical and occasionally extravagant, as he always was, and paid a price in some of life's comforts, but his complaints that he was approaching destitution were exaggerated.[22]

The distance from Europe was hardest to take. "We live here a life without a trace of external events," Popper wrote Kaufmann. "You have no idea how physical distance, something rather abstract, becomes profoundly and terribly concrete here in New Zealand. One lives a sort of pseudolife, outside the world."[23] New Zealand was calm; the Germans were well liked. No one thought of war. But Popper was losing sleep over events in Europe. Both he and Hennie were worried about relatives in Austria. They had no hope of visiting them: The trip took five weeks in each direction, and a return ticket for a couple cost about half his annual salary. Correspondence was the single means of keeping in touch. His friends on the other side encouraged him to write. Kaufmann and the Hempels wrote regularly, Carnap, Hayek, Tarski, and Woodger occasionally.[24] The Hempels sent two postcards from the second Paris congress in August 1937 with greetings from everyone: Carnap, Neurath, Oppenheim, Tarski. During his first year

---

[20] But radio and gramophone were never a priority. (In postwar years, Karl would rarely listen to the radio, once a year, perhaps.) Neighbors lent them an old gramophone.

[21] Hennie Popper to Ernst and Ilse Gombrich, 29 July 1943; Popper to Gombrich, 24 October 1944 and 2 July 1945; Popper's correspondence with Carl and Eva Hempel, especially 5 July 1943, all in Popper Archives (300, 2; 300, 3, 4; 306, 2, respectively); correspondence with Carnap, April 1937–July 1943, Carnap Collection; and with Kaufmann, April 1937–August 1938, esp. Hennie Popper to Kaufmann, 6 August 1938, *Kaufmann Nachlaß*.

Communication from both Peter Munz and Colin Simkin corrected my earlier dire picture of the Poppers' life in New Zealand in "Karl Popper in Exile," *Philosophy of the Social Sciences* 26 (1996): 452–91. I am grateful to both.

[22] The complaints would continue well into retirement, ceasing only in the 1980s when returns on his books, his being awarded prizes with cash attached to them, and the sale of his house at Penn finally put him at ease. He then became a rare-book collector, making up for (competing with?) his father's lost library. (*The Library of Sir Karl Popper* [London: Sotheby's, 1995].) For an academic, he left a substantial estate.

[23] Popper to Kaufmann, 27 November 1937, *Kaufmann Nachlaß*.

[24] He also corresponded regularly with his mother and uncle, Walter Schiff, but their correspondence has not reached the archives yet.

in New Zealand, Popper went out of his way to keep his correspondence up, but he was a terrible correspondent, and gradually slackened. Already in November, Eva Hempel was urging him to "please write! You cannot complain about the evil antipode if you make no effort to keep in touch!"[25] He continued to write for a while more, then stopped. His first two articles in English, on probability and the dialectic, appeared in *Mind* without his ever receiving the proofs. Moore, the editor, was not always organized, but, more importantly, he could not wait three months for corrections to be returned. For an engaged scholar, New Zealand was, as Hennie described, "halfway to the moon."

"I was sorry to hear that you were so unhappy on your arrival in New Zealand, and that you regret going so far away from Europe," wrote Woodger to Popper in May 1938.[26] Popper wanted to leave for the United States after only a few months. He planned to write, or translate into English, a couple of essays, and then go on a lecture tour of the United States during his summer break. He was hoping that an English translation of *Logik der Forschung* would soon appear, improving his chances for an American job. Meanwhile, he was working on probability, on a logic textbook, and, of course, on his courses. He found that there was no adequate logic textbook for beginners and thought he might quickly pull together an introductory text.[27] Little came of his writing, translation, and American tour plans. After March 1938, he was busy procuring visas for Austrian émigrés. Hearing the desperate cries from Europe, he recognized how much better off he was. He may not have wanted to compete with émigrés for American jobs. The outbreak of the war put his American plan to rest. He was in New Zealand to stay, at least for the war.

In September 1937, Hodge of London undertook, at Hayek's initiative, to translate and publish *Logik der Forschung*.[28] Stebbing chose the translator spoken of since 1934, Miss Gabain. Three months and sixty pages into the project, Gabain decided that schedule and the library conditions (in Bristol) would not permit completion in a timely manner.[29] (Apparently, she also undertook to translate a book by Ludwig von Mises.) Hodge took some time before picking a new translator, who sent about half the book to

[25] Eva Hempel to Popper, 29 November 1937, Popper Archives (306, 2).

[26] Woodger to Popper, 30 May 1938, Popper Archives (363, 17).

[27] He consulted Carnap: Popper to Carnap, June 1937 (n.d.), Carnap Collection.

[28] Hayek first tried unsuccessfully to interest C. K. Ogden, editor of Routledge's International Library of Psychology, Philosophy, and Scientific Method. (Hayek to Popper, 7 December and 28 December 1936; 9 June, 21 September, and 24 December 1937, Popper Archives [305, 12].) Hodge purchased the translation rights from Springer for £17, of which Popper received £2. (Otto Lange [Springer] to Hodge, 11 November 1937, and to Popper, 12 July and 12 October 1937, Popper Archives [352, 1].)

[29] Hodge to Hayek, 29 September 1937; Hodge to Popper, 28 December 1937 and 19 August 1938 (20, 17); Hayek to Popper, 12 March 1938 (305, 12); Springer to Popper, 25 July 1939 (352, 1).

Popper in May 1939. Popper found the translation unreadable.[30] A sample sent by another translator in the summer of 1940 still failed to satisfy him: He was particular about translations. The war complicated things further. Popper suggested that the translation be done under his supervision in New Zealand, but wanted Hodge to guarantee rapid publication. Hodge, who moved during the blitz to Edinburgh, responded after many months that paper restrictions made any definite publication date impossible. Popper, who contemplated various changes anyway – a new introduction and a rewriting of the chapters on probability and quantum theory – asked Hodge to sell him the translation rights. After some negotiations that showed Popper, for once, an astute businessperson, Hodge sold him, in October 1942, the option of purchasing the translation rights so that he could approach an American publisher.[31] By that time, Popper was all absorbed in getting *The Open Society* published. It would take another seventeen years, three complete translations, and futile waiting for the accompanying *Postscript* for *Logik* finally to appear in English.

After two years of job search and emigration, during which he could do no work, Popper now resumed orderly writing. Early in the summer break in November 1937, he completed a formal system of axioms for probability. It was one of the first attempts (the first, he thought) to lay out formally (that is, mathematically) the axioms underlying probability, and to demonstrate their independence, noncontradictory character, and sufficiency for derivation of probability statements. From a mathematical perspective, the advantage of formalization and axiomatization was obvious, and Popper took pride in his achievement. All known probability systems, he told Kaufmann – his own, Keynes's, Mazurkiewicz's, Waismann's – were compatible with his formalization, and appeared as specific interpretations of it.[32] In later years, he would suggest that he had a broader goal in mind, demonstrating eventually that corroboration was incompatible with probability.[33] At the time, it seems, he was mostly displaying his logistical wares.

He sent the brief work to *Nature*, which rejected it, in December 1937, as too specialized.[34] He resent it immediately to *Mind*, via Woodger. Meanwhile, he worked on it further, and sought Tarski's advice.[35] Tarski failed to

---

[30] Popper to translator, 12 September 1938; translator to Popper, 31 May and 22 August 1939; Popper to Hodge, 9 May 1940; Hodge to Popper, 28 May 1940, reporting that James Hodge, the firm's head, had been in the air force since August 1939, and that they had chosen a new translator (20, 17).

[31] Popper to Hodge, 12 December 1940, 21 May 1941, 8 September 1941, 28 July 1942; Hodge to Popper, 9 July 1941, 23 April 1942, 10 October 1942 (20, 17).

[32] Popper to Kaufmann, 27 November 1937.

[33] Popper, *The Logic of Scientific Discovery* (London: Hutchinson, 1959), Appendix *II, where Popper also pointed to later improvements (simplification) in his formalized system.

[34] Popper Archives (27, 5).

[35] Popper apparently wrote Tarski three times before receiving an answer (Tarski to Popper, 30 May

respond in a timely fashion, but Popper himself introduced some improvements (and discovered misprints). He sent his corrections to Woodger and Hayek only to learn that Moore had already sent the essay to print.[36] Tarski finally provided extensive criticism, and Popper continued to work on probability throughout the 1938 school year. He told Carnap in March, just a few days before the Anschluss, that he had also written forty pages of his logic textbook over the summer.[37]

The Nazi occupation of Austria in March 1938 disrupted his work once again, and changed its course. He attempted to get all the news he could about his family, and what he heard was terrible.[38] His cousin Georg Schiff was arrested, taken to Berlin for interrogation and, notwithstanding relatives' efforts on his behalf, never heard about again. His friend Otto Haas was sent to Dachau.[39] Other friends, Joseph Burstein, Peter Hilferding, and Felix Schafer, were thrown into concentration camps or prison. Max Spitzer, husband of a paternal cousin, was under police custody.[40] His sick mother died in May 1938, and his sister escaped to Paris in June, without a passport or money. His youngest uncle, Arthur Schiff, died the year after, in June 1939 (possibly a suicide).[41] Other relatives and friends were scrambling to leave the country, to England, France, anywhere – even New Zealand. Their desperate cries for help reached Popper. "Ready to undertake any job," stated all letters, some from people whom Popper barely knew.

Immediately upon hearing of the Anschluss, even before the stream of

---

1938). He urgently needed a copy of Mazurkiewicz's work on probability. (Tarski referred to Mazurkiewicz, his Warsaw colleague, in an *Erkenntnis* essay. Popper eventually received a photocopy from Carnap.) Tarski was giving Popper some of his own medicine, a rare spectacle. Like Popper, he was a prima donna, a chronic complainer, always "overworked," "did not receive letters," and the like. (He was in dire conditions in Warsaw, but his conduct did not change when he became universally recognized as a genius in the postwar United States.) Popper was infinitely understanding, as most people had to be with him.

[36] Karl Popper, "A Set of Independent Axioms for Probability," *Mind* 47 (1938): 275–7. Moore to Hayek, 10 March 1938; Hayek to Popper, 12 March 1938 (305, 12); Woodger to Popper, 30 May 1938 (363, 17).

[37] Popper to Carnap, 7 March 1938 and c. June 1938 (n.d.), Carnap Collection.

[38] Popper to Carnap, c. June 1938; Popper to Tarski, draft of July 1938 (354, 8); Hennie Popper to Kaufmann, 6 August 1938; Hayek to Popper, 22 August 1938 (305, 12); Popper to Hayek, c. October 1938, Hayek Archives (44, 1).

[39] Eventually put on trial for subversive activities before a Viennese court, Haas was executed in 1944.

[40] He later managed to obtain an exit visa and left with his wife and child, going first to Czechoslovakia, then to France, and from there to Argentina and the United States. I am grateful to Joyce Spitzer for an informative phone conversation on May 11, 1995. See also questionnaire for Robert Spitzer (1927–90), Research Foundation for Jewish Immigration, *Zentrum für Antisemitismusforschung*, Technische Universität, Berlin.

[41] Meldearchiv, Wiener Stadt- und Landesarchiv. Popper wrote Hayek (22 August 1974) that Arthur Schiff, like his wife Margarethe (née Breuer) and their two daughters, Hanna and Lili, "became direct or indirect victims of Hitler." Economist Erich Schiff (1901–92), who emigrated to the United States, was the family's sole survivor.

letters began, Popper and his friend Otto Frankael organized a Refugee Emergency Committee to secure immigration permits to New Zealand for Austrians. The obstacles were many. New Zealand was in the midst of a depression. Farm workers, mechanics, and engineers could get permits fairly easily, but how many of those were among potential immigrants? Medical doctors required three years' retraining before they could practice. Architects were needed, but not welcomed. For artists and academics there were virtually no positions. Opposition to immigration ran high. Elections were to be held in October 1938, and few government officials cared about the tragedy of people of whom they knew nothing. What could a committee led by two recent émigré intellectuals, with no political connections, do? Still, Popper managed to mobilize R. M. Campbell, of the New Zealand High Commission in London, behind their cause. In the fall, things started moving more quickly. By early 1939, the committee secured thirty-one refugee permits, and by the outbreak of the war thirty-six. Peter Hilferding, who was released from prison through Campbell's intervention, got one.[42] Economist Felix Schafer and physician Joseph Burstein, released from camps, got two others. Twice as many applications were denied as were approved. Popper felt helpless and depressed.[43]

Popper mentioned the committee only briefly in the *Autobiography*, and understated his role and achievement. Thirty-odd visas were not much, but they would not have been there without him. This was the one time in his adult life when he was involved in public affairs, and he surely saved lives. Yet, he seemed to take only limited pride in it. He was aware as much of the lives lost as of those saved. In April, Eva Hempel told him confidentially that Carnap and his colleagues were wavering about whether to help the people still in Austria get out, or to secure first the position of those who had left and were facing uncertain prospects.[44] Popper, too, had to decide which cases to push and which to leave aside. These were life-and-death decisions. That he pushed hardest for friends was likely and natural.

---

[42] Popper knew well both Peter and Karl Hilferding (1905–42). He tutored Peter for an external *Matura* in 1929, and apparently helped Karl with his studies, too. Peter changed his name to Milford while serving in the British army in Egypt during World War II (to avoid the liability of "Hilferding," should he be captured). His father, brother, and mother perished. He returned to Austria in 1947, and Popper attempted to promote his career. Later, in 1985–6, while in Vienna for a year, Popper supervised the dissertation of Milford's son, Karl (b. 1950), on Carl Menger – one of the few threads connecting progressive Vienna's past and present. (Milford's subject file and correspondence, Popper Archives [390, 5 and 327, 12]; Popper to R. M. Campbell, 8 July 1945, Popper Archives [366, 4].) Jeremy Shearmur first drew my attention to Peter Milford, Karl Milford facilitated my interview with his father, and Colin Simkin discussed further details with me.

[43] Popper, draft of *Autobiography* (holograph, 137, 1); Hennie Popper to Kaufmann, 6 August 1938, *Kaufmann Nachlaß;* Popper to Hayek, c. October 1938, Hayek Archives (44, 1); Popper to Carnap, 25 December 1938 and 17 February 1939, Carnap Collection; Popper to Gombrich, 28 April 1943, Popper Archives (300, 2).

[44] Eva Hempel to Popper, 25 April 1938 (306, 2).

Hennie complained that everyone wanted out with little regard for their prospects in New Zealand. This sounded discordant in light of Popper's emotional pleas just over a year earlier under less urgent circumstances. Her complaints reflected their frustration, despair, and guilt. "We could help our friends so little," she told Kaufmann.[45] "Deported to Theresienstadt on 25 May 1943 from the old-age home on Seegasse," says the Viennese registration record for Popper's Aunt Hellie.[46] In a draft of his *Autobiography*, Popper reckoned his losses: "Sixteen members of my family – cousins, uncles, aunts – died as a consequence of Nazism."[47]

"WHAT IS DIALECTIC?"

European events, then a global war, redirected Popper from natural to social science, and from logic to politics. Throughout 1938 and early 1939, he continued to work on probability, but gradually his interest in social science increased, as did his conviction that he had an important political message. Almost as a diversion, he began working in 1938 on two essays: "The Poverty of Historicism" and "What is Dialectic?" The first was a result of discussions with colleagues of themes that he had already mulled over in Brussels and London. Young economist Harold Larsen persuaded him to dictate an outline of "Poverty" to the economics secretary, producing a first draft.[48] Composition, however, became protracted. Popper sought to revolutionize social science, just as he did natural science, and had to think his way through it. In contrast, "What is Dialectic?" was a self-contained project – a critique of Marxist views on the relationship between logic and dialectic. It originated as a "popular lecture" that he gave on a number of occasions, first, probably, in his seminar in 1937 or 1938.[49] He edited it for publication rather quickly. It most likely went to *Mind* by the end of his 1938–9 summer break.

"What is Dialectic?" was Popper's first major essay in English.[50] The manuscript had surely been gone over by a colleague, but the English,

---

[45] Hennie Popper to Felix Kaufmann, 6 August 1938, *Kaufmann Nachlaß*.

[46] Meldearchiv, Wiener Stadt- und Landesarchiv.

[47] Draft of *Autobiography* (135, 1). Inexplicably, Popper erased this statement from the final version.

[48] Popper to Larsen, 23 August 1945, Popper Archives (319, 1). Jeremy Shearmur kindly directed me to this source.

[49] In *Autobiography*, p. 218 (n. 166), Popper referred to it as his "opening talk to my first seminar." (However, the Canterbury College file [366, 21] includes notes to a different lecture for the first seminar, on the Vienna Circle.) In *Conjectures and Refutations* (New York: Basic Books, 1963), p. 312, Popper said simply: "a philosophy seminar . . . in 1937." To Carnap, he wrote (10 December 1940): "a popular lecture I gave here in 1938." He probably spoke on the dialectic on a number of occasions.

[50] Popper, "What is Dialectic?" *Mind* 49 (1940): 403–26; reprinted, revised, in *Conjectures and Refutations*, pp. 312–35. I used also the original typescript, Popper Archives (27, 8).

crystal clear though it is, does not match the stylistic elegance of Popper's later work. It is difficult to trace the essay's composition. Popper mentioned it in none of his letters until he sent an offprint to Carnap in December 1940. (Was he uncertain whether *Mind* would publish a "popular" piece, outside his field of expertise?) The archives contain no correspondence with Moore (and no proofs). He was long familiar with Marxist positions on logic and the dialectic, and may have brushed up on his arguments against them, as well as on Hegel's *Logic*, for his introductory logic course.[51] He told economist J. B. Condliffe in May 1943 that he had sent the article to England in 1938 and "did not hear about it until 1941 [*sic*]."[52] Economist Colin Simkin (1915–98), who worked with him closely on "Poverty" and *The Open Society*, recalls Popper discussing "Dialectic" in a seminar, but believes it to have been complete by the time he arrived at Canterbury.[53] They began their collaboration, which included minute editing of Popper's drafts, in March or April 1939, and so "Dialectic" had likely been finished by then. Hennie's correspondence indicates that teaching and emigration affairs left Karl no time at all during the 1938 school year.[54] He told Carnap on December 25, 1938, that now that he was finally on vacation, he was working well. He did not specify the subject. Until early December, he was working on his axiomatization of probability. He told Carnap that he had sent it for publication. He was most likely writing "What is Dialectic?" from December 1938 to February 1939.

"What is Dialectic?" is instructive about the origins of Popper's political philosophy. It was probably provoked by the confusion of logic and dialectic, theory and history, causal explanation and biological metaphors among Viennese socialists, and Marxist social theorists and scientists (especially evolutionary biologists). Popper used here, for the first time, the rubric of "trial and error" to describe his own philosophy, and posed it as an alternative to the dialectic. He targeted Hegelian dialectic as "the worst of all absurd and incredible philosophic theories," foreshadowing *The Open Society*, and focused on its detrimental effects for Marx's sociological analysis, foreshadowing "The Poverty of Historicism."[55] Whereas *The Open Society* provided a political critique and historical interpretation of historicism, and "Poverty" a methodological critique, in "Dialectic" Marxist logic and Hegelian epistemology were at the center. In time and themes, "Dialec-

[51] Popper Archives (366, 19, 24). In "Dialectic," Popper also argued against Jeans's views on a mathematical-like universe, based on a description in L. Susan Stebbing, *Philosophy and the Physicist* (London: Methuen, 1937), and against H. Jeffreys's views on logic in "The Nature of Mathematics," *Philosophy of Science* 5 (1938).

[52] Popper to Condliffe, 19 May 1943, Popper Archives (28, 4).

[53] E-mail communication from Simkin, 28 May 1997. The question remains: Who helped Popper with editing? Larsen left in November 1938, and Simkin did not arrive until February or March 1939.

[54] Hennie Popper to Felix Kaufmann, 6 August 1938.

[55] Popper, "What is Dialectic?": 420.

tic" is the closest among his political works to Vienna and the philosophy of science.

Popper professed to have little problem with a "dialectical view" of the history of thought, that is, with the assumption that science and philosophy developed through a conflict between thesis and antithesis, issuing in a synthesis.[56] (He cautioned, however, that a synthesis did not always occur, and, at any event, its character could not be predicted by examining thesis and antithesis.) Already in his 1931 essay on the psychology of learning, he had likened the dialectic to the growth of knowledge through trial and error. Now he reaffirmed that the dialectic was a good approximation to "*trial and error . . .* the same method as that applied by living organisms in the process of adaptation."[57] More consciously developed, trial and error became the scientific method, permitting the survival of the fittest theory. The struggle among political ideologies was similar. People often perished with their belief intact, but occasionally turned against an ideology whose weaknesses had been demonstrated. The growth of knowledge was rarely, if ever, continuous, slow, and steady.

The problem with the dialectic was that Hegel and the Marxists extended its use from the history of ideas to history in general, and even to nature. Marxists spoke loosely of contradictions as explaining historical development. Marx said that capitalism "produced" its antithesis, thereby leading to socialism. Engels used biological metaphors to show that the growth of a plant followed the dialectic of nature. The seed was a thesis, the tree's germination an antithesis, and the production of new seeds a synthesis. Any child can understand that, said Engels. The confusion of social and biological metaphors with causal analysis reflected a dangerous misconception. Marxists assumed that the dialectic set the laws of history and nature.[58]

The root problems were a misunderstanding of the scope of logic and an absurd epistemology, the philosophy of identity (of reason and reality). Logic did not set, as Hegel assumed, "the laws of thinking," but merely formal rules of deduction. (Such as: If both "p or q" and "not p" are true, then "q.") Everyone, including dialecticians, made use of these rules. They presupposed the impossibility of admitting a contradiction. (If any two con-

---

[56] This was the popular rendering of Hegelian and Marxist dialectic, but an oversimplification. Engels described the dialectic in this manner (and provided Popper with his best examples), but Hegel and Marx, as a rule, did not.

[57] Popper, "What is Dialectic?": 403.

[58] Actually, Hegel and Engels applied the dialectic to nature; Marx confined it to history. Engels (*Anti-Dühring*) provided Popper's best examples: "The negation of the negation . . . [is the] law of development of nature, history, and thought." The best Popper could do with Marx was *Capital*, I, chap. 24: "[C]apitalism begets, with the inexorability of a law of Nature, its own negation." But certain Marxist evolutionary biologists, expressing contemporary conventions of leftist political discourse, established the identity of historical and biological laws. So Popper was on target nonetheless.

tradictory propositions were admitted, Popper showed, all propositions were.) Scientific progress depended on detecting contradictions and eliminating them. Theories that proved self-contradictory, or were contradicted by another theory that scientists accepted, were considered refuted, and dropped. Marxists did not help things by speaking of contradictions as "productive." Of course, they were productive, but precisely because everyone did their best to eliminate them. "The only 'force' which promotes the dialectic development [of ideas] is *our reluctance* to accept, and to put up with, the contradiction between the thesis and the antithesis," wrote Popper.[59] But Hegel and the Marxists regarded contradictions as conflicting historical trends, thus explaining them away. If the contradictions that abounded in reality were introduced into scientific reasoning, all criticism and progress would come to an end. Refutation would be impossible. "It is therefore about as inappropriate to take dialectic as part and parcel of logic, or else as being opposed to logic, as it would be so to take, say, the theory of evolution," contended Popper.[60]

Contradictions in themselves produced nothing. A thesis by itself did not produce an antithesis. Marxists could think this way because they inherited Hegel's identity theory that identified reason (and the laws of thinking, hence logic) with reality (and historical laws). Kant had set boundaries to knowledge by limiting philosophy to the realm of possible experience, ruling out "pure rationalism," or speculative metaphysics. (Popper suggested that he be modernized: Let testability delimit philosophy's boundaries.) Hegel, wishing to overcome Kant's limits and salvage "rationalism," contended that we could know reality because it was the mind's creation.[61] Faced with the resulting antinomies – contradictory metaphysical systems that were undecidable – Hegel said "they did not matter," because he could explain them historically as stages in the progress of reason.[62] Rationalism and empiricism, subjectivism, and objectivism, each found their place as moments in his historical scheme, but refutation became impossible. His reinforced dogmatism was a philosophical and political disaster. Identity theory allowed him to extend the dialectic from thought to reality, from the history of philosophy to history itself. The "laws of thinking" became nature's and history's laws. The new "science of logic," the dialectic, became an irrefutable science of history.

[59] "What is Dialectic?": 407.

[60] Ibid., 412. (Minor editorial changes to typescript, p. 12.) Popper tried to show that admitting even one contradictory statement amounted to admitting any statement whatsoever. (If the contradiction "p & $-p$" is admitted, then from "p or q" and "$-p$" we can deduce "q" for any q whatsoever.)

[61] This is an oversimplified view of Hegel's epistemology, but it is not wrong.

[62] Popper used Hegel's *Logic*, sec. 81. This was not quite fair. Hegel did not abandon the logical rule prohibiting contradiction, but explained contradictions historically. Nonetheless, the effect was the same: immunization to criticism. The fault was not, however, with historical explanation. The problem was theodicy: Hegel refused to accept that history could turn wrong. His historicization reflected complicity in history's judgment. Popper was correct in regarding this as dangerous.

The result was modern historicism: a theory of inexorable laws of historical development that delivered prophecies of the future course of history. Hegel's rebellious young student, Marx, rejected his idealism, but retained the dialectic. Marx's materialism had a progressive potential. (If I had to choose between materialism and idealism, said Popper, I would go for the first.) It sought to apply the methods of natural science in sociology and rejected social science's claims to be dealing with spirit. Although his "economism," the view that the relations of production determined consciousness, underestimated scientific ideas' role in history, it was an effective antidote to Hegel and a step forward for sociology. But the dialectic undermined these achievements by redirecting Marx away from natural science to the so-called historical method. Nowadays, everyone recognized that this method was overrated, but it still retained a hold on social science. (I criticized historicism in another paper, "The Poverty of Historicism," to be published soon, said Popper.) The relationship between the dialectic and the history of ideas was now severed, and, instead, economic and sociological laws became historical and dialectical. The dialectic was the law of the motion of society.

Marxist prophecies failed crucial tests. In *Capital*, Marx predicted that an "irresolute and non-resisting bourgeoisie" would make the transition from capitalism to socialism less painful than the industrial revolution. But the bourgeoisie, said Popper acerbically, did not prove so irresolute after all: Fascism was evidence enough. The dialectic, however, managed to explain away any failure of prophecy. There was always an "auxiliary hypothesis" to explain special circumstances, and postpone capitalism's collapse to the future. Any criticism was rejected as class bias. "As a rule, critics are denounced as not understanding dialectic, or as unable to understand proletarian science, or as traitors," wrote Popper.[63] Marxism, which began as an antidogmatic philosophy emphasizing knowledge's progressive nature, ended up as reinforced dogmatism: a philosophy claiming to explain all of reality, immune to criticism and to refutation by experience. "Scientific Marxism" duplicated Hegelianism, cultivating intolerance and undermining progress. "The whole development of dialectic should be a warning against speculative philosophy. . . . Philosophy must not be made a basis for any sort of scientific system and philosophers should be much more modest in their claims. For their task," Popper concluded, "is the study of the methods of science."[64]

Popper aspired to a radical reform of socialist modes of thinking. His leftist sympathies were obvious. He commended Marx's progressive poli-

---

[63] "What is Dialectic?": 425. The dialectic was sometimes essential to Popper's argument, at other times not. He did not quite explain how it was responsible for Marxist dogmatism. The use of auxiliary hypotheses (special historical conditions) to explain away refutation seems to me independent of it.

[64] Ibid., 426. (Typescript, p. 30, reads: "One task . . . is the study of the methods of science.") This is the strongest statement Popper ever made against metaphysics and it came close to positivism. It is

tics and sociological achievement and presented Hegel as servant of protototalitarian Prussia. However, the essay was interspersed with choice liberal phrases, and not always progressive ones. He spoke of free competition of theories as essential to scientific progress, likened it to the struggle of political ideologies, and suggested that the result was "the survival of the fittest," a Social Darwinian theme. Was Popper, still a socialist, a liberal unbeknownst to himself? Both "Poverty" and *The Open Society* demonstrated that he thought the two perfectly compatible. He always distinguished between the survival of theories and people. The "market" was allowed free operation with regard to the first, but not the latter. Freedom, too, required planning. Competition of ideas was no cure-all.

"What is Dialectic?" introduced Popper's political project. The scientific model of *Logik der Forschung* guided his critique of the dialectic as it would the critique of historicism. Already here he had made a subtle shift from "dialectical materialism" to "historicism." He was eager to get to Marx's method, its pseudoscientific claims, and its disastrous political consequences, whether such discussion was integral to the dialectic or not. The "resilient fascist bourgeoisie" that had sent him into exile and had just carried the Anschluss was very much on his mind. Generalizing his method as "trial and error," he made it flexible enough for applications to politics. He was thinking big: "It would be best, perhaps, not to use [the term "dialectic"] at all – we can always use the clearer terminology of a trial and error development."[65]

"THE POVERTY OF HISTORICISM," 1935–1940

Having sent "What is Dialectic?" to press, Popper returned to the rough draft he had of "The Poverty of Historicism," his treatise on social science methodology. No other nontechnical work of Popper is as difficult to

---

difficult to know what triggered it, but he was complaining to Kaufmann that the absurdities he encountered in teaching logic and ethics "could turn one into a positivist." (Popper to Kaufmann, 27 November 1937.) He was also lonely in exile, in need of support from his positivist friends.

Radical antiessentialism accompanied his opposition to metaphysics, especially to identity philosophy. Theories did *not* grasp anything about the world; they merely described it. Scientific languages, such as mathematics, were different modes of description. Saying that the mind understood the world because the world was mindlike (Hegel), or mathematical-like (Jeans), was senseless. Kant was implicated – if the mind imposed its forms on the world (making experience possible), the disagreement with Hegel was a matter of degree – but Popper toned down his idealism, emphasizing instead that he limited philosophy to possible (i.e., empirical) experience. The question of why some theories proved better than others, or "corresponded" to reality, Popper left in suspense. He answered it in the 1950s by envisioning a universe of propensities, thereby moving from modified conventionalism to modified essentialism. Throughout, he was inclined to defer the question to a biological a priori: We are programmed to explore the universe.

[65] Ibid., 412. (Typescript, p. 13, reads: "of the method of trial and error.")

understand. Published first as a series of three articles in *Economica* in 1944–5, then as a book in 1957, "Poverty" contains his clearest arguments against sociological determinism and historical laws.[66] It became popular during the cold war in the context of debates on Marxism.[67] Methodologists of economics and the social sciences have discussed it ever since.[68] Popper attributed the difficulties in understanding the work to his stodgy English, but his arguments were clear. It was the target of his critique and the context for its application that were obscure. My account of the work's formation may clarify them.

"HISTORICISM": THE PROBLEM OF INTERPRETATION

In "The Poverty of Historicism," Popper used the model of natural science that he had developed in *Logik der Forschung* to reshape social science methodology. He attempted to resolve most of the outstanding questions raised in British and Central European methodological debates for more than a century. When he began "Poverty," Popper was only vaguely familiar with the historical background, but he was sure that the terrain was murky, and he was going to clear it up. He had no intention of abiding by previous methodological frameworks. Rather, he intended to start anew. Using the model of *Logik der Forschung* as a thread through the maze of social science discourses, he extracted methodological issues out of their original theoretical contexts, and constructed a universal theoretical countermodel. He labeled this model "historicism," argued that it was responsible for a range of methodological and political catastrophes, and proceeded to demolish it. Against it, he offered *Logik der Forschung* as an alternative.

Popper's procedure resulted in major difficulties in understanding the work. "Poverty" included no clear historical reference to any historical context, political or intellectual. "Historicism" was unfamiliar, and some readers were unable to make heads or tails of arguments that purported to be applicable to history and politics but remained abstract.[69] The protracted process of the work's composition complicated matters further. Popper first conceived of the project in 1936 and worked on it between 1938 and 1940. *The Open Society* spun in an unexpected manner from "Poverty" in

---

[66] Karl Popper, "The Poverty of Historicism, I, II, III," *Economica* 11–12 (1944–5): 86–103, 119–37, 69–89; *The Poverty of Historicism* (London: Routledge, 1957).

[67] Two examples: Isaiah Berlin, *Four Essays on Liberty* (New York: Oxford University Press, 1969); E. H. Carr, *What is History?* (New York: Knopf, 1962).

[68] John O'Neill, ed., *Modes of Individualism and Collectivism* (London: Heinemann, 1973); Joseph Agassi and Ian Jarvie, eds., *Rationality* (Boston: Kluwer, 1987); Neil de Marchi, ed., *Post-Popperian Methodology of Economics* (Boston: Kluwer, 1992).

[69] For example, J. G. A. Pocock, "Review of *The Poverty of Historicism*," *The Cambridge Review* (23 November 1957): 200–1; Hans Meyerhoff, ed., *The Philosophy of History in Our Time* (New York: Doubleday, 1959), pp. 299–301.

1940.[70] Absorbed for the next three years in *The Open Society*, Popper put "Poverty" aside. Hayek published, with minor changes, Part I (currently, Parts I and II) of the 1940 manuscript in 1944, but Popper rewrote Part II (currently III and IV) completely in 1944 and early 1945. "Poverty" thus went through three stages of composition in different environments. Popper modified his intentions and arguments several times, creating tensions between the work's earlier and later parts, and making his intentions elusive.

The tension between the contexts of formation and reception of "Poverty" exacerbated the problem of reading. "Poverty's" formative experience was socialism's failure in Central Europe. Popper's initial charge against Marxism was impotence, not totalitarianism. He considered Central European socialists (and Marxian British intellectuals) misguided democrats, and directed his critique of Marxist historicism at them. He offered his technological social science and social engineering as an alternative to historicism. But "Poverty" appeared as a book in 1957, in the context of growing disenchantment on the left with the Soviet Union (Khrushchev's speech, Hungary, Poland). The primary context of reception was postwar Western Europe and the United States. From a cold-war perspective, Popper's critique was read as an attack on communism and a warning against social planning. This interpretation left large parts of the work inexplicable, but in the absence of a historical reading, it became predominant.

If contextual and historical problems in the interpretation of "Poverty" were not enough, the work's design itself suffered from tensions. Popper's conviction that his methodological and political projects were one was problematic. To him, the critique of historicism exposed both methodological fallacies and the danger of utopian politics. He provided a platform for reforming both social science and progressive politics, but the two projects pulled "Poverty" in different directions. The first required that he collect all methodological views opposed to *Logik*, whether relevant to politics or not, and join them into a countermodel, "historicism." The second required that he select methodological doctrines with dangerous political potential, exclude the rest (a majority), and elaborate the connections between methodology and politics. Popper refused to choose. He artfully drew connections between historicist methodology and utopian politics but, for the most part, developed the methodological project with little regard to politics. The discussion of piecemeal social engineering thus seemed tacked on to the methodological critique. Historical fragmentation, theoretical tensions, and philosophical abstraction all compounded the difficulties in reading the work.

Popper defined "historicism" as "a methodology of the social sciences

---

[70] Karl Popper, *The Open Society and Its Enemies*, 2 vols. (London: Routledge, 1945).

that emphasizes their historical character and aims at *historical prediction*."[71]
He divided historicist doctrines into two groups: "pro-naturalist" and "antinaturalist."[72] The first assumed that natural science method (which, in
Popper's view, they understood poorly) applied to social science; the latter
that it did not. Both argued that social science must become "historical."
"Poverty" consisted of four parts: In the first two, Popper limited himself
to exposition of historicist doctrines; in the last two, he criticized them. All
through, he did "not hesitate to construct arguments which have never, to
my knowledge, been brought forward by the historicists themselves, whenever I found that I could thereby strengthen their position."[73]

The term "historicism" had had no significant uses prior to "Poverty."[74]
Popper's "historicism" shared certain properties with German *Historismus*,
but the two were not identical.[75] He constructed his model as universally
as he could, identifying historical individuals with components of historicism, but none with the model as a whole:

> I am building up a theory which has often been maintained in parts, but
> hardly ever in the fully developed form presented here. This is why I have
> deliberately chosen the somewhat unfamiliar name "historicism." By intro-
> ducing it I hope to avoid discussions on merely verbal questions; for example,

[71] Karl Popper, "The Poverty of Historicism, I," *Economica* 11 (1944): 86 (henceforth "Poverty, I," which includes parts I and II); *The Poverty of Historicism*, p. 3 (henceforth *Poverty*): "an approach to the social sciences which assumes that historical prediction is their principal aim, and which assumes that this aim is attainable by discovering the 'rhythms' or the 'patterns', the 'laws' or the 'trends' that under-lie the evolution of history."

[72] Initially, he called them the "positive" and "negative" claims" of historicism. The manuscript of "Poverty, I" that Moore rejected in March 1943 was entitled: "The Claims of Historicism." (Moore to Popper, 12 March 1943, Popper Archives [329, 29].) Popper divided "Poverty, I" into parts I and II when he sent the manuscript to Hayek in November 1943. (Popper to Hayek, 17 October, 2 November, and 15 November 1943, Popper Archives [305, 13] and Hayek Archives [44, 1].) He asked Hayek to change "positive" and "negative claims" into "pro- and anti-naturalist claims" shortly there-after. (Popper to Hayek, 6 January 1944, Hayek Archives [44, 1].) Felix Kaufmann used the "natu-ralist/antinaturalist" distinction in *Methodenlehre der Sozialwissenschaften* (Vienna: Springer, 1936), and the terminology was fairly standard in social science literature. Popper did not change "claims" to "doctrines" until revising for the book.

[73] "Poverty, I": 86; *Poverty*, p. 3.

[74] Only after World War II has it become common to translate *Historismus* as "historicism." (Alan Donagan, "Popper's Examination of Historicism," in *The Philosophy of Karl Popper*, ed. Paul Arthur Schilpp [La Salle, Ill.: Open Court, 1974], pp. 905–24.) By now, this is the most common usage, and it aggravates the confusion over Popper's use. *Historismus* was translated as "historicism" in the English edition of Karl Mannheim, *Ideology and Utopia* (London: Routledge, 1936). (Popper used, however, the German edition.) Italian "storicismo" (Croce's) appeared as "historicism" in some English works prior to World War II. Still, the term was rarely used.

[75] Popper distinguished between them: "Poverty, I": 91; *Poverty*, p. 17. (See also: *The Open Society*, vol. 2, p. 196.) I shall leave *Historismus* untranslated to distinguish it from Popper's "historicism." For a genealogy of "historicism," see: Dwight Lee and Robert Beck, "The Meaning of 'Historicism,' " *American Historical Review* 59 (1954): 568–77; Georg Iggers, "Historicism," *Dictionary of the History of Ideas*, vol. 2 (New York: Scribner's, 1973), pp. 456–68.

whether a certain argument may be correctly described as a part of this methodology.[76]

The wish to avoid verbal quibbles was understandable for a philosopher who condemned language philosophy for its preoccupation with definitions. (It also relieved him of the burden of history, that is, from having to refer to historical debates he did not know well.) But, as one reviewer wondered: "[W]ho are or were the men called historicists? It is not to fall into the trap of asking what historicism 'really or properly means' to remark that there must be something in the real world to which the model corresponds."[77] Not one well-known historical figure subscribed to all, or even most, of the doctrines that Popper described as "historicist."[78] In *The Open Society*, the identity of the historicist enemies was clear: Plato, Hegel, and, notwithstanding his best intentions, Marx. But who were the historicists whom Popper had in mind in "Poverty"?[79]

There is significant evidence – textual, biographical, and contextual – that Marxism was "Poverty's" target.[80] Popper designed the title as a pun on Marx's critique of Proudhon in *The Poverty of Philosophy* (1847).[81] He spoke of "Poverty" on many occasions, including an interview with me, as directed at Marxist friends and the Austrian socialists.[82] He began writing

[76] "Poverty, I": 87; *Poverty*, p. 3: "I have tried to perfect a theory which has often been put forward, but perhaps never in a fully developed form. . . . I shall avoid merely verbal quibbles: for nobody, I hope, will be tempted to question whether any of the arguments here discussed really or properly or essentially belong to historicism."

[77] J. G. A. Pocock, *The Cambridge Review* (23 November 1957): 200–1. See also Charles Taylor's polemics, "The Poverty of *The Poverty of Historicism*," *The Universities and Left Review* (summer 1958): 77–8. Historicism, he charged, was "a vaguely mischaracterized straw-man."

[78] Lee and Beck, "The Meaning of 'Historicism,'" 568–77; Leon Goldstein, "Review of *The Poverty of Historicism*," *Ethics* 68 (1958): 296–7; Leonard Krieger, *Time's Reasons* (Chicago: University of Chicago, 1989), p. 107; Hans Meyerhoff, *The Philosophy of History*, pp. 299–301.

[79] Alan Donagan, "Popper's Examination of Historicism," defends Popper's right to construct a theoretical model, comprised of positions held by different thinkers at different times. But model construction does not seem to me to explain Popper's dehistoricization of historicism. Dehistoricization calls for biographical and contextual explanation, not for theoretical criticism or defense.

[80] Many reviewers read *Poverty* this way when it appeared as a book in 1957. Richard Wollheim, "Prosecuting the Myth," *New Statesman* (4 January 1958) credited Popper for having saved British intellectuals from the Marxist follies of the French. Maurice Cranston expressed a similar viewpoint in "The Open Future," *The Listener* (5 December 1957): 947–8. In contrast, Geoffrey Barraclough, "Tinkering with History," *The Spectator* (6 December 1957): 836 condemned the work as a right-wing "pugnacious counter-attack . . . directed against every variety of 'progressive' from Marx via Comte and Mannheim to Toynbee." Charles Taylor followed suit ("Poverty of *Poverty*": 200): *Poverty* expressed "the view of liberal non-interventionism, an apology for an utterly negative view of freedom." It used the haunting spectre of "the concentration camps" to advance a reactionary agenda. Herbert Marcuse, too, saw Popper's critique as directed at Hegel, Marx, and revolutionary socialism: "Karl Popper and the Problem of Historical Laws," in his *Studies in Critical Philosophy* (Boston: Beacon Press, 1973).

[81] Popper, "Preface: 1959" to *Poverty*, p. viii.

[82] Interview with Karl Popper, 26 January 1984; *Autobiography*, p. 113; "Gespräch mit Karl Popper," in *Theorie und Politik aus kritisch-rationaler Sicht*, ed. Georg Lührs et al. (Berlin: Dietz, 1978), pp. 24–6; Fritz Kolb, "Karl Popper und der Sozialismus," in *Theorie und Politik*, pp. 33–8.

it in the wake of the Anschluss to show where the Marxists had gone wrong. His critique of utopian planning in Sections 15 to 24 included Marxist socialization.[83] Still, he targeted less socialization and more progressive planning, less Marx and more Karl Mannheim, who, by Popper's admission, was only "Marxist inspired."[84] Some historicist doctrines could not be imputed to Marx. Many sections read like social science methodology, with little or no relationship to him. The thinker Popper criticized most often was a liberal, John Stuart Mill.[85] He conducted, in Parts III and IV, a long and respectful dialogue on social engineering with Hayek.[86] Marxism provided a frequent and important target, but there were clearly others.

In *Autobiography*, Popper suggested that "Poverty" criticized both Marxism and fascism.[87] He dedicated the book edition to the "memory of the countless men, women and children of all creeds or nations or races who fell victims to the fascist and communist belief in Inexorable Laws of Historical Destiny."[88] In *The Open Society*, he used "historicism" to designate both fascism and Marxism. In "Poverty," he made allusions to fascism and national socialism, and implied the totalitarian potential of utopian planning.[89] In later years, he recalled the influence of right-wing historicists, especially Oswald Spengler, during interwar years.[90] Still, "Poverty" was not an early manifestation of "totalitarianism," the cold-war paradigm emphasizing similarities between communism and fascism. Allusions to communism, if any, were vague. References to fascism were few. Spengler was mentioned once; when criticizing the cyclical view of history, Popper preferred arguing against the English historian Arnold Toynbee.[91] Neither Marxism nor totalitarianism explains the range of methodological issues that Popper engaged.

Ignoring politics, methodologists made better sense of "Poverty" than critics who searched for its historical targets. Popper used *Logik*'s model of

[83] Popper, "Poverty, I," 99–103; "The Poverty of Historicism, II. A Criticism of Historicist Method," *Economica* (1944): 119–33 (henceforth "Poverty, II," which includes Part III); *Poverty*, pp. 42–92.

[84] "Poverty, II," secs. 21–4, 26; Popper, "Replies to My Critics," in *The Philosophy of Karl Popper*, pp. 1173–4.

[85] "Poverty, II," secs. 22, 26; "Poverty, III," secs. 27–8, 32.

[86] "Poverty, II," secs. 19–23; "Poverty, III," secs. 27, 29.

[87] *Autobiography*, p. 113.

[88] *Poverty*, p. iv.

[89] Popper, "Poverty, I," sec. 10; "Poverty, II," secs. 23–4.

[90] Popper, "Replies to My Critics," pp. 1172–3; "Vorwort" to the German edition, *Das Elend des Historizismus* (Tübingen: Mohr, 1965), p. viii. The "anti-naturalist" doctrines of historicism also included *Historismus*. Contemporary Austrian intellectuals (e.g., Friedrich Hayek and Ludwig von Mises) and, more recently, historians of Germany, drew connections between *Historismus* and national socialist trends. Popper was not closely familiar with their works, but he admired Aurel Kolnai's *The War Against the West* (London: Victor Gallancz, 1938). Kolnai argued that German intellectual life had been permeated with national socialist ideals well before the rise of Hitler.

[91] Popper, "The Poverty of Historicism, III," *Economica* 12 (1945): 70–2, 84–5; (henceforth "Poverty, III," which includes Part IV); *Poverty*, pp. 109–13, 147–8.

natural science to form an antimodel: historicism. This was "Poverty's" single source of theoretical coherence. Critics complained that "rather than being the name of some systematically organized exposition in the philosophy of history and social science, 'historicism' is the name of a class, the members of which are those notions about history and social science to which Popper takes exception."[92] Having expressed their irritation and bewilderment, however, methodologists could still debate the viability of Popperian social science with little reference to history or politics. "Poverty's" methodological contribution had been splendidly illuminated in this fashion.[93] But historicism's identity and the political concerns that gave rise to the work have remained obscure.

SHIFTING HORIZONS: VIENNA, BRUSSELS, COPENHAGEN, CANTERBURY, AND THE MAKING OF "POVERTY," 1935–1939

"Your basic idea that the so-called *Geisteswissenschaften* [human sciences] are natural sciences is entirely persuasive," wrote Popper to Julius Kraft in January 1935.[94] He had just picked up his head from *Logik der Forschung*, and Kraft was urging him for months to read his recent book, *Die Unmöglichkeit der Geisteswissenschaft* (The Impossibility of the Human Science).[95] Kraft assailed German idealist concepts of *Geisteswissenschaft* that separated history and social science from natural science. He argued that when *Geist* or society became objects of science, they manifested "nature." Even history was a "natural science," insofar as it used sociological laws. He rejected positivism, however, and offered his own methodological unity of the "science of experience" (*Erfahrungswissenschaft*) as an alternative. In the course of his discussion, he raised the problems of values and objectivity in science, understanding (*Verstehen*) social action, and historical laws. Popper was of two minds. He accepted Kraft's orientation, a nonpositivist methodological unity of the sciences. (This remained his position to the end.) Moreover, he held Kraft's "distinction between descriptive and theoretical sciences to be fundamental." It corresponded, he said, to his own distinction between "laws" and "initial conditions" in causal explanation. (Theoretical science was interested in laws, descriptive science in unique conditions.) But he found Kraft difficult to follow, at points unclear. They were continuing their earlier skirmishes, but over a new terrain, which,

---

[92] Leon Goldstein, *Ethics* 68 (1958): 296–7.

[93] Ian Jarvie, "Popper on the Difference between the Natural and the Social Sciences," in *The Pursuit of Truth*, ed. Paul Levinson (Atlantic Highlands, N.J.: Humanities Press, 1982).

[94] Popper to Julius Kraft, 11 January 1935, Popper Archives (316, 24, under Victor Kraft).

[95] Julius Kraft, *Die Unmöglichkeit der Geisteswissenschaft* [1934], 2d ed. (Frankfurt: Öffentliches Leben, 1957). Theodor Gomperz had translated John Stuart Mill's "moral science" (*A System of Logic* [New York: Harper, 1846], Book 6) as *Geisteswissenschaft*. With Dilthey, the German term acquired new life and meaning.

Popper readily acknowledged, he little knew and had to think his way through.

He had little time to do so in 1935: He was fighting probability and quantum physics battles in the aftermath of *Logik*. But, as he was desperately searching for a job abroad, he was convinced that his pitiful situation resulted from socialism's failure. He had long thought that Marxism was a pseudoscience, responsible for suicidal socialist policies. When, precisely, it dawned on him that *Logik*, or his views on method, provided insight into the Central European catastrophe is not clear. It could not have been later than early January 1936. On his way to England through Brussels, he had been the guest of Alfred and Hilde Braunthal. On the evening of January 9, a group of friends gathered at their house: Carl and Eva Hempel, Paul Oppenheim, Karl Hilferding (studying at the time in Louvain, under Jesuit influence), and a "friend of Mannheim."[96] Alfred Braunthal, who had been educated in Marxist and German historical economics, had been publishing since 1920 on Marxist philosophy and economics.[97] Reacting to the socialist failures in Central Europe, he was now moving away from social democratic orthodoxy. Everyone in the audience was socialist; Oppenheim may have considered himself communist. But for Braunthal, they were interested in natural, not social, science.

The conversation turned to historical laws. Popper may have taken the lead.[98] In his *Autobiography*, he recalled distinguishing between scientific and historical explanations, to the effect that history was not interested in laws or prediction but in singular events. Historical explanations presupposed universal laws (or theories), but historians never tested them. History was not a science.[99] Hilferding apparently drew their attention to the relation-

---

[96] Popper recalled the occasion, and those attending, in his later correspondence with Braunthal (Popper to Braunthal, 21 May 1943 and 19 July 1944). Eva Hempel wrote to Ina Carnap (27 January 1936, Carnap Collection): "On January 8, Peter's [Carl Hempel's] birthday, . . . Popper of all people came through Brussels for two days. We had to spend most of the day at Oppenheim. I found Popper much nicer this time, not so terribly arrogant. It seems that the partial recognition he received for his book did him good. Discussions were quite nice, but always in the presence of Oppenheim, whom I find too courtly." She did not mention the meeting at Braunthal's the next evening, but Popper, in a later chronology (Popper Archives [405, 1]), remembered two "lectures" in the private circles of Oppenheim and Braunthal, and so their accounts agree.

[97] Alfred Braunthal, *Karl Marx als Geschichtsphilosoph* (Berlin: Cassirer, 1920); idem, *Die Entwicklungstendenzen der kapitalistischen Wirtschaft* (Berlin: Laub, 1927); idem, *Die Wirtschaft der Gegenwart und ihre Gesetze: ein sozialistisches Lehrbuch der Nationalokonomie* (Berlin: Laubsche, 1930).

[98] It appears that there was no formal "lecture," but informal conversation. (The "Historical Note," *Poverty*, p. v, gives the impression of a formal paper.) Popper's early recollections (Popper to Braunthal, 21 May 1943) were of "our talks in Brussels," transformed a year later (19 July 1944) into "my talk in Brussels." Hempel reported later to Carnap (27 January 1936) Popper's comments on his "definition of concept" in *Syntax*, and so conversations in Brussels ranged over many topics, and social science was by no means the center.

[99] *Autobiography*, p. 117; "Poverty, III," Section 30. See also: *The Open Society*, chap. 25, sec. 2 (pp. 248–52) and n. 7 (pp. 342–4), added in September 1944. All this must be treated cautiously not only because

ship between Popper's comments and his account of causality in *Logik*: Causal explanation was deduction of a statement (an "event") from a universal law subject to initial conditions.[100] History was interested in unique conditions, science in laws. In correspondence with Braunthal in 1943, Popper suggested that Chapter 5 of *The Open Society* also grew out of concerns raised in Brussels. The chapter discussed fact and (moral) value in relation to so-called historical or sociological law. Popper's Kantian position had been for long that no value could be derived from fact, and so no guide to action could emerge from "historical law," as Marxists argued. In this context, perhaps, Popper also criticized Mannheim, who was popular among some of his friends for his sociology of knowledge.[101] (Mannheim regarded all social knowledge as historical, and provided prescriptions for reconstructing ideology based on the historical laws operating in modern society.) It is unlikely that Popper, or anyone, used the term "historicism" to designate Mannheim's, or the Marxists' position: They spoke German, and German had, at the time, no equivalent term. The discussion, it seems, was wide ranging, all discussants contributing from their own perspectives.

Popper was now persuaded that *Logik* could explain much that had gone wrong with social science and socialist politics. Bad (Marxist) sociology was the root of evil. The problem was not simply Marxist pseudoscience. Social science method was at issue. In September 1935 in Paris, he heard Neurath lecture on "Man and Society in Science," drawing conclusions from unified science, physicalism, and protocols for sociological method.[102] He could not but disagree, but Neurath made it clear that the natural science issues dividing them had broader ramifications. In search of a job, Popper would do well to emphasize these ramifications. In the spring of 1936, in Hayek's seminar, he spoke on "The Poverty of Historicism." This was a formal presentation, and so he must have had at least notes.[103] In a letter seeking to

---

of possible memory failure after so many years but also Popper's eagerness to establish priority on "causal explanation" against Hempel ("The Function of General Laws in History," *Journal of Philosophy* 39 [1942]: 35–48) whom he charged with plagiarizing *Logik*. I shall discuss this issue further in Chapter 10.

[100] *Logik der Forschung*, sec. 12, pp. 26–8. Popper said that Hilferding's comments had focused on what later became "Poverty, III": 75–6; *Poverty*, pp. 122–4. Hilferding published shortly after a detailed account of *Logik*, comparing Popper and Reichenbach on probability and confirmation, and trying to arbitrate between the two: "Le fondement empirique de la science," *Revue des questions scientifiques* 110 (1936): 85–116. He expounded on Popper's causal explanation, but made no reference to historical explanation.

[101] Popper to Braunthal, 21 May 1943 and 19 July 1944 (Popper mentioned especially Fritz Hellin as a Mannheim admirer); my interview with Popper.

[102] Otto Neurath, "Mensch und Gesellschaft in der Wissenschaft," *Actes du Congrès International de Philosophie Scientifique*, 8 vols. (Paris: Hermann & Cie, 1936), 2: 32–40.

[103] Popper to Gombrich, 28 April 1943 (300, 2); Popper to Braunthal, 19 July 1944; Abba Lerner to Popper, 1951 (no exact date), Popper Archives (260, 1).

promote his candidacy for American jobs, he described the paper to Carnap as dealing with the "methods of sociology." This was the only occasion prior to New Zealand during which Popper formally lectured on social science.

In Copenhagen, social science was again on the agenda. Neurath's lectures to the congress were historicism embodied. His opening speech called on physicists not to overestimate the achievements of physics or impose their precision requirements on sociology. The historical science of sociology defied any absolute laws.[104] His second lecture, "Soziologische Prognosen," called for relativizing and historicizing science. He rejected the distinction between nomothetic and idiographic sciences, that is, between sciences interested in generalization and those interested in the unique.[105] (Popper had argued this distinction with respect to science and history.) Against the positivist effort to dissolve social into natural science, Neurath suggested that natural science become more historically conscious. Sociological predictions, limited to historical periods, were traditionally thought incompatible with astronomical predictions. But physics may have something to learn from sociology, said Neurath. Prediction effected results not only in social science (for example, market predictions), but in natural science, too: Personal interest influenced theory formation and testing. Sociology showed that absolutist dicta about verification and falsification had no place in science.[106]

"Soziologische Prognosen" was only the tip of Neurath's historicist iceberg. He had done extensive work on social science methodology in the early 1930s.[107] He conceived of sociology as a historical science, formulating "laws" in physicalist language. He hoped to put sociology in the service of progressive politics. While emphasizing the problems in projecting historical development, he regarded projections as sociology's major task. His arguments on sociological prediction and historical laws were precisely those Popper later labeled historicist.

Sociology, said Neurath, was not an autonomous theoretical science. The possibility of sociological prediction emerged from particular historical situations that suggested to scientists the shape of the future. Theory and practice were closely connected. Science was a public enterprise, the sociologist

[104] *Erkenntnis* 6 (1936): 289.

[105] *Locus classicus*: Wilhelm Windelband, "Geschichte und Naturwissenschaft" [1894], *Präludien*, vol. 2 (Tübingen: Mohr, 1921), pp. 136–60.

[106] "Soziologische Prognosen," *Erkenntnis* 6 (1936): 398–405. This was a direct challenge to Popper. There is no record of his response – he had much else to fight over with Neurath in Copenhagen – but the congress may have reinforced his sense that he would have to engage social science. He quoted "Soziologische Prognosen" in "Poverty, II": 66 n. 5; *Poverty*, p. 103 n. 1. John Somerville (New York) gave a second lecture on sociology in Copenhagen: "Logical Empiricism and the Problem of Causality in Social Science."

[107] Otto Neurath, *Empirische Soziologie* (Vienna: Springer, 1931); "Soziologie im Physikalismus," *Erkenntnis* 2 (1931): 393–431.

a member of a class, theory a form of practice, scholarship a mode of action. Sociological predictions were part of the class struggle: "Solidarity of fate leads to solidarity of behavior, and fosters scientific sociology, which tells the masses what the future will bring them."[108] Sociologists must be cautious in their predictions: Theoretical failure may mean disappointment to the working class and a political setback. Not all phenomena were the proper subject for prognosis. The prediction of an individual's future was impossible. Sociology dealt exclusively with collective entities: groups, classes, societies. Its predictions were "indefinite on many points." Historical and social complexity, the impossibility of considering all relevant facts, and acceptance of untested assumptions and initial conditions made predictions imprecise. Moreover: "Sociological predictions . . . are preconditions to what they predict. Predicting an eclipse of the sun does not influence the eclipse, but, surely, predicting market conditions can raise prices on the stock exchange, and asserting that a revolution will occur can influence the coming of revolution."[109] Scientists ought to be politically astute, take their predictions' effects into consideration, and use them to mobilize the masses. Science is an instrument of liberation. The end result of scientific prediction is transformation of the present.

No view of science aroused Popper's indignation as much as Neurath's. It was not so much that they disagreed. To be sure, in "Poverty," he would reject each and every one of Neurath's tenets: Sociology was not a historical science; there were no historical laws or theoretical history; history's course was impossible to predict. But these disagreements do not quite explain his outrage. More was at stake. Since his youthful involvement with communism, he had developed an intense dislike for intellectuals who took it upon themselves to transform the world. When they engaged in prediction of the future, he was beside himself. He thought they arrogated to themselves expert knowledge that they did not have and were elitist, presumptuous, and callous: false prophets. He held them responsible for the Central European catastrophe. He wrote "Poverty" to expose their methodological fallacies and political irresponsibility, and to present his own alternative: a technological social science, instrument of gradual peaceful reform.

"Poverty" had to wait, however. After Copenhagen, Popper, desperate to escape Central Europe, was in no state to focus on Neurath or social science. But he took with him to New Zealand Felix Kaufmann's recent book, *Methodenlehre der Sozialwissenschaften* (Methodology of the Social Sciences).[110] It was a comprehensive work, discussing three generations of

---

[108] Neurath, *Empirische Soziologie*, reprinted in *Gesammelte philosophische und methodologische Schriften*, vol. 1 (Vienna: Hölder-Pichler-Tempsky, 1981), p. 519.

[109] Ibid., p. 516.

[110] Felix Kaufmann, *Methodenlehre der Sozialwissenschaften* (Vienna: Springer, 1936). Popper's archives (Kaufmann subject file [432, 8]) also contain an offprint of "Die Bedeutung der logischen Analyse

Central European methodological debates. Kaufmann's virtues were amazing erudition, clarity of thinking, and the capacity to create dialogue between conflicting traditions.[111] He would identify antagonistic philosophical positions, show where presuppositions went wrong, and clarify the methodological rules obtaining. Popper was working his way through *Methodenlehre* in 1937, repeatedly informing Kaufmann that it proved useful for this subject or that student. It familiarized him with a field in which he had come to have aspirations, but about which he knew, as he testified in *The Poverty of Historicism*, "next to nothing."[112]

Together with Alfred Schütz, Kaufmann was the foremost Viennese disciple of phenomenologist philosopher Edmund Husserl (1858–1939). Phenomenology provided a method for grasping and analyzing meaning. Kaufmann believed that it resolved most epistemological problems. Phenomenological reduction, the *epoché*, restricted one's attention to the immediately given contents of consciousness, and rendered phenomena's essential meaning. Intellectual, or categorical, intuition (*Wesensschau*) grasped universals. After having read *Logik*, Kaufmann emphasized that intuition was subject to intersubjective confirmation.[113] But to Popper, this was all dangerous nonsense. He had not rejected Fries's "immediate knowledge" to accept Husserl's worse version. If intuition was subject to intersubjective criticism, then it had no epistemological significance. That it somehow reached an "essence" was an epistemological fallacy that he would assail in "Poverty."

"Many of the sharpest methodological controversies in the social sciences are ready for resolution," stated Kaufmann in *Methodenlehre*.[114] The central question was the applicability of the methods of physics to social

---

für die Sozialwissenschaften," *Actes du huitième Congrès International de Philosophie* [1936] (Nendeln, Liechtenstein: Kraus Reprint, 1968), pp. 209–16. The article introduced the book and provided an overview.

[111] Kaufmann's interests as a young student were in mathematics and the philosophy of physics, but as he was working toward a law degree, he specialized in the philosophy of law. He was Kelsen's beloved student, and became a *Privatdozent* in 1922. Somehow, he managed to combine an academic position with a full-time business job, regular participation in Kelsen's, Mises's, and Schlick's seminars, and publications in the philosophy of mathematics, legal theory, and the methodology of economics. Shortly after the Anschluss, he received an invitation to the New School for Social Research and emigrated. Alfred Schütz, "Felix Kaufmann, 1895–1949," *Social Research* 17 (1950): 1–7. Harry P. Reeder, *The Work of Felix Kaufmann* (Lanham, Md.: University Press of America, 1991) includes an overview of his work, a bibliography, and a directory to his archives.

[112] *Poverty*, p. 138. "Poverty, III": 81 states merely that when he had developed his natural science method, he "disregarded the social sciences altogether."

[113] Kaufmann's reception of Husserl is clearest in "Phenomenology and Logical Empiricism," trans. Dorion Cairns, in *Philosophical Essays in Memory of Edmund Husserl*, ed. Marvin Farber (Cambridge, Mass.: Harvard University Press, 1940), pp. 124–42. The basic Husserl text here is *Logical Investigations*, trans. J. N. Findlay, 2 vols. (New York: Humanities Press, 1970).

[114] Kaufmann, *Methodenlehre*, p. iii.

science. Kaufmann distinguished between naturalist and antinaturalist doctrines. Like Popper, he thought that misunderstanding of natural science
(as well as of logic and mathematics) was responsible for methodological
confusion. The book had two parts: the first, an exposition of social science's
basic concepts; the second, a discussion of controversial issues, with particular reference to economics and law. The first part did not help Popper
much. Some chapters went over material familiar to him: epistemology,
logic and mathematics, causality and law, science and metaphysics. Other
chapters, "life and consciousness" and the "concept of value," elaborated on
unfamiliar discourses of ethics and criminal law. Popper found them difficult. "I cannot simply learn from your book," he told Kaufmann. "I must
attempt to rethink everything, and it is not easy."[115] Kaufmann represented
philosophical traditions that Popper had no intention of trying to understand fully. Reluctant to express disapprobation, he tried to use *Methodenlehre* as a textbook. It did not always work.

The second part, in contrast, proved a rich source for the history of
methodology and historicist arguments. Kaufmann outlined the doctrines
of *Historismus*: Social science was historical; laws were developmental and
formed inductively from historical facts; their applicability was limited to
periods; the scientist's own historicity influenced laws' formation. He used
sociologists Max Scheler and Karl Mannheim as examples (and was critical of them). The key issue was, he said, whether social laws were universal, as the laws of physics were. He first established prerequisites for physical
laws (including exactitude, simplicity, and universality), then argued that the
difference between social and natural laws was one of degree, not quality.
He relaxed requirements for social laws. (Popper would allow no such relax-
ation.) He also discussed the great debate between the Austrian economists
(Menger) and the German historical school (Schmoller); meaning and
interpretation in social science; nomothetic versus idiographic sciences; the
"objectivity of values" (especially the southwest German school, Windelband, Rickert, and Weber); imputation of value in Austrian economics; and
the priority of social collectives to individuals (he dismissed both the question and fascist sociologist Othmar Spann). Most importantly, Chapter 6
provided a detailed account of Weber's ideal-types and purposeful (goal-
oriented) rationality. Kaufmann thought that, with few revisions, Weber
offered a viable method, solving the problem of social laws.

This was all valuable to Popper. To be sure, it was not enough. When he
read Hayek's methodological essays in 1943, and recognized how little he
knew about the history of social science, he apologized, and rushed to

---

[115] Popper to Kaufmann, mid-June 1937, referring to the chapter on the concept of value. Kaufmann's
American colleagues later shared Popper's difficulties. "He is German language in action," complained Arthur Bentley. "He sees *Geist, Vernunft, Verstand* as mental operations." (Ingeborg Katharina
Helling, "Felix Kaufmann," in *Vertriebene Vernunft II: Emigration und Exil österreichischer Wissenschaft
1930–1940*, ed. Friedrich Stadler [Vienna: Jugend und Volk, 1988], p. 450.)

rewrite the critical parts of "Poverty." But Kaufmann was a beginning. He supplied much of the historical information and some of the terminology for "Poverty." By providing a catalog of objectionable doctrines, he made it possible for Popper to set up the historicist model. Still, Popper told Kaufmann the truth when he said that he was trying to think social science anew. No one directed his social science inquiries the way Gomperz and Nelson had done with epistemology. Kaufmann gave a history of questions badly posed. Popper would not engage this history but start anew.

In the fall of 1937, Popper read Hayek's "Economics and Knowledge." With the possible exception of discussions in Menger's colloquium, this was his single introduction to the interwar debate on prediction among Austrian economists. His interest in economics was limited and his knowledge of it sketchy. He had read Austrian economist Böhm-Bawerk's critique of Marx and his theory of capital, and had learned some marginal utility economics from it. He had also heard much about Carl Menger (1840–1921), founder of Austrian economics, but knew neither his work nor that of other Austrian economists.[116] He complimented Hayek on his essay but, apparently, expressed also some reservation. Hayek told him that he wished they could have the opportunity to discuss the issues.[117]

Hayek's libertarian politics was intertwined with his conception of economics as an interpretive, nonpredictive science. Both he and his teacher Mises argued that human action should be understood "purposefully," in terms of its goals, not causally. The facts of social science were not physical or psychic, but values people attached to objects, and beliefs about the likely consequences of actions. The task of economics was not to formulate general laws of economic life; no such laws existed. Human preferences were always in flux and human actions changed accordingly. Rather, economics interpreted human action and the values people ascribed to commodities. Meaning and value were subjective, and their interpretation required intuitive understanding. Economics was a subjectivist science. This did not rule out theoretical generalization or economic trends. Economic theory explained the unintended consequences of human action, or better, of social interaction. But the patterns of economic life never assumed the character of laws, and predicting economic development, or market performance, was impossible. All social planning, founded on market prediction and control, was futile, simply irrational.[118]

---

[116] E-mail communication (18 March 1997) and letter (23 April 1997) from Colin Simkin.

[117] Hayek to Popper, 24 December 1937, Popper Archives (305, 12): He received Popper's letter of November 19. "Herzlichen Dank für den Bericht über Ihr Befinden und besonders für die freundlichen Worte bezüglich meines Aufsatzes. Ich wünschte wir hätten Gelegenheit, diese Dinge mündlich zu diskutieren." See also: *The Open Society*, chap. 10, n. 63.

[118] Ludwig von Mises, *Epistemological Problems of Economics* [1933] (Princeton, N.J.:Van Nostrand, 1960); *Human Action*, 3d ed. (Chicago: Regnery, 1966); Friedrich Hayek, editor's introduction to *Collectivist Economic Planning* (London: Routledge, 1935); "The Facts of Social Science," *Ethics* 54 (1943): 1–13;

Mises had exerted influence through a biweekly private seminar that met every other Friday from 1920 to 1934.[119] Among the members were Hayek and Morgenstern. During the 1920s, both had spent time in American universities and become familiar with business-cycle theory that provided investors with forecasts of future market performance. The Austrians were skeptical. They viewed the market as a communication system, relaying incomplete information to economic agents. No one agent possessed complete information. However, improvements in providing economic statistics could contribute to stability. The more rational investors were, the less the likelihood of sharp market turns. With private business funds, Mises and his students established, in 1927, the Austrian Institute for Trade Cycle Research (*Österreichisches Institut für Konjunkturforschung*). Hayek was the first director and Morgenstern his successor. One of the institute's first publications was Morgenstern's treatise on the limits of economic prediction.[120] He argued that statistical methods failed to come to grips with "economic facts." Prices were not physical phenomena subject to mathematical calculation, but provisional reference points for human action, reflecting ongoing rearrangement of priorities by economic agents. Predicting trade cycles influenced public behavior. Forecasts became either self-fulfilling prophecies or exercises in self-refutation. Economic forecasting was impossible.

As an alternative, Morgenstern began experimenting, in the early 1930s, with general equilibrium analysis. Hayek was unhappy. In "Economics and Knowledge," he probed the presuppositions of equilibrium theory. It was, he said, an unrealistic representation of the market, a series of tautologies without empirical relevance. There was, to be sure, an empirically observed tendency toward equilibrium, but the "pure logic of choice" underlying equilibrium analysis did not reflect market interaction and negotiation, and did not show how equilibrium came about. It assumed a static economy, perfect foresight, compatibility of individual preferences, and realization of all plans. It ignored both the time moment – individuals modified their plans (and preferences) every moment in response to changing conditions – and the uneven distribution of information, forcing agents to make decisions based on partial information. The market operated as a communication system in which it was impossible for anyone

Paul Silverman, "Law and Economics in Interwar Vienna" (Ph.D. diss., University of Chicago, 1984), esp. pp. 289–348.

[119] Martha Steffy Browne, "Erinnerungen an das Mises-Privatseminar," *Wirtschaftspolitische Blätter* 4 (1981): 110–20; Anton Amann, "Soziologie in Wien: Entstehung und Emigration bis 1938," in *Vertriebene Vernunft I*, pp. 214–37; Karl Müller, "Die Idealwelten der österreichischen Nationalökonomen," ibid., pp. 238–75.

[120] Oskar Morgenstern, *Wirtschaftsprognose: Eine Untersuchung ihrer Voraussetzungen und Möglichkeiten* (Economic forecasting: An investigation of its preconditions and possibilities) (Vienna: Springer, 1928).

to gather all information. The data required for equilibrium analysis was ever in flux. Its ephemeral character imposed epistemological limits on economics.[121]

Popper seemed to be of two minds. He liked Hayek's exploration of the logic of choice. It probably invited his first reflections on social science models, their premises, construction, and testing. But he disagreed with Hayek's methodological conclusions. Their orientations diverged radically: Popper was enthusiastic about mathematical economics, subscribed to the methodological unity of the sciences, and sought to develop a technological social science. Hayek harbored serious reservations about the first, and made it his life mission to combat the other two. The essay disclosed at various points Hayek's preference for nonpredictive, nonquantitative social science, using intuitive understanding and historical ideal types. These were all doctrines Popper classified as antinaturalist historicism. Without mentioning Hayek by name, he referred to him, in "Poverty, I," as a "writer with strong anti-historicist views" who had come to support the historicist position that the special character of "social facts" made use of quantitative methods impossible.[122] In a draft of "Poverty," he defended, in principle, the possibility of economic forecasts. He conceded that they were unfeasible only on account of science's public character.[123] Hayek remained, however, a secondary target of criticism until Popper read his methodological essays in 1943–4. Things then changed radically. "Poverty, II" and "III" engaged Hayek in lengthy dialogues.

On his first summer break (1937–8), Popper was preparing lectures for the next year and beginning his logic textbook. Both required intensive engagement with Mill's *Logic*. Book III, on induction, was an expected target of Popper's criticism. But it was the final Book VI, "on the logic of the moral sciences," that was a surprise. Mill, the prophet of liberalism, had subscribed to the cardinal historicist heresy: belief in historical laws that explained society's progress throughout the ages. Much like Marx, he hoped to discover the laws of social progress so that humanity could hasten their operation. Taking astronomy – a predictive, but largely nonexperimental science – as a model for sociology, he opted for long-term, large-scale, if

---

[121] Hayek, "Economics and Knowledge," *Economica* 4 (1937): 33–54.

[122] "Poverty, I": 93; *Poverty*, p. 24. "Poverty, III," Section 29, explained why equilibrium analysis was legitimate. The "pure logic of choice" reflected the rationality principle underlying social science models. (It may entail complete knowledge.) Models registered empirical deviations from perfect rationality.

[123] Hayek eliminated this part of Section 5 in proof. (Hayek's proofs, Popper Archives [47, 4], p. 35.) He likewise eliminated two paragraphs (proofs, pp. 41–2) in Section 9, defending the use of statistical methods. (Jeremy Shearmur has recently published the parts cut in "Popper, Hayek, and the Poverty of Historicism Part I," *Philosophy of the Social Sciences* 28 [1998]: 442–3, 445–6.) Hayek could legitimately see the cuts as superfluous, or less well argued, but he was also especially alert. He left untouched the fundamental critiques.

imprecise, predictions. Following Comte, he searched for social dynamics, forces producing social change, creating future "states of society." This fit well not only with Marx but also with the evolutionist vogue that Popper could recall from his "meeting at the windmill" with the leftist biologists. Both they and Mill used biological (organic) and physical (dynamic) metaphors for society.[124] Mill and Marx were as one: "naturalist" historicists who subscribed to the nineteenth-century belief in "inevitable" progress, informed by evolutionary theory. Popper no longer had any doubt about the malaise's wide spread. Progressive naturalists and conservative antinaturalists, a spectrum from Mill and Marx on the left to Spann and Spengler on the right, shared historicism and retarded social science. He could show where they had gone wrong.

Popper began discussing "Poverty" with economist Harold Larsen in 1938. Larsen recognized that he was having a difficult time starting to write, and astutely had him dictate an outline to the economics secretary, then edited it.[125] Shortly after, in November 1938, he left for London. When Simkin first saw "Poverty," in the antipodal fall of 1939, it was about "one third the size of the essay eventually published," still "in rough shape regarding English, not too clear in argument, in need of rearrangement and revision."[126] Popper was struggling to write in English.[127] He told Hempel shortly after arrival in New Zealand that he would no longer publish in German.[128] Unlike most émigrés, he sought a clean break with the German language and culture, which were tainted, he thought, with obscurantism and nationalism. "I cannot help thinking – *and* hoping – that the English language is more important, intellectually, than the German language," he told Hayek years later.[129] By 1940, when he switched to English in his correspondence (probably because of wartime censorship),

---

[124] A caveat: This is the way Popper viewed Mill's social science in 1938. (Mill, *Logic*, Book 6, chaps. 1, 3, 6–7, 10.) I am not sure, however, that he associated Mill's physical metaphors (dynamics, orbit, trajectory) with the biologists' organic ones until 1944 ("Poverty, II," sec. 22; "Poverty, III," sec. 27). In "Poverty, I" (sec. 3) he seemed to separate the two. Likewise, the emphasis on Mill's "holism," i.e., his efforts to grasp the "laws" determining the "state of society," seems to have come in 1941–2 (*The Open Society*, vol. 2, pp. 83–4). In "Poverty, I," "holism" seemed primarily a right-wing affair. Implicating Mill in Marx's effort to "shorten the birth pangs" of historical periods may have come only in 1944 ("Poverty, III," sec. 22, and corrections to *The Open Society*, chap. 13, n. 16: Popper to Gombrich, 9 September 1944 [28, 16]).

[125] Popper to Larsen, 23 August 1945, Popper Archives (319, 1). Popper made no mention of "Poverty" in his correspondence before the war. (He mentioned "Poverty" once, in "What is Dialectic?": 423.) But in 1945 he provided a brief history of his political project to Larsen, who had returned to New Zealand from military service. Jeremy Shearmur kindly directed me to the letter.

[126] E-mail communication from Simkin, 28 May 1997.

[127] He went around campus with Fowler's *Modern English Usage*, his main recreational reading. Colin Simkin, "The Birth of *The Open Society*," in his *Popper's Views on Natural and Social Science* (Leiden: Brill, 1993), p. 185.

[128] Popper to Hempel, 2 June 1937, Popper Archives (306, 2).

[129] Popper to Hayek, 24 October 1969, Popper Archives (305, 15).

his writing was almost flawless. In 1949, Waismann told him that he was never able to switch to English and was considering a return to Vienna.[130] Popper never contemplated such a return. This partially explains both his efforts and success at linguistic adjustment. But it was a measure of the difficulties he faced that "Poverty, I" remains his "stodgiest piece of writing."[131]

Popper's syllabi for his 1939 courses reflected his growing interest in social science and social planning. His course for the Canterbury Workers' Educational Association focused on "scientific methodology, both of the natural and social sciences." It included a discussion of "causality in physics and in the social sciences," comparisons of the experimental and statistical methods in sociology and physics, and deliberations on the relationship between physics and history, sociology and economics, and sociology and biology. The final theme was the methodological unity of science. The 1939 ethics syllabus had "planned action in the realm of the individual and social life" as one topic under "moral responsibility." Social philosophy now became Popper's central concern and would remain so until the end of World War II.[132]

Beginning in 1939, Simkin, a twenty-four-year-old lecturer in economics, became Popper's closest collaborator on "Poverty." Popper made great demands on his time but rewarded him with a postgraduate education in scientific method, probability, and mathematics. Popper professed to know little social science, and so Simkin helped not only with English but also economics. They discussed marginal utility theory, Austrian and Marxist value theory, and Keynesian macroeconomics. Popper received papers from Jacob Marschak, an émigré economist who became a major innovator in econometrics, and passed them on to Simkin. (Popper had met Marschak in Oxford, and they kept in touch after the latter moved to the United States.)[133] Mathematical economics figured prominently in their discussions. Popper was convinced of its importance and encouraged Simkin to improve his mathematical skills. He helped him with the mathematical aspects of Allen's and Hick's value theory, Tinbergen's statistics of the business cycle, and *Econometrica* articles.[134] Popper rarely read the works, but they discussed them with a view to method. Whereas economic paradigms, especially Keynesianism, captivated Simkin's interest, Popper remained

[130] Waismann to Popper, 14 February 1949, Popper Archives (359, 6).

[131] *Autobiography*, pp. 113–14.   [132] Popper Archives (366, 16, 24).

[133] Marschak to Popper, 27 April 1937, Popper Archives (324, 14).

[134] J. R. Hicks and R. G. D. Allen, "A Reconsideration of the Theory of Value," *Economica* 1 (1934): 52–76, 196–219; J. R. Hicks, *Value and Capital* (Oxford: Clarendon Press, 1939); Jan Tinbergen, *Statistical Testing of Business-Cycle Theories*, 2 vols. (Geneva: League of Nations, 1938–9); Colin Simkin: "John and Ursula Hicks: A Personal Recollection," *Indian Journal of Applied Economics* 7, no. 4 (1998): 5–14. Popper helped also with R. G. D. Allen, *Mathematical Analysis for Economists* (London: Macmillan, 1938), the only mathematics textbook he did not treat with contempt.

focused on mathematical models.[135] All the same, the economic context for his social science was econometrics in the service of Keynesian economic management, a stark contrast to Hayek's libertarianism.

Popper's vision of technological social science took shape in discussions with Simkin that continued into 1941–2, when he was already writing *The Open Society*. Simkin was working on problems of monopoly and counter-cyclical fiscal management.[136] They discussed social planning and how science could help. Popper distinguished between prediction of an event, or "prophecy," and preventive prediction, contingent upon conditions humans may change. The former was common in astronomy, the latter in the experimental sciences. Historicists mistakenly modeled social science on the former, rather than the latter. This accounted for their passivity. Concerned with predicting an "inevitable" future, they interpreted history instead of changing it. Popper thought that social science must be an instrument of progressive reform and design human institutions. He called preventive prediction "technological." Simkin suggested that he make "social technology" the rubric of his methodological revolution. Popper, eager to emphasize its experimental character, preferred "social engineering." Simkin drew his attention to the emergence of the welfare state in Switzerland and Scandinavian countries.[137] Together with New Zealand's welfare reforms, the New Deal, and English labor legislation, they provided historical models for social engineering. Popper hoped that his new social science would advance planning further.

The surprising feature of "Poverty's" development from 1939 on was the Central European context's rapid recession into the background. Neither technological social science nor social engineering was an original idea. They predominated in progressive Vienna. But exceedingly little of the Viennese background made its way into "Poverty." Commenting in *The Open Society* on the origin of "social engineering," Popper stated:

> For the term "social engineering," cp. M[ax] Eastman, *Marxism: Is it Science?* (1940). I read Eastman's book after the text of my own book was written; my term "social engineering" is, accordingly, used without any intention of alluding to Eastman's terminology. . . . The term "social technology" has been suggested to me by C. G. F. Simkin.[138]

---

[135] He took pride in working out mathematical solutions to economic problems, then comparing them to the literature, sometimes devoting hours to tasks that had no other purpose but proving once again his mathematical abilities. This seemed a good part of his fascination with economics. E-mail communication from Simkin, 28 May 1998.

[136] Colin Simkin, "Budgetary Reform" and "Budgetary Reform for New Zealand," *Economic Record* (1941–2): 192 ff., 16 ff., respectively. He also wrote a paper on Swedish cooperatives that remained unpublished.

[137] He had Popper read M. W. Childs, *Sweden: The Middle Way* (New Haven, Conn.: Yale University Press, 1936) and E. D. Simon, *The Smaller Democracies* (London: Gollancz, 1939).

[138] Popper, *The Open Society*, chap. 3, n. 9 (p. 185 of the first edition).

After the book had been published, readers alerted Popper to other Anglo-American uses of "social engineering." He kept adding them to his reference. The fifth edition reads:

> The term "social engineering" seems to have been used first by Roscoe Pound, in his *Introduction to the Philosophy of Law* (1922, p. 99; Brian Magee tells me now that the Webbs used it almost certainly before 1922). [Eastman reference] As the first social engineer one might describe the town-planner Hippodamus of Miletus.[139]

Eastman, Pound, Simkin, the Webbs, Hippodamus of Miletus: Did Popper suffer from amnesia? Every progressive intellectual living in Vienna was familiar with *Sozialtechnik*. Why did Popper dissociate his social science from the Viennese past?

Popper did not always recognize his intellectual debts, certainly not to disliked rivals, but he would not knowingly have covered up the origins of his work, or provided misleading references.[140] The Viennese past receded into the background less because he falsely claimed originality and more because his intellectual horizons were shifting. Even before he left Vienna, he had begun filtering his recollections of socialization and social science through natural science methodology. He had an amazing capacity, when preoccupied with a project, to regard everything happening around him through the prism of his work. Earlier socialization arguments made it into "Poverty" only if they had direct bearing on *Logik*'s application to social science. He knew progressive literature on social engineering, and referred to it in *The Open Society*. (He suggested that Lenin and the Marxists would have done well to consult both Joseph Popper-Lynkeus and Anton Menger because they represented a promising beginning of social engineering.)[141] But the progressives did not use such ideas as preventive prediction. He did not see their social engineering as germane to his project. He thought he was breaking new ground.

Still, the arguments Popper used to rebut the Marxists echoed those advanced by Lynkeus and his students. They argued that Marxism was pseudoscientific. Heinrich Löwy, Lynkeus's friend and literary executor, suggested that Marxist forecasts were not scientific predictions but prophecies, calls for political action to bring about a revolution. Social reform required

---

[139] Popper, *The Open Society*, 5th ed. (London: Routledge, 1966), pp. 210–11. See also: chap. 9, n. 1 and n. 4 (pp. 284, 286).

[140] This corrects my previous view ("The Making of the Open Society" [Ph.D. diss., Columbia University, 1993], esp. pp. 571–2) that Popper intervened in Viennese debates but covered his tracks. I am indebted to vigorous criticism by Popper's students, especially Jeremy Shearmur, as well as to the opened archives.

[141] Popper, *The Open Society*, chap. 13, n. 7. See also: chap. 10, n. 7. Josef Popper-Lynkeus, *Die Allgemeine Nährpflicht als Lösung der sozialen Frage*, 2d ed. (Vienna: Rikola, 1923); Anton Menger, *Neue Staatslehre* (Jena: Fischer, 1904).

faith, and historical determinism provided just that. Marx was a moral critic more than a scientist. He provided no prescription for moving from capitalism to socialism, thereby opening the road to communist violence. Socialism's rise reflected the ethical imperative of reform. It was not a testimony to Marxism's scientific character.[142] Popper was not active in Lynkeus's circle, but these arguments circulated in progressive discourse. If he was familiar with them, he reworked them, by the 1930s, into his own critique. The similarity of ideas and vocabulary revealed how much his philosophy owed to progressive Vienna, but it was now *his* philosophy. Or so, at least, he felt.

Progressive social planning was even closer to home. Popper's uncle, Walter Schiff, had advised the government on socialization in 1919–20, and Popper argued with him over it. In the mid-1920s, he confronted socialization issues again in Polanyi's seminar. If his interest in social questions later waned, he nonetheless had fierce arguments with his uncle once the latter had worked out a blueprint for the planned society.[143] Walter Schiff moved, in the early 1930s, toward the communists: "When I [Popper] was a communist, he told me: as a scientist, I can assure you that communism is false. When he became a communist, I told him: as a scientist, I cannot assure you that communism is false, but false it is!"[144] These episodes echoed in "Poverty" but did not provide a focus for discussion. To Popper, socialization amounted to nothing but talk, and progressive engineering needed improvement. His technological social science would show the way to the progressive dream. He was not going to get mired down in old arguments the futility of which became obvious when the Nazis marched into Austria. He was designing an alternative.

Much of the terminology of "Poverty" can be found in another proponent of social engineering: Neurath.[145] Planning, social technology *(Gesellschaftstechnik)*, historical prophecy, utopianism, collectivism, all appear in his pamphlets on socialization from 1919 to 1920.[146] Neurath formed the link between historicist social science and utopian socialization that Popper considered deadly. Social engineers, he said, were engaged in constructing utopia. "What yesterday counted as dreamers' work, today

---

[142] Popper-Lynkeus, "Über den Marxismus," in *Allgemeine Nährpflicht*, pp. 109–29; idem, *Gespräche*, ed. Margit Ornstein and Heinrich Löwy (Vienna: Löwit, 1924), pp. 10–28 (reports of encounters with communists); Heinrich Löwy, "Marxismus und Allgemeine Nährpflicht," in *Gespräche*, pp. 69–74.

[143] Walter Schiff, *Die Planwirtschaft und ihre ökonomischen Hauptprobleme* (The planned economy and its major problems) (Berlin: Heymanns, 1932).

[144] "Gespräch mit Sir Karl Popper (1991)," in Friedrich Stadler, *Studien zum Wiener Kreis* (Frankfurt: Suhrkamp, 1997), p. 541. Popper said that he made his uncle drop a chapter of the book.

[145] Popper carefully dissociated Lynkeus from Neurath: "Memories of Otto Neurath," in Otto Neurath, *Empiricism and Sociology*, ed. Marie Neurath and Robert S. Cohen (Boston: Reidel, 1972), pp. 51–2. He admired Lynkeus and pretended that his critique of utopianism did not apply to him.

[146] Even the distinction between holistic and piecemeal reform, which Popper would shortly make, appeared in Neurath in the form of total and partial socialization.

appears as preliminary scientific work for shaping the future: . . . [U]topias arise . . . as prophecies that want, at the same time, to become the causes of their own realization."[147] History provided social engineers with a blueprint of the future utopia:

> If we learn to evaluate contemporary phenomena from a different theoretical perspective, we shall enter the realm of social technology and its aspirations, and, at the same time, the realm of knowledge of prophecy, utopia, and history. The age of *Historismus* will come to an end, the age of Utopianism will begin.[148]

Scientific prediction and historical prophecy were one. This was precisely the argument Popper brought under fire in "Poverty." He reversed Neurath on social engineering and utopia, separating scientific prediction from historical prophecy, and applied technology from utopia.

Popper read some of Neurath's early publications and was familiar with his arguments. However, by the late interwar years, he no longer identified the arguments on utopia and planning specifically with Neurath. He criticized them as part of Marxist discourse. He recalled Neurath's sociology better and used "Soziologische Prognosen." Carnap also sent him *Empirische Soziologie.*[149] If he read it, he could not fail to recognize that Neurath embodied the politico-methodological syndrome of historicism. He was the single thinker who combined the naturalist and antinaturalist doctrines of historicism, synthesizing positivism, Marxism, and *Historismus.* Still, Neurath was not the issue; the syndrome was. Popper underestimated him, as the circle's members did. He thought of him as a politician, not a thinker.[150] His name did not come up in discussions of "Poverty" with Simkin.[151] He was part of the background, but Popper would not waste his time arguing against him when he could argue against Marx and Mill.

To be sure, Neurath stood for everything that was wrong with progressive and Marxist intellectuals. Nothing about him seemed right, neither the person nor his philosophy nor his politics. To Hayek, Popper wrote "in

---

[147] Neurath, "Die Utopie als gesellschaftstechnische Konstruktion," in *Durch die Kriegswirtschaft zur Naturalwirtschaft* (Munich: Callwey, 1919), pp. 228, 229.

[148] Idem, *Vollsozialisierung* (Jena: Diederichs, 1920), p. 33. Neurath modeled his method on *Historismus.* He suggested that comparative historical study would show societies to be at different stages in humanity's development. Generalization was impossible, but a universal history was not. Popper complained that historicists began by urging caution about theoretical generalization, and insisting that it must be historically grounded, but ended up constructing universal histories and utopian programs.

[149] Carnap to Popper, 29 December 1937; Popper to Carnap, 7 March 1938; Eva Hempel to Popper, 25 April 1938, all in Carnap Collection.

[150] "Gespräch mit Sir Karl Popper (1991)," pp. 536–7.

[151] He mentioned him once to Simkin as a secondary circle figure, editing the Encyclopedia series. E-mail communication from Colin Simkin, 18 March 1997.

confidence," in 1943, that his "little hit against Neurath is more than deserved by him, for the driving force is here: power. (This is why I instinctively dissociated myself, from the beginning, from all of his 'movements' whether 'logical positivism,' 'physicalism,' or 'encyclopaedism,' etc.)"[152] Searching for camaraderie with Hayek by expressing hostility to Neurath, Popper inadvertently disclosed, however, the limits of his memory. He had everything to gain by telling Hayek that he opposed Neurath on socialization. He had just sent Hayek "Poverty, I," and knew that it included views that ran contrary to his. It would endear "Poverty" to Hayek if he learned that it had been written, even in part, against Neurath. Popper's silence meant that, at least by 1943, he did not regard "Poverty" as criticizing Neurath. His mention of Neurath's post-1929 "movements" as "the beginning" meant that he remembered only vaguely the young Neurath.[153] The intellectual horizons of the middle-aged social scientist did not correspond to those of the youth. They shifted first from socialism to natural science, then from Central Europe to the trans-Atlantic world. They expanded in some respects, narrowed down in others. "Poverty" reflected the shifts.

Shifting horizons made it easier for Popper to claim that he was breaking completely new ground. He used terminology and ideas of Viennese progressives, but wore thick blinders. Simkin's "social technology" should have evoked vivid memories. It did not. Popper was in a new world, with bad memories of the old. He was imparting lessons of the Central European catastrophe, but he trying to make them relevant to an English audience. Neither Neurath nor Central European debates interested that audience. Social science methodology and planning did. Dehistoricization, or abstraction of Central European issues from their original context, was a strategy Popper pursued almost instinctively. It made him comfortable: His knowledge of the background was poor, and he was ambivalent about attacking Viennese friends. It also made his arguments relevant far beyond interwar Central Europe, in contexts he had never imagined.

THE STATE OF "POVERTY," 1939–1940

Popper undertook to reshape social science, and render it politically useful, when he knew little about it. He planned to carry out his revolution in one extensive essay, to be written in a language he was still acquiring. This was a tall order. Most intellectuals having similar aspirations would be well advised to seek medical help, but Popper was repeating a life pattern that had led to spectacular achievements (and failures). "Poverty, I," product of

[152] Popper to Hayek, 16 December 1943, Popper Archives (305, 13).
[153] His Neurath memories from the mid-1960s were unspecific about Neurath's views on socialization, but clear on the philosophy of science.

early 1940, does not measure up in style or argument to the rest of his work. During the next couple of years, however, he mastered a set of social science problems. "Poverty, II" and "III" cut through the problem of historical laws with unsurpassed clarity and virtuosity. Popper may not have reshaped social science, but he made a major contribution to it.

His plans for "Poverty" got derailed late in 1939. His critique of "essentialism" – a term which he coined and used in much the same way as poststructuralists do today – included comments on the totalitarian implications of Greek ontology and epistemology. Colleagues found them puzzling. He elaborated them. Soon, the critique became too long, a diversion from methodology. He decided that a second article, "Marginal Notes on the History of Historicism," was necessary, and cut the historical comments out of "Poverty." For a few months, he worked on both essays, giving increasing attention to the second. After May or June 1940, he laid "Poverty" aside and focused on the historical essay that grew into *The Open Society*.[154] While writing *The Open Society*, he made major theoretical and linguistic strides. Looking again at "Poverty" late in 1942, he realized that the essay was underdeveloped and was unhappy with it. Still, in October 1942, he sent "Poverty, I" to *Mind*, under the title: "The Claims of Historicism." *Mind* rejected it.[155] He resent it to *Economica* in November 1943, telling Hayek that he had introduced only stylistic changes since 1938.[156] Simkin remembers more substantial changes, but none came after mid-1940. "Poverty, II" and "III" seem as if coming from a different universe. There are still structural anomalies, created by adapting the new sections, containing novel ideas, to the original structure, but the writing flows, and the theoretical sophistication is stunning.

"Poverty, I" set up the historicist model. The model pulled together ten "negative," or antinaturalist, historicist claims, and six or seven "positive," or naturalist, ones. The antinaturalist doctrines proffered that natural science method was not applicable to social science, the naturalist ones that it was. Both agreed that social science must be historical. Precisely this claim Popper denied.

The antinaturalist doctrines posited that history's changeful character and complexity ruled out generalization, experiments, and precise predictions. Objectivity, too, was impossible in social science: Scientists were historical agents, part of the context they studied, their predictions influencing the outcome of events. The objects of inquiry were different in social science: not individual atoms, or a constellation thereof, but holistic entities of organic nature, such as society or economy. These did not allow for quan-

---

[154] Colin Simkin, "The Birth of *The Open Society*," and E-mail communication, 28 May 1997.
[155] Moore to Popper, 12 March 1943, Popper Archives (329, 29).
[156] Popper to Hayek, 17 October, 2 November, and 15 November 1943, Popper Archives (305, 13) and Hayek Archives (44, 1).

tification, or causal explanation, only for understanding by analogy, or intuitive interpretation of historical significance. Most importantly, natural science was methodologically nominalist, social science essentialist. Essentialism upheld the "real" existence of universals and their irreducibility to their composite elements. Social scientists grasped the nature of holistic phenomena, the universal essence underlying historical change. They pursued "what is" questions, for example, "What is a state?" They considered individual phenomena, having "many accidental features, . . . of no interest to science."[157]

The naturalist doctrines tried to model social science on astronomy, but retain its historical character. Social facts were exclusively historical; hence, social science's large-scale forecasts were historical, too. Just as dynamics explained planetary movements in physics, so did social dynamics, the mechanics of historical forces, explain historical motion in sociology. Social science sought to establish developmental historical laws that linked different historical periods. These laws were inexorable. Historical prediction, or prophecy, was inevitable. This left little, if any, room for social engineering. Whether historicists admitted it or not, social science interpreted the world; it could not change it.

Marx, Mill, and Neurath were Popper's major sources for naturalist doctrines. *Historismus*, as described by Kaufmann and practiced by Neurath, was a source for many antinaturalist doctrines, but there were others. Spann and Spengler, together with Hegel and, possibly, Marxist evolutionary biologists, were likely major targets in "holism." They were all implicated in "intuitive understanding," too, as were Dilthey, Weber, and Mannheim. Mannheim was most likely a major source for the problem of "objectivity." Hayek and the Austrian economists were one target of the critique in "quantitative methods," and, possibly, also in "the inexactitude of prediction." (In both these last sections, however, Popper constructed arguments on behalf of historicism that had never been put.) Finally, under "essentialism," Popper criticized Aristotle, Plato, and Husserl, but also Weber, whose "ideal-types" he (mistakenly) considered essentialist.[158]

There is no way of knowing for certain what the original critical part of "Poverty," which was later rewritten as "Poverty, II" and "III," looked like in 1940, but there is sufficient information for educated guesses.[159] Its length was just below two-thirds of "Poverty, I" (26 typescript pages, compared to 41).[160] "Poverty, II" and "III" were thus almost three times as long as the

---

[157] "Poverty, I": 94; *Poverty*, p. 28.

[158] Hayek's proofs, Popper Archives (47, 4), p. 44; Jeremy Shearmur, "Popper, Hayek, and the Poverty of Historicism," 445–6.

[159] Although Popper had at least three copies, he included none in his archives, and there is no trace of them elsewhere.

[160] Popper to Hayek, 2 November 1943, Hayek Archives (44, 1).

original. Significant parts of "Poverty, II" and "III" (the dialogues with Hayek, the critique of Mannheim) responded to works published, or read by Popper, after 1940. They introduced new distinctions (piecemeal versus holistic social engineering) and terminology (that is, methodological individualism) that did not appear in "Poverty, I." It is sometimes possible to date Popper's acquisition of new ideas by tracing them either to the final manuscript of *The Open Society* (October 1942, vol. 1; February 1942, vol. 2), or to the corrections that he introduced from June to October 1944. His exposition of historicism in "Poverty, I" sometimes suggests what arguments he intended to pursue in his critique, and what arguments of "Poverty, II" and "III" were *not* available to him at the time.[161]

This much is clear: Popper argued for the methodological unity of natural and social science.[162] He insisted that there were no special difficulties in tracing regularities, formulating theories, and establishing universal laws in social science. Historicists were wrong to argue that the uniqueness, complexity, and rapidity of historical change rendered predictions in social science inexact, prevented experiments, or confined generalizations to specific historical periods. Nature was at least as diverse as history. (His belief in universal humanity spoke.) Changes in nature were at least as rapid and complex, and they constantly created unique situations. Neither in physics nor in sociology did scientists proceed by generalization: Inductive inference was an illusion. Scientists began with problems, and their theories offered solutions. They did not know "for sure" that the proposed theories, or laws, were universal. They were always open to refutation, but to give up on their universality was to forgo science.[163]

Historicists misconceived social science because they misunderstood natural science, especially prediction. They mistakenly compared the artificial conditions of physical experiments with historical reality, concluding that the latter made experiments impossible and prediction inexact. But prediction was commonly possible only in artificial environments. Nature was no more predictable than history. With the exception of astronomy and meteorology, physics rarely predicted natural events. In both natural and social science, scientists created controlled experimental conditions, artificially insulated, then followed up with testing. Occurrence of an event prohibited by a theory, under specified initial conditions, constituted a

---

[161] This is especially the case for the proofs. (Popper Archives [47, 4].) Hayek initially sent "Poverty, I" to print "as is," then went over the page proofs and cut them down by about 15 percent. (Hayek to Popper, 28 April 1944, Hayek Archives [44, 1].) Jeremy Shearmur recounts the story in detail in "Popper, Hayek, and the Poverty of Historicism Part I," 434–50.

[162] My account of Popper's critique of historicism in 1940 goes beyond what is available in "Poverty, I," and relies on "Poverty, II" and "III," in conjunction with *The Open Society*. But I have been careful to include only arguments for which there is evidence that they existed in Popper's intellectual universe in 1940. When I am in doubt, I say so.

[163] "Poverty, I," secs. 1–5; "Poverty, II," sec. 26; "Poverty, III," sec. 29.

refutation. Prediction commonly ruled out an event, rather than specified a particular outcome of a situation. Science related what cannot happen, rather than what will.[164]

Given this account of prediction, there was no sense in demanding of sociology that it predict future events. History, made by human hopes and actions, was conditioned by the growth of knowledge, and could not be predicted. There were historical tendencies, but they did not make prediction of the future possible, and should not be construed as laws.[165] Neither in nature nor in history did one set of laws explain a concrete succession of events. Searching for developmental laws in history was sheer insanity. No science ever came close to explaining simpler successions. Moreover, applying physical and biological metaphors, such as "movement," "force," "organic," to history was misguided:

> The idea of the movement of society itself – the idea that society, like a physical body, can move *as a whole* along a certain path and in a certain direction – is merely a holistic confusion. . . . No series of, say, three or four causally connected phenomena proceeds according to any one law of nature.[166]

Theoretical history was impossible. The historical discipline had no interest in laws or prediction, but focused on description of unique events. Descriptions were not testable or falsifiable because historical events were nonrepeatable. Historicists were wrong to demand that social science adopt the historical method. Social science was theoretical and not historical, engaged in constructing and testing theories, not in reconstructing history.[167]

Still, unlike nature, social movements and institutions were human made. Could scientists understand collective social entities as they did individual physical atoms? Popper balked at both "holism" and "intuitive understanding." Methodological nominalism recognized that, like nature, society and history remained inaccessible in their totality. Scientists focused on selected aspects. Even the "wholes" of Gestalt psychologists, structures of coordinated elements, represented particular properties of their constituents. Collective entities were interactive systems, always reducible to their

---

[164] "Poverty, I," sec. 15; "Poverty, II," sec. 25; "Poverty, III," sec. 28.

[165] This much, I think, was clear by 1940. The explanation of the difference between law and trend, and the reformulation of historicism's problem as inability to distinguish between the two, did not come until late in 1944. "Poverty, I," secs. 8, 14, 16 (note that the book edition introduced "trends" on pp. 24 and 36, and italicized them on p. 45); "Poverty, III," secs. 27–8.

[166] "Poverty, III": 72, 73; *Poverty*, pp. 114, 117. I am not certain that this last argument was in the 1940 manuscript. My guess is that it was, but it gained much clarity once Popper explained the difference between trend and law.

[167] Again, this much, I think, was clear by 1940. The distinction between theory and interpretation came in 1942 (it required Popper's reflections on his own historical work). (*The Open Society*, chap. 25, secs. 1 and 3. These existed already in the February 1943 MS: Popper Archives [28, 14].)

constituents, for example, to individuals. They were not causal agents. (One may talk of society, class, and their social effects as a form of shorthand, but one must show how their effects were mediated through concrete social agents.)[168] Whatever differences there were between natural and social objects, they had no bearing on method.[169] Intuitive understanding played a role in social science, but it did so also in physics. It had no methodological consequences. Intersubjective testing was the single validity criterion. Sociology and economics were as objective as physics.[170]

Popper believed that his methodological reform had major political ramifications. Historicism retarded technological social science, obstructed social engineering, and deterred political activism. Instead of making history, historicists searched for inexorable historical laws, hoping to ride them. Instead of planning institutions, they prophesied the collapse of capitalism. This was a prescription for inaction. After each failure, socialists revised their interpretation. Meanwhile, the fascists acted. (The Anschluss was still fresh on Popper's mind.) "The philosophers have only interpreted the world," declared Marx; "the point, however, is to change it." But Marxists were in contradiction with themselves. Marx's "'activist' exhortation" was "in conflict with the most significant claims of historicism. . . . The historicist can only *interpret* social development and aid it in various ways; his point, however, is that *nobody can change* it."[171] Dreaming of revolution, the Marxists succumbed to reaction. Popper denied them any concept of planning or social technology. He had not yet formulated the distinction between "piecemeal" and "utopian social engineering." Marxism was not potentially totalitarian; it was impotent. He intended to save the Marxists from themselves. His technological social science would make good on Marx's exhortation.

Popper first conceived of "utopian engineering" as he was writing *The Open Society*. The connection between methodological holism and utopian engineering he formulated only in 1944, in "Poverty, II."[172] He then also wrote his critique of Mannheim's holistic planning. There were other major additions to "Poverty, II" and "III." Popper's engagement with Mill expanded significantly. In "Poverty, I," neither Mill's holism ("states of

---

[168] With the possible exception of the last sentence (a formulation I owe to Ian Jarvie), this critique of "holism" (Section 23) was available prior to the introduction of methodological individualism in 1944 (Section 29).

[169] Having read Hayek more carefully in 1943–4, Popper conceded that the constantly changing parameters in economic analysis made measurement more difficult. Application of quantitative methods was essential, all the same. Moreover, as human interaction was permeated with rationality, social facts (actions and beliefs) were more accessible, and social situations less complicated and more predictable than in physics. Social science models, based on the assumption of complete rationality, compensated for difficulties in constructing experimental situations. ("Poverty, III," sec. 29.)

[170] "Poverty, I," secs. 6–9; "Poverty, II," sec. 23; "Poverty, III," sec. 29.

[171] "Poverty, I": 102; *Poverty*, p. 52.

[172] *The Open Society*, chap. 9; "Poverty, II," secs. 22–4.

society"), nor his two sociologies (historicist and "technological"), nor his confusion of law and trend were a subject of criticism.[173] Popper sensed that both evolution and historical progress were trends, not laws, but as he had not yet clarified the presuppositions of "historical explanation," he could not fully explain the difference between trend and law.[174] Basic social science terminology was absent from "Poverty, I." Instead of "methodological individualism" and "collectivism," Popper used his own "methodological nominalism" and "holism."[175] He remembered writing on the "zero-method" and "situational logic" in 1938, but there is no evidence of social science models in "Poverty, I."[176] He added his institutional theory of progress (scientific progress depended on free institutions) in 1944–5.[177] It required both situational logic and the distinction between law and trend. In short, the original version of "Poverty" did not include some of the work's major contributions.

Even in its underdeveloped form, "Poverty" was a considerable achievement. Popper clarified scientific prediction in an original and brilliant fashion that completely transformed the debate and challenged a central tenet of interwar leftist culture. He concurred with the Austrian economists against Mill, Neurath, and the Marxists that social science was theoretical, not historical, but against the economists he argued that prediction was essential to natural and social science alike. It was just that science did not make the predictions both sides thought it did. It did not predict natural or historical events but excluded possible events in insulated experiments. (This also answered Neurath's and Morgenstern's argument that prediction could become a self-fulfilling prophecy.) Science was not omnipotent. Clearing out natural science myths, Popper reformed social science.

Popper retained autonomy and predictive power for science by disengaging prediction from history. *Pace* Neurath, scientists qua scientists were not political agents. Their predictions did not make history. But qua citizens, they could make technological social science an effective reform instrument. Their predictions could help design social institutions to protect society against historical vicissitudes. Popper did not separate theory and praxis, but he reformulated their relationship. Science informed planners

---

[173] "Poverty, II," sec. 22, "Poverty, III," secs. 28, 32.

[174] The first evidence that Popper thought through "historical explanation" was his corrections to *The Open Society* (chap. 25, sec. 2 and n. 7), 2 September 1944 (Popper to Gombrich [28, 16]). He first explained the difference between trend and law in "Poverty, III," Sections 27–8, after he had formulated in detail his view of historical explanation. However, all components of "historical explanation" had existed in his discourse since *Logik*.

[175] The conventional terms appeared in "Poverty, III" after Popper had read Hayek's "Scientism and the Study of Society, I," "II," and "III," *Economica* 9–11 (1942–4).

[176] *Autobiography*, pp. 116–17; "Poverty, III," secs. 29–31; corrections to *The Open Society*, chap. 14, pp. 90–2, 30 August 1944 (Popper to Gombrich [28, 16]). These methods will be explained in Chapter 10.

[177] "Poverty, III," sec. 32.

how they might prevent social ills. The decision whether and how to proceed was free. History did not tell one way or the other. How scientific activity was organized, a reform consensus molded, and reforms politically applied was of no concern to Popper in 1940. Working on *The Open Society*, then reading Hayek on methodology and politics, he recognized that planning presented major political problems. He never addressed them fully, and eventually they undermined his reform, but originally, his social engineering was progressive and activist. The intellectual universe from which "Poverty" emerged was decidedly leftist, ambivalent, perhaps, about Marxism, but at virtual loggerheads with Hayek's libertarianism.[178]

By 1940 Popper had already cut his ties to the old world but was not quite yet a member of the new. He always lived in between cultures, but never more so than during his early years in exile. "Poverty" emerged from this liminal period. His cultural transition was rapid. To the extent that he could find a political and cultural home anywhere, he had found it. If the failure of Austrian socialism gave rise to his critique of historicism, and Viennese progressivism informed his inquiries, he was already thinking about his new audience and new contexts for application. This, as well as his meager social science background, reinforced his proclivity to reformulate the methodological problem situation by abstracting Central European arguments from their historical context. As a result, "Poverty" had an ephemeral quality. That its critique of Marxism was later read as an attack on communism is not incomprehensible.

In the 1990s, historical contingency is an article of faith, and universal histories are vilified and ridiculed. It is difficult to imagine the interwar leftist milieu where belief in inexorable laws was as predominant as contingency is today. Popper was a critic of this culture. During his early years in exile, he was in his most "poststructuralist" mood – radically antiessentialist, suspicious of metaphysics, sensitive to the contours of ideology, excelling at deconstructing holistic entities, delighting in dissolving progressive narratives, insisting on the plurality (and ultimate subjectivity) of histories, refusing to admit anything but ruthless criticism as a foundation for social life. To be sure, his "methodological nominalism" did not dissolve the individual into discourse as poststructuralists do today, not only because the individual was integral but also because s/he was a good departure point for analysis. Individuals may be socially (and discursively) shaped, but the

---

[178] This agrees with Jeremy Shearmur, *The Political Thought of Karl Popper* (London: Routledge, 1996). Unlike Western commentators, Austrian historians recognize that *Poverty* was not an anticommunist treatise, but one reflecting ambivalence about Austrian socialism. Still, they judge *Poverty* by Popper's postwar proximity to Hayek, rather than by his interwar heterodox socialism: Friedrich Stadler, "Denkmuster und Lebenslinien: Karl R. Poppers Intellektuelle Autobiographie," and Johann Dvorak, "Karl Popper und die Wissenschaft von der Geschichte in der Epoche des Faschismus," both in *Versuche und Widerlegungen offene Probleme im Werk Karl Poppers* (Vienna: Geyer, 1986). See also the essays by Karl Müller in the same volume, edited by Müller, Stadler, and Friedrich Wallner.

discourses allegedly creating them present greater risks of mystical holism than they do. Nominalism purged them.

Contrary to appearances, poststructuralism did not banish "historicism" from the academy. The constant efforts that academics are making to catch the trend and keep ahead of the pack recapitulate interwar endeavors to ride the train of history. Popper is an effective antidote. He calls attention to the futility and danger of such efforts.

Chapter 9

The Open Society, *1940–1942*

With the outbreak of World War II Popper offered to enlist in the New Zealand armed forces.[1] Fortunately for him, the army, and political philosophy, his application was denied. He soon began to regard his political project as a contribution to the war effort, and invested it with a fighting soldier's zeal. *The Open Society* was his single major work in political philosophy, and the most popular one. It consists of three controversial critiques of Plato, Hegel, and Marx that trace totalitarianism to humankind's "venerated intellectual leaders." Popper opined that the fascist drive to return to "tribal" society fed on anxieties arising from rapid changes in open societies. He found these anxieties expressed in Plato and Hegel. Marx and the socialists, in contrast, were progressive democrats, but their scientific pretensions, the belief in historical inevitability, weakened their ability and resolve to confront fascism, leaving Central European democracies defenseless. Popper also discussed a large range of epistemological, ethical, and political problems, defining the major issues at stake in the war and the principles for social reconstruction thereafter. He completed *The Open Society* in February 1943, but it remained unpublished until November 1945. Once published, it became a success overnight. It has remained in print for over half a century, and has been translated into more than thirty languages and reissued in numerous editions and reprints.[2]

The attacks on Plato and Hegel as the fountainhead of totalitarianism and on Marx as a false prophet immediately created a stir. Controversies continued for years, reaching a peak with the 1950 American edition. Most classicists regarded Popper's totalitarian Plato as scandalous; Hegel scholars dismissed his Hegel as a myth; and Marxists attacked him as a liberal apologist. The experts' skepticism was drowned in the general public's enthusiasm and the praise of noted philosophers and historians.[3] Whether read in the context of the struggle against fascism or communism, *The Open*

---

[1] "Interview: Sir Karl Popper," *Sunday Times*, 12 July 1992, sec. 2.

[2] Karl Popper, *The Open Society and Its Enemies*, 2 vols. (London: Routledge, 1945). All references are to the first edition, unless otherwise indicated. As a rule, chapter and footnote numbers did not change between editions. I refer to them, rather than to page numbers, whenever possible.

[3] Isaiah Berlin, in Bibliography *Karl Marx*, 2d ed. (New York: Oxford University Press, 1948), Bertrand Russell, "Philosophy and Politics," *Unpopular Essays* (London: Allen & Unwin, 1950), p. 15, and testimonial and correspondence with Popper, 1946, Popper Archives, Hoover Institute (27, 14; 345, 14); reviews by Gilbert Ryle, *Mind* 56 (1947): 167–72 and Hugh Trevor-Roper, *Polemic* 3 (1946): 58–65.

Society responded to the central concerns of the educated public in Western Europe and the United States, and, later, in Central and Eastern Europe (where *samizdat* editions were popular). Written in amazingly clear language, its philosophical arguments were accessible to an audience not commonly used to discuss politics on such a level. Ever since, it has informed debate on democracy and discussions of Plato and Marx. Terms Popper coined or defined – Open Society, social engineering, essentialism – have become part of professional and popular discourse.[4] Few philosophical works have left a comparable impression.

THE POLITICAL PROJECT

Popper's despair at the course of European events and his resignation to the prospect of a long exile were reflected in his diminishing correspondence with friends. His long silence, lasting from early in 1939 until late in 1942 when he began writing friends concerning publication of *The Open Society*, complicates efforts to trace the origins and development of his political philosophy. He made no mention of his political project in his correspondence prior to 1940 and did not elaborate on it until 1942–3.[5] By that time he had already completed *The Open Society* and had had a draft of "The Poverty of Historicism" for more than four years. The archives contain no manuscript of *The Open Society* prior to October 1942.[6] Popper's *Autobiography* provides only a general tentative account of his project's development. A few letters from 1940 to 1942, containing brief statements about his current work, and a 1945 letter to a former colleague, including an ex post facto chronology, constitute additional evidence. Selected syllabi, lectures on logic, science, and religion, and notes taken at his 1941 course on the history of philosophy provide further signposts for his political education.[7] *The Open Society*'s rich references, compared with the early and later parts of "Poverty," likewise testify to his progress.

Popper's teaching had much to do with the direction his political philosophy took. His interest in Plato most likely emerged from his intro-

---

[4] Christian Fleck, "Sieg der *Offenen Gesellschaft?*" in *Heinrich Gomperz, Karl Popper und die Österreichische Philosophie*, ed. Martin Seiler and Friedrich Stadler (Amsterdam: Rodopi, 1994), pp. 201–22, includes some statistics.

[5] Popper to Carnap (four letters: 1939, 1940, 1942), Carnap Collection; Popper to Hayek, 16 September 1940, Hayek Archives (44, 1). It seems that Popper attempted to keep his political project confidential until it was complete.

[6] Manuscripts of vol. 1 (28, 12; 29, 1) probably date back to October 1942 with corrections (in blue ink) most likely introduced between February and April 1943. Manuscripts of vol. 2 (28, 13–14; 29, 2) date back to February 1943 with corrections introduced February–April 1943. The manuscript sent to Gombrich in late April (28, 15–16) included, retyped, all of these corrections.

[7] Canterbury College file, Popper Archives (366, 16, 19, 20, 24).

ductory ethics lectures in 1938–9. He complained profusely to Carnap, Hempel, and Kaufmann about having to teach the course, especially English ethics: "awful rubbish, enough to make one a positivist," he said.[8] The Greeks were essential to both his logic and ethics courses, and he did extensive readings in Greek logic and ethics. His antipathy to Plato was long-standing, but his observations on his historicism and totalitarianism were new. So was also his discovery of Aristotelian essentialism, the cardinal doctrine of historicist social science. In Section 10 of "Poverty," he criticized Aristotle and added cryptic remarks on Plato's historicism, as well as a few observations on his totalitarianism. He may also have mentioned Parmenides' doctrine of the One and Many that regarded difference and change in the universe as illusory and claimed that divine unity underlay opposites. He was chagrined that the University of New Zealand's final exams required students to recite such doctrines without exploring their antidemocratic implications. He showed his criticism to friends, including Henry Dan Broadhead, lecturer in classics, and they were mystified. An elaboration became necessary, and soon Popper found himself working on an essay on the history of historicism, leading in time to *The Open Society*.[9]

Popper's 1939 ethics syllabus already contained the historical framework for *The Open Society* and an outline of the first volume. The introduction to the course presented ethics as a normative, nondescriptive science and urged the adoption of the scientific attitude to it. The course next considered "facts of moral development: early group life and the beginning of morality, technical development and its social and moral implications, and social development – tribe, nation, humanity." The following section outlined moral theory from the rise of philosophy to Socrates: ethical relativism, the sophists, Socrates, Plato and Aristotle, the "Socratic" schools. The course then surveyed the empiricist and rationalist traditions in ethics, leaping from Democritus to the utilitarians, and from Pythagoras to Kant. It next considered the relationship between psychology and ethics, focusing on responsibility and "planned action in individual and social life," then moved to the "social aspects of ethics: individualism, nationalism, socialism; war and nationalism; internationalism." Finally, the course discussed "optimism and pessimism: moral progress and scientific progress."[10]

The course clarifies how Popper became interested in Plato and the Greeks. Certain features of his historical narrative had been present in his early work: nationalism to (socialist) internationalism, collectivism to individualism. Others were not: the transition from the closed to the open

[8] Popper to Kaufmann, 27 November 1937, *Kaufmann Nachlaß*: "Schrecklicher Quatsch (man konnte dabei ein Positivist werden)."

[9] *Autobiography*, pp. 113–14; *The Open Society*, chap. 3, n. 30; E-mail communication with Colin Simkin.

[10] Canterbury College box, Popper Archives (366, 16).

society and the trajectory: tribe to nation to humanity.[11] The progress from tribe to civil society had been a familiar sociological theme since the Scottish enlightenment, and reappeared in Marx, Engels, and nineteenth-century anthropologists. Popper joined it to two progressive narratives: Kant's and Nelson's account of the transition from nationalism to cosmopolitanism and his own account of the transition from magic to science. In his W.E.A. (Workers' Educational Association) course, "Science in the Making," given the same year, he contrasted the magical and humanistic attitudes toward science. He argued that modern views of science as a "body of knowledge" still reflected old magic. Scientific discovery did not unveil the truth but invented hypotheses that solved practical problems. Theory began and ended with efforts to shape the world.[12] Philosophy, science, technological progress, and ethical conventionalism became the Open Society's markers.

Eduard Meyer's *Geschichte des Altertums* (History of the ancient world) may have provided the crucial link between Greece and the anthropological narrative. Popper used Meyer extensively to familiarize himself both with classical Greece and the history of the ancient East.[13] Meyer (1855–1930) was the most influential German ancient historian of his time. He thought of himself as writing in an anthropological vein, carrying out the project of Karl Lamprecht's cultural history. He spoke of the transition from *Stamm* to *Staat, ethnos* to *polis*, in early Greek history. A nationalist, antidemocratic, and antiparliamentarian mandarin, he emphasized that both tribe and state were superior to the individual. Popper picked up on *Stamm*, which carried the primitive and nationalist connotations he wished to convey. As Meyer alluded to the close relationship between *polis* politics and the national state, Popper naturally assumed that nation followed tribe, then added humanity as a third and final stage, converting Meyer's reactionary narrative into a progressive cosmopolitan one.

Aside from the early Greeks, the Jews were the tribe par excellence. The racial *Stamm* played here especially well. Almost all enlightenment thinkers

[11] Popper still did not use the terms *open* and *closed society*. The term *Open Society*, he said later, expressed his feeling after he had arrived in England from fascist Austria. ("On Reason and the Open Society," *Encounter* 38 [1972]: 13–14.) Henri Bergson had used the terms *open society* and *closed society* in *Les deux sources de la morale et de la religion* (Paris: Presses Universitaires de France, 1932) (*Two Sources of Morality and Religion* [London: Macmillan, 1935].) In his "Note to the Introduction" (added in April 1944), Popper took pains to distinguish his view from Bergson's. He pursued the discussion further in chap. 10, n. 6 (rewritten April–May 1944) and n. 59 (2) (added June 1944: Popper to Gombrich, 27 June 1944 [300, 3]). For comparisons of Popper and Bergson: *The Open Society in Theory and Practice*, ed. Dante Germino and Klaus von Beyme (The Hague: Martinus Nijhoff, 1974), esp. essays by Dante Germino, Anthony Parel, and Melvin Richter.

[12] "The Sciences Natural and Physical: What is Science?" [Popper did not prohibit yet as essentialist "what is" questions], Popper Archives (366, 24).

[13] Eduard Meyer, *Geschichte des Altertums*, 2d ed., 5 vols. (Stuttgart: Cotta, 1915); *The Open Society*, chap. 10, nn. 8 and 39.

and liberal Protestant theologians shared the view that Christianity carried a cosmopolitan message which overcame Jewish ethnic exclusivity and ritual, that is, overcame tribalism.[14] Popper encountered this view once again in Meyer. The "chosen people" became for Popper a chosen race. This fit nicely with another work that shaped Popper's political horizons, Aurel Kolnai's *The War Against the West*. Kolnai (1900–73) was a Hungarian émigré (of Jewish origin), who studied in Vienna during the interwar period under Bühler, Gomperz, and Schlick (as well as under Husserl in Freiburg). Popper had met him at Polanyi's seminar but they did not keep in close touch. Kolnai regarded Nazism as a renewed tribal attack on the West, a pagan revival, seeking to obliterate Christian belief in the individual soul. He challenged Popper to rethink what was unique to the West and what was at stake in the war.[15] Popper's critique of Plato used Kolnai's terminology, "tribal egotism," "inequalitarianism," and the "soul," albeit in different senses from Kolnai. Austrian conceptions of nationality shaped both Popper's and Kolnai's views. Imperial Austria made *Volksstamm* (tribe, race, ethnicity) the basis of claims for *Nationalität* and cultural autonomy. Popper spoke of "tribal nationalism" (in current parlance, "ethnonationalism"). Tribe, nation, humanity became stages in the history of civilization.

Once Popper had decided, sometime late in 1939, to cut out the historical critique from "Poverty," the latter began taking shape as an exclusively social science work. It "was too abstract for wide appreciation," and so Popper decided to write a companion essay, "Marginal Notes on the History of Historicism." Both essays progressed slowly through the first eight months of the war.[16] The fall of France was a turning point. "I remember our sense of despair for Europe when listening together to a BBC report of Paul Reynaud's final appeal to the U.S. as France was succumb-

---

[14] The taboos of early Greek religion most likely evoked Jewish laws, especially dietary laws. (*The Open Society*, chap. 10, n. 38.)

[15] Aurel Kolnai, *The War Against the West* (New York: Viking, 1938). In postwar years, Popper regarded the conservative Kolnai as a worthy critic. (Correspondence with Kolnai, 1952–5 [316, 9]; Aurel Kolnai's subject file, Popper Archives [387, 25].) See also: "Aurel Kolnai: Prefatory Note," in *Structure and Gestalt*, ed. Barry Smith (Amsterdam: John Benjamins, 1981), pp. 393–5.

[16] In November 1939, Popper completed "Interpretation of Nebular Red-Shifts," *Nature* 145 (13 January 1940): 69–70. Nebular red-shifts had preoccupied him since they corroborated (in Eddington's eclipse observations) Einstein's theory in 1919. His brief piece responded to Gheury de Bray's previous note (*Nature* 144 [1939]: 285), which discussed "the possibility of explaining the red-shifts by assuming that the velocity of light is constant throughout the universe at any given time but decreases with time." Popper sought to show that "the proffered hypothesis . . . is one of three alternative ways of formulating the hypothesis of the expanding universe" (69). "The three . . . agree in regard to the observable effects they describe, . . . are logically equivalent, and do not describe alternative *facts*, but the same facts in alternative *languages*." This is the only occasion I know where Popper showed that a scientific dispute was mostly verbal. He usually considered this a positivist trick, and sought to demonstrate that disputes involved genuine problems. The note was highly technical, and Simkin surmises that Popper discussed it with Parton or White.

ing to Hitler," recalls Colin Simkin.[17] From then on, Popper seemed to have been possessed by his political mission. He worked ceaselessly on his historical essay, thinking at times that he might be writing the testament for Western civilization. He believed that his message was all-important: He had diagnosed Western civilization's malaise. His tone was strident, the connections he drew between historicist philosophy and fascist politics unnuanced. He identified the Western democracies with his own philosophy and personal fortunes. As always when at work on a monumental project, he was happy, if tense. His joy was a stark contrast to the stream of grim news from Europe.[18] He followed anxiously the efforts of relatives and friends, including his sister Annie, to escape from France. He feared for Britain, was relieved when Hitler attacked Russia instead, but remained apprehensive lest Russia succumb. Hearing of the Japanese attack on Pearl Harbor, he rejoiced: The U.S. entry meant that "the War will be won."[19]

The political project got, as usual, out of hand. Before long Popper was working on a series of essays on historicism's major prophets. Plato and Marx were the project's core from the start. His 1941 course in the history of philosophy reveals him working his way through Hegel, to whom he devoted the final eight lectures. It is unlikely that this was his original design: He would not have planned to spend a third of his course on a despised enemy, or to end the course with him – Hegel was always a transition to Marx. The sprawling and polemical Hegel lectures presented a marked contrast to the structured and judicious ones on empiricism and rationalism, and on Kant's epistemology and ethics.[20] Like his project, his course got out of control. He was traversing unfamiliar territory, lecturing

---

[17] Colin Simkin, "The Birth of *The Open Society*," in his *Popper's Views on Natural and Social Science* (Leiden: Brill, 1993), p. 185. Also: E-mail communication from Simkin, 9 June 1997.

[18] Popper to Carnap, 16 December 1940, Carnap Collection.

[19] *Autobiography*, pp. 114–15; draft of *Autobiography*, Popper Archives (135, 1).

[20] A student, perhaps an assistant, took notes, which were later typed (366, 24, under W.E.A. syllabus). The first six lectures contrasted empiricism and rationalism in early modern philosophy and presented Kant as a successful arbitrator. The next six focused on Kant's epistemology and another four on his ethics, providing first evidence that Popper was rethinking Kantian ethics. (See also 366, 14.) He was surefooted, but the lectures were less neatly organized, perhaps because, unlike the ones on epistemology, they were not borrowed from introductory courses he had taught before. He concluded with brief comments on Kant's politics, describing him as an ardent democrat, calling "Perpetual Peace" "one of the great[est] human documents," and expressing a mild reservation about "Universal History with a Cosmopolitan Purpose": Conjectural history was fine, but in Herder, Schlegel, and Hegel, the project ended in historicism (23 July 1941, p. 33).

The lectures were also significant in that they first included the bucket and the searchlight metaphors for human reason – the bucket theory viewed the mind as passively impressed with sensations, the searchlight as actively pursuing solutions to problems (pp. 16, 24, 45; "The Bucket and the Searchlight: Two Theories of Knowledge" [1948], *Objective Knowledge* [Oxford: Clarendon Press, 1972], pp. 341–61). The lectures also included the distinction between two types of philosophers, those interested in concepts and definitions and those interested in words and sentences (9 July 1941, p. 29). The former were essentialists. Popper would later identify them with language philosophers (*The Open Society*, chap. 11, sec. 2 and nn. 40–54; *Autobiography*, sec. 7).

on Hegel's philosophy of history and politics, reflecting recent readings that convinced him of Hegel's pervasive influence not only in Germany but in England as well: Broad (on McTaggart), Joad, Macmurray, Toynbee.[21] Elaborated and reorganized, the lectures became the Hegel chapter in *The Open Society*. As late as May 1941, Popper still conceived of his project as consisting of separate essays on the history of historicism that would join with "The Poverty of Historicism" and "What is Dialectic?" to form a collection on The Foundations of Political Science.[22] By the end of the course, in October 1941, he may have realized that he was writing a book. Hegel now provided an essential link in a historical narrative leading from Plato to Marx.

During the first half of 1942, the Japanese were advancing down the Pacific toward Australia. Popper began a mad rush to finish the book before they closed down on New Zealand. He worked feverishly, making ever-increasing demands on his colleagues. He had encouragement from Canterbury natural scientists, Broadhead helped him with Plato and classical Greece, and Simkin assisted with Marxist economics and corrected everything he had written. In May 1942, when Simkin entered the air force, the Marx part was done, and a draft of the manuscript, with the exception of the last chapter and many footnotes, almost ready. Margaret Dalziel, an assistant in classics and English, took Simkin's place, and Popper rewrote the entire manuscript with her. In May and June 1942, the battles of the Coral Sea and Midway removed the immediate danger for New Zealand, and, even before the battle of Stalingrad, Popper realized that Hitler had lost the Russian war. His relief must have been immense, but he did not let up on his work. *The Open Society* was his war effort, and he was almost apprehensive that the war would be over before the book was out. He now thought of it as also providing guidelines for postwar reconstruction. In October 1942 he completed what would become Volume 1 of *The Open Society,* and with an early version of Volume 2, he sent it to two U.S. publishers, hoping for a quick contract. Meanwhile, during the summer break of 1942–3, he worked literally night and day without sleep to revise the second volume and complete the footnotes. He managed to do so by the end of the break. In February 1943 the complete book went to the United States under the title: False Prophets: Plato – Hegel – Marx.

[21] C. D. Broad, *Examination of McTaggart's Philosophy*, 2 vols. (Cambridge: The University Press, 1933). "McTaggart was the most able and clear of Hegelians" (p. 44), yet provided an easy target for critics. Popper commended C. E. M. Joad's judgment of Hegel: *Guide to the Philosophy of Morals and Politics* (New York: Random House, 1938). He also used Schopenhauer's and Kierkegaard's critiques of Hegel, long familiar to him. John Macmurray, *The Clue to History* (New York: Harper, 1939) represented the worst amalgam of Christianity, Hegelian philosophy, and Marxist socialism. Arnold Toynbee's influential *A Study of History*, 3 vols. (London: Oxford University Press, 1934) embodied historicism. Throughout, Popper was flippantly dismissive of Hegel.

[22] Popper to Hodge, 21 May 1941, Popper Archives (20, 17).

"There is nothing to tell from our private life," wrote Popper discourteously to the Hempels in July 1943, "since we have nothing of this sort."[23] They never had much of a life apart from his work, but least of all when he was absorbed in *The Open Society*. Hennie was his only typist. She continued to type numerous drafts of his chapters for the next couple of years. In her free time, she tried to recreate Austria in exile, with little success. She socialized a little with Austrian émigrés and cultivated her garden, looking out at the Southern Alps. They went on a few skiing trips to Arthur's Pass and did some mountaineering. She took an interest in Karl's friends and students but had limited interaction with them: Social conversation stopped the moment he entered the room.[24] She adapted her friendships to suit his work, becoming close friends with Margaret Dalziel and Elise Simkin. When correspondence with women, or letters with a human touch, could help him, she was often the one to write.[25] She was melancholic at all times, worried about her mother and people close to her in Vienna. When they first had Simkin at their place for dinner early in 1939, both seemed wistful about life in Vienna before the Nazis.[26]

Popper was, however, an unqualified English "patriot." He preached to his students the superiority of British institutions, literature, and language to anything found in Central Europe. He was convinced that the decent, democratic, yet innocent English did not recognize their political and intellectual superiority to the wretched but pretentious Germans. His relentless attack on Plato and Hegel as totalitarian magicians, leading democrats astray, responded to English naïveté. He transferred this attitude to real life, too. A German Jewish refugee, Binswanger (relative of the renowned existential psychologist), came to lecture at Canterbury. Popper attacked him as a representative of pernicious German traditions that, once admitted by the English, would destroy rationality. He did his best to prevent Binswanger from getting a job at the college.[27] Chauvinism was, however, a deadly weapon, not to be wielded by outsiders. In June 1940, his senior colleague, Sutherland, spread rumors that cast doubt on his "loyalty to the British cause" and his right to instruct students on "war issues." (He alleged that Popper had attended a party given by an émigré to celebrate the fall of Holland to the Germans.) Popper was scared. As an enemy alien, he was exposed. Without the five- (or seven-) year residency requirement, New

[23] Popper to Carl and Eva Hempel, 5 July 1943, Popper Archives (306, 2).

[24] E-mail communication from Peter Munz, 3 February 1997; Agassi, *A Philosopher's Apprentice* (Amsterdam: Rodopi, 1993) reports the same pattern for postwar years.

[25] Popper to *Logik's* translator, 12 September 1938, indicating that Hennie would be writing to the cotranslator (the translator's wife), Popper Archives (20, 17); Hennie Popper to Ernst and Ilse Gombrich, 29 July 1943 (300, 2).

[26] E-mail communication from Colin Simkin, 9 June 1997.

[27] E-mail communication from Peter Munz, 25 February 1997.

Zealand had refused him naturalization in 1938, recognizing him only as a stateless person, with residence rights. Whether as a matter of routine or as a result of information Sutherland supplied, the police interviewed Popper. Nothing came of it, of course. Rector Hight wrote Popper a warm letter, testifying to his "loyalty and strong ethical appeal," and this ended the affair.[28]

Hight left Canterbury late in 1943, and, in the late war years, Popper remained without advocates on the college council. Still, he led a fulfilling intellectual life. He formed relationships with bright students, like Peter Munz. Munz began attending his lectures in 1941 and Popper invited him for Saturday sessions at his home, and played the role of the father figure, warning him about sex and giving advice about his relationships.[29] He greatly enriched Munz's life and the life of many others. In July 1941, Popper participated, with Simkin and other colleagues, in a series of broadcasts on New Zealand radio: "The Changing Bases of Society: Trends Likely to Influence the Future." The discussion was popular in character, and Popper played the pessimist against Simkin the optimist, giving Simkin the opportunity to elaborate on Swedish countercyclical budgetary policies and social engineering.[30] In the antipodal fall of 1943, he taught a course on research methods, primarily for agricultural chemists, organized by the Royal Society of New Zealand. It focused on practical research problems and had, he thought, excellent results. He enjoyed it: "It is comforting to find that philosophy can be of some practical use!" he wrote Carnap.[31]

In 1943 or 1944, Popper also gave four lectures in a university extension course, "Religion: Some Modern Problems and Developments." (The lecturers were mostly clergy.) He argued that his view of fallible science prevented a collision between science and religion, but observed that science, too, was a religion, demanding that all be sacrificed for truth. (Unbeknownst to Popper, he was echoing Nietzsche.) Science was a proper antidote to evil totalitarian religions, and so was also cooperation between Christians and non-Christians. Using Reinhold Niebuhr, Popper cautioned against political efforts to enforce morals, and he inveighed against collec-

---

[28] Popper to Hight, 17 June 1940; Hight to Popper, n.d. (366, 5). John Watkins discusses the episode in "Karl Raimund Popper 1902–1994," *Proceedings of the British Academy* 94 (1997): 654. On 29 September 1941, Popper received a "friendly alien" status. (Statement, LSE application, Hayek Archives [44, 1].)

[29] "She is more talented than you are, and you are hurting her career," he told Munz on one occasion. So much for his sexism, but also for his parenting. E-mail communication from Munz, 25 February 1997; Peter Munz, "Transformation in Philosophy Through the Teaching Methods of Wittgenstein and Popper," in *The Search for Absolute Values and the Creation of the New World* (New York: International Cultural Foundation, 1982).

[30] Popper Archives (27, 11).

[31] Popper to Carnap, 5 July 1943, Carnap Collection; Popper to Fritz Hellin, 20 July 1943, Popper Archives (28, 7).

tivism, utopianism, and historicism.[32] His lectures reflected *The Open Society*. He was living his work at all times and, for all his complaining, loving it.

HISTORICISM AND TOTALITARIANISM:
POPPER AND SOVIET COMMUNISM

Writing on Plato, Hegel, and Marx, Popper entered fields in which he had no expertise. His Greek could not have been good when he started the project. The *Realgymnasium's* curriculum included no Greek, and so whatever Greek he had, he had picked up either during his years at the humanistic gymnasium or on his own. He was familiar with the *Republic* and other Platonic dialogues, but he was not a classicist. He despised Hegel, but knew him little. He had thought over Marx for many years, but was not well read in recent Marxist theory. He now expanded his reading in ancient philosophy and history, charting his own interpretive course. He later explained lacunae in his scholarship by the limited library resources in New Zealand. He implied that he read whatever was available.[33] In many cases, he did. In others – Aristotle and Hegel were cases in point – he did not think the issues interesting enough to warrant further research. In Marx's case, he thought that he had gotten him right without the mediation, or obfuscation, of disciples. Thus, although he was a philosopher of natural science, he undertook to reshape the history of philosophy on his own. That the results were occasionally unscholarly was to be expected. That he achieved his goal, transforming the scholarly discussion of Plato and the public debate on Marx, is remarkable, a tribute to his imagination, daring, and ability to master new fields in a short time.

The Open Society offered a provocative hypothesis on the origins of historicism and totalitarianism and the relationship between them. Popper traced historicism to Heraclitus and the Presocratics and totalitarianism to Plato and classical Athens, then followed the development of historicism and totalitarianism up to Hegel and Marx. If historicism tied *The Open Society* to "Poverty" and methodological questions, totalitarianism gave it its distinct character as political philosophy. Popper sharply defined the differences between totalitarian and democratic polities: The first he associated with authority, spurious collective interest, and fear of change; the latter with freedom, individualism, critical discussion, and reform. Historicism's "myth of historical destiny" led to totalitarianism, a desperate effort to arrest or control change. It reflected the "strain of civilization," the anxiety accom-

---

[32] Popper Archives (366, 20). Popper dated the course to 1940, but his bibliography included Bertrand Russell, *Let the People Think* (London: Watt, 1941), and so 1942 was the earliest possible date. As his lectures reflected a completed *The Open Society*, the date was more likely 1943, possibly 1944.

[33] *Autobiography*, pp. 118–19.

panying "tribal society's" dissolution and the Open Society's emergence, the fear of change and instability created by social progress, the wish to return to the primitive community. The wish was futile, said Popper, and must be fought: "We must go on into the unknown, courageously."[34]

Most theories of totalitarianism emphasized modern dictatorship's novelty and the relationship between technology and mass terror, but Popper argued that totalitarianism "was as old as civilization itself."[35] Plato described all history as degeneration and conspired to halt the economic development of Athens and substitute an authoritarian regime for democracy. Unable to withstand the pressures and conflicts of Athens's open society, and startled by the execution of his mentor Socrates, he planned to return "to the cage of the closed society."[36] Plato's totalitarianism may not have directly inspired modern fascists, but it influenced Hegel, modern totalitarianism's prophet. Hegel recognized that one could not return to tribal society: His historicism was "progressive" in that it made history into destiny. He twisted humanitarian philosophy and politics so that they fit the mold of Prussian absolutism and "tribal nationalism." "Nearly all the more important ideas of modern totalitarianism are directly inherited from Hegel," wrote Popper.[37] Through Marxism, Hegelianism penetrated the humanitarian camp, corrupting intellectuals and workers. In impairing the defenses against fascism, Marxist historicism, too, was responsible for totalitarianism.

Of historicism and totalitarianism, Popper had a model of the first alone. Its application to the history of philosophy was not free of difficulties, as many aspects of historicism proved irrelevant to Plato, Marx, and Hegel. Popper focused on the historicist belief in destiny, tying it to such notions as the "chosen people," class, and race. Still, historicism was a well-defined concept. The same could not be said of totalitarianism. Popper never explained what it was. He assumed that the context – the fascist state and Nazi terror – was sufficient to clarify its meaning. He was right: Read in the context of fascism, his intentions were clear. Read in the context of the cold war, however, conceptual imprecision allowed for different interpretations as the meaning of totalitarianism in public discourse shifted to communism.

Mussolini first used "totalitarianism" in 1925, and his liberal and Catholic critics borrowed the term, using it to criticize fascist terror.[38] Italian

---

[34] *The Open Society*, vol. 1, p. 177.

[35] The most famous postwar statements were Hannah Arendt, *The Origins of Totalitarianism* (New York: Harcourt, Brace, 1951); Carl Friedrich and Zbigniew Brzezinski, *Totalitarian Dictatorship and Autocracy* (Cambridge, Mass.: Harvard University Press, 1956.)

[36] *The Open Society*, chap. 10, n. 70 (n. 71 in later editions).   [37] Ibid., vol. 2, p. 58.

[38] Martin Jänicke, *Totalitäre Herrschaft* (Berlin: Duncker & Humblot, 1971), p. 20. Mussolini spoke often of the fascists' "fierce totalitarian will" (*feroce volontà totalitaria*). Added in proof: Michelle-Irene Brundy has just shown me that the opposite is true. Mussolini appropriated the term from his liberal and Catholic critics, lending it a positive meaning. The liberal Giovanni Amendola first used "sistema

philosopher Giovanni Gentile turned the totalitarian state into a pillar of fascist philosophy.[39] Fascism and totalitarianism became interchangeable. With the triumph of national socialism, the concept was extended to Germany, and the focus of political analyses shifted from Mussolini to Hitler. In contrast to Italian fascism, Nazi ideology placed *Volk* rather than *Staat* at the center, and the Nazis gradually weeded out theorists, like Carl Schmitt, who used the "total state" to justify the *Gleichschaltung,* the "night of the long knives," and the Nuremberg Laws. Populist, emphatically racist, ideologists took the lead.[40] To observers, however, German politics seemed to exemplify totalitarianism. Terror, the end of civil and political liberties, and the seemingly unified state invading all spheres of life were "totalitarian."[41] Public discourse fused the "total state" with racism, hypernationalism, and imperialism into "totalitarianism."[42] This was "totalitarianism" as Popper used it in *The Open Society*: not an analytic model, but a rubric that captured those aspects of fascism inspiring the greatest horror, revulsion, and fear.[43]

Scholarly analyses of totalitarianism were not lacking. Many works written during the 1930s made a lasting contribution to understanding modern dictatorship. In *The Era of Tyrannies,* Élie Halévy analyzed the interplay of war and revolution, nationalism and socialism, in the formation of tyranny, and the "organization of enthusiasm" and corporatist economy in communist and fascist regimes.[44] His student Raymond Aron emphasized

totalitario" to criticize fascist electoral reform in May 1923, and the term was common among liberal and Catholic critics of fascism from then on. For complete references, see Michelle-Irene Brundy, "Le totalitarisme: Histoire du terme et statut du concept," *Communisme* 47–8 (1996): 13–32.

[39] Giovanni Gentile, "The Philosophical Basis of Fascism," *Foreign Affairs* 6 (January 1928): 290–304, an article directed at the foreign intelligentsia, but consistent with Gentile's works.

[40] Carl Schmitt, *The Concept of the Political* [1932], trans. George Schwab (New Brunswick, N.J.: Rutgers University Press, 1976); *Verfassungsrechtliche Aufsätze aus den Jahren 1924–1954* (Berlin: Duncker & Humblot, 1958).

[41] Historians from Ernst Frankael, *The Dual State* (New York: Oxford University Press, 1941) to Martin Broszat, *The Hitler State* [1969] (London: Longmans, 1981) to Hans Mommsen, "Die Realisierung des Utopischen: Die 'Endlösung der Judenfrage' im 'Dritten Reich,'" *Geschichte und Gesellschaft* 9 (1983): 381–420 have pointed out the disunity, competition, and confusion among Nazi agencies, which belied the unity projected by Nazi ideology. Hannah Arendt, *The Origins of Totalitarianism*, was most adamant that totalitarianism had nothing to do with the "total state" and that it contradicted the traditional state structure. This has now become the predominant view.

[42] "Symposium on the Totalitarian State," *Proceedings of the American Philosophical Society* 82 (1940), published separately in December 1939; Benjamin Alpers, "Understanding Dictatorship and Defining Democracy in American Public Culture, 1930–1945" (Ph.D. diss., Princeton University, 1994).

[43] Critics noted that Popper's totalitarianism was vague: Carl Friedrich, Michael Curtis, and Benjamin Barber, *Totalitarianism in Perspective* (New York: Praeger, 1969), essay by Barber. Even sympathetic reviewers professed confusion: Richard Robinson, "Dr. Popper's Defense of Democracy," *Philosophical Review* 60 (1951): 487–507, esp. 503.

[44] Élie Halévy, *The Era of Tyrannies* [1938] (Garden City, N.Y.: Anchor Books, 1965), esp. pp. 265–316.

the revolutionary and anti-Marxist character of totalitarian dictatorships.[45] Erich Voegelin explained the function of totalitarian ideologies as "political religions."[46] Emil Lederer, a German socialist economist disenchanted with Marxism, suggested that traditional state apparatus and social classes dissolved under totalitarianism.[47] Franz Neumann analyzed the contradiction between state and economy, administrative and cumulative needs, in the Nazi "totalitarian monopolistic economy."[48] Not all these works received immediate recognition, and most were probably unavailable to Popper in New Zealand, but he showed no sign of having read more popular studies either.[49] When he stated that his interest in social science method "was greatly stimulated by the rise of totalitarianism, and by the failure of the various social sciences and social philosophies to make sense of it," he could not have been making a well-informed statement.[50]

With few exceptions, public discourse until the end of World War II referred to fascist regimes alone as totalitarian. The concept, however, invited comparisons between fascism and communism.[51] Italian liberals and Catholics compared Soviet "red fascism" and Italian "white bolshevism." The liberals emphasized the state's control of economic life in both countries, the Catholics the repression of religion.[52] To Halévy, tyrannies emerging in the aftermath of World War I represented varieties of "national socialism."[53] Libertarian Austrian economists Ludwig von Mises and Friedrich Hayek condemned fascist and communist regimes alike as socialist and totalitarian.[54] Critics of bolshevism and Nazism invented the

---

[45] Raymond Aron, "Une révolution antiprolétarienne: Idéologie et réalité du national-socialisme" [1936] and "Etats démocratiques et Etats totalitaires" [1939], *Commentaire* 8 (1985): 299–310 and 6 (1983): 701–19, respectively.

[46] Eric Voegelin, *Die politischen Religionen* (Vienna: Bermann-Fischer, 1938).

[47] Emil Lederer, *The State of the Masses: The Threat of the Classless Society* (New York: Norton, 1940).

[48] Franz Neumann, *Behemoth: The Structure and Practice of National Socialism* (New York: Oxford University Press, 1942).

[49] Alfred Cobban, *Dictatorship: Its History and Theory* (New York: Scribner, 1939); Daniel Guérin, *Fascism and Big Business* (New York: Pioneer, 1939); Hermann Rauschning, *The Revolution of Nihilism* (New York: Longmans, Green & Co., 1939).

[50] *The Open Society*, vol. 2, p. 2. Could Popper's statement reflect primarily his response to Marxism and Karl Mannheim's *Man and Society in an Age of Reconstruction* (New York: Harcourt, Brace, 1940)?

[51] Les K. Adler and Thomas G. Paterson, "Red Fascism: The Merger of Nazi Germany and Soviet Russia in the American Image of Totalitarianism, 1930s–1950s," *American Historical Review* 75 (1970): 1046–64; Abbot Gleason, *Totalitarianism: The Inner History of the Cold War* (New York: Oxford University Press, 1995); Ernst Nolte, "Vierzig Jahre Theorien über den Faschismus," in *Theorien über den Faschismus*, ed. Ernst Nolte (Cologne: Kiepenheuer & Witsch, 1967), pp. 15–75; Walter Schlangen, *Die Totalitarismus-Theorie: Entwicklung und Probleme* (Stuttgart: Kohlhammer, 1976).

[52] Francesco Nitti, *Bolshevism, Fascism and Democracy* (New York: Macmillan, 1927); Luigi Sturzo, *Italy and Fascism* [1926] (New York: Fertig, 1967).

[53] Élie Halévy, *The Era of Tyrannies*.

[54] Ludwig von Mises, *Kritik des Interventionismus* (Jena: Fischer, 1929); Friedrich Hayek, *The Road to Serfdom* (Chicago: University of Chicago, 1944). Hayek used Halévy extensively.

concept of "political religion" almost concurrently.[55] American diplomats and journalists joked about "fascism" in Moscow. But the most sophisticated indictment of the Soviet Union as totalitarian emerged from among Marxist critics of Stalinism. Mensheviks and German socialists, especially members of *Neu Beginnen,* a German group straddling communism and social democracy, debated Stalinism at great length, and their exchanges were published in the parties' presses in exile. Rudolf Hilferding argued that Stalinist Russia was not "state-capitalism" but a totalitarian state economy not dissimilar to Nazi Germany. Former Mensheviks provided some of the cold war's earliest statements on Soviet totalitarianism.[56]

With the cold war, "totalitarianism" began dominating anticommunist Western rhetoric. Postwar historians and social scientists used it as the major analytic paradigm for Soviet Russia. The concept was both analytical and polemical, and always controversial. The New Left regarded it as mere propaganda. Yet, "totalitarianism" was primarily an antifascist concept in interwar years, and Marxists were responsible for the greatest conceptual innovation. It was conceived, elaborated, and argued prior to the cold war. Had this been recognized, the exchange on cold war liberalism during the 1960s and 1970s would have been more civilized.[57]

Prior to 1945, Popper did not use totalitarianism to describe communism even once. Like many liberals and socialists, he withheld judgment on Soviet Russia. He was unwilling to renounce civil liberty by supporting dictatorship, but, hopeful about Russia's future and mindful of its backwardness and autocratic past, he would not condemn it either. He saw both the French and Russian revolutions as marking human progress, but opposed political violence for anything other than defending democracy. Finding it highly problematic to justify immoral action for the future's sake, he denied that the socialist future justified the dictatorship of the proletariat. He felt ambivalent.

---

[55] Waldemar Gurian, *Bolshevism: Theory and Practice* (New York: Macmillan, 1932); Eric Voegelin, *Die politischen Religionen.*

[56] Rudolf Hilferding, "State Capitalism or Totalitarian State Economy?" [1940], *Modern Review* 1 (1947): 266–71; Raphael Abramovitch, "From Socialist Utopia to Totalitarian Empire," ibid., 249–65. André Liebich, "Marxism and Totalitarianism: Rudolf Hilferding and the Mensheviks" (Washington, D.C.: Wilson Center, 1987); William David Jones, *The Lost Debate: German Socialist Intellectuals and Totalitarianism* (Urbana, Ill.: University of Illinois Press, 1999).

[57] Christopher Lasch's strident "The Cultural Cold," in his *The Agony of the American Left* (New York: Vintage, 1969) did much to evoke the debate on totalitarianism. Some contributions: Ernest Menze, *Totalitarismus und Faschismus: Eine wissenschaftliche und politische Begriffskontroverse* (Munich: Oldenburg, 1980); *Totalitarismes,* ed. Guy Hermet (Paris: Economica, 1984) (the essay by Pierre Hassner, "Le totalitarisme vu de L'Ouest," pp. 15–41, is the best short review of the concept I know); *Totalitarian Democracy and After* (Jerusalem: Israel Academy, 1984), esp. the essay by Löwenthal; and Walter Laqueur, "Is There Now, or Has There Ever Been Such a Thing as Totalitarianism?" *Commentary* 80 (October 1985): 29–35.

In Popper's view, the Russian communists, full of "irrational faith," carried out a revolution, contrary to Marxist prescriptions, in an agricultural country. Against all odds, they won a bloody civil war. Faced with enormous social reconstruction, they stumbled upon piecemeal social engineering. The NEP (New Economic Policy) partially restored private enterprise, and the communists wisely waited for economic growth before collectivizing agriculture and introducing heavy industry. Reports on the first Five Year Plan, arriving in the midst of the Great Depression, projected a vital society confronting industrialization under adverse conditions. Popper knew little about the terror and the mass starvation accompanying collectivization, and concluded that the Five Year Plans were successful. He could not pretend, as he did with the NEP, that they were experiments in piecemeal social engineering, especially since he was not willing to see such experiments taking place elsewhere. At the same time, he did not wish to condemn them outright. He settled temporarily on seeing them as large-scale, undisciplined, partially scientific experiments that, by using propaganda and coercion, sometimes produced very good results, at enormous cost in life and liberty.[58]

The great purge trials coincided with the Popular Front, and with Russia assuming, after 1935, the leading role in resisting fascism. The Nazi–Soviet pact was a shock, but within two years, Russia was again on the Allies' side, carrying the brunt of the war. Popper's mute criticism of the Soviet Union in *The Open Society* reflected his wish not to damage the war effort, but such considerations would not explain his warm rhetoric about Soviet social engineering. He had still not made up his mind about the Soviet experiment. Urged by Alfred Braunthal to say more about it, he protested that "I do not know enough about Russia; and some views I held have been proved wrong."[59] Only the cold war set firmly and permanently his anti-Soviet position.

Popper was not blind to analogies between the Soviet and Nazi purges, but this did not sway his judgment that "totalitarianism" was a right-wing affair, an irrational, hypernationalist, romantic, racist, reactionary movement, not a revolutionary, progressive, and humanitarian one. The ancient model was Sparta, cast in Nazi Germany's image, a military aristocracy that wished to arrest change, maintain serfdom, and preserve the warrior's ethics against Athenian egalitarianism, democracy, and cosmopolitanism. Left and right historicism were not equivalent: The Marxists, mistaken as they were, belonged in the progressive camp fighting totalitarianism. The Soviet economy was "state-capitalism," and might develop into "totalitarian

---

[58] *The Open Society*, vol. 1: pp. 138–47; chap. 9, n. 6; chap. 10, n. 6; vol. 2: pp. 28, 78–9, 101–2, 133–4, 195; chap. 13, n. 7; chap. 16, n. 13. In later editions, his critique became more explicitly anti-Soviet. He also grew more reserved about the French Revolution, and focused on the terror rather than on 1789.

[59] Popper to Braunthal, 14 December 1943, Popper Archives (28, 2).

state-capitalism."[60] But he was anxious to turn the critique away from Russia, and veiled his criticism:

> Is it true that the workers' victory must lead to a classless society? I do not think so. . . . The most likely development is that those actually in power at the moment of victory – those of the revolutionary leaders who have survived the struggle for power and the various purges, together with their staff – will form the new ruling class of the new society, a kind of new aristocracy or bureaucracy; and it is most likely that they will attempt to hide this fact. This they can do, most conveniently, by retaining as much as possible of the revolutionary ideology . . . [especially] if they combine it with appeals to the fear of counter-revolutionary developments. In this way, the revolutionary ideology will serve them for apologetic purposes; as a vindication of the use they make of their power, and as a means of stabilizing it – in short, as a new "opium for the people."[61]

He pretended that this was a hypothetical situation, rather than historical analysis: "It is not my task here to make historical prophecies (or to interpret the past history of many revolutions). I merely wish to show that Marx's conclusion, the prophecy of the coming of a classless society, does not follow from the premises."[62]

Popper ridiculed the fascist "bogey of Bolshevism." He had not envisioned Soviet expansion or the division of Europe. He anticipated a postwar revival of fascism and Marxism in Central Europe, and thought that they would derive from national and regional traditions and lead to conflicts similar to those he had experienced in interwar years. He wanted all democratic forces, liberals and socialists alike, to coalesce to countervail fascism. Marxists would have to learn from interwar mistakes. Social planning was the key to designing new institutions. Whatever achievement the Soviet Union had, they were a result of applied social technology, not Marxism. His critique of Marxism had the Soviet experience at its margins. The center was occupied by projections for postwar reconstruction in Central and Western Europe.[63]

---

[60] *The Open Society*, chap. 18, nn. 5 and 9.

[61] Ibid., vol. 2, p. 127. These astute observations echo Bakunin, as well as Mensheviks and Trotskyists of the late 1930s. Popper most likely knew nothing about them. He may have read James Burnham (a former Trotskyist), *The Managerial Revolution* (New York: John Day, 1941): He criticized prophecies about "managerialism" and bureaucratic "technocracy." Later Bryan Magee pointed out the similarities to Milovan Djilas's theory of the New Class: *The Open Society*, vol. 2, chap. 18, n. 6; Milovan Djilas, *The New Class* (New York: Praeger, 1957).

[62] *The Open Society*, vol. 2, pp. 127–8.

[63] Ibid., "Introduction" and "Preface to the Second Edition"; *Autobiography*, p. 115; my interview with Popper, 26 January 1984.

PLATO, SOCRATES, CLASSICAL ATHENS,
AND THE "WEST"

Popper found in Plato the first and most comprehensive totalitarian program in Western philosophy. His interpretation shattered the traditional consensus regarding Plato as a fountainhead of Western humanism, and created a scandal among classicists. Most responded with critical and polemical reviews, and at least two wrote monographs to answer Popper.[64] He offered a rejoinder to them in a 1961 addendum to *The Open Society.* Scholarly controversy reverberated in the public sphere, and Plato was taken off his pedestal. He was never the same again. Popper had transformed a field.

SCHOLARSHIP AND POLITICS IN POPPER'S
INTERPRETATION OF PLATO

Plato was held in high regard both in Vienna, where Popper received his classical education, and in England and America, where his major audience was. The two contexts were linked. Progressive English and Viennese classicists conducted intensive exchanges during the Victorian period. Theodor Gomperz, whose *Greek Thinkers* popularized classical Greece in fin-de-siècle Vienna, was responsible for translating John Stuart Mill into German. In Mill's circle, he encountered George Grote, the foremost Victorian historian of classical Greece. Grote and Gomperz were both utilitarian reformers and read their struggles against aristocracy and church into the *polis,* identifying with classical democracy. They were not blind to Plato's authoritarianism, but their criticism was mild and respectful, never questioning his humanitarianism.[65] Cornford continued the tradition of progressive

---

[64] Critical reviews: G. C. Field, *Philosophy* 21 (1946): 271–6, as well as chapter 10 of *The Philosophy of Plato* (New York: Oxford University Press, 1949); R. Hackforth, *Classical Review* 61 (1947); Eric Unger, "Contemporary Anti-Platonism," *The Cambridge Journal* 2 (1949): 643–59; and G. J. de Vries, *Antisthenes Redivivus: Popper's Attack on Plato* (Amsterdam: North Holland Pub., 1952). See also: Hans Meyerhoff, "Plato among Friends and Enemies," *Encounter* (December 1961): 45–50 and John Plamenatz, *British Journal of Sociology* 3 (1952): 264–73. (Meyerhoff and Plamenatz were not classicists, but they wrote on Plato.) More balanced and sympathetic were Ernest Barker, "From Plato to Marx," *Sunday Times,* 9 December 1945; A. D. Lindsay, "The Open Society," *Manchester Guardian,* 25 January 1946; and Richard Robinson, "Dr. Popper's Defense of Democracy," *The Philosophical Review* 60 (1951): 487–507. See also: Gilbert Ryle, *Mind* 56 (1947): 167–72. Renford Bambrough, ed., *Plato, Popper and Politics:* (New York: Barnes and Noble, 1967) collected the most important reviews. Monographs: Ronald Levinson, *In Defense of Plato* (Cambridge, Mass.: Harvard University Press, 1953); John Wild, *Plato's Modern Enemies and the Theory of Natural Law* (Chicago: University of Chicago, 1953). See also his "Popper's Interpretation of Plato," in *The Philosophy of Karl Popper,* ed. Paul Arthur Schilpp (La Salle, Ill.: Open Court, 1974), vol. 2, pp. 859–75.

[65] George Grote, *Plato and Other Companions of Socrates* (London: John Murray, 1865); Theodor Gomperz, *Griechische Denker,* 3 vols. (Leipzig: Veit, 1896–1906). (*Greek Thinkers,* trans. Laurie Magnus and G. G. Berry, 4 vols. [London: Murray, 1901–12].) On the Gomperz–Mill connection: Adelaide

classical scholarship during the first half of the twentieth century, but in both Victorian and Edwardian England, the progressives were a minority. The conservative majority admired Plato and Aristotle, and shared their reservations about democracy. In the late Victorian period, Platonism enjoyed a revival in British universities, and Plato was upheld as a prophet, educator, moralist, and political reformer. At Oxford, Benjamin Jowett and Walter Pater raised three generations in awe of Plato. John Burnet, A. E. Taylor, and Ernst Barker continued, in Edwardian England, the tradition that regarded Plato as the founder of humanism and idealism, a Christian before Christ. Conservatives and progressives alike shared enormous respect for Plato.[66]

Twentieth-century dictatorship inspired a major reassessment of Plato. During the 1930s, harsh critiques came out, linking the *Republic* to Soviet and Nazi totalitarianism. Philosopher Werner Fite, classicist Alban Winespear, and Labor intellectual Richard Crossman attacked Plato from liberal and Marxist perspectives. All three saw the *Republic* as responding to the crisis of Athenian democracy, and argued that Plato opted to reestablish a "feudal" aristocracy in Athens, modeled on Sparta. All three denied that Plato had concern for the individual's moral development, or the citizens' welfare. Fite deplored Plato's "eugenics," especially his encouragement of "Dorian homosexual practices" to control breeding. Crossman focused on Plato's moral absolutism, censorship, and belief in revolution.[67]

Popper became familiar with much of this background. His intensive

---

Weinberg, *Theodor Gomperz and John Stuart Mill* (Geneva: Droz, 1963). On Grote's influence on German scholarship: Arnaldo Momigliano, "George Grote and the Study of Greek History," in his *Studies in Historiography* (London: Weidenfeld and Nicolson, 1966). Popper was also familiar with Eduard Zeller, whose work was critical of Plato and Aristotle. Zeller was widely read in Germany and later in translation in England: *Outlines of the History of Greek Philosophy* (1883), rev. by Wilhelm Nestle (New York: Humanities Press, 1951).

[66] Benjamin Jowett, *The Dialogues of Plato*, 3d ed., 5 vols. (Oxford: Oxford University Press, 1924); Walter Pater, *Plato and Platonism* (New York: Macmillan, 1894); John Burnet, *Greek Philosophy from Thales to Plato* (London: Macmillan, 1914); A. E. Taylor, *Plato* (London: Methuen, 1929). See also: Frank M. Turner, *The Greek Heritage in Victorian Britain* (New Haven, Conn.: Yale University Press, 1981). There were a few exceptions to the admiration for Plato. Macaulay criticized the idols of idealist philosophy, chief among which were Platonic truth, beauty, and good. James Martineau, a Unitarian intellectual, attacked Plato in *Types of Ethical Theory* (Oxford: Clarendon Press, 1885) for suppressing the individual. They remained, however, solitary voices.

[67] Werner Fite, *The Platonic Legend* (New York: Scribner, 1934); Alban Winespear, *The Genesis of Plato's Thought* (New York: Dryden, 1940); Richard Crossman, *Plato Today* [1937] (New York: Oxford University Press, 1939). Popper read and used Crossman and was eager to emphasize his independence: *The Open Society*, vol. 2, pp. 75, 114, 122, 149; chap. 3, n. 31; chap. 6, n. 2. In an early manuscript (Popper Archives [29, 3]), he mentions (chap. 6, n. 10) that he argued "the discrepancy between Plato's and the popular Greek idea of justice . . . in lectures since 1937" and included a question about it in the University of New Zealand final exam in 1941.

reading program brought him up to date on the scholarship.[68] He brushed up on his Greek and began translating Platonic excerpts, which, in his view, had been distorted by efforts to humanize him. His interpretation reflected the virtues and vices of an outsider's perspective. He upset long-held views in a manner unlike that of a classicist, rendering Greek terms in modern equivalents that most classicists found questionable. Still, a Plato scholar, Richard Robinson, agreed that it was not outrageous for him to redress the balance.[69] His view of the relationship between Socrates and Plato might be unacceptable, but he engaged classicists in an erudite fashion, and Robinson commended his discussion of the Socratic Problem (the progression of Plato's dialogues) as the most "clearly and persuasively set out" ever.[70] More so than historians, perhaps, Popper lacked a sense of what was feasible in classical Athens (an abolitionist movement, for example). But reading contemporary politics into the polis was a long practice. Popper just pushed it to its limits.

For a generation no longer educated in the classics, it is difficult to imagine earlier periods' intense engagement with the Greeks. German historians rewrote Athenian history each time Germany went through a major political change, taking sides in Athenian domestic and foreign conflicts.[71] Meyer thought of Athens under Themistocles as an ideal *Reich,* and regarded its decline as a result of democracy gone wild. He chastised Grote

[68] He read Grote, Gomperz, Meyer, Zeller, Burnet and Taylor, and their successors, Field and Morrow, Cornford, and Tarn. (G. C. Field, *Plato and his Contemporaries* [London: Methuen, 1930]; Glenn Morrow, "Plato and Greek Slavery," *Mind* 48 [1939]: 186–201; Francis M. Cornford, *Before and After Socrates* [Cambridge: Cambridge University Press, 1932] and Cornford's edition of the *Republic;* W. W. Tarn, "Alexander the Great and the Unity of Mankind," *Proceedings of the British Academy* 19 [1933]: 123–66.) He also used the standard collection of pre-Socratic fragments: Hermann Diels, *Die Fragmente der Vorsokratiker* (Berlin: Weidmannsche Buchhandlung, 1922). There were some lacunae: Jaeger's *Paideia* and Nettleship's and Shorey's works on Plato were, perhaps, the obvious ones. (Werner Jaeger, *Paideia* [1934], trans. Gilbert Highet, 3 vols. [New York: Oxford University Press, 1939–1944]; R. L. Nettleship, *Lectures on the Republic of Plato* [New York: Macmillan, 1929]; Paul Shorey, *What Plato Said* [Chicago: University of Chicago, 1933], as well as Shorey's *Republic*, which Popper regretted not having.)

[69] See the debate on paragraphs 942a–c of Plato's *Laws* (which served as an epigram to *The Open Society's* first volume). Plato urged that "no man, and no woman, be ever suffered to live without an officer set over them, [so as] to teach one's soul the habit of never so much as thinking to do one single act apart from one's fellows" (trans. A. E. Taylor, *The Collected Dialogues of Plato*, ed. Edith Hamilton and Huntington Cairns [Princeton, N.J.: Princeton University Press, 1963]). Was Plato's statement limited to military life, or did it extend, as Popper suggested, to daily life? (*The Open Society*, vol. 2, pp. 5, 89–91, and addendum to the 4th edition [London: Routledge & Kegan Paul, 1962], pp. 338–42; Levinson's critique: *In Defense of Plato*, pp. 531–4; Robinson's discussion: "Dr. Popper's Defense of Democracy": 490–2.)

[70] *The Open Society*, chap. 10, n. 56; Robinson, "Dr. Popper's Defense of Democracy": 494.

[71] Beat Näf, *Von Perikles zu Hitler?* (Bern: Peter Lang, 1985). For German artists, philosophers, and poets: Eliza Marian Butler, *The Tyranny of Greece Over Germany* (Cambridge: Cambridge University Press, 1935). For the archaeologists: Suzanne Marchand, *Down from Olympus: Archaeology and Philhellenism in Germany, 1750–1970* (Princeton, N.J.: Princeton University Press, 1996).

for his partiality toward the Athenian democrats and naval imperialism. (Periclean Athens resembled the British Empire too much.) Popper countered by exposing Meyer's antidemocratic bias and Prussian predilection for Roman militarism. For Grote and Gomperz, Sparta and the Athenian oligarchs were archenemies, and the sophists, the cynics, and the epicureans philosophical heroes. Popper followed in their footsteps: Their heroes and enemies were his, but he placed them in the context of the contemporary global struggle against totalitarianism. The democratic West's war with Nazi Germany recapitulated Athens's war with Sparta. The basic terms of Popper's interpretation emerged from contemporary politics, not classical Athens. Heinrich Gomperz warned repeatedly of the danger of false similarities between the classical and modern world.[72] Popper read his work but refused his skepticism, which would have rendered *The Open Society* impossible. He made Greek intellectual and political life speak directly to the present. The result was an anachronistic interpretation that diminished the past's alterity, but one that was scholarly well supported.

Sophisticated anachronism is difficult to criticize. Popper's critics, often avowed Platonists, found that they needed to argue their case issue by issue. Short reviews proved inadequate, and so they wrote volumes of formidable scholarship. When seeking to restore Plato to classical Greece, they used powerful arguments, but they ignored the contribution that Popper made to Plato scholarship by raising questions that ought to have been raised long before. Endeavoring to explain away Plato's harshest statements, the critics ran into problems similar to those plaguing Popper. Every translation renders the alien familiar. The line separating legitimate translation of Greek ideas into modern language from distortion of "otherness" is thin. Popper crossed this line, but so did most classicists. And he provided at least as much in return.

The myth of historical destiny, the idea that natural or divine forces shape history and it is futile for humans to attempt to do so, had prevailed among the early Greeks, said Popper. Even the pre-Socratic philosophers of sixth-century B.C. Ionia, originators of Western philosophy, did not break with it. They, especially Heraclitus, formulated central tenets of Plato's historicism. "Everything is in flux, and nothing is at rest," said Heraclitus; "one cannot step twice into the same river." Natural change had social corollaries: Political regimes rose and fell; laws and social norms were in flux. Pre-Socratic explanations disclosed ambivalence about change. Change was decay, but a cyclical historical law governed it. It was merely appearance, leaving the harmony of the universe undisturbed. The world was a unity of opposites, a mystical whole. Strife and war reflected opposites in conflict, but in the larger order of things, opposites coexisted harmoniously.

---

[72] Heinrich Gomperz, *Philosophical Studies* (Boston: Christopher, 1953).

Harmony was evident to those who unveiled the universal cycle. Modern historicists sought to control relativism by turning history into a final judge, Heraclitus by entrusting a cyclical law with arbitrating change, in an eternal and harmonious universe.

Pre-Socratic historicism reflected the transition from myth to critical philosophy. Like modern historicists, Heraclitus lived in a rapidly changing world. Democracy was on the rise, and the aristocratic regime of his home-town Ephesus was in trouble. Unable to deny change, he sought to control it by falling back on the myth of destiny. Historicism reflected fear of change, impotent efforts to contain progress. In later years, Popper was kinder to the pre-Socratics, arguing that they established the tradition of critical philosophy. By inventing hypotheses, rejecting them, then forming counterhypotheses, they liberated themselves from myth. He contrasted them with the dogmatic and mystical Pythagoreans who influenced Plato. Critical and dogmatic philosophy had been in conflict from the start.[73]

Plato shared the pre-Socratic conviction that change spelled decay, and appropriated the cyclical view of history. He regarded Athenian democracy as a degenerate form of government, a mere shadow of the ideal state of the golden age. Book VIII of the *Republic* described the stages of deterioration through which the ideal city had passed: timocracy, oligarchy, democracy, and tyranny. Contrary to most classicists, Popper insisted that the description was historical. Unlike the pre-Socratics, Plato determined to interrupt the cycle of destruction by arresting political change. His own ideal city might overcome the tendency toward deterioration.[74] Paradoxically, a pessimistic vision of destiny gave rise to activist historicism.

Plato combated the sophists, teachers of rhetoric active in fifth-century Athens. They broke decisively with the closed society and emphasized the relativity, contingency, and diversity of social norms. Primitive ethics, opined Popper, tended toward "naive monism," or biological naturalism. It regarded natural laws and social norms, *physis* and *nomos*, as identical. The

---

[73] Popper, "Back to the Presocratics," in *Conjectures and Refutations* (New York: Basic Books, 1963), pp. 136–65. See also his *The World of Parmenides: Essays on the Presocratic Enlightenment* (London: Routledge, 1998) and *In Search of a Better World* (London: Routledge, 1992), chaps. 7–8. For *The Open Society*, Popper consulted Wilhelm Nestle, *Die Vorsokratiker* (Jena: Diederichs, 1905) (chap. 2, n. 3). The historiography of Archaic Greece has made progress since, especially due to archaeological evidence. For an attempt to place the pre-Socratics in this context, see Anthony Snodgrass, *Archaic Greece* (Berkeley: University of California, 1980). For the pre-Socratics: G. S. Kirk and J. Raven, *The Presocratic Philosophers* (New York: Cambridge University Press, 1962). For another influential hypothesis about the invention of rationality and democracy: Jean Pierre Vernant, *The Origins of Greek Thought* (Ithaca, N.Y.: Cornell University Press, 1982).

[74] For the classical argument against the historicity of Plato's scheme, see A. E. Taylor, "The Decline and Fall of the State in Republic VIII," *Mind* 48 (1939): 23–38. On the connections between Plato and Heraclitus, see T. H. Irwin, "Plato's Heracleiteanism," *Philosophical Quarterly* 27 (1977), 1–13. In the *Metaphysics* 987a–32, Aristotle reported that Plato had been acquainted with the Heraclitean philosopher Cratylus "from his youth."

sophists rejected this view, and contrasted the unity of physis with the diversity of nomos. Protagoras, Antiphon, and others reached a position close to "critical dualism." They assumed that norms were made by humans and subject to change: The members of society were responsible for its laws. No moral decision could be derived from facts, and no normative law deduced from sociology. Historical trends could not instruct one how to act. There was an unbridgeable gap between facts and decisions. All this was becoming clear to the sophists. Some of them mistakenly assumed that critical dualism implied ethical relativism. A disconcerted Plato reacted by reestablishing monism and ethical absolutism.

Plato introduced the Forms. Worldly, sensible things as perceived by the common person were mere shadows, semblances of lesser or greater proximity to the heavenly Forms, essences of the intelligible world. Appearances changed, but real or true nature was eternal: "The changing visible world was only a decaying copy of an unchanging invisible world." Parmenides's One complemented the Forms. Being was One: We cannot think or speak of that which is not. To the extent that we think or speak of differences or changes, they must be illusory. Diversity was misleading: Particulars reflected essential, universal, divine unity. Plato identified the Forms of the good, beauty, and justice with Parmenides's One, turning his metaphysical doctrine into an ethical one. Unity was superior to diversity, and the closer individuals embodied the ideal city, the closer the *polis* was to the universal, eternal, and divine.[75] To these Plato added Pythagorean "number-mysticism." Impressed by the accuracy of mathematics and the power of equations, and convinced that numerical relations expressed formal properties of the universe, he set out to design an ideal humanity based on mathematical principles. The centerpiece was a breeding program that depended on a mysterious true number. The philosopher alone knew the number, and s/he alone could stop historical decline.[76]

For his city, Plato planned a strict division of "classes," based on "racial" differences. Each class had different social roles, rights, and duties. He abolished private property among the elite, the guardians, to prevent conflicts.[77] Authoritarian education ensured the elite's cohesion. Harsh censorship, heavy propaganda, and repressive measures enforced conformity, stemming dissent, critical thought, and innovation. A eugenics program bred warriors

---

[75] Popper sought to dissociate Socrates from Plato's Forms and Parmenides' One. Yet, for the Forms to emerge, all Plato had to do was identify Socrates' God, who was identical with the good, justice, and holiness, with Parmenides' One. After Socrates' execution, Plato and his students left Athens for a while and settled in Megara. He may have adopted Parmenides from Eucleides of Megara.

[76] Plato may have encountered Pythagorean number theory during his journey to Italy, recounted in the autobiographical Seventh Letter, *The Collected Dialogues*, pp. 1574–98.

[77] Popper insisted that Plato's socialism was merely instrumental in nature and did not reflect humanitarian ideals. He dismissed Plato's proposal for abolishing the family and transforming gender roles among the elite as "nothing new."

and rulers, a tribal aristocracy. This was a distinctly totalitarian program, but Plato misled his audience, packaging it in a humanitarian language. He called the ruling class "guardians," or sometimes "shepherds." (Popper turned them into "herdsmen" and "watch dogs.") He called the majority "flock." (Popper turned them into "human cattle.") He knew that he could not directly attack democratic ideals; they had taken root in Athens. He used democratic and sophistic terms, but perverted their meaning. His plot succeeded: His totalitarianism went unrecognized. Interpreters Christianized and idealized him. His ideas spread among well-meaning intellectuals, corrupting philosophy and damaging society.

Totalitarian "justice" was Plato's greatest perversion. Athenian democrats had a modern egalitarian concept of justice. They spoke of *isonomia,* equality before the law. Socrates (or Plato) himself seemed to argue for isonomia in the *Gorgias,* an early Platonic dialogue. But Plato defected. In the first book of the *Republic,* he used a young sophist, Thrasymachus, as an individualist bogey, to convince the reader that individualism, or egalitarian justice, was identical with egotism, and collectivist justice with altruism. He then presented a spurious argument about spheres in the human soul that corresponded to the division of labor in society. "[B]y means of a dramatic display of verbal fireworks, [Plato diverts the reader's] attention from the intellectual poverty of this masterly piece of dialogue," and reaches the conclusion that justice means separation of classes in accordance with the division of labor.[78] To Plato, continued Popper:

> The criterion of morality is the interest of the state. Morality is nothing but political hygiene. This is the collectivist, the tribal, the totalitarian theory of morality: "Good is what is in the interest of my group; or my state." . . . Totalitarianism is not simply amoral. It is the morality of the closed society – of the group, or of the tribe; it is not individual but collective selfishness.[79]

Plato also "corrupted and confused the theory and practice of education," turning it into an instrument of moral control, military training, and political selection (of leaders).[80] He prohibited the teaching of dialectics to youth and the disclosure to them of the secrets of the Forms, and limited educational opportunities to the upper caste. To persuade the common people to acquiesce, he invented racial myths, "noble lies" of a humanity generated by the earth, made of different metals, each with different qualities. Popper translated "metal" as "blood," and "earth" as "soil," and called the "noble lie" the "Myth of Blood and Soil" – Plato's lie as if out of Goebbels's propaganda. Recognizing that he would encounter dissent, Plato appointed, in his last dialogue, the *Laws,* a "Nocturnal Council" of inquisitors (the terms are again Popper's). It put dissenters under arrest, attempted to reform them, and executed the recalcitrant for religious impiety. Athens

---

[78] *The Open Society,* vol. 1, p. 86.   [79] Ibid., pp. 94–5.   [80] Ibid., p. 111.

put Socrates to death for impiety. To remedy its deficiencies, Plato designed a totalitarian state in which Socrates himself would not have survived. The *Republic* and the *Laws* would have "liquidated" Socrates.

"Why does Plato demand that the philosophers should be kings?" asked Popper. If "the king must . . . use lies," why would the lover of truth be king?[81] The philosopher-king's sole political knowledge was the mysterious nuptial Number. He was an expert in mathematical eugenics, a medicine man, a tribal sorcerer creating Greek supermen. He was actually none other than Plato himself. Having witnessed social conflicts in Athens toward the end of the Peloponnesian War, and the execution of his beloved and just teacher, Socrates, shortly thereafter, Plato opted for radical reconstruction of the city. Sparta's totalitarian system was his model, but it could offer no instruction on restoring order to a society that had already become open. The foundations of the Open Society had to be obliterated: commercial economy, imperial expansion, political competition, and, above all, critical discussion. Unable to bear the strain of civilization, the cultural anxiety generated by economic and political change, Plato set out to rescue his fellow citizens from the Open Society, even against their wishes, and recreate a closed tribal society that projected unity, homogeneity, and collective happiness. Socrates embodied the Open Society, and so Plato never renounced it openly. Pretending to elaborate Socrates, he distorted his teaching, bequeathing to the West a totalitarian blueprint, veiled in humanitarian and democratic language.

Popper's central thesis required that he demonstrate that Plato's historicism was responsible for his totalitarianism. Was Plato a historicist? Popper conceded that his "belief that it is possible for us to break the iron law of destiny and to avoid decay by arresting all change, shows that his historicist tendencies had definite limitation."[82] Did he believe in a "law of destiny" at all? The *Timaeus* suggested that the creation was perfect, and imperfections were due to historical change, but there was no pattern of moral and political degeneration.[83] In *Laws* 904c, the major speaker, the Athenian Stranger, describes an exhortation to an impious youth:

> Thus all things that have part in soul change, for the cause of change lies within themselves, and as they change they move in accord with the ordinance and law of destiny. If their changes of character are unimportant and few, they are transformed over the surface of the soil; if they are more and in the direction of grave wickedness, they fall into the depths and the so-called underworld.[84]

The descent of the soul into Hades, said Popper, demonstrated that the

---

[81] Ibid., p. 127.   [82] Ibid., p. 17.   [83] *Timaeus*, trans. Jowett, *The Collected Dialogues*, 30 ff.
[84] *Laws* 904c–d.

greater the change, the farther the fall from the creation's perfection.[85] But, a few lines later, the youth is reminded of the ascent of the just soul, "when by mingling with a divine virtue it . . . is borne along a hallowed path to some other better place."[86] The choice between a life of vice and virtue thus decided between degeneration and regeneration.[87] There was no law of destiny.

Plato's myths expressed wistfulness about the lost golden past, but the past did not include anything like the ideal city described in *Republic* VIII, and could not be recovered. His utopia did not retrieve a primitive past, but reformed an advanced civilization.[88] Popper argued against the historicists that individual moral choice made all the difference: Humans shaped destiny, not the other way round. Plato would have concurred. By Popper's own definition, he was not a historicist.[89] Popper later conceded as much. When J. D. Mabbott wrote him in 1947, arguing that Plato was an antihistoricist par excellence, he accepted his judgment with surprising equanimity. It left his main argument concerning Plato's totalitarianism untouched, he said.[90]

Was Plato totalitarian? He was vehement in opposing "individualism." Most individuals needed moral guidance, and allowing them to follow their

[85] *The Open Society*, chap. 4, section 1 and n. 3, 2d edition (London: Routledge & Kegan Paul, 1952). Popper rewrote this section to answer J. D. Mabbott's objections (8 July 1947, Popper Archives [28, 10]).

[86] *Laws* 904e.

[87] Plato's myths revealed his hope for regeneration and his conviction that the choice of a virtuous life was crucial: the *Statesman*, trans. J. B. Skemp, in *The Collected Dialogues*, 269b–274d; Aristophanes' tale in the *Symposium*, trans. Alexander Nehamas and Paul Woodruff (Indianapolis, Ind.: Hackett, 1989), 189c–193d; the myth of Er, the *Republic*, trans. G. M. A. Grube and C. D. C. Reeve (Indianapolis, Ind.: Hackett, 1992), Book X.

[88] Conrary to Popper, the ideal city was not a primordial city subject to a law of decline. He argued that, in *Laws* III, Sparta's ancient "tribal society" resembled the ideal city of *Republic* VIII. The evidence was weak. (The same was true for the mythical tales in *Timaeus* 24a–b describing ancient Athens and Egypt that were destroyed by the flood: *The Open Society*, pp. 38–43, chap. 4, nn. 27–32; also: chap. 3, n. 6.) Plato recounted the rise and decline of cities, good and bad: The ideal city never appeared as their origin. In discussing the Spartan and Cretan constitutions, the Athenian Stranger, the major speaker in the *Laws*, suggested that they had undergone improvements: There was no consistent degeneration (*Laws* 676c–686b). *Republic* II founded the *Kallipolis*, the good city of the guardians, prior to the philosopher-king. The *Kallipolis* emerged from a commercial civilization. Glaucon called the earlier, primitive, happy settlement the "city of pigs." It was not the ideal city (*Republic* 369a–374c).

[89] My critique was helped by Ronald Levinson, *In Defense of Plato*, esp. Appendixes X and XIV, pp. 612–15, 622–9, and John Wild, "Popper's Interpretation of Plato," in *The Philosophy of Karl Popper*, vol. 2, esp. pp. 861–2.

[90] Mabbott wrote (8 July 1947, Popper Archives [28, 10]) that Plato rejected Heraclitus and devised the Forms against him. He believed that the universe remained always permeated with reason (god) and, hence, could not degenerate into disorder, unlike individuals and societies who sometimes, but not always, did. Popper answered that even if Plato was no historicist, for the book's "unity," it was sufficient that he responded to Heraclitus and had a theory of political decay. (It is not clear that Popper ever completed and sent the letter: 9 November 1947 [28, 10].)

desires spelled disaster.[91] They would be selfish, shortsighted, and quarrelsome, and drag the city into anarchy. The common good was not the accumulation of individual interests; it was conformity to the moral order. There were big differences in human capacities, and his city recognized and institutionalized them, among others through eugenics. He made allowances for class mobility, but provided no machinery for it.[92] He was more concerned that a guardian with a merchant's soul would not rule than that common people with guardians' souls would have a fair chance. There has been a good amount of debate on his views on slavery, but there is no doubt that he regarded the absence of a clear distinction between citizens and slaves as indicative of democratic disorder.[93] If these were necessary and sufficient conditions for totalitarianism, then Popper proved his case.

I am not sure they are. Plato was not racist in the fascist sense. Good breeding created a potential for physical, intellectual, and moral virtues, but these were acquired through education. Education formed character and shaped hereditary "data." Mobility among classes, however limited, showed that classes were not "racial."[94] Neither the "master-race" nor the state was the measure of things. Both had to conform to the cosmic order, to universal standards. These excluded "might is right" and "collective selfishness." The elite's welfare was of no concern to Plato. The ultimate good was "getting the city into a certain condition which he wanted" for its perfection, beauty, and justice, precisely the aesthetic utopian vision that Popper described.[95] The city was not "organic," but "planned." Individuals, especially leaders, determined its character. Justice meant moral relations among them. Contrary to Popper, Plato was no aggressive militarist either. War resulted from an uncontrolled passion for luxuries. His autarky implied refusal to expand by either land or sea.[96] The city needed to defend itself, but planned no imperial expansion. Given current practice and prejudices, it was surprising not that he permitted enslavement of barbarian war prisoners, but rather that he suggested that his ideal city might exist among

---

[91] See Plato's description of life under democracy and tyranny in *Republic* VIII 557a–564a.

[92] *Republic* 434a–d, 466b–c. Popper thought that these paragraphs vacated 423c–d, which described class mobility. I do not think so.

[93] *Republic* 563b; *Laws* 777d–778a. Scholars debate whether slavery existed in the *Republic:* It had no institutional presence and did not seem necessary, but 433d, which mentioned a slave performing duties, may suggest that it was taken for granted. In *Laws* 776b–778a, Plato discussed slavery at length. The gist of his position was that slaves ought not to be abused, but that the social distinction between owners and slaves should be strictly maintained.

[94] *Republic* 423c–d. Popper read Nazi racial purity into *Republic* 546e–547a, which designated the intermingling of metals as the cause for the ideal city's decline. This seems unreasonable: It was ignorance of proper breeding *within* the ruling class (and deterioration of education) that Plato held responsible for decline, not racial interbreeding. The intermingling of races meant that guardians and philosophers included people who should not be rulers (*Republic* 545d–547b).

[95] Richard Robinson, "Dr. Popper's Defense of Democracy": 493.

[96] *Republic* 372e–373e.

the barbarians.[97] All his myths about the origin of humankind pointed to their common roots.[98] The idea of a universal humanity was not foreign to him. Totalitarian tendencies Plato certainly had; a fascist ideologue he was not.[99]

To Plato, education was about having the right desires. The end was the rule of the soul's rational part over the appetitive part. Popper found the idea incomprehensible. He subscribed to procedural rather than substantive rationality (criticism, not results, were rational). He was averse to judging desire, and had little use for the soul.[100] Plato's concepts appeared mystical and illiberal. The gap between progressive *Volksbildung* and Platonic education was unbridgeable. As a result, Popper did not appreciate, and resolved too easily, paradoxes of Platonic education. How could the education of myth and "noble fictions" create philosophers? How could a philosopher-king emerge from among brainwashed guardians? To Popper, Plato never intended to educate critical philosophers. Most interpreters suggest, however, that philosophically oriented youth would gradually shed myth and recognize the reasons for their education.[101] Others regard this as one paradox among many that demonstrate that Plato never intended to establish the Republic.[102]

Plato stated that his project depended on an unlikely, but not impossible, coalescence of philosophy and power: the fortunate birth of a prince with a philosophic soul, who, upon coming to power, would reform the

---

[97] *Republic* 469b–471b, 499a–d.

[98] The myth of metals proclaimed the siblinghood of all citizens (*Republic* 414c–415d).

[99] In developing my critique of Popper's view of Plato's racism, I was again much helped by Ronald Levinson, *In Defense of Plato*, esp. pp. 424–31, 450–9, 535–43, and John Wild, "Popper's Interpretation of Plato," pp. 864–6.

[100] *The Open Society*, vol. 1, pp. 166–7; chap. 10, n. 44 for the soul; chap. 5, n. 18 for moral judgment. Popper fought value relativism but took exception to absolutism, and thought it improper to judge other people's way of life. Jeremy Shearmur, *The Political Philosophy of Karl Popper* (London: Routledge, 1996), chap. 4, intelligently discusses some problems of his ethics.

[101] C. D. C. Reeve, *Philosopher-Kings* (Princeton, N.J.: Princeton University Press, 1988).

[102] Allan Bloom ("Interpretive Essay," *The Republic of Plato* [New York: Basic Books, 1968]) and John H. Randall (*Plato: Dramatist of the Life of Reason* [New York: Columbia University Press, 1970]) argued, from different perspectives, that consistent irony ran through the *Republic*, making the project's unfeasibility obvious.

Popper did not think of the dialogues as literary and dramatic works. "A critical interpretation must take the form of a rational reconstruction, and must be systematic," he said. "It must try to reconstruct the philosopher's thought as a consistent edifice" (*The Open Society*, chap. 5, n. 45). Perhaps, but ironies and ambiguities may then easily be lost. Popper spoke of Platonic irony in the *Menexenus* (pp. 83, 174; chap. 6, n. 19; chap. 8, n. 48). His wooden treatment of it convinced Richard Robinson that he partially failed "to grasp the nature of Plato's irony. . . . The *Menexenus* is a baffling mixture of the serious and the ironical, scoffing and love, compounded of Plato's love for Athens and his hate of democracy, which were so intertwined as to baffle Plato himself as well as his readers" ("Dr. Popper's Defense of Democracy": 490). Had Popper recognized the dialogues as literature and drama, he may have been less inclined to charge Plato with dishonesty, subversion, and manipulation.

city (beginning by expelling all adults).[103] In the decade prior to the *Republic* (c. 380 B.C.), and during the 360s, he educated a prospective king and a tyrant.[104] At least in the second case, he no longer hoped for the ideal city, only for improving governance. In his last dialogue, the *Laws* (c. 350), he opted for superior laws, not superior people. The Republic remained a heavenly model that made Adeimantus, Glaucon, and other youth recoil at the misfortune of a disordered humanity, attracted them to a virtuous life, and taught them how to answer the likes of Thrasymachus.[105]

The conscious utopianism of the *Republic* makes Popper's observations on totalitarianism problematic, but it does not invalidate them. If Plato thought that "utopian social engineering" was possible only under fortuitous circumstances, it was Popper's view that it had no chance of success whatsoever, and was bound to end up in totalitarianism. Even as a pattern in the sky, the *Republic* reflected dangerous illiberal tendencies. Historian Leonard Krieger has suggested that "enlightened despotism" had always been less a political program, more a dangerous mode of wishful thinking: If only philosophy and power coalesced![106] From the beginning, philosophers claimed entitlement to power by virtue of superior knowledge. Certain of possessing truth, they justified executing heretics. Assured about heavenly patterns, they did not recoil from violence in constructing them on earth. Today, liberals and poststructuralists concur on the danger of such claims of truth. Popper sounded the alarm first.

CLASSICAL ATHENS: THE HEAVENLY CITY OF A PROGRESSIVE PHILOSOPHER

To Popper, classical Athens was the first Open Society, the first to break from "tribalism," overcome myth, magic, and custom and to found politics on *logos* and law. He surmised that, originally, the Greeks lived in tribes. Taboo and ritual ruled. Social hierarchy was considered natural, sanctioned by religion and tradition. No change of mores was permitted, no consistent effort to improve life expected. Primitive unity prevailed, and social conflict was dreaded. Law did not check the warmth and brutality of personal bonds.[107] Economic and intellectual developments in Archaic Greece

---

[103] *Republic* 498d–502c. Allan Bloom ("Interpretive Essay") suggested that the *Republic*, properly read, teaches the dangers of utopianism and the limits of reform.

[104] Dion I, brother-in-law of Dionysius I, and Dionysius II, both of Syracuse in Sicily. "Letter VII: To the Friends and Companions of Dion," *The Collected Dialogues*.

[105] For the ideal city as a heavenly model, see the beautiful paragraph in *Republic* 592b. On the utopian genre: Judith Shklar, *Men and Citizens* (New York: Cambridge University Press, 1969).

[106] Leonard Krieger, *An Essay on the Theory of Enlightened Despotism* (Chicago: University of Chicago, 1975).

[107] Popper recognized some of his "anthropological" account's limits: "[T]here is no standardized 'tribal way of life' " (*The Open Society*, vol. 1, p. 151). He intended it as a model, authorizing the distinction between the closed and the Open Society.

gradually dissolved the tribes. Colonization expanded geographical and intellectual horizons, and monetary economy and naval commerce created new modes of social interaction.[108] Critical investigation of nature and society led to recognition that norms, laws, and institutions were human made. Arguments about the best constitution began, democratic voices became vigorous, and social conflicts erupted. The privileged classes responded anxiously, looking back to the golden age when their position had been secure and social unity had prevailed. The strain of civilization began taking its toll.

Athens embodied the Open Society: secular, commercial, democratic, and cosmopolitan. Between the Persian and Peloponnesian Wars (479 B.C.–431 B.C.), it went from triumph to triumph, building a commercial empire and developing a flourishing culture. Pericles' Funeral Speech, recounted in Thucydides' *History of the Peloponnesian War,* was its greatest testimony. It praised Athenian liberty, equality, imperial magnanimity, cultural achievement, cosmopolitanism, and, above all, individualism. There were other testimonies to Athenian progressivism: the speeches of Hippias and Protagoras in the *Protagoras;* the theories of justice developed by the "School of Gorgias," and, above all, Socrates' philosophy. All were monuments to the Great Generation of philosophers and politicians who lived in Athens before and during the Peloponnesian War.

Popper constructed Athenian democracy in the mold of Viennese progressivism. He brushed off evidence conflicting with this view and, on occasion, speculated where none existed. Athenian intolerance, he opined, was a myth, an invention of democracy's aristocratic enemies. Slavery regrettably existed in Athens, but so did also an abolitionist movement. Athens was famous for its liberal treatment of slaves. Athenian imperialism was mild and cosmopolitan. Athens's allies maintained their autonomy and constitution, only paying a tribute. Thucydides and other conservatives were responsible for imperialism's bad reputation: They opposed it because it threatened the landed aristocracy:

> I am far from defending everything that Athens did in building up her empire, and I certainly do not wish to defend wanton attacks (if such have occurred), or acts of brutality. . . . But it is necessary, I believe, to see that tribalist exclusiveness and self-sufficiency could be superseded only by some form of imperialism.[109]

---

[108] Historians have recently concluded that there was no commercial economy motivated by profit in Archaic Greece. The major advances were in politics, religion, and the military. The *polis* emerged as a community of warriors when common cults worshiped in a central temple. This is a far cry from Popper's *doux commerce*. See Anthony Snodgrass, *Archaic Greece*; Jean Pierre Vernant, *The Origins of Greek Thought*; Victor D. Hanson, *The Other Greeks* (New York: Free Press, 1995).

[109] *The Open Society,* vol. 1, p. 158.

Popper interpreted extant literary sources in a manner many classicists found questionable. His reading of Pericles' Funeral Oration was paradigmatic of his approach. He assumed both that Thucydides accurately reported Pericles' speech and that it faithfully described Athenian life. Neither the speech's literary role in Thucydides nor the funeral oration's ideological role in Athenian life deterred him.[110] He ignored the parts of the speech that contradicted his interpretation and Pericles' two other orations in the *History* that reflected power politics.[111] Contrary to Popper, it is unlikely that Pericles, or any classical Greek, articulated an "individualist" view of the *polis,* liberal concepts of liberty and justice, or a cosmopolitan vision of international politics.[112] To be sure, Thucydides' Pericles contrasted favorably the Athenians' leisurely private business with the Spartans' regimented life. But to him, democracy's magic was the voluntary and spontaneous service individuals rendered to the city, their ability to move swiftly between private and military life. Thucydides' Pericles never questioned the subordination of individual to polis. Indeed, Athenian political grandeur was "Pericles'" central theme. Thus, in the Funeral Oration:

> Mighty indeed are the marks and monuments of our empire. . . . Future ages will wonder at us, as the present age wonders at us now . . . for everywhere we have left behind us everlasting memorials of good done to our friends or suffering inflicted on our enemies.
>
> This, then, is the kind of city for which these men . . . died. It is only natural that every one of us who survive them should be willing to undergo hardships in her service.[113]

Popper also turned the sophists into critical rationalists. Based on two brief fragments attributed to the sophist Lycophron, he drew a portrait of a fifth-century liberal democrat. Lycophron's statements were recorded by Aristotle. The first quoted him to the effect that the polis was "a guarantor of men's rights against one another."[114] Law and justice were

---

[110] Nicole Loraux, *The Invention of Athens: The Funeral Oration in the Classical City,* trans. A. Sheridan (Cambridge, Mass.: Harvard University Press, 1986).

[111] Thucydides, *History of the Peloponnesian War,* trans. R. Warner (New York: Penguin, 1972), I 140–4, II 35–46, 60–4; *The Open Society,* vol. 1, pp. 82, 162–4, chap. 6, n. 16.

[112] To use Isaiah Berlin's terminology, the Greeks did not possess a concept of "negative liberty," the idea that individual freedom should be protected against state and society. Isaiah Berlin, "Two Concepts of Liberty," in *Four Essays on Freedom* (New York: Oxford University Press, 1969). For the opposite view: M. H. Hansen, *The Athenian Democracy at the Age of Demosthenes* (Oxford: Blackwell, 1991).

[113] Thucydides, *History* II 41. Athenian "individualism" was, indeed, one of Thucydides' themes, but he understood it differently from Popper: "[E]ach man cultivates his own intelligence with a view to doing something notable for his city" (I 70). For Thucydides, see Peter Pouncey's wonderful *The Necessities of War* (New York: Columbia University Press, 1980).

[114] Aristotle, *Politics* 1280b 8, trans. Ernest Barker (New York: Oxford University Press, 1946). Aristotle argued that, unless one agreed that the *polis* "must devote itself to the end of encouraging goodness . . . law becomes a mere covenant – or (in the phrase of the sophist Lycophron) 'a guarantor of men's rights against one another' – instead of being, as it should be, a rule of life such as will make the members of the *polis* good and just."

conventional, the results of a contract among the citizens to protect the rights of each against the other. Popper surmised that Lycophron's view was close to his own antihistorical "protectionist" theory of justice. As opposed to Plato's naturalist, collectivist, and totalitarian theory, Popper's was conventionalist, egalitarian, and individualist. Justice presupposed free and equal individuals seeking to protect their interests. It had no foundation in nature. It was not about cultivating virtue. No historical account of justice, no original contract, was relevant to the evaluation of current needs.[115] Lycophron must have recognized, thought Popper, that morality depended on freedom to choose, and that state intervention in private affairs in virtue's name corrupted morality.

The second Lycophron quotation appeared in Aristotle's discussion of noble birth. Aristotle quoted "Lycophron the sophist" to the effect that it was "something altogether trivial. . . . The attractiveness of good birth is obscure, and its dignity a matter of words. . . . The preference for it is a matter of opinion, and in truth there is no difference between the low-born and the well-born."[116] Since Lycophron dismissed good birth as "trivial" and propounded both a contractual view of the polis and an egalitarian theory of justice, he must have believed, thought Popper, in a universal humanity. He considered distinctions between citizen and slave, Greek and barbarian, superficial and opposed slavery.[117] Egalitarian, individualist, and cosmopolitan, Lycophron was Athens's Popper.

It was impossible for Athenian progressives, thought Popper, to remain silent in the face of slavery. He elicited antislavery sentiments from sophists Alcidamas and Antisthenes through similar procedures. They were reputed, like Lycophron, to have been influenced by Gorgias. Popper established, therefore, the "School of Gorgias." The school embodied the Great Generation's ideals and led the Athenian abolitionist movement.[118] Other intellectuals joined. Sophists Hippias and Protagoras were members. They delivered speeches in the *Protagoras* about humanity's common origins and individuals' equal share in justice and political knowledge. (Neither Hippias nor Protagoras made any explicit reference to slaves or barbarians.)[119] Socrates was a member, too: Did he not recognize the rationality of a slave

---

[115] *The Open Society*, vol. 1, pp. 80–105; chap. 6, nn. 45–52. It was important for Popper to establish that Lycophron was not a "historicist" because he argued that Plato distorted sophistic justice by presenting it as a historical account of the state's origins. He insisted that Callicles in the *Gorgias* was actually arguing against Lycophron, and, hence, Plato must have known Lycophron's theory. By having Adeimantus present "Lycophron's theory" in the *Republic* as a historicist theory, Plato made the job of refutation easy, and the way to totalitarian justice was open.

[116] Aristotle, "On Good Birth" (Fragments), *Works*, ed. David Ross (Oxford: Clarendon Press, 1952), vol. 12, p. 59.

[117] *The Open Society*, vol. 1, pp. 58–9, 97–101, 161–2; chap. 6, n. 45. This argument is discussed well in Ronald Levinson, *In Defense of Plato*, pp. 418–24.

[118] *The Open Society*, vol. 1, pp. 58–9, 100–3, 133–4, 161–2; chap. 8, n. 48.

[119] *Protagoras*, trans. W. K. C. Guthrie, *The Collected Dialogues*, 320d–323a (Protagoras's myth of common origins), 337d–338a (Hippias on "kinship by nature").

in the *Meno* by using him to prove an axiom in geometry?[120] The attacks by the Old Oligarch, Plato, and Aristotle on slaves' unruliness in Athens proved the strength of Athenian abolitionism. They combined criticism of Athenian pluralism with reproaches for Athenian indulgence toward slaves and foreigners.[121] They knew well that cosmopolitanism gave rise to abolitionism.[122]

In his quest for progressive Athens, Popper underestimated the social limits of Athenian criticism. Athenian philosophers and dramatists may have recognized the conventional nature of slavery, perhaps even its injustice, but we have no record of opposition to slavery in Athens, political or intellectual. Aristotle contested the conventionalist (that is, antinaturalist) view of slavery in the *Politics*, and so it was likely a competing discourse.[123] Plato questioned gender roles in the *Republic* and proposed abolishing the family. Such recognition of the social construction of fundamental distinctions could conceivably extend to slavery.[124] In his tragedies, Euripides showed women, children, and slaves as noble heroes, and gods and men as brutes. In the *Bacchae,* he reversed all distinctions of gender, age, and race considered essential to the polis.[125] If he could turn social hierarchy upside down and reverse social roles in his plays, it is not inconceivable that he, and others, entertained doubts about slavery. Yet, the debate on the injustice of slavery that was possible in principle did not take place historically: We are left with hints of heretical thoughts that intellectuals may have entertained. Slavery was essential to the polis, especially to the economically developed democratic *poleis.*[126] A city without slaves was utopian. Abolition would be tantamount to discarding private property and would probably necessitate the wide introduction of serfdom, along the Spartan model. Theoretical reflections about the justice of slavery were possible; practical abolitionist proposals were not. An Athenian abolitionist movement was highly improbable.[127]

Searching for a cosmopolitan empire, Popper may also have exaggerated

---

[120] *Meno* 82b, trans. Grube, *Five Dialogues* (Indianapolis, Ind.: Hackett, 1981).

[121] Pseudo-Xenophon (Old Oligarch), *The Constitution of the Athenians*, in *Aristotle and Xenophon on Democracy and Oligarchy*, trans. J. M. Moore (Berkeley: University of California, 1975), i 10–12, ii 7–8; Plato, *Republic* 557b–e, 562e–563b; Aristotle, *Politics* 1313b 11.

[122] *The Open Society*, vol. 1, pp. 35–6, 58–9, 161–7; chap. 5, n. 13; chap. 8, n. 48.

[123] *Politics* 1225a–b.   [124] *Republic* 453a–461e.

[125] Euripides, *Alcestis, Bacchae, Trojan Women, Iphigineia in Aulis, The Complete Greek Tragedies*, ed. David Grene and Richmond Lattimore, 4 vols. (Chicago: University of Chicago Press, 1959–60).

[126] Moses Finley, "Was Greek Civilization Based on Slavery?" in his *Economy and Society in Ancient Greece* (New York: Viking, 1982).

[127] "[Philosopher Michael] Foster (who worked out all your references) and [Roman historian Ronald] Syme . . . both maintained that your picture of a humanitarian liberal equalitarian movement in Athens had no foundation. . . . [B]oth thought you had read back nineteenth-century liberalism into an era where there was not the faintest gleam of it as a political force or a 'movement.' " J. D. Mabbott to Popper, 8 July 1947 (Popper Archives [28, 10]).

the cultural openness of Athens. Athens proved more receptive to foreign influences than did other Greek cities: Commercial traffic through the Piraeus brought foreigners with different dialects and dress to the city. Conservative critics drew the same connections Popper did among commercialism, cosmopolitanism, cultural diversity, and democracy. Popper took their sarcastic portrayals of Athenian cosmopolitanism literally. Athenian liberties were far more precarious than he conceded. Athens permitted unprecedented freedom of speech, but did not legally protect it. The audience decided the limits of tolerance. Philosophers and dramatists wrote, spoke, and performed at their own risk. They could, and were, sued for impiety. Popper regarded Socrates' execution as a single fateful aberration. It was not. Protagoras and Euripides both ended up in exile, possibly after judicial proceedings. Athenian intolerance was not just a myth created by democracy's enemies.[128]

Popper's idealization of Athenian imperialism flew in the face of evidence of brutality. Athenian rule was not mild, but as harsh as Athens deemed necessary to accomplish its objectives: political hegemony and financial exploitation.[129] Thucydides remains our major literary source on Athenian imperialism. He recorded and analyzed its growing harshness during the Peloponnesian War. He described two memorable episodes, Mytilene (427 B.C.) and Melos (416 B.C.). In the first, the Athenians almost put to death, or reduced to slavery, the population of a rebellious ally. In the second, they actually did so to a small island that refused to join their empire. Thucydides dramatized the episodes and may have omitted information explaining Athenian actions, but his testimony of the brutality remains incontrovertible.[130] Popper doubted it and decided to overlook it. Even if "wanton attacks" occurred, they should not obscure the glory of cosmopolitan imperialism.

Popper's unabashed support for Athens is less surprising than the aspects of Athenian politics and culture that he chose to emphasize. Why attempt at all cost to find in Athens an abolitionist movement, insist on Athenian cosmopolitanism, and defend Athenian imperialism? He seems to have read his hopes for Central Europe into Athens. The Habsburg Empire's disintegration doomed the Viennese progressives' longing for a democratic empire. No agent for cosmopolitanism existed any longer. In his exile, Popper wrote to vindicate progressive dreams against fascism. Classical Athens was both a democracy and an empire. So was Britain: a liberal maritime

---

[128] A. H. M. Jones, "The Athenian Democracy and Its Critics," *The Historical Journal* 11 (1953): 1–26 thinks otherwise. His sympathetic account of Athenian freedoms is close to Popper's.

[129] Moses Finley, "The Athenian Empire: A Balance Sheet," in *Economy and Society*.

[130] Thucydides, *History* III 2–50, V 84–116. Both A. H. M. Jones, "The Athenian Democracy," and Moses Finley, "The Melian Dialogue," in Thucydides, *History*, Appendix 3, believe that Athens behaved in accordance with Greek norms. They challenge Thucydides' anti-Athenian bias and question his narrative of growing harshness. They do not dispute, however, his reports of Athenian brutality.

commonwealth, fighting a continental totalitarian enemy.[131] Sparta – a military caste ruling over serfs, closing the borders to foreign influences, maintaining an autarkic rural economy – was the epitome of the closed society. To Popper, it resembled Nazi Germany. Like many before him, he imagined ancient wars and philosophical disputes in the frame of modern politics. The Peloponnesian War became World War II. He divided Greek *poleis*, politicians, and intellectuals into two camps, democratic and totalitarian, and fought the war of one against the other. Theodor Gomperz had already made Athens the site of the Greek enlightenment, and, together with the English progressives, idealized its democracy. Popper discovered his cosmopolitan empire. It mattered little that it happened two millennia ago and far from Central Europe. Where the Habsburg Empire failed, Athens succeeded, if only for a brief moment. Progressive imperialism triumphed over tribal nationalism. Against the "conservative critics" of Athens, he defended his vision: a democratic cosmopolitan empire advancing human emancipation. Where he found success once, the exile could hope, amid global ruins, for another.

SOCRATES' JUDAS: BIOGRAPHY AND AUTOBIOGRAPHY IN
THE OPEN SOCIETY

Popper drew contrasting portraits of Socrates and Plato: Socrates was a democrat, Plato a totalitarian. Socrates was lovingly critical of Athens; Plato perverted his teaching and betrayed Athens. This was highly controversial. In the history of philosophy so far, Socrates had been intertwined with Plato. No one prior to Popper had suggested that Plato was a traitor to his master.

Socrates left no written record. Sources on his life and work are limited. In addition to the Platonic dialogues, there are four Socratic discourses by the Athenian general Xenophon, Aristophanes' parody *The Clouds,* and scattered references to Socrates in Aristotle.[132] There are also fragments of speeches mentioning Socrates' trial. These leave no doubt that he was a major figure in Athenian intellectual life, and his trial was a major event. The public identified him with the sophists. A number of his disciples became powerful politicians: Alcibiades led the expedition to Sicily in 415, defected to Sparta, and collaborated with the Persians, and Critias and Charmides led the murderous thirty tyrants who ruled Athens under

---

[131] Steven Beller suggested to me the British-Athenian parallel and emphasized that it must have informed *The Open Society.*

[132] Xenophon, *Memorabilia, Oeconomicus, Symposium, Apology*, trans. E. C. Marchant (Cambridge, Mass.: Harvard University Press, 1923); Aristophanes, *The Clouds*, trans. Moses Hadas, *The Complete Plays of Aristophanes* (New York: Bantam Books, 1962); Aristotle, *Politics; Nichomachean Ethics*, trans. Terence Irwin (Indianapolis, Ind.: Hackett, 1985); *Metaphysics*, trans. W. D. Ross, 2 vols. (Oxford: Clarendon Press, 1924).

Spartan auspices in 403. To Athenian democrats, Socrates had come to represent the enemy's *Geist*. They used his questioning of Athenian civic religion to bring charges of impiety and corruption of youth against him in 399.[133] Rather than go into exile, Socrates chose death. Works commemorated his life, trial, and death.[134]

There is no clear path to the historical Socrates. The portrayals of Aristophanes, Plato, and Xenophon have little in common, and there is no sure way to judge among them. Even Plato's *Apology*, the only dialogue anchored in a historical event, the trial, was not a transcription of Socrates' defense, possibly not even a reconstruction. Reporting played little role in ancient commemoration, and so the public character of speech was no guarantee of the historical accuracy of Plato's representation.[135] Aristophanes depicted Socrates' popular image but provided no reliable record of his views. Xenophon appears not to have been a member of Socrates' circle and had little to say about him as a philosopher. Aristotle was born fifteen years after Socrates' death and derived his information about him from his students. He did distinguish between Socrates and Plato, and scholars use him as a guide in interpreting the dialogues, but the boundaries between Socrates and his students were already dim when he recorded their views. Problematic as their use is, the Platonic dialogues provide the only account of Socrates by a disciple who was present at his trial and execution, a philosopher himself.

Socrates appears in all of Plato's dialogues, with the exception of the *Laws,* and is the major speaker in all, save the last four. Scholars have discerned changes in "Socrates" through the dialogues and attribute them to Plato's intellectual development. They generally agree that the Forms were Platonic, rather than Socratic, and that the mathematical ordering of the universe reflected Pythagorean influence on Plato after Socrates' death. Socrates had, however, a predominant influence on Plato. The question is where and how to draw the line between Socrates and Plato. This is the "Socratic Problem."

---

[133] Plato's *Apology* (as well as *Euthyphro*) and Xenophon's *Apology* mentioned the charges. One Meletus brought them, but Plato recognized Anytus, the second-ranking democrat, as standing behind (*Apology* 28a).

[134] A good number of apologies (defenses) and accusations of Socrates appeared, and half a century later orators still used his trial in court cases. Aeschines' speech in court in 345 B.C. mentioned Socrates: "You put to death Socrates the sophist, fellow citizens, because he was shown to have been the teacher of Critias, one of the Thirty who put down democracy." (Quoted in Barry Strauss, *Athens After the Peloponnesian War* [Ithaca, N.Y.: Cornell University Press, 1987], p. 3.) Polycrates' popular "Accusation of Socrates" is lost.

[135] Heinrich Gomperz, "Sokrates Haltung vor seinen Richtern," *Wiener Studien* 54 (1936): 32–43. Xenophon justified his Apology by remarking "that others have written about this, and all have reproduced the loftiness of Socrates' works . . . but they have not shown clearly that he had now come to the conclusion that for him death was more to be desired than life" (*Apology* 1). Commemoration meant shaping Socrates' legacy, not documentation.

Classicists distinguish between the early dialogues – the *Apology*, *Crito*, *Euthyphro*, and, later, *Gorgias* and *Protagoras* – and the late ones – the *Statesman*, *Timaeus*, and *Laws*; the *Republic* and the *Symposium*, written around 380, are considered middle. In the earlier, and often shorter, dialogues, Socrates does not present his own philosophy, but rather questions the traditional view of virtue and Athenian beliefs about ethics, religion, and politics. His method of questioning is the *elenchos*. He asks the interlocutor to define the nature of justice, piety, courage, moderation, wisdom, and other virtues and, then, subjects the definition to a scrutiny from which it never emerges unscathed. Socrates' own views do not receive a programmatic presentation. They seem to be that virtue is knowledge and vice is due to ignorance (no one acts unjustly knowingly and willingly); that virtue is one (wisdom is justice, beauty, and holiness); and that politics is an art requiring expertise. Socrates focuses, however, on demonstrating the incoherence of the sophists' and the Athenians' views. In the late dialogues, the *elenchos* virtually disappears, and Socrates develops his cosmology, epistemology, and politics. How does the transformation of "Socrates" between the early and late dialogues reflect on the historical Socrates?

Most classicists believe that the earlier dialogues reflect more closely the Socratic method and views, and that the later ones represent mostly Plato's own ideas. Popper endorsed this view and carried it to an extreme: That which other scholars regarded as Plato's development of Socratic ideas, Popper regarded as perversion. He suggested that the *Apology* (the first dialogue) and the *Laws* (the last one) were paradigmatic of Socrates and Plato: To the extent that Socrates conformed to the *Apology* in other dialogues, they were Socratic; to the extent that he conformed to the *Laws*, Platonic. Against Burnet and Taylor, who argued for the Socratic character of the *Republic* and the proximity of Platonic and Socratic views, Popper mobilized an arsenal of traditional arguments, adding some, less convincing perhaps, of his own. He answered Burnet and Taylor in a tightly argued, seven-page footnote, a masterpiece of erudition, clarity, and cogency.[136]

---

[136] *The Open Society*, chap. 10, n. 56. Burnet (*Greek Philosophy*) and Taylor (*Plato*) made Plato into a Christian humanist. Their revisionism is no longer popular but had a following during the first half of this century. They assumed that the dialogues were historical, and that Plato described Socrates' development from youth to old age. Only the *Sophist*, *Statesman*, and *Timaeus*, where Socrates plays no major role, and the *Laws*, where he is absent, were Platonic. The *Republic* and the *Symposium* were Socratic, as were the Forms.

Popper insisted that Socrates of the *Apology* and the *Crito* represented the "real" Socrates. The other early dialogues also reflected, to a lesser extent, the historical Socrates. The *Meno* and the *Gorgias* came early, the *Phaedo* – an account of the soul and the Forms – later. The *Euthyphro*, where Socrates was critical of Athenian courts, was later than assumed, and the *Theaetetus*, where Socrates expressed belief in the common origin of humankind, earlier (chap. 8, n. 50 [6], added to the second edition, and addendum to the fourth edition, "The Dating of the *Theaetetus*"). The late dialogues, *Republic* included, were Platonic. Socrates was a literary phantom, a product of Plato's deformed imagination.

To Popper, Socrates was "the greatest apostle of individualist ethics of all times."[137] He called Socrates' view that virtue was knowledge "moral intellectualism." It promoted egalitarianism and individualism: Anyone could learn. Socrates rejected privilege, sought to protect rights, and recognized all individuals as deserving respect. His concept of the soul transcended the *psyche*, the animating principle. The virtuous person was self-sufficient, happy even when suffering social hostility, never harming anyone, not even the unjust. Socrates' "teaching that it is better to suffer [violent] acts than to do them is indeed very similar to Christian teaching, and his doctrine of justice fits in excellently with the spirit of Pericles."[138] His criticism of democracy was intended – much like Popper's criticism of socialism – to reform democracy, not destroy it. His refusal to cooperate with the Thirty proved his loyalty. In the *Apology*, he mentioned a close democratic friend, Chaerophon. In the *Crito*, he refused to save his own life by violating democracy. He associated with young aristocrats to reform them, not to support oligarchic designs. His statement in the *Crito* that the constitutions of Sparta and Crete were superior to Athens was a Platonic interpolation.[139] He may well have thought that the best people should rule, that common people lacked political expertise, and that those in need of enlightenment sought it least and required guidance to achieve it. But this potential authoritarianism was rendered harmless by his critical disposition. Authority could only be established by personal example. He demonstrated what authority should be like: self-critical, in dialogue, repelled by dogma, repulsed by violence.

Socrates was the first philosopher to embody the scientific attitude that emphasized criticism and self-criticism. His statement that wisdom consisted in knowledge of one's ignorance encapsulated critical rationalism. His life was a search for the truth, an unending inquiry. He knew that truth was difficult to come by and refused to abide by convention or dogma: The unexamined life, he told the jury, was not worth living. He died for freedom of political criticism, science, and philosophy. Plato betrayed him, turning philosophy from criticism into dogma, reinforced by authority. Against Socratic ignorance, Plato posed an omniscient philosopher-king. Socrates engaged the youth in critical dialogue, persuading them to examine their life; Plato prohibited teaching them philosophy. Having transformed critical rationalism into reinforced dogmatism, Plato ended up in totalitarianism.

Popper's Socrates was as anachronistic as his "classical Athens." "Moral intellectualism" implied neither egalitarianism nor individualism.[140]

---

[137] *The Open Society*, vol. 1, p. 112.   [138] Ibid., p. 91.

[139] Ibid., chap. 10, n. 53. For Socrates' disobedience of the Thirty: Plato's *Apology* 32c–d; Chaerophon: *Apology* 20e–21a; the Spartan preference: *Crito* 52e–53a.

[140] In the *Gorgias*, "Socrates" used "the view of the many that justice means equal shares" against Callicles, but expressed neither agreement nor disagreement with it (*Gorgias* 488b–489a).

Socrates did not believe that all people had equal capacities to be virtuous.[141] His view that it was worse to behave unjustly than suffer injustice was "individualist" to the extent that it allowed the just person happiness apart from the community, but it did not imply a denial of collective justice or good. Neither Socrates nor any Greek likely had a Kantian conception of legal impartiality, believed in inalienable individual rights protected by law, or assumed that all people should be treated as ends rather than means. The language, the concepts, the concerns were not quite there.

There is no compelling evidence for Socrates' democratic disposition, and much to tell against it. The closest he came to endorsing Athenian institutions was in justifying his refusal to escape from prison: "You must either persuade [your country]," he told Crito, "or obey it."[142] He then praised Athenian laws for having "given you birth, nurtured you, educated you, [and] given you a share of all the good things."[143] Obedience to laws was a universal requirement for "well-governed" and "civilized" polities. Thebes and Megara (which did not have democratic constitutions) would look at him suspiciously as a breaker of laws, if he escaped to them.[144] He had no right to disobey Athenian laws if he "did not choose to go to Sparta or Crete which [he] always said were well-governed."[145] Thus, in the dialogue in which "Socrates" was most accepting of Athenian laws, and in which a preference for democracy over other constitutions would have supported his argument against going into exile, "Socrates" nowhere expressed support for democracy and stated his high opinion of nondemocratic polities.

Other dialogues corroborate Socrates' antidemocratic sympathies. In the *Protagoras*, he wondered why the general opinion was that politics, unlike other crafts, required no expertise. Politics crafted souls: Why were people willing to entrust their souls to the ignorant? Why did they assume that all citizens were qualified politicians?[146] In the *Apology*, he expressed distrust of the majority:

> Be sure, gentlemen of the jury, . . . no man will survive who genuinely opposes you or any other crowd and prevents the occurrence of many unjust

---

[141] "Socrates" used a slave in the *Meno* to demonstrate the human ability to learn something not previously known (a geometrical theorem), but did not treat him as a free agent (*Meno* 82b–85c). Incidentally, a "Platonic Socrates," not a "progressive" one, conversed with the slave. "Socrates" used the slave to prove the Platonic theory of knowledge as recollection (*anamnesis*).

[142] *Crito* 52b. Was Socrates endorsing the democratic assembly, where citizens argued, debated, and passed laws, thus suggesting that one must obey the law to which one had given consent? Possibly, but it is more likely that he was referring to the opportunity defendants had to persuade the jury.

[143] *Crito*, 51c–d.   [144] *Crito*, 53b.

[145] *Crito*, 52e–53a. I do not assume the historicity of the *Crito*, the *Apology*, or any early dialogue. I merely dispute Popper's interpretation of the political import of "Socrates' " statements.

[146] *Protagoras* 319b–d.

and illegal happenings in the city. A man who really fights for justice must lead a private, not a public, life if he is to survive for even a short time.[147]

He was confident, however, that "it is wicked and shameful . . . to disobey one's superior, be he god or man."[148] Knowledge and virtue established a hierarchy. Democratic polities neither recognized nor conformed to it.

Socrates' political associations were antidemocratic. If he mentioned a democratic friend in his defense to prove his political neutrality, the young aristocrats attending court, willing to testify on his behalf and pay the fine, easily offset his profession of neutrality.[149] He emphasized his refusal to carry out the Thirty's order to bring in General Leon of Salamis for execution, but his presence at the center of oligarchic power, when the democrats were hiding, in exile, or plotting their return in the Pireaus, as well as the charge with which the tyrants entrusted him, could be evidence of guilt by association.[150] Not one democratic philosopher or statesman, *pace* Popper's view of Antisthenes, can be found among his disciples. None left us a record of his democratic convictions or sentiments. Socrates could hardly have been the democrat Popper described.[151]

He could not be a critical rationalist either. Popper transplanted Socrates' "I know what I do not know" from Greek ethics into modern epistemology.[152] Socrates reinterpreted the Greek "know thyself": Recognize your power's limits and do not fall into hubris (illusion of divine grandiosity). The injunction was moral, not epistemological. Self-knowledge entailed intellectual modesty, but the search for virtue was not infinite. It ended with the just and virtuous life. Socrates did not share Popper's agnosticism: "criticism" was a means to an end. Contrary to the opinion of Popper, the pursuit of truth was not, in itself, the good life. Like many martyrs, Socrates died for the truth as he saw it, not for the freedom of criticism and inquiry.

Why did Plato betray Socrates? Popper provided a psychological explanation that showed uncommon sensitivity to the relationship between biography and work. Few of his imaginative conjectures seem tenable, but the

---

[147] *Apology* 31d–32a. Also *Apology* 28a–b, *Crito* 44c, 47a–48a, and *Gorgias* 471e–472c.

[148] *Apology* 29b.   [149] *Apology* 20c–21a, 33d–34a, 38b.   [150] *Apology*, 32c–e.

[151] A. K. Rogers, *The Socratic Question* (New Haven, Conn.: Yale University Press, 1933) thinks otherwise. For a recent consideration: Gregory Vlastos, "The Historical Socrates and Athenian Democracy," *Political Theory* 2 (1983): 495–516. I have found Ronald Levinson, *In Defense of Plato*, pp. 635–45 helpful in developing my critique.

[152] *Apology* 21d.

[153] Three examples: He suggested that "Socrates' " account of his intellectual development in the *Phaedo* reflected neither Socrates' nor Plato's biographies. Rather, Plato constructed Socrates' biography so that it justified his move from Socratic agnosticism to Pythagorean absolutism (chap. 7, n. 9). In the *Parmenides*, the young Socrates is rebuffed for inadequate knowledge of epistemology. This reflected Plato's effort to explain his prohibition of dialectics to youth in the *Republic:* His construction of Socrates in one dialogue responded to his need to justify his break with Socrates in another (2d. ed., p. 134). In the *Charmides* and the *First Alcibiades* (the latter's authenticity is in doubt), Alcibiades'

artistry is wonderful.[153] Plato, he said, belonged to an aristocratic family deeply involved in oligarchic politics.[154] The oligarchs undermined Athens during the Peloponnesian War, and when the war was lost, they came to power with Sparta's support. Plato's uncle, Critias, led the oligarchic revolution of 403 B.C. Plato had hopes for it and was disappointed when it turned into a murderous tyranny that killed thousands of Athenians. After eight months the democrats returned and, in 399, tried and executed Socrates. Plato was beside himself. He blamed the tragedy on democracy and the Open Society and determined to build a polity in which such abuse could not happen. Mathematical knowledge, unavailable to Socrates, would provide the design. He somehow convinced himself that in overthrowing democracy and making philosophers into rulers, he was fulfilling Socratic ideals. He also had personal political ambitions. To Popper, his "beautiful portrait of the sovereign is a self-portrait."[155]

Yet, Plato was a divided soul: He felt the humanitarian and democratic passion on the one hand and the closed society's appeal on the other. No wonder his dialogues contained both humanitarian and totalitarian sentiments. No wonder the transformation of Socratic concepts was slow, uneven, ambiguous.[156] "[I]n the depths of his soul," said Popper, Plato felt "that Socrates' teaching was very different indeed from his presentation, and that he was betraying Socrates. And I think that Plato's continuous efforts to make Socrates re-interpret himself are at the same time Plato's effort to quiet his own bad conscience."[157]

Plato's theory of justice as the proper balance among the soul's contending parts (_Republic_ IV) reflected his desperate effort to control, nay suppress, conflict through rationality: "That Plato, with his longing for unity and harmony, visualized the structure of the human soul as analogous to that of a class-divided society shows how deeply he must have suffered."[158] The tension between the wishes for harmony, even if repressive, and openness, even if discordant, characterized not only Plato but open societies in general. This was Plato's dangerous appeal: "Plato's influence can partly be explained by the fascination of this conflict between two worlds in one soul. . . . This struggle touches our feelings, for it is still going on within ourselves."[159]

Whence Popper's sensitivity to Plato's psychology? He attempted no

---

and Charmides' conversion to Socratic ideals reflected Plato's own experience, and his wish to leave a testimony, if an indirect one, to the influence Socrates had on youth (chap. 10, n. 47).

[154] The Old Oligarch's violent attack on democracy, Popper suggested, reflected their aspirations. Pseudo-Xenophon, _The Constitution of the Atheneans_.

[155] _The Open Society_, vol. 1, p. 137; _Republic_ 493e–497c. In later editions, Popper used Hans Kelsen's psychoanalysis of Plato's lust for power as supporting evidence (chap. 8, n. 60).

[156] Popper turned to advantage the contradictions which his theory introduced into the dialogues. In the _Menexenus_, Plato could not help but confess the profound impression which Pericles' Funeral Oration left on him.

[157] _The Open Society_, vol. 1, pp. 172–3.   [158] Ibid., p. 173. Also: chap. 10, n. 59 (1).   [159] Ibid., p. 173.

such psychologization of Socrates but, rather, shaped Socrates in his own image. To quip: "The beautiful portrait of [Socrates] is a self-portrait." In Socratic "self-sufficiency of the good man" (understood as Kantian autonomy), Popper found vindication of his solitary life: a self-sufficient philosopher. In Socrates' philosophy, he found affirmation of both critical rationalism and his self-image as a radical democratic critic. His relationship to Plato, in contrast, was ambivalent. He attributed to him political ambitions "reaching for the stars."[160] He had none himself. In his old age he confided to young admirers, with a mysterious look on his face, the advice he had given world leaders, but this was innocuous self-importance, not ambition. He wanted to be recognized as this century's greatest philosopher, but this was not tantamount to the pursuit of political power. Throughout his life he regarded political ambition negatively. The grandiose ambitions he attributed to young communist friends he read into Plato, who was, like them, a utopian revolutionary. He had the last laugh: "Plato," he said acerbically, "had to be satisfied with establishing the first professorship, instead of the first kingship, of philosophy."[161]

The closed society had no appeal to Popper. In this respect, his reconstruction of Plato's emotional life had little to do with his own. But his sensitivity to tormented souls had much to do with his life. He described Plato as experiencing "exhilarating and extravagant hopes of success, alternating with periods of despair."[162] He himself swung radically between hope and despair throughout life. His belief in rationality and progress collided with his nonfoundationism. He passionately called, at one and the same time, for commitment and criticism. Was he himself not a divided soul? He did not identify with "Plato," but he drew heavily on his own emotional life in imagining him.

Popper castigated "vulgar Marxist" conspiracy theories as gross simplifications of history, but his history of philosophy made wide use of such theories.[163] Great philosophers rarely got their message across: Epigones' conspiracies and disciples' betrayals distorted them beyond recognition. Plato betrayed Socrates; Hegel and the Romantics betrayed Kant; the positivists and, later, Popper's own students distorted critical rationalism. Popper's explanation of intellectual change had less to do with the "logic of the situation" and more with "wickedness [that was] responsible for all the evils we suffer from."[164] It reflected deep distrust of the world and was

---

[160] Ibid., p. 136.   [161] Ibid., p. 137.   [162] Ibid., p. 136.

[163] Popper's critique of conspiracy theories is in ibid., vol. 2, pp. 93–4, chap. 17, n. 17, and 2d. ed., pp. 94–6, where it is developed in accordance with situational logic.

[164] Ibid., 2d. ed., vol. 3, p. 95. The dissonance between his political philosophy and his history of philosophy (as well as his complaints about the reception of his ideas) grew ever greater. Jeremy Shearmur drew my attention to his 1956 critique of Russell's view that moral failure, or "wickedness," was the source of the current human predicament: "The History of Our Time: An Optimist's View," in *Conjectures and Refutations*, pp. 365–6.

self-defeating: If critical exchange had rarely taken place in history, critical rationalism was in trouble. Popper needed to be saved from his own history of philosophy.

Concluding two volumes of the Library of Living Philosophers dedicated to his philosophy, Popper explained, in "Replies to My Critics," his special relationship to Socrates: "I regard myself as a disciple of Socrates, that is, of the speaker of the *Apology*, and I love the man."[165] He defended his treatment of the Socratic Question in *The Open Society*.[166] "If we reject Plato's *Apology* as an essentially valid historical testimony, then . . . the Socratic problem becomes insoluble," he wrote, and the Socratic legend created by Aristophanes may remain alive.[167] Why should this be so distressing? "Aristophanes and the Socratic Legend" preceded "The Popper Legend." Just as Aristophanes distorted Socrates' teaching and smeared his reputation among the Athenians, so contemporary philosophers created the legend of a positivist Popper. Just as Socrates' defense failed to dispel the Socratic legend, so Popper's refutation of critics was to no avail. Indeed, this reply, too, was probably doomed to failure. Yet, he was determined to try once more to set the record straight, for himself and for Socrates:

> Nothing could be further from my mind than comparing myself to Socrates. But by showing that even the teaching of such a person as myself has given rise to a legend – and to a legend which is a perverse distortion of the truth – I may perhaps make a contribution to the destruction of the Socratic legend due to Aristophanes.[168]

This was slightly disingenuous: Popper used the Socratic legend to dispel the Popper legend, not the other way round. Socrates was a two-page introduction to a two-hundred-page reply to critics, setting aright Popper's place in contemporary philosophy. In Popper's account of both legends, the philosopher was a lone crusader for truth, dedicating his life to the enlightenment of humankind. In both cases, the philosopher's message was distorted: He was misunderstood, ridiculed, persecuted, and, in Socrates' case, martyred. The true philosopher was a crusader and a martyr. The Socratic legend vindicated Popper's philosophical mission and legacy and thereby created a new Popper legend.

THE OPEN SOCIETY, ATHENIAN DEMOCRACY, AND "WESTERN CIVILIZATION"

Well before critiques of Western humanism became popular, Popper showed that philosophy was entangled with totalitarianism from its origin.

---

[165] Popper, "Replies to My Critics," *The Philosophy of Karl Popper*, p. 962. Popper's 1978 introduction to *Die beiden Grundprobleme* described the work as elaborating on Socratic "not knowing."

[166] He made, however, a significant concession: Plato did not intend the dialogues as historical documents of Socrates. If so, the arguments about deception and manipulation would need to be modified.

[167] "Replies to My Critics," p. 962.   [168] Ibid., p. 963.

He exposed not only a master but also a tradition. Reviewers who objected that English Platonism was benevolent, or that the fascists had no use for Plato, partially missed the point.[169] Popper argued less the direct transmission of Platonic ideas and more that these ideas permeated Western philosophy. Not the radical right alone was implicated but classical liberal education, too. Popper was right on target when he zeroed in on the danger of utopian communal harmony, repressive and antipluralist. He showed also that utopianism, intellectual conceit, and political ambition were intertwined among philosophers. Presumption of knowledge, certitude where doubt was appropriate, could lead to totalitarianism. Popper was anachronistic, but could anyone read Plato's proposals for emptying the city of adults who were attached to the old ways, and for eliminating recalcitrant dissenters as hopelessly sick, and not conjure up the worst episodes in contemporary history? And was this not a radical departure from "Socrates," the dissenter of the *Apology* and the *elenchos*? In a scholarly world where Grote and Cornford drew the boundaries of acceptable criticism, the postwar debate on totalitarianism and ancient philosophy would not have taken place.[170] Popper made it possible.

Popper's critique of Western philosophy should have endeared *The Open Society* to poststructuralists. It did not. Although Popper exposed philosophy's dark sides, he continued to believe in the "West" and in the Greeks' crucial role in its formation. He never made his assumptions clear, but he distinguished between the historical and the "ideal" West and identified the latter with the Open Society, rationality (that is, critical discussion), and Athenian democracy.[171] Against the ideal West he posited the closed society. All societies that had not developed critical discourse were closed. Advanced polities had both closed and open dimensions, but have gotten furthest from the closed society. People entered relationships and formed groups based on choice and preference, not blood relations. Change in the Open Society was rapid and conflict permanent, but there was no way back: "[W]e must go on into the unknown."[172]

A strange teleology dominated Popper's Western history: "Our western civilization originated with the Greeks. They were, it seems, the first to make the step from tribalism to humanitarianism," and promoted the individualism that, "united with altruism, has become the basis of our western

---

[169] A. D. Lindsay, "The Open Society," *Manchester Guardian*, 25 January 1946.

[170] By now the pendulum may have swung too far. Having used Popper for my introductory classes in American colleges, I can testify that students find his view of Plato's fascism so persuasive that it is difficult to convince them to take the *Republic* seriously.

[171] He quoted approvingly Richard Crossman (*Plato Today*, p. 93): "Socrates showed that philosophy is nothing else than conscientious objection to prejudice and unreason. . . . All that is good in our Western culture has sprung from this spirit. . . . [This] is the only force which can break the dictatorship of force and greed" (chap. 7, n. 12).

[172] *The Open Society*, vol. 1, p. 177.

civilization."[173] "An open society can only go on, or be arrested and forced back into the cage, i.e., to the beasts."[174] The West could either fulfill that which it was already by definition – rational, humanitarian, cosmopolitan – or decay into the Other, its origin. Popper seemed to discount diverse patterns. This was historicism (and essentialism), but it was innocuous because it was nondeterminist and nontriumphalist.[175] Progress was possible, but regress, given history, more likely. The narrative's major problem was not Western superiority but potential defeatism. Whence hope? From nowhere, said Popper, but we must fight nonetheless.

The West claimed to be universal, opening its gates to Greeks and barbarians alike. Was it capable of accommodating diversity? Popper's Athens offered an equivocal answer. It was culturally pluralistic, but its cosmopolitanism expressed itself most strongly in imperialism. A universal empire seemed a precondition to the Open Society: Alexander, the Romans, Napoleon, the Habsburgs. Popper's recollection of imperialist episodes was selective. It did not include Cortés, the Middle Passage, or Nazi *Lebensraum*. Imperialism represented cosmopolitanism's possibility; this was enough. But cosmopolitan identity seemed abstract and unreal. Popper himself conceded that "concrete groups" – families, churches, voluntary associations, possibly even ethnic communities – would remain even in the Open Society. They would continue to fulfill some of the functions that kinship groups had in the "closed society." Indeed, they were essential: People, Popper said unsympathetically, will "try to satisfy their emotional social needs as well as they can."[176] But "emotional social needs" remained foreign to him, implicated with fascism. When criticism conflicted with traditional life and belief, his stance was clear: Openness and tolerance required that custom and authority give way. He never negotiated between the closed and the Open Society, or showed their possible convergence in the future.

There was no room for negotiation with fascism. Popper's categorical rejection of the claims of closed communities against the cosmopolitan Open Society ought to be understood in the context of fascism. Popper acknowledged "diversity" and – with the exception of Jewish religion and nationality which, he insisted, must be given up – assailed any effort to suppress difference. He defended minorities' rights.[177] To be sure, he thought that ethnic and religious differences were insignificant. Diversity existed, but unlike universal humanity, it was no cause for celebration. His refusal

---

[173] Ibid., pp. 151, 89, respectively.   [174] Ibid., chap. 5, n. 45 (2).

[175] John Watkins, "A Whiff of Hegel in *The Open Society*?" in *Popper's Open Society After 50 Years*, ed. Ian Jarvie and Sandra Pralong (London: Routledge, 1999) notices the historicism.

[176] *The Open Society*, 2d ed., vol. 1, p. 175.

[177] In one of his last public appearances, he acerbically suggested that Germany's and France's "homogenous populations" were due to "political and educational means of suppressing minorities or dialects": "Prague Lecture," www.lf3.cuni.cz/aff/p2_e.html (access through The Karl Popper Web: www.eeng.dcu.ie/~tkpw/).

to celebrate diversity reflected determination not to eliminate difference but to ensure it does not infringe on universal humanity. The first response to the racist argument that those who are different are inferior and cannot be members of the nation is *not* that we ought to respect difference; it is that we are all equally human and entitled to equal rights as citizens.

Popper's universalism did have blind spots. Current observers may note especially his blindness to gender. As classicists at the time had rather fanciful ideas about Athenian women's liberties (based on their roles in Athenian drama), Popper could not have known much about them.[178] He gave short shrift, however, to Plato's proposal for abolishing the family and granting nearly equal roles to guardian women. Plato's "liberation" of women, he thought, was a mere result of abolishing the family and private property, and, as such, irrelevant to equality between the sexes.[179] Still, the *Republic* discussed at length women's potential for military, philosophical, and political careers. Popper was indifferent. Viennese progressives were in the forefront of feminism. Popper thought there were more important issues.[180]

All the same, in modern Europe, the Open Society opened its gates to constituencies previously ignored and reassessed its requirements for inclusion. Will progress continue? Popper was not sure. His history of the West was one of terror and persecution interrupted by humanitarian efforts. The West had barely made progress over two millennia: "Plato was a child of a time which is still our own. (We must not forget that it is, after all, only a century since the abolition of slavery in the United States, and even less since the abolition of serfdom in Central Europe.)"[181] Such progress as had been made over the last century was now once more threatened by the return of the repressed, the fascist closed society. Popper and critics of Western humanism were in agreement about the West's failure, but he

---

[178] J. Gould, "Law, Custom and Myth: Aspects of the Social Position of Women in Classical Athens," *Journal of Hellenic Studies* 100 (1980): 38–59; Roger Just, *Women in Athenian Law and Life* (London: Routledge, 1989); John Winkler, *The Constraints of Desire* (London: Routledge, 1989).

[179] "Since all property is common property, there must also be a common ownership of women and children. . . . The family must be destroyed, or rather, extended to cover the whole warrior class" (p. 48). This is also Susan Okin's view: *Women in Western Political Thought* (Princeton, N.J.: Princeton University Press, 1979). Still, Plato could have achieved the same effect of (male) bonding by treating women as common property, or slaves, rather than elevating them to equal partnership. Gregory Vlastos, "Was Plato a Feminist?" *Times Literary Supplement*, 17–23 March 1989, 276 ff.; Julia Annas, "Plato's *Republic* and Feminism," *Philosophy* 51 (1976): 307–21.

[180] One exception: His denunciation of the Glauconic Edict that permitted those who excelled on the battlefield to choose their partner for intercourse, regardless of the other party's wishes (*Republic* 468c). The rule presumably applied to men and women soldiers alike, and they could choose sexual partners of either sex, but it institutionalized rape. Popper protested against the "brutal law" (p. 132).

Popper thought that Plato encouraged "Dorian homosexuality" "to recapture, in the life of the war-horde, an emotional satisfaction which had been largely destroyed by the breakdown of tribalism" (2d ed., chap. 10, n. 7). Popper had gay students who became close friends, but on family and sex, he remained a traditional bourgeois.

[181] *The Open Society*, vol. 1, p. 173.

upheld an ideal "West" that remained immune to history's atrocities. In the midst of the West's greatest catastrophe ever, he envisioned the Open Society that sustained hope. As hope could not be sustained without example, he searched history. He found Socrates, Pericles, and classical Athens. He saw his world in theirs and did his best to bring out the similarities, creating a vision of what the "West" could be like, never was, and likely never will be.

CRITICAL RATIONALISM BETRAYED:
POPPER'S ATTACK ON HEGEL

Popper devoted to Plato and Marx ten chapters each, only one lengthy chapter to Hegel. "I neither could nor wished to spend unlimited time upon deep researches into the history of a philosopher whose work I abhor."[182] He wrote on Hegel in "scherzo-style" as an intermezzo between Plato and Marx. He read only selections of Hegel and virtually no scholarly work on him.[183] Hegel is notoriously difficult, and Popper's animosity was such that he made only moderate effort to understand him. No Hegel scholar has taken Popper seriously, and even critics of Hegel dissociated themselves from him.[184] He implicated a philosopher, and a tradition, in national socialism without giving them a fair hearing. Nonetheless, his attack did not meet (as his critique of Plato had) with outrage.[185] Hegel's

---

[182] Ibid., Addendum to the 4th edition, vol. 2, p. 394.

[183] He used mostly *Hegel Selections*, ed. Jacob Loewenberg, The Modern Student's Library of Philosophy (New York: Scribner's, 1929). "This excellent and easily accessible selection contains a great number of the most characteristic passages from Hegel, so it was possible in many cases to choose the quotations from them" (*The Open Society*, vol. 2, p. 290). The book included selections from *The Phenomenology of the Mind* and the *Encyclopaedia*, and brief excerpts from the *Lectures on Aesthetics*, *The Philosophy of History*, and *The Philosophy of Right*. Popper did consult *The Philosophy of Right* to identify paragraph numbers for the Loewenberg quotation. In later editions, he (or his assistants) added references to Hegel's *Sämtliche Werke*, ed. Hermann Glockner, 26 vols. (Stuttgart: Frommanns, 1927–40).

   As for scholarship, Popper used J. H. Stirling's introduction and annotations to Albert Schwegler, *Handbook of the History of Philosophy*, 14th ed. (Edinburgh: Oliver & Boyd, 1890) and Edward Caird, *Hegel* (Philadelphia: Lippincott, 1883) (*The Open Society*, vol. 2, pp. 7, 25, 31–2; chap. 11, n. 23; chap. 12, nn. 14–17 and 81). (Schwegler was Hegel's student, and both Caird and Stirling were Victorian Hegelians.) After having completed *The Open Society*, Popper read Michael Foster, *The Political Philosophies of Plato and Hegel* (Oxford: Oxford University Press, 1935) (chap. 12, n. 46, and chap. 25, n. 19, both added in September 1944: Popper Archives [28, 16]).

[184] Carl J. Friedrich, "Introduction" to *The Philosophy of Hegel* (New York: Modern Library, 1953), esp. pp. xv, 546–9 (nn. 1, 2, 44); Sidney Hook, "Hegel Rehabilitated," in Walter Kaufmann, ed., *Hegel's Political Philosophy* (New York: Atherton, 1970), esp. p. 56.

[185] A notable exception: Walter Kaufmann, "The Hegel Myth and Its Method," *The Philosophical Review* 60 (1951): 459–86. Logical positivists and British empiricists, long hostile to German Idealism, were Popper's major sympathetic audience. Rudolf Carnap, "Überwindung der Metaphysik durch logische Analyse der Sprache," *Erkenntnis* 2 (1932): 219–41; Bertrand Russell, "Philosophy and Politics," in his *Unpopular Essays* (London: Allen and Unwin, 1950), pp. 9–34.

reputation as a reactionary Prussian had been firmly established in England and North America since World War I.[186] When the Nazis seized power, Hegel became a Nazi philosopher.[187] Popper's attack exemplified the genre. It was less criticism, more abuse. Critical rationalism presupposes that an enemy's worthiness cannot be prejudged (not even his being an enemy). Criticism is a precondition to delegitimization. Popper failed a crucial test.

As Hegel's sharp exchanges with critics from the right (von Haller) and left (Fries) showed, he was a controversial thinker throughout his life. The struggle over his legacy began shortly after his death. On the left, the young Hegelians formulated critiques of religion and politics that gave rise to Marxism.[188] On the right, theologian J. E. Erdmann of Halle (1805–92) declared Hegel's state an organic ethical unity.[189] Prussian liberal Karl Rosenkrantz (1805–79) commemorated Hegel in his biography as an enlightened philosopher of the Prussian state.[190] Rudolf Haym criticized this portrait in *Hegel und seine Zeit*, a critique which, through Nelson, informed Popper's view of Hegel.[191] Several mandarins celebrated Hegel as the Second Reich's national philosopher, but his academic fortunes in Germany declined throughout the second half of the nineteenth century. From Ranke to Meinecke, German historians rejected his universal history in favor of individuality and *Historismus*.

During the first decade of this century, Dilthey led an academic revival of Hegel studies.[192] The conservative mandarins transformed Hegel during the interwar years into an authoritarian nationalist philosopher, their efforts disclosing ambivalence about the Nazis. They were glad to undermine Weimar with an authoritarian "Hegel."[193] Some even made him into a

[186] John Dewey, *German Philosophy and Politics* (New York: Holt, 1915); L. T. Hobhouse, *The Metaphysical Theory of the State* (London: Allen & Unwin, 1918); C. E. Vaughan, *Studies in the History of Political Philosophy* (Manchester: University Press, 1925); E. F. Carritt and T. M. Knox, an exchange on "Hegel and Prussianism," *Philosophy* (January, April, and July 1940), reprinted in *Hegel's Political Philosophy*, ed. Kaufmann.

[187] W. H. McGovern, *From Luther to Hitler* (Boston: Houghton Mifflin, 1941).

[188] John Toews, *Hegelianism* (New York: Cambridge University Press, 1980); David McLellan, *The Young Hegelians and Karl Marx* (London: Macmillan, 1969); Nicholas Lobkowicz, *Theory and Practice* (Notre Dame, Ind.: University of Notre Dame, 1967); and an older work, Sidney Hook, *From Hegel to Marx* (London: Gollancz, 1936).

[189] J. E. Erdmann, *Philosophische Vorlesungen über den Staat* (Halle: Schmidt, 1851).

[190] Karl Rosenkrantz, *Georg Wilhelm Friedrich Hegels Leben* [1844] (Darmstadt: Wissenschaftliche Buchgesellschaft, 1977).

[191] Rudolf Haym, *Hegel und seine Zeit*, ed. Hans Rosenberg, 2d ed. (Leipzig: Heims, 1927). See my discussion in Chapter 3.

[192] Wilhelm Dilthey, *Die Jugendgeschichte Hegels* [1905], *Gesammelte Schriften* (Leipzig: Teubner, 1921), vol. 4. See also: Kuno Fischer, *Hegels Leben, Werke und Lehre*, 2 vols. (Heidelberg: Winter, 1901). After the publication of Hegel's early theological writings (Hermann Nohl, ed., *Hegels theologische Jugendschriften* [Tübingen: Mohr, 1907]), a number of important works came out, among them, Franz Rosenzweig, *Hegel und der Staat*, 2 vols. (Munich: Oldenbourg, 1920).

[193] Martin Busse, *Hegels Phänomenologie des Geistes und der Staat* (Berlin: Junker und Dunnhaupt, 1931); Theodore Haering, *Hegel: Sein Wollen und sein Werk*, 2 vols. (Leipzig: Teubner, 1929).

totalitarian philosopher, but few went the extra step, turning his ethical community into a racial "blood and earth" one.[194] Whichever the case, it turned out to make little difference for the Nazis. They refused to recognize Hegel as an intellectual ancestor, making no effort to appropriate him for Nazi politics, and some ideologues, Rosenberg, for example, were downright hostile to him.

Marxists considered Hegel the greatest bourgeois philosopher. Marx insisted to the end that he was Hegel's student, and Engels spoke of Marxism as turning the Hegelian dialectic "on its head."[195] This was not good intellectual history, but it accorded Hegel a place in the Marxist pantheon. When the wooden dialectical materialism of Plekhanov and the Russian communists threatened Marxism's idealist heritage, György Lukács revived it in *History and Class Consciousness* (1923).[196] With Stalinism triumphant in Moscow, however, only Western Marxists were free to experiment with Hegel. The Frankfurt School, Adorno, Horkheimer, and Marcuse, engaged Hegel critically. Marcuse's *Reason and Revolution* (1941) was the only book in English for many years to take note of Hegel's recently published early writings, the Jena *Realphilosophie*.[197] He defended Hegel against interpretations implicating him in national socialism. In France, Alexandre Kojève, a German-educated Russian émigré who fancied himself a Stalinist, introduced a generation of French intellectuals to Hegel's *Phenomenology*.[198] His Heideggerian-Marxist interpretation of Hegel resonated among Existential Marxists: Beauvoir, Merleau-Ponty, Sartre, and others. Until postmodernism swept the Western academies in the 1980s, Hegel's fortunes on the left remained secure.[199]

---

[194] Julius Binder, *System der Rechtsphilosophie*, 2d. ed. (Berlin: Stilke, 1937); Karl Larenz, "Volksgeist und Recht," *Zeitschrift für deutsche Kulturphilosophie* 1 (1935). My account of Hegel's reception in the German academy owes much to Henning Ottmann, *Individuum und Gemeinschaft bei Hegel* (Berlin: Gruyter, 1977), vol. 1.

[195] For Marx, the *locus classicus* is the 1873 "Afterword" to the second German edition of *Das Kapital:* "I therefore openly showed myself the pupil of that mighty thinker." (*Capital*, trans. Samuel Moore and Edward Eveling, 2 vols. [London: Sonnenschein, Lowrey, 1887.]) For Engels: *Ludwig Feuerbach and the End of Classical German Philosophy* (Moscow: Foreign Languages Publishing House, 1962), vol. 2, pp. 386–7.

[196] Trans. Rodney Livingstone (Boston: MIT, 1971); Georg Lukács, *Geschichte und Klassenbewußtsein* (Berlin: Malik, 1923).

[197] Herbert Marcuse, *Reason and Revolution* (Boston: Beacon, 1941). The *Jenenser Realphilosophie* was a series of lectures at Jena from 1803 to 1806 (ed. Johannes Hoffmeister, 2 vols. [Leipzig: Meiner, 1931–2]). A more recent evaluation: Shlomo Avineri, "Labor, Alienation, and Social Classes in Hegel's *Realphilosophie*," *Philosophy and Public Affairs* 1 (1971): 96–119.

[198] Alexandre Kojève, *Introduction à la Lecture de Hegel*, ed. Raymond Queneau (Paris: Gallimard, 1947). On Kojève, Hyppolite, and Weil: Michael Roth, *Knowing and History: Appropriations of Hegel in Twentieth Century France* (Ithaca, N.Y.: Cornell University Press, 1988).

[199] There were exceptions: The Austro-Marxists were one; Louis Althusser another: *Pour Marx* (Paris: Maspero, 1965).

Hegel's influence outside of Germany was by no means limited to the Marxist left. In late Victorian England, his philosophy inspired liberals and conservatives. Liberal T. H. Green emphasized the state's moral responsibility for its citizens. Conservatives voiced demands for restoring the state's moral authority to counter democratization. In Italy, Croce developed Hegel's philosophy of history. His student, Giovanni Gentile, used his philosophy to show that the fascist state transcended liberalism. Everywhere, confrontation with Hegel stimulated divergent philosophies. Kierkegaard, Heidegger, and Dewey were cases in point. Hegel had irreconcilable enemies, too, and nowhere more so than in Vienna. Schopenhauer's vituperative attack on Hegel was popular there, and Popper used it extensively.[200] The Fries–Nelson tradition reinforced his anti-Hegelianism as well. Throughout the book, his suggestion that a thinker was influenced by Hegel meant a short dismissal. He was aware of some of Hegel's influences, ignorant of others, but interested only in two: his influence on Marx and on national socialism.

To bridge two millennia of historicist thought between Plato and Hegel, Popper provided a historical outline of the struggle between totalitarianism and democracy.[201] Alexander's empire and Hellenistic schools, the cynics and epicureans, kept the Socratic legacy alive, and the Roman Empire opened closed societies. The Jews, the quintessential tribe, reacted by rigidly reformulating biblical laws. Early Christianity protested their worship of the Word and spread a universalist message, but the Roman Empire took advantage of the new religion, turning the church into a state instrument. With Justinian's religious persecutions of non-Christians, the Middle Ages began. Medieval Christianity absorbed Platonic-Aristotelian totalitarian ideas, the Inquisition being their ultimate expression. First the Renaissance, then the Enlightenment weakened the medieval church, but its political counterpart, feudalism, reinforced by the Reformation, existed until the French Revolution. The revolution recovered classical individualism, egalitarianism, and cosmopolitanism, and began again the fight for the Open Society. The feudal monarchies resisted, and

---

[200] Arthur Schopenhauer, Preface to the second edition of *Die Welt als Wille und Vorstellung, Sämmtliche Werke* (Leipzig: Brockhaus, 1922), vol. 2; Appendix to "Skitze einer Geschichte der Lehre vom Idealen und Realen," *Parerga und Paralipomena, Sämmtliche Werke*, vol. 5, pp. 22–32. Popper criticized Schopenhauer for his reactionary politics, but praised his intellectual integrity. "His critique of Kant is perhaps the most lucid and worthwhile philosophical writing in [the] German language": Popper to Gombrich, 23 August 1943 (300, 2). See also: *The Open Society*, vol. 2, chap. 12, pp. 30–1 and nn. 12–13.

[201] The chapter was titled "The Aristotelian Roots of Hegelianism," but there was little in it on either Aristotle or Hegel. Popper expressed a low opinion of Aristotle, and devoted a mere six pages to his teleology and essentialism, which provided building blocks for Hegel's philosophy. He devoted thirteen pages to a critique of language philosophy, denouncing its preoccupation with definitions as "essentialism."

[w]hen in 1815 the reactionary party began to resume its power in Prussia, it found itself in dire need of an ideology. Hegel was appointed to meet this demand, and he did so by reviving the ideas of the first great enemies of the open society, Heraclites, Plato, and Aristotle. . . . Hegel . . . represents the "missing link," as it were, between Plato and the modern form of totalitarianism.[202]

Just as Plato had converted Socrates' critical philosophy into dogmatism, so Hegel (along with Fichte, Schelling, Schlegel, and other German romantics) transformed Kant's liberalism into reactionary historicism. Hegel "bowed and twisted Kant's view into its opposite." Kant limited state power to assure the greatest possible liberty for all. Law was universal, citizens' rights and duties equal. Hegel suggested that Kantian liberty and equality were "subjective," "abstract," one-sided, mere aspects of the broader liberty and equality realized in Prussia. Liberty was not freedom to act as one chose, but obedience to law; equality did not mean equal treatment, but recognition of gender, age, and wealth differences. The constitution was a fine idea, but Hegel limited access to government and retained full authority for the monarch. The state became "God's march through the world," setting the standards of morality and truth. It demanded unswerving loyalty and service. No individual counted when state interest was at stake. Even freedom of thought had to give way. Contemporary Prussia, the reactionary Prussia of Friedrich Wilhelm III, represented the pinnacle of freedom.

Hegel converted German nationalism from liberalism to Prussian absolutism. German nationalism originated in a "tribal reaction" to the French empire, but for a short period, it was identical with popular sovereignty, and the movement seemed liberal. Hegel "tamed nationalism not by outspoken opposition but by transforming it into a well-disciplined Prussian authoritarianism. And it so happened that he brought back a powerful weapon into the camp of the closed society, where it fundamentally belonged," wrote Popper.[203] Hegel joined nationalism and the absolutist state together. National states were tested in war, their subjects proving their worth in battle, leading heroic lives. To Hegel:

if I wish "to emerge into Existence" . . . then I must "assert my personality." This . . . leads . . . to a new justification of the theory of slavery [and] has

[202] *The Open Society*, vol. 2, pp. 28–9. Karl Milford believes that there is more to the "Platonic and Aristotelian roots of Hegelianism" than meets the eye. Nineteenth-century German political economists and historians revealed a combination of Aristotelian and historicist themes, and classical education provided the background against which both Spengler and interwar socialists developed their historicist theories. Popper, argues Milford, need not have been familiar with particular authors and works to be impressed by the convergence of Aristotelian and Hegelian themes in the Viennese milieu. "It was in the air" (conversation with author, 3 October 1999).

[203] Ibid., pp. 53–4.

. . . its counterpart in Hegel's theory of international relations. Nations must assert themselves on the stage of History; it is their duty to attempt the domination of the world.[204]

Victory determined justice. "The litany of private virtues . . . must not be raised" against historical destiny.[205] This was modern totalitarianism: authoritarian leadership, total mobilization, propaganda, and heroic life.

Hegel's philosophy conveyed idealism: He "talk[ed] more loudly about 'reason' than any man before or after him."[206] His manner of reconciling contradictions immunized his philosophy to criticism. His convoluted style gave the impression of profundity and made exposing his charlatanism difficult. Still, he would never have made it without government support. As Prussia's official philosopher, he extended patronage to his students, and they, in turn, promoted his philosophy. Marx fell into the trap. Hegelianism entered the Marxist camp as a fifth column, weakening the resolve to combat nationalism and war: "[T]he formula of the fascist brew is in all countries the same: Hegel plus a dash of nineteenth-century materialism (especially Darwinism)."[207] The fascists may emphasize race and people *(Volk)*, rather than state, but Hegel himself regarded the state as the "Spirit of the People." He did not speak of race, but the fascists translated spirit into blood, establishing race conflict as the motor of history. Hegel and the fascists were at one. The hysterical cries: "We want our history! We want out destiny! We want our fight! We want our chains! resound through the edifice of Hegelianism."[208]

To demonstrate Hegel's influence on German culture, Popper quoted an array of intellectuals: Nazi (Krieck and Rosenberg), Nazi fellow travelers (Freyer and Heidegger), "Prussian socialists" (Spengler), even anti-Nazi (Jaspers).[209] Both Heidegger and Jaspers, he said, were nihilists. Heidegger sought to overcome anguish of death by surrender to the *Führer* and national destiny. Jaspers proposed that life's meaning was clear only to those facing annihilation. This was "the philosophy of the gambler – of the gangster."[210] Schopenhauer suggested that "if one wishes to dull the wits of a boy and make it impossible for him to think, there is no better tested method than a thorough study of Hegel."[211]

---

[204] Ibid., pp. 7–8. [205] Ibid., p. 64. [206] Ibid., p. 70. [207] Ibid., p. 57. [208] Ibid., p. 72.

[209] He did not read them, but relied on Aurel Kolnai's *The War Against the West*. "I am greatly indebted to Kolnai's work, which has made it possible for me to quote . . . a considerable number of authors who would otherwise have been inaccessible to me. (I have, however, not always followed the wording of Kolnai's translations)" (chap. 12, n. 71). He also found Julius Kraft, *Von Husserl zu Heidegger* [1932], 2nd ed. (Frankfurt: Öffentliches Leben, 1957) and Alfred Zimmern, ed., *Modern Political Doctrines* (New York: Oxford University Press, 1939) helpful.

[210] *The Open Society*, vol. 2, p. 74.

[211] Loc. cit. Schopenhauer, "Anhang" zu "Lehre vom Idealen und Realen," p. 25. (I modified slightly Popper's translation.)

German intellectuals studied Hegel, and he had a disastrous effect on them.

Hegel held the philosophy chair in Berlin from 1818 to his death in 1831, and was Rector for a number of years during the 1820s. As Schopenhauer and Popper pointed out, Prussian university professors were appointed and paid by the education ministry, and so he was technically a "paid agent of the Prussian government." His political formation was, however, distinctly non-Prussian. His intellectual maturation took place in Württemberg, and later at Jena. Both had distinctly non-Prussian civic and religious traditions.[212] In his 1802 essay "The German Constitution," Hegel bemoaned the fate of a divided reactionary Germany. He delighted in the Prussian defeat at Jena in 1806, as it enabled the French to introduce reforms throughout southern and western Germany. In the aftermath of defeat, Prussian reformers Stein and Hardenberg transformed Prussia into a modern state. They abolished serfdom, introduced a universal draft, granted municipal autonomy, streamlined the bureaucracy, reformed the educational system, and established a new university in Berlin. Their reform impetus died in the wake of the renewed struggle against Napoleon, but the battle between reactionaries and reformers continued in the early Restoration years, and Hegel was called to Berlin as the progressives' candidate. *The Philosophy of Right* (1821) reflected his high hopes for Prussia: One day, he told Hardenberg, it may become the ideal state he described.[213] In the preface, he attacked Fries, the nationalist students' idol. Public disorder was a major threat. Reforms had to be introduced from above, not through protests and pressure.

Hegel's hopes for Prussia were dashed. The reactionaries in the Prussian court gained ground during the 1820s. Many of them were unhappy with Hegel, censored his work, and put him and his students under police surveillance. But, mandarin that Hegel was, he did not become an outspoken critic. His anxieties focused on public disorder and the commercialization of culture, not on political oppression. For all the intelligent apologies of his modern admirers, his growing conservatism was evident. In his last political essay, he rejected the British Reform Bill that abolished an absurd electoral system and extended suffrage to the urban middle class. The new system, he reasoned, signaled the triumph of civil society over the state, allowing merchants to become the nation's legislators. In the more liberal European countries, it seemed, constitutional reform progressed beyond what Hegel was willing to allow. Still, Popper's portrayal of him as a

---

[212] Laurence Dickey, *Hegel: Religion, Economics and the Politics of the Spirit, 1770–1807* (New York: Cambridge University Press, 1987).

[213] He was less reserved in his 1818 inaugural address: He praised Prussia's leadership in the struggle against foreign tyranny. Having become Prussia's prominent philosopher, he forgot his earlier endorsement of the French occupation.

reactionary Prussian was unfair. He was, to be sure, an antidemocrat, and had misgivings about liberalism, but he represented Prussian reform, not reaction.[214]

Hegel felt that morality and politics would not survive the chasm that Kant had opened between moral freedom and natural necessity, ethical absolutes and historical contingency, the Kingdom of Ends and contemporary politics. He tried to close the gap. Popper argued that his closure left no room for criticism. He used Hegel's famous statement in *The Philosophy of Right* to buttress this argument:

What is rational is actual
And what is actual is rational.[215]

To Popper, if the actual was rational, then reality was rational. Kaufmann pointed out, however, that Hegel distinguished between the real (*real*), which reflected historical contingency, and the actual (*wirklich*), which meant potentiality fulfilled.[216] Hegel did not sanction the Prussian government, which was a historical accident, but the actual state, Prussia as it could become. The tension between the two left room for change. Still, did Hegel take advantage of it? Moderately, and progressively less as he got older. He queried insightfully radical platforms, but unfailingly found them deficient. He recognized the gap between his ideals and the current order, but was incapable of direct criticism, to say nothing of public protest. He somehow hoped that *Bildung*, educating a new generation of mandarins, would eventually translate into political change. He entrusted history with the closing of the gap he saw widening before his eyes. Admitting failure would mean that history had gone wrong. Hegel could not bear such a result. He aimed to justify history.

Hegel criticized liberal and democratic views of the constitution. Popper thought that he perverted constitutionalism. In the three excerpts from the *Encyclopedia*, *The Philosophy of History*, and *The Philosophy of Right* that Popper used, Hegel opposed the view that constitutions could be "made" by people, pointing out that they grew out of historical conditions.[217] The

---

[214] *Hegel: Political Writings*, eds. Laurence Dickey and H. B. Nisbet (Cambridge: Cambridge University Press, 1999) is an excellent collection. The introduction includes an extensive historiographical discussion and offers a spirited defense of Hegel. For the older debate, see Avineri's, Kaufmann's, and Pelczynski's responses to Hook in *Hegel's Political Philosophy*, ed. Kaufmann, and in Shlomo Avineri, *Hegel's Theory of the Modern State* (New York: Cambridge University Press, 1972).

[215] "Was vernünftig ist, das ist wirklich; und was wirklich ist, das ist vernünftig": "Vorrede" zu *Grundlinien der Philosophie des Rechts*, *Sämtliche Werke*, vol. 7, p. 33; "Preface" to *Elements of the Philosophy of Right*, ed. Allen Wood, trans. H. B. Nisbet (New York: Cambridge University Press, 1991), p. 20.

[216] Walter Kaufmann, "The Hegel Myth and Its Method": 469. See Allen Wood's comment to the same effect, *Philosophy of Right*, pp. 389–90.

[217] *Enzyklopädie der philosophischen Wissenschaften* [1817], trans. William Wallace and A.V. Miller, *The Philosophy of Mind* (New York: Oxford University Press, 1971), Sections 540–2; *Vorlesungen über die Philosophie der Geschichte*, *Sämtliche Werke*, vol. 11, pp. 80–2; *Philosophy of Right*, Sections 273–81.

question was not how to make, but rather how to change a constitution. The constitution was not an agreement among the citizens on restricting liberty through law. This was "subjective," "abstract," fictive. "Objective liberty" was embodied in law and in a plurality of governing institutions. They included representative bodies (to which Hegel was disinclined to give legislative power), but also a hereditary monarch. "Objective liberty" did not obliterate "subjective liberty": "We established earlier the two moments: first, the idea of freedom as an absolute final aim; second, its means, the subjective side of knowledge and will. . . . [T]he State [is] . . . the objective unity of these two moments . . . [that] are intimately connected."[218] Democrats and liberals would not endorse Hegel's constitutionalism, but he did not endorse a totalitarian state.

German nationalists from Fries to Haym regarded Hegel as an enemy, a protagonist of the confederation established by the Congress of Vienna. Hegel's early essay on "The German Constitution" (1802) supported unification, but this reflected nationalism less than it did the recognition that unification was the precondition to modernization and political reform. To the very end, he admired Napoleon as a harbinger of progress, and resisted the nationalist frenzy of the Battle of Nations. With Prussia and the German states reformed, he also lost interest in unification. Prussia was, during the Restoration, the mortal enemy of German nationalism. Hegel's "nation-state" was not as aggressive as Popper alleged.[219] War was a test of national vigor, and individual sacrifice expressed devotion to universal ideals, but culture, not war, was the modern state's *telos*. Hegel did not sanction imperialism and did not promote "heroic experience."[220] His problem was not nationalism but theodicy: the endeavor to show that the wars plaguing the world somehow had meaning and were worth it.

Popper misinterpreted not only Hegel but also contemporary German intellectuals as well.[221] He had limited knowledge of German intellectual life, and used Kolnai's *The War Against the West* as a shortcut. Kolnai argued

---

[218] *Philosophie der Geschichte*, p. 82. Popper quoted this paragraph in part (chap. 12, n. 43[1]), but saw it as the ultimate hypocrisy: "Thus we begin with freedom and end with the totalitarian state. One can hardly present the twist more cynically."

[219] Hegel's view of the human search for recognition did not sanction aggressive pursuits either. Precisely because slaves could not "assert their personality," they did not grant their masters recognition, and neither master nor slave was free. The unfulfilled search for recognition through domination ended in the modern state that recognized all citizens, yet demanded universal obedience. Like Popper, Hegel saw abolition as the acid test for progress. Hegel, *Phänomenologie des Geistes*, 6th ed. (Hamburg: Meiner, 1952), esp. pp. 138–50.

[220] *Philosophy of Right*, Sections 321–40.

[221] Heidegger was a Nazi, and his philosophy was implicated in fascism, but he surely did not believe that " 'Pure Being' and 'Pure Nothingness' are identical" (*The Open Society*, vol. 2, p. 76). If Jaspers represented "an esoteric group of intellectuals, who have surrendered their reason and with it their humanity," how come he opposed the Nazis and, after the war, was one of the few to call upon Germans to admit their war guilt (p. 78)? His was not (chap. 12, n. 89) "a hysterical romanticism, combined with a brutal barbarism and . . . professorial pedantry."

that antihumanitarianism and anticosmopolitanism pervaded German culture. German tribal egotism, historical relativism, nationalism, and anti-intellectualism could be traced back to the attack on the Roman Empire. He paid little attention to Hegel, but Popper read his perspective on contemporary Germany into Hegel, thus showing Hegel's "influence."[222]

It was not a coincidence that Kolnai and Popper shared a wholesale condemnation of German intellectuals. Both regarded the Habsburg monarchy's dissolution as an unmitigated disaster and blamed it on nationalism. They contrasted Prussian nationalism with Austrian cosmopolitanism. Nazi racism was nationalism's highest stage. There was no good and bad nationalism: They rejected cultural *Deutschtum* as much as the ethnic one. The only nation Popper recognized was a political one, founded on the French Revolution's concept of citizenship. Ethnic origins, religious affiliation, and cultural difference were irrelevant. Alone among liberals of his generation, he challenged national self-determination and the national state. Nationalities did not exist. German thinkers from Herder to Fichte to Hegel invented them to serve the interests of reactionary states:

> The idea that there exist natural units like nations or linguistic or racial groups is entirely fictitious. . . . The principle of the national state . . . owes its popularity solely to the fact that it appeals to tribal instincts.[223] . . . None of the theories which maintain that a nation is united by common origin, or a common language, or a common history, is acceptable, or applicable in practice. The principle of the national state . . . is a myth. It is an irrational, a romantic and Utopian dream.[224]

Wilson's and Masaryk's "well meant" effort to apply national self-determination consistently throughout Central Europe – "one of the most mixed of all the thoroughly mixed regions of Europe" – was an incredible folly that brought about the failure of Versailles: "An international federation in the Danube basin might have prevented much."[225] The only remedy was recognizing state boundaries as conventional, sanctioning the status quo, and establishing an armed international organization to guarantee peace.[226] Nationalities were false, reactionary, and utopian. Individuals, empires, and cosmopolitan federations were true, progressive, and

---

[222] Kolnai decried Hegel's totalitarian state in his critique of Othmar Spann's holism and corporatism. (*The War Against the West*, pp. 127–8, 391–3, 400, 576–7.)

[223] *The Open Society*, chap. 9, n. 7(1).   [224] Ibid., vol. 2, p. 49.   [225] Ibid., chap. 12, n. 53.

[226] Ibid., chap. 5, n. 13(2); chap. 6, n. 44 (in later editions Popper expanded this note to rebut Hans Morgenthau's dismissal of an international legal order); chap. 9, n. 7; vol. 2: p. 238; chap. 12, nn. 19 53; chap. 13, n. 2(1); idem., "Kant's Critique and Cosmology," in *Conjectures and Refutations*, esp. p. 182; idem., "Epistemology and Industrialization," in *The Myth of the Framework* (London: Routledge, 1994), pp. 185–7; idem., "On Culture Clash," in *In Search of a Better World* (London: Routledge, 1992), pp. 118–21. In his last public lecture, Popper blamed ethnic terrorism in Bosnia on national self-determination, and warned that if the principle did not lose its authority, postcommunist Central Europe would fall prey to the same: "Prague Lecture," www.lf3.cuni.cz/aff/p2_e.html.

possible. Hegel represented the nation-state, Kant cosmopolitanism. No wonder Popper saw Hegel as the origin of modern totalitarianism.

Defending his commitment to rationalism, Popper stated that "[r]ationalism is bound up with the idea that the other fellow has a right to be heard, and to defend his arguments."[227] Furthermore, it "is an attitude of readiness to listen to critical arguments . . . admitting that 'I may be wrong and you may be right, and by an effort, we may get nearer to the truth.' "[228] This is one of the nicer descriptions of critical rationalism, emphasizing dialogue and cooperation, rather than ruthless criticism and competition. Dialogue participants share a desire to learn and reach the truth. In the case of dead philosophers, readers must assume that they may be right, and, at the very least, that there is something to be learned from them. Popper's critique of Hegel violated these maxims: "In order to discourage the reader beforehand from taking Hegel's bombastic and mystifying cant too seriously, I shall quote some of the amazing details which he discovered about sound [his failed attempt to develop a dialectical natural science]."[229] Popper distorted Hegel's arguments by, literally, cutting them short, discouraging readers from following them carefully, and justifying the procedure with a character assassination:

> I have radically abbreviated [Hegel's] argument; and I must warn the reader that I shall have to do the same throughout the chapter; for only in this way is it at all possible to present, in a readable manner, his verbosity and the flight of his thoughts (which, I do not doubt, is pathological).[230] [His] method of burying thoughts under a heap of words . . . is one symptom of hysteria[,] . . . an excellent object for psychoanalysis.[231]

Tortuous as Hegel's prose was, his works exemplified moderation in tone and disposition. He manifested no hysteria. One could not say the same about Popper's attack on him. Critics called Popper to task on his limited knowledge, biased reading, and ad hominem attack. He responded: "I am still surprised that serious philosophers were offended by my admittedly partly playful attack upon a philosophy which I am still unable to take seriously . . . and can only regard with a mixture of contempt and horror."[232] The strictures of critical rationalism did not apply to Hegel: One did not need to take his arguments seriously. He stood outside the community of reason. Exclusion is always dangerous, but, certainly, one could not exclude Hegel before his arguments were understood and criticized. No "feeling of conviction" or "indubitable certainty" could justify that, "no more than thumping the table."[233] Popper more than thumped the table. He used

[227] *The Open Society*, vol. 2, p. 225.   [228] Ibid., p. 213.   [229] Ibid., p. 26.   [230] Ibid., p. 42.
[231] Ibid., chap. 11, n. 25.   [232] Ibid., Addendum to the 4th edition, p. 394.
[233] Popper, *The Logic of Scientific Discovery* (London: Hutchinson, 1959), pp. 46, 105.

propaganda techniques to caricature Hegel. He twisted his ideals into their opposite, attributed to him false motives, denounced him as pathological. On all major issues dividing Popper and Hegel, I stand with Popper. Hegel's theodicy, his premature reconciliation of liberty and power, favored the status quo and represented a long and dangerous German intellectual tradition.[234] All the same, he was neither totalitarian nor nationalist and deserved a serious critique, not a caricature. Popper's attack remains a showpiece of intolerance and narrow-mindedness. Writing in the midst of a war that would decide civilization's fate, Popper understandably "did not mince words," but this should have reinforced, not waived, critical rationalist maxims. Resorting to manipulation to delegitimize Hegel, Popper betrayed critical rationalism.

CRITICAL RATIONALISM AND MARXISM

Popper considered Marx and the Marxists fellow progressives. He criticized Marx's historicism, not his totalitarianism. The critique's tone was moderate, the evaluation balanced. He had read a fair amount of Marx, and some Engels and Lenin, but remained unaware of most Marxist interpretive traditions.[235] His "Marx" was the Austrian socialists' Marx – the Marx of the *Arbeiter-Zeitung*, the young communists of 1919, socialist friends during the 1920s. This was the Old, not the Young Marx: a determinist economist and evolutionary sociologist, not a revolutionary idealist.

During the last two decades of Marx's life, socialist movements appropriated his ideas. He was rarely happy with the appropriations and, in his

---

[234] Leonard Krieger, *The German Idea of Freedom* (Chicago: University of Chicago, 1957).

[235] Popper seriously studied *Das Kapital*, and referred to the Everyman's Library edition of the first volume (trans. Eden and Cedar Paul, 2 vols. [London: Dent, Dutton, 1930] and the German edition of the second and third volumes (ed. Friedrich Engels [Hamburg: Meissner, 1894]). For the rest, he relied on *A Handbook of Marxism*, ed. Emile Burns (New York: International Publishers, 1935) that contained selections from Marx, Engels, Lenin, and Stalin. Selections included *The Communist Manifesto*, "Preface to *A Contribution to the Critique of Political Economy*," "Address of the Central Committee to the Communist League," "Theses on Feuerbach," *The Poverty of Philosophy*, *The Eighteenth Brumaire of Louis Bonaparte*, and *The Civil War in France*, and a very short fragment of *The German Ideology*. No work earlier than "Theses on Feuerbach" (1845) was included. Popper seemed not to have known the early Marx.

Selections from Engels included, among others, excerpts from *Anti-Dühring*, *Ludwig Feuerbach and the End of Classical German Philosophy* and *The Origin of the Family, Private Property and the State*. Selections from Lenin included *What Is to Be Done?*, *Materialism and Empirio-Criticism*, *Imperialism: the Highest Stage of Capitalism*, *The State and Revolution*, and *Left-Wing Communism*. In later editions Popper referred to the *Marx–Engels Gesamtausgabe* and the Little Lenin Library (London: Lawrence and Wishart, 1929). As secondary readings, Popper admired H. B. Parkes, *Marx: A Post Mortem* (London: Allen & Unwin, 1945) and used Lucien Laurat, *Marxism and Democracy* (London: Gollancz, 1940). This seemed to have exhausted his readings on Marx at the time he was writing *The Open Society*.

writings and correspondence, notably in the "Critique of the Gotha Program," complained about misunderstandings of his theory. For more than a decade after his death, Engels represented his legacy. He pushed Marxism further in the evolutionary direction, emphasized its scientific character, and developed a materialist metaphysics. In 1891, German socialist Eduard Bernstein initiated the revisionist controversy by disposing of revolution and dictatorship, and advocating reforms, parliamentary action, and trade unionism. Kautsky and the orthodox Marxists opposed Bernstein, and maintained the Engelsian balance between evolution and revolution. In practice, however, the German socialists were a parliamentary party, reliant on the trade unions, with a large bureaucracy and institutional network. A group of young radicals, led by Rosa Luxembourg, protested against the decline of the revolutionary spirit, but the party, the largest in Europe, remained unified until 1917 when it split over the war.

Marxism first entered the Russian populist movement in the 1880s. Plekhanov viewed Marxism as a deterministic scientific philosophy, and he coined the term dialectical materialism. Lenin adopted his view but, as a political leader of action, found a place in his determinist system for a professional revolutionary party of the intelligentsia. He reasoned that at certain historical moments, historical conditions created the opportunity for revolutionary intervention, and the avant-garde could push the proletariat into action. This was, in Lenin's view, the situation in October 1917 in Russia, and the Bolshevik gamble proved successful. An intensive debate ensued throughout Europe between the communists, who wished to imitate the Bolsheviks, and the social democrats, who urged working within the parliamentary system. The socialist camp split permanently.

The Old Marx, the genealogy Marx–Engels–Lenin, and communist-socialist debates circumscribed the Marxist universe familiar to Popper. He did not know *The Economic and Philosophical Manuscripts of 1844* that first came out in German in 1932, attracting little attention.[236] In postwar years, the *Manuscripts* ushered in major renovations of Marxism, and nowadays they are considered essential to understanding the Young Marx. The *Grundrisse* of political economy, a preparatory work for *Capital* that demonstrated how crucial the Hegelian heritage remained for the Old Marx, was not available until 1939 (and in English, not until 1959).[237] Popper's horizons were even more confined. In the early 1920s, Lukács frequented the barracks where Popper was living, but Popper seemed unfamiliar with *History and Class Consciousness* (1923) and the controversy surrounding it. He knew

---

[236] *Karl Marx Friedrich Engels historisch-kritische Gesamtausgabe* (Berlin: Marx–Engels Verlag, 1932), vol. 3; Karl Marx, *The Economic and Philosophical Manuscripts of 1844*, trans. Martin Milligan (New York: International Publishers, 1964).

[237] Karl Marx, *Grundrisse der Kritik der politischen Ökonomie*, 2 vols. (Moscow: Verlag für Fremdsprächige Literatur, 1939–41); *Grundrisse: Foundations of the Critique of Political Economy*, trans. Martin Nicolaus (New York: Vintage, 1973).

of Rosa Luxemburg and witnessed the council movement in Vienna, but there was no trace of them in *The Open Society*. He ignored the Austro-Marxists: Adler, most of Bauer, Hilferding, and Renner. One could hear echoes of Bauer's political essays, but that was all. The brilliance of Popper's critique of Marx was due less to his thorough knowledge of Marxism, more to his application of Ockham's razor to a popular Marx.

Popper focused on methodology first. He compared Marxism with the social science that he had elucidated in "The Poverty of Historicism" and asked how Marx measured up as a critical rationalist. He found much to commend, but the virtues that he adumbrated had less to do with Marxism and more with critical rationalism. This was especially clear in Chapter 14, "The Autonomy of Sociology." He took as his point of departure Marx's view that "it is not the consciousness of human beings that determines their existence; rather, it is their social existence that determines their con-sciousness." He used it to form a critique of psychologism: "The greatest achievement of Marx as a sociologist" was recognizing that "legal relation-ships [and] political structures cannot . . . be explained by . . . 'the progres-siveness of the human mind.' "[238] Explanation of social phenomena in terms of their origin and development, or in terms of human nature [Mill], was invalid. Structure and function alone counted. Marx focused on the unin-tended consequences of human interaction and on institutional arrange-ments emerging from such interaction. He had an "institutionalist" view of sociology, broke with historicism, and rejected "conspiracy theories of history" that attributed social ills to individuals' or groups' evil intentions. He was concerned with the "logic of the situation," the emergence of pat-terns of human behavior under specific circumstances, explained by the rationality of human action. In short, Marx's sociologism was close to Popper's own social science.

Popper acknowledged that he was imputing to Marx designs that he had not had. Marx attributed little significance to intentions because, as a his-torical materialist, he thought that people entered social relationships inde-pendently of their will. He criticized German idealism, not psychologism. His interest in social structure did not exclude historical development. But Popper wished to correct and improve Marx, and he used the critique to elucidate his own social science. Using "Poverty," he argued that historical determinism was not essential to scientific prediction, and historical ten-dencies were not of concern to social science. He assumed, correctly, that historical materialism was not an epistemological doctrine, and Marx did not oppose metaphysical dualism (body and mind). Historical materialism, said Popper, was "economism," and economism ought to be understood loosely as the logic of social situations, not strictly as "class interest,"

---

[238] *The Open Society*, vol. 2, p. 84. Both quotations are from Marx's "Preface" to *A Contribution to the Critique of Political Economy*, trans. Salo Ryazanskaya (New York: International Publishers, 1970).

"economic motives," or denial of ideas' historical influence. The Soviet Union showed that socialist ideas could contribute to economic revolution and planning. Class conflicts always existed in society and always would. Marx brilliantly analyzed class relations under laissez-faire capitalism, but his statement that "all history is a history of class struggles" was an oversimplification. Classes were not indivisible, and not all political conflicts were class conflicts.

Insofar as the Austrian socialists' "Marx" was concerned, Popper's critique of determinism was on target, but he did less than justice to Marx. Marx occasionally referred to his theory of history as "science," spoke of inexorable historical laws, and used deterministic metaphors, such as structure-superstructure. But, alongside these, there were nuanced analyses of the interaction of ideas, agents, and classes. Popper's footnotes indicated that he was well aware of them. In *Capital*, Marx spoke of the state, at one point, as an economic force, and parts of *Capital* read more like a study of tendencies than of laws, of probable, not inevitable, history. Popper concluded, correctly I believe, that the more extreme formulas should not be taken as Marx's last word (and, again correctly, that Engels was more determinist).[239] He ignored the more subtle formulas because contemporary Marxism, not the historical Marx, was of primary importance. Still, his critique eliminated Marxist tentativeness precisely where it was appropriate. Marx wavered on the autonomy he was willing to concede to politics and ideas. He never allowed them as much autonomy as Popper wished, but when Popper urged readers not to take seriously extreme "economism," he did not necessarily disagree with Marx.

To Marx, economic structure, interest, and motive were one. Giving up on the class struggle would radically change Marxism, precisely Popper's wish. Was it imperative? Marx insisted that historical explanation be reduced, in the last analysis, to class relations, but was sensitive to divisions within classes and the complex relations among them.[240] Popper's alternative to class was never clear. He accurately pinpointed Marx's problematic suppositions, but preferred to leave situational logic open. Marxist situational logic remains, at its best, to be superseded. (Again, Popper did not disagree.) The surgical operation that aimed to save Marxism's living parts for critical rationalism may have been unnecessary, but it was, all the same, instructive. It showed two paradigms in dialogue, informing each other, a rare sight.

All fraternity disappeared when Popper discussed Marxist concepts that he held responsible for the failure of Central European socialism, first and foremost the concept of the state. To Marx, "the executive of the modern

---

[239] *The Open Society*, pp. 314–15 (chap. 17, n. 28 [n. 30 in later editions]).

[240] *The German Ideology*, trans. Salo Ryazanskaya (Moscow: Foreign Languages Publishing House, 1968); *The Eighteenth Brumaire of Louis Bonaparte*, trans. Eden and Cedar Paul (New York: International Publishers, 1926); *Critique of the Gotha Programme* [1875] (New York: International Publishers, 1966).

state is merely a committee managing the economic affairs of the whole bourgeoisie."[241] The state translated class domination into legal terms. Marx showed well how economics shaped legislation under unrestrained capitalism, but failed to see that democratization could transform the situation. Only the bourgeoisie's revolutionary overthrow, he insisted, would end oppression. The dictatorship of the proletariat was a necessary transition between capitalism and socialism. Marx was not concerned about temporary increase of state power because the abolition of classes would result in the state's withering away. In Russia, however, the state showed no sign of withering. The communists ended up with a dictatorship. Social democratic parties did not conform to revolutionary prescriptions, but failed to recognize the possibilities and dangers of political power. They fell prey to fascism.

Popper was right. Even when astute and pragmatic in daily politics, Marxists remained utopian about the future state. However, when Bernstein and Bauer explained that the state could become autonomous in particular contexts, Popper argued that their views were no longer Marxist.[242] Why? The formulations they used were, by Popper's own admission, Marxist. To him, Marxism was "economism," the only alternative his own politics. Throughout life, he denied that economic interest groups, or social classes, shaped contemporary political agendas.[243] He professed agnosticism about historical trends, emphasized technological and scientific progress, and insisted on humanity's freedom to shape its destiny. This seems to me neither a convincing view nor one that can help historiography. Popper had no credible alternative to sophisticated Marxism that made the relationship between state and economy contingent on circumstances.

Marx predicted capitalism's inevitable collapse, revolution, and socialism. Popper sought to prove that his predictions did not follow from his premises, and, in any case, historical events had refuted them. Socialism's inevitability was based on two ill-founded premises: one, that capitalism and socialism were the only alternatives; two, that the revolution would result in a classless society. Marx assumed that laissez-faire capitalism could not be reformed. He was wrong: The platform at the end of *The Communist Manifesto* had been realized in most advanced capitalist societies. Unrestrained capitalism had given way to political interventionism. When Marx admitted that political action could "shorten the birth pangs" of a new period, history became unpredictable: Technology and science made varieties of social organization possible. Revolution would not necessarily bring forth socialism: "[C]lass struggle as such does not always produce lasting solidarity among the oppressed. . . . [I]t is quite possible that groups of

---

[241] *The Open Society*, vol. 2, p. 112. Popper was quoting the *Manifesto*.

[242] Ibid., pp. 111–12, 131–2, chap. 19, n. 13.

[243] "On Reason and the Open Society," *Encounter* 38 (1972): 13–18.

workers may obtain privileges which amount to an exploitation of less fortunate groups."[244] Socialism may be a moral imperative, and if the workers' solidarity lasted long enough to introduce new institutions, socialism might be possible, but there was nothing inevitable about it. As anticipated by Marx, classless society was utopian, its aesthetic perfectionism representing wishful thinking, not critical reasoning: "[S]cientific prophecy [provided] an escape from our present responsibilities into a future paradise."[245]

Marx assumed that society would progressively bifurcate into two opposing classes, a huge proletariat and an ever smaller bourgeoisie. With growing misery, class tension would eventually erupt. But misery, observed Popper, could lead to defeatism, and neither success nor misery guaranteed unity: The Marxist search for scapegoats to explain divisions within the working class was evidence enough. Economic growth under capitalism made a mockery of increasing misery. The middle class had expanded, and "statistics no longer show[ed] any tendency for the number of industrial workers to increase in relation to the other classes."[246] The working class needed political alliances, and the revolution constituted an insurmountable obstacle. Humanitarian socialism could serve as a basis for cooperation between socialist and bourgeois parties. The working class would not cease exerting pressure for reform – reforms were always introduced under pressure – but the socialists would need to compromise, and, above all, renounce violence.

Popper's showpiece was a lengthy critique of Marx's prediction of capitalism's inevitable collapse, focusing on *Capital*. Marx detected correctly, said Popper, capitalist tendencies toward increased productivity and accumulation of wealth. He was wrong about concentration of wealth and growing misery, and failed to see that legislative intervention could counteract tendencies. His essentialist labor theory of value was at fault. He assumed that some objective quality in the commodity explained its price, and capitalists extracted surplus value. But the labor theory was insufficient to explain exploitation. The capitalists paid starvation wages only because chronic overpopulation created a large industrial reserve. Once supply and demand determined wages (or the cost of labor), what point was there in insisting that the amount of labor put into the product determined its value? Marx described correctly, and movingly, surplus population's effect on wages, and his moral outrage at human exploitation was admirable. Even Marx admitted, however, that his description was accurate only for laissez-faire capitalism. Once trade unions became legal, collective bargaining a practice, and strikes legitimate, the so-called iron law of wages was broken. Moreover, even under perfect competition, the market did not necessarily

---

[244] *The Open Society*, vol. 2, p. 128.

[245] Loc. cit. See also: chap. 18, n. 4. I explained the Austrian context for this critique in Chapter 7 and wish to repeat here neither my caveats nor my sense that Popper was basically right.

[246] Ibid., p. 145.

push labor's value down. Nothing prevented capitalists from increasing production, whereby competition would develop over labor, pushing wages higher. Lower wages and underemployment still required explanation, but Popper's (liberal) hunch was that they were due to low productivity and imperfect competition.

Popper was intrigued by Marx's theory of the trade cycle. Not only was the theory essential to prophecies of capitalism's collapse, but trade cycles were also a major concern of Viennese economists in interwar years, and countercyclical management, exemplifying social engineering, was a major subject of discussion between Simkin and Popper from 1939 to 1942.[247] To Marx, capitalist production created ever more frequent and severe depressions. By investing in machinery to increase productivity, driving wages down to maintain competitiveness, and expanding production to a maximum, capitalism created chronic overproduction in an ever-shrinking market. Popper considered the theory a great achievement, but he argued that cycles involved more factors than Marx allowed and that economists did not know enough about them. Society was not helpless in confronting depressions. Countercyclical policies, including extension of credit and Swedish-type budgetary management, might help. Unemployment insurance and social legislation might alleviate hardship. As for the consistent decline in the rate of profit, increased production might compensate for it. Even if Marx was correct, declining profits did not spell increasing misery. The same amount of reinvestment capital could still be generated through expansion of production and increased employment. In the long run, piecemeal social engineering might solve the trade-cycle problem.

Having rejected Marx's law of increasing misery, Popper turned to auxiliary hypotheses explaining the failure of Marxist prophecy. He focused on imperialism and traced the theory's development from Marx to Engels to Lenin. He accorded Engels and Lenin none of the respect he showed toward Marx. The exploitation of "the natives through colonization" was appalling, but it did not increase the working class's standard of living in the metropolis.[248] The United States, the Scandinavian countries, and Switzerland had few or no colonies but just as high living standards as Britain. Capitalist countries generally experienced growing affluence and were nowhere engulfed in revolutionary turmoil. Only in Russia, suffering from the typical misery of capitalist infancy, did the revolution succeed, and there, only because of the peasants and the defeat in the war. Marx's prophecy failed. No auxiliary theory could save it.

[247] Popper, *The Open Society*, chap. 9, n. 3; chap. 20, n. 30, referring to Simkin's two articles on "Budgetary Reform," *Economic Record* (1941–2): 192 ff., 16 ff.

[248] *The Open Society*, vol. 2, p. 177. In *Capital* Marx noted the higher rate of profit in the colonies. Engels ascribed to it the bourgeoisification of the British proletariat: Colonial exploitation made concessions at home possible. Lenin concurred, and regarded imperialism as the highest stage of capitalism.

Marxist and liberal economists alike had reservations about Popper's critique. Marx assumed endemic overproduction under capitalism. In *Capital* IV, he distinguished between local short-range crises, as described by liberal political economy, and the general crisis of capitalism, when all factors of production would merge at one time to bring the system to a halt. It was not clear that Popper's suggestions about a competitive market pushing wages up, expansion of production to overcome decline in profit, and countercyclical policies to cushion depressions answered Marx's objections.[249] Some liberal economists dissented from his acceptance of the Marxist trade cycle and his critique of laissez-faire.[250] Still, he had no intention of offering an alternative to Marxist economics, only pinpointing problems in Marxist inevitability and their political consequences. This he did well. His critique went to the heart of Marxist problems and did so in a manner facilitating exchange with Marxists. He may not have broken new ground on all points, but he was unusually precise and clear. Marxists considered him their most formidable critic. Fifteen years after his retirement from the London School of Economics, when the remnants of the New Left, faculty and students, were holding the last line against Margaret Thatcher's assault, Popper was still the liberal critic to contend with, the one most feared and respected.

In his *Autobiography*, Popper expressed admiration for the Viennese workers: "Their leaders were able to inspire them with a marvelous faith in their mission, . . . the liberation of mankind. . . . The whole movement was inspired by . . . an ardent religious and humanitarian faith."[251] This was surprising: As a good Viennese progressive, Popper had nothing nice to say about religion. He delegitimized historical prediction by calling it prophecy. Was the religious element in Marxism a source of strength or weakness? In *The Open Society* he wrote that

> Marx's prophecies might well have come true. A faith like the progressivist optimism of the nineteenth century can be a powerful political force; it can help to bring about what it has predicted. . . . Looking back at the course of events from 1864 to 1930, I think that but for the somewhat accidental fact that Marx discouraged research in social technology, European affairs might possibly have developed, under the influence of this prophetic religion, towards a socialism of a non-collectivist type. . . . But this would not

[249] *Theorien über den Mehrwert* (Theories of surplus value, referred to as *Capital* IV), 4 vols. (Stuttgart: Dietz, 1905). In translating Marxist propositions into liberal political economy, Popper sometimes deprived them of their social dimension. The labor theory of value was not just a theory of prices but an explanation of the social relations of production. (Maurice Cornforth, *The Open Philosophy and the Open Society* [New York: International Publishers, 1968], pp. 188–214.)

[250] Hayek and Robbins wanted him to compress his critique of Marx and eliminate the discussion of value theory: Hayek to Popper, 29 January 1944, Hayek Archives (44, 1); Gombrich to Popper, 17 March 1944, Popper Archives (300, 3).

[251] *Autobiography*, pp. 35–6.

have been a corroboration of a scientific prophecy. It would have been the result of a religious movement, and fundamentally of the faith in humanitarianism, together with a critical use of our reason. . . .

But things developed differently. The prophetic element in Marx's creed was dominant in the minds of his followers. It swept everything else aside, banishing the power of cool and critical judgment and, outside Russia at any rate, destroying the belief that by the use of reason we may change the world.[252]

The critique of Marxism ended on a very different note than that of *The Open Society* as a whole. Rather than condemning Marxism as secular religion and pseudoscience, Popper maintained that Marxism's failure was the result of an improper synthesis of faith and reason, prophecy and science. He did not suggest that the Marxists dispense completely with their prophecies – this would slow down social reform – only that their prophecies be accompanied by a positive attitude toward social technology. Had the Marxists' faith in humanitarianism been accompanied by critical reason, they would have realized the noncollectivist socialist society. They failed because their prophecies were insufficiently balanced by critical rationalism. The prophetic element in Marxism undermined the critical, scientific one, and "destroyed the *belief* that by the use of *reason* we may change the world." (False) prophecy undermined (true) belief in scientific rationality. Pseudoscience, or false belief, undermined science, true belief.[253]

Viennese progressivism, Austrian socialism, and Marxism were all animated by "the progressive optimism of the nineteenth century." So also was critical rationalism. Yet, progressivism could not withstand Popper's criticism. He demolished all grand narratives, denying scientific status to his own history: It was one interpretation among many. Competing historical narratives were criticizable and debatable, but ultimately undecidable. The progressive optimism animating his philosophy succumbed to his critique. His ethics reinforced philosophical austerity. He rejected value relativism, but had no way of grounding "religious humanitarianism." Like Kant, he found it difficult to sustain hope in humanity and history. Both resorted to "belief in reason," or "rational belief" (*Vernunftglaube*), but it was belief that ran against their critiques.[254]

The limits of "rational belief" handicapped Popper's reform politics.

---

[252] Vol. 2, pp. 185–6.

[253] Ian Jarvie objects here (E-mail communication to author, 8 March 1999): "[Y]our free use of 'belief' and 'true belief' is most questionable, since Popper said he was not a belief-philosopher. If you think he was, then you should say so. I do not think he ever said science was true belief. That is the justificationist view." I think that Popper is a "belief-philosopher" in the same way Kant was: Rational belief (or belief in reason) may not be essential to their projects, but it greatly facilitates them. Historically, their projects were contingent on such belief.

[254] *The Open Society*, chaps. 22, 25, and Addendum to the 4th edition, "Facts, Standards and Truth." Immanuel Kant, "Was heißt: Sich im Denken orienti[e]ren?" in *Gesammelte Schriften* (Berlin: Reimer, 1912), vol. 8, pp. 131–47.

Historically, "the power of cool and critical judgment" rarely coexisted with religious humanitarian faith. If faith was necessary in politics, what were the boundaries between reason and faith? If the public sphere did not abide by critical discourse, but was also an arena for religious struggle, how could Popper hope for consistent application of social technology?[255] How could conflicts between political religions be arbitrated? Democracy ruled out force, but, other than encouraging dialogue, and perhaps compromise, critical rationalism provided no guidelines. All it offered was its own splendid example of arguing for a humanitarian vision and reconciling faith and reason, commitment and criticism.

Popper was aware of the dilemmas of progressivism, but nonfoundationism limited his options. A generation of postwar liberals shared his dilemmas. Wishing to preserve as large a domain for individual liberty as was compatible with public order, they were anxious to leave value conflicts unresolved, apprehensive that philosophical absolutism might eventually translate into coercion. Like Popper, they limited the public consensus to democratic rules, construing the consensus as broadly as possible. They knew that value conflicts were rarely resolvable and chose to live in suspense. Their dilemmas remain our own.

---

[255] Popper recognized that politics was subject to "irrational forces." Social engineers would have to take them into consideration when planning for freedom. They were one reason that reforms had to be introduced in a piecemeal fashion, so that errors could be corrected. But, if politics was an arena for religious struggle, and scientific reform itself was motivated by a religious ethos, then the consensus for social engineering presupposed the converting of believers in prophecies, e. g., the Marxists, to belief in science. If such a conversion did not occur, and some fragile reform consensus was nonetheless achieved, prophecies would continue to be influential, and scientific planning would have to tailor itself to prophetic influences. Scientists would utilize, perhaps even realize, prophecies, rather than criticize them. Piecemeal social engineering would become the handmaid of religion.

Chapter 10

The Rebirth of Liberalism in Science and Politics, 1943–1945

Popper's war effort ended up influencing the course of the wrong war. *The Open Society* addressed the problems confronting the Western democracies fighting fascism, but, published in November 1945, it made a significant contribution, albeit unintended, to the cold-war mobilization against communism. Popper discussed long-standing issues in the history of liberalism, the relevance of which only increased with the cold war. *The Open Society* became a foundational text for postwar liberalism.

As Popper got the first responses to his book, he realized that he had accomplished something he had not anticipated. "I attempted to destroy the unreal and metaphysical gulf that separates reasonable and liberal people in the various camps of the left," he told Alfred Braunthal. "To my own amazement, this seems to be no empty dream. A leader of a liberal anti-socialist individualism such as Hayek has expressed his complete agreement, and so has, apart from yourself, an English socialist leader of a strong color [Harold Laski]."[1] By "showing how much of [Marxism] must be dropped, if we are to bridge the gulf which at present . . . paralyses the camp of those who have the will to build a better future," he wrote Hyman Levy and Ernst Gombrich, he tried to "consolidate what might be called 'the left'" against fascism.[2] Instead, Popper ended up constructing a cold-war coalition – liberals and social democrats – against communism.

The Open Society articulated the Social Democratic Consensus of postwar years and provided a social-reform platform for the welfare state.[3] Notwithstanding Hayek's enthusiasm for *The Open Society*, he, and the libertarians, did not belong in the consensus, consistently challenged it, and eventually helped dismantle it. Already in 1943, Hayek was wondering how Laski could be so enthusiastic about *The Open Society*. He must not have read the book to the end, he suggested. Ernst Gombrich, who became Popper's major correspondent in 1943, thought that this was intellectual malice.[4] He and Popper felt that Hayek, an established conservative academic, belonged

---

[1] Popper to Alfred Braunthal, 12 December 1943, Popper Archives (28, 2).

[2] Popper to Hyman Levy, 22 July 1943, Popper Archives (300, 2); Popper to Ernst Gombrich, 13 December 1943, Popper Archives (300, 2).

[3] Ralf Dahrendorf, "The End of the Social-Democratic Consensus?" in his *Life Chances* (Chicago: Chicago University Press, 1979); Richard Löwenthal, "Beyond the Social-Democratic Consensus," in his *Social Change and Cultural Crisis* (New York: Columbia University Press, 1984).

[4] Gombrich to Popper, 11 March 1944 (300, 3).

to different social and political circles than their own. But Hayek ended up influencing the direction of Popper's political philosophy. Popper wrote *The Open Society* as a non-Marxist socialist, impatient with laissez-faire, but he published it, nearly three years later, as a welfare liberal, sensitive to libertarian concerns. In between, in 1943–4, he read Hayek's methodological essays and *The Road to Serfdom*. His political shift was not radical, but it was noticeable, and it became pronounced in postwar years. Hayek convinced him that both socialism and the enthusiasm for scientific planning could undermine liberty, and he lost some confidence in his progressivism. From 1942 to 1944, he referred to his war project as a comprehensive, unified, political philosophy, founded on a reform of the "methodology of the social sciences."[5] By 1945, he expressed regret that upon his return to London, he would have to continue to focus on social questions.[6] He actually never did. His long-term interests were in natural science methodology, but Hayek, too, contributed to his political timidity.

Hayek's influence was not all negative. Responding to his challenge, Popper refined both his social science methodology and social engineering. Before Popper made the final transition to the cold-war West, Hayek's writings had taken him, one last time, back to Central Europe. Hayek had reworked a century-long methodological debate, and Popper rewrote "Poverty, II" and "III" in its light. The revised "Poverty" reflected his move from heterodox socialism to reform liberalism. In *The Open Society*'s final chapters, and in "Poverty, III," he explored the analogies between his philosophy of science and politics. The result was a rebirth of liberalism in science, ethics, and politics.

PUBLICATION WOES

On the date of the El Alamein battle, 23 October 1942, Popper sent *The Open Society* to the United States. His English publisher, Hodge, had notified him that war conditions, especially paper shortage, would delay indefinitely the publication of *Logik der Forschung*. Popper surmised that prospects for quick publication of his new book were better in the United States. As he had neglected his correspondence for years, he was sure of the U.S. address of only one friend, Viennese musician Fritz Deutsch (Freder-

---

[5] Popper to Carnap, 15 October 1942, Carnap Collection, Archives of Scientific Philosophy; Popper to Gombrich, 28 April 1943, and to Braunthal, 21 May 1943. In the summer of 1944, he contemplated additional political essays: "Public and Private Virtues," "The Refutation of Determinism," and "The Logic of Freedom." (Popper to Gombrich, 28 October 1944.) The first two exist as a postwar lecture and a draft article, Popper Archives (39, 17; 15, 25–29, respectively). He first mentioned the "logic of freedom" in *The Open Society* (chap. 10, n. 63), and his thoughts on it may have contributed to his reworking of (liberal) democratic theory for the American edition (1950).

[6] Popper to Woodger, 25 September 1945, Popper Archives (363, 17).

ick Dorian), living in Pittsburgh. (He had known Dorian and his family from social events at the Schiffs' Pressbaum villa in pre–World War I days, the Schoenberg circle, and private performances in interwar years.) He also had the addresses of Carnap and other academics, but he was anxious about preventing a repeat of *Logik*'s "plagiarism." He sent the book to Dorian and gave him a strict warning not to show it to anyone but publishers. Dorian was to send the manuscript to a set list of publishers. Should it be rejected, it would be returned to him (rather than to New Zealand) and sent to the next publisher on the list. Determined to control publication details from afar, Popper enclosed minute instructions for proofreading and printing.

Popper was convinced of his book's significance, but insecure about its scholarly merits. He had attacked respected authorities, and made a foray into fields where he had no expertise, without the benefit of a major library or criticism by leading scholars. "In the economic field I am a typical dilettante," he wrote Hayek.[7] Only a publisher who found the book an eye opener was likely to publish it. He preferred a good trade publisher to an academic press, so that his message would reach the "common person." In mid-November, he sent a manuscript directly to Macmillan and, three weeks later, another one to Harper.[8] In mid-October, he also sent "The Poverty of Historicism, I" to *Mind*, under the title: "The Claims of Historicism." Breaking his long silence, he told correspondents of his grand political project, his war effort.

This was no way of getting a publisher. Macmillan and Harper rejected the hefty manuscript out of hand. The three copies landed on Dorian's table. Dorian barely glanced at them; he had other things on his mind than fighting Popper's battles. He contacted a mutual friend, Fritz Hellin, who had arrived in the United States in 1941 after a harrowing trip from France. Hellin was a talented but irresponsible floater, a close friend of Popper since the socialist colony of 1919. He was now a research assistant of Carl Friedrich, a Harvard professor of government, and could solicit his help with publishers. Hellin called on Alfred Braunthal for help. Braunthal was at the time director of the hatters' union, as well as a researcher on postwar reconstruction for labor unions. The three, Braunthal, Dorian, and Hellin, conferred in New York in May 1943, and then decided that early rejections had showed that publisher connections were essential. Hellin cavalierly ignored Popper's request that the manuscript not be shown to other scholars and gave Friedrich a copy, leaving his precise expectations for help unclear. He also contacted Felix Kaufmann, who was completing a book

---

[7] Popper to Hayek, 26 October 1943, Hayek Archives, Hoover Institute (44, 1).

[8] Popper used D. K. Roberts, ed., *The Authors, Playwrights & Composers Handbook* (London: John Lane, 1938) for instruction on publication. Popper to "Friend" (Dorian), 23 October and 18 November 1942, Popper Archives (28, 6, under Hellin).

on the methodology of the social sciences, and solicited his help. Kaufmann, familiar with Popper's litanies about plagiarism of *Logik*, declined to read the manuscript, but he referred Hellin to Columbia philosopher Ernest Nagel. Braunthal cabled Popper: "Hellin working on publication assisted by Friedrich." Hellin related some of the developments in a letter to a Viennese friend in New Zealand, and followed up with a haughty letter to Popper, dismissing his concerns and indicating that both stylistic changes and shortening of the manuscript would be necessary to facilitate publication.[9]

Popper was in despair. His cables asking for clarification of the manuscripts' fate remained without response for months.[10] "It is a terrible strain, to have worked so hard, to know how urgent and important the matter is, and to be cut off far away on an island . . . for so many months without a reasonable word concerning the book," he wrote Hellin.[11] A Dorian cable indicated that publishers regarded publication as "untimely," and Carnap, whom Popper notified of his project, was alarmed by the title (False Prophets: Plato – Hegel – Marx), cautioning Popper not to give comfort to Marx's enemies. Popper concluded that his title was the reason for rejection, and proposed changing it to A Social Philosophy for Everyman, or A Critique of Political Philosophy. After El Alamein, he recognized that Hitler's defeat was a matter of time, and wrote a new preface and introduction, emphasizing his contribution to reconstruction issues, rather than just the war effort. Recognizing that his name was unknown to English readers, he even claimed, in a brief biographical enclosure for

---

[9] Hellin to Burstein, excerpt, dated 23 March 1943, but posted in early May; Hellin to Popper, 22 May 1943 (28, 6). (Popper did not receive the latter for at least half a year. In fairness, Popper did not treat a manuscript that Hellin had sent him for publication any better. They were critical of each other, and neither took the other's requests seriously.) Hellin insisted that an "in" connection was a must, that Friedrich would never plagiarize, and that Popper should wait for a publisher's advice on the title. He mentioned Popper's dismissal of Aristotle as problematic. Friedrich may have uttered something to this effect. Popper reported (*Autobiography*, p. 118) that his friends had submitted the manuscript to a noted authority who thought "the irreverence toward Aristotle" made it unfit for publication. There is no archival trace other than the above. An anxious Popper may have exaggerated Hellin's remark. Popper's Aristotle left him vulnerable to criticism, for his scholarly apparatus was thin. A critic irritated by the tenor of his argument could choose the easy way out, rather than confront his Plato.

[10] After Popper had cabled, Dorian informed him twice of Macmillan's and Harper's rejections, without adding any further information. Popper could not confirm the arrival of the revised MS (Volume 2, with complete notes for the entire book), which he had sent Dorian in February 1943, until Hellin cabled him on July 18. Dorian kept two manuscripts without informing Braunthal (the latter collected them in the summer of 1944) and gave Hellin the third, as well as the February manuscript. (Hellin forwarded the last two to Friedrich.) Consequently, Ernst Papanek, a Viennese friend (from school-reform days), whom Popper cabled in desperation in May, mentioned only two manuscripts (19 May cable), increasing Popper's anxiety. (Popper to Braunthal, 21 May 1943 [28, 2].) Dorian said (26 June 1943 [28, 6]) that both he and Hellin had previously written and cabled concerning the manuscripts, but Hellin's letters of May 1943 suggest no earlier communication.

[11] Popper to Hellin, 21 May and 29 June 1943 (28, 6).

publishers, to have been "a member of the Viennese Circle of Philosophers." Isolated in New Zealand, he was fighting nightmares that he himself had conjured.

In mid-April, Popper received Dorian's first letter and realized that he had done nothing. He looked for alternatives. He had lost touch with Ernst Gombrich during the war because, typically, he had not responded to his letters. Somehow, he got his address. He cabled, asking whether he might send the manuscript. Gombrich responded warmly, and Popper sent three manuscripts, two with notes only for Chapters 1 to 3. He wrote Hayek and Susan Stebbing at the same time, and Hyman Levy a few months later, soliciting their help. He asked Gombrich not to show the manuscript to anyone except Stebbing. Another venue for publication opened. This was a much-needed encouragement because sometime in late April, Popper also received *Mind*'s rejection of "Poverty, I."[12]

Popper still expected U.S. publication to be easier, if he could only move his friends into action. In mid-May, he learned from Braunthal's cable that Hellin had taken charge of publication efforts, but he had neither Hellin's nor Braunthal's address. Searching for connections, he fell upon J. B. Condliffe, an established economist, friend of Karl Polanyi, previously of Canterbury College, now in the United States. He sent him an updated manuscript (with partial notes), and suggested that if Condliffe was not inclined to recommend it to Norton, he could forward it to Braunthal. Condliffe, having better things to do, gave the manuscript to Braunthal, and advised him that publication through an academic press, partially financed by the author, offered the best prospects.[13] On May 19, Popper finally obtained both Hellin's and Braunthal's addresses. He cabled Hellin urging that his instructions be followed and confidentiality observed, canceled Dorian's power of attorney, and wrote both Hellin and Braunthal, enclosing another updated manuscript. Earlier, he had asked that Braunthal not be shown the manuscript. Now he was eager for him to read it and take charge.[14]

"Be patient, await letters," Hellin cabled Popper on July 18. This was impossible for Popper, especially since things were moving slowly. He received no letters from Hellin. In October, he heard, through Braunthal, that Hellin had shown the book to mathematician Paul Boschan and

---

[12] Dorian to Popper, 8 February 1942; Popper to Gombrich, 16 and 28 April 1943 (300, 2). Popper sent his first cable on 14 April, and posted the manuscripts consecutively on 29 April (with full instructions), 21 May, 15 June 1943. Popper to Hayek, 26 April 1943, Hayek Archives (44, 1); Popper to Levy, 22 July 1943, Popper Archives (300, 2); Stebbing to Gombrich, 30 June 1943, Popper Archives (406, 6); Moore to Popper, 12 March 1943, Popper Archives (329, 28).

[13] Popper to Condliffe, 19 May 1943; Condliffe to Popper, 27 July 1943 (28, 4); Braunthal to Popper, 25 July 1943 (28, 2).

[14] Popper to Dorian, 20 April (draft not sent) and 18 May 1943; Popper to Hellin, 16 May, 19 May, and 21 May 1943 (28, 6).

economist Peter Drucker. He angrily asked Hellin to transfer all manuscripts to Braunthal, and to withdraw.[15] Having tried to control all details of publication from afar, everything now seemed out of control, his manuscripts floating around the United States, circulating among people he did not trust, their whereabouts a mystery. Things improved when Braunthal took charge. Having read the book in August, he recognized immediately its powerful appeal. It was, he told Popper, a revelation, coming precisely when his own disillusion with Marxism and German idealism had left him drifting intellectually. He thought, however, that the manuscript was too long, and the separation between texts and notes awkward. He suggested that Popper cut down the Plato part, eliminate name calling (Aristotle a mediocrity, Fichte an impostor, Hegel a charlatan), and give him *plein pouvoir* to integrate text and notes. Determined to do his best to promote the book, he approached publisher John Day. The editor, Walsh, seemed willing to publish a shorter manuscript. Drucker had connections to Yale University Press. Yale, too, was willing to consider a manuscript about half the size of *The Open Society*. Braunthal urged Popper to accept major cuts. It was now, he said, up to Popper.[16]

Popper's responses to Braunthal reflected his precarious emotional state and opened a window to his psychology. He cabled Braunthal immediately, rejecting cuts, then waited for three weeks for news from Cambridge University Press in England before answering him. When Cambridge's rejection became obvious, he poured his frustration and self-pity on Braunthal in two ungracious and self-absorbed letters. He was "rather ill all the time," he said. Braunthal could not realize, having read the book only once, how much work he had invested in it, experimenting with models, rearranging, rewriting, "burying" his efforts, "concealing" his labor. "The idea that anybody can simply break up and re-assemble what has been built up with so much deliberation is rather startling."[17] Braunthal had no right to substitute his for Popper's judgment and disregard instructions. His strategy with Walsh was self-defeating: Instead of defending Popper against cuts, he proposed them. (Braunthal categorically denied that.) He was sorry to criticize Braunthal, but personal feelings should be of no concern to friends fighting for a common cause.[18] His book's publication was not a personal matter: Life and death might depend on it. The book could revolutionize social science and "have amazing practical results fairly quickly."

He had an "obligation" toward his book, his "spiritual child," he said.[19] "I consider the destruction of the awe of the Great Names, the Great Intellectual Authorities, one of the necessary prerequisites of a recuperation of

[15] Popper to Hellin, 29 June and 12 October 1943.

[16] Braunthal to Popper, 25 August and 11 November 1943; Popper to Braunthal, 19 October 1943 (28, 2). Braunthal's letter to Popper of 4 September 1943 is not in the archives.

[17] Popper to Braunthal, 12 October 1943.   [18] Popper to Braunthal, 19 October 1943.

[19] Popper to Braunthal, 23 August 1943.

mankind," he wrote Hellin in another letter. He did not intend "to put anybody else, or myself, in the place of these Great Names." Rather, the "pretentiousness with which the business of philosophy is glorified must disappear." The book was exceptional for its range and clarity, not for being a "statement of a new great philosophy": It was a "direct development of the much abused 19th century philosophy (in a similar vein to Russell)." It "will not easily find support from those who are 'arrived,' or from those who hope to arrive one day." "This [confession] may perhaps convince you [Hellin] that my attitude toward the book is free of any touch of megalomania."[20]

Popper's letters reflected courage, perceptiveness, and sound judgment, combined with egoism, hypocrisy, and self-delusion. From his incomplete psychology thesis to *Grundprobleme* to *Logik* to *The Open Society*, he expected his works to become world transformative. Most were exceptionally important, but, his denials notwithstanding, he was engaged in self-aggrandizement. He correctly judged *The Open Society*: a much-needed rehabilitation of nineteenth-century progressive liberalism when its fortunes were at a nadir. But he was blind to the self-aggrandizement involved in his transgression against intellectual authorities. From positivism to Platonism, he posed as a giant killer. Critical rationalism undermined authority without putting Popper in charge, but was he not a new (anti)prophet? He claimed to separate philosophy and person, but at each and every point, he closely guarded his interests, advancing proprietary claims to his ideas. After his retirement from the London School of Economics, he complained to Ernest Gellner that the school no longer taught enough of his philosophy. "He didn't mind for himself," he said, "but he had a duty to his thought."[21] Blindness bordered on hypocrisy: His letters to Gombrich showed him a brilliant observer of his own psychology – when his interests were not at stake. Few of his friends owed him much. He never did for Braunthal or Gombrich half of what they did for him, but he expected them to recognize his importance and selflessly devote themselves to his philosophy. His genius, he would be the first to admit, justified no claim to superior treatment. He remained to the end a spoiled child who threw temper tantrums when he did not get his way. Fortunately, he usually got his way in the end – to our enormous benefit.

Braunthal was busy, had limited connections, and got nowhere, but he behaved like a true friend. His response to Popper, though perturbed, was kind.[22] He felt for him, he said. His exhaustion and isolation were the cause of his mistrust of friends. He could not expect them to act as agents, or automatons. They had the right to suggest changes. There was no

---

[20] Popper to Hellin, 29 June 1943 (28, 6).
[21] Ernest Gellner, "The Rational Mystic," *The New Republic*, 19 April 1993, 35–8.
[22] Braunthal to Popper, 25 November 1943 (28, 2).

authorial infallibility. Now that he had refused cuts, Braunthal would do as he asked, and he did just that. He urged Hellin to ask Friedrich to recommend an unshortened manuscript to Harvard. Friedrich declined.[23] Braunthal, Boschan, and Kaufmann decided to offer the book to an expanding publisher, the University of North Carolina. Early in April 1944, Braunthal sent it, accompanied by a warm recommendation from Kaufmann. UNC declined. During the winter of 1943–4, Braunthal was too busy to write for months, and Popper, aware that his friends in the United States considered him a major pain, apologized and expressed despair in his letters.[24] His apologies were not completely sincere. In correspondence with Gombrich, he remained bitter about Braunthal. Once he received news of the contract with Routledge and had no need for Braunthal, his letters became formal, curt, cool. He never forgave him. In his *Autobiography*, he spoke of the disappointment that his American friends had been to him.[25]

His experience with his friends in England was happier from the start. "In time of physical exhaustion and deep depression [your letters] really saved me from despair," he wrote to Gombrich in July 1943.[26] Gombrich admired him, accommodated his unreasonable requests, and dedicated himself to publishing his book. He was working at a night post for the BBC German Monitoring Service, and kept a loose affiliation with the Warburg Institute, occasionally publishing scholarly pieces. He began devoting his daytime to Popper. Around him clustered Austrian émigrés, many of whom had known and respected Popper since colony- and school-reform days. Gombrich continuously assured Popper of their good wishes. Popper was not forgotten, he said; indeed, philosophy students at Cambridge often mentioned him.[27] Stebbing and Levy, too, tried to help, though Stebbing was ill and died in September, and Levy was unsuccessful. Hayek proved crucial. He was everything Popper was not – a well-connected academic, sociable, caring about people he liked, and tolerant of differences as long as they served his goal, the fight against socialism. He approached R. B. Braithwaite, a member of the Cambridge University Press board who

---

[23] Friedrich to Hellin, 7 October and 17 December 1943; Hellin to Friedrich, 1 December 1943, enclosing Braunthal's letter of 28 November 1943, Harvard University Archives (HUG[FP] 17.12, box 19). Friedrich told Hellin that he could not assure Harvard that the book would sell. He later wrote Popper (12 September 1949) that he "greatly appreciated" the book (Popper Archives [297, 25]), but gave the American edition a mixed review (*Southwestern Social Science* [March 1951]). Academic duplicity is second to none.

[24] Popper to Braunthal, 14 December 1943 (28, 2); 7 and 15 February, and 1, 9, 25 March 1944 (28, 3); Braunthal to Popper, 19 and 28 March, and 2, 9, 16, 23 April 1944 (28, 3).

[25] Popper to Braunthal, 11 April, 12 May, 19 June, and 19 July 1944; Braunthal to Popper, concerned about his health and offering financial help, 19 and 31 May, July 29 1944 (28, 3); *Autobiography*, p. 119.

[26] 22 July 1943 (300, 2). Most airgraphs sent 1943–4 were photominiaturized to save on space and weight and can be difficult to decipher.

[27] Gombrich to Popper, 11 May, 28 June, and 21 August 1943.

remembered Popper and was encouraging. Popper was revived by the news, his gratitude to Hayek overwhelming: "I have done nothing to deserve your kindness."[28]

Gombrich and Hayek both read the book over the summer and wrote Popper appreciatively about it. Gombrich offered some valuable criticism, especially of the Hegel section, and observed that Popper's insistence that there was no history, only a plurality of constructed histories, belied his commitment to progress. Popper was concerned about Hayek's reaction: He knew that Hayek's libertarianism conflicted with his social engineering. When Hayek chose to regard him as an ally who could appeal to the left, he was immensely relieved. Hayek showed the book to his colleagues, sociologist Morris Ginsberg, Lionel Robbins, and LSE director Carr-Saunders. All were impressed. Harold Laski, a leading socialist intellectual and LSE political theorist, was likewise enthusiastic. Popper rejoiced: Both socialists and liberals endorsed his philosophy.[29]

All the same, a grueling publication struggle lay ahead. Cambridge rejected the book on September 24; it was too long, and "a university press ought not to publish a book that is so disrespectful of Plato."[30] Levy offered the book to Nelson, who turned it down, notwithstanding Laski's support. Hayek spoke to Unwin, who was not willing to commit to a publication date because of the paper shortage. Hayek trusted Robbins to recommend the book to Macmillan.[31] Robbins insisted, however, that Popper first radically compress the Marx part. Hayek delicately suggested to Popper that Robbins might be right. He, too, seemed to think Popper's critique of Marxist economics superfluous and probably took exception to his attack on laissez-faire. Popper responded in a series of emotional airgraphs that explained why he could not rewrite Marx – "Don't think I am hysterical if I say that it is physically impossible" – and invited Hayek to do part of the job. He indicated, as he had done earlier with Yale, that he would rather have the Plato volume published separately than introduce major revisions.[32] Hayek seemed to be running into precisely the same difficulties as

[28] Popper to Hayek, 23 August 1943, Hayek Archives (44, 1). See also: Hayek to Popper, 12 July and 28 July 1943, Popper Archives (305, 13); Hayek to Gombrich, 28 June, 21 July, and 25 July 1943, Popper Archives (406, 6); Gombrich to Hayek, n.d., 14 July, 21 July, and 28 July 1943 (44, 1); Gombrich to Popper, 28 July 1943, Popper Archives (300, 2). Gombrich most likely received Popper's cabled permission to give the manuscript to Hayek on July 13 or 14.

[29] Gombrich to Popper, 17 July, 25 July, 11 August, 15 November 1943 (300, 2), 12 January, 16 January, 1 April 1944 (300, 3); Hayek to Popper, 12 November, 27 December 1943, Hayek Archives (44, 1); Popper to Braunthal, 12 December 1943; Popper to Gombrich, 13 December 1943.

[30] Gombrich to Popper, 13 October 1943.

[31] Levy to Gombrich, 11 October 1943 (406, 6); Gombrich to Popper, 28 October 1943, 16 January 1944; Gombrich to Hayek, 10 January 1944; Hayek to Gombrich, 14 January 1944, Hayek Archives (44, 1).

[32] Hayek to Popper, 29 January 1944, Hayek Archives (44, 1); Popper to Hayek, 14 March, 15 March 1944, Popper Archives (305, 13) and Hayek Archives (44, 1); Popper to Braunthal, 12 December 1943; Popper to Gombrich, 14 March 1944.

Braunthal. Exhausted and depressed early in 1944, Popper was approaching a complete physical and psychological collapse.

Against Popper's and Gombrich's predilections, Hayek submitted the manuscript to Routledge. Popper surmised that inasmuch as Routledge had published Mannheim and he, Popper, had attacked him, it was not a promising venue. But Routledge editor, Herbert Read loved the book. It was, he said, "the only new book of its kind which in recent years has given me a real thrill."[33] He convinced his colleagues to take a chance. On March 11 in a meeting at the Reform Club, "amidst gilded columns and white haired gentlemen with magnificent pink but angular faces" (wartime shortages presumably left the affluent and powerful alone "pink"), Gombrich – a young and subdued outsider – met Hayek and Read. (The club, he related to Popper, was where those who were "in" cut deals that decided authors' fate.) Read suggested publishing the book in two volumes under the title The Open Society and Its Antagonists.[34] He recommended only minor corrections. Gombrich sent a cable with the good news, but it did not reach Popper. When another cable with news of the actual contract came on April 10, Popper's joy was boundless: "I was very near to giving up all hope. . . . [I]t is amazing how one's outlook on life can change in a few minutes."[35]

Popper's instinct proved right: An editor who recognized the book's appeal made publication possible. But it is unlikely that Popper would have ever reached Read had his instructions been followed. "[O]f all my suggestions regarding the course to be taken in finding a publisher, *not one* turned out to be of any use!" he confessed to Gombrich. "All my letters were therefore not only of no help, but must have been a real nuisance to you. I realize this with great regret."[36] Having said that, he immediately launched into a discussion of editorial questions, trying again to control the uncontrollable. His recognition of personal failings made no difference in his behavior. "I doubt very much whether I am worthy of all you have so lavishly bestowed on me," he said to Gombrich, "your goodwill, your good humor, and the ease with which you give (contrasting so sharply with my narrow and egotistical prepossession with a definite aim)."[37] He knew himself all too well. He just could not help it.

Gombrich and Hayek, Popper said, "saved his life," but his spirits did not

[33] Read to Hayek, 7 March 1944, Hayek Archives (44, 1).

[34] Gombrich to Popper, 29 February and 11 March 1943. Popper had discussed the title "The Open Society and Its Enemies" since October 1943, increasingly setting his mind on it: Popper to Hayek, 11 October 1944, Hayek Archives (44, 1). Hayek did not like it: 4 December 1943; Popper to Braunthal, 2 November 1943; Popper to Gombrich, 14 March 1944. John Findlay may have convinced Popper to switch to this title: John Watkins, "Karl Raimund Popper 1902–1994," *Proceedings of the British Academy* 94 (1997): 659.

[35] Popper to Gombrich, 10 April 1944 (300, 3).   [36] Popper to Gombrich, 22 April 1944.

[37] Popper to Gombrich, 10 April 1944.

remain high for long. The book's writing and protracted publication took a physical and emotional toll. During the first half of 1944, he suffered from a series of illnesses accompanied by depression. The causes were partially physical. He apparently lost nine teeth, suffered from acute exhaustion, and had an abnormally low blood pressure. He was diagnosed with a deficiency of the adrenal glands and treated with injections, possibly of an early form of cortisone. These, together with two short vacations in the Southern Alps that included piano playing, appeared to have revived him. He denied emphatically that he had had a nervous breakdown, speaking instead of collapse and depression. Without his medical records, it is difficult to fathom what his problems were, but he told Hayek in May 1944 that he could barely understand what he was reading. By mid–August 1944, he was again himself, but, the following spring, he burned his back in an accident and could not lie on his back or sit straight for six weeks. With early summer vacations and complete rest, he recovered by the holidays. Trouble continued in 1945. He had a series of bad colds, his moods swinging radically. Not hearing from the LSE through April 1945, he "was ill again . . . very weak. My doctor insisted that I should go to the mountains. . . . I was first pretty miserable there, but after two days I had a marvelous recovery."[38] On his return he heard about his LSE appointment, and the world looked rosy again.

　　Some of Popper's students and friends have suggested that more often than not, he was hypochondriacal rather than ill.[39] This rings true. Even as a young man, he would frequently open his letters by complaining that he had been working awfully hard and was ill.[40] He undoubtedly felt sick, but his complaints were partially manipulative, excuses for neglecting friends, refusing visitors, and the like. He also endeavored to make himself into a martyr: His labor, especially his war effort, seemed all the more noble if it made him sick. Still, this leaves unexplained his work pattern: periods of

---

[38] Popper to Gombrich, 12 June 1945 (300, 4). See also: Popper to Hellin, 16 May 1943; Popper to Braunthal, 1 March and 19 June 1944; Popper to Hayek, 26 October 1943, 14 March, 16 May, 24 September 1944, Hayek Archives (44, 1); Popper to Gombrich, 5 June, 27 June, and 8 August 1944, 9 April and 16 April 1945 (300, 3, 4).

[39] Joseph Agassi, *A Philosopher's Apprentice* (Amsterdam: Rodopi, 1993); Herbert Feigl, circular letter, 16 September 1954, Ernest Nagel Papers, Columbia University (box 1); E-mail communication from Peter Munz, 3 February 1997.

[40] Popper told Berti Wiesner (22 May 1932, Popper Archives [362, 8]) that he was sick all winter with chronic appendicitis and eventually went through an operation. An appendectomy for "chronic appendicitis" was a common procedure in interwar years whenever a patient complained about unspecific abdominal pain. Studies later discovered that few patients improved, and "chronic appendicitis" became a controversial diagnosis. It has recently made a return, but for a far more limited class of patients. (Peter Mattei, Juan E. Sola, and Charles J. Yeo, "Chronic and Recurrent Appendicitis are Uncommon Entities Often Misdiagnosed," *Journal of the American College of Surgeons* 178 [1994]: 385–9. Dr. Roger Mell, St. Luke's Hospital, St. Louis, provided me with the reference.) Popper complained about stomach ailments all his life. In 1932, the doctors probably operated to explore the source and, finding nothing, diagnosed "chronic appendicitis" and performed an appendectomy.

high-spirited, incredibly intense labor followed by collapse and depression, the doctors being unable to find what was wrong. Neither Popper nor his doctors were likely to declare his fatigue psychologically induced, especially when he reported that his work drove him to exhaustion. On occasion, perplexed doctors hospitalized him for tests, as when he had felt weak in early December 1936 in Vienna. (He had had a trying year abroad, had lost his house and job, and had then abandoned hope for a Cambridge invitation or a position abroad.)[41] On other occasions, they ordered vacations. This is not to say that he did not suffer, at points, from serious medical problems, but they, too, often produced medically inexplicable results, such as months of prolonged weakness. He ended up outliving all of his peers, most of his doctors, and some of his students, enjoying bad health to the ripe old age of 92.

The melancholic Hennie could not but reinforce Popper's depression. She was an incredible source of support and advice, but deepened his bleak vision. His work drove her, too, to exhaustion: "[T]he more distance I gain from the last nightmare years of typing, the less I can understand how on earth I managed it."[42] Writing to the Gombrichs in July 1943, she described their life in such gloomy terms that it greatly alarmed their friends in England. During the summer, she said, they ate only "home grown" vegetables raised in the garden she cultivated with much toil on the dry and rocky slope of their quarter-acre house. (Simkin testifies that this was impossible; the garden was too small.) The rest of the year they subsisted on a diet of rice and carrots. (Munz suggests that this was partially because she hated to cook and Popper felt that anything but vegetables, chocolate cake, and milk shakes irritated his stomach.) Their house constantly required costly and laborious maintenance. In winters, she said, it was damp and cold because they saved on fuel. (Simkin opined later that the house was more upscale than those of other lecturers. When visitors wondered how they could afford it, Hennie responded that it was their bacon and eggs.) In short, she described their New Zealand exile as poor and miserable.[43]

They were undoubtedly in financial straits in 1943. They not only had large mortgage and insurance payments but also sent some money for Annie through the Red Cross, and incurred unexpected publication expenses. Popper had sent twelve cables by July 1943, and the pace picked up during his correspondence with Gombrich. At six to nine shillings each, the telegrams dug deeply into his limited resources. (He claimed that each was

---

[41] Popper to Kaufmann, 12 December 1936, *Kaufmann Nachlaß, Sozialwissenschaftliches Archiv*, University of Constance.

[42] Hennie Popper to the Gombrichs, 24 October 1944 (300, 3).

[43] Hennie Popper to the Gombrichs, 29 July 1943 (300, 2). See also: Popper to Hellin, 29 June 1943 (28, 6); Popper to Hempel, 5 July 1943, Popper Archives (306, 2); Popper to Carnap, 5 July 1943, Carnap Collection.

almost equivalent to his weekly income after deducting taxes, insurance, mortgage, and utilities from his salary.) Still, things were not quite as bad as Hennie described. In March 1944 she told the Gombrichs that "we have peace and plenty of food, and you have bombs and, to put it mildly, a very restricted diet, and other hardships."[44] Their complaints reflected their state of mind, rather than their material circumstances. Hennie made the book's fate her own, and the American saga depressed her. When the telegram informing them of the book contract was read to Popper over the phone, she performed a "silent Indian dance" behind, and the walls she needed to whitewash, she told Gombrich, suddenly shrank.[45] New Zealand was exile, and her husband's work a constant predicament. This, not bad housing and food, was the source of the Poppers' misery.

Worsening departmental relations made Popper's life more difficult. His senior colleague, Sutherland, increasingly frowned upon his research, first making him pay for typing paper for the book's many versions at a time when he could least afford it, then insinuating that he was neglecting his teaching duties. (As Popper was exhausted, ill, and pushing himself with revisions to "Poverty" and *The Open Society*, it would not be surprising if he did not devote full attention to college affairs.) In the summer of 1944, things came to a head when Popper proposed curricular revision that shifted the emphasis to scientific philosophy and required psychology students to take logic, and Sutherland denied him his fair share in examination fees when he was short on money. Popper complained to the new rector, Tocker, but no permanent solution seems to have been reached.[46] He was immensely bitter about not receiving a salary increase. He told Gombrich that when friends inquired of college administrators, they were told that Canterbury recognized that he was too good for them, and if he wished to move elsewhere, he was welcome to do so. He was a difficult person who made some enemies, but the majority of faculty and students seemed to like him well, and this helped.[47]

There was no respite from work once he completed his book. During the school year of 1943, he was working again on long-neglected mathematics papers: a set of postulates for Boolean algebra, the foundations of probability, and other papers on mathematical logic published in postwar years. Work proceeded slowly and painfully.[48] He soon had to return to social science methodology. Hayek inquired about "Poverty" and tentatively

---

[44] Hennie Popper to the Gombrichs, 28 March 1944.

[45] Hennie Popper to the Gombrichs, 10 April 1944.

[46] Popper to Registrar (via Rector Tocker), 9 November 1944; Tocker to Popper, 11 December 1944 (366, 5). See also: Popper to Hayek, 26 October 1943.

[47] Popper to Gombrich, 24 October 1944, 28 March, 9 April, and 2 July 1945.

[48] Popper to Hellin, 16 May 1943; Popper to Hayek, 17 October 1943, Hayek Archives (44, 1); Popper to Gombrich, 13 December 1943 and 24 October 1944; "An Independent Set of Axioms for Lattices," summer 1943–4 (27, 12).

offered to publish it even before seeing the manuscript. Popper sent him "Poverty, I" with only minor corrections in mid-November 1943, but determined to rewrite the critical part. Hayek mentioned to him his own works on the subject, especially "The Counter-Revolution of Science" and "Scientism and the Study of Society," and sent him other recent reprints. Popper read them in the spring of 1943, and they opened his eyes. He discovered a range of discourse on social science unknown to him. For a moment, he seemed thrown off balance, but he was quickly back on his feet, pushing social science methodology forward. The years 1944 and 1945 saw the culmination of Popperian social science.

HISTORY, SOCIAL SCIENCE, AND THE POLITICS OF PLANNING, 1944–1945

Popper's conception of "Poverty" changed as he was writing *The Open Society*. His methodological essay became part of a comprehensive political philosophy. In the book he introduced ideas later incorporated into "Poverty" in 1944–5, significantly, the distinction between "piecemeal" and "utopian social engineering." Confronting Plato's *Republic*, or, perhaps, Hayek's 1939 pamphlet *Freedom and the Economic System*, he recognized that he was incorrect to deny planning to historicists.[49] Historicists planned, but their programs suffered from fundamental errors. In *The Open Society*, he argued that Plato's *Republic* (and, by implication, Marxist socialization) advanced an aesthetic vision that required dictatorship. Utopian engineering's collectivist and centralist nature remained implied, rather than explicit, in his work until he wrote "Poverty, II" in 1944.

In *The Open Society*, Popper confronted thinkers who contributed to his further development of social science method. He challenged Mill repeatedly, criticizing his psychologism, theory of democracy, and historicist sociology. He engaged Max Weber on historical explanation and model building. He may have first delved into Weber's methodological exchange with historian Eduard Meyer, and was thereby led to his other essays. He found himself more in agreement with Weber than he had anticipated, but this did not change his view that Weber was a historicist.

The major influence on "Poverty, II" and "III" was, however, Hayek. Reading him, Popper recognized that "Poverty" constituted an intervention in a century-old Central and Western European debate. Throughout the 1930s and early 1940s, Hayek reshaped these debates, drawing their ramifications for contemporary Europe. This explains why he understood immediately the thrust of "Poverty" (whereas *Mind*'s editor, Moore, did not). Popper debated Hayek at length in "Poverty, II" and "III." Under-

---

[49] Friedrich Hayek, *Freedom and the Economic System* (Chicago: University of Chicago, 1939).

standing the intellectual universe he now entered requires a digression to the Central European *Methodenstreit*.

METHODENSTREIT: AUSTRIAN ECONOMICS AND THE GERMAN HISTORICAL SCHOOL

The *Methodenstreit* of the 1880s pitted Gustav Schmoller and the German historical school against Carl Menger and the Austrian school of economics. It established two national traditions in economics and social science that clashed over the next half century. The conflict was both methodological and political, and involved academic power struggles and arguments on national policy and social reform. Time and again, Austrian intellectuals reinterpreted it to address contemporary issues: socialization, economic planning, interpretive and positivist social science.

In his *Investigations Into the Methods of the Social Sciences* (1883), Menger attacked the historical paradigm in German economics. He targeted three major figures: Wilhelm Roscher of Leipzig, Bruno Hildebrand of Jena, and Karl Knies of Heidelberg. Between the 1840s and the 1860s, they had established German historical economics. They became known later as the old historical school, and generations of scholars were unkind to them. Menger, Mises, and Hayek presented them as theoretically inept; Schmoller and the young historical school paid them little respect; and Weber launched his methodological essays with a stringent critique of their method. In fact, they were innovative, erudite, and judicious scholars, responsible for German economists' high reputation.

In his 1843 *Grundriss zu Vorlesungen über die Staatswirtschaft* (Outline of Lectures on Political Economy), Roscher set out to imitate Savigny's accomplishment in jurisprudence and transform political economy (*Nationalökonomie*) into a historical science.[50] He accepted the English economists' notion of economic lawfulness, but sought to historicize its laws and extend its concepts to cameralism.[51] Each political economy, he argued, was a growing organism, and economics involved governing people and evaluating their actions. The economist must have knowledge of social life and constitutional and cultural history. Roscher seemed to distinguish between two types of laws: The "physiological" processes of specific economies gave rise to "relative" economic laws, typical of

---

[50] Wilhelm Roscher, *Grundriss zu Vorlesungen über die Staatswirtschaft. Nach geschichtlicher Methode* (Göttingen: Dieterichsche Buchhandlung, 1843); Karl August von Savigny, *On the Vocation of Our Age for Legislation and Jurisprudence* [1831] (New York: Arno, 1975); *Geschichte des Römischen Rechts im Mittelalter* [1834–1851], 2nd ed. (Aalen: Scientia, 1986).

[51] He rejected, however, cameralist assumptions about the *Polizeistaat*'s complete control of the economy. *Staatswirtschaft* became the major branch of *Staatswissenschaft*. Keith Tribe, *Governing Economy: The Reformation of German Economic Discourse, 1750–1840* (Cambridge: Cambridge University Press, 1988).

particular stages of historical development. Absolute laws of economic development called for historical comparisons among different societies. Roscher was in search of a universal history, founded on the laws of economic development.[52]

This universal history, or laws of "the total development of humankind," remained elusive. Hildebrand and Knies disposed of Roscher's absolute laws, but accepted wholeheartedly his historical, empiricist, and holistic approach. Knies argued that all economic theories were products of their time and, like changes in economic conditions, reflected "the entire organism of a human and historical epoch."[53] The universal laws of political economy, for which classical economics searched, did not exist. Theoretical absolutism in political economy was a passing phase. Economic "laws" testified only to one period's understanding of history, and to "the progressive manifestation of the truth" in the succession of historical periods, but "neither in their totality nor in their formulation may they be regarded as something final."[54] A universal history was impossible, and Knies came close to questioning laws of any kind.

Methodological holism, opposition to the methodological unity of science, historical rather than theoretical social science, rejection of universal laws: The methodological pronouncements of the old historical school read like a list of historicism's "anti-naturalist" doctrines. Sections of "Poverty" read almost as a direct response to Roscher and Knies. By 1945, Popper was aware of their significance – he criticized Friedrich Engel-Janosi's book on German historicism for ignoring them – but it is doubtful that he read them.[55] He did not need to: Later generations of Austrian and German economists and sociologists developed their methodologies confronting the old historical school, and Kaufmann and Hayek summarized their positions for him.

---

[52] Roscher, *Grundriss*, esp. the Preface; *Principles of Political Economy*, 13th ed. (Chicago: Callaghan, 1882); Albion Small, *The Origins of Sociology* (Chicago: University of Chicago Press, 1924), pp. 154–66, 194–203.

[53] Karl Knies, *Die Politische Ökonomie vom Standpunkte der geschichtlichen Methode*, 2nd ed. (Brunswick: Schwetschke, 1883), p. 23. (Translation is Small's: *The Origins of Sociology*, p. 200.)

[54] Loc. cit. Samuel Bostaph, "The Methodological Debate between Carl Menger and the German Historicists," *Atlantic Economic Journal* 7 (1978): 9–11.

[55] "Review of Friedrich Engel-Janosi, *The Growth of German Historicism* (Baltimore: Johns Hopkins, 1944)," in *Economica* 12 (1945): 259–61. Popper criticized Janosi for not discussing Roscher, Knies, and Hildebrand, "the founders of the Historical School of German Political Economy . . . even though the first, at least, did not only write on the theory of historiography, but was also a historian himself." Karl Milford insists (conversation with author, 27 January 1999) that Popper was more aware of the nineteenth-century methodological background than I allow here, if only indirectly. Popper still remembered, in the 1980s, Gottlieb Hufeland's letters to Kant. Hufeland had already developed in 1807 a subjectivist theory of values (prices), grounded in "ontological individualism." See Karl Milford, "Roschers historische Methode," in Erich Streissler et al., *Wilhelm Roscher als führender Wirtschaftstheoretiker* (Düsseldorf: Verlag Wirtschaft und Finanzen, 1994).

Unlike Hildebrand and Knies, Gustav von Schmoller (1838–1917), leader of the young historical school, had no deep antipositivist convictions, but, like them, he denied historical laws. The context-bound, "relative" laws of historical economics were tentative and subject to historical change and scientific refinement. He shared the old school's distaste for theory, proclivity for empirical research, and methodological collectivism.[56] In his own studies, he focused on social institutions, historical change in economic and political organizations, and the state's role in economic affairs.[57] The absence of historical laws meant that economies were subject to human regulation, the state being the chief economic agent. He was vituperative in attacking "Manchesterism," the laissez-faire doctrines and policies associated with Britain. Germany, he was convinced, should choose a different path to greatness, that of an economy geared toward social welfare and national solidarity, protected from the stronger British economy by tariffs. He managed to translate these convictions into a program for academic research and a platform for political action. In a series of meetings in 1872–3, he established, together with Adolf Wagner and Lujo Brentano, the *Verein für Socialpolitik*, which lobbied the government to introduce welfare policies. The association became the most powerful academic organization in Germany and acquired substantial political influence.[58] It was not, however, uncontroversial: Some old national liberals dubbed Schmoller and his colleagues *Kathedersozialisten* (Socialists of the Lectern), and the aging historian Heinrich von Treitschke started a campaign against "academic socialism."[59] The polemics subsided in the late 1870s, the *Verein* becoming part of the Prussian establishment, but its reputation for socialism survived.

Later generations of Austrian economists argued that intimate connections existed between the historical school's methodology and politics. Mises and Hayek regarded Schmoller and the Verein as a fountainhead of German statist socialism, culminating in national socialism. As Mises and Hayek were engaged in an intellectual crusade against Marxism and economic planning, they argued that left- and right-wing socialism both led to totalitarian dictatorship. The politics of the Verein thus became

---

[56] Joseph Schumpeter coined the term in a 1926 review of Schmoller: "Gustav Schmoller und die Probleme von Heute," in his *Dogmenhistorische und biographische Aufsätze* (Tübingen: Mohr, 1954).

[57] Gustav Schmoller, *Grundriss der allgemeinen Volkswirtschaftslehre*, 2 vols. (Munich: Duncker & Humblot, 1920), esp. prefaces to both volumes; idem, "Die Schriften von K. Menger und W. Dilthey zur Methodologie der Staats- und Sozialwissenschaften," in his *Zur Literaturgeschichte der Staats- und Sozialwissenschaften* (Leipzig: Duncker & Humblot, 1888), pp. 275–304.

[58] Fritz Ringer, *The Decline of the German Mandarins: The German Academic Community, 1890–1933* (Cambridge, Mass.: Harvard University Press, 1969), pp. 143–62; James Sheehan, *German Liberalism in the 19th Century* (Chicago: University of Chicago Press, 1978), pp. 151–8.

[59] Heinrich von Treitschke, *Der Socialismus und seine Gönner* [1875] (Berlin: Reimer, 1989). Schmoller responded in "Über einige Grundfragen des Rechts und der Volkswirtschaft," in his *Über einige Grundfragen der Sozialpolitik*, 2d edition (Leipzig: Duncker & Humblot, 1904).

integral to the *Methodenstreit*; *Historismus* and national socialism became siblings.[60]

Enter Menger. His *Principles of Economics* (1871) is nowadays considered a foundation of marginalist economics.[61] He believed that it offered a new method, stating that "I have endeavored to reduce the complex phenomena of human economic activity to the simplest elements that can still be subjected to accurate observation . . . and to investigate the manner in which the more complex economic phenomena evolve from their elements according to definite principles."[62] This method, which Menger and his disciples called "atomistic" or "compositive," marked "methodological individualism," the Austrian school's distinctive approach.[63] One progressed from individual to composite and complex phenomena, endeavoring to find causal connections, or laws, obtaining among the phenomena.[64] Collective entities were composite in nature, the result of interaction of multiple individuals, not "holistic," unified wholes. In "Poverty, III," Popper commended methodological individualism as the only legitimate scientific procedure.[65]

Menger was, at the same time, an "essentialist." Whenever he mentioned the reduction of complex phenomena to their individual constituents, he advocated, as the next step, abstracting *das Wesen*, grasping a phenomenon's nature, its inherent characteristics. Abstracting the essence meant disposing of contingencies. This was the precondition to reconstituting causal relations among individual phenomena, that is, establishing scientific laws explaining the operation of composite wholes (for example, the market).[66] Causal laws expressed phenomena's essential nature. Menger adhered to the cardinal historicist heresy, and it was shared by the Austrian school. Popper ignored it; he associated "essentialism" with methodological collectivism alone.[67]

On the methodological unity of science, the central issue of "Poverty," Menger took a nuanced stance.[68] He insisted that the economic realm –

[60] Ludwig von Mises, *The Historical Setting of the Austrian School of Economics* (New Rochelle, N.Y.: Arlington House, 1969) and Friedrich Hayek, *The Road to Serfdom* (Chicago: University of Chicago, 1944).

[61] Carl Menger, *Principles of Economics* (Glencoe, Ill.: Free Press, 1950); *Grundsätze der Volkswirthschaftslehre* (Vienna: Wilhelm Braumüller, 1871).

[62] *Principles of Economics*, pp. 46–7.

[63] Joseph Schumpeter coined the term in *Das Wesen und der Hauptinhalt der theoretischen Nationalökonomie* (Leipzig: Duncker & Humblot, 1908). It has been widely used ever since.

[64] Menger, *Principles of Economics*, pp. 55, 194.   [65] Popper, "Poverty, III": 80–2; *Poverty*, pp. 136–43.

[66] Menger, *Principles of Economics*, pp. 46–7, 55–67.

[67] Popper, "Poverty, III": 80; *Poverty*, p. 136. Popper may have been unaware of Menger's essentialism.

[68] Menger, *Principles of Economics*, p. 47. Economics shared many methodological principles with natural science, but there were laws peculiar to each field of knowledge, and those of economics still needed to be established. Once each field's unique laws were established, scientists could proceed to investigate the connections among the various fields and establish methodological unity, but for the time, such attempts were premature and bound to end in grave errors.

production, consumption, market relations – was subject to causal laws, just as nature was to physical laws. Economic concepts, such as usefulness (or utility), value, exchange, and good, were as independent of human will as natural phenomena were. His "subjectivism" in the determination of value was tempered by his conviction that human need (*Bedürfnis*) and action were on the whole predictable and could be scientifically determined. The status of economics as an exact science and its objectivity, or "value-free" character, depended on "the conformity to definite laws that condition the outcome of the economic activity of men and are entirely independent of human will."[69] Mises and Hayek felt uncomfortable with the "objectivist," or positivist, elements in Menger, and pushed Austrian economics further toward "subjectivism."[70] Popper, in contrast, expressed sympathy with Menger.[71] He claimed that falsifiability and intersubjectivity answered both Menger's and Hayek's objections to science's methodological unity.

The hegemony of historical economics in Germany made it increasingly difficult for Menger to promote his approach. By the early 1880s, he had decided to attack the historical school, and focused on the declining old figures, above all Roscher.[72] He contrasted his own "exact-theoretical" approach with the historical school's "empirical-historical" one, and argued that the two were mutually exclusive. His own approach represented economics (*Volkswirtschaft*) proper: "There were two great classes of scientific knowledge": the "individual," or historical, dealing with concrete phenomena in their "full empirical reality," and the "general," or theoretical, investigating the typical relationships of phenomena. Historical economists confused descriptions of historical phenomena in "their full empirical reality" with phenomena's universal nature. When they engaged in theory, they constructed "real types": historical patterns and regularities – or, to use Menger's terms, "empirical laws" – that were limited to particular contexts and periods. Such real types were appropriate to historical economics, but offered no substitute for theory, which required exact, absolute, universal laws.[73] History abounded in circumstances of little relevance to lawfulness. No economic theory could provide an adequate description of

---

[69] Ibid., p. 40.

[70] For "subjectivism": Wolfgang Grassl, "Markets and Morality: Austrian Perspectives on the Economic Approach to Human Behavior," in *Austrian Economics*, ed. Wolfgang Grassl and Barry Smith (New York: New York University Press, 1986), pp. 139–81; Israel Kirzner, "Ludwig von Mises and Friedrich von Hayek: The Modern Extension of Austrian Subjectivism," in *Die Wiener Schule der Nationalökonomie*, ed. Norbert Leser (Vienna: Böhlau, 1986), pp. 133–56; and Erich Streissler and Wilhelm Weber, "The Menger Tradition," in *Carl Menger and the Austrian School of Economics*, ed. J. R. Hicks and W. Weber (Oxford: Clarendon Press, 1973), pp. 226–31.

[71] Popper, "Poverty, III": 78; *Poverty*, pp. 130–1.

[72] Carl Menger, *Investigations into the Method of the Social Sciences with Special Reference to Economics* [1883] (New York: New York University Press, 1985).

[73] Ibid., p. 58: "The realistic orientation of theoretical research excludes in principle the possibility of arriving at strict (exact) theoretical knowledge."

empirical reality, and none could predict with exactitude and certainty economic development. All exact theories, all laws, were nonempirical and nontestable:

> There are no strict types in "empirical reality." . . . The circumstance that people are not guided exclusively by self-interest prohibits the strict regularity of human action in general, and of economic action in particular. . . . Testing the exact theory of economy by the full empirical method is simply a methodological absurdity . . . analogous to that of a mathematician who wants to correct the principles of geometry by measuring real objects.[74]

Economic theory had limited applicability, but it explained the world, all the same.[75]

Menger was a household name in Vienna in interwar years. Popper discussed marginalist economics with Polanyi, and it informed his critique of Marx, but it is unlikely that he had ever read Menger. The original edition of *Principles* went out of print, and a second edition, edited by Menger's son Karl, was apparently difficult to use. Until Hayek edited Menger's *Collected Works* in the 1930s, Menger had been known primarily through his disciples.[76] Popper regarded him as the greatest of economists, but did not mention him (or methodological individualism) in "Poverty, I" and "II." Having read Hayek's "Scientism" late in 1943, he recognized Menger's bearing on his theory. His references in "Poverty, III" indicated that he now had a general knowledge of Menger's procedures for constructing theories.[77] Still, in 1986, supervising Karl Milford's dissertation on Menger, he was gratified to discover how close the *Investigations* were to him. Asked in postwar years about the affinity between his social science models and marginal utility theory, he explained (correctly, I believe) that marginalist economics was "in the air" in interwar Vienna. One need not have read Menger to be a marginalist.[78]

Popper expressed agreement with Menger on methodological individualism, the causal, formal, and exact nature of scientific theory, and the methodological unity of science. He could have added their agreement on the distinction between history and social science; history's nontheoretical nature; and economic theory's concern with unintended consequences. He

[74] Ibid., pp. 56, 84, 64, respectively.   [75] Ibid., pp. 33–40, 54–73, 82–9, 95–101, 203–13.

[76] *Grundsätze der Volkswirthschaftslehre*, 2d ed. (Vienna: Hölder-Pichler-Tempsky, 1923); Volume 1 of *The Collected Works of Carl Menger*, 4 vols. (London: London School of Economics and Political Science, 1934). Economist Bruce Caldwell of the University of North Carolina at Greensboro kindly provided me with this information.

[77] Popper, "Poverty, III": 74, 78, 81, 82; *Poverty*, pp. 120, 131, 139, 141. The issues discussed: empirical and exact types; the methodological unity of science; complexity of situations in natural and social science and the need for theoretical abstraction; and the compositive method (in connection with Popper's "zero-method"). In *The Open Society*, chap. 14, n. 14, rewritten in August 1944, Popper challenged Menger's "subjectivism."

[78] Colin Simkin, E-mail communication, 18 March 1997.

limited his open dissent to Menger's distinction between exact and empirical types, but, in fact, they disagreed on crucial methodological issues.[79]
Not only was Menger an "essentialist," but his argument that exact theories were nonempirical and non–testable also made them metaphysical at
best, spellbinding at worst. Providing precise and definite (short-range)
forecasts for testing was crucial to Popper. This was just what Menger
denied that exact theory could do.

Menger was, however, a venerable Viennese economist. Hayek admired
him, and Popper would not split hairs with friends. John Stuart Mill,
holding positions similar to Menger, had already provided a target for
Popper's criticism. When Popper could note an agreement with Menger,
he did so; when he could use him to support a disagreement with Hayek
(on the methodological unity of science), he did so, too. Otherwise, he
ignored Menger's problematic, even historicist, positions.

Schmoller's lengthy review of Menger's *Investigations* had long been decried
by Austrian economists as a narrow-minded dismissal of a brilliant theoretician by a powerful German academician. It actually provided a cogent
defense of historical economics and struck at the core of Menger's problem
– the latitude given the economic theorist to establish nontestable universal laws. Schmoller acknowledged that constructing types began with individual elements and involved abstraction from the phenomena, but insisted
that reaching the "very simplest individual elements" was no simple matter.
No theoretician could isolate a phenomenon's essential aspects without first
subjecting it to an exhaustive examination. Transition between empirical
description and abstraction was gradual, and the empirical bent of economics was appropriate to its premature state. Historical economic theories that would eventually emerge would not resemble "exact types," or
claim universality. Patterns certainly existed in history, and economics captured them, but laws (and theories) were human made and grasped no
"essential nature."[80]

Contrary to Schmoller's expectations, theory never emerged from
historical economics. Twenty years later, Weber showed why it never would.
Popper agreed with Weber and Menger on this, but in all other respects,
his views were strangely closer to the historicist Schmoller than to Menger.
Schmoller's rejection of unfalsifiable, nonempirical laws and his insistence
that scientific laws were open to revision eloquently expressed Popperian
principles. He was "collectivist" but not "holist": He always placed
individuals a in network of relationships, or "the whole," but he rejected

---

[79] Popper did not distinguish between levels of generality. All theories involved universal statements. Empirical data could not give rise to theory; theory was prior to experience. Empirical types simply did not exist. He also opposed Menger's psychologism (which may have had its roots in Mill).

[80] Gustav Schmoller, "Die Schriften von K. Menger and W. Dilthey," in *Zur Literaturgeschichte der Staatsund Sozialwissenschaften*, pp. 278–94.

Roscher's organic view of society as mystical.[81] He was no historicist. The sole cord linking Popper to the Austrian economists' fight against *Historismus* was his opposition to turning economics into a historical science. He never read Schmoller, but even a cursory reading would have reaffirmed his wisdom in constructing historicism as an abstract, theoretical, ahistorical model. It simply did not apply to the young historical school.

In 1884 Menger published a furious response to Schmoller, and Schmoller returned his review copy with an offensive letter, later published in his journal.[82] The exchange thereby came to a close, the lines of battle now sharply drawn, but the *Methodenstreit* continued for the next half century. In Germany, historical economics became virtually unchallenged, but Austrian economics emerged as a school that enjoyed international reputation. By the mid-1880s, Eugen von Böhm-Bawerk and Friedrich von Wieser, Menger's disciples, published their first works. They defended the Austrian approach in American journals, and foreign scholars thus became familiar with the Methodenstreit.[83] Henry Seager, an American economics student, visited Europe during the academic year 1891–2 and again in 1892–3. Having spent one semester in Berlin and another in Vienna, he reported his impressions:

> To these four men, Menger, Schmoller, Böhm-Bawerk and Wagner the eyes of the economists of all nations are at present directed as to the most conspicuous representatives of our science. . . . The great universities in Berlin and Vienna are at present time magnets attracting economics students from all countries.[84]

For Austrian economics, the Methodenstreit gave a set of methodological doctrines, a distinct intellectual identity, an enemy, and a clear sense of mission. Even Hayek, who thought, like Schumpeter, that the Methodenstreit was an unfortunate distraction from the serious business of theoretical economics, found himself constantly returning to it.[85] Popper entered the debate as an outsider, a natural science methodologist. The issues that stirred the economists did not interest him, and he had grave reservations about "subjectivism," but his sympathies and allegiance lay with

---

[81] Review of Roscher, *Zur Literaturgeschichte.*

[82] Menger, *Die Irrthümer des Historismus in der deutschen Nationalökonomie* (The errors of Historismus in German economics) (Vienna: Hölder, 1884). The short book consisted of "sixteen letters to a friend." Schmoller, "Antwortbrief," *Schmollers Jahrbuch* 8 (1884).

[83] Eugen von Böhm-Bawerk, "The Austrian Economists," *Annals of the American Academy of Political and Social Science* 1 (1891): 361–84; "The Historical vs. the Deductive Method in Political Economy," ibid. 1 (1890): 244–71; Friedrich von Wieser, "The Theory of Value," ibid. 2 (1892): 24–52; "The Austrian School and the Theory of Value," *Economic Journal* 1 (1891): 108–21.

[84] Henry Seager, "Economics at Berlin and Vienna," *Journal of Political Economy* 1 (1893): 238.

[85] Joseph Schumpeter, *A History of Economic Analysis* (London: Allen and Unwin, 1954), pp. 808–9; Friedrich Hayek, "Carl Menger," *Economica* 1 (1934): 393–420; "Scientism and the Study of Society, I," "II," "III," *Economica* 9–11 (1942–4): 267–91, 34–63, 27–39, respectively.

the Austrians against the Germans. Menger may have made historicist mistakes, but he was a founding father. Schmoller may have been a Humean empiricist, but he was a historicist enemy.

Weber was the one distinguished German intellectual who took Menger, and other Austrian economists, seriously.[86] The Austrians reciprocated in kind. Mises admired him, formulated his economics in dialogue with his work, and put him constantly on his private seminar's agenda in interwar years.[87] Popper recognized him as the most influential social science methodologist. Weber entered the Methodenstreit having already confronted a number of German social science approaches. Of those familiar to Popper, Dilthey and the Neo-Kantians were important.

In his *Introduction to the Human Sciences,* Wilhelm Dilthey (1833–1911) sought to contain what he regarded as the assault of positivism and natural science on the autonomy of human life.[88] He distinguished between natural and human science. The two had different interests in their objects of study, and different relationships obtained in them between scientist and objects. Human science's objects were not simply physical data; they were invested with meaning. The historical world was an objectification of life, a product of labor and communication, a creation of people's interaction, an expression of inner selves. The knowing subject, or scientist, was also a historical being, involved in the world of meaning investigated. No radical break as the one between *Geist* and nature, scientist and physical atoms, existed.

This had methodological ramifications. The mechanical explanations of physics could never address meaning or account for human action, social institutions, and historical events. The task of *Geisteswissenschaft* was not causal explanation (*Erklären*), but understanding (*Verstehen*) and interpretation (*Deutung*) of meaning. Understanding was possible because,

---

[86] He read Menger carefully, defended him against Lujo Brentano's charge of "psychologism," and criticized the historical school for their hostile reception. He chose Friedrich von Wieser as the author for a volume on economic theory to be included in the incomplete *Grundriss der Sozialökonomik.* In 1903, he recommended Böhm-Bawerk for an honorary doctorate at Heidelberg, knowing that Schmoller was the other candidate. In *Economy and Society,* he commended Mises's theory of money. Max Weber, "Die Grenznutzlehre und das 'psychophysische Grundgesetz,'" *Gesammelte Aufsätze zur Wissenschaftslehre,* 2d ed. (Tübingen: Mohr, 1951), pp. 384–99; Friedrich Tenbruck, "Zur Genese der Methodologie Max Webers," in *Kölner Zeitschrift für Soziologie und Sozialpsychologie* 11 (1959): 573–630; Manfred Schön, "Gustav Schmoller and Max Weber," in *Max Weber and His Contemporaries,* ed. Wolfgang Mommsen and Jürgen Osterhammel (London: Allen and Unwin, 1987), pp. 59–70.

[87] Paul Silverman, "Law and Economics in Interwar Vienna: Kelsen, Mises, and the Regeneration of Austrian Liberalism" (Ph.D. diss., University of Chicago, 1984), 292–303.

[88] Trans. Ramon J. Betanzos (Detroit, Mich.: Wayne State University Press, 1988); *Einleitung in die Geisteswissenschaften* [1883], *Gesammelte Schriften,* vol. 1. (Leipzig: Teubner, 1922).

in contrast to natural science, scientists or historians could "relive" (*Erleben*) experiences of other humans, comprehend their action and interaction, and interpret their context. Interpretation's success depended on a clear distinction between meanings attributed by the historian and those attributed by the inquiry's subject. The *Geisteswissenschaften* – the humanities, history, economics, and even psychology – all engaged in interpretation and were, according to Dilthey, hermeneutical in nature.[89]

Popper had mentioned the *Einleitung* in his early works on psychology in the 1920s. His favorable disposition towards *Geisteswissenschaft* changed into negative evaluation in "Poverty," where he criticized Dilthey for "intuitive understanding." In postwar years, he mentioned Dilthey's relativism in connection with the "historicist climate" of interwar Vienna, associating him with Spengler. He combined, he said, essentialism and intuitive understanding.[90] He argued that *Erleben* had limited value and thought that situational logic, or context construction, provided an alternative.

In conscious opposition to Dilthey's interpretive science, the Neo-Kantians of the Southwest German School – Wilhelm Windelband (1848–1915), Heinrich Rickert (1863–1936), and Emil Lask (1875–1915) – began developing their methodology in the 1890s. Windelband's inaugural address in 1894 in Strasbourg sounded to contemporaries like a call to arms against positivism.[91] History and natural science, he said, represented mutually exclusive modes of scientific inquiry, idiographic and nomothetic. Scientists were interested in phenomena for their common characteristics, historians for their uniqueness. Natural science abstracted from individual phenomena to disclose their shared properties, repetition and regularity, and to form universal laws. Individual phenomena were of interest to it only insofar as they exemplified general laws. Yet, humans ascribed value to the unique, and historians selected phenomena based on values people ascribed to them. History focused on the individual.[92]

Rickert accepted much of Windelband and pushed for a distinct methodology for the "cultural sciences" (*Kulturwissenschaften*). Following his student Lask, he emphasized the unbridgeable gap between knowledge and the world, concept and reality. Reality was irrational: It could never be

[89] My account is based mostly on the *Einleitung,* but includes notions developed in later works, especially *Der Aufbau der geschichtlichen Welt in den Geisteswissenschaften* [1911] (The construction of the historical world in the human sciences), vol. 7 of *Gesammelte Schriften* (1927). See also Larry Frohman's "Liberalism, Modernity, and Social Theory in the Work of Wilhelm Dilthey: From Transcendentalist Idealism to Phenomenological Hermeneutics" (Ph.D. diss., University of California, Berkeley, 1991), esp. pp. 1–28.

[90] Karl Popper, "Replies to My Critics," in *The Philosophy of Karl Popper* (La Salle, Ill.: Open Court, 1974), p. 1173.

[91] Wilhelm Windelband, "Geschichte und Naturwissenschaft" [1894], *Präludien* (Tübingen: Mohr, 1921), 2:136–60.

[92] Windelband, "Geschichte und Naturwissenschaft"; Guy Oakes, *Weber and Rickert: Concept Formation in the Cultural Sciences* (Cambridge, Mass.: MIT, 1988), pp. 41–8.

known in its totality. It presented "an infinite manifold of single events." Contrary to both positivists and the historical school, theoretical repro-duction of reality was impossible. Ascription of value was the precondition to historical knowledge. Scientists identified phenomena as subjects of interest through their "value relevance" (*Wertbeziehung*), then used concepts to simplify and organize the phenomena into knowledge. The concepts of natural and cultural science differed in their relationship to reality. In natural science, concepts reflected not the phenomena but their laws. Natural science was *Begriffswissenschaft*: The concepts, not the phenomena, were of interest. In contrast, cultural sciences were, as Simmel suggested, *Wirk-lichkeitswissenschaften*, maintaining closer proximity to reality, the phenom-ena themselves of interest. Rickert left the precise relationship undefined, and Weber's ideal-type clarified it.

Rickert agreed with Windelband that humans attributed value to the unique, but he pointed out that historical inquiry moved between indi-viduality and generality. To be of interest, individuals had to represent cul-tural trends. Historians illuminated historical actors' ideas and actions against the cultural context. Objectivity hinged on historians' separation of their own judgment from their subjects' values. Yet, which values moved historians in selecting phenomena and constructing contexts? Rickert insisted that science presupposed certain objective values – scientific truth was one – having Kantian transcendental validity.[93] Weber broke radically with Rickert on this issue, but Popper thought the question superfluous: "Value relevance" added nothing "to the methodological analysis."[94] Sci-entists were interested in phenomena for multiple reasons, and this made no difference for procedure. Popper adopted and amplified the distinction between idiographic history and nomothetic science, but denied that cul-tural science was historical, and rejected the distinction between social and natural science.

In the 1900s, Weber published a series of critiques that arbitrated the Methodenstreit and developed his social science methodology: Roscher (1903), Knies (in two parts, 1905 and 1906), Meyer (1906), and legal theorist Rudolf Stammler (1907). His famous "'Objectivity' in Social Science" (1904) discussed Menger.[95] He accepted the Neo-Kantian view

[93] Heinrich Rickert, *Die Grenzen der naturwissenschaftlichen Begriffsbildung,* 3d ed. (Tübingen: Mohr, 1921); Guy Oakes, *Weber and Rickert,* pp. 49–110.

[94] Karl Popper, *The Open Society,* chap. 25, n. 9.

[95] "Roscher und Knies und die logischen Probleme der historischen Nationalökonomie," *Gesammelte Aufsätze zur Wissenschaftslehre,* pp. 1–145; "'Objectivity' in Social Science and Social Policy" and "Studies in the Logic of the Social Sciences" (critique of Meyer), in *The Methodology of the Social Sciences,* ed. and trans. Edward Shils and Henry Finch (New York: Free Press, 1949), pp. 50–112, 113–88, respectively; "R. Stammlers 'Überwindung' der materialistischen Geschichtsauffassung," *Wis-senschaftslehre,* pp. 291–359. On Max Weber and the historical school, see Wilhelm Hennis, "A Science of Man," in *Max Weber and His Contemporaries,* ed. Mommsen and Osterhammel, pp. 25–58.

that "value relevance" constituted the objects of social research, and he sought to challenge the historical school's view that theory reproduced reality. Rather than confront Schmoller, he uncovered his methodology's origin in Roscher and Knies. Their protests against the abstract theories of classical economics reflected, he said, not only naive belief in representation but also Hegelian and Comtean philosophies. They clung to a science that would discover the laws of historical development, a metareality underlying empirical history.[96] His argument was not persuasive, but Austrian economists adopted it. The unity of *Historismus*, positivism, and Hegelianism became a popular idea among them. Popper's historicism, too, lumped the three. Moreover, Popper condemned as "essentialist" doctrines similar to those that Weber had attacked as "emanationist" (for example, Knies's "holism"). His critique of "intuitive understanding" was also reminiscent of Weber's arguments against "intuitionism."[97] Popper probably did not have Weber's critique in mind when he developed his historicist model, but mysterious knots in his historicism appear almost as commonplace in the context of Weber and the Austrian economists.

Weber credited Menger with establishing, well before Rickert, the difference between a science aiming at general laws (*Gesetzwissenschaft*) and one aiming at historical reality (*Wirklichkeitswissenschaft*), "exact" and "empirical" types. Empirical observation alone never gave rise to general laws. But Menger failed to recognize, said Weber, the special character of phenomena investigated by social science: They were meaningful. He mistakenly assumed that economics could become, like physics, a *Gesetzwissenschaft*, whereas marginal utility theory and its concepts – price, interest, rent – were actually mere theoretical constructs, ideal-types, that emphasized aspects of capitalism.[98] Ideal-type was "a conceptual construct which is neither historical reality nor even the 'true' reality," but a "concept [abstracted from concrete phenomena] with which the real situation or action is compared and surveyed for the explication of certain of its significant components."[99] Contrary to Menger, social science was both theoretical and historical, closer to reality than he imagined – it explained concrete historical phenomena – and further removed from it – it formed analytic constructs, not essential laws.

To Weber, social science was interpretive (*verstehende*), but he rejected

[96] In Roscher, Hegelianism converged with naturalism and organicism. The national economy was an organism whose laws of development could be expressed in quasi-physiological terms. In Knies, methodological holism, collective action, and the "concrete individual" manifested "anthropological emanatism." Even his opposition to positivism and Hegelianism – Knies decried natural-historical laws – did not liberate him from Hegelian "pan-logicism." Weber, "Roscher und Knies," esp. pp. 138–45.

[97] "Poverty," Sections 8, 29; Weber, "Roscher und Knies," pp. 118–26.

[98] Worse, Menger hoped – and in this he shared Schmoller's prejudice – to reduce the "laws" of economic behavior to psychological motivations, a position Weber thought untenable: "Die Grenznutzlehre und das 'psychophysische Grundgesetz,'" 394–7.

[99] "'Objectivity' in Social Science," p. 93.

Dilthey's and Rickert's separation between causal explanation and interpretation of meaning. Ideal-types were both interpretive and causal. They ruled out a large number of facts as contingent and accentuated others, and so causality was ever implied. Still, the patterns they established could always be reduced to human behavior and be understood in terms of its meaning. Social science was interested in concrete phenomena, the "historical individual," but even explanation of individual phenomena required general laws. To be sure, these laws were not universal – their degree of generality was pragmatically determined. They established historical patterns that could, on occasion, be further abstracted and formulated as laws, but they never became universal: Natural science's radical abstraction, or "bracketing," of individual phenomena's unique qualities was inappropriate for social science. Ideal-types provided conceptual tools for "analysis of historically unique configurations, or their individual components."[100]

Weber was a "methodological individualist." Culture and institutions consisted of individuals' interaction and the meaning they ascribed to it. Model construction began with explanation of action and required both understanding (*Verstehen*) of motives and interpretation of subjective meaning, that is, meaning attributed by actors to their behavior and setting. Scientists searching for patterns inquired after "meaning adequacy": Given the goals individuals pursued and the means available to them, did they attribute "correct" meaning to their action? To the extent they did, their action was "rational" and their behavior typical. Like Rickert, Weber assumed that only "value-relevance" made reality manageable by designating aspects of reality as objects of study. Unlike Rickert, he insisted that not subjective meaning alone determined value relevance, but the scientists' own interest and culture as well. Ideal-types translated subjective meaning into cultural significance (*Bedeutung*). Interpretation, or translation, was always done from a particular perspective. Concept formation in social science was an unending process, reflecting changing concerns and conflicting perspectives. This did not mean free reign for "value-judgments": Model construction was subject to empirical evidence, and subjective meaning was a necessary, if insufficient, condition to the judging of cultural significance. Still, no Rickertian transcendental values guaranteed ideal-types' validity.[101]

"Poverty" and *The Open Society* contained a good number of references to Weber's *Gesammelte Aufsätze zur Wissenschaftslehre*. Popper and Weber agreed on many principles, but Popper noted only the proximity of their views on historical explanation and psychologism, and failed to enlist Weber against "essentialism" and "holism."[102] He regarded Weber as a historicist

---

[100] Loc. cit.   [101] "'Objectivity' in Social Science," pp. 112–13.

[102] "Poverty, III": 83–4; *Poverty*, pp. 145–7; *The Open Society*, vol. 2, p. 90; chap. 14, n. 14; chap. 25, n. 7. Popper disagreed with Weber that historical laws had a lower degree of generality: Laws were universal, or they were not laws.

enemy, not an ally. He believed that "ideal-types largely correspond to the essences of Aristotle and Husserl," and that *verstehende* sociology used "intuitive understanding" as its method.[103] He made short shrift of Weber's argument on the meaningful nature of social science phenomena. He even suggested that Weber and Rickert did not recognize – as he did – that there was no such thing as a single "history," only multiple histories written from different perspectives.[104] This was, however, precisely Weber's point.

Popper's uncharitable view was partially a result of Weber's reception in Vienna. Whatever Popper knew of "subjectivist" method in economics he found objectionable. Weber's historical relativism, nuanced though it was, classified him as historicist. Popper also had little patience with Weber's "objectivity." Public criticism was necessary and sufficient for objectivity; other considerations were irrelevant. Weber upheld science's methodological unity, but only with qualifications. His social science was historical. This sufficed, in Popper's view, to regard him a historicist. All the same, Popper's and Weber's views on social science models were close, and in postwar years, Popper would draw still closer to Weber by developing the "rationality principle." Weber was an ally against historicism. Popper just did not recognize him as such.

METHODENSTREIT, HISTORICISM, AND SOCIAL
ENGINEERING: MISES, HAYEK, POPPER

During the interwar debate on socialization, the Austrian economists joined Marx to the enemy camp that Weber created: Hegelianism, *Historismus*, positivism. Marxism, they argued, exemplified the historical school. The Methodenstreit now became openly political, focusing on socialism. Popper, too, incorporated Hegel, the positivists, the historists, and the Marxists into his model of historicism. Reading Hayek in 1943, he discovered that they had developed, separately from each other, similar arguments on the relationship between politics and methodology, but disagreed on major issues. In his correspondence with Hayek over the next couple of years, he was unusually respectful and eager to please, but he was also his usual self, passionately argumentative. His reflections on Hayek led both to methodological advances and to political shifts in his philosophy.

Already in the late 1890s, Böhm-Bawerk had criticized Marx's value theory, and Hilferding responded to him in *Der Kampf*'s first issue in 1904.[105] In 1919, Mises presented Böhm-Bawerk as the official Austrian critic of Marx and socialism. Austrian economists, he argued, had long

---

[103] *The Open Society*, chap. 3, n. 30; chap. 11, n. 44 (2).   [104] Ibid., chap. 25, n. 9.

[105] Eugen von Böhm-Bawerk, *Karl Marx and the Close of His System* [1896] and Rudolf Hilferding, *Böhm-Bawerk's Criticism of Marx* [1904], ed. Paul M. Sweezy (New York: Augustus Kelly, 1966). See also Böhm-Bawerk, "Control or Economic Law?" (trans. of *Macht oder ökonomischen Gesetz?*), in *Shorter Classics of Eugen von Böhm-Bawerk* (South Holland, Ill.: Libertarian Press, 1961), 1:139–200.

opposed Marxist and Prussian socialism, now threatening to engulf Europe.[106] This was problematic: The Austrian economists represented diverse political views, and Mises's and Hayek's libertarianism was unprecedented. They did not continue a liberal antisocialist tradition; they created it. The interwar calculation debate consolidated their libertarian turn, but only their emigration West, and the discredit their colleagues in Austria brought upon themselves by cooperating with the Nazis, made libertarianism predominant in the Austrian school.

Mises's 1920 article, "Economic Calculation in the Socialist Commonwealth," was a dramatic attack on the socialization plans currently debated among progressives and socialists.[107] In the absence of a capitalist market, he argued, production costs and commodity values could not be determined. A central planning board could neither measure costs nor determine prices. Prices reflected not inherent values but changing human preferences. They were a means of communication among consumers, producers, and distributors. By measuring consumer preferences, they provided producers and distributors necessary information for planning production and distribution (costs of materials, wages, transportation, and so forth): "It is precisely in market dealings that market prices are formed, [then] taken as the bases of calculation for all kinds of goods and labor. Where there is no free market, there is no pricing mechanism; without a pricing mechanism, there is no economic calculation."[108] And without economic calculation, no rational planning of production could take place.

Economic and technological rationality diverged. Human needs could not be objectively measured or determined. Even if an alternative measuring of preferences were found, results would be to no avail. With markets no longer determining monetary values, money would cease operating as valuating means. What common valuation unit would a planning board use to impute value to commodities and determine production costs? "The administration may know exactly what goods are most urgently needed. But it has . . . dispensed with the valuation of the means of production . . . [and will] find it impossible to use money as an expression of the price of the factors of production (including labor)."[109]

Mises triggered a debate that lasted for two decades and moved from Central to Western Europe. Initially, exchanges took place primarily in the *Archiv*, and involved Austrian economists (Mises, Hayek, Schumpeter), progressives (Neurath, Schiff), and socialists (Karl Polanyi, Otto Leichter). With the Central European emigration to England, and Hayek's growing

---

[106] Ludwig von Mises, *Nation, State, and Economy* (New York: New York University Press, 1983), esp. pp. 177–221 on "Socialist Imperialism."

[107] Ludwig von Mises, "Wirtschaftsrechnung in der Gemeinwirtschaft," *Archiv für Sozialwissenschaft und Sozialpolitik* 47 (1920): 86–121; "Economic Calculation in the Socialist Commonwealth," in *Collectivist Economic Planning*, ed. Friedrich Hayek (London: Routledge, 1935), pp. 87–130.

[108] Mises, "Economic Calculation," p. 111.   [109] Ibid., pp. 107–8.

influence at the LSE in the 1930s, the debate moved to British journals, involving both émigrés (Hayek, Lange) and British economists (Robbins, H. D. Dickinson, Maurice Dobb). Schumpeter, Polanyi, Leichter, Dickinson, and Dobb defended, from different perspectives, the possibility of socialist calculation. Neurath and Schiff argued for a planned administrative economy, Oskar Lange and Abba Lerner (both at the LSE) for a socialist market economy.[110] This was a rehearsal for the postwar debate on the welfare state. Popper was familiar with the early calculation debate – Polanyi's seminar discussed it – but not much taken by it. He knew of Mises and his circle, but it is unlikely that he read Mises closely.[111] He strongly disliked subjectivism and libertarianism. He "first met Mises early in 1935 in Vienna, owing to his interest in my first book. . . . Both he and I were aware of a strong opposition between our views in the field of the theory of knowledge and methodology. Mises saw me as a dangerous opponent."[112] Popper and Hayek entered the Methodenstreit from opposite political directions.

Socialists pointed out that a central planning authority could imitate the market by using advanced technology and mathematical formulae to calculate and impute values. In response, Hayek reformulated, in the early 1930s, Mises's argument. The market was an efficient communication system. Attempts to imitate it raised practical problems, likely to make economic operation cumbersome and reduce productivity. The planning board would have to collect information on all aspects of the changing economy, centralize and command it, then redistribute it to producers. This bordered on the absurd: The socialists refused to admit that "we are not intellectually equipped to improve the working of our economic system by 'planning' . . . without very considerably impairing productivity."[113]

Both Mises and Hayek believed that the root of planning was the technological outlook on economic problems:

> The increasing preoccupation of the world with problems of engineering character tends to blind people to the totally different character of the economic problem. . . . Central economic planning is nothing but an applica-

[110] Oskar Lange, "On the Economic Theory of Socialism," *Review of Economic Studies* 4 (1936–7): 136–44. Lange raised the possibility of a socialist market, presaging social democratic theories of the welfare state. Abba Lerner, "Economic Theory and Socialist Economy," *Review of Economic Studies* 2 (1933–4): 51–61.

[111] Popper's outline for the *Autobiography* included Mises (Popper Archives [134, 4]). He referred to the Mises circle in correspondence.

[112] Karl Popper, "The Communist Road to Self-Enslavement," *Cato Policy Report* 14 (1992): 10. (I owe this reference to Jeremy Shearmur.) In 1992, Popper claimed to have accepted Mises's free market principle. This was true, with caveats, for the old Popper, but not for *The Open Society*'s author.

[113] Friedrich Hayek, "The Current State of the Debate," in *Collectivist Economic Planning*, p. 241; "The Trend in Economic Thinking," *Economica* 13 (1933), 132–3; "The Use of Knowledge in Society," in his *Individualism and Economic Order* (Chicago: University of Chicago, 1948), pp. 77–91.

tion of engineering principles to the whole of society, based on the assumption that a complete concentration of all relevant knowledge is possible.[114]

Engineering was the product of positivism, or, as Hayek called it, "scientism": applying natural science methods to social science.

Seeking to anchor themselves in tradition, Hayek and Mises rewrote the Methodenstreit. Menger, too, they said, had been fighting their war. The historical school abolished the distinction between theoretical and historical science and emulated natural science in social science.[115] As historical methods failed to produce theories, historical economists moved in opposing directions: On the one hand, they denied historical patterns and the possibility of social theory; on the other, they doubled their efforts to distill laws of social development. Comte and Marx reentered historical economics through the back door. Rejected for their positivism, materialism, and, in Marx's case, cosmopolitanism and socialism, the historical school unwittingly resurrected their Hegelian-style universal history.[116] Mises and Hayek ascribed to the historical school, one by one, the pronaturalist (scientistic) doctrines of historicism that Popper brought under fire in "Poverty."

Mises and Hayek condemned historical determinism and any "law" of historical development. There was no theoretical science of history; no prediction of history was possible. They rejected historical relativism and the sociology of knowledge: Human preferences were subjective, yet theory was universally valid. They denounced methodological collectivism, especially the use of class, nation, and historical period as entities, or individual "wholes." They censured behaviorism, physicalism, and "objectivist" approaches to social science because they treated social facts as physical objects and explained human behavior in causal terms, ignoring its purposeful character. Against "objectivism" they proffered "subjectivist" interpretive social science, grounded in "intuitive understanding" of human action. Objectivism (positivism), collectivism, historism: This was the unholy trinity Popper discovered in Hayek in 1943–4.[117]

The Methodenstreit, Mises and Hayek argued, was from the beginning a confrontation between liberal and authoritarian politics. Unbeknownst to Menger, he, too, had been fighting against Prussian socialism. They traced

---

[114] Hayek, "The Nature and History of the Problem," in *Collectivist Economic Planning*, p. 4; "Scientism and the Study of Society, III," *Economica* 11 (1944): 36.

[115] Hayek, "Scientism and the Study of Society, II," *Economica* 10 (1943): 51.

[116] Mises, *A Critique of Interventionism* [1929] (New Rochelle, N.Y.: Arlington House, 1977), pp. 102, 137–8; *The Historical Setting of the Austrian School of Economics*, pp. 28–30; Hayek, "The Nature and History of the Problem," pp. 10–14; "Scientism, II": 50–63.

[117] Mises, *Epistemological Problems of Economics* [1933] (Princeton, N.J.: Van Nostrand, 1960), pp. 1–22, 35–51, 68–145; Hayek, "The Trend in Economic Thinking"; "The Facts of Social Science" [1943], in *Individualism and Economic Order*, pp. 57–75; "Scientism and the Study of Society, I," *Economica* 9 (1942) and "Scientism, II."

national socialism to the historical school. They did not stop here: Marxism and Historismus were one:

> In many respects the most powerful school of socialism the world has so far seen is essentially a product of . . . *Historismus*. . . . Marx wholeheartedly accepted the central contention of the historical school that most of the phenomena of economic life were not the result of permanent causes, but only the product of special historical development. It is no accident that the country where the historical school had had its greatest vogue was also the country where Marxism was wholeheartedly accepted.[118]

Historicist and Marxists were at one in their impatience with the market and their utopian economic management. An adequate legal framework to protect orderly competition was all the "planning" necessary. The rest was pseudoscientific utopia.[119]

Popper had known little of this when, in October 1943, he received Hayek's first letter, accompanied by two brief articles in which Hayek attacked leftist biologists (Bernal, Haldane, Hogben) for scientism. Hayek also mentioned "Counter-Revolution" and "Scientism." He suspected that Popper would dissent from his critique of scientism, but hoped they might reach an understanding. They had respect for each other and felt vulnerable in the other's field of expertise: Hayek in natural science, Popper in economics and, to a lesser extent, in social philosophy. Popper's first response, upon reading Hayek's reprints, was to recognize the biologists' fallacies – they would soon become his target of criticism in "Poverty" – but argue that his methodological unity of science did not fall under Hayek's criticism.[120] By December he had read "Counter-Revolution" and "Scientism" and, shortly thereafter, Hayek's other essays on the calculation debate and social science. His excitement was great. Both he and Hayek argued from methodology to politics, and their enemies seemed identical: the positivists, the Marxists, the historicists. To Popper's delight, Hayek reaffirmed his instinct that the three actually were one – historicism.

Not that Popper agreed with Hayek on methodology or politics. Quite the contrary: Hayek adhered to most of the antinaturalist doctrines of "historicism." To Popper, economics was not "subjectivist" or "interpretive." Human action's purposeful character did not rule out lawfulness, and unique and changing events did not exclude controlled experiments. Pre-

[118] Hayek, "The Nature and History of the Problem," p. 10.

[119] Hayek, "The Trend in Economic Thinking"; "The Nature and History of the Problem," and "The Present State of the Debate," in *Collectivist Economic Planning*; Mises, *Nation, State, and Economy*; Joseph Schumpeter, "The Sociology of Imperialism" [1919], in his *Imperialism and Social Classes* (New York: Kelley, 1951).

[120] Hayek to Popper, 12 July 1943; Popper to Hayek, 17 October 1943, Popper Archives (305, 13). Hayek's articles appeared in *Nature* and *The Liberal Review*. "The Counter-Revolution of Science, I," "II," and "III" appeared in *Economica* 8 (1941): 9–36, 119–50, 281–320.

diction was essential, and quantitative methods and mathematical models were indispensable. When Hayek used organic metaphors for society to argue against planning, or spoke of "intuitive understanding," Popper's hair surely stood on end. But he was careful in the manner he formulated his criticism. Hayek was considering "Poverty" for publication, helping to find a publisher for *The Open Society*, and trying to get him to the LSE. Moreover, Hayek brought home to him the danger of "scientism." Having read in January 1944 Waddington's *Science and Ethics*, Popper concluded that the evolutionist vogue easily degenerated into historicist ethics, sanctioning history's judgment. He was convinced that Hayek's opposition to applying natural science in economics was rooted in misconception of natural science. Surely, if Hayek recognized that natural science, too, was hypothetical and deductive, never predicting concrete developments (only excluding certain events), and that intuitive understanding played as great a role in physics as in economics, surely then Hayek would not object to methodological unity.[121]

Hayek's response to *The Open Society* was encouraging. Having adumbrated the manuscript's virtues, he added that he had no objection to methodological unity the way Popper defined it, or to "interventionism" and "partial engineering," although he himself would not use the terms.[122] They were fighting the same enemies, but on different fronts, and Popper's terminology could appeal to leftists who shut their ears to him. Popper passed the test: "The book has convinced me that fundamentally we are thinking alike," and it would be profitable for him to work in close contact with Popper. Popper was grateful, but could not conceal his disagreements or dissimulate for long. He expressed enthusiasm about "Counter-Revolution" and "Scientism," and told Hayek that his critique of behaviorism was the best he had read, but he criticized "subjectivism":

> We certainly must not attempt to discount what we know about ourselves. *But only such knowledge of "subjective" character (in your sense) becomes significant in the social sciences as can ultimately be used to construct "compositively" (observable or) testable theories of social behavior (i.e., "objective" theories in your sense).* . . . You might rejoin: No, for we don't know the inside of the atoms! My answer: *But we proceed in physics as if we did.* . . . In the social sciences . . . we have the advantage of knowing the "inside of the atoms." But this is replaced by the uncertainty as to the ("objective") social relevance of any particular piece of such knowledge.[123]

---

[121] In "Poverty, III": 80–2; *Poverty*, pp. 137–43, Popper went to great lengths to reconcile Hayek's position with his own, interpreting Hayek in a way that made his views compatible with *Logik der Forschung*.

[122] Hayek to Popper, 12 November 1943.

[123] Popper to Hayek, 16 December 1943, Popper Archives (305, 13).

Hayek could not become Popper's methodological guide, but he did encourage creative rethinking and brought out the antiscientistic potential of "Poverty". Popper had previously thought the evolutionist vogue implicated in historicism, but harmless. He now recognized that his critique of Marx and Mill applied equally to "evolutionism": "Even though all this only means a very slight change of emphasis in my theoretical attitude, it does mean a practical change, viz., a change in the personnel to be attacked."[124] Rewriting his critique of historical laws (Section 27 of "Poverty"), he denied that evolution was a "theory" proper, and decried its abuse in history and social science. Rethinking "law," he clarified the distinction between law and trend. Reacting to the emerging debate on historical explanation, he elaborated on the differences between historical and theoretical explanation. These were some of the outstanding achievements of "Poverty", and they reflected a shift of emphasis from the critique of antinaturalism to the critique of naturalism.

Still, Hayek contributed more to the politics of "Poverty" than to its methodology. He alerted Popper to the "collectivist" potential of social technology and fostered his suspicion of bureaucracy. Popper still wanted social technology to "design institutions," but he had to refine his technological science. Rewriting "Poverty, II" during the antipodal summer and fall of 1944, he tried, in vain, to square his differences with Hayek. He adopted Hayek's idea of designing the legal framework to regulate social interaction as an alternative to administrative control, but gave legal reform a broad institutional interpretation, assigning it tasks far exceeding Hayek's intentions, equivalent, at a minimum, to the welfare state. He suggested that not engineering itself but historicism was responsible for collectivism: "Where the scientistic enthusiasts fail . . . is, rather, the *holistic* exaggeration" of planning.[125] Just as historicists insisted on methodological holism, they opted for a total transformation of society:

> The strongest element in the alliance between historicism and Utopianism is, undoubtedly, the holistic approach which is common to both. Historicism is interested in the development, not of aspects of social life, but of "society as a whole"; and Utopian engineering is similarly holistic. Both overlook the important fact . . . that "wholes" in this sense can never be the object of scientific inquiry. Both are dissatisfied with "piecemeal tinkering" and "muddling through": they wish to adopt more radical methods.[126]

---

[124] Popper to Hayek, 17 January 1944. See also: Popper to Hayek, 6 January 1944 (305, 13).

[125] Popper to Hayek, 7 February 1944 (305, 13). Jeremy Shearmur writes (E-mail communication to author, 22 May 1999): "It is important not to read Hayek's later views into the Hayek of the 1940s. He was, at the time, much less obviously far from Popper than he might later have seemed." I have meanwhile read Shearmur's *After Hayek* (London: Routledge, 1996), which discusses the gradual changes in Hayek's views. This wonderful book has made Hayek an interesting thinker for me for the first time.   [126] "Poverty, II": 126; *Poverty*, p. 74.

Wishing to control all historical change, each and every aspect of social transformation, historicists entrusted full authority to a central planning board. Scientific engineering required trial and error, but collectivist planning did not allow for it. Lest criticism undermined their blueprint, holists silenced criticism. Holism issued in totalitarianism.[127]

In contrast, methodological individualism was equivalent to progressive liberalism. Recognition of methodological limits was conducive to political moderation. All reforms had unintended consequences, and so learning from errors was essential. As the "totality" of society remained inaccessible to scientists, piecemeal social engineers focused on limited reforms. They introduced reforms cautiously, reexamining their effects, correcting themselves in midcourse. "Social tinkering" might grow into a planned society, but through cumulative improvement. Technological social science subjected reform to science's "standards of clarity and practical testability." Piecemeal social engineering constituted the social application of *Logik der Forschung*.[128]

As Popper was trying to use anticollectivism to construct a bridge between libertarianism and progressivism, he fell upon a mutual adversary of Hayek and himself, Karl Mannheim. He had already criticized Mannheim's sociology of knowledge in *The Open Society*. Now he found all the marks of historicist, collectivist, utopian planning in his project for reconstructing democracy. Popper structured his critique of holistic planning around Mannheim's *Man and Society in an Age of Reconstruction*.[129] Mannheim had left Germany for England in 1933, becoming a lecturer at the L.S.E. His writings sounded as urgent a note as *The Open Society*: Totalitarianism was threatening to become liberal democracy's destiny. His analysis of totalitarianism found totalitarianism's roots in the masses' alienation. Society failed to solve modernity's problems. The solution lay in a transformation from current "plan-less regulation" to the planned society. Sociological knowledge should be used to reconstruct society and plan for freedom.[130] Overcoming the fissure between state and society was essential to democratization, as were education for citizenship and reconstitu-

---

[127] "Poverty, II," Sections 20–4. See also *The Open Society*, chap. 9, n. 4, chap. 18, n. 15 (rewritten September 1944); chap. 20, n. 26 where engagement with Hayek is still limited to *Freedom and the Economic System*.

[128] "Poverty, II," Sections 21–4; "Poverty, III," Section 32.

[129] Karl Mannheim, *Man and Society in an Age of Reconstruction* [1935], rev. ed. (New York: Harcourt, Brace, 1940). Popper explained his focus on Mannheim by the scale of Mannheim's project and his popularity among his friends: "Poverty, II": 123; *Poverty*, p. 67; "Replies to My Critics," *The Philosophy of Karl Popper*, pp. 1173–4.

[130] Mannheim, *Man and Society*; "The Democratization of Culture," in his *Essays on the Sociology of Culture* (London: Routledge and Kegan Paul, 1956) (the essay was written in the early 1930s); *Diagnosis of Our Time: Wartime Essays of a Sociologist* (London: Routledge, 1943), chaps. 1, 4–6; *Freedom, Power and Democratic Planning*, pt. 1 (London: Routledge and Kegan Paul, 1951) (posthumously published).

tion of communal bonds. Popper regarded these proposals as dangerous, if well-intentioned, efforts to do away with the limits of authority and the safeguards of liberty. Holistic social engineering was the method of both revolutionary and reactionary dictatorships.[131]

Hayek made Popper recognize the impossibility of concentrating knowledge in one planning agency. Popper responded that a "principle of democratic lucidity" (Simkin's term), presupposing a dispersal of knowledge, underlay his engineering. (He offered to drop the term "engineering" altogether, but did not do so.)[132] He emphasized indirect intervention and use of private, rather than public, agencies for reform in order to avoid an increase in state power. He sought to convince Hayek that although he himself was unsympathetic to laissez-faire, social technology was politically neutral. Just as theories proscribed certain events, technological social science pointed out the limits of the possible: It told social engineers what they could not do.[133] As he grew conservative in later years, his science left engineers progressively less to do, but in 1944, his progressive origins were still evident, and he was struggling with Hayek's growing influence on his politics. He acknowledged that he had grossly underestimated the danger of scientism and that his own philosophy had been tinged with it.[134] All the same, he insisted that noninterventionism was impossible:

> If we aim at democracy, then we must avoid certain measures, and adopt others. . . . [W]e do use means to keep crime under control, and child labor; and we may be able to end wars by similar means. All this is no doubt legitimate; and so is the attempt to control poverty and one-sided exploitation, and to try to eliminate it.[135]

Hayek showed Popper that "unbridled [as opposed to critical] rationalism is not only inconsistent in theory, but bound to choose inconsistent ends, if applied to the practical tasks of politics."[136] Yet, Popper felt that his task was "to fight irrationalism, especially since I always had, and still have, the feeling that there is something in 'scientism' [that is] not only in [Comte's] unity of method [and emphasis on prediction], but also in the idea (shared by Marx, Mannheim, etc.) of the rational control of our social . . . environment."[137] "I still cherish a faith . . . that it is our task to progressively rationalize the irrational," and use science to transform the world:

[131] "Poverty, II," Sections 21–4. See also *The Open Society*, chap. 9 (where Mannheim makes no appearance yet).

[132] Popper to Hayek, 14 March and 1 June 1944, Popper Archives (305, 13).

[133] "Poverty, II," Section 20.

[134] Popper to Hayek, 15 March 1944 (1st continuation), Popper Archives (305, 13).

[135] Popper to Hayek, 7 February 1944 (305, 13).

[136] Popper to Hayek, 28 May 1944, Hayek Archives (44, 1).

[137] Popper to Hayek, 16 December 1943, 7 February 1944.

The anxiousness of our time to help the poor and to eliminate unemployment is one of the best motives. . . . [M]ass unemployment is [not] due simply to clumsy interventionism. . . . [I]t is just as necessary to emphasize the need of rational interference . . . for the avoidance of unemployment as it is to emphasize the danger of collectivism. . . . We cannot "plan" civilization, and especially the growth of reason. . . . "[G]rown institutions," such as language or the market, never have been consciously invented, [but] they should not be considered sacrosanct.[138] . . . The piecemeal technologist recognizes that only a minority of social institutions are consciously designed, while the vast majority have just "grown", as the undesigned results of human actions. But, however strongly he may be impressed by this important fact, as a technologist or engineer, he will look upon them from a functional or instrumental point of view. He will see them . . . as convertible to the service of certain ends, as machines rather than as organisms.[139]

This was a radical departure from Hayek's understanding of social institutions as organic and spontaneous. Popper and Hayek represented divergent Austrian traditions. Progressivism and libertarianism simply did not mesh.

This was not Popper's last word. Having completed "Poverty, II" in mid-May 1944, he read *The Road to Serfdom*, "one of the most important political books I have ever seen," he wrote Hayek. It left an indelible impression on him. Hayek elaborated a series of paradoxes that became typical of cold-war liberalism. Popper had so far radically separated socialism and fascism, scientism and irrationalism. There were misguided people but no enemies on the left. Good intentions counted most. Hayek now showed that good intentions might lead to hell: "The very moral idealism of our politics inspires us to a tremendous effort in digging the grave of civilization"; he also showed "the continuity of socialist and fascist thought." To Gombrich Popper wrote that Hayek "has seen very much sharper than I have: . . . socialism itself leads directly to totalitarianism."[140] To be sure, Popper's avowal that "your interpretation is much more convincing" was too quick and radical to hold. *The Open Society* argued differently, and he never seriously modified it.[141] Nor did he second Hayek in his postwar writings. The closest he came was suggesting in his *Autobiography* that he would have remained a socialist had socialism not put liberty at risk. In speeches, he reaffirmed the old line that "ethical collectivism leads not so much to

[138] Popper to Hayek, 28 May 1944. I did not keep the original order of phrases in the letter.

[139] "Poverty, II": 122–3; *Poverty*, pp. 64–5.

[140] Popper to Hayek, 28 May and 1 June 1944; Popper to Gombrich, 5 June 1944, respectively.

[141] He told Hayek on June 1 that he would tone down his criticism of laissez-faire. Rewriting Chapter 17 of *The Open Society* in August 1944, he did tone down the emotional indictment, and cautioned that careless planning could increase the power of the state and threaten freedom. (*The Open Society*, pp. 121–3 [chap. 17, sec. 6].) In future editions, he substituted "unrestrained capitalism" for "*laissez-faire* capitalism" and elaborated the "paradox of economic planning" (2d. ed., pp. 131–3 [chap. 17, sec. 7]). All the same, his call for consistent interventionism remained unchanged.

socialism and communism, but to Fascism." Marx's and socialists' ultimate aim was individualism. The radical nationalists – the Italian fascists and German Nazis – were the real collectivists.[142] All the same, Carnap astutely observed that "Poverty, II" no longer seemed a work of a heterodox socialist.[143] Hayek badly shook Popper's progressivism.

"I think that I have learnt more from you than from any other living thinker, except perhaps Alfred Tarski," Popper wrote Hayek. Hayek did not make him into a libertarian, but he began arguing for reform less for its social benefits, more to prevent a collectivist revolution. Interventionism was necessary to overcome "the fatal split in the humanitarian camp and unite the vast majority of liberals and socialists."[144] Hayek must compromise:

> [I]f we present the matter too much as an alternative between scientistic rationalism and a humility which considers [social] formations as sacrosanct, then *freedom will be lost*. . . . If we do not constantly emphasize that [protectionist] ideals can be realized by individualistic methods, [we shall] fail to win the confidence of those misguided idealists who press . . . for collectivism. What we need is peace and mutual confidence within the camp of humanitarianism, and the great majority of socialists is in this camp.[145]

In 1944–5, Popper remained committed to reform, but he wavered on the practical direction that it might take. His commitment diminished progressively during the postwar years, but to the end, he diverged from Hayek. When Hayek spoke of egalitarian ideals as nonsense, an argument flared up. Popper considered him, however, the more profound social philosopher and, returning to the philosophy of science, left social theory to him. When the cold-war coalition and the welfare state faced difficulties, Popper remained quiet. He and his students never dedicated themselves to resolving reform's problems. Hayek had little influence on his methodology, but he stymied the growth of his political philosophy. As a methodologist of science, Popper was unrivaled. He absorbed the Methodenstreit into his theoretical framework and forged ahead. But Hayek managed to corrupt his socialism.

HISTORY AND SCIENCE IN POPPER

Popper began his political project of radically separating history and social science, a defensive move against historicism. This seemed an anomaly in his otherwise unified universe of knowledge, and it did not hold. In September 1944, revising Chapter 25 of *The Open Society*, he developed his account of "historical explanation." From December 1944 to March 1945,

---

[142] Popper, "Ethical and Methodological Individualism" (12, 1).
[143] Carnap to Popper, 17 November 1946, Carnap Collection.
[144] Popper to Hayek, 15 March 1944.   [145] Popper to Hayek, 28 May 1944.

he rewrote "Poverty, III," distinguishing between law and trend, and explaining models in social science and history. The result was surprising: Brilliantly rebutting the evolutionist vogue, he narrowed, at the same time, the gap that he had opened between history and science. His postwar ideas on model construction and situational logic closed the gap almost completely.

Evolution, argued Popper, was a brilliant hypothesis about humankind's common ancestry. The evolutionary process was a unique and complex historical sequence of events. It could not be tested because no other universe in which to test it was available. As the explanation of even a simple succession of events involved multiple laws and limiting conditions, there could be no "law of evolution." It was not a universal theory proscribing events but a singular (or particular) historical (existential) statement. One had to distinguish between universal laws and unique trends. Trends depended on initial conditions, and their length could not be predicted because changing conditions might result in reversal. There were historical trends; evolution was one. Historicists confused trends with laws. If initial conditions sustaining trends were regarded as permanent, or long-term, they might have systematic impact, as many trends playing a role in evolution had. Still, they depended on particular conditions persisting, and this is what historicists, like Mill, ignored with their developmental historical laws. Nineteenth-century progressivist optimism was to blame for the confusion. Popper challenged it with "poststructuralist" insistence on contingency.[146]

Yet, he himself wrote a teleological history and felt compelled to account for its scientific status. In 1942, he formulated the distinction between theory and interpretation. Both historical and scientific descriptions represented points of views, but scientific theories were testable and falsifiable, and historical interpretations rarely so. More than one interpretation corresponded to records, and there were no new facts, no test to decide between them. Interpretations represented complementary perspectives: His narrative of progress from closed to Open Society did not clash with a narrative of regress. This did not mean that there were no better and worse interpretations; records could contradict an interpretation, too many auxiliary hypotheses ruled it out, and so forth. But there was no history "as it actually happened." Narratives depended on perspective to provide a method for selecting data. The imperatives for good history meant selecting an interesting viewpoint and being aware of it.

---

[146] "Poverty, III," Sections 27–8. Popper went into detail to demonstrate that Mill confounded laws and trends. Allan Megill thinks that this is unfair. Mill may be, on occasion, confused, but he is resolved to combat tendencies endangering liberty. Mill was, like Popper, a progressivist, but antihistoricist. (Allan Megill, "J. S. Mill's Religion of Humanity and the Second Justification for the Writing of *On Liberty,*" *Journal of Politics* 34 [1972]: 612–24 and E-mail communication to author, 22 March 1999.)

As Popper investigated trend and law, it appeared that theories, too, commonly incorporated limiting conditions, their universality reduced, their contingency increasing. Universal laws were infrequent; natural and social science explained trendlike regularities. This drew natural and social science closer, reinforcing their methodological unity, but it also drew science closer to history. In 1942, Popper insisted that history described the unique, and science explained the universal. By 1944, confronting Hempel's "historical explanation" and Mill's "historicist" effort to reduce trend to law, he conceded that history both explained and described.[147] It explained typical events but described their uniqueness. Popper came close to the Neo-Kantian "historical individual."

The logic of (causal) explanation in natural, social, and historical science was unified: A singular event was deduced from a universal law (theory), subject to initial conditions. Explanation always involved prediction, although scientists spoke of it only when subjecting a theory to a test. The question was: What did scientists find of interest and consider problematic? If a prognosis was readily available, but its initial conditions or universal laws were problematic, scientists spoke of "explanation." If they had interest in new information, or application, or wished to test a problematic premise (law or conditions), they spoke of "prediction," or "test." Social science formed theories; history explained singular (specific) events. Explaining events involved laws, but they were not historians' major interest, were usually trivial, and could never be subject to test. In contrast, a singular hypothesis (prediction), deduced from other initial conditions and unproblematic universal laws, then confronted with documents (test), was common. Like historians, practitioners applying laws to particular conditions were also not interested in laws.[148] "[A]ll causal explanation of a singular event can be said to be historical," he reasoned.[149] Theoretical science alone tested events for the sake of universal laws. History and science represented different interests in scientific explanation, but even these

---

[147] Popper thought that the debate had originated with Hempel's plagiarism of "causal explanation" from *Logik* (Section 12, on causal explanation). (*The Open Society*, chap. 25, n. 7 [1] and [3]; "Poverty, III": 83.) Hempel borrowed, indeed, his causal explanation, but other than Popper's report on the meeting in Brussels on January 9, 1936, there is no evidence of his interest in historical explanation prior to 1944. It was likely a response to Hempel and Mill. Unlike Hempel's positivist "covering law model," Popper's historical explanation allowed for diversity of interests, but the literature focused on Hempel, not Popper, and he was bitter. (*Autobiography*, p. 117.) For Hempel's 1942 article, see his *Aspects of Scientific Explanation and Other Essays in the Philosophy of Science* (New York: Free Press, 1965), pp. 231–43. See also: Donald Davidson, "Actions, Reasons, and Causes," in his *Essays on Actions and Events* (Oxford: Clarendon Press, 1980), pp. 3–19; Fritz Ringer, "Causal Analysis in Historical Reasoning," *History and Theory* 28 (1989): 152–72; Wesley Salmon, *Four Decades of Scientific Explanation* (Minneapolis, Minn.: University of Minnesota Press, 1989). Everyone has difficulty finding laws from which historical events can be deduced. If Popper's view is adopted, the riddle is solved: These laws are implied, never specified, usually trivial, and history has no interest in them.

[148] This may limit social science's relevancy to social engineering. In later years, Popper spoke of piecemeal social engineering as helpful to science, rather than the other way around.

[149] "Poverty, III": 83; *Poverty*, p. 144. "Cause" is understood here as a single initial condition.

interests no longer appeared exclusive, with practical science closer to history than to theoretical science. The universe of knowledge was drawn closer.

In "Poverty, III," Popper recognized some differences between natural and social science. To overcome the difficulty of creating artificial experimental conditions in a social environment, Popper suggested constructing models of human interaction – groups, institutions, market – based on the individuals' perfect rationality and perfect knowledge. The "zero method" would then be used to measure deviation from the model, and exceeding the limits of permissible deviation would falsify it.[150] Model construction was easier in social than in natural science because social situations had rationality imbedded in them: "Our actions are to a very large extent explicable in terms of the situation in which they occur." As Weber suggested, "when we speak of 'rational behavior' or of 'irrational behavior' then we mean behavior which is, or which is not, in accordance with the logic of that situation."[151] Social science explained interaction among individuals that gave rise to institutions and traditions and, in turn, constrained agents.[152]

[150] Popper conceded that changing economic parameters made applying quantitative methods, especially measurement, difficult, but insisted that these methods were crucial and that statistical methods might overcome the difficulties. "Poverty, III": 82; *Poverty*, p. 142–3.

[151] *The Open Society*, p. 90 (added in August 1944). Popper used Weber and situational logic to criticize psychologism. Intentions and motivations counted little, not only because, as he said in an earlier draft of *The Open Society*, social science dealt with unwanted consequences, but also because the situation itself determined action. He reevaluated his position on Weber's antipsychologism. In the 1942 draft he called Weber's "meaning adequacy," or rationality criterion, an interesting argument against psychologism, but different from his. In August 1944, he made it his own. His dialogue with Weber thus contributed to the developing of situational logic. (Compare chap. 14, esp. n. 13, in manuscript, Popper Archives [29, 3], with *The Open Society*, chap. 14, pp. 90–2 and nn. 13 and 14.) Weber's influence has been argued by Struan Jacobs, "Popper, Weber and the Rationalist Approach to Social Explanation," *British Journal of Sociology* 41 (1990): 559–70.

[152] Popper's economic models exemplified situational logic, but I am not sure that the opposite is true, historically or theoretically. Popper stated that situational logic developed Hayek's "pure logic of choice," and, in *Autobiography*, p. 117, that it generalized the method of marginal utility theory. The first occurrence of situational logic in his work, however, is Plato's logic of power (*The Open Society*, chap. 10, n. 63). Popper did identify it with Hayek's "logic of choice," but his model was political and institutional. He developed situational logic further in August 1944, using Weber's "rationality" to argue against psychologism (*The Open Society*, chap. 14, pp. 90–2 and nn. 13 and 14; Popper Archives [29, 1, 3]). The context was sociological. Only in 1945, in "Poverty, III," did he use economic models and the zero method as examples of situational logic. (As Peter Hedström, Richard Swedberg, and Lars Udéhn point out in "Popper's Situational Analysis and Contemporary Sociology," *Philosophy of the Social Sciences* 28 [1998]: 344–6, Popper did not even identify the zero method [Section 29] with situational logic [Section 31], although, given *The Open Society*, the identification is noncontroversial.) In "The Logic of the Social Sciences" [1962], in Theodor Adorno et al., *The Positivist Dispute in German Sociology* (London: Heinemann, 1976), p. 102, Popper presented situational logic as the method of both *verstehende Soziologie* (interpretive sociology) and economics. This was not inconsistent. Weber thought that Menger provided exemplary social science models. Both Weber and Popper conceived of marginal utility theory as exemplifying interpretive sociological models using the rationality principle.

Plato was the first to see that the logic of power explained tyrants' moves, as well as the unanticipated consequences of their policies. Contrary to their intentions, tyrants facilitated democracy, rather than a return to the closed society. Likewise, the logic of international power explained states' foreign policies. (Democrats should opt for developing a logic of freedom, shaping institutions in such a manner that freedom was protected.) Historians widely used situational models, explaining the "necessity" of events, actions, and policies. More was needed:

> We need studies . . . of the social institutions through which ideas may spread and captivate individuals, of the way in which new traditions may be created, and of the way in which traditions work and break down. . . . [I]ndividualistic and institutionalist models of such collective entities as nations, or governments, or markets, will have to be supplemented by models of political situations and social movements.[153]

His own interest was in using "situational logic" to explain the rise of rationalism and the scientific tradition.[154] His "institutional theory of progress" proposed that only a polity promoting freedom of criticism could hope for sustained growth of knowledge.

"Poverty" was Popper's single major pronouncement on social science, but on a few occasions in postwar years, he returned to situational logic, models, and the rationality principle, and offered second thoughts on social science method. Reading Collingwood, he suggested that constructing problem situations to explain intellectual development could largely substitute for hermeneutics.[155] Reenactment (*Erleben*) was useful in interpretation, but it was possible in various degrees, and its goal was always to construct an explanatory context open to criticism. Social science and history "combin[ed] intuitive understanding of reality with the objectivity of rational criticism."[156] In his 1961 Frankfurt address – Habermas's response to which rekindled the "positivism dispute" (*Positivismusstreit*) in German sociology – Popper spoke of situational logic as the method of *verstehende*

---

[153] "Poverty, III": 85; *Poverty*, p. 149.

[154] "Toward a Rational Theory of Tradition" [1949], in *Conjectures and Refutations*, pp. 120–35; "Back to the Presocratics" [1958], ibid., pp. 136–53; "A Pluralist Approach to the Philosophy of History" [1969], in his *The Myth of the Framework*, ed. M. A. Notturno (London: Routledge, 1994), pp. 154–84. He also used the "logic of power" to criticize the "conspiracy theory of society," which he regarded as a variety of psychologism: *The Open Society*, 2d ed., vol. 2, pp. 93–7.

[155] Collingwood used both, but emphasized "re-enactment," the significance of which Popper wished to diminish, but not abolish. Popper equated "re-enactment" with Dilthey's *Erleben*. Allan Megill suggested to me (E-mail communication, 22 March 1999) that reenactment actually entailed "rethinking" rather than "re-experiencing," hence was compatible with Popper and the construction of problem situations. Popper, "On the Theory of the Objective Mind," in his *Objective Knowledge* (Oxford: Clarendon Press, 1972), esp. pp. 186–90; "A Pluralist Approach to the Philosophy of History."

[156] *Objective Knowledge*, p. 190.

Soziologie.[157] He ended up accepting both Weber's purposeful human behavior and his ideas on model construction.

His major postwar statement on social science models was a 1963 Harvard political economy lecture, "Models, Instruments, and Truth."[158] As he moved from a causal deterministic universe to a probabilistic one, he concluded that in natural and social science alike, theories were commonly probabilistic, not causal: "Strict causal laws are limiting, and rather rare, cases of scientific explanations."[159] Astronomy's causal laws were an exception, due to planetary systems' isolation. When multiple variables were involved, causality was impossible. He gave up on any universal (i.e., timeless) social laws, but still hoped for probabilistic ones.[160] "Historical explanation," he decided (correctly, I believe), was not the major contribution of "Poverty" to history; situational logic was.[161]

In natural, social, and historical science alike, models, not laws, most easily explained regularities, or types of events. Social science explained events in terms of human actions and social situations by constructing models of the social situations in which agents were acting. To explain pedestrians' movements, one attributed to them the aim of "crossing the street" and described physical obstacles and traffic rules. A rationality principle "animated" the situational model.[162] It did not imply that people always behaved rationally; indeed, they did not. Models were never true but, rather, an oversimplification of reality that increasingly approached truth as their accuracy improved. "Rationality" was methodological, a question of the adequacy of the agent's behavior to the situation a model described. (Even explanation of mad behavior required rational reconstruction.) It was sound policy never to blame a model's failure on the failure of rationality (that is, never to declare the rationality principle itself false), for that would rule out models.[163] History's problem situations, too, represented (rarely testable)

---

[157] "The Logic of the Social Sciences," p. 102.

[158] "Models, Instruments, and Truth: The Status of the Rationality Principle in the Social Sciences," in *The Myth of the Framework.* (For the lecture's circumstances, see Hedström, Swedberg, and Udéhn, "Popper's Situational Analysis and Contemporary Sociology": 361.) An extract was published as "La rationalité et le statut du principe de rationalité," in *Les fondements philosophiques des systèmes économiques,* ed. Emil M. Classen (Paris: Payot, 1967) ("The Rationality Principle," in *A Pocket Popper,* ed. David Miller [Glasgow: Fontana, 1983]). See also drafts and revisions, Popper Archives (6, 8; 71, 3–10; 72, 1–10).

[159] Colin Simkin, *Popper's Views on Natural and Social Science* (Leiden: Brill, 1993), p. 65.

[160] Ibid., p. 126.   [161] *Autobiography,* pp. 117–18.

[162] To use Popper's terminology for causal explanation, models roughly represented typical initial conditions and relations among them. Some mechanism of interaction, a law, was necessary to "move" the model. As causal laws were hardly ever applicable in social science, the rationality principle was the single "universal law" making movement, or interaction among the model's parts, possible.

[163] The rationality principle remained, however, problematic, as Popper claimed both that it was methodological *and* that it was *empirically* false but approaching truth. He later recognized as much, opted for the second (empirical) view, but insisted that it was wise not to implicate the rationality principle in model failure. (See Noretta Koertge, "The Methodological Status of Popper's

models. Scientists had greater interest in models themselves, historians in particular facts, but they were methodologically close.

Science's methodological unity now appeared very real. Popper began by insisting on causal nonhistorical social science, but ended up with non-causal science, social models that were historical in all but name, and a method similar to Weber's. This was not the end. Simkin reported in 1993 that Popper recognized that economic models could not generate even probabilistic laws – there were too many difficulties in measurement; rather, they were quantitative examples of situational analysis, relating to periods and contexts of relatively short duration.[164] Only with great luck was progress possible. This pessimism contrasted with Popper's conviction in "Poverty" that he would revolutionize social science. It was far from dev-astating, however, to his philosophy, for toward the end of his life, he deter-mined that not hypothetico-deductive structure, causal explanation, testing, or refutability marked theory, but critical discussion and progress from one problem to another, a deeper one. In this emphatically nonscientistic uni-verse of knowledge, history and science coexisted peacefully, striving for elusive progress.

"Poverty" accomplished its negative aims, but not the positive ones. Popper's exposition of scientific and historical explanation was brilliant and his critique of historical laws devastating. Sociologists and biologists would continue the evolutionist vogue, but only at their peril. However, neither a new theoretical social science nor a technological one has emerged from "Poverty." A methodological critique, offering *Logik der Forschung*'s natural science model, and suggesting a few stratagems for models, was simply not enough. Situational logic remained underdeveloped, even Popper's 1963 lecture unpublished until 1994. Popper did not revolution-ize social science.

Economists do not seem to have widely read "Poverty," but Popper has become a household name among them.[165] In his influential *Essays in Pos-itive Economics* (1950), Milton Friedman proposed that absence of testing

Rationality Principle," *Theory and Decision* 10 [1979]: 83–95 for a discussion.) He distinguished between three "rationalities": "the situation as it actually was" (objective); "the situation as the agent actually saw it" (subjective); and "the situation as the agent could (and possibly ought to) have seen it." As Weber recognized, the third was crucial for judging meaning adequacy and constructing models. Tensions between the first and second rationalities, the objective situation and the agent's subjective view of it, played a key role in historical explanation.

[164] Simkin, *Popper's Views on Natural and Social Science*, p. 177.

[165] Mark Blaug, *Economic Theory in Retrospect*, 3d. ed. (Homewood, Ill.: Irwin, 1978), p. 714, suggests that although Popper has had a great influence on economists, few have read him, and most have relied on Friedman's report of his views. Terence Hutchinson, however, read *Logik* early, and hailed testability: *The significance and Basic Postulates of Economic Theory* (London: Macmillan, 1938). Karl Milford suggests that I have underestimated the influence of Popperian ideas, especially situational logic and methodological individualism, on the making of postwar social science in Central Europe, especially on the New Institutionalism.

and falsification in contemporary economics retarded its development, and offered Popper as an answer.[166] During the 1950s, a group of economics students at the LSE, informed by Joseph Agassi, rebelled against Robbins's a-priorism, and attempted to apply Popper's causal explanation. They encountered difficulties testing statistical hypotheses – they were not aware of Popper's suggestions for testing probability statements – and desisted. Neil de Marchi suggests that their difficulties were partially due to the absence of any connection between econometrics and economics at the LSE until 1963, but economists have generally had difficulty testing.[167] All the same, Popper increased their methodological awareness.[168]

Social scientists have made no consistent effort to apply situational logic, but rational choice theory, which has become popular among sociologists and political scientists in the last two decades, has used similar models, borrowed from economics.[169] As Richard Swedberg and Egon Matzner point out, Popper could exercise a moderating influence on such "economic imperialism."[170] He refused to take the profit maximizing (or interest calculating) individual as a given, and his models opted to shift the analysis to the institutional setting. To the individual with stable economic preferences, he counterposed an interactive situation. His individual was less predictable, his methodological individualism more moderate. Herein lies his models' great promise *and* problem: Scholars encounter difficulties moving between analysis of individuals and the institutional setting. If institutions and traditions represent unintended consequences of interaction *and*

---

[166] (Chicago: University of Chicago, 1950). Of course, Friedman's work is not fully Popperian. Indeed, Alan Musgrave showed him to be an instrumentalist (or a conventionalist), and his views thus conflict with Popper: "'Unreal Assumptions' in Economic Theory: The F-Twist Untwisted," *Kyklos* 34 (1981): 377–87. I wish to thank Bruce Caldwell, Karl Milford, and Jeremy Shearmur for their comments and the reference.

[167] Neil de Marchi, ed., *The Popperian Legacy in Economics* (Cambridge: Cambridge University Press, 1988).

[168] Mark Blaug *The Methodology of Economics* (New York: Cambridge University Press, 1980), chaps. 1–2, argues that Popper's methodological individualism made macroeconomics virtually impossible. Other economists criticized the rationality principle. See Neil de Marchi, ed., *Post-Popperian Methodology of Economics* (Boston: Kluwer, 1992); Jack Birner, "A Roundabout Solution to a Fundamental Problem in Menger's Methodology and Beyond," in *Carl Menger and His Legacy*, ed. Bruce Caldwell (Durham, N.C.: Duke University Press, 1990), pp. 241–62. Birner attempts to use Noretta Koertge's "Popper's Rationality Principle" to improve on Popper.

[169] James Coleman developed rational choice sociology: *Foundations of Social Theory* (Cambridge, Mass.: Harvard University Press, 1990). Gary Becker's *The Economic Approach to Human Behavior* (Chicago: University of Chicago Press, 1976) represents the most recent effort to generalize economic models as social science method. For an earlier (simplistic) example: Anthony Downs, *An Economic Theory of Democracy* (New York: Harper & Row, 1957).

[170] "Introduction to the Special Issue on Situational Analysis," *Philosophy of the Social Sciences* 28 (1998): 333–8. Swedberg and Mazner credit Popper with inventing "economic imperialism," but correctly emphasize his differences with rational choice theory. "Imperialism," then, concedes too much. As Popper regarded economics as the most advanced of social sciences, he sought to lend its prestige to his social science models. He did a disservice to himself. Situational logic did not represent economic imperialism but the sociologization of economics.

constrain individual action, then they must have a modus operandi of their own that, nonetheless, must be explained, in the last analysis, through individuals' interaction.[171] This is a tall order. What is institutional quasi-existence like? How does one transform interacting individuals into an institution, or a tradition? The models Popper actually constructed always represented a single agent in an institutional setting, not interaction. Could interactive models mediate between individuals and institutions and move between micro- and macroanalysis? Nowhere has the problem been satisfactorily resolved.[172]

Just as Popper suggested, situational logic has been most successfully used in history, historians often being unconscious of the models they use, and rarely, if ever, constructing them. Problem situations have played a major role in contextual intellectual history and the history of science. For the Cambridge school of political theory, the linguistic, or rhetorical, situation explains the moves a thinker makes. Like Weber and Popper, Quentin Skinner has settled on "the situation as agents could (and possibly ought to) have seen it" as the yardstick for ascribing meaning to their utterance.[173] Historians, too, have had success mostly in explaining an individual, or a small group of thinkers. Broad discursive change has proved too complex, or elusive, for explanation in detail. To be sure, historians have constructed social and cultural contexts to explain discursive shifts, but moving between agents and paradigmatic change, showing how individual utterances created discursive shifts, remains problematic. No historical school regards Popper's situational logic as having inspired their work, but he elucidated wonderfully, if all too briefly, the premises underlying widely used practices in history and social science.

Prior to the 1970s, no prominent politician or social reformer espoused

---

[171] Popper spoke ("The Logic of the Social Sciences," p. 103) of the "quasi-action of institutions." Joseph Agassi discusses the problem in "Methodological Individualism," *British Journal of Sociology* 11 (1960): 244–70; "Institutional Individualism," ibid. 26 (1975): 144–55. See also Hedström, Swedberg, and Udéhn, "Popper's Situational Analysis and Contemporary Sociology," especially 353–4, and Ian Jarvie, "Situational Logic and Its Reception," *Philosophy of the Social Sciences* 28 (1998): 365–80.

[172] See, however, Ian Jarvie's suggestion in *Concepts and Society* (London: Routledge, 1972) that the concept of "role" may mediate between individuals and institutions. Many of Popper's students and friends had a major interest in social science, and he left an indelible mark on their work. A few examples: Joseph Agassi and Ian Jarvie, eds., *Rationality* (Boston: Kluwer, 1987); Ralf Dahrendorf, "Uncertainty, Science and Democracy," in his *Essays in the Theory of Society* (Stanford, Calif.: Stanford University Press, 1968); Ernest Gellner, "Nationalism," in his *Thought and Change* (London: Weidenfeld and Nicholson), chap. 7; Ernst Gombrich, "The Logic of Vanity Fair," in *The Philosophy of Karl Popper*, pp. 925–57; Joseph Agassi's and J. W. N. Watkins' essays in *Modes of Individualism and Collectivism*, ed. John O'Neill (London: Heinemann, 1973). Writers for *Philosophy of the Social Sciences* since 1971 often betray a debt to Popper.

[173] See the discussion of Skinner's "Meaning and Understanding in the History of Ideas," in *Meaning and Context: Quentin Skinner and His Critics*, ed. James Tully (Princeton, N.J.: Princeton University Press, 1989).

piecemeal social engineering, but in the mid-1970s, politicians in all three major West German parties declared that their programs represented Popperian principles.[174] Popper articulated well the postwar Social Democratic Consensus, extending from the Christian Democrats to the Social Democrats, supporting the welfare state, hostile to communism. At the same time, Popper was unhappy with most reforms. They did not represent trial and error but an interplay of political interests and social groups. Democracy did not resemble an ideal scientific community. Marx and Mannheim were not the only utopians. Popper, too, had utopian expectations of scientific social reform.

For the intellectual historian, "Poverty" is a rewarding challenge: shifting intentions, fragmented composition, and changing contexts. Once "Poverty" is historicized, the intellectual worlds of Vienna and Central Europe come alive through it, showing discourses adapting to radically new contexts across a century and over continents. Although the Methodenstreit came to an end with World War II, antihistoricism and piecemeal reform acquired new life during the cold war. In "Poverty," familiar figures in British philosophy (Mill) and academic life (Mannheim) displaced Central European intellectuals (Neurath). This facilitated the reception of "Poverty" in postwar Europe, but disguised its original targets. When Routledge & Kegan Paul published "Poverty" as a book in 1957, it was almost a foregone conclusion that it would be read primarily as a critique of communism. Few Western intellectuals were familiar with the Methodenstreit, or debates on socialization in Vienna. The title's pun on Marx and Popper's record as his critic assured that the work's anti-Marxist arguments would receive the most attention. Should any doubt have existed, Popper's dedication removed it: "In memory of the countless men, women and children of all creeds or nations or races, who fell victim to the fascist and communist belief in Inexorable Laws of Historical Destiny." The author himself sanctioned the appropriation of "Poverty" for the new context.

POPPER AND POSTWAR EUROPEAN LIBERALISM

The Open Society came out in November 1945, just a few months after the end of World War II. Within two years, Europe was engulfed in a cold war that expanded to the entire globe. In the preface to *The Open Society*'s American edition (1950), Popper acknowledged the changing context: "Seen in the darkness of the present world situation, the criticism of Marxism . . . is liable to stand out as the main point of the book. This view of it is not wholly wrong and perhaps unavoidable, although the aims of the book are much wider." Popper's views on democracy and social reform

---

[174] Helmut Spinner, *Popper und die Politik* (Berlin: Dietz, 1978) peruses the phenomenon.

fit neatly within a liberal discourse that reached full development in postwar years, a product of a generation of liberal intellectuals who had fought fascism, then shifted to containing communism. As *The Open Society* contributed significantly to postwar liberalism, it was commonly misread as anticommunist. Reviewers often noted its origins in the struggle against fascism, then spoke, in the same breath, of the critique of totalitarianism and Marxism. The new context shaped the reading, to Popper's delight. He made relatively few public pronouncements on the cold war, but there was no mistaking his anticommunist stance.[175] With *The Open Society*'s success, he became a recognized public intellectual. His return to England facilitated his rise to fame.

RETURN TO LONDON

"I am personally anxious to get Dr. Popper to this School," wrote Hayek to Gombrich in July 1943, "but . . . unless I can convince some of my colleagues that he [has] active interest in the . . . social sciences, I have little chance. With the MS [of *The Open Society*] in my hand, I might do a little more."[176] He did. Three weeks later, he wrote LSE director Carr-Saunders, who was vacationing in Cornwall, and presented Popper as an ideal candidate for a major readership in logic and scientific method. Since Abraham Wolf had vacated his part-time LSE professorship (shared with University College) in 1941, the LSE had been without a philosophy faculty. Under war exigencies, and with the LSE moving to Cambridge (the Hostel, Peterhouse), new appointments were suspended. Now that they were contemplating the move back to London, Hayek suggested that they convert the half-time professorship to a full-time readership and consider Popper. He spoke highly of Popper's philosophical achievements and, significantly, his interest in social science. The LSE needed someone, he thought, thoroughly versed in scientific philosophy, yet critical of logical positivism, who would develop social science methodology.[177] Popper would not fulfill Hayek's hopes for a new social science, but he would build a new department in logic and the scientific method at the LSE, exceeding expectations in other respects.

Carr-Saunders was noncommittal, and Hayek began drafting faculty behind his plan, showing them Popper's manuscript. Morris Ginsberg,

---

[175] Three examples: "The History of Our Time: An Optimist's View," in his *Conjectures and Refutations* (New York: Basic Books, 1963), pp. 364–76; "Zum Thema Freiheit," *Die Philosophie und die Wissenschaften*, ed. Ernst Oldemeyer (Meisenheim am Glan: Anton Hain, 1967), pp. 1–12; "What Does the West Believe In?" [1959], in his *In Search of a Better World* (London: Routledge, 1994), pp. 204–22.

[176] 12 July 1943, Popper Archives (305, 13).

[177] Hayek to Carr-Saunders, 7 August 1943; Hayek to Popper, 5 November 1943; Hayek to Horton (chair of the appointment committee), 14 March 1945, all in Hayek Archives (44, 1).

professor of sociology, was essential. He liked the chapter on the autonomy of sociology (against psychologism) and lent Hayek his support. Harold Laski first declined to join, but upon reading the manuscript in October, changed his mind, endorsing Popper.[178] The timid Carr-Saunders liked the book, and so did Robbins when he read it around the New Year. In November, Hayek wrote Popper officially, inquiring whether he would be interested. The airgraph, received on December 8, had a "bombshell effect" on the Poppers. Of course he would like to be considered, he told Hayek, and he would be ready to leave New Zealand on short notice. He was apprehensive, however, lest his publications prove insufficient and blamed their paucity on political circumstances in Austria and library conditions and teaching duties in New Zealand.[179] Hayek hastened to alert him that the appointment process was likely to be slow and long – he should not pack – but expressed his confidence about the final results.

Even Hayek did not imagine how arduous the process would be. Popper submitted virtually all application materials by February 1944 for Hayek's review and advice, authorizing Gombrich to apply for him.[180] The material stayed with Hayek nearly a year, the university taking no action until late in the fall of 1944. Popper was growing impatient, but meanwhile he had his hands full with "Poverty" and revisions to *The Open Society.* He did most revisions to Volume 1 from late April to the end of June 1944, at which time he felt ill, then collapsed for the rest of the antipodal winter. In late August, he began work on extensive revisions to Volume 2, sending, until mid-October, more than seventy airgraphs to Gombrich, with a rewritten Chapter 17, additional sections to Chapters 24 and 25, and many new paragraphs and notes, bringing *The Open Society* up to date with his recent social science methodology. Gombrich hired two assistants to introduce the revisions and check the proofs, and Ilse Barea did the index.[181] By early December, all revisions were back with Routledge, and Popper could begin his usual litanies about the publisher taking his time and not keeping the contract.

Meanwhile, he was pursuing other jobs. His friend John Findlay vacated a well-paid philosophy chair at the University of Otago in Dunedin, and faculty, especially neurophysiologist John Eccles in the medical school,

---

[178] Hayek to Laski, 28 September 1943; Laski to Hayek, 29 September 1943; Hayek to Popper, 12 November 1943, all in Hayek Archives (44, 1).

[179] Popper to Hayek, 8 and 9 December 1943, Hayek Archives (44, 1); Popper to Gombrich, 13 December 1943.

[180] Gombrich to Hayek, 7 February 1943, Hayek Archives (44, 1); Hayek to Gombrich, 14 February and 28 October 1944, Popper Archives (406, 6).

[181] The Popper–Gombrich correspondence (300, 3) contains a few of the revisions to vol. 1, and box 28, file 16 has all revisions to vol. 2. The 1942 manuscript (28, 12; 29, 1) can be compared with the first edition for the remaining revisions to vol. 1.

encouraged him to apply.[182] He preferred the LSE, but needed a backup. In January he applied for a professorship in Perth (Australia) and a lecturship in Sydney. In early March, he read in the papers that questions were being raised in the Australian parliament about the appointment of a foreigner, one Popper, at Sydney. He cabled his withdrawal but was urged to reconsider, wavered for two months hoping to hear from London, then declined a second time in early May. Next, he applied for a fellowship at Balliol College, Oxford, and a position at the University of Durham, but got neither: Beyond the circle of philosophers familiar with *Logik*, he was still unknown. Before the bad news arrived, he had heard from London.[183]

The advertisement for the LSE readership came out in early January 1945. In addition to the vice-chancellor and principal (ex-officio), the committee included four LSE members – Carr-Saunders, Ginsberg, Hayek, and Tawney; one internal expert, Spinoza scholar H. F. Hallett; and two external experts, Oxford moral philosopher and Aristotle scholar David Ross and philosopher L. J. Russell.[184] Hayek had warned Popper and Gombrich that as a committee member, he would have to be discreet, but he continued advising Gombrich to the end. Gombrich applied on February 5, submitting Popper's statement detailing his studies, teaching, and publications; three testimonials (Findlay, Hight, Bohr); and three references (Braithwaite, Moore, Woodger).[185] The committee was to meet for interviews and a decision on March 21, but a fortnight before, the date was moved ahead a day or two. Hayek's scheme almost fell apart. He had to leave for the United States (to promote his book) in a war convoy on the meeting's date, and he heard some bad news. Having read "Poverty, I" and "II," Ginsberg withdrew his support, taken aback by what he regarded as Popper's hubris and dogmatism. Hallett, the internal expert, was against Popper. There were nine candidates, including Friedrich Waismann. Hayek sent the chair a detailed evaluation, concluding that Popper was the only possibility. To his

[182] Popper to Hayek, 23 October 1944, Hayek Archives (44, 1).

[183] Popper to Gombrich, 26 January, 14 February, and 4 May 1945; Gombrich to Popper, 28 April 1945; cable declining Sydney, 8 march 1945 (300, 1); Gombrich to Hayek, 12 March 1945; Popper to Hayek, 11 April 1945, Hayek Archives (44, 1).

[184] The registrar's letter (Hayek Archives [44, 1]) indicated Sir Malcolm Dougal, not Tawney, as a member, but John Watkins, "Karl Raimund Popper 1902–1994": 657–60, had access to the LSE. records, and offers the composition in my text. Most of the LSE staff was drafted; Robbins was serving in the war cabinet's economic section. Hayek, who had only occasional war assignments, was free to engage in academic politics.

[185] Popper's statement (Hayek Archives [44, 1]) represented a straight intellectual and professional path. He avowed consistent interest in the rational foundation of science since studying with Hahn in the early 1920s, and indicated that he qualified as a teacher in 1926 with a thesis on axiomatics in geometry. (He qualified first in 1924, requalified at the institute in 1927, and completed the thesis in 1929.) Braithwaite wrote an outstanding reference for Popper's application to Dunedin: Popper to Gombrich, 14 February 1945.

surprise, the external experts endorsed Popper, and the committee agreed.[186] Popper was appointed.

Hayek had requested that Popper be notified by cable, but the university would put nothing in writing before the senate approved. Gombrich's desperate inquiries remained unanswered. Upon his return on May 16, Hayek cabled Popper, reaching him on May 21, aboard a bus in a remote village, on his trip back from Mt. Cook.[187] Popper's joy was immense. Gombrich had wondered earlier whether Popper really wanted to return to a London that had suffered war damage and was depressive, expensive, and tumultuous, especially when a better-paid position in calm Dunedin was within grasp. Hennie had grown to like New Zealand's peace, quiet, outdoor life, and inoffensive politics, and feared London's bustle and social obligations: "I hate meeting new people, and tea parties." Still, she worried about her sick mother in Salzburg, and "the thought of returning to the Old World is very attractive, though God knows what it will be like." Besides, they must return for Karl.[188] He was never in doubt. He wanted a new life in England, and began preparing for departure even before receiving notification of his appointment.

Before he departed New Zealand, he left a further impression on its academic life. In late May, he gave a series of lectures on scientific philosophy at Otago Medical School in Dunedin and drew crowds. (John Eccles, with whom he had formed a close friendship and research collaboration in his final years in New Zealand, had arranged for his visit, with a view to the job opening in philosophy.) Throughout the winter of 1945, Popper launched a reform movement that eventually transformed the University of New Zealand into a respectable research institution. As the university was preparing to assess its postwar aims, it solicited faculty input on research. Popper led faculty from three colleges in laying out a reform platform. They criticized current conditions in light of European universities, and argued that only confrontation with research problems would keep teaching and teachers' minds alive. In July 1945, they published a pamphlet signed by faculty in Canterbury, Otago, and Auckland, all Popper's friends. The pamphlet was excerpted in various New Zealand papers. "Popper's impact on the academic life of the College," testified a historian of the

---

[186] If Popper were to have declined the position, Casimir Lewy, a young mathematician, was to be offered a lectureship. Hayek's evaluation and his communication with Gombrich and Popper are in his archives (44, 1), but my knowledge of other committee members is due to Watkins, "Karl Raimund Popper 1902–1994": 657–60.

[187] Hayek to Vice-Chancellor Horton, 15 March 1945; Gombrich to Hayek, 17 May 1945; Popper to Hayek, 3 June 1945, all in Hayek Archives (44, 1); Hayek to Popper, 19 March and 26 May 1945, Popper Archives (305, 13); Hayek to Gombrich, 16 May 1945, Popper Archives (406, 6); Gombrich to Popper, 17 May 1945; Popper to Gombrich, 12 June 1945.

[188] Gombrich to Popper, 11 December 1944; Hennie Popper to the Gombrichs, 12 June and 4 May 1945, respectively.

University of Canterbury, "was greater than that of any person, before or since. . . . [His] most significant achievement was to force the research door open[;] . . . the movement he fathered was to become an irresistible force in the postwar years."[189]

Popper's major worries throughout the severe winter of 1945 were selling his house; shipping furniture; and obtaining exit permits, passports, entry visas into Britain, and shipping passages, apportioned by the military. He showed acumen in contacting R. M. Campbell at the New Zealand high commissioner's office in London and in calling on his New Zealand MP, and he drowned Hayek in a stream of letters requesting his assistance. Concerned about moving expenses that, together with back taxes he owed, amounted to his annual New Zealand salary, he inquired with Hayek about his future salary and status. Hayek sprang into action; Popper would start with a "major readership" at £850, going up in biannual increments to £950. By early September, he had sold his house, arranged for shipping some furniture, and procured exit permits and passports, only to be shocked by the arrival of entry permits limited to twelve months. He balked. He would qualify for New Zealand naturalization when the practice was reintroduced after the war and would not risk his right to live in the Commonwealth, and possibly be forced to return to Austria. Eventually he obtained a one-year leave from Canterbury, without resigning, and, just before he left, his MP ensured that he and Hennie would be the first New Zealanders to benefit from the reintroduction of naturalization. (Britain would naturalize him on November 1, 1946, and he would become a citizen in 1949. Austria would restore his citizenship a few decades later.) On October 16 they left Christchurch for Auckland, where they fought for freighter berths (in separate cabins, each converted from two to four passengers) through early November, finally getting space on a ship departing December 5. They sailed around Cape Horn, arriving in Britain on January 5, 1946. The Gombrichs waited at the docks, with a copy of *The Open Society*.[190]

[189] W. J. Gardner, E. T. Beardsley, and T. E. Carter, *A History of the University of Canterbury, 1873–1973* (Christchurch, N.Z.: University of Canterbury, 1973), p. 262. See also: ibid., pp. 260–8, 307–8, 393; R. S. Allan et al., "Research and the University: A Statement by a Group of Teachers in the University of New Zealand" (Christchurch, N.Z.: Caxton Press, 1945); Karl Popper, "Some Comments on the University of New Zealand and Comparisons with European Universities" (discussion of university problems by the council and staff, 6 September 1945), Popper Archives (366, 12); John Eccles, "My Living Dialogue with Popper," in *The Pursuit of Truth*, ed. Paul Levinson (Atlantic Highlands, N.J.: Humanities Press, 1982), esp. pp. 221–3.

[190] Popper read Morgenstern's and Neumann's *The Theory of Games and Economic Behavior* aboard, a further inspiration for his belief in mathematical-economic models. Popper–Hayek and Popper–Gombrich correspondence, June–December 1945; Popper to Campbell, 8 July 1945 (366, 4); Popper to Canterbury Council, 15 September 1945; Registrar to Popper, 25 September 1945 (366, 4); Gombrich, *The Open Society and Its Enemies: Remembering Its Publication Fifty Years Ago* (London: Tymes Court, 1995).

Popper was on the receiving end in his lifelong friendships with Gombrich and Hayek alike, but he was the leader in the first, reluctant follower in the second. In his postwar correspondence with Hayek, he expressed gratitude to him in terms reminiscent of prayers of thanks to the Lord for having delivered his people from exile and slavery in Egypt and led them through the wilderness:

> When I was in New Zealand, out of the world and buried by all my philosophical colleagues, you remembered me. It was through you that I came back into the world. It was through you (and Ernst Gombrich) that *The Open Society* was published, after a period (before you interfered) which led Hennie and me almost to despair. And when I came to the LSE, through you, you gave me so much encouragement and help, . . . There cannot be, ever, equality or reciprocity between you and me. I never could do anything for you, and it is extremely unlikely that I ever shall. . . . I do not consider myself intellectually your equal. . . . I know that you have broken new ways quite beyond my reach.[191]

In fact, he never accepted Hayek's superiority (and need not have; he was the more important and capable thinker). Their relationship was not free of competition, and he sought to distance himself from Hayek and guard his independence. To free *The Open Society* from association with *The Road to Serfdom* (and prevent charges of plagiarism), he inserted a note, indicating that the first volume was completed in October 1942, the second in February 1943.[192] He declined Hayek's offer to write a preface to *The Open Society:* "I am too proud," he wrote Gombrich, and "it would brand the book and myself."[193] Notwithstanding profuse thanks and adoration, he never accepted Hayek's, or anyone's, authority, or even politely concealed disagreements he considered essential. When Hayek drafted him to the libertarian Mont Pèlerin Society during the early postwar period, Popper suggested that it be turned into a wide cold-war coalition, including socialists. Since it was precisely the Social Democratic Consensus and the welfare state that Hayek wanted to challenge, his advice was subversive.[194] When he did not care much about his differences with Hayek, he expressed his criticism only surreptitiously: "[It] is not communism's lack of efficiency

---

[191] Popper to Hayek, 20 October 1964, Hayek Archives (40, 2). Popper was responding to Hayek's offer to dedicate a book to him. Compare the Jewish Saturday morning prayer נשמת כל חי (Every Creature's Soul): "Thou hast delivered us fron Egypt, Lord our God, and redeemed us from slavery. Thou hast nourished us in famine and provided us with plenty. Thou hast rescued us from violent death, made us escape the plague, and freed us from severe and lasting diseases. Until now thy mercy has helped us, and thy kindness has not abandoned us; mayest thou, Lord our God, never forsake us." It is unlikely that Popper ever saw this Jewish prayer, but there are Protestant equivalents.

[192] Popper to Gombrich, 5 June and 27 June 1944; *The Open Society*, vol. 2, p. 346 (end of notes).

[193] Gombrich, *The Open Society and Its Enemies*, p. 15.

[194] Hayek to Popper, 28 December 1946; Popper to Hayek, 11 January 1947, Popper Archives (305, 13).

that we decry [this was precisely Hayek's argument] but its lack of freedom."[195] When he disagreed strongly – with Hayek's psychology – he argued forcefully in their correspondence.[196]

In a 1984 letter, Popper spoke of Hayek as a father, and reflected on their relationship with his typical mix of psychological perceptiveness and blindness:

> I have created myself a kind of generational gulf between you and myself. Although you were only 3 years when I was born, you became, as I now realize, a kind of father figure; fortunately not in the Freudian sense – there never was a trace of this in the relation to my own father, whom I loved and greatly admired. However, you became certainly a Respectsperson [*sic*], and even now, when I am 82, and we have been friends for so many years, you still are! And, strangely enough, you yourself . . . described your feelings towards me as those towards a young man who has made good.[197]

To become a surrogate father, Hayek measured up to Popper's unreasonable expectations of protection and support and overcame his chronic suspicions about friends' loyalty. Popper did not always reciprocate. He was an unreliable correspondent, and rarely went out of his way, or interrupted his schedule, to meet Hayek. Fathers and gods, it seems, also needed to abide by the demands of Popper's philosophy.

THE DILEMMAS OF POSTWAR EUROPEAN LIBERALISM

Postwar liberals provided the intellectual core of the Social Democratic Consensus prevailing in European politics until 1968. They overcame traditional apprehensions about a state-regulated economy, and accepted a measure of socialization. Some were enthusiastic about social legislation and unsympathetic – at least until the 1970s – to libertarian litanies. Popper's political philosophy articulated their social vision. He presented piecemeal social engineering as an alternative to revolutionary socialism. No revolutionary transformation was necessary because unrestrained capitalism was gone, *The Communist Manifesto*'s major goals were achieved, and a framework for reforms existed. Marxism was superfluous.

Postwar liberals were convinced of an imminent communist threat to liberal democracy and attempted to form as broad an anticommunist consensus as they could.[198] The position a socialist party took on revolution

---

[195]   Popper, *Vorwort* to Fritz Kolb, *Es kam ganz anders* (Vienna: ÖBV, 1981).

[196]   Correspondence between Popper and Hayek, October 1952 to February 1953, Popper Archives (305, 14) and Hayek Archives (44, 1).

[197]   Popper to Hayek, 30 April 1984, Popper Archives (305, 17).

[198]   The CIA occasionally supported their efforts, channeling funds to the Congress for Cultural Freedom and *Encounter*. (The U.S. Congress would not second a progressive coalition of socialists and liberals.) Peter Coleman, *The Liberal Conspiracy* (New York: Free Press, 1989).

determined whether it was part of the consensus, or potentially totalitarian. Postwar socialist parties in Western and Central Europe – including the Austrian and, at least after 1959, the German – passed the liberal test. *The Open Society* helped establish the standard. In interwar years, Popper had argued that fascism, not capitalism, was the major problem facing Austrian socialists. In postwar years, communism became the enemy, but his call for an alliance to defend democracy retained its vitality. It was essential to convince socialists and unions that the central issue was not capitalism versus socialism, but democracy versus totalitarianism. Most socialists recognized the communist threat without liberal prompting, but *The Open Society*'s reform rhetoric made forging the consensus easier.

For all of Popper's passionate reform rhetoric, his "protectionism" and "interventionism" reflected liberal ambiguities. These were evident already in "Poverty, II," but became more pronounced in postwar years. By "protectionism" he meant the state protecting the freedoms of all members, freedom understood broadly as expansive social rights and economic security. Laissez-faire, he argued,

> faces the problem: What freedom should the state protect? The freedom of the labor market, which amounts to the freedom of the rich to oppress the poor, or the freedom of the poor to unite? Whichever decision is taken, it leads to state-intervention, to the use of organized political power . . . in the field of economic conditions. . . . [A] free market is paradoxical. If the state does not interfere, then other semi-political organizations, such as monopolies, trusts, unions, etc. may interfere, reducing the freedom of the market to a fiction.[199]

Society had a moral responsibility to alleviate suffering, and modern technology made resolving all major social problems possible, above all eliminating poverty: "We must not blame anybody else any longer, nor cry out against the sinister economic demons behind the scenes. For . . . [w]e can tame them."[200] Taming demons was not, however, without risk. At points, Popper argued that

> the alleged clash between freedom and security . . . turns out to be a chimera. For there is no freedom if it is not secured by the state; and conversely, only a state which is controlled by the free citizens can offer them any reasonable security. . . . The important and difficult question of the limitation of freedom cannot be solved by a cut and dried formula.[201]

Later, he voiced concern lest growing state power endanger liberty. Upholding the Kantian distinction between legal impartiality and individual authority, he hoped to introduce reforms "of the 'institutional

---

[199] *The Open Society*, vol. 2, p. 167, and chap. 20, n. 26.   [200] Ibid., vol. 2, p. 120.
[201] Ibid., vol. 2, pp. 97–8.

framework' [rather than] give officials power to intervene." This was "a corner stone of democratic political theory."[202] He somehow believed that such reforms would be sufficient to realize his comprehensive welfare agenda.

A look at these reforms may clarify why Popper could be so sanguine: limit exploitation (by shortening the working day); insure the workers (and all citizens) against disability, unemployment, and old age; guarantee livelihood to everybody willing to work, and so forth. Should these be enacted, said Popper, "the protection of the freedom of the citizen from economic terrorism will approach completeness."[203] At no point did he concede that socialization was necessary. Put on the spot by Carnap – "[W]ould you agree . . . that it is necessary to transfer at least the bulk of the means of production from private into public hands?" – he quibbled: "I am neither prosocialization nor against it. . . . There is a need for a much greater equalization of incomes than in any state I know," but there are means short of socialization, such as increased productivity and taxation, to address the problem. Business monopolies are politically dangerous, and, if they cannot be broken, "I am even rather strongly in favor of . . . socialization," provided socialization's "serious dangers" were recognized, and it was not regarded as a "cure-all."[204] This marked him clearly as an antilibertarian, a firm supporter of the mixed economy and the welfare state, even a mild social democrat. Still, there was nothing radical about his reforms. Many had already been introduced in Western and Central Europe by World War II; the rest required no significant institutional adjustment. For the most part, advanced capitalist societies had already deployed social technology. "What Marx called 'capitalism' . . . has completely 'withered away' in the twentieth century," superseded by collectivist interventionism in Russia, democratic interventionism in the smaller democracies, the New Deal in America, and fascism.[205] Popper was most passionate about social reforms that had already been achieved.

Late-nineteenth-century social liberals recognized that freedom meant little to the economically deprived and educationally disadvantaged. Many liberals preferred to carry out social reforms through voluntary associations and cooperatives, but were willing to extend state power as well. To some, social reform was a vehicle to unify the nation for the imperialist struggle; to others, a fulfillment of a moral religious mission; yet to others, a product of a humanistic or scientific vision.[206] Viennese progressivism represented

---

[202] Popper to Hayek, 1 June 1944, Popper Archives (305, 13).

[203] *The Open Society*, vol. 2, p. 118.

[204] Carnap to Popper, 17 November 1946; Popper to Carnap, 6 January 1947, Carnap Collection.

[205] *The Open Society*, chap. 18, n. 9.

[206] For the British: L. T. Hobhouse, *Liberalism* [1911] (New York: Oxford University Press, 1964) and J. A. Hobson, *The Crisis of Liberalism* [1909] (New York: Barnes & Noble, 1974). Secondary works: Stefan Collini, *Liberalism and Sociology* (Cambridge: Cambridge University Press, 1979); Peter Clarke,

the entire spectrum from nationalists to statists to cosmopolitans and social engineers. Popper rethought the progressive platform, but did not advance beyond it. "Interventionism" was premised on the liberal state as protector of liberty, not on equality. In his famous essay, "Citizenship and Social Class" (1949), T. H. Marshall argued that citizenship did not require eliminating all socioeconomic differences, but those relevant to the exercise of citizenship had to disappear.[207] Popper never made a similar argument. Like many social liberals who lived to see the Beveridge Report of 1943 and postwar labor governments, he felt uncomfortable with broad socialization, unions' expanded role, high rates of taxation, and, above all, the expanding civil service. Together with the social liberals, but at a younger age, he switched to the conservatives. In 1946, he warned Hayek that "should your proposition [that 'individual freedom is incompatible with a full satisfaction . . . of distributive justice'] be true[,] . . . then a real tragic conflict exists, and freedom must destroy itself. . . . I shall not easily be convinced." In his old age, he was convinced. A genuine dilemma existed, and "liberty before equality."[208]

In postwar years, Popper no longer demonstrated commitment to reform. His two goals, reduction in government and social legislation, were often in tension.[209] In *The Open Society*, he glossed it over and upheld both socialist and liberal ideals. The balance gradually shifted. He never disavowed piecemeal engineering, but he argued that its purpose was to decrease, not increase, state power. He also showed growing sympathy toward libertarianism, and did little to stop the conservative onslaught of the 1980s.[210] To be sure, he never believed in the market, and continuously warned that permitting high unemployment would undermine democracy. With the fall of communism, Hayek urged a rapid transition to a market economy. Popper advised a gradual transition that would guard against deterioration of living standards and permit, first and

---

Liberals and Social Democrats (Cambridge: Cambridge University Press, 1978); and James T. Kloppenberg, *Uncertain Victory* (New York: Oxford University Press, 1986). William Logue traces similar tendencies in France: *From Philosophy to Sociology* (Chicago: Northern Illinois University Press, 1983). For Germany: James Sheehan, *German Liberalism in the Nineteenth Century* (Chicago: University of Chicago Press, 1978).

[207] T. H. Marshall, "Citizenship and Social Class," in his *Class, Citizenship and Social Development* (Chicago: University of Chicago Press, 1977).

[208] *Autobiography*, p. 36; idem, "Freiheit vor Gleichheit," in the *Frankfurter Allgemeine Zeitung*, 24 December 1976; my interview with Popper.

[209] *The Open Society*, pp. 121–3 (chap. 17, sec. 6), and 2d. ed., pp. 131–3 (chap. 17, sec. 7), "the paradox of economic planning": If reformers were not cautious, planning could inadvertently end up limiting liberty by increasing state power.

[210] In a 1982 interview with Franz Kreuzer, *Offene Gesellschaft–offenes Universum* (Vienna: Deuticke, 1982), p. 20, Popper even expressed some sympathy with anarchism, which he had dismissed in *The Open Society*, chap. 17, n. 8, and chap. 18, n. 4. It was, he said, an unrealizable ideal, but the closest we can get to it, the better off freedom is. See also: "Gespräch" in *Theorie und Politik aus kritisch-rationaler Sicht*, ed. Georg Lühr et al. (Berlin: Dietz, 1978), pp. 21–5.

foremost, establishing the rule of law.[211] He was wiser than Hayek, as was his liberal cohort, but he never made good on his reform rhetoric; they sometimes did.

To postwar liberals, mass politics seemed to put liberty at risk, parliament incapable of protecting it. Fascist and communist parties took advantage of parliamentary and electoral politics, enjoying the support of significant constituencies. As universal suffrage was a fait accompli, postwar liberals had to rethink the relationship of liberalism and democracy. Popper's solution was simple: He redefined democracy as liberalism: "I suggest the term 'democracy' for a government of which we can get rid without bloodshed: . . . the social institutions provide means by which the rulers may be dismissed by the ruled, and the social traditions ensure that these institutions will not easily be destroyed by those . . . in power."[212] Democracy was a mechanism for orderly removal of rulers. This conformed to nineteenth-century liberal ideals, and was close to Schumpeter's definition of modern democracy as competition for power among elites, but it had nothing to do with the common understanding of democracy: equal participation, self-determination, republicanism.[213] Popper was open about it:

> Seen in this light, the theory of democracy is not based upon the principle that the majority should rule; rather, the various equalitarian methods of democratic control, such as general elections and representative government, are to be considered as no more than well-tried and, in the presence of a wide-spread tradition of distrust of tyranny, reasonably effective institutional safe-guards against tyranny.[214]

Liberals traditionally regarded representative government and, later, universal suffrage, as the modern equivalent of political participation in the *polis*. Popper thought that they were mere instruments to prevent dictatorship. Democracy served liberalism.

Not that Popper had elitist sentiments; throughout his life he disparaged those who claimed superiority to fellow humans. The common person was as good a judge of political affairs as intellectuals and politicians, and often a better one: "I hold, with Kant, that it must be the principle of all

---

[211] Karl Popper, "Advice to Russian Readers of *The Open Society*," in Colin Simkin, *Popper's Views on Natural and Social Science*, Appendix 3, pp. 198–9.

[212] Popper, *The Open Society*, 2d ed., vol. 1, p. 124.

[213] Germaine de Staël, *Considérations sur la Révolution française* [1817] (Paris: Tallandier, 1983); Benjamin Constant, "Principles of Politics Applicable to All Representative Governments," in *Political Writings*, trans. Biancamaria Fontana (New York: Cambridge University Press, 1988); John Stuart Mill, *Considerations on Representative Government* (London: Longman, 1865); Joseph Schumpeter, *Capitalism, Socialism and Democracy* (New York: Harper, 1942), chap. 22.

[214] Popper, *The Open Society*, 2d ed., vol. 1, p. 125. Note that Popper added this nonmajoritarian, liberal theory of democracy only in 1950.

morality that no man shall consider himself more valuable than any other person. I assert that this is the only acceptable principle, considering the notorious impossibility of judging oneself impartially."[215] Political equality was a function of this moral principle: Laws, rights, and duties ought to apply equally to all citizens. Popper could have chosen to extend this principle further, and argue for equal access to political power. He could have found some support for it in Kant's views on self-determination and lawfulness, but he chose not to pursue this, and regarded arrangements for apportioning political power as pragmatic. Instead of Kant's republicanism, he emphasized his "liberalism," especially his ideal of "a constitution that achieves the greatest possible freedom of human individuals by framing the laws in such a way that the freedom of each can co-exist with that of all others."[216]

This return to old-fashioned liberalism reflected the totalitarian experience. Before World War I, progressive liberals had thought it possible to endorse popular sovereignty and secure civil liberties. Mass support for fascism gave Popper pause. He concluded that the paradox of democracy was real: If the majority was sovereign, then it could decide it no longer wished a democratic government. It could, as a third of the German electorate did, vote the fascists into power. All theories of sovereignty were internally contradictory. He proposed to forgo questions about authority's source. Rather than "who should rule," ask "how can we so organize political institutions that bad or incompetent rulers can be prevented from doing too much damage."[217] No sovereignty should go unchecked.

Popper did not realize it, but he was borrowing a chapter from Constant and other liberals.[218] But, unlike them, he offered no palliative to the illiberal electorate. He neither could nor wished to limit suffrage to those social classes likely to support a liberal constitution. Should liberals "live to see the day when the majority vote destroys the democratic institutions, then this sad experience will tell them only that there does not exist a foolproof method of avoiding tyranny."[219] He could outlaw illiberal movements. Although this was difficult for a liberal government, he suggested that it was an inevitable consequence of the paradox of tolerance:

---

[215] *The Open Society*, chap. 6, n. 20 (3).   [216] Ibid., chap. 6, n. 4.   [217] Ibid., vol. 1, p. 107.

[218] Constant, *Political Writings*; Germaine de Staël, *Considérations*; François Guizot, *Histoire des origines du Gouvernement Représentatif en Europe*, 2 vols. (Paris: Didier, 1851); Alexis de Toqueville, *Democracy in America* (New York: Doubleday, 1975). Popper did not know the French liberals (but he read Mill and T. H. Green and expressed agreement with their views). His contemporaries, notably Raymond Aron (1905–80), Isaiah Berlin (1909–98), and Jacob Talmon (1916–80), thought that the original liberal problem – the defense of liberty against absolutism and Jacobin, or plebiscitary, democracy – reflected their own predicament, and they emphasized their affinities with nineteenth-century liberals.

[219] Popper, *The Open Society*, 2d ed., vol. 1, p. 125.

Unlimited tolerance must lead to the disappearance of tolerance. . . . I do not imply . . . that we should always suppress the utterance of intolerant philosophies; as long as we can counter them by rational argument and keep them in check by public opinion, suppression would certainly be most unwise. But we should claim the *right* to suppress them. . . . [A]ny movement preaching intolerance places itself outside the law.[220]

Popper did not limit suppression to political activities, but extended it to speech. He had in mind the fascists, their terror, and hysterical speeches, but it was not difficult to extend the principle to communists. His proposal acquired ominous meaning during the cold war, especially in the context of McCarthyism.[221] He never openly seconded restrictions on communists (and was harassed on account of his past communist associations when he applied for a U.S. visa in 1956).[222] But he did not offer second thoughts on the paradox of tolerance, either. He would do what was necessary to guard liberty, even at liberty's cost.

Suppression was a last resort. How did one pursue democracy? Against abundant evidence that liberal democratic politics did not permit effective articulation of marginal groups' interests, postwar liberals insisted that popular participation and representation were viable. They developed the New Democratic Theory, which regarded modern politics as a competition of elites over the vote and of organized interests over allocation of political and economic resources. Individual participation and representation might be fictitious, but organized citizens had a fair chance. Radical critics claimed that this was wishful thinking: Elites circumvented or manipulated channels, and adverse demands got entangled.[223] Liberals usually dodged the radical critiques. Whereas civil liberties elicited their loyalty and passion, political and social equality did not. In stating his indifference to classical democracy openly, Popper expressed a belief most of his liberal cohort kept quiet.[224]

Popper and postwar liberals recognized socialist ideals as enlightened and humanitarian, but insisted that utopian socialism was bound to end in totalitarianism. The idea of "inevitable revolution" reflected eschatological and chiliastic expectations for the end of history, a messianic vision of a heavenly kingdom descending on earth. Such a vision, said Popper, "only succeeds in making a hell – that hell which man alone prepares for his fellow man."[225] Raymond Aron and Jacob Talmon echoed Popper. Talmon argued

[220] Ibid., chap. 7, n. 4, added either between February and April 1943, or between April and June 1944.

[221] On the same issue, see Sidney Hook, *Heresy, Yes: Conspiracy, No!* (New York: John Day, 1953).

[222] Popper to Hayek, 14 August 1956, Hayek Archives (44, 1).

[223] For a new democratic theorist turned critic: Charles Lindblum, *Politics and Markets* (New York: Basic Books, 1977).

[224] *The Open Society*, 2d ed., vol. 1, pp. 124–5. See also: "On Reason and the Open Society," *Encounter* 38 (1972): 13–18.

[225] *The Open Society*, 1st ed., vol. 2, p. 148.

that both the French Revolution, in its Jacobin phase, and Marxist socialism reflected secularized and politicized messianism, searching for salvation
in this world. Encountering resistance, revolutionaries rarely hesitated
resorting to the worst repression: The future of humanity was at stake; no
sacrifice seemed too high. The irrational yearning for a harmonic social
order was the source of a messianic neurosis. To Aron, Marxism responded
to the emotional needs of alienated intellectuals, promising liberation, providing a key to history, convincing believers of its inevitability. Marxist
culture created myths that had little to do with reality, or even with Marx,
and remained immune to criticism: an ideal Revolution, a unified Left, and
the Proletariat. These myths excused the worst Stalinist atrocities. The
majority of the French intelligentsia cast their lot with totalitarianism.
Marxism was the opium of the intellectuals: a secular religion shielding its
believers from reality, demanding total belief and obedience, sanctioning
murder.[226]

Postwar liberals fought the nightmares of the death camps and the gulags,
but their rhetoric of "nonviolence" had a long and respectable tradition.
As liberalism emerged in response to the Jacobin terror and Napoleon's
imperialism, control of violence was its major concern. De Staël and Constant regarded Jacobinism and imperialism as disastrous attempts to revive
ancient military virtues. Commerce had a civilizing effect (*doux commerce*)
on modern society, rendering warfare obsolete, establishing alternative
modes of communication and interaction.[227] To Thierry and Guizot,
modern constitutions domesticated violence: Parliament substituted speech
and debate for armed struggle.[228] Reason, or compromise, prevailed over
force. Around the turn of the century, Weber and Pareto suggested that this
was wishful thinking: The state merely contained and monopolized violence, then rechanneled it to international politics. Their *Realpolitik*
informed postwar liberalism – Aron's work on international relations, for
example – but insofar as domestic politics was concerned, liberals insisted

---

[226] Raymond Aron, *The Opium of the Intellectuals* (New York: Doubleday, 1957); Jacob Talmon, *The Origins of Totalitarian Democracy* (London: Secker and Warburg, 1952); *Political Messianism* (London: Secker and Warburg, 1960).

[227] Germaine de Staël, *De la littérature considérée dans ses rapports avec les institutions sociales*, 2 vols. (Geneva: Droz, 1959); Constant, "The Spirit of Conquest and Usurpation (1813–15)," *Political Writings*. De Staël and Constant distinguished between ancient democracy, whose virtues were military, and modern society, which permitted enjoyment of personal liberties. The Jacobins emulated Sparta. (Talmon argued the same.) Until the 1970s, postwar liberals defended consumer culture against complaints that it weakened Western resolve to fight communism. Republican critics of commerce have argued since the seventeenth century that commerce "effeminized." Liberals responded that "civilized" did not mean effeminate – they remained masculine – and, at the same time, ascribed to femininity much of the progress in civilization and morals.

[228] Lionel Gossman, "Augustin Thierry and Liberal Historiography," *History and Theory*, Beiheft 15 (1976): 3–83.

that politics adequately, even justly, arbitrated social conflicts, and the use of (revolutionary) violence was criminal.

Carl Schmitt, a fascist critic of liberalism, observed that liberalism displaced conflict from the military to the economic and intellectual spheres, rechanneling violence into competition.[229] Popper's philosophy is a fine example of such displacement. Resisting dictatorship was the sole goal justifying violence. Democracy provided effective mechanisms for changing rulers, resolving conflicts, and persuading opponents. (In the future, an international order would do the same.) Yet, democracy depended on a culture of critical debate that assumed the character of war: "[I]t is the great tradition of Western rationalism to fight our battles with words rather than with swords."[230] Popper defended the weak by regulating economic competition, but expected ruthless intellectual rivalry, a Darwinian struggle of ideas. Whence the hope that a democratic consensus would emerge from ruthless criticism, or that competing interests would yield to the force of better argument? Schmitt complained that never-ending parliamentary debate made decision impossible and consensus unlikely, and that deals were actually cut behind closed doors. Popper did not answer the complaint.

Shaping a democratic political culture could answer Schmitt, but Popper had no way of doing it, leaving democracy too fortuitous. Should voters fail to see freedom's blessings, he threw his hands in the air. Tocqueville emphasized the crucial role of communal organizations, political participation, and religion in forming a democratic consensus. Mill believed that secular education may enlighten the lower classes. Popper did not avail himself of earlier liberal solutions, and had none of his own. His focus remained negative liberty: freedom from political, religious, and scientific authority.[231] To be sure, critical discussion implied beliefs and attitudes that Popper called rational and humanitarian. They required cultivation, but he deprived himself of the means of promoting them, refusing any foundational vision of the good society and declining to use education to cultivate virtues. He offered no guidelines, informed by sociology, psychology, or history, for molding a democratic consensus. Nonfoundationism became the distinctive mark of a new liberalism the strengths and appeal of which were matched only by its problems.

[229] Carl Schmitt, *Die geistesgeschichtliche Lage des heutigen Parlamentarismus*, 2d. ed. (Berlin: Duncker & Humblot, 1926); *The Concept of the Political* [1932] (New Brunswick, N.J.: Rutgers University Press, 1976).

[230] *The Open Society*, vol. 2, Addendum to the 4th ed., p. 396.

[231] Isaiah Berlin, "Two Concepts of Liberty" [1958], in his *Four Essays on Liberty* (New York: Oxford University Press, 1968), pp. 118–72. Popper admired Berlin's essay, but he argued that "only those who have, more or less, adopted [the] Socratic way of life can fully understand . . . negative freedom. . . . [M]ay not the search for truth – *sapere aude* – be part of a positive idea of self-liberation?" (Popper to Berlin, 17 February 1959 [276, 10].) This shows that he had a vision of the good life and understood that liberalism was anchored in it. Like God, however, it remained a subject of silence.

ETHICS, SCIENCE, AND DEMOCRACY

Popper's moral theory modified Kant, emphasizing the subjective dimensions of his ethics and narrowly defining the scope of issues falling under the categorical imperative (the command of reason, thou shall do *x*). Following Kant, Popper argued that morality could not be derived from human nature, and moral virtue was not identical with self-interest. "Ethical naturalism," whether Aristotelian–Thomistic natural law or modern natural right, was wrong. "Ethical positivism," the view that existing laws determined morality, was pernicious, equivalent to "might is right." "The existence of moral ideals *is* a sort of practical refutation of moral positivism."[232] Morality and legality must be separated: "What we need and what we want is to moralize politics, and not to politicize morals."[233] Popper encouraged the "scientific attitude toward ethics," but maintained that there was no "scientific ethics": A scientifically derived moral judgment would end freedom, hence morality. He radicalized Kant's defense of autonomy (against determinism), purging Kant of naturalistic and psychologistic residues. At points, he said, Kant thought that he could deduce the categorical imperative logically, at points psychologically; at others he recognized that it was not deducible. Truly, the categorical imperative could be justified neither by "rational nature" nor by pure motives. Just as Kant's transcendental deduction failed in epistemology, it failed in ethics; it presupposed universality and lawfulness that could not be proven. Things were fairly simple: As no synthetic statement could be proved, no science of ethics was possible.[234]

Popper declined Kant's "moral good" as well. Any definition, or judgment, of the good was superfluous. Even if the good were determinable – which it was not; it evoked immediately the question of the authority declaring something to be good – why the good ought to be of concern to us still needed to be answered. Moreover, "preoccupation with the

---

[232] Popper, "A Non-Psychological Justification of the Categorical Imperative" (366, 14). This is problematic: Popper did not believe that the existence of scientific theories is "a sort of practical refutation" of skepticism. Why are things different with ethics? Jeremy Shearmur, *The Political Thought of Karl Popper* (London: Routledge, 1996), p. 197, n. 4, is skeptical that this Canterbury typescript, attributed to "Professor Popper," was indeed his ("some of the terminology in which the argument is developed does not seem characteristic of Popper"), but regards it as reflecting Popper's concerns at the time. Possibly, it was a student's transcript. (Someone typed notes taken at Popper's lectures in 1941 [366, 24]. They were, on occasion, less than coherent. "A Non-Psychological Justification" is a more finished product, but this may be its origin.)

[233] *The Open Society*, vol. 2, p. 99.

[234] Ibid., chap. 5, n. 18 (1); philosophy lectures, Canterbury College, 1941, pp. 25–30 (under W.E.A. course, 366, 24). At points, however, Popper's objections seemed directed less at Kant's derivation of the imperative and more at his injecting it with content. He himself seemed to suggest the argument he criticized. If there were ethics, he said, the categorical imperative would be its necessary and sufficient condition. As there was . . . But, of course, was there? Popper was thinking his way.

motives of actions is misguided and harmful in ethics." It was precisely the anticipated consequences of one's actions, which Kant excluded in pure motives' name, that ought to guide moral decision. (In Shaw's *Saint Joan*, the accuser breaks down, alas too late, when witnessing Joan of Arc burning at the stake, saying: I did not intend it.) Nor was application of the categorical imperative to complex situations as easy and simple as Kant imagined. Indeed, the ethic of pure motives (*Gesinnungsethik*) did not exist at all." 'Act from a pure moral motive' is, from a pragmatic point of view, self-contradictory."[235]

In *The Open Society*, Popper devoted most of his attention to historicist moral theory. He correctly observed that Marx did not develop ethics, but proceeded to fill in the gap. Marx dangerously combined relativism, determinism, and political activism, depriving individuals of agency and judgments of universality: Historical conditions determined "correct" judgment. Marx faced a problem: Having reduced morality to historical necessity, what judgment remained for agents to make, and what actions to take? Marxists bridged the gap between historicism and activism: "[H]elp bring about the inevitable future." Socialism was both historical and (fortunately) moral necessity, and historical agents "can actively assist in shortening and lessening [the] birth-pangs" of socialism.[236] Popper rejected this outright. Moral decision could not be derived from knowledge of the future. Even if people could know what history's judgment would be, they would still have to decide whether to abide by it; history's judgment was notoriously wrong. Values or standards could never be deduced from facts, and moral norms could no more be derived from history than from nature. Moral decisions depended, to be sure, on background and context, but they were not determined by it. People growing up in similar circumstances made different decisions, learned from mistakes, and changed their views. Like Isaiah Berlin and other postwar liberals, Popper sought to save a measure of individual autonomy and agency in the sphere of morality.[237]

This was an eloquent defense of the moral individual, but Popper's moral agnosticism could degenerate into subjectivism and value relativism. If neither nature nor history provided moral standards, what informed

---

[235] Popper, "A Non-Psychological Justification." Kant recognized as much, suggesting in *Grounding for the Metaphysics of the Morals* that even if pure moral action had never taken place, this made no difference to morality and pure motive. Popper's stance was identical to Weber's ethics of responsibility (*Verantwortungsethik*). His brief critique of Kant's *Gesinnungsethik* showed, in my view, excellent judgment.

[236] *The Open Society*, vol. 2, p. 192.

[237] Isaiah Berlin, "Historical Inevitability," in his *Four Essays on Liberty*, pp. 41–117. According to Popper, the anticipated consequences of one's actions appropriately influenced moral decision. Could "Marxist ethic" not be justified by the long-term consequences of collective interaction? Yes, but such long-term calculation was both unscientific and harmful to individual decision.

individual "moral" decisions? At a minimum, Popper needed an alternative justification for the categorical imperative, the universal moral rule. He found it in the community of reason. He extended "intersubjectivity" from scientific testing to public criticism and established it as rationality's criterion. Just as intersubjective criticism was a necessary and sufficient condition for science, so it was for ethics. It implied equality and impartial truth: One must be willing to subject one's judgment to criticism and change it; other people had the right to be heard. Values were reasonable beliefs, subject to criticism and argument: "We can learn in the realm of standards just as well as in the realm of facts."[238] Only communicable and criticizable positions were ethical: "We cannot deduce synthetic moral principles from the mere idea of ethics; we can only infer from it that if there is an ethics, then it must have this impartial, impersonal character."[239]

Already in *Logik der Forschung*, the community of reason was essential to Popper's redefinition of scientific "objectivity." Since he disposed of foundationism, science became intersubjective and involved communal acceptance and rejection of experiments. To function properly, it needed a critical public, but in *Logik der Forschung*, Popper paid no attention to institutions. He discussed the logic of science, not the sociology of the scientific community. When he spoke of observation, experiment, and refutation, he made no distinction between the individual scientist and the community. The logic of science applied equally to both. He seemed to take the Central European community of scientists and philosophers as a matter of course. He presupposed a Republic of Science but did not formulate a vision of it.

Ethics and politics forced Popper to focus on science's public character. Seeking an alternative criterion for moral and political rationality, and a vindication of the moral individual and the Open Society against fascism, he recognized similarities between his scientific, moral, and political ideals. Critical discussion demarcated science, ethics, and politics. His 1941 lectures on Kant's ethics provided a first glimmer of intersubjective criticism as a criterion of rationality, and his critique of the sociology of knowledge in *The Open Society* provided his first view on the "social aspects of knowledge [and] scientific method."[240] He had long been skeptical about Marx's critique of ideology and about unmasking opponents' class bias. In *Ideology and Utopia*, Mannheim extended Marx's critique to Marxism itself and

---

[238] *The Open Society*, vol. 2, Addendum to the 4th ed., p. 386.

[239] Popper, "A Non-Psychological Justification," p. 5. Jeremy Shearmur (*The Political Thought of Karl Popper*, p. 91) points out that this still provided no guidance to moral judgment, and it remained unclear how judgments were morally constrained. Even in the 1961 Addendum to *The Open Society* (p. 386), combating value relativism, Popper could only advise "that cruelty is always 'bad'; that it should always be avoided where possible; that the golden rule is a good standard which can perhaps even be improved by doing unto others, wherever possible, as *they* would be done by."

[240] *The Open Society*, vol. 2, p. 205.

entrusted intellectuals with initiating a dialogue that would increase awareness of multiple perspectives and synthesize them, thereby producing objective science. Intellectuals' understanding of ideas' social conditioning – their own included – would contribute, he hoped, to creating a "total ideology."[241] Such an approach, argued Popper, misunderstood scientific objectivity and "destroyed the basis of rational discussion."[242] Science was not

> a process in the mind or "consciousness" of the individual scientist. . . . If scientific objectivity were founded . . . upon the individual scientist's impartiality or objectivity, then we should have to say good-bye to it. . . . Science and scientific objectivity . . . result . . . from the co-operation of many scientists, . . . the inter-subjectivity of scientific method.[243]

Science's social institutions – laboratories, periodicals, congresses – furthered critical openness. They provided a model for politics. If political institutions and discussions could be modeled on scientific ones, the Open Society would be forthcoming. The Open Society emulated the Republic of Science and, in turn, guaranteed the freedom essential to scientific progress. Totalitarianism would put an end to free criticism, destroying science.

The defense of science and the Open Society was one. Against the irrationalism, romanticism, and mysticism that Popper associated with the fascist attack on democracy, he developed his own critical rationalism. Public discussion was its core, and trust in it was the Open Society's philosophy. Humanitarianism and egalitarianism were most compatible with the scientific ethos of criticism. This brought together Popper's philosophy of science, ethics, and politics, *Logik der Forschung* and *The Open Society*:

> Critical rationalism . . . with its emphasis upon argument and experience, with its device "I may be wrong and you may be right, and by an effort we may get nearer to the truth," is . . . closely akin to the scientific attitude. It is bound up . . . with the idea that the other fellow has a right to be heard, and to defend his arguments. . . . In this way, rationalism is linked up with the recognition of the necessity of social institutions to protect freedom of criticism [and with] something like a moral obligation towards . . . practical social engineering – piecemeal engineering, of course – . . . for the ratio-

---

[241] Karl Mannheim, *Ideologie und Utopie* (Bonn: Cohen, 1929). Popper's reading of Mannheim was not unfair, but ungenerous. Mannheim strove to make the social conditioning of political perspectives part of the scientific dialogue. He assumed that such a conversation would facilitate understanding of opponents' perspectives and discussion of opposing truth claims. The sociology of knowledge cannot be entrusted, *pace* Mannheim, with arbitrating truth claims, but it can facilitate, *pace* Popper, the critical discussion that does.

[242] Popper, *The Open Society*, vol. 2, p. 204.

[243] Ibid., p. 205. (In later editions Popper emphasized: "the *friendly-hostile co-operation* of many scientists.")

nalization of society. . . . [Moreover, it implies] a common language of reason
. . . [and] recognizes the unity of human reason.[244]

Thinkers from Kant to Habermas hit upon the critical public as guarantor of rationality.[245] They also shared its dilemmas. Popper's public
remained an ideal, an *ought* rather than an *is*. How did the public, or intersubjective criticism, really work? It was not clear that access was available
to all, certainly not equal access. (Popper's difficulties at getting his own
books published could have alerted him to that.) Once ideas entered the
public sphere, who won? Did the logic of science and social reform really
set discussion rules? Without a sociology of science and politics, the public
remained a regulative ideal at best. Popper's rejection of the sociology of
knowledge and his reservations about class analysis foreclosed any arbitration between logical and sociological factors in the making of the scientific and political consensus. We have no better standard for scientific and
political rationality than his. He successfully constructed critical rationalism as a liberal democratic philosophy, and eloquently defended the Open
Society against totalitarianism, but he did not show that open scientific and
political communities actually existed. And he left us no instructions on
how to get there.

"The foundation of all knowledge," said Popper, "is a matter of free
choice of a goal that cannot be rationally justified."[246] "Only those sharing
the same goal can rationally argue over differences of opinion."[247] How,
then, did a consensus on basic scientific and political values emerge? Popper
never answered. A scientific consensus existed, and a political one was
within reach, if the fascists were defeated. He could try to persuade opponents of critical rationalism and democracy, but it was not his task to explore
how a consensus might be formed. His indifference was mistaken. He
himself recognized that if the scientific community failed to agree on test
statements, testing was in jeopardy: "If someday it should no longer be possible for scientific observers to reach agreement about basic statements, this
would amount to the failure of language as a means of universal communication . . . a new 'Babel of Tongues.' . . . The soaring edifice of science
would soon lie in ruins."[248] Scientific discourse was at the mercy of sociological and psychological factors. They could prove more consequential

---

[244] Ibid., pp. 224–6. The quotation represents selections from one lengthy paragraph.

[245] The Enlightenment's "public sphere" (*Öffentlichkeit*), as transformed by Habermas into the "ideal
speech situation," represents Popper's critical discussion and intersubjective criticism at their best.

[246] Popper, *Die beiden Grundprobleme der Erkenntnistheorie* (Tübingen: Mohr, 1979), p. 395.

[247] Popper, *Logik*, p. 10. "[E]inen vernüftigen, argumentierenden Meinungsstreit kann es jedoch nur
zwischen denen geben, die denselben Zweck verfolgen." In *LSD*, p. 37, n. *5, Popper retracted this
statement: Rational discussion (not agreement!) was always possible between interested parties. This
made consensus possible in principle, but did not contribute to its formation.

[248] *Logik*, p. 61; *LSD*, p. 104. (Popper's translation here is rather free, but nicely captures the rhetorical bent of the original.)

to science than logic and methodology. How much truer this would be of politics!

Popper was aware of some dimensions of the problem, unaware of others, and to none did he find satisfactory solutions. He viewed the democratic state as guarantor of the public sphere, and insisted that moral virtues were none of its business. Most critics of democracy

> do not understand what democratic institutions may be expected to do. . . . Democracy . . . provides the institutional framework for reform, . . . [for] the use of reason in the designing of new institutions and the adjusting of old ones. It cannot provide reason. . . . (The idea that the problem [of the intellectual and moral standard of the citizen] can be tackled . . . by . . . educational control is mistaken.) . . . It rests with us to improve matters. The democratic institutions cannot improve themselves.[249]

He opposed state involvement in education beyond the basic provision of schools, and wished for education to destroy authority, not build consensus. Appeal to the teacher's authority, teaching of science as a dogma, inculcation of values, all were illegitimate. Teachers could stimulate their students' interest in values, but this presupposed a friendship that both sides could terminate. Under present conditions, such efforts would impose and do more harm than good. He recommended intensifying (potentially iconoclastic) scientific education at the expense of (conservative) classical education.[250]

"The question of the intellectual and moral standard of [the] citizens is to a large degree a personal problem," believed Popper (as did many postwar liberals).[251] This was not the only possible liberal position. Liberalism always strove to protect a private sphere from state and society, but during the second half of the nineteenth century, two generations of English and French liberals, from T. H. Green to L. T. Hobhouse in England and Charles Renouvier to Emile Durkheim in France, endeavored to form a liberal civic culture that would enshrine individual liberties and egalitarian citizenship. The threat of totalitarianism restored the primacy of "negative liberty," but left postwar liberals with no means of forging a democratic consensus. They could no longer avail themselves of religion and education: They were apprehensive lest "education for democracy" turn into indoctrination, and, as an avowedly secular cohort (including many cosmopolitan Jews), they neither wished to cultivate established religions nor were sanguine about their beneficial effects, especially given their record in fascist Europe. Durkheim's "civic religion" they viewed with suspicion.[252]

---

[249] *The Open Society*, vol. 2, pp. 110–11. For the first clause, I used the 2d ed., p. 126.

[250] Ibid., vol. 1, pp. 97–8, 110–11, 115; vol. 2, pp. 262–4.   [251] Ibid., vol. 1, p. 110.

[252] Emile Durkheim, "The Principles of 1789 and Sociology" and "Individualism and the Intellectuals," in *Emile Durkheim on Morality and Society*, ed. Robert Bellah (Chicago: University of Chicago, 1973); *Professional Ethics and Civic Morals* (Glencoe, Ill.: Free Press, 1958).

"Secular religion" (Marxism) was a subject of denunciation, not endorsement; a threat, not a solution.

Intermediary organizations between state and individual could help, perhaps, arbitrate a consensus. Liberal sociologists and political theorists from Tocqueville to Durkheim to Robert Dahl recognized that for modern democracy to be effective, active participation in voluntary groups, organizations, and communities was necessary. Popper remained silent about voluntary associations, partially because he suspected that they represented closed societies, not democratic forums. His theory of the "abstract society," added in 1950 to *The Open Society*, described it as a society where people "practically never meet face to face – in which all business is conducted by individuals in isolation who communicate by typed letters or by telegrams, and who go about in closed motor cars. (Artificial insemination would allow even propagation without a personal element.)"[253] He emphasized that the abstract society was a model that exaggerated modernity's features, but he was far from unsympathetic to it. What has been lost in the intimacy of contact, he argued, has been gained in freedom and choice. The Open Society had both "abstract" and communal elements, but more categorically than any liberal, he rejected the latter's claims.

Could Popper envision a consensus beyond the bare "protectionist" minimum? Like most of his postwar cohort, he was suspicious of any "positive aim" of liberalism, any vision of ideal citizenship. Behind such visions always lurked the dogmatism and radicalism sustaining totalitarianism. "Monolithic social ends," he declared, "would mean the death of freedom."[254] His pluralism was radical, different in focus, perhaps, from postmodernism (race and gender virtually ignored), but not in principle. Radical pluralism had its cost: helplessness in the face of challenges to the liberal consensus. Liberals became ever more aware of the unique conditions enabling liberal democracy in the West, ever more pessimistic about its prospect elsewhere. When consensus failed, they could be persuaded to sanction military intervention: Aron supported de Gaulle's semicoup in 1958. In *The Open Society*, Popper spoke of Western colonialism as one of humanity's darkest chapters. Toward the end of his life, he bemoaned colonialism's precipitous end because it did not permit the gradual growth of democratic traditions.[255] Postwar liberals lived on edge, apprehensive about any sign of a weakening consensus, counting their blessings for living in a period of economic growth that facilitated democratic stabilization.

Popper did offer some guidelines for a reform consensus. Aware that the utilitarian formula "the greatest happiness for the greatest number" posited an ideal transcending "protectionism" and threatening freedom, Popper

---

[253] Ibid., 2d ed., p. 174 (p. 170 of the American ed.).

[254] *The Open Society*, vol. 2, Addendum to the 4th ed., p. 396.

[255] Interview, in *Der Spiegel*, June 1992, trans. in *Ha-aretz*, 27 September 1992.

suggested an alternative. Instead of "maximize happiness," "minimize suffering":

> [F]rom the moral point of view, suffering and happiness must not be treated as symmetrical; . . . the promotion of happiness is in any case much less urgent than rendering help to those who suffer. . . . [H]uman suffering makes a direct moral appeal . . . for help; . . . there is no similar call to increase the happiness of [one] doing well.[256]

Still, just as corroboration and falsification had a different logical status, but relied on the scientific consensus, so happiness and suffering had a different moral status, but required a political consensus. Defining the task of reform negatively may have eased, but not resolved, the problem of forming a consensus.[257]

Underlying Popper's conviction that public debate would give rise to a consensus in science, ethics, and politics was Kant's *Vernunftglaube*, belief in reason:

> Some may perhaps ask how an individual can demand devotion to any cause, and especially to such an abstract cause as scientific inquiry. But . . . I do not think that devotion should be *demanded*, only . . . *encouraged*. I believe that devotion to certain institutions, for instance, to those of the democratic state, and even to certain traditions, may fall well within the boundaries of individualism.[258]

Certainly; but how does one encourage such devotion to democracy and critical debate? Popper conceded that the basic choice, for or against rationalism, was "irrational": He could not argue with a Nazi youth who told him – "I do not argue; I shoot."[259] How did one cultivate

---

[256] *The Open Society*, vol. 2, chap. 5, n. 6 (2); chap. 9, n. 2.

[257] In an early postwar lecture, "Public and Private Virtues" (Popper Archives [39, 17]), Popper used negative utilitarianism to formulate a reform agenda, which, he hoped, would be acceptable to both socialists and liberals. Jeremy Shearmur argues that Popper's ethical individualism pushed toward libertarianism rather than toward negative utilitarianism that required imposition to relieve suffering: "Popper developed his ideas about protectionism and negative utilitarianism in terms of an agenda for public policy without discussing its relationship with the exercise of individual freedom, and individual moral responsibility, which he is so concerned to protect." Libertarian and socialist ideals were in conflict, Popper attempting to uphold both. (*The Political Thought of Karl Popper*, p. 103.)

[258] *The Open Society*, vol. 1, chap. 7, n. 23.

[259] William Bartley, David Miller, and Jeremy Shearmur suggest that this was an unnecessary concession to irrationalism. Critical rationalism needed to "justify" nothing. Any critical exchange already presupposed intersubjectivity. If someone did not want to engage in a dialogue, but shoot, there was nothing Popper could do, but this did not undermine philosophy or ethics, or require that he pronounce a commitment to "rationalism." Everything was open. Nazis threatening to shoot deprived themselves of ethical justification. Should they try to persuade, they had already accepted the premise of critical rationalism. (Bartley, *The Retreat to Commitment* [London: Chatto & Windus, 1962], esp. pp. 146–7; Miller, *Critical Rationalism* [Chicago: Open Court, 1994], chap. 4; Shearmur,

an irrational commitment to rationalism? This was a key question on which the political fortunes of Popper's philosophy (and postwar liberalism) could founder. When, in the wake of 1968, the Social Democratic Consensus disintegrated, postwar liberals were baffled and helpless, and they joined conservatives in lamenting the increasing demands for sharing a diminishing economic pie and the lack of resolve to combat totalitarian threats. They had no strategy for remolding the liberal consensus.

Postwar liberals felt uncomfortable with the conservative–liberal alliance of the Reagan–Thatcher era. Some joined; most remained critical. Popper never openly endorsed it, but he was not unsympathetic. Hayek, who had been considered obsolete in postwar years, became the New Right's prophet. To him, libertarianism grew out of *Logik* and *The Open Society*. In "The Use of Knowledge in Society," he suggested that the market was a systematic "discovery process": Decisions of consumers, producers, and distributors were subject to constant "testing" and correction through trial and error. Economic success depended on quick response to changing circumstances and learning from error. Markets constituted an ideal education for humanity and a model for political interaction and decision making. Discovery and testing, freedom and competition, were characteristics of science, politics, and capitalism. Scientific freedom, liberal politics, and the free market were guarantors of the open and prosperous society.[260]

Popper challenged this equation. He pointed out that productivity and justice, even liberty and justice, may conflict.[261] The analogues of science, market, and politics had only limited validity. In science, "our hypotheses die for us"; scientific revolutions were harbingers of progress. Politics and the market dealt with humans who ought never to be put at risk. Science was revolutionary, politics reformist, and the market malleable. Under ethical guidance, politics used science to shape markets. It could do so because, contrary to the opinion of Hayek, human reason was potent. Notwithstanding the catastrophes that he had witnessed – World War I, the collapse of democracy, totalitarianism, genocide – Popper remained optimistic. Pessimism was an indulgence. Those who sought a better world had to maintain Kant's *Vernunftglaube*. Only those believing

---

The Political Thought of Karl Popper, esp. p. 107.) Bartley's critique was a major advance for critical rationalism, but, historically, it *was* Popper's irrational commitment to rationalism that gave rise to his philosophy. Bartley wisely disposed of the justificationist ladder once he had seen the world aright.

[260] Hayek, "The Use of Knowledge in Society" [1945]; *Markt, Plan, Freiheit. Franz Kreuzer im Gespräch mit Friedrich von Hayek und Ralf Dahrendorf* (Vienna: Deuticke, 1983), p. 18. Jeremy Shearmur develops the argument for the market as a "system of learning" by trial and error in *The Political Thought of Karl Popper,* esp. pp. 116–19.

[261] Popper to Hayek, 28 April 1977, Popper Archives (305, 16); Popper, Preface to *Miseria dello storicismo,* 2d ed. (Milan: Feltrinelli, 1975).

could hope that the life of reason would give rise to a scientific, ethical, and political consensus that was supported by little else. The problems that our generation has faced with forming a reform consensus did not compare to those Popper had witnessed. What right did we have to lose belief so easily?

Epilogue: Popper in the Postwar World, 1946–1994

"Would you ever consider . . . returning to Vienna?" asked Carnap of Popper shortly before he departed New Zealand. "No, never!" answered Popper.[1] Alas, one does not cut ties to the homeland so easily. Popper remained ambivalent about Vienna to his last days. In 1946–7, he was sending food packages to needy Austrian relatives and friends, constantly warning his English colleagues that unless the Allies improved conditions, they were likely to witness a resurgence of political extremism. In 1948, Victor Kraft probed whether Popper might accept a professorship in Vienna.[2] Popper used the prospective offer primarily to enhance his chances of an LSE professorship, but it may have also given him pause. Conditions in Austria were still tough, but Hennie wanted badly to be back near her sick mother in Salzburg. They returned there periodically, on special permits, until her mother's death in 1949 or thereabouts. Beginning in 1948, Popper taught in the Alpbach summer school in Tyrol, established by members of the Austrian resistance to educate youth in the pan-European spirit. Their visits extended to Vienna, and Hennie enjoyed them thoroughly. Being called *Frau Professor* in her hometown, she related to Joseph Agassi, was a treat. Yet they never stayed for a long period, always hastening back to England. In 1960, trusting the most in Austrian doctors, Popper had a serious, and successful, eye operation in Vienna. In 1965 the City of Vienna awarded him the *Geisteswissenschaften* prize. The wounds of the past, it seemed, were beginning to heal.

Writing to director Otto Lange of the Springer publishing house in 1946, Popper said that "after ten years, I had lost completely my stylistic touch in German, as if I tried to set a fine instrument going with numb

---

In the Epilogue, I have tried to sketch the impact that Popper's earlier life had on his later career and point out the importance of his philosophy for current concerns. I have thus traced through the postwar period some of the salient themes of his earlier life, indicating both change and continuity. I have made no attempt to provide anything approaching a biography of the late Popper, or to convey the vast range of issues, especially scientific ones, that engaged him. The mature Popper is better known than the young one, and I look forward to future biographies of his life in England. The Epilogue is precisely what I called it – an epilogue, tying together some of the earlier themes, not endeavoring to open new ones.

[1] Carnap to Popper, 20 May 1945; Popper to Carnap, 23 June 1945, Carnap Collection.

[2] Correspondence between Victor Kraft and Popper, 1948, Popper Archives (316, 24).

fingers."[3] As his beautiful German demonstrated, he had not quite lost his touch. Rather, he did not like German. To him, the language was tainted by obscurantism and nationalism. When, in 1969, Hayek asked him to come to Salzburg where they would both receive lucrative professorships, he explained to Hayek his ambivalence about Austria and German culture in words he had never used before, or after, in his correspondence:

> Anti-Semitism is still strong in Austria. . . . I think that people of Jewish origin, like I [*sic*] (Hennie is of Lower Austrian peasant origins) should keep away, in order to allow the feeling to die down. When we considered a few years ago . . . where to settle when I retire, we thought of returning to Austria . . . but we decided against it, because of Anti-Semitism. It is, Hennie thinks, worse in Salzburg; and a university position is, clearly, more exposed than a simple retirement.[4]

His explanation reflected his ambivalence toward Austria and the problematic relationship that assimilated Viennese Jews had with their country. Popper would have had a homeland if it had not been for anti-Semitism. Austria *was* his home – that is where Hennie and he would rather have lived – and yet it was not, because Jews were singled out from among Austrians as objects of hatred. Deprived of one *Heimat*, Popper created another: cosmopolitan philosophy. He was reluctant to put it at risk by going back to Austria: "The influence of my ideas [may] be undermined by my leaving the English-speaking world," he wrote Hayek in the same letter. "I shall write even worse English . . . and I cannot help thinking – and hoping – that the English language is more important, intellectually, than the German language."

In the late 1970s, the Second Republic hesitantly began to repatriate exiles and claim their intellectual heritage as its own. The Poppers got back their Austrian citizenship in 1976, but they had no intention of returning. They wished to ensure a pension for Hennie, should Karl die first. Vienna celebrated his eightieth birthday with symposia and awards to the "great Austrian philosopher." In 1985–6, he found himself in Vienna for a year, the first time in half a century. The circumstances were somber. Hennie, suffering from terminal cancer, chose to die in Vienna, in her old neighborhood. She passed away in November 1985 and was buried with her father and maternal grandparents in the tiny Lainzer Friedhof. For a few months afterward, Popper toyed with the idea of staying in Austria. To Colin

---

[3] 25 April 1946 (352, 1): "Nach 10 Jahren habe ich das Stilgefühl im Deutschem völlig verloren, als ob man versuchen würde ein feines Instrument mit erstarrt, gefühllosen Fingern anzufassen."

[4] Popper to Hayek, 24 October 1969, Popper Archives (305, 15). Popper also discussed the financial inadvisability of such a move. Salzburg was a conservative Catholic bulwark, but the philosophy department included some Popper disciples. However, there was some opposition to his appointment. (I owe this information to Friedrich Stadler.) Hayek found Salzburg inhospitable and eventually left.

Simkin, who spent time with him in Vienna, he spoke wistfully of the Habsburg Empire.[5] His Austrian friends, including Health Minister Franz Kreuzer, sought to reestablish a bond between him and Vienna. He was to become the head of a new Ludwig Boltzmann Institute, to be opened in his Hietzing residence. He became an honorary professor at the University of Vienna, the dream of every interwar Viennese Jewish intellectual. But the time for reconciliation with the old Heimat had passed. The Vienna he knew, with its vibrant assimilated-Jewish culture, was no longer there. His friends and home were in England. He was a stranger in his own land. He left for England.[6]

England had become a second home, if there was ever any. Popper's return to London in January 1946 had meant that the worst of exile was over. The first couple of years were exhilarating. He was a rising star. *The Open Society* threw him overnight into the public eye. At the LSE, he drew large audiences, competing with Laski for popularity. He had not yet settled into their East Barnet residence before he received the first invitations for major meetings of British philosophers. On October 25, 1946, he confronted Wittgenstein in a now-famous Moral Sciences Club meeting in Cambridge. Leading British philosophers, present and future, attended. He challenged Wittgenstein by insisting that there existed genuine philosophical problems, not mere linguistic puzzles. He offered induction, infinity, and the validity of moral rules as examples. Wittgenstein dismissed these as logical and mathematical problems, or as linguistic confusion, and eventually left the room. Bertrand Russell wrote Popper later that he was appalled by the reception the Wittgensteinians had accorded him, and was completely on his side. He kept silent, he said, because Popper so ably defended himself. The next day, Russell apparently told American philosopher Hiriam McLendon that Popper had more learning and erudition than all those present. Popper felt that he had won the giants' battle.[7]

The English idyll did not last. In January 1949, after Popper had threatened to leave for a chair in New Zealand, the LSE appointed him professor. Shortly after, he received an invitation to give the William James Lectures at Harvard in 1949 and 1950. He enjoyed his time in the United States and had a rosy picture of it. (The blacks were a "depressed class," he said, but they were the least depressed minority he had seen – one wonders by what standard.) In Princeton he had a moment of glory when Bohr and Einstein attended his lecture on quantum theory and, long after the audience had left, continued the discussion for hours. Back in England, however, things took a turn for the worse. Hayek left the LSE for Chicago

---

[5] Colin Simkin to author, 23 April 1997 (letter), 9 June 1997 (E-mail).

[6] Karl Milford kindly provided information on Popper's sojourn in Vienna, 1985–6 (conversation, 31 January 1999).

[7] John Watkins, "Karl Raimund Popper 1902–1994," *Proceedings of the British Academy* 94 (1997): 660–3; "The Truth Will Out," *The Philosophers' Magazine*, Spring 1999.

in 1948. A scandalized Lionel Robbins cooled his relations with Popper, who stood by his friend. Popper's enthusiasm for teaching was waning. He still delivered his lectures impromptu (or, at most, from sparse notes), using no syllabus or course plan, speaking on problems that interested him at the moment, somehow always clear and organized, leaving listeners mesmerized. But his audience was now smaller, younger (no released soldiers), and, he thought, immature. He began feeling alienated in his own school.

Using the money he had received from the William James Lectures as a down payment, and taking out an all-too-big mortgage, the Poppers bought Fallowfield, a house in need of repair, surrounded by a large garden, on the rural western outskirts of London in Penn, Buckinghamshire. They would live there until Hennie's death in 1985. They made Fallowfield into a beautiful, serene residence, isolated from the world's turmoils, where Popper could focus on his work. Renovations in 1951–2 were, however, difficult, and the difficulties were exacerbated by Karl's and Hennie's depression. Even after they had recovered, life did not return to the previous routine. With a reduced teaching load – at times only two courses per term, one a lecture, the other a seminar – Popper showed up at the LSE only one day a week. The rest he spent working at home. He worked day and night, with infrequent respites taken for piano playing, novel reading (Jane Austen and Anthony Trollope), or an occasional visitor. Research assistants brought books from the library. To meet him for a serious discussion, one had to travel to his residence. (Agassi, who worked with him closely in the mid-1950s, had to live close by.) He read the paper and listened to the radio only rarely and had no television. His legendary seclusion in Penn had begun.[8]

Seclusion from urban life was accompanied by withdrawal from political philosophy. In the immediate postwar period, Popper still engaged political and social issues, developing *The Open Society*'s and *Poverty*'s main themes in lectures, papers, and essays. He continued to think through the relationship between liberalism and socialism and began exploring the social preconditions for a deliberative democracy – the formation of a critical rationalist tradition.[9] His explorations remained preliminary. He never quite abandoned political philosophy, but after 1950, it was never his major concern. "Public Opinion and Liberal Principles" (1954) reflected growing conservative moralism, but also the recognition that *The Open Society*'s ideal

[8] Here, and elsewhere, the epilogue is indebted to Joseph Agassi, *A Philosopher's Apprentice* (Amsterdam: Rodopi, 1993); David Miller, "Sir Karl Raimund Popper," *Biographical Memoirs of Fellows of the Royal Society* 43 (1997): 367–409; John Watkins, "Karl Raimund Popper" and "Karl Popper: A Memoir," *The American Scholar* 66 (1997): 205–19.

[9] "Public and Private Virtues," lecture and draft article (39, 17; 15, 25–9, respectively); "Speech on the Principles of *The Open Society*" (27, 7); "Utopia and Violence," "Prediction and Prophecy in the Social Sciences," "Toward a Rational Theory of Tradition," all in *Conjectures and Refutations* (New York: Basic Books, 1963), pp. 355–63, 336–46, 120–35, respectively.

critical public was problematic.[10] He posed a series of queries essential to the realization of liberal ideals, but never pursued them. His political essays over the next fifteen years lived off of old capital. They strike this reader as irritatingly self-congratulatory, the "West" declared unambiguously the best society that had ever existed. Anxious lest calls for unilateral disarmament by Russell and other intellectuals – "better red than dead" – weaken Western resolve and precipitate Soviet threats, and thinking that his voice, too, might be heard in Moscow, he countered with "better dead than red": Life without liberty was not worth living.[11] Read in the context of the cold war and the political irresponsibility of segments of the leftist intelligentsia, his statements are not as outrageous as they seem today, but they are disturbing all the same.

In 1950, Popper added the theory of the abstract society to *The Open Society*. His theoretical imagination was likely informed as much by his own life and aspirations as by observations on modern life. Human contact was time-consuming and, unless contributing to his philosophy, a burden. He became progressively isolated among British philosophers. It did not take long before his tactless conduct brushed against their easy sociability.[12] Many admired his seriousness and abilities but found him insufferable. They would have gladly accepted him, if he had been a better listener, more generous, less self-righteous. He had little interest in accomodating them, or taking part in their activities. He did not think much of most of them and believed their concerns, particularly linguistic ones, trivial. He preferred his study, his disciples, his seminar. In 1951, he participated in founding the *British Journal for the Philosophy of Science*, and served as chair of the Philosophy of Science Group the year after. His public engagement diminished in later years: Having often responded negatively to invitations to conferences, he found them dwindling. He surmised that there was an academic conspiracy to exclude him and consign his works to oblivion. The nightmare that he conjured tended to become a self-fulfilling prophecy.

Herbert Feigl visited Popper in Penn in the summer of 1954 and described, to friends in the United States, his "splendid isolation" in Fallowfield, "an impressive country manor, with a beautiful terrace and park-like gardens." Popper played a gracious host but complained that members

---

[10] *Conjectures and Refutations*, pp. 347–54.

[11] "The History of Our Time," ibid., pp. 364–76; "What Does the West Believe In?" in *In Search of a Better World* (London: Routledge, 1992), pp. 204–22; "Zum Thema Freiheit," in *Die Philosophie und die Wissenschaften*, ed. Ernst Oldemeyer (Meisenheim am Glan: Anton Hain, 1967), pp. 1–12. Popper's criticism of Russell is open in the second essay, as well as in: "Science: Problems, Aims, Responsibilities," in *The Myth of the Framework* (London: Routledge, 1994), pp. 82–111. He expressed his opposition to unilateral disarmament also in "The Moral Responsibility of the Scientist," ibid., pp. 121–9.

[12] Popper's friend, philosopher and politician Bryan Magee, recalls: "My chief impression of him at our early meetings [1959] was of an intellectual aggressiveness such as I had never encountered before. Everything we argued about he pursued relentlessly, beyond the limits of acceptable aggression in conversation." (*Confessions of a Philosopher* [New York: Random House, 1997], p. 182.)

of the circle had repeatedly plagiarized *Logik*. Feigl found him "hard to bear": "more autistic than ever," "paranoic," and "megalomaniac." At the same time, he urged his colleagues to examine closely Popper's recent arguments on probability and confirmation. His playful report of two philosophical conferences in Oxford and Zurich – combination of academic gossip and high-handed criticism – ended abruptly when he got to Popper. The tone became serious and respectful: One encountered, in Feigl's words, "great brilliance and originality," or differently said, a superior mind.[13]

Popper's brilliance attracted a small group of exceptionally intelligent students at the LSE who constituted the inner Popperian circle. Popper had first met Paul Feyerabend in Alpbach in 1948. Feyerabend came to study with him in 1952 but left after a year. Agassi came in 1953 from Israel, becoming Popper's research assistant when Feyerabend left, and, for the next five years, he and Popper were inseparable. He became lecturer in 1957. John Watkins had first heard Popper lecture in the fall of 1947. He participated in Popper's seminar for many years, then, in 1958, became reader in logic and scientifc method. Ian Jarvie crossed over from anthropology in 1957; William Bartley arrived from Harvard in 1958; Imre Lakatos, a Hungarian émigré studying at Cambridge, first gave a paper to the seminar in the spring of 1958, collaborated with Popper's students thereafter, then joined as lecturer after Agassi's departure in 1960. Polish émigrés Czeslaw Lejewski and Jerzy Giedymin attended Popper's seminars, as did, for short periods, Ralf Dahrendorf, Ernest Gellner, and A. I. Sabra (later a Harvard historian of science and an Arabist). Hans Albert came for visits from Germany. The Popperians were a distinctly cosmopolitan circle, an international gathering of brilliant cultural outsiders.

Agassi's autobiography, *A Philosopher's Apprentice*, wonderfully describes the intellectual excitement Popper generated around him. It centered on his (in)famous Tuesday evening seminar, attended by graduate students and guest scholars. Usually a student, or a guest, read a paper. They often did not get through the better part of the paper because Popper (and others) constantly interrupted with criticism. Debates were heated. Everyone (but Popper, who remained in control) had to leave their egos at the door because criticism could be crushing. Popper was oblivious to the power dynamics obtaining in rhetorical exchange and could be blind to the psychology of learning, too. He detected immediately when listeners disagreed, or were confused, but he took no notice of the effect he caused when he humiliated interlocutors. He enforced clarity of ideas and simplicity of speech with an iron hand.[14] He thought that his seminar was

---

[13] Circular letter to Carnap, Frank, Hempel, Morris, and Nagel, 16 September 1954, Ernest Nagel Papers (box 1), Columbia University, Rare Books and Manuscripts.

[14] Joseph Agassi, *A Philosopher's Apprentice*, chaps. 2–6; William Bartley, *Unfathomed Knowledge, Unmeasured Wealth* (La Salle, Ill.: Open Court, 1990), chap. 9.

exemplary of free criticism. An American visitor observed, in contrast, that it resembled the House Committee on Un-American Activities. Many participants found it exhilarating and enriching and would rather not have changed it, even if they could. Still, the atmosphere did not encourage free debate. Insecure or timid students found it difficult to contribute, and self-confidence has (or should have) nothing to do with the search for truth.

From the mid- to the late 1950s, Popper was writing a companion volume to the English translation of *Logik der Forschung*. Hennie was convinced that his philosophy of science, and not political philosophy, represented his major legacy, and beseeched him to prepare a translation. (In addition to the failed translations of the late 1930s, Henry Woodger prepared a complete translation under the title "Hypothesis and Confirmation," and Feyerabend apparently prepared another – neither to Popper's complete satisfaction.)[15] Popper reworked a translation by Julius and Lan Fried, and added to the book twelve new appendixes of historical and technical interest (mostly improvements on probability). Altogether, over a third of the volume was new. He also added numerous footnotes, indicating where he no longer agreed with the original, or had improved on it. The notes referred repeatedly to the companion volume, *Postscript: After Twenty Years*, which was conceived as an essay but, typically, expanded into a book. It was virtually complete by the end of Popper's tenure at the Center for Behavioral Sciences in Stanford in 1956–7, and in proofs by 1959, but abandoned after 1962, and published, with further additions, only twenty years later, under Bartley's editorship, in three volumes.

The *Postscript* elaborated a new cosmology. Popper propounded an indeterministic universe where chance was real, but not random. The forces obtaining at each conjuncture created propensities, but they did not determine results. Different future states were possible but not equally likely. Physical probabilities reflected objective propensities. Popper's metaphysical realism was now pronounced. Epistemological theories, he insisted, were, like other metaphysical theories, criticizable, even if not empirically testable. He could explain his preferences for subject–object and mind–body dualism over sensationalist and linguistic monism and his support of an objective-fallibilist view of science against essentialism and instrumentalism (conventionalism). Science, he acknowledged, was shot through with metaphysics, the distinction between scientific and nonscientific knowledge a blur. Knowledge always grew through learning from mistakes, and this held true for daily problems no less than for philosophical and scientific problems.

Popper's radical anti-inductivism conflicted not only with scientific

---

[15] Woodger's translation is in Popper Archives (12, 13). Joseph Agassi told me of Feyerabend's translation.

prejudice and "common sense" but also, it seemed, with Popper's own conviction about the growth of knowledge. Science seemed all too chaotic and random to allow for growth. All theories were likely "false," "all empirical statements about the world equally uncertain," eventually to be replaced.[16] Corroboration was no appraisal of truth or certainty. There were no rules to protect a well-corroborated theory any more than a haphazard guess from a decisive refutation. Chance could play havoc, leading to a quick refutation of a "good" theory, leaving a "bad" one untouched for ages. Why should anyone play the scientific game? As Lakatos noted, the abyss· of skepticism opened, and the young Popper refused to close it: "*One has to choose between some sort of methodological falsificationism and irrationalism.* [The methodological falsificationist] offers a game in which one has little hope of winning, but claims that it is still better to play than to give it up."[17]

The number of philosophers and scientists willing to play with little chance of winning was never great. In the late 1950s, Popper did something about it. He began speaking of science as aiming at theories of growing approximation to the truth, or verisimilitude, truth-likeness. As the truth content of a theory increased, so did its degree of verisimilitude. The growth of knowledge entailed the substitution of theories of greater verisimilitude for ones with a lower degree. Popper added methodological provisions to protect well-corroborated theories. New theories had to be simple, independently testable, and pass "some new, and severe, tests" before being accepted. The growth of knowledge now seemed more orderly.[18]

Popper presented these ideas as elaborating *Logik der Forschung*. Most of his students thought that they were new, and gave them a mixed reception. Agassi, ever suspicious of corroboration, rejected the new methodological requisites as resurrecting verificationism.[19] Lakatos, in contrast, came to regard verisimilitude, in the late 1960s, as a welcomed turning point in Popper's philosophy. He wanted to push it further, and correlate verisimilitude and corroboration by conceding a weakened inductive principle,

[16] John Watkins, "Hume, Carnap, and Popper," *The Problem of Inductive Logic*, ed. Imre Lakatos (Amsterdam: North Holland Pub. Co., 1968), pp. 277–8.

[17] Imre Lakatos, "Falsification and the Methodology of Scientific Research Programmes," in *Criticism and the Growth of Knowledge*, ed. Imre Lakatos and Alan Musgrave, *Proceedings of the International Colloquium in the Philosophy of Science, London 1965* (Cambridge: The University Press, 1970), 4:91–195. Quotation is from p. 113.

[18] Popper, "Truth, Rationality, and the Growth of Knowledge," *Conjectures and Refutations*, pp. 215–50; "The Aim of Science" [1957], *Objective Knowledge* (Oxford: Clarendon Press, 1972), pp. 191–205.

[19] One learned from refutation rather than from corroboration. For a recent statement, see "Celebrating *The Open Society*," *Philosophy of the Social Sciences* 27 (1997): 486–525: "Refutation is advancement[;] . . . the very elimination of obstacles is progress. The corroboration of a theory . . . is a failure . . . to eliminate error – unless the corroborated theory happens to be true" (495). Watkins, too, believes that verisimilitude let inductivism in through the back door: *Science and Scepticism* (Princeton, N.J.: Princeton University Press, 1984).

recognizing repeated corroboration in severe tests as cumulative certainty.[20] Without it, he said, verisimilitude could not help Popper distinguish his "fallibilism" from skepticism and relativism. Popper could not even provide a rationale for leaving a high-rise building by the elevator rather than the window. (Not quite. Corroboration did inspire confidence, but could not provide a precise measure of certainty. The elevator may one day break down and prove just as treacherous as leaving by the window.) It turned out that verisimilitude could not do even the modest job Popper assigned it. David Miller refuted Popper's formulation in 1974, and has recently conceded that "although realists are confident that it makes good sense to claim that one theory (say, general relativity) is objectively closer to the truth than is another (say, classical mechanics), and hence an instance of scientific progress, no one can give a logically watertight account of what such progress amounts to."[21]

Lakatos presented his proposals as the only way to save Popper from Feyerabend's theoretical anarchism. Feyerabend married skepticism to the political rebellion of the 1960s. It did not take much. He needed only to push Popper's views to their limit: the subjective and intuitive character of discovery, theoretical adventure and revolution, anti-inductivism and antiverificationism. At the same time, he disposed of falsification and corroboration (as well as consensus), rejected methodology *tout court*, and dismissed critical rationalism as traditional philosophy's last stand. Precisely the violation of rules, he tried to show, permitted, historically, theoretical advances. (Popper never suggested that following rules always produced success.) "There is only *one* principle that can be defended under *all* circumstances," he said: " 'anything goes.' "[22] Popper's students, it seemed, were pulling apart his brilliant synthesis of subjectivism and objectivism, conventionalism and absolutism, consensus and logical certainty, scientific tradition and revolutionary change, corroboration and falsification. Some began pushing it "right" toward conservative conventionalism, others "left," toward anarchism. Will the synthesis hold?

Critical rationalism cannot find a cure for skepticism, or "theoretical

---

[20] To Lakatos, one needed to resurrect some inductive principle to explain "why we play the game of science." Scientific progress required defense of current theories no less than their revolutionary overthrow. He endeavored to bring Popper closer to conservative conventionalists, by blocking early refutation of "scientific research programs," enabling them to "overcome infantile disease," "allowing scientists time to ponder any refutation."

[21] David Miller, "Sir Karl Raimund Popper": 393. Miller has recently tried to improve on verisimilitude: *Critical Rationalism* (Chicago: Open Court, 1994), chap. 10.

[22] Paul Feyerabend, *Against Method: Outline of an Anarchistic Theory of Knowledge* (London: NLB, 1975), p. 28. Recognizing later that in espousing this principle he found himself in a performative contradiction, he suggested that he "wrote in a rather ironical vein." ("Preface" to rev. ed. [London: Verso, 1988].) The revised edition also provides a "Sketch of the Main Argument." Rhetoric aside, there is little in the "Sketch" with which Popper would disagree, or which would force him to change his position.

anarchism," in any measure of certainty. It was precisely Lakatos's search for certitude in progress, rather than hope for progress, that Popper denied. As uncertainty destabilizes received opinion, it risks a turn to fideism or skepticism. Popper's methodological proposals reflect hope that rational debate will lead to improvement. One can encourage but not force such hope. His proposals also reflect the conviction that criticism entails responsibility – we know little, so we should acknowledge refutation and change course; politics should safeguard critical debate. Such responsibility can be encouraged, but cannot be forced, either. As Agassi and Bartley have repeatedly pointed out, skeptics and fideists are invited to join the critical debate, and often do, and scientists and philosophers cannot proceed without such a debate, if their enterprise is to be intersubjective. Whether Popper's methodological proposals are always conducive to learning (hence, to scientific progress) is, of course, debatable. Critical rationalists have diverged on particulars. "How one hypothesis may be appraised as better than the other hypotheses under discussion," says Watkins, "and what a future hypothesis would need to do for it to be even better than this one – this is what Popper's methodology is about."[23] Feyerabend dismissed the methodological debate as irrelevant. As a historian, I cannot contribute to it, let alone arbitrate it, but I am perplexed why many on the left still regard Feyerabend's easy dismissal as a hard-won truth, and the Popperians' efforts to debate as hopeless.

Feyerabend did not, however, represent the major challenge to Popper; Thomas Kuhn did. *The Structure of Scientific Revolution* (1962) exposed the gap between Popper's ideal science and scientific practice. It was not an altogether unfamiliar problem to Popper. Neurath had already argued in 1935 that Popper's scientific model did not conform to scientific practice. (Neurath's current partisans, Nancy Cartwright and Jordi Cat, concur.) Both Neurath and Popper were more sensitive to science's extralogical dimensions than were other circle members, but Neurath, a social reformer even when speaking of science, emphasized, more than Popper, science's collective character. As the sociology of science did not yet exist, both Neurath's and Popper's observations were preliminary. *Logik der Forschung* was a book on scientific method, not on scientists or the scientific community. Popper acknowledged extralogical criteria for scientific decisions, but they were of no concern to him. Method applied precisely the same way to the individual scientist and to the community. The psychological and sociological conditions making intersubjectivity possible were irrelevant. During his exile in New Zealand, he added an important proviso. Political freedom made criticism possible; hence, it was essential to science, but he resisted any temptation to carry the investigation further. Science's institutions and public processes were essential, but he took them for

[23] "Hume, Carnap, and Popper," pp. 277–8.

granted – they existed because science did. He assumed the public character of science, but never investigated it.

This was a problem. As Popper discarded foundationism, intersubjective
criticism became objectivity's new grounds. Criticism and testing operated
by consensus and convention. How did intersubjective criticism really
work? It was not clear that access was available to the whole public, certainly not equal access. Once ideas entered the public sphere, who won?
Did the logic (or methodology) of science really set the rules of discussion? Without a sociology of science, public criticism remained a regulative ideal at best. Moreover, Feyerabend and Kuhn charged that Popper
could not account for most "correct" historical decisions in favor of better
theories. If the key to scientific progress was the psychology, sociology, and
routine of scientific communities, not criticism and testing, then Popper's
effort to erect a rational edifice of science and explain the growth of knowledge as a rational process was problematic.

As a graduate student at Harvard, Kuhn attended Popper's seminar in
1950, but, like Michael Polanyi, he drew a picture of science dominated by
tradition, "tacit knowledge," and "routine," the formulation of problems and
testing of theories severely limited by conventions and beliefs.[24] "Normal
Science" did not test theories; rather, it solved puzzles within established
paradigms. The growth of knowledge was the cumulative solutions of
puzzles within a paradigm, not the substitution of one theory for another.
Adventurous experimentation and testing on a grand scale, of the sort envisioned by Popper (Eddington's experiment), were largely limited to short,

---

[24] Popper complained that Kuhn described him as a naive falsificationist. It is not clear how carefully
Kuhn read *The Logic of Scientific Discovery.* (*The Structure of Scientific Revolutions,* 2d ed. [Chicago: University of Chicago, 1970], pp. 146–7; Popper, "Replies to My Critics," *The Philosophy of Karl Popper,*
ed. Schilpp, pp. 1144–5, 1149.) Popper felt, as usual, that Kuhn had plagiarized his ideas. For Kuhn's
view of their relationship, see "Logic of Discovery or Psychology of Research?" in *Criticism and the
Growth of Knowledge,* ed. Imre Lakatos and Alan Musgrave, pp. 1–23.

In the preface to his book, Kuhn acknowledged the formative influence of an unknown monograph that has meanwhile become a classic in the sociology of science, Ludwik Fleck's *Entstehung
und Entwicklung einer wissenschaftlichen Tatsache* (Basel: Benno Schwabe, 1935) (*The Genesis and Development of a Scientific Fact* [Chicago: University of Chicago Press, 1979]). Fleck (1896–1961), a Polish-
Jewish microbiologist, developed a sociological understanding of scientific method as a collective
style of thought (*Denkstil*). He emphasized the collective framing and historically contingent character of "scientific fact" and provided a history of syphilis that showed the definition of the disease
to depend on collective, culturally contingent thought structures. His work addressed Carnap and
the Vienna Circle critically. Schlick recommended his book to Springer, but nothing came of the
recommendation. Fleck's concern with the socio-historical making of science explains the changing fortunes of his work. Unlike *Logik der Forschung,* it did not speak directly to the methodological and linguistic concerns of the Vienna Circle, but it did address Kuhn's interest in the actual
historical working of science (whereas *Logik* had little to say about it). It is *not* that what Fleck says
conflicts with Popper's methodological views; rather, historians and sociologists of science bracket
the question of the methodological "ought" in a manner that Popper and the Vienna Circle philosophers were unwilling to do.

extraordinary periods of scientific crisis, when the reigning paradigm ran into difficulties because of repeated failures to solve puzzles. Two or more paradigms – each with its own problem situation and methodology – competed. This was not a rational affair, not a critical debate. Communication between proponents of the two was limited, as if they belonged to different language communities, requiring arduous translation from one to the other. Acceptance of one paradigm was not the result of falsification – what counted for experiment in one paradigm did not in the other – but was closer to a religious conversion. "Progress" between paradigms might occur, but it was not linear: The new paradigm better solved contemporary problems, but Einstein seemed, in some respects, closer to Aristotle than to Newton. Scientific revolutions, the core of Popper's Great Science, were not rational, at least not the way Popper understood rationality. Tacit acceptance of the paradigm was a precondition to the critical debate Popper envisioned.[25]

Popper was disheartened. Normal science did not resemble his heroic, audacious, revolutionary project, embodying the Enlightenment. Yet, Kuhn revealed dimensions of science of which he had been unaware: "Normal Science was, indeed, an eye opener for me, even though I do not care very much for what I see. . . . I not only dislike the phenomenon, but I think that it has only recently become very important and, in my opinion, a danger to science."[26] Kuhn's appeal to history, psychology, and sociology to explain science seemed to undo *Logik der Forschung*: "I regard it as disappointing because it shows that all I have said before against sociologistic and psychologistic tendencies was in vain."[27]

This was no answer, and he could do, and did do, better. In his beautiful "The Myth of the Framework," he denied Kuhn's incommensurability of paradigms. No doubt revolution implied a *Gestalt* switch, but it rendered neither comparison nor criticism impossible. (The astronomies of Aristarchus and Copernicus were not incomparable.) Total ideologies, reflecting closed systems and ways of life, made communication difficult, but they did not make it impossible, and it was worth it. He provided examples of paradigmatic shifts in mathematics and physics, above all, theories of the constitution of matter (for example, atomism), arguing that the shifts involved criticism and were not irrational. Conversions and fashions existed, of course, but rational discussion was not limited to periods of crisis, and, indeed, crisis versus paradigm did not adequately describe science.

---

[25] Thomas Kuhn, *The Structure of Scientific Revolutions*; "Logic of Discovery or Psychology of Research?"; Michael Polanyi, *Personal Knowledge: Towards a Post-Critical Philosophy* (London: Routledge & Kegan Paul, 1958).

[26] Karl Popper, "Replies to My Critics," p. 1145.

[27] Popper, "Normal Science and Its Dangers," in *Criticism and the Growth of Knowledge*, p. 58.

Popper's response remained constrained, however – more a *credo* than historical observation – because of his reluctance to open the history of science to contextual considerations that he regarded as "sociological" or "psychological." It is not that sociology or psychology can enlighten us about "the aims of science and its possible progress." Popper provided the yardstick, and we have no better prescription for rationality and progress than his. Rather, history and sociology can clarify the obtacles to the realization of his ideal scientific community. He himself feared "Big Science," and felt an alien in a world of governmental and corporate projects, driven by budgets, markets, and technology. In his view, much of contemporary science was trivial, "normal scientists" not really scientists. How was he planning to fight them without having a firm grip on their practices? How could he hope to rationalize scientific debate (and democratize the scientific community) without knowing the obstacles in his way, without understanding how they operated, how scientific consensus and hegemony were *really* formed? Any future leftist project to realize Popper's liberal utopia will have to appropriate modes of investigation from history, sociology, and science studies (while often disposing of much of their ethos).[28]

   The new history of science seems to me less damaging to Popper than to traditional inductivist accounts, much less so than Popperians may fear, or science studies practitioners imagine. To be sure, if methodologically irrelevant criteria alone determined choice among theories, Popper's account would be in jeopardy. But the new history seems less to advance such a claim and more to suspend the question of "truth" and shift the inquiry to the rhetoric through which scientists claimed authority and to the reception that made one theory's triumph over another possible.[29] It often presupposes the traditional narrative of crucial experiments, rather

---

[28] To persuade opponents of the rationality of scientific progress, Popper turned instead to evolutionary epistemology: "The Rationality of Scientific Revolutions" [1975], in *The Myth of the Framework*, pp. 1–32. For an interesting attempt to develop a Popperian sociology of knowledge, see Ian Jarvie's forthcoming *The Republic of Science*.

[29] When Steven Shapin and Simon Schaffer (*Leviathan and the Air-Pump: Hobbes, Boyle, and the Experimental Life* [Princeton, N.J.: Princeton University Press, 1985]) explore Robert Boyle's creation of the modern scientific notions of "fact," "experiment," and "publicity," they historicize the basic notions to which scientists still adhere (or appeal). They do not, in my view, undermine them. When Jan Golinski (*Science as Public Culture: Chemistry and Enlightenment in Britain, 1760–1820* [New York: Cambridge University Press, 1992], chaps. 4–6) explores the extrascientific contexts for the triumph of oxygen over phlogiston – competing ideals of scientific, political, and national community – he accepts as a given Antoine Laurent Lavoisier's combustion theory and *experimentum crucis*. Popper would not have been surprised that the controversy over Lavoisier's experiment focused on the accuracy of his measurement and the appropriateness of his instruments. This is precisely the argumentation *Grundprobleme* and *Logik* explored. To Golinski, Lavoisier's complex and expensive experiment signaled a triumph for institutionalized elitist science over Joseph Priestley's enlightenment ideal of scientific public culture, where cheap repetitive experiments popularized science. Popper regretted such developments and protested, more emphatically and innocently than Golinski, against the authority of experts.

than dispose of it, opens it up to broader social and intellectual contexts, rather than substitute for it.[30] To be sure, at some point, historians must bring together in one account the internal logic of science and the "logics" of the various contexts.[31] If social and political theory have their own internal logic, it would be strange to deny it to scientific theory. It is just that in choosing to bracket internal logic (and "truth"), the new historians made it seem, at times, as if it had disappeared. It did not, and precisely here lies the most challenging work for historians, and for those wishing to transform science in light of Popperian ideals.

The early 1960s saw the onset of Popper's evolutionary epistemology. He now spoke openly of the "natural selection" of hypotheses, and described biological evolution itself as a process of error elimination. He sought to build a measure of voluntarism and indeterminism (commonly associated with Lamarckism) into Darwinian evolution by surmising organisms' active role in natural selection (without influencing genetic structure). He distinguished between organisms' aim structure and skill structure, and suggested that aims could develop, for a while, independently of skills, preparing the grounds for selection among mutations affecting skills: The development of the woodpecker's beak became easier once the bird had acquired a taste for bugs living in tree bark. Humans could do better, consciously modifying both aims and the environment. From the amoeba to Einstein there was one step, a crucial one: the "consciously critical attitude towards [one's] own ideas." The amoeba died when it made a mistake. Humans no longer died while improving. Criticism substituted for physical annihilation as a correction mechanism: Our theories died for us; the growth of knowledge continued.[32]

Popper's efforts to read a measure of agency into natural selection and guard, at one and the same time, objectivity and freedom led to broader reflections on the mind–body problem and the manner by which humans shaped their environment. Indeterminism, he recognized, was not enough. He was a dualist, but Cartesian dualism had left unresolved the problem of how minds could shape bodies. Moreover, it had not raised the question

---

[30] For the traditional narrative of Lavoisier and the revolution of chemistry, see Herbert Butterfield, *The Origins of Modern Science, 1300–1800* (London: Bell, 1949), chap. 11. See also Kuhn's interesting comments in *The Structure of Scientific Revolutions*, pp. 147–9: "Though neither Priestley's nor Lavoisier's theory agreed precisely with existing observations, few contemporaries hesitated more than a decade in concluding that Lavoisier's theory provided the better fit of the two."

I would like to thank the members of my 1998 and 1999 graduate colloquia in the historiography and methodology of intellectual history at Duke for discussions of the history of science that have informed these comments.

[31] On correlating internal and external explanations, see my "Leonard Krieger: Historicization and Political Engagement in Intellectual History," *History and Theory* 35 (1996): 80–130.

[32] Popper, "Evolution and the Tree of Knowledge" [1961], in *Objective Knowledge*, pp. 256–84; "The Rationality of Scientific Revolutions."

of "how such non-physical things as *purposes, deliberations, plans, decisions, theories, intentions,* and *values,* can play a part in bringing about physical changes in the physical world."[33] Behaviorists and materialists reduced the nonphysical to the physical, ending up in a "determinist nightmare." Popper sought to use a reformed evolutionary theory to offer an alternative. In 1965, he conjectured that language and consciousness evolved as parts of a hierarchy of "plastic" mental controls that best enabled humans to confront environmental tasks. He could not explain precisely how mental controls and physical bodies interacted, but his conjecture gave "good evolutionary (or functional) reasons in favour of interaction."[34]

This did not resolve the ontological status of "mental controls." It made no sense to reduce them to the "physical," but language (and theories) clearly went beyond subjective mental states. In 1967, Popper offered his three-worlds theory, "the philosophy of my old age," suggesting that the products of human mental activity belonged in a Third World (or World 3). Minds (World 2) created this world, and it shaped the physical world (World 1) through their intervention, but it existed autonomously. Knowledge (3) became relevant when historical agents (2) drew on it to solve problems (3) emerging from their interaction with the physical world (1). Positivists, and observers steeped in the "scientific worldview," raised an eyebrow as they saw the philosopher who demarcated science from metaphysics turning to ontology. When, fifteen years later, he delved into the origin of life, and spoke emphatically of teleology in evolutionary biology, observers charged that he was resurrecting romantic *Naturphilosophie.* Popper acknowledged that his World 3 was close to his two implacable enemies, Plato and Hegel, but his third-world Forms were neither static nor eternal, nor did they ever reach the Absolute Spirit's finality. All the same, Neurath would have felt vindicated in his prediction (to Carnap) that Popper would become a metaphysician – not a judgment that Popper would have cared to dispute.[35]

Having brought several sciences and branches of philosophy together in a unified cosmology, Popper was convinced of the utmost importance of his philosophy. At points, he even seemed to suggest that the survival of Western democracy and science depended on acceptance of his ideas. He received recognition. He became a Fellow of the British Academy in 1958, and was knighted in 1965. He always had admirers among scientists and Nobel laureates, including, to name a few, biologist Peter Medawar (who

---

[33] "Of Clouds and Clocks: An Approach to the Problem of Rationality and the Freedom of Man" [1965], *Objective Knowledge,* pp. 206–55. Quotation is on p. 229.

[34] Ibid, p. 255; comment added in 1974.

[35] "Epistemology Without a Knowing Subject" [1968] and "On the Theory of the Objective Mind," in *Objective Knowledge,* pp. 106–52, 153–90, respectively; "Knowledge and the Shaping of Reality" [1982], *In Search of a Better World,* pp. 3–29; Ernest Gellner, "The Rational Mystic," *The New Republic,* 19 April 1993, 35–8.

thought him "incomparably the greatest philosopher of science ever"); neurophysiologist John Eccles; biochemist Jacques Monod; physicists Alfred Landé, Hermann Bondi, Erwin Schrödinger, and Jean-Pierre Vigier; animal psychologists Donald Campbell and Konrad Lorenz. Many of them felt that his philosophy illuminated their practice and reinvigorated it like no other. Their friendship and admiration meant a lot to him. He was enormously gratified when finally elected (on Medawar's initiative) a Fellow of the Royal Society in 1976, and disappointed to discover that this had been done under a section permitting appointment of nonscientists (politicians included). By the 1960s, he was known, if not popular, among the intelligentsia in North America and Britain. In Germany, Hans Albert promoted his ideas. The *Positivismusstreit* evoked a lively exchange on his social science methodology, but his influence was no match for that of the Frankfurt school. He had admirers in Latin America, India, and Japan. All the same, he felt that both he and his philosophy had not received their due.

The late 1960s should have been a time of celebration. He planned to retire in 1969, vigorous as ever, and devote himself to his *Autobiography* and to responses to his critics in *The Philosophy of Karl Popper*, a volume of the Library of Living Philosophers dedicated to his philosophy. It did not work out this way. First he discovered that his income upon retirement would be insufficient. Then in the fall of 1969, he went to teach, for a semester, at Brandeis University and "make some money." He had a miserable time. To Gombrich he complained about what he considered the unpleasant characteristics of rich American Jews.[36] (He would never write this way to anyone but assimilated Jewish friends. Hayek never got such letters.) When he left London for Brandeis, the LSE was in shambles. Student protests had begun early in 1967 over Walter Adams's appointment as director.[37] The protests died down for a year, then resurged in the fall of 1968, reaching their peak on January 24, 1969, when the LSE "gates," designed to prevent occupation of the "old building," were brought down with pickaxes. The school closed for four weeks, the faculty badly split, some siding with the students. Secluded in Penn, Popper never fully understood the events, but Watkins, his lieutenant and successor at the LSE, and philosopher Alan Musgrave, his student and a lecturer, took a leading role in confronting the students. To the New Left, Popper became, on account of his critique of Marx and the confrontation, the establishment philosopher par excellence. For the next fifteen years, he was the philosopher to contend with among

---

[36] Popper to Gombrich, 25 September 1969 (300, 7).

[37] Popper felt that he partially owed his life to Walter Adams, who, as head of the Academic Assistance Council, had facilitated his New Zealand appointment. As principal of the University College of Rhodesia, Adams apparently colluded in some segregationist practices. Popper and Watkins were out of sympathy with the students from the beginning, but Watkins, a member of the academic board, thought Adams's appointment a mistake. (Ralf Dahrendorf, *LSE: A History of The London School of Economics and Political Science, 1895–1995* [Oxford: Oxford University Press, 1995], pp. 443–75.)

Marxist students at the LSE (and throughout Britain). They distrusted his politics and feared his brilliance.

To Colin Simkin, Popper wrote in June 1969 in a confidential letter that they were witnessing the decline of the West.[38] Marxists had infiltrated all the English newspapers (but the *Daily Telegraph*), and even *The Times* supported the students. Socialism was running triumphant. The arms and space race (begun with the Sputnik) had brought government control of scientific and economic life in Europe and the United States. Freedom was lost. His unusually dark vision (and bad judgment) reflected incomprehension and fear in face of the surprising events. At Brandeis, where the threat was not as close to home, he was more sympathetic to the students. The students, he thought, were rebelling against the self-important nonsense that they had been taught: "The Revolution is no more than the older generation of university teachers deserve."[39] The students misunderstood the root of evil: It was not capitalism but academic hypocrisy. He was trying to enlighten them. Of course, this did not mean theoretical or political concessions. Feyerabend, he wrote Hayek, had lost his head, becoming a leftist agitator, encouraging African-American students to overthrow Western science and opt for black magic.[40] A year later, German television organized a debate between Popper and Herbert Marcuse. He complained to a friend that he would now have to waste time reading Marcuse. The debate might as well have taken place among the deaf, as he and Marcuse talked past each other.[41]

The worst turn of events was his deteriorating relations with his students. He left an indelible impression on every student with whom he worked closely, and on many who just attended his seminars, or regularly conversed with him (Ralf Dahrendorf, Ernest Gellner, Bryan Magee). He could be generous toward his students, not only contributing of his time but also arranging for financial assistance and promoting their careers, but he expected an enormous amount in return. He turned his talented students into apprentices working to develop *his* philosophy. Inevitably, questions of both autonomy and priority emerged, and he was not generous in granting either. "One is envious of everyone except of one's own son and student," said a Jewish sage.[42] He treated his students like children (or thought he did), but was jealous of his priority all the same. His students used his philosophy as their point of departure. As he preached openness to criticism, they began by trying to improve on it. They found him unreceptive to any published criticism and ungracious in his responses. He felt that they had betrayed him.

---

[38] Undated (350, 15).   [39] Popper to Gombrich, 25 September 1969 (300, 7).

[40] Popper to Hayek, 15 December 1969 (305, 15).

[41] The debate was not face to face. The interviewer presented both a set of questions: *Revolution oder Reform? Herbert Marcuse und Karl Popper – Eine Konfrontation*, ed. Franz Stark (Munich: Kösel, 1972).

[42] *Babylonian Talmud, Sanhedrin*, 105b: "בבל אדם מתקנא חוץ מבנו ותלמידו".

He quarreled endlessly with his students (as they often did among themselves). First there came, in the early 1960s, a near break in his relationship with Agassi (the final break came in 1971), then in 1965 the break with Bartley, in 1969 with Lakatos, in 1982 with Watkins. All acknowledged his enormous contribution to their life and philosophy and expressed their gratitude. (Feyerabend seemed to be the only one who concealed his debt and denigrated him.) But the breaks often resembled, as Popper himself perceived, "father-killing," and they were painful. Early in 1971, overworked and depressed, he was trying, and failing, to write his responses to critics for the Schilpp volume. His relations with Agassi and Lakatos, and their criticism, were haunting him. He collapsed. A short vacation in Corfu in April revived him, and with utmost effort, the support of younger students – David Miller and Jeremy Shearmur – and an army of typists, he brought the volume to completion.[43] His bitterness, cantankerousness, and suspicion only increased, however. Bartley made up with him in the late 1970s, but Popper neither forgot nor forgave. Miller seems to have been the only student who worked closely with him for three decades without a major crisis (and, this, some observe, at a tremendous cost to his own career). Others have gone through cycles of discipleship and rebellion, presenting, to critical observers, a spectacle reminiscent of a sect, encircled by a hostile world, engaged in internal struggles over authority and doctrinal purity.

Intellectual fashions change quickly. The mid-1970s witnessed Popper's rise to prominence in Germany ("of all places – I do not like Germany"). The *Tendenzwende*, the change of political and intellectual currents in Germany after 1973, signaling waning socialist reformism and emerging neoconservatism, created renewed interest in Popper. Two small volumes on critical rationalism and social democracy appeared in 1975, followed by a third in 1978.[44] Socialist Chancellor Helmut Schmidt wrote the introduction, and publication was heralded as "the opening of a new phase in the history of social democracy." A festival of critical rationalism began: articles in newspapers, interviews, publications on Popper, new editions of his works, a critical edition of *Die beiden Grundprobleme der Erkenntnistheorie.* Popper had not written a major work in political theory for three decades, but *The Open Society* seemed to acquire new life among young and old, left and right. Marxist socialists, on both sides of the border, seemed the only dissenters. Helmut Spinner, an astute Popper student and

---

[43] Popper to Schilpp, 22 January, 29 March, 9 April, 18 April, 16 August, 23 August, 25 August 1971 (334, 3). David Miller, "Sir Karl Raimund Popper": 397 describes the volume's completion. Students' accounts of their relations with Popper: Joseph Agassi, *A Philosopher's Apprentice*; William Bartley, *Unfathomed Knowledge*; John Watkins, "Karl Raimund Popper" 673–8 (on Lakatos; compare Miller: 397–8) and "Karl Popper: A Memoir": 216–17 (his own rift).

[44] Georg Lührs et al., eds., *Kritischer Rationalismus und Sozialdemokratie* (Berlin: Dietz, 1975), 2 vols.; Georg Lührs et al., eds., *Theorie und Politik aus kritisch-rationaler Sicht* (Berlin: Dietz, 1978).

bemused observer, pointed out that Popper's philosophy addressed the problems of interwar Central Europe, and its current applications were not a simple matter.[45] Popper himself was reluctant, for a while, to express his views on contemporary German politics. (The Greens and the opposition to American nuclear missiles in the early 1980s brought him out. He made some of his least balanced statements in support of science and nuclear deterrence.) All this mattered little. The festival eventually subsided, but Popper became a familiar public figure in Germany, rarely seen but often talked about.

Interest in Popper surged in France and Italy as well. His major works were translated into Italian in the 1970s, and *Logik der Forschung* into French in 1973.[46] Numerous works on his life and thought appeared. The Austrians finally caught on.[47] Vienna celebrated his eightieth birthday with radio and newspaper interviews and two international congresses.[48] The exile, who had run away from his homeland in fear for his life, suddenly became "the great Austrian philosopher" – the only way a young generation could legitimize and repatriate representatives of interwar culture, still regarded as alien by the elders. German and Austrian socialists and left-leaning Italian publishers spearheaded the Popper revival, but both moderate socialists and conservatives used Popper to counter the New Left and reinforce anticommunism. Popper himself remained aloof from the struggle over his legacy, but to the extent that he intervened, he legitimized the conservative, and not the socialist, appropriation.

Popper left a major mark in Eastern Europe, too. There, the Open Society had an immediate appeal that it lacked in the West. The liberal utopia provided two generations of anticommunist revolutionaries with a guiding vision. Communists feared Popper more than most Western theoreticians because his political philosophy and philosophy of science eschewed easy ideological dismissal. Cambridge historian Istvan Hont recalls how, in the mid-1960s, his philosophy mentor in Budapest directed him to the library's cellar where *The Open Society* and *Poverty* were locked. *Samizdat* translations of Popper began circulating widely in Poland in the

---

[45] Helmut Spinner, *Popper und die Politik* (Berlin: Dietz, 1978), esp. pp. 1–80. Ralf Dahrendorf concurred (see p. 45).

[46] On Popper's reception in Italy, see Stefano Gattei, *Critica della ragione incerta: Introduzione al pensiero di Karl Popper* (Rome: Societa aperta, 1996).

[47] It is strange that Chancellor Bruno Kreisky, the epitome of socialist reformism and assimilationist politics, delayed initiatives. He disliked Popper, mostly because he associated him with Hayek's attack on the welfare state. Friedrich Stadler kindly provided this information.

[48] *Offene Gesellschaft, offenes Universum – Franz Kreuzer im Gespräch mit Karl R. Popper* (Vienna: Deuticke, 1982) (a series of radio interviews); Friedrich Wallner, ed., *Karl Popper – Philosophie und Wissenschaft: Beiträge zum Popper-Kolloquium* (Vienna: Braumüller, 1985) (see Wallner's "Vorwort" for details on the May 1983 symposium); Karl Müller, Friedrich Stadler, and Friedrich Wallner, eds., *Versuche und Widerlegungen offene Probleme im Werk Karl Poppers* (Vienna: Geyer, 1986) (see "Vorwort" for details on the 1983 festivities).

1970s. "The little revolution in my country in 1980–81 had its theoretician," wrote a Polish student to Popper in 1982; "it was you, Sir."[49]

Popper would have likely ended on the political right even without the New Left, but perhaps not as solidly. Winds of détente blew from his "Note on the Cold War" of the late 1960s.[50] In "The Open Society and the Democratic State" (1963), he expressed concern about the accumulation of riches. It reflected, however, not criticism of the growing gap between rich and poor – in 1989 he stated openly that the gap did not matter as long as there was enough for everyone, a retraction of his earlier position (as late as the early postwar years) – but moral indictment of the pursuit of wealth.[51] He was worried not about social injustice but about what Tocqueville, in his most reactionary mood, called "the democratic disease of envy." He thought that Hayek's *The Constitution of Liberty* (1960) was excellent, especially his suggestion of an upper house to constrain reckless popular legislation. (This went back on his firm democratic and egalitarian commitments.) His sentiments against big government, big science, and academic authority strangely resembled the New Left's hatred of the military-industrial complex and scientists' collusion in it, but, then, conservatives and the New Left could often sound similar notes in their attack on the Social Democratic Consensus. The New Left, the British public health system (a subject of unending complaints for him and Hennie), and the British labor unions' suicidal tactics in the late 1970s brought out his conservatism in the extreme.

It was not a well informed conservatism. Isolated in Penn, he was out of touch not only with recent intellectual trends but also with historical developments. He relied on friends to keep him appraised of political events. They needed to draw his attention to the fact that his epistemological term "Third World" already carried a set of political meanings (and he had best change it to World 3). It had not occurred to him. When, in his final years, he watched a little television, he was horrified by both the programs and the media's power, and suggested controlling them in a manner that violated liberal principles.[52] His political and intellectual universe was circumscribed by fin-de-siècle Viennese progressivism, interwar socialism, and early postwar Atlantic liberalism. It closed there-

---

[49] Adam Chmielewski to Popper (284, 6). David Miller, "Karl Raimund Popper," 400 directed me to this source.

[50] (6, 8).

[51] (5, 3 and 7). This was a speech that Popper delivered in Delhi, India. See also "Ethical and Methodological Individualism" (12, 1) and the introduction to *In Search of a Better World*.

[52] *La télévision: Un danger pour la démocratie* (Paris: Anatolia Editions, 1994). Already in *The Open Society* (chap. 17, n. 27), Popper was proposing to regulate election campaigns so that programmatic discussions would prevail, and not propaganda. Many will consider his proposals illiberal. They certainly showed a distrust of the electorate that is not altogether compatible with the Open Society. But, then, Popper was frustrated with fascist success at manipulating political debate. He was determined to rationalize it.

after. Internal development still took place, but the context, especially politics, made only infrequent rude intrusions.[53]

This was too bad, for in the aftermath of the New Left, liberty and reason encountered formidable challenges, not original ones, perhaps, but ones that poststructuralism brought acutely to consciousness. Further development of Popper's ideas could have answered these challenges, and answered them well, but neither Popper nor his students seem to me to have taken the necessary routes. Poststructuralists question the possibility of a critical dialogue, to say nothing of agreement or compromise, between communities that do not share Popper's conception of rationality. They warn that an effort to impose, or even promote, Popper's rationality would be tantamount to a search for Western hegemony, authorizing as universal a historically contingent concept. Does Popper have an answer?

While responding to Kuhn (and Wittgenstein) in the late 1970s and early 1980s, Popper spoke nostalgically of Habsburg (and classical Athenian) multiculturalism, praising culture clash as productive of great intellectual advances.[54] Culture clash was conducive to critical dialogue that transformed identities, transgressed boundaries, and changed communities. But Popper underestimated the difficulty of creating a situation that would make such a dialogue possible. Culture clash under conditions of unequal power does not always create dialogue, or advance cosmopolitanism. It may result in oppression. This had happened to the Czechs and Jews in Vienna under his eyes. All the same, he held fast to culture clash's emancipatory potential. He had seen its wonderful effect, he thought, among German-acculturated Viennese Jews. They had liberated themselves from traditional small-town Jewish life and became a cultural elite. Surely under the conditions of Western liberty such a result could be duplicated. Culture clash would expand horizons and open closed communities. It would advance recognition of rationality in relativity, unity in diversity, cosmopolitanism in multiculturalism. It might set humanity on the way to the Open Society.

Popper took it for granted that the conditions for cross-cultural dialogue already existed in Western societies. He was convinced that any culture clash would take place on a fairly level playing field. Freedom of expression was necessary and sufficient for a productive clash. At times, he seemed aware that this was not quite the case. He noted that

> culture clash may lose some of its great value if one of the clashing cultures
> regards itself as universally superior, and even more so if it is so regarded
> by the other: this may destroy the greatest value of culture clash, [the

---

[53] This agrees with Bryan Magee, *Confessions of a Philosopher*, pp. 200–1.

[54] "On Culture Clash" and "On a Little-Known Chapter of Mediterranean History," in *In Search of a Better World*, pp. 117–25, 107–16, respectively; "Der wichtigste Beitrag seit Aristoteles," *Wissenschaft aktuell* 1 (September 1980) (an interview with Peter Weibel on Kurt Gödel and the Vienna Circle, August 1978, Alpbach).

development of] a critical attitude. . . . The critical attitude of trying to learn
from the other will be replaced by a kind of blind acceptance. . . . Ontological relativity . . . can prove of immense value: . . . the partners in the
clash may liberate themselves from the prejudices of which they are unconscious. . . . Such a liberation may be a result of criticism awakened by culture
clash. [55]

Other than the moral injunction *not* to assume a superior attitude, however,
Popper had no suggestion as to how to promote such ontological relativity. He himself was not free of superior attitudes toward closed communities and Jewish and non-Western cultures.[56] To be sure, dialogue can
disabuse participants of superior attitudes. Self-criticism cannot be made a
condition for exchange; it is one of its ends. But dialogue's power is limited.
For optimal criticism, an ideal speech situation must be approximated.
Popper and his students did not investigate the social and cultural conditions promoting critical exchange. They have made it easy for critics of
liberalism to deny the vital dialogue that opens closed communities one
to another.

In *The Open Society*, Popper recognized that participants' "irrational
commitment to rationalism" was the precondition to dialogue.[57] Bartley
showed later that no irrational commitment was necessary; dialogue itself
contained all the rules, and they who participated necessarily followed
them. This did not solve the problem of encouraging people to debate and
accept criticism. Popper insisted that the sociology of knowledge was of
no help. It was rooted in the wrong assumption — shared even by Kant —
"that presuppositions . . . can neither be changed by decision nor refuted
by experience."[58] True, but then how does one promote such transformative experience? Karl Mannheim's central concern was creating dialogue
among conflicting perspectives that may facilitate resolution of social conflicts. He pointed out the limits that ideologies imposed on dialogue, but
hoped that intellectuals, uniquely positioned to recognize the diversity and
historical contingency of ideologies, could facilitate it. He shared with

---

[55] Popper, "The Myth of the Framework," in his *The Myth of the Framework*, p. 51.

[56] Yet in some respects, he was remarkably free of ethnic prejudice. Julius Kraft, a much kinder person
than Popper was, complained to Popper bitterly in 1958 about his daughter's engagement to an
Indian (not an uncommon attitude among German Jews). Popper was unsympathetic: "[T]he news
itself is, really, not more worrying than if she had announced her engagement to, say, a wealthy busi-
nessman of Scottish extraction. . . . You must wait till you meet the man: he may make a great
impression on you, and they may be very happy. One of my nicest students was an Indian." (Popper
to Kraft, 2 June 1958, Julius Kraft papers, State University of New York at Albany.) This may not
seem a crushing attack on ethnic prejudice, but it was an effective rebuke.

[57] Popper, *The Open Society*, vol. 2, p. 218. "[W]hoever adopts the rationalist attitude does so because
without reasoning he has adopted some decision, or belief, or habit, or behavior, which therefore
in its turn must be called 'irrational,' . . . an irrational *faith in reason*."

[58] Ibid., p. 208.

Popper the liberal ideal of rational communication, and sought to domesticate conflict through debate. His hopes for the intelligentsia are no more vindicated by contemporary American intellectuals than they were by the Germans, but in awkwardly investigating the conditions that would make dialogue possible, Mannheim pursued a line of inquiry that Popperians should have undertaken, not rejected.[59]

Commitment to reason is insufficient, of course. Any dialogue is better than none – as celebrants of liberal democracy never fail to remind us – but, for an ideal speech situation, power must be so neutralized that it has minimal influence on dialogue. Radical critics have shown, at least to my satisfaction, that socially disadvantaged groups do not have a fair chance of being heard, let alone prevailing, in the so-called democratic political process. Organized elites and corporate interests block, manipulate, and circumvent the channels. Just as the young Popper believed – all the way through his correspondence with Carnap in 1946 – a fairly egalitarian socioeconomic structure and public control of corporations are preconditions to effective democratic dialogue. Any effort to realize Popperian ideals would involve radical social reform aimed at approximating an ideal speech situation for political debate.

Neoconservative critics have moved, since the 1970s, in the opposite direction. Such a debate, they began arguing, is not feasible at all. Carl Schmitt had already denounced parliamentary debate as a farce. Debate produced neither consensus nor compromise. Deals were cut behind closed doors. Politics required arbitrary decision. Both Heinrich Gomperz and Popper pointed out that decision was always based on partial information at best, neither time nor expediency allowing for exhaustive consideration. To Schmitt, it was the final location of authority – who made the decision – that counted. Similarly, neoconservatives complained that conflicting social demands overwhelmed the political process, the state unable to negotiate them effectively. Too much democracy, not too little, was the problem. They sought to relieve the pressure by blocking access to the process. The more astute and generous among them began looking for alternatives to centralized decision making, suggesting that if regional and local institutions negotiated the demands overwhelming the central government, both democracy and efficiency might be enhanced. As Jürgen Habermas noted in his response to Daniel Bell, radicals and conservatives could open a

---

[59] Karl Mannheim, *Ideology and Utopia* (New York: Harcourt, Brace, 1936). I have used here Richard Ashcraft's "Political Theory and Political Action in Karl Mannheim's Thought: Reflections upon *Ideology and Utopia* and its Critics," *Comparative Studies of Society and History* 23 (1981): 23–50. Like most interpreters, Popper dismissed Mannheim's sociological determinism and Hegelian universal class (the free-floating intellectuals). He is not incorrect, but he ignored Mannheim's liberal political concerns and his usefulness for investigating the preconditions of rational communication.

productive debate on "renegotiating the social contract" based on similar democratic proposals.[60]

The debate has never taken place because in the wake of the Reagan–Thatcher revolution, the left, especially in the United States, has despaired of rationalizing politics and found consolation in a largely barren (and misguided) cultural politics, the conservatives only too happy to fight the "tenured radicals" on the new grounds and draw on the gender and racial prejudices of the population to defeat them. To the extent that it has been seeking to influence politics, the left for two decades has promoted the particular (and sometimes conflicting) interests of minorities and middle-class women. Here it can point to achievements (though rarely of its own making), but they appear against the backdrop of the welfare state's retreat, increasingly divergent distribution of wealth, and, worse, their growing legitimization, which would make future reversal difficult. There are excellent Popperian grounds to promote minorities and women. Not only are social justice and equality values in themselves, but free (autonomous) social agents also render critical debate a reality rather than an ideal, with empowerment of the disadvantaged signaling progress toward an ideal speech situation. Put this way, promotion of disadvantaged groups becomes part of a general program for democratization and rationalization. This program would require resumption of the debate that Habermas and Bell began.

Such a debate means reconstituting a liberal framework for reform and ending the indiscriminate (and irresponsible) attack on the "Enlightenment." Critics have ignored the benefits that varieties of enlightenment have conferred upon different minorities. (I consider myself to have been a beneficiary.) They seek to create a protective environment where minorities are free to expand "their" culture without a challenge from the "hegemonic" one. (This would have left me a member of a fairly closed community, not someone predisposed to write on Popper.) To the extent that preemptory validation of a "minority culture" prevents criticism, it hinders progress. The recent assault on the *Haskalah* (Jewish enlightenment) has delegitimized the *maskilim's* criticism of traditional Judaism and the ghetto. The underlying assumption seems to be an unconditional acceptance of an oppressed minority's culture. In contrast, efforts to improve, even transform, a minority are viewed with great suspicion. Enlightenment is decried; the ghetto vindicated.

Celebration of the diversity of closed communities is a poor substitute for diversity in an open society: shifting boundaries, changing conventions,

---

[60] "Neoconservative Culture Criticism in the United States and West Germany: An Intellectual Movement in Two Political Cultures," in *Habermas and Modernity*, ed. Richard J. Bernstein (Cambridge, Mass.: MIT Press, 1985), pp. 78–94. This was, in part, a response to Daniel Bell, *The Cultural Contradictions of Capitalism* (New York: Basic Books, 1976).

destabilized beliefs. Fascism, Popper thought, was fear of change. Culture clash is the salt of diversity. The dilemmas of liberal universalism may not lend themselves to an easy solution, but the imperative of diversity provides no alternative. It derives, in the last analysis, from enlightenment universalism, the respect of humanity qua humanity. We are forever condemned to negotiate between the closed community and the Open Society. Liberal universalism may threaten difference, but it has devised several ways of negotiating the threat. One of them is: reason about it.

Can we reason over differences, especially ethnic and religious differences? Popper thought that it was difficult, but possible, and that we do it all the time, although we rarely reach agreement.[61] It is true that when he initially envisioned critical dialogue, he expected it to take place among people sharing a significant background, or, at the very least, accepting unproblematically debate and argumentation. It is also true that ruthless criticism, not to mention the culture of debate that he promoted in his own seminars, is ill suited to intercultural (or political) dialogue. Yet, at times, Popper proposed a more generous discourse ethic:

> Rationalism is the attitude of readiness to listen to critical arguments and to learn from experience: . . . [the] hope that by such means as argument and careful observation, people may reach some kind of agreement on many problems of importance . . . and reach a compromise which because of its equity is acceptable to most. . . . The attitude of reasonableness is . . . that in the search for truth we need cooperation.[62]

Participants in debate must recognize others as equal, make a genuine effort to listen, understand, and learn, and attempt to reach agreement and compromise. Popper did not distinguish, as Habermas does, between scientific and political discourse, cognitive interest and symbolic interaction, instrumental and communicative rationality. Understanding and compromise played roles in the formation of the scientific and political consensus alike. He did seem to distinguish, however, between criticism and "the attitude of reasonableness." In intercultural dialogue, understanding is especially important, and in politics, compromise is perhaps more important than critical judgment. "The attitude of reasonableness" allows for some differentiation between spheres, although not as sharp as the one Habermas proposes.

Only in a deliberative democracy (or the Open Society) are intersubjective criticism and politics proximate. We do not yet live in such a democracy, and if we ever come close, there will be communities that do not accept intersubjective criticism. In domestic and international politics alike, discourse communities, often widely divergent, compete. Reconciling their claims requires negotiation. Negotiating is debating, but there is no

[61] "The Myth of the Framework." [62] *The Open Society*, vol. 2, p. 225.

use pretending that the rules of critical exchange apply. The best compromise possible, given prevailing disagreements, may substitute as a guideline for the best argument. Not all situations admit of an acceptable compromise, and so liberals (or critical rationalists) must often decide whether a compromise comes close enough to the best argument (or proposal) as they emerge (or would have emerged) from intersubjective criticism, or not. Liberal communicative ideals remain valid, as does Popper's rationality criterion. They tell us where we should head. But they provide no guidelines for evaluating political proposals. Popper did not address the problems emerging from the divergence between ideal and real politics, intersubjective criticism and negotiation for compromise. He did not suggest how we might proceed in situations that do not admit of intersubjective criticism. This already appeared as a difficulty in his account of science, but it is an especially acute problem in politics where we may not even hope for a (methodological) consensus over criteria for evaluating proposals. If critical rationalism is to remain politically vital, not merely a regulative ideal for a utopian cosmopolitan age, Popperians need to develop guidelines for political evaluation.

Popper attributed, correctly I believe, current disenchantment with reason to expecting too much of it. Debate does take place, but it rarely emulates intersubjective criticism; agreement is rare, and compromise seems inadequate, even judged by relaxed standards. There is, however, no alternative. Some critics of "rationality" have proposed refounding discourse ethics on empathy, rather than on criticism. More recently, progressives who recognize the dead end to which poststructuralist politics have led – how can they protect disempowered minorities in oppressive cultures once universal standards are proscribed? – hope to find in emotives the universal structure they have failed to find in reason. This, too, is a dead end. Not only do they use "reason" to argue universal emotives, but they will also need to arbitrate conflicting emotives. Discourse intervenes, so does dialogue, so does intersubjective criticism. We are back where we started.[63]

Popper recognized that multiple closed communities, from families where affective relations predominate to religious associations where tradition and belief reign supreme, flourish in any open society. These communities need not make critical debate their principle (although, as a rule, the larger the room they give it, the healthier the Open Society), but

---

[63] Theories of emotives may help manage affective relations, cultivate those we cherish, and restrain those we discourage, but only critical discussion can tell us what sort of relationships to cherish and how we might manage them. Popper, to be sure, underestimated affective relations, especially their significance for forming attitudes and beliefs sustaining the Open Society. Emotions seemed to him suspicious, irrational, implicated with fascism, responsible for disrupting debate and compromise. Working out the uses of a theory of emotives for critical rationalism may be one task Popperians will undertake.

they need to endorse it to regulate their relations with other communities. The Open Society respects their relative autonomy, but it claims the right to intervene in their affairs when they prevent their members from fully participating in society. Intervention legitimately includes the terminating of practices that enforce extreme gender and race oppression, from female "circumcision" to depriving youth of education that would enable them to participate in critical debate. Retaining closure to protect communal culture and identity is not an acceptable defense strategy. Communal hierarchies of class, gender, and race must give in to the Open Society. The questions of whether, when, and how the Open Society may intervene to open closed communities is to be pragmatically decided. That such questions constitute permanent dilemmas for progressives and rarely admit of satisfactory resolution is obvious. That they can, and have, led to abuse – universalist rhetoric mobilized to break communal structures obstructing modern forms of economic and political domination – is all too true. That there is any escape from the dilemmas I very much doubt.

Popper, as I have pointed out at various junctures, was oblivious to feminism, and yet his ideas emerged from a progressive feminist milieu and could be used to promote women's emancipation. In the last two decades, however, certain strains of feminism have challenged liberal emancipationist ideals.[64] They have argued that liberal universalism is masculine in character; "apparently universal categories, such as the 'individual,' . . . are sexually particular, constructed on the basis of male attributes, capacities and modes of activity." Moreover, the separation between the private and public spheres entrenches patriarchy; "the masculine public world of . . . rights, contract, reason, . . . gains . . . significance only in contrast with . . . the private world of natural subjection, inequality . . . and femininity."[65] This line of reasoning essentializes liberalism, ignoring evidence that liberals disturbed established categories of masculine and feminine as much as affirmed them, and that they reshuffled the private–public distinction, rather than reified it.

Critics have traditionally complained that liberals devalued the public and elevated the private, that they diminished participatory politics and privileged "private" relationships, whether economic, discursive, or familial.[66] Liberals' anxiety about political authority is notorious. They endeavored to construct the private sphere as a bulwark against violation of liberty. (That they mobilized the state to realize their programs, when they

---

[64] Carole Pateman, *The Sexual Contract* (Stanford, Calif.: Stanford University Press, 1988); Joan Scott, *Gender and the Politics of History* (New York: Columbia University Press, 1988).

[65] Carole Pateman, "The Theoretical Subversiveness of Feminism," in *Feminist Challenges: Social and Political Theory*, ed. Carole Pateman and Elizabeth Gross (Boston: Northeastern University Press, 1987), p. 6.

[66] Pateman herself advanced such a critique in *Participation and Democratic Theory* (Cambridge: Cambridge University Press, 1970).

could, and often violated their own principles is no evidence that their anxiety was disingenuous, or unjustified.) Liberal idealization of the private sphere as an oasis in times of political trouble reflected, to be sure, comfort with unchallenged patriarchy. Few liberals, notably John Stuart Mill, scrutinized private patriarchy. But liberals transformed both "private" and "public" so that they were no longer identical with the traditional rendering of masculine and feminine. Viewing themselves, in the aftermath of the French Revolution, as victims of political violence and ideological extremism, liberals found themselves identifying with the feminine. This is no twentieth-century projection: Civic humanists charged liberals with effeminizing the public sphere, and liberals denied it with one voice, then wrote histories showing women's role in civilizing a barbarian feudal world with the other.[67] Their own efforts to domesticate political violence mimicked, on occasion, imagined feminine strategies. The birth of liberalism signaled the introduction of the "feminine" into politics, or, put boldly, the end of "masculine" politics.

Liberal universalism does not reflect masculine abstraction; it challenges it. If liberal concepts, such as citizenship, were, or are, tinged with sexual particularity, the best way to refashion them is through public criticism. In the Open Society, masculine and feminine are constantly remade; gender differences are ever shifting. Debate is essential to negotiating and managing them equitably. Popper did not deny, or affirm, sexual difference; he insisted that shared humanity be made grounds for political participation. The efforts liberals made throughout the nineteenth century to exclude women and workers from participation in public discourse only testify to the force of a vision the full implications of which they were trying to avoid. Openness and publicity have historically benefited the underdogs whose increasing share in public debate is a major indicator of progress. This has very much been the case for women. Liberal universalism contains genuinely universalist moments. The point is to capitalize on them, not to destroy liberalism.

Having returned in the summer of 1986 from Vienna to London, after his wife's death, Popper sold Fallowfield and moved to Kenley (Surrey), south of London, again to a secluded house, with speed bumps on his private road making visits to his residence all the more arduous. His secretary, Melitta Mew, filled in for Hennie, managing every aspect of his life. (Together with her husband, she would also become his executor.) He enjoyed the growing international recognition, making official visits to heads of state and receiving former premiers (Schmidt) at his residence. His influence spread to China and, after communism's fall, the Soviet Union,

[67] François Guizot, *Histoire des origines du Gouvernement Représentatif en Europe*, 2 vols. (Paris: Didier, 1851), Lecture 1; *L'histoire de la civilisation en Europe* (Paris: Didier, 1868), esp. Lecture 5; Lionel Gossman, "Augustin Thierry and Liberal Historiography," *History and Theory, Beiheft* 15 (1976).

his works reaching every corner of the globe. In 1982, financier George Soros established The Open Society Institute (originally a fund), dispensing stipends to black South African students and impoverished Eastern European scholars, and supporting academic projects of social significance. In 1991, Soros founded the Central European University in Budapest, Prague, and Warsaw. Popper's cosmopolitanism served as inspiration.

Popper continued to work hard to the end, his prose beautiful as ever. In his late eighties, however, he recognized that he could no longer prepare for publication any of the major manuscripts that he had earlier contemplated. He relented, and was happier for it. Indeed, those close to him report that in his final years, even without Hennie, he was happier than he had ever been before, more secure in his reputation, less pressured by his work. Visitors now found him eager to talk about politics. He seemed obsessed with Khrushchev's conspiracy to subdue the West through a nuclear threat, and admired Kennedy's management of the Cuban missile crisis. (In the 1980s, however, he was disappointed in Kennedy, just as he had been in Marx, when he discovered that they both had had mistresses. This offended him more than anything they said or did.) He was concerned about the global dispersal of Russia's nuclear arsenal, blasted the Greens for their crusade against science, proposed an all-out struggle to stem population growth in the Third World and thought that the Catholic Church might be persuaded to acquiesce in it, and suggested that decolonialization had come too early, without preparing the colonized to assume responsibility ("as if the children were permitted to run the kindergarten," he said). His comments still showed, on occasion, his youthful combination of foresight and good judgment; at other times they disclosed his forty-year seclusion in Fallowfield, naïveté, and the prejudices of past ages.[68]

Some visitors inquired about his Viennese background. They found him reluctant to recollect the past, irritated when they persisted in their questions. He would much rather talk about the postwar world, where he was recognized and felt safe, and not about interwar Vienna, where he had struggled for recognition and felt that his life as an intellectual of Jewish origin was in danger. His students respected his privacy and never asked about his family. A pair of scholars, Hans-Joachim Dahms and Friedrich Stadler, discovered, however, that when they asked specific questions about events, places, and people, Popper would suddenly remember. Their interview, soon to be published in full, gives glimpses of the life I have endeavored to recount in this biography.[69]

---

[68] *The Lesson of This Century: With Two Talks on Freedom and the Democratic State: Karl Popper interviewed by Giancarlo Bosetti*, trans. Patrick Camiller (London: Routledge, 1996); Eugene Yue-Ching Ho, "At 90, and Still Dynamic: Revisiting Sir Karl Popper and Attending His Birthday Party," *Intellectus* 23 (July–September 1992): 1–5 (available also through The Karl Popper Web); Interview, *Der Spiegel*, June 1992, trans. in הארץ *Ha-aretz*, 27 September 1992.

[69] Excerpts were published as "Popper und der Wiener Kreis – Aus einem Gespräch mit Sir Karl Popper (1991)," in Friedrich Stadler, *Studien zum Wiener Kreis* (Frankfurt: Suhrkamp, 1997), pp. 525–45.

Popper died on September 17, 1994, and was cremated near London. Cremation befitted him, a philosopher who lived in permanent exile, who had no homeland in life or death. He asked for his ashes to be placed in an urn in Hennie's grave.[70] This, too, was appropriate. Not only did she represent his most significant human attachment; their relationship, which transcended ethnonational divisions, also testified to the vitality of the cosmopolitan idea. Still, Popper's final homecoming was strange. None of his relatives were buried in the same small Catholic cemetery. His ashes lie with three generations of Henningers and Gussls, of whose history, culture, and life he knew little. Cremated rather than buried, occupying his wife's family grave rather than his own, he is as much a sojourner in Austria in death as he was in life.

The pain of alienation and exile that shaped *The Open Society* strikes one with awe and fear. Enlightenment cosmopolitanism provided a vision of a home to refugees of the worst disaster that befell humanity in the twentieth century. Popper immortalized their dreams in the Open Society. He believed that he had witnessed some progress toward the fulfillment of his visions. Communism's collapse and the progress of European unity pleased him. He regarded the members of the Atlantic Alliance as "the best societies that humankind has known." Yet, in truth, they fell short of his philosophy's standards. Access to the public sphere remained restricted through mechanisms and processes to which he was insensitive. The Jewish problem, the source of his cosmopolitanism, did not reach a solution compatible with the Open Society. One need not echo his outright rejection of Jewish statehood to recognize as much. Little during the twentieth century pointed to the realization of his visions. Everywhere the Open Society remained elusive.

The widespread disenchantment with the Enlightenment and the Open Society is thus not surprising. The political and philosophical dilemmas of Vienna 1900 are still with us, from Bosnia to Israel, from the Collège de France to Duke University. The New Left represented the last great Western movement trying, in skewed ways, to realize an enlightenment vision. It brought disrepute not only on itself but also on liberalism, because conservatives understand well what the left often ignores – the underlying unity of liberal and Marxist emancipation. Throughout this century, each disappointment with totalitarianism, right or left, each recoil in horror from a grand narrative that proved not only false but murderous, brought with it its own "poststructuralism," its own challenge to the possibility of truth, knowledge, and rational politics. If this biography is not free of *ira et studium*, it is because one expects better judgment and greater resilience from intellectuals. In the wake of the New Left's demise and the New Right's rise, few on the left retained commitment to the reforging of a democratic

[70] Ian Jarvie and David Miller kindly provided me with this information.

consensus for reform; most, without acknowledging past political mistakes, delighted in deconstructing enlightenment emancipation.

I offer Popper as an alternative. He articulated with unsurpassable clarity the dilemmas of Vienna 1900 and made continuous struggle with them possible. I have tried to show that he worked his way through most post-structuralist problems – rationality, linguistic self-referentiality, foundation-ism, grand narrative, progress – and provided brilliant solutions, the only viable solutions I know. He has also made a significant contribution to lib-eralism by providing a compelling defense against totalitarianism (when one was badly lacking), general guidelines for social reform (emerging from a dialogue with Marxism), and a vision of a cosmopolitan public sphere that becomes all the more appealing with globalization. He insisted that critical awareness and political commitment were compatible. If his own conduct was, on occasion, a living contrast to his philosophy, he was also steadfast in refusing academic fashion, faithful to his ideas to the end. Amid the Central European ruins he kept faith, and he urged a continued fight for a better future. Where there is struggle there is hope. This is Popper's rejoinder to postmodernism.

Hope does not come cheap, but only those least in need of it – well fed and self-satisfied Western academics – can easily dispose of it. I have often wondered why few historians who have studied the twentieth century's greatest tragedies have despaired of the possibility for political improvement in the way that many contemporary intellectuals have. I have also won-dered why I, myself, having first grown up in an area of deteriorating ethnic conflicts, then studying a vanished culture, have not despaired. Nowadays, one walks the streets of Vienna with unremitting dread. They are a con-stant reminder of the erasure of a culture and the genocide of a people. The familiar buildings are there, untouched by the catastrophe, but the people and the vital intellectual life are gone. One is faced with a vivid demonstration of what Popper called "radical evil."[71] By the nature of their projects, historians cannot directly address contemporary problems and can rarely make a major theoretical contribution, but they can call attention to historical moments that represent unfulfilled promises, ready to be recov-ered, appropriated, and drawn again into the struggle for a better world. Fin-de-siècle progressivism and Red Vienna represent such moments, and Popper represents one of their greatest accomplishments. Looking over a century that knew two world wars and put the survival of civilization in question, I have sought to rescue, from amid the ruins, hope and vision for the next century. Popper is their embodiment.

[71] Edward Zerin, "Karl Popper on God. The Lost Interview" [1969], *Skeptic* 6, no. 2 (1998): 48.

Bibliography

This bibliography lists all works cited in the notes. It does not, however, contain works that have informed my methodology or provided historical and philosophical background. (In particular, I have omitted references to theoretical debates in intellectual history.) I have divided the bibliography into two sections: archives and published works. The short bibliographical essay provides a brief description of the archival sources.

ARCHIVES

The Hoover Institute, Stanford University, is the main repository for the Popper papers. The archives include manuscripts of Popper's works from 1927 to 1986, correspondence from 1932 to 1987, teaching materials from 1937 to 1970, conference proceedings, letters of reference, and additional biographical material (including photographs). The archives are superbly organized. The register can be accessed electronically through The Karl Popper Web: www.eeng.dcu.ie/~tkpw/. The British Library of Political and Economic Science (LSE), the Karl Popper Institut (Vienna), the *Karl-Popper-Sammlung* (University of Klagenfurt, Austria), and The Popper Project (Central European University, Budapest) have microfilmed copies of the Hoover originals. The University of Klagenfurt also has Karl Popper's library, containing, among other things, remnants of his father's library and books annotated with his comments.

The Hoover Archives do not yet include Popper's personal correspondence, but I am not sure how much of it is extant. Popper apparently expressed the wish that all material be made public after his death. This also includes his writings from 1981 on, as well as earlier material that had been overlooked. I think it is important that this material be made available to scholars expeditiously.

I have used the archives of the following members and associates of the Vienna Circle: Rudolf Carnap, Herbert Feigl, Felix Kaufmann, Karl Menger, Richard von Mises, Otto Neurath, Hans Reichenbach, and Moritz Schlick. The Archives of Scientific Philosophy, University of Pittsburgh, have the Carnap and Reichenbach Collections (as well as copies of the Feigl, Neurath, and Schlick papers). The extensive Carnap Collection includes correspondence with Popper and with members of the circle. The correspondence between Carnap and Neurath, as well as between Ina Carnap and Eva Hempel, often pertains to Popper. The Reichenbach Collection includes correspondence with Popper (1932–5). The Feigl Collection (original at the Center for the Philosophy of Science, the University of Minnesota, Minneapolis) includes postwar correspondence between Popper and Feigl. The *Felix Kaufmann Nachlaß* includes correspondence with Popper (1935–8), as well as correspondence pertaining to Popper with Carnap, Hempel, and Neurath. I have used the microfilmed copy at the *Sozialwissenschaftliches Archiv*, University of Constance, Germany. (The original at the Center for Advanced Research in Phenomenology at Wilfred Laurier University, Waterloo, Ontario, is less accessible. The archives' register is published; see under

Harry P. Reeder in the next section.) Karl Menger's papers at Duke University include some postwar correspondence with Popper and a draft of "Kriterium" (1932). The Richard von Mises papers in the Harvard University Archives include some correspondence with Abraham Wald pertaining to Popper. The *Wiener Kreis Stichting*, Haarlem, the Netherlands has the Neurath and Schlick *Nachlässe*. (I used, however, the microfilmed copies in the *Philosophisches Archiv*, the University of Constance.) The *Neurath Nachlaß* includes correspondence with Popper, as well as correspondence pertaining to Popper with Carnap, Philipp Frank, Jørgen Jørgensen, Tadeusz Kotarbinski, Heinz Neider, Reichenbach, and L. S. Stebbing. The *Schlick Nachlaß* includes correspondence with Carnap, Feigl, Frank, and Springer (Otto Lange) pertaining to *Logik der Forschung*.

The Hoover Institute Archives contain the Friedrich Hayek papers that include extensive correspondence with Popper from 1938 on. The Carl Friedrich papers in the Harvard University Archives include correspondence with Fritz Hellin (and a letter from Alfred Braunthal) concerning publication of *The Open Society*. The papers of G. E. Moore in the Cambridge University Library contain some correspondence with Popper. Julius Kraft's papers at the State University of New York, Albany, contain correspondence with Popper, mostly from 1958 to 1960 (but also a 1925 letter). The Ernest Nagel papers at Columbia University include correspondence with members of the Vienna Circle, occasionally touching on Popper. The Paul Lazarsfeld papers at Columbia University do not have correspondence with Popper, but they contain material relevant to the Pädagogisches Institut. The archives at the Karl Polanyi Institute, Concordia University, Montreal, contain a manuscript by Felix Schafer, describing Polanyi's 1920s seminar in Vienna, his intellectual circle, and Popper's participation. The diary of Oscar Morgenstern, in his papers at Duke University, includes a reference to Popper (9 December 1934) and information on Menger's *Mathematisches Kolloquium* and the Mises circle. The Papers of the Society for the Protection of Science and Learning (SPSL), Bodleian Library, Oxford University, contain Popper's 1936 application to the academic council.

The Wiener Stadt- und Landesarchiv, City Hall, Vienna can provide basic residential (post 1910) and biographical information on Popper and his family. *Matrikelamt 8* is the residential *Meldearchiv; Matrikelamt 61* contains the *Verlassenschaftsakten* of Simon Popper and Max Schiff. The *Isrealitische Kultusgemeinde Wien* has marriage and burial records for Viennese Jews, but most of the pre–World War II material, including some tax records, is in the Central Archives for the History of the Jewish People, The Hebrew University of Jerusalem. The Research Foundation for Jewish Immigration, *Zentrum für Antisemitismusforschung*, Technische Universität, Berlin, has an informative questionnaire that Popper filled out in 1980 for the *International Biographical Dictionary of Central European Emigrés, 1933–1945*.

PUBLISHED SOURCES

Abramovitch, Raphael. "From Socialist Utopia to Totalitarian Empire." *Modern Review* 1 (1947): 249–65.
Actes du Congrès International de Philosophie Scientifique. 8 vols. Paris: Hermann & Cie, 1936.
Adam, Erik. "Austromarxismus und Schulreform." In *Die Schul- und Bildungspolitik der österreichischen Sozialdemokratie in der Ersten Republik*, edited by Erik Adam, Primus-Heinz Kucher, Eva Reitmann, and Josef Weidenholzer. Vienna: ÖBV, 1983.
Adler, Alfred. *Studie über Minderwertigkeit von Organen.* Berlin: Urban & Schwarzenberg, 1907.

Über den nervösen Charakter: Grundzüge einer vergleichenden Individual-Psychologie und Psychotherapie. 4th ed. Munich: Bergmann, 1928.

What Life Should Mean to You. Boston: Little, Brown, 1931.

Adler, Kurt. "Ursprünge und Ausstrahlungen der Individualpsychologie." In *Das geistige Leben Wiens in der Zwischenkriegszeit,* edited by Norbert Leser. Vienna: ÖBV, 1981.

Adler, Les K., and T. G. Paterson. "Red Fascism: The Merger of Nazi Germany and Soviet Russia in the American Image of Totalitarianism, 1930s–1950s." *American Historical Review* 75 (1970): 1046–64.

Adler, Max. *Kant und der Marxismus.* Berlin: Laub, 1925.

Neue Menschen. Berlin: Laub, 1924.

Adorno, Theodore W., Karl Popper, Ralf Dahrendorf, Jürgen Habermas, Hans Albert, and Harold Pilot. *The Positivist Dispute in German Sociology.* Translated by Glyn Adey and David Frisby. London: Heinemann, 1976.

Agassi, Joseph. "Celebrating *The Open Society.*" *Philosophy of the Social Sciences* 27 (1997): 505.

"Institutional Individualism." *British Journal of Sociology* 26 (1975): 144–55.

"Methodological Individualism." *British Journal of Sociology* 11 (1960): 244–70.

"Modified Conventionalism." In *Science in Flux.* Boston: Reidel, 1975.

A Philosopher's Apprentice. Amsterdam: Rodopi, 1993.

"Sensationalism." *Mind* 75 (1966): 1–24.

"To Salvage Neurath." *Philosophy of the Social Sciences* 28 (1998): 83–101.

Agassi, Joseph, and Ian Jarvie, eds. *Rationality.* Boston: Kluwer, 1987.

Agnon, Shmuel Yosef. *Tmol Shilshom* (Heretofore). Tel Aviv: Schocken, 1968.

Allan, R. S., et al. "Research and the University: A Statement by a Group of Teachers in the University of New Zealand." Christchurch, N.Z.: Caxton Press, 1945.

Allen, R. G. D. *Mathemetical Analysis for Economists.* London: Macmillan, 1938.

Alpers, Benjamin. "Understanding Dictatorship and Defining Democracy in American Public Culture, 1930–1945." Ph.D. diss., Princeton University, 1994.

Althusser, Louis. *Pour Marx.* Paris: Maspero, 1965.

"Sur le jeune Marx." In *Pour Marx.* Paris: Maspero, 1965.

"Sur l'évolution du jeune Marx." In *Éléments d'autocritique.* Paris: Hachette, 1974.

Amann, Anton. "Soziologie in Wien: Entstehung und Emigration bis 1938." In *Vertriebene Vernunft: Emigration und Exil österreichischer Wissenschaft 1930–1940.* Edited by Friedrich Stadler. Vol. 1. Vienna: Jugend und Volk, 1987.

Amendola, Giovanni. *L'Aventino contro il Fascismo: Scritti politici.* Milano: Ricciardi, 1976.

American Philosophical Society. "Symposium on the Totalitarian State." *Proceedings of the American Philosophical Society* 82 (1940).

Anderson, Harriet. *Utopian Feminism: Women Movements in Fin-de-siècle Vienna.* New Haven, Conn.: Yale University Press, 1992.

Annas, Julia. "Plato's *Republic* and Feminism." *Philosophy* 51 (1976): 307–21.

Anon. Review of *Logik der Forschung. Revue des sciences philosophiques et théologiques* 24, no. 4 (1935).

Applegate, Celia. *A Nation of Provincials: The German Idea of Heimat.* Berkeley, Calif.: University of California Press, 1990.

Arendt, Hannah. *The Origins of Totalitarianism.* New York: HBJ, 1951.

Aristophanes. *The Clouds,* in *The Complete Plays of Aristophanes.* Translated by Moses Hadas. New York: Bantam Books, 1962.

Aristotle. *Metaphysics.* Translated by W. D. Ross. 2 vols. Oxford: Clarendon Press, 1924.

Nichomachean Ethics. Translated by Terence Irwin. Indianapolis, Ind.: Hackett, 1985.

"On Good Birth" (Fragments). Vol. 12 in *Works*, edited by David Ross. Oxford: Clarendon Press, 1952.

Politics. Translated by Ernest Barker. New York: Oxford University Press, 1946.

Aron, Raymond. "États démocratiques et états totalitaires" [1939]. *Commentaire* 6 (1983): 701–19.

The Opium of the Intellectuals. New York: Doubleday, 1957.

"Une révolution antiprolétarienne: Idéologie et réalité du national-socialisme" [1936]. *Commentaire* 8 (1985): 299–310.

Aschheim, Steven. *Brothers and Strangers: The Eastern European Jew in German and German Jewish Consciousness, 1800–1923.* Madison, Wis.: University of Wisconsin Press, 1983.

Ash, Mitchell. "Psychology and Politics in Interwar Vienna: The Vienna Psychological Institute, 1922–1942." In *Psychology in Twentieth-Century Thought and Society*, edited by Mitchell Ash and William Woodward. New York: Cambridge University Press, 1987.

Ashcraft, Richard. "Political Theory and Political Action in Karl Mannheim's Thought: Reflections upon *Ideology and Utopia* and its Critics." *Comparative Studies of Society and History* 23 (1981): 23–50.

Auner, Joseph. "Schoenberg's Handel Concerto and the Ruins of Tradition." *Journal of the American Musicological Society* 49 (1996): 264–313.

Austriacus, Prof. Dr. (Johann Sauter). "Der Fall des Wiener Professors Schlick – eine Mahnung zur Gewissenserforschung." *Schönere Zukunft*, 12 July 1936; reprinted in Friedrich Stadler, *Studien zum Wiener Kreis*. Frankfurt: Suhrkamp, 1997.

Avineri, Shlomo. *Hegel's Theory of the Modern State.* New York: Cambridge University Press, 1972.

"Labor, Alienation, and Social Classes in Hegel's *Realphilosophie.*" *Philosophy and Public Affairs* 1 (1971): 96–119.

Ayer, A. J. *Language, Truth and Logic.* London: Gollancz, 1936.

Ayer, Alfred, ed. *Logical Positivism.* New York: Free Press, 1959.

Babylonian Talmud. 21 vols. Vilna: Romm, 1880–92.

Bachelard, Gaston. *Le nouvel esprit scientifique.* Paris: Felix Alcan, 1934.

La philosophie du non. Paris: Presses Universitaires de France, 1940.

Review of *Logik der Forschung. Recherches Philosophiques* 5 (1936): 447.

Bailyn, Bernard, and Donald Fleming, eds. *The Intellectual Migration.* Cambridge, Mass.: Harvard University Press, 1969.

Ballod, Karl. *Die Zukunftsstaat – Produktion und Konsum im Sozialstaat.* 2d ed. Stuttgart: Dietz, 1919.

Bambrough, Renford, ed. *Plato, Popper and Politics.* New York: Barnes and Noble, 1967.

Barash, Asher. *Kitve Asher Barash* (Collected Works). 3 vols. Tel Aviv: Massada, 1952.

Barker, Ernest. "From Plato to Marx." *Sunday Times*, 9 December 1945.

Greek Political Theory. 4th ed. London: Methuen, 1951.

Barraclough, Geoffrey. "Tinkering with History." *The Spectator*, 6 December 1957, 836.

Bartley, William W., III. "Rehearsing a Revolution: Music and Politics" (extract from "Karl Popper: A Life"). Paper presented at the Pacific Regional Meeting of the Mont Pèlerin Society, Christchurch, New Zealand, 27–30 November 1989.

"Theory of Language and Philosophy of Science as Instruments of Educational Reform: Wittgenstein and Popper as Austrian School Teachers." In *Methodological and Historical Essays in the Natural and Social Sciences*, edited by Robert S. Cohen and Marx W. Wartofsky. Boston Studies in the Philosophy of Science 14. Boston: Reidel, 1974.

The Retreat to Commitment. London: Chatto & Windus, 1962.

Unfathomed Knowledge, Unmeasured Wealth. La Salle, Ill.: Open Court, 1990.

Wittgenstein. Philadelphia: Lippincott, 1973.

Bauer, Otto. *Der Aufstand der österreichischen Arbeiter.* Prague: Verlag der deutschen sozialdemokratischen Arbeiterpartei in der Tschechoslowakischen Republik, 1934.

The Eighteenth Brumaire of Louis Bonaparte. Translated by Eden and Cedar Paul. New York: International Publishers, 1926.

"Der Faschismus." *Der Sozialistische Kampf* 1 (1938): 75–83.

Kapitalismus und Sozialismus nach dem Weltkrieg. Vienna: Wiener Volksbuchhandlung, 1931.

Die Nationalitätenfrage und die Sozialdemokratie. Vienna: Volksbuchhandlung, 1924.

Die österreichische Revolution. Vienna: Wiener Volksbuchhandlung, 1923. *(The Austrian Revolution.* London: Parsons, 1925.)

Der Weg zum Sozialismus. Vienna: Wiener Volksbuchhandlung, 1919.

Zwischen zwei Weltkriegen? Bratislava: Eugen Prager, 1936.

Bauman, Sygmunt. "Strangers: The Social Construction of Universality and Particularity." *New German Critique* 78 (1989): 7–42.

Beaglehole, J. C., et al. [A. E. C., R. M. C., J. M. McE.] "I. L. G. Sutherland, 1897–1952." *Journal of Polynesian Society* 61 (1952): 120–9.

Becker, Gary. *The Economic Approach to Human Behavior.* Chicago: University of Chicago Press, 1976.

Bein, Alex. *Theodore Herzl.* Philadelphia: Jewish Publication Society of America, 1941.

Belke, Ingrid. *Die sozialreformerischen Ideen von Josef Popper-Lynkeus (1838–1921) in Zusammenhang mit allgemeinen Reformbestrebungen des Wiener Bürgertums um die Jahrhundertwende.* Tübingen: Mohr, 1978.

Bell, Daniel. *The Cultural Contradictions of Capitalism.* New York: Basic Books, 1976.

Bellamy, Edward. *Looking backward, 2000–1887.* New York: Regent, 1887. (*Ein Rückblick aus dem Jahre 2000 aus 1887.* Leipzig: Philipp Reclam, 1890.)

Beller, Steven. *Vienna and the Jews: A Cultural History, 1867–1938.* New York: Cambridge University Press, 1989.

"Patriotism and the National Identity of Habsburg Jewry, 1860–1914." *Leo Baeck Institute Year Book* 41 (1996): 215–38.

Benedikt, Heinrich, ed. *Geschichte der Republik Österreich.* Munich: Oldenbourg, 1954.

Benetka, Gerhard. *Psychologie in Wien: Sozial- und Theoriegeschichte des Wiener Psychologischen Instituts 1922–1938.* Vienna: WUV-Universitätsverlag, 1995.

Berg, Alban. "Statement of Aims for the 'Society for Private Music Performances in Vienno.'" In Joan Allen Smith. *Schoenberg and His Circle: A Viennese Portrait.* New York: Macmillan, 1986.

Bergson, Henri. *Les deux sources de la morale et de la religion.* Paris: Presses Universitaires de France, 1932. *(Two Sources of Morality and Religion.* London: Macmillan, 1935.)

Berkson, William, and John Wettersten. *Learning from Error: Karl Popper's Psychology of Learning.* La Salle, Ill.: Open Court, 1984.

Berlin, Isaiah. *Four Essays on Freedom.* New York: Oxford University Press, 1969.

Four Essays on Liberty. New York: Oxford University Press, 1969.

Karl Marx. 2d ed. New York: Oxford University Press, 1948.

Bernal, J. D. *The Social Function of Science.* London: Routledge, 1939.

Bernfeld, Siegfried. *Kinderheim Baumgarten: Bericht über einen ernsthaften Versuch mit neuer Erziehung.* Berlin: Jüdischer Verlag, 1921.

"Sozialistische Erziehungskritik." *Sozialistische Erziehung* 6 (May 1926): 106–8.

Bettauer, Hugo. *Die Stadt ohne Juden.* Vienna: Gloriette, 1922.

Binder, Julius. *System der Rechtsphilosophie.* 2d ed. Berlin: Stilke, 1937.

Birner, Jack. "A Roundabout Solution to a Fundamental Problem in Menger's Methodology and Beyond." In *Carl Menger and His Legacy,* edited by Bruce Caldwell. Durham, N.C.: Duke University Press, 1990.

Black, Max. Review of *Logik der Forschung. Mind* 45 (1936): 104–6.

Blackmore, John T. *Ernst Mach: His Life, Work, and Influence.* Berkeley, Calif.: University of California, 1972.

Blanshard, Brand. Foreword to *Socratic Method and Critical Philosophy,* by Leonard Nelson. Translated by Thomas K. Brown III. New Haven, Conn.: Yale University Press, 1949.

Blaug, Mark. *Economic Theory in Retrospect.* 3d. ed. Homewood, Ill.: Irwin, 1978.

The Methodology of Economics. New York: Cambridge University Press, 1980.

Bloch, Joseph. *Israel and the Nations.* Berlin: Harz, 1927.

Der nationale Zwist und die Juden in Österreich. Vienna: Gottlieb, 1886.

"Nichts gelernt und nichts vergessen." *Oesterreichische Wochenschrift,* 22 June 1917, 390.

Bloom, Allan. Interpretive essay. In *The Republic of Plato,* translated by Allan Bloom. New York: Basic Books, 1968.

Blumberg, Albert, and Herbert Feigl. "Logical Positivism: A New Movement in European Philosophy." *Journal of Philosophy* 28 (1931): 281–96.

Böhm-Bawerk, Eugen von. "The Austrian Economists." *Annals of the American Academy of Political and Social Science* 1 (1891): 361–84.

"Control or Economic Law?" (trans. of *Macht oder ökonomischen Gesetz?.*) In vol. 1 of *Shorter Classics of Eugen von Böhm-Bawerk.* South Holland, Ill.: Libertarian Press, 1961.

"The Historical vs. the Deductive Method in Political Economy." *Annals of the American Academy of Political and Social Science* 1 (1890): 244–71.

Karl Marx and the Close of His System. Edited by Paul M. Sweezy. New York: Augustus Kelly, 1966.

Bolzano, Bernard. *Bernard Bolzanos Wissenschaftslehre.* 4 vols. 2d ed. Leipzig: Felix Meiner, 1929–31.

Borkenau, Franz. *World Communism: A History of the Communist International.* Ann Arbor, Mich.: University of Michigan, 1962.

Born, Max. *Einstein's Relativity Theory.* Translated by Henry L. Brose. London: Methuen, 1924.

Die Relativitätstheorie Einstein und ihre physikalischen Grundlagen. 3d ed. Berlin: Julius Springer, 1922.

Bostaph, Samuel. "The Methodological Debate between Carl Menger and the German Historicists." *Atlantic Economic Journal* 7 (1978): 3–16.

Bottomore, Tom, and Patrick Goode, eds. *Austro-Marxism.* Oxford: Clarendon Press, 1978.

Boyarin, Daniel. *Unheroic Conduct: The Rise of Heterosexuality and the Invention of the Jewish Man.* Berkeley, Calif.: University of California Press, 1997.

Boyer, John. *Culture and Political Crisis in Vienna: Christian Socialism in Power, 1897–1918.* Chicago: Chicago University Press, 1995.

"Freud, Marriage, and Late Viennese Liberalism." *Journal of Modern History* 50 (1978): 72–102.

Political Radicalism in Late Imperial Vienna. Chicago: University of Chicago Press, 1981.

Braunthal, Alfred. *Die Entwicklungstendenzen der kapitalistischen Wirtschaft.* Berlin: Laub, 1927.

Karl Marx als Geschichtsphilosoph. Berlin: Cassirer, 1920.

Die Wirtschaft der Gegenwart und ihre Gesetze: Ein sozialistisches Lehrbuch der Nationalökonomie. Berlin: Laubsche, 1930.

Braunthal, Julius. *In Search of the Millenium.* London: Gollancz, 1945.

Brentano, Franz. *Psychologie vom empirischen Standpunkt.* 2 vols. Leipzig: Felix Meiner, 1924–5. (*Psychology from an Empirical Standpoint.* Translated by Antos Rancurello, D. B. Terrell, and Linda McAlister. London: Routledge, 1995.)

Breytenbach, Breyten. "The Long March from Hearth to Heart." *Social Research* 58 (1991): 69–83.

Broad, C. D. *Examination of McTaggart's Philosophy.* 2 vols. Cambridge: The University Press, 1933.

Broszat, Martin. *The Hitler State.* London: Longmans, 1981.

Browne, Martha Steffy. "Erinnerungen an das Mises-Privatseminar." *Wirtschaftspolitische Blätter* 4 (1981): 110–20.

Bugental, James, ed. "Symposium on Karl Bühler's Contributions to Psychology." *The Journal of General Psychology* 75 (1966): 181–219.

Bühler, Charlotte, *Kindheit und Jugend.* Leipzig: Hirzel, 1928.
Das Seelenleben des Jugendlichen. 4th ed. Jena: Fischer, 1927.
"Selbstdarstellung." In *Psychologie in Selbstdarstellungen,* edited by Ludwig Pongratz, Werner Traxel, and Ernst Wehner. Bern: Huber, 1972.

Bühler, Charlotte, Hildegard Hetzer, and Beatrix Tudor-Hart. *Soziologische und psychologische Studien über das erste Lebensjahr.* Jena: Fischer, 1927.

Bühler, Karl. *Abriß der geistigen Entwicklung des Kindes.* Leipzig: Quelle and Meyer, 1919. (*The Mental Development of the Child.* New York: Harcourt, Brace & Company, 1930.)
Die geistige Entwicklung des Kindes. 3rd ed. Jena: Fischer, 1922.
Die Krise der Psychologie. Jena: Fischer, 1927.
Sprachtheorie. Jena: Fischer, 1934.
"Tatsachen und Probleme zu einer Psychologie der Denkvorgänge." *Archiv für die gesamte Psychologie* 9 (1907): 297–365; 12 (1908): 1–23, 24–92, 93–123.

Bürger, Eduard. *Arbeitspädagogik: Geschichte, Kritik, Wegweisung.* 2d ed. Leipzig: Engelmann, 1923.

Burnet, John. *Greek Philosophy from Thales to Plato.* London: Macmillan, 1914.

Burnham, James. *The Managerial Revolution.* New York: John Day, 1941.

Burns, Emile, ed. *A Handbook of Marxism.* New York: International Publishers, 1935.

Busse, Martin. *Hegels Phänomenologie des Geistes und der Staat.* Berlin: Junker und Dunnhaupt, 1931.

Butler, Eliza Marian. *The Tyranny of Greece Over Germany.* Cambridge: Cambridge University Press, 1935.

Butterfield, Herbert. *The Origins of Modern Science, 1300–1800.* London: Bell, 1949.

Cahnman, Werner. "Adolf Fischhof and his Jewish Followers." *Leo Baeck Institute Year Book* 4 (1959).

Caird, Edward. *Hegel.* Philadelphia: Lippincott, 1883.

Carnap, Rudolf. "Die alte und die neue Logik." *Erkenntnis* 1 (1930): 12–26.
"Intellectual Autobiography." In *The Philosophy of Rudolf Carnap,* edited by Paul Arthur Schilpp. La Salle, Ill.: Open Court, 1963.
Der logische Aufbau der Welt. Berlin: Weltkreis, 1928. (*The Logical Structure of the World and Pseudoproblems in Philosophy.* Berkeley, Calif.: University of California, 1967.)
Logische Syntax der Sprache. Vienna: Julius Springer, 1934.
"Die physikalische Sprache als Universalsprache der Wissenschaft." *Erkenntnis* 2 (1932): 432–65.
"Psychologie in physicalischer Sprache." *Erkenntnis* 3 (1932): 107–42.

"Testability and Meaning." *Philosophy of Science* 3 (October 1936): 419–71; 4 (January 1937): 1–40.

"Über Protokollsätze." *Erkenntnis* 3 (1932): 215–28.

"Überwindung der Metaphysik durch logische Analyse der Sprache." *Erkenntnis* 2 (1932): 219–41.

Carnap, Rudolf, Hans Hahn, and Otto Neurath. *Wissenschaftliche Weltauffassung: Der Wiener Kreis.* Vienna: Wolf, 1929. ("The Scientific Conception of the World: The Vienna Circle." In Otto Neurath, *Empiricism and Sociology,* edited by Marie Neurath and Robert S. Cohen. Boston: Reidel, 1972.)

Carr, E. H. *What is History?* New York: Knopf, 1962.

Carritt, E. F., and T. M. Knox. An exchange on "Hegel and Prussianism." In *Hegel's Political Philosophy,* edited by Walter Kaufmann. New York: Atherton, 1970. [First published in *Philosophy* (January, April, and July 1940).]

Cartwright, Nancy, Jordi Cat, Lola Fleck, and Thomas Uebel. *Otto Neurath: Philosophy between Science and Politics.* Cambridge: Cambridge University Press, 1996.

Castle, Edward. "Unterrichtsreform." In vol. 1 of *Geschichte der deutschen Literatur in Österreich-Ungarn im Zeitalter Franz Joseph I,* edited by Edward Castle. Vienna: Earl Fromme, 1936.

Cat, Jordi. "The Popper–Neurath Debate and Neurath's Attack on Scientific Method." *Studies in History and Philosophy of Science* 26 (1995): 219–50.

Childs, M. W. *Sweden: The Middle Way.* New Haven, Conn.: Yale University Press, 1936.

Clarke, Peter. *Liberals and Social Democrats.* Cambridge: Cambridge University Press, 1978.

Cobban, Alfred. *Dictatorship: Its History and Theory.* New York: Scribner, 1939.

Coleman, James. *Foundations of Social Theory.* Cambridge, Mass.: Harvard University Press, 1990.

Coleman, Peter. *The Liberal Conspiracy.* New York: Free Press, 1989.

Collini, Stefan. *Liberalism and Sociology.* Cambridge: Cambridge University Press, 1979.

Constant, Benjamin. "Principles of Politics Applicable to All Representative Governments." In *Political Writings,* translated by Biancamaria Fontana. New York: Cambridge University Press, 1988.

"The Spirit of Conquest and Usurpation." In *Political Writings,* translated by Biancamaria Fontana. New York: Cambridge University Press, 1988.

Cornford, Francis M. *Before and After Socrates.* Cambridge: Cambridge University Press, 1932.

Cornforth, Maurice. *The Open Philosophy and the Open Society.* New York: International Publishers, 1968.

Cranston, Maurice. "The Open Future." *The Listener,* 5 December 1957, 947–8.

Crossman, Richard. *Plato Today.* New York: Oxford University Press, 1939.

Dahrendorf, Ralf. "The End of the Social-Democratic Consensus?" In *Life Chances.* Chicago: Chicago University Press, 1979.

LSE: A History of The London School of Economics and Political Science, 1895–1995. Oxford: Oxford University Press, 1995.

"Uncertainty, Science and Democracy." In *Essays in the Theory of Society.* Stanford, Calif.: Stanford University Press, 1968.

Davidson, Donald. "Actions, Reasons, and Causes." In *Essays on Actions and Events.* Oxford: Clarendon Press, 1980.

Day, Anne. *Fünf gläserne Särge.* Munich: Lentz, 1974.

Getrennt und doch vereint, Jüwellen-Roman 879 (1961).

Liane: Das Mädchen aus dem Urwald. Bayreuth: Heros, 1958.

Liane: Zwischen zwei Welten. Bayreuth: Heros, 1958.

Deák, István. *Beyond Nationalism: The Social and Political History of the Habsburg Officer Corps, 1848–1918.* New York: Oxford University Press, 1990.

"The Habsburg Army in the First and Last Days of World War I: A Comparative Analysis." In *East Central European Society in World War I,* edited by B. K. Király and N. F. Dreisinger. New York: Columbia University Press, 1985.

de Marchi, Neil, ed. *The Popperian Legacy in Economics.* Cambridge: Cambridge University Press, 1988.

Post-Popperian Methodology of Economics. Boston: Kluwer, 1992.

de Staël, Germaine. *Considérations sur la Révolution française.* 1817. Reprint, Paris: Tallandier, 1983.

De la Littérature considerée dans ses rapports avec les institutions sociales. 2 vols. Geneva: Droz, 1959.

de Vries, G. J. *Antisthenes Redivivus: Popper's Attack on Plato.* Amsterdam: North Holland, 1952.

Dewey, John. *German Philosophy and Politics.* New York: Holt, 1915.

Diamant, Alfred. *Austrian Catholics and the First Republic: Democracy, Capitalism, and the Social Order, 1918–1934.* Princeton, N.J.: Princeton University Press, 1960.

Dickey, Laurence. *Hegel: Religion, Economics and the Politics of the Spirit, 1770–1807.* New York: Cambridge University Press, 1987.

Diels, Hermann. *Die Fragmente der Vorsokratiker.* Berlin: Weidmannsche Buchhandlung, 1922.

Dilthey, Wilhelm. *Der Aufbau der geschichtlichen Welt in den Geisteswissenschaften. Gesammelte Schriften.* Vol. 7. Leipzig: Teubner, 1927.

Introduction to the Human Sciences. Translated by Ramon J. Betanzos. Detroit, Mich.: Wayne State University Press, 1988. [Originally published as *Einleitung in die Geisteswissenschaften* (1883).]

Die Jugendgeschichte Hegels. Gesammelte Schriften. Vol. 4. Leipzig: Teubner, 1921.

Dingler, Hugo. *Der Zusammenbruch der Wissenschaft und der Primat der Philosophie.* Munich: Reinhardt, 1926.

Djilas, Milovan. *The New Class.* New York: Praeger, 1957.

Donagan, Alan. "Popper's Examination of Historicism." In *The Philosophy of Karl Popper,* edited by Paul Arthur Schilpp. La Salle, Ill.: Open Court, 1974.

Downs, Anthony. *An Economic Theory of Democracy.* New York: Harper & Row, 1957.

Duhem, Pierre. *La Théorie physique: Son objet et sa structure.* Paris: Chevalier & Rivière, 1906. (German edition: *Ziel und Struktur der physikalischen Theorien.* Translated by Friedrich Adler. Leipzig: Barth, 1908.)

Durand-Barthez, Manuel. *Être Autrichien: La problématique de la faute chez les écrivains autrichiens du début du siècle.* Bern: Peter Lang, 1997.

Durkheim, Emile. *Emile Durkheim on Morality and Society.* Edited by Robert Bellah. Chicago: University of Chicago Press, 1973.

Professional Ethics and Civic Morals. Glencoe, Ill.: Free Press, 1958.

Dvorak, Johann. "Karl Popper und die Wissenschaft von der Geschichte in der Epoche des Faschismus." In *Versuche und Widerlegungen offene Probleme im Werk Karl Poppers,* edited by Karl Müller, Friedrich Stadler, and Friedrich Wallner. Vienna: Geyer, 1986.

Eccles, John. "My Living Dialogue with Popper." In *The Pursuit of Truth,* edited by Paul Levinson. Atlantic Highlands, N.J.: Humanities Press, 1982.

Edmondson, C. Earl. *The Heimwehr and Austrian Politics, 1918–1936.* Athens, Ga.: University of Georgia, 1978.

Einstein, Albert. *Geometrie und Erfahruung*. Berlin: Julius Springer, 1921.

"Induktion und Deduktion in der Logik." *Berliner Tageblatt*, 25 December 1919.

Relativity: The Special and the General Theory. Translated by Robert Lawson. London: Methuen, 1920.

Über die spezielle und die allgemeine Relativitätstheorie: (Gemeinverständlich). 9th ed. Braunschweig: Friedrich Vieweg, 1920.

Einstein, Albert, Boris Podolsky, and Nathan Rosen. "Can Quantum-Mechanical Description of Physical Reality be Considered Complete?" *Physical Review* 47 (1935): 777–80.

Elon, Amos. *Herzl*. New York: Holt, Rinehart and Winston, 1975.

Engels, Friedrich. *Ludwig Feuerbach and the End of Classical German Philosophy*. Moscow: Foreign Languages Publishing House, 1962.

Erdmann, J. E. *Philosophische Vorlesungen über den Staat*. Halle: Schmidt, 1851.

Eschbach, Achim. "Karl Bühler: Sematologist." Editor's introduction to Karl Bühler, *Theory of Language*, translated by Donald Fraser Goodwin. Amsterdam: John Benjamins, 1990.

Euripides. *Alcestis, Bacchae, Trojan Women, Iphigineia in Aulis: The Complete Greek Tragedies*. Edited by David Grene and Richmond Lattimore. 4 vols. Chicago: University of Chicago Press, 1959–60.

Fadrus, Viktor. "Die Neugestaltung der Lehrerbildung in Deutschland und Österreich." *Schulreform* 5 (1926): 1–42.

Feigl, Herbert. *Theorie und Erfahrung in der Physik*. Karlsruhe: Braun, 1929.

"The 'Wiener Kreis' in America." In *The Intellectual Migration: Europe and America, 1930–1960*, edited by Donald Fleming and Bernard Bailyn. Cambridge, Mass.: Harvard University Press, 1969.

Felkin, Henry and Emmie. "Biography of Herbart." In Johann Friedrich Herbart, *The Science of Education*. Boston: Heath, 1908.

Felt, Ulrike. "Lire de la science à Vienne, 1900–1938." In *La science populaire dans la presse et l'édition, XIXe et XXe siecles*, edited by Bernadette Bensaude-Vincent and Anne Rasmussen. Paris: CNRS éditions, 1997.

Feyerabend, Paul. *Against Method: Outline of an Anarchistic Theory of Knowledge*. London: NLB, 1975. Rev. ed., London: Verso, 1988.

"Herbert Feigl." In *Mind, Matter, and Method*, edited by Paul Feyerabend and Grover Maxwell. Minneapolis, Minn.: University of Minnesota, 1966.

Field, G. C. Review of *The Open Society*. *Philosophy* 21 (1946): 271–6.

The Philosophy of Plato. New York: Oxford University Press, 1949.

Plato and His Contemporaries. London: Methuen, 1930.

Finley, Moses. *Economy and Society in Ancient Greece*. New York: Viking, 1982.

Fischel, Hans. "Zweck und Form der Schulgemeinde." In vol. 2 of *Mittelschülerbewegung und Schulgemeinde*. Vienna: Vereinigung sozialistischer Mittelschüler, 1919.

Fischer, Ernst. *Erinnerungen und Reflexionen*. Reinbek bei Hamburg: Rowohlt, 1969.

Fischer, Kuno. *Hegels Leben, Werke und Lehre*. 2 vols. Heidelberg: Winter, 1901.

Fischer, Ruth. *Stalin and German Communism*. Cambridge, Mass.: Harvard University Press, 1948.

Fite, Werner. *The Platonic Legend*. New York: Scribner, 1934.

Fleck, Christian. *Rund um "Marienthal"*. Vienna: Gesellschaftskritik, 1990.

"Sieg der *Offenen Gesellschaft*?" In *Heinrich Gomperz, Karl Popper und die Österreichische Philosophie*, edited by Martin Seiler and Friedrich Stadler. Amsterdam: Rodopi, 1994.

Fleck, Lola. "A Life Between Science and Politics." In Nancy Cartwright et al., *Otto Neurath: Philosophy between Science and Politics*. Cambridge: Cambridge University Press, 1996.

Fleck, Ludwik. *Entstehung und Entwicklung einer wissenschaftlichen Tatsache.* Basel: Benno Schwabe, 1935. (*The Genesis and Development of a Scientific Fact.* Chicago: University of Chicago Press, 1979.)

Forsthoff, Ernst, ed. *Rechtstaatlichkeit und Sozialstaatlichkeit: Aufsätze und Essays.* Darmstadt: Wissenschaftliche Buchgesellschaft, 1968.

Foster, Michael. *The Political Philosophies of Plato and Hegel.* Oxford: Oxford University Press, 1935.

Frankael, Ernst. *The Dual State.* New York: Oxford University Press, 1941.

Fränkel, Hermann Ferdinand. *Wege und Formen frühgriechischen Denkens.* Edited by Franz Tietze. Munich: Beck, 1955.

Frankel, Jonathan, and Steven Zipperstein, eds. *Assimilation and Community: The Jews in Nineteenth-Century Europe.* Cambridge: Cambridge University Press, 1992.

Frege, Gottlob. *The Foundation of Arithmetic: A Logico-Mathematical Enquiry into the Concept of Number.* Oxford: Basil Blackwell, 1968.

Freidenreich, Harriet Pass. *Jewish Politics in Vienna, 1918–1938.* Bloomington, Ind.: Indiana University Press, 1991.

Freud, Sigmund. *The Interpretation of Dreams.* Translated by John Strachey. New York: Avon Books, 1965.

Freundlich, Erwin. *The Foundations of Einstein's Theory of Gravitation.* Translated by Henry Brose. 2d ed. London: Methuen, 1924.

Die Grundlagen der Einsteinschen Gravitationstheorie. Berlin: Julius Springer, 1916.

Friedman, Milton. *Essays in Positive Economics.* Chicago: University of Chicago Press, 1950.

Friedrich, Carl J. "Introduction" to *The Philosophy of Hegel.* New York: Modern Library, 1953.

Review of *The Open Society. Southwestern Social Science* (March 1951).

Friedrich, Carl, and Zbigniew Brzezinski. *Totalitarian Dictatorship and Autocracy.* Cambridge, Mass.: Harvard University Press, 1956.

Friedrich, Carl, Michael Curtis, and Benjamin Barber. *Totalitarianism in Perspective.* New York: Praeger, 1969.

Fries, Jakob Friedrich. *Die Geschichte der Philosophie, dargestellt nach den Fortschritten ihrer wissenschaftlichen Entwickelung. Sämtliche Schriften,* vols. 18–19. Aalen: Scientia, 1978.

Neue oder anthropologische Kritik der Vernunft. 2d ed. 3 vols. Heidelberg: Winter, 1828–31.

"Über die Gefährdung des Wohlstandes und Charakteres der Deutschen durch die Juden." *Heidelberger Jahrbücher* 16–17 (1816).

Von deutschem Bund und deutscher Staatsverfassung. Heidelberg: Mohr und Winter, 1816.

Frijda, Nico, and Adriaan De Groot, eds. *Otto Selz: His Contribution to Psychology.* The Hague: Mouton, 1982.

Frohman, Larry. "Liberalism, Modernity, and Social Theory in the Work of Wilhelm Dilthey: From Transcendentalist Idealism to Phenomenological Hermeneutics." Ph.D. diss., University of California, Berkeley, 1991.

Fuchs, Albert. *Geistige Strömungen in Österreich, 1867–1918.* Vienna: Löcker, 1949.

Furtmüller, Karl. *Auf dem Weg zur Schulgemeinde.* Vienna: Jugend und Volk, 1926.

Gardner, W. J., E. T. Beardsley, and T. E. Carter. *A History of the University of Canterbury, 1873–1973.* Christchurch, N.Z.: University of Canterbury, 1973.

Gattei, Stefano. *Critica della ragione incerta: Introduzione al pensiero di Karl Popper.* Rome: Società aperta, 1996.

Gay, Peter. *Weimar Culture.* New York: Harper, 1968.

Gehlen, Arnold. "Antropologische Ansicht der Technik." In *Technik im technischen Zeitalter,* edited by Hans Freyer, Johannes C. Papalekas, and Georg Weippert. Düsseldorf: Schilling, 1965.

Gellner, Ernest. "The Rational Mystic." *The New Republic*, 19 April 1993, 35–8.

Thought and Change. London: Weidenfeld and Nicholson.

Gentile, Giovanni. "The Philosophical Basis of Fascism." *Foreign Affairs* 6 (January 1928): 290–304.

Gerlich, Rudolf. *Die gescheiterte Alternative: Sozialisierung in Österreich nach dem Ersten Weltkrieg.* Vienna: Braumüller, 1980.

Germino, Dante, and Klaus von Beyme, ed. *The Open Society in Theory and Practice.* The Hague: Martinus Nijhoff, 1974.

Gerschenkron, Alexander. *An Economic Spurt That Failed.* Princeton, N.J.: Princeton University Press, 1977.

Geymonat, Ludovico. "Logica e filosofia delle scienze." *Rivista di filosofia* 28 (1936): 3–16.

Gilman, Sander. *Jewish Self-Hatred.* Baltimore, Md.: Johns Hopkins University Press, 1985.

Glaser, Ernst. *Im Umfeld des Austromarxismus.* Vienna: Europaverlag, 1981.

Gleason, Abbot. *Totalitarianism: The Inner History of the Cold War.* New York: Oxford University Press, 1995.

Glettler, Monika. *Die Wiener Tschechen um 1900.* Munich: Oldenbourg, 1972.

Glöckel, Otto. *Drillschule, Lernschule, Arbeitsschule.* Vienna: Organisation Wien der Sozialdemokratischen Partei, 1928.

Selbstbiographie; sein Lebenswerk: Die Wiener Schulreform. Zurich: Genossenschaftsdrukerei, 1939.

Das Tor der Zukunft. Vienna: Verein Freie Schule, 1917.

Gobetti, Piero. *La Rivoluzione liberale.* Turin: Einaudi, 1969.

Gödel, Kurt. "Über formal unentscheidbare Sätze der Principia Mathematica und verwandter Systeme I." *Monatshefte für Mathematik und Physik* 38 (1931): 173–98.

Goldstein, Leon. Review of *The Poverty of Historicism. Ethics* 68 (1958): 296–7.

Golinski, Jan. *Science as Public Culture: Chemistry and Enlightenment in Britain, 1760–1820.* New York: Cambridge University Press, 1992.

Gombrich, Ernst. "The Logic of Vanity Fair." In *The Philosophy of Karl Popper*, edited by Paul Arthur Schilpp. 2 vols. La Salle, Ill.: Open Court, 1974.

The Open Society and Its Enemies: Remembering Its Publication Fifty Years Ago. LSE Discussion Paper Series. London: Tymes Court, 1995.

Gomperz, Heinrich. *Die Idee der überstaatlichen Rechtsordnung.* Vienna: Strache, 1920.

The Limits of Cognition and the Exigencies of Action. Berkeley, Calif.: University of California, 1938.

Philosophical Studies. Edited by Daniel S. Robinson. Boston: Christopher Publishing House, 1953.

Philosophie des Krieges in Umrissen. Gotha: Perthes, 1915.

"Sokrates Haltung vor seinen Richtern." *Wiener Studien* 54 (1936): 32–43.

Weltanschauungslehre. Ein Versuch die Hauptprobleme der allgemeinen theoretischen Philosophie geschictlich zu entwickeln und sachlich zu bearbeiten. Vol. 1, *Methodologie.* Vol. 2, Part 1, *Noologie – Einleitung und Semasiologie.* Jena: Diederichs, 1905–8.

"Die Wissenschaft und die Tat." In *Werturteilsstreit*, edited by Hans Albert and Ernst Topitsch. Darmstadt: Wissenschaftliche Buchgesellschaft, 1971.

Gomperz, Theodor. *Essays und Errinerungen.* Stuttgart: Deutsche Verlags-Anstalt, 1905.

Griechische Denker. 3 vols. Leipzig: Veit, 1896–1906. (*Greek Thinkers.* Translated by Laurie Magnus and G. G. Berry. 4 vols. London: Murray, 1901–12.)

Gossman, Lionel. "Augustin Thierry and Liberal Historiography." *History and Theory, Beiheft* 15 (1976): 3–83.

Gould, J. "Law, Custom and Myth: Aspects of the Social Position of Women in Classical Athens." *Journal of Hellenic Studies* 100 (1980): 38–59.

Grassl, Wolfgang. "Markets and Morality: Austrian Perspectives on the Economic Approach to Human Behavior." In *Austrian Economics*, edited by Wolfgang Grassl and Barry Smith. New York: New York University Press, 1986.

Grelling, Kurt. Review of *Logik der Forschung. Theoria* 1 (1937): 134–43.

Grote, George. *Plato and Other Companions of Socrates.* London: John Murray, 1865.

Gruber, Helmut. *Red Vienna: Experiment in Working-Class Culture, 1919–1934.* New York: Oxford University Press, 1991.

Grünebaum, Ludwig. "Führerschaft, Demokratie, Ethik: Eine Kritik von Leonard Nelsons *Demokratie und Führerschaft.*" *Zeitschrift für die gesamte Staatswissenschaft* 107 (1951): 36–89.

Güdemann, Moritz. *Jüdische Apologetik.* Glogau: Flemming, 1906.

  Nationaljudentum. Leipzig: Breitenstein, 1897.

Guérin, Daniel. *Fascism and Big Business.* New York: Pioneer, 1939.

Guizot, François. *L'Histoire de la civilisation en Europe.* Paris: Didier, 1868.

  Histoire des origines du Gouvernement Représentatif en Europe. 2 vols. Paris: Didier, 1851.

Gulick, Charles. *Austria: From Habsburg to Hitler.* 2 vols. Berkeley, Calif.: University of California, 1948.

Gurian, Waldemar. *Bolshevism: Theory and Practice.* New York: Macmillan, 1932.

Habermas, Jürgen. *Communication and the Evolution of Society.* Translated by Thomas McCarthy. Boston: Beacon Press, 1974.

  Faktizität und Geltung: Beiträge zur Diskurstheorie des Rechts und des demokratischen Rechtsstaats. Frankfurt: Suhrkamp, 1992.

  "Neoconservative Culture Criticism in the United States and West Germany: An Intellectual Movement in Two Political Cultures." In *Habermas and Modernity*, edited by Richard J. Bernstein. Cambridge, Mass.: MIT Press, 1985.

  "A Positivistically Bisected Rationalism." In *The Positivist Dispute in German Sociology*, by Theodor Adorno et al. London: Heinemann, 1976.

  Technik und Wissenschaft als "Ideologie." Frankfurt: Suhrkamp, 1968.

  The Theory of Communicative Action. 2 vols. Boston: Beacon Press, 1984–7.

Hackforth, R. Review of *The Open Society. Classical Review* 61 (1947). [Critical reviews re Popper's Plato theories.]

Hacohen, Malachi. "Dilemmas of Cosmopolitanism: Karl Popper, Jewish Identity, and 'Central European Culture.'" *Journal of Modern History* 71 (1999): 105–49.

  "Karl Popper in Exile: The Viennese Progressive Imagination and the Making of *The Open Society.*" *Philosophy of the Social Sciences* 26 (December 1996): 452–91.

  "Leonard Krieger: Historicization and Political Engagement in Intellectual History." *History and Theory* 35 (1996): 80–130.

  "The Making of the Open Society." Ph.D. diss., Columbia University, 1993.

Haering, Theodore. *Hegel: Sein Wollen und sein Werk.* 2 vols. Leipzig: Teubner, 1929.

Hainisch, Michael. *Die Zukunft der Deutsch-Österreicher.* Vienna: Deuticke, 1892.

Haldane, J. B. S. *The Marxist Philosophy and the Sciences.* New York: Random House, 1939.

Halévy, Élie. *The Era of Tyrannies.* Garden City, N.Y.: Anchor Books, 1965.

Haller, Rudolf. "Einleitung." In *Fragen zu Wittgenstein und Aufsätze zur Österreichischen Philosophie.* Amsterdam: Rodopi, 1986.

"Der Erste Wiener Kreis." In *Fragen zu Wittgenstein und Aufsätze zur Österreichischen Philosophie*. Amsterdam: Rodopi, 1986.

"Gibt es eine Österreichische Philosophie?" In *Fragen zu Wittgenstein und Aufsätze zur Österreichischen Philosophie*. Amsterdam: Rodopi, 1986.

"The Neurath Principle." In *Rediscovering the Forgotten Vienna Circle*, edited by Thomas Uebel. Boston: Kluwer, 1991.

"Philosophy and the Critique of Language: Wittgenstein and Mauthner." In *Questions on Wittgenstein*. Lincoln, Nebr.: University of Nebraska Press, 1988.

Questions on Wittgenstein. Lincoln, Nebr.: University of Nebraska Press, 1988.

"Wittgenstein and Austrian Philosophy." In *Questions on Wittgenstein*. Lincoln, Nebr.: University of Nebraska Press, 1988.

"Zur Historiographie der Österreichischen Philosophie." In *From Bolzano to Wittgenstein: The Tradition of Austrian Philosophy*, edited by J. C. Nyíri. Vienna: Hölder-Pichler-Tempsky, 1986.

Haller, Rudolf, and Friedrich Stadler, eds. *Ernst Mach*. Vienna: Hölder-Pichler-Tempsky, 1988.

Wien–Berlin–Prag: Der Aufstieg der wissenschaftlichen Philosophie. Vienna: Hölder-Pichler-Tempsky, 1993.

Hansen, M. H. *The Athenian Democracy at the Age of Demosthenes*. Oxford: Blackwell, 1991.

Hansen, Troels Eggers, ed. *Die beiden Grundprobleme der Erkenntnistheorie*. Tübingen: Mohr, 1979.

"Popper's Early Work on the Theory of Knowledge." (Unpublished) *Ringvorlesung* (30 October 1998), *Karl Popper Institut*, Vienna.

Hanson, Victor D. *The Other Greeks*. New York: Free Press, 1995.

Hassner, Pierre. "Le totalitarisme vu de l'Ouest." In *Totalitarismes*, edited by Guy Hermet. Paris: Economica, 1984.

Hautmann, Hans. *Die verlorene Räterepublik: Am Beispiel der Kommunistischen Partei Deutschösterreichs*. Vienna: Europa, 1971.

Hautmann, Hans, and Rudolf Kropf. *Die österreichische Arbeiterbewegung vom Vormärz bis 1945*. Vienna: Europa, 1974.

Hayek, F. A. "Carl Menger." *Economica* 1 (1934): 393–420.

"The Counter-Revolution of Science, I, II, III" *Economica* 8 (1941): 9–36, 119–50, 281–320.

"Economics and Knowledge." *Economica* 4 (1937): 33–54.

"The Facts of Social Science." *Ethics* 54 (1943): 1–13.

Freedom and the Economic System. Chicago: University of Chicago Press, 1939.

Hayek on Hayek. Edited by Stephen Kresge and Leif Wenar. Chicago: University of Chicago Press, 1988.

Individualism and Economic Order. Chicago: University of Chicago Press, 1948.

Markt, Plan, Freiheit. Franz Kreuzer im Gespräch mit Friedrich von Hayek und Ralf Dahrendorf. Vienna: Deuticke, 1983.

The Road to Serfdom. Chicago: University of Chicago Press, 1944.

"Scientism and the Study of Society, I." *Economica* 9 (1942): 267–91.

"Scientism and the Study of Society, II." *Economica* 10 (1943): 34–63.

"Scientism and the Study of Society, III." *Economica* 11 (1944): 27–39.

"The Trend in Economic Thinking." *Economica* 13 (1933): 121–37.

Hayek, F. A., ed. *Collectivist Economic Planning*. London: Routledge, 1935.

Haym, Rudolf. *Hegel und seine Zeit*. Edited by Hans Rosenberg. 2d ed. Leipzig: Heims, 1927.

Hedström, Peter, Richard Swedberg, and Lars Udéhn. "Popper's Situational Analysis and Contemporary Sociology." *Philosophy of the Social Sciences* 28 (1998): 339–64.

Hegel, G. W. F. *Elements of the Philosophy of Right*. Edited by Allen Wood. Translated by H. B. Nisbet. New York: Cambridge University Press, 1991.

Hegel Selections. Edited by Jacob Loewenberg. The Modern Student's Library of Philosophy. New York: Scribner's, 1929.

Hegel: Political Writings. Edited by Laurence Dickey and H. B. Nisbet. Cambridge: Cambridge University Press, 1999.

Hegels theologische Jugendschriften. Edited by Hermann Nohl. Tübingen: Mohr, 1907.

Jenenser Realphilosophie. Edited by Johannes Hoffmeister. 2 vols. Leipzig: Meiner, 1931–2.

Phänomenologie des Geistes. 6th ed. Hamburg: Meiner, 1952.

The Philosophy of Mind. Translated by William Wallace and A. V. Miller. New York: Oxford University Press, 1971.

The Philosophy of Right. Translated by T. M. Knox. New York: Oxford University Press, 1967.

Sämtliche Werke. Edited by Hermann Glockner. 26 vols. Stuttgart: Frommanns, 1927–40.

Hegselmann, Rainer. "Otto Neurath – Emiristischer Aufklärer und Sozialreformer." Editor's introduction to *Otto Neurath: Wissenschaftliche Weltauffassung, Sozialismus und Logischer Empirismus*. Frankfurt: Suhrkamp, 1979.

Heisenberg, Werner. *Die physikalischen Prinzipien der Quantentheorie*. Leipzig: Hirzel, 1930.

"Über quantentheoretische Umdeutung kinematischer und mechanischer Beziehungen." *Zeitschrift für Physik* 33 (1925): 879–93.

Helling, Ingeborg Katharina. "Felix Kaufmann." In vol. 2 of *Vertriebene Vernunft: Emigration und Exil österreichischer Wissenschaft 1930–1940*, edited by Friedrich Stadler. Vienna: Jugend und Volk, 1988.

Hempel, Carl G. *Aspects of Scientific Explanation and Other Essays in the Philosophy of Science*. New York: Free Press, 1965.

"The Function of General Laws in History." *Journal of Philosophy* 39 (1942): 35–48.

"On the Logical Positivists' Theory of Truth." *Analysis* 2 (1935): 49–59.

Review of *Logik der Forschung*. *Deutsche Literaturzeitung* 58 (1937): 309–14.

Hennis, Wilhelm. "A Science of Man." In *Max Weber and His Contemporaries*, edited by Wolfgang Mommsen and Jürgen Osterhammel. London: Allen and Unwin, 1987.

Herbart, Johann Friedrich. *Outlines of Educational Doctrine*. New York: Macmillan, 1909.

Hermann, Grete. Review of *Logik der Forschung*. *Physikalische Zeitschrift* 13 (1935): 481–2.

Hermet, Guy, ed. *Totalitarismes*. Paris: Economica, 1984.

Hertz, Frederick. *The Economic Problems of the Danubian States: A Study in Economic Nationalism*. 1947. Reprint, New York: Howard Fertig, 1970.

Hertzka, Theodor. *Freiland. Ein sociales Zukunftsbild*. 4th ed. Dresden: Pierson, 1890.

Herzl, Theodor. *A Jewish State*. Translated by Sylvie d'Avigdor. London: Nutt, 1896.

Der Judenstaat. Leipzig: Breitenstein, 1896.

Hetzer, Hildegard. *Kindheit und Armut*. Leipzig: Hirzel, 1929.

Heřman, Jan. "The Evolution of Jewish Population in Bohemia and Moravia, 1754–1953." In *Papers in Jewish Demography, 1973*, edited by U. O. Schmelz, P. Glikson, and S. Della Pergolia. Jerusalem: Hebrew University of Jerusalem, 1977.

Hicks, J. R. *Value and Capital*. Oxford: Clarendon Press, 1939.

Hicks, J. R., and R. G. D. Allen. "A Reconsideration of the Theory of Value." *Economica* 1 (1934): 52–76, 196–219.

Hilbert, David. *Grundlagen der Geometrie*. 6th ed. Leipzig: Teubner, 1923.

Hilferding, Karl. "Le fondement empirique de la science." *Revue des questions scientifiques* 110 (1936): 85–116.

Hilferding, Rudolf. *Böhm-Bawerk's Criticism of Marx.* Edited by Paul M. Sweezy. New York: Augustus Kelly, 1966.

"State Capitalism or Totalitarian State Economy?" *Modern Review* 1 (1947): 266–71.

Ho, Eugene Yue-Ching. "At 90, and Still Dynamic: Revisiting Sir Karl Popper and Attending His Birthday Party." *Intellectus* 23 (July–September 1992): 1–5. [Also available through The Karl Popper Web].

Höbelt, Lothar. *Kornblume und Kaiseradler: Die deutschfreiheitlichen Parteien Altösterreichs 1882–1918.* Vienna: Verlag für Geschichte und Politik, 1993.

Hobhouse, L. T. *Liberalism.* 1911. Reprint, New York: Oxford University Press, 1964.

The Metaphysical Theory of the State. London: Allen & Unwin, 1918.

Hobson, J. A. *The Crisis of Liberalism.* 1909. Reprint, New York: Barnes & Noble, 1974.

Holleis, Eva. *Die Sozialpolitische Partei: Sozialliberale Bestrebungen in Wien um 1900.* Munich: Oldenbourg, 1978.

Holzapfel-Gomperz, Bettina. *Reisnerstraße 13. Meine Jugend im Wien der Jahrhundertwende.* Vienna: Österreichische Verlagsanstalt & Schroll, 1980.

Hook, Sidney. *From Hegel to Marx.* London: Gollancz, 1936.

"Hegel Rehabilitated." In *Hegel's Political Philosophy,* edited by Walter Kaufmann. New York: Atherton, 1970.

Heresy, Yes: Conspiracy, No! New York: John Day, 1953.

Horak, Roman, Wolfgang Maderthaner, and Michaela Maier, eds. *Wiener Beiträge zur Moderne.* Vienna: WUV, 1999.

Hubert, Rainer. "Freimaurerei in Österreich 1871 bis 1938." In *Zirkel und Winkelmass.* Vienna: Eigenverlag der Museen der Stadt Wien, 1984.

Hubert, Rainer, and Ferdinand Zörrer. "Die östereichischen Grenzlogen." *Quatuor Coronati Jahrbuch* (1983): 143–66.

Hume, David. *A Treatise of Human Nature.* Oxford: Oxford University Press, 1960.

Husserl, Edmund. *Logical Investigations.* Translated by J. N. Findlay. 2 vols. New York: Humanities Press, 1970.

Hutchinson, Terence. *The Significance and Basic Postulates of Economic Theory.* London: Macmillan, 1938.

Iggers, Georg. "Historicism." In vol. 2 of *Dictionary of the History of Ideas.* Edited by Philip W. Wiener. New York: Scribner's, 1973.

"Interview: Sir Karl Popper." *Sunday Times,* 12 July 1992, section 2.

Irwin, T. H. "Plato's Heracliteanism." *Philosophical Quarterly* 27 (1977): 1–13.

Jacob, Margaret. *Living the Enlightenment.* New York: Oxford University Press, 1991.

Jacobs, Struan. "Popper, Weber and the Rationalist Approach to Social Explanation." *British Journal of Sociology* 41 (1990): 559–70.

Jaeger, Werner. *Paideia.* Translated by Gilbert Highet. 3 vols. New York: Oxford University Press, 1939–44.

Jaffé, Edgar. "Die Militarisierung unseres Wirtschaftsleben." *Archiv für Sozialwissenschaft und Sozialpolitik* 40 (1915): 511–47.

Jahoda, Marie, and Hans Zeisel. *Die Arbeitslosen von Marienthal.* Leipzig: Hirzel, 1933.

Jammer, Max. *The Philosophy of Quantum Mechanics.* New York: John Wiley, 1974.

Jänicke, Martin. *Totalitäre Herrschaft.* Berlin: Duncker & Humblot, 1971.

Janik, Allan, and Stephen Toulmin. *Wittgenstein's Vienna.* New York: Touchstone, 1972.

Jarvie, Ian. *Concepts and Society.* London: Routledge, 1972.

"Popper on the Difference between the Natural and the Social Sciences." In *The Pursuit of Truth*, edited by Paul Levinson. Atlantic Highlands, N.J.: Humanities Press, 1982.

"Situational Logic and Its Reception." *Philosophy of the Social Sciences* 28 (1998): 365–80.

Jaspers, Karl. *Psychologie der Weltanschauungen.* 3d ed. Berlin: Julius Springer, 1925.

Jelavich, Barbara. *Modern Austria: Empire and Republic, 1800–1986.* New York: Cambridge University Press, 1987.

Jellinek, Adolf. *Aus der Zeit: Tagesfragen und Tagesbegebenheiten.* Budapest: Markus, 1886.

Bezelem Elohim: Fünf Reden über die israelitische Menschenlehre und Weltanschauung. Vienna: Beck, 1871.

"Jüdisch-österreichisch," *Die Neuzeit,* 15 June 1883, 225.

Jenks, William A. *Austria under the Iron Ring, 1879–1893.* Charlottesville, Va.: University of Virginia, 1965.

Joad, C. E. M. *Guide to the Philosophy of Morals and Politics.* New York: Random House, 1938.

Jodl, Friedrich. *Geschichte der Ethik als philosophischer Wissenschaft.* 4th ed. 2 vols. Darmstadt: Wissenschaftliche Buchgesellschaft, 1965.

Jodl, Margarete Forster. *Friedrich Jodl.* Stuttgart: Cotta, 1920.

Johnston, William. *The Austrian Mind: An Intellectual and Social History, 1848–1938.* Berkeley, Calif.: University of California, 1972.

"Neo-Idealists from Austria 1870–1938." *Modern Austrian Literature* 4 (1971): 7–17.

Jones, A. H. M. "The Athenian Democracy and Its Critics." *The Historical Journal* 11 (1953): 1–26.

Jones, William David. *The Lost Debate: German Socialist Intellectuals and Totalitarianism.* Urbana, Ill.: University of Illinois Press, 1999.

Jørgenson, Jørgen. *The Development of Logical Empiricism.* Chicago: University of Chicago Press, 1951.

Jowett, Benjamin. Introduction to *The Dialogues of Plato.* 3d ed. 5 vols. Translated by Benjamin Jowett. Oxford: Oxford University Press, 1924.

Judson, Pieter. *Exclusive Revolutionaries.* Ann Arbor, Mich.: University of Michigan Press, 1996.

Just, Roger. *Women in Athenian Law and Life.* London: Routledge, 1989.

Kanitz, Otto. "Alfred Adler und die sozialistische Erziehung." *Sozialistische Erziehung* 10 (1930).

Kant, Immanuel. *Critique of Judgement.* Oxford: Clarendon Press, 1952.

Critique of Pure Reason. Translated by Norman Kemp Smith. New York: Macmillan, 1929.

"Der Streit der Fakultäten (1798)." In vol. 7 of *Gesammelte Schriften (Akademieausgabe).* Berlin: Reimer, 1912.

"Über den Gemeinspruch: Das mag in der Theorie richtig sein, taugt aber nicht für die Praxis (1793)." In vol. 8 of *Gesammelte Schriften (Akademieausgabe).* Berlin: Reimer, 1912.

"Was heißt: Sich im Denken orienti(e)ren?" In vol. 8 of *Gesammelte Schriften (Akademieausgabe).* Berlin: Reimer, 1912.

"Zum ewigen Frieden." In vol. 8 of *Gesammelte Schriften (Akademieausgabe).* Berlin: Reimer, 1912.

Katz, Jacob. *Jews and Freemasons in Europe, 1723–1939.* Cambridge, Mass.: Harvard University Press, 1970.

Kaufmann, Felix. *Methodenlehre der Sozialwissenschaften.* Vienna: Julius Springer, 1936.

"Phenomenology and Logical Empiricism." Translated by Dorion Cairns. In *Philosophical Essays in Memory of Edmund Husserl*, edited by Marvin Farber. Cambridge, Mass.: Harvard University Press, 1940.

Kaufmann, Walter. "The Hegel Myth and Its Method." *Philosophical Review* 60 (1951): 459–86.

Kaufmann, Walter, ed. *Hegel's Political Philosophy*. New York: Atherton, 1970.

Kelsen, Hans. *General Theory of Law and State*. Cambridge, Mass.: Harvard University Press, 1945.

Kernbauer, Hans, Eduard März, and Fritz Weber. "Die wirtschaftliche Entwicklung." In *Österreich 1918–1938. Geschichte der Ersten Republik*, edited by Erika Weinzierl and Kurt Skalnik. 2 vols. Graz: Styria, 1983.

Kerschensteiner, Georg. *Der Begriff der Arbeitsschule*. 2d ed. Leipzig: Teubner, 1913.

Das einheitliche deutsche Schulsystem. 2d ed. Leipzig: Teubner, 1922.

Staatsbürgerliche Erziehung der deutschen Jugend. 5th ed. Erfurt: Villaret, 1911.

Kestenberg-Gladstein, Ruth. "The Jews between Czechs and Germans in the Historic Lands, 1848–1918." In vol. 1 of *The Jews of Czechoslovakia*. Philadelphia Pa.: Jewish Publication Society, 1966.

Keynes, John Maynard. *A Treatise on Probability*. London: Macmillan, 1921. (German: *Über Wahrscheinlichkeit*. Leipzig: Barth, 1926.)

Kierkegaard, Søren. *The Concept of Anxiety, Kierkegaard's Writings*. Translated by Howard and Edna Wong. Princeton, N.J.: Princeton University Press, 1980.

Fear and Trembling, Kierkegaard's Writings. Translated by Howard and Edna Wong. Princeton, N.J.: Princeton University Press, 1983.

Journals and Papers. 5 vols. Bloomington, Ind.: Indiana University Press, 1970.

Stages on Life's Way, Kierkegaard's Writings. Translated by Howard and Edna Wong. Princeton, N.J.: Princeton University Press, 1988.

Kieval, Hillel. *The Making of Czech Jewry*. New York: Oxford University Press, 1988.

Kirk, G. S., and J. Raven. *The Presocratic Philosophers*. New York: Cambridge University Press, 1962.

Kirzner, Israel. "Ludwig von Mises and Friedrich von Hayek: The Modern Extension of Austrian Subjectivism." In *Die Wiener Schule der Nationalökonomie*, edited by Norbert Leser. Vienna: Böhlau, 1986.

Kitchen, Martin. *The Coming of Austrian Fascism*. London: Croom Helm, 1980.

Klemperer, Klemens von. *Ignaz Seipel: Christian Statesman in a Time of Crisis*. Princeton, N.J.: Princeton University Press, 1972.

Klemperer, Victor. *Ich will Zeugnis ablegen bis zum letzten*. 2 vols. Berlin: Aufbau, 1995.

Kloppenberg, James T. *Uncertain Victory*. New York: Oxford University Press, 1986.

Knies, Karl. *Die Politische Ökonomie vom Standpunkte der geschichtlichen Methode*. 2d ed. Brunswick: Schwetschke, 1883.

Knight, Helen. "Philosophy in Germany." *Philosophy* 11 (January 1936).

Koelbl, Herlinde. *Jüdische Portraits: Photographien und Interviews*. Frankfurt: Fischer, 1989.

Koertge, Noretta. "The Methodological Status of Popper's Rationality Principle." *Theory and Decision* 10 (1979): 83–95.

Koestler, Arthur. *Darkness at Noon*. New York: Bantam Books, 1941.

Köhler, Elsa. *Die Personlichkeit des dreijahrigen Kindes (Annchen)*. Leipzig: Hirzel, 1926.

Kohn, Gustav. Address to a meeting concerning the coming parliamentary elections, 20 February 1897. *Mittheilungen der Oesterreichisch-Israelitischen Union* 9, no. 92 (March 1897): 2–6.

Kojève, Alexandre. *Introduction à la Lecture de Hegel*. Edited by Raymond Queneau. Paris: Gallimard, 1947.

Kolb, Fritz. "Erziehung zur Revolution." *Sozialistische Erziehung* 6 (September 1926): 208–10.

Es kam ganz anders. Vienna: ÖBV, 1981.

"Karl Popper und der Sozialismus." In *Theorie und Politik aus kritisch-rationaler Sicht*, edited by Georg Lührs et al. Berlin: Dietz, 1978.

"Klares Wollen!" *Sozialistische Erziehung* 4 (January 1924): 2–5.

Kolnai, Aurel. *Structure and Gestalt*. Edited by Barry Smith. Amsterdam: John Benjamins, 1981.

The War Against the West. London: Victor Gallancz, 1938.

Kraft, Julius. "Introduction" to Leonard Nelson, *Socratic Method and Critical Philosophy*. Translated by Thomas K. Brown III. New Haven, Conn.: Yale University Press, 1949.

"Introduction" to selections from *Hegel und seine Zeit, Ratio* 2 (1960): 42–3.

Die Unmöglichkeit der Geisteswissenschaft. 2d ed. Frankfurt: Öffentliches Leben, 1957.

Von Husserl zu Heidegger. 2d ed. Frankfurt: Öffentliches Leben, 1957.

Kraft, Victor. "Popper and the Vienna Circle." In *The Philosophy of Karl Popper*, edited by Paul Arthur Schilpp. 2 vols. La Salle, Ill.: Open Court, 1974.

The Vienna Circle. New York: Philosophical Library, 1953.

Kraft, Viktor. *Die Grundformen der Wissenschaftlichen Methoden*. Vienna: Hölder-Pichler-Tempsky, 1925.

Kraus, Karl. *Eine Krone für Zion*. Vienna: Frisch, 1898.

Die letzten Tage der Menschheit. 1922. Reprint, Zurich: Pegasus, 1945.

Krauss, Samuel. *Joachim Edler von Popper: Ein Zeit- und Lebensbild aus der Geschichte der Juden in Böhmen*. Vienna: Selbstverlag des Verfassers, 1926.

Die Wiener Geserah vom Jahre 1421. Vienna: Braumüller, 1920.

Krieger, Leonard. *An Essay on the Theory of Enlightened Despotism*. Chicago: University of Chicago Press, 1975.

The German Idea of Freedom. Chicago: University of Chicago Press, 1957.

"Kant and the Crisis of Natural Law." *Journal of the History of Ideas* 26 (1965): 191–210.

Time's Reasons. Chicago: University of Chicago Press, 1989.

Krohn, Claus-Dieter. *Intellectuals in Exile*. Amherst, Mass.: University of Massachusetts Press, 1993.

Krüger, Dieter. *Nationalökonomen im wilhelmischen Deutschland*. Göttingen: Vandenhoeck & Ruprecht, 1983.

Kuéss, Gustav, and Bernhard Scheichelbauer. *200 Jahre Freimaurerei in Österreich*. Vienna: Kerry, 1959.

Kuhn, Thomas. "Logic of Discovery or Psychology of Research?" In *Criticism and the Growth of Knowledge*, edited by Imre Lakatos and Alan Musgrave. Vol. 4 of *Proceedings of the International Colloquium in the Philosophy of Science, London 1965*. Cambridge: The University Press, 1970.

The Structure of Scientific Revolutions. 2d ed. Chicago: University of Chicago, 1970.

Külpe, Oswald. *Outlines of Psychology (1893)*. Translated by Edward Bradford Titchener. New York: Macmillan, 1895.

Vorlesungen über Psychologie. 2d ed. Leipzig: Hirzel, 1922.

Lagerlöf, Selma. *Wunderbare Reise des kleinen Nils Holgersson mit den Wildgänsen*. 3 vols. Munich: Langen, 1907–9.

Lakatos, Imre. "Falsification and the Methodology of Scientific Research Programmes." In *Criticism and the Growth of Knowledge*, edited by Imre Lakatos and Alan Musgrave. Vol. 4 of *Proceedings of the International Colloquium in the Philosophy of Science, London 1965*. Cambridge: The University Press, 1970.

Lange, Oskar. "On the Economic Theory of Socialism." *Review of Economic Studies* 4 (1936–7): 136–44.

Laqueur, Walter. "Is There Now, or Has There Ever Been Such a Thing as Totalitarianism?" *Commentary* 80 (October 1985): 29–35.

Larenz, Karl. "Volksgeist und Recht." *Zeitschrift für deutsche Kulturphilosophie* 1 (1935).

Lasch, Christopher. "The Cultural Cold." In *The Agony of the American Left.* New York: Vintage, 1969.

Laurat, Lucien. *Marxism and Democracy.* London: Gollancz, 1940.

Laurence, Richard. "Bertha von Suttner and the Peace Movement in Austria to World War I." *Austrian History Yearbook* 23 (1992): 181–201.

Lazarsfeld, Paul. "An Episode in the History of Social Research." In *The Intellectual Migration*, edited by Bernard Bailyn and Donald Fleming. Cambridge, Mass.: Harvard University Press, 1969.

Lazarsfeld, Paul, ed. *Jugend und Beruf.* Jena: Fischer, 1931.

Lazarsfeld, Paul, and Ludwig Wagner. *Gemeinschaftserziehung durch Erziehungsgemeinschaften.* Vienna: 1924.

Lebzeltern, Gustav. "Karl Bühler – Lebens und Werke." In *Die Uhren der Lebewesen*, by Karl Bühler, edited by Gustav Lebzeltern. Vienna: Böhlau, 1969.

Lederer, Emil. *The State of the Masses: The Threat of the Classless Society.* New York: Norton, 1940.

Lee, Dwight, and Robert Beck. "The Meaning of 'Historicism.'" *American Historical Review* 59 (1954): 568–77.

Leinfellner, Elisabeth. "Fritz Mauthner im historischen Kontext der empiristischen, analytischen und sprachkritischen Philosophie." In *Fritz Mauthner*, edited by Elisabeth Leinfellner and Hubert Schleichert. Vienna: Böhlau, 1995.

Lenin, Vladimir Ilich. *Materialism and Empirio-Criticism.* 4th ed. Moscow: Progress Publishers, 1964.

Leonard, Robert J. "From Parlor Games to Social Science: Von Neumann, Morgenstern and the Creation of Game Theory, 1928–1944." *Journal of Economic Literature* 33 (1995): 730–61.

Le Rider, Jacques. *Modernité viennoise et crises de l' identité.* Paris: Presses universitaires de France, 1990.

Lerner, Abba. "Economic Theory and Socialist Economy." *Review of Economic Studies* 2 (1933–4): 51–61.

Leser, Norbert. *Zwischen Reformismus und Bolschewismus: Der Austromarxismus als Theorie und Praxis.* 2d ed. Vienna: Böhlaus, 1985.

Levinson, Ronald. *In Defense of Plato.* Cambridge, Mass.: Harvard University Press, 1953.

Levy, Hyman, and Julian Huxley, eds. *Science and Social Needs.* New York: Harper, 1935.

Liebich, André. "Marxism and Totalitarianism: Rudolf Hilferding and the Mensheviks." Occasional Paper, Kenan Institute for Advanced Russian Studies, Woodrow Wilson International Center. Washington, D.C.: Wilson Center, 1987.

Lindblum, Charles. *Politics and Markets.* New York: Basic Books, 1977.

Lindsay, A. D. "The Open Society." *Manchester Guardian*, 25 January 1946.

Link, Werner. *Die Geschichte des Internationalen Jugend-Bundes (IJB) und des Internationalen Sozialistischen Kampf-Bundes (ISK).* Meisenheim am Glan: Hain, 1964.

Lobkowicz, Nicholas. *Theory and Practice.* Notre Dame, Ind.: University of Notre Dame, 1967.

Loewenberg, Peter. "Otto Bauer as an Ambivalent Party Leader." In *The Austrian Socialist Experiment: Social Democracy and Austromarxism, 1918–1934*, edited by Anson Rabinbach. Boulder, Colo.: Westview Press, 1985.

Logue, William. *From Philosophy to Sociology*. Chicago: Northern Illinois University Press, 1983.

Loos, Adolf. *Richtlinien für ein Kunstamt* (Guidelines for a ministry of art). Vienna: Lanyi, 1919.

Loraux, Nicole. *The Invention of Athens: The Funeral Oration in the Classical City*. Translated by A. Sheridan. Cambridge, Mass.: Harvard University Press, 1986.

Löwenthal, Richard. "Beyond the Social-Democratic Consensus." In *Social Change and Cultural Crisis*. New York: Columbia University Press, 1984.

Löwy, Heinrich. "Marxismus und Allgemeine Nährpflicht." In *Gespräche*, edited by Margit Ornstein and Heinrich Löwy. Vienna: Löwit, 1924.

Luft, David. *Robert Musil and the Crisis of European Culture*. Berkeley, Calif.: University of California, 1980.

Lührs, Georg, Thilo Sarrazin, Frithjof Spreer, and Manfred Tietzel, eds. *Kritischer Rationalismus und Sozialdemokratie*. 2 vols. Berlin: Dietz, 1975.

Theorie und Politik aus kritisch-rationaler Sicht. Berlin: Dietz, 1978.

Lukács, Georg. *Geschichte und Klassenbewußtsein*. Berlin: Malik, 1923.

Lukács, György. *History and Class Consciousness*. Translated by Rodney Livingstone. Boston: MIT, 1971.

MacDonald, Mary. *The Republic of Austria, 1918–1934*. London: Oxford University Press, 1946.

Mach, Ernst. *Die Analyse der Empfindungen und das Verhaltniss des Physischen zum Psychischen*. 2d ed. Jena: Fischer, 1900.

Die Geschichte und die Wurzel des Satzes von der Erhaltung der Arbeit. Prague: Calve, 1872.

"Die ökonomische Natur der physikalischen Forschung." In *Populärwissenschaftliche Vorlesungen*. 3d ed. Leipzig: Barth, 1903.

Magee, Bryan. *Confessions of a Philosopher*. New York: Random House, 1997.

Macmurray, John. *The Clue to History*. New York: Harper, 1939.

Malcolm, Norman. *Nothing Is Hidden*. Oxford: Basil Blackwell, 1986.

Mannheim, Karl. *Diagnosis of Our Time: Wartime Essays of a Sociologist*. London: Routledge, 1943.

Essays on the Sociology of Culture. London: Routledge and Kegan Paul, 1956.

Freedom, Power and Democratic Planning. London: Routledge and Kegan Paul, 1951.

Ideologie und Utopie. Bonn: Cohen, 1929. (*Ideology and Utopia*. New York: Harcourt, Brace, 1936).

Man and Society in an Age of Reconstruction. Rev. ed. New York: Harcourt, Brace, 1940.

"The Problem of Generations." In *Essays on the Sociology of Knowledge*. New York: Oxford University Press, 1952.

Marchand, Suzanne. *Down from Olympus: Archaeology and Philhellenism in Germany, 1750–1970*. Princeton, N.J.: Princeton University Press, 1996.

Marcuse, Herbert. "Karl Popper and the Problem of Historical Laws." In *Studies in Critical Philosophy*. Boston: Beacon Press, 1973.

Reason and Revolution. Boston: Beacon, 1941.

Marshall, T. H. "Citizenship and Social Class." In *Class, Citizenship and Social Development*. Chicago: University of Chicago Press, 1977.

Martineau, James. *Types of Ethical Theory*. Oxford: Clarendon Press, 1885.

Marx, Karl. *Capital*. Translated by Samuel Moore and Edward Eveling from the 3d German ed. 2 vols. London: Sonnenschein, Lowrey, 1887.

A Contribution to the Critique of Political Economy. Translated by Salo Ryazanskaya. New York: International Publishers, 1970.

Critique of the Gotha Programme. New York: International Publishers, 1966.

The Economic and Philosophical Manuscripts of 1844. Translated by Martin Milligan. New York: International Publishers, 1964.

The German Ideology. Translated by Salo Ryazanskaya. Moscow: Foreign Languages Publishing House, 1968.

Grundrisse der Kritik der politischen Ökonomie. 2 vols. Moscow: Verlag für Fremdsprächige Literatur, 1939–41.

Grundrisse: Foundations of the Critique of Political Economy. Translated by Martin Nicolaus. New York: Vintage, 1973.

Das Kapital. Translated by Eden and Cedar Paul. Vol. 1 of Everyman's Library edition (English). London: Dent, Dutton, 1930.

Das Kapital. Edited by Friedrich Engels. Vols. 2 and 3. Hamburg: Meissner, 1894.

Theorien über den Mehrwert (Theories of surplus value, referred to as *Capital IV*). 4 vols. Stuttgart: Dietz, 1905.

"Zur Kritik der Hegelschen Rechtsphilosophie. Einleitung." Vol. 1 of *Werke*. Berlin: Dietz, 1961.

Marx, Karl, and Friedrich Engels. *Karl Marx Friedrich Engels historisch-kritische Gesamtausgabe.* Vol. 3. Berlin: Marx-Engels Verlag, 1932.

Mattei, Peter, Juan E. Sola, and Charles J. Yeo. "Chronic and Recurrent Appendicitis Are Uncommon Entities Often Misdiagnosed." *Journal of the American College of Surgeons* 178 (1994): 385–9.

Mattl, Siegfried. "Politik gegen den Tod: Der Stellenwert von Kunst und Kultur in der frühen sozialdemokratischen Bewegung. Eine Skizze." In *Die Bewegung*, edited by Erich Fröschl, Maria Mesner, and Helge Zoitl. Vienna: Passagen, 1990.

Matzner, Egon, and Ian Jarvie. "Introduction to the Special Issue on Situational Analysis." *Philosophy of the Social Sciences* 28 (1998): 333–8.

Mauthner, Fritz. *Beiträge zu einer Kritik der Sprache.* 3d ed. Leipzig: Felix Meiner, 1923.

Die Sprache. Frankfurt: Rütten and Loening, 1907.

Mayer-Hillebrand, Franziska. "Franz Brentano: Der Werdegang seines philosophischen Denkens." *Wissenschaft und Weltbild* 21 (July–September 1968): 12–30.

McCormick, B. J. *Hayek and the Keynesian Avalanche.* New York: St. Martin's, 1992.

McGovern, W. H. *From Luther to Hitler.* Boston: Houghton Mifflin, 1941.

McGrath, William. *Dionysian Art and Populist Politics in Austria.* New Haven, Conn.: Yale University Press, 1974.

McGuinness, Brian. *Wittgenstein: A Life.* Berkeley, Calif.: University of California, 1988.

McGuinness, Brian, ed. *Unified Science.* Boston: Reidel, 1987.

Wittgenstein and the Vienna Circle: Conversations Recorded by Friedrich Waismann. Oxford: Basil Blackwell, 1979.

McLellan, David. *The Young Hegelians and Karl Marx.* London: Macmillan, 1969.

Mendelsohn, Ezra. *On Modern Jewish Politics.* New York: Oxford University Press, 1993.

Menger, Anton. *Neue Staatslehre.* Jena: Fischer, 1904.

The Right to the Whole Produce of Labor. Translated by M. E. Tanner. 1899. Reprint, New York: Augustus Kelley, 1962.

Menger, Carl. *The Collected Works of Carl Menger.* 4 vols. London: London School of Economics and Political Science, 1934.

Grundsätze der Volkswirthschaftslehre. Vienna: Wilhelm Braumüller, 1871.

Investigations into the Method of the Social Sciences with Special Reference to Economics. New York: New York University Press, 1985.

Die Irrthümer des Historismus in der deutschen Nationalökonomie. Vienna: Hölder, 1884.

Principles of Economics. Glencoe, Ill.: Free Press, 1950.

Menger, Karl. "The Formative Years of Abraham Wald." *Annals of Mathematical Statistics* 23 (1952): 18–19.

"Memories of Moritz Schlick." In *Rationality and Science,* edited by Eugene Gadol. New York: Springer, 1982.

"The Role of Uncertainty in Economics." In *Selected Papers in Logic, Foundations, Didactics, Economics.* Boston: Reidel, 1979.

Menger, Karl, ed. *Ergebnisse eines Mathematischen Kolloquiums.* 8 vols. 1931–7.

Menze, Ernest. *Totalitarismus und Fascismus: Eine wissenschaftliche und politische Begriffskontroverse.* Munich: Oldenburg, 1980.

Meyer, Eduard. *Geschichte des Altertums.* 2d ed. 5 vols. Stuttgart: Cotta, 1915.

Meyerhoff, Hans, ed. *The Philosophy of History in Our Time.* New York: Doubleday, 1959.

"Plato among Friends and Enemies." *Encounter* (December 1961): 45–50.

Milford, Karl. "Roschers historische Methode." In *Wilhelm Roscher als führender Wirtschaftstheoretiker,* by Erich Streissler, Peter Rosner, Franz Baltzarek, and Karl Milford. Düsseldorf: Verlag Wirtschaft und Finanzen, 1994.

Mill, John Stuart. *Considerations on Representative Government.* London: Longman, 1865.

A System of Logic. New York: Harper, 1846.

Miller, David. *Critical Rationalism.* Chicago: Open Court, 1994.

"Sir Karl Raimund Popper." *Biographical Memoirs of Fellows of the Royal Society* 43 (1997): 367–409.

Mises, Ludwig von. *A Critique of Interventionism.* New Rochelle, N.Y.: Arlington House, 1977.

"Economic Calculation in the Socialist Commonwealth." In *Collectivist Economic Planning,* edited by Friedrich Hayek. London: Routledge, 1935.

Epistemological Problems of Economics. Princeton, N.J.: Van Nostrand, 1960.

The Historical Setting of the Austrian School of Economics. New Rochelle, N.Y.: Arlington House, 1969.

Human Action. 3d ed. Chicago: Regnery, 1966.

Kritik des Interventionismus. Jena: Fischer, 1929.

Nation, State, and Economy. New York: New York University Press, 1983.

"Wirtschaftsrechnung in der Gemeinwirtschaft." *Archiv für Sozialwissenschaft und Sozialpolitik* 47 (1920): 86–121.

Mises, Richard von. "Fundamentalsätze der Wahrscheinlichkeitsrechnung." *Mathematische Zeitschrift* 5 (1919): 52–99.

Wahrscheinlichkeit, Statistik, und Wahrheit. Vienna: Julius Springer, 1928.

Wahrscheinlichkeitsrechnung und ihre Anwendung in der Statistik und theoretischen Physik. Leipzig: Deuticke, 1931.

Moellin, Jacob ben Moses. *Sheelot u-Teshuvot Maharil.* Jerusalem: Mifal Torah Hakhame Ashkenaz, 1979.

Momigliano, Arnaldo. "George Grote and the Study of Greek History." In *Studies in Historiography.* London: Weidenfeld and Nicolson, 1966.

Mommsen, Hans. "Die Realisierung des Utopischen: Die 'Endlösung der Judenfrage' im 'Dritten Reich.'" *Geschichte und Gesellschaft* 9 (1983): 381–420.

"Theorie und Praxis des österreichischen Ständestaats 1934 bis 1938." In *Das geistige Leben Wiens in der Zwischenkriegzeit*, edited by Norbert Leser. Vienna: ÖBV, 1981.

Monk, Ray. *Ludwig Wittgenstein*. New York: Free Press, 1990.

Morgenstern, Oskar. *Selected Writings of Oskar Morgenstern*, edited by Andrew Schotter. New York: New York University Press, 1976.

Wirtschaftsprognose: Eine Untersuchung ihrer Voraussetzungen und Möglichkeiten (Economic forecasting: An investigation of its preconditions and possibilities). Vienna: Julius Springer, 1928.

Morrow, Glenn. "Plato and Greek Slavery." *Mind* 48 (1939): 186–201.

Müller, Karl. Essays in *Versuche und Widerlegungen offene Probleme im Werk Karl Poppers*, edited by Karl Müller, Friedrich Stadler, and Friedrich Wallner. Vienna: Geyer, 1986.

"Die Idealwelten der österreichischen Nationalökonomen." In vol. 1 of *Vertriebene Vernunft: Emigration und Exil österreichischer Wissenschaft 1930–1940*, edited by Friedrich Stadler. Vienna: Jugend und Volk, 1987.

Müller, Karl, Friedrich Stadler, and Friedrich Wallner, eds. *Versuche und Widerlegungen offene Probleme im Werk Karl Poppers*. Vienna: Geyer, 1986.

Munz, Peter. *Our Knowledge of the Growth of Knowledge*. London: Routledge and Kegan Paul, 1985.

"Transformation in Philosophy Through the Teaching Methods of Wittgenstein and Popper." In *The Search for Absolute Values and the Creation of the New World*. Vol. 2 of *Proceedings of the Tenth International Conference on the Unity of the Sciences*. New York: International Cultural Foundation, 1982.

Musil, Robert. *Der Mann ohne Eigenschaften, Roman*. Hamburg: Rowohlt, 1952.

Näf, Beat. *Von Perikles zu Hitler?* Bern: Peter Lang, 1985.

Nagel, Ernest. Review of *Logik der Forschung*. *Journal of Philosophy* 32 (1935): 107–8.

Natkin, Marcel. "Einfachheit, Kausalität und Induktion." Ph.D. diss., University of Vienna, 1928.

Neider, Heinrich. "Persönliche Erinnerungen an den Wiener Kreis." *Conceptus* 11 (1977): 21–56.

Nelson, Leonard. "Jakob Friedrich Fries und seine jüngsten Kritiker." In vol. 1 of *Gesammelte Schriften*. 9 vols. Hamburg: Felix Meiner, 1970.

"Die Kritische Methode und das Verhältnis der Psychologie zur Philosophie." In vol. 1 of *Gesammelte Schriften*. Hamburg: Felix Meiner, 1970.

Politics and Education. London: Allen & Unwin, 1928.

Progress and Regress in Philosophy: From Hume and Kant to Hegel and Fries. Edited by Julius Kraft. Translated by Humphrey Palmer. 2 vols. Oxford: Basil Blackwell, 1970.

Die Rechtswissenschaft ohne Recht (Jurisprudence without justice). Leipzig: Veit, 1917.

Socratic Method and Critical Philosophy. Translated by Thomas K. Brown, III. New Haven, Conn.: Yale University Press, 1949.

Spuk. Einweihung in das Geheimnis der Wahrsagerkunst Oswald Spenglers. In vol. 3 of *Gesammelte Schriften*. Hamburg: Felix Meiner, 1970.

Über das sogennante Erkenntnisproblem. Göttingen: Vandenhoeck und Ruprecht, 1908.

"Die Unmöglichkeit der Erkenntnistheorie." In vol. 2 of *Gesammelte Schriften*. Hamburg: Felix Meiner, 1973.

Nemeth, Elizabeth. *Otto Neurath und der Wiener Kreis: Revolutionäre Wissenschaftlichkeit als politischer Anspruch*. Frankfurt: Campus, 1981.

Nestle, Wilhelm. *Die Vorsokratiker*. Jena: Diederichs, 1905.

Nettleship, R. L. *Lectures on the Republic of Plato*. New York: Macmillan, 1929.

Neumann, Franz. *Behemoth: The Structure and Practice of National Socialism*. New York: Oxford University Press, 1942.

Neumann, John von, and Oskar Morgenstern. *Theory of Games and Economic Behavior*. 2d ed. Princeton, N.J.: Princeton University Press, 1947.

Neumann, Sigmund. *Modern Political Parties*. Chicago: University of Chicago Press, 1956.

Neurath, Otto. *Le développement du Cercle de Vienne et l'avenir de l'empirisme logique*. Paris: Hermann & Cie, 1936.

———. *Durch die Kriegswirtschaft zur Naturalwirtschaft*. Munich: Callwey, 1919.

———. "Einheit der Wissenschaft als Aufgabe." *Erkenntnis* 5 (1935): 16–22.

———. "Einheitswissenschaft und Psychologie." In vol. 2 of *Gesammelte philosophische und methodologische Schriften*. Vienna: Hölder-Pichler-Tempsky, 1981.

———. "Einzelwissenschaften, Einheitswissenschaft, Pseudorationalismus." In vol. 1 of *Actes du Congress Internationale de Philosophie Scientifique*. Paris: Hermann & Cie, 1936.

———. *Empirische Soziologie* (Empiricism and sociology). Vienna: Julius Springer, 1931.

———. "L'encyclopédie comme 'modèle.'" *Revue de Synthèse* 12 (1936): 187–201.

———. "Une encyclopédie internationale de la science unitaire." In vol. 2 of *Actes du Congrès International de Philosophie Scientifique*. Paris: Hermann & Cie, 1936.

———. "Experiences of Socialization in Bavaria." In *Empiricism and Sociology*, edited by Marie Neurath and Robert S. Cohen. Boston: Reidel, 1972.

———. "From Vienna Method to Isotope." In *Empiricism and Sociology*, edited by Marie Neurath and Robert S. Cohen. Boston: Reidel, 1972.

———. "Mensch und Gesellschaft in der Wissenschaft." In vol. 2 of *Actes du Congrès International de Philosophie Scientifique*. Paris: Hermann & Cie, 1936.

———. "Physikalismus." In vol. 1 of *Gesammelte philosophische und methodologische Schriften*. Vienna: Hölder-Pichler-Tempsky, 1981.

———. "Protokollsätze." *Erkenntnis* 3 (1932): 205.

———. "Pseudorationalismus der Falsifikation." *Erkenntnis* 5 (1935): 353–65. (English: "Pseudorationalism of 'Falsification.'" In *Philosophical Papers*, edited and translated by R. S. Cohen and Marie Neurath. Boston: Reidel, 1983.)

———. "Radikaler Physikalismus und 'wirkliche Welt.'" *Erkenntnis* 4 (1934): 346–62.

———. "Soziologie im Physikalismus." *Erkenntnis* 2 (1931): 393–431.

———. "Soziologische Prognosen." *Erkenntnis* 6 (1936): 398–405.

———. "Die Utopie als gesellschaftstechnische Konstruction." In *Durch die Kriegswirtschaft zur Naturalwirtschaft*. Munich: Callwey, 1919.

———. *Vollsozialisierung*. Jena: Diederichs, 1920.

Nimmerrichter, Alfred. *Loge Humanitas – Chronik des Überlebens, Quatuor-Coronati-Berichte*, vol. 17. Forthcoming.

Nitti, Francesco. *Bolshevism, Fascism and Democracy*. New York: Macmillan, 1927.

Nolte, Ernst. "Vierzig Jahre Theorien über den Faschismus." In *Theorien über den Faschismus*, edited by Ernst Nolte. Cologne: Kiepenheuer & Witsch, 1967.

Oakes, Guy. *Weber and Rickert: Concept Formation in the Cultural Sciences*. Cambridge, Mass.: MIT, 1988.

Okin, Susan. *Women in Western Political Thought*. Princeton, N.J.: Princeton University Press, 1979.

Oldroyd, David. *The Arch of Knowledge*. New York: Methuen, 1987.

Olechowski, Richard. "Schulpolitik." In vol. 1 of *Österreich 1918–1938. Geschichte der Ersten Republik*, edited by Erika Weinzierl and Kurt Skalnik. 2 vols. Graz: Styria, 1983.

O'Neill, John, ed. *Modes of Individualism and Collectivism*. London: Heinemann, 1973.

Österreichische Gesellschaft für Kulturpolitik and Meidlinger Kulturkreis. *Mit uns zieht die neue Zeit: Arbeiterkultur in Österreich 1918–1934*. Vienna: Habarta, 1981.

Ottmann, Henning. *Individuum und Gemeinschaft bei Hegel*. Vol. 1. Berlin: Gruyter, 1977.

Oxaal, Ivar, and Walter Weitzmann. "The Jews of Pre-1914 Vienna." *Leo Baeck Institute Yearbook* 30 (1985): 395–432.

Papanek, Ernst. *The Austrian School Reform*. New York: Fell, 1962.

Parkes, H. B. *Marx: A Post Mortem*. London: Allen & Unwin, 1945.

Pateman, Carole. *Participation and Democratic Theory*. Cambridge: Cambridge University Press, 1970.

  The Sexual Contract. Stanford, Calif.: Stanford University Press, 1988.

  "The Theoretical Subversiveness of Feminism." In *Feminist Challenges: Social and Political Theory*, edited by Carole Pateman and Elizabeth Gross. Boston: Northeastern University Press, 1987.

Pater, Walter. *Plato and Platonism*. New York: Macmillan, 1894.

Pauley, Bruce. *From Prejudice to Persecution: A History of Austrian Antisemitism*. Chapel Hill, N.C.: University of North Carolina, 1992.

  Hitler and the Forgotten Nazis: A History of Austrian National Socialism. Chapel Hill, N.C.: University of North Carolina, 1981.

Pauthier, J. L. "Les catholiques sociaux et les démocrates-chretiens français devant l'Italie fasciste, 1932–1935." Ph.D. diss., Paris, 1981.

Pears, David. *Wittgenstein*. London: Fontana, 1969.

Pflug, Siegmund [Simon Popper]. *Anno Neunzehnhundertdrei in Freilichtmalerei*. Leipzig: Eisenstein, 1904.

Plamenatz, John. Review of *The Open Society*. *British Journal of Sociology* 3 (1952): 264–73.

Plato. *The Collected Dialogues of Plato*. Edited by Edith Hamilton and Huntington Cairns. Princeton, N.J.: Princeton University Press, 1963.

  Five Dialogues. Translated by G. M. A. Grube. Indianapolis, Ind.: Hackett, 1981.

  Laws. Translated by A. E. Taylor. In *The Collected Dialogues*.

  Protagoras. Translated by W. K. C. Guthrie. In *The Collected Dialogues*.

  Republic. Translated by G. M. A. Grube and C. D. C. Reeve. Indianapolis, Ind.: Hackett, 1992.

  The Statesman. Translated by J. B. Skemp. In *The Collected Dialogues*.

  Symposium. Translated by Alexander Nehamas and Paul Woodruff. Indianapolis, Ind.: Hackett, 1989.

Pocock, J. G. A. Review of *The Poverty of Historicism*. *The Cambridge Review* (23 November 1957): 200–1.

Poincaré, Henri. *La Science et l'hypothèse*. Paris: Flammarion, 1903. (German edition: *Wissenschaft und Hypothese*. Leipzig: Teubner, 1906.)

Polanyi, Karl. "Die funktionelle Theorie der Gesellschaft und das Problem der sozialistische Rechnungslegung." *Archiv für Sozialwissenschaft und Sozialpolitik* 52 (1924): 218–28.

  The Great Transformation. New York: Farrar and Rinehart, 1944.

  "Neue Erwangungen zu unserer Theorie von Praxis (1925)." In *Austromarxistische Positionen*, edited by Gerald Mozetic. Vienna: Böhlau, 1983.

  Primitive, Archaic, and Modern Economies: Essays of Karl Polanyi. Garden City, N.Y.: Anchor, 1968.

  "Sozialistische Rechnungslegung." *Archiv für Sozialwissenschaft und Sozialpolitik* 49 (1922): 377–418.

Polanyi, Michael. *Knowing and Being.* Chicago: University of Chicago Press, 1969.
  Personal Knowledge: Towards a Post-Critical Philosophy. London: Routledge & Kegan Paul,
  1958.
Polanyi-Levitt, Kari, ed. *The Life and Work of Karl Polanyi.* Montreal: Black Rose, 1990.
Popper, Karl. "Advice to Russian readers of *The Open Society.*" In Colin Simkin, *Popper's
  Views on Natural and Social Science.* Leiden: Brill, 1993.
  "Against Big Words." In *In Search of a Better World.* London: Routledge, 1992.
  "The Aim of Science." In *Objective Knowledge.* Oxford: Clarendon Press, 1972.
  Ausgangspunkte (Autobiography). Hamburg: Hoffman und Campe, 1979.
  "Back to the Presocratics." In *Conjectures and Refutations.* New York: Basic Books, 1963.
  Die beiden Grundprobleme der Erkenntnistheorie [1930–33]. Edited by Troels Eggers Hansen.
  Tübingen: Mohr, 1979.
  "The Bucket and the Searchlight: Two Theories of Knowledge." In *Objective Knowledge.*
  Oxford: Clarendon Press, 1972.
  "The Communist Road to Self-Enslavement." *Cato Policy Report* 14 (1992).
  Conjectures and Refutations. New York: Basic Books, 1963.
  "The Demarcation between Science and Mataphysics." In *Conjectures and Refutations.* New
  York: Basic Books, 1963.
  "Einleitung 1978." In *Die beiden Grundprobleme der Erkenntnistheorie,* edited by Troels
  Eggers Hansen. Tübingen: Mohr, 1979.
  "Epistemology and Industrialization." In *The Myth of the Framework.* London: Routledge,
  1994.
  "Epistemology without a Knowing Subject." In *Objective Knowledge.* Oxford: Clarendon
  Press, 1972.
  "Erinnerungen an Schlick" [1984]. Hoover Institute Archives, Karl Popper Papers, box
  252, file 1.
  "Evolution and the Tree of Knowledge." In *Objective Knowledge.* Oxford: Clarendon Press,
  1972.
  "Freiheit vor Gleichheit." In *Frankfurter Allgemeine Zeitung,* 24 December 1976.
  "Die Gedächtnispflege unter dem Gesichtpunkt der Selbsttätigkeit." *Die Quelle* 81 (1931):
  607–19.
  "Gespräch mit Karl Popper." In *Theorie und Politik aus kritisch-rationaler Sicht,* edited by
  Georg Lührs et al. Berlin: Dietz, 1978.
  "Gespräch mit Sir Karl Popper (1991)." In Friedrich Stadler, *Studien zum Wiener Kreis.*
  Frankfurt: Suhrkamp, 1997.
  "The History of Our Time: An Optimist's View." In *Conjectures and Refutations.* New York:
  Basic Books, 1963.
  "An Independent Set of Axioms for Lattices." (Summer 1943–44.) Hoover Institute
  Archives, Karl Popper Papers, box 27, file 12.
  "'Induktionslogik' und 'Hypothesenwahrscheinlichkeit.'" *Erkenntnis* 5 (1935): 170–
  2.
  "In Memory of Hans Hahn." In vol. 1 of *Hans Hahn: Collected Works.* Vienna: Springer,
  1995.
  In Search of a Better World. London: Routledge, 1992.
  "Interpretation of Nebular Red-Shifts." *Nature* 145, 13 January 1940, 69–70.
  Interview in *Der Spiegel* (June 1992), translated in *Ha-aretz,* 27 September 1992.
  Interview with Franz Kreuzer. In *Offene Gesellschaft – offenes Universum.* Vienna: Deuticke,
  1982.

"Julius Kraft, 1898–1960." *Ratio* 4 (1962): 2–15.

"Knowledge and the Shaping of Reality." In *In Search of a Better World*. London: Routledge, 1992.

"Ein Kriterium des empirischen Charakters theoretischer Systeme." *Erkenntnis* 3 (1933): 426–7. (Published in English as "A Criterion of the Empirical Character of Theoretical Systems." *The Logic of Scientific Discovery*. London: Hutchinson, 1959.)

"Language and the Body-Mind Problem." In *Conjectures and Refutations*. New York: Basic Books, 1963.

The Lesson of This Century: With Two Talks on Freedom and the Democratic State: Karl Popper interviewed by Giancarlo Bosetti. Translated by Patrick Camiller. London: Routledge, 1996.

The Logic of Scientific Discovery. Translated by Karl Popper. London: Hutchinson, 1959.

"The Logic of the Social Sciences" [1962]. In *The Positivist Dispute in German Sociology*, by Theodor Adorno et al, translated by Glyn Adey and David Frisby. London: Heinemann, 1976.

Logik der Forschung: Zur Erkenntnistheorie der modernen Naturwissenschaft. Vienna: Julius Springer, 1935.

"Memories of Otto Neurath." In Otto Neurath, *Empiricism and Sociology*, edited by Marie Neurath and Robert S. Cohen. Boston: Reidel, 1972.

Miseria dello storicismo. 2d ed. Translated by Carlo Montaleone. Milan: Feltrinelli, 1975.

"Models, Instruments, and Truth: The Status of the Rationality Principle in the Social Sciences." In *The Myth of the Framework*. London: Routledge, 1994.

"The Moral Responsibility of the Scientist." In *The Myth of the Framework*. London: Routledge, 1994.

The Myth of the Framework. London: Routledge, 1994.

"The Myth of the Framework." In *The Myth of the Framework*. London: Routledge, 1994.

"Normal Science and Its Dangers." In *Criticism and the Growth of Knowledge*, edited by Imre Lakatos and Alan Musgrave. vol. 4 of *Proceedings of the International Colloquium in the Philosophy of Science, London 1965*. Cambridge: The University Press, 1970.

Objective Knowledge. Oxford: Clarendon Press, 1972.

"Of Clouds and Clocks: An Approach to the Problem of Rationality and the Freedom of Man." In *Objective Knowledge*. Oxford: Clarendon Press, 1972.

Offene Gesellschaft – offenes Universum: Franz Kreuzer im Gespräch mit Karl R. Popper. Vienna: Deuticke, 1982.

"On a Little-Known Chapter of Mediterranean History." In *In Search of a Better World*. London: Routledge, 1992.

"On Culture Clash." In *In Search of a Better World*. London: Routledge, 1992.

"On Reason and the Open Society." *Encounter* 38 (1972): 13–18.

"On the Theory of the Objective Mind." In *Objective Knowledge*. Oxford: Clarendon Press, 1972.

The Open Society and Its Enemies. 2 vols. London: Routledge, 1945.

The Open Society and its Enemies. 2d ed. London: Routledge & Kegan Paul, 1952.

The Open Society and its Enemies. 4th ed. London: Routledge & Kegan Paul, 1962.

The Open Society and its Enemies. 5th ed. London: Routledge & Kegan Paul, 1966.

The Open Universe: An Argument for Indeterminism. London: Hutchinson, 1981.

"Pädagogische Zeitschriftenschau." *Die Quelle* 82 (1932): 712–33.

"A Pluralist Approach to the Philosophy of History." In *The Myth of the Framework*, edited by M. A. Notturno. London: Routledge, 1994.

Postscript to The Logic of Scientific Discovery: Realism and the Aim of Science; The Open Universe; Quantum Theory and the Schism in Physics. 3 vols. London: Hutchinson, 1981–2.

"The Poverty of Historicism, I, II, III," *Economica* 11–12 (1944–5): 86–103, 119–37, 69–89.

The Poverty of Historicism. London: Routledge & Kegan Paul, 1957.

"Prediction and Prophecy in the Social Sciences." In *Conjectures and Refutations.* New York: Basic Books, 1963.

"The Propensity Interpretation of Probability." *British Journal for the Philosophy of Science* 10 (1959): 25–42.

"The Propensity Interpretation of the Calculus of Probability, and the Quantum Theory." In *Observation and Interpretation,* edited by Stephen Körner. London: Butterworths, 1957.

"Public Opinion and Liberal Principles." In *Conjectures and Refutations.* New York: Basic Books, 1963.

Quantum Theory and the Schism in Physics. London: Hutchinson, 1981.

"La rationalité et le statut du principe de rationalité." In *Les Fondements philosophiques des systemes economiques,* edited by Emil M. Classen. Paris: Payot, 1967. (English version, "The Rationality Principle," in *A Pocket Popper,* edited by David Miller. Glasgow: Fontana, 1983.)

"The Rationality of Scientific Revolutions." In *The Myth of the Framework.* London: Routledge, 1994.

Realism and the Aim of Science. London: Hutchinson, 1982.

"Reason or Revolution?" In *The Positivist Dispute in German Sociology,* by Theodor Adorno et al. London: Heinemann, 1976.

"Replies to My Critics." In vol. 2 of *The Philosophy of Karl Popper,* edited by Paul Arthur Schilpp. La Salle, Ill.: Open Court, 1974.

"Review of Friedrich Engel-Janosi, *The Growth of German Historicism.* (Baltimore: Johns Hopkins, 1944)." *Economica* 12 (1945): 259–61.

"Science: Conjectures and Refutations." In *Conjectures and Refutations.* New York: Basic Books, 1963.

"Science: Problems, Aims, Responsibilities." In *The Myth of the Framework.* London: Routledge, 1994.

"A Set of Independent Axioms for Probability." *Mind* 47 (1938): 275–7.

La télévision: Un danger pour la démocratie. Paris: Anatolia Editions, 1994.

"Three Views Concerning Human Knowledge." In *Conjectures and Refutations.* New York: Basic Books, 1963.

"Toleration and Intellectual Responsibility." In *In Search of a Better World.* London: Routledge, 1992.

"Toward a Rational Theory of Tradition." In *Conjectures and Refutations.* New York: Basic Books, 1963.

"Truth, Rationality, and the Growth of Knowledge." In *Conjectures and Refutations.* New York: Basic Books, 1963.

"Über die Stellung des Lehrers zu Schule und Schüler. Gesellschaftliche oder individualistische Erziehung?" *Schulreform* 4 (1925): 204–8.

"Über nachwirkungsfreie Folgen." *Ergebnisse eines Mathematischen kolloquiums* 7 (1936): 12.

Unended Quest: An Intellectual Autobiography. La Salle, Ill.: Open Court, 1976.

"Utopia and Violence." In *Conjectures and Refutations.* New York: Basic Books, 1963.

"Vorwort" to Fritz Kolb, *Es kam ganz anders. Betrachtungen eines alt gewordenen Sozialisten.* Vienna: ÖBV, 1981.

"Vorwort." *Das Elend des Historizismus.* Tübingen: Mohr, 1965.

"What Does the West Believe in?" In *In Search of a Better World*. London: Routledge, 1992.

"What is Dialectic?" *Mind* 49 (1940): 403–26.

"Der wichtigste Beitrag seit Aristoteles." *Wissenschaft aktuell* 1 (September 1980).

The World of Parmenides: Essays on the Presocratic Enlightenment. London: Routledge, 1998.

A World of Propensities. Bristol: Thoemmes, 1990.

Die Zukunft ist offen. Edited by Franz Kreuzer. Munich: Piper, 1985.

"Zum Thema Freiheit." In *Die Philosophie und die Wissenschaften*, edited by Ernst Oldemeyer. Meisenheim am Glan: Anton Hain, 1967.

"Zur Kritik der Ungenauigkeitsrelationen." *Die Naturwissenschaften* 22 (30 November 1934): 807.

"Zur Methodenfrage der Denkpsychologie." Ph.D. diss., University of Vienna, 1928.

"Zur Philosophie des Heimatgedankens." *Die Quelle* 77 (1927): 899–908.

Popper, Karl, and John Eccles. *The Self and Its Brain*. New York: Springer, 1977.

Popper-Lynkeus, Josef. *Die Allgemeine Nährpflicht als Lösung der sozialen Frage*. 2d ed. Vienna: Rikola, 1923.

Gespräche. Edited by Margit Urnstein and Heinrich Löwy. Vienna: Löwit, 1924.

Mein Leben und Wirken. Dresden: Carl Reissner, 1924.

Die technischen Fortschritte nach ihrer aesthetischen und kulturellen Bedeutung. Leipzig: Carl Reissner, 1888.

Pouncey, Peter. *The Necessities of War*. New York: Columbia University Press, 1980.

Pseudo-Xenophon. *The Constitution of the Athenians*. In *Aristotle and Xenophon on Democracy and Oligarchy*, translated by J. M. Moore. Berkeley, Calif.: University of California, 1975.

Pulzer, Peter. *The Rise of Political Antisemitism in Germany and Austria*. Rev. ed. Cambridge, Mass.: Harvard University Press, 1988.

Rabinbach, Anson. *The Crisis of Austrian Socialism: From Red Vienna to Civil War, 1927–1934*. Chicago: University of Chicago Press, 1983.

Randall, John H. *Plato: Dramatist of the Life of Reason*. New York: Columbia University Press, 1970.

Rauschning, Hermann. *The Revolution of Nihilism*. New York: Longmans, Green & Co., 1939.

Rechter, David. "Neither East nor West: Viennese Jewish Politics in World War One." Ph.D. diss., Hebrew University of Jerusalem, 1994.

Reeder, Harry P. *The Work of Felix Kaufmann*. Lanham, Md.: University Press of America, 1991.

Reeve, C. D. C. *Philosopher-Kings*. Princeton, N.J.: Princeton University Press, 1988.

Reichenbach, Hans. "Axiomatik der Wahrscheinlichkeitsrechnung." *Mathematische Zeitschrift* 34 (1932): 568–619.

"Bemerkung." *Erkenntnis* 3 (1933): 426–7.

"Kausalität und Wahrscheinlichkeit." *Erkenntnis* 1 (1930): 158–88.

"Über Induktion und Wahrscheinlichkeit. Bemerkungen zu Karl Poppers *Logik der Forschung*." *Erkenntnis* 5 (1935): 267–84.

"Wahrscheinlichkeitslogik." *Sitzungsberichte der Preussischen Akademie der Wissenschaften, Physik.-mathem. Klasse* 29 (1932): 476–90.

Reichmayr, Johannes. "Sozialistische Erziehung und Psychoanalyse in der Ersten Republik." In *Die Österreichische Reformpädagogik 1918–1938*, edited by Erik Adam. Vienna: Böhlau, 1981.

Reininger, Robert. "Das Causalproblem bei Hume und Kant." *Kant Studien* 6 (1901): 427–58.

Metaphysik der Wirklichkeit. Vienna: Braumüller, 1931.

Philosophie der Wirklichkeitsnähe: Festschrift zum 80. Geburtstag Robert Reiningers. Vienna: Sexl, 1949.

Das psycho-physische Problem. Vienna: Braumüller, 1916.

Reiter, Wolfgang. "The Year 1938 and Its Consequences for the Sciences in Austria." In *Vertreibung der Vernunft: The Cultural Exodus from Austria*, edited by Friedrich Stadler and Peter Weibel. 2d ed. New York: Springer, 1995.

Rickert, Heinrich. *Die Grenzen der naturwissenschaftlichen Begriffsbildung.* 3d ed. Tübingen: Mohr, 1921.

Ringer, Alexander. *Arnold Schönberg: The Composer as Jew.* Oxford: Clarendon, 1990.

Ringer, Fritz. "Causal Analysis in Historical Reasoning." *History and Theory* 28 (1989): 152–72.

The Decline of the German Mandarins: The German Academic Community, 1890–1933. Cambridge, Mass.: Harvard University Press, 1969.

Roberts, D. K., ed. *The Authors, Playwrights & Composers Handbook.* London: John Lane, 1938.

Robinson, Richard. "Dr. Popper's Defense of Democracy." *Philosophical Review* 60 (1951): 487–507.

Röd, Wolfgang. "Alois Riehl und der Herbartianismus in Österreich." In *From Bolzano to Wittgenstein: The Tradition of Austrian Philosophy*, edited by J. C. Nyíri. Vienna: Hölder-Pichler-Tempsky, 1986.

Rogers, A. K. *The Socratic Question.* New Haven, Conn.: Yale University Press, 1933.

Rorty, Richard. *Philosophy and the Mirror of Nature.* Princeton, N.J.: Princeton University Press, 1979.

Roscher, Wilhelm. *Grundriss zu Vorlesungen über die Staatswirtschaft. Nach geschichtlicher Methode.* Göttingen: Dieterichsche Buchhandlung, 1843.

Principles of Political Economy. 13th ed. Chicago: Callaghan, 1882.

Rose, Paul. *Revolutionary Antisemitism in Germany: From Kant to Wagner.* Princeton, N.J.: Princeton University Press, 1990.

Rosenkrantz, Karl. *Georg Wilhelm Friedrich Hegels Leben.* 1844. Reprint, Darmstadt: Wissenschaftliche Buchgesellschaft, 1977.

Rosenzweig, Franz. *Hegel und der Staat.* 2 vols. Munich: Oldenbourg, 1920.

Roth, Joseph. *Radetzkymarsch.* Berlin: Kiepenheuer, 1932.

Roth, Michael. *Knowing and History: Appropriations of Hegel in Twentieth Century France.* Ithaca, N.Y.: Cornell University Press, 1988.

Rothenberg, Gunther. "The Habsburg Army in the First World War: 1914–1918." In *East Central European Society in World War I*, edited by B. K. Király and N. F. Dreisinger. New York: Columbia University Press, 1985.

Rozenblit, Marsha. *The Jews of Vienna: Identity and Assimilation, 1867–1914.* Albany, N.Y.: State University of New York Press, 1983.

Russell, Bertrand. *Let the People Think.* London: Watt, 1941.

"The Limits of Empiricism." *Proceedings of the Aristotelian Society* 36 (1936): 131–50.

"Philosophy and Politics." In *Unpopular Essays.* London: Allen and Unwin, 1950.

Rykwert, Joseph. "House and Home," *Social Research* 58 (Spring 1991): 51–62.

Ryle, Gilbert. "Review of *The Open Society.*" *Mind* 56 (1947): 167–72.

Salmon, Wesley. *Four Decades of Scientific Explanation.* Minneapolis, Minn.: University of Minnesota Press, 1989.

Sandall, Roger. "Karl Popper." *Salisbury Review* 15 (1996): 12–17.

Sauer, Werner. *Österreichische Philosophie zwischen Aufklärung und Restauration. Beiträge zur*

Geschichte des Frühkantianismus in der Donaumonarchie. Amsterdam: Rodopi, 1982.

Savigny, Karl August von. *Geschichte des Römischen Rechts im Mittelalter.* 2d ed. Aalen: Scientia, 1986.

On the Vocation of Our Age for Legislation and Jurisprudence. New York: Arno, 1975.

Scheu, Friedrich. *Ein Band der Freundschaft: Schwarzwald-Kreis und die Entstehung der Vereinigung Sozialistischer Mittelschüler.* Vienna: Böhlau, 1985.

Schiff, Walter. *Die Planwirtschaft und ihre ökonomischen Hauptprobleme.* Berlin: Heymanns, 1932.

Schlangen, Walter. *Die Totalitarismus-Theorie: Entwicklung und Probleme.* Stuttgart: Kohlhammer, 1976.

Schlick, Moritz. *Allgemeine Erkenntnislehre.* 2d ed. Berlin: Julius Springer, 1925.

"Die Kausalität in der gegenwärtigen Physik." *Die Naturwissenschaften* 19 (1931): 145–62. ("Causality in Contemporary Physics." In vol. 2 of *Philosophical Papers*, edited by H. L. Mulder and B. van de Velde-Schlick. Boston: Reidel, 1979.)

"Über das Fundament der Erkenntnis." *Erkenntnis* 4 (1934): 79–99. ("On the Foundation of Knowledge." In vol. 2 of *Philosophical Papers*, edited by H. L. Mulder and B. van de Velde-Schlick. Boston: Reidel, 1979.)

"Die Wende in der Philosophie." *Erkenntnis* 1 (1930): 4–11.

Schmitt, Carl. *Der Begriff des Politischen.* Hamburg: Hanseatische Verlagsanstalt, 1933. (Published in English as *The Concept of the Political.* Translated and introduced by George Schwab. New Brunswick, N.J.: Rutgers University Press, 1976.)

Die geistesgeschichtliche Lage des heutigen Parlamentarismus. 2d ed. Berlin: Duncker & Humblot, 1926.

Verfassungsrechtliche Aufsätze aus den Jahren 1924–1954. Berlin: Duncker & Humblot, 1958.

Schmoller, Gustav. "Antwortbrief." *Schmollers Jahrbuch* 8 (1884).

Grundriss der allgemeinen Volkswirtschaftslehre. 2 vols. Munich: Duncker and Humblot, 1920.

"Die Schriften von K. Menger und W. Dilthey zur Methodologie der Staats- und Sozialwissenschaften." In *Zur Litteraturgeschichte der Staats- und Sozialwissenschaften.* Leipzig: Duncker and Humblot, 1888.

"Über einige Grundfragen des Rechts und der Volkswirtschaft." In *Über einige Grundfragen der Sozialpolitik.* 2d ed. Leipzig: Duncker and Humblot, 1904.

Schnitzler, Arthur. *My Youth in Vienna.* New York: Holt, Rinehart and Winston, 1970.

Schoenberg, Arnold. *Style and Idea: Selected Writings of Arnold Schoenberg.* Edited by Leonard Stein. London: Faber, 1975.

Schön, Manfred. "Gustav Schmoller and Max Weber." In *Max Weber and His Contemporaries*, edited by Wolfgang Mommsen and Jürgen Osterhammel. London: Allen and Unwin, 1987.

Schönberg, Arnold. "Musik." In *Stil und Gedanke: Aufsätze zur Musik.* Frankfurt: Fischer, 1976.

Von Neuer Musik. Cologne: Marcan, 1924.

Schopenhauer, Arthur. Appendix to "Skitze einer Geschichte der Lehre vom Idealen und Realen." In *Parerga und Paralipomena.* Vol. 5 of *Sämmtliche Werke.* 2d ed. Leipzig: Brockhaus, 1922.

Preface. *Die Welt als Wille und Vorstellung.* Vol. 2 of *Sämmtliche Werke.* 2d ed. Leipzig: Brockhaus, 1922.

Schorske, Carl. *Fin-de-siècle Vienna: Politics and Culture.* New York: Knopf, 1980.

"Generational Tension and Cultural Change: Reflections on the Case of Vienna." *Daedalus* (fall 1978): 111–22.

Schumpeter, Joseph. *Capitalism, Socialism and Democracy*. New York: Harper, 1942.

"Gustav Schmoller und die Probleme von Heute." In *Dogmenhistorische und biographische Aufsätze*. Tübingen: Mohr, 1954.

A History of Economic Analysis. London: Allen and Unwin, 1954.

"The Sociology of Imperialism." In *Imperialism and Social Classes*. New York: Kelley, 1951.

Das Wesen und der Hauptinhalt der theoretischen Nationalökonomie. Leipzig: Duncker and Humblot, 1908.

Schütz, Alfred. "Felix Kaufmann, 1895–1949." *Social Research* 17 (1950): 1–7.

Scott, Joan. *Gender and the Politics of History*. New York: Columbia University Press, 1988.

Seager, Henry. "Economics at Berlin and Vienna." *Journal of Political Economy* 1 (1893).

Selz, Otto. *Die Gesetze der produktiven und reproduktiven Geistestätigkeit*. Bonn: Cohen, 1924.

Über die Gesetze des geordneten Denkverlaufs. Stuttgart: Spemann, 1913.

Shapin, Steven. *Leviathan and the Air-pump: Hobbes, Boyle, and the Experimental Life*. Princeton, N.J.: Princeton University Press, 1985.

Shaw, George Bernard. *Zurück zu Methusalem: Ein Metabiologischer Pentateuch*. Berlin: Fischer, 1922.

Shearmur, Jeremy. *The Political Thought of Karl Popper*. London: Routledge, 1996.

"Popper, Hayek, and the Poverty of Historicism Part I." *Philosophy of the Social Sciences* 28 (1998): 434–50.

Sheehan, James. *German Liberalism in the Nineteenth Century*. Chicago: University of Chicago Press, 1978.

Shklar, Judith. *Men and Citizens*. New York: Cambridge University Press, 1969.

Shorey, Paul. *What Plato Said*. Chicago: University of Chicago Press, 1933.

Siegel, Carl. "Philosophie." In vol. 1 of *Geschichte der deutschen Literatur in Österreich-Ungarn im Zeitalter Franz Joseph I*, edited by Edward Castle. Vienna: Earl Fromme, 1936.

Silverman, Paul. "Law and Economics in Interwar Vienna: Kelsen, Mises and the Regeneration of Austrian Liberalism." Ph.D. diss., University of Chicago, 1984.

Simkin, Colin. "The Birth of *The Open Society*." In *Popper's Views on Natural and Social Science*. Leiden: Brill, 1993.

"Budgetary Reform" and "Budgetary Reform for New Zealand." (Australian) *Economic Record* (1941): 192 ff.; (1942): 16 ff.

"John and Ursula Hicks: A Personal Recollection." *Indian Journal of Applied Economics* 7, no. 4 (1998): 5–14.

Popper's Views on Natural and Social Science. Leiden: Brill, 1993.

Simon, E. D. *The Smaller Democracies*. London: Gollancz, 1939.

Simons, Peter. "The Anglo-Austrian Analytic Axis." In *From Bolzano to Wittgenstein: The Tradition of Austrian Philosophy*, edited by J. C. Nyíri. Vienna: Hölder-Pichler-Tempsky, 1986.

Smaldone, William. *Rudolf Hilferding: The Tragedy of a German Social Democrat*. DeKalb, Ill.: Northern Illinois University Press, 1998.

Small, Albion. *The Origins of Sociology*. Chicago: University of Chicago Press, 1924.

Smith, Joan Allen. *Schoenberg and His Circle: A Viennese Portrait*. New York: Macmillan, 1986.

Snodgrass, Anthony. *Archaic Greece*. Berkeley, Calif.: University of California, 1980.

Sorkin, David. *The Transformation of German Jewry, 1770–1840*. New York: Oxford University Press, 1987.

Sotheby's. *The Library of Karl Popper* (sale catalogue). London: Sotheby's, 1995.

Sozialdemokratische Arbeiterspartei Deutschösterreichs. *Protokoll des sozialdemokratischen Parteitages 1926*. Vienna: Volksbuchhandlung, 1926.

Spinner, Helmut. *Popper und die Politik.* Berlin: Dietz, 1978.

Stadler, Friedrich. "Aspekte des gesellschaftlichen Hintergrunds und Standorts des Wiener Kreises am Beispiel der Universität Wien." In *Wittgenstein, The Vienna Circle and Critical Rationalism,* edited by H. Berghel et al. Vienna: Hölder-Pichler-Tempsky, 1979.

"Denkmuster und Lebenslinien: Karl R. Poppers Intellektuelle Autobiographie." In *Versuche und Widerlegungen offene Probleme im Werk Karl Poppers,* edited by Karl Müller, Friedrich Stadler, and Friedrich Wallner. Vienna: Geyer, 1986.

"Heinrich Gomperz und Karl Popper im Kontext des Logischen Empirismus." In *Heinrich Gomperz, Karl Popper und die Österreichische Philosophie,* edited by Martin Seiler and Friedrich Stadler. Amsterdam: Rodopi, 1994.

"Otto Neurath – Moritz Schlick." In *Grazer Philosophische Studien* 16–17 (1982): 451–63.

"Popper und der Wiener Kreis – Aus einem Gespräch mit Sir Karl Popper (1991)." In Friedrich Stadler, *Studien zum Wiener Kreis.* Frankfurt: Suhrkamp, 1997.

"Spätaufklärung und Sozialdemokratie in Wien, 1918–1938." In *Aufbruch und Untergang: Österreichische Kultur zwischen 1918 und 1938,* edited by Franz Kadrnoska. Vienna: Europaverlag, 1981.

Studien zum Wiener Kreis. Frankfurt: Suhrkamp, 1997.

Vom Positivismus zur "Wissenschaftliche Weltauffassung." Vienna: Löcker, 1982.

Stadler, Friedrich, ed. *Vertriebene Vernunft: Emigration und Exil österreichischer Wissenschaft 1930–1940.* 2 vols. Vienna: Jugend und Volk, 1987–8.

Stadler, Friedrich, and Peter Weibl, eds. *Vertreibung der Vernunft: The Cultural Exodus from Austria.* 2d ed. New York: Springer, 1995.

Stark, Franz, ed. *Revolution oder Reform? Herbert Marcuse und Karl Popper – Eine Konfrontation.* Munich: Kösel, 1972.

Stebbing, L. Susan. *Philosophy and the Physicist.* London: Methuen, 1937.

Steine, Patricia. *Hunderttausende Steine.* Vienna: Falter, 1993.

Stirling, J. H. Introduction and annotations to Albert Schwegler, *Handbook of the History of Philosophy.* 14th ed. Edinburgh: Oliver & Boyd, 1890.

Stourzh, Gerald. "Ethnic Attribution in Late Imperial Austria: Good Intentions, Evil Consequences." *Austrian Studies* 5 (1994): 67–83.

"Galten die Juden als Nationalität Altösterreichs?" In *Prag-Czernowitz-Jerusalem,* by Anna Drabek, Mordechai Eliav, and Gerald Stourzh. Eisenstadt: Roetzer, 1984.

Die Gleichberechtigung der Nationalitäten in der Verfassung und Verwaltung Österreichs 1848–1918. Vienna: Österreichische Akademie, 1985.

Strauss, Barry. *Athens After the Peloponnesian War.* Ithaca, N.Y.: Cornell University Press, 1987.

Streissler, Erich, and Wilhelm Weber. "The Menger Tradition." In *Carl Menger and the Austrian School of Economics,* edited by J. R. Hicks and W. Weber. Oxford: Clarendon Press, 1973.

Struve, Walter. *Elites Against Democracy: Leadership Ideals in Bourgeois Political Thought in Germany, 1890–1933.* Princeton, N.J.: Princeton University Press, 1973.

"Leonard Nelson: The Rule of the Just." In *Elites Against Democracy: Leadership Ideals in Bourgeois Political Thought in Germany, 1890–1933.* Princeton, N.J.: Princeton University Press, 1973.

Sturzo, Luigi. *Italy and Fascism.* 1926. Reprint, New York: Fertig, 1967.

Sutherland, I. L. G., ed. *The Maori People Today: A General Survey.* London: Oxford University Press, 1940.

The Maori Situation. Wellington, N.Z.: Tombs, 1935.

Sztéjnbarg, Dina. Review of *Logik der Forschung*. *Rocznika Przeglądau Filozoficznego* 37 (1935): 269–78.

Talmon, Jacob. *The Origins of Totalitarian Democracy*. London: Secker and Warburg, 1952. *Political Messianism*. London: Secker and Warburg, 1960.

Tarn, W. W. "Alexander the Great and the Unity of Mankind." *Proceedings of the British Academy* 19 (1933): 123–66.

Tarski, Alfred. *Einführung in die Mathematische Logik und die Methodologie der Mathematik*. Vienna: Julius Springer, 1937.
"Der Wahrheitsbegriff in den formalisierten Sprachen." *Studia Philosophica* 1 (1935): 261–405.

Tartakower, Arieh. "Jewish Migratory Movements in Austria in Recent Generations." In *The Jews of Austria: Essays on Their Life, History and Destruction*. London: Vallentine, 1967.

Taschwer, Klaus. "Wissenschaft für alle. 'Volksuniversitäten' als Vermittlungsorte zwischen Wissenschaft und Öffentlichkeit im Wien um 1900." Ph.D. diss., University of Vienna, 1999.

Taylor, A. E. "The Decline and Fall of the State in Republic VIII." *Mind* 48 (1939): 23–38. *Plato*. London: Methuen, 1929.

Taylor, Charles. "The Poverty of *The Poverty of Historicism*." *The Universities and Left Review* (summer 1958): 77–8.

Tenbruck, Friedrich. "Zur Genese der Methodologie Max Webers." *Kölner Zeitschrift für Soziologie und Sozialpsychologie* 11 (1959): 573–630.

Thucydides. *History of the Peloponnesian War*. Translated by R. Warner. New York: Penguin, 1972.

Tinbergen, Jan. *Statistical Testing of Business-Cycle Theories*. 2 vols. Geneva: League of Nations, 1938–9.

Toews, John. *Hegelianism*. New York: Cambridge University Press, 1980.

Topitsch, Ernst. "Kant in Österreich." In *Philosophie der Wirklichkeitsnähe: Festschrift zum 80. Geburtstag Robert Reiningers*. Vienna: Sexl, 1949.

Toqueville, Alexis de. *Democracy in America*. New York: Doubleday, 1975.

Totalitarian Democracy and After. Jerusalem: Israel Academy, 1984.

Toynbee, Arnold. *A Study of History*. 3 vols. London: Oxford University Press, 1934.

Treitschke, Heinrich von. *Der Socialismus und seine Gönner*. Berlin: Reimer, 1989.

Trevor-Roper, Hugh. Review of *The Open Society*. *Polemic* 3 (1946): 58–65.

Tribe, Keith. *Governing Economy: The Reformation of German Economic Discourse, 1750–1840*. Cambridge: Cambridge University Press, 1988.

Tsarek, Anton. "Die praktische Arbeit in der Erziehungsbewegung IV." *Sozialistische Erziehung* 4 (January 1924): 194–8.

Tully, James, ed. *Meaning and Context: Quentin Skinner and His Critics*. Princeton, N.J.: Princeton University Press, 1989.

Turner, Frank M. *The Greek Heritage in Victorian Britain*. New Haven, Conn.: Yale University Press, 1981.

Uebel, Thomas. *Overcoming Logical Positivism from Within*. Amsterdam: Rodopi, 1992.

Uitz, Helmut. *Die österreichischen Kinderfreunde und Roten Falken 1908–1938: Beiträge zur sozialistischen Erziehung*. Vienna: Geyer, 1975.

Unger, Eric. "Contemporary Anti-Platonism." *The Cambridge Journal* 2 (1949): 643–59.

Utley, Philip. "Siegfried Bernfeld's Jewish Order of Youth, 1914–1922." *Leo Baeck Institute Year Book* 24 (1979): 349–68.

Vaihinger, Hans. *Die Philosophie des als ob*. 4th ed. Leipzig: Meiner, 1920.

Vaughan, C. E. *Studies in the History of Political Philosophy.* Manchester: University Press, 1925.

Vernant, Jean Pierre. *The Origins of Greek Thought.* Ithaca, N.Y.: Cornell University Press, 1982.

Vital, David. *The Origins of Zionism.* New York: Oxford University Press, 1975.

Vlastos, Gregory. "The Historical Socrates and Athenian Democracy." *Political Theory* 2 (1983): 495–516.

"Was Plato a Feminist?" *Times Literary Supplement,* 17–23 March 1989, 276 ff.

Voegelin, Eric. *Die politischen Religionen.* Vienna: Bermann-Fischer, 1938.

Waddington, C. H. *The Scientific Attitude.* London: Penguin, 1941.

Waismann, Friedrich. *The Principles of Linguistic Philosophy.* London: Macmillan, 1965.

"Logische Analyse des Wahrscheinlichkeitsbegriffs." *Erkenntnis* 1 (1930): 228–48.

Wald, Abraham. "Die Widerspruchsfreiheit des Kollektivbegriffes der Wahrscheinlichkeitsrechnung." *Ergebnisse* 8 (1937): 38–72.

Wallner, Friedrich. "Popper und die österreichische Philosophie." In *Karl Popper – Philosophie und Wissenschaft: Beiträge zum Popper-Kolloquium,* edited by Friedrich Wallner. Vienna: Braumüller, 1985.

Wandruszka, Adam. "Deutschliberale und deutschnationale Strömungen." In *Das geistige Leben Wiens in der Zwischenkriegszeit,* edited by Norbert Leser. Vienna: ÖBV, 1981.

"Das 'nationale Lager.'" In vol. 1 of *Österreich 1918–1938. Geschichte der Ersten Republik,* edited by Erika Weinzierl and Kurt Skalnik. 2 vols. Graz: Styria, 1983.

Watkins, John. "Hume, Carnap, and Popper." In *The Problem of Inductive Logic,* edited by Imre Lakatos. Amsterdam: North Holland Pub. Co., 1968.

"Karl Popper: A Memoir." *The American Scholar* 66 (1997): 205–19.

"Karl Raimund Popper 1902–1994." *Proceedings of the British Academy* 94 (1997): 645–84.

Science and Scepticism. Princeton, N.J.: Princeton University Press, 1984.

"The Truth Will Out." *The Philosophers' Magazine,* Spring 1999.

"A Whiff of Hegel in The Open Society?" In *Popper's Open Society After 50 Years,* edited by Ian Jarvie and Sandra Pralong. London: Routledge, 1999.

Weber, Fritz. "Hauptprobleme der wirtschaftlichen und sozialen Entwicklung Österreichs in der Zwischenkriegzeit." In *Aufbruch und Untergang: österreichische Kultur zwischen 1918 und 1938,* edited by Franz Kadrnoska. Vienna: Europaverlag, 1981.

Weber, Max. "Die Grenznutzlehre und das 'psychophysische Grundgesetz.'" *Gesammelte Aufsätze zur Wissenschaftslehre.* 2d ed. Tübingen: Mohr, 1951.

"'Objectivity' in Social Science and Social Policy." In *The Methodology of the Social Sciences,* edited and translated by Edward Shils and Henry Finch. New York: Free Press, 1949.

"R. Stammlers 'Überwindung' der materialistischen Geschichtsauffassung." In *Gesammelte Aufsätze zur Wissenschaftslehre.* 2d ed. Tübingen: Mohr, 1951.

"Roscher und Knies und die logischen Probleme der historischen Nationalökonomie." In *Gesammelte Aufsätze zur Wissenschaftslehre.* 2d ed. Tübingen: Mohr, 1951.

"Studies in the Logic of the Social Sciences." In *The Methodology of the Social Sciences,* edited and translated by Edward Shils and Henry Finch. New York: Free Press, 1949.

Wegs, J. Robert. *Growing Up Working Class: Continuity and Change Among Viennese Youth, 1890–1938.* London and University Park: Pennsylvania State University Press, 1989.

Weiler, Gershon. *Mauthner's Critique of Language.* Cambridge: Cambridge University Press, 1970.

Weinberg, Adelaide. *Theodor Gomperz and John Stuart Mill.* Geneva: Librairie Droz, 1963.

Weinberg, Julius. Review of *Logik der Forschung. Philosophical Review* 45 (1936): 511–14.

Weininger, Otto. *Geschlecht und Charakter*. Vienna: Braumüller, 1903.

Weintraub, E. Roy. "On the Existence of a Competitive Equilibrium: 1930–1954." *Journal of Economic Literature* 21 (1983): 1–39.

Weinzierl, Erika. "Hochschulleben und Hochschulpolitik zwischen den Kriegen." In *Das geistige Leben Wiens in der Zwischenkriegszeit*, edited by Norbert Leser. Vienna: ÖBV, 1981.

Weinzierl, Erika, and Kurt Skalnik, eds. *Österreich 1918–1938. Geschichte der Ersten Republik*. 2 vols. Graz: Styria, 1983.

Weissel, Erwin. *Die Ohnmacht des Sieges: Arbeiterschaft und Sozialisierung nach dem Ersten Weltkrieg in Österreich*. Vienna: Europaverlag, 1976.

Wettersten, John. *The Roots of Critical Rationalism*. Amsterdam: Rodopi, 1992.

Whitehead, Alfred North, and Bertrand Russell. *Principia Mathematica*. 3 vols. Cambridge: The University Press, 1910–13.

Whiteside, Andrew. *The Socialism of the Fools*. Berkeley, Calif.: University of California, 1975.

Wieser, Friedrich von. "The Austrian School and the Theory of Value." *Economic Journal* 1 (1891): 108–21.

  "The Theory of Value." *Annals of the American Academy of Political and Social Science* 2 (1892): 24–52.

Wild, John. *Plato's Modern Enemies and the Theory of Natural Law*. Chicago: University of Chicago Press, 1953.

  "Popper's Interpretation of Plato." In vol. 2 of *The Philosophy of Karl Popper*, edited by Paul Arthur Schilpp. La Salle, Ill.: Open Court, 1974.

Windelband, Wilhelm. "Geschichte und Naturwissenschaft." In vol. 2 of *Präludien*. Tübingen: Mohr, 1921.

Winespear, Alban. *The Genesis of Plato's Thought*. New York: Dryden, 1940.

Winkler, John. *The Constraints of Desire*. London: Routledge, 1989.

Winter, Eduard. *Bernard Bolzano – Ein Lebensbild*. Stuttgart: Frommann, 1969.

Winter, Eduard, ed. *Robert Zimmermanns Philosophische Propädeutik und die Vorlagen aus der Wissenschaftslehre Bernard Bolzanos*. Vienna: Österreichische Akademie, 1975.

Winter, Ernst Karl. "Die Staatskrise in Österreich." *Wiener Politische Blätter* 1 (16 April 1933).

Wistrich, Robert. *The Jews of Vienna in the Age of Franz Joseph*. New York: Oxford University Press, 1990.

  Socialism and the Jews: The Dilemmas of Assimilation in Germany and Austria-Hungary. London: Associated University Presses, 1982.

Wittelshöfer, Otto. *Politische und wirtschaftliche Gesichtspunkte in der österreichischen Nationalitätenfrage*, Preußische Jahrbücher 76, no. 3 (1894).

Wittgenstein, Ludwig. *Philosophical Investigations*. Edited by G. E. M. Anscombe and Rush Rhees. London: Macmillan, 1958.

  Tractatus Logico-Philosophicus. Translated by C. K. Ogden. 1922. Reprint, London: Routledge, 1990. (Originally published in German as "Logisch-Philosophische Abhandlung." *Annalen der Naturphilosophie* 14 [1921]: 185–262.)

Wolf, Karl. "Der Grazer Schule: Gegenstandstheorie und Wertlehre." *Wissenschaft und Weltbild* 21 (July–September 1968): 31–56.

Wollheim, Richard. "Prosecuting the Myth." *New Statesman*, 4 January 1958.

Woodger, Joseph Henry. *The Axiomatic Method in Biology*. With appendices by Alfred Tarski and W. F. Floyd. Cambridge: The University Press, 1937.

Xenophon. *Memorabilia, Oeconomicus, Symposium, Apology*. Translated by E. C. Marchant. Cambridge, Mass.: Harvard University Press, 1923.

Zeisel, Hans. "The Vienna Years." In *Qualitative and Quantitative Social Research*, edited by Robert Merton, James Coleman, and Peter Rossi. New York: Free Press, 1979.

Zeller, Eduard. *Outlines of the History of Greek Philosophy*. Revised by Wilhelm Nestle. New York: Humanities Press, 1951.

Zeman, Z. A. B. *The Break-Up of the Habsburg Empire, 1914–1918*. New York: Oxford University Press, 1961.

Zerin, Edward. "Karl Popper on God. The Lost Interview." *Skeptic* 6, no. 2 (1998): 46–9.

Zilsel, Edgar. *Das Anwendungsproblem*. Leipzig: Barth, 1916.

——— "Der einführende Philosophieunterricht an den neuen Oberschulen." *Volkserziehung, Pädagogischer Teil* 2 (1921): 324–41.

——— Review of *Logik der Forschung*. *Die Naturwissenschaften* 23 (1935): 531 f.

Zilsel, Paul. "Über Edgar Zilsel." In vol. 2 of *Vertriebene Vernunft: Emigration und Exil österreichischer Wissenschaft 1930–1940*, edited by Friedrich Stadler. Vienna: Jugend und Volk, 1988.

Zimmermann, Robert. "Philosophie und Philosophen in Österreich." *Österreichisch-Ungarische Revue* 6 (1889): 177–98.

Zimmern, Alfred, ed. *Modern Political Doctrines*. New York: Oxford University Press, 1939.

Zoitl, Helge. "Akademische Festkultur." In *Aufbruch und Untergang: Österreichische Kultur zwischen 1918 und 1938*, edited by Franz Kadrnoska. Vienna: Europaverlag, 1981.

Zolo, Danilo. *Reflexive Epistemology: The Philosophical Legacy of Otto Neurath*. Boston: Reidel, 1989.

Zweig, Stefan. *The World of Yesterday*. New York: Viking, 1943.

Index

References to Karl Popper within entries are abbreviated "KP"